Lecture Notes in Computer Science 10614

Commenced Publication in 1973
Founding and Former Series Editors:
Gerhard Goos, Juris Hartmanis, and Jan van Leeuwen

Editorial Board

More information about this series at http://www.springer.com/series/7407

Alessandra Lintas · Stefano Rovetta
Paul F.M.J. Verschure · Alessandro E.P. Villa (Eds.)

Artificial Neural Networks and Machine Learning – ICANN 2017

26th International Conference on Artificial Neural Networks
Alghero, Italy, September 11–14, 2017
Proceedings, Part II

 Springer

Editors

Alessandra Lintas
University of Lausanne
Lausanne
Switzerland

Stefano Rovetta
University of Genoa
Genoa
Italy

Paul F.M.J. Verschure
Universitat Pompeu Fabra
Barcelona
Spain

Alessandro E.P. Villa
University of Lausanne
Lausanne
Switzerland

ISSN 0302-9743   ISSN 1611-3349 (electronic)
Lecture Notes in Computer Science
ISBN 978-3-319-68611-0   ISBN 978-3-319-68612-7 (eBook)
https://doi.org/10.1007/978-3-319-68612-7

Library of Congress Control Number: 2017956064

LNCS Sublibrary: SL1 – Theoretical Computer Science and General Issues

Printed on acid-free paper

This Springer imprint is published by Springer Nature
The registered company is Springer International Publishing AG
The registered company address is: Gewerbestrasse 11, 6330 Cham, Switzerland

Preface

This volume is part of the two-volume proceedings of the 26th International Conference on Artificial Neural Networks (ICANN-2017), held during September 11–14, 2017 in Alghero, Italy. ICANN 2017 was organized with the support of the Department of Architecture of the University of Sassari, the Neuroheuristics Research Group of the University of Lausanne, and the European Neural Network Society (ENNS).

The ICANN conference is the flagship annual conference of the European Neural Network Society. The ICANN series of conferences was initiated in 1991 and soon became the major European gatherings of experts in the field of neural networks and related areas. The unique character of this conference is its transdisciplinarity, beyond the interdisciplinarity of machine learning, bringing together researchers from all horizons, i.e., mathematics, physics, information and computer sciences, engineering, as well as theoretical and experimental neurosciences. The conference is organized in partnership with ENNS with its governance fully committed to not-for-profit procedures that allow us to keep the congress fees low compared with international standards. This policy granted the participation of a significant number of undergraduate and master students, who accounted for 18% of the scientific delegates. The ICANN governance model consolidated the practice to include membership of ENNS, valid through December of the calendar year of the conference, for all ICANN participants who present a scientific communication. Last, but not least, two best paper awards are distributed, along with ten travel grants sponsored by ENNS.

Following the practice of the ICANN conference series since 2011, the ICANN 2017 conference was organized following a dual-track stream of oral talks lasting 20 minutes each, one track including seven sessions of mainly ANN and machine-learning-inspired presentations, and one track including seven sessions of mainly bio-inspired presentations. A tutorial on the capabilities of shallow and deep networks supported by ENNS President Vera Kurkova and a special session organized on the topic of neural networks and applications to environmental sciences were organized on the first day of the conference, before the opening of the main program. Poster sessions have always played a key role in successful ICANN conferences. This year, the time and space allocated to nine poster sessions was further expanded, and posters were left on display throughout the entire duration of the conference. The scientific program was completed by five keynote lectures from world-renowned scholars: Professor Moshe Abeles talking about temporal information in neural coding; Professor Marco Gori about the computational framework associated with the emergence of inference rules; Professor Elisabeth André about emotional intelligence in human–computer interaction; Professor David Ríos about adversarial machine learning; and Professor Michele Giugliano about information transmission in weakly coupled large-scale neural ensembles.

Out of approximately 270 papers submitted to ICANN 2017, the Program Committee selected 128 full and 63 short papers. It is interesting to note that about half of the accepted short papers were initially submitted as full papers. Although these papers did not get through the strict reviewing process for full papers, their authors prepared a short paper version for presentation at ICANN. Because of its reputation as a high-level conference, ICANN rarely receives papers of poor quality, and the fact that one third of the scientific delegates chose to submit short papers is certainly a proof of the vitality and attractiveness of the ICANN conference. The type of submission was not the ultimate criterion in assigning the submitters to an oral or a poster presentation. Short papers account for 19/79 oral presentations and 44/112 poster presentations.

The number of accepted papers necessitated publishing the proceedings in two volumes. The contributions (oral and posters) were grouped following the respective track: Volume I for Artificial Neural Networks and Biological Inspiration and Volume II for Formal Models and Their Applications. The proceedings of the short papers have been grouped, following the rules of the publisher, at the end of each volume. The presenting authors came from 33 countries all over the world: 87 from Europe, 74 from Asia, 26 from the Americas, three from Oceania and one from Africa. China (39) and Germany (33) were the most represented countries.

It is our pleasure to express our gratitude to everybody who contributed to the success of the conference and the publication of the proceedings. In particular, we thank the members of the Executive Committee of the ENNS and the president, Vera Kurkova, for entrusting us with the organization of the conference. We would like to express our sincere gratitude to the members of the Program Committee and all the reviewers, who did a tremendous job under time constraints during the review process. We thank all members of the local Organizing Committee and the local staff for the great effort and assistance in the organization of the conference, in particular, Antonello Monsù Scolaro (Department of Architecture in Alghero of the University of Sassari), Eugenio Lintas (Sassari), and Anna Mura (SPECS, Universitat Pompeu Fabra, Barcelona). We are greatly indebted to Dr. Paolo Masulli for his commitment as ENNS interim secretary and ICANN communication chair along all phases of the organization. We would also like to thank the publisher, Springer, for their cooperation during the publishing process that was under strict time limitations. Finally, we thank all authors who contributed to these volumes for sharing their ideas, their results, and their spirit with the community during the scientific and social programs of the conference. We are sure that the participants of ICANN 2017 maintained the enthusiasm of the founders of ENNS and initial organizers of the ICANN conferences and that they will continue to generate new ideas and innovative results in the field of neural networks and related areas.

August 2017

Alessandra Lintas
Stefano Rovetta
Paul F.M.J. Verschure
Alessandro E.P. Villa

Organization

General Chair

Alessandro E.P. Villa   University of Lausanne, Switzerland

General Co-chair

Alessandra Lintas   University of Lausanne, Switzerland

Local Co-chairs

Stefano Rovetta   University of Genoa, Italy
Paul F.M.J. Verschure   SPECS-Universitat Pompeu Fabra, Spain

Communication Chair

Paolo Masulli   University of Lausanne, Switzerland

Local Organizing Committee

Paolo Enrico   University of Sassari, Italy
Alessandra Lintas   University of Lausanne, Switzerland
Eugenio Lintas   Sassari
Antonello Monsù Scolaro   University of Sassari, Italy
Anna Mura   SPECS-Universitat Pompeu Fabra, Barcelona, Spain

Scientific and Reviewing Committee

Jérémie Cabessa   Université Panthéon-Assas - Paris 2, France
Petia Koprinkova-Hristova   Bulgarian Academy of Sciences, Sofia, Bulgaria
Věra Kůrková   Czech Academy of Sciences, Prague, Czech Republic
Alessandra Lintas   University of Lausanne, Switzerland
Paolo Masulli   University of Lausanne, Switzerland
Francesco Masulli   University of Genoa, Italy
Paul F.M.J. Verschure   SPECS-Universitat Pompeu Fabra, Spain
Antonio Javier Pons Rivero   Universitat Politècnica de Catalunya, Spain
Yifat Prut   Hebrew University Jerusalem, Israel
Stefano Rovetta   University of Genoa, Italy
Antonino Staiano   University of Naples Parthenope, Italy
Igor V. Tetko   Helmholtz Zentrum München, Germany
Alessandro E.P. Villa   University of Lausanne, Switzerland

Program Committee

Lydia Fischer	Honda Research Institute Europe, Germany
Věra Kůrková	Czech Academy of Sciences, Prague, Czech Republic
Alessandra Lintas	University of Lausanne, Switzerland
Francesco Masulli	University of Genoa, Italy
Stefano Rovetta	University of Genoa, Italy
Antonino Staiano	University of Naples Parthenope, Italy
Alessandro E.P. Villa	University of Lausanne, Switzerland

Secretariat and Communication

Alessandra Lintas	University of Lausanne, Switzerland
Paolo Masulli	University of Lausanne, Switzerland

ENNS Travel Grant Committee

Cesare Alippi	Politecnico di Milano, Italy
Jérémie Cabessa	Université Panthéon-Assas - Paris 2, France
Barbara Hammer	University of Bielefeld, Germany
Petia Koprinkova-Hristova	Bulgarian Academy of Sciences, Sofia, Bulgaria
Věra Kůrková	Czech Academy of Sciences, Prague, Czech Republic
Paolo Masulli	University of Lausanne, Switzerland
Jaakko Peltonen	University of Tampere, Finland
Antonio Javier Pons Rivero	Universitat Politècnica de Catalunya, Spain
Yifat Prut	Hebrew University Jerusalem, Israel
Igor V. Tetko	Helmholtz Zentrum München, Germany
Paul F.M.J. Verschure	SPECS-Universitat Pompeu Fabra, Spain
Francisco Zamora-Martínez	University of Pamplona, Spain

Additional Reviewers

Tayfun Alpay	University of Hamburg, Knowledge Technology, WTM, Germany
Pablo Barros	University of Hamburg, Germany
Lluis Belanche	Universitat Politècnica de Catalunya, Spain
Michael Biehl	University of Groningen, The Netherlands
Giacomo Boracchi	Politecnico di Milano, Italy
Hans Albert Braun	University of Marburg, Germany
Li Bu	China
Guido Bugmann	Plymouth University, UK
Jérémie Cabessa	Université Panthéon-Assas, Paris 2, France
Francesco Camastra	University of Naples Parthenope, Italy
Angelo Cangelosi	Plymouth University, UK
Giovanna Castellano	University of Bari, Italy
Marta Castellano	Institute of Cognitive Sciences, Germany

Davide Chicco	University of Toronto, Canada
Angelo Ciaramella	University of Naples Parthenope, Italy
Jorg Conradt	TU München, Germany
David Coufal	Insitute of Computer Science AS CR, Czech Republic
Jose Enrique De Tomas	University of Alicante, Spain
Marc Deffains	Hebrew University Jerusalem, Israel
Sergey Dolenko	D.V. Skobeltsyn Institute of Nuclear Physics, M.V. Lomonosov Moscow State University, Russia
Jose Dorronsoro	Universidad Autonoma de Madrid, Spain
Wlodzislaw Duch	Nicolaus Copernicus University, Poland
David Díaz-Vico	Universidad Autónoma de Madrid, Spain
Lambros Ekonomou	City University London, UK
Anna Maria Fanelli	University of Bari, Italy
Andreas Fischer	University of Fribourg, Switzerland
Lydia Fischer	Honda Research Institute Europe
Giorgio Gnecco	IMT Lucca, Italy
José Luis González-de-Suso	das-Nano, Spain
Claudius Gros	Goethe University of Frankfurt, Germany
Ankur Gupta	University of British Columbia, Canada
Tatiana V. Guy	Institute of Information Theory and Automation, Czech Republic
Frantisek Hakl	Institute of computer Science, Czech Republic
Barbara Hammer	Bielefeld University, Germany
Stefan Heinrich	Universität Hamburg, Germany
Katsuhiro Honda	Osaka Prefecture University, Japan
Brian Hyland	University of Otago, New Zealand
Lazaros Iliadis	Democritus University of Thrace, Greece
Maciej Jedynak	University Grenoble Alpes, Grenoble Institute of Neuroscience, France
Marika Kaden	HS Mittweida, Germany
Fotis Kanellos	National Technical University of Athens, Greece
Juha Karhunen	Aalto University, Finland
Matthias Kerzel	Universität Hamburg, Germany
Mario Koeppen	Kyushu Institute of Technology, Japan
Stefanos Kollias	National Technical University of Athens, Greece
Ján Koloda	das-Nano, Spain
Petia Koprinkova-Hristova	Bulgarian Academy of Sciences, Bulgaria
Irena Koprinska	University of Sydney, Australia
Vera Kurkova	Institute of Computer Science, Academy of Sciences of the Czech Republic, Czech Republic
Giancarlo La Camera	SUNY Stony Brook, USA
Alessandra Lintas	University of Lausanne, Switzerland
Ling Luo	University of Sydney, Australia
Iván López-Espejo	University of Granada, Spain
Sven Magg	Universität Hamburg, Germany
Miroslaw Malek	USI-Lugano, Switzerland

Petr Marsalek	Charles University in Prague, Czech Republic
Francesco Masulli	University of Genoa, Italy
Paolo Masulli	University of Lausanne, Switzerland
Joshua Mati	Hebrew University Jerusalem, Israel
Corrado Mencar	University of Bari A. Moro, Italy
George Mengov	Sofia University, Bulgaria
Valeri Mladenov	Technical University of Sofia, Bulgaria
Juan Manuel Moreno	Universitat Politecnica de Catalunya, Spain
Anna Mura	SPECS-UPF Barcelona, Spain
Roman Neruda	Institute of Computer Science, ASCR, Czech Republic
Nathan Netanyahu	Bar-Ilan University, Israel
Francesca Odone	University of Genoa, Italy
Luca Oneto	University of Genoa, Italy
Sebastian Otte	University of Tübingen, Germany
Joan Pastor Pellicer	Universitat Politècnica de València, Spain
Riccardo Pecori	eCampus, Italy
Jaakko Peltonen	Aalto University, Finland
Vincenzo Piuri	University of Milan, Italy
Mirko Polato	University of Padova, Italy
Antonio Javier Pons Rivero	Universitat Politècnica de Catalunya, Barcelona, Spain
Yifat Prut	Hebrew University Jerusalem, Israel
Federico Raue	University of Kaiserslautern, Germany
Francesco Regazzoni	Università della Svizzera Italiana, Switzerland
Marina Resta	University of Genoa, Italy
Jean Roaut	University of Québec Sherbrooke, Canada
Manuel Roveri	Politecnico di Milano, Italy
Stefano Rovetta	University of Genoa, Italy
Alessandro Rozza	Waynaut, Italy
Marcello Sanguineti	University of Genoa, Italy
Wolfram Schenck	Bielefeld University of Applied Sciences, Germany
Friedhelm Schwenker	University of Ulm, Germany
Jordi Soriano	Universitat de Barcelona, Spain
Alessandro Sperduti	University of Padova, Italy
Antonino Staiano	University of Naples Parthenope, Italy
Michael Stiber	University of Washington Bothell, USA
Aubin Tchaptchet	Philipps University of Marburg, Germany
Igor Tetko	HMGU, Germany
Yancho Todorov	Aalto University, Finland
Alberto Torres-Barrán	Universidad Autónoma de Madrid, Spain
Jochen Triesch	Frankfurt Institute for Advanced Studies, Germany
Francesco Trovo	Politecnico di Milano, Italy
Georgi Tsvetanov Tsenov	Technical University Sofia, Bulgaria
Antonio Vergari	University of Bari, Italy
Paul F.M.J. Verschure	SPECS-Universitat Pompeu Fabra, Spain
Petra Vidnerová	Czech Academy of Sciences, Czech Republic
Alexander Vidybida	Bogolyubov Institute for Theoretical Physics, Ukraine

Contents – Part II

Games and Strategy

Boltzmann Machines and Phase Transitions

Context Information Learning and Self-Assessment
in Advanced Machine Learning Models

Representation and Classification

Clustering

Learning from Data Streams and Time Series

Image Processing and Medical Applications

Advances in Machine Learning

Short Papers

Contents – Part I

From Neurons to Networks

Neuromorphic Hardware

Brain Topology and Dynamics

Synaptic Plasticity and Learning

Neural Networks Meet Natural and Environmental Sciences

Short Papers

Convolutional Neural Networks

Spiking Convolutional Deep Belief Networks

Jacques Kaiser[✉], David Zimmerer, J. Camilo Vasquez Tieck, Stefan Ulbrich,
Arne Roennau, and Rüdiger Dillmann

FZI Research Center for Information Technology, 76131 Karlsruhe, Germany
{jkaiser,zimmerer,tieck,sulbrich,roennau,dillmann}@fzi.de

Abstract. Understanding visual input as perceived by humans is a
challenging task for machines. Today, most successful methods work by
learning features from static images. Based on classical artificial neural
networks, those methods are not adapted to process event streams as
provided by the Dynamic Vision Sensor (DVS). Recently, an unsupervised learning rule to train Spiking Restricted Boltzmann Machines has
been presented [9]. Relying on synaptic plasticity, it can learn features
directly from event streams. In this paper, we extend this method by
adding convolutions, lateral inhibitions and multiple layers. We evaluate
our method on a self-recorded DVS dataset as well as the Poker-DVS
dataset. Our results show that our convolutional method performs better and needs less parameters. It also achieves comparable results to
previous event-based classification methods while learning features in an
unsupervised fashion.

Keywords: Spiking neural network · Convolutional Restricted Boltzmann Machine · event-based Contrastive Divergence

1 Introduction

Extracting features from visual input is an important topic of computer vision.
It allows reducing the redundancy in pixel intensities, so that images can be
described with fewer parameters. However, finding good features to represent
natural images is complicated, and today most feature extractors are learned.
While there are many methods to learn features from an image dataset, only few
methods learn features from event streams as provided by the Dynamic Vision
Sensor (DVS) [8].

In this paper, we present a method to learn event-based features in an unsupervised fashion called Spiking Convolutional Deep Belief Network (SCDBN).
The core component of our method is the Spiking Convolutional Restricted
Boltzmann Machine (SCRBM), which convolves input spike trains and learns
with event-based Contrastive Divergence (eCD) [9]. We evaluate our method
against previously presented event-based feature extractors by ranking it on the
Poker-DVS dataset [12]. The main contribution of this paper is the addition of
convolutions and lateral inhibitions to the original method [9], as proposed in
[6] for classical non-spiking RBMs.

© Springer International Publishing AG 2017
A. Lintas et al. (Eds.): ICANN 2017, Part II, LNCS 10614, pp. 3–11, 2017.
https://doi.org/10.1007/978-3-319-68612-7_1

2   Related Work

The Convolutional Restricted Boltzmann Machine (CRBM) was invented simultaneously in [3,6,10]. In similarity to Convolutional Neural Networks (CNNs), it can be seen as the advancement of an energy-based model adapting to compositional data. Unlike a normal RBM, the visible and hidden layer in a CRBM are connected in a convolutional manner instead of being fully connected.

In contrast to CNNs, due to their local learning rule, RBMs can not be explicitly trained to perform max pooling operations. Thus a softmax based probabilistic max pooling is introduced in [6] to enforce local sparseness in the hidden activations, on which a pooling layer can be stacked. Since RBMs have been described as the most biologically plausible deep learning architecture [1], there were many attempts to adapt them to spiking networks. Indeed, recent studies suggest that information is encoded in the brain as representations of probability distributions and probabilistic interference [5,7,14].

A first framework which proposed how spiking neurons can perform Markov chain Monte Carlo (MCMC) sampling and approximate a Boltzmann distribution was introduced in [2]. A neuron is regarded as a random variable with a binary state defined by whether it is firing or not. Since the firing of a neuron is instantaneous, after a neuron has fired it is set to the firing state for a time period τ. A common choice for τ is the refractory period of the neuron τ_{ref}. Consequently, one way to characterize the firing probability of a neuron is to take the relative time a neuron has spent in the firing state. Thus for a given timestep, the state of the network is defined by the states of the individual neurons.

This model is improved in [11] by replacing the stochastic neuron model by conductance based LIF neurons, a more common and biologically inspired neuron model. Indeed, under high frequency (Poisson) noise, a conductance-based LIF neuron reaches a high conductance state of its membrane potential. In this high conductance state, the neuron shows stochastic firing of sigmoidal shape, determined by the input current and the noise frequency.

This neural sampling framework was further extended by a synaptic plasticity rule to perform Contrastive Divergence (CD) in continuous time [4,9]. The approach presented in [9], called event-based Contrastive Divergence (eCD), relies on bidirectional synapses and an adapted symmetric Spike-Timing-Dependent Plasticity (STDP) variant, which alternates between Long-Term Potentiation (LTP) and Long-Term Depression (LTD) to model the positive and negative phases of the CD algorithm respectively. The same network can therefore perform an arbitrary number of CD steps. In this paper, we use the eCD learning rule presented in [9] to train Spiking Convolutional Restricted Boltzmann Machine (SCRBM) and stack them into Spiking Convolutional Deep Belief Network (SCDBN).

3   Architecture

In this section we describe the architecture of our SCRBM, how we tune the synaptic weights and stack them to form a SCDBN. For the convolution

(Sect. 3.1), we highlight the differences between our method and the method proposed in [6], which relies on classical artificial neurons. For the learning rule (Sect. 3.2), we highlight the differences between our method and the method proposed in [9], which does not consider convolutions or multi-layer architectures.

3.1 Spiking Convolutional Layer

Convolution in neural networks stands for weight sharing over receptive fields in structured data. It reduces the number of parameters to tune by applying the same processing to all receptive fields. Convolution is now a widely adopted concept to process images with neural networks.

The architecture of our SCRBM is similar to the one presented in [6]. The hidden layer is splitted into feature maps defined by kernels. A kernel represents the weights that are shared across receptive fields in a feature map. Adjacent receptive fields are overlapping and the output neurons have the same topology as their input regions, see Fig. 1a.

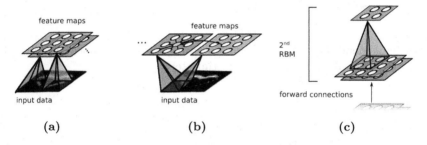

Fig. 1. Schema of the architectures for the proposed SCDBN. (a) The hidden layer of a SCRBM is organized in feature maps convolving the input. (b) The feature maps have inhibitory connections from one to another to encourage feature discrimination, and across local neighborhood for sparsity. (c) A SCDBN consisting of two stacked SCRBMs, connected with a purely feedforward layer.

Unlike [6], our network consists of spiking neurons, where each synapse has its own dynamics. Therefore, each synapse has its own weight on which it performs local updates following the STDP learning rule. We synchronize all weight updates within a feature map at regular timesteps.

3.2 Learning Rule

To train a SCRBM, we adapt the eCD rule proposed in [9]. The original eCD rule can be expressed as:

$$\frac{\mathrm{d}}{\mathrm{d}t} w_{ij} = g(t) \cdot \mathrm{STDP}(v_i(t), h_j(t)), \tag{1}$$

where $v_i(t)$ and $h_j(t)$ are the spike trains of the visible and hidden units v_i and h_j, $g(t) \in \mathbb{R}$ is the global signal determining positive and negative phases of CD and $STDP(v, h)$ is a symmetric LTP rule on the bidirectional synapse.

The original division into four training phases has similarities to persistent CD since the activity of the hidden layer of the previous step is used as starting state for the next step. Therefore, we extend the learning rule with a fifth phase, where the network is "flushed" thus enabling normal CD (see Fig. 2).

Fig. 2. The five phases of eCD for a training step. The input stream is only clamped to the visible units during the burn-in phase. In the second phase, we learn the data by activating LTP. Learning is then deactivated in the burn-out phase. In the fourth phase, we unlearn the model with LTD. Unlike [9], we add a fifth phase to flush the network. A training step is simulated for $T_{\text{step}} = 168\,\text{ms}$, the learning phases last 8%, the burn phases 36% and the flush phase 12%.

We implement the weight sharing by averaging the synaptic weights of a kernel within a feature map at discrete timesteps:

$$w_{\text{shared}} \leftarrow \frac{\sum\limits_{w \in W_{\text{group}}} w}{|W_{\text{group}}|} \tag{2}$$

$$\forall w \in W_{\text{group}}, \quad w \leftarrow w_{\text{shared}},$$

with W_{group} the set of shared synaptic weights within a feature map.

3.3   Lateral Inhibition

Classical Convolutional Neural Networks often alternate between convolutional layers and max pooling layers. A softmax based probabilistic max pooling was proposed in [6] to introduce local sparseness in the hidden activations. However, this approach requires information about neighboring neuron activations at discrete timesteps and is therefore not suited for networks of spiking neurons. In contrast to [6], we enforce sparseness in the hidden layer by introducing lateral inhibitions. Specifically, we introduce two types of lateral inhibition: between all neurons within the same feature map, and between all neurons having the same location across different feature maps, see Fig. 1b. The former increases sparsity in a feature map by reducing the probability of a neighbor neuron to fire when another already fired, similar to probabilistic max pooling. The latter enforces the learning of discriminative features by reducing the correlation between different kernels, see Fig. 1b. Let $w_{ijk}^{i'j'k'}$ be the weight between two hidden-layer neurons x_{ijk} and $x_{i'j'k'}$ at position i,j and i',j' at feature map k and k' respectively. We have:

$$
w_{ijk}^{i'j'k'} = \begin{cases} \beta_1, & \text{for } |i-i'| < b_d \text{ , } |j-j'| < b_d \text{ and } k \neq k', \\ \beta_2, & \text{for } |i-i'| < b_s \text{ , } |j-j'| < b_s \text{ and } k = k', \\ 0, & \text{otherwise,} \end{cases} \tag{3}
$$

where b_d and b_s are the neighborhood size in different feature maps and within the same feature map respectively, and $\beta_1, \beta_2 \leq 0$ are inhibitory weights. This removes one advantage of RBMs since the hidden units are no longer independent, which makes it harder to sample from the true Boltzmann distribution. However, since the spiking network continuously performs sampling steps, the approximation has shown to be sufficient if the weights are not too strong and prevent changes of different modes, see Fig. 3.

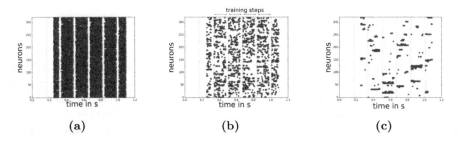

Fig. 3. Spike trains of neurons in the hidden layer during many training steps with varying lateral inhibitions. As the lateral inhibition increases, the activity becomes more sparse, preventing mode switching. We set inhibition size $b_d = b_s = 1$ and weights $\beta_1 = \beta_2 = \beta$, see Eq. 3. (a) No lateral inhibitions $\beta = 0$. (b) Weak lateral inhibitions: $\beta = -1$. (c) Strong lateral inhibitions: $\beta = -10$.

3.4   Spiking Convolutional Deep Belief Network

With networks of classical artificial neurons, several RBMs are stacked upon each other to form a DBN, which has more representational power thanks to its hierarchy of layers. More precisely, a RBM is trained greedily on the whole dataset, which is then entirely converted to hidden layer activations after a forward pass. The converted dataset is then used to train the next RBM in the stack, and so forth. During testing, the resulting DBN can then abstract the data by performing one forward pass per layer. In other words, layers are sampled one by one with respect to the previous one in a bottom-up fashion.

Unfortunately, spiking RBMs can not sample a layer with respect to another one and ignore all other top-down connections from the next layer. Instead, one-way forward connections between the hidden layer of the previous RBM and the visible layer of the next RBM (see Fig. 1c) must be added. This approach only allows the abstraction of data (forward passes) and prevents the reconstruction over more than one layer (downward passes). Bidirectional synapses can therefore also be replaced with forward synapses to save computational power.

4 Results

In contrast to networks of classical artificial neurons which are trained on images, we train our network of spiking neurons on event-based data captured by a DVS [8]. We evaluate the quality of the learned features in two ways. Firstly, we quantitatively evaluate the ability of our SCDBN to abstract event-based data on a classification task. We show how convolutions improve the performance on a self-recorded dataset, where objects are not properly centered in the event stream. We then compare our method against other event-based classification methods by ranking it on the popular Poker-DVS dataset [12]. Secondly, we qualitatively evaluate the ability of our method to reconstruct a partially occluded stream of events.

4.1 Experimental Setup

We evaluate our approach on two different event-based datasets. **Ball-Can-Pen**: Motivated by different grasp types [13], we recorded ball, can and pen images flashing on a screen with a DVS. The set consists of 90 samples for each of the three classes, each sample lasting 100ms. The samples were further downscaled from 128×128 to 16×16 pixels. In this dataset, the objects do not have the same location on the images, making them harder to classify. **Poker-DVS Dataset** [12]: we further downsample the extracted Poker patches to a size of 16×16 pixels and only consider spikes in the first 8 ms.

4.2 Classification

We quantitatively compare our method to other event-based classification methods. The architecture of our SCDBN consists of two layers. The first layer is convolutional with ten filters of size 10×10 and performs the feature extraction. The second layer is fully connected and performs the association between the extracted features and the correct labels. The complete architecture is depicted in Fig. 4b. For both datasets, each layer is trained over 600 randomly drawn samples. The final accuracy is calculated over the training set.

To outline the benefits of our convolutional architecture, we compare the performance against a similar architecture but without any convolutions, with ten fully connected hidden units for extracting features. This non-convolutional architecture is similar as the one used in [9], with an additional layer. Due to the lower number of parameters in convolutional layer, the convolutional model is less prone to overfitting than the non-convolutional one. The number of parameters and the classification accuracy can be seen in Table 1 and in Fig. 4c. Even with fewer parameters, the convolutional architecture has a higher classification accuracy. Moreover, our model reaches 90% accuracy on Poker-DVS.

Table 1. Classification accuracy of our method on two event-based datasets. Due to the small amount of training samples, testing is performed on the training set. Despite fewer parameters for the convolutional architecture, runtime is longer due to the shared synapses having their own dynamics.

	Accuracy	Parameters in 1st layer	Runtime/Sample
Ball-Can-Pen without convolution	0.82	2560	4.8 s
Ball-Can-Pen with convolution	1.0	1000	6.2 s
Poker-DVS with convolution	0.90	1000	6.2 s
Poker-DVS Spiking CNN [12]	0.91	600 (trained offline)	-
Poker-DVS H-First [12]	0.975	0 (hard coded)	-

4.3 Reconstruction

In this section, we qualitatively evaluate the quality of our learned features by reconstructing missing data in the event stream input. Specifically, we start by streaming events in the visible layer of the first SCRBM, and after streaming is done, we record the spikes of the visible layer. We also corrupt the stream of data by spatially removing half of the events. The results indicate that the network is not just able to reconstruct complete data samples but is also able to fill in missing information, see Fig. 4d.

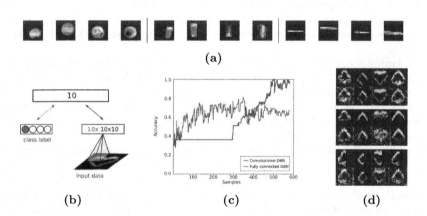

Fig. 4. Experimental evaluation of our SCDBN. (a) Samples of balls, cans and pens from our self-recorded Ball-Can-Pen dataset. Event-streams are aggregated to images for visualization. (b) The SCDBN consists of 16 × 16 visible neurons, 10 feature maps of size 10 × 10 and 10 association neurons. (c) Classification accuracy on the Ball-Can-Pen dataset of our method against a similar network without convolutions, as presented in [9]. (d) Reconstructed event-stream from the first SCRBM in the SCDBN stack. Top: full input, middle: horizontal crop, bottom: vertical crop.

5   Conclusion

In this paper, we introduce the Spiking Convolutional Deep Belief Network (SCDBN), a new method to learn high-level features from event-based data. Relying on event-based contrastive divergence [9], our network is trained with synaptic plasticity directly within the spiking network. We demonstrate that by adding convolutions to the original method, we can improve the performance while reducing the number of parameters to learn (Fig. 4c). Moreover, we show that the performance of our method is comparable to previous event-based classification methods while learning features in an unsupervised fashion. The main bottleneck of our method is the runtime required for training, see Table 1. It could be reduced by using neuromorphic hardware. However, bidirectional synapses, shared weights and global phases are currently technically difficult to implement on such hardware.

Acknowledgments. The research leading to these results has received funding from the European Union Horizon 2020 Programme under grant agreement n.720270 (Human Brain Project SGA1).

References

1. Bengio, Y., Lee, D.H., Bornschein, J., Lin, Z.: Towards Biologically Plausible Deep Learning. arXiv preprint arXiv:1502.0415, p. 18 (2015)
2. Buesing, L., et al.: Neural dynamics as sampling: a model for stochastic computation in recurrent networks of spiking neurons. PLoS Comput. Biol. **7**(11), e1002211 (2011)
3. Desjardins, G., et al.: Empirical evaluation of convolutional RBMs for vision. Technical report 1327, Département d'Informatique et de Recherche Opérationnelle, Université de Montréal (2008)
4. Diehl, P.U., et al.: Fast-classifying, high-accuracy spiking deep networks through weight and threshold balancing. In: International Joint Conference on Neural Networks (IJCNN), vol. 2015 (2015)
5. Griffiths, T.L., Kemp, C., Tenenbaum, J.B.: Bayesian models of cognition. In: Sun, R. (ed.) Cambridge Handbook of Computational Cognitive Modeling. Cambridge University Press, Cambridge (2008)
6. Lee, H., et al.: Convolutional deep belief networks for scalable unsupervised learning of hierarchical representations. In: International Conference on Machine Learning, pp. 609–616 (2009)
7. Lee, T.S., Mumford, D.: Hierarchical Bayesian inference in the visual cortex. J. Opt. Soc. Am. **20**(7), 1434–1448 (2003)
8. Lichtsteiner, P., et al.: A 128 × 128 120 dB 15us latency asynchronous temporal contrast vision sensor. IEEE J. Solid-state Circuits **43**(2), 566–576 (2008)
9. Neftci, E., et al.: Event-driven contrastive divergence for spiking neuromorphic systems. Front. Neurosci. **7**, 1–14 (2014)
10. Norouzi, M., Ranjbar, M., Mori, G.: Stacks of convolutional restricted boltzmann machines for shift-invariant feature learning. In: Conference on Computer Vision and Pattern Recognition (CVPR), pp. 2735–2742. IEEE (2009)

11. Petrovici, M.A.: Form Versus Function: Theory and Models for Neuronal Substrates. Springer, New York (2016)
12. Serrano-Gotarredona, T., et al.: Poker-DVS and MNIST-DVS: Their history, how they were made, and other details. Front. Neurosci. **9**, 1–10 (2015)
13. Vasquez Tieck, J.C., et al.: Towards grasping with spiking neural networks for an anthropomorphic robot hand. In: International Conference on Artificial Neural Networks (ICANN) (2017)
14. Yang, T., Shadlen, M.N.: Probabilistic reasoning by neurons. Nature **447**(7148), 1075–1080 (2007)

Convolutional Neural Network for Pixel-Wise Skyline Detection

Darian Frajberg[✉], Piero Fraternali, and Rocio Nahime Torres

Politecnico di Milano, Piazza Leonardo da Vinci, 32, Milan, Italy
{darian.frajberg,piero.fraternali,rocionahime.torres}@polimi.it

Abstract. Outdoor augmented reality applications are an emerging class of software systems that demand the fast identification of natural objects, such as plant species or mountain peaks, in low power mobile devices. Convolutional Neural Networks (CNN) have exhibited superior performance in a variety of computer vision tasks, but their training is a labor intensive task and their execution requires non negligible memory and CPU resources. This paper presents the results of training a CNN for the fast extraction of mountain skylines, which exhibits a good balance between accuracy (94,45% in best conditions and 86,87% in worst conditions), memory consumption (9,36 MB on average) and runtime execution overhead (273 ms on a Nexus 6 mobile phone), and thus has been exploited for implementing a real-world augmented reality applications for mountain peak recognition running on low to mid-end mobile phones.

1 Introduction

Convolutional Neural Networks (CNNs) are a powerful tool for addressing hard object recognition tasks, and have achieved significant improvements outperforming previous computer vision techniques in many benchmarks. In particular, detection problems such as biomedical images analysis [3] and edges extraction [9] require solutions with high precision at pixel level. An emerging field of application of CNNs is the implementation of *Augmented Reality (AR)* systems, in which the users are offered an interface that enriches the view of real objects with computer-generated information [5]. AR applications are normally implemented on portable, low power devices, such as smart glasses or even mobile phones. Examples are found in tourism (e.g., PeakLens[1]), astronomy (e.g., Star Chart[2]), games (e.g., PokemonGo[3]), etc. The main challenge of developing a computer vision component for an AR application for low power devices is the need of providing high recognition accuracy, real-time performance, with acceptable memory and battery consumption. These competing objectives require adequate training of the CNN, minimization of the model, and reduction of the

---

[1] http://www.peaklens.com.
[2] http://www.sites.google.com/site/starchartuserguide.
[3] http://www.pokemongo.com.

© Springer International Publishing AG 2017
A. Lintas et al. (Eds.): ICANN 2017, Part II, LNCS 10614, pp. 12–20, 2017.
https://doi.org/10.1007/978-3-319-68612-7_2

overall application fingerprint. This paper presents the training and evaluation of a CNN for a pixel-wise mountain skyline detection task and reports the result of its usage in the development of PeakLens [4], an AR mobile app for mountain peaks identification. PeakLens relies on the alignment between a virtual panorama visible from the current user's location, computed from the GPS coordinates, from the compass orientation, and from a Digital Elevation Model (DEM) of the Earth, and the mountain skyline extracted from the camera view. Such alignment must be done precisely and in real-time and thus requires very high accuracy of the extracted skyline and fast execution. For training and evaluating the skyline detection CNN, we executed a crowd-sourcing task and manually annotated 8.940 mountain images, fetched from Flickr and from over 2.000 publicly available touristic web-cams. Images in the data set are complex, diverse, and contain a variety of obstacles occluding the skyline horizon.

The focus of this paper is the description of the CNN model and of its training, and the evaluation of the resulting pixel-level classifier for mountain images taken in uncontrolled conditions. The training data set consists of positive and negative patches automatically sampled from the annotated mountain photo collection. For evaluation, we noted that the CNN accuracy obtained at patch level does not represent well the quality of the output for an entire image; thus, we defined metric functions that assess the quality of the mountain skylines extracted with the CNN at the whole image level, and computed such functions with the help of the manually annotated ground truth skylines. The contributions of the paper are the following:

- We recall the mountain skyline extraction problem, as defined in the relevant literature (e.g., [2]).
- We illustrate a mountain skyline extraction pipeline that exploits a CNN for evaluating the probability of pixels to belong to the skyline, and a post-processing step for extracting the actual skyline from pixel probabilities.
- We define whole image metrics for evaluating the quality of an extracted skyline with respect to the gold standard created with annotations.
- We evaluate the designed pipeline quantitatively, in terms of precision and execution overhead (time and memory). Precision is evaluated on two classes of images: without occlusions and with occlusions.
- We discuss the use of the realized component in a real world mobile app (www.peaklens.com), with very demanding accuracy, speed and memory constraints.

The paper is organized as follows: Sect. 2 briefly surveys the related work on pixel-wise feature and objected detection and on the specific problem of mountain skyline extraction; Sect. 3 explains the proposed CNN models and the method to train it; Sect. 4 presents the evaluation methods and results of the accuracy and performance of the trained skyline extraction component and also discusses a real-world case study where the component is embedded in a mobile app for mountain peak detection; finally, Sect. 5 concludes and gives an outlook on the future work.

2   Related Work

Skyline extraction is a sub-problem of image-to-terrain alignment; early works, such as [1,2], tackled the problem by computing the alignment between the digital elevation model (DEM) and skylines extracted from mountain images. All documented methods work offline and at the server-side.

Heuristic methods. To extract skylines, [2] proposed an automatic approach exploiting an edge-based heuristics, whereas [1] applied sky segmentation techniques based on dynamic programming, which required manual support for challenging pictures. The authors of [1] also released a data set that contains 203 images with ground truth information (including segmentation masks). Feature-based heuristic methods (e.g., based on edge detection) work well on images taken in good conditions, but do not address bad weather and skyline occlusions adequately. In these cases, a cloud, a high voltage cable, or a roof impact negatively the heuristic edge filter, e.g., a cloud edge would be treated as skyline and the mountain slope below would be erroneously regarded as noise.

CNN methods. Skyline extraction problems can also be addressed with CNNs, which have exhibited superior performance in a variety of computer vision tasks, such as object recognition and semantic segmentation. In [8] the authors used the data set of [1] to extract the skyline with a deconvolutional neural network for image segmentation; their approach treats an input image as a foreground-background segmentation problem and does not single out obstacles. Pixel-level CNN methods have been experimented successfully e.g., in biomedical images analysis. In [3] the authors proposed a novel binary pixel-based CNN for the detection of mitosis in breast cancer histology images. The network is trained with patches extracted from the images, classified as mitosis or non-mitosis based on the probability of the center pixel of being close to the centroid of a mitosis. Pixel-wise CNNs are also used for edges extraction problems. In [9] the authors take image patches as input and predict if their central pixels belong to an edge.

Our skyline detection approach is inspired by [3] and works at pixel-level. We consider an image as a map of patches and analyze the local context around each center pixel to predict whether it belongs to the skyline or not. Differently from [3,9] we specialize the CNN for mountain skyline detection; differently from [8], we train the network on a large data set of images (8.940) taken in uncontrolled conditions including samples with many different types of obstacles, and we evaluate the obtained precision quantitatively (94,45% in best conditions and 86,87% in worst conditions). Differently from all the mentioned works, we target the fast execution of the CNN on low power devices, in real time and at the client side, and report the performance of skyline extraction (273 ms per image on a Nexus 6 mobile phone).

3   Skyline Extraction with CNN

We defined the CNN architecture presented in Table 1, which is an adaptation of the well known LeNet model [7]. The main difference is that we do not consider

Table 1. CNN architecture

Layer	Type	Input	Filter	Stride	Pad	Output
Layer 1	Conv	$29 \times 29 \times 3$	$6 \times 6 \times 3 \times 20$	1	0	$24 \times 24 \times 20$
Layer 2	Pool (max)	$24 \times 24 \times 20$	2×2	2	0	$12 \times 12 \times 20$
Layer 3	Conv	$12 \times 12 \times 20$	$5 \times 5 \times 20 \times 50$	1	0	$8 \times 8 \times 50$
Layer 4	Pool (max)	$8 \times 8 \times 50$	2×2	2	0	$4 \times 4 \times 50$
Layer 5	Conv	$4 \times 4 \times 50$	$4 \times 4 \times 50 \times 500$	1	0	$1 \times 1 \times 500$
Layer 6	Relu	$1 \times 1 \times 500$	Max(0,x)	1	0	$1 \times 1 \times 500$
Layer 7	Conv	$1 \times 1 \times 500$	$1 \times 1 \times 500 \times 2$	1	0	$1 \times 1 \times 2$
Layer 8	Softmaxloss	$1 \times 1 \times 2$	-	1	0	$1 \times 1 \times 2$

28×28 gray-scaled inputs, but 29×29 RGB inputs. The output of our architecture considers 2 classes, which represent whether the center pixel of the input image is part of the skyline (1) or not (0). In the sequel, we will consider the probability of a pixel to be part of the skyline.

To create the input data set, we conducted an internal crowdsourcing task and manually annotated the skyline of 8.940 mountain images fetched from Flickr and from over 2.000 publicly available touristic web-cams. Images in the data set are complex, diverse and contain a variety of obstacles occluding the skyline horizon. The data set images were split: 65% for training, 25% for validation and 10% for test. The preparation of the training data set consisted in the extraction of positive and negative patches from the mountain photo collection. To sample patches with the most informative content, we applied to each image a soft Canny filter, computed the edge map, and selected only candidate patches with an edge pixel at their center. Patches are then labeled as positive or negative based on their central pixel: if this matches an annotated pixel, the patch is considered positive; otherwise, it is considered negative. Since non-skyline points are much more numerous than skyline points, we generated an unbalanced data set by randomly extracting 100 positive and 200 negative patches from each image. The CNN model was trained using the Caffe framework [6] on a machine with an NVIDIA GeForce GTX 1080. It took 61 min to complete and the total number of learned parameters of the resulting model is 428.732. At execution time, the fully convolutional network is fed with whole images and returns a spatial map for each image, in which each pixel is assigned a probability of being positive.

Post-processing. Post-processing is executed over the output of the CNN to select at most N pixels per column (PPC). $0 \ldots 1$ values are mapped to the $0 \ldots 255$ range, a small erosion is applied and all pixels with scores lower than a predefined threshold (THR) are removed. We tested also another subsequent extra post-processing step (EPS), in which the CNN output is multiplied by a Canny edge map extracted from the original image (see Tables 2 and 3 for an evaluation).

4   Evaluation

Accuracy. The maximum accuracy achieved by the CNN model over the test data set **at patch level** was 95,05%, obtained with a threshold value for positive probability of 0,4644. However, accuracy measured at patch level does not intuitively represent the quality of the output for an entire image. Therefore, we defined metric functions that assess image level quality by comparing the skyline extracted with the CNN with the one manually annotated in the ground truth. Then we evaluated such functions on the test data set images, which were resized down to 321 pixels of width and corresponding height. For sake of tolerance, the ground truth annotations were slightly dilated to 9 pixels of size. The following image-level metric functions have been used:

Average Skyline Accuracy (ASA) measures the fraction of image columns that contain ground truth skyline pixels and in which at least one of the positive (i.e., above threshold) pixels extracted by the CNN matches one of the ground truth pixels; **Average No Skyline Accuracy (ANSA)** measures the fraction of columns that do not contain any ground truth skyline pixel (due to obstacles) and for which also the CNN output does not contain positive pixels; this metric evaluates false positives in images with an interrupted skyline; **Average Accuracy (AA)** measures the fraction of columns in which the ground truth and the CNN skyline agree, considering agreement when none contain pixels or otherwise at least one of the CNN pixels matches one of the ground truth pixels.

Let $CNN(i, j)$ be a function that returns 1 if the image pixel at coordinates (i,j) belongs to the skyline extracted by the CNN (0 otherwise) and let $GT(i, j)$ be a function that returns 1 if the pixel (i,j) belongs to the ground truth skyline (0 otherwise).

$$ASA = \sum_{j=1}^{cols} I_{GT \wedge CNN}(j) / \sum_{j=1}^{cols} I_{GT}(j) \tag{1}$$

$$ANSA = \sum_{j=1}^{cols} I_{\overline{GT} \wedge \overline{CNN}}(i, j) / (cols - \sum_{j=1}^{cols} I_{GT}(j)) \tag{2}$$

$$AA = \frac{1}{cols} \sum_{j=1}^{cols} I_{agree}(j) \tag{3}$$

where:
$I_{GT}(j) := 1 \; if \; \exists i| \; GT(i, j) = 1; \; 0 \; otherwise$
$I_{GT \wedge CNN}(j) := 1 \; if \; \exists i| \; GT(i, j) = 1 \wedge \; CNN(i, j) = 1; \; 0 \; otherwise$
$I_{\overline{GT} \wedge \overline{CNN}}(j) := 1 \; if \; \forall i| \; GT(i, j) = 0 \wedge \; CNN(i, j) = 0; \; 0 \; otherwise$
$I_{agree}(j) \; := 1 \; if \; I_{GT \wedge CNN}(j) = 1 \vee I_{\overline{GT} \wedge \overline{CNN}}(j) = 1; \; 0 \; otherwise$

Figure 1 shows a mountain image with the ground truth annotation in red (left) and the quality metrics calculated on the output produced by a CNN with a regular post-processing that selects 1 PPC. On the right, pixels in white represent the ground truth annotation, pixels in green represent correctly predicted skyline pixels, while pixels in red represent incorrect ones.

Fig. 1. Evaluation of image with interrupted skyline. Average Skyline Accuracy: 98%. Average No Skyline Accuracy: 73%. Average Accuracy: 94%. (Color figure online)

To evaluate the quality loss due to occlusions that produce non continuous skylines, we performed two evaluation rounds. First, we assessed the 462 images of the test data set (51,68%) with no interruptions. As shown in Table 2 Average Accuracy is 94,45% with 1 PPC (row 1) and 97,04% with 3 PPC (row 6). The threshold was set to 0 to maximize the chances of selecting at least one CNN pixel per column. The loss of accuracy is only due to pixels that the CNN positions at a different row w.r.t. the ground truth. In the second round, we considered the entire test data set of 894 images, in which 8% of all the columns correspond to interrupted skyline. Results are reported in Table 3: the maximum Average Accuracy decreases to 86,87% for 1 PPC (row 7) and 89,36% for 3 PPC (row 12): occlusions that interrupt the skyline impact the accuracy by introducing false positives and false negatives. A threshold of 100 proved the most suitable value to maximize the AA metric. Different post-processing methods were also evaluated, as shown in the other rows of Tables 2 and 3: overall the use of the CNN with EPS achieved the highest result with 1 PPC (Table 2, row 1: 94,45%; and 3 row 7: 86,87%), such values improve when the multiplication between the CNN output and Canny is used, achieving the best results with 3 PPC (Table 2, row 6: 97,04% and Table 3, row 12: 89,36%); the multiplication between the extracted skyline and the edge map obtained with a Gaussian Blur followed by a Canny filter is always outperformed.

Table 2. Evaluation on test data set with only continuous skyline images

V	PPC	THR	EPS	ASA	ANSA	AA
1	1	0	No	94,45%	-	**94,45%**
2	1	0	(Blur + Canny)	92,69%	-	92,69%
3	1	0	Canny	93,73%	-	93,73%
4	3	0	No	95,92%	-	95,92%
5	3	0	(Blur + Canny)	96,72%	-	96,72%
6	3	0	Canny	97,04%	-	**97,04%**

Table 3. Evaluation on complete test data set

V	PPC	THR	EPS	ASA	ANSA	AA
7	1	100	No	92,45%	20,14%	**86,87%**
8	1	100	(Blur + Canny)	90,11%	28,77	85,31%
9	1	100	Canny	91,55%	23,19%	86,21%
10	3	100	No	94,25%	18,83%	88,41%
11	3	100	(Blur + Canny)	93,97%	28,65%	88,83%
12	3	100	Canny	95,07%	22,54%	**89,36%**

Runtime Performance. The execution of the CNN model in desktop PCs has negligible execution time per image. To evaluate the suitability for an AR application on low power mobile devices, where not only a high recognition accuracy is needed, but also a real-time performance, we assessed the execution time per image in smart phones of different categories. To this end, we selected an input image of dimensions 321×241 pixels. While most smart-phones support capturing frames of larger size, after different experimental trials we observed that this dimension has the best balance of accuracy, memory consumption (9,36 MB on average), and execution time, on a broad spectrum of devices. The evaluation was performed by repeating skyline extraction on a test image 1.000 times in each device, taking as result the average execution time. As shown in Table 4, the execution time in low power mobile devices is much higher than in a PC, where skyline extraction can be performed at a frequency of 13 images per second: the best smart-phone of the test could process around 3 images per second, whereas computation took something less than 2 s in the devices with lowest hardware. Processing images at the rates shown in Table 4 is compatible with the usability requirements of a real-time AR application. Image processing is done in background with respect to the user interface; if the camera view movements are not too sudden, as one expects in a mountain peak recognition use case, the skyline extraction and the subsequent DEM alignment step could be done at a frequency lower that the 15 frame per second normally considered viable for video play; the price to pay is some jitter in the camera view, when the skyline extraction and DEM alignment execute and require an update of the peak positions in the camera view. However, this limitation on low power mobile phones did not seem to impact users too much, as discussed next.

Usage experience. The skyline extraction CNN described in the paper is embedded in the PeakLens AR mobile app, which provides real-time mountain peak identification by processing camera frames at the maximum allowed speed and overlaying onto them the icons of the visible mountain peaks. Peaks are fetched by an annotated DEM, queried online, when Internet connectivity is available, or offline on board of the mobile phone, where it is stored in a compressed format. The initial peak positioning is done using only the DEM and the GPS and compass sensors: the virtual panorama in view is estimated and peaks

Table 4. Time required to execute the skyline extraction

Device	Time(ms)
MacBook Pro - 2,9 GHz Intel Core i5 (2 cores) - 16 GB	73
Nexus 6 - 2,65 GHz Qualcomm Snapdragon 805 (4 cores) - 3 GB	273
One Plus A0001 - 2,46 GHz Qualcomm Snapdragon 801 (4 cores) - 3 GB	296
Nexus 5X - 1,82 GHz Qualcomm Snapdragon 808 (6 cores) - 2 GB	437
Moto G4 PLUS - 1,52 GHz Qualcomm Snapdragon 617 (8 cores) - 2 GB	472
Asus Z00D - 1,6 GHz Intel Atom z2560 (2 cores) - 2 GB	1128
Galaxy Nexus - 1,2 GHz TI OMAP 4460 (2 cores) - 1 GB	1775

are projected onto the camera frame based on where they are in the virtual panorama. Obviously, such method is extremely prone to the frequently occurring errors in the DEM, GPS and compass. Here is where the skyline extraction component is exploited, by updating the peak positions based on the registration of the camera view skyline extracted by the CNN and the skyline of the virtual panorama. Thanks to such registration, PeakLens is able to automatically correct substantial errors in the DEM, GPS position and compass, in real-time.

5 Conclusions and Future Work

In this paper we have discussed a CNN model for mountain skyline extraction, trained with a large set of annotated images taken in uncontrolled conditions, and capable of supporting an AR mountain peak recognition app also on low-end mobile phones. Future work will concentrate on the optimization of the CNN model, to make its execution faster on phones with less than 1GB RAM and support usage even without the compass, which requires the very fast alignment of the camera view with a 360° virtual panorama.

References

1. Baatz, G., Saurer, O., Köser, K., Pollefeys, M.: Large scale visual geo-localization of images in mountainous terrain. In: Fitzgibbon, A., Lazebnik, S., Perona, P., Sato, Y., Schmid, C. (eds.) ECCV 2012. LNCS, pp. 517–530. Springer, Heidelberg (2012). doi:10.1007/978-3-642-33709-3_37
2. Baboud, L., Čadík, M., Eisemann, E., Seidel, H.P.: Automatic photo-to-terrain alignment for the annotation of mountain pictures. In: 2011 IEEE Conference on Computer Vision and Pattern Recognition (CVPR), pp. 41–48. IEEE (2011)
3. Cireşan, D.C., Giusti, A., Gambardella, L.M., Schmidhuber, J.: Mitosis detection in breast cancer histology images with deep neural networks. In: Mori, K., Sakuma, I., Sato, Y., Barillot, C., Navab, N. (eds.) MICCAI 2013. LNCS, vol. 8150, pp. 411–418. Springer, Heidelberg (2013). doi:10.1007/978-3-642-40763-5_51

4. Fedorov, R., Frajberg, D., Fraternali, P.: A framework for outdoor mobile augmented reality and its application to mountain peak detection. In: De Paolis, L.T., Mongelli, A. (eds.) AVR 2016. LNCS, vol. 9768, pp. 281–301. Springer, Cham (2016). doi:10. 1007/978-3-319-40621-3_21

5. Jain, P., Manweiler, J., Roy Choudhury, R.: Overlay: practical mobile augmented reality. In: Proceedings of the 13th International Conference on Mobile Systems, Applications, and Services, pp. 331–344. ACM (2015)

6. Jia, Y., Shelhamer, E., Donahue, J., Karayev, S., Long, J., Girshick, R., Guadarrama, S., Darrell, T.: Caffe: convolutional architecture for fast feature embedding. In: Proceedings of 22nd ACM International Conference on Multimedia, pp. 675–678. ACM (2014)

7. LeCun, Y., Boser, B., Denker, J.S., Henderson, D., Howard, R.E., Hubbard, W., Jackel, L.D.: Backpropagation applied to handwritten zip code recognition. Neural Comput. 1(4), 541–551 (1989)

8. Porzi, L., Rota Bulò, S., Ricci, E.: A deeply-supervised deconvolutional network for horizon line detection. In: Proceedings of ACM Multimedia Conference, pp. 137–141. ACM (2016)

9. Wang, R.: Edge detection using convolutional neural network. In: Cheng, L., Liu, Q., Ronzhin, A. (eds.) ISNN 2016. LNCS, vol. 9719, pp. 12–20. Springer, Cham (2016). doi:10.1007/978-3-319-40663-3_2

1D-FALCON: Accelerating Deep Convolutional Neural Network Inference by Co-optimization of Models and Underlying Arithmetic Implementation

Partha Maji[✉] and Robert Mullins

Computer Laboratory, University of Cambridge,
15 JJ Thomson Avenue, Cambridge CB3 0FD, UK
{partha.maji,robert.mullins}@cl.cam.ac.uk

Abstract. Deep convolutional neural networks (CNNs), which are at the heart of many new emerging applications, achieve remarkable performance in audio and visual recognition tasks, at the expense of high computational complexity, limiting their deployability. In modern CNNs it is typical for the convolution layers to consume the vast majority of the compute resources during inference. This has made the acceleration of these layers an important research and industrial goal. In this paper, we examine the effects of co-optimizing the internal structures of the convolutional layers and underlying implementation of fundamental convolution operation. We demonstrate that a combination of these methods can have a big impact on the overall speed-up of a CNN, achieving a tenfold increase over baseline. We also introduce a new class of fast 1-D convolutions for CNNs using the Toom-Cook algorithm. We show that our proposed scheme is mathematically well grounded, robust, does not require any time-consuming retraining, and still achieves speed-ups solely from convolutional layers with no loss in baseline accuracy.

Keywords: Convolutional neural network · Deep learning · Computational optimization · Hardware implementation

1 Introduction

Convolutional neural networks (CNNs) are becoming a mainstream technology for an array of new embedded applications including speech recognition, language translation, image classification and numerous other complex tasks. This breakthrough has been made possible by recent progress in deep learning. But, these deep models typically require millions of parameters and billions of operations to produce human level accuracy [1,8,18]. The memory and compute requirements especially complicate the deployment of deep neural networks on low power embedded platforms as they have a very limited compute and power budget. To avoid running end-to-end inference on embedded systems, the current state-of-the-art solutions enable this type of application by off-loading the

© Springer International Publishing AG 2017
A. Lintas et al. (Eds.): ICANN 2017, Part II, LNCS 10614, pp. 21–29, 2017.
https://doi.org/10.1007/978-3-319-68612-7_3

computation to cloud-based infrastructures where server-grade machines (GPUs and other manycore processors) perform the heavy number crunching. Unfortunately, the cloud assisted approach is limited due to the implications on the privacy, latency, and scalability of mobile applications [18].

In this paper, we propose a robust and easy-to-implement acceleration scheme, named 1-D FALCON (Fast Approximate Low-rank CONvolution), which can be applied on readily available state-of-the-art pre-trained models. Our proposed scheme exploits the inherent redundancy present in the convolution layers in order to reduce the compute complexity of deep networks. Additionally, we decompose each convolution layer into low-rank vectors to exploit row stationary computing [18]. We then apply a modified version of the Toom-Cook algorithm to compute the convolution on 1-D vectors to further reduce the number of multiplications in discrete convolution.

Although many earlier studies have focused on reducing overall memory footprint by compression, only a few have aimed at speeding up convolutional layers. Unlike many previously proposed pruning and regularization techniques, our scheme does not involve any time-consuming iterative retraining cycle. Furthermore, since rank selection and decomposition are only dependent on individual layer's inherent property, each convolution layer can be approximated in parallel. Our approximation scheme is mathematically well grounded, robust and thus easily tunable using numerical formulation and without sacrificing baseline accuracy. To the best of our knowledge, this paper is the first to study a co-optimization scheme that combines both the one-shot low-rank model approximation technique and a fast arithmetic scheme that exploits convolutions by separability.

2   Related Work

Model pruning has been used both to reduce over-fitting and memory footprint. Optimal brain damage [3] and optimal brain surgeon [9] are early examples of pruning which aimed at reducing the number of connections within a network. Recently, Han et al. proposed a pruning scheme for CNNs which aims at reducing the total number of parameters in the entire network [7,8]. However, the authors in this paper mentioned that it is challenging to achieve any significant runtime speed-up of convolutional network with conventional direct implementation. In addition, pruning involves a very long iterative prune and retraining cycle. For example, it took seven days to retrain the pruned five (convolution) layer AlexNet [8], which is not practical for fast time-to-market products.

Liu et al. [14] proposed a Sparse Convolutional Neural Networks (SCNN) model that exploits both inter-channel and intra-channel redundancy to maximize sparsity in a model. This method is very effective for number of parameter reduction in the fully-connected layers. The retraining stage with a modified cost function is very time-consuming.

Denton et al. showed in a recent research that the generalized eigendecomposition based truncation can help to reduce parameters from the fully-connected layers [4]. Although, the authors didn't consider the compute heavy convolutional layers. Jaderberg *et al.* proposed a singular value decomposition based technique for layer-by-layer approximation [10]. Their methodology uses iterative steps where a layer can only be approximated after the previous layer has been compressed. The author used an updated loss function to learn the low-rank filters which is again a time consuming process. The author also reported that simultaneous approximation of all the layers in parallel is not efficient. Mamalet *et al.* design the model to use low-rank filters from scratch and combine them with pooling layer [15]. However, their technique cannot be applied to general network design. Sironi *et al.* showed that learning-based strategies can be used to obtain seperable (rank-1) filters from multiple filters, allowing large speedups with minimal loss in accuracy [17]. We build our methodology on this fundamental idea. Instead of learning separable filters, we use a one-shot approach which can be applied statically.

Gupta *et al.* [5] studied the effect of limited precision data representation in the context of training CNNs. They observed that CNNs can be trained using only 16-bit wide fixed-point number representation with little to no degradation in the classification accuracy. A number of optimization schemes have been proposed recently that recommend use of fewer bits to represent the parameters and datapaths [2,6,7]. Our proposed scheme is orthogonal to these techniques and can be combined with quantization to further reduce the compute complexity and storage requirement.

Cong *et al.* showed that by using Strassen's algorithm computation complexity in convolutional layers can be reduced by up to 47% [1]. Vasilache *et al.* used a FFT based scheme to speed up convolutions, which are not very effective for small filters [19]. Recently, both nVidia's cuDNN and Intel's MKL library added support for Winograd's algorithm to speed up convolutions, which was originally proposed by Lavin *et al.* [12]. Although combining sparse methods and Winograd's convolution holds the potential to achieve significant speed up, pruning Winograd kernels to induce sparsity poses challenges.

3 Methodology

Sze *et al.* in their Eyeriss research project showed that a row stationary (RS) 1-D convolution is optimal for throughput and energy efficiency than traditional tiled 2-D implementation [18]. Our methodology follows the principles of 1-D row-stationary convolution. To achieve this we first approximate each layer to the necessary level to reduce compute complexity and then decompose each convolutional filter bank into two rank-1 filter banks by introducing an intermediate layer in between. If the classification accuracy drops at this stage we fine-tune the model using the training dataset. Then we apply a modified version of the Toom-Cook algorithm, which computes each 1-D convolution for a chosen set of distinct data points, to further reduce the number of strong operations (in this case multiplications). We will show that the combined application of these two schemes results into significant reduction in compute complexity.

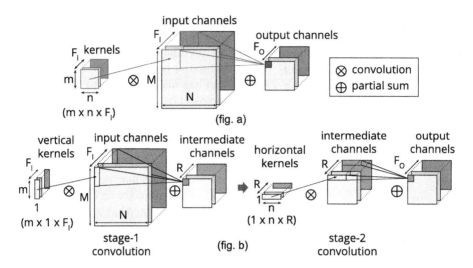

Fig. 1. (a) The original convolution with a $(m \times n)$ kernel. (b) The two-stage approximate convolution using a $(m \times 1)$ column kernel in stage-1 followed by a $(1 \times n)$ row kernel in stage-2. There are R channels in the intermediate virtual layer.

3.1   Layerwise Approximation and Convolution by Separability

In CNNs, multiple layers of convolutional filter (also known as kernel) banks are stacked on top of each other followed by a non-linear activation function. A significant redundancy exists between those spatial filter dimensions and also along cross-channel feature maps. Most of the previous research has focussed on either exploiting approximation along spatial filter dimensions or along one of the feature channel dimension. In our approach, we aim at approximating the redundancy across both the input and output feature maps.

Let us assume, in a convolutional neural network, a 4-dimensional kernel can be represented as $\mathcal{W} \in \mathbb{R}^{F_I \times (m \times n) \times F_O}$, where spatial 2-dimensional kernels are of size (mxn) and F_I, F_O are the input and output channels within a layer, respectively. We can also represent an input feature map as $\mathcal{X} \in \mathbb{R}^{M \times N \times F_I}$ and corresponding kernels as $\mathcal{W}_i \in \mathbb{R}^{m \times n \times F_I}$ for i-th set of weights, where each input feature map is of size (MxN). The original convolution for the i-th set of weights in a given layer now becomes

$$\mathcal{W}_i * \mathcal{X} = \sum_{f=1}^{F_I} \mathcal{W}_i^f * x^f \tag{1}$$

Our goal is to find an approximation of kernel $\mathcal{W}_i$, such that $\mathcal{W}_i = \widetilde{\mathcal{W}}_i + \mathcal{E}$. Using the concept of separable filters [17], let us assume for a small error $\mathcal{E}$, the chosen rank is R. How the rank R is chosen will be explained in the next section. The modified kernel now can be represented by the Eq. (2), where $\mathcal{V} \in \mathbb{R}^{R \times (m \times 1 \times F_I)}$ is the approximate column kernel, and $\mathcal{H} \in \mathbb{R}^{F_O \times (1 \times n \times R)}$ is the approximate row kernel.

$$\mathcal{W}_i * \mathcal{X} \simeq \sum_{r=1}^{R} h_i^r * \mathcal{V}^r = \sum_{r=1}^{R} h_i^r * (v_r * x) = \sum_{r=1}^{R} h_i^r * (\sum_{f=1}^{F_I} v_r^f * x^f) \qquad (2)$$

Figure 1 depicts the idea of re-constructing the convolution layer using the newly constructed column and row low-rank kernels and compares them with the original 2-D direct convolution. We compute the column and row kernels $(\mathcal{V}, \mathcal{H})$ statically using generalized eigenvalue decomposition by minimizing the error $\mathcal{E}$. Since we decide the magnitude of the approximation statically, we avoid long running time from learning based techniques. Additionally, as the approximation is an inherent property of each layer, we can restructure all the convolutional layers in a CNN in parallel, which also saves time. If the accuracy of a model drops at this stage after approximating all the layers, we fine-tune the complete model for once using the training dataset.

3.2   Rank Search and Layer Restructuring Algorithm

The rank R is chosen by the one-shot minimization criterion described before. We apply singular value decomposition on the 2-D tensor $\mathbb{R}^{(F_I m) \times (n F_O)}$, which we obtain from the original 4-D tensor $\mathbb{R}^{F_I \times m \times n \times F_O}$. Unlike other minimization criterion such as Mahalanobis distance metric or data covariance distance metric [4], our simple criterion gives us an exact decomposition. Algorithm 1 describes the main steps of our low-rank approximation and CNN layer restructuring scheme.

Algorithm 1. Rank Approximation and Layer Restructuring Algorithm

---

1 **function LayerwiseReduce** (M, C, W);

    Input   : Target ConvNet model: M, Kernel Dimension: p_i,

                      Compression factor of each layer: $[c_1, c_2, .., c_n]$,

                      Pre-trained weights of individual layer:$[w_1, w_2, .., w_n]$

    Output: Reduced ConvNet Model: M^*,

                      Reduced weights of each layer: $[v_1, v_2, .., v_n], [h_1, h_2, .., h_n]$

2 **for** $i \leftarrow 1$ **to** *Layers* **do**

3   **if** $layerType == Conv$ **then**

4         $targetRank \leftarrow \frac{p_i F_I F_O}{c_i (F_I + F_O)}$;

5         $U \Lambda V^T \leftarrow SVD(w_i)$;

6         $disconnectLayers(w_i)$;

7         $v_i \leftarrow U \sqrt{\Lambda}$;

8         $h_i \leftarrow V \sqrt{\Lambda}$;

9         $addNewLayer(targetRank)$;

10        $M^* \leftarrow reconstructModel(M, v_i, h_i)$;

11   **end**

12 **end**

3.3   The Modified Toom-Cook's Fast 1-D Convolution

Once we have obtained newly constructed multi-stage 1-D convolution layers, we then apply a modified version of the Toom-Cook algorithm to reduce number of multiplication further. In the Toom-Cook method, a linear convolution can be written as product of two polynomials in the real field [20].

$$s(p) = w(p)x(p), \quad where \quad deg[x(p)] = N - 1 \, , \quad deg[w(p)] = L - 1$$

The output polynomial $s(p)$ has degree $L + N - 2$ and has $L + N - 1$ different coefficients. Instead of explicitly multiplying the polynomials $w(p).x(p)$ using the discrete convolution, the Toom-Cook algorithm evaluates the polynomials $w(p)$ and $x(p)$ for a set of data points β_i and then multiplies their values $s(\beta_i) = w(\beta_i)x(\beta_i)$. Afterwards the product polynomials $s(p)$ is constructed using Lagrange interpolation. The algorithm consists of four steps:

1. Choose $L + N - 1$ distinct data points $\beta_0, \beta_1,...,\beta_{L+N-2}$.
2. Evaluate $w(\beta_i)$ and $x(\beta_i)$ for all the data points.
3. Compute $s(\beta_i) = w(\beta_i)x(\beta_i)$.
4. Finally, compute $s(p)$ by Lagrange interpolation as follows

$$s(p) = \sum_{i=0}^{L+N-2} s(\beta_i) \frac{\prod_{j \neq i}(x - \beta_j)}{\prod_{j \neq i}(\beta_i - \beta_j)} \tag{3}$$

Since, $(L+N-1)$ distinct data points are chosen in step 1, total $(L+N-1)$ multiplications are required in step 3. The Toom-Cook algorithm can also be viewed as a method of factoring matrices and can be expressed as the following form ($\odot$ denotes element-wise multiplication)

$$s(p) = S[\{Ww(p)\} \odot \{Xx(p)\}] \tag{4}$$

where W, X and S are the transform matrix for kernels, input, and output respectively. The cost of computing $\{Ww(p)\}$ gets amortized over reuse of the result for many input slices. The matrices X and S consist of small integers $(0, \pm1, \pm2, ..)$, making it possible to realize them by a number of pre- and post-additions. The only dominant cost over here are $(L + N - 1)$ elementwise multiplications.

4   Results and Analysis

In order to evaluate the effectiveness of our scheme we compared it against several popular networks targeting MNIST, CIFAR-10 and ImageNet dataset. In this paper, we demonstrate our result for VGG-16 model, which won the ImageNet challenge in 2014. VGG-16 is a deep architecture and consists of 13 convolutional layers out of a total 16 layers. To make a comparison with wide variety of speedup techniques we chose a direct 2-D convolutional scheme [18], a low-rank scheme based on Tucker decomposition [11], two popular pruning techniques [8,16], a sparsification scheme [13], and Winograd's filtering scheme [12]. We used three main metrics for comparison: *(i)* **MULs:** Total number of strong operations in the convolutional layers, *(ii)* **Speed-up:** Total speed-up achieved compared to baseline 2-D convolution, and *(iii)* **Fine-Tuning Time:** Average fine-tuning time in number of epochs. As can be seen from the Table 1, our FALCON scheme achieves significant speed-up compared to any other scheme and does not require long fine-tuning time. The overall speed-up comes from combined application of both low-rank approximation scheme and fast 1-D convolution technique.

Table 1. A comparison of speed-up of VGG-16 using different schemes

Optimization scheme	#MULs	Speed-up	Fine-tuning time
2-D convolution [18]	15.3G	1.0x	None
Groupwise sparsification [13]	7.6G	2.0x	>10 epochs
Iterative pruning [16]	4.5G	3.4x	60 epochs
Winograd [F($4 \times 4, 3 \times 3$)], [12]	3.8G	4.0x	None
Pruning+Retraining [8]	3.0G	5.0x	20–40 epochs
Tucker decomposition [11]	3.0G	5.0x	5–10 epochs
1-D FALCON [Ours]	1.3G	11.4x	1–2 epochs

Speed-up from Low-rank Approximation: The computational cost of the baseline 2-D direct convolution is $\mathcal{O}(F_I MNmnF_O)$. But, using our 1-D FALCON approximation scheme, the computational cost for vertical-stage and horizontal-stage are $\mathcal{O}(F_I MNmR)$, $\mathcal{O}(RMNnF_O)$, respectively, resulting a total computational cost of $\mathcal{O}((mF_I + nF_O)MNR)$. If we choose R such that $R(mF_I + nF_O) << mn(F_I F_O)$, then computational cost can be reduced. Our evaluation on VGG-16 showed an average speed-up of 3–5x in all layers and a maximum 8–9x speed-up on many individual layers.

Speed-up from Toom-Cook Algorithm: The 1-D Toom-Cook algorithm requires a $(N + L - 1)$ number of multiplications compared to a direct implementation which will require NxL number of multiplications, where N, L are the dimensions of input feature slice and 1-D filter, respectively. In case of VGG-16 model, we chose $N = 4$ and $L = 3$, resulting a 2x savings in each 1-D stage. As our modified VGG-16 model has vertical and horizontal stages, it achieves a total 4x saving in multiplication.

Efficient Use of Memory Bandwidth and Improved Local Reuse: The 1-D convolution by separability in our FALCON scheme also aims to maximize the reuse and accumulation at the local storage level for all types of data including weights, activations and partial sums. In case of padded convolution unnecessary data loads are also avoided due to the fact that halo regions are now needed only either at the vertical or horizontal edges.

5   Conclusions

In this work we demonstrated that co-optimization of internal structure of models and underlying detailed implementation together can help to achieve significant speed-up in convolutional neural network based inference tasks. We have introduced an easy-to-implement and mathematically well grounded scheme to aim at row stationary 1-D convolution, which can be applied on any pre-trained model statically. Unlike many pruning and regularization techniques, our scheme does not require any time consuming fine-tuning. Our evaluation showed that using our 1-D FALCON scheme, a significant speed-up can be achieved in the convolutional layers without sacrificing baseline accuracy.

References

1. Cong, J., Xiao, B.: Minimizing computation in convolutional neural networks. In: Wermter, S., Weber, C., Duch, W., Honkela, T., Koprinkova-Hristova, P., Magg, S., Palm, G., Villa, A.E.P. (eds.) ICANN 2014. LNCS, vol. 8681, pp. 281–290. Springer, Cham (2014). doi:10.1007/978-3-319-11179-7_36
2. Courbariaux, M., Bengio, Y.: Binarynet: training deep neural networks with weights and activations constrained to +1 or −1. CoRR abs/1602.02830 (2016)
3. Cun, Y.L., Denker, J.S., Solla, S.A.: Optimal brain damage. In: Advances in Neural Information Processing Systems, pp. 598–605 (1990)
4. Denton, E., Zaremba, W., Bruna, J., LeCun, Y., Fergus, R.: Exploiting linear structure within convolutional networks for efficient evaluation. In: NIPS (2014)
5. Gupta, S., Agrawal, A., Gopalakrishnan, K., Narayanan, P.: Deep learning with limited numerical precision. CoRR abs/1502.02551 (2015)
6. Gysel, P., Motamedi, M., Ghiasi, S.: Hardware-oriented approximation of convolutional neural networks. CoRR abs/1604.03168 (2016)
7. Han, S., Mao, H., Dally, W.J.: Deep compression: compressing deep neural network with pruning, trained quantization and huffman coding. In: ICLR (2016)
8. Han, S., Pool, J., Tran, J., Dally, W.J.: Learning both weights and connections for efficient neural networks. In: NIPS (2015)
9. Hassibi, B., Stork, D.G.: Second order derivatives for network pruning: optimal brain surgeon. In: NIPS (1993)
10. Jaderberg, M., Vedaldi, A., Zisserman, A.: Speeding up convolutional neural networks with low rank expansions. CoRR abs/1405.3866 (2014)
11. Kim, Y., Park, E., Yoo, S., Choi, T., Yang, L., Shin, D.: Compression of deep convolutional neural networks for fast and low power mobile applications. In: EMDNN (2016)
12. Lavin, A.: Fast algorithms for convolutional neural networks. In: CVPR (2016)
13. Lebedev, V., Lempitsky, V.: Fast convnets using group-wise brain damage. In: CVPR (2016)
14. Liu, B., Wang, M., Foroosh, H., Tappen, M., Pensky, M.: Sparse convolutional neural networks. In: CVPR, June 2015
15. Mamalet, F., Garcia, C.: Simplifying convnets for fast learning. In: Villa, A.E.P., Duch, W., Érdi, P., Masulli, F., Palm, G. (eds.) ICANN 2012. LNCS, vol. 7553, pp. 58–65. Springer, Heidelberg (2012). doi:10.1007/978-3-642-33266-1_8
16. Molchanov, P., Tyree, S., Karras, T., Aila, T., Kautz, J.: Pruning convolutional neural networks for resource efficient transfer learning. In: EMDNN (2016)

17. Rigamonti, R., Sironi, A., Lepetit, V., Fua, P.: Learning separable filters (2013)
18. Sze, V., Chen, Y., Emer, J.S., Suleiman, A., Zhang, Z.: Hardware for machine learning: challenges and opportunities. CoRR abs/1612.07625 (2016)
19. Vasilache, N., Johnson, J., Mathieu, M., Chintala, S., Piantino, S., LeCun, Y.: Fast convolutional nets with fbfft: A GPU performance evaluation. In: ICLR (2015)
20. Wang, Y., Parhi, K.: Explicit cook-toom algorithm for linear convolution. In: ICASSP (2000)

Shortcut Convolutional Neural Networks for Classification of Gender and Texture

Ting Zhang, Yujian Li$^{(\boxtimes)}$, and Zhaoying Liu

College of Computer Science, Beijing University of Technology,
Beijing 100124, China
zhangting08@emails.bjut.edu.cn,
{liyujian,zhaoying.liu}@bjut.edu.cn

Abstract. Convolutional neural networks are global trainable multi-stage architectures that automatically learn translation invariant features from raw input images. However, in tradition they only allow adjacent layers connected, limiting integration of multi-scale information. To further improve their performance in classification, we present a new architecture called shortcut convolutional neural networks. This architecture can concatenate multi-scale feature maps by shortcut connections to form the fully-connected layer that is directly fed to the output layer. We give an investigation of the proposed shortcut convolutional neural networks on gender classification and texture classification. Experimental results show that shortcut convolutional neural networks have better performances than those without shortcut connections, and it is more robust to different settings of pooling schemes, activation functions, initializations, and optimizations.

Keywords: Convolutional neural networks · Multi-scale · Shortcut connections · Gender classification · Texture classification

1 Introduction

Image classification (e.g. of gender and texture) has been a long standing problem in computer vision and machine learning. It is a very challenging task from the viewpoint of classical feature extraction, requiring image features ideally designed to capture important, distinctive and robust information in images [1]. However, deep learning can demonstrate excellent performance, especially using convolutional neural networks (CNNs).

Traditionally, a standard CNN is composed of convolutional layers (CLs), pooling layers (PLs) and fully-connected layers (FCLs). CLs and PLs are exploited to extract features from different scales, with FCLs working as a classifier. For convenience, we refer to a CL or a PL as a CPL. In fact, a CNN may have a number of CPLs, followed by several FCLs. Note that a CL/PL may consist of many convolutional/pooling feature maps. Strictly speaking, a standard CNN has no shortcut connections across layers. Thus, although such a CNN

© Springer International Publishing AG 2017
A. Lintas et al. (Eds.): ICANN 2017, Part II, LNCS 10614, pp. 30–39, 2017.
https://doi.org/10.1007/978-3-319-68612-7_4

can work very well in many applications, it is limited to integrate multi-scale information from an image.

To make use of discriminative information from non-topmost CPLs, we present a new architecture, called shortcut convolutional neural network (S-CNN). An S-CNN can integrate multi-scale features through shortcut connections from a number of CPLs to the FFCL. It is well admitted that human vision is a multi-scale process [2]. Therefore, it would be reasonable to integrate different levels of image features for robust classification.

2   Shortcut CNNs

In this section, we describe a specific architecture of S-CNNs and the learning algorithm in detail.

2.1   Model Description

As displayed in Fig. 1, the S-CNNs alternately stack three convolutional layers and three max-pooling layers, followed by a fully-connected layer to concatenate multi-scale features, and the softmax output layer indicating classes. The input size is $32 \times 32 \times 1$, and the dimension of the output layer is the number of classes.

All convolutional layers can be represented as:

$$\mathbf{h}_{k,j} = f\left(\mathbf{u}_{k,j}\right) = f\left(\sum_i \mathbf{h}_{k-1,j} * \mathbf{W}_{ij}^k + \mathbf{b}_j^k\right), k = 1, 3, 5. \tag{1}$$

Note that $\mathbf{W}_{ij}^k$ is the weight matrix between $\mathbf{h}_{k-1,i}$ and $\mathbf{h}_{k,j}$, and $\mathbf{b}_j^k$ is the bias of $\mathbf{h}_{k,j}$. $\mathbf{h}_{k,j}$ denotes the j-th feature map in the k-th convolutional layer. $*$ stands for convolution and f for activation function. By default, f is chosen as the rectified linear unit (ReLU). As a convolutional feature map, $\mathbf{h}_{k,j}$ can learn

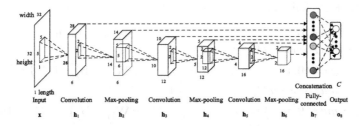

Fig. 1. A specific architecture of S-CNNs. Cuboids stand for the input and all convolutional and max-pooling layers. The length of a cuboid denotes the number of maps, and its width $\times$ height denotes the map dimension. The inside small cuboids and squares denote the 3D convolution kernel sizes and the pooling region sizes of convolutional and max-pooling layers, respectively. The fully-connected layer is the concatenation of some lower-hidden-layer activations. The neuron number of the output layer equals C, i.e. the number of classes.

a spatial level of features from its input. These features are usually different in different maps, and would be more abstract for higher levels.

In each max-pooling layer, we use the stride of 2 for all feature maps. The max-pooling function has the expression:

$$\mathbf{h}_{k,j} = maxpooling\{\mathbf{h}_{k-1,j}\}, k = 2,4,6. \tag{2}$$

where $\mathbf{h}_{k,j}$ denotes the j-th feature map in the k-th pooling layer. Its function is to progressively reduce the spatial size of the representation to reduce the amount of parameters and computation in the network, and hence to also control overfitting.

The fully-connected layer is the concatenation of two or more CPL activations through shortcut connections, forming the entire discriminative vector of multi-scale features [3]. It takes the form:

$$\mathbf{h}_7 = (a_1\mathbf{h}_1, a_2\mathbf{h}_2, a_3\mathbf{h}_3, a_4\mathbf{h}_4, a_5\mathbf{h}_5, \mathbf{h}_6). \tag{3}$$

where $\mathbf{h}_k$ denotes the k-th hidden layer ($1 \leq k \leq 5$). Let $A = a_1a_2a_3a_4a_5$ be a binary string indicating the style of shortcut connections. For example, $A = 11111$ indicates that all the five associated CPLs have shortcut connections to the FCL. $A = 00000$ means no shortcut connections at all, meaning the standard CNN. In practice, the shortcut style is configured manually.

The actual output is a C-way softmax with the form:

$$\mathbf{o}_8 = softmax(\mathbf{u}_8) = softmax(\mathbf{W}^8\mathbf{h}_7 + \mathbf{b}^8). \tag{4}$$

where $\mathbf{W}^8$ and $\mathbf{b}^8$ denote the weight and bias of the output layer, with $softmax_i(x) = \exp(x_i)/\sum_j \exp(x_j)$.

2.2 Learning Algorithm

For the l-th sample, the S-CNNs compute the activations of each hidden and the actual outputs as follows:

$$\begin{cases} \mathbf{h}^l_{1,j} = max(\mathbf{0}, \mathbf{u}^l_{1,j}) = max(\mathbf{0}, x^l * \mathbf{W}^1_j + \mathbf{b}^1_j), 1 \leq j \leq 6 \\ \mathbf{h}^l_{2,j} = maxpooling\{\mathbf{h}^l_{1,j}\}, 1 \leq j \leq 6 \\ \mathbf{h}^l_{3,j} = max(\mathbf{0}, \mathbf{u}^l_{3,j}) = max(\mathbf{0}, \sum_{i=1}^{6}\mathbf{h}^l_{2,i} * \mathbf{W}^3_{ij} + \mathbf{b}^3_j), 1 \leq j \leq 12 \\ \mathbf{h}^l_{4,j} = maxpooling\{\mathbf{h}^l_{3,j}\}, 1 \leq j \leq 12 \\ \mathbf{h}^l_{5,j} = max(\mathbf{0}, \mathbf{u}^l_{5,j}) = max(\mathbf{0}, \sum_{i=1}^{12}\mathbf{h}^l_{4,i} * \mathbf{W}^5_{ij} + \mathbf{b}^5_j), 1 \leq j \leq 16 \\ \mathbf{h}^l_{6,j} = maxpooling\{\mathbf{h}^l_{5,j}\}, 1 \leq j \leq 16 \\ \mathbf{h}^l_7 = (a_1\mathbf{h}^l_1, a_2\mathbf{h}^l_2, a_3\mathbf{h}^l_3, a_4\mathbf{h}^l_4, a_5\mathbf{h}^l_5, \mathbf{h}^l_6) \\ \mathbf{o}^l_8 = softmax(\mathbf{u}^l_8) = softmax(\mathbf{W}^8\mathbf{h}^l_7 + \mathbf{b}^8) \end{cases} \tag{5}$$

Let $\mathbf{y}^l = (y^l_1, y^l_2, ..., y^l_C)^T$ be the desired output and $\mathbf{o}^l_8 = (o^l_{8,1}, o^l_{8,2}, ..., o^l_{8,C})^T$ the actual output. Taking the objective function of cross entropy loss, namely,

$$E(\mathbf{y}^l, \mathbf{o}^l_8) = -\sum_{l=1}^{N}\sum_{c=1}^{C} y^l_c \log(o^l_{8,c}) \tag{6}$$

we can compute the sensitivities $\boldsymbol{\delta}_k^l$ $(1 \le k \le 8)$ of each layer as follows:

$$\begin{cases} \boldsymbol{\delta}_8^l = \mathbf{o}_8^l - \mathbf{y}^l \\ \boldsymbol{\delta}_7^l = \left[(\mathbf{W}^8)^T \boldsymbol{\delta}_8^l \right] \circ softmax'\left(\mathbf{u}_8^l\right) \\ \left(\boldsymbol{\delta}_{1,FC}^l \boldsymbol{\delta}_{2,FC}^l \boldsymbol{\delta}_{3,FC}^l \boldsymbol{\delta}_{4,FC}^l \boldsymbol{\delta}_{5,FC}^l \boldsymbol{\delta}_{6,FC}^l\right) = \boldsymbol{\delta}_7^l \\ \boldsymbol{\delta}_6^l = \boldsymbol{\delta}_{6,FC}^l \\ \boldsymbol{\delta}_{5,j}^l = max'\left(\mathbf{0}, \mathbf{u}_{5,j}^l\right) \circ upmax\left\{\boldsymbol{\delta}_{6,j}^l\right\} + a_5\boldsymbol{\delta}_{5,FC,j}^l, 1 \le j \le 16 \\ \boldsymbol{\delta}_{4,j}^l = \boldsymbol{\delta}_{5,j}^l \, \widehat{*} \, rot180\left(\mathbf{W}_{ij}^5\right) + a_4\boldsymbol{\delta}_{4,FC,j}^l, 1 \le j \le 12 \\ \boldsymbol{\delta}_{3,j}^l = max'\left(\mathbf{0}, \mathbf{u}_{3,j}^l\right) \circ upmax\left\{\boldsymbol{\delta}_{4,j}^l\right\} + a_3\boldsymbol{\delta}_{3,FC,j}^l, 1 \le j \le 12 \\ \boldsymbol{\delta}_{2,j}^l = \boldsymbol{\delta}_{2,j}^l \, \widehat{*} \, rot180\left(\mathbf{W}_{ij}^3\right) + a_2\boldsymbol{\delta}_{3,FC,j}^l, 1 \le j \le 6 \\ \boldsymbol{\delta}_{1,j}^l = max'\left(\mathbf{0}, \mathbf{u}_{1,j}^l\right) \circ upmax\left\{\boldsymbol{\delta}_{2,j}^l\right\} + a_1\boldsymbol{\delta}_{1,FC,j}^l, 1 \le j \le 6 \end{cases} \quad (7)$$

where $\boldsymbol{\delta}_8^l$ stands for the sensitivity (or backpropagation error) of the output layer, $\boldsymbol{\delta}_1^l, \boldsymbol{\delta}_2^l, \cdots, \boldsymbol{\delta}_7^l$ represent the sensitivities of the first, second, ... , and seventh hidden layers, respectively. $\boldsymbol{\delta}_{k,FC}^l$ $(1 \le k \le 6)$ is the part of the seventh hidden layer (i.e. the fully-connected layer) that corresponds to the k-th hidden layer. Additionally, $upmax\{\cdot\}$ is the upsampling function for the max-pooling. Moreover, $\widehat{*}$ denotes the full version of convolutional operation, $rot180(\cdot)$ indicates flipping a matrix horizontally and vertically. $softmax'(\cdot)$ stands for the derivative of the softmax function.

Using (6) and (7), we can compute the derivatives with respect to each parameter (i.e., weights and biases) as follows:

$$\begin{cases} \frac{\partial E}{\partial \mathbf{W}^8} = \sum_{l=1}^{N} \boldsymbol{\delta}_8^l \left(\mathbf{h}_7^l\right)^T, \frac{\partial E}{\partial \mathbf{b}^8} = \sum_{l=1}^{N} \boldsymbol{\delta}_8^l, \\ \frac{\partial E}{\partial \mathbf{W}_{ij}^k} = \sum_{l=1}^{N} \boldsymbol{\delta}_{k,j}^l * \mathbf{h}_{k-1,i}^l, \frac{\partial E}{\partial \mathbf{b}_j^k} = \sum_{l=1}^{N} \boldsymbol{\delta}_{k,j}^l, k = 1, 3, 5 \end{cases} \quad (8)$$

Based on (5)–(8), we design a training algorithm of gradient descent for the S-CNN model illustrated in Fig. 1, as shown in Algorithm 1. Note that $maxepoch$ stands for the number of training iterations.

Algorithm 1. BP for the S-CNN

Input : Training set, network architecture, $maxepoch$;
Output: $\mathbf{W}_j^1, \mathbf{b}_j^1(1 \le j \le 6), \mathbf{W}_{ij}^3, \mathbf{b}_j^3(1 \le j \le 12), \mathbf{W}_{ij}^5, \mathbf{b}_j^5(1 \le j \le 16), \mathbf{W}^8, \mathbf{b}^8$.

1 Randomly initialize the weights and biases of the S-CNN;
2 **for** $epoch=1$ to $maxepoch$ **do**
3   **for** $l=1$ to N **do**
4   Compute the activations and the actual outputs by (5);
5   Compute the sensitivities of each layer by (7);
6   Compute the derivatives by (8);
7   Update all the weights and biases with gradient descent;
8   **end**
9 **end**

---

3   Results

In this section, we evaluate S-CNNs for gender classification on three benchmark datasets: AR, FaceScrub, CelebA, and for texture classification on one benchmark dataset: CUReT. The basic information and the setup of experiments are described in Subsect. 3.1, with gender classification, texture classification, and different settings shown in Subsects. 3.2, 3.3 and 3.4, respectively. In experiments on each dataset, we train all S-CNNs together with the CNN, and then give the results of all different shortcut styles.

3.1   Datasets and Setup

Table 1 gives the information of datasets in experiments. Figure 2 shows examples from the above datasets. It should be noted that for each of the first four datasets, all images for any single subject are either in the training set or the testing set, but not both. In our experiments, all images were resized to 32×32 and converted to gray scale. The CNN and S-CNNs were implemented with the stochastic version of Algorithm 1 by the GPU-accelerated CNN library Caffe. The weights were initialized using the "Xavier" method [4] with a momentum of 0.9, a weight decay of 0.004, a mini-batch size of 100, a fixed learning rate of 0.001 for weights and double for biases. On a desktop PC equipped with E5-2643 V3 CPU, 64 GB memory and a NVIDIA Tesla K40c, the training iterations of the four datasets are 5000, 50000, 60000, and 60000, respectively.

3.2   Gender Classification

We compare performances of the CNN and S-CNNs on the three datasets of AR, FaceScrub and CelebA. The styles (S) and accuracy (Acc) of gender classification

Table 1. Number of training samples and testing samples of the datasets.

Dataset	Training set			Testing set		
	Training number	Female	Male	Testing number	Female	Male
AR	2080	1040	1040	520	260	260
FaceScrub	61817	30169	31648	8151	4081	4070
CelebA	160000	80000	80000	8000	4000	4000
CUReT	11285			915		

(a)   (b)   (c)   (d)

Fig. 2. Images examples from the AR dataset(a), the FaceScrub dataset(b), the CelebA dataset(c) and the CUReT dataset(d).

are reported in Tables 2, 3 and 4, respectively. And the highest accuracies are bolded.

In Table 2, all S-CNNs outperform the CNN (92.30%) in terms of accuracy. With only one shortcut CPL, i.e. the styles of 10000, 01000, 00100, 00010 and 00001, S-CNNs gradually have slightly worse performance. With two shortcut CPLs, the highest accuracy of S-CNNs is 95.23% obtained by the 01010 style, and the lowest is 93.65% by the 00011 style. With three shortcut CPLs, the highest accuracy is 94.83% obtained by the 01101 style, and the lowest is 93.84% by the 11010 style. With four shortcut CPLs, the highest accuracy is 94.64% obtained by the 01111 style, and the lowest is 93.85% by the 11011 style.

In Table 3, all S-CNNs have higher accuracies than the CNN (78.57%). With one shortcut CPL, the highest accuracy of S-CNNs is 80.98% reached by the style of 00100, and the lowest is 79.98% by 10000. With two shortcut CPLs, the highest accuracy is 82.14% reached by 01001, and the lowest is 80.01% by 11000. With three shortcut CPLs, the highest accuracy is 81.37% reached by 11010, and the lowest is 80.52% by 10011 and 00111. With four shortcut CPLs, the highest accuracy is 81.58% reached by 10111, and the lowest is 79.79% by 11011.

Table 2. Test accuracies (%) of the CNN and S-CNNs on the AR dataset.

S	Acc	S	Acc	S	Acc	S	Acc
00000	92.30	10010	93.85	11100	94.05	01011	94.45
10000	94.26	10001	93.84	11010	93.84	00111	94.24
01000	94.25	01100	94.46	11001	94.06	11110	94.62
00100	94.21	01010	**95.23**	10110	93.85	11101	94.42
00010	93.70	01001	95.22	10101	94.06	11011	93.85
00001	93.47	00110	94.44	10011	94.05	10111	94.61
11000	93.68	00101	93.86	01110	94.83	01111	94.64
10100	93.86	00011	93.65	01101	94.42	11111	94.44

Table 3. Test accuracies (%) of the CNN and S-CNNs on the FaceScrub dataset.

S	Acc	S	Acc	S	Acc	S	Acc
00000	78.57	10010	80.04	11100	80.55	01011	80.67
10000	79.98	10001	80.53	11010	81.37	00111	80.52
01000	80.68	01100	80.96	11001	80.79	11110	80.72
00100	80.98	01010	81.10	10110	81.07	11101	80.56
00010	80.60	01001	**82.14**	10101	80.57	11011	79.79
00001	80.97	00110	80.85	10011	80.52	10111	81.58
11000	80.01	00101	80.99	01110	81.21	01111	80.80
10100	80.37	00011	80.93	01101	80.74	11111	80.59

Table 4. Test accuracies (%) of the CNN and S-CNNs on the CelebA dataset.

S	Acc	S	Acc	S	Acc	S	Acc
00000	84.21	10010	86.62	11100	86.73	01011	86.39
10000	86.30	10001	86.20	11010	**87.19**	00111	86.19
01000	85.95	01100	86.62	11001	86.15	11110	86.73
00100	85.92	01010	86.57	10110	87.06	11101	86.67
00010	85.81	01001	86.29	10101	86.74	11011	86.64
00001	85.72	00110	86.26	10011	86.63	10111	86.62
11000	86.18	00101	86.17	01110	86.54	01111	86.75
10100	86.89	00011	86.54	01101	86.40	11111	87.00

In Table 4, all S-CNNs have accuracies exceeding the CNN (84.21%). With one shortcut CPL, S-CNNs perform slightly worse gradually for the styles of 10000, 01000, 00100, 00010 and 00001. With two shortcut CPLs, the highest accuracy of S-CNNs is 86.89% attained by 10100, and the lowest is 86.17% by 00101. With three shortcut CPLs, the highest accuracy is 87.19% attained by 11010, and the lowest is 86.15% by 11001. With four shortcut CPLs, the highest accuracy is 86.75% attained by 01111, and the lowest is 86.62% by 10111.

Overall, the S-CNNs get the highest accuracies of 95.23% on AR, 82.14% on FaceScrub, and 87.19% on CelebA. Compared to the CNN, these accuracies gain a relative increase of 3.17%, 4.54%, and 3.54%, respectively. This is probably because the S-CNNs can integrate multi-scale features from many CPLs, leading to a more suitable model.

3.3 Texture Classification

We also compare performance of the CNN and S-CNNs on the CUReT dataset for texture classification. The results are reported in Table 5, where all S-CNNs

Table 5. Test accuracies (%) of the CNN and S-CNNs on the CUReT dataset.

S	Acc	S	Acc	S	Acc	S	Acc
00000	66.17	10010	69.95	11100	73.42	01011	77.35
10000	66.97	10001	72.44	11010	73.58	00111	77.24
01000	71.70	01100	76.86	11001	70.39	11110	74.00
00100	73.42	01010	74.38	10110	71.87	11101	75.81
00010	74.91	01001	70.24	10101	74.69	11011	75.14
00001	75.12	00110	75.97	10011	75.49	10111	75.38
11000	64.87	00101	77.34	01110	76.13	01111	73.00
10100	72.13	00011	78.86	01101	**79.00**	11111	74.72

have higher accuracies than the CNN (66.17%). And the highest accuracy is bolded. For 1–4 shortcut CPLs, the highest accuracies of S-CNNs are 75.12%, 78.86%, 79.00% and 75.81% with the lowest of 66.97%, 64.87%, 70.39% and 73.00%, respectively. The highest ones are achieved by the styles of 00001, 00011, 01101 and 11101, and the lowest by 10000, 11000, 10110 and 01111.

Overall, on CUReT the highest accuracy of S-CNNs is 79.00%, relatively increased by 19.39% in comparison with the CNN. This means that the S-CNNs could be more suitable than the CNN for text classification by integration of multi-scale features. However, in general the best style is not 11111, with which the S-CNN gets 74.72%.

3.4 Different Settings

We further compare the CNN and S-CNNs with different settings of pooling schemes, activation functions, initializations, and optimizations on the AR dataset. The results are reported in Tables 6, 7, 8 and 9, with the best accuracies bolded.

Table 6. Test accuracies (%) of the CNN and S-CNNs with average pooling on the AR dataset.

S	Acc	S	Acc	S	Acc	S	Acc
00000	88.50	10010	93.66	11100	93.27	01011	93.68
10000	93.66	10001	93.67	11010	93.44	00111	94.45
01000	93.48	01100	93.13	11001	93.48	11110	93.86
00100	92.90	01010	94.42	10110	93.67	11101	93.85
00010	92.88	01001	94.45	10101	93.67	11011	92.73
00001	92.12	00110	94.46	10011	94.45	10111	93.28
11000	93.08	00101	93.48	01110	**94.85**	01111	94.24
10100	93.27	00011	92.13	01101	93.31	11111	94.05

Table 7. Test accuracies (%) of the CNN and S-CNNs with sigmoid function on the AR dataset.

S	Acc	S	Acc	S	Acc	S	Acc
00000	67.67	10010	93.65	11100	94.45	01011	91.34
10000	93.68	10001	93.64	11010	94.41	00111	85.05
01000	93.00	01100	94.06	11001	94.22	11110	**94.85**
00100	88.10	01010	94.00	10110	93.67	11101	94.84
00010	67.93	01001	92.00	10101	93.70	11011	94.27
00001	67.67	00110	85.60	10011	93.70	10111	94.25
11000	94.26	00101	90.23	01110	94.00	01111	90.29
10100	93.70	00011	69.29	01101	91.78	11111	94.06

Table 8. Test accuracies (%) of the CNN and S-CNNs with Mara initialization on the AR dataset.

S	Acc	S	Acc	S	Acc	S	Acc
00000	91.49	10010	94.35	11100	94.25	01011	93.32
10000	93.47	10001	94.24	11010	94.21	00111	93.49
01000	94.04	01100	94.24	11001	93.86	11110	94.06
00100	92.53	01010	94.24	10110	93.73	11101	94.05
00010	91.97	01001	92.70	10101	93.66	11011	93.86
00001	91.90	00110	92.52	10011	93.56	10111	92.90
11000	93.67	00101	93.69	01110	94.02	01111	92.13
10100	**94.62**	00011	93.49	01101	92.91	11111	93.85

Table 9. Test accuracies (%) of the CNN and S-CNNs with Adam optimization on the AR dataset.

S	Acc	S	Acc	S	Acc	S	Acc
00000	91.35	10010	94.23	11100	94.04	01011	**94.84**
10000	93.37	10001	93.66	11010	93.65	00111	92.72
01000	93.88	01100	93.47	11001	93.09	11110	94.80
00100	93.47	01010	93.09	10110	93.09	11101	94.43
00010	93.45	01001	92.34	10101	93.03	11011	94.04
00001	93.27	00110	94.06	10011	92.89	10111	92.70
11000	93.85	00101	93.86	01110	94.07	01111	92.33
10100	94.23	00011	91.53	01101	93.86	11111	92.52

Table 6 shows the performance of the CNN and S-CNNs with average pooling instead of max-pooling. Compared to 92.30% in Table 2, the CNN has a relative reduction of 4.12% in accuracy, whereas to 95.23%, the highest accuracy of S-CNNs is 94.85%, relatively reduced by 0.40%.

In Table 7, we describe their performance with ReLU replaced by sigmoid. With a relative reduction of 26.68%, the accuracy of the CNN decreases from 92.30% to 67.67%, whereas the highest accuracy of S-CNNs drops from 95.23% to 94.85%, relatively reduced by 0.40%.

In Table 8, we depict their performance with a different initialization of Msra [5] from Xavier. It can be seen that the CNN has a relative 0.88% reduction, from 92.30% to 91.49%. However, the S-CNN has a relative 0.64% reduction in terms of the highest accuracy, from 95.23% to 94.62%.

In Table 9, we delineate their performance with the Adam [6] optimization. We clearly get that, the CNN achieves the 91.35% accuracy, and the S-CNNs obtain the best performance of 94.84%. They respectively have a relative reduction of 1.03% and 0.41% in comparison with 92.30% and 95.23%.

Overall, on the AR dataset the S-CNNs have a smaller accuracy reduction than the CNN with different settings, especially of the sigmoid function, indicating that our S-CNN has a more stable performance than the standard CNN.

4 Conclusion

We have presented a novel architecture of shortcut convolutional neural networks to improve the performance of standard CNNs. Moreover, we compared performance of the standard CNN and S-CNNs on gender and texture classification. Additionally, we evaluated their performance with different settings. Experimental results show that S-CNNs can achieve higher accuracies than the standard CNN by concatenating multi-scale features from many CPLs. Meanwhile, the performance of S-CNNs are more stable in different choices of pooling schemes, activation functions, initializations, and optimizations. Although the best shortcut style is generally data-dependent, it is helpful to improve CNNs in accuracy. As future work, we would focus study on more general S-CNNs and related shortcut methods in theory and practice.

Acknowledgments. This work was supported in part by the National Natural Science Foundation of China under grant 61175004,China Postdoctoral Science Foundation funded project(2015M580952), and Beijing Postdoctoral Research Foundation (2016ZZ-24).

References

1. Lowe, D.G.: Distinctive image features from scale-invariant keypoints. Comp. Visi. **60**(2), 91–110 (2004)
2. Donoho, D.L., Huo, X.: Beamlets and multiscale image analysis. In: Barth, T.J., Chan, T., Haimes, R. (eds.) Multiscale and Multiresolution Methods, vol. 20, pp. 149–196. Springer, Heidelberg (2001)
3. Sermanet P., Y. Lecun Y.: Traffic sign recognition wit multi-scale convolutional networks. In: IEEE International Joint Conference on Neural Networks, pp. 2809–2813 (2011)
4. Glorot, X., Bengio, Y.: Understanding the difficulity of training deep feedforward neural networks. J. Mach. Learn. Res. **9**, 249–256 (2010)
5. He, K., Zhang, X., Ren, S., Sun, J.: Delving deep into rectifiers: surpassing human-level performance on ImageNet classification. In: IEEE Internatioal Conference on Computer Vision, pp. 1026–1034 (2015)
6. Kingma, D.F., Ba, J.L.: Adam: a method for stochastic optimization. In: 3rd IEEE International Conference on Learning Representation (2015)

Word Embedding Dropout and Variable-Length Convolution Window in Convolutional Neural Network for Sentiment Classification

Shangdi Sun and Xiaodong Gu$^{(\boxtimes)}$

Department of Electronic Engineering, Fudan University, Shanghai, China
`xdgu@fudan.edu.cn`

Abstract. Recently the research on sentiment analysis has been attracting growing attention because of the popularity of opinion-rich resources, such as internet movie databases and e-commerce websites. Convolutional neural network(CNN) has been widely used in sentiment analysis to classify the polarity of reviews. For deep convolutional neural networks, dropout is known to work well in the fully-connected layer. In this paper, we use dropout technique in the word embedding layer, and proof it is equivalent to randomly picking activation based on a multinomial distribution at training time. Empirical results also support this and show that using dropout in the word embedding layer can reduce overfitting. Meanwhile, we investigate the effect of convolution window size on the classification results, and use variable-length convolution window in proposed method. Experimental results show that our method obtains a state-of-the-art performance on ASR. Compared with other similar architectures, the accuracies of our method in this paper are also competitive on IMDB and Subj.

Keywords: Sentiment classification · Convolutional neural network · Word embedding dropout · Variable-length convolution window

1 Introduction

Nowadays, people have been accustomed to buying goods on the online shopping platform, and booking movie tickets on the movie information website. With the increase in the number of users, as well as the emergence of a variety of social media, the number of reviews is extremely large and the source is becoming more and more widely. However, the huge number reviews with diverse forms resulting in the inconvenience for the potential consumers to read, the users will neither spend a lot of time to read these redundant comments nor find useful information. It is very important to dig out the information that users are interested in and can really help. Sentiment Analysis(SA), also called Opinion Mining(OM), is the cardinal technology in this field. It analyzes the product reviews, social trends and other text data, in order to find out the user's views, emotions, attitudes, opinions on any object. Sentiment analysis is a cross field of

© Springer International Publishing AG 2017
A. Lintas et al. (Eds.): ICANN 2017, Part II, LNCS 10614, pp. 40–48, 2017.
https://doi.org/10.1007/978-3-319-68612-7_5

data mining and statistical machine learning, and now it is a hot topic in deep learning and artificial intelligence. It can be divided into three levels: document level, sentence level, entity and aspect level. In this paper, we focus on the classification of document level and sentence level. The research object of this paper is the movie reviews and commodity reviews, which will be divided into positive/negative or subjective/objective.

Convolutional neural network (CNN) is currently achieving a brilliant success in computer vision [1] and computer speech. Motivated by the terrific discriminative capability of deep convolutional features, CNN also is used in many traditional Natural Language Processing(NLP) tasks [2] and other NLP areas such as information retrieval [3]. In comparison with one-hot representation, words are encoded as low-dimensional vector which called distributed representation by CNN.

Convolutional neural network has got some competitive results in sentiment classification, but compared with the traditional method, the accuracy has no clear superiority. One of the important reasons is over-fitting. Because of the particularity of text data, we use dropout technique in the embedding layer which is an unique layer in the text categorization. That means that some terms are discarded randomly and their corresponding weights in the word embedding layer will not be updated in the training period. The experimental results show that dropout can prevent over-fitting in word embedding layer just as it does in the fully-connected layer. In addition, we explore the effect of convolution window size on the classification accuracy. In general, most of the papers chose 3 as their window size, which is an empirical value, especially for English text, the window size can get good results. Under the premise of not changing the total number of filter, we employ a combination of different lengths of window and verify that the association of multiple window sizes can improve the classification accuracy. In experiment, word embedding dropout and variable-length convolution window are used simultaneously, we obtain some competitive results on IMDB, Subj. and ASR.

2   Word Embedding Layer Dropout

Convolutional neural network have far been known to produce remarkable performance on MNIST [4]. But like other types of neural networks, CNN was not the focus of the machine learning academia in the 1990 s and 2000 s. SVM was the most popular choice because it could achieve a pretty good outcome in most of the tasks. With the revival of deep learning [5–7], convolutional neural networks and other deep models regained attention in the field of machine learning and artificial intelligence. As with other depth networks, improper training of deep convolutional neural networks can create many problems. The computation time and over-fitting are two main issues. In recent years, GPUs help a lot by speeding up computation significantly to solve the former problem. Over-fitting has been a obstacle which restricts the convolutional neural network to get better results.

2.1   Regularization and Dropout

Thanks to the local-connectivity and shared-filter architecture in convolutional layers, CNN have much fewer connections and need training fewer parameters compared to regular feed-forward networks with similarly-sized layers. At the same time, pool operation makes the network select the maximum response. It provides a form of translation invariance and thus benefits generalization. So compared with the traditional neural network, convolutional neural network is far less prone to over-fitting problem. However, when the number of layers of the convolution network is large enough or the training sample is not enough, the over-fitting phenomenon still occurs.

In general, there are two traditional ways to resist over-fitting: (1) Reduce the features and retain the most important features. (2) Penalty the weights of unimportant features. For the first kind of method, it usually selects the features using feature engineering. The typical method is Principal Component Analysis(PCA), it extracts the main factors from multiple features and can get the most important variables. In fact, in CNN structure, the multiple convolution kernels are responsible for getting enough features. The pooling operation selects the strongest responses and most important features. For idea (2), in deep learning or other tasks with huge features, it is really difficult to select major features, so that we can not according to the thought of (1) to reduce the feature, so we can only start from another perspective: give smaller weights to the important features. This is the regularization. A simple and effective regularization method is to impose a L2 regularization to penalty the weights to constrain the solution space.

In addition, early stopping which will terminate the training when the loss function of the validation set does not fall, to prevent the phenomenon of over-fitting. Bayesian fitting smooths the prediction using the posterior probability distribution [8]. Weight elimination prunes redundant weights in the network [9]. Data augmentation makes additional diversification to the original data to increase the training samples. In practical applications, employing these techniques to train a larger neural network can get better results than using any regularization technique to train a small network.

Dropout is a radically different technique for regularization, which is widely used in deep learning. The idea is not the same as the above methods, it does not modify the loss function to limit the weight, nor does it change the weight itself. Instead, it modifies the network directly, the procedure is like averaging the effects of a very large number of different networks. Dropout is similar to the bagging proposed in 1996 [10]. In the case of dropout training, some neurons in the network are deleted randomly (and temporarily), so there are many possibly trained models, and these models share the same parameters, but the number of trained models is uncertain. Actually, the number of explicitly trained models is not larger than $N \times E$, where N is the number of training examples, and E is the training epochs. And the number of possibly trained models is 2^n, where n is the number of neural units in a layer which will adopt dropout.

Dropout was first used in the full-connected layer [11]. Then, dropout in the convolutional layer [12] and the pooling layer [13] can also improve the generalization ability.

2.2 Dropout Training in Word Embedding Layer

The role of the word embedding layer is to convert One-hot representation to distributed representation. Let $l \in R$ be the sentence length, $|V| \in R$ be the vocabulary size and $W \in R^{k \times |V|}$ be the embedding matrix of k-dimensional word vectors. The i-th word in a sentence is transformed into a k-dimensional vector w_i by matrix-vector product:

$$w_i = W \times x_i. \tag{1}$$

Here x_i is the one-hot representation for the i-th word.

For every mini-batch, we generate a column vector M and the dimension is the same with x_i which is equal to $|V|$. The m_i of each dimension in the vector are subject to the Bernoulli distribution, that is, the probability of 0 is P, the probability of 1 is $1 - P$:

$$m_i \sim B(1, 1 - P). \tag{2}$$

Thus, the column vector M is a vector of $|V|$ dimensions, and the value of each dimension is set to 0 by probability P. The vector M is applied to Eq. (1):

$$w_i = W \times (x_i \circ M). \tag{3}$$

Here $\circ$ is the Hadamard product, that means two vectors of the same length are multiplied by the corresponding positions.

After such an operation, "1" in the x_i may be set to "0". The word x_i will be removed, which is equivalent to cutting off the connection with the corresponding weight, and the word vector formed by these weights will not be expressed. For this mini-batch, the word vector corresponding to these "missing term" will not be updated. In the test phase, all the word vector weights are preserved, so we subtract the weight of the word embedding layer by the retain probability $1 - P$ during the test phase.

3 Variable-Length Convolution Window

The related parameters of the convolutional kernel (or filter) are mainly initialization, the number and the size of kernel. The initialization is generally taken to random initialization, because if the initialization by adding too much manual design, that the process of extracting features is more like "feature engineering" approach, deviated from the essence of deep learning. Therefore, the adjustment of the parameters of the kernel is mainly concentrated in the number and the size. Since the dimension of the word vector is fixed, the convolution window length becomes the only factor in determining the size of the kernel, that is, how many consecutive words are convoluted.

We think that a single length of the window is too simple. Some common phrases which express strong emotional may be two words or four words or more, so take a combination of different window lengths is very necessary. Figure 1 is our multi-length convolution window model.

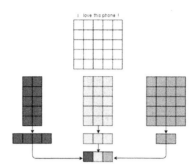

Fig. 1. The window lengths are 2, 3, 4 with one feature map each. The window length of the red one is 2. Since the length of the sentence is 5 and the stride is 1, the red kernel will generate 4 different convolutional value. The yellow and blue kernels do the same procedure. Then, max pooling takes the maximum value generated by each kernel and the features of "I love this phone!" are obtained. (Color figure online)

4   Experiments

We conduct sentiment classification experiments on three datasets. Detailed statistics are shown in Table 1.

Table 1. Dataset statistics

Dataset	(N_+, N_-)	$|V|$	l	CV
IMDB	(25k,25k)	392K	231	N
Subj	(5000,5000)	24K	23	10
ASR	(1731,830)	6K	17	10

The first one is IMDB, a large movie review dataset with 50k length reviews [14]. Subj. is our second dataset, the subjectivity dataset with subjective reviews and objective plot summaries [15]. The third dataset called ASR (Amazon Smartphone reviews) which introduced in [16]. (N_+, N_-): number of positive and negative examples. $|V|$: the vocabulary size. l: average number of words per example. CV: number of cross-validation splits, or N for train/test split.

Our network has a convolutional layer, a max-pooling layer and a fully-connected layer with 200 hidden neurons. We use rectified linear units as activation functions for convolutional layer and hidden layer, and sigmoid function for output layer. The weights in all layers are initialized from a zero-mean Gaussian distribution with 0.1 as standard deviation and the constant 0 as the neuron biases. The dropout rate in hidden layer is 0.5 which is a typical value [11]. The settings of hyper-parameters on the network are shown in Table 2.

Table 2. Network parameters

Hyper-parameters	Value
Word embedding dimension	50
Convolution window size	3
Number of convolution kernels	120
Mini-batch	50

4.1 Results of Word Embedding Dropout

Cross-entropy loss is used as loss function. Figure 2 shows the value of loss function on training set and test set.

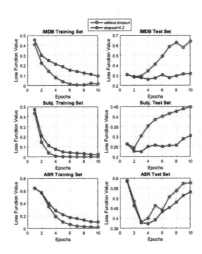

Fig. 2. The results of word embedding dropout on three datasets.

The dropout rate of word embedding layer is $0.2(P = 0.2)$, other value like 0.3 and 0.5 also could weaken over-fitting, but we achieved the most obvious effect on three datasets under the value of 0.2. We can see that the loss function on the training set drops rapidly and approaches 0 without dropout. The training set does not fit perfectly for every sample after adding the word embedding dropout. However, in the testing phase, with the increase in the number of epoch, the loss function value of the test set without dropout increases rapidly and the over-fitting phenomenon occurs. The blue curve which has dropout always maintain at a small loss value on the test set. For ASR, the over-fitting is more serious probably because the dataset is too small. But even so, the word embedding dropout weakened the over-fitting to a certain extent.

4.2   Combination of Different Window Lengths

In this experiment, we keep the total number of convolution kernels at 120. We use word embedding dropout and other parameters are same as last experiment. We change the length of the convolution window to make a different combination. The specific combinations are shown in Table 3.

Table 3. Classification accuracy of convolution window combinations with different lengths

Combination methods	IMDB	Subj.	ASR
3 with 120 feature maps	89.03	91.80	83.05
3,4 with 60 feature maps each	89.32	91.90	83.27
2,3 with 60 feature maps each	89.11	92.10	84.44
2,3,4 with 40 feature maps each	**89.76**	**92.40**	**85.60**
Baseline(BoWSVM)	89.39	91.95	83.05

The experimental results prove that the combination of multi-length convolution windows is better than windows with length of 3. Although the optimal combination scheme of different datasets is different, the combination of variable-length convolution window can really achieve higher classification accuracy. The results under the combination of 2,3,4 with 40 feature maps each are better than the baseline (BoWSVM) [15]. The 85.60% is currently the best classification results on ASR. The accuracy compared with other similar architectures are also competitive on IMDB and Subj.

5   Conclusions

In this paper, we propose to add dropout to the word embedding layer in order to reduce the over-fitting of standard CNN. Every term will be discarded by probability in training time, and the word vector weights are not updated. In this way, the effect of a single term on the positive and negative attributes of the sample is reduced. It encourages our network to learn a useful feature without relying on specific term. Experiments show that the dropout of the word embedding layer can effectively prevent over-fitting. In addition, we change the original fixed length of the window to a combination of variable-length convolution window and achieve the best or near optimal sentiment classification accuracy in three datasets. The result under the combination of 2,3,4 with 40 feature maps each obtains the state-of-the-art sentiment classification accuracy on ASR. So the convolution window size can have a large effect on performance. Each dataset has its own optimal combination and should be tuned.

Acknowledgments. This work was supported in part by National Natural Science Foundation of China under grant 61371148.

References

1. Szegedy, C., Liu, W., Jia, Y., Sermanet, P., Reed, S., Anguelov, D., Erhan, D., Vanhoucke, V., Rabinovich, A.: Going deeper with convolutions. In: IEEE Conference on Computer Vision and Pattern Recognition, pp. 1–9. IEEE Computer Society, Boston (2015)
2. Collobert, R., Weston, J., Bottou, L., Karlen, M., Kavukcuoglu, K., Kuksa, P.: Natural language processing (almost) from scratch. J. Mach. Learn. Res. **12**, 2493–2537 (2011)
3. Shen, Y., He, X., Gao, J., Deng, L., Mesnil, G.: A latent semantic model with convolutional-pooling structure for information retrieval. In: 23rd ACM International Conference on Conference on Information and Knowledge Management, pp. 101–110. ACM, Shanghai (2014)
4. LeCun, Y., Bottou, L., Bengio, Y., Haffner, P.: Gradient-based learning applied to document recognition. Proc. IEEE **86**(11), 2278–2324 (1998)
5. Bengio, Y., Courville, A., Vincent, P.: Representation learning: a review and new perspectives. IEEE Trans. Pattern Anal. Mach. Intell. **35**(8), 1798–1828 (2013)
6. Hinton, G.E., Salakhutdinov, R.R.: Reducing the dimensionality of data with neural networks. Science **313**(5786), 504–507 (2006)
7. LeCun, Y., Bengio, Y., Hinton, G.E.: Deep learning. Nature **521**(7553), 436–444 (2015)
8. Mackay, D.J.: Probable networks and plausible predictions: a review of practical Bayesian methods for supervised neural networks. Netw. Comput. Neural Syst. **6**(3), 469–505 (1995)
9. Ledoux, M., Talagrand, M.: Probability in Banach Spaces: Isoperimetry and Processes. Springer Science & Business Media, New York (2013)
10. Breiman, L.: Bagging predictors. Mach. Learn. **24**(2), 123–140 (1996)
11. Hinton, G.E., Srivastave, N., Krizhevsky, A., Sutskever, I., Salakhutdinov, R.R.: Improving neural networks by preventing co-adaption of feature detectors. arXiv preprint arXiv:1207.0580 (2012)
12. Srivastava, N., Hinton, G.E., Krizhevsky, A., Sutskever, I., Salakhutdinov, R.: Dropout: a simple way to prevent neural networks from overfitting. J. Mach. Learn. Res. **15**(1), 1929–1958 (2014)
13. Wu, H., Gu, X.: Towards dropout training for convolutional neural networks. Neural Netw. **71**, 1–10 (2015)
14. Maas, A.L., Daly, R.E., Pham, P.T., Huang, D., Ng, A., Potts, C.: Learning word vectors for sentiment analysis. In: 49th Annual Meeting of the Association for Computational Linguistics: Human Language Technologies, vol. 1, pp. 142–150. ACL, Portland (2011) Portland (2011)

15. Pang, B., Lee, L.: A sentimental education: sentiment analysis using subjectivity summarization based on minimum cuts. In: 42nd Annual Meeting of the Association for Computational Linguistics, pp. 271–278. ACL, Barcelona (2004)
16. Sun, S., Gu, X.: Sentiment analysis using extreme learning machine with linear kernel. In: 25th International Conference on Artificial Neural Networks, pp. 547–548. Springer, Barcelona (2016)

Reducing Overfitting in Deep Convolutional Neural Networks Using Redundancy Regularizer

Bingzhe Wu[1,2(✉)], Zhichao Liu[1], Zhihang Yuan[1,2], Guangyu Sun[1], and Charles Wu[2]

[1] CECA, Peking University, Beijing 100871, China
wubingzhe@pku.edu.cn
[2] Otureo Technologies (Beijing) Co., Ltd., Beijing 100080, China

Abstract. Recently, deep convolutional neural networks (CNNs) have achieved excellent performance in many modern applications. These high performance models normally accompany with deep architectures and a huge number of convolutional kernels. These deep architectures may cause overfitting, especially when applied to small training datasets. We observe a potential reason that there exists (linear) redundancy among these kernels. To mitigate this problem, we propose a novel regularizer to reduce kernel redundancy in a deep CNN model and prevent overfitting. We apply the proposed regularizer on various datasets and network architectures and compare to the traditional L2 regularizer. We also compare our method with some widely used methods for preventing overfitting, such as dropout and early stopping. Experimental results demonstrate that kernel redundancy is significantly removed and overfitting is substantially reduced with even better performance achieved.

1 Introduction

Recently, various deep CNN architectures have been widely proposed for modern applications, such as image classification and semantic segmentation. Most state-of-the-art CNN models tend to employ a lot of stacked layers along with a huge number of parameters, such as deep residual network [3], which has included more than 100 layers. Normally, it is easier to result in overfitting with more parameters included, especially on small training datasets. Thus, it has become one obstacle to apply these complicated models on many practical problems.

In the past few years, research works have been proposed to prevent overfitting by reducing Co-dependence in deep CNNs. Hinton et al. [4] introduced "dropout" to prevent overfitting. Srivastava et al. [10] show that dropout has a regularizing effect, leading to less correlated features. Cogswell et al. [1] find correlation between the cross-covariance of hidden unit activations. Then, they propose a loss function termed *DeCov* to prevent overfitting, which is based on the covariance matrix of the activation. Inspired by these works, we propose a novel regularizer to prevent overfitting in this work. Different from prior approaches, we concentrate on reducing the kernel redundancy instead of Co-dependence in deep networks. More specifically, we propose a new regularizer

A. Lintas et al. (Eds.): ICANN 2017, Part II, LNCS 10614, pp. 49–55, 2017.
https://doi.org/10.1007/978-3-319-68612-7_6

called *correlation*$_{loss}$, which encourages kernels that have less (linear) correlation. In addition, this regularizer is applied to convolutional layers rather than fully-connected layers.

We apply the proposed regularizer on different network architectures using various datasets, which include CIFAR10/100 and ImageNet. Experimental results show that kernel redundancy is significantly removed and overfitting is substantially reduced. Comparison with L2 penalty demonstrate the advantage of using our approach over traditional approaches. In addition, we even achieve a higher accuracy on CIFAR100 dataset than the previous state-of-the-art result (81.03 % vs. 75.72 %).

The rest of this paper is organized as follows. In Sect. 2, we present how to calculate correlation coefficients between two kernels. Based on this, we visualize features and convolutional kernels to show kernel redundancy. In Sect. 3, we propose our novel regularizer termed *correlation*$_{loss}$. In Sect. 4, we provide comprehensive experimental results over a range of datasets, followed by a conclusion in Sect. 5.

2   Exploring Kernel Redundancy in Deep CNNs

In this section, we first quantitatively define redundancy between two convolution kernels using correlation coefficient. Then, we demonstrate kernel redundancy in real CNN models.

2.1   Correlation Between Two Kernels

First, we explain how to compute the correlation coefficient between two vectors denoted as x, y. Let $f_{cor}(x, y)$ denote the Pearson's correlation coefficient [7] of two vectors,

$$f_{cor}(x, y) = \frac{\sum_i (x_i - \overline{x})(y_i - \overline{y})}{\sqrt{\sum_i (x_i - \overline{x})^2 \sum_i (y_i - \overline{y})^2}}, \tag{1}$$

where $\overline{x}$ and $\overline{y}$ denote the average of elements in vector x and y, respectively.

Here we denote two given convolutional kernels as $S1$ and $S2$. We first flatten $S1, S2$ to $S1_{flatten}, S2_{flatten}$. The correlation is computed between two flattened vectors. We use the computed correlations as a metric of similarity between two kernels. For simplicity, we denote $cor(S1, S2)$ as the similarity metric. The computing formula is listed as follows:

$$cor(S1, S2) = f_{cor}(S1_{flatten}, S2_{flatten}) \tag{2}$$

2.2   Distribution of Correlations in a Real CNN Model

We apply the proposed $cor(Si, Sj)$ on a VGG19 [9] model trained on ImageNet. We calculate the correlation coefficients among all pairs of kernels i and j from the same layer in VGG19. The histogram of correlation coefficients for all kernel pairs is shown in Fig. 1. For the first convolution layer, we can observe that the distribution of $cor(Si, Sj)$ is zero centered. But a number of kernel pairs gather at both ends in the histogram. This indicates that there are many kernel pairs, which have high correlation coefficients in the first convolution layer of the VGG19 model. While going deeper into the network, we find that the numbers of high correlation kernel pairs decrease sharply. An interesting observation is that this trend is similar to that found in Shang's work [8]. Shang et al. propose a new activation to eliminate this phenomenon. In this work, we will address this issue by minimizing the $correlation_{loss}$ (will be introduced in Sect. 3).

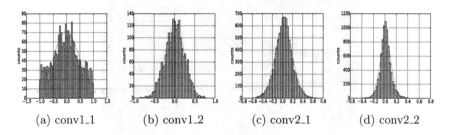

(a) conv1_1   (b) conv1_2   (c) conv2_1   (d) conv2_2

Fig. 1. Histograms of the correlation coefficients from conv1_1 to conv2_2 in VGG19. There are many kernel pairs with high correlation coefficient in conv1_1. Numbers of high-correlation pairs gradually decrease when going deeper into the network.

2.3   Visualizing High-Similarity Kernels and Features

Based on the above observation, we select some high-correlation kernel pairs for visualization in Fig. 2. We put kernel pairs with high-correlation together and we find that they have a similar pixel distributions. For comparison, we select some high-similarity kernel pairs from VGG19 [9] and AlexNet [6] in Figs. 3 and 4, respectively.

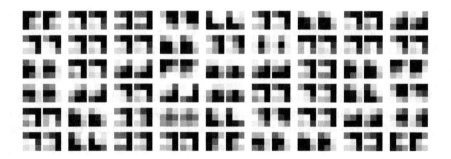

Fig. 2. Illustration of kernel pairs with high-correlation.

Fig. 3. Some high-correlation pairs of kernels from the same layer of AlexNet.

In Fig. 4, column 2 and column 3 demonstrate the features that extracted by the kernels from high-similarity pairs. It is difficult for human to distinguish two generated features from the same image.

Fig. 4. Demonstrate the features extracted by high-similarity pair of kernels.

Inspired by these observations, we can treat these pairs with high correlation as a (linear) redundancy in deep CNNs. To address this issue, we minimize the $correlation_{loss}$ to eliminate the (linear) redundancy of convolution layer in deep CNNs. The $correlation_{loss}$ will be introduced in next section.

3 $Correlation_{loss}$

We collect correlation coefficients among all pairs of kernels from same convolution layer and form a matrix G listed as follows. Si and Sj represent the i-th kernel and j-th kernel of a convolution layer in a deep CNN.

$$G_{i,j} = cor(Si, Sj) \tag{3}$$

As discussed in last section, we try to minimize the correlations among these kernels. Thus, we can treat the Frobenius norm of G as a regularizer. Since the diagonal of G is the self-correlation coefficients, we can subtract the term from the matrix norm to calculate a final penalty term as follows:

$$correlation_{loss} = \frac{1}{2}(\|G\|_F^2 - \|diag(G)\|_2^2) \tag{4}$$

where $\|\cdot\|_F$ is the Frobenius norm.

We can find that $correlation_{loss}$ is different from L_{DeCov} introduced in [1]. Instead, it is similar to the L_2 or L_1 regularizers because it is a function purely based on weight vectors. We can simply implement the regularizer and apply it to any layer in a deep CNN. We add this loss with classification loss and get total loss with following equation. l represents the l-th layer in a deep CNN model.

$$total_{loss} = L_{classification} + \lambda * \sum_l correlation_{loss} \qquad (5)$$

4   Experiment Results

4.1   CIFAR10 and CIFAR100

CIFAR10 and CIFAR100 datasets each consist of 50,000 training and 10,000 testing images evenly drawn from 10 and 100 classes respectively. For preprocessing, we subtracted the mean and divide by the variance. We also use random horizontal flip and change the contrast for data augmentation.

We conduct experiments with VGG16 [9] and 34 layers Res-Net [3] on these two datasets. We add batch normalization [5] after each convolutional layers. For $correlation_{loss}$, we set $\lambda = 0.01$ in Eq. (5).

We refer cor_{loss} to $correlation_{loss}$ in the result table for simplicity. In this paper, we use the gap between train and test accuracy for evaluating overfitting. We conduct a serial of experiments to compare different strategies for preventing overfitting. Firstly, we compare our proposed regularizer with the traditional L2 regularizer. In Tables 1 and 2, we observe a significant improvement when using $correlation_{loss}$ on these two models. We see that using $correlation_{loss}$ instead of $L2$ weight decay has obviously decreased the gap (between train accuracy and test accuracy) while obtaining a better test accuracy.

Table 1. Results on CIFAR10

Model	cor_{loss}	L2	Train	Test	Train-test
VGG16	No	Yes	98.78	85.45	13.33
VGG16	Yes	No	95.24	90.28	4.96
ResNet-34	No	Yes	100	91.13	8.87
ResNet-34	Yes	No	99.45	93.45	6.00

To compare our method with previous methods for preventing overfitting, We conduct experiments with 34 layers ResNet [5] on cifar10 dataset. For fair comparison, we add L2 regularizer in all these experiments. Table 3 shows the results.

From the experimental results in Table 3, our method has a slight improvement compared to dropout. We find that using both our method and dropout can further improve the accuracy.

We also combine early stopping with our method and dropout to see if it can provide improvement. In our experiment, 10% of the original training set is split into a validation set. We find that using early stopping doesn't improve the generation of such a complicated deep convolutional neural network. In [10], the authors also mentioned this issue.

Table 2. Results on CIFAR100

Model	cor_{loss}	L2	Train	Test	Train-test
VGG16	No	Yes	99.45	75.50	8.01
VGG16	Yes	No	85.34	81.03	4.31
ResNet-34	No	Yes	100	66.6	33.4
ResNet-34	Yes	No	95.43	72.24	23.19

Table 3. Comparative Experiments with dropout based on Resnet-34.

Dataset	cor_{loss}	Dropout	Early stopping	Train	Test	Train-test
Cifar10	No	Yes	No	98.97	93.02	5.95
Cifar10	Yes	No	No	98.22	93.20	5.02
Cifar10	Yes	Yes	No	97.32	94.18	3.14
Cifar10	Yes	Yes	Yes	97.12	93.41	3.71

4.2   ImageNet

Imagenet [2] is a large labeled dataset. In our experiment, we select the validation set of ImageNet2012 as testing dataset and the ILSVRC12's training data as the training dataset. We test our new regularizer on VGG19 [9] and find once again that the cor_{loss} gives improvement over the baseline model with L2 regularizer.

Table 4. ImageNet Benchmark set results

Models	Top1	Top5	Train-val (Top1)
VGG19 with L2	68.44	88.37	15.27
VGG19 with cor_{loss}	69.52	88.47	11.84

Even more interesting thing is that we observe the phenomenon discussed in Sect. 3 vanishes when we use the $correlation_{loss}$ instead of the $L2$ regularizer. It proves that this new regularizer is effective for reducing the (linear) kernel redundancy.

5 Conclusion

In this paper, we propose a new regularizer called $correlation_{loss}$, which explicitly penalizes correlations among kernels in convolutional layers. Our new regularizer has demonstrated a strong ability to prevent overfitting. We show that using $correloation_{loss}$ achieves better performance than traditional regularizer with different datasets and model architectures.

Acknowledgments. This work is supported by National Natural Science Foundation of China (No. 61572045).

References

1. Cogswell, M., Ahmed, F., Girshick, R., Zitnick, L., Batra, D.: Reducing overfitting in deep networks by decorrelating representations. ICLR (2016)
2. Deng, J., Dong, W., Socher, R., Li, L.-J., Li, K., Fei-Fei, L.: Imagenet: a large-scale hierarchical image database. In: IEEE Conference on Computer Vision and Pattern Recognition, 2009, CVPR 2009, pp. 248–255. IEEE (2009)
3. He, K., Zhang, X., Ren, S., Sun, J.: Deep residual learning for image recognition. CoRR, abs/1512.03385 (2015)
4. Hinton, G.E., Srivastava, N., Krizhevsky, A., Sutskever, I., Salakhutdinov, R.R.: Improving neural networks by preventing co-adaptation of feature detectors. arXiv preprint arXiv:1207.0580 (2012)
5. Ioffe, S., Szegedy, C.: Batch normalization: accelerating deep network training by reducing internal covariate shift. arXiv preprint arXiv:1502.03167 (2015)
6. Krizhevsky, A., Sutskever, I., Hinton, G.E.: Imagenet classification with deep convolutional neural networks. In: Advances in Neural Information Processing Systems, pp. 1097–1105 (2012)
7. Pearson, K.: Note on regression and inheritance in the case of two parents. Proc. R. S. London **58**, 240–242 (1895)
8. Shang, W., Sohn, K., Almeida, D., Lee, H.: Understanding and improving convolutional neural networks via concatenated rectified linear units. arXiv preprint arXiv:1603.05201 (2016)
9. Simonyan, K., Zisserman, A.: Very deep convolutional networks for large-scale image recognition. Eprint Arxiv (2014)
10. Srivastava, N., Hinton, G.E., Krizhevsky, A., Sutskever, I., Salakhutdinov, R.: Dropout: a simple way to prevent neural networks from overfitting. J. Mach. Learn. Res. **15**(1), 1929–1958 (2014)

An Improved Convolutional Neural Network for Sentence Classification Based on Term Frequency and Segmentation

Qi Wang[✉], Jungang Xu, Ben He, and Zhengcai Qin

University of Chinese Academy of Sciences, Beijing, China
397254703@qq.com

Abstract. Recently, Sentence classification is a ubiquitous Natural Language Processing (NLP) task and deep learning is proved to be a kind of methods that has a significant effect in this area. In this work, we propose an improved Convolutional Neural Network (CNN) for sentence classification, in which a word-representation model is introduced to capture semantic features by encoding term frequency and segmenting sentence into proposals. The experimental results show that our methods outperform the state-of-the-art methods.

Keywords: Sentence classification · CNN · Term frequency · Segmentation

1 Introduction

With the popularity of Internet and the rapid development of intelligent terminals, Internet users generate a lot of information everyday, including original articles, news, reviews, etc. This information is spreading in the form of text and is used to judge whether information is effective and whether it is attractive. So in recent years, sentence classification has been an active research filed in NLP. Traditional sentence classification methods are mainly based on statistical principles, and which are almost classic machine learning methods.

Currently, deep learning models have achieved remarkable results in computer vision [1], speech recognition [2] and NLP [3]. And CNN has proved to be very effective in achieving state-of-the-art results for sentence classification tasks. In a sentence classification task, the aim is to predict class label information for one or more sentences. For example, we classify the movie reviews into positive or negative. However, the input for CNN is just concatenated by the word embeddings, so some semantic features for a sentence may be lost.

In this paper, an improved CNN model for sentence classification based on term frequency and sentence segmentation is proposed. Our contributions are as follows. First, the term frequency embedding to encode the frequency of each word is introduced. Second, sentence segmentation is added when forming the word embedding matrix. Last, the term frequency and the sentence segmentation results are taken as a CNN input.

© Springer International Publishing AG 2017
A. Lintas et al. (Eds.): ICANN 2017, Part II, LNCS 10614, pp. 56–63, 2017.
https://doi.org/10.1007/978-3-319-68612-7_7

This paper is organized as follows. Section 2 introduces related works on neural networks in NLP. Section 3 describes our novel approach for sentence classification. Section 4 discusses the experiments for validating our proposed method. Finally, Sect. 5 concludes the work and suggests the future work.

2   Related Works

Language modeling is the first application for neural networks in NLP, and which has been useful to learn distributed representations for words [3–7]. These word embeddings have guided the new direction for NLP tasks. So neural networks are using more extensively in NLP. In addition to the above mentioned, a class of recursive neural networks and neural tensor networks are proposed for paraphrase detection [8], parsing [9], sentiment analysis [10], knowledge base completion [11], question answering [12], etc.

Much prior work has exploited deep neural networks to model sentence. A general class of basic sentence model is Neural Bag-of-Words (NBOW) model, and which includes a projection layer and one or more fully connected layers. The model using an external parse tree is the Recursive Neural Network (RecNN) [13]. And the Recurrent Neural Network (RNN) [14] is a special case of recursive networks. The RNN can be used as a language model and also can be viewed as a sentence model with a linear structure. The CNN is also introduced into sentence modeling. A simple one layer CNN model [15] combines softmax to achieve sentence classification tasks. A CNN typically has one or more convolutional layers and a final fully-connected layer, and there will be a pooling layer between every two layers. Combined with the characteristics between CNN and Time-Delay Neural Networks (TDNN) [3], the Dynamic Convolutional Neural Networks (DCNN) [16] are using for sentence modeling and have a good performance on many datasets.

3   Model Description

Our proposed model based on CNN is shown in Fig. 1. The whole model consists of four main layers: (i) sentence representation, (ii) convolution, (iii) pooling and (iv) logistic regression.

3.1   Input

To extract sentence-level features of the input for our improved CNN, we propose two methods as follows.

- **Addition of term frequency (TF):** It is necessary to specify which words are frequently appear in sentences. Therefore, the TF is proposed, which is defined as the word's frequency in the whole dataset. The value of TF is the normalization of the term count. In addition, the term frequency of stop word is set to zero.

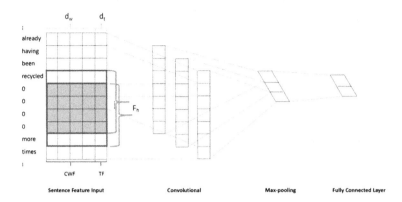

Fig. 1. Model architecture with term frequency and segmentation for sentence classification. (Color figure online)

– **Segmentation:** Each input sentence is split into several parts as proposals. Thus more internal/edge features can be extracted. The length of a sentence decides how many proposals a sentence could have.

As shown in Fig. 1, the sentence feature input module contains two parts, Context-Word Feature (CWF) [17] and TF feature. CWF is the vector of each word transformed by looking up word embeddings [15,16,18]. TF feature is the term frequency of each word.

The whole sentence can be represented by $x = [x_1, x_2, ..., x_n]$, where x_i is the i-th word in the sentence and n is the length of the input sentence. Set d_t as the width of term frequency embedding, and set d_w as the width of the word embedding. So the whole width of the i-th word in the sentence is defined as d.

$$d = d_t + d_w \tag{1}$$

Each word in a sentence is replaced with its vector representation, a sentence matrix $\mathbf{X} \in \mathbb{R}^{n \times d}$ can be obtained.

Next, the step size of segmentation m is calculated by Eq. 2.

$$m = \lfloor \frac{k}{n} \rfloor \tag{2}$$

Here, k is a fixed parameter. A window of length m is used to split each sentence from the beginning into w parts, where

$$w = \lceil \frac{n}{m} \rceil \tag{3}$$

Several zeros are inserted between w proposals to separate them. The number of zero is decided by the height of max filter window. The number of padding zeros is defined as z,

$$z = (w - 1) \times (max(F(h)) - 1) \tag{4}$$

where $F(h)$ denotes the height of filter windows.

As shown in Fig. 1, the red box represents the filter window. When we need to separate two proposals, several zeros should be inserted between them. Only in this way, a convolutional window which only contains one proposal content at some moment in convolution process can be ensured. The number of zeros depends on the height of max filter window. As the filter windows of 3, 4, 5 in our experiments are used, at least 4 zeros need to be inserted between proposals as shown in Fig. 1 to achieve our method. So the reason that the $(max(F(h))-1)$ is used to denote the number of padding zeros between proposals is that neither can separate proposals exactly to get more internal/edge features nor can cause redundancy.

Thus, the sentence feature input in Fig. 1 can be described as matrix $\mathbf{X} \in \mathbb{R}^{(n+z) \times d}$.

3.2 Convolution

The convolution layer is aiming to capture the compositional semantics of an entire sentence and compress these valuable semantics into feature maps.

Concretely, the following operator is used to obtain another sequence c:

$$c = f(F \cdot x_{i:i+h-1} + b) \tag{5}$$

where a filter $F \in \mathbb{R}^{h \times d}$ and b is a bias term, and f is an activation function, such as tanh or rectifier linear unit (ReLU).

3.3 Pooling

To extract the most remarkable features(max value) within each feature maps, a max-over-time pooling [15,16,18] operation over feature map is applied. The approach takes one feature map as a pool and get one max value for each feature map.

For each filter F, its score sequence c is passed through the max function to produce a single number,

$$P_F = \max\{c\} = \max\{c_1, c_2, ..., c_{n-h+1}\} \tag{6}$$

which is used to estimate the possibility n-gram of F appears in the context.

3.4 Regularization and Classification

Finally, the pooling scores for every filter are concatenated into a single feature vector o to represent the sentence.

$$o = [P_1, P_2, ...P_q] \tag{7}$$

Here, q is the number of filters in the model and P_i is the pooling score of the i-th filter. Then, a dropout [15,19] is employed to prevent the co-adaptation of hidden units by randomly dropping out a proportion p of the hidden units during forward and backpropagation. The weights whose l_2-norms exceed a hyperparameter as Kim [15] are also rescaled.

4   Experiments

4.1   Datasets

To evaluate the performance of our proposed method, The summary of the selected datasets are listed in Table 1. Here, a is the number of target classes, l is the average sentence length, N is the dataset size, $|V|$ is the vocabulary size, $|V_{pre}|$ is the number of words presented in the set of pre-trained word vectors.

Table 1. Summary of the datasets after tokenization.

Dataset	a	l	N	$|V|$	$|V_{pre}|$
MR	2	20	10662	18765	16448
CR	2	19	3775	5340	5046

- **MR**: Movie reviews with one sentence per review. Classification involves detecting positive/negative reviews [20].
- **CR**: Customer reviews of various products (camera, MP3 etc.). Task is to predict positive/negative reviews [21].

4.2   Hyperparameters and Training

For all datasets we use rectified linear units, filter windows $(F(h))$ of 3, 4, 5 with 100 feature maps each, dropout rate (r) of 0.5, l_2 constraint (s) of 3, parameter k of 300, mini-batch size of 50 and static model. The static model is that all words are pre-trained from word2vec and they are kept static during the experiments.

4.3   Pre-trained Word Vectors

The word embedding we used is word2vec which is trained on 100 billion tokens of Google News dataset. The vectors have 301 dimensions including term frequency embedding and word embedding. If words do not appear in the pre-trained words, they are initialized randomly.

4.4   Experimental Results and Analysis

Experimental results are listed in Table 2. The first four works in the top section have good results on sentence classification. The method NBSVM [22] uses Naive Bayes SVM and MNB [22] uses multinomial Naive Bayes with uni-bigrams to achieve sentence classification. The G-Dropout [23] uses Gaussian Dropout training for classification and Tree-CRF [24] presents a dependency tree-based method using conditional random fields with hidden variables. The next three works in the middle section are state-of-the-art methods. The CNN-static [15] is a model with pre-trained vectors from word2vec and all words are kept static and only the

Table 2. Results of our CNN models against other methods.

Model	MR	CR
NBSVM [22]	79.4	81.8
MNB [22]	79.0	80.0
G-Dropout [23]	79.0	82.1
Tree-CRF [24]	77.3	81.4
CNN-static [15]	81.0	84.7
CNN-non-static [15]	81.5	84.3
CNN-multichannel [15]	81.1	85.0
CNN-TF	81.3	85.0
CNN-TF-Segmentation	**81.8**	**85.1**

other parameters are learned. The CNN-non-static [15] is the same as CNN-static but the pre-trained vectors are fine-tuned for each task. The CNN-multichannel [15] uses two sets of word vectors and each set is treated as a channel. The works in the bottom section are our methods. The results of our methods are significantly better than that of above methods. Note that static CNN model which does not allow the input embeddings to be updated during training is used in our experiment to explored the performance of our methods which introduced TF and sentence segmentation.

When using the CNN-TF, it can achieve better results than most of other methods except CNN-non-static in MR and CNN-multichannel in CR. One possible reason is that TF plays an important role in extracting the sentence semantic features. TF represents the frequency of one word which determines this word is necessary or not. If a word appears frequently (except the stop words) in a dataset, its weights should be higher.

When using the CNN-TF-Segmentation, it can achieve the best results in MR and CR. These results show that the internal/edge features can be extracted through sentence segmentation. These features play important roles in sentence classification. So the term frequency and internal/edge features are necessary for sentence classification.

5   Conclusions

In this paper, an improved CNN method for sentence classification is proposed. On one hand, the term frequency is introduced to be an important feature. The higher term frequency one word has, the more important the word is. On the other hand, sentence segmentation is introduced to produce more sentence proposals, and the sentence proposals are presented to learn more internal features and edge features and the features are much valuable for classification. The effectiveness of our approach is verified by applying it to sentence classification on two benchmark datasets: a movie review dataset called MR and a customer review dataset called CR. Experimental results show that our methods perform better than the state-of-the-art methods on both datasets.

Our future work will concentrate on how to extract more semantic features, improving CNN further and extending the improved CNNs to other applications.

Acknowledgements. This work is supported by the Beijing Natural Science Foundation under Grant No. 4162067.

References

1. Krizhevsky, A., Sutskever, I., Hinton, G.E.: ImageNet classification with deep convolutional neural networks. In: Proceedings of the 26th Annual Conference on Neural Information Processing Systems, pp. 1097–1105 (2012)
2. Graves, A., Mohamed, A.R., Hinton, G.E.: Speech recognition with deep recurrent neural networks. In: Proceedings of the 38th International Conference on Acoustics, Speech and Signal Processing, pp. 6645–6649. IEEE Press, New York (2013)
3. Collobert, R., Weston, J.: A unified architecture for natural language processing: deep neural networks with multitask learning. In: Proceedings of the 25th International Conference on Machine Learning, pp. 160–167. ACM, New York (2008)
4. Bengio, Y., Ducharme, R., Vincent, P.: A neural probabilistic language model. J. Mach. Learn. Res. **3**(6), 1137–1155 (2003)
5. Mnih, A., Hinton, G.E.: A scalable hierarchical distributed language model. In: Proceedings of the 22nd Annual Conference on Neural Information Processing Systems, pp. 1081–1088 (2008)
6. Turian, J., Ratinov, L., Bengio, Y.: Word representations: a simple and general method for semi-supervised learning. In: Proceedings of the 48th Annual Meeting of the Association for Computational Linguistics, pp. 384–394. ACL Press, Stroudsburg (2010)
7. Mikolov, T., Sutskever, I., Chen, K., Corrado, G., Dean, J.: Distributed representations of words and phrases and of words and phrases and their compostionality. In: Proceedings of the 27th Annual Conference on Neural Information Processing Systems, pp. 3111–3119 (2013)
8. Socher, R., Pennington, J., Huang, E.H., Ng, A.Y., Manning, C.D.: Semi-supervised recursive autoencoders for predicting sentiment distributions. In: Proceedings of the 8th Conference on Empirical Methods in Natural Language Processing, pp. 151–161. ACL Press, Stroudsburg (2011)
9. Socher, R., Perelygin, A., Wu, J.Y., Chuang, J., Manning, C.D., Ng, A.Y., et al.: Recursive deep models for semantic compositionality over a sentiment treebank. In: Proceedings of the 10th Conference on Empirical Methods in Natural Language Processing, pp. 1631–1642. ACL Press, Stroudsburg (2013)
10. Socher, R., Bauer, J., Manning, C.D., Ng, A.Y.: Parsing with compositional vector grammars. In: Proceedings of the 51st Annual Meeting of the Association for Computational Linguistics, pp. 455–465. ACL Press, Stroudsburg (2013)
11. Socher, R., Chen, D., Manning, C.D., Ng, A.Y.: Reasoning with neural tensor networks for knowledge base completion. In: Proceedings of the 27th Annual Conference on Neural Information Processing Systems, pp. 464–469 (2013)
12. Iyyer, M., Boyd-Graber, J., Claudino, L., Socher, R., Iii, H.D.: A neural network for factoid question answering over paragraphs. In: Proceedings of the 11th Conference on Empirical Methods in Natural Language Processing, pp. 633–644. ACL Press, Stroudsburg (2014)

13. Socher, R., Huang, E.H., Pennington, J., Ng, A.Y., Manning, C.D.: Dynamic pooling and unfolding recursive autoencoders for paraphrase detection. In: Proceedings of the 25th Annual Conference on Neural Information Processing Systems, pp. 801–809 (2011)
14. Mikolov, T., Kombrink, S., Burget, L., Cernocky, J.H.: Extensions of recurrent neural network language model. In: Proceedings of the 36th IEEE International Conference on Acoustics, Speech and Signal Processing, pp. 5528–5531. IEEE Press, New York (2011)
15. Kim, Y.: Convolutional neural networks for sentence classification. In: 11th Conference on Empirical Methods in Natural Language Processing, pp. 1746–1751. ACL Press, Stroudsburg (2014)
16. Kalchbrenner, N., Grefenstette, E., Blunsom, P.: A convolutional neural network for modelling sentences. In: Proceedings of the 52nd Annual Meeting of the Association for Computational Linguistics, pp. 655–665. ACL Press, Stroudsburg (2014)
17. Chen, Y., Xu, L., Liu, K., Zeng, D., Zhao, J.: Event extraction via dynamic multipooling convolutional neural networks. In: Proceedings of the 53rd Annual Meeting of the Association for Computational Linguistics and 7th International Joint Conference on Natural Language Processing of the Asian Federation of Natural Language Processing, pp. 167–176. ACL Press, Stroudsburg (2015)
18. Collobert, R., Weston, J., Bottou, L., Karlen, M., Kavukcuoglu, K., Kuksa, P.: Natural language processing (almost) from scratch. J. Mach. Learn. Res. **12**(1), 2493–2537 (2011)
19. Hinton, G.E., Srivastava, N., Krizhevsky, A., Sutskever, I., Salakhutdinov, R.R.: Improving Neural Networks by Preventing Co-adaptation of Feature Detectors. CoRR, abs/1207.0580 (2012)
20. Pang, B., Lee, L.: Seeing stars: exploiting class relationships for sentiment categorization with respect to rating scales. In: Proceedings of the 43rd Annual Meeting of the Association for Computational Linguistics, pp. 115–124. ACL Press, Stroudsburg (2005)
21. Hu, M., Liu, B.: Mining and summarizing customer reviews. In: Proceedings of the 10th ACM SIGKDD International Conference on Knowledge Discovery and Data Mining, pp. 168–177. ACM, New York (2004)
22. Wang, S., Manning, C.D.: Baselines and bigrams: simple, good sentiment and topic classification. In: Proceedings of the 50th Annual Meeting of the Association for Computational Linguistics, pp. 90–94. ACL Press, Stroudsburg (2012)
23. Wang, S., Manning, C.D.: Fast dropout training. In: Proceedings of the 30th International Conference on Machine Learning, pp. 118–126 (2013)
24. Nakagawa, T., Inui, K., Kurohashi, S.: Dependency tree-based sentiment classification using CRFs with hidden variables. In: Proceedings of the 48th Annual Meeting of the Association for Computational Linguistics, pp. 786–794 (2010)

Parallel Implementation of a Bug Report Assignment Recommender Using Deep Learning

Adrian-Cătălin Florea[1](✉), John Anvik[2], and Răzvan Andonie[1,3]

[1] Electronics and Computers Department, Transilvania University of Braşov,
Braşov, Romania
acflorea@unitbv.ro
[2] Department of Mathematics and Computer Science, University of Lethbridge,
Lethbridge, AB, Canada
john.anvik@uleth.ca
[3] Computer Science Department, Central Washington University,
Ellensburg, WA, USA
andonie@cwu.edu

Abstract. For large software projects which receive many reports daily, assigning the most appropriate developer to fix a bug from a large pool of potential developers is both technically difficult and time-consuming. We introduce a parallel, highly scalable recommender system for bug report assignment. From a machine learning perspective, the core of such a system consists of a multi-class classification process using characteristics of a bug, like textual information and other categorical attributes, as features and the most appropriate developer as the predicted class. We use alternatively two Deep Learning classifiers: Convolutional and Recurrent Neural Networks. The implementation is realized on an Apache Spark engine, running on IBM Power8 servers. The experiments use real-world data from the Netbeans, Eclipse and Mozilla projects.

1 Introduction

Bug report triage is the process by which bug reports submitted to a software project's "bug tracker", a form of issue tracking system, are analyzed to determine if the report will result in development activity. As large software development projects can receive hundreds of bug reports per day [4,5], bug report triage is a significant software maintenance problem, as it can take substantial time and resources [8]. Bug report assignment is an important bug report triage decision, as errors can result in delays to the project [4,5,7].

Deep Learning techniques are a modern tool that provides highly promising results in a vast area of applications [10]. They have the drawback of long training times and complex architectures which often do not scale well. The high complexity of such models has so far lead to their low adoption rate in the area of recommender systems.

We present a highly scalable parallel Deep Learning-based implementation of a bug report assignment recommender system. To the best of our knowledge,

© Springer International Publishing AG 2017
A. Lintas et al. (Eds.): ICANN 2017, Part II, LNCS 10614, pp. 64–71, 2017.
https://doi.org/10.1007/978-3-319-68612-7_8

no previous attempts have been made in using Deep Learning techniques for bug report assignment recommendations. Our main focus is not the execution time itself, but the scalability of the system on a cluster. This is measured by the speedup (the ratio of the sequential execution time to the parallel execution time) and parallel efficiency (speedup divided by the number of processors/cores). In a cluster architecture, these are important metrics. Our contributions are the following:

- *The first Deep Learning-based approach for automated bug report assignment in large software projects*, with prediction performance on par with the state of the art.
- *A highly scalable, parallel implementation* that alleviates the problem of a long training time and model size.

The paper proceeds as follows: Sect. 2 gives a brief overview of the existing work in the context of Deep Learning for recommender systems and previous attempts of using machine learning techniques for bug report assignment recommendation. We then describe our recommender system in Sect. 3. In Sect. 4, we discuss the results obtained using three real-world datasets from the Netbeans, Eclipse and Mozilla projects. The paper is concluded in Sect. 5.

2   Related Work

We restrict our focus to Deep Learning architectures used to train recommender systems. The following are some of the results which are related to the recent high interest in Deep Learning.

Salakhutdinov *et al.* [17] proposed one of the first approaches, where they integrate an instance of a two-layer Restricted Boltzmann Machines (RBM) into a Collaborative Filtering type recommender to be able to handle large datasets. They tested their model on the Netflix dataset, consisting of over 100 million user/movies rating. Although the approach outperformed the existing models at that time, it used as input exclusively the ratings and it was found to be not deep enough. Wang *et al.* [20] proposed a hierarchical Bayesian model called Collaborative Deep Learning (CDL) and used movie review text along with the ratings to alleviate the cold-start problem. Reviews were converted into a numerical representation using the Bag Of Words (BOW) technique, and this numerical data were fed into a Deep Auto Encoder to obtain a lower dimensional feature space [19]. The model gave good results, but it suffered from losing the semantic information embedded in the text, as well as from ignoring the word order.

There have been other attempts to integrate different types of Deep Neural Networks into recommender systems. As a potential solution to deal with the cold start problem, Wang *et al.* used a Convolutional Neural Network (CNN) to develop a hybrid recommender that considers real-world users information and high-level representation of audio data [21]. Kyo-Joong *et al.* [16] developed a personalized news recommender system based on a three-layer perceptron in which they integrated several numerical features extracted from textual data.

Tomar *et al.* [18] used a Word2Vec [6] model to provide hashtag recommendations for English tweets[1]. The obtained word representation was then fed into a deep feedforward neural network.

Given the large amount of data, as well as the large number of parameters required to build deep learning models, leveraging the resources of a cluster to optimize the training is gaining a lot of attention. With Apache Spark offering a dense and intuitive API for building parallel applications, combining Spark and Deep Learning is an emerging research direction. Stoica *et al.* [13] developed the SparkNet framework that uses Apache Spark to train multiple instances of Caffe models, distributed over a cluster using data parallelism[2]. Even though it is not a recommender system per se, SparkNet can provide the backbone of such a system. Similar attempts of using Apache Spark to parallelize deep learning were also reported by Abu Alsheikh [2]. Their work focused on using Deep Learning for mobile data analytics.

In the area of bug report assignment recommendation, standard machine learning techniques have been employed, including Naïve Bayes [14], SVM [9], and C4.5 [3]. Some of these techniques were also used in combination with dimensionality reduction, such as LSI [1], X^2 [5,9] and LDA [9,15]. The first parallel bug report assignment recommender systems was implemented by Florea *et al.* [9] and used a distributed version of a SVM on a Spark cluster.

3   Deep Learning Bug Report Assignment Recommender

This section presents our recommender system. As shown in Fig. 1, the input to the recommender system consists of MySQL database dumps. The data is filtered and pre-processed as described in Sect. 3.2. We export the pre-processed data as input for building a Paragraph2Vec [12] model which we later feed into either a CNN or a Long Short Term Memory (LSTM) network [10].

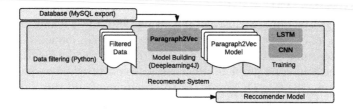

Fig. 1. Recommender system macro architecture.

We describe in the following sections: the datasets used for evaluation, the cleansing and pre-processing phases, the training algorithm, and the implementation.

3.1   Datasets

To evaluate the performance of our recommender system, we use real data from the following three software projects: **Eclipse** and **Netbeans** - both datasets available from the 2011 Working Conference on Mining Software Repositories Data Challange webpage,[3] and **Mozilla** - made available to us by the Mozilla Foundation. All of the datasets were in the form of anonymized MySQL dumps of the respective Bugzilla database. From these data dumps, we extract data from the fields of the following tables: `bugs` (`bug_id`, `creation_ts`, `bug_status`, `product_id`, `resolution`, `component_id`, `bug_severity`), `bugs_activity` (`who`, `bug_when`), `longdescs` (`bug_id`, `thetext`) and `duplicates` (`dupe`). The `bugs` table stores essential details of a bug including its id, severity, creation date, and current bug status. The `bugs_activity` table stores the activity logs, including all of the changes in the bug status. The `duplicates` table contains information about duplicate bug reports. The bug report's textual information is kept in the `longdescs` table.

3.2   Data Preparation

To prepare the data, we apply similar data cleansing steps as described by Anvik and Murphy [4] and Florea *et al.* [9]. Among all the CLOSED bugs (`bugs.bug_status = 'CLOSED'`), we consider exclusively the reports marked as FIXED (`bugs.resolution = 'FIXED'`). Based on project heuristics, as detailed by Anvik and Murphy [4], we consider the developer who fixed a report as the one marking it as FIXED in `bugs_activity`. To be able to produce effective predictions, we restrict our input both in terms of training data and in terms of target classes (developers). We consider a developer to be active in the project if, and only if, she fixed an average of three or more bug reports per month over the last three months. Doing so eliminates developers with only occasional contributions to the project. We also remove those that have an exceptionally high frequency of marking reports FIXED (more than $mean + 2 * stddev$), on the assumptions that these represent project managers and not developers. For each bug report, we use a normalized version of its textual representation obtained by converting the text to lower case, removing any non-alphanumerical characters, and concatenating the text from the report's title, description, and comments. In addition to textual data, we use the `component_id`, `product_id` and `bug_severity` fields as one-hot-encoded categorical variables.

We use the Distributed Bag of Words version of Paragraph Vector (PV-DBOW) [12] to obtain numerical values for features from our textual data. For each dataset, we train a model with 100 features for 20 epochs, with no hard-coded stopwords, using a window size of 5. The input for the PV-DBOW model is the text retrieved from all of the reports in the database. This is done as each term can contain valuable semantic information, regardless of the report status, resolution or age. For training, we restrict the data to bugs marked as

---

[3] http://2011.msrconf.org/msr-challenge.html.

FIXED during the most recent 240 days, considering that the most recent data is also the most relevant data.

3.3 Recommender Training

We are interested in predicting recent data based on older one. Therefore, we order the data based on most recent change date and split it into 80% training, 10% validation and 10% test. We tune the recommender using the validation data and report the results obtained on the test data. We train the recommender on an Apache Spark[4] cluster using either a CNN or a LSTM network.

Convolutional Neural Network. To induce a level of spatiality between words from a certain paragraph, for CNN, we split the textual representation of bugs into **n** equal sequences and compute their PV-DBOW representation individually. Our network of choice consists of two pairs of convolution and average pooling layers, followed by two dense layers, as shown in Fig. 2. The "C" layers $(C(k_i, 1)(1, 1)f_i)$ represent convolution layers with a $(k_i, 1)$ size kernel, a stride of $(1, 1)$ and f_i filters. "P" layers are pooling layers, while "D" layers are dense layers. For our recommender system, we set the value of **n** to five and (k_i) to two for both of the "C" layers. The first dense layer has 500 neurons and uses ReLU $(f(x) = max(0, x))$ activation. For the second dense layer, we use the softmax $(\sigma(z)_j = \frac{e^{z_j}}{\sum_{k=1}^{K} e^{z_k}})$ activation.

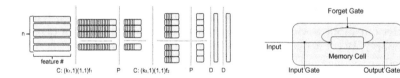

Forget Gate

Input   Output

Memory Cell

Input Gate   Output Gate

Fig. 2. The CNN architecture   **Fig. 3.** An LSTM cell

Long Short Term Memory. For LSTM, no further data preprocessing is required. The data is fed to a two-layer Recurrent Neural Network. The first layer is a "Graves" [11] RNN unidirectional layer with 250 output neurons, a dropout of 0.5 and the softsign $(f(x) = \frac{x}{1+|x|})$ activation. Each cell is a typical memory cell as shown in Fig. 3. The output layer uses the softmax activation.

3.4 Implementation Details

The recommender system is developed in Scala 2.11.8, with the exception of the data cleansing phase, which is implemented in Python 2.7.11. We use Deeplearning4j[5] to build and train the neural networks. We train both the CNN and LSTM

---
[4] http://spark.apache.org/.
[5] https://deeplearning4j.org/about.

networks on an Apache Spark engine. Each Spark cluster consists of one master node and 4, 8 or 12 workers. Data is distributed among the workers and the training starts with the initial set of parameters. Once every n iterations, the new parameter values are sent back to the master which averages and re-distributes them to the worker nodes. Training continues with the new parameter values and the process repeats for a predefined number of steps or until certain convergence criteria are met.

We train and test our recommender on two IBM Power8 8001-22C (Briggs) servers with Ubuntu 16.04 LTS installed, using the IBM. version of Spark 1.6.3. Each server has 2 processors with 20 cores each and 512GB of RAM. The code is publicly available on GitHub[6].

4 Results

Table 1 shows the precision, recall and F1-measure values obtained by the LSTM and CNN recommenders compared to the distributed SVM-based results reported in Florea *et al.* [9]. The CNN recommender version shows comparable results across all projects in terms of classification performance when compared to the parallel SVM implementation. Although LSTM has, in most of the cases, a

Table 1. Precision, recall and F1-measure after 100 epochs with batch sizes of 10 and 25 samples compared to the parallel SVM implementation. Best values are in bold.

Dataset	Netbeans					Eclipse					Mozilla				
Architecture	LSTM		CNN		SVM	LSTM		**CNN**		SVM	LSTM		CNN		SVM
Batch size	10	25	10	25	-	10	25	10	25	-	10	25	10	25	-
Precision	0.86	0.85	**0.90**	0.88	0.89	0.73	0.67	**0.80**	**0.80**	0.78	0.59	0.62	**0.78**	0.77	0.77
Recall	0.83	0.83	0.87	0.86	**0.88**	0.70	0.68	0.75	0.75	**0.77**	0.70	0.71	**0.75**	**0.75**	**0.75**
F1-measure	0.84	0.84	**0.88**	0.87	**0.88**	0.71	0.67	**0.77**	**0.77**	**0.77**	0.64	0.66	**0.76**	0.75	0.73

Table 2. Network average training time per epoch (in seconds), speedup and efficiency with increasing number of workers as compared to a 4 cores execution baseline.

Dataset	Netbeans				Eclipse				Mozilla			
Architecture	LSTM		CNN		LSTM		CNN		LSTM		CNN	
Batch size	10	25	10	25	10	25	10	25	10	25	10	25
Average training time	408	212	442	175	1192	492	1411	525	3347	1028	3636	1579
Speedup 8 cores	1.83	2.93	2.85	1.84	2.02	2.14	2.34	2.16	2.84	1.66	2.01	1.82
Efficiency 8 cores	0.92	1.47	1.42	0.92	1.01	1.07	1.17	1.08	1.42	0.83	1.00	0.91
Speedup 12 cores	2.53	4.06	4.31	4.12	2.52	2.69	3.96	3.67	5.23	3.12	2.94	3.06
Efficiency 12 cores	1.27	2.03	2.15	2.06	1.26	1.35	1.98	1.84	2.62	1.56	1.47	1.53

---

[6] https://github.com/acflorea/deep-columbugus,mariana-triage.

significantly lower training time, as shown in Table 2, it yields worse performance results for all projects. Of the four sample sizes (10, 25, 100 and 250) examined, 100 and 250 samples led to notably worse classification performance for LSTM when compared to sample sizes of 10 or 25. However, for CNN, increasing the sample size resulted in only a small performance degradation.

Both network architectures have good scalability. The speedup and efficiency values for training the recommender are depicted in Table 2.

5   Conclusions

A highly scalable parallel Deep Learning-based implementation of a bug report assignment recommender system was introduced, with both the CNN and LSTM approaches explored. Using a parallel implementation, we trained the recommender relatively fast, considering that deep network training is generally slow. Although the CNN recommender achieves results on par with the parallel SVM implementation, the SVM approach remains superior in terms of training speed.

This work opens further research directions both in terms of optimizing the training speed (e.g., use GPUs instead of CPUs) and prediction performance (e.g., identify more efficient CNN architectures).

Acknowledgments. The authors are grateful to the Mozilla Foundation for providing a dump of their Bugzilla database and to IBM Client Center, Poughkeepsie, NY, USA for allowing us to use their infrastructure.

References

1. Ahsan, S.N., Ferzund, J., Wotawa, F.: Automatic software bug triage system (bts) based on latent semantic indexing and support vector machine. In: Fourth International Conference on Software Engineering Advances, ICSEA 2009, pp. 216–221, September 2009
2. Alsheikh, M.A., Niyato, D., Lin, S., Tan, H., Han, Z.: Mobile big data analytics using deep learning and apache spark. CoRR abs/1602.07031 (2016). http://arxiv.org/abs/1602.07031
3. Anvik, J., Hiew, L., Murphy, G.C.: Who should fix this bug? In: Proceedings of the 28th International Conference on Software Engineering, ICSE 2006, NY, USA, pp. 361–370 (2006). http://doi.acm.org/10.1145/1134285.1134336
4. Anvik, J., Murphy, G.C.: Reducing the effort of bug report triage: recommenders for development-oriented decisions. ACM Trans. Softw. Eng. Methodol. **20**(3), 10:1–10:35. http://doi.acm.org/10.1145/2000791.2000794
5. Banitaan, S., Alenezi, M.: Tram: an approach for assigning bug reports using their metadata. In: 2013 Third International Conference on Communications and Information Technology, pp. 215–219, June 2013
6. Bengio, Y., Ducharme, R., Vincent, P., Janvin, C.: A neural probabilistic language model. J. Mach. Learn. Res. **3**, 1137–1155. http://dl.acm.org/citation.cfm?id=944919.944966

7. Bhattacharya, P., Neamtiu, I., Shelton, C.R.: Automated, highly-accurate, bug assignment using machine learning and tossing graphs. J. Syst. Softw. **85**(10), 2275–2292 (2012)
8. Cavalcanti, Y.A.C., da Mota Silveira Neto, P.A., do Carmo Machado, I., de Almeida, E.S., de Lemos Meira, S.R.: Towards understanding software change request assignment: a survey with practitioners. In: Proceedings of the 17th International Conference on Evaluation and Assessment in Software Engineering, pp. 195–206 (2013)
9. Florea, A.-C., Anvik, J., Andonie, R.: Spark-based cluster implementation of a bug report assignment recommender system. In: Rutkowski, L., Korytkowski, M., Scherer, R., Tadeusiewicz, R., Zadeh, L.A., Zurada, J.M. (eds.) ICAISC 2017. LNCS, vol. 10246, pp. 31–42. Springer, Cham (2017). doi:10.1007/978-3-319-59060-8_4
10. Goodfellow, I., Bengio, Y., Courville, A.: Deep Learning. MIT Press, Cambridge (2016). http://www.deeplearningbook.org
11. Graves, A.: Supervised Sequence Labelling with Recurrent Neural Networks. Studies in Computational intelligence, New York (2012). http://opac.inria.fr/record=b1133792
12. Le, Q.V., Mikolov, T.: Distributed representations of sentences and documents. CoRR abs/1405.4053 (2014). http://arxiv.org/abs/1405.4053
13. Moritz, P., Nishihara, R., Stoica, I., Jordan, M.I.: SparkNet: training deep networks in spark. ArXiv e-prints, November 2015
14. Nasim, S., Razzaq, S., Ferzund, J.: Automated change request triage using alpha frequency matrix. In: Frontiers of Information Technology (FIT), pp. 298–302 (2011)
15. Nguyen, T.T., Nguyen, A.T., Nguyen, T.N.: Topic-based, time-aware bug assignment. SIGSOFT Softw. Eng. Notes **39**(1), 1–4. http://doi.acm.org/10.1145/2557833.2560585
16. Oh, K.J., Lee, W.J., Lim, C.G., Choi, H.J.: Personalized news recommendation using classified keywords to capture user preference. In: 16th International Conference on Advanced Communication Technology, pp. 1137–1155 (2014)
17. Salakhutdinov, R., Mnih, A., Hinton, G.: Restricted boltzmann machines for collaborative filtering. In: Proceedings of the 24th International Conference on Machine Learning, ICML 2007, NY, USA, pp. 791–798 (2007). http://doi.acm.org/10.1145/1273496.1273596
18. Tomar, A., Godin, F., Vandersmissen, B., Neve, W.D., de Walle, R.V.: Towards twitter hashtag recommendation using distributed word representations and a deep feed forward neural network. In: 2014 International Conference on Advances in Computing, Communications and Informatics, Delhi, India, September 24–27, 2014 (2014). http://dx.doi.org/10.1109/ICACCI.2014.6968557
19. Vincent, P., Larochelle, H., Lajoie, I., Bengio, Y., Manzagol, P.A.: Stacked denoising autoencoders: Learning useful representations in a deep network with a local denoising criterion. J. Mach. Learn. Res. **11**, 3371–3408. http://dl.acm.org/citation.cfm?id=1756006.1953039
20. Wang, H., Wang, N., Yeung, D.: Collaborative deep learning for recommender systems. CoRR abs/1409.2944 (2014). http://arxiv.org/abs/1409.2944
21. Wang, X., Wang, Y.: Improving content-based and hybrid music recommendation using deep learning. In: Proceedings of the 22nd ACM International Conference on Multimedia, MM 2014, NY, USA, pp. 627–636 (2014). http://doi.acm.org/10.1145/2647868.2654940

A Deep Learning Approach to Detect Distracted Drivers Using a Mobile Phone

Renato Torres[1,2]($\boxtimes$), Orlando Ohashi[3], Eduardo Carvalho[4,5],
and Gustavo Pessin[5]

[1] Institute of Exact and Natural Sciences, Federal University of Pará,
Belém, PA, Brazil
renato.hidaka@ifpa.edu.br
[2] Informatics Department, Federal Institute of Pará, Paragominas, PA, Brazil
[3] Cyberspace Institute, Federal Rural University of Amazônia, Belém, PA, Brazil
[4] SENAI Institute of Innovation in Minerals Technologies, Belém, PA, Brazil
[5] Applied Computing Lab, Vale Institute of Technology, Belém, PA, Brazil

Abstract. Detect distracted driver is an essential factor to maintain road safety and avoid the risk of accidents and deaths. Studies of the World Health Organization shows that the distraction caused by mobile phones can increase the crash risk by up to 400%. This paper proposes a convolutional neural network that is able to monitor drivers video surveillance, more specifically detect and classify when the driver is using a cell phone. The experiments show an impressive accuracy, achieving up 99% of accuracy detecting distracted driver.

Keywords: Convolutional neural network (CNN) · Driver behavior · Driver distraction · Driver's monitoring

1 Introduction

According to World Health Organization (WHO), the road traffic accident is one of the ten most frequent causes of death in the world [1]. In 2005, WHO published the report *The Global Burden of Disease* [2] that shows that more than 1.2 million people died and 50 million were injured in traffic accidents worldwide only in 2014. Traffic accidents cost US$ 518 billion every year. If nothing changes, in 2030, traffic accident will be the fifth cause of death in the world. In 2010, the United Nations (UN) created the program *Global Plan for Decade of Action for Road Safety 2011–2020* [3]. The program main goal is to reduce the road traffic fatalities by 50% and save 5 million lives in ten years. UN proposes five main lines of action: (i) road safety management; (ii) safer roads and mobility; (iii) safer vehicles; (iv) safer road users and (v) post-crash response.

The UN invited WHO to continuously monitoring the traffic safety. WHO created a *Global Status Report on road safety and special series*. The reports provide a snapshot of the gaps and needs of the road safety situations. Among the reports already published by WHO, the report Mobile Phone Use: a growing

© Springer International Publishing AG 2017
A. Lintas et al. (Eds.): ICANN 2017, Part II, LNCS 10614, pp. 72–79, 2017.
https://doi.org/10.1007/978-3-319-68612-7_9

problem of driver distraction (2011) [4] highlights the impact of cell phone use on driving performance. This report shows that the use of mobile phone can increase the drivers crash risk by a factor of four and if a driver is sending or retrieving text messaging, the amount of time that it spent with their eyes off the road increase by up to 400%. The use of mobile phone causes slower reaction times to detect and respond to driving-related events as, slower reactions to traffic signals and aggressive breaking.

In this context, we understand that automatically detect driver's distraction is an essential task in maintaining a safer traffic, one of the programs created by UN. In this paper, we propose a deep learning solution that automatically processes images from internal video surveillance system, with the aim to detect distracted drivers associated with the use of mobile phone. More specifically the proposed approach is a convolutional neural network (CNN) that detect if a driver is using or not a mobile phone, and the specific action, if the driver is sending/reading text messaging or talking on the phone.

2 Related Studies

There is a vast literature on detect driver distraction. Usually, driver's distraction is classified as internal and external to the vehicle. Regarding the internal distraction, the object of study this paper, we can highlight some related research.

Wollmer et al. [5] developed a long short term memory (LSTM) recurrent neural network to detect eight type of distraction based on modeling contextual information in driving and head tracking data captured during test drivers in real traffic. The approach used an interface of controller area network (CAN) and a head tracking system to obtain the necessary features to the model. The results show that the LSTM enable a reliable subject-independent detection of inattention with an accuracy of up to 96.6%.

Craye and Karry [6] proposed a computational model to detect distracted drivers. The model consists of four Kinect modules that are responsible for tracking: the eye behavior, arm position, head orientation and facial expressions. These features analyzed by these modules were used in two different classification strategies: AdaBoost classifier and Hidden Markov Model. The results show that the model achieved 85% of accuracy for the type of distraction and 90% for distraction detection.

Liu et al. [7] explored a semi-supervised method for driver distraction detection in real driving conditions to alleviate the cost of the labeling training data. The authors developed a Laplacian support vector machine and a semi-supervised extreme learning machine that use eyes and head movements to classify alert and distracted drivers. The main benefits of this work are that it reduces the necessity manual labeling of the data. The authors show that the approach improves the detection accuracy as compared with traditional supervised methods.

The work of Fernández et al. [8] show a review of the role of computer vision technology applied to the development of monitoring systems to detect distraction. The main methods for face detection, face tracking and detection of facial landmarks are summarized in this paper showing that they are a key component in many of the video-based inattention monitoring systems.

Unlike previous studies that require specialized equipment to detect distracted drivers, by analyzing specific behaviors such as eye tracking, head orientation, arms positions and facial expressions. In this work, we propose a methodology that uses surveillance camera and CNN to analyze driver's distraction. Our proposal does not require any additional equipment and achieved impressive results. Research as Wang et al. [9] and Bejiga et al. [10] are examples of the power of the CNN in correlated areas.

3   The Problem

The task of detect distracted drivers can be summarized as a binary classification problem. The driver is driving safely, or it's distracted. By contrast, if the goal is to identify the cause of the distraction, it's a multiclass classification problem. In this paper, we address both tasks, we classify the type of distraction, associated with the use of the mobile phone and we also classify as a binary problem combining the types of distraction in one major class.

We have used the StateFarm database [12] in our experiments. StateFarm was a database employed in a public kaggle contest[1]. The objective of the competition is to classify nine types of driver distraction, that are: C_1 - texting right; C_2 - talking on the phone right; C_3 - texting left; C_4 - talking on the phone left; C_5 - operating the radio; C_6 - drinking; C_7 - reaching behind; C_8 - hair and make-up; C_9 - talking to a passenger. Besides C_0 class that refers to non-distracted drivers.

In this research, we restrict to the classes associated with the use of mobile phone. The drivers can be classified in one of the following situations: C_0 - safe driving; C_1 - texting right; C_2 - talk on the phone right; C_3 - texting left and C_4 - talk on the phone left (see Fig. 1). The issue to classify distracted drivers consists, at each sample define the correct class C_i such that $i = \{1, 2, 3, 4\}$. On the other hand, the problem of detecting distracted drivers can be summarized as, if the sample is in C_0 or not. If it doesn't belong, means that the driver is distracted.

4   Methodology

In this section, we present the pre-processing methodology realized in this work, the architecture design of convolutional neural network (CNN) developed and the experiments that were accomplished to measure the accuracy of the model.

In the pre-processing stage, each image was loaded and resized to 150×150 pixels. These images were storage in a $150 \times 150 \times 3$ matrix. The 3D matrix was necessary because of the RGB color model. Each cell of the matrix kept a value between 0 to 255. We use Min-Max transformation to normalize the values of the matrix. Each value between 0 to 255 was transformed to values in the 0 to 1 range.

---

[1] https://www.kaggle.com/c/state-farm-distracted-driver-detection.

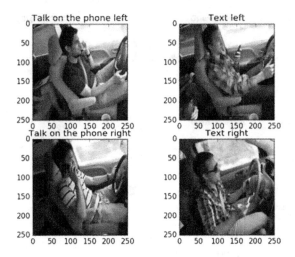

Fig. 1. Types of distractions.

4.1 Convolutional Neural Network

Convolutional neural networks (CNN) are structures divided into two parts: convolution layer and fully connected layer. According to Goodfellow, Bengio and Courville [11], the convolutional layer is responsible for extracting the features using a combination of linear and nonlinear activation functions such as pooling, that summarizes the output of the layer. The second structure of the network is a fully connected layer that is responsible for using the extracted features of the convolutional layer to realize the prediction or classification. Normally, the fully connected layer is build using a Multilayer Perceptron (MLP).

Figure 2 shows the CNN architecture developed in this work. We can see that each convolution layer is composed of a 3-upla <Convolution, Nonlinear activation function, Pooling>. The first and second convolution layer are setting with 32 kernels of 3×3, ReLU activation function, and MaxPooling of 2×2. In the third layer, we used a convolution with 64 kernels of 3×3, ReLU activation function and MaxPooling of 2×2. In the fully connected layer, we used a Multilayer Perceptron with 64 neurons and ReLU activation function in the hidden layer and 5 neurons and sigmoid activation function in the output layer. We used the Keras[2] framework implementations to build this architecture.

4.2 Experiments

The main purpose this research is to detect and classify distracted driver's associated with the use of the mobile phone, we use only the samples referring to the classes C_0, C_1, C_2, C_3 and C_4 of the original problem [12]. Table 1 shows the number of pictures used for the training and validation of each class.

---

[2] https://keras.io/.

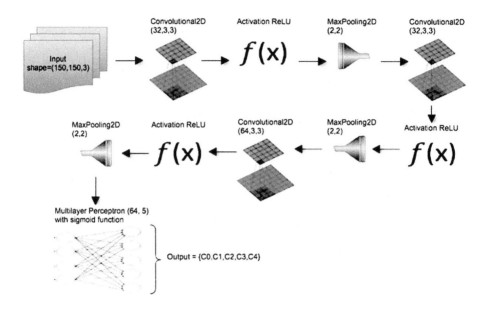

Fig. 2. CNN architecture developed.

Table 1. Number of samples to training and validate.

	C_0	C_1	C_2	C_3	C_4	Total
Training	2088	1864	2065	1936	1888	9841
Validation	401	403	252	410	438	1904
Total	2489	2267	2317	2346	2326	11745

From the 9841 training samples, we used 6593 (67%) for the training of the network and 3248 (33%) for the validation of each epoch. We set the number of epochs in the training of the CNN to 13 and the batch size to 32. Since we are dealing with a multiclass classification problem, we used the loss function categorical cross entropy and the optimizer RMSprop.

To run the experiments, we use a computer with the following settings: 2,9 GHz Intel Core i7 processor, 8 GB 1600 MHz DDR3 memory and Intel HD Graphics 4000 of 1536 MB. CNN training lasted about an hour and the accuracy of training and validation set were, respectively, $acc = 0.9841$ and $acc\_val = 0.9926$. Figure 3 shows the learning curve of the 13 training epochs in function of the error. In this graphic, we can see that in the last epoch we have the lowest error rates in both the training set and test set. These characteristics inform that we have a low bias and variance and that our proposed approach can realize the necessary generalization to reduce the possibility of overfitting.

To demonstrate the generalization of the model the next step of the experiment was to perform the classification of the 1904 test samples. The accuracy

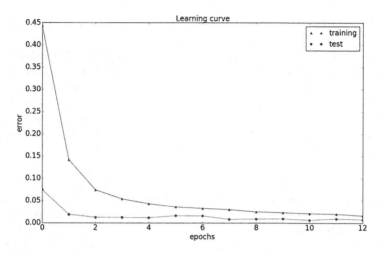

Fig. 3. Learning curve of the 13 training epochs in function of the error.

obtained was 0.9952 and can be observed in detail in the confusion matrix of Fig. 4. In this confusion matrix, we can see that we had only nine wrong classifications. These level of accuracy show that the proposed model was able to successfully realize the generalization in the task of classifying distracted driver's associated with the mobile phone use.

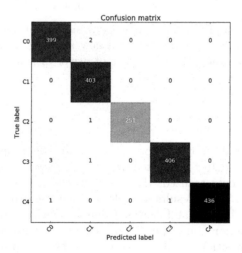

Fig. 4. Confusion matrix

Considering the binary classification task of detecting distracted drivers, recognize if the sample is in C_0 or not. We modify the confusion matrix for the binary problem. In this case, the cause of distraction is not relevant, we merge all the types of distracted classes, C_1, C_2, C_3 and C_4 in one major class called C_x.

As expected in this new confusion matrix, the number of misclassification reduced. Two misclassifications are false negative and four are false positive. The false negative indicates the sample that is of the C0 type but was classified as Cx type, i.e., two situations where the driver was driving safely, but the model classified as distracted. On the other hand, the false positive indicates the number of samples that are of the Cx type but were incorrectly classified as C0 type. In this case, were four situations where the driver was distracted but was not detected by the model.

Using the number of false positives and negatives it is possible to calculate precision and recall measures. Precision has the purpose of measure the proportion of elements that were classified as C0 in relation to false positives. By contrast, recall has the aim of the measure the proportion of elements that were classified as C0 in relation to false negatives. These two measures indicate that the closer to one, better the level of generalization performed by the model. Equation 1 summarizes precision, recall, and accuracy calculated from the confusion matrix.

$$precision = \frac{TP}{TP+FP} = \frac{399}{399+4} = 0.99$$
$$recall = \frac{TP}{TP+FN} = \frac{399}{399+2} = 0.995 \tag{1}$$
$$accuracy = \frac{TP+TN}{n} = \frac{399+1499}{1904} = 0.9968$$

The experiments and analyses carried out show that the developed model was able to successfully perform the necessary learning to detect and classify with an excellent accuracy, the four types of driver distraction associated with the mobile phone use.

5   Conclusion

The results presented in this paper shows that the proposed approach is extremely efficient to detect distracted drivers associated with the mobile phone use. In the experiments realized, the convolutional neural network presented an accuracy of 99%. These results are relevant because driver's distraction is a risk factor to traffic injuries and deaths. Comparing with correlated works that detect driver distraction using specific and expensive hardware, like Kinect as eye behavior, arm position, head orientation and facial expressions. This excellent accuracy combined with the fact that our solution requires a minimal setup, a standard video camera. Allow our proposed solution to be applied in industrial scale. Therefore, we concluded that our solution is promising and, for this reason, as future work, we will create an application so that people can use our solution.

References

1. World Health Organization: Global Status Report on Road Safety (2015). http://www.who.int/violence_injury_prevention/publications/road_traffic/en/
2. World Health Organization: The global burden of disease. http://www.who.int/healthinfo/global_burden_disease/2004_report_update/en/
3. United Nations: Global Plan for the Decade of Action for Road Safety 2011–2020. http://www.who.int/roadsafety/decade_of_action/plan/en/
4. World Health Organization: Mobile phone use: a growing problem of driver distraction. http://www.who.int/violence_injury_prevention/publications/road_traffic/distracted_driving/en/
5. Wollmer, M., Blaschke, C., Schindl, T., Schuller, B., Farber, B., Mayer, S., Trefflich, B.: Online driver distraction detection using long short-term memory. IEEE Trans. Intell. Transp. Syst. **12**(2), 574–582 (2011)
6. Craye, C., Karray, F.: Driver distraction detection and recognition using RGB-D sensor. In: Computer Vision and Patter Recognition. Cornel University Library (2015). https://arxiv.org/abs/1502.00250
7. Liu, T., Yang, Y., Huang, G., Yeo, Y., Lin, Z.: Driver distraction detection using semi-supervised machine learning. IEEE Trans. Intell. Transp. Syst. **17**(4), 1108–1120 (2016)
8. Fernández, A., Usamentiaga, R., Cars, J.L., Casado, R.: Driver distraction using visual-based sensors and algorithms. Sensors **16**(11), 1805 (2016). doi:10.3390/s16111805. (Basel, Switzerland)
9. Wang, R., Xu, Z.: A pedestrian and vehicle rapid identification model based on convolutional neural network. In: Proceedings of the 7th International Conference on Internet Multimedia Computing and Service (ICIMCS 2015). NY, USA, Article 32. ACM, New York (2015)
10. Bejiga, M., Zeggada, A., Nouffidj, A., Melgani, F.: A convolutional neural network approach for assisting avalanche search and rescue operations with UAV imagery. Sensors **9**(2), 100 (2017). doi:10.3390/rs9020100
11. Goodfellow, I., Bengio, Y., Courville, A.: Deep Learning. MIT Press. http://www.deeplearningbook.org/
12. StateFarm: State Farm Distracted Driver Detection. https://www.kaggle.com/c/state-farm-distracted-driver-detection/data

A Multi-level Weighted Representation for Person Re-identification

Xianglai Meng$^{(\boxtimes)}$, Biao Leng, and Guanglu Song

School of Computer Science and Engineering, Beihang University, Beijing, China
mengxianglai@buaa.edu.cn

Abstract. The introduction of deep neural networks (DNN) into person re-identification tasks has significantly improved the re-identification accuracy. However, the substantial characteristics of features extracted from different layers of convolutional neural networks (CNN) are infrequently considered in existing methods. In this paper, we propose a multi-level weighted representation for person re-identification, in which features containing strong discriminative powers or rich semantic meanings are extracted from different layers of a deep CNN, and an estimation subnet evaluates the quality of each feature and generates quality scores used as concatenation weights for all multi-level features. The features multiplied by their weights are concatenated together to the final representations which are improved eventually by a triplet loss to increase the inter-class distance. Therefore, the representation exploits the various benefits of different level features jointly. Experiments on the iLIDS-VID and PRID 2011 datasets show that our proposed representation significantly outperforms the baseline and the state of the art methods.

Keywords: Deep learning · Multi-level · Weighting scheme · Person re-identification

1 Introduction

Person re-identification is a task of matching a person captured by non-overlapping cameras. It is crucial for smart surveillance systems and has attracted enormous attentions to promote the re-identification accuracy. A typical resolution for person re-identification contains two central parts: a discriminative feature extraction method and a distance metric learning approach. In spite of considerable efforts in recent years, this problem is still challenging as a consequence of large appearance variations caused by massive changes of environments and viewpoints.

Recently, many works tend to use deep convolutional neural networks and achieves outstanding performances compared with traditional hand-crafted features [8,10,11]. However, the majority of works using CNN concentrate on digging up information from features of multiple images or from features of multiple parts of an image, while the substantial characteristics of multi-level features

© Springer International Publishing AG 2017
A. Lintas et al. (Eds.): ICANN 2017, Part II, LNCS 10614, pp. 80–88, 2017.
https://doi.org/10.1007/978-3-319-68612-7_10

extracted from different layers of CNN are generally disregarded. Advantages of using multi-level CNN features have been explored in visual tracking tasks, and experiments show that features of a top convolutional layer contains more abstract and semantic meanings and that features of a lower layer are more discriminative to separate instances of the same class [11]. Studies [9,14] on visualization and understanding of convolutional networks can support this argument as well.

Inspired by the situation, multi-level features of CNN are utilized to construct a more discriminative representation in this work. Furthermore, an estimation of the features extracted from different layers should be implemented to estimate their contributions to the final representation, as the values of different level features are diverse. However, it's nearly impossible to establish a standard assessment of features' qualities or to get score labels of features' discriminative powers, which leaves an explicit supervised feature-quality-score generating hard to perform. As a consequence, a weighting scheme using triplet loss is proposed to address this issue by taking the scores generated by the estimation subnet as weights when multi-level features are concatenated together to construct the final representation of person re-identification.

The contribution of this paper is twofold. First, we exploit the discriminative and semantic characteristics of multi-level CNN features in person re-identification task and achieved the state of the art performance. Second, we propose an estimation subnet under a weighting scheme to generate the quality scores of different level features which is used to improve the holistic accuracy. Experiments on the iLIDS-VID and PRID 2011 datasets show that our multi-level weighted representation outperforms the state of the art and baseline methods.

2 Related Work

Most works [3,4,6,12,13] on person re-identification task concentrate on either extracting discriminative and robust features or on establishing an enhanced feature similarity metric. And recently, inspired by the successful applications of DNN in various areas of computer-vision [5,8,10], DNN have been used in the person re-identification task [1,7,15]. However, most of these methods ignore the importance of multi-level information in the person re-identification task. Our proposed approach differs significantly from all these methods, as the multi-level information extracted from different layers of the convolutional network is used in the construction of our representation, and an estimation subnet is developed to generate quality scores of multi-level features under a weighting scheme for a better accuracy. In addition, an aggressive data augmentation method demonstrates the robustness of our representation and improves the performance on iLIDS-VID dataset which has many heavily occluded images.

3   Method

3.1   The Proposed Representation Construction Network

A diagram of our multi-level weighting network is shown in Fig. 1. As illustrated in the figure, the proposed re-id method uses triplet images as inputs for the final triplet loss during the training process. In each triplet, there are two different images of one same person and the third image of another person, with images of camera one and of camera two mixed together. In our architecture, each frame is firstly processed by a deep convolutional network, and then multi-level features are extracted from different layers of the network and supervised with softmax losses so that the qualities of extracted features can be guaranteed. After that, estimation subnets perform a quality evaluation of features, which generate quality scores for each extracted feature. All features are multiplied by weights via the weighting layer. The weighted features are then concatenated together in the channel dimension and sliced in the num dimension according to the triplet they belong to. After an L2 normalization layer, these concatenated features are sent into a low-margin triplet loss layer, as our experiments show that it's easy to see overfitting problems with a high margin as a consequence of the small scale of person re-id datasets.

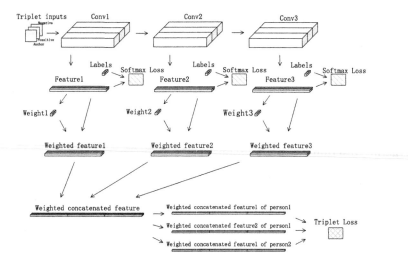

Fig. 1. The multi-level weighted training network. Triplet training images are fed into a deep CNN from which multi-level features are extracted. These features are supervised with the softmax loss and estimated to generate quality scores. Subsequently, the features are multiplied with their scores and concatenated together in the channel dimension. The final representation is supervised with a triplet loss.

3.2   Quality Estimation Subnets

We proposed two quality estimation structures to evaluate the extracted features and to generate quality scores.

The first structure is shown in Fig. 2(b), in which a fully-connected layer is used to perform the assessment of multi-level features and followed by a sigmoid layer to produce a projection to the interval of 0 and 1 since the outputs of subnets are used as weights. This subnet is intuitively devised with an intention to estimate the features directly and thus the fully-connected layer is straightly connected to the extracted features. The structure is straightforward but short of enough information for the estimation of the features with such connection. Experiments prove that the performance of this uncomplicated structure is unstable.

To address this issue, the structure in Fig. 2(a) is proposed. With a convolutional layer connected to the convolutional feature maps from which the multi-level features are extracted, the estimation subnet obtains more information about the multi-level features. Experiments show that representation constructed with this subnet achieves higher and steadier performance than the former subnet.

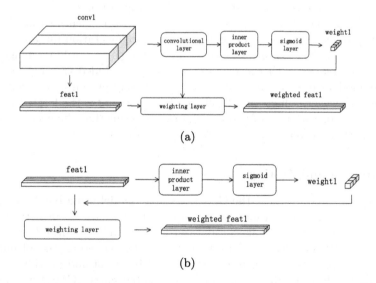

(a)

(b)

Fig. 2. Two proposed quality estimation subnets for the evaluation of each feature and for the generation of quality scores.

3.3   Weighting Scheme with Triplet Loss

With the quality estimation subnet, we propose to train a network for the evaluation of features' qualities and the generation of quality scores. However, there is no quality score label and it's hard to establish such an assessment by hand, which means an explicit supervision of the quality estimation subnet is unattainable. Thus, the estimation subnet is settled in a weighting scheme in which the quality scores generated by subnets are taken as weights of the extracted features when the final representations are concatenated from the weighted multi-level features. Under the supervision of a triplet loss, the inter-class distance of the final representation is improved and the quality estimation subnet is trained indirectly during back propagations.

4   Experiments

4.1   Datasets and Data Augmentation

The iLIDS-VID dataset involves 300 different pedestrians observed across two disjoint camera views at an airport arrival hall, in which the images contain cluttered backgrounds, frequent occlusions, and large variations of lighting conditions and cameras' viewpoints. We use the 178 persons of the PRID 2011 dataset who appear in both two cameras with more than 27 clean frames in our experiments. Persons in each dataset are randomly split into the training set and the testing set in equal amounts, and all experiments are repeated 10 times with 10 different splits of datasets to get the average results.

Occlusion is one of the major difficulties in person re-identification task. To solve this problem, we utilize an aggressive data augmentation method to fabricate pseudo-occlusion instances by covering a large part of original images with a mean value block. With the increase of heavily occluded training instances, the CNN model can learn more about how to classify person images with large occlusions. However, a huge disadvantage of this method is the large divergence and the severe disturbance of training data, as a result that the accuracy of the baseline method decreases with this data augmentation.

4.2   Training and Testing

In our experiments, we chose the GoogLeNet [10] model using batch normalization [2] as our baseline method and the convolutional part of our network. The pre-trained model on the ImageNet dataset is used, and the initial learning rate was set to 0.001 and decreased by multi-steps. The covering rate of our data augmentation process was set to one-third both in height and in width.

During the testing stage, the cumulative match curve (CMC) was used to quantitatively evaluate our models. Features of all images in a sequence were extracted and averaged for one final representation of a person in that camera, with the first camera chosen as the probe and the second camera as the gallery, and the simple cosine similarity metric was used to rank the features and to match the same person in different cameras.

4.3   Comparison with the Baseline and the State of the Art

In this experiment, we investigate the performances of our weighted multi-level feature on the iLIDS-VID and PRID 2011 datasets. In Table 1, *Ours* represents our multi-level weighted representation using the subnet in Fig. 2(a), and *aug* signifies that the features are trained with the data augmentation in Sect. 4.1.

Due to the great discriminative power of GoogLeNet with batch normalization, our baseline method has achieved the same performance with the state of the art. And our proposed method significantly outperforms the state of the art and the baseline method on both datasets. With the use of our aggressive data augmentation in the training stage, a significant degeneration of the baseline method can be observed as a consequence of the deficiency of robustness, while our method improves the rank 1 accuracy remarkably by 7.5% on the iLIDS-VID dataset which contains numerous heavily occluded images.

Table 1. Comparison of our feature with related methods and baseline on iLIDS-VID and PRID 2011. *Ours* represents the weighted multi-level feature using the estimation subnet in Fig. 2(a) and *aug* means the features are trained with our data augmentation described in Sect. 4.1.

Datasets	iLIDS-VID				PRID 2011			
CMC rank (%)	1	5	10	20	1	5	10	20
Ours+aug	80.1	94.2	97.3	98.8	83.8	96.2	98.0	100
Ours	72.6	87.8	92.2	95.4	83.8	96.6	97.8	99.8
Baseline+aug [2]	53.3	77.8	88.0	94.9	81.3	93.9	96.6	98.7
Baseline [2]	58.3	79.4	87.1	92.0	79.1	94.8	97.8	99.3
CNN+RNN [7]	58	84	91	96	70	90	95	97
CNN+XQDA [15]	53.0	81.4	89.7	95.1	77.3	93.5	95.7	99.1
TDL [13]	56.3	87.6	95.6	98.3	56.7	80.0	87.6	93.6
STA [6]	44.3	71.7	83.7	91.7	64.1	87.3	89.9	92.0
eSDC [12]	41.3	63.5	72.7	83.1	48.3	74.9	87.3	94.4
KISSME [4]	36.5	67.8	78.8	87.1	34.4	61.7	72.1	81.0

4.4   Comparison of Weighted Multi-level Feature and Non-weighted Multi-level Feature

To evaluate our quality estimation subnets, we compare the performances on the iLIDS-VID dataset of our multi-level weighted features implemented with the two estimation subnets in Fig. 2 and the non-weighted multi-level feature. In the experiments, our aggressive data augmentation is performed during the training stage, and Fig. 3 shows the CMC curves of these features.

As shown in the diagram, the weighted multi-level features achieve an improvement by about 2.5% on average in accuracy compared with the non-weighted multi-level feature, and the quality estimation subnet in Fig. 2(a)

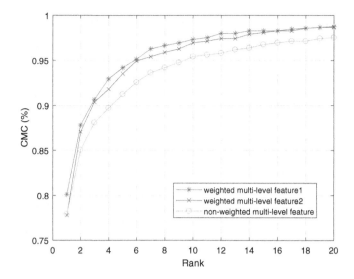

Fig. 3. CMC curves for the iLIDS-VID dataset, comparing weighted multi-level feature1 using the subnet in Fig. 2(a), weighted multi-level feature2 using the subnet in Fig. 2(b), and non-weighted multi-level feature. Our data augmentation in Sect. 4.1 is used for training.

behaves more accurate and steady than the subnet in Fig. 2(b). The results show the effectiveness of our quality estimation weighting scheme.

4.5   Cross-Dataset Testing

A cross-dataset testing is more meaningful to value the method's performance in real-world applications. Hence, a cross-dataset testing was performed using the whole iLIDS-VID dataset as training set and using the PRID 2011 dataset as the testing set. The results of the cross-dataset testing shown in Table 2 show that our multi-level weighted representation significantly outperforms the related methods and the baseline by large margins, which demonstrates the strong robustness of our presentation for person re-id.

Table 2. Cross-dataset testing results. CD [1] is trained on Shinpuhkan 2014 dataset and other methods are trained on iLIDS-VID. CNN+RNN [7] is tested on 50% of the PRID 2011 dataset and other methods are tested on the whole PRID 2011 dataset.

CMC rank (%)	1	5	10	15	20	30
Ours	43.8	69.1	81.5	84.8	89.3	94.4
Baseline [2]	32.6	57.3	67.4	73.0	80.9	87.1
CNN+RNN [7]	28	57	69	–	81	–
CD [1]	16.8	–	43.3	–	52.4	56.8

5   Conclusion

In this paper, we have presented a novel multi-level weighted representation for person re-identification. In our architecture, multi-level features are firstly extracted from different layers of a deep CNN and then evaluated by a subnet which generates quality scores for all multi-level features. Due to the lack of quality score labels and of explicit supervisions, the subnet is settled to be trained indirectly in a weighting scheme in which the scores are taken as weights of the extracted features. These features multiplied with their weights are eventually concatenated together to the final representations which are supervised with a triplet loss for a holistic improvement. With the comprehensive consideration of multi-level features and the effective quality estimation weighting approach, our representation outperforms the baseline and the state of the art methods on two standard datasets by large margins.

Acknowledgment. This work is supported by the National Natural Science Foundation of China (No. 61472023).

References

1. Hu, Y., Yi, D., Liao, S., Lei, Z., Li, S.Z.: Cross dataset person re-identification. In: Jawahar, C.V., Shan, S. (eds.) ACCV 2014. LNCS, vol. 9010, pp. 650–664. Springer, Cham (2015). doi:10.1007/978-3-319-16634-6_47
2. Ioffe, S., Szegedy, C.: Batch normalization: accelerating deep network training by reducing internal covariate shift, pp. 448–456 (2015)
3. Khamis, S., Kuo, C., Singh, V.K., Shet, V., Davis, L.S.: Joint learning for attribute-consistent person re-identification, pp. 134–146 (2014)
4. Kostinger, M., Hirzer, M., Wohlhart, P., Roth, P.M., Bischof, H.: Large scale metric learning from equivalence constraints, pp. 2288–2295 (2012)
5. Krizhevsky, A., Sutskever, I., Hinton, G.E.: Imagenet classification with deep convolutional neural networks, pp. 1097–1105 (2012)
6. Liu, K., Ma, B., Zhang, W., Huang, R.: A spatio-temporal appearance representation for viceo-based pedestrian re-identification, pp. 3810–3818 (2015)
7. Mclaughlin, N., Rincon, J.M.D., Miller, P.: Recurrent convolutional network for video-based person re-identification, pp. 1325–1334 (2016)
8. Schroff, F., Kalenichenko, D., Philbin, J.: Facenet: a unified embedding for face recognition and clustering, pp. 815–823 (2015)
9. Simonyan, K., Vedaldi, A., Zisserman, A.: Deep inside convolutional networks: visualising image classification models and saliency maps (2013)
10. Szegedy, C., Liu, W., Jia, Y., Sermanet, P., Reed, S., Anguelov, D., Erhan, D., Vanhoucke, V., Rabinovich, A.: Going deeper with convolutions, pp. 1–9 (2015)
11. Wang, L., Ouyang, W., Wang, X., Lu, H.: Visual tracking with fully convolutional networks, pp. 3119–3127 (2015)
12. Wang, T., Gong, S., Zhu, X., Wang, S.: Person re-identification by discriminative selection in video ranking. IEEE Trans. Pattern Anal. Mach. Intell. **38**(12), 2501–2514 (2016)
13. You, J., Wu, A., Li, X., Zheng, W.: Top-push video-based person re-identification, pp. 1345–1353 (2016)

14. Zeiler, M.D., Fergus, R.: Visualizing and understanding convolutional networks. In: Fleet, D., Pajdla, T., Schiele, B., Tuytelaars, T. (eds.) ECCV 2014. LNCS, vol. 8689, pp. 818–833. Springer, Cham (2014). doi:10.1007/978-3-319-10590-1_53
15. Zheng, L., Bie, Z., Sun, Y., Wang, J., Su, C., Wang, S., Tian, Q.: MARS: a video benchmark for large-scale person re-identification. In: Leibe, B., Matas, J., Sebe, N., Welling, M. (eds.) ECCV 2016. LNCS, vol. 9910, pp. 868–884. Springer, Cham (2016). doi:10.1007/978-3-319-46466-4_52

Games and Strategy

DeepAPT: Nation-State APT Attribution Using End-to-End Deep Neural Networks

Ishai Rosenberg, Guillaume Sicard, and Eli (Omid) David[✉]

Deep Instinct Ltd., Tel Aviv, Israel
{ishair,guillaumes,david}@deepinstinct.com

Abstract. In recent years numerous advanced malware, aka *advanced persistent threats* (APT) are allegedly developed by nation-states. The task of attributing an APT to a specific nation-state is extremely challenging for several reasons. Each nation-state has usually more than a single cyber unit that develops such advanced malware, rendering traditional authorship attribution algorithms useless. Furthermore, those APTs use state-of-the-art evasion techniques, making feature extraction challenging. Finally, the dataset of such available APTs is extremely small.

In this paper we describe how deep neural networks (DNN) could be successfully employed for nation-state APT attribution. We use sandbox reports (recording the behavior of the APT when run dynamically) as raw input for the neural network, allowing the DNN to learn high level feature abstractions of the APTs itself. Using a test set of 1,000 Chinese and Russian developed APTs, we achieved an accuracy rate of 94.6%.

1 Introduction

While malware detection is always a challenging research topic, a special challenge involves nation-state advanced persistent threats (APT), highly sophisticated and evasive malware. Since the usage of such cyber weapons might be considered an act of war [10], the question "which country is responsible?" could become critical.

In this paper we use raw features of dynamic analysis to train a nation-state APT attribution classifier. The main contribution of this paper is providing the first nation-state APT attribution classifier, which achieves a high accuracy on the largest test set of available nation-state developed APTs ever collected, successfully attributing new malware families.

The rest of the article is structured as follows: Sect. 2 contains the relevant related work to our use cases. Section 3 specifies the problem definition and the unique challenges in this domain, both with nation-state APT attribution in general and especially when using feature engineering. Section 4 contains our nation-state APT attribution classifier implementation and the experimental results. Section 5 contains our concluding remarks.

2 Background and Related Work

There are numerous topics related to authorship attribution, such as plagiarism detection, books authorship attribution, source code authorship attribution and

© Springer International Publishing AG 2017
A. Lintas et al. (Eds.): ICANN 2017, Part II, LNCS 10614, pp. 91–99, 2017.
https://doi.org/10.1007/978-3-319-68612-7_11

binary program authorship attribution. [15] provides a broad review of many of those topics, including the natural language processing (NLP) and traditional machine learning (ML) algorithms and the relevant features used, for example lexical (e.g., word frequencies), syntactic (e.g., sentence structure), semantic (e.g., synonyms), and application specific (such as a specific structure, for instance HTML).

In the following sub-sections, we focus only on the ones relevant to our work (and ignoring those that are irrelevant, such as source code authorship attribution, which cannot be used in our case since a source code is not available for the APTs).

2.1 Binary Code Authorship Attribution

Certain stylistic features can survive the compilation process and remain intact in binary code, which leads to the feasibility of authorship attribution for binary code. Rosenblum et al. [13] extracted syntax-based and semantic-based features using predefined templates, such as idioms (sequences of three consecutive instructions), n-grams, and graphlets. Machine learning techniques are then applied to rank these features based on their relative correlations with authorship. Alrabaee et al. [1] extracted a sequence of instructions with specific semantics and to construct a graph-based on register manipulation, where a machine learning algorithm is applied afterwards. Caliskan et al. [5] extracted syntactical features present in source code from decompiled executable binary.

Though these approaches represent a great effort in authorship attribution, it should be noted that they were not applied to real malware. Furthermore, some limitations could be observed including weak accuracy in the case of multiple authors, being potentially thwarted by light obfuscation, and their inability to decouple features related to functionality from those related to authors styles.

2.2 Malware Attribution

The difficulty in obtaining ground truth labels for samples has led much work in this area to focus on clustering malware, and the wide range of obfuscation techniques in common use have led many researchers to focus on dynamic analysis rather than static features (i.e., instead of examining the static file, focus on the report generated after running the file dynamically in a sandbox).

The work of Pfeffer et al. [12] examines information obtained via both static and dynamic analysis of malware samples, in order to organize code samples into lineages that indicate the order in which samples are derived from each other. Alrabaee et al. [2] have used both features extracted from the disassembled malware code (such as idioms) and from the executable itself, used mutual information and information gain to rank them, and built an SVM classifier using the top ranked features. Those methods require a large amount of pre-processing and manual domain-specific feature engineering to obtain the relevant features.

The malware attribution papers mentioned so far are applicable only to cases where a malware is an evolution of another malware (e.g., by mutation), or from the same family, functionality-wise. These methods are not effective when completely different families of malware are examined. Our paper presents a novel application of DNN for APT attribution, specifying which nation has developed a specific APT, when the APTs in question are not derivatives of one another, and belong to completely different families.

The work of Marquis-Boire et al. [4] examines several static features intended to provide credible links between executable malware binary produced by the same authors. However, many of these features are specific to malware, such as command and control infrastructure and data exfiltration methods, and the authors note that these features must be extracted manually. To the best of our knowledge, this is the only available paper that explicitly dealt with nation-state APTs detection (using features common in them, such as APTs). However, those use cases are limited, and no accuracy or other performance measures were provided. In addition, the paper did not deal with classifying which nation developed the malware, and rather mentioned that one could use the similarities between a known (labeled) nation-state APT to an unknown one to infer the attribution of the latter.

3   Problem Definition: Nation-State APT Attribution

Given an APT as an executable file, we would like to determine which nation state developed it. This is a multi-class classification problem, i.e., one label per candidate nation-state.

3.1   The Challenges of Nation-State Attribution

Trying to classify the nation that developed an APT can be an extremely challenging task for several reasons that we cover here.

Each nation-state has usually more than a single cyber unit developing such products, and there is more than a single developer in each unit. This means that the accuracy of traditional authorship attribution algorithms, which associates the author of source code or program using stylistic features in the source code, or such features that have survived the compilation, would be very limited.

These APTs also use state-of-the-art evasion techniques, such-as anti-VM, anti-debugging, code obfuscation and encryption ([16]), making feature extraction challenging.

Moreover, the number of such available APTs is small, since such APTs tend to be targeted, used for specific purposes (and, unlike common criminal malware, not for monetary gain) and therefore are not available on many computers. Their evasion mechanisms make them hard to detect as well. This results in a further decrease in the training set size from which to learn.

Finally, since nation states are aware that their APTs can be caught, they commonly might try to fool the security researchers examining the APT to think that another malware developer group (e.g., another nation) has developed it (e.g., by adding the APT strings in a foreign language, embedding data associated with a previously published malware, etc.). That is, unlike traditional authorship attribution problems, in this case the "authors" are actively trying to evade attribution and encourage false attribution.

Despite these issues, manual nation-state APT attribution is performed, mostly based on functional similarities, shared command and control servers (C&Cs, which provide an accurate attribution), etc. For example, the APTs Duqu, Flame and Gauss were attributed to the same origin as Stuxnet following a very cumbersome advanced manual analysis ([3]). The question is: How can we overcome these challenges and create an automated classifier (that does not require lengthy manual analysis)?

3.2 Using Raw Features in DNN Classifications in the Cyber Security Domain

One of Deep Neural Networks (DNN) greatest advantages is the ability to use raw features as input, while learning higher level features on its own during the training process. In this process, each hidden layer extracts higher level features from the previous layer, creating a hierarchy of higher-level features.

This is the reason why deep learning classifiers perform better than traditional machine learning classifiers in complex tasks that requires domain-specific features such as language understanding [6], speech recognition, image recognition [17], etc. In such a framework the input is not high level features, which are derived manually based on limited dataset, thus not necessarily fitting the task at hand. Instead, the input is raw features (pixels in image processing, characters in NLP, etc.). The DNN learns a high-level hierarchy of the features during the training phase. The deeper the hidden layer is the higher the abstraction level of the features (higher-level features).

While most previous work on applying machine learning to malware analysis relied on manually crafted features, David et al. [7] trained DNN on raw dynamic analysis reports to generate malware signatures for use in a malware family classification context. In this paper we similarly train a DNN on raw dynamic analysis reports but the goal is obtaining a different functionality (APT attribution rather than signature generation).

The benefits of using raw features are:

(1) Cheaper and less time consuming than manual feature engineering. This is especially true in the case of nation-state APTs, where the code requires a lot of time to reverse engineer in-order to gain insights about features, due to obfuscation techniques commonly used by it, as mentioned above.
(2) Higher accuracy of Deep Learning classifiers, since important features are never overlooked. For instance, in our nation-state APT attribution classifier, mentioned in the next section, we have used the technique suggested in [11] to assess the contribution of each of our features, by multiplying (and summing up) their weights in the network, where the highest value indicates the most significant feature. We have seen that, besides the expected API

calls and IP strings of C&C servers, arbitrary hexadecimal values were surprisingly some of the most important features. A security researcher might throw such addresses away, since they are useless. However, those values were the size of data of specific PE section which contained encrypted malicious shellcode, identifying a specific malware family.

(3) More flexibility due to the ability to use the same features for different classification objectives. For instance, our nation-state APT attribution classifier uses the same raw features of the malware signature generator implemented in [7]. Therefore, we could implement both, using only a single feature extraction process.

4   Implementation and Experimental Evaluation

The challenges mentioned in the previous section require a novel approach inorder to mitigate them. As mentioned before, the problem at hand is not a regular authorship attribution problem, since more than a single developer is likely to be involved, some of them might be replaced in the middle of the development. This makes regular authorship attribution algorithms, using personal stylistic features irrelevant. Another approach would be to consider all of the same nation state APTs as a part of a single malware family. The rationale is that common frameworks and functionality should exist in different APTs from the same nation. However, this is also not accurate: each nation might have several cyber units, each with its own targets, frameworks, functionality, etc. Thus, it would be more accurate to look at this classification task as a malicious/benign classifier: each label might contain several "families" (benign web browsers, malicious ransomware, etc.) that might have very little in common. Fortunately, DNN is known to excel in such complex tasks.

This brings us to the usage of raw features: since we do not know how many "actual APT families" are available in the dataset, we need to use raw features, letting the DNN build its feature abstraction hierarchy itself, taking into account all available APT families, as mentioned in Sect. 1.

4.1   Raw Features Used

A sandbox analysis report of an executable file can provide a lot of useful information, which can be leveraged for many different classification tasks. In order to show the advantages of using raw features by a DNN classifier, we have chosen raw features that can be used for different classification tasks.

Cuckoo Sandbox is a widely used open-source project for automated dynamic malware analysis. It provides static analysis of the analyzed file: PE header metadata, imports, exports, sections, etc. Therefore, it can provide useful information even in the absence of dynamic analysis, due to, e.g., anti-VM techniques used by nation-state APTs. Cuckoo Sandbox also provides dynamic analysis and monitors the process system calls, their arguments and their return value. Thus, it can provide useful information to mitigate obfuscation techniques used by nation-state APTs. We have decided to use Cuckoo Sandbox reports as raw data for our classifiers due to their level of detail, configurability, and popularity. We used Cuckoo Sandbox default configuration.

Our purpose was to let our classifiers learn the high-level abstraction hierarchy on their own, without involving any manual or domain-specific knowledge. Thus, we used words only, which are basic raw features commonly used in the text analysis domain. Although Cuckoo reports are in JSON format, which can be parsed such that specific information is obtained from them, we did not perform any parsing. In other words, we treated the reports as raw text, completely ignoring the formatting, syntax, etc. Our goal was to let our classifiers learn everything on their own, including JSON parsing, if necessary. Therefore, the markup and tagged parts of the files were extracted as well. For instance, in "api: CreateFileW" the terms extracted are "ap" and "CreateFileW", while completely ignoring what each part means.

Specifically, our method follows the following simple steps to convert sandbox files into fixed size inputs to the neural network:

(1) Select as features the top 50,000 words with highest frequency in all Cuckoo reports, after removing the words which appear in all files. The rationale is that words which appear in all files, and words which are very uncommon do not contain lots of useful information.
(2) Convert each sandbox file to a 50,000-sized bit string by checking whether each of the 50,000 words appear in it. That is, for each analyzed Cuckoo report, feature[i]=1 if the i-th most common word appears in that cuckoo report, or 0 otherwise.

In other words, we first defined which words participated in our dictionary (analogous to the dictionaries used in NLP, which usually consist of the most frequent words in a language) and then we checked each sample against the dictionary for the presence of each word, thus producing a binary input vector.

4.2   Network Architecture and Hyper-Parameters

We trained a classifier based on Cuckoo reports of samples of APT which were developed (allegedly) by nation-states. Due to the small quantity of available samples, we used only two classes: Russia and China (which are apparently the most prolific APT developers).

Our training-set included 1,600 files from each class (training set size of 3,200 samples) of dozens of known campaigns of nation-developed APTs. 200 samples from the training set were used as a validation set. The test set contained additional 500 files from each class (test set size of 1,000 files). The labels (i.e., ground-truth attribution) of all these files are based on well-documented and extended manual analyses within the cyber-security community, conducted during the past years.

Note that the above-mentioned separation between training and test sets completely separates between different APT families as well.

That is, if an APT family is in test set, then all its variations are also in test set only. This makes the training challenge much more difficult (and more applicable to real-world), as in many cases inevitably we will be training on APT developed by one group of developers, and testing on APT developed by a completely different group.

Our DNN architecture is a 10-layers fully-connected neural network, with 50,000-2,000-1,000-1,000-1,000-1,000-1,000-1,000-500-2 neurons, (that is, 50,000 neurons on the input layer, 2,000 in the first hidden layer, etc.), with an additional output softmax layer. We used a dropout ([14]) rate of 0.5 (ignoring 50% of the neurons in hidden layers for each sample) and an input noise (zeroing) rate of 0.2 (ignoring 20% of input neurons) to prevent overfitting. A ReLU ([8]) activation function was used, and an initial learning rate of 10^{-2} which decayed to 10^{-5} over 1000 epochs. These hyper-parameters were optimized using the validation set.

4.3   Experimental Evaluation

Following the training phase, we tested the accuracy of the DNN model over the test set. The accuracy for the nation-state APT attribution classifer was **94.6%** on the test set, which contained only families that were not in the training set.

These are test accuracies are surprising in light of the complete separation of malware families between train and test sets. Inevitably in many cases the developers or even the developing units of the APT in train and test sets are different (e.g., APTs in train set developed by one Chinese cyber unit, and APTs in test set developed by another Chinese cyber unit).

Given this strict separation, and in light of the high accuracy results obtained, the results lead to the conclusion that each nation-state has (apparently) different sets of methodologies for developing APTs, such that two separate cyber units from nation A are still more similar to each other than to a cyber unit from nation B.

5   Concluding Remarks

In this paper we presented the first successful method for automatic APT attribution to nation-states, using raw dynamic analysis reports as input, and training a deep neural network for the attribution task. The use of raw features has the advantages of saving costs and time involved in the manual training and analysis process. It also prevents losing indicative data and classifier accuracy, and allows flexibility, using the same raw features for many different classification tasks.

Our results presented here lead to the conclusion that despite all the efforts devoted by nation states and their different cyber units in developing unattributable APTs, it is still possible to reach a rather accurate attribution. Additionally, different nation-states use different APT developing methodologies, such that the works of developers in separate cyber units are still sufficiently similar to each other that allow for attribution.

While the work presented here could help facilitate automatic attribution of nation-state attacks, we are aware that nation-states could subvert the methods presented here such that they would modify their new APTs to lead to their misclassification and attribution to another nation-state. For example, using deep neural networks themselves, they could employ generative adversarial networks (GAN)[9] to modify their APT until it successfully fools our classifier into attributing it to another nation-state. Applying GAN for APT modification would prove very difficult, but theoretically possible.

In our future works in this area we will examine additional nation state labels (multi-class classifier), once larger datasets of such APTs become available.

References

1. Alrabaee, S., Saleem, N., Preda, S., Wang, L., Debbabi, M.: Oba2: an onion approach to binary code authorship attribution. Digit. Invest. **11**, S94–S103 (2014)
2. Alrabaee, S., Shirani, P., Debbabi, M., Wang, L.: On the feasibility of malware authorship attribution. arXiv preprint arXiv:1701.02711 (2017)
3. Bencsath, B., Pek, G., Buttyan, L., Felegyhazi, M.: The cousins of stuxnet: duqu, flame, and gauss. In: Proceedings of Future Internet (2012)
4. Marquis-Boire, M., Marschalek, M., Guarnieri, C.: Big game hunting: the peculiarities in nation-state malware research. In: Proceedings of Black Hat USA (2015)
5. Caliskan-Islam, A., Yamaguchi, F., Dauber, E., Harang, R., Rieck, K., Greenstadt, R., Narayanan, A.: When coding style survives compilation: de-anonymizing programmers from executable binaries. arXiv preprint arXiv:1512.08546 (2015)
6. Collobert, R., Weston, J., Bottou, L., Karlen, M., Kavukcuoglu, K., Kuksa, P.: Natural language processing (Almost) from scratch. J. Mach. Learn. Res. **12**, 2493–2537 (2011)
7. David, O.E., Netanyahu N.S.: DeepSign: deep learning for automatic malware signature generation and classification. In: Proceedings of the International Joint Conference on Neural Networks (IJCNN), pp. 1–8 (2015)
8. Glorot, X., Bordes, A., Bengio. Y.: Deep sparse rectifier neural networks. In: Proceedings of 14th International Conference on Artificial Intelligence and Statistics, pp. 315–323 (2011)
9. Goodfellow, I.J., Pouget-Abadie, J., Mirza, M., Xu, B., Warde-Farley, D., Ozair, S., Courville, A.C., Bengio, Y.: Generative adversarial nets. In: Advances in Neural Information Processing Systems (NIPS), pp. 2672–2680 (2014)
10. Hathaway, O.A., Crootof, R.: The Law of Cyber-Attack. Faculty Scholarship Series. Paper 3852 (2012)
11. Olden, J.D., Jackson, D.A.: Illuminating the 'black-box': a randomization approach for understanding variable contributions in artificial neural networks. Ecol. Model. **154**, 135–150 (2002)
12. Pfeffer, A., Call, C., Chamberlain, J., Kellogg, L., Ouellette, J., Patten, T., Zacharias, G., Lakhotia, A., Golconda, S., Bay, J., Hall, R., Scofield, D.: Malware analysis and attribution using genetic information. In: Proceedings of the 7th IEEE International Conference on Malicious and Unwanted Software (2012)

13. Rosenblum, N., Zhu, X., Miller, B.P.: Who wrote this code? identifying the authors of program binaries. In: Atluri, V., Diaz, C. (eds.) ESORICS 2011. LNCS, vol. 6879, pp. 172–189. Springer, Heidelberg (2011). doi:10.1007/978-3-642-23822-2_10

14. Srivastava, N., Hinton, G., Krizhevsky, A., Sutskever, I., Salakhutdinov, R.: Dropout: a simple way to prevent neural networks from overfitting. J. Mach. Learn. Res. **15**, 1929–1958 (2014)

15. Stamatatos, E.: A survey of modern authorship attribution methods. J. Am. Soc. Inf. Sci. Technol. **60**(3), 538–556 (2009). ISSN 1532–2882

16. Virvilis N., Gritzalis D.: The big four - what we did wrong in protecting critical ICT infrastructures from advanced persistent threat detection? In: Proceedings of the 8th International Conference on Availability, Reliability & Security, pp. 248–254. IEEE (2013)

17. Zeiler, M.D., Fergus, R.: Visualizing and understanding convolutional networks. In: Fleet, D., Pajdla, T., Schiele, B., Tuytelaars, T. (eds.) ECCV 2014. LNCS, vol. 8689, pp. 818–833. Springer, Cham (2014). doi:10.1007/978-3-319-10590-1_53

Estimation of the Change of Agents Behavior Strategy Using State-Action History

Shihori Uchida[1(⊠)], Sigeyuki Oba[1], and Shin Ishii[1,2]

[1] Kyoto University, Yoshidahonmachi 36-1, Sakyo-ku, Kyoto-city, Japan
uchida-s@sys.i.kyoto-u.ac.jp
[2] ATR Cognitive Mechanism Laboratories, Kyoto, Japan
http://ishiilab.jp/kyoto/en/

Abstract. Reinforcement learning (RL) provides a computational model to animal's autonomous acquisition of behaviors even in an uncertain environment. Inverse reinforcement learning (IRL) is its opposite; given a history of behaviors of an agent, IRL attempts to determine the unknown characteristics, like a reward function, of the agent. Conventional IRL methods usually assume the agent has taken a stationary policy that is optimal in the environment. However, real RL agents do not necessarily take stationary policy, because they are often on the way of adapting to their own environments. Especially when facing an uncertain environment, an intelligent agent should take a mixed (or switching) strategy consisting of an exploitation that is best at the current situation and an exploration to resolve the environmental uncertainty. In this study, we propose a new IRL method that can identify both of a non-stationary policy and a fixed but unknown reward function, based on the behavioral history of a learning agent; in particular, we estimate a change point of the behavior policy from an exploratory one in the agent's early stage of the learning and an exploitative one in its later learning stage. When applied to a computer simulation during a simple maze task of an agent, our method could identify the change point of the behavior policy and the fixed reward function, only from the agent's history of behaviors.

Keywords: Reinforcement learning · Inverse reinforcement learning · Behavior strategy · Change point · Maximum likelihood estimation

1 Introduction

Reinforcement learning (RL) [1] provides a computational model to animal's acquisition of behaviors even in an uncertain environment, based on its trial and error. Especially when the environment is unknown or uncertain, an RL agent needs to take a behavior policy that is not necessarily the best in the current situation but is good for getting new information to know the environment or to resolve the uncertainty thereof. There are two major strategies to characterize the behavioral policy; an exploitation policy determines the next action such to maximize the current value function, and an exploration policy determines

© Springer International Publishing AG 2017
A. Lintas et al. (Eds.): ICANN 2017, Part II, LNCS 10614, pp. 100–107, 2017.
https://doi.org/10.1007/978-3-319-68612-7_12

the next action so to resolve the uncertainty of the environment. The agent can take a balance of the two strategies above, by, for example, ϵ-greedy policy and soft-max policy.

Recently, inverse reinforcement learning (IRL) has been emerged, in which the unknown characteristics, like a reward function, of an agent are determined, given a history of behaviors of the agent [1]. In this study, we propose a new IRL method that can track the strategy change of the behaving agent, under the assumption that the reward function is consistent; in particular, we estimate the change point of behavior policy using the history of states and actions even from learning processes of an RL agent. Conventional IRL methods often assumed the agent has taken a stationary policy that is optimal in the environment. A previous study presented an idea to apply IRL to learning, so non-stationary, processes of an RL agent, in which the agent's learning strategy was still fixed [7]. Since such strategies of a learning agent are represented as hyper-parameters, our topic can be said as *meta* inverse reinforcement learning. When applied to our computer simulation, our method successfully identified not only the change point of the behavior policy, but also other agent's characters, like the consistent reward function, only from the agent's behavioral history.

2   Background

2.1   Reinforcement Learning

RL is a computation model of animal's decision making such to adapt to its environment, in terms of maximization of the expected accumulation of rewards provided by the environment. The learner (agent) observes a state $s_t \in \mathcal{S}$ and selects an action $\pi(s_t) = a_t \in \mathcal{A}$ using its policy $\pi(s_t)$. The state is updated from s_t to s_{t+1} according to a Markovian process $P(s_{t+1}|s_t, a)$, and the agent receives a reward $R(s_t, a_t, s_{t+1}) \in \mathbb{R}$. The agent may learn a value function, an estimated accumulation of rewards to be obtained toward the future;

$$Q^{\pi}(s, a) = \mathbb{E}_{\pi}\left[\sum_{t=0}^{\infty} \gamma^t R(s_t, a_t, s_{t+1})|s_0 = s, a_0 = a\right]. \tag{1}$$

2.2   Model-Free Reinforcement Learning

In this study, we employ SARSA(λ) learning, a model-free RL algorithm to estimate the action-value function $Q(s, a)$ in an unknown environment [1]. The algorithm is as follows:

$$e(s_t, a_t) \leftarrow e(s_t, a_t) + 1$$
$$Q(s, a) \leftarrow Q(s, a) + \alpha e(s, a)\{R(s_t, a_t, s_{t+1}) + \gamma Q(s_{t+1}, a_{t+1}) - Q(s_t, a_t)\}(\forall s, a)$$
$$e(s, a) \leftarrow \gamma \lambda e(s, a), \tag{2}$$

where $e(s, a)$ denotes an eligibility trace, an approximate number of visits of the state-action pair (s, a).

When we use the action value function as a utility function, a soft-max (Boltzmann) policy is given as

$$\pi(a|s) = \frac{\exp(\beta Q(s, a))}{\sum_{a' \in \mathcal{A}} \exp(\beta Q(s, a'))}, \tag{3}$$

where $\beta > 0$ is a hyper-parameter, called an 'inverse temperature', that controls the randomness of action selection [1]. When β is large the agent chooses an action that maximizes the action value with a large probability, whereas a small β facilitates the agent to choose its actions at random. We call β as 'temperature' in this article for simplicity.

2.3   The Change of Action Policy During Learning Situation

In RL, there are two major strategies to determine behavioral policy, exploration and exploitation [6]. If the value function has been well estimated, a policy that selects a 'greedy' action at each state is the best to get the largest reward: this is called an exploitation. When the value function is poorly estimated because of the lack of environmental information, on the other hand, the agent needs additional trials and errors to well identify the value, hence non-optimal actions based on the current, temporal value function: this is called an exploration.

When facing an uncertain environment, a natural way for an animal to adapt to it is to take an exploration policy, which is appropriate to get knowledge of the environment in its early stage of learning, and then to turn to exploitation, which is best to get much rewards based on the well-identified value function in its later stage of learning. Although these two strategies can be mixed so that the mixing rate can be gradually changed like simulated annealing, in this study, we assume there is an unknown timing to switch from the early explorative policy to the later exploitive policy, which is characterized by a change point of the policy's hyper-parameter.

2.4   Inverse Reinforcement Learning

Inverse Reinforcement Learning (IRL) estimates reward function based on an agent history of behaviors; it is called IRL because it solves an inverse problem of RL. The original development of IRL was to estimate a reward function and hence the purpose of animals [3], and later was extended into apprenticeship learning [4].

On the other hand, there are some factors, like policy hyper-parameters, that determine the character of the agent, other than the reward function. A typical example is the temperature. Although existing studies proposed an estimation method of the policy hyper-parameter based on the animals behaviors [5] and its dynamic control method to adapt uncertain environments [6], there has been no study to estimate such hyper-parameters within the framework of IRL.

2.5   Previous Work

Although the most IRL studies have assumed that the agent is taking optimal, and hence stationary policy, Sakurai et al. extended the conventional framework into such to include behaviors even in a learning process of the target agent [7]. Assuming that an agent performs an RL with a soft-max policy based on the value function and the value learning by SARSA(λ), they estimated the unknown reward function based on the agent's learning behaviors. Given the observed behavioral history of the RL agents, the log likelihood becomes

$$J = \sum_{t=0}^{T} J_t(Q_t(s_t, a_t)),$$

$$J_t(Q_t(s_t, a_t)) = Q_t(s_t, a_t) - \log \sum_{a \in \mathcal{A}} \exp(Q_t(s_t, a_t)), \tag{4}$$

where J_t is the logarithm of probability to observe a state-action pair (s_t, a_t) at time t under the current action-value $Q_t(s_t, a_t)$. Calculating the gradient of the log-likelihood above with respect to the reward function $R(s, a, s')$ and the initial action-value $Q_0(s, a)$, they estimated those unknowns according to a stochastic gradient method.

3   Proposed Method

In this study, we extend the IRL method above to such to include a dynamic change of policy hyper-parameter $\beta(t)$, so that the log-likelihood becomes

$$G = \sum_{t=0}^{T} G_t(Q_t(s_t, a_t), \beta(t)),$$

$$G_t(Q_t(s_t, a_t), \beta(t)) = \beta(t)Q_t(s_t, a_t) - \log \sum_{a} \exp(\beta(t)Q_t(s_t, a_t)). \tag{5}$$

The unknowns in our new IRL are the reward function $R(s, a, s')$, the initial action-value $Q_0(s, a)$, and the time-dependent temperature hyper-parameter $\beta(t)$. However, there is obvious indeterminancy among these due to the co-linear dependency on the policy, we need some additional constraints to solve the maximum likelihood problem.

3.1   Derivation of the Gradient

Here, we present a matrix form of the log-likelihood:

$$G_t(\mathbf{Q}_t, \beta) = \beta \mathbf{X}_t^{\mathrm{T}} \mathbf{Q}_t + \log(\mathbf{Y}_t^{\mathrm{T}} \mathbf{F}_t'), \tag{6}$$

where $\mathbf{Q}_t$ denotes a vector-formed action-value function whose i-th element is $[\mathbf{Q}_t]_i = Q_t(s^i, a^i)$. $\mathbf{X}_t$ is a vector such that $[\mathbf{X}_t]_i = 1, [\mathbf{X}_t]_{k \neq i} = 0$ holds, where

i indexes the state-action pair (s_t, a_t). $\mathbf{Y}_t$ is a vector such that $[\mathbf{Y}_t]_{k \in \mathcal{H}} = 1, [\mathbf{Y}_t]_{k \notin \mathcal{H}} = 0$ holds, where $\mathcal{H}$ is a set of such state-action pairs that can lead to the next state s_t. $\mathbf{F}_t$ is a vector whose l-th element is $\exp([\beta \mathbf{Q}_t]_l)$, where l takes any index for every possible state-action pair. Using these vector notations, the SARSA learning, Eq. (2), is rewritten as

$$
\begin{aligned}
\mathbf{Q}_{t+1} &= \mathbf{Q}_t + \alpha \mathbf{E}_t (\mathbf{A}_t \mathbf{R} + \gamma \mathbf{B}_{t,t+1} \mathbf{Q}_t - \mathbf{B}_{t,t} \mathbf{Q}_t) \\
&= \{\mathbf{I} + \alpha \mathbf{E}_t (\gamma \mathbf{B}_{t,t+1} - \mathbf{B}_{t,t})\} \mathbf{Q}_t + \alpha \mathbf{E}_t \mathbf{A}_t \mathbf{R},
\end{aligned} \tag{7}
$$

where $\mathbf{E}_t$ is the eligibility trace whose update rule is also given as a matrix form:

$$
\mathbf{E}_t = \lambda \gamma \mathbf{E}_{t-1} + \mathbf{B}_{t,t}. \tag{8}
$$

Here, $\mathbf{R}$ is a vector whose each element corresponds to the reward value received by taking an action a at state s. $\mathbf{B}_{t,t}$ is a diagonal matrix whose i-th diagonal element $[\mathbf{B}_{t,t}]_{(i,i)}$ is 1 and all the other elements are 0, where i indicates the current state-action pair $(s, a) = (s_t, a_t)$. Similarly, $\mathbf{B}_{t,t+1}$ is a diagonal matrix whose j-th diagonal element is 1 and all the other elements are 0, where j indicates the next state-action pair $(s, a) = (s_{t+1}, a_{t+1})$. $\mathbf{A}_t$ is a matrix such that $[\mathbf{A}_t \mathbf{R}]_i = R(s_t, a_t, s_{t+1})$ holds. Accordingly, the gradient of the log-likelihood with respect to β is given by

$$
\frac{\partial G_t}{\partial \beta} = \mathbf{Q}_t^{\mathrm{T}} \mathbf{X}_t - \frac{\mathbf{Y}_t^{\mathrm{T}} (\mathbf{F}_t' \otimes \mathbf{Q}_t)}{\mathbf{Y}_t^T \mathbf{F}_t'}. \tag{9}
$$

3.2 Estimation of Change of Temperature Hyper-parameter

The above formulation aims at estimating the time-course of the temperature hyper-parameter $\beta(t)$. Although it is possible by introducing an appropriate dynamical model onto the temperature profile, in this study, we assume for simplicity that the temperature parameter β may be switched at a single change point $t = T_{\text{switch}}$ and $\beta_1 < \beta_2$ holds, where β_1 and β_2 are the temperature values before and after the change point, respectively. Thus, the log-likelihood becomes

$$
G = \sum_{t=0}^{T_{\text{switch}}} G_t(Q(s_t, a_t), \beta_1) + \sum_{t=T_{\text{switch}}}^{T} G_t(Q(s_t, a_t), \beta_2),
$$

$$
G_t(Q_t(s_t, a_t, \beta_i)) = \beta_i Q_t(s_t, a_t) - \log \sum_a \exp(\beta_i Q_t(s_t, a_t)) \qquad (i = 1, 2)(10)
$$

Our unknowns are the reward function, the change point T_{switch}, and the temperature hyper-parameters before and after the change point, β_1 and β_2, which are all estimated by maximizing the log-likelihood, equation (10).

4   Results

4.1   Experiment Setting

We generated state-action sequences by simulating an RL agent that tries to reach the right-bottom corner from the left-upper corner in a simple 3×3 maze (Fig. 2(a)). The agent with the optimal policy takes four actions from the start to the goal, $N_{short} = 4$. The state transitions are deterministic. The RL agent (i.e., the target agent) performed the value learning of SARSA(0) and the soft-max policy whose temperature hyper-parameter may change in time.

4.2   Simultaneous Estimation of the Values and the Change Point

Before the main experiments, we checked the basic behaviors of our IRL algorithm. We confirmed our algorithm could estimate (1) fixed β over learning episodes, (2) changing timing of β when the true values of β before and after the change point are known, with high accuracy.

Here, we simultaneously estimated the reward function, a single change point of the temperature, and a pair of unknown temperature values, β_1 and β_2, by assuming that the ratio $\beta_2/\beta_1 = 10$ was known by our IRL. We used the state-action history data of a learning agent, consisting of 200 and 200 episodes before and after the change point. In the actual IRL estimation, we used a sequential estimation heuristics; we divided the simultaneous estimation into the following four steps: (1) Assuming the constant temperature, we estimated the reward function and the constant temperature based on the method in Sect. 3.1. (2) Based on the consistent temperature estimated in step 1, we set the initial estimates of β_1 and β_2 such to satisfy the known ratio of them, i.e., $\beta_2 = 10\beta_1$. (3) We estimated the change point, with a fixed pair of the temperature values as in step 2. (4) After separating the learning episodes into before and after the change point estimated in step 3, we re-estimated β_1 and β_2 individually based on the separated behavior data.

Figure 1 shows the average and variance of the likelihood obtained in step 3 above, over 10 learning runs. We can see our IRL algorithm could exactly estimate the change point of the temperature hyper-parameter for all 10 runs. Next, we show how our IRL works for estimating the temperature β. The target agent used $\beta_1 = 0.1$ and $\beta_2 = 1.0$, before and after the change point, respectively. After step 2 above, our IRL estimated the temperature values as 0.18 and 1.0, before and after the change point. After step 4, they were improved as $\beta_1 = 0.193$ and $\beta_2 = 0.88$.

Figure 2 partly shows the estimated reward function that is assumed to be consistent between before and after the change point. The estimated reward increased as the corresponding state-action was approaching the goal. Also, there was variance in the estimation, due to the ill-posedness in the IRL-based reward estimation problem and the insufficiency of samples produced the target agent.

Next, we attempted to evaluate the proposed method in terms of the reproducibility of the target agent behaviors. The log-likelihood is a mutual entropy

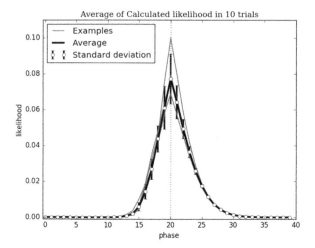

Fig. 1. Estimation of change points of the policy over 10 IRL runs. Horizontal and vertical axes denote the possible change point (1 phase = 10 episodes) and the likelihood of change point respectively. Average and standard deviation among 10 runs, and three examples out of the 10 runs are shown. The likelihood was maximal at the true change point (the 200-th episode) for all runs.

G	1	2
3	4	5
6	7	S

R(S,A)	Estimated reward
R(1,←)	2.87 ± 0.255
R(1,→)	−1.30 ± 0.448
R(4,→)	−0.839 ± 0.177
R(7,↑)	1.77 ± 0.452

(a) **Maze setting**   (b) **Examples of estimated reward**

Fig. 2. (a) A 3×3 maze task. These are no obstacles other than the outer walls (thick lines); moves rushing into the wall and returning to the start square are not allowed. When an agent arrives at the goal square, it receives a positive reward, is returned to the start square, and an episode ends. At other squares, it does not receive any reward. The objective of the RL agent is to acquire the optimal policy by repeating the episodes. (b) A part of reward function estimated by our IRL. We actually estimated a reward function in the form of $R(s, a, s')$, but it is equivalent to $R(s, a)$, because of the deterministic nature of our maze setting. SD is over 10 IRL runs. The variance varies according to the ill-posedness of the IRL and the short of samples produced by the target agent. The reward function was estimated as increasing as the action was effective in approaching the goal. For example, moving left at square 1, $R(1, \leftarrow)$, was much better than moving right at the same square, $R(1, \rightarrow)$. Some example of reward. We assume the deterministic state transition,thus the reward function $R(s, a, s')$ is expressed in the form of $R(s, a)$.

between the empirical distribution of the target agent's behaviors and the predictive distribution estimated by our IRL, so can be seen as the criterion of the accuracy of the reproducibility of the target agent behaviors, even it was still on the way of learning. When evaluating our method in terms of the behavior reproducibility, we used the previous IRL method (Sakurai et al. [7]) as a baseline, because our method is an extended version of that method. In Fig. 1, the horizontal coordinate of phase 0 corresponds to the previous method, because it does not incorporate any change in the temperature, although the constant temperature value was estimated based on the target agent's behaviors. Apparently, the likelihood calculated by the proposed method that assumed a single change point at phase = 20 was higher than that of the baseline method, suggesting our method showed higher reproducibility in the target agent's behaviors than the baseline method. From this result, we conclude the proposed method can be used for estimating wider range of behavioral strategies.

5   Conclusion

We proposed a new IRL method that can estimate both the unknown reward function and the unknown characteristics of RL agents. This method is applicable to non-optimal or non-stationary agents. Our computer simulation showed that our method successfully identified not only the reward function, but also the timing of the policy change and the policy hyper-parameters before and after the change point, only from the agent's behaviors. Since the current experiment was for a very simple maze task, an extensive experiment using various nonlinear problems would be necessary. Moreover, identification and mimicking animal's adaptation in unknown or changing environments are our particular interests that should be tackled in a near future.

References

1. Sutton, R.A., Barto, A.G.: Reinforcement Learning: An Introduction. MIT Press, Cambridge (1998)
2. Ramachandran, D., Amir, E.: Bayesian inverse reinforcement learning. Urbana **51**(61801), 1–4 (2007)
3. Russell, S.: Learning agents for uncertain environments. In: Proceedings of the Eleventh Annual Conference on Computational Learning Theory, pp. 101–103. ACM, July 1998
4. Abbeel, P., Ng, A.Y.: Apprenticeship learning via inverse reinforcement learning. In: Proceedings of the Twenty-First International Conference on Machine Learning, p. 1. ACM, July 2004
5. Samejima, K., Doya, K., Ueda, Y., Kimura, M.: Estimating internal variables and paramters of a learning agent by a particle filter. In: Neural Information Processing Systems (NIPS), pp. 1335–1342, December 2003
6. Ishii, S., Yoshida, W., Yoshimoto, J.: Control of exploitation-exploration meta-parameter in reinforcement learning. Neural Netw. **15**(4), 665–687 (2002)
7. Sakurai, S., Oba, S., Ishii, S.: Inverse reinforcement learning based on behaviors of a learning agent. In: Arik, S., Huang, T., Lai, W.K., Liu, Q. (eds.) ICONIP 2015. LNCS, vol. 9489, pp. 724–732. Springer, Cham (2015). doi:10.1007/978-3-319-26532-2_80

Boltzmann Machines and Phase Transitions

Generalising the Discriminative Restricted Boltzmann Machines

Srikanth Cherla, Son N. Tran$^{(\boxtimes)}$, Artur d'Avila Garcez, and Tillman Weyde

School of Mathematics, Computer Science and Engineering, City University London,
Northampton Square, London EC1V 0HB, UK
{srikanth.cherla.1,son.tran.1,a.garcez,t.e.weyde}@city.ac.uk

Abstract. We present a novel theoretical result that generalises the Discriminative Restricted Boltzmann Machine (DRBM). While originally the DRBM was defined assuming the $\{0,1\}$-Bernoulli distribution in each of its hidden units, this result makes it possible to derive cost functions for variants of the DRBM that utilise other distributions, including some that are often encountered in the literature. This paper shows that this function can be extended to the Binomial and $\{-1,+1\}$-Bernoulli hidden units.

Keywords: Restricted Boltzmann Machine · Discriminative learning · Hidden layer activation function

1 Introduction

The restricted Boltzmann machine (RBM) is a generative latent-variable model which models the joint distribution of a set of input variables. It has gained popularity over the past decade in many applications, especially for pretraining deep neural network classifiers [3,7]. One of its applications is as a standalone classifier, referred to as the Discriminative Restricted Boltzmann Machine (DRBM) [5]. As the name might suggest, the DRBM is a classifier obtained by carrying out discriminative learning in the RBM and it directly models the conditional distribution one is interested in for prediction. This bypasses one of the key problems faced in learning the parameters of the RBM generatively, which is the computation of the intractable *partition function*. In the DRBM this partition function is cancelled out in the expression for the conditional distribution thus simplifying the learning process.

It is often the case that a new type of activation function results in an improvement in the performance of an existing model or in a new insight into the behaviour of the model itself. In the least, it offers researchers with the choice of a new modelling alternative. In fact, different type of units such as bipolar Bernoulli [1], Gaussian [11], Binomial [10] and rectified linear [8] have been studied. However, we observe that while effort has gone into enhancing

---

Srikanth and Son contribute equally.

© Springer International Publishing AG 2017
A. Lintas et al. (Eds.): ICANN 2017, Part II, LNCS 10614, pp. 111–119, 2017.
https://doi.org/10.1007/978-3-319-68612-7_13

the performance of a few other connectionist models by changing the nature of their hidden units, this has not been attempted with the DRBM. So in this paper, we first describe a novel theoretical result that makes it possible to generalise the model's cost function. The result is then used to derive two new cost functions corresponding to DRBMs containing hidden units with the Binomial and $\{-1, +1\}$-Bernoulli distributions respectively. These two variants are evaluated and compared with the original DRBM on the benchmark MNIST and USPS digit classification datasets, and the 20 Newsgroups document classification dataset. We find that each of the three compared models outperforms the remaining two in one of the three datasets, thus indicating that the proposed theoretical generalisation of the DRBM may be valuable in practice. Applications of such models can be classification tasks such as handwritten digit recognition, document categorisation.

In the next Section, we explain the generalisation of the discriminative function in RBMs. It is followed by Sect. 3 that shows how to implement this idea. Experimental results are discussed in Sects. 4 and 5 presents a summary, together with potential extensions of this work[1].

2   Generalising the Discriminative Learning in RBMs

The Restricted Boltmzann Machine (RBM) [9] is an undirected bipartite graphical model. In the case for classification, it contains a set of visible units $\mathbf{v} = \{\mathbf{x} \in \mathbb{R}^{n_x}, \mathbf{y} \in \mathbb{R}^{n_y}\}$, where $\mathbf{x}$ is the input vector, and $\mathbf{y}$ is the one-hot encoding of the class-label; and a set of hidden units $\mathbf{h} \in \mathbb{R}^{n_h}$. The two layers are fully inter-connected but there exist no connections between any two hidden units, or any two visible units. Additionally, the units of each layer are connected to a bias unit whose value is always 1. The edge between the ith input x_i and the jth hidden unit h_j is associated with a weight w_{ij}. All these weights are together represented as a weight matrix $W \in \mathbb{R}^{n_x \times n_h}$. Similarly, $U \in \mathbb{R}^{n_y \times n_h}$ is the weight matrix between labels $\mathbf{y}$ and the hidden layer $\mathbf{h}$. The weights of connections between input and label units and the bias unit are contained in bias vectors $\mathbf{a} \in \mathbb{R}^{n_x}$, $\mathbf{b} \in \mathbb{R}^{n_y}$ respectively. Likewise, for the hidden units there is a hidden bias vector $\mathbf{c} \in \mathbb{R}^{n_h}$. The RBM is characterized by an energy function: $E(\mathbf{x}, \mathbf{y}, \mathbf{h}) = -\mathbf{a}^\top \mathbf{x} - \mathbf{b}^\top \mathbf{y} - \mathbf{c}^\top \mathbf{h} - \mathbf{x}^\top W \mathbf{h} - \mathbf{y}^\top U \mathbf{h}$ to represent the joint probability of every possible pair of visible and hidden vectors as: $P(\mathbf{x}, \mathbf{y}, \mathbf{h}) = \frac{1}{Z} e^{-E(\mathbf{x}, \mathbf{y}, \mathbf{h})}$ where Z is the partition function, $Z = \sum_{\mathbf{x}, \mathbf{y}, \mathbf{h}} e^{-E(\mathbf{x}, \mathbf{y}, \mathbf{h})}$.

In this paper, we are interested in the conditional function which is important for classification:

$$P(y|\mathbf{x}) = \frac{\sum_{\mathbf{h}} \exp\left(-E\left(\mathbf{x}, \mathbf{y}, \mathbf{h}\right)\right)}{\sum_{\mathbf{y}^*} \sum_{\mathbf{h}} \exp\left(-E\left(\mathbf{x}, \mathbf{y}^*, \mathbf{h}\right)\right)} \tag{1}$$

The denominator sums over all class-labels $\mathbf{y}^*$ to make $P(\mathbf{y}|\mathbf{x})$ a probability distribution. In the original RBM, $\mathbf{x}$ and $\mathbf{y}$ together make up the visible layer.

---

[1] Another version of this work is stored online at https://arxiv.org/abs/1604.01806.

The model is learned discriminatively by maximizing the log-likelihood function based on the expression of the conditional distribution above. Normally, such RBMs have binary states $\{0, 1\}$ for the hidden units. We will show how to extend the conditional distribution with different type of hidden units.

Proposition 1. *If an RBM whose hidden units have K states $\{s_k | k = 1 : K, K \in \mathbb{Z}\}$ then its conditional distribution in (1) can be computed analytically as:*

$$P(y|\mathbf{x}) = \frac{\exp\left(b_y\right) \prod_j \sum_k \exp\left(s_k \alpha_j\right)}{\sum_{y^*} \exp\left(b_{y^*}\right) \prod_j \sum_k \exp\left(s_k \alpha_j^*\right)} \tag{2}$$

where $\alpha_j = \sum_i x_i w_{ij} + u_{yj} + c_j$

Proof. We consider the term containing the summation over $\mathbf{h}$ in (1):

$$\sum_{\mathbf{h}} \exp\left(-E\left(\mathbf{x}, \mathbf{y}, \mathbf{h}\right)\right) = \sum_{\mathbf{h}} \exp\left(\sum_{i,j} x_i w_{ij} y_j + \sum_j u_{yj} h_j + \sum_i a_i x_i + b_y + \sum_j c_j h_j\right)$$

$$= \exp\left(\sum_i a_i x_i + b_y\right) \sum_{\mathbf{h}} \exp\left(\sum_j h_j \sum_i x_i w_{ij} + u_{yj} + c_j\right) \tag{3}$$

Now consider only the second term of the product in (3). We simplify it by re-writing $\sum_i x_i w_{ij} + u_{yj} + c_j$ as α_j. Thus, we have:

$$\sum_{\mathbf{h}} \exp\left(\sum_j h_j \sum_i x_i w_{ij} + u_{yj} + c_j\right) = \prod_j \sum_k \exp\left(s_k \alpha_j\right) \tag{4}$$

where s_k is each of the k states that can be assumed by each hidden unit j of the model. The last step of (4) results from re-arranging the terms after expanding the summation and product over $\mathbf{h}$ and j in the previous step respectively. The summation $\sum_{\mathbf{h}}$ over all the possible hidden layer vectors $\mathbf{h}$ can be replaced by the summation $\sum_k$ over the states of the units in the layer. The number and values of these states depend on the nature of the distribution in question. The result in (4) can be applied to (3) and, in turn, to (1) to get the following general expression of the conditional probability $P(y|\mathbf{x})$:

$$P(y|\mathbf{x}) = \frac{\exp\left(b_y\right) \prod_j \sum_k \exp\left(s_k \alpha_j\right)}{\sum_{y^*} \exp\left(b_{y^*}\right) \prod_j \sum_k \exp\left(s_k \alpha_j^*\right)}$$

Proposition 1 generalises the conditional probability of the DRBM first introduced in [5]. The term inside the summation over k can be viewed as a product between α_j corresponding to each hidden unit j and each possible state s_k of this hidden unit. Knowing this makes it possible to extend the original DRBM to be governed by other types of distributions in the hidden layer, as what will be discussed in the next section.

3   Extensions to Other Hidden Layer Distributions

We first use the Proposition 1 to derive the expression for the conditional probability $P(y|\mathbf{x})$ in the original DRBM [5]. This will be followed by its extension, first to the $\{-1, +1\}$-Bernoulli distribution (referred to here as the *Bipolar DRBM*)and then the Binomial distribution (the *Binomial DRBM*).

DRBM: The $\{0,1\}$-Bernoulli DRBM corresponds to the model originally introduced in [5]. In this case, each hidden unit h_j can either be a 0 or a 1, i.e.
$s_k = \{0,1\}$. This reduces $P(y|\mathbf{x})$ in (2) to

$$P_{\text{ber}}(y|\mathbf{x}) = \frac{\exp(b_y) \prod_j (1 + \exp(\alpha_j))}{\sum_{y^*} \exp(b_{y^*}) \prod_j (1 + \exp(\alpha_j^*))} \tag{5}$$

which is identical to the result obtained in [5].

Bipolar DRBM: A straightforward adaptation to the DRBM involves replacing its hidden layer states by $\{-1, +1\}$ as previously done in [1] in the case of
the RBM. This is straightforward because in both cases the hidden states of the
models are governed by the Bernoulli distribution, however, in the latter case
each hidden unit h_j can either be a -1 or a $+1$, i.e. $s_k = \{-1, +1\}$. Applying
this property to (2) results in the following expression for $P(y|\mathbf{x})$:

$$P_{\text{bip}}(y|\mathbf{x}) = \frac{\exp(b_y) \prod_j (\exp(-\alpha_j) + \exp(\alpha_j))}{\sum_{y^*} \exp(b_{y^*}) \prod_j (\exp(-\alpha_j^*) + \exp(\alpha_j^*))} \tag{6}$$

Binomial DRBM: It was demonstrated in [10] how groups of N (where N is
a positive integer greater than 1) stochastic units of the standard RBM can be
combined in order to approximate discrete-valued functions in its visible layer
and hidden layers to increase its representational power. This is done by replicating each unit of one layer N times and keeping the weights of all connections
to each of these units from a given unit in the other layer identical. The key
advantage for adopting this approach was that the learning algorithm remained
unchanged. The number of these "replicas" of the same unit whose values are
simultaneously 1 determines the effective integer value (in the range $[0, N]$) of
the composite unit, thus allowing it to assume multiple values. The resulting
model was referred to there as the Rate-Coded RBM (RBMrate).

The intuition behind this idea can be extended to the DRBM by allowing
the states s_k of each hidden unit to assume integer values in the range $[0, N]$.
The summation in (2) would then be $S_N = \sum_{s_k=0}^{N} \exp(s_k \alpha_j)$, which simplifies
as below:

$$S_N = \sum_{s_k=0}^{N} \exp(s_k \alpha_j) = \frac{1 - \exp((N+1)\alpha_j)}{1 - \exp(\alpha_j)} \tag{7}$$

in (2) to give

$$P_{\text{bin}}(y|\mathbf{x}) = \frac{\exp(b_y) \prod_j \frac{1 - \exp((N+1)\alpha_j)}{1 - \exp(\alpha_j)}}{\sum_{y^*} \exp(b_{y^*}) \prod_j \frac{1 - \exp((N+1)\alpha_j^*)}{1 - \exp(\alpha_j^*)}} \cdot \tag{8}$$

4 Experiments

We evaluated the Bipolar and the Binomial DRBMs on three benchmark machine learning datasets. These are two handwritten digit recognition datasets — USPS and MNIST, and one document classification dataset — 20 Newsgroups.

4.1 MNIST Handwritten Digit Recognition

The MNIST dataset [6] consists of optical characters of handwritten digits. Each digit is a 28×28 pixel gray-scale image (or a vector $\mathbf{x} \in [0,1]^{784}$). Each pixel of the image corresponds to a floating-point value lying in the range $[0,1]$ after normalisation from an integer value in the range $[0,255]$. The dataset is divided into a single split of pre-determined training, validation and test folds containing $50,000$ images, $10,000$ images and $10,000$ images respectively.

Table 1 lists the classification performance on this dataset of the three DRBM variants derived above using the result in (2). The first row of the table corresponds to the DRBM introduced in [5]. We did not perform a grid search in the case of this one model and only used the reported hyperparameter setting in that paper to reproduce their result[2]. It was stated there that a difference of 0.2% in the average loss is considered statistically significant on this dataset.

Table 1. A comparison between the three different variants of the DRBM on the USPS dataset. The Binomial DRBM in this table is the one with $n_{bins} = 2$.

Model	Average loss (%)
DRBM ($n_{hid} = 500$, $\eta_{init} = 0.05$)	**1.78** (± 0.0012)
Bipolar DRBM ($n_{hid} = 500$, $\eta_{init} = 0.01$)	1.84 (± 0.0007)
Binomial DRBM ($n_{hid} = 500$, $\eta_{init} = 0.01$)	1.86 (± 0.0016)

Going by this threshold of difference, it can be said that the performance of all three models is equivalent on this dataset although the average accuracy of the DRBM is the highest, followed by that of the Bipolar and the Binomial DRBMs. All three variants perform best with 500 hidden units. It was observed that the number of bins n_{bins} didn't play as significant a role as first expected. There seemed to be a slight deterioration in accuracy with an increase in the number of bins, but the difference cannot be considered significant given the threshold for this dataset. These results are listed in Table 2.

4.2 USPS Handwritten Digit Recognition

The USPS dataset [2] contains optical characters of handwritten digits. Each digit is a 16×16 pixel gray-scale image (or a vector $\mathbf{x} \in [0,1]^{256}$). Each pixel

---

[2] We obtained a marginally lower average loss of 1.78% in our evaluation of this model than the 1.81% reported in [5].

Table 2. Classification performance of the Binomial DRBM with different values of n_{bins} on the MNIST dataset. While the performance does show a tendency to worsen with the number of bins, the difference was found to be within the margin of significance for this dataset.

n_{bins}	n_{hid}	η_{init}	Average loss (%)
2	500	0.01	**1.86**
4	500	0.01	1.88
8	500	0.001	1.90

of the image corresponds to a floating-point value lying in the range $[0, 1]$ after normalisation from an integer value in the range $[0, 255]$. The dataset is divided into a single split of pre-determined training, validation and test folds containing $7,291$ images, $1,458$ images and $2,007$ images respectively.

Table 3 lists the classification performance on this dataset of the three DRBM variants derived above using the result in (2). Here the Binomial DRBM (of $n_{bins} = 8$) was found to have the best classification accuracy, followed by the Bipolar DRBM and then the DRBM. The number of hidden units used by each of these models varies inversely with respect to their average loss.

Table 3. A comparison between the three different variants of the DRBM on the USPS dataset. The Binomial DRBM in this table is the one with $n_{bins} = 8$.

Model	Average loss (%)
DRBM ($n = 50$, $\eta_{init} = 0.01$)	6.90 ($\pm$0.0047)
Bipolar DRBM ($n = 500$, $\eta_{init} = 0.01$)	6.49 ($\pm$0.0026)
Binomial DRBM (8) ($n = 1000$, $\eta_{init} = 0.01$)	**6.09** ($\pm$0.0014)

Table 4 shows the change in classification accuracy with a change in the number of bins. In contrast to the observation in the case of MNIST, here an increase in n_{bins} is accompanied by an improvement in accuracy.

Table 4. Classification average losses of the Binomial DRBM with different values of n_{bins}.

n_{bins}	η_{init}	n_{hid}	Average loss (%)
2	0.01	50	6.90 ($\pm$0.0047)
4	0.01	1000	6.48 ($\pm$0.0018)
8	0.01	1000	**6.09** ($\pm$0.0014)

4.3   20 Newsgroups Document Classification

The 20 Newsgroups dataset [4] is a collection of approximately $20,000$ newsgroup documents, partitioned evenly across 20 different categories. A version of the dataset where the training and the test sets contain documents collected at different times is used here. The aim is to predict the correct category of a document published after a certain date given a model trained on those published before the date. We used the $5,000$ most frequent words for the binary input features to the models. This preprocessing follows the example of [5], as it was the second data used to evaluate the DRBM there. We made an effort to adhere as closely as possible to the evaluation methodology there to obtain results comparable to theirs despite the unavailability of the exact validation set. Hence a validation set of the same number of samples was created[3].

Table 5 lists the classification performance on this dataset of the three DRBM variants derived above using the result in (2). Here the Bipolar DRBM outperformed the remaining two variants, followed by the Binomial DRBM and the DRBM.

Table 5. A comparison between the three different variants of the DRBM on the 20 Newsgroups dataset. The Binomial DRBM in this table is the one with $n_{bins} = 2$.

Model	Average loss (%)
DRBM $(n = 50, \eta_{init} = 0.01)$	$28.52\,(\pm 0.0049)$
Bipolar DRBM $(n = 50, \eta_{init} = 0.001)$	**$27.75\,(\pm 0.0019)$**
Binomial DRBM $(n = 100, \eta_{init} = 0.001)$	$28.17\,(\pm 0.0028)$

Table 6 shows the change in classification accuracy with a change in the number of bins.

Table 6. Classification performance of the Binomial DRBM with different values of n_{bins}.

n_{bins}	η_{init}	n_{hidden}	Average loss (%)
2	0.001	100	**$28.17\,(\pm 0.0028)$**
4	0.001	50	$28.24\,(\pm 0.0032)$
8	0.0001	50	$28.76\,(\pm 0.0040)$

---

[3] Our evaluation resulted in a model with a classification accuracy of 28.52% in comparison with the 27.6% reported in [5].

5   Conclusions and Future Work

This paper introduced a novel theoretical result that makes it possible to generalise the hidden layer activations of the Discriminative RBM (DRBM). This result was first used to reproduce the derivation of the cost function of the DRBM, and additionally to also derive those of two new variants of it, namely the Bipolar DRBM and the Binomial DRBM. The three models thus derived were evaluated on three benchmark machine learning datasets — MNIST, USPS and 20 Newsgroups. It was found that each of the three variants of the DRBM outperformed the rest on one of the three datasets, thus confirming that generalisations of the DRBM may be useful in practice.

It was found in the experiments in Sect. 4, that the DRBM achieved the best classification accuracy on the MNIST dataset, the Bipolar DRBM on the 20 Newsgroups dataset and the Binomial DRBM on the USPS dataset. While this does indicate the practical utility of the two new variants of the DRBM introduced here, the question of whether each of these is better suited for any particular types of dataset than the rest is to be investigated further.

Given the application of the result in (2) to obtain the Binomial DRBM, it is straightforward to extend it to what we refer to here as the *Rectified Linear DRBM*. This idea is inspired by [8], where the Rate-coded RBM [10] (analogous to the Binomial DRBM here) is extended to derive an RBM with Rectified Linear units by increasing the number of replicas of a single binary unit to infinity. Adopting the same intuition here in the case of the DRBM, this would mean that we allow the states s_k to assume integer values in the range $[0, \infty)$ and thus extend the summation S_N in the case of the Binomial DRBM to an infinite sum S_∞.

References

1. Freund, Y., Haussler, D.: Unsupervised learning of distributions on binary vectors using two layer networks. In: Advances in Neural Information Processing Systems, pp. 912–919 (1992)
2. Hastie, T., Tibshiran, R., Friedman, J., Franklin, J.: The Elements of Statistical Learning: Data Mining, Inference and Prediction. Springer Series in Statistics. Springer, New York (2005). Chap. 1
3. Hinton, G.E., Osindero, S., Teh, Y.W.: A fast learning algorithm for deep belief nets. Neural Comput. 18(7), 1527–1554. doi:10.1162/neco.2006.18.7.1527
4. Lang, K.: Newsweeder: learning to filter netnews. In: Proceedings of the 12th International Conference on Machine Learning, pp. 331–339 (1995)
5. Larochelle, H., Bengio, Y.: Classification using discriminative restricted Boltzmann machines. In: International Conference on Machine Learning, pp. 536–543. ACM Press (2008)
6. LeCun, Y., Bottou, L., Bengio, Y., Haffner, P.: Gradient-based learning applied to document recognition. Proc. IEEE 86(11), 2278–2324 (1998)
7. Mohamed, A.R., Dahl, G., Hinton, G.: Acoustic modeling using deep belief networks. IEEE Trans. Audio Speech Lang. Process. 20(1), 14–22 (2012)

8. Nair, V., Hinton, G.: Rectified linear units improve restricted boltzmann machines. In: Proceedings of the 27th International Conference on Machine Learning (ICML2010), pp. 807–814 (2010)
9. Smolensky, P.: Information processing in dynamical systems: foundations of harmony theory. In: Parallel Distributed Processing: Explorations in the Microstructure of Cognition, vol. 1, pp. 194–281. MIT Press (1986)
10. Teh, Y.W., Hinton, G.: Rate-coded restricted boltzmann machines for face recognition. In: Advances in Neural Information Processing Systems, pp. 908–914 (2001)
11. Welling, M., Rosen-Zvi, M., Hinton, G.: Exponential family harmoniums with an application to information retrieval. In: Advances in Neural Information Processing Systems, pp. 1481–1488 (2004)

Extracting M of N Rules from Restricted Boltzmann Machines

Simon Odense[(✉)] and Artur d'Avila Garcez

City, University of London, London EC1V 0HB, UK
{simon.odense,artur.garcez}@city.ac.uk

Abstract. Rule extraction is an important method seeking to understand how neural networks are able to solve problems. In order for rule extraction to be comprehensible, good knowledge representations should be used. So called M of N rules are a compact way of representing knowledge that has a strong intuitive connection to the structure of neural networks. M of N rules have been used in the past in the context of supervised models but not unsupervised models. Here we present a novel extension of a previous rule extraction algorithm for RBMs that allows us to quickly extract accurate M of N rules. The results are compared on simple datasets showing that M of N extraction has the potential to be an effective method for the knowledge representation of RBMs.

Keywords: Rule extraction · M of N · RBM · Neural networks

1 Introduction

Despite being effective tools for classification and prediction, neural networks suffer from the black box problem. Although it might be able to solve a problem, a neural network by itself does not offer much insight into the solution. Many techniques to extract the implicit knowledge of neural networks and represent it using more interpretable logical structures have been developed. The two important factors to weigh when considering these techniques are accuracy and representation. On one hand, we would like the extracted logical rules to accurately capture the behaviour of the network. On the other hand, we want the rules to be easily understood by people and represented in a compact way. These two issues represent a trade off, generally the more accurate your extracted rules the less compact/comprehensible they will be. Consider the two extreme cases, at one end we have a large rule set calculating the expected output of the neural network for every possible combination of inputs, the output of these rules will match the output of the network 100% of the time for a deterministic network but will be incomprehensible. The other extreme case is when we have a trivial rule with a constant output, this is very easy to understand but it doesn't faithfully represent the network at all. With this in mind we would ideally use representations that closely resemble the network itself but are more comprehensible. In many applications decision trees are used to capture the behaviour

© Springer International Publishing AG 2017
A. Lintas et al. (Eds.): ICANN 2017, Part II, LNCS 10614, pp. 120–127, 2017.
https://doi.org/10.1007/978-3-319-68612-7_14

of a network. These models are easy to understand but are not always powerful enough to accurately represent a network. Perhaps the most basic way of representing extracted knowledge from a neural network is with Horn clauses [10], that is rules of the form $a \leftarrow x_1 \wedge ... \wedge x_n$. Here a is called the head of the clause and $x_1 \wedge ... \wedge x_n$ the body. Horn clauses are appealing for their simplicity and their connection to logic programming. However, it can be difficult for them to accurately capture the behaviour of a network. The problem is that in a neural network, the structure of the input data is irrelevant when the total input to a neuron is already known, whereas a Horn clause depends on the exact structure of the input. A more intuitive representation of a neural network is the M of N rule. The purpose of this paper is to develop a method for extracting M of N rules that can be applied to unsupervised and probabilistic networks such as the RBM. An M of N rule is a generalization of a Horn clause in which the body consist of a set of literals (Boolean variables or their negation) $(x_1, ..., x_N)$ and a positive integer M. The head of an M of N rule is true iff M of the literals are true. For example 2 of (a, b, c) is true if $a \wedge b$ or $a \wedge c$ or $b \wedge c$ is true. There is a strong link between M of N rules and neural networks since an M of N rule can be thought of as a "weightless perceptron" by considering a simple perceptron with weights identically 1 and with a bias of M. The similarity to the structure of neural networks allows M of N rules to accurately represent neural networks in a more compact way than simple Horn clauses as illustrated by the following example. Consider a simple perceptron with a single output node with bias -30 and 100 input nodes all with weight 10. Any three input nodes being on is sufficient to predict an output of 1, however a Horn clause needs to specify exactly which three. A single Horn clause cannot represent this network accurately at all, instead we need $\binom{100}{3}$ Horn clauses, each with 3 literals in the body to accurately represent this network. By contrast a single M of N rule will do the trick, 3 of the set of input neurons. This is a single rule with 101 parameters verses $\binom{100}{3}$ rules each with 3 parameters. The comparison of Horn clauses to M of N rules is reminiscent of the comparison between traditional circuits and linear threshold circuits. It can be shown that in some cases there is an exponential gap in compactness between threshold circuits and traditional AND-OR-NOT circuits [11]. Clearly M of N rules have huge potential to provide a compact representation of a neural network. However, to the author's knowledge, M of N rules have only been applied to the supervised and deterministic case.

M of N rules were first derived in the context of the KBANN model [4]. This method clustered the weights and looked for combinations of weights which exceeded the threshold of the output neuron. Shortly after, M of N rules were used in conjunction with decision trees in ID2-of-3 and then TREPAN [3,5]. Here M of N rules were constructed using a hill climbing search (a greedy search considering $M+1$ of N and $M+1$ of $N+1$ at each step) to maximize the difference in entropy. The combination of M of N rules with decision trees can be a powerful way of representing a network, however, interpretability suffers [9]. Another M of N extraction algorithm using clustering, MofN3 [6], first extracts DNF rules from supervised networks using the X2R algorithm [8] before converting them to M of N rules. All of these algorithms were developed for supervised networks. MofN3 crucially uses class labels for clustering and calculating the difference in entropy on a split for an unsupervised probabilistic models like the RBM is intractable. One approach would be to find another function on which to perform hillclimbing, the obvious one being the expected value of the error between the rules and the network. This however is still intractable and as we will see in the experiments not optimal anyways. Instead we take a decompositional approach.

A decompositional algorithm for extracting conjunctive rules from RBMs along with associated confidence values was developed in [1]. We will proceed by extending this algorithm using techniques similar to the original M of N extraction algorithms in order to give a fast and accurate method for extracting M of N rules from RBMs which could in principle be applied to any neural network. Section 2 will give an overview of the method for extracting conjunctive rules from RBMs given in [1], Sect. 3 we will present an algorithm which uses conjunctive rules with confidence values to generate M of N rules for RBMs, we'll conclude by testing the two algorithms along with a third greedy algorithm on networks trained on small datasets and show that extracting M of N rules represents a significant advantage in terms of accuracy over purely conjunctive rules.

2 Extracting Conjunctive Rules from RBMs

Here we outline the algorithm presented in [1] for extracting Conjunctive rules from RBMs (see [13] for example for details about RBMs). By conjunctive rules we mean rules of the form $h_j \leftarrow x_1 \wedge x_2 \wedge ... \wedge \neg x_k \wedge ... \wedge \neg x_n$. Furthermore this algorithm gives, for each rule, an associated confidence value $c_j \in \mathbb{R}^+$. We interpret the confidence value in a way similar to penalty logic [7], that is it is a measure of how confident we are that the rule is true. Given all possible conjunctive rules of the network each with a confidence value, The confidence can be thought of as a degree of belief in the rule. This somewhat mitigates the inherent issue of comparing deterministic rules with a probabilistic network. In order to achieve this, the algorithm works by minimizing the loss function given below

$$I_{loss} = \sum_{i,j} \frac{1}{2} |w_{i,j} - c_j S(i,j)|^2 \tag{1}$$

where $S(i,j) = 1$ if x_i is in the rule corresponding to h_j, $S(i,j) = -1$ if $\neg x_i$ is in the rule corresponding to h_j, and $S(i,j) = 0$ otherwise. The algorithm begins by setting $S(i,j) = 1$ if $w_{i,j} \geq 0$ and $S(i,j) = -1$ if $w_{i,j} < 0$. Then we can set each confidence to the value that minimizes I_{loss}. It is not hard to see that this is simply

$$c_j = \frac{\sum_i w_{i,j} S(i,j)}{\sum_i S(i,j)^2} \tag{2}$$

From there we want to set $S(i,j) = 0$ if it will decrease (1), this is true iff $c_j \geq 2|w_{i,j}|$.

The algorithm proceeds by iteratively choosing c to minimize (1) and then updating $S(i,j)$ based on the previous condition until no improvements are seen. This results in a set of purely conjunctive rules, one for each hidden neuron, each of which has an associated confidence value, c_j. This algorithm can be extended to deep networks by using the fact that deep networks can be learned greedily with stacks of RBMs [12]. This is done by first applying the algorithm to each layer to produce a hierarchical set of inference rules each with a confidence value. Then, given a set of inputs each with an associated confidence value, we can propagate through the layers by inferring the confidence value of each successive layer from the extracted rules and the confidence values of the previous layer.

3   Extracting M of N Rules from RBMs

We want to extend the previous algorithm in a way that will produce M of N rules instead of purely conjunctive ones. We can make a conjunctive rule into an M of N rule simply by choosing a value, M, for that rule. Given a set of conjunctive rules, all we need to do is choose a value,M_j, for every rule. We use a method similar to the one found in [2] by setting M_j to be the minimum value so that $M_j \cdot c_j \geq T_j$ where T_j is some threshold. Consider the minimum possible input to h_j, this is just $I_{min,j} := b_j + \sum_{i:w_{i,j}<0} w_{i,j}$. Then since $P(h_j = 1|x) > 0.5$ if the total input to h_j is greater than 0 and we want our rule to predict 1 in this case, we should set M_j to be the minimum value such that $M_j \cdot c_j + I_j \geq 0$ In other words $T_j = -I_j$. For the case that no value of M can exceed T_j we proceed by attempting to add a literal to the rule and recalculating c_j according to (2), we choose the literal to add to be the one corresponding to the neuron with the highest absolute weight in the set of literals not in the rule. If there is nothing to add and we still cannot exceed T_j then we output the rule $N + 1$ of N, in other words the rule which always outputs 0. To illustrate we consider a simple example. Take an RBM with a single hidden unit and two visible units with weights $w_{1,h} = 1, w_{2,h} = -1, h_b = 0$. Then minimizing (1) gives us the rule $h \leftarrow x_1 \wedge \neg x_2$ with confidence $c = 1$. Then we set the threshold $T = 1$ and since $1 \cdot 1 \geq 1$ we set $M = 1$ giving us the rule 1 of $(x_1, \neg x_2)$. To summarize, our algorithm is as follows.

Data: A neural network, $\mathcal{N}$
Result: A set of M of N rules R
Run the algorithm from the previous section on $\mathcal{N}$ to get an initial set of rules R;
for *Each hidden neuron* $h_j \in \mathcal{N}$ **do**
$\quad M_j = N + 1$
$\quad W_{j,to\_add} = \{w_{i,j} : S(i,j) = 0\}$
$\quad$ **while** $W_{j,to\_add} \neq \emptyset$ **and**$\{M : M \cdot c_j \geq -b_j - \sum\limits_{i:w_{i,j}<0} w_{i,j}\} = \emptyset$ **do**
$\quad\quad k = \arg \max\{|w_{\cdot,j}| : S(i,j) = 0\}$
$\quad\quad S(k,j) = sign(w_{k,j})$
$\quad\quad W_{j,to\_add} = W_{j,to\_add} \setminus w_{k,j}$
$\quad\quad$ Update c_j according to (2)
$\quad$ **end**
$\quad$ **if** $\{M : M \cdot c_j \geq -b_j - \sum\limits_{i:w_{i,j}<0} w_{i,j}\} \neq \emptyset$ **then**
$\quad\quad M_j = \min\{M : M \cdot c_j \geq -b_j - \sum\limits_{i:w_{i,j}<0} w_{i,j}\}$;
$\quad$ **end**
end

Algorithm 1. Extracting M of N rules from a network using a set of conjunctive rules with confidence values as a starting point

4   Experiments

4.1   Experimental Setup

Three different rule extraction algorithms were tested on 12 different RBMs each trained on a different small dataset generated using logical functions. The datasets were generated by taking every possible combination of the first $n - 1$ visible units and setting the nth visible unit to the output of the first $n - 1$ visible units with the function. For example the XOR (3 vis) dataset has the first two variables free and the third calculated as x_1 XOR x_2 giving us $(0,0,0),(0,1,1),(1,0,1),(1,1,0)$. Since the datasets are small, we are able to get an exact measure of the accuracy of the extracted rules by calculating their expected error. This is just the expected value of the difference between the output of our rules and the output of the network for a single hidden unit, averaged over all hidden units. To be precise the expected error is

$$\frac{1}{m} \sum_i \sum_{v \in V} (p(h_i = 1|v)|1 - r(v)| + P(h_i = 0|v)|r(v)|) \tag{3}$$

Here V is the space of visible configurations, $r(v)$ is the output of our rule on input v, and m is the number of hidden neurons. Note that this is equivalent to measuring the expected error of the rule compared to the whole network when using the Hamming distance. The maximum error possible is 1 and the minimum is 0. Again note that we are comparing deterministic rules to a probabilistic network which is why we look at the error as a random variable dependent on the output of the network, also note that the M of N rules generated also have associated confidence values which we can take into consideration when looking over the set of generated rules. We also report the average value of M and N in order to gain some insight into how interpretable these rules might be, if N scales linearly with the size of the input data then large datasets will give us totally incomprehensible rules (Table 1).

Table 1. Comparing hill climbing with expected error (hcee) to the optimal confidence algorithm presented in [1] and the M of N version of the optimal confidence algorithm

Network	hcee			optmial confidence		
	M/N	Error	Time(s)	M/N	Error	Time(s)
XOR(3 vis 10 hid)	2.1/2.7	0.0991	0.322	2.7/2.7	0.2279	0.09
XOR(6 vis 20 hid)	2.65/3.4	0.1095	7.819	4.55/4.55	0.3344	0.014
XOR(9 vis 30 hid)	3.36/4.03	0.1035	89.158	5.8/5.8	0.2766	0.036
NAND(3 vis 10 hid)	1.4/1.4	0.1277	0.222	2.6/2.6	0.2302	0.007
NAND(6 vis 20 hid)	2.35/2.65	0.1206	5.248	3.6/3.6	0.2540	0.022
NAND(9 vis 30 hid)	2.93/3.3	0.1227	74.511	5.4/5.4	0.2723	0.034
OR(3 vis 10 hid)	1.6/2.1	0.1424	0.095	2.4/2.4	0.2328	0.004
OR(6 vis 20 hid)	2.4/2.8	0.1132	5.429	3.6/3.6	0.2665	0.021
OR(9 vis 30 hid)	2.53/3.26	0.1369	74.209	5.13/5.13	0.3614	0.036
AND(3 vis 10 hid)	2.0/2.2	0.0884	0.249	2.4/2.4	0.1735	0.007
AND(6 vis 20 hid)	2.5/2.85	0.1068	3.584	3.5/3.5	0.2439	0.021
AND(9 vis 30 hid)	3.26/3.93	0.1052	87.367	5.4/5.4	0.2819	0.035

MofN optimal confidence

Network	M/N	Error	Time(s)
XOR(3 vis 10 hid)	2.4/2.8	0.1149	0.009
XOR(6 vis 20 hid)	3.35/4.75	0.1067	0.023
XOR(9 vis 30 hid)	4.86/6.06	0.1234	0.043
NAND(3 vis 10 hid)	2.3/2.8	0.1562	0.011
NAND(6 vis 20 hid)	3.3/3.9	0.1312	0.026
NAND(9 vis 20 hid)	4.53/5.56	0.1300	0.039
OR(3 vis 10 hid)	1.8/2.5	0.1614	0.004
OR(6 vis 20 hid)	3.1/3.75	0.1223	0.024
OR(9 vis 30 hid)	3.83/5.2	0.1440	0.038
AND(3 vis 10 hid)	2.2/2.4	0.1042	0.007
AND(6 vis 20 hid)	3.4/4.05	0.1125	0.029
AND(9 vis 30 hid)	4.6/5.6	0.1240	0.040

4.2 Experimental Results

Here we tested three different rule extraction algorithms on small RBMs trained on datasets constructed from Boolean functions. We tested the original optimal confidence algorithm along with the M of N optimal confidence algorithm and with the expected error.

Each Network was trained for 10000 iteration using contrastive divergence with 10 Gibbs steps. It is clear that overall the M of N optimal confidence algorithm gives the best trade off for time and accuracy. As expected the most accurate method is the hill climb using the expected error but this sums over all visible states and is thus exponential. We see that the time it takes grows quite quickly whereas the time it takes the M of N optimal confidence algorithm to finish grows relatively slowly. In addition the expected error for the M of N optimal confidence algorithm is more or less in line with hill climbing, in some cases even beating it, which implies that hill climbing is not optimal for finding the minimum expected error.

Speed wise the optimal confidence algorithm is the fastest with the M of N optimal confidence algorithm being only slightly slower. Also interesting things to note is that for all algorithms the expected error is relatively consistent as the dataset increasing in size. This is encouraging. Finally notice that M and N appear to increase slower than the dimension of the test set in all cases although they grow slowest with hill climbing. For larger datasets the expected error will be intractable and instead we will have to rely on test error over a sample set to evaluate the accuracy.

5   Conclusion

Even in the probabilistic context, deterministic rule extraction can provide us with rules that accurately capture the network's behaviour. The representation used for the rule extraction is crucial. The results show that M of N rules represent a significant potential advantage in accuracy for rule extraction from RBMs. This is in addition to the advantage of the more compact representation compared to purely conjunctive rules. We see that our simple extension of the optimal confidence algorithm is almost on par with hill climbing in terms of accuracy. Since hill climbing directly minimizes the expected error it is not surprising that it beats the optimal confidence methods, however, the fact that computing the expected error is exponential in the number of visible units makes hill climbing impossible for the vast majority of real world datasets. The fact that MofN optimal confidence is close to, and in some cases even beats hill climbing, shows that it is possible to extract accurate M of N rules quickly using this algorithm. Furthermore, the fact that in some cases our algorithm *beats* hill climbing suggests that hill climbing might not be the best method for constructing M of N rules in general. It is possible that you can find another loss function which can be calculated faster than the expected error but it is implausible that performing hill climbing on this new loss function could result in rules that are better, or even on par with, the rules generated by hill climbing using the expected error itself. We can see too that M of N extraction represents a significant improvement to the accuracy of the extracted rules versus the standard optimal confidence algorithm. This shows that using M of N extraction in the probabilistic, unsupervised context can be advantageous compared to standard optimal confidence rule extraction both in terms of accuracy and compactness. Future work to be done is defining rules for composing M of N rules with confidence values so that we can apply this algorithm in a greedy way to create rules for deep networks.

References

1. Son, T., d'Avila Garcez, A.: Deep logic network: inserting and extracting knowledge from deep belief networks. IEEE Trans. Neural Netw. Learn. Syst. **PP**(99), 1–13 (2016)
2. Towell, G.G., Shavlik, J.W.: The extraction of refined rules from knowledge-based neural networks. Mach. Learn. **13**(1), 71–101 (1993)
3. Craven, M.: Extracting comprehensible models from trained neural networks. Ph.D. thesis, University of Wisconsin-Madison (1996)
4. Towell, G.G.: Symbolic knowledge and neural networks: insertion, refinement and extraction. Ph.D. thesis, University of Wisconsin - Madison (1991)
5. Murphy, P., Pazzani, M.: ID2-of-3: constructive induction of M-of -N concepts for discriminators in decision trees. In: Machine Learning: Proceedings of the Eighth International Workshop (1991)
6. Setiono, R.: Extracting M of N rules from trained neural networks. IEEE Trans. Neural Netw. Learn. Syst. **11**(2), 512–519 (2000)
7. Pinkas, G.: Reasoning, connectionist nonmonotonicity and learning in networks that capture propositional knowledge. Artif. Intell. **77**, 203–247 (1995)
8. Liu, H., Tan, S.: X2R: a fast rule generator. In: IEEE International Conference on Systems, Man and Cybernetics, Intelligent Systems for the 21st Century (1995)
9. Percy, C., d'Avila Garcez, A., Dragičević, S. França M., Slabaugh, G., Weyde, T.: The need for knowledg extraction: understanding harmful gambling behaviour with neural networks. In: 22nd European Conference on Artificial Intelligence, pp. 974–981 (2016)
10. d'Avila Garcez, A., Lamb, L., Gabbay, D.: Neural-Symbolic Cognitive Reasoning. Springer, New York (2009)
11. Kautz, W.: The realization of symmetric switching functions with linear-input logical elements. IRE Trans. Electron. Comput. **EC–10**(3), 371–378 (1961)
12. Hinton, G.E., Osindero, S., Teh, T.W.: A fast learning algorithm for deep belief nets. Neural Comput. **18**(7), 1527–1554 (2006)
13. Smolensky, P.: Information proessing in dynamical systems: foundations of harmony theory. In: Parallel Distributed Processing, vol. 1, pp. 194–281. Foundations. MIT Press, Cambridge (1986)

Generalized Entropy Cost Function in Neural Networks

Krzysztof Gajowniczek$^{(\boxtimes)}$, Leszek J. Chmielewski,
Arkadiusz Orłowski, and Tomasz Ząbkowski

Faculty of Applied Informatics and Mathematics – WZIM,
Warsaw University of Life Sciences – SGGW,
Nowoursynowska 159, 02-787 Warsaw, Poland
krzysztof_gajowniczek@sggw.pl

Abstract. Artificial neural networks are capable of constructing complex decision boundaries and over the recent years they have been widely used in many practical applications ranging from business to medical diagnosis and technical problems. A large number of error functions have been proposed in the literature to achieve a better predictive power. However, only a few works employ Tsallis statistics, which has successfully been applied in other fields. This paper undertakes the effort to examine the q-generalized function based on Tsallis statistics as an alternative error measure in neural networks. The results indicate that Tsallis entropy error function can be successfully applied in the neural networks yielding satisfactory results.

Keywords: Neural networks · Tsallis entropy error function · Classification

1 Introduction and Problem Statement

Artificial neural networks (ANNs) are flexible and powerful statistical learning models used in many applications. They have been extensively and successfully applied in areas such as signal processing, pattern recognition, machine learning, system control, and many business problems including marketing and finance [1–5]. Several features of artificial neural networks make them very popular and attractive for practical applications. First, they possess an ability to generalize, even in the case of incomplete or noisy data. Second, neural networks are non-parametric which means that they do not require any a-priori assumptions about the distribution of the data. Third, they are good approximators able to model continuous function to a desired accuracy.

From a pattern recognition perspective, the goal is to find the required mapping from input to output variables in order to solve the classification or the regression problem. The main issue in neural networks application is to find the correct values for the weights between the input and output layer using a supervised learning paradigm (training). During the training process the difference between the prediction made by the network and the correct value for the output is calculated, and the weights are changed in order to minimize the error.

The form of the error function is one of the factors in the weight update process. For the successful application it is important to train the network with an error function that

© Springer International Publishing AG 2017
A. Lintas et al. (Eds.): ICANN 2017, Part I, LNCS 10614, pp. 128–136, 2017.
https://doi.org/10.1007/978-3-319-68612-7_15

reflects the objective of the problem. The mean square error (MSE) is the most commonly used function although it has been suggested that it is not necessarily the best function to be used, especially in classification problems [6–8]. A number of alternative error functions have been proposed in the literature and the maximum likelihood (cross entropy) function was particularly reported as a more appropriate function for classification problems [7, 8].

In this paper we undertake the effort to examine an alternative error function such as the q-generalized function based on Tsallis statistics. In particular the properties of the function and its impact on the neural network classifiers is analyzed as well as a careful analysis of the way in which the error function is introduced in the weight update equations is presented. To the best of our knowledge the proposed error function was never examined before in the context of the neural network learning.

The rest of this paper is organized as follows. In the second section the literature review on similar problems is presented. An analysis of the way the error function is incorporated in the training algorithm is presented in section three. The fourth section deals with the experiments carried out and their results are presented. The paper ends with concluding remarks in the last section.

2 Literature Review on Similar Problems

The research on neural networks is considerable and the literature around this filed is growing rapidly. While the method becomes a more and more substantial part of the state-of-the-art automatic pattern recognition systems applicable in a variety of fields, different questions arise considering the network architecture and the fundamentals of training process.

Usually, the works include modifications and improvements of the neural network structure, weights initialization [9], weights updating procedure [10], error functions [11, 12] and activation functions [13, 14]. The training of artificial neural networks usually requires that users define an error measure in order to adapt the network weights to meet certain model performance criteria. The error measure is very important and in certain circumstances it is essential for achieving satisfactory results. Different error measures have been used to train feedforward artificial neural networks, with the mean-square error measure (and its modifications) and cross-entropy being the most popular ones.

It can be shown that the true posterior probability is reaching a global minimum for both the cross-entropy and squared error criteria. Thus, in the theory an ANN can be trained equally well by minimizing each of the functions, as long as it is capable of approximating the true posterior distribution arbitrarily close. When it comes to the modelling of distribution, squared error is bounded and the optimization is therefore more robust to outliers than minimization of cross-entropy. However, in practice, cross-entropy mostly leads to quicker convergence resulting better quality in terms of classification error rates. Hence, squared error became less popular over the last years [8, 15]. In the literature, the previous works on the error functions have usually been evaluated on rather small datasets.

When it comes to applications under the nonextensive statistics with Tsallis distributions, called q-distributions, formed by maximizing Tsallis entropy with certain constraints – such distributions have applications in physics, astronomy, geology, chemistry and finance [16]. However, these q-distributions remain largely unnoticed by the computer science audience, with only a few works applying them to ANNs, not necessary as the error functions [17]. For instance, [17] introduces q-generalized RNNs (random neural network) for classification where parametrized q-Gaussian distributions are used as activation functions. These distributions arise from maximizing Tsallis entropy and have a continuous real parameter q – the entropic index – which represents the degree of nonextensivity.

In this paper, in order to address the identified literature gap, we present an investigation on the properties of the q-entropic error criteria for training of ANNs. The theoretical analysis of the error bounds was supported by experimental evaluation with properly trained networks taking into account classification accuracy measures.

3   Theoretical Framework

As a general measure of diversity of objects, a Shannon entropy is often used which is defined as:

$$H_S = -\sum_{i=1}^{n} t_i \log t_i,$$

(1)

where t_i is the probability of occurrence of an event x_i being an element of the event X that can take values $x_i, \ldots, x_n$. The value of the entropy depends on two parameters: (1) disorder (uncertainty) and it is maximum when the probability t_i for every x_i is equal; (2) the value of n. Shannon entropy assumes a tradeoff between contributions from the main mass of the distribution and the tail. To control both parameters a generalizations was proposed by Tsallis:

$$H_{T_q} = \frac{1}{q-1}\left(1 - \sum_{i=1}^{n} t_i^q\right).$$

(2)

With Shannon entropy, events with high or low probability have equal weights in the entropy computation. However, using Tsallis entropy, for q > 1, events with high probability contribute more to the entropy value than those with low probabilities. Therefore, the higher is the value of q, the higher is the contribution of high probability events in the final result.

It can be shown that q-Tsallis relative entropy is a generalization of the Kullback-Leibler entropy (in the limit of q → 1 the q-Tsallis relative entropy becomes the Kullback-Leibler entropy). It refers to two probability distributions $\{t_i\}$ and $\{y_i\}$, $i = 1$ to n, over the same alphabet, and is defined as [18]:

$$H_{T_q}(t_i \| y_i) = \frac{1}{1-q}\left(1 - \sum_{i=1}^{n} t_i^q y_i^{1-q}\right). \tag{3}$$

At the limit $q = 1$, one has $H_{T_i}(t_i \| y_i) = \sum_{i=1}^{n} t_i \log(\frac{t_i}{y_i})_i$, i.e., the Kullback-Leibler relative entropy [19]. For any order $q \neq 0$, the Tsallis relative entropy $H_{T_q}(t_i \| y_i)$ of the above Eq. (3) vanishes if and only if $t_i = y_i$ for all $i = 1$ to n. For any $q > 0$, the Tsallis relative entropy $H_{T_q}(t_i \| y_i)$ is always nonnegative. In this regime of $q > 0$, the Tsallis relative entropy $H_{T_q}(t_i \| y_i)$ behaves much like the conventional Kullback-Leibler relative entropy, yet in a generalized form realized by the additional parameterization by q.

In the present paper we have used a variant of gradient descent method known as Broyden-Fletcher-Goldfarb-Shanno (BFGS) optimization algorithm [20], in order to train a neural network (multilayer perceptron). To make use of BFGS, the function being minimized should have an objective function that accepts a vector of parameters, input data, output data, and should return both the cost and the gradients. In these circumstances the cost function which implements the Tsallis entropy is defined as:

$$C(t, y) = \frac{1}{1-q}\left(1 - t^q y^{1-q} - (1-t)^q (1-y)^{1-q}\right), \tag{4}$$

where t and y stand for the true value and output of the neural network, respectively.

Figure 1 shows the general behavior of the error function for different values of parameter q.

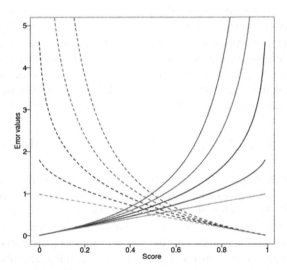

Fig. 1. Error entropy values for different q values in terms of different score values. Color denotes the value of the parametr q as follows: 0 – green, 0.5 – blue, 1 – black, 1.5 – red, 2 – purple. The difference between the solid and dashed lines is explained in the main text. (Color figure online)

The solid lines show entropy values for the growing score (outcome of ANN) in case if the true value is 0. It could be clearly seen that if the score tends to 1 the error function increases; in other words, this is an undesirable situation for a given case. In contrast, the dashed lines show entropy values for the growing score in case if the true value is 1. Once again, entropy values increase when the ANN network outcome is inconsistent with the true value.

4 Numerical Experiment

4.1 Implementation

In our case, all the numerical calculations were performed on a personal computer with the following parameters: Ubuntu 16.04 LTS operating system and Intel Core i5-2430 M 2.4 GHz, 2 CPU * 2 cores, 8 GB RAM. R-CRAN [21], which is an advanced statistical package, as well as an interpreted programming language, was used as the computing environment. For training neural networks we used the BFGS algorithm, available in the *nnet* library [21]. A logistic function was used to activate all of the neurons in the neural network and initial weights vector was chosen randomly using a uniform distribution.

To compare the neural networks obtained for different values of q we define two measures. These are: (1) AUC (area under the ROC curve) and (2) classification accuracy. Those measures are related to efficiency and effectiveness of the ANN and they have been often used for evaluation of classification models in the context of various practical problems such as credit scoring, income and poverty determinants or customer insolvency and churn [22, 23].

The starting point for the numerical experiments was the randomly selected split of the examined datasets into two parts, which corresponded to the training and validation with the following proportions: training 70%, validation 30%. The main criterion taken into account while learning the models was to gain good generalization of knowledge with the least error. The most commonly used measure to assess the quality of binary classification problem is AUC. Therefore, to find the best parameters for all models and to assure their generalization, the following function was maximized:

$$f(AUC_T, AUC_W) = -\frac{1}{2}|AUC_T - AUC_W| + \frac{1}{2}AUC_W, \tag{5}$$

where AUC_T and AUC_W stand for the training and validation errors, respectively.

In contrast to other machine learning algorithms, ANN required special preparation of the input data. The vector of continuous variables were standardized, while the binary variables were converted such that the value of 0 was transformed into -1.

Each time, 15 neural networks were learned with various parameters (the number of neurons in the hidden layer from 1 to 15). To avoid overfitting, after the completion of each learning iteration (with a maximum of 50 iterations), the models were checked for the error measure defined in Eq. (5). At the end, the ANN characterized by the smallest error was chosen as the best model. In order to achieve robust estimation of models' error, for each number of hidden neurons, ten different ANN were learned with different initial weights vector. Final estimation of the error was computed as the average value over ten models and for each number of hidden neurons.

4.2   Results

Our research was conducted on several benchmarking data sets which are freely available. However, due to limited room, results for two datasets only are shown. We conducted the simulations using the dataset known as Churn (3333 observations 19 predictors [24]) and Hepatitis [25] (155 observations and 19 predictors). Moreover, only relevant results related to the best performance in terms of Eq. 5 are discussed. For both datasets the networks with at least 10 hidden units delivered the robust results as provided in Tables 1 and 2.

Table 1. The results for the Churn dataset.

q-value	Number of hidden neurons	Avg number of iterations	Training sample		Validation sample		AUC Equation No 5
			Accuracy	AUC	Accuracy	AUC	
1.0	10	20.3	0.904	0.895	0.888	0.874	0.852
1.2	10	14.8	0.913	0.906	0.899	0.886	0.867
1.4	10	13.5	0.906	0.893	0.898	0.880	0.867
1.0	11	17.7	0.921	0.915	0.904	0.891	0.868
1.2	11	14.8	0.922	0.912	0.905	0.891	0.869
1.4	11	14.9	0.909	0.896	0.901	0.884	0.871
1.0	12	18.3	0.919	0.909	0.903	0.891	0.872
1.2	12	15.0	0.913	0.906	0.901	0.894	0.882
1.4	12	16.2	0.900	0.904	0.902	0.891	0.878

Table 2. The results for the Hepatitis dataset.

q-value	Number of hidden neurons	Avg number of iteration	Training sample		Validation sample		AUC Equation No 5
			Accuracy	AUC	Accuracy	AUC	
1.0	11	5.4	0.773	0.841	0.762	0.837	0.832
1.2	11	4.1	0.772	0.838	0.755	0.835	0.832
1.4	11	4.7	0.774	0.837	0.758	0.834	0.829
1.0	12	6.0	0.778	0.844	0.756	0.837	0.830
1.2	12	5.5	0.775	0.841	0.756	0.836	0.829
1.4	12	5.1	0.770	0.836	0.754	0.833	0.827
1.0	13	4.6	0.769	0.838	0.748	0.832	0.825
1.2	13	4.3	0.771	0.836	0.746	0.830	0.824
1.4	13	4.1	0.768	0.835	0.745	0.831	0.826

In particular, the results can be summarized as follows:

- The best results were obtained for q-value equal to 1.0, 1.2 and 1.4; significant drop in classification accuracy was in general observed for $q > 2$ (due to the limit of pages and the goal of the article set for the best results, data not shown).
- Behavior of error function with q-parameter greater than 1 is more non-linier (see Fig. 1) than behavior of error function based on Shannon entropy ($q \approx 1$);
- ANN learned with $q > 1$ required less iteration to achieve convergence in terms of Eq. (5);
- Overall performance depends on number of input variables (input neurons) and number of hidden neurons; The choice of the proper network structure should be based on solid experiments, since this may lead to unwanted effects influencing the stability and performance of the training algorithm and the trained network as a whole.

5 Summary and Concluding Remarks

The results of this study indicate that in classification problems, Tsallis entropy error function can be successfully applied in the neural networks yielding satisfactory results in terms of the number of iterations required for training, and the generalization ability of the trained network.

The contribution of this study provides the proof that the q-entropy can substitute other standard entropic error functions like the Shannon's one with satisfactory results, leading to less epochs and delivering the same percentage of correct classifications. The choice of the error function is indeed an important factor to be examined with great care when designing a neural network for a specific classification problem.

Possible future research on this topic could consider two streams. Firstly, comparative study on the impact of various error functions, including mean square error and the mean absolute error, used for various classification problems [26–28], should be made. Secondly, the effect of the proposed error functions on other types of neural network architectures, including application on a variety of real datasets, should be studied.

References

1. Paliwal, M., Kumar, U.A.: Neural networks and statistical techniques: a review of applications. Expert Syst. Appl. **36**(1), 2–17 (2009)
2. Bishop, C.M.: Neural Networks for Pattern Recognition. Clarendon Press, Oxford (1995)
3. Szupiluk, R., Wojewnik, P., Ząbkowski, T.: Prediction improvement via smooth component analysis and neural network mixing. In: Kollias, S., Stafylopatis, A., Duch, W., Oja, E. (eds.) ICANN 2006. LNCS, vol. 4132, pp. 133–140. Springer, Heidelberg (2006). doi:10.1007/11840930_14
4. Gajowniczek, K., Ząbkowski, T.: Data mining techniques for detecting household characteristics based on smart meter data. Energies **8**(7), 7407–7427 (2015)

5. Ząbkowski, T., Szczesny, W.: Insolvency modeling in the cellular telecommunication industry. Expert Syst. Appl. **39**, 6879–6886 (2012)
6. Kalman, B.L., Kwasny, S.C.: A superior error function for training neural networks. In: International Joint Conference on Neural Networks, pp. 49–52 (1991)
7. White, H.: Artificial Neural Networks: Approximation and Learning Theory. Blackwell, Cambridge (1992)
8. Golik, P., Doetsch, P., Ney, H.: Cross-entropy vs squared error training: a theoretical and experimental comparison. In: 14th Annual Conference of the International Speech Communication Association "Interspeech-2013", pp. 1756–1760, France (2013)
9. Waghmare, L.M., Bidwai, N.N., Bhogle, P.P.: Neural network weight initialization. In: Proceedings of IEEE International Conference on Mechatronics and Automation, pp. 679–681 (2007)
10. Ramos, E.Z., Nakakuni, M., Yfantis, E.: Quantitative measures to evaluate neural network weight initialization strategies. In: IEEE Computing and Communication Workshop and Conference (CCWC), pp. 1–7 (2017)
11. Falas, T., Stafylopatis, A.G.: The impact of the error function selection in neural network-based classifiers. In: International Joint Conference on Neural Networks, pp. 1799–1804 (1999)
12. Shamsuddin, S.M., Sulaiman, M.N., Darus, M.: An improved error signal for the backpropagation model for classification problems. Int. J. Comput. Math. **76**(3), 297–305 (2001)
13. Narayan, S.: The generalized sigmoid activation function: competitive supervised learning. Inf. Sci. **99**(1–2), 69–82 (1997)
14. Kamruzzaman, J., Aziz, S.M.: A note on activation function in multilayer feedforward learning, In: Proceedings of the 2002 International Joint Conference on Neural Networks, IJCNN 2002, pp. 519–523 (2002)
15. Kline, D.M., Berardi, V.L.: Revisiting squared-error and cross-entropy functions for training neural network classifiers. Neural Comput. Appl. **14**(4), 310–318 (2005)
16. Picoli, S., Mendes, R.S., Malacarne, L.C., Santos, R.P.B.: Q-distributions in complex systems: a brief review. Braz. J. Phys. **39**(2A), 468–474 (2009)
17. Stosic, D., Stosic, D., Zanchettin, C., Ludermir, T., Stosic, B.: QRNN: q-generalized random neural network. IEEE Trans. Neural Netw. Learn. Syst. **28**(2), 383–390 (2016)
18. Tsallis, C.: Introduction to Nonextensive Statistical Mechanics. Springer, New York (2009)
19. Cover, T.M., Thomas, J.A.: Elements of Information Theory. Wiley, New York (1991)
20. Dai, Y.H.: Convergence properties of the BFGS algorithm. SIAM J. Optim. **13**(3), 693–701 (2002)
21. R Core Team: A language and environment for statistical computing, R Foundation for Statistical Computing, Vienna, Austria (2015)
22. Gajowniczek, K., Ząbkowski, T., Szupiluk, R.: Estimating the ROC curve and its significance for classification models' assessment. Quant. Methods Econ. **15**(2), 382–391 (2014)
23. Chrzanowska, M., Alfaro, E., Witkowska, D.: The individual borrowers recognition: single and ensemble trees. Expert Syst. Appl. **36**(3), 6409–6414 (2009)
24. Churn dataset. http://www.dataminingconsultant.com/DKD.htm. Last Accessed 12 Jan 2017
25. Hepatitis dataset. https://archive.ics.uci.edu/ml/datasets/Hepatitis. Last Accessed 12 Jan 2017

26. Gajowniczek, K., Ząbkowski, T., Orłowski, A.: Entropy based trees to support decision making for customer churn management. Acta Phys. Pol., A **129**(5), 971–979 (2016)
27. Gajowniczek, K., Karpio, K., Łukasiewicz, P., Orłowski, A., Ząbkowski, T.: Q-entropy approach to selecting high income households. Acta Phys. Pol., A **127**(3A), 38–44 (2015)
28. Gajowniczek, K., Ząbkowski, T., Orłowski, A.: Comparison of decision trees with renyi and tsallis entropy applied for imbalanced churn dataset. Ann. Comput. Sci. Inf. Syst. **5**, 39–43 (2015)

Learning from Noisy Label Distributions

Yuya Yoshikawa[(✉)]

Software Technology and Artificial Intelligence Research Laboratory (STAIR Lab),
Chiba Institute of Technology, Narashino, Japan
yoshikawa@stair.center

Abstract. In this paper, we consider a novel machine learning problem, that is, learning a classifier from noisy label distributions. In this problem, each instance with a feature vector belongs to at least one group. Then, instead of the true label of each instance, we observe the label distribution of the instances associated with a group, where the label distribution is distorted by an unknown noise. Our goals are to (1) estimate the true label of each instance, and (2) learn a classifier that predicts the true label of a new instance. We propose a probabilistic model that considers true label distributions of groups and parameters that represent the noise as hidden variables. The model can be learned based on a variational Bayesian method. In numerical experiments, we show that the proposed model outperforms existing methods in terms of the estimation of the true labels of instances.

Keywords: Probabilistic generative model · Variational Bayesian methods · Demographic estimation

1 Introduction

In this paper, we consider a novel machine learning problem, that is, learning a classifier from noisy label distributions. Figure 1 illustrates the assumptions for this problem. There are N groups and U instances. Each instance has a feature vector and true single label. Each group consists of a subset of all instances. Then, for each group, the *true label distribution*, that is, the distribution of the true labels of the instances associated with the group, can be calculated. However, the true labels and true label distribution cannot be observed. Instead, we observe the *noisy label distribution*, that is, the label distribution such that the true label distribution is distorted by an unknown noise. Our goals are to (1) estimate the true label of each instance, and (2) learn a classifier that predicts the true label of a new instance.

We propose a generative probabilistic model that considers the true label distributions of groups and parameters that represent the noise as hidden variables. The model can be learned based on a variational Bayesian method [1]. In numerical experiments, we show that, using a synthetic dataset generated based on the problem, the proposed model outperforms existing methods in terms of the estimation of the true labels of instances.

© Springer International Publishing AG 2017
A. Lintas et al. (Eds.): ICANN 2017, Part II, LNCS 10614, pp. 137–145, 2017.
https://doi.org/10.1007/978-3-319-68612-7_16

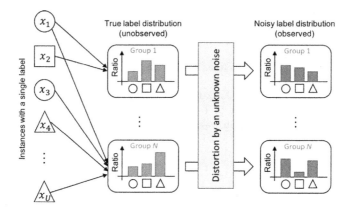

Fig. 1. Assumptions for learning a classifier from noisy label distributions. The shape of each instance indicates its label. The edge connecting an instance to a group indicates that the instance belongs to the group.

As a particular example of this problem, we consider the demographic estimation of individuals, which is the estimation of gender, age, occupation, race, and living place using individuals' features [2,6,9]. In social networking services (SNS) on the web, marketing and developing advertisement delivery systems are conducted using the demographic information of users. However, because such demographic information cannot be obtained in many cases, its estimation is required. A typical approach to demographic estimation using machine learning is to first annotate the demographic information for individuals and then learn a classifier that predicts the demographics for unknown individuals using the annotated demographic information. However, it is difficult and expensive to annotate the information manually.

Instead, using the machine learning approach, we can use the proposed model for demographic estimation. For the case of demographic estimation, each instance corresponds to a user on SNS, and its feature vector and label are the content created by the user and the demographic label of the user, respectively. Then, we use corporate accounts on SNS as groups and regard the users who follow the corporate accounts as members of the groups. Because the demographic labels of the users are unknown, we cannot also observe the true label distributions of the groups. Instead, we use the demographic distributions of visitors to corporate websites, which can be obtained easily and cheaply from audience measurement services, such as Quantcast[1]. Because the demographic distributions of websites differ from those of SNS, we use the distributions as noisy label distributions in our problem. Finally, by learning the proposed model, it is expected that the demographics of the users in SNS can be estimated without annotating demographic information.

---

[1] https://www.quantcast.com/.

2   Related Work

To the best of our knowledge, there is no study that addresses the problem contained in this paper. However, this problem may be considered to be similar to or a type of multiple instance learning (MIL) [5,7]. In standard MIL, the sets that consist of pairs of instances and their binary labels are given. Each of the sets is labeled positive if at least one positive label is included in the set, and negative otherwise. Then, the goal of MIL is to learn a classifier that predicts whether a new set that consists only of instances is positive or negative. There are two main differences between our problem and MIL. First, our problem assumes that the label of each instance is unobserved. Second, the goal of our problem is to learn a classifier that predicts a label of a newly given instance rather than a set of instances.

Note that our problem is inspired by the demographic estimation method of Culotta et al. [3,4]. They considered the situation described in the last paragraph of Sect. 1. Then, they proposed learning a demographic classifier of SNS users directly using the demographic distributions of website visitors. However, their method implicitly assumes that the demographic distributions of SNS users and website visitors are identical.

In this study, we formalize the problem of Culotta et al. as a general machine learning problem. Then, the proposed model can capture the difference between two distributions, such as the demographic distributions of SNS users and website visitors, by modeling the process by which they are distorted by an unknown noise.

3   Proposed Method

In this section, we propose a probabilistic model to address the problem described in the first paragraph of Sect. 1. First, we explain the formulation of the proposed model. Then, we explain how to learn the proposed model based on a variational Bayesian method.

3.1   Model Formulation

In the problem, there are N groups and U instances. Each instance has a D-dimensional feature vector and true label. Let $\mathbf{x}_u \in \mathbb{R}^D$ be the feature vector of the uth instance and $y_u \in \{1, 2, \cdots, M\}$ be the true label of the uth instance, where M is the number of classes. For convenience, we define a set of all feature vectors and set of all true labels as $\mathcal{X} = \{\mathbf{x}_u\}_{u=1}^{U}$ and $\mathcal{Y} = \{y_u\}_{u=1}^{U}$, respectively. Each group consists of a subset of all instances. We denote the set of instances associated with the ith group by $G_i \subseteq \{u\}_{u=1}^{U}$. Then, for each group, the *true label distribution*, that is, the distribution of the true label of the instances associated with the group, can be calculated. In particular, we denote the true label distribution of the ith group by $\mathbf{z}_i \in \mathbb{R}^M$, where $\mathbf{z}_i = \frac{1}{|G_i|} \sum_{u \in G_i} \mathrm{vec}(y_u)$ and $\sum_{m=1}^{M} z_{im} = 1$, where $\mathrm{vec}(y_u)$ returns a vector whose y_uth element is one and other elements are zero. Note that, the true label of each instance and true label distribution of each group are unobserved. Instead, we observe the *noisy label distribution*, that is, a label distribution such that the true label distribution is distorted by an unknown noise. We denote the noisy label distribution of the ith group by $\mathbf{s}_i \in \mathbb{R}^M$, where $\sum_{m=1}^{M} s_{im} = 1$.

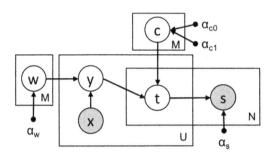

Fig. 2. Graphical representation of the proposed model. The white and the gray circles represent hidden and observed variables, respectively. The edges represent the dependency between the variables. The dots are hyper-parameters determined manually before training.

Figure 2 illustrates the graphical representation of the proposed model. The generative process of the proposed model is as follows:

1. For each class $m = 1, 2, \cdots, M$:
   (a) Draw weight vector $\mathbf{w}_m \sim \mathcal{N}(\mathbf{0}, \alpha_w^{-1}\mathbf{I}_D)$.
   (b) Draw confusion vector $\mathbf{c}_m \sim \mathrm{Dir}(\beta_m)$.
2. For each instance $u = 1, 2, \cdots, U$:
   (a) Draw true label $y_u \sim \mathrm{Softmax}([\mathbf{w}_m^\top \mathbf{x}_u]_{m=1}^{M})$.
   (b) For each group $i = 1, 2, \cdots, N$:
      i. Draw group-dependent label $t_i \sim \mathrm{Cat}(\mathbf{c}_{y_u})$.
3. For each group $i = 1, 2, \cdots, N$:
   (a) Draw noisy label distribution $\mathbf{s}_i \sim \mathcal{N}(\mathbf{t}_i, \alpha_s^{-1}\mathbf{I}_M)$,
      where $\mathbf{t}_i = \frac{1}{|G_i|} \sum_{u \in G_i} \mathrm{vec}(t_{iu})$.

In the proposed model, the true label y_u of each instance u is generated from the distribution calculated based on the inner product of weight vector $\mathbf{w}_m$ and feature vector $\mathbf{x}_u$. Weight vector $\mathbf{w}_m$ for each class m is generated from an isotropic Gaussian with zero mean and covariance matrix $\alpha_w^{-1}\mathbf{I}_D$, where $\mathbf{I}_D$ is a D-dimensional identity matrix. The distribution is normalized using a softmax function. Although this is the same idea as multi-class logistic regression, in the proposed model, the true label is unobserved and considered as a hidden variable.

The true label distribution (unobserved) and noisy label distribution (observed) are different because of the distortion by an unknown noise. To capture such a phenomenon, the proposed model has confusion vector $\mathbf{c}_m \in \mathbb{R}_+^M$

for each class m, where the lth element of $\mathbf{c}_m$ represents the probability with which class m is changed to class l by an unknown noise. We assume that confusion vector $\mathbf{c}_m$ for each class m is generated from the Dirichlet distribution, with parameter $\beta_m \in \mathbb{R}_+^M$. To incorporate the magnitude of the noise as prior knowledge into the proposed model, we parameterize β_m as follows:

$$\beta_{ml} = \begin{cases} \alpha_{c_0} & (m \neq l) \\ \alpha_{c_1} & (m = l). \end{cases} \tag{1}$$

When a large magnitude of noise is expected, we set α_{c_0} to a larger value than α_{c_1}.

Then, the noisy label distribution of each group is generated. In particular, for each instance $u \in G_i$ associated with the ith group, group-dependent label $t_{iu} \in \{1, 2, \cdots, M\}$ is generated from the categorical distribution, with parameter $\mathbf{c}_{y_u}$. We define $\mathbf{t}_i = \frac{1}{|G_i|} \sum_{u \in G_i} \mathrm{vec}(t_{iu})$. Note that, because the instance can belong to multiple groups, the group-dependent labels of the instance may vary according to the groups. Finally, the noisy label distribution of the ith group is generated from a Gaussian distribution, with $\mathbf{t}_i$ as a mean vector and $\alpha_s^{-1}\mathbf{I}_M$ as a covariance matrix.

3.2   Inference Based on Variational Bayesian Method

We introduce the inference method of the proposed model based on a variational Bayesian method [1].

First, the logarithm of the marginal posterior of weight matrix $\mathbf{W}$ and confusion matrix $\mathbf{C}$ is given by

$$\log p(\mathbf{W}, \mathbf{C}|\mathbf{X}, \mathbf{S}, \alpha) \propto \log \sum_{\mathbf{T}, \mathbf{Y}} p(\mathbf{S}|\mathbf{T}, \alpha_s) p(\mathbf{T}|\mathbf{Y}, \mathbf{C}) p(\mathbf{Y}|\mathbf{W}, \mathbf{X})$$
$$+ \log p(\mathbf{W}|\alpha_w) + \log p(\mathbf{C}|\alpha_{c_0}, \alpha_{c_1}). \tag{2}$$

According to the generative process, the factors in (2) are defined as follows:

$$p(\mathbf{S}|\mathbf{T}, \alpha_s) = \prod_{i=1}^{N} \mathcal{N}(\mathbf{s}_i|\mathbf{t}_i, \alpha_s^{-1}\mathbf{I}_M), \tag{3}$$

$$p(\mathbf{T}|\mathbf{Y}, \mathbf{C}) = \prod_{i=1}^{N} \prod_{u \in E_i} c_{y_u, t_{iu}}, \tag{4}$$

$$p(\mathbf{Y}|\mathbf{W}, \mathbf{X}) = \prod_{u=1}^{U} \frac{\exp(\mathbf{w}_{y_u}^\top \mathbf{x}_u)}{\sum_{m=1}^{} \exp(\mathbf{w}_m^\top \mathbf{x}_u)}, \tag{5}$$

$$p(\mathbf{W}|\alpha_w) = \prod_{m=1}^{M} \mathcal{N}(\mathbf{w}_m|\mathbf{0}, \alpha_w^{-1}\mathbf{I}_D), \tag{6}$$

$$p(\mathbf{C}|\alpha_{c_0}, \alpha_{c_1}) = \prod_{m=1}^{M} \frac{\Gamma\left(\sum_{l=1}^{M} \beta_{ml}\right)}{\prod_{l=1}^{M} \Gamma(\beta_{ml})} \prod_{l=1}^{M} c_{ml}^{\beta_{ml}-1}. \tag{7}$$

The goal of inference is to obtain $\mathbf{W}$ and $\mathbf{C}$ such that 2 is maximized. However, considering all possible combinations of $\mathbf{T}$ and $\mathbf{Y}$ is impossible in terms of the complexity of computational time. Therefore, we derive the following variational lower bound $\mathcal{L}(\Theta)$ for (2) according to Jensen's inequality:

$$\log p(\mathbf{W}, \mathbf{C}|\mathbf{X}, \mathbf{S}, \alpha) \geq \sum_{\mathbf{T}, \mathbf{Y}} q(\mathbf{T}, \mathbf{Y}) \log \frac{p(\mathbf{S}|\mathbf{T}, \alpha_s)p(\mathbf{T}|\mathbf{Y}, \mathbf{C})p(\mathbf{Y}|\mathbf{W}, \mathbf{X})}{q(\mathbf{T}, \mathbf{Y})}$$

$$+ \log p(\mathbf{W}|\alpha_w) + \log p(\mathbf{C}|\alpha_{c_0}, \alpha_{c_1})$$

$$= \mathcal{L}(\Theta). \tag{8}$$

Then, we optimize the variational lower bound (8) instead. For convenience, we define $\Theta = \{\mathbf{W}, \mathbf{C}, \zeta, \eta\}$. With variational distribution $q(\mathbf{T}, \mathbf{Y})$, we assume the following factorization: $q(\mathbf{T}, \mathbf{Y}) = q(\mathbf{Y}|\zeta)q(\mathbf{T}|\eta)$, where

$$q(\mathbf{Y}|\zeta) = \prod_{u=1}^{U} \zeta_{uy_u}, \quad q(\mathbf{T}|\eta) = \prod_{i=1}^{N} \prod_{u=1}^{U} \eta_{iut_{iu}}. \tag{9}$$

Next, we derive the update rules for $\mathbf{W}$, $\mathbf{C}$, ζ, and η.

Update $\mathbf{W}$. Because $\mathbf{W}$ cannot be updated in closed form, we calculate the gradient with respect to $\mathbf{W}$ as follows:

$$\frac{\partial \mathcal{L}(\Theta)}{\partial \mathbf{w}_m} = \sum_{u=1}^{U} \left(\zeta_{um} - \frac{\exp(\mathbf{w}_m^\top \mathbf{x}_u)}{\sum_{l=1}^{M} \exp(\mathbf{w}_l^\top \mathbf{x}_u)} \sum_{l=1}^{M} \zeta_{ul} \right) \mathbf{x}_u - \alpha_w \mathbf{w}_m. \tag{10}$$

Then we update $\mathbf{W}$ using a gradient-based optimization method, such as the quasi-Newton method.

Update $\mathbf{C}$. Because of the constraint that $\sum_{l=1}^{M} c_{ml} = 1$ for each class m, we derive the update rule for $\mathbf{C}$ according to the Lagrange multiplier method as follows:

$$c_{ml} = \frac{\sum_{i=1}^{N} \sum_{u=1}^{U} \zeta_{um}\eta_{ium} + \beta_{ml} - 1}{\sum_{m'=1}^{M} \sum_{i=1}^{N} \sum_{u=1}^{U} \zeta_{um'}\eta_{ium'} + \sum_{l'=1}^{M} \beta_{ml'} - M}. \tag{11}$$

Update ζ. Because of the constraint that $\sum_{m=1}^{M} \zeta_{um} = 1$ for each instance u, we derive the update rule for ζ according to the Lagrange multiplier method as follows:

$$\zeta_{um} \propto \exp \left\{ \sum_{i=1}^{N} \sum_{l=1}^{M} \eta_{iul} \log c_{ml} + a_{um} - \log \sum_{m'=1}^{M} \exp(a_{um'}) \right\}, \tag{12}$$

where $a_{um} = \mathbf{x}_u^\top \mathbf{w}_m$. After calculating (12), the values are normalized such that $\sum_{m=1}^{M} \zeta_{um} = 1$.

Update η. Because of the constraint that $\sum_{m=1}^{M} \eta_{ium} = 1$ for the pair of each group i and each instance u, we derive the update rule for η according to the Lagrange multiplier method. However, because the update rule cannot be calculated in closed form, we derive the gradients with respect to η_{ium} and multiplier parameter λ_{iu} as follows:

$$\frac{\partial \mathcal{L}(\Theta)}{\partial \eta_{ium}} = -\frac{\alpha_s}{|G_i|} \left(s_{im} - \mathbb{E}[t_i]_m \right) + \sum_{l=1}^{M} \zeta_{ul} \log c_{lm} - \log \eta_{ium} - 1 + \lambda_{iu}, \quad (13)$$

$$\frac{\partial \mathcal{L}(\Theta)}{\partial \lambda_{iu}} = \sum_{m=1}^{M} \eta_{ium} - 1. \quad (14)$$

and then we alternatively update the parameters using these gradients, where $\mathbb{E}[t_i]_m = \frac{1}{|G_i|} \sum_{u \in G_i} \eta_{ium}$.

We continue to update the parameters $\mathbf{W}$, $\mathbf{C}$, ζ, and η sequentially until the value of (8) converges. The hyper-parameters α are determined by cross-validation.

4   Experiments

To confirm the effectiveness of the proposed model in the scenario shown in Fig. 1, we performed numerical experiments on a synthetic dataset.

We considered a four-class classification problem. The synthetic dataset was generated according to the generative process of the proposed model described in Sect. 3.1. Note the following:

- The feature vector of each instance was generated from an isotropic Gaussian with zero mean and a variance equal to one.
- We set the number of instances to $U = 100$ and the number of groups to $N = 1,000$, and each group consisted of 30 randomly chosen instances.
- We defined β according to (1), where we set $\alpha_{c_0} = 1$ and $\alpha_{c_1} \in \{1, 10, 100\}$.

For comparison, we used two methods proposed by Culotta et al. [4]. These methods learn a regression function that predicts the values of the noisy label distribution of each group from the feature vector of each instance associated with the group. After learning, they calculate the label distribution of a newly given instance, and then output the label with the highest value of the label distribution as a prediction result. Culotta et al. used a multi-task elastic net (MTEN) that captured the relationship among each dimension of the distribution, and a ridge regression that predicted the value of each dimension of the distribution independently. For MTEN and ridge regression, we used the implementation of scikit-learn [8] in the same way as Culotta et al.

Table 1 shows the accuracy of the true label estimation on three synthetic datasets with different α_{c_1}. When α_{c_1} was small, the difference between the true label distribution and the noisy label distribution was large. As a result, the

Table 1. Accuracy of true label estimation on a synthetic dataset.

	$\alpha_{c_1} = 1$	$\alpha_{c_1} = 10$	$\alpha_{c_1} = 100$
Proposed	**0.43**	**0.52**	**0.45**
MTEN [4]	0.32	0.51	0.31
Ridge [4]	0.24	0.48	0.24

accuracy of the existing method, for example, ridge regression, was much the same as a random choice, that is, $1/4 = 0.25$. By contrast, because the proposed model could capture the difference by learning confusion matrix $\mathbf{C}$, it could estimate the true labels accurately. Moreover, when α_{c_1} was large, the proposed model consistently outperformed existing methods.

5   Conclusion

We considered a novel machine learning problem, that is, learning a classifier from noisy label distributions. To address this problem, we proposed a generative probabilistic model, which can be inferred based on a variational Bayesian method. In numerical experiments, we showed that, the proposed model outperformed existing methods in terms of the estimation of the true labels of instances.

In future work, we will confirm the effectiveness of the proposed model in demographic estimation using real datasets provided by Culotta et al. [3]. Additionally, because the proposed model only captured a single pattern of noise, we will extend the proposed model so that it captures multiple patterns of noise.

References

1. Bishop, C.M.: Pattern Recognition and Machine Learning. Springer, Heidelberg (2006)
2. Cheng, Z., Caverlee, J., Lee, K.: You are where you tweet : a content-based approach to geo-locating twitter users. In: Proceedings of the 19th ACM International Conference on Information and Knowledge Management, pp. 759–768 (2010)
3. Culotta, A., Kumar, N.R., Cutler, J.: Predicting twitter user demographics using distant supervision from website traffic data. J. Artif. Intell. Res. **1**, 389–408 (2016)
4. Culotta, A., Ravi, N.K., Cutler, J.: Predicting the demographics of twitter users from website traffic data. In: Proceedings of the Twenty-Ninth AAAI Conference on Artificial Intelligence, pp. 72–78 (2015)
5. Dietterich, T.G., Lathrop, R.H., Lozano-Pérez, T.: Solving the multiple instance problem with axis-parallel rectangles. Artif. Intell. **89**, 31–71 (1997)
6. Li, J., Ritter, A., Hovy, E.: Weakly Supervised User Profile Extraction from Twitter. In: Association of Computational Linguistics, pp. 165–174 (2014)
7. Maron, O., Lozano-Pérez, T.: A framework for multiple-instance learning. In: Advances in Neural Information Processing, pp. 570–576 (1997)

8. Pedregosa, F., Varoquaux, G., Gramfort, A., Michel, V., Thirion, B., Grisel, O., Blondel, M., Prettenhofer, P., Weiss, R., Dubourg, V., Vanderplas, J., Passos, A., Cournapeau, D., Brucher, M., Perrot, M., Duchesnay, É.: Scikit-learn: machine learning in python. J. Mach. Learn. Res. **12**, 2825–2830 (2011)
9. Rao, D., Yarowsky, D., Shreevats, A., Gupta, M.: Classifying latent user attributes in twitter. In: Proceedings of the 2nd International Workshop on Search and Mining User-Generated Contents (2010)

Phase Transition Structure of Variational Bayesian Nonnegative Matrix Factorization

Masahiro Kohjima[✉] and Sumio Watanabe

Department of Mathematical and Computing Science, Tokyo Institute of Technology,
G5-19, 4259 Nagatsuta, Midori-ku, Yokohama 226-8502, Japan
koujima.m.aa@m.titech.ac.jp, swatanab@c.titech.ac.jp

Abstract. In this paper, we theoretically clarify the phase transition structure of the variational Bayesian nonnegative matrix factorization (VBNMF). By asymptotic analysis of the objective functional in variational inference, we find that the variational posterior distribution of the VBNMF is drastically changed by hyperparameters; we call this phenomenon *phase transition* of the VBNMF. We also discuss a numerical experiment demonstrating our theoretical results.

Keywords: Nonnegative matrix factorization · Variational Bayes · Phase transition · Asymptotic analysis · Hyperparameter design

1 Introduction

Nonnegative matrix factorization (NMF) [1,2] is a ubiquitous tool used in various research fields including signal processing, pattern recognition, and data mining [3]. NMF is formulated as the method which decomposes an input matrix into the product of factor matrices with nonnegative values (Fig. 1(a)). Thanks to the nonnegativity constraint, extracted factors are readily interpretable. NMF is frequently used for extracting latent structure and patterns.

The standard algorithms for NMF such as majorization minimization [1] and variational Bayes (VB) [4], require the setting of the number of factors. Since the *true* number of factors of the input matrix is unknown, the chosen number of factors may be larger than the true one. This setting frequently appears in practical model selection scenarios. In this case, the factorization result cannot be uniquely determined, as shown in Fig. 1(a). Because both Result case 1, in which redundant factors vanish, and Result case 2, in which redundant factors remain, can exactly reconstruct the input matrix, we cannot distinguish which result is better from the difference from the input matrix. In order to compare the results, the factorization results should be evaluated by the value of hyperparameters.

In this paper, we theoretically prove the following two results. (i) The factorization results of the variational Bayesian NMF algorithm (VBNMF) are changed according to hyperparameters. (ii) Its critical line is explicitly given by the size of the input matrix. Figure 1(b) shows our theoretical results. Depending on whether the hyperparameters are in the area above or below the critical line

© Springer International Publishing AG 2017
A. Lintas et al. (Eds.): ICANN 2017, Part II, LNCS 10614, pp. 146–154, 2017.
https://doi.org/10.1007/978-3-319-68612-7_17

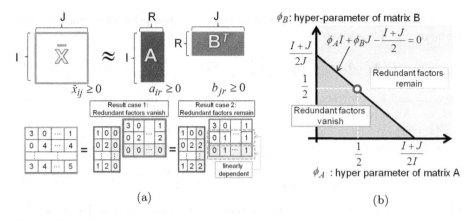

(a)   (b)

Fig. 1. (a) NMF and example of factorization results when redundant factor exists. (b) Phase transition diagram obtained by our analysis

$\phi_A I + \phi_B J = (I + J)/2$, the factorization results drastically change, where I and J are sizes of the input matrix and ϕ_A and ϕ_B are hyperparameters. We call this phenomenon *phase transition* of the VBNMF. Clarification of the phase transition structure provides useful insight in the hyperparameter design.

These results are derived by analyzing the minimum value of the objective function of the VBNMF, which is called the variational free energy (VFE). In this paper, we consider the setting that the amount of data (the number of observed matrices) is sufficiently large and identify the optimal number of factors through an asymptotic analysis. Note that the setting where multiple matrices are observed arises in recent application, e.g., purchase data analysis [5] and traffic data analysis [6]. The analysis of VFE itself is also important topic in the literature of statistical learning theory [7–9].

The rest of this paper is organized as follows. Section 2 is the preliminary section. We briefly discuss NMF, the VB algorithm, and VFE. In Sect. 3, we present the main theoretical results and proof. We also provide an interpretation of the results. In Sect. 4, we discuss a numerical experiment and we conclude the paper in Sect. 5.

2 Preliminaries

2.1 Variational Bayesian Nonnegative Matrix Factorization

Let $\boldsymbol{X} \in \mathbb{R}_+^{I \times J}$ be an $I \times J$ matrix whose elements are all nonnegative real values. We also denote a set of matrices $\boldsymbol{X}_1, \boldsymbol{X}_2, \cdots, \boldsymbol{X}_n$ as $\boldsymbol{X}^n$, where n is the number of matrices. The x_{ij}^m represents the (i, j)-th element of the m-th matrix $\boldsymbol{X}_m$. With NMF, it is assumed that each matrix can be approximated by a product of nonnegative factor matrices $\boldsymbol{A} \in \mathbb{R}_+^{I \times R}$ and $\boldsymbol{B} \in \mathbb{R}_+^{J \times R}$. By modeling that the elements of $\boldsymbol{X}$ are subject to Poisson distribution, the probability distribution of generating $\boldsymbol{X}^n$ is given by

$$P(\boldsymbol{X}^n|\boldsymbol{A},\boldsymbol{B}) = \prod_{m=1}^{n} \prod_{i,j=1}^{I,J} \mathcal{PO}\Big(x_{ij}^m \Big| \sum_{r=1}^{R} a_{ir}b_{jr}\Big), \tag{1}$$

where a_{ir} and b_{jr} represent the (i,r)-th element of $\boldsymbol{A}$ and the (j,r)-th elements of $\boldsymbol{B}$, respectively. $\mathcal{PO}$ is Poisson distribution, $\mathcal{PO}(x|\mu) = \exp\{-\mu + x\log(\mu) - \log\Gamma(x+1)\}$. We introduce a hidden variable $\boldsymbol{S}^n$ whose element s_{ijr}^m represents the contribution of the r-th factor to x_{ij}^m. The joint distribution is given by

$$P(\boldsymbol{X}^n,\boldsymbol{S}^n|\boldsymbol{A},\boldsymbol{B}) = \prod_{m=1}^{n} \prod_{i,j=1}^{I,J} \delta\big(x_{ij}^m - s_{ij\cdot}^m\big) \prod_{r=1}^{R} \mathcal{PO}\big(s_{ijr}^m|a_{ir}b_{jr}\big). \tag{2}$$

Note that a dot index means the corresponding one is summed out: $s_{ij\cdot} = \sum_{r=1}^{R} s_{ijr}, s_{\cdot jr} = \sum_{i=1}^{I} s_{ijr}, s_{i\cdot r} = \sum_{j=1}^{J} s_{ijr}$. We use the conjugate gamma priors on $\boldsymbol{A}$ and $\boldsymbol{B}$.

$$P(\boldsymbol{A}) = \prod_{i,r=1}^{I,R} \mathcal{G}(a_{ir}|\phi_A,\eta_A/\phi_A), \; P(\boldsymbol{B}) = \prod_{j,r=1}^{J,R} \mathcal{G}(b_{jr}|\phi_B,\eta_B/\phi_B), \tag{3}$$

where ϕ_A, η_A, ϕ_B, and η_B are hyperparameters. $\mathcal{G}$ denotes Gamma distribution, $\mathcal{G}(x|\phi,\eta) = \exp\{(\phi-1)\log x - x/\eta - \log\Gamma(\phi) - \phi\log\eta\}$. As shown in Fig. 2, a_{ir} and b_{jr} tend to be small as ϕ_A and ϕ_B decrease. Using them together, the joint distribution is $P(\boldsymbol{X}^n,\boldsymbol{S}^n,\boldsymbol{A},\boldsymbol{B}) = P(\boldsymbol{X}^n,\boldsymbol{S}^n|\boldsymbol{A},\boldsymbol{B})P(\boldsymbol{A})P(\boldsymbol{B})$.

The variational Bayesian (VB) algorithm is used to estimate the variational distribution, which approximates a posterior distribution of parameters and hidden variables. The VB algorithm for NMF with Poisson distribution was derived by Cemgil [4][1]. The variational distribution $q(\boldsymbol{A},\boldsymbol{B},\boldsymbol{S}^n)$ is optimized by minimizing the functional $\bar{\mathcal{F}}[q]$, which is defined by

$$\bar{\mathcal{F}}[q] = \mathbb{E}_{q(\boldsymbol{A})q(\boldsymbol{B})q(\boldsymbol{S}^n)} \left[\log \frac{q(\boldsymbol{A})q(\boldsymbol{B})q(\boldsymbol{S}^n)}{p(\boldsymbol{X}^n,\boldsymbol{S}^n,\boldsymbol{A},\boldsymbol{B})}\right], \tag{4}$$

under the constraint that variational distribution is independent: $q(\boldsymbol{A},\boldsymbol{B},\boldsymbol{S}^n) = q(\boldsymbol{A})q(\boldsymbol{B})q(\boldsymbol{S}^n)$. Note that $\mathbb{E}_{q(\boldsymbol{A})q(\boldsymbol{B})q(\boldsymbol{S}^n)}$ denotes the expectation w.r.t. $\boldsymbol{A},\boldsymbol{B}$ and $\boldsymbol{S}^n$ following the variational distribution. Minimizing the functional $\bar{\mathcal{F}}[q]$ is equivalent to minimizing the Kullback-Leibler divergence between posterior and variational distributions. From the optimality condition derived from the variational method, the variational distribution of $\boldsymbol{A}$ and $\boldsymbol{B}$ is a gamma distribution and that of $\boldsymbol{S}$ is a multinomial distribution:

$$q(\boldsymbol{A}) = \prod_{i,r} \mathcal{G}(a_{ir}|\alpha_{ir}^A,\beta_{ir}^A), \quad \alpha_{ir}^A \equiv \phi_A + n\bar{s}_{i\cdot r}, \; \beta_{ir}^A \equiv \big(\phi_A/\eta_A + n\bar{b}_{\cdot r}\big)^{-1}, \tag{5}$$

$$q(\boldsymbol{B}) = \prod_{j,r} \mathcal{G}(b_{jr}|\alpha_{jr}^B,\beta_{jr}^B), \quad \alpha_{jr}^B \equiv \phi_B + n\bar{s}_{\cdot jr}, \; \beta_{jr}^B \equiv \big(\phi_B/\eta_B + n\bar{a}_{\cdot r}\big)^{-1}, \tag{6}$$

$$q(\boldsymbol{S}^n) = \prod_{m,i,j} \mathcal{M}\big(s_{ij}|x_{ij}^m, \{p_{ijr}^S\}\big), \; p_{ijr}^S \propto \rho_{ijr} \equiv \exp\big(\mathbb{E}_{q(\boldsymbol{A})q(\boldsymbol{B})} [\log a_{ir} + \log b_{jr}]\big). \tag{7}$$

---

[1] More precisely, Cemgil derived the VB when $n = 1$ [4]. For the asymptotic analysis provided in the next section, we slightly modify the algorithm for arbitral n.

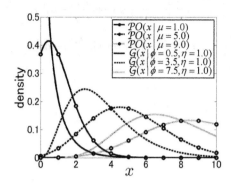

Fig. 2. Density function of Poisson and Gamma distributions.

Table 1. Definition of symbols

Symbol	Description
$\bar{\mathcal{F}}$	Functional to be minimized using VB
$\bar{\mathcal{F}}_{vb}$	Variational free energy (VFE)
$\mathcal{E}$	Empirical entropy
R^*	Nonnegative rank of true matrix $\boldsymbol{X}^*$
R^*_{vb}	Optimal number of factors that minimize VFE
R	Number of factors used in VBNMF
$\hat{R}$	Effective number of factors, which remain in result of VBNMF

The statistics in above equations are computed as $\bar{a}_{ir} = \alpha^A_{ir}\beta^A_{ir}$, $\bar{b}_{jr} = \alpha^B_{jr}\beta^B_{jr}$, $\bar{s}_{ijr} = \bar{x}_{ij}p^s_{ijr}$, $\bar{x}_{ij} = \frac{1}{n}\sum_{m=1}^n x^m_{ij}$, $\mathbb{E}_{q(\boldsymbol{A})}[\log a_{ir}] = \Psi(\alpha^A_{ir}) + \log(\beta^A_{ir})$, $\mathbb{E}_{q(\boldsymbol{B})}[\log b_{jr}] = \Psi(\alpha^B_{jr}) + \log(\beta^B_{jr})$, where $\Psi(\cdot)$ denotes the digamma function. The VB algorithm is the recursive iteration of Eqs. (5), (6), and (7).

2.2 Variational Free Energy (VFE)

To analyze the result of the VBNMF, we need to investigate the objective functional. The minimum value is referred to as the variational free energy (VFE), $\bar{\mathcal{F}}_{vb} = \min_{q(\boldsymbol{A})q(\boldsymbol{B})q(\boldsymbol{S}^n)} \bar{\mathcal{F}}[q]$. This indicates the objective value at the (optimal) output of the VB algorithm. Investigation of this value enables us to investigate the factorization result of the VBNMF. Note that the reason the term "free energy" is used is that the VFE is an upper bound of free energy: $\mathcal{F} = -\log \int p(\boldsymbol{X}^n, \boldsymbol{S}^n, \boldsymbol{A}, \boldsymbol{B})d\boldsymbol{A}d\boldsymbol{B}d\boldsymbol{S}^n$. Analogous to the role of free energy[2], the smaller VFE indicates the better choice of the model.

The VFE of NMF has an analytic form. In the next section, we use the following decomposition.

$$\bar{\mathcal{F}}_{vb} = F_A + F_B + F_X, \tag{8}$$

---

[2] Since free energy is a sign inversion of the log marginal likelihood, a lower free energy means a higher log-likelihood of the model.

$$F_A = \sum_{i,r} \left\{ (\alpha_{ir}^A - \phi_A)\Psi(\alpha_{ir}^A) - \phi_A \log(\beta_{ir}^A) + (\frac{\phi_A}{\eta_A})\bar{a}_{ir} + \log\frac{\Gamma(\phi_A)}{\Gamma(\alpha_{ir}^A)} + \phi_A \log(\frac{\eta_A}{\phi_A}) - \alpha_{ir}^A \right\},$$

$$F_B = \sum_{j,r} \left\{ (\alpha_{jr}^B - \phi_B)\Psi(\alpha_{jr}^B) - \phi_B \log(\beta_{jr}^B) + (\frac{\phi_B}{\eta_B})\bar{b}_{jr} + \log\frac{\Gamma(\phi_B)}{\Gamma(\alpha_{jr}^B)} + \phi_B \log(\frac{\eta_B}{\phi_B}) - \alpha_{jr}^B \right\},$$

$$F_X = \sum_{i,j} \left\{ \sum_r n\bar{a}_{ir}\bar{b}_{jr} + \sum_m \log\Gamma(x_{ij}^m + 1) - n\bar{x}_{ij}\log(\sum_r \rho_{ijr}) \right\}.$$

3   Theoretical Analysis

3.1   Main Result

This section provides our main theoretical result. In the proof of the theorem, we assume that the following assumption is satisfied.

Assumption 1. *The true probability distribution, which generates observed matrices X^n, is given by $P(X^n|X^*) = \prod_{m=1}^n \prod_{i,j=1}^{I,J} \mathcal{PO}\left(x_{ij}^m \middle| (X^*)_{ij}\right)$. We denote the nonnegative rank [10] of the true matrix X^*, i.e., true number of factors, as R^{*}[3].*

Our main theorem clarifies the effect of hyperparameters on the result of the VBNMF.

Main Theorem. *Suppose Assumption 1 is satisfied and R is not less than R^*. Then, as the number of observed matrices $n \to \infty$, the R_{vb}^*, which minimizes the VFE, is given by*

$$R_{vb}^* = \begin{cases} R^* & (\text{if } \phi_A I + \phi_B J < (I+J)/2), \\ R & (\text{otherwise}). \end{cases} \tag{9}$$

Moreover, the asymptotic form of the VFE is given by[4]

$$\bar{F}_{vb} = \mathcal{E} + \lambda_{vb}\log(n) + \mathcal{O}_p(1), \tag{10}$$

$$\lambda_{vb} = \begin{cases} (\phi_A I + \phi_B J)(R - R^*) + \frac{I+J}{2}R^* & (\text{if } \phi_A I + \phi_B J < \frac{(I+J)}{2}) \\ \frac{I+J}{2}R & (\text{otherwise}), \end{cases} \tag{11}$$

where $\mathcal{E}$ is the empirical entropy defined by $\mathcal{E} = -\log p(X^n|X^*)$.

The proof is shown in the following subsection. Here, we provide an interpretation of the theorem. Equation (9) shows that the optimal number of factors R_{vb}^* is determined by the hyperparameters. Figure 1(b) is the diagram that describes

---

[3] Nonnegative rank is defined as the smallest number of "nonnegative" rank-1 matrix into which the matrix can be decomposed. Nonnegative rank does not generally equal "standard" rank. For more details, see [11].

[4] $\mathcal{O}_p$ is the order notation of random variables. A sequence of random variables X_n is said to be $\mathcal{O}_p(1)$ if it is bounded in probability [12].

the relation of hyperparameters and R_{vb}^*, which we call *phase transition*. In the area under the critical line $\phi_A I + \phi_B J = (I + J)/2$, R_{vb}^* equals the *true* number of factors, R^*. On the other hand, above the critical line, the optimal number of factors equals the number of factors used in the algorithm, R. Since ϕ_A and ϕ_B are the parameters of the gamma prior, our result fits the fact smaller values make A and B sparse. Analogous to the optimal number of factors, Eqs. (10) and (11) show that the behavior of VFE is also changed whether the hyperparameters are above or under the critical line.

This theorem provides useful application to the hyperparameter design. Let us consider the case in which the redundant factors are required to vanish. In this case, Eq. (9) shows that it is not enough to set a small value to either ϕ_A or ϕ_B. This setting is sometimes done by researchers who try to obtain a *sparse* matrix A and *dence* matrix B. The following example shows how the theorem is used to determine the setting of hyperparameters.

Example: Let $I = 10$, $J = 90$ and consider setting $\phi_A = 0.1$. To remove redundant factors, $\phi_A I + \phi_B J = 1 + 90\phi_B < 50 = (I + J)/2$ must be satisfied then $\phi_B < (50 - 1)/90 \approx 0.54$. Therefore, $\phi_A = 0.1, \phi_B = 0.5$ is recommended.

3.2   Proof of Main Theorem

Finally, this subsection provides the proof of main theorem.

Theorem 1. *As the number of matrices* $n \to \infty$, *the asymptotic form of the VFE* $\bar{\mathcal{F}}_{vb}$ *is given by* $\bar{\mathcal{F}}_{vb} = \mathcal{E} + \{\min_{R^* \leq \hat{R} \leq R} \Lambda(R, \hat{R})\} \log(n) + \mathcal{O}_p(1)$, *where* $\Lambda(R, \hat{R}) = (\phi_A I + \phi_B J) R - (\phi_A I + \phi_B J - \frac{I+J}{2}) \hat{R}$.

Note that $\hat{R}$ is *the effective number of factors*, which does *not* vanish. The main theorem is immediately obtained from Theorem 1.

Proof of Main Theorem. *From the definition of* $\Lambda(R, \hat{R})$, *in the case of* $\phi_A I + \phi_B J < (I + J)/2$, *the smaller* $\hat{R}$ *is, the smaller* $\bar{\mathcal{F}}_{vb}$. *Therefore,* $R_{vb}^* = R^*$. *In the another case, a larger* $\hat{R}$ *is better, and* $R_{vb}^* = R$. *Substituting* R_{vb}^* *into* $\hat{R}$, *Eq. (11) is obtained.* □

Thus, we need to prove Theorem 1. It requires following three lemmas, Lemmas 1, 2, and 3. The proofs of these lemmas are provided in the Appendix.

Lemma 1. *As the number of matrices* $n \to \infty$, *the first and second terms of Eq. (8),* F_A *and* F_B, *are given by* $F_A = \{\phi_A IR - (\phi_A - \frac{1}{2})I\hat{R}\} \log(n) + \mathcal{O}_p(1)$ *and* $F_B = \{\phi_B JR - (\phi_B - \frac{1}{2})J\hat{R}\} \log(n) + \mathcal{O}_p(1)$.

Lemma 2. F_X *in Eq. (8) is given by* $F_X = -\log P(X^n|\bar{A}, \bar{B}) + \mathcal{O}_p(1)$.

Lemma 3. *Suppose Assumption 1 is satisfied and* R *is not less than* R^*. *Then,* $\mathcal{F}[q]$ *is minimized if and only if* $\hat{R}$ *satisfies* $R^* \leq \hat{R} \leq R$. *Moreover, as the number of matrices* $n \to \infty$, *the asymptotic form of* F_X *is given by* $F_X = \mathcal{E} + \mathcal{O}_p(1)$.

By applying Lemmas 1, 2, 3, Theorem 1 is proven.

Proof (Theorem 1). *From Eq. (8), $\bar{\mathcal{F}}_{vb} = F_A + F_B + F_X$ holds. Using the Lemmas 1, 2 and 3, we can obtain the asymptotic form with $\hat{R}$. Since the VFE with $\hat{R}$ is minimized when $\hat{R}$ minimizes the $\Lambda(R, \hat{R})$, we complete the proof.* □

4 Experiment

In this section, we confirm the validity of the main theorem through numerical experiment. We prepared the true matrix $\boldsymbol{X}^* = \{x_{ij}^*\} \in \mathbb{R}_+^{5 \times J}$ as $x_{ij}^* = \max{(4 - (j\%5), 1)}$ if $i = 0, 1, 2$ and otherwise, $x_{ij}^* = \max{((j\%5) - 1, 1)}$. Note that $c\%d$ denotes the remainder when c is divided by d. Obviously, nonnegative rank of $\boldsymbol{X}^*$, $R^* = 2$. Using this matrix, we generated matrices $\boldsymbol{X}^n$ following Eq. (1) and applied the VBNMF. Using the matrices and the result of the VBNMF, we computed the empirical entropy $\mathcal{E}$ and the experimental value of the VFE $\bar{\mathcal{F}}_{vb}$. To obtain the experimental values, we ran the VBNMF 2000 times with a random initialization and set the maximum number of iterations to 1000. We checked whether the asymptotic value of VFE in the main theorem was satisfied since it is the key of our theoretical results. We conducted an experiment involving varying the size of input matrices and the number of factors.

Figure 3 shows the results when the hyperparameters were set to $\phi_A = \eta_A = \phi_B = \eta_B = 1.0$. The horizontal axis represents the number of observed matrices with log scale. The solid line represents the theoretical value $\lambda_{vb} \log(n)$, and the angle corresponds to λ_{vb}. The marked point represents the experimental value $\bar{\mathcal{F}}_{vb} - \mathcal{E}$. The dashed line represents the linear regression line to the experimental values. Since Eq. (10) contains the $\mathcal{O}_p(1)$ constant term, there exists a small difference between the solid and dashed lines. Therefore, we need to focus on the angle of the solid and dashed lines since it indicates the coefficient with respect to $\log(n)$. We can easily confirm that the angles of the lines are almost the same. This means our theory effectively explains the experimental results.

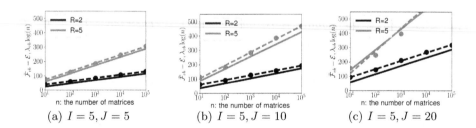

(a) $I = 5, J = 5$ (b) $I = 5, J = 10$ (c) $I = 5, J = 20$

Fig. 3. Comparison of experimental and theoretical values of VFE.

5 Conclusion

We theoretically clarified the phase transition structure of VBNMF through the asymptotic analysis of VFE. The numerical experiments support the validity of our analysis. Future work includes an extension of our analysis to the case where different probability distributions or different factorization form is adopted.

Appendix: Proof Sketch of Lemmas 1, 2, and 3

For the proof of the Lemmas 1 and 2, we apply following two inequalities of the digamma and log-digamma functions [13]: for $x > 0$, $\frac{1}{2x} < \log(x) - \Psi(x) < \frac{1}{x}$, $0 \leq \log \Gamma(x) - \{(x - \frac{1}{2}) \log(x) - x + \frac{1}{2} \log 2\pi\} \leq \frac{1}{12x}$. Without loss of generality, we can assume $\bar{s}_{i \cdot r} = \bar{s}_{\cdot jr} = 0$ is satisfied for all r, $\hat{R} < r \leq R$, the proof is completed.

For the Lemma 3, two different strategies are needed for deriving upper bound and lower bound. We first show the upper bound. From the definition of the VFE and the results of Lemmas 1 and 2, VFE can be written as $\bar{\mathcal{F}}_{vb} = \Lambda(R, R_{vb}^*) \log(n) - \log P(\boldsymbol{X}^n | \bar{\boldsymbol{A}}, \bar{\boldsymbol{B}}) + \mathcal{O}_p(1)$. Since VFE is the minimum value of $\bar{\mathcal{F}}[q]$, VFE satisfies

$$\bar{\mathcal{F}}_{vb} = \Lambda(R, R_{vb}^*) - \log P(\boldsymbol{X}^n | \bar{\boldsymbol{A}}, \bar{\boldsymbol{B}}) + \mathcal{O}_p(1) \leq \Lambda(R, R_{vb}^*) + \mathcal{E} + \mathcal{O}_p(1). \quad (12)$$

Then, $-\log P(\boldsymbol{X}^n | \bar{\boldsymbol{A}}, \bar{\boldsymbol{B}}) \leq \mathcal{E} + \mathcal{O}_p(1)$ is shown. The lower bound is derived by using the classical statistical learning theory. Let us define the probabilistic model that has a parameter of Poisson distribution for all the elements of matrix (i, j), $\tilde{\boldsymbol{\mu}} = \{\tilde{\mu}_{ij}\}_{i,j=1}^{I,J}$. By using this model, the probability of generating matrix $\boldsymbol{X}_m$ can be written as $\tilde{P}(\boldsymbol{X}_m | \tilde{\boldsymbol{\mu}}) = \prod_{(i,j)} \mathcal{PO}(x_{ij}^m | \tilde{\mu}_{ij})$. From the property of the maximum likelihood estimator (MLE) $\tilde{\boldsymbol{\mu}}_{ML}$ and the definition of the MLE,

$$\frac{1}{n} \sum_{m=1}^{n} \log \frac{P(\boldsymbol{X}_m | \boldsymbol{X}^*)}{\tilde{P}(\boldsymbol{X}_m | \tilde{\boldsymbol{\mu}}_{ML})} = \frac{C}{n} + \mathcal{O}_p(\frac{1}{n}), \quad \sum_{m=1}^{n} \log \frac{P(\boldsymbol{X}_m | \boldsymbol{X}^*)}{P(\boldsymbol{X}_m | \bar{\boldsymbol{A}}, \bar{\boldsymbol{B}})} \geq \sum_{m=1}^{n} \log \frac{P(\boldsymbol{X}_m | \boldsymbol{X}^*)}{\tilde{P}(\boldsymbol{X}_m | \tilde{\boldsymbol{\mu}}_{ML})}$$

$$(13)$$

holds, where C is a constant term. Then, we obtain $-\log P(\boldsymbol{X}^n | \bar{\boldsymbol{A}}, \bar{\boldsymbol{B}}) \geq -\log P(\boldsymbol{X}^n | \boldsymbol{X}^*) + C + \mathcal{O}_p(1) = \mathcal{E} + \mathcal{O}_p(1)$.

References

1. Lee, D.D., Seung, H.S.: Algorithms for non-negative matrix factorization. In: Advances in Neural Information Processing Systems, pp. 556–562 (2001)
2. Lee, D.D., Seung, H.S.: Learning the parts of objects by non-negative matrix factorization. Nature **401**(6755), 788–791 (1999)
3. Cichocki, A., Zdunek, R., Phan, A.H., Amari, S.: Nonnegative Matrix and Tensor Factorizations: Applications to Exploratory Multi-way Data Analysis and Blind Source Separation. Wiley, Chichester (2009)
4. Cemgil, A.T.: Bayesian inference for nonnegative matrix factorisation models. Comput. Intell. Neurosc. **2009**, 17 (2009). doi:10.1155/2009/785152. Article ID: 785152
5. Kohjima, M., Matsubayashi, T., Sawada, H.: Probabilistic non-negative inconsistent-resolution matrices factorization. In: Proceedings of the 24th ACM International Conference on Information and Knowledge Management, pp. 1855–1858 (2015)
6. Deng, D., Shahabi, C., Demiryurek, U., Zhu, L., Yu, R., Liu, Y.: Latent space model for road networks to predict time-varying traffic. In: Proceedings of the 22nd ACM SIGKDD International Conference on Knowledge Discovery and Data Mining, pp. 1525–1534 (2016)

7. Watanabe, K., Watanabe, S.: Stochastic complexities of Gaussian mixtures in variational Bayesian approximation. J. Mach. Learn. Res. **7**, 625–644 (2006)
8. Watanabe, K., Shiga, M., Watanabe, S.: Upper bound for variational free energy of bayesian networks. Mach. Learn. **75**(2), 199–215 (2009)
9. Nakajima, S., Sato, I., Sugiyama, M., Watanabe, K., Kobayashi, H.: Analysis of variational Bayesian latent dirichlet allocation: weaker sparsity than map. In: Advances in Neural Information Processing Systems, pp. 1224–1232 (2014)
10. Cohen, J.E., Rothblum, U.G.: Nonnegative ranks, decompositions, and factorizations of nonnegative matrices. Linear Algebra Appl. **190**, 149–168 (1993)
11. Vavasis, S.A.: On the complexity of nonnegative matrix factorization. SIAM J. Optim. **20**(3), 1364–1377 (2009)
12. Van der Vaart, A.W.: Asymptotic Statistics, vol. 3. Cambridge University Press, Cambridge (2000)
13. Alzer, H.: On some inequalities for the gamma and psi functions. Math. Comput. Am. Math. Soc. **66**(217), 373–389 (1997)

Link Enrichment for Diffusion-Based Graph Node Kernels

Dinh Tran-Van[1], Alessandro Sperduti[1], and Fabrizio Costa[2($\boxtimes$)]

[1] Department of Mathematics, Padova University, Padua, Italy
{dinh,sperduti}@math.unipd.it
[2] Department of Computer Science, University of Exeter, Exeter, UK
f.costa@exeter.ac.uk

Abstract. The notion of node similarity is key in many graph processing techniques and it is especially important in diffusion graph kernels.
However, when the graph structure is affected by noise in the form of
missing links, similarities are distorted proportionally to the sparsity of
the graph and to the fraction of missing links. Here, we introduce the
notion of *link enrichment*, that is, performing link prediction in order to
improve the performance of diffusion-based kernels. We empirically show
a robust and large effect for the combination of a number of link prediction and a number of diffusion kernel techniques on several gene-disease
association problems.

Keywords: Graph kernels · Diffusion kernels · Link prediction

1 Introduction

A powerful approach to process large heterogeneous sources of data is to use
graph encodings [1,8] and then use graph-based learning systems. In these systems the notion of node similarity is key. A common approach is to resort to
graph node kernels such as diffusion-based kernels [2] where the graph node kernel measures the proximity between any pair of nodes by taking into account
the paths that connect them. However, when the graph structure is affected by
noise in the form of missing links, node similarities are distorted proportionally
to the sparsity of the graph and to the fraction of missing links. Two of the main
reasons for this are that (1) the lower the average node degree is, the smaller the
number of paths through which information can travel, and (2) missing links can
end up separating a graph into multiple disconnected components. In this case,
since information cannot travel across disconnected components, the similarity
of nodes belonging to different components is null. To address these problems we
propose to solve a link prediction task prior to the node similarity computation
and start studying the question: *how can we improve node similarity using link
prediction?* In this work we review both the link prediction literature and the
diffusion kernel literature, select a subset of approaches in both categories that
seem well suited, focus on a set of node predicting problems in the bioinformatics

© Springer International Publishing AG 2017
A. Lintas et al. (Eds.): ICANN 2017, Part II, LNCS 10614, pp. 155–162, 2017.
https://doi.org/10.1007/978-3-319-68612-7_18

domain and empirically investigate the effectiveness of the combination of these approaches on the given predictive tasks. The encouraging result that we find is that all the strategies for link prediction we examined consistently enhance the performance on downstream predictive tasks, often significantly improving state of the art results.

2 Notation and Background

Let us consider an undirected graph $G = (V, E)$ in which V represents a set of entities (vertices) and E characterizes the entity relationships (links). The adjacency matrix A is a symmetric matrix used to describe the direct links between vertices v_i and v_j in the graph. Any entry A_{ij} is equal to 1 when there exists a link connecting v_i and v_j, and is 0 otherwise. The Laplacian matrix L is defined as $L = D - A$, where D is the diagonal matrix with non-null entries equal to the summation over the corresponding row of the adjacency matrix, i.e. $D_{ii} = \sum_j A_{ij}$.

Graph Node Kernels. A graph node kernel is a kernel which defines the similarity between nodes in a graph. Formally, a graph node kernel, $k(\cdot, \cdot)$, is defined as $k : V \times V \longrightarrow \mathbb{R}$ such that k is symmetric positive semidefinite. Graph node kernels have been successfully applied in various domains ranging from recommendation systems to disease gene prioritization. The most popular graph node kernels can be classified in: (1) diffusion-based or (2) decomposition graph node kernels.

Diffusion-based graph node kernels derive from the Laplacian diffusion kernel [2]. These kernels measure the node proximity between pairs of nodes on the basis of the paths that connect them. They achieve state-of-the-art performance on dense graphs because of their ability to define a good notion of global similarity. However, their performance degrades for sparse graphs, especially in the presence of disconnected components. Among the most popular diffusion-based graph node kernels, there are:

- *Laplacian exponential diffusion kernel (LEDK)* [2]: This kernel is based on heat diffusion phenomenon: imagine to initialize each vertex with a given amount of heat and let it flow through the edges until an arbitrary instant of time. The similarity between any vertex couple v_i, v_j is the amount of heat starting from v_i and reaching v_j within a given time. The LEDK kernel matrix is computed by:

$$K_{LEDK} = e^{-\beta L} , \tag{1}$$

where β is the diffusion parameter used to control the rate of diffusion, and $e^X = \sum_{k=0}^{\infty} \frac{1}{k!} X^k$ refers to the matrix exponential for matrix X. Choosing a consistent value for β is very important: on the one side, if β is too small, the local information cannot be diffused effectively and, on the other side, if it is too large, the local information will be lost. K_{LEDK} is positive semi-definite as proved in [2].

– *Markov exponential diffusion kernel (MEDK)* [3]: In LEDK, similarity values between high degree vertices is generally higher compared to that between low degree ones. This could be problematic since peripheral nodes have unbalanced similarities with respect to central nodes. To make the strength of individual vertices comparable, a modified version of LEDK is introduced:

$$K_{MEDK} = e^{-\beta M} , \tag{2}$$

where $M = (D - A - nI)/n$ and n, I are the total number of vertices in graph and identity matrix, respectively.

– *Markov diffusion kernel (MDK)* [10]: MDK exploits the idea of diffusion distance, which is a measure of how similar the pattern of heat diffusion is between a pair of initialized nodes. In other words, it expresses how much nodes "influence" each other in a similar fashion. From the transition matrix P ($P = D^{-1}A$), we define $Z(t) = \frac{1}{t}\sum_{\tau=1}^{t} P^\tau$. MDK kernel matrix is then computed as follows:

$$K_{MDK} = Z(t)Z^\top(t) . \tag{3}$$

– *Regularized Laplacian kernel (RLK)* [4]: It represents a normalized version of the random walk with restart model. The kernel matrix is defined as:

$$K_{RLK} = \sum_{n=0}^{\infty} \beta^n(-L)^n , \tag{4}$$

where β is again the diffusion parameter. RLK counts the paths connecting two nodes on the graph induced by taking $-L$ as the adjacency matrix, regardless of the path length. Thus, a non-zero value is assigned to any couple of nodes as long as they are connected by any indirect path.

In decomposition graph node kernels [5] the similarity notion between two graphs is obtained by decomposing each graph into all the possible subgraphs belonging to a predetermined class and by devising a valid kernel between the resulting simpler subgraphs. It is possible to convert a decomposition graph kernel into a node kernel simply by extracting a subgraph to associate to each node, such as the neighborhood subgraph rooted at the node under consideration. An advantage of decomposition kernels is that they can autonomously address the case of nodes belonging to distinct graph components. A recent decomposition graph node kernel is the Conjunctive Disjunctive Node Kernel (CDNK), proposed in [6], based on the extension of a neighborhood graph kernel [7] to the dense graph case.

Link Prediction. Link prediction is the task of recovering missing links or predicting links that are going to be present in the future state of an evolving graph. A link prediction algorithm allows to score all non-observed links and rank them from the most to the least probable. Several link prediction algorithms have been proposed in literature and have been applied to different domains ranging from recommendation systems, to bioinformatics, to network security. Following [9], we can classify these methods in: *similarity-based algorithms*, *maximum likeli-hood methods*, and *probabilistic models*. Similarity-based methods assign for each non-observed link a score and this score is then directly used as the proximity between starting and ending nodes of that link. In maximum likelihood methods, some organizing principles of the graph structure are assumed. Then, we com-pute the likelihood of non-observed links based on the corresponding rules and parameters. Probabilistic models intent to make the abstract of observed graph structure and then the missing link prediction process is made by employing a trained model. Given a graph, the probabilistic model works by optimizing a built target function in order to form a model composed of a set of parameters that best fits the observed data of the graph.

The similarity-based methods are popular since they are simpler and compu-tationally more efficient than maximum likelihood and probabilistic models. To define a notion of similarity, we can use vertices' attributes. However, these attributes are normally hidden. Therefore, most similarity-based approaches are based on the structured similarity. Among similarity-based methods, global ones normally outperform local and semi-local similarity-based algorithms since global methods are able to capture the global similarity between nodes of graph. It is important to notice that all graph node kernels belong to similarity group, and all graph node kernels described in previous section: LEDK, MEDK, MDK, RLK, CDNK, are global ones. Therefore, in this paper, we employ graph node kernels also for link prediction task. Given a graph, in order to use a graph node kernel for link prediction we first use kernel to compute a kernel matrix which encodes the similarity between any couple of nodes of the graph. The values inside the achieved matrix are used as the scores for non-observed links to be considered as link of the graph.

3   Method

Often the relational information that defines the graph structure is incomplete because certain relations are not known at a given moment in time or have not been yet investigated. When this happens the resulting graphs tend to become sparse and composed of several disconnected components. Diffusion-based ker-nels are not suited in these cases and show a degraded predictive capacity. Our key idea is to introduce a *link enrichment phase* that can address both issues and enhance the performance of diffusion-based systems.

Given a link prediction algorithm M, a diffusion-based graph node kernel K and a sparse graph $G = (V, E)$ in which $|V| = n$ and $|E| = m$, with $m \approx n$ the link enrichment method consists of two phases:

- enrichment: the link prediction algorithm M is used to score all possible $\frac{n(n-1)}{2} - m$ missing links. The top scoring t links are added to E to obtain E' that defines the new graph $G' = (V, E')$.
- kernel computation: the diffusion-based graph node kernel K is applied to graph G' to compute the kernel matrix K' which captures the similarities

between any couple of nodes, possibly belonging to different components in the graph G.

The kernel matrix K' can be used directly by a kernelized learning algorithm, such as a support vector machine, to make predictive inferences.

4   Empirical Evaluation

To empirically study the answer to the question: *how can we improve node similarity using link prediction?* we would need to define a taxonomy of prediction problems on graphs that make use of the notion of node similarity and analyze which link prediction strategies can be effectively coupled with specific node similarity computation techniques for each given class of problems. In addition we should also study the quantitative relation between the degree of missingness and the size of the improvement offered by prepending the link prediction to the node similarity assessment. In this paper we start such endeavor restricting the type of predictive problems to that of node ranking in the sub-domain of gene-disease association studies with a fixed but unknown degree of missingness given by the current medical knowledge. More in detail, the task, known as *gene prioritization*, consists in ranking candidate genes based on their probabilities to be related to a disease on the basis of a given a set of genes experimentally known to be associated to the disease of interest. We have studied the proposed approach on the following 4 datasets:

BioGPS: a gene co-expression graph (7311 nodes and 911294 edges) constructed from the BioGPS dataset, which contains 79 tissues, measured with the Affymetrix U133A array. Edges are inserted when the pairwise Pearson correlation coefficient (PCC) between genes is larger than 0.5.

HPRD: a database of curated proteomic information pertaining to human proteins. It is derived from [13] with 9,465 vertices and 37,039 edges. We employ the HPRD version used in [12] that contains 7311 nodes and 30503 edges.

Phenotype similarity: we use the OMIM [11] dataset and the phenotype similarity notion introduced by Van Driel et al. [14] based on the relevance and the frequency of the Medical Subject Headings (MeSH) vocabulary terms in OMIM documents. We built the graph linking those genes whose associated phenotypes have a maximal phenotypic similarity greater than a fixed cut-off value. Following [14], we set the similarity cut-off to 0.3. The resulting graph has 3393 nodes and 144739 edges.

Biogridphys: this dataset encodes known physical interactions among proteins. The idea is that mutations can affect physical interactions by changing the shape of proteins and their effect can propagate through protein graphs. We introduce a link between two genes if their products interact. The resulting graph has 15389 nodes and 155333 edges.

4.1 Evaluation Method

To evaluate the performance of the diffusion kernels, we follow [3]: we choose 14 diseases with at least 30 confirmed genes. For each disease, we construct a positive set $\mathcal{P}$ with all confirmed disease genes. To build the negative set $\mathcal{N}$, we randomly sample a set of genes that are associated at least to one disease class, but not related to the class which defines the positive set such that $|\mathcal{N}| = \frac{1}{2}|\mathcal{P}|$. We replicate this procedure 5 times[1]. We assess the performance of kernels via a 3-fold CV, where, after partitioning the dataset $\mathcal{P} \cup \mathcal{U}$ in 3 folds, we use one fold for training model using SVM and the two remaining folds for testing. For each test gene g_i, the model returns a score s_i proportional to the likelihood of being associated to the disease. Next a decision score q_i is computed as the top percentage value of s_i among all candidate gene scores. We collect all decision scores for every test genes to compute the area under the curve for the receiver operating characteristic (AUC-ROC). The final performance on the disease class is obtained by taking average over 3 folds × 5 trials.

Model Selection: The hyper-parameters of the various methods are set using a 3-fold on training set in which one fold is used for training the model and two remaining folds are used for validation. We try the values for LEDK and MEDK in $\{0.01, 0.05, 0.1\}$, time steps in MDK in $\{3, 5, 10\}$ and RLK parameter in $\{0.01, 0.1, 1\}$. For CDNK, we try for the degree threshold value in $\{10, 15, 20\}$, clique size threshold in $\{4, 5\}$, maximum radius in $\{1, 2\}$, maximum distance in $\{2, 3, 4\}$. The number of links used for the enrichment are chosen in $\{40\%, 50\%, 60\%, 70\%\}$ of the number of existing links. Finally, the regularization tradeoff C for the SVM is chosen in $\{10^{-4}, 10^{-3}, 10^{-2}, 10^{-1}, 1, 10, 10^2, 10^3, 10^4\}$.

5 Results and Discussion

In Table 1 we report a synthesis of all the experiments. Each row represent a different disease, in the columns we consider the different sources of information used to build the underlying graph (BioGPS, Biogridphys, Hprd, Omim). Note that each resource yields a graph with different characteristic sparsity and number of components. We compare the average AUC-ROC scores in two cases: plain diffusion kernel (denoted by a "−" symbol) and diffusion kernel on a modified graph G' (denoted by a "+" symbol) which includes the novel edges identified by a link prediction system. Here we report the aggregated results (a detailed breakdown is available in *Appendix*[2]) where we have averaged not only across a random choice of negative genes, but also among the type of diffusion kernel and the type of link prediction. The noteworthy result is how consistent the result is: each link prediction method improves each diffusion kernel algorithm, and on average using link prediction yields a 15% to 20% relative error reduction

---

[1] Note that the positive set is held constant, while the negative set varies.
[2] https://github.com/dinhinfotech/ICANN/blob/master/appendix.pdf.

Table 1. Predictive performance on 14 gene-disease associations using four different graphs induced by the BioGPS, Biogridphys, Hprd and Omim. We report the average AUC-ROC (%) and standard deviations for all diffusion-based kernels with (+) and without (−) link enrichment.

Disease	BioGPS −	BioGPS +	Biogridphys −	Biogridphys +	Hprd −	Hprd +	Omim −	Omim +
1	60.3 ± 1.5	63.4 ± 1.0	73.1 ± 4.1	77.1 ± 2.9	75.5 ± 0.2	77.5 ± 0.9	85.3 ± 1.1	86.9 ± 1.5
2	53.7 ± 1.4	63.4 ± 3.8	56.6 ± 3.4	61.3 ± 4.1	57.1 ± 0.9	60.2 ± 1.8	75.0 ± 2.2	76.5 ± 2.4
3	50.2 ± 0.4	58.6 ± 3.0	58.9 ± 5.9	67.5 ± 7.7	61.8 ± 3.6	70.7 ± 3.8	77.3 ± 1.8	83.1 ± 0.9
4	61.5 ± 0.9	72.2 ± 2.2	65.7 ± 4.1	74.6 ± 4.2	67.3 ± 1.1	71.9 ± 2.2	90.2 ± 1.2	92.1 ± 1.2
5	55.1 ± 0.4	61.7 ± 0.9	54.2 ± 4.8	60.7 ± 4.0	57.7 ± 1.6	67.0 ± 1.8	76.4 ± 0.8	81.9 ± 1.5
6	60.8 ± 0.9	67.9 ± 2.2	60.6 ± 3.6	65.9 ± 3.5	66.8 ± 1.3	71.9 ± 2.3	79.9 ± 2.4	83.3 ± 1.2
7	68.1 ± 1.4	73.4 ± 0.7	57.7 ± 3.2	63.7 ± 4.0	68.9 ± 2.1	72.5 ± 1.2	81.0 ± 1.2	84.1 ± 1.0
8	69.2 ± 2.3	74.0 ± 2.2	68.1 ± 3.6	72.6 ± 2.5	76.6 ± 2.2	80.3 ± 2.8	85.4 ± 2.2	91.0 ± 1.0
9	62.0 ± 1.6	64.5 ± 1.4	68.7 ± 4.6	71.7 ± 4.3	68.4 ± 2.5	75.0 ± 3.2	78.5 ± 0.2	80.6 ± 0.6
10	67.5 ± 2.9	72.9 ± 1.8	58.8 ± 3.2	66.1 ± 3.8	65.8 ± 3.4	74.4 ± 2.6	86.1 ± 0.6	87.8 ± 0.3
11	58.7 ± 1.8	62.3 ± 1.5	58.2 ± 1.2	61.6 ± 1.7	60.1 ± 1.1	64.2 ± 1.5	82.0 ± 1.4	83.6 ± 0.9
12	64.0 ± 1.3	73.6 ± 1.7	59.3 ± 2.1	67.0 ± 2.8	60.8 ± 1.1	68.8 ± 2.8	82.0 ± 1.8	85.9 ± 1.7
13	56.5 ± 0.9	63.3 ± 2.4	55.8 ± 1.1	65.1 ± 4.2	66.4 ± 1.3	71.8 ± 1.7	83.1 ± 2.8	87.5 ± 2.5
14	55.2 ± 0.3	62.3 ± 1.2	55.6 ± 1.6	63.5 ± 4.0	66.3 ± 2.3	71.1 ± 2.8	97.4 ± 0.1	99.0 ± 0.4
$\overline{AUC}$	60.2 ± 0.3	66.7 ± 1.2	60.8 ± 1.6	67.0 ± 4.0	65.7 ± 2.3	71.2 ± 2.8	82.8 ± 0.1	86.0 ± 0.4

for diffusion-based methods. What varies is the amount of improvement, which depends on the coupling between the four elements: the disease, the information source, the link prediction method and the diffusion kernel algorithm. In specific we obtain that the largest improvement is obtained for disease 3 (connective) where we have a maximum improvement of 20% ROC points, while the minimum improvement is for disease 8 (immunological) with a minimal improvement of 0% ROC points (see in the detailed report). On average the largest improvement is of 13% ROC points, while the smallest improvement is on average of 1% ROC point. Such stable results are of interest since diffusion-based methods are currently state-of-the-art for gene-disease prioritization tasks, and hence a technique that can offer a consistent and relatively large improvement can have important practical consequences in the understanding of disease mechanisms.

6   Conclusion and Future Work

In this paper we have proposed the notion of *link enrichment* for diffusion kernels, that is, the idea of carrying out the computation of information diffusion on a graph that contains edges identified by link prediction approaches. We have discovered a surprisingly robust signal that indicates that diffusion-based node kernels consistently benefit from the coupling with similarity-based link prediction techniques on large scale datasets in biological domains.

In future work we will carry out a more fine grained analysis, defining a taxonomy of prediction problems on graphs that make use of the notion of node similarity and analyze which link prediction strategies can be effectively coupled with specific node similarity computation techniques for a given problem class. In addition we will study the quantitative relation between the degree of missingness and the size of the improvement offered by prepending the link prediction to the node similarity assessment. Finally, we will extend the analysis to the more complex case of kernel integration and data fusion, i.e. when multiple heterogeneous information sources are used jointly to define the predictive task.

Acknowledgments. This work was supported by the University of Padova, Strategic Project BIOINFOGEN.

References

1. Huang, Z., et al.: A graph-based recommender system for digital library. In: Proceedings of the 2nd ACM/IEEE-CS Joint Conference on Digital Libraries. ACM (2002)
2. Kondor, R.I., Lafferty, J.: Diffusion kernels on graphs and other discrete structures. In: Proceedings of the 19th International Conference on Machine Learning (ICML 2002) (2002)
3. Chen, B., et al.: Disease gene identification by using graph kernels and Markov random fields. Sci. China Life Sci. **57**(11), 1054 (2014)
4. Chebotarev, P., Shamis, E.: The matrix-forest theorem and measuring relations in small social groups. Autom. Remote Control **58**(9), 1505–1514 (1997)
5. Haussler, D.: Convolution kernels on discrete structures. Technical report UCS-CRL-99-10, UC Santa Cruz (1999)
6. Tran-Van, D., Sperduti, A., Costa, F.: Conjunctive disjunctive node kernel. In: Proceedings of 25th European Symposium on Artificial Neural Networks, Computational Intelligence and Machine Learning (2017)
7. Costa, F., Kurt, D.: Fast neighborhood subgraph pairwise distance kernel. In: Proceedings of the 26th International Conference on Machine Learning. Omnipress (2010)
8. Ramadan, E., Sadiq, A., Rafiul, H.: Network topology measures for identifying disease-gene association in breast cancer. BMC Bioinform. **17**(7), 274 (2016)
9. Lu, L., Tao, Z.: Link prediction in complex networks: a survey. Phys. A **390**(6), 1150–1170 (2011)
10. Fouss, F., et al.: An experimental investigation of kernels on graphs for collaborative recommendation and semisupervised classification. Neural Netw. **31**, 53–72 (2012)
11. McKusick, V.A.: Mendelian inheritance in man and its online version, OMIM. Am. J. Hum. Genet. **80**(4), 588–604 (2007)
12. Chatr-Aryamontri, A., et al.: The BioGRID interaction database: 2015 update. Nucleic Acids Res. **43**(D1), D470–D478 (2015)
13. Prasad, T.S.K., et al.: Human protein reference database - 2009 update. Nucleic Acids Res. **37**(Database), D767–D772 (2009)
14. Van Driel, M.A., et al.: A text-mining analysis of the human phenome. Eur. J. Hum. Genet. **14**(5), 535–542 (2006)

Context Information Learning and Self-Assessment in Advanced Machine Learning Models

Classless Association Using Neural Networks

Federico Raue[1,3]([✉]), Sebastian Palacio[3], Andreas Dengel[1,3],
and Marcus Liwicki[2]

[1] Computer Science Department, University of Kaiserslautern,
Kaiserslautern, Germany
{federico.raue,andreas.dengel}@dfki.de
[2] MindGarage, University of Kaiserslautern, Kaiserslautern, Germany
liwicki@cs.uni-kl.de
[3] Smart Data and Knowledge Services,
German Research Center for Artificial Intelligence (DFKI), Kaiserslautern, Germany
sebastian.palacio@dfki.de

Abstract. The goal of this paper is to train a model based on the relation between two instances that represent the same *unknown* class. This task is inspired by the *Symbol Grounding Problem* and the *association learning* between modalities in infants. We propose a novel model called *Classless Association* that has two parallel Multilayer Perceptrons (MLPs) with a EM-training rule. Moreover, the training relies on matching the output vectors of the MLPs against a statistical distribution as alternative loss function because of the *unlabeled* data. In addition, the output classification of one network is used as target of the other network, and vice versa for learning the agreement between both *unlabeled* sample. We generate four *classless* datasets based on MNIST, where the input is two different instances of the same digit. Furthermore, our *classless association* model is evaluated against two scenarios: totally supervised and totally unsupervised. In the first scenario, our model reaches a good performance in terms of accuracy and the classless constraint. In the second scenario, our model reaches better results against two clustering algorithms.

1 Introduction

Infants are able to learn the binding between *abstract concepts* to the real world via their sensory input. For example, the abstract concept *ball* is binding to the visual representation of a rounded object and the auditory representation of the phonemes /b/ /a/ /l/. This scenario can be seen as the *Symbol Grounding Problem* [6]. Moreover, infants are also able to learn the *association* between different sensory input modes while they are still learning the binding of the abstract concepts. Several results have shown a correlation between object recognition (visual) and vocabulary acquisition (auditory) in infants [1,2]. One example of this correlation is the first words that infants have learned. In that case, the words are mainly nouns, which are *visible concepts*, such as, dad, mom, ball, dog, cat [5].

© Springer International Publishing AG 2017
A. Lintas et al. (Eds.): ICANN 2017, Part II, LNCS 10614, pp. 165–173, 2017.
https://doi.org/10.1007/978-3-319-68612-7_19

Furthermore, we can define the previous scenario in terms of a machine learning task. More formally, the task is defined by learning the association between two parallel streams of data that represent the same *unknown* class. Note that this task is different from the *supervised* association where the data has labels. First, the classes are *unknown* in our scenario whereas the classes are known in the supervised case. Second, both classifiers need to agree on the same coding scheme (i.e. one-hot encoding) for each sample pair during training. In contrast, the coding-scheme is already pre-defined before training in the supervised case.

Usually, classifiers require labeled data for training. However, the presented scenario needs an alternative training mechanism. One way is to train based on statistical distributions. Casey [3] proposed to solve the OCR problem using language statistics for inferring form images to characters. Later on, Knight *et al.* [9] applied a similar idea to machine translation. Recently, Sutskever *et al.* [13] defined the *Output Distribution Matching (ODM)* cost function for dual autoencoders and generative networks.

In this paper[1], we are proposing a novel model that is trained based on the association of two different samples of the same *unknown* class. The presented model has two parallel Multilayer Perceptrons (MLPs) with an Expectation-Maximization (EM) [4] training rule that matches the network output against a statistical distribution. Moreover, both networks agree on the same classification because one network is used as target of the other network, and vice versa. This work is an extension of Raue *et al.* [11] where the authors proposed a symbolic association, which is based on representing the input samples with *soft labels* (labels without the vectorial representation of the association). In contrast, our model does only require a statistical distribution instead of labels for training. Our contributions in this paper are

- We define a novel training rule based on *matching* the output vectors of the presented model and a statistical distribution. Note that the output vectors are used as symbolic features similar to the *Symbol Grounding Problem*. Furthermore, the proposed training rule is based on an *EM-approach* and classified each sample based on generated *pseudo-classes* (Sect. 2).
- We propose a novel architecture for learning the association in the *classless* scenario. Moreover, the presented model uses two parallel MLPs, which require to agree on the same class for each input sample. This association is motivated by the correlation between different sensory input signals in infants development. In more detail, one network is the target of the other network, and vice versa. Also, note that our model is gradient-based and can be extended to deeper architectures (Sect. 2).
- We evaluate our *classless* association task against two cases: totally supervised and totally unsupervised. In this manner, we can verify the range of our results in terms of supervised and unsupervised cases since our model is neither totally supervised nor totally unsupervised. We compare against a MLP trained with labels as the supervised scenario (upper bound) and two

---

[1] a preliminary draft of this paper was submitted elsewhere [12].

clustering algorithms (K-means and Hierarchical Agglomerative) as the unsupervised scenario (lower bound). First, our model reaches better results than the clustering. Second, our model shows promising results with respect to the supervised scenario (Sects. 3 and 4).

2 Classless Association Model

In this work, we present a novel model that is trained based on the association between two different instances of the same *unknown* class. More formally, $x^{(1)} \in R^{n1}$ and $x^{(2)} \in R^{n2}$ are feature vectors for each input, and the task is to classify both input vectors with the same *pseudo-class* $c^{(1)} = c^{(2)}$, where $c^{(1)}, c^{(2)} \in R^{n3}$. With this in mind, our model has two parallel *Multilayer Perceptrons(MLPs)* with an EM-training rule [4] that does not rely on *labeled* data. In contrast, our training rule uses a statistical constraint as alternative loss function for training each network. As a result, we have introduced a *weighting vector* (γ) for learning the statistical matching. In addition, each MLP generates *pseudo-classes* during training based on the statistical constraint. The *pseudo-classes* are used for learning the agreement between both MLPs, which relies on using the *pseudo-classes* of one MLP as target of the other MLP, and vice versa. Figure 1 shows a general view of our model.

Initially, all input samples $x^{(1)}$ and $x^{(2)}$ have random *pseudo-classes* $c^{(1)}$ and $c^{(2)}$, which have the same desired statistical distribution $\phi \in R^{n3}$ (i.e. uniform distribution). Both, the *weighting vectors* $\gamma^{(1)} \in R^{n3}$ and $\gamma^{(2)} \in R^{n3}$ are initialized to one. Note that the *E-step* and *M-step* are applied to each MLP indepently.

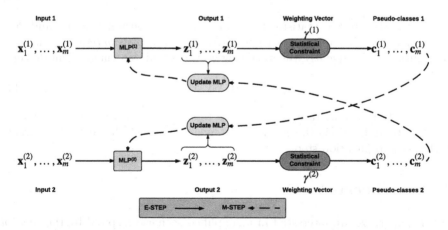

Fig. 1. Overview of the presented model for classless association of two input samples that represent the same unknown classes. The association relies on matching the network output and a statistical distribution. In addition, our model uses the pseudo-classes obtained by $MLP^{(1)}$ as targets of $MLP^{(2)}$, and vice versa.

The *E-step* generates the *pseudo-classes* for each MLP and calculates the current statistical distribution of network output $z^{(1)} \in R^{n3}$ and $z^{(2)} \in R^{n3}$ and weighting vectors[2]. In this case, an approximation of the distribution is obtained by the following equation

$$\hat{z} = \frac{1}{M} \sum_{i=1}^{M} power(z_i, \gamma) \tag{1}$$

where γ is the weighting vector, z_i is the output vector of the network, M is the number of elements, and the function $power$[3] is the element-wise power operation between the output vector z_i and the weighting vector γ. We have used the *power function* because the output vectors are quite similar at the initial state of the network, and the *power function* provides an initial boost for learning to separate the input samples in different *pseudo-classes* in the first iterations. Moreover, the output classification is retrieved by the maximum value of the following equation

$$c^* = arg\ max_c\ power(z_i, \gamma) \tag{2}$$

where c^* is the *pseudo-class*, which is used in the *M-step* for updating the MLP weights. Note that the *pseudo-classes* are not updated in an online manner, but after a certain number of iterations since the network requires a number of iterations to learn the common features.

The *M-step* updates the weighting vector and the MLP parameters. The cost function is the variance between the distribution and the desired statistical distribution, which is defined by

$$cost = (\hat{z} - \phi)^2 \tag{3}$$

where $\hat{z}$ is the current statistical distribution of the output vectors, and $\phi \in R^{n3}$ is a vector that represents the desired *statistical distribution*, e.g. uniform distribution. Consequently, the weighting vector is updated via gradient descent

$$\gamma = \gamma - \alpha\ *\nabla_\gamma cost \tag{4}$$

where α is the learning rate and $\nabla_\gamma cost$ is the derivative w.r.t γ. Also, the MLP weights are updated via the generated *pseudo-classes*, which are used as targets in the backpropagation step.

3 Experiments

In this paper, we are interested in a simplified scenario inspired by the *Symbol Grounding Problem* and the association learning between sensory input signal

---

[2] From now on, we drop the super-indexes (1) and (2) for explanation purposes.
[3] We decide to use *power* function instead of z_i^γ in order to simplify the index notation.

in infants. We evaluated our model in four *classless* datasets that are generated from MNIST. The procedure of generating *classless datasets* from *labeled datasets* have been already applied in [7,13]. Each dataset has two disjoint sets *input 1* and *input 2*. The first dataset (*MNIST*) has two different instances of the same digit. The second dataset (*Rotated-90 MNIST*) has two different instances of the same digit, and all input samples in *input 2* are rotated 90°. The third dataset (*Inverted MNIST*) follows a similar procedures as the second dataset, but the transformation of the elements in *input 2* is the invert function instead of rotation. The last dataset (*Random Rotated MNIST*) is more challenging because all elements in *input 2* are randomly rotated between 0 and 2π. All datasets have a uniform distribution between the digits and the dataset size is 21,000 samples for training and 4,000 samples for validation and testing.

The following parameters turned out being optimal on the validation set. For the first three datasets, each internal MLP relies on two fully connected layers of 200 and 100 neurons respectively. The learning rate for the MLPs was set to start at 1.0 and was continuously decaying by half after every 1,000 iterations. We set the initial *weighting vector* to 1.0 and updated after every 1,000 iterations as well. Moreover, the best parameters for the fourth dataset were the same for $MLP^{(1)}$ and different for $MLP^{(2)}$, which has two fully connected layers of 400 and 150 neurons respectively and the learning rate stars at 1.2. The target distribution ϕ is uniform for all datasets. The decay of the learning rate for the *weighting vector* was given by $1/(100 + epoch)^{0.3}$, where *epoch* was the number of training iterations so far. The mini-batch size M is 5,250 sample pairs (corresponding to 25% of the training set) and the mean of the derivatives for each mini-batch is used for the back-propagation step of MLPs. Note that the mini-batch is quite big comparing to common setups. We infer from this parameter that the model requires a sample size big enough for estimating the uniform distribution and also needs to learn slower than traditional approaches.

To determine the baseline of our *classless constraint*, we compared our model against two cases: totally supervised and totally unsupervised. In the supervised case, we used the same MLP parameters and training for a fair comparison. In the unsupervised scenario, we used K-means and Agglomerative Clustering to each set (*input 1* and *input 2*) independently. The clustering algorithm implementation are provided by scikit-learn.

4   Results and Discussion

In this work, we have generated ten different folds for each dataset and report the average results. We introduce the *Association Accuracy* for measuring association, and it is defined by the following equation

$$Association\ Accuracy = \frac{1}{N} \sum_{i=1}^{N} \mathbb{1}(c_i^{(1)} = c_i^{(2)}) \tag{5}$$

where the *indicator function* is one if $c_i^{(1)} = c_i^{(2)}$, zero otherwise; $c_i^{(1)}$ and $c_i^{(2)}$ are the *pseudo-classes* for $MLP^{(1)}$ and $MLP^{(2)}$, respectively (N is the number of elements). In addition, we also reported the *Purity* of each set (*input* 1 and *input* 2).

Table 1 shows the *Association Accuracy* between our model as well as the supervised association task and the *Purity* between our model and two clustering algorithms. First, the supervised association task performs better that the presented model. This was expected because our task is more complex in relation to the supervised scenario. However, we can infer from our results that the presented model has a good performance in terms of the classless scenario and supervised method. Second, our model not only learns the association between input samples but also finds similar elements covered under the same *pseudo-class*. Furthermore, we evaluated the purity of our model and found that the performance of our model reaches better results than both clustering methods for each set (*input* 1 and *input* 2).

Figure 2 illustrates an example of the proposed learning rule. The first two columns ($MLP^{(1)}$ and $MLP^{(2)}$) are the output classification (Eq. 2) and each row represents a *pseudo-class*. We have randomly selected 15 output samples for each MLP (not cherry picking). Initially, the *pseudo classes* are random selected for each MLP. As a result, the output classification of both networks does not show any visible discriminant element and the initial purity is close to random choices (first row). After 1,000 iterations, the networks start learning some features in order to discriminate the input samples. Some groups of digits are grouped together after 3,000 iterations. For example, the first row of $MLP^{(2)}$

Table 1. Association accuracy (%) and purity (%) results. Our model is compared to the supervised scenario (class labels are provided) and to K-means and Hierarchical Agglomerative clustering (no class information).

Dataset	Model	Association Accuracy (%)	Purity (%) input 1	input 2
MNIST	Supervised association	96.7 ± 0.3	96.7 ± 0.2	96.6 ± 0.3
	Classless association	86.1 ± 3.2	89.6 ± 4.5	89.0 ± 4.2
	K-means	-	63.9 ± 2.2	62.5 ± 3.7
	Hierarchical Agglomerative	-	64.9 ± 4.7	64.3 ± 5.5
Rotated-90 MNIST	Supervised association	93.2 ± 0.3	96.4 ± 0.2	96.6 ± 0.2
	Classless association	86.5 ± 2.5	82.9 ± 4.5	82.9 ± 4.3
	K-means	-	65.0 ± 2.8	64.0 ± 3.6
	Hierarchical Agglomerative	-	65.4 ± 3.5	64.1 ± 4.1
Inverted MNIST	Supervised association	93.2 ± 0.3	96.5 ± 0.2	96.5 ± 0.2
	Classless association	89.2 ± 2.4	89.0 ± 6.8	89.1 ± 6.8
	K-means	-	64.8 ± 2.0	65.0 ± 2.5
	Hierarchical Agglomerative	-	64.8 ± 4.4	64.4 ± 3.8
Random Rotated MNIST	Supervised association	88.0 ± 0.5	96.5 ± 0.3	90.9 ± 0.5
	Classless association	69.3 ± 2.2	75.8 ± 7.3	65.3 ± 5.0
	K-means	-	64.8 ± 2.6	14.8 ± 0.4
	Hierarchical Agglomerative	-	65.9 ± 2.8	15.2 ± 0.5

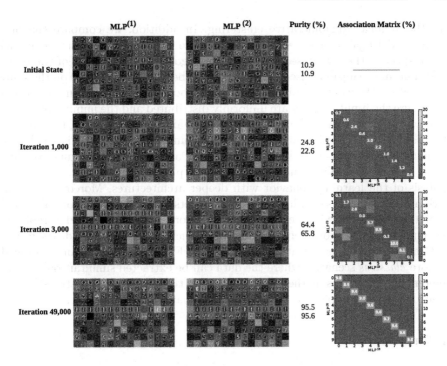

Fig. 2. Example of the presented model during *classless* training. In this example, there are ten *pseudo-classes* represented by each row of $MLP^{(1)}$ and $MLP^{(2)}$. Note that the output classification is randomly selected (not cherry picking). The *classless association* model slowly start learning the features and grouping similar input samples. Afterwards, the output classification of both MLPs slowly agrees during training, and the association matrix shows the relation between the occurrences of the *pseudo-classes*.

shows several digits *zero*, whereas $MLP^{(1)}$ has not yet agreed on the same digit for that *pseudo-class*. In contrast, both MLPs have almost agree on digit *one* at the fifth row. Finally, the association is learned using only the statistical distribution of the input samples and each digit is represented by each *pseudo-class*.

5   Conclusion

In this paper, we have shown the feasibility to train a model that has two parallel MLPs under the following scenario: pairs of input samples that represent the same unknown classes. This scenario was motivated by the *Symbol Grounding Problem* and association learning between sensory input signal in infants development. We proposed a model based on gradients for solving the *classless association*. Our model has an EM-training that matches the network output against a statistical distribution and uses one network as a target of the other network, and vice versa. Our model reaches better performance than K-means and Hierarchical Agglomerative clustering. In addition, we compare the presented model against a supervised method. We find that the presented model with respect to the supervised method reaches good results because of two extra conditions in the unsupervised association: unlabeled data and agree on the same *pseudo-class*. We want to point out that our model was evaluated in an optimal case where the input samples are uniformly distributed and the number of classes is known. However, we will explore the performance of our model if the number of classes and the statistical distribution are unknown. One way is to change the number of *pseudo-classes*. This can be seen as changing the number of clusters k in K-means. With this in mind, we are planning to do more exhaustive analysis of the learning behavior with deeper architectures. Moreover, we will work on how a small set of labeled classes affects the performance of our model (similar to semi-supervised learning). Furthermore, we are interested in replicating our findings in more complex scenarios, such as, multimodal datasets like TVGraz [8] or Wikipedia featured articles [10]. Finally, our work can be applied to more *classless* scenarios where the data can be extracted simultaneously from different input sources at the same time. Also, transformation functions can be applied to input samples for creating the association without classes.

References

1. Asano, M., Imai, M., Kita, S., Kitajo, K., Okada, H., Thierry, G.: Sound symbolism scaffolds language development in preverbal infants. Cortex **63**, 196–205 (2015)
2. Balaban, M.T., Waxman, S.R.: Do words facilitate object categorization in 9-month-old infants? J. Exp. Child Psychol. **64**(1), 3–26 (1997)
3. Casey, R.G.: Text OCR by Solving a Cryptogram. International Business Machines Incorporated, Thomas J. Watson Research Center, New York (1986)
4. Dempster, A., Laird, N., Rubin, D.: Maximum likelihood from incomplete data via the EM algorithm. J. R. Stat. Soc. **39**(1), 1–38 (1977)
5. Gershkoff-Stowe, L., Smith, L.B.: Shape and the first hundred nouns. Child Dev. **75**(4), 1098–114 (2004)
6. Harnad, S.: The symbol grounding problem. Phys. D **42**(1), 335–346 (1990)
7. Hsu, Y.C., Kira, Z.: Neural network-based clustering using pairwise constraints. arXiv preprint arXiv:1511.06321 (2015)
8. Khan, I., Saffari, A., Bischof, H.: Tvgraz: multi-modal learning of object categories by combining textual and visual features. In: AAPR Workshop, pp. 213–224 (2009)
9. Knight, K., Nair, A., Rathod, N., Yamada, K.: Unsupervised analysis for decipherment problems. In: Proceedings of the COLING/ACL on Main Conference Poster Sessions, pp. 499–506. Association for Computational Linguistics (2006)
10. Rasiwasia, N., Costa Pereira, J., Coviello, E., Doyle, G., Lanckriet, G., Levy, R., Vasconcelos, N.: A new approach to cross-modal multimedia retrieval. In: ACM International Conference on Multimedia, pp. 251–260 (2010)
11. Raue, F., Palacio, S., Breuel, T.M., Byeon, W., Dengel, A., Liwicki, M.: Symbolic association using parallel multilayer perceptron. In: Villa, A.E.P., Masulli, P., Pons Rivero, A.J. (eds.) ICANN 2016. LNCS, vol. 9887, pp. 347–354. Springer, Cham (2016). doi:10.1007/978-3-319-44781-0_41

12. Raue, F., Palacio, S., Dengel, A., Liwicki, M.: Classless association using neural networks. In: ICLR 2017 (2017, submitted). https://openreview.net/forum?id=ryh_8f9lg&noteId=ryh_8f9lg
13. Sutskever, I., Jozefowicz, R., Gregor, K., Rezende, D., Lillicrap, T., Vinyals, O.: Towards principled unsupervised learning. arXiv preprint arXiv:1511.06440 (2015)

Shape from Shading by Model Inclusive Learning Method with Simultaneous Estimation of Parameters

Yasuaki Kuroe[1(✉)] and Hajimu Kawakami[2]

[1] Kyoto Institute of Technology, Matsugasaki, Sakyo-ku, Kyoto 606-8585, Japan
kuroe@kit.ac.jp
[2] Department of Electronics and Informatics, Ryukoku University, 1-5, Yokotani, Ohe-cho, Seta, Ohtsu 520-2194, Japan
kawakami@rins.ryukoku.ac.jp

Abstract. The problem of recovering shape from shading is important in computer vision and robotics. It is essentially an ill-posed problem and several studies have been done. In this paper, we present a versatile method of solving the problem by neural networks. The proposed method introduces the concept of the model inclusive learning with simultaneous estimation of unknown parameters. In the method a mathematical model, which we call 'image-formation model', expressing the process that the image is formed from an object surface, is introduced and is included in the learning loop of a neural network. The neural network is trained so as to recover the shape with simultaneously estimating unknown parameters in the image-formation model. The performance of the proposed method is demonstrated through experiments.

Keywords: Model inclusive learning · Neural network · Shape from shading · Parameter estimation

1 Introduction

The problem of surface-shape recovery of an object from a single intensity image is an important problem in computer vision and robotics and so on. The problem was first formulated in the general setting by Horn and several studies have been done based on the formulation [1,2]. The problem is essentially ill-posed and reduced to a nonlinear-function approximation problem.

In recent years, there have been increasing research interests of artificial neural networks and many efforts have been made on applications of neural networks to various fields. The most significant features of artificial neural networks are the extreme flexibility due to the learning capability of nonlinear function approximation and the generalization ability. It is expected, therefore, that neural networks make it possible to easily solve the ill-posed problem of shape from shading by their learning and generalization ability. Wei and Hirzinger presented a solution of the problem by using a multilayer feedforward network

© Springer International Publishing AG 2017
A. Lintas et al. (Eds.): ICANN 2017, Part II, LNCS 10614, pp. 174–182, 2017.
https://doi.org/10.1007/978-3-319-68612-7_20

[3]. Motivated by the work [3], we already proposed a versatile method of solving the problem of recovering shape from shading by neural networks [4]. The proposed method is versatile in the sense that it can solve the problem in various circumstances. In order to realize the versatility, we introduced the concept of model inclusive learning of neural networks [5]. In the model inclusive learning a priori knowledge and inherent properties of a target are incorporated into the formulation of learning problem, which could regularize an ill-posed problem and could improve learning and generalization ability of neural networks. It has been extended to a method which realizes recovering surface shape with simultaneously estimating the parameters of reflections [6] and illumination directions [7].

In this paper, we present a method of solving the shape from shading problem by introducing the concept of the model inclusive learning with simultaneous estimation of unknown parameters. In order to realize recovering shape and estimating all the unknown parameters simultaneously we propose a method of dividing the learning procedure into some steps and determining the order of those steps based on the sensitivity analysis of the parameters. The performance of the proposed method is demonstrated through experiments.

2   Model Inclusive Learning Method with Simultaneous Estimation of Unknown Parameters

Supervised learning is one of the most popular learning methods. Figure 1 shows a block diagram that illustrates its general framework. There are a lot of learning problems of neural networks, where teaching signals are not given directly to the output of neural networks, to which supervised learning cannot be applied. We have developed a learning method that can cope with those problems by incorporating a priori knowledge and inherent properties of a target, which we call model inclusive learning [5]. Figure 2 shows a block diagram that illustrates its general framework. In the method we construct a mathematical model for the

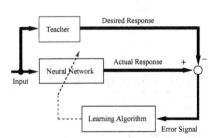

Fig. 1. General framework of supervised learning (learning with a teacher).

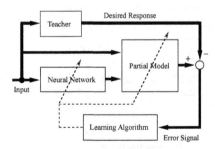

Fig. 2. General framework of model inclusive learning method of neural networks with simultaneous estimation of unknown parameters.

knowledge and inherent properties, which we call a partial model of the target, and include it in the learning loop of a neural network. The neural network is trained so as to minimize the error between the teaching signal (desired response) and the corresponding output of the partial model. If there are parameters whose values are unknown in the partial model, not only values of the weight coefficients of the neural network but also those of the unknown parameters are adjusted in the learning, which is the model inclusive learning method with simultaneous estimation of unknown parameters.

3   General Framework of Proposed Shape from Shading by Model Inclusive Learning Method

An image of a three-dimensional object taken by a camera in an imaging condition depends on its geometric structure (shape), its reflectance properties and the imaging conditions (the distribution of light sources etc.). The image formation process can be illustrated as shown in the upper part of Fig. 3. The process can be regarded as a mapping from the geometric structure of the surface to the image. We call the mathematical model of the mapping 'image-formation model'. Note that the image-formation model, denoted by $\hat{F}$, depends on the reflectance properties and the imaging conditions. We assume that, in the image-formation model $\hat{F}$, the mathematical models of reflectance properties and the imaging conditions are known. This problem can be solved by the model inclusive learning of neural networks shown in Fig. 2, as follows.

The schematic diagram of the proposed method is shown in Fig. 3. Suppose that an image of a three-dimensional target object is formed through an image formation process shown in the upper part of Fig. 3. Let $G(x, y)$ denote the brightness at a position (x, y) on the image. We formulate the learning problem

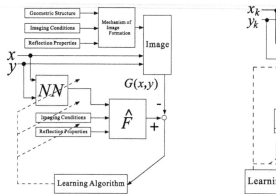
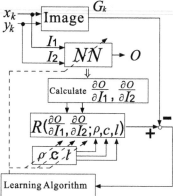

Fig. 3. General framework of proposed shape from shading by model inclusive learning of a neural network.

Fig. 4. Block diagram of proposed model inclusive learning algorithm.

of a neural network such that it recovers the geometric structure of the surface of the object as its input and output relation. In the formulation the neural network is trained with including the image-formation model $\hat{F}$ as follows. As shown in Fig. 3, we input a position (x, y) on the image to the neural network (NN), and we also input the corresponding output of the neural network to the image-formation model $\hat{F}$ together with the reflection properties and the imaging conditions. If the neural network is successfully trained so that the geometric structure of the surface of the object is realized as its input and output relation, the output of the image-formation model $\hat{F}$ becomes equal to the brightness $G(x, y)$. Therefore, training the neural network so as to reduce the error between the output of the image-formation model $\hat{F}$ and the brightness $G(x, y)$ over all the data points to zero would make it possess the geometric structure of the surface as its input and output relation. Noting that, if there are unknown parameters in the imaging conditions and reflection properties, we adjust not only values of the neural network parameters but also those unknown parameters, as shown in Fig. 3, so as to minimize the error between the output of the image-formation model $\hat{F}$ and the brightness $G(x, y)$ over all the data points. If the error can be reduced sufficiently by the adjustments of the parameters, the surface recovery and the estimation of the unknown parameters are achieved simultaneously.

4   Problem Formulation and Proposed Learning Method

4.1   Problem Formulation

Suppose that the surface of an object is represented by

$$z = f(x, y) \tag{1}$$

in a camera coordinate system x - y - z, with the x - y plane coinciding with the image plane, and z axis coinciding with the optical axis of the camera. It is known that, assuming that orthographic projection and uniform reflectance property of the object, the brightness at a position (x, y) on the image plane can be described as

$$G(x, y) = R(p, q ; l), \qquad p = \frac{\partial f}{\partial x}, \quad q = \frac{\partial f}{\partial y} \tag{2}$$

where $l = (l_1, l_2, l_3)$ is the illuminant direction and (p, q) is the surface gradient at (x, y). Equation (2) is called image irradiance equation. $R(p, q ; l)$ is called the reflectance map and represents reflection properties. Note that the image irradiance Eq. (2) is corresponding to the image-formation model $\hat{F}$. In general the image formation model is known to be composed of the specular reflection $\Phi(\theta(p, q; l), c)$ and the diffuse reflection $\cos \phi(p, q; l)$ as follows:

$$R(p, q ; \rho, c, l) = \rho \cdot \Phi(\theta(p, q; l), c) + (1 - \rho) \cdot \cos \phi(p, q; l) \tag{3}$$

where $\theta(p, q; l) = \cos^{-1} \frac{pl_1 + ql_2 - (l_3 - 1)}{\sqrt{p^2 + q^2 + 1}\sqrt{l_1^2 + l_2^2 + (l_3 - 1)^2}}$, $\cos \phi(p, q; l) = \frac{pl_1 + ql_2 - l_3}{\sqrt{p^2 + q^2 + 1}}$, ρ ($0 \leq \rho \leq 1$) is the ratio parameter and c is the parameter describing extent of the specular reflection. Note that in (3) we use the expression $R(p, q; \rho, c, l)$ to represent the reflectance map in (2) in order to clarify that it also depends on reflection parameters ρ and c. There have been several models proposed for the specular reflection $\Phi(\theta(p, q; l), c)$, a typical representative of which is the Torrance-Sparrow Model [9]:

$$\Phi(\theta(p, q; l), c) = \exp(-c^2\theta^2(p, q; l)) \tag{4}$$

The illumination direction $l = (\ell_1, \ell_2, \ell_3)$ is expressed as follows:

$$\ell_1 = \sin\theta\cos\varphi, \quad \ell_2 = \sin\theta\sin\varphi, \quad \ell_3 = \cos\theta \tag{5}$$

where θ is the polar angle and φ is the azimuth.

The objective here is to recover the geometric structure of the surface (1) from a single image. In this paper we propose a model inclusive learning method to solve the problem under the following conditions: (A1) the mathematical expression of the reflectance map $R(p, q; \rho, c, l)$ is known, (A2) values of the reflection parameters ρ and c are unknown, and values of the illuminant direction $l = (\ell_1, \ell_2, \ell_3)$, that is, θ and φ in (5) are unknown.

4.2   Proposed Learning Method

Figure 4 shows the schematic diagram of the proposed model inclusive learning method of neural networks. Let G_k denote the brightness which is observed at a position (x_k, y_k) from an image taken from an object surface. We prepare a neural network (NN) with two inputs denoted by $I = [I_1, I_2]^T$ and one output denoted by O and consider that the input $I = [I_1, I_2]^T$ and the output O correspond to the position (x, y) on the image and the depth z of the surface, respectively. For an observed brightness G_k, we give its position (x_k, y_k) on the image to the input $I = [I_1, I_2]^T$ of the neural network and derive the derivatives of the output of the neural network with respect to the input, and obtain the values of the derivatives at $[I_1, I_2]^T = (x_k, y_k)^T$:

$$\left.\frac{\partial O}{\partial I}\right|_{I=(x_k,y_k)} = (\left.\frac{\partial O}{\partial I_1}\right|_{I=(x_k,y_k)}, \left.\frac{\partial O}{\partial I_2}\right|_{I=(x_k,y_k)})^T. \tag{6}$$

Note that those derivatives become equal to the surface gradient (p, q) at the position (x_k, y_k) if the input and output relation of the neural network exhibits the geometric structure (1) of the object. We substitute the values of the derivatives (6) into the surface gradient (p, q) of the image-formation model $R(\cdot, \cdot; \rho, c, l)$. The obtained $R(\partial O/\partial I_1, \partial O/\partial I_2; \rho, c, l)$ corresponds to the outputs of the image formation model $\hat{F}$ in Fig. 3 and is to be coincided with the brightness G_k. Accordingly, training the neural network so as to reduce the error between the brightness G_k and $R(\partial O/\partial I_1, \partial O/\partial I_2; \rho, c, l)$ over all the data points to zero, we can obtain the geometric structure of the surface as the input and output relation of the neural network. Note that we assume that values of the reflection parameters ρ and c are unknown and those of the parameters of the illumination direction $l = (\ell_1, \ell_2, \ell_3)$ (i.e. θ and φ) are unknown. In the model inclusive learning we adjust not only values of the neural-network parameters but also those of the reflection parameters ρ and c and the illumination direction $l = (\ell_1, \ell_2, \ell_3)$ so as to minimize the error between the brightness G_k and $R(\partial O/\partial I_1, \partial O/\partial I_2; \rho, c, l)$ as shown in Fig. 4. Note also that the reflectance map $R(p, q; \rho, c, l)$ contains unknown parameters l (θ and φ), ρ and c, in the calculation of $R(\partial O/\partial I_1, \partial O/\partial I_2; \rho, c, l)$ we use their current estimated values.

Define the performance index by

$$
J = \frac{1}{2} \sum_{(x_k, y_k) \in D_G} \left\{ R \left(\left. \frac{\partial O}{\partial I_1} \right|_{I=(x_k, y_k)}, \left. \frac{\partial O}{\partial I_2} \right|_{I=(x_k, y_k)} ; \rho, c, l \right) - G_k \right\}^2 \quad (7)
$$

where D_G is a set of data points (x_k, y_k) at which the brightness G_k is observed from the image. Note that J is the square error between G_k and $R(\partial O/\partial I_1, \partial O/\partial I_2; \rho, c, l)$ over the data points D_G. The problem is now reduced to finding values of parameters of the neural network and also those of the parameters of the illumination direction l (θ and φ) and the reflection parameters ρ and c that minimize the performance index J, a solution of which could achieve simultaneously recovering shape and estimating the illumination direction and the reflection parameters.

In order to search values of the network parameters and the unknown parameters which minimize J, the gradient based methods can be used, in which several useful algorithms are available: the steepest descent algorithm, the conjugate gradient algorithm, the quasi-Newton algorithm and so on. The main problem associated with these algorithms is the computation of the gradients of J with respect to the parameters of the neural network and the unknown parameters l (θ and φ), ρ and c. Note that, as previously stated, the derivatives of the output with respect to the input of the neural network $\partial O/\partial I$ are also needed to be calculated. Efficient algorithms to calculate these gradients and the derivatives can be derived by introducing adjoint models of the neural network [8]. The derivation is omitted.

It is important to note that, in the minimization of the performance index J by the use of an appropriate gradient based algorithm, it may not succeed to converge if all the parameters, that is, the parameters of the neural network and the unknown parameters l (θ and φ), ρ and c, are simultaneously adjusted from the beginning of the optimization. In order to solve the problem we divide the learning procedure into some steps. In order to determine the order of those steps we perform the sensitivity analysis of those parameters ρ, c and l (θ and φ). Evaluating the sensitivities of the performance index (7) with respect to those unknown parameters l (θ and φ), ρ and c, we obtain the following result. For the parameters of the illumination direction, $\frac{\partial J}{\partial \theta}$ and $\frac{\partial J}{\partial \varphi}$ are of order 10^{-2} and of order 10^{-3}, respectively. For the reflection parameters, $\frac{\partial J}{\partial \rho}$ is of order 10^{-4} and $\frac{\partial J}{\partial c}$ is order of 10^{-4}. Hence we divide the learning procedure into three steps; in the first step we adjust only the parameters of the neural network, and in the second step we adjust the parameters of the neural network together with the reflection parameters, and in the third step we adjust all the parameters simultaneously. The three-step optimization procedure is summarized as follows:

Step 1: Give an appropriate initial guess of the values of the illumination direction l (θ and φ) and the reflection parameters ρ and c. Adjust only the parameters of the neural network according to an appropriate gradient based algorithm with the parameters of the illumination direction and the reflection parameters being kept constant at the initial guess. The adjustment is repeated until it converges and the tentative surface shape of the target object is obtained. We call it the initial surface shape.

Step 2: Starting from the initial surface shape, adjust the parameters of the neural network together with the parameters of illumination direction l (θ and φ) according to an appropriate gradient based algorithm. The adjustment is continued until it converges.

Step 3: Adjust the parameters of the neural network together with all the unknown parameters l (θ and φ), ρ and c according to an appropriate gradient based algorithm until the adjustment converges.

5   Experiment

In this section we show the results of the experiment in order to demonstrate the performance of the proposed method. In the following experiment a four-layer feedforward neural network with 15 hidden units is used, the structure of which is determined by preparatory experiments. We utilize the quasi-Newton method with the Davidon-Fletcher-Powell algorithm [10] in Step 1, 2 and 3.

In the experiment the image we used is a Venus statue which is made up of curved surfaces shown in Fig. 5. The experiment was performed by using the image of size 71×51 shown in Fig. 6 which is the right eye of the Venus statue in Fig. 5. In Step 1 of the three-step optimization procedure we give the initial guess of the parameters of illumination direction and the reflection parameters as $\theta = 2.98[rad]$, $\varphi = 0.95[rad]$, $\rho = 0.407$ and $c = 0.317$, which are obtained by the preparatory calibration experiment.

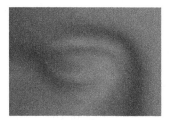

Fig. 5. Venus statue consisted of curved surfaces.

Fig. 6. Real images of the right eye of the Venus statue.

Figure 7 shows the recovered surface obtained by the proposed method. In the lower part of the figure the contour map of the surface is shown. Figure 8 shows the recovered surface obtained by the model inclusive learning method without estimating the unknown parameters l (θ and φ), ρ and c, that is, only the Step 1 is performed until it converges. It is observed by comparing those figures that the result of Fig. 7 can captures the fine structure much more than that of Fig. 8, which reveals the effectiveness of the proposed model inclusive learning method with simultaneous estimation of unknown parameters. Figure 9 shows an example of the convergence behavior of the proposed learning method in which the result in Fig. 7 is obtained, and Fig. 10 shows that in which the result in Fig. 8 is obtained. In those figures the variations of the performance index J versus the number of the learning iterations are plotted. It can be seen that the value of J in Fig. 9 converges to the value much smaller than that in

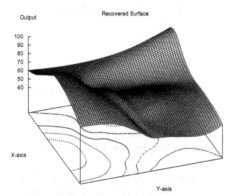

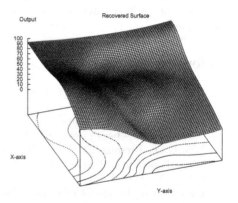

Fig. 7. Recovered eye-surface obtained by the proposed method.

Fig. 8. Recovered eye-surface obtained by the method without estimating the unknown parameters.

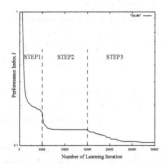

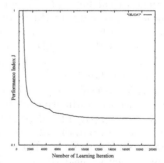

Fig. 9. An example of convergence behaviour of J during the learning iteration obtained by the proposed method.

Fig. 10. An example of convergence behaviour of J during the learning iteration obtained by the method without estimating the unknown parameters.

Fig. 10. Note that the value of J in Fig. 9 begins to decrease again just after the optimization iteration switches from Step 1 to 2 and also from Step 2 to 3 although it converges during the previous step. This fact reveals the effectiveness of the proposed three-step optimization procedure.

6   Conclusion

The problem of recovering shape from shading is important in computer vision and robotics and many studies have been done. This paper presented a versatile method of solving the problem by neural networks introducing the concept of the model inclusive learning with simultaneous estimation of unknown parameters. In order to realize recovering shape and estimating parameters simultaneously we proposed a method of dividing the learning procedure into three steps and determining the order of those steps based on the sensitivity analysis of parameters. The performance of the proposed method was demonstrated through experiments.

References

1. Horn, B.K.P., Brooks, M.J. (eds.): Shape from Shading. The MIT Press, Cambridge (1989)
2. Klette, R., et al.: Computer Vision: Three-Dimensional Data From Images. Springer, Heidelberg (1998). pp. 263–345
3. Wei, G.Q., Hirzinger, G.: Learning shape from shading by a multilayer network. IEEE Trans. Neural Netw. **7**(4), 985–995 (1996)
4. Kuroe, Y., Kawakami, H.: Versatile neural network method for recovering shape from shading by model inclusive learning. In: Proceedings of International Joint Conference on Neural Networks, pp. 3194–3199 (2011)
5. Kuroe, Y., Kawakami, H.: Estimation method of motion fields from images by model inclusive learning of neural networks. In: Alippi, C., Polycarpou, M., Panayiotou, C., Ellinas, G. (eds.) ICANN 2009. LNCS, vol. 5769, pp. 673–683. Springer, Heidelberg (2009). doi:10.1007/978-3-642-04277-5_68
6. Kuroe, Y., Kawakami, H.: Shape from shading by model inclusive learning with simultaneously estimating reflection parameters. In: Wermter, S., Weber, C., Duch, W., Honkela, T., Koprinkova-Hristova, P., Magg, S., Palm, G., Villa, A.E.P. (eds.) ICANN 2014. LNCS, vol. 8681, pp. 443–450. Springer, Cham (2014). doi:10.1007/978-3-319-11179-7_56
7. Kuroe, Y., Kawakami, H.: Model inclusive learning for shape from shading with simultaneously estimating illumination directions. In: Arik, S., Huang, T., Lai, W.K., Liu, Q. (eds.) ICONIP 2015. LNCS, vol. 9489, pp. 501–511. Springer, Cham (2015). doi:10.1007/978-3-319-26532-2_55
8. Kuroe, Y., Nakai, Y., Mori, T.: A learning method of nonlinear mappings by neural networks with considering their derivatives. In: Proceedings of the IJCNN, Nagoya, Japan, pp. 528–531 (1993)
9. Torrance, K.E., Sparrow, E.M.: Theory for off-specular reflection from roughened surfaces. J. Opt. Soc. Am. **57**(9), 1105–1114 (1967)
10. Luenberger, D.G.: Introduction to Linear and Nonlinear Programming. Addison-Wesley, Boston (1973). pp. 194–197

Radius-Margin Ratio Optimization for Dot-Product Boolean Kernel Learning

Ivano Lauriola$^{(\boxtimes)}$, Mirko Polato, and Fabio Aiolli

Department of Mathematics, University of Padova,
Via Trieste, 63, 35121 Padova, Italy
ivanolauriola@gmail.com, {mpolato,aiolli}@math.unipd.it

Abstract. It is known that any dot-product kernel can be seen as a linear non-negative combination of homogeneous polynomial kernels. In this paper, we demonstrate that, under mild conditions, any dot-product kernel defined on binary valued data can be seen as a linear non-negative combination of boolean kernels, specifically, monotone conjunctive kernels (mC-kernels) with different degrees. We also propose a new radius-margin based multiple kernel learning (MKL) algorithm to learn the parameters of the combination. An empirical analysis of the MKL weights distribution shows that our method is able to give solutions which are more sparse and effective compared to the ones of state-of-the-art margin-based MKL methods. The empirical analysis have been performed on eleven UCI categorical datasets.

Keywords: Multiple kernel learning · Radius-margin optimization · Boolean kernels

1 Introduction

In the context of kernel machines, the choice of the kernel function is a key step to build good predictors. Kernel learning (KL), and the multiple kernel learning (MKL) paradigm in particular, aims at learning the best representation, i.e., the kernel function, directly from data. In the case of MKL, the used kernel is a combination of many base kernels. There exists several methods for combining kernels. In this paper, we consider only linear non-negative combinations of base kernels, in the form $\kappa(\mathbf{x}, \mathbf{z}) = \sum_{r=0}^{R} \mu_r \kappa_r(\mathbf{x}, \mathbf{z})$, $\mu_r \geq 0$.

Learning is usually supported by a validation step, where a user estimates the effectiveness of different kernels on a subset of training data, namely the validation set. More recently, alternative criteria have been proposed to estimate the goodness of a representation [4]. An important example of these strategies is the minimization of the radius-margin bound [2], that is the ratio between the radius of the minimum enclosing ball (MEB) and the margin observed on training data. In [5], for example, this strategy has been used for MKL optimization.

It is well known [3,8] that any *dot-product kernel* (DPK) of the form $\kappa(\mathbf{x}, \mathbf{z}) = f(\langle \mathbf{x}, \mathbf{z} \rangle)$ can be seen as a *dot product polynomial* (DPP), that is a non-negative linear combination of *homogeneous polynomial kernels* (HP-kernels),

© Springer International Publishing AG 2017
A. Lintas et al. (Eds.): ICANN 2017, Part II, LNCS 10614, pp. 183–191, 2017.
https://doi.org/10.1007/978-3-319-68612-7_21

i.e., $\kappa(\mathbf{x}, \mathbf{z}) = \sum_{d=0}^{D} a_d \langle \mathbf{x}, \mathbf{z} \rangle^d$, with appropriate coefficients $a_d \geq 0$. Recently, it has been shown that it is possible to generalize any DPK by making this combination non-parametric and by optimizing the coefficients a_d from data via a maximum margin MKL algorithm in both binary [3] and multiclass [6] contexts.

A first important contribution of the present paper is an extension of the above-mentioned result in the case of boolean input vectors $\mathbf{x}, \mathbf{z} \in \{0, 1\}^n$. Specifically, we demonstrate that any DPK defined on boolean vectors can be seen as a non-negative linear combination of *monotone conjunctive kernels* (mC-kernels) of different degrees. The mC-kernel of degree d basically counts the number of common true d-degree (positive) conjunctions of variables in the two input vectors and can be easily computed by a binomial coefficient $\kappa_{\wedge}^d(\mathbf{x}, \mathbf{z}) = \binom{\langle \mathbf{x}, \mathbf{z} \rangle}{d}$. The combination is referred to as *monotone conjunctive kernel polynomial* (mCKP).

Similarly to [3], here we propose to optimize the coefficients of a general mCKP via MKL. However, in our case, we propose a new gradient-descent method able to effectively minimize the exact radius-margin ratio. A similar kind of minimization have been proposed in [5] for MKL. However, in that work, different approximations were made to make the problem tractable.

We compare the proposed MKL algorithm (here dubbed RM-GD) in terms of AUC and the obtained radius-margin ratio on several categorical datasets, against two MKL baselines. Interestingly, we observed that, in almost every dataset, the distribution of the weights obtained by our MKL algorithm is very sparse and typically picked around two (one low degree and one high degree) mC-kernels. Hence, we refine our proposal by giving another simpler version of the algorithm that combines just one conjunctive kernel of a given degree with the identity matrix. This version has the advantage to be easily parallelizable.

2   Notation and Background

Let $\mathbf{X} \in \{0, 1\}^{l \times n}$ be the binary training matrix, and let $\mathbf{y} \in \{+1, -1\}^l$ be the vector of labels. We denote by $\kappa_{\wedge}^d(\mathbf{x}, \mathbf{z}) = \binom{\langle \mathbf{x}, \mathbf{z} \rangle}{d}$ and $\kappa_{HP}^d(\mathbf{x}, \mathbf{z}) = \langle \mathbf{x}, \mathbf{z} \rangle^d$ the d-degree monotone conjunctive kernel (mC-kernel) and the d-degree homogeneous polynomial kernel (HP-kernel) between $\mathbf{x}$ and $\mathbf{z}$, respectively.

The normalized version of a given kernel κ, here denoted $\tilde{\kappa}$, can also be considered. Note that, when needed, it can be easily computed by means of the well-known formula $\tilde{\kappa}(\mathbf{x}, \mathbf{z}) = \kappa(\mathbf{x}, \mathbf{z}) / \sqrt{\kappa(\mathbf{x}, \mathbf{x}) \kappa(\mathbf{z}, \mathbf{z})}$.

Given a training kernel matrix $\mathbf{K}$ such that $\mathbf{K}_{i,j} = \kappa(\mathbf{x}_i, \mathbf{x}_j)$, it can be shown that the margin obtained by a (hard-margin) SVM using that kernel can be computed as $\rho^2 = \min_{\gamma \in \Gamma} \gamma^\top \mathbf{Y} \mathbf{K} \mathbf{Y} \gamma$, where $\mathbf{Y}$ is the diagonal matrix of training labels $\mathbf{Y} = diag(\mathbf{y})$ and $\Gamma = \{\gamma \in \mathbb{R}_+^l \mid \sum_{i:y_i=+1} \gamma_i = 1 \wedge \sum_{i:y_i=-1} \gamma_i = 1\}$.

Furthermore, it can be seen that, when a kernel is normalized, the radius of the MEB enclosing training data in feature space can be obtained by solving $R^2 = 1 - \min_{\alpha \in \mathcal{A}} \alpha^\top \mathbf{K} \alpha$ where $\mathcal{A} = \{\alpha \in \mathbb{R}_+^l, \sum_i \alpha_i = 1\}$.

Finally, given $\mathbf{x} \in \mathbb{R}^n$ and $\mathbf{p} \in \mathbb{N}_0^n$, the symbol $\mathbf{x}^\mathbf{p}$ will denote the product among variables exponentiated component-wise, that is $\mathbf{x}^\mathbf{p} = x_1^{p_1}, \ldots, x_n^{p_n}$.

3   DPKs as Linear Combinations of mC-kernels

The feature space of the HP-kernel of a given degree d is formed by all the monomials of degree d, each weighted by some coefficient. When the input vectors are binary, then many of these monomials collide in a single value, since the factors of the monomials x_i^p will have the same value for every $p \geq 1$. This observation allows us to give the following results concerning the relationship between HP-kernels and mC-kernels.

Theorem 1. *Given* $\mathbf{x}, \mathbf{z} \in \{0,1\}^n$, *then any HP-kernel can be decomposed as a finite non-negative linear combination of mC-kernels (a mCKP) of the form:*

$$\kappa_{HP}^d(\mathbf{x}, \mathbf{z}) = \sum_{s=0}^{d} h(s,d)\, \kappa_{\wedge}^s(\mathbf{x}, \mathbf{z}), \qquad h(s,d) \geq 0.$$

Proof. Given $\mathbf{x}, \mathbf{z} \in \{0,1\}^n$, by definition:

$$\kappa_{\wedge}^s(\mathbf{x}, \mathbf{z}) = \binom{\langle \mathbf{x}, \mathbf{z} \rangle}{s} = \sum_{\mathbf{b} \in \mathbb{B}_s} \mathbf{x}^{\mathbf{b}} \mathbf{z}^{\mathbf{b}} \tag{1}$$

where $\mathbb{B}_s \equiv \{\mathbf{b} \in \{0,1\}^n \mid \|\mathbf{b}\|_1 = s\}$. Moreover, we have:

$$\kappa_{HP}^d(\mathbf{x}, \mathbf{z}) = \langle \mathbf{x}, \mathbf{z} \rangle^d = \left(\sum_{i=1}^{n} x_i z_i\right)^d = \sum_{\mathbf{p} \in \mathbb{P}_d} \underbrace{\left(d! \prod_{p_i \in \mathbf{p}} \frac{1}{p_i!}\right)}_{q(\mathbf{p},d)} \mathbf{x}^{\mathbf{p}} \mathbf{z}^{\mathbf{p}} = \sum_{\mathbf{p} \in \mathbb{P}_d} q(\mathbf{p},d) \mathbf{x}^{\mathbf{p}} \mathbf{z}^{\mathbf{p}}, \tag{2}$$

with $\mathbb{P}_d \equiv \{\mathbf{p} \in \mathbb{N}_0^n \mid \|\mathbf{p}\|_1 = d\}$. Hence, Eq. 2 can be written as

$$\kappa_{HP}^d(\mathbf{x}, \mathbf{z}) = \sum_{s=0}^{d} \sum_{\mathbf{p} \in \mathbb{P}_d^s} q(\mathbf{p},d) \mathbf{x}^{\mathbf{p}} \mathbf{z}^{\mathbf{p}}, \tag{3}$$

where $\mathbb{P}_d^s \equiv \{\mathbf{p} \in \mathbb{P}_d \mid \sum_{i=1}^{n} [\![p_i > 0]\!] = s\}$ and $[\![\cdot]\!]$ the indicator function.

Let us now partition the set $\mathbb{P}_d^s$ in such a way to have two vectors taken from $\mathbb{P}_d^s$ in the same class of equivalence if and only if they share the same components greater than zero. Specifically, given $\mathbf{b} \in \mathbb{B}_s$, then $\mathbb{P}_d^s(\mathbf{b}) \equiv \{\mathbf{p} \in \mathbb{P}_d^s \mid \forall i : p_i > 0 \iff b_i = 1\}$. With this notation, we can rewrite Eq. 3 as:

$$\kappa_{HP}^d(\mathbf{x}, \mathbf{z}) = \sum_{s=0}^{d} \sum_{\mathbf{b} \in \mathbb{B}_s} \mathbf{x}^{\mathbf{b}} \mathbf{z}^{\mathbf{b}} \sum_{\mathbf{p} \in \mathbb{P}_d^s(\mathbf{b})} q(\mathbf{p},d). \tag{4}$$

Now, we can observe that, when s is fixed, then $\sum_{\mathbf{p} \in \mathbb{P}_d^s(\mathbf{b})} q(\mathbf{p},d)$ is constant over the elements $\mathbf{b} \in \mathbb{B}_s$. This is because the terms of the summations are the same. So, by taking any representative $\mathbf{b}_s \in \mathbb{B}_s$, we can rewrite Eq. 4 as:

$$\kappa_{HP}^d(\mathbf{x}, \mathbf{z}) = \sum_{s=0}^{d} \underbrace{\left(\sum_{\mathbf{p} \in \mathbb{P}_d^s(\mathbf{b}_s)} q(\mathbf{p},d)\right)}_{h(s,d)} \left(\sum_{\mathbf{b} \in \mathbb{B}_s} \mathbf{x}^{\mathbf{b}} \mathbf{z}^{\mathbf{b}}\right) = \sum_{s=0}^{d} h(s,d)\, \kappa_{\wedge}^s(\mathbf{x}, \mathbf{z}). \qquad \blacksquare$$

In the following we will show that, assuming boolean input vectors with the same number of active variables, a similar result of Theorem 1 also holds when using normalized monotone conjunctive kernels.

Theorem 2. *Given* $\mathbf{x}, \mathbf{z} \in \{0,1\}^n$ *such that* $\|\mathbf{x}\|_1 = \|\mathbf{z}\|_1 = m$, *then any HP-kernel can be decomposed as a finite non-negative linear combination of normalized mC-kernels, that is:*

$$\kappa_{HP}^d(\mathbf{x}, \mathbf{z}) = \sum_{s=0}^{d} h(m, s, d) \, \widetilde{\kappa}_{\wedge}^s(\mathbf{x}, \mathbf{z}), \qquad h(m, s, d) \geq 0.$$

Proof. Consider the normalized mC-kernel, defined as follows:

$$\widetilde{\kappa}_{\wedge}^s(\mathbf{x}, \mathbf{z}) = \frac{\binom{\langle \mathbf{x}, \mathbf{z} \rangle}{s}}{\binom{\langle \mathbf{x}, \mathbf{x} \rangle}{s}^{\frac{1}{2}} \binom{\langle \mathbf{z}, \mathbf{z} \rangle}{s}^{\frac{1}{2}}}.$$

Since we assume $\|\mathbf{x}\|_1 = \|\mathbf{z}\|_1 = m$, we can write:

$$\widetilde{\kappa}_{\wedge}^s(\mathbf{x}, \mathbf{z}) = \frac{\binom{\langle \mathbf{x}, \mathbf{z} \rangle}{s}}{\binom{m}{s}^{\frac{1}{2}} \binom{m}{s}^{\frac{1}{2}}} = \frac{1}{\binom{m}{s}} \kappa_{\wedge}^s(\mathbf{x}, \mathbf{z})$$

where we used the fact that for binary vectors $\| \cdot \|_1 = \| \cdot \|_2^2$ always holds and hence, by Theorem 1 we can conclude:

$$\kappa_{HP}^d(\mathbf{x}, \mathbf{z}) = \sum_{s=0}^{d} \underbrace{h(s, d) \binom{m}{d}}_{h(m,s,d)} \widetilde{\kappa}_{\wedge}^s(\mathbf{x}, \mathbf{z}) = \sum_{s=0}^{d} h(m, s, d) \, \widetilde{\kappa}_{\wedge}^s(\mathbf{x}, \mathbf{z}).$$

■

As discussed by Donini and Aiolli in [3], under mild conditions, any DPK of the form $\kappa(\mathbf{x}, \mathbf{z}) = f(\langle \mathbf{x}, \mathbf{z} \rangle)$ can be seen as a DPP, that is $\kappa(\mathbf{x}, \mathbf{z}) = \sum_{d=0}^{+\infty} a_d \kappa_{HP}^d(\mathbf{x}, \mathbf{z})$. Exploiting this result and the theorems above, we can get the following corollary.

Corollary 1. *Given* $\mathbf{x}, \mathbf{z} \in \{0,1\}^n$ *such that* $\|\mathbf{x}\|_1 = \|\mathbf{z}\|_1 = m$, *then any DPK can be decomposed as a finite non-negative linear combination of normalized mC-kernels:*

$$\kappa(\mathbf{x}, \mathbf{z}) = f(\langle \mathbf{x}, \mathbf{z} \rangle) = \sum_{s=0}^{m} g(m, s) \, \widetilde{\kappa}_{\wedge}^s(\mathbf{x}, \mathbf{z}), \qquad g(m, s) \geq 0$$

Proof (sketch). By using Theorem 1 we can see that $\kappa_{HP}^d(\mathbf{x}, \mathbf{z})$ can always be seen as a non-negative linear combination of the first m mC-kernels (since $\kappa_{\wedge}^s(\mathbf{x}, \mathbf{z}) = 0$ always holds when $s > m$). Hence, using the result in [3] and Theorem 2, the claim can be easily demonstrated.

■

4 The Proposed Algorithm

In the previous section we have shown that any DPK defined on binary vectors can be seen as a parametric linear combination of mC-kernels (a mCKP). In this section, we propose to make the combination non-parametric and to learn the coefficients of the mCKP by optimizing the radius-margin ratio of the combined kernel. Basically, we search on the kernel space $\kappa(\mathbf{x}, \mathbf{z}) = \sum_s^d \mu_s \tilde{\kappa}_\wedge^s(\mathbf{x}, \mathbf{z})$, where $\mu_s \geq 0$, $\sum_s \mu_s = 1$ are the parameters to optimize. In this space we want to obtain the kernel that minimizes the radius-margin ratio.

First of all, we perform a change of variables by introducing a new vector of variables $\boldsymbol{\beta}$ and replacing $\mu_s(\boldsymbol{\beta}) = e^{\beta_s}/(\sum_r e^{\beta_r})$. This allows us to obtain an unconstrained problem easier to optimize. Specifically, we are now able to write the radius-margin ratio minimization problem as in the following:

$$
\min_{\boldsymbol{\beta}} \Psi(\boldsymbol{\beta}), \text{ where } \Psi(\boldsymbol{\beta}) = \frac{1 - \hat{\boldsymbol{\alpha}}(\boldsymbol{\beta})^\top \left(\sum_{r=1}^R \mu_r(\boldsymbol{\beta})\mathbf{K}_r\right) \hat{\boldsymbol{\alpha}}(\boldsymbol{\beta})}{\hat{\boldsymbol{\gamma}}(\boldsymbol{\beta})^\top \mathbf{Y} \left(\sum_{r=1}^R \mu_r(\boldsymbol{\beta})\mathbf{K}_r\right) \mathbf{Y}\hat{\boldsymbol{\gamma}}(\boldsymbol{\beta})},
$$

$$
\hat{\boldsymbol{\alpha}}(\boldsymbol{\beta}) = \arg\min_{\boldsymbol{\alpha}\in\mathcal{A}} \boldsymbol{\alpha}^\top \left(\sum_{r=1}^R \mu_r(\boldsymbol{\beta})\mathbf{K}_r\right) \boldsymbol{\alpha} \text{ and } \hat{\boldsymbol{\gamma}}(\boldsymbol{\beta}) = \arg\min_{\boldsymbol{\gamma}\in\Gamma} \boldsymbol{\gamma}^\top \mathbf{Y} \left(\sum_{r=1}^R \mu_r(\boldsymbol{\beta})\mathbf{K}_r\right) \mathbf{Y}\boldsymbol{\gamma}.
$$

By definition $\sum_{r=1}^R \mu_r(\boldsymbol{\beta}) = 1$, so

$$
\Psi(\boldsymbol{\beta}) = \frac{\sum_{r=1}^R e^{\beta_r} \overbrace{\left(1 - \hat{\boldsymbol{\alpha}}(\boldsymbol{\beta})^\top \mathbf{K}_r \hat{\boldsymbol{\alpha}}(\boldsymbol{\beta})\right)}^{a_r(\boldsymbol{\beta})}}{\sum_{r=1}^R e^{\beta_r} \underbrace{\left(\hat{\boldsymbol{\gamma}}(\boldsymbol{\beta})^\top \mathbf{Y}\mathbf{K}_r \mathbf{Y}\hat{\boldsymbol{\gamma}}(\boldsymbol{\beta})\right)}_{b_r(\boldsymbol{\beta})}} \approx \frac{\langle e^{\boldsymbol{\beta}}, \mathbf{a}\rangle}{\langle e^{\boldsymbol{\beta}}, \mathbf{b}\rangle} = \bar{\Psi}(\boldsymbol{\beta}),
$$

where $e^{\boldsymbol{\beta}} = [e^{\beta_1}, \ldots, e^{\beta_R}]$, $\mathbf{a} = [a_1, a_2, \ldots, a_R]^\top$, $\mathbf{b} = [b_1, b_2, \ldots, b_R]^\top$ and we assume $\mathbf{a}, \mathbf{b}$ constants around a given $\boldsymbol{\beta}$. In order to optimize the function $\Psi(\boldsymbol{\beta})$ we then perform a series of steps of gradient descent on the approximated function $\bar{\Psi}(\boldsymbol{\beta})$ followed by a new computation of $\mathbf{a} = \mathbf{a}(\boldsymbol{\beta})$, and $\mathbf{b} = \mathbf{b}(\boldsymbol{\beta})$. The gradient step can be easily found as $\forall r \in \{1, \ldots, R\}$ we have the following:

$$
\frac{\partial \bar{\Psi}(\boldsymbol{\beta})}{\partial \beta_r} = \frac{a_r e^{\beta_r}\langle e^{\boldsymbol{\beta}}, \mathbf{b}\rangle - b_r e^{\beta_r}\langle e^{\boldsymbol{\beta}}, \mathbf{a}\rangle}{\langle e^{\boldsymbol{\beta}}, \mathbf{b}\rangle^2} = \frac{e^{\beta_r}(a_r\langle e^{\boldsymbol{\beta}}, \mathbf{b}\rangle - b_r\langle e^{\boldsymbol{\beta}}, \mathbf{a}\rangle)}{\langle e^{\boldsymbol{\beta}}, \mathbf{b}\rangle^2}
$$

Summarizing, starting from $\boldsymbol{\beta} = \mathbf{0}$ and $\boldsymbol{\mu}(\boldsymbol{\beta})$ the uniform distribution over base kernels, at each iteration, the kernel combination $\mathbf{K}$ is computed using the current $\boldsymbol{\mu}(\boldsymbol{\beta})$ and then the vectors $\mathbf{a} = \mathbf{a}(\boldsymbol{\beta})$ and $\mathbf{b} = \mathbf{b}(\boldsymbol{\beta})$ can be computed as described above. Finally, the update of $\boldsymbol{\beta}$ and $\boldsymbol{\mu}(\boldsymbol{\beta})$ are performed as follows:

$$
\beta_r \leftarrow \beta_r - \eta \frac{e^{\beta_r}\sum_s e^{\beta_s}(a_r b_s - a_s b_r)}{\langle e^{\boldsymbol{\beta}}, \mathbf{b}\rangle^2} \quad \forall r \in \{1, \ldots, R\}, \qquad \boldsymbol{\mu} \leftarrow \frac{1}{\sum_r e^{\beta_r}} e^{\boldsymbol{\beta}}
$$

where η is the learning rate. This iterative procedure continues until a maximum number of iterations (max_iter) is reached.

5   Experimental Assessment

Experiments have been performed using 11 binary and categorical datasets obtained from the UCI Machine Learning Repository [7]. The datasets have different sizes and characteristics, which are reported in Table 1. A preprocessing phase has been performed to make all these datasets binary. In particular, categorical features have been mapped into binary features by *one-hot* encoding, examples with missing values have been removed, and multiclass problems (audiology, zoo, primary-tumor, soybean, dna) transformed to binary ones by manually splitting the original classes in two groups. Different MKL settings for the combination of normalized mC-kernels have been compared. Namely:

Table 1. AUC score (1st row) and radius-margin ratio (2nd row) for all the methods. In the case of $K_{C,id}^{RM-GD}$ the average parameters obtained in validation, i.e. average of degrees and average of the weights given to the identity matrix, are also indicated. For each dataset, in parenthesis, the information about #examples, #features and type of the dataset: binary ('b') or categorical ('c').

Dataset	K_C^{avg}	K_C^{MKL}	K_C^{RM-GD}	$K_{C,id}^{RM-GD}$
audiology	$99.99_{\pm0.04}$	$99.99_{\pm0.04}$	$100.00_{\pm0.00}$	$100.00_{\pm0.00}(2.64, 0.0023)$
(92,84,c)	$6.08_{\pm0.33}$	$5.99_{\pm0.32}$	$5.38_{\pm0.25}$	$5.41_{\pm0.25}$
zoo	$100.00_{\pm0.00}$	$100.00_{\pm0.00}$	$100.00_{\pm0.00}$	$100.00_{\pm0.00}(2.10, 0.0021)$
(101,21,c)	$3.01_{\pm0.23}$	$2.62_{\pm0.28}$	$2.24_{\pm0.32}$	$2.27_{\pm0.34}$
promoters	$96.37_{\pm1.99}$	$96.38_{\pm1.96}$	$95.83_{\pm1.93}$	$95.82_{\pm1.95}(1.00, 0.0068)$
(106,228,c)	$11.27_{\pm0.25}$	$11.02_{\pm0.32}$	$8.77_{\pm0.63}$	$8.79_{\pm0.65}$
primary-tumor	$72.55_{\pm4.37}$	$72.69_{\pm4.30}$	$74.58_{\pm4.58}$	$75.53_{\pm4.76}(1.38, 0.7079)$
(132,24,c)	$15.87_{\pm1.30}$	$15.05_{\pm0.87}$	$14.31_{\pm0.72}$	$14.37_{\pm0.69}$
house-votes	$99.11_{\pm0.41}$	$99.10_{\pm0.42}$	$99.20_{\pm0.41}$	$99.21_{\pm0.45}(2.30, 0.1992)$
(232,16,b)	$8.90_{\pm1.13}$	$8.90_{\pm1.17}$	$8.49_{\pm1.13}$	$8.60_{\pm1.12}$
soybean	$99.73_{\pm0.19}$	$99.73_{\pm0.19}$	$99.70_{\pm0.25}$	$99.69_{\pm0.25}(3.30, 0.0008)$
(266,88,c)	$11.49_{\pm0.73}$	$11.32_{\pm0.82}$	$10.86_{\pm0.96}$	$10.93_{\pm0.98}$
spect	$82.01_{\pm3.14}$	$82.06_{\pm3.02}$	$83.39_{\pm3.10}$	$83.81_{\pm3.11}(1.04, 0.5154)$
(267,23,b)	$18.91_{\pm1.32}$	$18.56_{\pm1.15}$	$17.53_{\pm1.08}$	$17.63_{\pm1.09}$
tic-tac-toe	$98.82_{\pm0.46}$	$99.04_{\pm0.39}$	$99.74_{\pm0.20}$	$99.76_{\pm0.20}(4.00, 0.0001)$
(958,27,c)	$73.39_{\pm1.57}$	$70.93_{\pm1.45}$	$60.75_{\pm1.49}$	$60.92_{\pm1.61}$
dna-bin	$98.46_{\pm0.21}$	$98.53_{\pm0.20}$	$98.71_{\pm0.18}$	$98.69_{\pm0.18}(2.00, 0.0001)$
(2000,180,b)	$118.49_{\pm1.98}$	$108.87_{\pm2.46}$	$103.45_{\pm2.43}$	$104.16_{\pm2.53}$
splice	$98.98_{\pm0.13}$	$99.04_{\pm0.12}$	$99.14_{\pm0.15}$	$99.08_{\pm0.13}(2.00, 0.0001)$
(3175,240,c)	$195.50_{\pm2.13}$	$143.85_{\pm2.99}$	$133.39_{\pm3.26}$	$134.35_{\pm3.30}$
kr-vs-kp	$99.90_{\pm0.05}$	$99.91_{\pm0.04}$	$99.92_{\pm0.04}$	$99.95_{\pm0.04}(3.80, 0.090)$
(3196,38,c)	$109.84_{\pm2.75}$	$109.19_{\pm2.89}$	$107.92_{\pm2.95}$	$112.28_{\pm2.79}$

- K_C^{avg}: the average of normalized mC-kernels of degrees 1 to 10, that is $\forall r, \mu_r = \frac{1}{10}$;
- K_C^{MKL}: the MKL solution where coefficients $\boldsymbol{\mu}$ are computed by the EasyMKL method [1] on normalized mC-kernels of degrees 1 to 10;
- $K_C^{RM\text{-}GD}$: the MKL solution of the gradient descent based algorithm proposed in this paper for the minimization of the radius-margin ratio when combining normalized mC-kernels of degrees 1 to 10;

For each MKL method, an SVM model has been trained using the obtained kernel. Available data have been split into training (50%) and test (50%); training data has been used to select the kernel and fit the SVM, then the AUC score has been calculated on the test set. To improve the statistical significance of the results, for each method, 50 runs with different splits (the same set for all the methods) have been performed. The average AUC in the test sets and the average ratio obtained in the training sets are reported in Table 1. Results show a significant AUC improvement of the proposed methodology $K_C^{RM\text{-}GD}$ with respect to MKL baselines, for the large majority of tasks.

In order to better evaluate the behaviour of the proposed algorithm for the radius-margin optimization, in Fig. 1 the distribution of weights is reported with

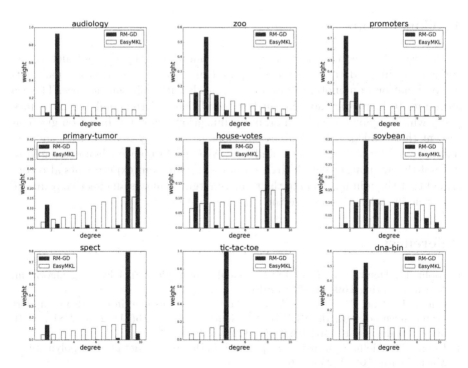

Fig. 1. Distribution of the weights obtained by EasyMKL (in white) and RM-GD (in blue) when combining mC-kernels of degrees 1 to 10 on nine UCI datasets. (Color figure online)

respect to the one of EasyMKL, a MKL algorithm which aims at maximizing the margin alone. From the figure it is self-evident that margin maximization can give very different results with respect to the minimization of the radius-margin ratio. We observe that the weight vectors learned by our algorithm are very sparse, and hence only a small subset of kernels are combined to form the final kernel. The most typical configuration sets only two coefficients with large values, one low degree mC-kernel and one high degree mC-kernel.

Given the considerations above, we tried to apply the same gradient-descent radius-margin ratio optimization algorithm using only one non trivial mC-kernel combined with the identity matrix (note that high degree mC-kernels approximates the identity matrix). The optimal degree of the mC-kernel to combine is then chosen by selecting the one with the best ratio of the combined kernel. The obtained results, together with the average parameter selected in validation (the degree of the mC-kernel selected and the weight given to the identity matrix), are presented in the last column of Table 1. Not surprisingly, the obtained ratio is always worse than the ratio obtained by considering all the kernels at once. However, the difference is not so significant and the AUC score obtained by this simplified method is comparable, with the advantage of being highly parallelizable.

6   Conclusions

In this work we showed that, under mild conditions, any dot-product kernel applied to binary data can be decomposed in a linear non-negative parametric combination of monotone conjunctive kernels with different degrees. Then, a procedure to learn the (non-parametric) coefficients of the combination is proposed which exploits a radius-margin optimization algorithm based on gradient descent (here called RM-GD). The solutions returned by RM-GD are generally characterized by high sparseness and high AUC performance when compared to state-of-the-art margin-based MKL methods. Finally, our experiments also confirmed that the minimization of the radius-margin bound is an effective principle to pursue in order to minimize the expected test error.

References

1. Aiolli, F., Donini, M.: EasyMKL: a scalable multiple kernel learning algorithm. Neurocomputing **169**, 215–224 (2015)
2. Chung, K., Kao, W., Sun, C., Wang, L., Lin, C.: Radius margin bounds for support vector machines with the RBF kernel. Neural Comput. **15**(11), 2643–2681 (2003). http://dx.doi.org/10.1162/089976603322385108
3. Donini, M., Aiolli, F.: Learning deep kernels in the space of dot product polynomials. Mach. Learn. **106**, 1–25 (2016)
4. Duan, K., Keerthi, S.S., Poo, A.N.: Evaluation of simple performance measures for tuning SVM hyperparameters. Neurocomputing **51**(Complete), 41–59 (2003)

5. Kalousis, A., Do, H.T.: Convex formulations of radius-margin based support vector machines. In: Proceedings of the 30th International Conference on Machine Learning, vol. 28, pp. 169–177 (2013)
6. Lauriola, I., Donini, M., Aiolli, F.: Learning dot-product polynomials for multi-class problems. In: Proceedings of the European Symposium on Artificial Neural Networks, Computational Intelligence and Machine Learning (ESANN) (2017)
7. Lichman, M.: UCI machine learning repository (2013). http://archive.ics.uci.edu/ml
8. Schoenberg, I.J.: Positive definite functions on spheres. Duke Math. J. **9**(1), 96–108 (1942)

Learning a Compositional Hierarchy of Disparity Descriptors for 3D Orientation Estimation in an Active Fixation Setting

Katerina Kalou[1(✉)], Agostino Gibaldi[1,2],
Andrea Canessa[1], and Silvio P. Sabatini[1]

[1] Department of Informatics, Bioengineering, Robotics and System Engineering,
University of Genoa, Genoa, Italy
aikaterini.kalou@edu.unige.it
[2] School of Optometry, University of California, Berkeley, Berkeley, CA, USA

Abstract. Interaction with everyday objects requires by the active visual system a fast and invariant reconstruction of their local shape layout, through a series of fast binocular fixation movements that change the gaze direction on the 3-dimensional surface of the object. Active binocular viewing results in complex disparity fields that, although informative about the orientation in depth (e.g., the slant and tilt), highly depend on the relative position of the eyes. Assuming to learn the statistical relationships between the differential properties of the disparity vector fields and the gaze directions, we expect to obtain more convenient, gaze-invariant visual descriptors. In this work, local approximations of disparity vector field differentials are combined in a hierarchical neural network that is trained to represent the slant and tilt from the disparity vector fields. Each gaze-related cell's activation in the intermediate representation is recurrently merged with the other cells' activations to gain the desired gaze-invariant selectivity. Although the representation has been tested on a limited set of combinations of slant and tilt, the resulting high classification rate validates the generalization capability of the approach.

Keywords: Active vision · Binocular disparity · Gaze direction · Biologically-inspired neural networks

1 Introduction

Recovering the 3D layout of an object or a scene from images is a well formalized problem [3], which, provided a sufficiently dense disparity information, allows a full reconstruction of the scene. Typically, in 3D reconstruction one assumes a vision system with a fixed parallel optical axis binocular geometry yielding to binocular disparities along the horizontal epipolar lines; if necessary including a rectification stage of the stereo image pairs. This is not the case for natural binocular vision systems, where the stereo images are acquired by pairs of eyes that are highly mobile and that continuously explore the scene

© Springer International Publishing AG 2017
A. Lintas et al. (Eds.): ICANN 2017, Part II, LNCS 10614, pp. 192–199, 2017.
https://doi.org/10.1007/978-3-319-68612-7_22

in a vergent geometry, by changing the fixation point on the visible surfaces of the 3D external world [2]. A vergent stereo imaging geometry is a powerful means for focusing the attention of a vision system on a particular 3D region of interest. However, the price we pay is a more complex geometric relationship between binocular corresponding points. This is especially true for visual exploration of the peripersonal space where large values of vergence occur [4]. The zero-disparity condition at fixation, granted by vergence movements, directly influences the visually-based information for the 3D position and orientation of the fixated object. Only the residual disparities elsewhere in the visual field are cues for stereopsis. Moreover, also how the system verges has an impact for the accuracy of stereopsis. Different eye positions can influence the local shape of the zero disparity surface near the fixation point and thus the mechanisms of perceptual vision. The momentarily existing fixation point, i.e. where the system verges, becomes a reference that can be parameterized by the relative orientations of the eyes. From this perspective, it is plausible that the visual system develops convenient visual descriptors of 3D shapes, concurrently with the capability of making binocular exploratory fixations on the surface of the observed objects. Towards this goal, using the data collected from a biologically inspired simulator of an active binocular visual system, we propose a hierarchical neural architecture that, starting from local disparity fields of 3D planar surfaces, learns to extract a set of invariant feature maps for reconstructing the plane orientation in depth across a number of different gaze directions.

2   State of the Art

There are several evidences of disparity-based representation for 3D surface perception along the cortical visual pathway. Area V3A, a part of the higher primary visual stream, is associated with disparity processing for 3D shape perception in both human and primates [15]. Ban and Welchman [1] in an fMRI experiment reported a sensitivity to the relative disparity of planar surfaces slanted about the horizontal axis. Furthermore, the middle temporal area (MT) has been reported to be responsible for gradient disparity processing [12]. Overall, findings in a large number of exstrastriate cortical areas have shown that populations of neurons exhibit selective responses to 3D shape and orientation encoded on the basis of global differential properties of the binocular disparity of elongated surfaces in depth [6].

These findings demonstrate the sensitivity of visual cortical neurons to the disparity gradient components elicited by the local shape's orientation that cannot be explained by the conventional tuning for frontoparallel disparities. It is worth noting that the majority of the experimental studies on 3D shape-from-disparity and their computational modeling counterparts consider the horizontal disparity component, only. In the present study, we do consider the gradient of the 2D disparity vector field as it naturally arises in an active binocular system setup [5]. As proposed by Koenderick and van Doorn [7], using both the vertical and horizontal components of disparity allows us to compute the differential geometric transformations of the vector field: divergence (div), rotation

(rot) and the two components for shear (def_1 and def_2). These disparity transformations have been found to be invariant with the viewing geometry and the
environmental noise and thus, an ideal input for a method that learns a set of
disparity-based gaze-invariant features for 3D orientation reconstruction [8].

By exploiting the vector field information induced by the motion parallax,
Liu and van Hulle [9] trained a multilayered recurrent network to reconstruct
the slant and tilt of a 3D plane from its 2D projected motion vectors. Following
a similar paradigm, in the present work we propose a hierarchical recurrent
architecture of interconnected layers trained to discriminate among four planar
orientation categories from the four-dimensional inputs of the local differentials
of the input disparity vector field maps using a sampled dataset of nine different
gaze directions.

3   Methods

3.1   Simulating the 3D Environment and the Fixation Geometry

For the collection of the disparity patterns corresponding to different oriented
planes in 3D, we use an active vision simulator, that implements the biological
principles of cyclopean binocular geometry as described by Hansard and Horaud
[5] modeled in an ideal stereo head. The fixation point F_0 was initialized in space,
defined in a Cartesian coordinates fixed reference frame with $(X_0, Y_0, Z_0) =
[0, 0, 350]$ mm referenced on the cyclopean nodal point $N = [0, 0, 0]$ mm. The
initial cyclopean gaze direction was defined as the unit vector $u_0 = \frac{F_0}{|F_0|}$ that
defined the direction from point N to the fixation point F_0 (Fig. 1). The initial
azimuth and elevation angles were computed as $\tan \alpha_0 = \frac{-Y_0}{Z_0}$ and $\sin \epsilon_0 =
\frac{X_0}{Z_0}$ respectively. Each new gaze direction u was expressed as a new pair of
(α, ϵ) angles, leading to the computation of a new fixation point F. During the
simulation, 9 different gaze directions on the surface of the 3D plane u_L with
$L = [1, 2, ..., 9]$ were implemented, so as the fixation points F_L were sampled in
a clockwise order on a 3×3 rectangular grid of approximately $10° \times 10°$ visual
degrees around the initial fixation point. The parameters used in this study are:
baseline $b = 70$ mm, focal length $f = 17$ mm and field of view equal to $20°$ that
approximate the biological structure of the human visual system.

After the visual parameter setup, the 3D geometry of the scene was created
by the simulator as a planar mesh rotated in space with a center fixed in $P_0 =
(0, 0, 350)$ mm and a size of 502×502 mm ($\simeq 70° \times 70°$ visual degrees). This size
was chosen to cover the whole visual field for every condition of slant, tilt and
gaze direction. Each plane was built by the simulator as a union of all the points
P_i in this virtual space that satisfy the equation $\mathbf{P} = \{P_i : n^T(P_i - P_0) =
0\}$ where n is the normal vector of the plane. The plane's rotation space was
finally parameterized, as a matrix: $\mathbf{R}_{XYZ}(\theta\sigma\tau) = \mathbf{R}_{Z(\tau)}\,\mathbf{R}_{Y(\sigma)}\,\mathbf{R}_{X(\theta)}$ where the
torsion (θ), slant (σ) and tilt (τ) orientation angles were expressed as rotations
around a fixed $[X, Y, Z]$ world reference frame. The disparity vector field was
then computed for each σ, τ and gaze direction L while the torsion angle was

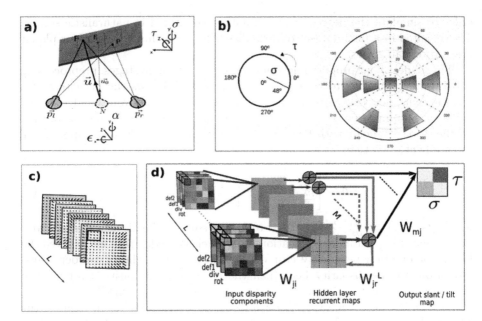

Fig. 1. The overall architecture of the model. (a): The active fixation geometry in the simulation environment with u representing the gaze direction characterized by the pair of elevation and azimuth angles (α, ϵ). (b): The planar 3D orientation parametric space where the slant (σ) and the tilt (τ) angles represent the latitude and longitude of a polar grid, respectively. (c): For each gaze direction L a disparity vector field is collected and transformed in the 4D elementary disparity field differentials, that were the input of a three layer recurrent network in (d) used for learning gaze-invariant disparity components in the slant/tilt parametric space.

kept at $\theta = 0$, as $\boldsymbol{\delta} = (\delta_H, \delta_V) = \boldsymbol{p}_l - \boldsymbol{p}_r$ where $p_l(x_l, y_l)$ and $p_r(x_r, y_r)$ are the two-dimensional projections of each of the points of the plane P on the left and right virtual eye, respectively.

3.2   Intermediate Representations

The input to the network was the disparity vector maps computed for the 144 unique sampling points of slant and tilt angles: 12 values of slant σ in the range $[3°, 42°]$ by steps of $3°$, and 12 values of tilt (τ) in the range $[30°, 330°]$ by steps of $30°$. Subsequently, such slant and tilt combinations were grouped into 4 categories of planar orientation samples so as to be used as the training set of our network. For each of the original 144 orientation points a 2D vector disparity map was computed with a 123×123 pixel ($\simeq 20° \times 20°$ visual degrees) resolution for each of the 9 different gaze directions - arrayed as inputs to the network with the same clockwise order as their spatial sampling on the 3×3 rectangular grid - resulting in a $2 \times 123 \times 123 \times 9$ training input vector. Furthermore, a white Gaussian noise (zero mean and $0 < \text{SD} < 1$) was added to the stimuli, in order to simulate the degree of uncertainty encountered in naturalistic setups. This resulted in a final dataset of 2880 disparity vector maps for all four planar orientation categories.

The model of our proposed network comprises two main stages: preprocessing and training. The preprocessing stage of our model follows the principles of a convolutional network with two non-trainable layers, a convolutional (c-layer) and a subsampling one (s-layer). The c-layer consists of a 2D spatial convolution on the disparity fields with Gaussian derivative kernels to locally approximate the gradient operation:

$$\nabla \boldsymbol{\delta} = \begin{bmatrix} \frac{\partial \delta_H}{\partial x} & \frac{\partial \delta_H}{\partial y} \\ \frac{\partial \delta_V}{\partial x} & \frac{\partial \delta_V}{\partial y} \end{bmatrix} \sim \begin{bmatrix} G_x * \delta_H & G_y * \delta_H \\ G_y * \delta_H & G_y * \delta_V \end{bmatrix} \tag{1}$$

where $(G_x, G_y) = (\frac{\partial G}{\partial x}, \frac{\partial G}{\partial y})$ are used to locally smooth the disparity derivatives. A Gaussian with a standard deviation of 12 pixels is used. Then, we followed the linear combination between vector differential to obtain the first-order transformations of the disparity field (i.e., the elementary disparity components): $\mathrm{div} = (\delta_H * G_x + \delta_V * G_y)/2$, $\mathrm{rot} = (\delta_V * G_y - \delta_H * G_y)/2$, $\mathrm{def}_1 = (\delta_H * G_x - \delta_V * G_y)/2$, and $\mathrm{def}_2 = (\delta_H * G_y + \delta_V * G_x)/2$. Each component was taken as an input to the s-layer where it was pooled by means of a 7×7 sliding Gaussian kernel resulting in the $5 \times 5 \times 4 \times 9$ dataset that was used as the input for the training module of the network. The data were finally normalized to have zero mean and $[-1\ 1]$ magnitude range, and divided in 70% and 30% for the training and test sets, respectively.

3.3   Training the Architecture

As shown in Fig. 1 the second stage of the network is a three-layer recurrent architecture with the input layer consisting of 9 diverse 4×4 hidden layer maps - one for each gaze direction. During the first step of the feed-forward process, each of the elementary disparity components 'gaze blocks' projects to its own hidden layer map with its own set of synaptic weights. The weights between each of the input units and their forward layer were initialized as a 2D Gaussian kernel acting as a smooth decreasing function of the distance between each input unit i and the respective hidden layer unit j; k refers to the specific disparity component:

$$W_{ji}^k = exp\left[-\left(\frac{(x_i^k - x_j)^2 + (y_i^k - y_j)^2}{2s^2}\right)\right] \tag{2}$$

where s models the size of the smoothing kernel.

Including the recurrent step, each hidden unit (h_j) receives an input from the activations a_r of all the units belonging to the same hidden layer map (i.e., gaze direction L) as well as the ones from the maps related to all the other gaze directions a_r^M, $M = 1, \ldots 9$, $M \neq L$. The intra-map weights W_{jr} as well as the weights W_{jr}^M between the different hidden unit maps were initialized as a difference of Gaussian functions, representing a pattern of localized excitatory and inhibitory synapses. As a whole, the activation function of each hidden layer unit j can be written as:

$$a_j = S \left(h_j + \sum_r W_{jr} a_r + \sum_{r,M} W_{jr}^M a_{rM} + b_j \right) \tag{3}$$

where $h_j = \sum_{i,k} W_{ji}^k z_i^k$ is the weighted sum of all the inputs z, $S(.)$ the sigmoid function and b_j the activation bias.

Finally, each hidden unit projects to the four output units encoding the possible combinations of slant and tilt plane orientation in an abstract parametric space. The weights W_{mj} between the hidden unit j and an output unit m were initialized with random positive values with uniform distribution and their activation was again characterized by the sigmoid function. At each iteration the weights were updated as: $W_{ji}^k \leftarrow W_{ji}^k + \lambda \frac{\partial E}{\partial W_{ji}^k}$, $W_{jr}^L \leftarrow W_{jr}^L + \lambda \frac{\partial E}{\partial W_{jr}^L}$, and $W_{mj} \leftarrow W_{mj} + \lambda \frac{\partial E}{\partial W_{mj}}$, until the logistic error E was below 0.1. The training algorithm was run for 500 iterations with a learning rate $\lambda = 0.2$. A modified version of the Backpropagation Through Time algorithm (BTT) is used to operate in batch mode as in Liu and van Hulle [9]. The BTT algorithm considers a special case of the general gradient descent backpropagation algorithm [13], where the weights are updated through a number of steps defined by the number of recurrent connections between their layers. For a given 3D orientation category, the desired output was 1 for the corresponding output unit and 0 for all other units (1-out-of-N coding).

4   Results and Conclusions

The accuracy of the algorithm at the end of training procedure, reached a level of 100% on the training and 94% on the test set. Since the random selection of the test data among the denoised data excludes any potential bias, the source of the 6% error is possibly the entrapment of the cost function in a local minima - a well known vulnerability of NN's with long recurrent temporal series [11]. Future work will include a probabilistic ordering of the gaze data series based on psychophysical data that will lead to a more informative representation of the 3D planar orientation across gaze directions.

Figure 2a shows examples of the weight pattern between the input and hidden layer, before and after the training. The initial input weight field (W_{ji} has a smooth spatial radially symmetric retinotopic (x,y) profile for all the gaze directions. However, it is worth noting that at the end of the training process the input weight field looses its local retinotopy, resulting in a more global weighting of the elementary disparity components all over the visual field, and for all gaze directions. Most importantly, Fig. 2b shows that the trained weight fields W_{mj} between the hidden and the output layer form a characteristic selectivity for their output slant/tilt class (class 2 in the example of Fig. 2), even if they were

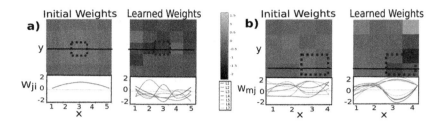

Fig. 2. Composition of the weight fields before and after training. (a): Weight fields between an elementary differential component of the disparity field (rot) and the hidden unit in the position corresponding to the position of the red square. (b): Weight fields between the hidden units and the output layer in the position corresponding to the position of the red square. The maps represent the field for a single gaze direction ($L = 1$) while the plots below show the cross-sections of the weight fields for all gaze directions. (Color figure online)

randomly initialized. As it can be seen in the plots at the bottom of Fig. 2b, this emerging selectivity appears to be a common feature across gaze directions. Furthermore, an interesting characteristic of the weight field development appears in Fig. 3. The weights between the hidden layer units for gaze direction $L = 1$ and each of the output units of the classification layer $m = [1, .., 4]$ tend to learn an emerging clustered connectivity pattern that directly maps to the slant and tilt parametric space.

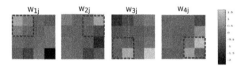

Fig. 3. Weight fields between the hidden units and the four-classes output units. The local patterns of connectivity point out an emerging clusterization of the slant and tilt information in the hidden representation. Here, only the case for gaze direction $L = 1$ is shown.

In conclusion, the results of the model demonstrate that, starting from a retinotopic multi-dimensional connectivity of locally-defined disparity components, it is possible to learn a set of globally-defined invariant descriptors that successfully encode the parametric space of slant and tilt orientation across a number of different gaze directions. The high accuracy results achieved and the short training time will allow us, as the next step, to study how the same model framework can incorporate the input disparity as the population activity of a large set of biologically-inspired disparity detectors.

References

1. Ban, H., Welchman, A.E.: fMRI analysis-by-synthesis reveals a dorsal hierarchy that extracts surface slant. J. Neurosci. **35**(27), 9823–9835 (2015)
2. Canessa, A., Gibaldi, A., Chessa, M., Fato, M., Solari, F., Sabatini, S.P.: A dataset of stereoscopic images and ground-truth disparity mimicking human fixations in peripersonal space. Sci. Data **4** (2017)
3. Dhond, U.R., Aggarwal, J.K.: Structure from stereo-a review. IEEE Trans. Syst. Man Cybern. **19**(6), 1489–1510 (1989)
4. Gibaldi, A., Canessa, A., Sabatini, S.P.: The active side of stereopsis: fixation strategy and adaptation to natural environments. Sci. Rep. **7**, 44800 (2017)
5. Hansard, M., Horaud, R.: Cyclopean geometry of binocular vision. JOSA A **25**(9), 2357–2369 (2008)
6. Hinkle, D.A., Connor, C.E.: Three-dimensional orientation tuning in macaque area V4. Nat. Neurosci. **5**(7), 665–670 (2002)
7. Koenderink, J.J., van Doorn, A.J.: The internal representation of solid shape with respect to vision. Biol. Cybern. **32**(4), 211–216 (1979)
8. Koenderink, J.J., van Doorn, A.J.: Facts on optic flow. Biol. Cybern. **56**(4), 247–254 (1987)
9. Liu, L., van Hulle, M.M.: Modeling the surround of MT cells and their selectivity for surface orientation in depth specified by motion. Neural Comput. **10**(2), 295–312 (1998)
10. LeCun, Y., Huang, F.J., Bottou, L.: Learning methods for generic object recognition with invariance to pose and lighting. In: 2004 Proceedings of the 2004 IEEE Computer Society Conference on Computer Vision and Pattern Recognition, CVPR 2004, vol. 2, pp. II–104. IEEE (2004)
11. Medsker, L.R., Jain, L.C.: Recurrent neural networks. Des. Appl. **5** (2001)
12. Nguyenkim, J.D., DeAngelis, G.C.: Disparity-based coding of three-dimensional surface orientation by macaque middle temporal neurons. J. Neurosci. **23**(18), 7117–7128 (2003)
13. Rumelhart, D.E., Hinton, G.E., Williams, R.J.: Learning internal representation by back propagation. Parallel Distrib. Process.: Explor. Microstruct. Cogn. **1** (1986)
14. Salinas, E., Abbott, L.F.: A model of multiplicative neural responses in parietal cortex. Proc. Nat. Acad. Sci. **93**(21), 11956–11961 (1996)
15. Tsao, D.Y., Vanduffel, W., Sasaki, Y., Fize, D., Knutsen, T.A., Mandeville, J.B., Wald, L.L., Dale, A.M., Rosen, B.R., Van Essen, D.C., Livingstone, M.S.: Stereopsis activates V3A and caudal intraparietal areas in macaques and humans. Neuron **39**(3), 555–568 (2003)

A Priori Reliability Prediction with Meta-Learning Based on Context Information

Jennifer Kreger[1(✉)], Lydia Fischer[2], Stephan Hasler[2],
Thomas H. Weisswange[2], and Ute Bauer-Wersing[1]

[1] Frankfurt University of Applied Sciences, Nibelungenplatz 1,
60318 Frankfurt am Main, Germany
j.kreger@fb2.fra-uas.de
[2] Honda Research Institute Europe GmbH,
Carl-Legien-Str. 30, 63073 Offenbach am Main, Germany

Abstract. Machine learning systems are used in a wide variability of tasks, where reliability is very important. Often from the output of these systems their reliability cannot directly be deduced. We propose an approach to predict the reliability of a machine learning system externally. We tackle this by using an additional machine learning component we call meta-learner. This meta-learner can use the original input as well as supplementary context information for its judgment. With this approach the meta-learner can make a prediction of the performance of the machine learner before this one is actually executed. Based on this prediction unreliable decisions can be rejected and the systems reliability is retained. We show that our method outperforms certainty-based approaches at the example of road terrain detection.

Keywords: Reliability prediction · Meta-learning · Rejection

1 Introduction

Lately machine learning and statistical classification techniques significantly gained in popularity and became an integral part of many daily life applications. Although machine learning algorithms perform well in many situations, sometimes they fail. Of course, wrong outputs have different impacts depending on the intended application, from e.g. user disappointment in the case of recommendation systems or automatic speech recognition systems, up to serious endangerment of life caused by safety critical systems such as self-driving cars or medical diagnosis systems. Hence, productive systems relying on machine learning methods must be able to estimate the reliability of the output in order to differentiate between situations where outputs are safe for further processing and those where failure is likely. Moreover, in real-time safety critical systems this decision has to be made fast.

Therefore research in the field calls more and more attention to reliability estimation of classification methods and efficient rejection strategies [1,8,14,15]

© Springer International Publishing AG 2017
A. Lintas et al. (Eds.): ICANN 2017, Part II, LNCS 10614, pp. 200–207, 2017.
https://doi.org/10.1007/978-3-319-68612-7_23

as an effective way to improve the system's overall performance. Many state-of-the-art rejection approaches are based on certainty measures indicating whether a given data point is classified correctly or not. Uncertain data points are rejected dependent on a predefined threshold, that is obtained by optimizing the so-called error-reject tradeoff [6]. However, to design a proper certainty measure, detailed knowledge of the machine learning algorithm itself is required.

Another approach that aims to improve the performance of machine learners by investigating the system and its output is *meta-learning* [3,10,13,16,17]. Additional data is gathered that is not considered mandatory to solve the original task. Meta-learning approaches seek to find and use correlations between this additional knowledge and the machine learner's performance. The internal goal is not simply to reject results, but also to feed back information about the learning process into the system. Hence, to enable the system to adapt to the current situation and improve its performance, e.g. by selecting the features most suitable to solve the task under the current circumstances.

Both approaches, certainty-based and meta-learning-based, depend on observations and evaluations of the specific machine learning algorithm and rely on detailed internal knowledge of the machine learner itself. This implies that a model which is able to judge the reliability of one algorithm cannot necessarily be transferred to another machine learning approach. Moreover, methods using the machine learner's outputs or internal state parameters to estimate its performance must definitely execute the machine learning algorithm, even if the result on a data sample turns out as unreliable. This can be time consuming and as a consequence, triggering a defined fall-back mechanism may be late in the case of real-time safety critical applications.

Here, we propose an approach to rapidly predict the reliability of a machine learner's output independent of its underlying algorithm. For this purpose, we adapted the meta-learning approach (cf. Fig. 1). We use only (i) the raw input sample and additional data from the environment that is available prior to processing of the machine learner and (ii) a performance measure that is derived from the output of the machine learner and the ground truth data associated with the input sample. The machine learner and its output are no direct part of the reject decision, i.e. the prediction phase remains completely unknown to the meta-learner. We test our approach exemplary on two different vision-based segmentation systems, RTDS [9] and Bayesian SegNet [11]. We assume that even with very good models these systems may fail in case of technical issues as strong over-/underexposure or dirt on the camera lense. Also, the systems will probably fail in unknown environments like unpaved roads. For both machine learning applications we demonstrate the suitability of our approach and compare it to a certainty-based rejection method as state-of-the-art alternative. Please note, that our approach is *generic*, i.e. is – in principle – applicable to machine learning systems where ground truth data is available and a suitable performance measure can be deduced. Preliminary results of the study have been published in [12].

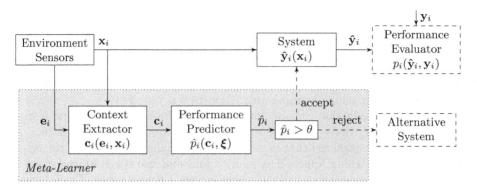

Fig. 1. Description of a general system (top row) enhanced with our *Meta-Learner* approach (gray box).

2   Methods

The structure of our approach is shown in Fig. 1. We assume to have a given *System* that generates output $\hat{\mathbf{y}}_i$ for input $\mathbf{x}_i$. Usually the *System* is a machine learner that was trained on a classification or regression task. Based on ground truth information $\mathbf{y}_i$ a performance measure p_i can be computed offline.

The aim of our *Meta-Learner* extension (Fig. 1: gray box) is to predict the performance of the *System* for the current input $\mathbf{x}_i$ at run time. For this it computes context features $\mathbf{c}_i$ on sensor measurements of the environment that are usually composed of the *System*'s input $\mathbf{x}_i$ and an additional input $\mathbf{e}_i$. These context features are used by the *Performance Predictor* to estimate a scalar value $\hat{p}_i$ that is later compared against a threshold θ to decide if the *System*'s output $\hat{\mathbf{y}}_i$ will be credible or not. In the latter case potentially an *Alternative System* could be used to handle the current situation. This *Alternative System* is usually more costly.

The important aspect of our *Meta-Learner* method is that it treats the *System* as a black box, i.e. it has no knowledge about the *System*'s inner structure and state. Furthermore, at run time the final decision of *accepting* or *rejecting* does not depend on the *System*'s output $\hat{\mathbf{y}}_i$. Therefore the *Meta-Learner* can perform an early reject decision and potentially save computation time.

In general, the *Performance Predictor* is a regression model that estimates the true performance of the *System*. Hence the regression parameters $\boldsymbol{\xi}$ are chosen as to minimize the prediction error between p_i and the estimated *System*'s performance $\hat{p}_i$ for a given training set $\{\mathbf{c}_i, p_i\}_{i=1}^{N}$. Again the *System*'s output $\hat{\mathbf{y}}_i$ is not used directly, but in its *abstract* form as a real-valued performance measure p_i. To compute p_i, ground truth information $\mathbf{y}_i$ is required.

For choosing an optimal threshold θ, the costs for a *reject* decision and a false *accept* decision have to be taken into account. Rejecting a sample should increase the *Evaluated Performance* for the remaining samples. Note that the costs of rejecting a sample directly depend on the *Alternative System*. An optimal threshold can only be chosen if all costs are known.

3   Application

We apply our meta-learning approach in the context of computer vision and image segmentation, precisely we focus on machine learning methods performing segmentation tasks on complex traffic scenes. In this setting a input data sample $\mathbf{x}_i$ is an RGB image, the output of the image segmentation systems $\hat{\mathbf{y}}_i$ is an array of class labels indicating for each pixel in $\mathbf{x}_i$, whether it belongs to e.g. road terrain or any other defined class that can occur in traffic scenes. Accordingly, we need a measure that takes the performance p_i accumulated over a whole image into account and that is later predicted by our meta-learner. We choose the *Quality* score [9] as performance measure:

$$p_i := p_i(\hat{\mathbf{y}}_i, \mathbf{y}_i) = \frac{TP}{TP + FN + FP} \in [0, 1] \tag{1}$$

where the quantities true positives (TP), false negatives (FN), and false positives (FP) are determined by comparing the system's output $\hat{\mathbf{y}}_i$ to labeled ground truth images $\mathbf{y}_i$ pixel-wise. The *Quality* score does not depend the true negatives (TN) and is therefore less biased by class imbalances. For multiple classes the quality is averaged over all classes.

To design a system for our scenarios that is computationally inexpensive and fast, we restrict the extraction of context features $\mathbf{c}_i$ to: (1) methods describing the image $\mathbf{x}_i$ holistically, and (2) methods resulting in low dimensional feature vectors. We therefore choose the global image descriptor Centrist [18] complemented with a color histogram. So far we do not consider further input $\mathbf{e}_i$ from the environment.

The first machine learning system we apply our meta-learner to is the road terrain detection system (RTDS [9]). It differentiates between road and non-road areas (Fig. 2a–d). RTDS returns a confidence value for each pixel indicating the probability of belonging to road area in a 2-dimensional bird's eye view. Thresholding on the confidence map generates the segmentation result $\hat{\mathbf{y}}_i^{\text{RTDS}}$ for road and non-road area of the corresponding input image $\mathbf{x}_i$. The original data set consists of $N_{\text{nat}} = 204$ raw natural images of traffic scenes for which hand-labeled ground-truth is available. Unfortunately, the original data set is biased and contains only few samples where RTDS has poor results. Since it is the overall goal to provide an efficient reject strategy, examples where the machine learning method fails are vital to our approach. Therefore, we artificially enriched the original data set: we added disturbances by applying different sorts of global noise to some of the natural images (γ-correction, Gaussian blur, and salt noise). In summary, we extend the original data set with a set of artificially disturbed images to $N_{\text{nat+art}} = 536$ images in total.

The second machine learning system is Bayesian SegNet[1] [11]. It is a segmentation system designed especially for traffic scene analysis and handles 11

---

[1] Available at: https://github.com/alexgkendall/caffe-segnet.

related classes. The output $\hat{\mathbf{y}}_i^{\mathrm{SegNet}}$ is a color coded image indicating the predicted classes. Additionally there is a certainty map for each class that are aver-
aged into a single certainty map (Fig. 2e–g). Bayesian SegNet is trained on the
CamVid data [4] with a test set of $N_{\mathrm{camvid}} = 232$ images.

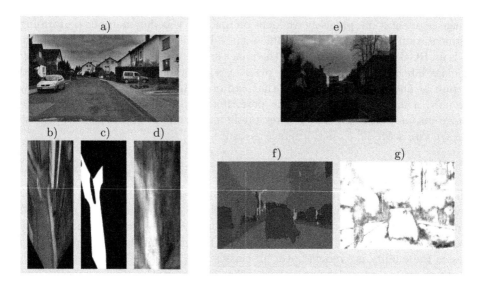

Fig. 2. RTDS input image (a), image transformed into a 2D bird's eye view (b), hand
labeled ground truth (c), output confidence matrix (d). Bayesian SegNet [11] input
image (e), output segmentation prediction (f), and certainty output (g), light means
high certainty. (Color figure online)

In the experiments we compare the rejection strategy based on the quality
predicted by our meta-learners against the true quality (ground truth) and a
state-of-the-art certainty-based approach [8]. We consider three different regression models for our meta-learner: (i) AdaBoost [7] with decision trees, known to
be robust and fast, (ii) support vector machines (SVM [5]), as a more sophisticated model, and (iii) k-nearest neighbor regression (KNN [2]), as a simple
model[2].

4   Experiments

To evaluate our meta-learner we plot the mean quality over the rate of rejected
samples. Therefor we iteratively increase the rejection threshold θ starting with
no rejection ($\theta = 0$, rejection rate $r = 0$) such that one more data sample is
rejected. When one data sample is remaining we stop the rejection.

---

[2] We use the implementations of scikit learn available at: http://scikit-learn.org/
   stable.

$$r(\theta) = \frac{1}{N} \sum \begin{cases} 1 & \hat{p}_i <= \theta \\ 0 & else \end{cases} \qquad (2)$$

After each rejection we compute the mean quality of the machine learner for the remaining data samples:

$$p_{\text{mean}}(\theta) = \frac{1}{N} \sum \begin{cases} p_i & \hat{p}_i > \theta \\ 0 & else \end{cases} \qquad (3)$$

Note that a small rejection rate causing a high increase of the mean quality is appreciated. Due to the small amount of available data we use leave-one-out cross validation averaging over 10 repetitions.

In Fig. 3 (top) we compare the rejection performance of different meta-learners using varying regression models (AdaBoost, SVM, KNN) to the ground truth and a certainty-based approach. For the related experiments we use the

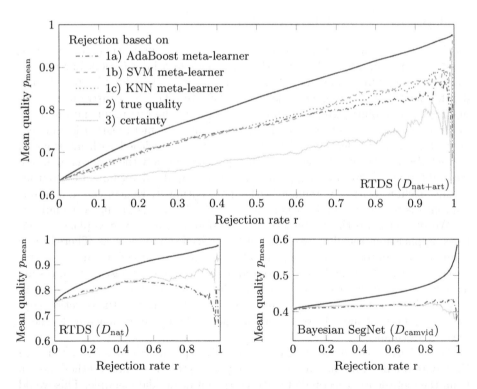

Fig. 3. Comparison of different rejection approaches. The worst sample is rejected dependent on (1) the prediction of the meta-learner, (2) the true quality, (3) the classification certainty. Top: comparison of different regression models – (a) Ada-Boost, (b) SVM, (c) KNN – on RTDS with $D_{\text{nat+art}}$. Bottom left: RTDS with D_{nat}. Bottom right: Bayesian SegNet with D_{camvid}.

data set $D_{nat+art}$ with artificial and natural images, as well as the obtained RTDS qualities. It can be seen that the meta-learners almost reach the best possible performance obtained with the true output quality for the interesting regime of small rejection rates ($<10\%$). For higher rates the difference increases but it is still outperforming the certainty-based approach. The results also state that there is nearly no difference between the analyzed meta-learners. Therefore we use AdaBoost in the following because it is known to deliver robust and fast results.

The bottom plots show the RTDS and SegNet results only using natural images. In both scenarios our approach provides similar results as the certainty-based approach. For the RTDS both rejection approaches reach a reasonable improvement of the mean quality on the natural images with low rejection rates. The difficulty on the Bayesian SegNet is the homogeneous distribution of the related quality values. Therefore both rejection approaches achieve only slight improvements of the mean output quality, but even the rejection based on the true quality values can barely achieve an increase of the quality.

5   Conclusion and Future Work

Machine learning methods are used in a wide field of applications wherein reliability is very important. Many of these methods lack information how reliable their output is. Often they are enhanced with a certainty estimation based on in depth knowledge of the machine learner itself. We relax this constraint by estimating the reliability externally only incorporating the raw input data and the machine learner's output performance for training. The meta-learner is independent of the machine learner. The input data can be enriched with information extracted from the environment. For the application solely the input is required. An additional benefit of this approach is that we rapidly determine if the output of the machine learner is reliable without executing it. Hence, the aim of our approach is to reject samples where the machine learner is predicted to fail.

We demonstrate the usefulness of our approach on two exemplary vision-based applications tackling two different traffic scene analysis tasks. Therefore we compare our approach with an optimal baseline and a state-of-the-art certainty-based approach. It turned out that our approach provides almost as good results as the baseline in the relevant regime of small rejection rates and shows a better or similar performance as the certainty-based rejection. Hence, the rejection approach based on the meta-learner's predictions can improve the machine learner's mean performance.

One future research direction could be to incorporate features extracted from the environment. A further interesting approach is to investigate whether one can train the meta-learner to predict the quality of a future data sample. This would be useful in applications dealing with image streams, especially for autonomous cars where a time dependency between data samples is guaranteed. In this case it might be beneficial as well to apply a more sophisticated rejection strategy, e.g. an adaptive threshold, that adjusts to the current data distribution, assuming an online learning scenario.

References

1. Alvarez, I., Bernard, S., Deffuant, G.: Keep the decision tree and estimate the class probabilities using its decision boundary. In: International Joint Conference on Artificial Intelligence, pp. 654–659 (2007)
2. Andoni, A., Indyk, P.: Near-optimal hashing algorithms for approximate nearest neighbor in high dimensions. In: Annual IEEE Symposium on Foundations of Computer Science, pp. 459–468. IEEE (2006)
3. Brazdil, P., Carrier, C.G., Soares, C., Vilalta, R.: Metalearning: Applications to Data Mining. Springer Science & Business Media, Berlin (2008)
4. Brostow, G.J., Fauqueur, J., Cipolla, R.: Semantic object classes in video: a high-definition ground truth database. Pattern Recogn. Lett. **30**(2), 88–97 (2008)
5. Chang, C.C., Lin, C.J.: LIBSVM: a library for support vector machines. ACM Trans. Intell. Syst. Technol. **2**(3), 1–27 (2011)
6. Chow, C.: On optimum recognition error and reject tradeoff. IEEE Trans. Inf. Theory **16**(1), 41–46 (1970)
7. Drucker, H.: Improving regressors using boosting techniques. In: International Conference on Machine Learning, vol. 97, pp. 107–115 (1997)
8. Fischer, L., Hammer, B., Wersing, H.: Efficient rejection strategies for prototype-based classification. Neurocomputing **169**, 334–342 (2015)
9. Fritsch, J., Kühnl, T., Kummert, F.: Monocular road terrain detection by combining visual and spatial information. IEEE Trans. Intell. Transp. Syst. **15**(4), 1586–1596 (2014)
10. Giraud-Carrier, C.: Metalearning-a tutorial. In: Tutorial at the International Conference on Machine Learning and Applications, pp. 11–13 (2008)
11. Kendall, A., Badrinarayanan, V., Cipolla, R.: Bayesian SegNet: model uncertainty in deep convolutional encoder-decoder architectures for scene understanding. arXiv:1511.02680 (2015)
12. Kreger, J., Fischer, L., Hasler, S., Bauer-Wersing, U., Weisswange, T.H.: Quality prediction for a road detection system. Mach. Learn. Rep. **04**(2016), 93–94 (2016)
13. Lemke, C., Budka, M., Gabrys, B.: Metalearning: a survey of trends and technologies. Artif. Intell. Rev. **44**(1), 117–130 (2015)
14. Lu, H., Wei, S., Zhou, Z., Miao, Y., Lu, Y.: Regularised extreme learning machine with misclassification cost and rejection cost for gene expression data classification. Int. J. Data Min. Bioinform. **12**(3), 294–312 (2015)
15. Pillai, I., Fumera, G., Roli, F.: Multi-label classification with a reject option. Pattern Recogn. **46**(8), 2256–2266 (2013)
16. Rossi, A.L.D., Carvalho, A.C., Soares, C.: Meta-learning for periodic algorithm selection in time-changing data. In: IEEE Brazilian Symposium on Neural Networks, pp. 7–12. IEEE (2012)
17. Vilalta, R., Drissi, Y.: A perspective view and survey of meta-learning. Artif. Intell. Rev. **18**(2), 77–95 (2002)
18. Wu, J., Rehg, J.M.: CENTRIST: a visual descriptor for scene categorization. IEEE Trans. Pattern Anal. Mach. Intell. **33**(8), 1489–1501 (2011)

Attention Aware Semi-supervised Framework for Sentiment Analysis

Jingshuang Liu[1], Wenge Rong[1(✉)], Chuan Tian[1], Min Gao[2], and Zhang Xiong[1]

[1] School of Computer Science and Engineering, Beihang University, Beijing, China
{jingshuangliu,w.rong,chuantian,xiongz}@buaa.edu.cn
[2] School of Software Engineering, Chonqing University, Chongqing, China
gaomin@cqu.edu.cn

Abstract. Using sentiment analysis methods to retrieve useful information from the accumulated documents in the Internet has become an important research subject. In this paper, we proposed a semi-supervised framework, which uses the unlabeled data to promote the learning ability of the long short memory (LSTM) network. It is composed of an unsupervised attention aware long short term memory (LSTM) encoder-decoder and a single LSTM model used for feature extraction and classification. Experimental study on commonly used datasets has demonstrated our framework's good potential for sentiment classification tasks. And it has shown that the unsupervised learning part can improve the LSTM network's learning ability.

Keywords: Sentiment analysis · Semi-supervised learning · Attention · Long short term memory · Encoder-decoder

1 Introduction

Nowadays, people tend to publish opinions and comments on goods, movies, and etc. through the Internet based services. As a result a large number of such documents have been collected, which makes it an important task to retrieve valuable information beneath these online collections [13]. Sentiment analysis is an effective method to investigate the polarity of online posted messages [13].

Many deep models have been introduced to the sentiment analysis tasks, among which Recurrent Neural Network (RNN) has shown its great power since it can learn the underlying relationships between the words [12]. However, RNN had the vanishing gradient problem [6]. To overcome this shortcoming, long short term memory (LSTM) with gates and cell mechanism has been proposed in the literature. It has proven its potential in maintaining the advantages of RNN while overcoming the problems of vanishing gradient [8].

Besides the more and more advanced model, for the classification tasks it is also believed that importing external knowledge from different domains can help to improve the model's performance [3]. Under this assumption, we proposed a framework which employs an unsupervised model for pre-training the parameters in the supervised model. At present, the encoder-decoder is a useful structure for

A. Lintas et al. (Eds.): ICANN 2017, Part II, LNCS 10614, pp. 208–215, 2017.
https://doi.org/10.1007/978-3-319-68612-7_24

unsupervised learning in natural language process (NLP) tasks [5], and attention mechanism is another valid promotion to the behaviour of unsupervised learning [4]. Therefore, we proposed to use an attention mechanism aware LSTM encoder-decoder to pre-train parameters in a unsupervised step. In this part, we applied unlabelled data for training. Then the supervised learning LSTM network is implemented for feature extraction and classification.

The rest of the paper is organized as follows: Sect. 2 will present the background knowledge about our research. The pipeline of our proposed semi-supervised model will be illustrated in Sect. 3. Finally, the experiment study and discussion will be discussed in Sect. 4 and Sect. 5 will conclude this paper and point out possible future directions.

2   Background

Currently sentiment analysis has gained much attention in both academic and industrial community [13]. Since a large amount of information can be collected through the social media network, sentiment analysis has witnessed a great development in analysing the information beneath the online documents. Due to its capability of analysing polarity of online documents, it has become a fundamental technique in a lot of applications [13].

For sentiment analysis, supervised learning has proven its success in many tasks [3]. However, in order to enhance the generalisation ability of the learning model, this kind of method need a large number of labelled corpus. At present, it is convenient to acquire abundant unlabelled corpus from the website. But the dataset are usually limited in quantity, quality, and coverage [2]. Meanwhile, in some cases, the supervised learning model was only randomly initialised and the parameters was likely to get into poor local minimums [3]. If the model can be initialised properly, the generalisation ability can be improved [3].

In machine learning, semi-supervised learning is a useful technique to use both the unlabelled and labelled data [2]. The most common way for semi-supervised learning is to split the training process into two parts [11]. The first part is the unsupervised learning using large unlabelled corpus. In this step, a set of parameters can be obtained. The second is using the retrieved parameters to initialise a supervised learning model. In this way, the parameters are fine tuned with the model globally using labelled data. In this research, we used the data crawled from website for unsupervised learning. For instance, we used the Amazon Review data which has high relevance to our experimental dataset. Therefore, we can acquire high quality parameters with these unlabelled dataset.

The encoder-decoder model has achieved great success in the tasks for NLP lately, such as machine translation, speech recognition, slot filling and text parsing [5]. In this approach, sequence models can be applied as an encoder to encode the input data into a state. Afterwards the state is used for the input of a decoder, which is also variable, to predict the output sequence. In our work, we used LSTM as both the encoder and decoder.

The attention mechanism has been proposed in recent years and has made great breakthroughs in fields like machine translation, video and image analysis

[4]. It can free the model from having to encode a whole sequence into a vector, and the decoder only needs to focus on the relevant information [4]. This mechanism can help enhance the accuracy of the unsupervised process greatly.

3   Methodology

The proposed sentiment analysis framework is shown in Fig. 1, where the first section is the unsupervised model to obtain the parameters for initialisation. The second section is a supervised LSTM network with a Softmax layer used to learn the hidden features of the instance and make prediction.

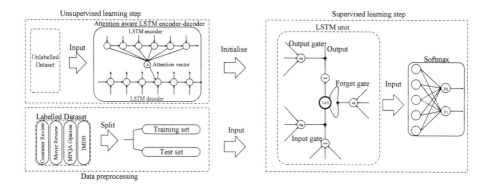

Fig. 1. Attention aware semi-supervised LSTM framework

3.1   Unsupervised Learning

Here we employed an attention aware LSTM encoder-decoder structure in the unsupervised learning step to pre-train the parameters. The LSTM encoder-decoder is used to reconstruct the input word sequence. For the encoding part, at each time step, a single word was inputted into the encoder until the model gets an $\langle EOS \rangle$ symbol. Finally the hidden state of the encoder could be gained. And for the decoding part, the hidden state acquired from former step worked as the initial state of the LSTM decoder. At each time step, the output was applied as the input for next time step until the model outputted an $\langle EOS \rangle$.

The attention mechanism is employed as follows: As shown in the unsupervised learning step in Fig. 1, a context vector a_t is added to the output layer of the LSTM decoder. The vector a_t was computed by:

$$e_{tj} = sim(s_{t-1}, h_j) \tag{1}$$

$$\alpha_{tj} = \frac{\exp(e_{tj})}{\sum_{i=1}^{T_x} \exp(e_{ti})} \tag{2}$$

$$a_t = \sum_{j=1}^{T_x} \alpha_{tj} h_j \tag{3}$$

where e_{tj} is the cosine similarity between the state of the memory cell in time step t_1 in the decoder s_{t-1} and the state of the memory cell in time step j of the encoder h_j. In the figure, we only take one attention vector for example for simplicity, and in fact there are a lot more context vectors (For instance, if the input length is 10, then there are 10 context vectors in total). With the context vector added, the values of the gates and cells in the LSTM decoder were computed as follows:

$$i = \sigma(x_t U^i + s_{t-1} W^i + a_t) \tag{4}$$
$$f = \sigma(x_t U^f + s_{t-1} W^f + a_t) \tag{5}$$
$$o = \sigma(x_t U^o + s_{t-1} W^o + a_t) \tag{6}$$
$$\hat{c}_t = \tanh(x_t U^c + s_{t-1} W^c + a_t) \tag{7}$$
$$c_t = c_{t-1} \circ f + \hat{c}_t \circ i \tag{8}$$
$$s_t = \tanh(c_t) \circ o \tag{9}$$

where x_t is the input to the memory cell. U^i, U^f, U^o, U^c, W^i, W^f, W^o, W^c are weight matrices. i, f, o stand for values of the input gate, forget gate, and output gate. $\hat{c}_t$ is the candidate value for states of the memory cell. c_t is the new state of memory cell and s_t is the output of hidden state at time step t. And a_t is added respectively.

In this part, we trained the unsupervised model with unlabelled dataset. After the unsupervised training process, we extracted the parameters of the LSTM encoder and used it in the later supervised training part.

3.2 Supervised Learning

Feature Extraction. We initialised the LSTM network with the parameters we obtained from the last part. In this step, we used the labelled instances as input. In the LSTM, the new state of memory cell c_t and the output of hidden state s_t are computed the same as Eqs. 8 and 9. The other values of gates and cells were computed like those we introduced before in Sect. 3.1 only without the attention vector a_t.

Prediction. In the last part, a Softmax classifier was attached to the LSTM network to predict whether the output of the LSTM network is positive or negative. After Implementing the framework, we trained the two parts respectively. The Cross Entropy was used as the cost function:

$$\text{Cost} = -\frac{1}{m} \sum_{i=1}^{m} [y_i \log \hat{y}_i + (1 - y_i) \log(1 - \hat{y}_i)] \tag{10}$$

where $\hat{y}_i$ is the predicted result and y_i is the label of the instance i, m is the number of the instances. In this research, we employed stochastic gradient descend (SGD) method to optimise the back propagation through time algorithm. Our algorithm was realized on the Theano platform. And in order to accelerate our training process, we referenced Bengio et al.'s approach to train compute the i, f, o, a_t in parallel [1].

4   Experiment Study

4.1   Datasets and Evaluation Metrics

In this research, in order to evaluate the proposed model and test the performance of different word embedding strategy, four public datasets are employed, i.e. the non-balanced dataset Customer Review[1], MPQA opinion corpus[2], and the balanced dataset Movie Review[3] and IMDB[4]. The four datasets have 3,772, 10,662, 10624, 50,000 instances respectively and the positive and negative instances rates are 0.64/0.36, 0.31/0.69, 0.5/0.5, 0.5/0.5. In this research, for the first three datasets, we randomly split the datasets into ten sets and adopt the 10-fold cross validation strategy to compute the average accuracy. And for IMDB, since the author has already split it into 50%/50% for training and testing, we just followed this common splitting approach.

To evaluate the proposed model's potential, the widely used measurement accuracy [9] is employed in this research and it is defined as:

$$Accuracy = \frac{\sum\limits_{i=1}^{n} 1\{y_i = p_i\}}{\#testdata} \tag{11}$$

where y_i stands for the true value that the instance is labelled, and p_i is the result predicted by our model. By evaluating the accuracy in testing set, we can see our model's performance towards generalised dataset.

To test the performance of the proposed model, several baselines in the literature are employed. For the Customer Review, MPQA Opinion Corpus and Movie Review, Bag-of-Words, Vote by lexicon, Rule-based reversal, Tree-Based CRF, word embedding based CNN, RNN and LSTM are employed [7,8,10,12]. While for IMDB dataset, LSA, LDA, MAAS Semantic, MAAS Full, word embedding based CNN, RNN and LSTM are used [7–9,12]. Also, for comparsion, we implemented a framework with random initialised parameters (without attention aware pre-training step).

4.2   Results and Discussion

The comparison of the proposed model against the baseline methods are displayed in Tables 1 and 2. It is found that the proposed model outperform the

---

[1] http://www.cs.uic.edu/~liub/FBS/sentiment-analysis.html.
[2] http://mpqa.cs.pitt.edu/.
[3] http://www.cs.cornell.edu/people/pabo/movie-review-data/.
[4] http://ai.stanford.edu/~amaas/data/sentiment/.

baseline methods in all the four datasets. The reason is that other baseline methods cannot learn the underlying relationships between words in great intervals. For instance, word embedding based CNN is not a time series model, Word embedding based RNN has the problem of vanishing gradient and WB+LSTM is not well pre-trained since it is a simple supervised learning model.

Table 1. Accuracy for customer review, MPQA opinion and movie review

Method	Customer review	MPQA opinion	Movie review
Bag-of-word	0.814	0.841	0.764
Voting by lexicon	0.742	0.817	0.631
Rule-based reversal	0.743	0.818	0.629
Tree-CRF	0.814	0.861	0.773
Word embedding based CNN	0.819	0.918	0.778
Word embedding based RNN	0.821	0.867	0.781
Word embedding based LSTM	0.764	0.922	0.774
Our framework (no attention aware)	0.830	0.921	0.784
Our framework (attention aware)	**0.846**	**0.928**	**0.797**

Table 2. Accuracy for IMDB

Method	IMDB
LSA	0.839
LDA	0.674
MAAS semantic	0.873
MAAS full	0.874
Word embedding based CNN	0.884
Word embedding based RNN	0.829
Word embedding based LSTM	0.835
Our framework (no attention aware)	0.891
Our framework (attention aware)	**0.901**

Besides, our framework surpasses the semi-supervised LSTM without attention mechanism. It indicates that the attention mechanism used in our framework can promote the performance of the LSTM encoder-decoder model. The reason is that the attention mechanism makes the LSTM encoder not have to encode a long sequence into a single vector. It helps the LSTM decoder focus on the relevant information and enhances the unsupervised process.

Comparing with other baseline methods, we find the proposed model gained satisfactory performance. The reason is probably mainly three folds: (1) the unsupervised step which pre-training the parameters for the LSTM network

214   J. Liu et al.

can really help to improve the performance of the LSTM; (2) the attention mechanism makes the LSTM encoder-decoder get better training ability; (3) the LSTM network behaves well in learning long-range dependencies of words as it can catch long sequence information.

Furthermore, we also compared different unlabelled dataset used for the pre-training step and the result is as shown in Fig. 2, where we set a LSTM with random initialised parameters (without pre-training) as the baseline. In this experiment, we found the Amazon review (256,479 sentences) attained the best result. And the model pre-trained by IMDB training set (25,000 sentences) also got better results than the randomly initialised LSTM. The reason is that the unlabelled dataset consists of exterior knowledge. And the Amazon Review includes highly relevant information to our experimental dataset since most of them are all reviews. As a result, the Amazon Review has more useful messages.

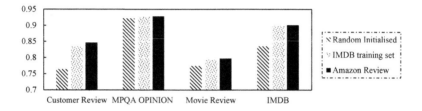

Fig. 2. Results of different datasets used in the unsupervised learning step

5   Conclusion and Future Work

In this paper, we proposed an attention aware semi-supervised LSTM framework. We first introduced the tasks of sentiment analysis and analysed the benefits of unsupervised learning for sentiment analysis. The attention mechanism made the unsupervised encoder-decoder LSTM to focus on the useful information and thus we can obtain the well pre-trained parameters for initialising the supervised LSTM. Afterwards, we presented our model in detail. We first employed an unsupervised learning model for pre-training the parameters. Then we constructed an LSTM network for feature extraction and prediction. The LSTM network was initialised by the parameters obtained in the unsupervised procedure. In our experiments, the proposed framework beat the baseline methods. The experimental results had proven the generalisation ability of framework for sentiment analysis tasks. Concerning to the future work, we plan to use different kinds of unlabelled data for the unsupervised learning process. And we will replace the LSTM encoder-decoder structure with other sequence model.

Acknowledgments. This work was partially supported by the National Natural Science Foundation of China (No. 61332018), and the Fundamental Research Funds for the Central Universities.

References

1. Bastien, F., Lamblin, P., Pascanu, R., Bergstra, J., Goodfellow, I.J., Bergeron, A., Bouchard, N., Warde-Farley, D., Bengio, Y.: Theano: new features and speed improvements. CoRR abs/1211.5590 (2012)
2. Cheng, Y., Xu, W., He, Z., He, W., Wu, H., Sun, M., Liu, Y.: Semi-supervised learning for neural machine translation. In: Proceedings of 54th Annual Meeting of the Association for Computational Linguistics, pp. 1965–1974 (2016)
3. Erhan, D., Bengio, Y., Courville, A.C., Manzagol, P., Vincent, P., Bengio, S.: Why does unsupervised pre-training help deep learning? J. Mach. Learn. Res. **11**, 625–660 (2010)
4. Firat, O., Cho, K., Bengio, Y.: Multi-way, multilingual neural machine translation with a shared attention mechanism. In: Proceedings of 2016 Conference of the North American Chapter of the Association for Computational Linguistics, pp. 866–875 (2016)
5. Gu, J., Lu, Z., Li, H., Li, V.O.K.: Incorporating copying mechanism in sequence-to-sequence learning. In: Proceedings of 54th Annual Meeting of the Association for Computational Linguistics, pp. 1631–1640 (2016)
6. Jozefowicz, R., Zaremba, W., Sutskever, I.: An empirical exploration of recurrent network architectures. In: Proceedings of 32nd International Conference on Machine Learning, pp. 2342–2350 (2015)
7. Krizhevsky, A., Sutskever, I., Hinton, G.E.: Imagenet classification with deep convolutional neural networks. In: Proceedings of 26th Annual Conference on Neural Information Processing Systems, pp. 1106–1114 (2012)
8. Lu, Y., Salem, F.M.: Simplified gating in long short-term memory (LSTM) recurrent neural networks. CoRR abs/1701.03441 (2017)
9. Maas, A.L., Daly, R.E., Pham, P.T., Huang, D., Ng, A.Y., Potts, C.: Learning word vectors for sentiment analysis. In: Proceedings of 49th Annual Meeting of the Association for Computational Linguistics, pp. 142–150 (2011)
10. Nakagawa, T., Inui, K., Kurohashi, S.: Dependency tree-based sentiment classification using CRFs with hidden variables. In: Proceedings of 2010 Annual Conference of the North American Chapter of the Association for Computational Linguistics, pp. 786–794 (2010)
11. Rasmus, A., Berglund, M., Honkala, M., Valpola, H., Raiko, T.: Semi-supervised learning with ladder networks. In: Proceedings of 29th Annual Conference on Neural Information Processing Systems, pp. 3546–3554 (2015)
12. Raza, K.: Recurrent neural network based hybrid model for reconstructing gene regulatory network. Comput. Biol. Chem. **64**, 322–334 (2016)
13. Zhao, J., Liu, K., Xu, L.: Sentiment analysis: mining opinions, sentiments, and emotions. Comput. Linguist. **43**(3), 595–598 (2016)

Chinese Lexical Normalization Based on Information Extraction: An Experimental Study

Tian Tian[(✉)] and WeiRan Xu

Pattern Recognition and Intelligent System Laboratory,
Beijing University of Posts and Telecommunications, Beijing 100876, China
tt1717@foxmail.com

Abstract. In this work, we described a novel method for normalizing
Chinese informal words to their standard equivalents. We form the task
as an information extraction problem, using Q & A community answers
as source corpus. We proposed several LSTM based models for the extraction task. To evaluate and compare performances of the proposed models,
we developed a standard dataset containing factoid generated by real-
world users in daily life. Since our method do not use any linguistic
features, it's also applicable to other languages.

Keywords: Text normalization · LSTM · Q & A community

1 Introduction

Social media, such as Twitter[1] and Weibo[2], has become an important topic in the
computational linguistic community. Unlike the formal text, the user-generated
text are littered with neologisms, abbreviations and phonetic substitutions. The
existence of informal word is problematic for many NLP systems which are
generally trained on clean and formal text. To handle this problem, One possible
way is retrain the NLP tools on data from the domain. However this approach
could be labor expensive and time consuming. Although the form of informal
words varied, an informal word often has a viable formal equivalent such as *tmrw*
is short for *tomorrow*. Thus an alternative approach is to mapping the informal
lexical variants back to their standard orthography [1,2].

Generally, the text normalization task in social media field can be decomposed into two subtasks: identify informal word in source corpus and mapping
informal word back to it's formal equivalent. In this study, we focus on the second sub-task assuming that the informal word has been identified already. The
inspiration for our work comes mainly from the work of Li and Yarowsky [3].
They tackle the problem of identifying informal/formal Chinese word pairs in the

---

[1] www.twitter.com.
[2] www.weibo.com.

© Springer International Publishing AG 2017
A. Lintas et al. (Eds.): ICANN 2017, Part II, LNCS 10614, pp. 216–223, 2017.
https://doi.org/10.1007/978-3-319-68612-7_25

Web domain. Given an informal word, They employ a general search engine[3] to collect sentences that illustrate the equivalence between informal/formal pairs, then generating candidate hypotheses from the sentences and further ranked using a conditional log-linear model. From our perspectives, data retrieved from a general search engine could be much noisy even with specially designed queries and a conditional log-linear model may not powerful enough to learn the complex mapping function between informal/formal pairs. In our work, we replace the general search engine with a Q & A community search engine. Given an Informal word, we search the Q & A community use designed questions, collecting answers that satisfy specific rules as evidence and from which we extract the informal word's corresponding formal equivalent. Thus we transfer the normalization task into an information extraction task. Formally, the task can be stated as follows:

Suppose we have an sentence which illustrate the equivalence between an informal-formal pairs, the sentence $x = \{x_1, \ldots, x_N\}$ consisting of N words and an informal word x_i exist in it, extract a sub-sequence $\{x_b, \ldots, x_e\}$, where $1 \leq b \leq e \leq N$, as the informal words formal equivalent that most consistent with the meaning of the evidence.

In the following sections, We will introduce the proposed LSTM based models for the extraction task. To evaluate and compare performances of the proposed models, we developed a standard dataset containing factoid generated by real-world users in daily life performance of each model will reported in later sections.

2 Proposed Models

2.1 LSTM Networks

Recurrent Neural Networks (RNN) is a neural network designed for modeling sequential information. Given an input sequence of vectors $\{x_1, \ldots, x_N\}$, RNN generates a sequence of hidden states $\{h_1, \ldots, h_N\}$, which computed as follows:

$$h_t = \tanh(W_h h_{t-1} + W_x x_t + b) \tag{1}$$

Theoretically, RNN is capable of learning long distance dependence, however in practice, it suffers from the gradient vanishing/exploding problems [4]. Long-short term memory networks (LSTM) [5] is a variant of RNN, introduced to cope with the gradient problems. By incorporating three gating functions and maintaining a memory cell, LSTM allows information to flow over long distances. Formally the hidden states in LSTM computed in the following ways:

$$
\begin{aligned}
f_t &= \sigma(W_f x_t + U_f h_{t-1} + b_f) \\
i_t &= \sigma(W_i x_t + U_i h_{t-1} + b_i) \\
o_t &= \sigma(W_o x_t + U_o h_{t-1} + b_o) \\
g_t &= \tanh(W_g x_t + U_g h_{t-1} + b_g) \\
c_t &= f_t \odot c_{t-1} + i_t \odot g_t \\
h_t &= o_t \odot \tanh(c_t)
\end{aligned}
\tag{2}
$$

---

[3] www.baidu.com.

where i_t, f_t, o_t, c_t represents the input, forget, output gates and memory cell, main mechanism fight against the gradient problem, $\sigma(\cdot)$ and $\tanh(\cdot)$ are the element-wise sigmoid and hyperbolic tangent function, and $\odot$ is the element-wise multiplication operator. We use x_t denotes both the word and its embeddings for simplicity.

In the first model, we use a standard LSTM networks to encode the evidence and derive the target sequence by predicting its beginning and ending indices independently. The probability distributions of the start index and end index over entire sentence are computed as:

$$p^s = \text{softmax}(v_s \boldsymbol{h}) \tag{3}$$

$$p^e = \text{softmax}(v_e \boldsymbol{h}) \tag{4}$$

where $\boldsymbol{h} = [h_1; ...; h_N]$, $H \in \mathbb{R}^{d \times N}$, is the hidden states generated by LSTM, v_s, $v_e \in \mathbb{R}^{1 \times d}$ are parameters to be learned.

During training, we minimize the following loss function based on training examples:

$$-\sum_{i=1}^{K} \log(p_{y_i^s}^s) + \log(p_{y_i^e}^e) \tag{5}$$

where y_i^s, y_i^e are the truth start and end indices of the i'th example, K is the number of examples in the training set, p_i represents the i'th element of vector $\boldsymbol{p}$.

During predicting, we choose the valid span (j, k) with maximum value of $p_j^s p_k^e$ as the target sequence:

$$(j, k) = \operatorname*{argmax}_{j \le k} p_j^s p_k^e \tag{6}$$

2.2   Bi-LSTM Networks

In the aforementioned LSTM based models, we use a standard LSTM processing the input sentence in one direction. At time step t, the hidden state h_t only contains information about previous time step. Bi-directional LSTM (Bi-LSTM) is designed to capture full contextual information from past and future context. BiLSTM network has two parallel standard LSTM layer, refer to as forward layer and backward layer. Given an input sequence $\boldsymbol{x}$, the forward layer process input sequence from left to right, generate a sequence of hidden states $\overrightarrow{\boldsymbol{h}}$, the backward layer process input sequence from right to left, generate a sequence of hidden states $\overleftarrow{\boldsymbol{h}}$. The final representation of hidden state at each time step is the concatenation of the two layers hidden states $h_t = [\overrightarrow{h_t}, \overleftarrow{h_t}]$. The BiLSTM based model in this section is similar with the aforementioned LSTM based model except that the LSTM layer is replaced by a Bi-LSTM layer.

2.3   Stacked Bi-LSTM

The proposed stacked Bi-LSTM has two layers of Bi-LSTM. The first layer process the input sequence in bi-direction and generates a sequence of hidden states $\boldsymbol{h}^1 = [h_1^1; ...; h_N^1]$, then the second layer takes $\boldsymbol{h}^1$ as input and outputs hidden states $\boldsymbol{h}^2 = [h_1^2; ...; h_N^2]$. $\boldsymbol{h}^1$ and $\boldsymbol{h}^2$ are used to compute the probability distributions of start index and end index individually.

$$p^s = \text{softmax}(v_s \boldsymbol{h}^1) \tag{7}$$

$$p^e = \text{softmax}(v_e \boldsymbol{h}^2) \tag{8}$$

2.4   LSTM with Chunk Encoding

In the previous models, we extract answer chunks by predicting the start and end indices separately. In this model, we encode a possible answer chunks within a maximum length into a fixed size representation and directly model the probability distribution over all possible answer chunks.

First, the input sentence $\boldsymbol{x}$ is encoded by a bi-directional LSTM resulting in hidden states $\overrightarrow{h}$ of the forward layer and $\overleftarrow{h}$ of the backward layer. For a certain candidate answer chunks $a = x_{i:j}$, which starting at position i and ending at position j, we encode it as:

$$h_a = [\overrightarrow{h_j}; \overleftarrow{h_k}] \tag{9}$$

Then the probability is modeled as:

$$p(a|\boldsymbol{x}) = \frac{\exp(vh_a)}{\sum\limits_{\tilde{a} \in A(\boldsymbol{x})} \exp(vh_{\tilde{a}})} \tag{10}$$

where $A(\boldsymbol{x})$ is the set of all possible candidate chunks.

In training, the following negative log likelihood is minimized:

$$-\sum_{i=1}^{K} \log P(a_i|\boldsymbol{x}_i) \tag{11}$$

where K is the number of examples, a_i is the golden answer of the i'th example.

3   Experiment

3.1   Data Collection

Baidu Zhidao[4] is the largest Chinese Q & A community. The website provides a search engine which can retrieve relevant questions along with peoples' answers according to the input query. Given an informal word, we search the community with designed queries like "what is the meaning of ___?", in which the slot is filled with the informal word. Then we download web pages returned in the first 3 result pages and extract answers as evidence with the following rules:

---

[4] www.zhidao.baidu.com.

- the informal word consist in both the question and the answer
- the selected answers should get high points of "agree"

The first rule aims to filter out irrelevant questions retrieved by the search engine, the second rule ensures that the answer is appropriate to our question. In most cases, answers selected under the restriction of these two rules, will contain an appropriate formal word that equivalent to the given informal word. To construct the dataset, we manually collect 858 informal words. Following this procedure, we finally get 2901 unique sentences[5]. Each sentence contains at least an informal-formal pair and has illustrated the equivalence between them. We employed LTP Toolkit[6] for sentence tokenization. An additional informal words dictionary is used to help the toolkit segment informal words correctly.

3.2   Implement Details

In the experiments, the first layer for all LSTM models are word embedding layer. The embedding layers are initialized with pre-trained 100-dimensional embeddings using skip-gram model [6] implemented by word2vec toolkit. The embeddings is trained on part of Chinese Gigaword corpus[7] and fixed during training. All words without pre-trained embedding are mapped to an $<unk>$ token. Especially, all given informal word are mapped to an $<informal>$ token to help the models identify the informal word's location.

The hidden size used in all LSTM is set to 50 and tune this parameter did not significantly influence the final result. All LSTM weights and feed-forward layers are initialized from a uniform distribution between (0.01, 0.01). For regularization, we adopt dropout with a probability of 0.2 in all LSTM layers and word embedding layer. All models are trained end-to-end using Adam with initial learning rate 0.0005. We employ gradient clipping when the norm of gradients exceeds 5. The batch size is set to 10. All models are implemented with Keras and Theano.

The sentences was split into training (80%) and test set (20%) with informal word as a key. During training, 10% of the training data form the validation set for the purpose of model evaluation and early stoping. We report result based on Exact Match (EM) and F-score. The EM metric measures the percentage of predictions that exact match the ground truth answers. The F-score is carry out on word level which measures the overlap between the prediction and ground truth answer. Word based F-score is a more relaxed metric than Exact Match.

3.3   Result and Discussion

Table 1 shows the performances of each models. From the results we observe that the stacked Bi-LSTM performs better than the other starting/ending prediction

---

[5] Our dataset is available at www.github.com/tiantian002/.

[6] www.ltp-cloud.com.

[7] www.catalog.ldc.upenn.edu/LDC2009T14.

Table 1. Evaluation results

Models	EM	Precision	Recall	F1	Parameters
LSTM	49.1	50.5	58.3	54.2	30.3K
Bi-LSTM	50.6	53.3	62.8	57.7	60.6K
Stacked Bi-LSTM	53.9	55.2	68.7	61.2	121K
LSTM with chunk encoding	55.3	57.3	68.4	62.5	60.5K

models. We believe that the two-layer stacked architecture can establish dependence between the begin and ending index to a certain degree. The Bi-LSTM model performs better than the LSTM model, since it benefit from the full contextual features. The chunk encoder performs best since it directly predict a answer chunk rather than predict it's starting/ending points. In experiment, we observed that, all start/ending prediction models performs better than the chunk encoding model when the target sequence contains only one word. However their performance drops rapidly when the length of target sequence increased. The performance of the chunk encoding model among each length of target sequence is relatively stable, since it encodes all chunks in a unified way.

Inherently, given a sentence contains N tokens, the number of possible candidates is in the order of $O(N^2)$. The first three models benefit from the simple independent assumption of predicting the beginning and ending points, which reduce the size of models softmax operation into $O(N)$ order. The chunk model reduce complexity by reusing outputs of the encoder layer and limiting the max length of candidates. With the max length of candidates set to M, the size of the softmax operation is $O(MN)$ order. Additionally, the models complexity is also affected by the different architectures of RNNs, the amount of trainable parameters of each model is shown in Table 1.

We analyse the error cases that all proposed models failed and find out that they mainly fall into two categories. Some answers contains more than one pair of informal-formal words, an example in English could be like *"tmr is often used for tomorrow, just like asap equals as soon as possible"*. In this case, the target sequence depends on the given informal words, *tomorrow* for *tmr* and *as soon as possible* for *asap*. This makes extraction be a target-depended task. An example of the second class could be like *"see you 2nite just is see you tonight"*, semantically the sentence defines two equivalent chunk *see you 2nite* and *see you tonight*, however it involved inference to know that *2nite* equals *tonight*. Designing model for this two problems should enhance the overall performance and we leave it to further research.

4   Related Works

Text normalization has been an important topic in text-to-speech and clinical text processing for a long time. In recently years, the researchers focused more on the field of social media. Many works are inspired by other tasks, such as machine translation [7], spell checking [2]. In [8] Liu et al. proposed a cognitively-inspired approaches, Beaufort et al. [9] incorporating rule with statistical based models, random walks also involved to solve the normalization task [10]. Due to the lack of annotated data, unsupervised or semi-supervised method [11–13] is also popular with the researchers.

In processing Chinese, Wang and Kan [14] proposed a model to process informal word detection and word segmentation jointly. In [15], they further extend their work into text normalization. By using context information, they generates candidates from large corpus, then classify the candidates with linguistic and statistic features. Li and Yarowsky [3] tackle the problem in the web domain by generating candidates from Baidu search engine and ranking using a conditional log-linear model. Qian et al. [16] proposed a joint model for segmentation, POS-tagging and normalization for Chinese microblogs. To meet the normalization task, they build up a noisy informal/formal pair dictionary with bootstrapping algorithm.

Recent years, neural networks have shown outstanding performance in various NLP tasks. Researchers start introduce neural techniques into social media normalization. In [17] word-level edits are predicted based on LSTM networks with character sequences and POS features. In [18], a hierarchical two layer forward feed neural networks was proposed to jointly predict whether a word should be normalized and the normalized token given an input token.

In addition, a thorough discussion of the effect of text normalization in social media could be seen in [19].

5   Conclusion

In this work, we tackle the lexical normalization task with information extraction method. We proposed several LSTM based models for the extraction. To evaluate and compare performances of the proposed models, we developed a standard dataset containing factoid generated by Q&A community users in daily life. We reported our experiment result and discussed advantages and disadvantages of each model. In future work, We want annotate more training data and introduce linguistic features to push the performance further and test our method on other languages.

Acknowledgments. This work was supported by 111 Project of China under Grant No. B08004, National Natural Science Foundation of China (61273217, 61300080, 61671078), the Ph.D Programs Foundation of Ministry of Education of China (20130005110004).

References

1. Han, B., Baldwin, T.: Lexical normalisation of short text messages: makn sens a Twitter. In: Proceedings of the 49th Annual Meeting of the Association for Computational Linguistics, Portland, pp. 368–378. ACL (2011)

2. Liu, F., Weng, F., Wang, B., Liu, Y.: Insertion, deletion, or substitution? Normalizing text messages without pre-categorization nor supervision. In: Proceedings of the 49th Annual Meeting of the Association for Computational Linguistics: Human Language Technologies, Portland, pp. 71–76. ACL (2011)

3. Li, Z., Yarowsky, D.: Mining and modeling relations between formal and informal Chinese phrases from web corpora. In: Proceedings of the Conference on Empirical Methods in Natural Language Processing, pp. 1031–1040 (2008)

4. Bengio, Y., Simard, P.: Learning long-term dependencies with gradient descent is difficult. IEEE Trans. Neural Netw. 5(2), 157–166 (1994)

5. Hochreiter, S., Schmidhuber, J.: Long short-term memory. Neural Comput. 9(8), 1735–1780 (1997)

6. Mikolov, T., Sutskever, I., Chen, K., Corrado, G.S., Dean, J.: Distributed representations of words and phrases and their compositionality. In: Proceedings of NIPS (2013)

7. Aw, A.T., Zhang, M., Xiao, J.: A phrase-based statistical model for SMS text normalization. In: Proceedings of COLING/ACL 2006, Sydney. ACL (2006)

8. Liu, F., Weng, F., Jiang, X.: A broad-coverage normalization system for social media language. In: Proceedings of the 50th Annual Meeting of the Association for Computational Linguistics, Jeju Island, pp. 1035–1044. ACL (2012)

9. Beaufort, R., Roekhaut, S., Cougnon, L.-A., Fairon, C.: A hybrid rule/model-based finite-state framework for normalizing SMS messages. In: ACL, pp. 770–779 (2010)

10. Hassan, H., Menezes, A.: Social text normalization using contextual graph random walks. In: Proceedings of ACL (2013)

11. Cook, P., Stevenson, S.: An unsupervised model for text message normalization. In: Proceedings of the Workshop on Computational Approaches to Linguistic Creativity, Boulder, pp. 71–78. ACL (2009)

12. Han, B., Cook, P., Baldwin, T.: Automatically constructing a normalisation dictionary for microblogs. In: Proceedings of the Joint Conference on Empirical Methods in Natural Language Processing and Computational Natural Language Learning, Jeju Island, pp. 421–432. ACL (2012)

13. Yang, Y., Eisenstein, J.: A log-linear model for unsupervised text normalization. In: Proceedings of the 2013 Conference on Empirical Methods in Natural Language Processing, Seattle, pp. 61–72. ACL (2013)

14. Wang, A., Kan, M.-Y.: Mining informal language from Chinese microtext: joint word recognition and segmentation. In: Proceedings of the 51st Annual Meeting of the Association for Computational Linguistics, pp. 731–741 (2013)

15. Wang, A., Kan, M.-Y., Andrade, D., Onishi, T., Ishikawa, K.: Chinese informal word normalization: an experimental study. In: Proceedings of IJCNLP, pp. 127–135 (2013)

16. Qian, T., et al.: A transition-based model for joint segmentation, POS-tagging and normalization. In: EMNLP (2015)

17. Min, W., Mott, B., Lester, J.: NCSU_SAS_WOOKHEE: a deep contextual long-short term memory model for text normalization. In: Proceedings of WNUT, Beijing (2015)

18. Leeman-Munk, S., Lester, J.: NCSU_SAS_SAM: deep encoding and reconstruction for normalization of noisy text. In: Proceedings of WNUT, Beijing (2015)

19. Baldwin, T., Li, Y.: An in-depth analysis of the effect of text normalization in social media. In: Conference of the North American Chapter of the Association for Computational Linguistics: Human Language Technologies (2015)

Analysing Event Transitions to Discover Student Roles and Predict Grades in MOOCs

Ángel Pérez-Lemonche$^{(\boxtimes)}$, Gonzalo Martínez-Muñoz, and Estrella Pulido-Cañabate

Escuela Politécnica Superior, Universidad Autónoma de Madrid, Madrid, Spain
angel.perezl@estudiante.uam.es, {gonzalo.martinez,estrella.pulido}@uam.es

Abstract. When interacting with a MOOC, students can perform different kinds of actions such as watching videos, answering exercises, participating in the course forum, submitting a project or reviewing a document. These actions represent the dynamism of student learning paths, and their preferences when learning in an autonomous mode. In this paper we propose to analyse these learning paths with two goals in mind. The first one is to try to discover the different roles that students may adopt when interacting with an online course. By applying k-means, six of these roles are discovered and we give a qualitative interpretation of them based on student information associated to each cluster. The other goal is to predict academic performance. In this sense, we present the results obtained with Random Forest and Neural Networks that allow us to predict the final grade with around 10% of mean absolute error.

Keywords: Learning analytics · Role clustering · Neural networks

1 Introduction

Massive Open Online Courses (MOOCs) generate loads of data that can be processed by using Learning Analytics to further exploration and comprehension of the courses. In [5], concepts, processes and potential applications of what Learning Analytics could bring are defined and developed in a theoretical way. Educational data mining can also be applied to educational data for extracting further knowledge of the learning processes [2]. In addition, as stated in [4] Educational Big Data also applies analysis techniques but in a time-efficient manner so that educational institutions can benefit from the analysis results and redesign their online courses accordingly.

In this sense, one way to explore MOOC data is to apply unsupervised or supervised machine learning algorithms in order to identify groups of students by their learning approaches or to predict their performance. This can help to understand the behaviour not only within the course given, but also in general, as a pedagogical instrument to know how people learn best and identify the roles that foster learning.

© Springer International Publishing AG 2017
A. Lintas et al. (Eds.): ICANN 2017, Part II, LNCS 10614, pp. 224–232, 2017.
https://doi.org/10.1007/978-3-319-68612-7_26

In [10], different techniques are reviewed for role discovering in social networks. Three approaches are described to solve this problem: graph-based analysis, feature-based analysis and a hybrid approach. Their experiments, that focus on a graph-based approach, identified persistent roles in different social networks. In the proposed work, we followed a feature-based approach, since the definition of a graph in the context of online learning is unclear.

Other study related to unsupervised learning in MOOCs is the analysis of discussion forums by applying word-based methods [6]. This study compares with the results obtained by using manual labelling. The authors identify seven clusters based on student interactions with the forum. In other studies [7,11], clustering techniques are applied to measure the engagement of students in the courses. In [7], they define a feature to measure the level of interaction with the course and then compute its value for each week of the course. These sequences of values are clustered for different users and courses to detect engagement patterns across courses.

In [11], they find three profiles based on the number of logins, assignment submissions and watched videos. However, most students were assigned to a cluster identified with those that carried out very few actions in the course. In our work, we preferred to discard students with a small number of interactions to better understand the behaviour of those interested in the course work.

Another important application of machine learning in MOOCs is grade prediction. The goal is to predict how well students will perform before they actually finish the course and to understand which factors affect academic performance. The results of this analysis can be useful to personalise and improve the course contents [9]. Some works such as [1] predict the grade based only on activity-related events. In [8] predictions are based on quizzes' results. In other study [12], timestamps of events are used to perform their predictions.

In contrast with existing work that analyses the number of events generated by students when interacting with online courses, in this paper we propose to add the temporal dimension and analyse the temporal sequence of events that we call *learning paths*. We extract the information contained in these temporal sequence of events by using the transitions between consecutive events as features.

We show that learning paths give information about students learning process that can help us to identify and understand the roles that students take when following an online course. Furthermore, they are also useful to predict students academic performance and can discriminate students that will achieve a high score from others not interested in getting a certificate.

2   Problem Description and Data Processing

The analysis presented in this work is based on log data obtained from the first edition of the MOOC *Playing with Android - Learn how to program your first app* offered by the Universidad Autónoma de Madrid in edX[1]. The goal of this course

---

[1] https://www.edx.org/school/uamx.

(taught in Spanish) is to understand the fundamental aspects of programming in Android and to be able to use these elements to develop a simple Android app.

The course is structured in seven weeks. The first six weeks introduce the contents of the course and propose programming activities. The last week is reserved for a final exam. During the six-week period, videos, short questions related to the video contents and programming activities are made available to students in a weekly basis. Each week's content is presented using an average of five short videos. After each video, a few short questions are proposed in order to check whether the main ideas explained in the videos have been understood. Each week also includes a programming activity intended for students to program some elements related to the topics covered during the week. Both questions and activities are evaluable and have a weight of 10% and 30% for the final grade, respectively. In addition, there is a programming project activity that runs throughout the course with a weight of 30% of the grade. The final exam accounts for the final 30% of the grade. All the documentation of the course is available in pdf format. In addition a general forum allows students to obtain help and interact with other students.

As the students progress through the elements of the course different events are recorded. The path that each student follows in the course is free within the weeks that are available. However the contents are organised sequentially and there is a suggested path that can be followed. From the myriad of events the edX platform generates, we have identified six that we consider able to describe the behaviour of students in the course. The identified events are **Video** — from all events related to student interaction with videos we have kept only the one related to the action of playing the video—, **Exercise** —event related to student answering a multiple choice question associated to a video—, **Activity** —student submission of a multiple choice question related to the programming activities of the week—, **Forum** —the event accounts for every possible student interaction with the course forum—, **Project** —student submission of one of the parts of the programming project—, and **Document** —student navigation through one of the text documents related to videos or downloading them—.

For each identified event, the following information is kept: student identifier, timestamp, content identifier and, in the case of evaluable content, the submitted value and the result of the submission. Note that, in addition to filtering the events, a cleaning phase was also applied to remove repeated events and events with missing information such as the id of the student generating the event, time, etc. Finally, events are sorted by time and grouped by student.

In order to model the progress of students through the course and to keep temporal information, transitions between consecutive events are extracted from the sorted series of events of each user. For each student, a transition matrix is generated where each row of the matrix corresponds to a starting event type, each column to the ending event and each cell value to the number of transitions from the event of the corresponding row to the given column. The event types are the ones described above, thus the matrix size is 6 by 6. Furthermore, students with less than 20 transitions were removed in order to avoid noisy patterns. After this whole process, we obtained transition matrices for 2,329 students.

Finally, these transition matrices were normalized by dividing each cell by the total number of events in the matrix. Preliminary experiments showed that working with normalized transition matrices provided more consistent results. This preliminary analysis also showed that many transitions were never, or very rarely, observed. Hence, instead of working with these rare features, we selected the features that accounted for more than 95% of the transitions. The remaining set of transitions were accumulated into a new feature. In total, from the 36 possible transitions we kept 13 of them and an additional one summarizing the rest, leaving the resulting features to use as: *Activity to Activity* (A2A), *Activity to Exercise* (A2E), *Activity to Video* (A2V), *Document to Document* (D2D), *Document to Video* (D2V), *Exercise to Activity* (E2A), *Exercise to Exercise* (E2E), *Exercise to Video* (E2V), *Forum to Forum* (F2F), *Video to Activity* (V2A), *Video to Document* (V2D), *Video to Exercise* (V2E), *Video to Video* (V2V) and *Rest* (Rest).

3   Experiments

In this section, the information related to student transitions between events, as described above, is used to carry out two experiments. In the first experiment, students are clustered based on transitions, in order to identify the different learning patterns that students follow in the course. The second experiment shows that the information about how students *move* through the course (i.e. the transitions) can be used to accurately predict the final grade.

For both experiments, the 14 previously identified features are used to describe the student interactions with the course.

In order to extract the different groups of students in relation to how they move in the course, several clustering algorithms were applied. Specifically, we tested: Mean Shift clustering, Hierarchical clustering, Gaussian Mixture Model and k-means.

Mean Shift and Hierarchical clustering grouped most students in one big cluster ($\approx$86% of students), one medium cluster ($\approx$13% of students) and one or several very small clusters ($<$1%). Gaussian Mixture Model finds rather balanced clusters, however, with very small inter-cluster distance. Small inter-cluster distance and highly unbalanced clusters makes the interpretation of the different patterns difficult.

The best and most interpretable results were given by k-means. We combined this method with BIC and with inter-cluster distance to select the number of clusters. Figure 1, shows the average inter-cluster distance (top plot) and BIC (bottom plot) with respect to the number of clusters. We identified six clusters as a reasonable number of k, which provides a small BIC and a good inter-cluster distance together with interpretability. By using higher values of k, the interpretability of clusters decreases with no significant improvement in the inter-cluster distance.

Table 1. Information associated to each cluster

	# of Students	Average grade	Avg. access time (Days)	Avg. time last event	Avg. # of transitions
Cluster 0	269	0.0 ± 0.1	20.8 ± 11.0	25.9 ± 10.8	45.5 ± 21.8
Cluster 1	395	0.2 ± 0.4	9.6 ± 6.9	15.6 ± 10.3	32.6 ± 14.4
Cluster 2	111	0.4 ± 1.0	19.3 ± 10.0	28.9 ± 10.0	45.2 ± 25.4
Cluster 3	324	1.2 ± 2.3	12.8 ± 7.7	23.0 ± 11.4	90.9 ± 71.5
Cluster 4	200	3.5 ± 3.5	16.9 ± 6.7	26.0 ± 10.1	103.1 ± 51.7
Cluster 5	1030	3.9 ± 3.5	15.5 ± 5.9	28.6 ± 10.2	132.2 ± 61.5

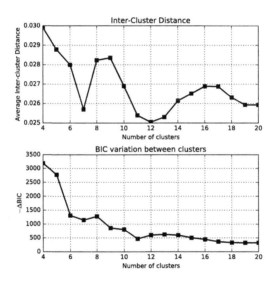

Fig. 1. (a) Inter-cluster distance for k-means algorithm. (b) BIC variation between clusters.

A similar number of clusters was found in other studies [6,7] that suggest using a number of clusters between 3 and 10.

Table 1 shows the statistics related to the students in those clusters. The table shows for each cluster: the number of students assigned to it, their average grade (ranged 0 to 10), average access time (average of event timestamps measured in days since the beginning of the course), the average time of the last event of each user (in days since the beginning), and the average number of transitions performed. The clusters are sorted by ascending average grade. Note that none of the clusters have an average grade greater than 5.0. This is due to the fact that only ≈25% of the analysed students actually finish the course and take the final exam.

In Fig. 2 the centroids of the clusters found are plotted as a radar chart in the 14-dimensions of the problem. Since vectors are normalized to sum one, they take values from 0 to 1, being 1 the centre of the plot.

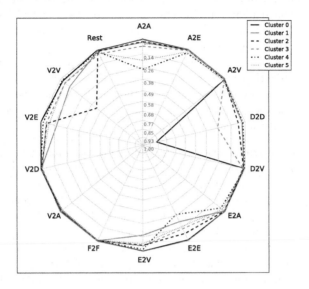

Fig. 2. Centroids position in the cluster.

Based on the information of Table 1 and Fig. 2, different kinds of students can be identified:

- **Cluster 0**: This cluster corresponds to the one with the highest peak in document to document transitions (D2D). In fact, students assigned to this cluster barely carry out any other activity. Hence, their final mark in average is 0.0. In addition, they perform their interaction with the course at the latest time with respect to all clusters on average, indicating that they wait until all contents are available to download the documents. They could be the ones whose aim is just downloading the course documents to read them later.
- **Cluster 1:** Students in this cluster distribute their activities among all transitions related to videos and exercises (V2V, V2E, E2V and E2E). They work at the beginning of the course as can be seen by the lowest average access time observed. These students could be identified as the ones that start the course but soon dropout.
- **Cluster 2:** This cluster presents the highest peak in video to video transitions (V2V) and smaller peaks in exercise related and document to document transitions (D2D). They barely perform any evaluable activity, as can be observed in their low final mark but this group is active along the whole course. They have one of the highest average access time. This group could be identified with students interested in the contents but not in the evaluation or certificate. This is the cluster with the lowest number of students assigned.

- **Cluster 3:** The students of this group dropout quite early in the course on average. They perform some activities and exercises and finally download the documents. This cluster could be identified with students that cannot follow the course but download the documents for reviewing them later.
- **Cluster 4:** The students in this cluster show peaks in activities (A2A) and exercises (E2E) and show a smaller number of interactions with the contents. Nevertheless, they perform quite well on average.
- **Cluster 5:** The students in this cluster also show peaks in activities (A2A) and exercises together with interactions with the content. This is the cluster with the largest number of students assigned. The students in this cluster could be seen as the *normal* students, that is, the ones that follow the course going through all the contents and activities.

In order to understand whether student transitions along the course could be used to predict the grade, a second experiment was carried out. For this experiment, a multilayer Neural Networks and Random Forest [3] regressors were applied to predict the grade in the range [0, 10]. The procedure followed in this experiment was the same for both methods: (i) Data were split using 10-fold cross-validation; (ii) For each train partition, the best parameter configuration was selected by applying a grid search with 10-fold cross-validation within the training set. For the Neural Network the following parameters were tested: the maximum number of iterations [100; 200; 500; 1,000], alpha [10e−2, 10e−4, 10e−6], and one and two hidden layers with [(5), (10), (50), (100), (5, 2), (10, 5), (50, 10), (100, 10)]. For Random Forest we used 500 estimators, unlimited maximum depth, and the number of features selected in each node using sqrt and log2 of the total number of features; (iii) After selecting the best parameter configuration over the train data, the model was trained using the full training data and (iv) finally, the test partition was used to obtain an estimation of the generalization error.

Two metrics were used to both select the optimum set of parameters and evaluate the models in test: the mean squared error (MSE) and the mean absolute error (MAE). The mean values obtained for both error metrics are shown in Table 2 together with the standard deviation given after the ± sign. For the Neural Network the median parameters chosen were the maximum number of iterations 500, alpha 0.001, and two hidden layers, the first one with 50 neurons and the second one with 10 neurons; whereas for Random Forest the median parameters chosen were 500 estimators, and the maximum number of features selected using square root of the number of features. The average results are shown in Table 2.

From Table 2, it can be observed that Random Forest achieves slightly better results for this task than Multilayer Neural Network. Both methods obtain an absolute mean error close to 1, which is a rather accurate prediction, only one point above or below, on average, of the student final mark.

Table 2. Average grade prediction error

	SME	MAE
Neural network	3.8 ± 0.7	1.3 ± 0.16
Random forest	3.3 ± 0.5	1.1 ± 0.15

4   Conclusions

In this paper we propose to model the progress of students through online courses as well as the associated temporal information by extracting the transitions between consecutive events from those generated by each student. By applying clustering and neural networks methods to data related to these event transitions we showed that it is possible to identify different student learning patterns and to predict student academic performance with around 10% of mean absolute error. This allows us to conclude that the analysis of event transitions can be a promising approach to understand and predict student behaviour.

Acknowledgments. The authors acknowledge financial support from the Spanish *Ministerio de Economa y Competitividad* (TIN2016-76406-P and from the UAM/IBM Chair).

References

1. Ashenafi, M.M., Riccardi, G., Ronchetti, M.: Predicting students' final exam scores from their course activities. In: 2015 IEEE Frontiers in Education Conference (FIE), pp. 1–9 (2015)
2. Baker, R.S., Inventado, P.S.: Educational data mining and learning analytics. In: Larusson, J.A., White, B. (eds.) Learning Analytics, pp. 61–75. Springer, New York (2014). doi:10.1007/978-1-4614-3305-7_4
3. Breiman, L.: Random forests. Mach. Learn. **45**(1), 5–32 (2001)
4. Ducange, P., Pecori, R., Sarti, L., Vecchio, M.: Educational big data mining: how to enhance virtual learning environments. In: Graña, M., López-Guede, J.M., Etxaniz, O., Herrero, Á., Quintián, H., Corchado, E. (eds.) ICEUTE/ SOCO/CISIS -2016. AISC, vol. 527, pp. 681–690. Springer, Cham (2017). doi:10. 1007/978-3-319-47364-2_66
5. Elias, T.: Learning Analytics: The Definitions, the Processes, and the Potential (2011)
6. Ezen-Can, A., Boyer, K.E., Kellogg, S., Booth, S.: Unsupervised modeling for understanding MOOC discussion forums: a learning analytics approach. In: Proceedings of the Fifth International Conference on Learning Analytics And Knowledge, LAK 2015, pp. 146–150. ACM (2015)
7. Ferguson, R., Clow, D.: Examining engagement: analysing learner subpopulations in massive open online courses (MOOCs). In: Proceedings of the Fifth International Conference on Learning Analytics and Knowledge, LAK 2015, pp. 51–58. ACM (2015)

8. Jiang, S., Williams, A., Schenke, K., Warschauer, M., O'dowd, D.: Predicting MOOC performance with week 1 behavior. In: Educational Data Mining 2014 (2014)
9. Lefevre, M., Guin, N., Marty, J.C., Clerc, F.: Personalization of MOOCs (2016)
10. Revelle, M., Domeniconi, C., Johri, A.: Persistent roles in online social networks. In: Frasconi, P., Landwehr, N., Manco, G., Vreeken, J. (eds.) ECML PKDD 2016. LNCS, vol. 9852, pp. 47–62. Springer, Cham (2016). doi:10.1007/978-3-319-46227-1_4
11. Tseng, S.F., Tsao, Y.W., Yu, L.C., Chan, C.L., Lai, K.R.: Who will pass? Analyzing learner behaviors in MOOCs. Res. Pract. Technol. Enhanced Learn. **11**(1), 8 (2016)
12. Xu, B., Yang, D.: Motivation classification and grade prediction for MOOCs learners. In: Computational Intelligence and Neuroscience 2016 (2016)

Applying Artificial Neural Networks on Two-Layer Semantic Trajectories for Predicting the Next Semantic Location

Antonios Karatzoglou[1,2($\boxtimes$)], Harun Sentürk[1], Adrian Jablonski[1], and Michael Beigl[1]

[1] Karlsruhe Institute of Technology, Karlsruhe, Germany
{antonios.karatzoglou,michael.beigl}@kit.edu,
antonios.karatzoglou@de.bosch.com,
{harun.sentuerk,adrian.jablonski}@student.kit.edu
[2] Robert Bosch GmbH, Corporate Sector Research and Advance Engineering, Stuttgart, Germany

Abstract. Location-awareness and prediction play a steadily increasing role as systems and services become more intelligent. At the same time semantics gain in importance in geolocation application. In this work, we investigate the use of artificial neural networks (ANNs) in the field of semantic location prediction. We evaluate three different ANN types: FFNN, RNN and LSTM on two different data sets on two different semantic levels each. In addition we compare each of them to a Markov model predictor. We show that neural networks perform overall well, with LSTM achieving the highest average score of 76,1%.

Keywords: Feed-forward-, Recurrent-, LSTM- Artificial Neural Networks · Markov chains · Semantic trajectories · Location prediction

1 Introduction

Knowing the location constitutes an important asset especially for location based management systems (LBMS) and services (LBS), whereby knowing both current, as well as the future location are equally important. In resource management systems for instance like intelligent traffic systems (ITS) and mobile communication, location prediction helps systems to look ahead in people's behavior and (pro-)act in an appropriate way. While predicting the location point (e.g. GPS coordinates) of a user is useful, knowing more about the particular location itself brings additional benefits. Having for instance knowledge about the location type ("home", "work", "restaurant", etc.) enables systems to better understand the logic behind users' movement patterns. This understanding results subsequently in deriving more sophisticated, high level rules and to provide consequently more accurate predictions. The use of semantics leads to the notion *semantic trajectories* described in Sect. 3. There exist many different location

© Springer International Publishing AG 2017
A. Lintas et al. (Eds.): ICANN 2017, Part II, LNCS 10614, pp. 233–241, 2017.
https://doi.org/10.1007/978-3-319-68612-7_27

prediction algorithms. Each approach points out certain advantages and disadvantages depending on its model and the nature and size of the available data. Artificial Neural Networks (ANNs) show generally a good performance in time series analysis and forecasting. Moreover, recurrent networks in particular, perform well when it comes to modeling sequences due to their nature. This makes them an ideal candidate for modeling spatio-temporal sequences. In addition, mobility analysis is generally considered to be a complex and nonlinear problem, which ANNs are also capable of handling well. In this paper we investigate the use of artificial neural networks in modeling semantic trajectories of mobile users and predicting their future semantic location. For this purpose we implement and compare three different types of neural networks: Feed-Forward, simple Recurrent and Long-Short-Term-Memory (LSTM), a special form of recurrent nets. The resulting models are trained and tested on two different data sets: a 3-month long single user data set and the multi-user MIT data set [3]. In addition, we compare their performance to the one of a typical probabilistic approach, Markov Chains. We show that neural networks perform overall well in predicting the next semantic locations with LSTM outperforming the competition. The rest of the paper is organized as follows; The related work is described in Sect. 2. Next, Sect. 3 gives a short insight in semantic trajectories. In Sect. 4 we will go deeper to the theoretical background and the implementation of our models. Section 5 gives a comprehensive view on our evaluation results, while lastly, Sect. 6 outlines our overall conclusions.

2   Related Work

Biesterfeld et al. were one of the first that used neural networks to address the topic location prediction. In their work [2], they investigated several variants of feed-forward and recurrent networks. They showed that neural networks perform generally well when it comes to motion pattern representation, with feed-forward achieving the best results. In [7], Vintan et al. within the scope of building an indoor location prediction system based on a 3-layer feed-forward perceptron investigated both separate models for each of the user, as well as a joint model composed of all of them. Their result indicate a higher accuracy on the part of the individualized models by showing an accuracy up to 92%. In 2012, Etter et al. compared three different models for solving a location prediction task [4]. A 3-layer feed-forward ANN achieved the best results, outperforming both the Dynamic Bayesian Network (DBN) and the Gradient Boosted Decision Trees (GBDT). Finally, Song et al. describe in their recent work [5] a deep LSTM based neural network architecture for simulating and predicting human mobility and transportation mode. They evaluated their system against Hidden Markov Model (HMM), Gaussian Model (GM) and a set of other neural networks variants. The deep LSTM was found to perform at best. The aforementioned research work dedicates itself to the use of ANNs on modeling and forecasting users' trajectories in general. However, recently there exists a small but growing research community, which takes the semantics behind the trajectories explicitly into consideration. Alvares et al. were one of the first in [1], who modeled and analyzed semantic trajectories. Some years later, in 2011, Ying et al. presented a first location prediction approach based on semantic trajectories [9]. They used prefix trees to model the respective trajectories and took both the popularity of the location, as well as the movement pattern similarity of users for estimating the future location. Semantic trajectories can also be found in (location) recommendation systems and/or location based social networks, where knowing the semantics of a location plays a major role. An interesting approach is given by Zheng et al. [10], who take different geographic levels into account by applying a tree-based hierarchical graph, whereby each level denotes a different geospatial scale (city, district, block) and thereby a different semantic interpretation accordingly. The recommended location itself is finally provided through a HITS-based inference model depending on the travel history of the user in the respective different levels. In our work we aim at exploring both the modeling of semantic trajectories with ANNs, as well as the notion of different semantic layers, while testing several ANN types at the same time.

3   Semantic Trajectories

Trajectories define spatio-temporal sequences, which describe the movement of objects. A typical (GPS) trajectory can be seen in formula 1. A single point is determined by its latitude, its longitude, the altitude and the corresponding time:

$$traj = (lat_1, long_1, alt_1, t_1), (lat_2, long_2, alt_2, t_2), ... \qquad (1)$$

Coordinates are not enough though for understanding the logic behind such movement patterns and the overall people's behavior; an understanding that promotes a more accurate estimation of their next steps. Spaccapietra et al. highlighted first the importance of *semantics* when modeling trajectories in order to understand the varying underlying meaning of them. So, in [6] they introduced a *conceptual view* over them by importing basic semantic elements such as *stops, moves, begin* and *end*. Yan et al. define a *semantic trajectory* in [8] as:

"*a structured trajectory where the spatial data (the coordinates) are replaced by geo-annotations and further semantic annotations*"

resulting to a sequence of *semantic episodes*:

$$traj_{sem} = se_1, se_2, se_3, ... \qquad (2)$$

There are many ways to describe a location depending on the semantic level to which is regarding to. Locations can be clustered and arranged in a type taxonomy. The higher the level, the wider becomes the definition. The location instance, that is the actual place itself that the user visits, lies at the very bottom. For instance *chinese restaurant in the 76th street $\rightarrow$ chinese restaurant $\rightarrow$ asian food restaurant $\rightarrow$ restaurant $\rightarrow$ food serving location*. Our work relies on this kind of semantic trajectories, while investigating different semantic levels at the same time.

4   Neural Network Based Semantic Location Prediction - Design, Implementation, and Parameter Selection

We implemented three different semantic location predictors in total, based on three different ANN architecture types respectively: Feed-Forward, simple Recurrent and LSTM. This section describes our implemented models and their corresponding parameters, while giving a short glimpse behind the theory of each at the same time. In order to have a fair comparison, we used the same 3-layer architecture (one hidden layer) for all. The number of input and output neurons $N_i = N_o = N$ complies with the number of different locations l_N found in each training and testing dataset respectively. We used *one-hot encoding* in order to represent the l semantic locations for both our input, as well as output vector. Our predictors were evaluated once with and once without taking temporal information (time and day) into account. In the case, in which time and day are being considered, our input vector grows by $7 + |timeslots|$.

4.1   Feed-Forward Neural Networks (FFNN)

Feed-Forward neural networks represent the simplest type of neural networks, but nonetheless they feature a good performance across multiple domains. A typical 3-layer FFNN similar to the one we implemented can be seen in Fig. 1. In the case of FFNN, we extended the input vector and hence the number of input neurons by l_{hist} for covering the movement history of the users resulting in a $l \times l_{hist}$ long vector. The sigmoid function and back propagation (BP) were used as activation function and learning algorithm accordingly.

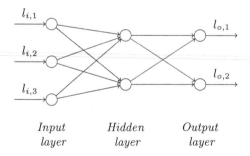

Input   Hidden   Output
layer   layer   layer

Fig. 1. Visualization of a typical 3-layer FFNN. $l_{i,j}$ represent current and previous visited semantic locations (depending on the set location history value). $l_{o,j}$ are the predicted semantic locations.

4.2   Recurrent Neural Networks (RNN)

Recurrent neural networks feature feedback loops that allow knowledge to be passed through the time from one step to the next. They are non-memoryless.

In particular, such loops are capable of pushing the output of a certain neuron in every time step either as an additional input to the same neuron itself, or to another neuron of the same or of a previous layer. This fact makes them ideal for modeling sequences. We used a similar 3-layer layout and encoding like the one by the FFNN, except that now, due to the nature of RNN, we don't have to explicitly extend the input vector by the previously visited places. Back propagation through time (BPTT) was selected to be our learning algorithm.

4.3   Long-Short-Term-Memory Neural Networks (LSTM)

LSTMs constitute a special type of recurrent neural networks, which are capable of storing longer sequences without showing the fading long-term dependency effect that appears in other RNNs. This is achieved by using so called *cells* that decide which and how many input sequences to keep or not.

4.4   Parameter Selection

In this work by taking primarily Vintan et al's results in [7] into consideration, who showed that individual models outperform a general model, we concentrate ourselves on creating personal models for each user. We applied 10-fold cross-validation on the single user dataset described in Sect. 5 as fitting optimization approach in order to find the best experimental setup for each of our models. Thus, we trained our models in 90% of the data and tested them on the remaining 10% for each possible combination of following parameter values: numbers of hidden neurons: [16, 32, 64, 128], epoch: [10, 20, 50, 100, 150], learning rate: [0.005, 0.01], history: [1, 2, ..., 16] and batch size: [1, 10, 50]. The training data set was build up through random selection of sequences with a length depending on the history that our model takes each time into consideration. The setup that led to the highest accuracy and f-score performance was selected for each ANN type respectively. This procedure took place twice, once for each semantic level (see Sect. 5). Table 1 summarizes the results.

5   Evaluation

We evaluated the following three models for predicting the next semantic location: FFNN, RNN and LSTM. All three models were evaluated on their performance they achieved on two different data sets: a 3-months long single-user data set and the multi-user Reality Mining data set [3]. Because of the sparseness and the partial inconsistency of the last, we preprocessed it first by removing duplicated entries and illogical outliers such as jumps to other countries. We selected furthermore the most conscientious users with the most check-ins, resulting in a total of 26 users over a time of 9 months. Each data set contains semantically labeled locations recorded by the users, like "Hilton hotel", "Media Lab", "MIT main campus", "Dentist" etc. Next, in order to investigate how different semantic levels affect the prediction, we processed both data sets to

Table 1. Final parameter setups obtained as described in Subsect. 4.4. MM refers to the Markov model, which is used as reference in our evaluation.

	ANN type	Hidden neurons (or cells)	Epoch	Learning rate	Weekday	Time	History	Batch size
Low sem. level	FFNN	32	100	0,01	No	No	2	1
	RNN	32	10	0,01	No	No	15	1
	LSTM	16	10	0,005	No	No	2	50
	MM	-	-	-	No	No	1	1
High sem. level	FFNN	32	10	0,01	No	No	9	1
	RNN	64	150	0,01	No	No	7	1
	LSTM	16	1,00	0,005	No	No	2	50
	MM	-	-	-	No	No	1	1

Table 2. Average statistic scores with and without taking time and day into account (1st and 2nd value respectively) (Reality Mining MIT data set)

	ANN type	Accuracy	Precision	Recall	f-Score
Low sem. level	FFNN	0,583 | 0,547	**0,272** | 0,251	0,260 | 0,239	0,248 | 0,231
	RNN	**0,611 | 0,626**	0,269 | 0,249	**0,286** | 0,268	**0,260** | 0,244
	LSTM	0,580 | 0,576	0,234 | 0,249	0,263 | 0,268	0,228 | 0,232
High sem. level	FFNN	0,679 | 0,664	0,378 | 0,437	0,387 | 0,377	0,379 | 0,387
	RNN	0,670 | 0,664	0,338 | 0,4124	0,370 | 0,383	0,351 | 0,382
	LSTM	**0,696 | 0,692**	**0,541** | 0,452	**0,483** | 0,458	**0,469** | 0,439

Table 3. Average and maximal accuracy scores (single-user data set)

	ANN type	Accuracy	Max value
Low sem. level	FFNN	0,411	0,594
	RNN	0,421	0,640
	LSTM	0,543	0,623
	MM	**0,611**	**0,942**
High sem. level	FFNN	0,634	0,787
	RNN	0,582	0,789
	LSTM	**0,761**	0,783
	MM	0,750	**1,00**

derive a higher conceptual view on them. For this purpose we applied a semantic clustering algorithm and assigned a *higher* label to each of the locations.

We oriented ourselves on the location taxonomy of *foursquare*[1], which led us to following higher semantic types: "home", "friend's home", "education", "medical", "transport", "shop", "square", "street", "(foreign) city", "entertainment", "center" and "other". These semantic annotations subsume the *lower* ones and represent therefore a higher location interpretation. We applied the same 10-fold cross-validation process in order to evaluate our predictors as we did for finding the optimal setup described in Sect. 4.4. Each predictor was trained and tested separately on each user, which led us to 26 individual models per predictor. The parameter setup for each predictor can be found in Table 1. Accuracy, precision, recall and f-score were used as metrics for our evaluation. Table 2 provides our summary statistics from the evaluation with the multi-user MIT data set. It contains the average ascertained results among all users. This table is quite revealing in many ways. What stands out is that in general temporal information does not lead to significant higher scores as one would expect. In contrary, in most of the cases, temporal information seems to affect negatively the scores. This justifies once more our parameter choice (time and weekday: "no") in Table 1. Thus, one could infer that it is not the absolute time and day that is important, but the sequence when it comes to semantic trajectory based prediction. Furthermore, it is apparent that all three models perform much better with semantically annotated locations of higher order. This can be attributed on the one hand to the fact that people move in space based on rules and patterns of higher semantical order. On the other hand, we must not forget that in the high level case, the models have to deal with clustered and therefore overall less locations. This favors additionally their performance. Closer inspection of the table shows that other than expected both recurrent networks do not stand out significantly over the FFNN. In the high semantic level case, LSTM outperforms the other two and RNN shows the worst performance, whereas the opposite is true for the lower one. Thus, the architecture type plays a significant role. Additionally, it must be mentioned that FFNN provided respectively high results with a much higher epoch value (100) than RNN and LSTM (both 10), which makes it more CPU-intensive and time-consuming. What is also striking about the figures in the table is that LSTM outperforms clearly the other models with regard to precision, recall and f-score. This means that it is not only more accurate, but also more consistent, that is its predictions scatter much less. This can be attributed partly to its solid memory-based architecture. Table 3 illustrates our findings of our evaluation with the single-user data set. In addition to the neural networks, we compared each model against a Markov model (MM) based predictor that serves as our reference. Table 1 shows the parameters of the Markov model that yield its best results and were used for our comparison. Furthermore, Table 3 contains the maximum recorded prediction accuracy (right column). The results correlate with the values in Table 2. The average scores achieved with the high level semantical data are again clearly higher compared to the low level ones. In addition, LSTM outperforms this time in both cases the FFNN and the simple RNN. LSTM outperforms even the Markov Model in the high level data case,

---

[1] https://developer.foursquare.com.

which interestingly shows similar high accuracy values. MM seem moreover to perform better than ANNs on low level location types. In individual cases MM achieved a 100% accuracy. A possible explanation might be the size of the available data. ANNs show their best performance in modeling big data and our data were probably not big enough.

6   Conclusion

The purpose of this work was to investigate the use of artificial neural networks in the field of semantic trajectory based location prediction. For this purpose three different neural network architectures were implemented: FFNN, RNN and LSTM. A two-(semantic)level evaluation was carried out on two different data sets, a 3-month long single-user data set and the MIT Reality Mining data set. In addition, we compared our models against a Markov Model based predictor. Our results illustrate a good average performance of the ANNs, especially on the higher semantic layer, with LSTM reaching an average accuracy of 76,1% outperforming the competition. Furthermore, our results indicate a significant contribution of high level semantic annotation of locations to the prediction. Overall this study strengthens the idea of using ANNs for location prediction and highlights the importance of semantics in this area. In our future work, we plan to extend the semantic knowledge that flows through the model by utilizing a.o. linked data libraries, and to experiment with other ANN types.

References

1. Alvares, L.O., Bogorny, V., Kuijpers, B., Moelans, B., Fern, J.A., Macedo, E., Palma, A.T.: Towards semantic trajectory knowledge discovery. In: Data Mining and Knowledge Discovery (2007)
2. Biesterfeld, J., Ennigrou, E., Jobmann, K.: Neural networks for location prediction in mobile networks. In: Proceedings of International Workshop on Applications of Neural Networks to Telecommunications, pp. 207–214 (1997)
3. Eagle, N., Pentland, A.S.: Reality mining: sensing complex social systems. Pers. Ubiquit. Comput. **10**(4), 255–268 (2006)
4. Etter, V., Kafsi, M., Kazemi, E.: Been there, done that: what your mobility traces reveal about your behavior. In: Proceedings of MDC by Nokia Workshop 10th PerCom (2012)
5. Song, X., Kanasugi, H., Shibasaki, R.: Deeptransport: prediction and simulation of human mobility and transportation mode at a citywide level. In: Proceedings of 25th International Joint Conference on Artificial Intelligence, pp. 2618–2624 (2016)
6. Spaccapietra, S., Parent, C., Damiani, M.L., de Macedo, J.A., Porto, F., Vangenot, C.: A conceptual view on trajectories. Data Knowl. Eng. **65**(1), 126–146 (2008)
7. Vintan, L., Gellert, A., Petzold, J., Ungerer, T.: Person movement prediction using neural nets. In: 1st Workshop on Modeling and Retrieval of Context, vol. 114, pp. 1–12 (2004)
8. Yan, Z., Chakraborty, D., Parent, C., Spaccapietra, S., Aberer, K.: Semantic trajectories: mobility data computation and annotation. ACM Trans. Intell. Syst. Technol. **4**(3), 49:1–49:38 (2013)

9. Ying, J.J.C., Lee, W.C., Weng, T.C., Tseng, V.S.: Semantic trajectory mining for location prediction. In: Proceedings of 19th ACM SIGSPATIAL, GIS 2011, pp. 34–43 (2011)

10. Zheng, Y., Zhang, L., Xie, X., Ma, W.Y.: Mining interesting locations and travel sequences from GPS trajectories. In: Proceedings of 18th International Conference on WWW, pp. 791–800 (2009)

Model-Aware Representation Learning for Categorical Data with Hierarchical Couplings

Jianglong Song[1](✉), Chengzhang Zhu[1,2], Wentao Zhao[1], Wenjie Liu[1], and Qiang Liu[1]

[1] College of Computer, National University of Defense Technology, Changsha, China
{songjl,wtzhao,liuwenjie15,qiangliu06}@nudt.edu.cn
[2] Advanced Analytics Institute, University of Technology Sydney, Ultimo, Australia
kevin.zhu.china@gmail.com

Abstract. Learning an appropriate representation for categorical data is a critical yet challenging task. Current research makes efforts to embed the categorical data into the vector or dis/similarity spaces, however, it either ignores the complex interactions within data or overlooks the relationship between the representation and its fed learning model. In this paper, we propose a model-aware representation learning framework for categorical data with hierarchical couplings, which simultaneously reveals the couplings from value to object and optimizes the fitness of the represented data for the follow-up learning model. An SVM-aware representation learning method has been instantiated for this framework. Extensive experiments on ten UCI categorical datasets with diverse characteristics demonstrate the representation via our proposed method can significantly improve the learning performance (up to 18.64% improved) compared with other three competitors.

Keywords: Categorical data · Model-aware representation learning · Hierarchical couplings

1 Introduction

Categorical data appears widely in our daily living, study, work and social activities. Compared with numerical data, analyzing categorical data is much harder due to the intrinsic complexities brought by its nominal values. A fundamental task for categorical data analytics is representing the nominal values in a numerical space, which largely determines the quality of data understanding and the flexibility of data mining.

Instead of the basic one-hot embedding method [5], there are two groups of methods for categorical data representation. One group of methods focuses on embedding intrinsic data complexities into vector or dis/similarity space. To capture the intra-attribute couplings, the work in [4,9] proposed the conditional probability and rough membership function based method, respectively. To reveal the inter-attribute couplings, the inter-attribute conditional probability in [1,6,8] and the co-occurrence frequency of highly interdependent attribute

© Springer International Publishing AG 2017
A. Lintas et al. (Eds.): ICANN 2017, Part II, LNCS 10614, pp. 242–249, 2017.
https://doi.org/10.1007/978-3-319-68612-7_28

in [7] were adopted. Some recently proposed methods [13,16] integrate the multiple types of relationship that show better representation strength. Another group of methods learns the representation of categorical data based on the final learning task or the follow-up learning model. One of the typical methods is value difference metric (VDM) [11], which embeds the categorical data to a similarity space based on the value distribution in class spaces. However, this method does not consider the embedded data distribution. In contrast, the method proposed in [15] learns a vector to maximize the inter-class margin of the represented data. To further consider the impact of the fed learning model, the heterogeneous support vector machine (HSVM) [10] has been proposed, which finds a representation to minimize the generalization error bound of SVM.

Although the aforementioned work showed some merits in categorical data embedding, they either ignore the complex interactions within data or overlook the relationship between the representation and its fed learning model. Failing to disentangle the complex interactions within data will cause the represented data lack of generalized ability [2], while decoupling from follow-up learning model will reduce the learnability of the whole learning system [12].

In this paper, we propose a **Mo**del-aware **re**presentation learning framework for **Cat**egorical data with **h**ierarchical couplings (MoreCatch) to simultaneously reveal the couplings from value to object and optimize the fitness of the represented data for the follow-up learning model. In particular, MoreCatch first leverages the value-level complex interactions as intra-attribute couplings, and combines it with attribute-level complex interactions as inter-attribute couplings to embed the object-level couplings into a similarity space. Then, it learns a representation by minimizing the generalization error bound of the follow-up learning model with the learned dis/similarity space as a regularization. Therefore, the represented data via MoreCatch will not only reflect the value-to-object couplings but also is adaptive to the specific learning model.

The key contributions made in this work are:

- A model-aware representation learning framework: this is the first framework to jointly learn the data and model characteristics for categorical data representation. This framework guarantees both the generalization ability and the fitness of the represented data.
- An SVM-aware representation learning method: an instantiation of the proposed MoreCatch has been proposed, which considers support vector machine (SVM) [12] as the fed classification. The method learns a vector representation by maximizing the radius margin bound of SVM with the regularization learned by coupled attribute similarity for objects (CASO) [13].
- We propose an efficient optimization algorithm for the SVM-aware representation learning instantiation. It has the capacity for parallelization, thus suits for the large amounts of data.

We compare the MoreCatch with several state-of-the-art and baseline categorical data representation methods on ten datasets with diverse characteristics. The experimental results demonstrate that MoreCatch significantly improves the learning performance (up to 18.64% improved).

2 Related Work

2.1 Support Vector Machine Generalization Error Estimation

Given a dataset $\{(x_i, y_i)\}_{i=1}^{n}$, we map an input vector x into higher dimensional feature space through the nonlinear function $\varphi(x)$. SVM finds a linear decision function by maximizing the margin between two different classes. The parameters w and b are obtained by solving the following convex optimization problem.

$$\min_{w,b} \frac{1}{2}||w||^2 + c \cdot \sum_{i=1}^{n} \xi_i \tag{1}$$
$$s.t. \quad y_i \cdot (w^T \cdot \varphi(x_i) + b) \geq 1 - \xi_i, \ \xi_i \geq 0, \ i = 1, 2, ...n,$$

where c is regularization parameter and ξ_i is a slack variable. The upper bound of radius margin error estimation is computed as in [12]:

$$T = \frac{R^2}{\gamma^2} = R^2 \cdot ||w||^2, \tag{2}$$

where R is the minimum radius of a sphere which contains all samples and γ is the maximal distance between the two different classes.

2.2 Coupled Attribute Similarity Metric

Coupled attribute similarity for objects (CASO) measure is proposed by Can Wang et al. CASO is an efficient data-driven similarity learning approach for categorical objects with attribute couplings to capture a global picture of attribute similarity [13]. It involves the intra-coupled similarity, the inter-coupled similarity and their integration on the object level. The intra-coupled similarity is obtained based on attribute value frequency distribution within an attribute and the inter-coupled similarity is calculated from value co-occurrences between attributes. In this paper, we apply the coupled attribute dissimilarity for objects (CADO) induced from CASO to investigate the intrinsic characteristics of data.

$$CADO(x_i^k, x_j^k) = \sum_{i=1}^{m} h_1(\delta_k^{Ia}(x_i^k, x_j^k)) \cdot h_2(\delta_k^{Ie}(x_i^k, x_j^k, \{X^q\}_{q \neq k})), \tag{3}$$

where x_i^k and x_j^k are current categorical values of k_{th} dimension of sample x_i and x_j. δ_k^{Ia} and δ_k^{Ie} are intra-coupled and inter-coupled attribute similarity for values. In addition, $h_1(t)$ and $h_2(t)$ are decreasing functions. Based on intra-coupled and inter-coupled similarities, $h_1(t)$ and $h_2(t)$ can be flexibly chosen to build dissimilarity measures according to specific requirements.

3 Model-Aware Representation Learning

3.1 The MoreCatch Framework

The proposed model-aware representation learning framework for categorical data with hierarchical couplings (MoreCatch) is presented in Fig. 1. It first combines the value-level intra-attribute couplings with attribute-level inter-attribute

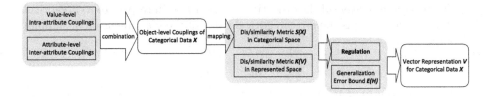

Fig. 1. Framework of MoreCatch

couplings as the object-level couplings, and then embeds it into a dis/similarity space. Finally, it learns the representation by minimizing the generalization error bound of the follow-up learning model with the learned dis/similarity as a regularization. Formally, given a classifier $\mathcal{H}$ with a generalization error bound $\mathbb{E}(\mathcal{H})$ and a categorical dataset $\mathbf{X}$, the objective of the MoreCatch learns a vector representation $\mathbf{V}$ for $\mathbf{X}$ that

$$\min_{\mathbf{V}} \ \mathbb{E}(\mathcal{H}) + \lambda \|S(\mathbf{X}) - K(\mathbf{V})\|^2, \tag{4}$$

where $S(\cdot)$ is the dis/similarity metric in the categorical data space that capturing the hierarchical couplings, $K(\cdot)$ is the dis/similarity metric in the represented space that will be used in the $\mathcal{H}$, and λ is a trade-off parameter to control the influence of the data and model characterises.

3.2   An SVM-Aware Representation Learning Method

We implement an SVM-aware representation learning method as an instantiation of the MoreCatch. It considers SVM as the follow-up classifier $\mathcal{H}$ of the represented categorical data. Inspired by the [10], it uses radius margin bound to instantiate the $\mathbb{E}(\mathcal{H})$. Meanwhile, the $S(\cdot)$ is implemented by the CADO since it can comprehensively leverage the couplings from value-level to object-level.

Correspondingly, we select Euclidean distance as the metric in the represented data space. Putting Eqs. (2) and (3) into Eq. (4), we have the objective function SVM-aware representation as follows:

$$L = R^2 \cdot \|w\|^2 + \lambda \sum_{i,j=1}^{n} \left(CADO(v_i, v_j) - D(x_i, x_j)\right)^2, \tag{5}$$

where $D(\cdot, \cdot)$ is the Euclidean distance between objects in represented data space. Minimize L can induce the vector representation of categorical data, $\mathbf{V}$.

3.3   Algorithm for the SVM-Aware Representation Learning

In this subsection, we propose an efficient stochastic gradient descent algorithm to optimize the Eq. (5).

The partial derivative of the objective function L with respect to a categorical attribute value a_p^k (a_p^k is the p_{th} categorical value of the k_{th} dimension of sample) is computed as

$$\frac{\partial L}{\partial a_p^k} = \frac{\partial L_1}{\partial a_p^k} + \frac{\partial L_2}{\partial a_p^k}, \tag{6}$$

where L_1 and L_2 refer to the radius error bound and similarity regularization, respectively. The partial derivative of the objective L_1 is computed as

$$\frac{\partial L_1}{\partial a_p^k} = R^2 \cdot \frac{\partial ||w||^2}{\partial a_p^k} + \frac{\partial R^2}{\partial a_p^k} \cdot ||w||^2. \tag{7}$$

The parameter w of traditional SVM can be obtained by solving its dual formula, and we can calculate the partial derivative of $||w||^2$ with respect to the categorical attribute value a_p^k as follows:

$$\frac{\partial ||w||^2}{\partial a_p^k} = \alpha^{*T} \cdot \frac{\partial K}{\partial a_p^k} \cdot \alpha^*, \tag{8}$$

where α^{*T} is the optimal solution $(\alpha_1 y_1, \alpha_2 y_2, ..., \alpha_n y_n)_{1 \times n}$. R is the minimum radius of a sphere which contains all samples in the feature space. It can be calculated based on the following formula:

$$R^2 = \beta \cdot diag(K) - \beta^T \cdot K \cdot \beta, \tag{9}$$

where β is the optimal solution to the dual problem, and K is a kernel matrix. $diag(K) = (K(x_1, x_1), K(x_2, x_2), ..., K(x_n, x_n))^T{}_{n \times 1}$. $\partial K(x_i, x_i)/\partial a_p^k$ equals zero in a regularization kernel function. Therefore, the partial derivative of radius R^2 can be simplified as follows:

$$\frac{\partial R^2}{\partial a_p^k} = -\beta^T \cdot \frac{\partial K}{\partial a_p^k} \cdot \beta. \tag{10}$$

Then, Eqs. (8) and (10) are taken into Eq. (7) to get the derivative of L_1:

$$\frac{\partial L_1}{\partial a_p^k} = R^2 \cdot (\alpha^{*T} \cdot \frac{\partial K}{\partial a_p^k} \cdot \alpha^*) - ||w||^2 \cdot (\beta^T \cdot \frac{\partial K}{\partial a_p^k} \cdot \beta). \tag{11}$$

The partial derivative of the Gaussian kernel matrix can be calculated as follows:

$$\frac{\partial K(x_i, x_j)}{\partial a_p^k} = K(x_i, x_j) \cdot (-\frac{v_i^k - v_j^k}{\sigma^2}) \cdot \begin{cases} +1, if\ v_i^k = a_p^k \\ -1, if\ v_j^k = a_p^k \\ 0,\ otherwise. \end{cases} \tag{12}$$

The value of CADO is calculated in the stage of data preprocessing and it is a constant that has no influence in the process of derivation. The partial derivative of the objective L_2 is computed as follows:

$$\frac{\partial L_2}{\partial a_p^k} = -4 \cdot \lambda \sum_{i,j=1}^{n} (CADO(x_i, x_j) - D(x_i, x_j)) \cdot (v_i^k - v_j^k) \cdot \begin{cases} +1, if\ v_i^k = a_p^k \\ -1, if\ v_j^k = a_p^k \\ 0,\ otherwise. \end{cases} \tag{13}$$

Algorithm 1. SVM-aware representation learning

Input: Categorical dataset $X = \{x_1, x_2, ..., x_n\}$
Output: A mapping table for each categorical attribute value and a classifier
Iteration:
1: $t \leftarrow 0$
2: Assign an initial real value for each categorical attribute a_p^k
3: **while** stop criteria not satisfied **do**
4:     Calculate $\|w\|^2$ and kernel matrix based on SVM
5:     Calculate radius R^2 based on Eq. (9)
6:     Calculate the Euclidean distance D between objects
7:     Calculate $\frac{\partial L_1}{\partial a_p^k}$ for categorical attribute value based on Eqs. (11) and (12)
8:     Calculate $\frac{\partial L_2}{\partial a_p^k}$ for each categorical attribute value based on Eq. (13)
9:     Calculate $\frac{\partial L}{\partial a_p^k}$ for each categorical attribute value based on Eq. (6)
10:     Update mapping value $(a_p^k)^{t+1} = (a_p^k)^t - \eta \cdot \frac{\partial L}{\partial a_p^k}$
11:     Calculate the error bound L
12:     $t \leftarrow t + 1$
13: **end while**

During the SVM-aware representation learning, the algorithm maps categorical attributes into a real number space by minimizing the generalization error bound with the dissimilarity regularization. The mapping is learned by a gradient descent scheme, which can randomly assign the initial real value, then iteratively update the assignments of categorical attributes until the generalization error bound converges to a minimum state. It is shown in Algorithm 1.

Here, we initialize each categorical attribute value by calculating its conditional probability in the manner as VDM (Value Difference Metric). VDM calculates the distance between categorical attributes by utilizing the label information of samples [14]. The more similar the frequencies of categorical attributes that appear in one class, the shorter is the distance between attributes.

It is noted that the coupled attribute dissimilarity for objects (CADO) is computed on the basis of original categorical attribute values which has no assignments in the real number space. And it is a constant during the process of representation learning. This algorithm also gets benefit from the parallel ability since the gradient of each value can be calculated separately.

4 Experiments and Analysis

Ten categorical datasets from the UCI machine learning repository are used in the experiments. The details of these datasets are shown in Table 1.

We compare the SVM-aware representation under MoreCatch framework (MoreCatch (SVM-aware), for short) with state-of-the-art categorical data representation method HSVM [10] and the baseline method VDM [11]. The represented data of the above methods is fed into SVM with Gaussian kernel for classification. The samples containing missing values are discarded in data preprocessing stage. We utilize one-against-all for multi-class tasks and evaluate the

Table 1. Predictive accuracy (%) of SVM with different representation methods

Dataset	Size	Attri.	Class	MoreCatch (SVM)	VDM	HSVM	Δ
molecular	106	57	2	**78.70 ± 9.75**	74.68 ± 8.43	41.66 ± 9.82	5.38
spect	267	22	2	**100**	79.38 ± 4.48	84.29 ± 4.10	18.64
solar flare1X	323	10	2	**100**	97.82 ± 2.15	**100**	0.00
vote	435	16	2	98.29 ± 2.41	96.53 ± 3.24	**98.72 ± 1.28**	0.00
tic-tac-toe	958	9	2	**100**	98.22 ± 0.72	**100**	0.00
chess	3196	36	2	**99.44 ± 0.40**	97.03 ± 0.20	98.89 ± 0.20	0.56
mushroom	8124	22	2	**100**	**100**	**100**	0.00
splice	3190	61	3	**99.90 ± 0.10**	97.20 ± 1.70	99.70 ± 0.30	5.88
soybean-small	47	35	19	**98.96 ± 2.23**	95.83 ± 2.00	98.33 ± 2.60	0.30
soybean-large	307	35	19	**85.39 ± 0.56**	82.50 ± 3.17	83.70 ± 1.68	1.96
Mean	-	-	-	**96.07**	91.92	90.53	4.51

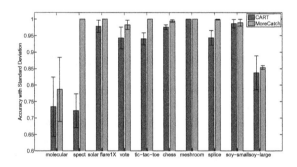

Fig. 2. MoreCatch-enabled SVM and CART comparison on ten datasets

algorithm based on 10-fold cross validation. The performance of representation learning method is evaluated by the accuracy of its enabled SVM.

The mean and standard deviation of accuracy are shown in Table 1 as *mean* ± *std*. Bold font has been used to mark the best method for each dataset. The last column of the table, Δ, stands for the improvement of the proposed method compared with the best one of the other three methods. As shown in Table 1, the accuracy of the MoreCatch (SVM) is superior to that of other algorithms. For the DNA data with complex couplings, the MoreCatch (SVM-aware) improves significantly compared with the state-of-the-art method HSVM. Such a high improvement is due to MoreCatch not only considers the model complexity, but also captures the intrinsic data characteristics.

To further demonstrate the performance of the proposed MoreCatch, we compare it with CART [3], which is a decision tree algorithm that can handle categorical data directly. The results are showed in Fig. 2. It demonstrates that MoreCatch is consistently better than CART. The key reason is our proposed MoreCatch can get benefit from the kernelized SVM for non-linear classification.

5   Conclusion

In this paper, a model-aware representation learning framework for categorical data with hierarchical couplings(MoreCatch) is proposed to jointly learn the data and model characteristics. Then, a SVM-aware representation learning method is proposed as an instantiation of MoreCatch. Experiments show that representation via our proposed method can significantly improve the learning performance compared with other three competitors.

References

1. Ahmad, A., Dey, L.: A method to compute distance between two categorical values of same attribute in unsupervised learning for categorical data set. Pattern Recogn. Lett. **28**(1), 110–118 (2007)
2. Bengio, Y., Courville, A., Vincent, P.: Representation learning: a review and new perspectives. IEEE Trans. Pattern Anal. Mach. Intell. **35**(8), 1798–1828 (2013)
3. Breiman, L., Friedman, J.H., Olshen, R., Stone, C.J.: Classification and regression trees. Biometrics **40**(3), 358 (1984)
4. Cao, F., Liang, J., Li, D., Bai, L., Dang, C.: A dissimilarity measure for the k-modes clustering algorithm. Knowl.-Based Syst. **26**, 120–127 (2012)
5. Grąbczewski, K., Jankowski, N.: Transformations of symbolic data for continuous data oriented models. In: Kaynak, O., Alpaydin, E., Oja, E., Xu, L. (eds.) ICANN/ICONIP -2003. LNCS, vol. 2714, pp. 359–366. Springer, Heidelberg (2003). doi:10.1007/3-540-44989-2_43
6. Ienco, D., Pensa, R.G., Meo, R.: From context to distance: learning dissimilarity for categorical data clustering. ACM Trans. Knowl. Discov. Data **6**(1), 1–25 (2012)
7. Jia, H., Cheung, Y.M., Liu, J.: A new distance metric for unsupervised learning of categorical data. IEEE Trans. Neural Netw. Learn. Syst. **27**(5), 1065–1079 (2016)
8. Le, S.Q., Ho, T.B.: An association-based dissimilarity measure for categorical data. Pattern Recogn. Lett. **26**(16), 2549–2557 (2005)
9. Ng, M.K., Li, M.J., Huang, J.Z., He, Z.: On the impact of dissimilarity measure in k-modes clustering algorithm. IEEE Trans. Pattern Anal. Mach. Intell. **29**(3), 503–507 (2007)
10. Peng, S., Hu, Q., Chen, Y., Dang, J.: Improved support vector machine algorithm for heterogeneous data. Pattern Recogn. **48**(6), 2072–2083 (2015)
11. Stanfill, C., Waltz, D.: Toward memory-based reasoning. Commun. ACM **29**(12), 1213–1228 (1986)
12. Vapnik, V.N.: Statistical Learning Theory, vol. 1. Wiley, New York (1998)
13. Wang, C., Dong, X., Zhou, F., Cao, L., Chi, C.H.: Coupled attribute similarity learning on categorical data. IEEE Trans. Neural Netw. Learn. Syst. **26**(4), 781 (2015)
14. Wilson, D.R., Martinez, T.R.: Improved heterogeneous distance functions. J. Artif. Intell. Res. **6**(1), 1–34 (1997)
15. Xie, J., Szymanski, B.K., Zaki, M.J.: Learning dissimilarities for categorical symbols. In: JMLR: Workshop on Feature Selection in Data Mining, pp. 2228–2238. JMLR.org (2013)
16. Zhang, K., Wang, Q., Chen, Z., Marsic, I., Kumar, V., Jiang, G., Zhang, J.: From categorical to numerical: multiple transitive distance learning and embedding. In: SIAM International Conference on Data Mining, pp. 46–54. SIAM (2015)

Perceptron-Based Ensembles and Binary Decision Trees for Malware Detection

Cristina Vatamanu[1,2(✉)], Doina Cosovan[1], Dragoş Gavriluţ[1,2], and Henri Luchian[1]

[1] Faculty of Computer Science, Alexandru Ioan Cuza University, Iaşi, Romania
{cvatamanu,dgavrilut}@bitdefender.com,
{doina.cosovan,hluchian}@info.uaic.ro
[2] Bitdefender Anti-Malware Laboratory, Bucharest, Romania

Abstract. Nowadays, security researchers witness an exponential growth of the number of malware variants in the wild. On top of this, various advanced techniques like metamorphism, server-side polymorphism, anti-emulation, commercial or custom packing, and so on, are being used in order to evade detection. It is clear that standard detection techniques no longer cope with the ongoing anti-malware fight. This is why machine learning techniques for malware detection are continually being developed and improved. These, however, operate on huge amounts of data and face challenges like finding an equilibrium between the three most desired requirements: low false positive rate, high detection rate, acceptable performance impact. This paper aims to reach this equilibrium by starting with an algorithm which has a zero false positive rate during the training phase and continuing by further improving it, in order to increase the detection rate without significantly altering the low false positive property.

Keywords: Linear classifier · Perceptron · Ensemble · One side class perceptron · Binary decision tree · Hybrid methods · False positive rate

1 Introduction

In the Cyber Security industry a false positive is by far more problematic than a false negative. It is easier to add detection later than to help customers recover their data. This is why reducing the number of false positives is our top priority. Our approach is to start with a classifier that has a zero false positive rate during the training phase and to continue by improving the detection rate while keeping the false positive rate as close to zero as possible. Of all the machine learning algorithms, we decided to use the perceptron because it has an acceptable performance impact and because we want to start with a low false positive algorithm and there is a perceptron variation, called the One Side Class Perceptron, which is able to obtain a zero false positive rate during the training phase. This paper tries to improve the One Side Class ensemble (OSC-BC) which was first introduced in [13]. An ensemble system was considered for improving the

© Springer International Publishing AG 2017
A. Lintas et al. (Eds.): ICANN 2017, Part II, LNCS 10614, pp. 250–259, 2017.
https://doi.org/10.1007/978-3-319-68612-7_29

detection rate. Though it managed to keep the false positive rate low (0.007%), the detection could not be improved more than 35%. Because of this, the data was first clustered with the help of the Binary Decision Tree (BDT) and then ensembles were trained on each cluster. This improved the detection up to 70%, keeping the false positive rate as low as 0.2%. This led us to the idea that the starting point (the OSC-BC algorithm) is good while the mechanism used to improve the detection rate could be improved. This paper proposes two techniques to achieve this: adapting perceptron parameters and intercalating the ensemble steps of OSC-BC with BDT clustering.

2   Related Work

Machine learning techniques are being rapidly adopted in malware detection field of research thanks to their ability to counter polymorphism, metamorphism, and packing techniques used by malware. Consequently, different authors tried to approach the problem of malware detection using various machine learning algorithms like Artificial Neural Networks (ANN), Bayesian Networks (BN), Naive Bayes (NB), Decision Tree (DT), k-Nearest Neighbor (kNN), Support Vector Machines (SVM), OneR, and so on. In this section, we are going to discuss the advances in malware detection in two different directions, both related to our research: perceptron variations and ensembles.

In [11], Rosenblatt introduced the perceptron. The idea behind it is very simple: first it computes a linear combination of the input applied to its synapses and then applies a sign function on the result in order to classify the element. Since then, perceptrons proved to be effective in solving various problems. Because each problem requires different aspects to be considered and optimized, a lot of perceptron variations, adaptations and enhancements appeared.

A perceptron variation, the voted-perceptron algorithm, is introduced in [3]. It combines Rosenblatt's perceptron algorithm with Helmbold and Warmuth's leave-one-out method and takes advantage of the data that are linearly separable with large margins. Used against malware detection in [1], it provides a 99% accuracy and a high detection rate. However their focus was not to minimize the false positive rate, thus making their algorithm difficult to use in practice.

A few papers have focused on budget-conscious perceptrons, which attempt to keep the number of support patterns small. The attractiveness of the idea comes from the improvements observed in both training and classification time, but also in the simplicity of the model. For example, in [2], the budget-conscious perceptron keeps track of the support patterns and discards the ones that become redundant as new, nearer to the separation plan examples are being received. In the same paper a budget-conscious aggressive algorithm perceptron is proposed. Although the authors in [12] argue that a perceptron with zero false positives during the training phase can not be developed, a solution is proposed in [5] and optimized in [4]. Since we use this perceptron in an ensemble, this section also presents various ensembles proposed in the literature for malware detection.

Some papers present and provide a detailed analysis of a single but new combination technique aiming at solving a specific problem [15], where individual decisions of PNN (Probabilistic Neural Networks) classifiers are combined using rules created in the frame of Dempster-Shafer theory.

Another example is [8], which introduces SVM-AR. This ensemble consists of an SVM component, which computes a hyper-plane classifying the samples as clean or malicious, and association rules, behaving as local optima filters for the records miss-classified by the SVM classifier.

Another SVM-based ensemble is proposed in [14], where SBMDS (interpretable String-Based Malware Detection System) is introduced. It uses Support Vector Machine (SVM) ensemble with Bagging in order to classify the samples.

The same combination of Support Vector Machine and Bagging is presented in [6]. First, individual SVMs are trained independently on samples randomly chosen through a bootstrap technique. Then, the obtained SVM classifiers are aggregated in various ways like Majority Voting, LSE (least squares estimation)-based weighting, and the double-layer hierarchical combining.

Other papers focus on comparing different well-known mechanisms of combining the algorithms in order to find the one best suiting a specific problem. For example, the authors in [9] combine 5 different classifiers (C4.5, kNN, VFI, OneR and Naive Bayes) using 8 different combination techniques (Best Classifier, Majority Voting, Performance Weighting, Distribution Summation, Bayesian Combination, Naive Bayes, Stacking, and Troika) for finding the best ensemble which classifies files, described by structural, API-based features, and n-grams.

The authors of [10], however, test various ensembles for Android detection. Algorithms like kNN, NNet, CART, and SVM variations (SVMLinear, SVMPoly, SVMRadical) are aggregated through Majority Voting and Stacking.

Most papers conclude that ensembles perform better than individual algorithms.

3   Algorithms

The One-Side Class Perceptron [4] (abbreviated OSCP) is a perceptron that satisfies the following property: given two classes, the hyper-plane will separate on one side only elements belonging to the first class and on the other - all the elements belonging to the second class and a few elements from the first class. In order to achieve this property, each perceptron iteration is followed by an adaptation of the hyper-plane in order to restore the property.

When used in malware detection, the OSCP can build a linear classifier with zero false positives during training (only malicious samples on one side of the hyper-plane and both clean and malicious - on the other side).

Further, in order to ensure a high detection rate along with the property of having a close to zero false positive rate (during testing), a combination of two One Side Class Perceptrons is proposed in [13]. If these two One Side Class Perceptrons are merged, then two correctly classified sets of data are obtained: one containing clean samples and the other - malicious samples.

Figure 1 illustrates on the upper left side the dataset containing clean (circles) and malicious (squares) samples. The first hyper-plane separates clean samples on one side and both clean and malicious samples on the other side (upper right side of the image). The second hyper-plane divides only malicious samples on one side and both clean and malicious samples - on the other side (lower left side of the image). Between the two hyper-planes there are data that could not be correctly classified (lower right side of the image).

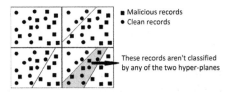

Fig. 1. Ensemble with both classes based on OSC perceptron

In order to deal with the incorrectly classified data, an ensemble was developed starting from the previously described combination of two One Side Class Perceptrons [13]. It is called One Side Class Perceptron ensemble with both classes and abbreviated ENS10-OSC-BC in the paper in which it is introduced, but, for simplicity, we abbreviate it ENS throughout this paper. Specifically, we can run this ensemble algorithm on the training data, save the obtained model (the two hyper-planes), discard the correctly classified elements and reiterate the same process on the misclassified elements. The algorithm stops either when all the data is correctly classified (no data remains between the two hyper-planes) or when the maximum number of iterations is reached (enforced in practice).

3.1 Parameter Adaptation

In our experiments [13], we have used 10 ensemble steps and for each ensemble step, 2 OSC algorithms were trained using 500 perceptron iterations. In order to choose the number of ensemble steps, we decided to try to execute the algorithm with as many steps as possible in order to correctly classify all the data. However, since the dataset is very big, we performed this test on a subset (332.404 records: 31.940 infected files and 300.464 clean ones). Unfortunately, at the 39th ensemble step, the algorithm couldn't produce a hyper-plane able to correctly classify and remove from the dataset at least one of the records. By doubling the number of perceptron iterations from this point on, we allowed the algorithm to continue beyond the 39th step. But seven steps later (at the 46th step), the algorithm was blocked again. Repeating the same operation on the perceptron iterations, the algorithm continued only 12 more steps (until the 58th step). Since in the last executed 5 ensemble steps only one record per step was correctly classified and discarded, with 113.560 records still unclassified, we came to the conclusion that the algorithm has and will continue to have a very slow decrease. The decrease can be seen in Fig. 2.

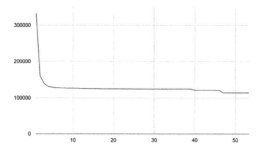

Fig. 2. Number of unclassified records during ensemble steps

Note how the first three ensemble steps managed to correctly classify and remove from the dataset more than half of the records. From the 6th step the decrease started to be and remained almost imperceptible with the exception of the 39th and 46th steps, which correspond to the two ensemble steps for which the number of perceptron iterations was doubled. Using 10 ensemble steps is a reasonable choice from three points of view. Firstly, the number of records correctly classified and removed from the dataset beyond the 10th step is not big in comparison to the remaining unclassified records. Secondly, the training time with 10 ensemble steps and 500 perceptron iterations allows the models to be train fast enough for the anti-virus product to have a quick response in the wild. Thirdly, the space needed to save the model trained with 10 steps is reasonable. At each ensemble step, the model needs to save (2 bytes for feature ID + 4 bytes for feature value) * 2 models * n features (n is minimum 500).

In order to train perceptrons on millions of samples in an acceptable amount of time, restrictions are usually set on the algorithm parameters. Given the way OSC-BC operates (at each step, the algorithm discards the samples correctly classified), the number of processed samples decreases with each step, which means the processing time will decrease as well. In order to take advantage of the gained processing time, the number of perceptron training iterations and/or the number of features can be increased with each ensemble step.

First, we tried to adapt the number of features used during the ensemble's steps. We came up with 5 ensembles of the form ENS-xF, which means $500 + step * x$ features per ensemble step, x taking on the values *0, 100, 200, 300, and 400*.

The ensemble ENS-100F improves significantly the detection of the initial ensemble ENS, but, unfortunately, it also doubles the number of false positives. By further increasing the number of used features for each ensemble step in ENS-200F, we notice that both the detection and the false positive rates increase, but the proportions are much smaller. However, by increasing the same parameter to 300 and 400 in ENS-300F and ENS-400F respectively, we observe that detection rate as well as false positive rate start to decrease.

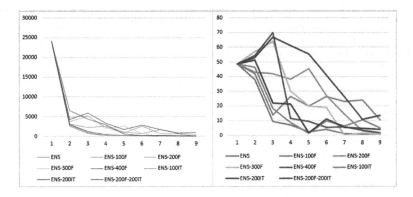

Fig. 3. Detection rate and false positive rate over 10 ensemble steps

Second, we tried to apply the same technique for the number of iterations of the OSC training, obtaining two ensembles ENS-xIT, which means the OSCs are trained for *500 + step * x*, *x* taking on the values *100 and 200*. For these last two tests, both the detection and false positive rates increased with a slower rate.

Studying these two methods we have decided to combine the algorithms that obtained the best detection results. In this way we came up with ENS-200F-200IT, which has *500 + step * 200* iterations per perceptron training and *500 + step * 200* features per ensemble step. It performs better than all the others regarding the detection rate, but worse than all of them regarding the false positive rate.

The Fig. 3 illustrates the way the number of records correctly classified respectively incorrectly classified decreases during the 10 steps performed by all defined ensembles: ENS, ENS-100F, ENS-200F, ENS-300F, ENS-400F, ENS-100IT, ENS-200IT, ENS-200F-200IT. It can be easily observed that ENS-200F-200IT has the smoothest decrease. This means that the number of correctly classified samples during the subsequent steps was improved by this technique.

3.2 BDT Steps

During the experiments conducted in [13], we observed that the OSC-BC algorithm performed well on the first ensemble step, but the number of records correctly classified and discarded in subsequent steps decreased significantly. In order to solve this problem, the present paper proposes a new way of combining the OSC-BC algorithm with the BDT. Instead of clustering all the data and applying the OSC-BC algorithm on each obtained cluster (as in [13]), this paper proposes to intercalate the ensemble steps of OSC-BC with BDT clustering for maximizing the number of records being discarded at each step.

First, we give more details regarding the steps performed by the ensemble disregarding both classes of correctly classified samples at each step, which may be observed in Algorithm 1. Note that this algorithm represents a single

---

Algorithm 1. Ensemble Both Classes Iteration Algorithm

1: $S \leftarrow \bigcup_{i=1}^{|R|} R_i$ - the records
2: **function** $EnsembleBothClassesIteration(S)$
3:     $NS \leftarrow \emptyset$
4:     $Model_{clean} \leftarrow OSC(S, clean)$
5:     $Model_{infected} \leftarrow OSC(S, infected)$
6:     **for** $i \leftarrow 1 \rightarrow |S|$ **do**
7:         **if** $IsCorrectlyClassified(Model_{clean}, S_i)$ **then**
8:             **if** $not\ IsCorrectlyClassified(Model_{infected}, S_i)$ **then**
9:                 $NS.push(S_i)$
10:             **end if**
11:         **else**
12:             **if** $IsCorrectlyClassified(Model_{infected}, S_i)$ **then**
13:                 $NS.push(S_i)$
14:             **end if**
15:         **end if**
16:     **end for**
17:     **return** $(Model_{clean},\ Model_{infected},\ NS)$
18: **end function**

---

step of the OSC-BC algorithm. It receives as parameter the dataset to be classified and returns the models computed using the One Side Class Perceptron ($Model_{clean}$ and $Model_{infected}$) and the incorrectly classified subset (NS, which contains the records correctly classified by $Model_{clean}$ and incorrectly classified by $Model_{infected}$ and the records correctly classified by $Model_{infected}$ and incorrectly classified by $Model_{clean}$).

Second, we review the BDT splitting and clustering mechanisms. The algorithm is parameterized with the records being classified, the feature set used to describe the records and the BDT maximum depth. The leaf nodes contain the final clusters, while the internal nodes are decision nodes and contain conditions used to split the current data in two groups as follows: if a record contains a specific feature, then it is sent to the right node/sub-cluster, otherwise, to the left node/sub-cluster. At each step in the BDT, the feature with the highest score is chosen, where the score is computed with the formula $\frac{(1-|\frac{countClean}{totalClean} - 0.5|)+(1-|\frac{countInfected}{totalInfected} - 0.5|)}{2}$, where totalClean/totalInfected is the total number of clean/infected files and countClean/countInfected is the number of clean/infected files for which the given feature is set to true.

The reason we use this score is because we want to split the data in 2 subsets so that both subsets have an equilibrium between the number of malicious and the number of clean samples. We don't want to choose a feature which is present in most clean samples and in a small number of malicious samples or vice-versa. On the contrary, the best feature according to this score would be the feature which is present in half of the clean samples and in half of the malicious samples. Such a feature is not useful when training a perceptron and might as well be used

Algorithm 2. Ensemble based on BDTs and Ensemble Steps with Both Classes

1: $S \leftarrow \bigcup_{i=1}^{|R|} R_i$ - the records
2: $F \leftarrow \bigcup_{j=1}^{|R.F|} R.F_j$ - the feature set
3: $MaxDepth$ - the maximum BDT level
4: $CountEns$ - the number of ensemble steps
5: $CurrentIteration \leftarrow 0$
6: **function** $BdtEnsembleBothClasses$(S, F)
7:      $(Model_{clean}, Model_{infected}, NS) = EnsembleBothClasses(S)$
8:      $Save(Model_{clean}, Model_{infected})$
9:      $CurrentIteration \leftarrow CurrentIteration + 1$
10:     **if** $CurrentIteration = CountEns$ **then**
11:         $return$
12:     **end if**
13:     $C \leftarrow GetBdtClust(NS, F, MaxDepth)$
14:     **for** $j \leftarrow 1 \rightarrow |C|$ **do**
15:         $BdtEnsembleBothClasses(C_j)$
16:     **end for**
17: **end function**

to split the dataset in 2 subsets which are easier classified with a perceptron, especially since after splitting the data in two according to a chosen feature, this feature is removed from the set of features of the resulted 2 subsets/nodes.

Another reason for using this score is that we have a smaller chance to obtain a very big cluster and a very small cluster at each splitting step, causing the final clusters to have similar sizes.

In this way, by increasing the number of features and decreasing the number of records, the chance to classify all the records is higher.

Third, the way the BDT Algorithm and the ensemble method are interlaced is illustrated in Algorithm 2. At each ensemble step, the algorithm computes the two hyper-planes ($Model_{clean}$ and $Model_{infected}$) using the Algorithm 1. The computed models are saved and BDT clustering is used to split the mis-classified samples in subsets. For each resulted subset, the mechanism is applied recursively.

4   Results

The dataset used in our experiments consists of 242.811 malicious and 2.105.896 clean samples collected during three months and one year respectively. Each sample is described by 6.275 boolean features obtained either in a static (file geometry and characteristics) or dynamic (behavior) manner. The 500 features used in the training process were selected using the F2 score [7]. Each algorithm was tested using a 3-fold cross validation. Table 1 illustrates the obtained results.

Table 1. Results for ensembles and the hybrid mechanisms

Algorithm	FP rate	Detection rate	Training time
ENS	0.0159%	34.9699%	4:25:27.031
ENS-100F	0.0334%	45.9307%	5:07:26.870
ENS-200F	0.0374%	49.9215%	6:07:44.738
ENS-300F	0.0342%	49.4652%	7:00:54.222
ENS-400F	0.0299%	48.5496%	7:51:11.673
ENS-100IT	0.0220%	36.1729%	6:49:06.055
ENS-200IT	0.0242%	36.6923%	9:16:27.555
ENS-200F-200IT	0.0537%	56.8767%	13:39:01.548
BDT4-ENS	0.2618%	70.07%	4:48:00.000
BDT4-ENS-200F-200IT	0.5990%	83.10%	5:11:00.000
ENS-BDT1-200F-200IT	0.8690%	84.02%	5:15:00.000

5   Conclusions

In comparison to our previous paper [13], in this paper we managed to obtain an increase in detection with almost 15% (from 70.07% to 83.10% for BDT4-ENS-200F-200T and 84.02% for ENS-BDT1-200F-200IT) while keeping a small number of false positives. When comparing BDT4-ENS-200F-200IT and ENS-BDT1-200F-200IT, it becomes clear that the detection increase for BDT4-ENS-200F-200IT comes at a significantly smaller cost regarding the false positive rate (0.5990% and respectively 0.8690%). The training time (around 5 h) is reasonable enough in order to use it in the cyber-security industry.

In search of an equilibrium between the 3 most important variables (detection rate, false positive rate and training time), from the industry point of view, the most desirable algorithm among those studied above is BDT4-ENS-200F-200IT.

References

1. Altaher, A., Ramadass, S., Ali, A.: Computer virus detection using features ranking and machine learning. J. Appl. Sci. Res. **7**(9), 1482–1486 (2011)
2. Crammer, K., Kandola, J.S., Singer, Y.: Online classification on a budget. In: Advances in Neural Information Processing Systems 16 [Neural Information Processing Systems, NIPS 2003, Vancouver and Whistler, British Columbia, Canada, 8–13 December 2003], pp. 225–232 (2003)
3. Freund, Y., Schapire, R.E.: Large margin classification using the perceptron algorithm. Mach. Learn. **37**(3), 277–296 (1999)
4. Gavrilut, D., Benchea, R., Vatamanu, C.: Optimized zero false positives perceptron training for malware detection. In: 14th International Symposium on Symbolic and Numeric Algorithms for Scientific Computing, SYNASC 2012, Timisoara, Romania, 26–29 September 2012, pp. 247–253 (2012)

5. Gavrilut, D., Cimpoesu, M., Anton, D., Ciortuz, L.: Malware detection using machine learning. In: Proceedings of the International Multiconference on Computer Science and Information Technology, IMCSIT 2009, Mragowo, Poland, 12–14 October 2009, pp. 735–741 (2009)
6. Kim, H.-C., Pang, S., Je, H.-M., Kim, D., Bang, S.-Y.: Support vector machine ensemble with bagging. In: Lee, S.-W., Verri, A. (eds.) SVM 2002. LNCS, vol. 2388, pp. 397–408. Springer, Heidelberg (2002). doi:10.1007/3-540-45665-1_31
7. Ng, K.L.S., Mishra, S.K.: De novo SVM classification of precursor microRNAs from genomic pseudo hairpins using global and intrinsic folding measures. Bioinform./Comput. Appl. Biosci. **23**(11), 1321–1330 (2007)
8. Lu, Y.-B., Din, S.-C., Zheng, C.-F., Gao, B.-J.: Using multi-feature and classifier ensembles to improve malware detection. J. C.C.I.T. **39**(2), 57–72 (2010)
9. Menahem, E., Shabtai, A., Rokach, L., Elovici, Y.: Improving malware detection by applying multi-inducer ensemble. Comput. Stat. Data Anal. **53**(4), 1483–1494 (2009)
10. Ozdemir, M., Sogukpinar, I.: An android malware detection architecture based on ensemble learning. Trans. Mach. Learn. Artif. Intell. **2**(3), 90–106 (2014)
11. Rosenblatt, F.: The perceptron: a probabilistic model for information storage and organization in the brain. Psychol. Rev. **65**(6), 386 (1958)
12. Tretyakov, K.: Machine learning techniques in spam filtering. Data Min. Prob.-Oriented Semin. **3**(177), 60–79 (2004)
13. Vatamanu, C., Cosovan, D., Gavriluţ, D., Luchian, H.: A comparative study of malware detection techniques using machine learning methods. Int. J. Comput. Electr. Autom. Control Inf. Eng. **9**(5), 1157–1164 (2015)
14. Ye, Y., Chen, L., Wang, D., Li, T., Jiang, Q., Zhao, M.: SBMDS: an interpretable string based malware detection system using SVM ensemble with bagging. J. Comput. Virol. **5**(4), 283–293 (2009)
15. Zhang, B., Yin, J., Hao, J., Zhang, D., Wang, S.: Malicious codes detection based on ensemble learning. In: Xiao, B., Yang, L.T., Ma, J., Muller-Schloer, C., Hua, Y. (eds.) ATC 2007. LNCS, vol. 4610, pp. 468–477. Springer, Heidelberg (2007). doi:10.1007/978-3-540-73547-2_48

Multi-column Deep Neural Network for Offline Arabic Handwriting Recognition

Rolla Almodfer[1], Shengwu Xiong[1,2], Mohammed Mudhsh[1],
and Pengfei Duan[1,2(✉)]

[1] School of Computer Science and Technology,
Wuhan University of Technology, Wuhan 430070, China
duanpf@whut.edu.cn
[2] Hubei Key Laboratory of Transportation Internet of Things,
Wuhan University of Technology, Wuhan 430070, China

Abstract. In recent years Deep Neural Networks (DNNs) have been successfully applied to several pattern recognition filed. For example, Multi-Column Deep Neural Networks (MCDNN) achieve state of the art recognition rates on Chinese characters database. In this paper, we utilized MCDNN for Offline Arabic Handwriting Recognition (OAHR). Through several settings of experiments using the benchmarking IFN/ENIT Database, we show incremental improvements of the words recognition comparable to approaches used Deep Belief Network (DBN) or Recurrent Neural Network (RNN.) Lastly, we compare our best result to those of previous state-of-the-arts.

Keywords: Multi-Column Deep Neural Networks · DNN · Offline Arabic handwriting recognition

1 Introduction

During the past decade, significant progress has been made in handwriting words recognition field. Applications like postal address and zip code recognition, passport validation, check processing are practical applications in handwriting recognition area. Numerous research results have been reported on handwriting recognition during last few decades. Although there are promising results for recognition Latin, Chinese and Japanese script, accuracies on recognition handwriting Arabic scripts fall behind. This is due to unlimited variation in human handwriting, the large variety of Arabic character shapes, the presence of ligature between characters and overlapping of the components. The different approaches of handwritten word recognition (HWR) fall into either the on-line or off-line category. In on-line HWR, the computer recognizes the words as they are written. Off-line recognition is performed after the writing is completed. We here focus on Off-line HWR which has traditionally been tackled by following two main approaches: (i) Analytic approach and (ii) holistic approach. The analytic approach [1, 2] a word is decomposed into a set of smaller components (e.g., characters, graphemes, allographs) and then features are extracted for each component. Finally, the word is transformed into sequential feature vectors suited for training and recognition. A large variety of techniques/classifiers have been employed for the

A. Lintas et al. (Eds.): ICANN 2017, Part II, LNCS 10614, pp. 260–267, 2017.
https://doi.org/10.1007/978-3-319-68612-7_30

analytic approach; we cite: HMM (hidden Markovian Models) [3], LVQ (Learning Vector Quantization) [4], SVM (Support Vector Machines) [5], and PGM (Probabilistic Graphical Models) [6]. Although being successful, the performance of such approaches has always been substantially dependent on the selection of right representing features, which is a difficult task for cursive writing. In a holistic approach, the entire word is recognized without prior decomposition of the word [7, 8]. In this case, the features vectors are extracted from the word as a whole.

Recently, Deep Neural Networks (DNN) has acquired a reputation for solving many computer vision problems, and its application to the field of HWR has been shown to provide significantly better results than traditional methods [9]. In this vein, the first reported successful use of DNN for Arabic handwritten word recognition was multidimensional recurrent neural networks [10]. The authors obtained 91.4% accuracy on IFN/ENIT database. Later, Elleuch et al. [11] presented a Convolutional Deep Belief Network (CDBN) to recognize Arabic words. The authors obtained 83.7 Accuracy rate on IFN/ENIT Database. In spite of the previous works, using Deep architectures on Arabic handwriting recognition are relatively scarce comparative to other languages.

Deep Neural Networks (DNN) brings about new breakthrough technology for Handwriting Chinese Character Recognition (HCCR) with great success. For example, the multi-column deep neural network (MCDNN) method proposed by Cireşan et al. [12, 13] shows remarkable ability in lots of applications and attains near-human performance on handwritten datasets. It has achieved state of the art recognition rates on Chinese characters from the ICDAR 2011 [14] and ICDAR 2013 [15] offline handwriting competitions, approaching human accuracy [16]. The MCDNN is a simple average voting ensemble model, composed of several standard DNNs.

In this paper, we utilized the successful Multi Column Deep Neural Network MCDNN for OAHR. In the proposed model, each of DNN is trained to predict word label using the same training data but normalized differently. Therefor we create additional datasets by normalizing word width to 100, 200, 300 pixels. The normalization helps to reduce both error rate and number of columns required to reach a good accuracy [13]. Through output averaging, three independently trained DNNs form a MCDNN with error rate 8.5% below the error rate of single DNN. We show that this is an effective technique to improve classification performance of the model.

2 Arabic Handwriting Characteristics and Challenges

Arabic cursive writing is unique compared to Latin, Chinese and Japanese. Arabic is composed of 28 main characters and written from right to left in both printed and handwritten forms. Each character has two or four different shapes depending on its position in the word, which will increase the number of classes to be recognized from 28 to 84. The number and position of dots dominate characters that have similar shapes [17, 18]. Fifteen characters have dots with the character and 52 basic character shapes without dots. Some challenging structural characteristics of the characters in the database are described below:

1. Arabic word consists of one or more connected components (sub-words), and each one contains one or more characters that can be overlapped with other characters or diacritics. Moreover, multiple characters can be combined vertically to form a ligature (Fig. 1a).
2. Some words have touching or broken characters (Fig. 1b).
3. Every writer has an individual writing style (Fig. 1c).
4. Some Arabic characters have diacritic marks (a diacritic may be placed above or below the body of the character). These diacritics can be overlapped (Fig. 1d).

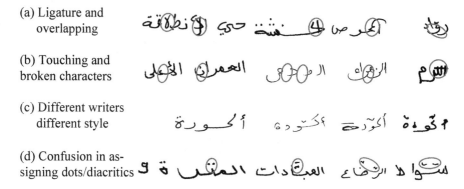

Fig. 1. Complexities in Arabic handwriting recognition

3   System Overview

In this section we briefly summarize a standard DNN. We then describe our proposed MCDNN for offline Arabic handwriting recognition (OAHR).

3.1   Deep Neural Networks

A DNN is one of the most advanced machine learning techniques, it consists of a succession of convolutional and max-pooling layers, and each layer receives connections from its preceding layer. The most popular image classification structure of DNN is constructed by three main processing layers: Convolutional Layer, Pooling Layer and Fully Connected Layer (or classification layer). DNN units are described below:

Convolutional Layer
Let $x_i^l \in \mathbb{R}^{M_l \times M_l}$ represents the ith map in the lth layer, j^{th} kernel filter in the lth layer connected to the ith map in the $(l-1)^{th}$ layer denoted $K_{ij}^l \in \mathbb{R}^{k_l \times k_l}$ and index maps set $M_j = \{i | i^{th}$ in the $(l-1)^{th}$ Layer map connected to j^{th} map in the lth layer$\}$. The convolution operation can be given by Eq. (1).

$$x_i^l = f\left(\sum_{i \in M_j} x_i^{l-1} * K_{ij}^l + b_j^l\right) \tag{1}$$

where $f\,(.)$ is non-linearity activation function and b_j^l is bias.

Max-Pooling Layer

The max-pooling layer abstracts the input feature into a lower dimensional feature. It has been shown that max-pooling can lead to faster convergence select superior invariant features, and improve generalization [19]. Pooling equation can be described in Eq. (2).

$$x_j^l = Max(x_i^{l-1}) \tag{2}$$

where $Max\,(.)$ is Max-sampling function to compute the max value of each $n \times n$ region in x_i^{l-1} map.

Classification Layer

The fully connected layer is used at the end of the network. After multiple convolutional and max-pooling layers, a shallow Multi-Layer Perceptron (MLP) is used to complete the DNN. The output maps of the last convolutional layer are either down-sampled to 1 pixel per map, or a fully connected layer combines the outputs of the topmost convolutional layer into a 1D feature vector. The last layer is always a fully connected layer with one output unit per class in the classification task. This layer may have a non-linear activation function or a *softmax* activation in order to output probabilities of class predictions.

3.2 MCDNN Architecture

The MCDNN was originally designed as an ensemble method to improve the performance of DNN for image classification [13]. In this model, each column (or single DNN) share the same network configuration and training data. They are randomly initialized, and the input data preprocessed differently for each column. The number of columns varied depending on the dataset used. Predictions from all columns are averaged to get the final output. Here, the original IFN/ ENIT data are normalized such that the height always equals 100 pixels. We normalized the words widths to 100, 200, 300 pixels (see Fig. 2). This is like seeing the data from different angles [13]. We trained one column (one DNN) per normalization, resulting in total of 3 columns for the MCDNN. Each column configured with seven layers, counting input and output layer. The number of maps per layer is 32. The last layer always has 937 neurons, i.e. one per class. The first column (*DNN A*) trained on 100×100 pixels images, the second column (*DNN B*) trained on 200×100 pixels images. The last column (*DNN C*) trained on 300×100 pixels images.

Given the outputs of the columns, we compute the prediction by averaging the output of each column:

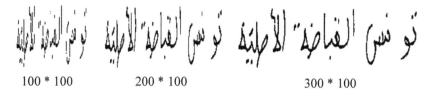

100 * 100   200 * 100   300 * 100

Fig. 2. Arabic word images with different normalization

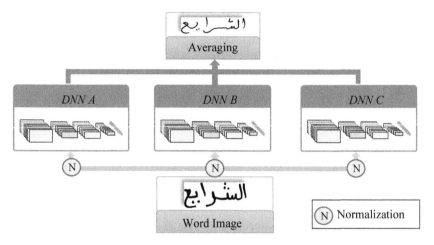

Fig. 3. MCDNN architecture, the final predictions are obtained by averaging individual predictions of each DNN

$$y_{MCDNN}^{N} = \frac{1}{N} \sum_{i=1}^{N} y_{DNN}^{i} \qquad (3)$$

where y_{DNN}^{i} corresponds to the prediction from i^{th} column DNN; N corresponds to the number of total columns. The architecture of MCDNN is depicted in Fig. 3.

4   Experiments Results

Dataset IFN/ENIT [7] contains 32492 binary images of Arabic words written by more than 400 writers. 19724 words for training and 12768 for testing. The handwritten words represent 937 Tunisian town/village names. The database is normalized before the training starts. The architecture of a single DNN is composed of two convolution layers and two max pooling layers. Each of the first two convolution layers is followed by a max pooling layer, with a pooling size of 2×2 and a stride of 2 pixels. No spatial zero padding is used in the convolution layer, and the convolution stride is fixed to 1 pixel. In Fig. 4 the 300×100 input image to *DNN C* was filtered by 32 convolution filters of size 5×5 in the first convolution layer, resulting in 32 feature maps of size

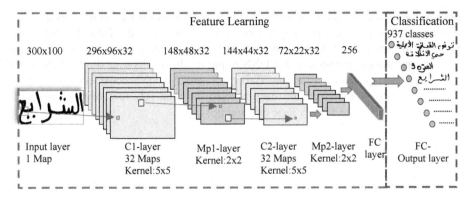

Fig. 4. The architecture of *DNN C*

296×96. After the first pooling layer, their sizes become 148×48. The first pooling layer's outputs are sent into the second convolution layer, which has a convolution filter size of 5×5, leading to 32 feature maps of size 144×44. After the second pooling layer, their sizes become 72×22 which brings out 32 feature maps of size 72×22. These features are then fed to a simple Multi- Layer Perceptron (MLP) with two layer. The first is fully connected layer size is 256. Finally the output layer has one neuron per class (937).

The three DNNs are trained using on-line gradient descent with a momentum of 0.9, and a weight of 0.0005 per iteration. The type of non-linearity used is Rectified Linear Unit (*ReLU*) which given as $f(x) = max (0, x)$. The reason for using it instead of other nonlinear functions like *tanh* ($f(x) = tanh(x)$) and sigmoid ($f(x) = (1 + e-x)-1$) is because training with gradient descent is comparatively much faster for *ReLU* than the other non-linearities functions [15], moreover it can be more easily developed by thresholding the matrix of activations at zero, without suffering from saturation. We used a *softmax* [6] activation function, thus each neuron's output represents the posterior class probability. *Softmax* activation function, is applied as an effective method for multi-class classification problem. The mini-batch size is 128 and the networks were trained for 200 epochs. The whole training procedure for a single network took at most 66 h on a desktop PC with an Intel i7 3770 processor, a NVidia GTX780 graphics card and 16 gigabytes of on-board RAM.

Table 1 compares the error rate of different methods [10, 11, 20] on IFN/ENIT. For a single DNN, *DNN C* gave about a 3% improvement over *DNN A* and *DNN B*. This

Table 1. Error rate for the IFN/ENIT database

Author	Model	Error rate%
Elleuch et al. [11]	CDBN	16.3%
Maalej and Kherallah [20]	MDLSTM	11.2%
Present work	DNN C	10.9%
Graves [10]	MDLSTM	8.6%
Present work	**MCDNN**	**8.5%**

improvement comes at a cost of increase in training and classification time, as the sizes of images fed to *DNN C* were bigger. Our lowest error rate in the Table 1 is 8.5%, not far from the result (8.6%) obtained by Graves et al. Nevertheless, our model is less complex and easy to implement. MCDNN improves the results over single DNN (*DNN C*) and achieves the lowest error rate. The error rate of MCDNN considers low to a very hard classification problem, with many classes and relatively few samples per class. The DNN suffers more from a lack of training samples.

5   Conclusion

In this paper, we have explored the applicability of MCDNN on Arabic handwritten recognition and demonstrated the efficiency applied on IFN/ENIT databases. We show incremental improvements of the word recognition comparable to approaches used DBN with an error rate of 16.3% or RNN with an error rate of 8.6%. Our results were promising with an error rate of 10.9% using single DNN and 8.5% using 3-columns MCDNN. As a future work, we plan to add more columns inspiring by the success from other applications used MCDNN, like Chinese characters recognition (8 columns with an error rate of 6.5%) and traffic signs recognition (25 columns with an error rate of 0.54%) [13]. Moreover, we will increase the depth of each DNN as deeper network can increase the classification accuracy [21].

Acknowledgments. This research was supported in part by Science & Technology Pillar Program of Hubei Province under Grant (#2014BAA146), Nature Science Foundation of Hubei Province under Grant (#2015CFA059), Science and Technology Open Cooperation Program of Henan Province under Grant (#152106000048).

References

1. Kim, K.K., Jin, H.K., Yun, K.C., et al.: Legal amount recognition based on the segmentation hypotheses for bank check processing. In: Proceedings of International Conference on Document Analysis and Recognition, pp. 964–967. IEEE Xplore (2001)
2. Vinciarelli, A.: A survey on off-line cursive word recognition. Pattern Recogn. **35**(7), 1433–1446 (2002)
3. Mohamad, A.H., Likformansulem, L., Mokbel, C.: Combining slanted-frame classifiers for improved HMM-based Arabic handwriting recognition. IEEE Trans. Pattern Anal. Mach. Intell. **31**(7), 1165–1177 (2009)
4. Ali, M.A.: Arabic handwritten characters classification using learning vector quantization algorithm. In: Elmoataz, A., Lezoray, O., Nouboud, F., Mammass, D. (eds.) ICISP 2008. LNCS, vol. 5099, pp. 463–470. Springer, Heidelberg (2008). doi:10.1007/978-3-540-69905-7_53
5. Elzobi, M., Al-Hamadi, A., Al Aghbari, Z., Dings, L., Saeed, A.: Gabor wavelet recognition approach for off-line handwritten arabic using explicit segmentation. In: Choras, R.S. (ed.) Image Processing and Communications Challenges 5, pp. 245–254. Springer, Heidelberg (2014). doi:10.1007/978-3-319-01622-1_29

6. Khemiri, A., Kacem, A., Belaid, A.: Towards Arabic handwritten word recognition via probabilistic graphical models. In: International Conference on Frontiers in Handwriting Recognition, pp. 678–683. IEEE (2014)
7. Madhvanath, S., Govindaraju, V.: The role of holistic paradigms in handwritten word recognition. IEEE Trans. Pattern Anal. Mach. Intell. **23**(2), 149–164 (2001)
8. Ruiz-Pinales, J., Jaime-Rivas, R., Castro-Bleda, M.J.: Holistic cursive word recognition based on perceptual features. Pattern Recogn. Lett. **28**(13), 1600–1609 (2007)
9. Wu, C., Fan, W., He, Y., et al.: Handwritten character recognition by alternately trained relaxation convolutional neural network. In: International Conference on Frontiers in Handwriting Recognition, pp. 291–296. IEEE (2014)
10. Graves, A.: Offline Arabic handwriting recognition with multidimensional recurrent neural networks. In: Advances in Neural Information Processing Systems, pp. 545–552 (2012)
11. Elleuch, M., Tagougui, N., Kherallah, M.: Deep learning for feature extraction of Arabic handwritten script. In: Azzopardi, G., Petkov, N. (eds.) CAIP 2015. LNCS, vol. 9257, pp. 371–382. Springer, Cham (2015). doi:10.1007/978-3-319-23117-4_32
12. Cireşan, D., Meier, U., Masci, J., et al.: Multi-column deep neural network for traffic sign classification. Neural Netw. **32**(1), 333 (2012)
13. Schmidhuber, J., Meier, U., Ciresan, D.: Multi-column deep neural networks for image classification, vol. 157, no. 10, pp. 3642–3649 (2012)
14. Liu, C.L., Yin, F., Wang, Q.F., et al.: ICDAR 2011 Chinese handwriting recognition competition. In: International Conference on Document Analysis and Recognition, pp. 1464–1469. IEEE (2011)
15. Yin, F., Wang, Q.F., Zhang, X.Y., Liu, C.L.: ICDAR 2013 Chinese handwriting recognition competition. In: ICDAR 2013 (2013)
16. Dan, C., Meier, U.: Multi-column deep neural networks for offline handwritten Chinese character classification. In: International Joint Conference on Neural Networks, pp. 1–6. IEEE (2015)
17. Aburas, A.A., Gumah, M.E.: Arabic handwriting recognition: challenges and solutions. In: International Symposium on Information Technology, pp. 1–6. IEEE (2008)
18. Srihari, S.N., Ball, G.: An assessment of arabic handwriting recognition technology. In: Märgner, V., El Abed, H. (eds.) Guide to OCR for Arabic Scripts, pp. 3–34. Springer, London (2012). doi:10.1007/978-1-4471-4072-6_1
19. Lecun, Y., Kavukcuoglu, K., Farabet, C.: Convolutional networks and applications in vision. In: International Symposium on Circuits and Systems, DBLP, pp. 253–256 (2010)
20. Maalej, R., Kherallah, M.: Improving MDLSTM for offline Arabic handwriting recognition using dropout at different positions. In: Villa, A.E.P., Masulli, P., Pons Rivero, A.J. (eds.) ICANN 2016. LNCS, vol. 9887, pp. 431–438. Springer, Cham (2016). doi:10.1007/978-3-319-44781-0_51
21. Simonyan, K., Zisserman, A.: Very deep convolutional networks for large-scale image recognition. Comput. Sci. (2014)

Using LSTMs to Model the Java Programming Language

Brendon Boldt[✉]

Marist College, 3399 North Rd., Poughkeepsie, NY, USA
brendon.boldt1@marist.edu

Abstract. Recurrent neural networks (RNNs), specifically long-short term memory networks (LSTMs), can model natural language effectively. This research investigates the ability for these same LSTMs to perform next "word" prediction on the Java programming language. Java source code from four different repositories undergoes a transformation that preserves the logical structure of the source code and removes the code's various specificities such as variable names and literal values. Such datasets and an additional English language corpus are used to train and test standard LSTMs' ability to predict the next element in a sequence. Results suggest that LSTMs can effectively model Java code achieving perplexities under 22 and accuracies above 0.47, which is an improvement over LSTM's performance on the English language which demonstrated a perplexity of 85 and an accuracy of 0.27. This research can have applicability in other areas such as syntactic template suggestion and automated bug patching.

1 Introduction

Machine learning techniques of language modeling are often applied to natural languages, but techniques used to model natural languages such as n-gram, graphed-based, and context sensitive models can be applicable to programming languages as well [1–3]. One such application of a language model is next-word prediction which can prove very useful for tasks such as syntactic template suggestion and bug patching [2,4]. There has been research into programming language models which use Bayesian statistical inference (n-gram models) to perform next-word prediction [1]. Yet some of the most successful natural language models have been built using recurrent neural networks (RNNs); their ability to remember information over a sequence of tokens makes them particularly apt for next-word prediction [5].

Specifically, long-short term memory (LSTM) RNNs have further improved the basic RNN model by increasing the ability of an RNN to remember data over a long sequence of input without the signal decaying quickly [5]. LSTMs are a sequence-to-word language model which means given a sequence of words (e.g., words in the beginning of a sentence), the model will produce a probability distribution describing what the next word in the sequence is.

© Springer International Publishing AG 2017
A. Lintas et al. (Eds.): ICANN 2017, Part II, LNCS 10614, pp. 268–275, 2017.
https://doi.org/10.1007/978-3-319-68612-7_31

In terms of the Java programming language, we are specifically investigating next-statement prediction in method bodies. While other parts of Java source code (e.g., class fields, import statements) do have semantic significance, method bodies make up the functional aspect of source code[1] and most resemble natural language sentences. Just as individual semantic tokens (words) comprise natural language sentences, statements, which can be thought of as semantic tokens, comprise method bodies. Furthermore, the semantics of individual natural language words coalesce to form the semantics of sentence just as the semantics of the statement in a method body form the semantics of the method as a whole. By this analogy, language modeling techniques which operate on sentences comprised of words could apply similarly to method bodies comprised of statements.

2 Tokenizing Java Source Code

We are specifically looking at predicting the syntactic structure of the next statement in within Java source code method bodies. The syntactic structure of a complete piece of source code can be represented as an abstract syntax tree (AST) where each node of the tree represents a distinct syntactic element (e.g., statement, boolean operator, literal integer). Method bodies are, in particular, comprised of statements which, more or less, represent a self-contained action. Each of these statements is the root of its own sub-AST which represents the syntactic structure of only that statement. In this way, statements are independent, semantically meaningful units of a method body which are suitable to be tokenized for input into the RNN.

Nguyen and Nguyen [2] studied a model for syntactic statement prediction called ASTLan which uses Bayesian statistical inference to interpret and predict statements in the form of sequential statement ASTs. While Bayesian statistical inference can be applied to statements directly in their AST form, RNNs operate on independent tokens such as English words. Thus, it is necessary that statement ASTs be flattened into a tokenized form in order to produce an RNN-based model.

2.1 Statement-Level AST Tokenization

The RNN model described in Zaremba et al. [5] specifically uses space-delimited text strings; hence, when the statement ASTs are tokenized, they must be represented as space-delimited text strings.

To show the tokenization of Java source, take the following Java statement: `int x = obj.getInt();`. The corresponding AST, as given by the Eclipse AST parser, appears in Fig. 1 [6]. This statement, in turn, would be transformed as follows[2]

---

[1] Functional insofar as method bodies describe the active (non-declarative) behavior of the program.

[2] `VariableDeclarationStatement` is not included in the tokenized version of the AST since the syntax is adequately represented by starting with the root node's children.

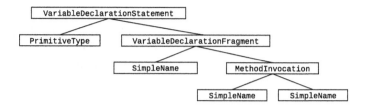

Fig. 1. The abstract syntax tree (AST) representation of the Java statement `int x = obj.getInt();`

```
_PrimitiveType_VariableDeclarationFragment(_SimpleName
_MethodInvocation(_SimpleName_SimpleName)))
```

```
_60(_39_59(_42_32(_42_42)))
```

The first token uses the AST node names while second token represents the same AST by instead using integer IDs corresponding to the AST node names as assigned by the Eclipse parser (e.g., 60 corresponds to "PrimitiveType" nodes and 42 corresponds to "SimpleName" nodes). Using integer IDs saves space and is the format used in the actual LSTM.

Individual AST nodes are separated by underscores ("_") and parentheses are used to denote a parent-child relationship so that the tree structure of the statement is preserved. In fact, it is possible to recreate the syntax of the original source code from the tokens; thus, this tokenization is lossless in terms of *syntactical* information yet lossy in other areas. For example, variable and function names are discarded during the translation to make the model independent of variable and function names.

2.2   Method-Level Tokenization

Consider the following Java method:

```
int foo() {
    int x = obj.getInt();
    if (x > 0) {
        x = x + 5;
    }
    return x;
}
```

Each statement in the method body is tokenized just as the single statement was above, and the resulting tokens are delimited using spaces. Braces, while not statements, are included (denoted by "{" and "}") to retain the semantic structure of the method body. The method above becomes the following sequence of tokens:

```
(_39_42 { _60(_39_59(_42_32(_42_42)))
_25(_27(_42_34) { _21(_7(_42_27(_42_
34))) } _41(_42) }
```

The sequence of these tokens forms a "sentence" which represents the body of a Java method. Sentences in the dataset are separated by the `<eos>` metatoken to mark the end of a sentence. These sentences of tokens will then comprise the corpus that the LSTM network uses to train and make predictions.

2.3   English and Java Source Corpora Used

Similarly to Zaremba et al. [5], we are using the Penn Treebank (PTB) for the English language corpus as it provides an effective, general sample of the English language. For the Java programming languages, four different corpora were each built by processing (as described above) a large repository of Java source code. The repositories used were the Java Development Kit (JDK), Google Guava, ElasticSearch, and Spring Framework. The JDK is a good reference for Java since it is a widely-used implementation of the Java language; the other three projects were selected based on their high popularity on GitHub in addition to the fact they are Java-based projects.

It is important to note that the PTB does not contain any punctuation while the tokenized Java source contains "punctuation" only in the form of statement body-delimiting curly braces ("{" and "}") since these are integral to the semantic structure of source code. All English and Java corpora use a metatoken to mark the end of a sentence.

2.4   Vocabulary Comparison

In addition to preserving the logical structure of the source code, another goal of the specific method of tokenization was to produce a vocabulary with a frequency distribution similar to that of the English corpus. If the same Java statement tokens appear too frequently, the tokenization might be generalizing the Java source too much such that it loses the underlying semantics. If the statement tokens, instead, all have a very low frequency it would be difficult to effectively perform inference on the sequence of tokens within the allotted vocabulary size.

In all of the Java corpora, the left and right curly braces comprise approximately 35% of the total tokens present. This a disproportionately high number in comparison to the rest of the tokens, but removing them from the frequency distribution, since they classify as punctuation, gives a more accurate representation of the vocabularies. The adjusted frequency distribution shown in Fig. 2 compares the PTB to the JDK source code. The rate of occurrence for the highest ranked words is significantly higher in the JDK than in the PTB, but the frequency distributions track closely together beyond the fifth-ranked words. Generally, all four Java corpora showed similar frequency distributions.

The statistical similarities between the English and the translated Java corpora suggest that the Java statement tokens have an adequate amount of detail

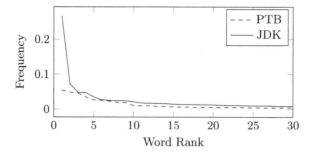

Fig. 2. Comparison of English and Java word frequency distributions. The y-axis represents the total proportion of the word with a given rank (specified by the x-axis).

in terms of mimicking English words. If the Java statement tokens were too detailed, their frequencies would be far lower than those of English words; if the Java statement tokens were not detailed enough, their frequencies would be much higher than those of English words (Table 1).

Table 1. Proportion and rank of the metatoken <unk>. Proportions and ranks are from the adjusted Java corpora with the left and right curly braces removed.

Corpus	Proportion	Rank
PTB	0.0484	2
JDK	0.0724	2
Guava	0.0476	5
ElasticSearch	0.1618	2
Spring framework	0.0873	2

Another consideration when comparing the English and Java corpora is the prevalence of the metatoken <unk> which denotes a token not contained in the language model's vocabulary. Due to the nature of LSTMs, the vocabulary of the language model is finite; hence, any word not contained in the vocabulary is considered unknown. We specifically used a vocabulary size of 10,000. A vocabulary size which is too small will fail to represent enough words in the corpus; the result is the LSTM seeing a high proportion of the <unk> metatoken. A vocabulary which is too large increases the computation required during training and inference. The proportion of <unk> tokens in both the English and the Java source data sets (save for ElasticSearch[3]) are <10% which indicates that the 10,000 word vocabulary accounts for approximately 90% of the corpus' words by volume. It is important that the Java corpora's <unk> proportion is not significantly higher than that of the PTB since that would suggest that 10,000 is too small a vocabulary size to describe the tokenized Java source code.

---

[3] ElasticSearch had a proportion of 16%.

3   Language Modeling

3.1   Neural Network Structure and Configuration

In order to make a good comparison between language modeling in English and Java, a model with demonstrated success at modeling English was chosen. The model selected was an LSTM neural network, a type of RNN, as described in Zaremba et al. [5]. This particular LSTM uses regularization via dropout to act as a good language model for natural languages such as English [5].

The LSTM's specific configuration was the same as the "medium" configuration described in Zaremba et al. [5] with the exception that the data was trained for 15 epochs instead of 39 epochs. Beyond 15 epochs (on both the English and Java datasets), the training cost metric (perplexity) continued to decrease while the validation cost metric remained steady. This suggests that the model was beginning to overfit the training data and that further training would not improve performance on the test data. Specifically, this model contains two RNN layers with a vocabulary size of 10, 000 words.

Each corpora was split into partitions such that 80% was training data and the remaining 20% was split evenly between test and validation data. Perplexity, the performance metric of the LSTM, is determined by the ability of the LSTM to perform sequence-to-word prediction on the test set of that corpus. Perplexity represents how well the prediction (in the form of a probability distribution) given by the LSTM matches the actual word which comes next in the sentence. A low perplexity means that the language model's predicted probability distribution matched closely the actual probability distribution, that is, it was better able to predict the next word. Perplexity is the same metric that is used in Zaremba et al. [5] to compare language models.

3.2   Language Model Metrics

We chose word-level perplexity as the metric for comparing the language models' performance on the given corpora since it provides a good measurement of the model's overall ability to predict words in the given corpus [7]. Perplexity for a given model is calculated by exponentiating (base e) the mean cross-entropy across all words in the test set. This is formally expressed as follows:

$$P(L) = \exp\left(\frac{1}{N} \sum_{i=1}^{N} H(L, w_i)\right),\qquad(1)$$

where N is the test data set size, L is the language model, w_i is the ith word in the test set, and $H(L, w_i)$ is the natural log cross-entropy from w_i to the prediction given by $L(w_i)$. A lower perplexity represents a language model with better predictive performance [8].

The cross-entropy is the opposite of summing the product of the probability of that word appearing, i.e., 1 for the correct word and 0 for all other incorrect words, and the natural logarithm of the output value of LSTM's softmax layer. The cross-entropy is defined as follows:

$$H(L, w) = -\sum_{i=1}^{V} p(w_i) \ln L(w_i), \tag{2}$$

where V is the vocabulary size and $p(w_i)$ is the probability of w_i being the correct word. Since the probability for incorrect words is 0 and the correct word is 1, the sum can be reduced to -1 times the natural log of the probability of the correct word as given by the LSTM. Thus, the cross-entropy is simply

$$H(L, w) = -\ln L_w(w). \tag{3}$$

$L_w(w)$ represents the LSTM's softmax output specifically for the word w. Additionally, mean word-level accuracy was calculated for each language model considering the top 1, 5, and 10 predictions made by the model.

4   Results

The perplexities achieved on the corpora by the LSTM are displayed in Table 2. The smallest perplexity for non-English data sets was measured for the Spring Framework, while the largest was for the JDK data. The table also indicates that all four Java data sets showed a drastic reduction in perplexity compared to the English data set. Nonetheless, the perplexity achieved on the English dataset is similar to that reported by Zaremba et al. [5]. These results indicate the superiority of LSTMs on both programming languages and a language as complex as the English language.

Table 2 shows the top-k accuracies for each corpora. Clearly, results suggest that the proposed LSTM model is able to more accurately model pre-processed Java source code than it can English. The table also indicates that, for the English data set, the use of a large number of predictors can dramatically increase the overall rate of predictors with the correct next word; e.g., increasing from one to ten predictors at least doubled the proportion of predictors. There is a similar effect over Java-based data sets; however, in these data sets the predictors start at a higher proportion than with English.

Table 2. Perplexities (P) given by Eq. 1. Proportion of predictions which had the correct word in their top-k predictions. "ElasticSearch" is written as "ES" and "Spring Framework" is written as "SF".

Corpus	P	Top 1	Top 5	Top 10	Language
PTB	85.288	0.269	0.470	0.552	English
JDK	21.808	0.474	0.652	0.716	Java
Guava	18.678	0.519	0.696	0.751	Java
ES	11.397	0.576	0.739	0.784	Java
SF	11.318	0.560	0.722	0.783	Java

5   Conclusion

In this paper, we have presented a way of modeling a predictive strategy over the Java programming language using an LSTM. Using datasets such as PTB, JDK, Guava, ElasticSearch, and Spring Framework we have shown that LSTMs are suitable in predicting the next syntactic statements of source code based on preceding statements. Results indicate that the LSTMs can achieve lower perplexities and, hence, produce more accurate models on the Java datasets than the English dataset.

The pre-processed Java code represents a very general and cursory representation of the original code as it does not include anything such as variable names or variable types. Future research along these lines could account for information such as variable types, variable names, etc. It would also be beneficial to compare the modeling of Java with other programming languages or to train the model across multiple repositories in one language.

Source code repositories:
LSTM model: https://github.com/brendon-boldt/lstm-language-model
Java translator: https://github.com/brendon-boldt/javalator

References

1. Allamanis, M., Sutton, C.: Mining source code repositories at massive scale using language modeling. In: Proceedings of the 10th Working Conference on Mining Software Repositories, MSR 2013, Piscataway, NJ, USA, pp. 207–216. IEEE Press (2013)
2. Nguyen, A.T., Nguyen, T.N.: Graph-based statistical language model for code. In: Proceedings of the 37th International Conference on Software Engineering, ICSE 2015, Piscataway, NJ, USA, vol. 1, pp. 858–868. IEEE Press (2015)
3. Asaduzzaman, M., Roy, C.K., Schneider, K.A., Hou, D.: A simple, efficient, context-sensitive approach for code completion. J. Softw.: Evol. Process **28**(7), 512–541 (2016). JSME-15-0030.R3
4. Kim, D., Nam, J., Song, J., Kim, S.: Automatic patch generation learned from human-written patches. In: Proceedings of the 2013 International Conference on Software Engineering, ICSE 2013, Piscataway, NJ, USA, pp. 802–811. IEEE Press (2013)
5. Zaremba, W., Sutskever, I., Vinyals, O.: Recurrent neural network regularization. CoRR, abs/1409.2329 (2014)
6. Eclipse Foundation: Eclipse documentation on the AST class (2016). http://help. eclipse.org/luna/index.jsp?topic=%2Forg.eclipse.jdt.doc.isv%2Freference%2Fapi% 2Forg%2Feclipse%2Fjdt%2Fcore%2Fdom%2FAST.html. Accessed 18 Aug 2016
7. Sundermeyer, M., Ney, H., Schlüter, R.: From feedforward to recurrent LSTM neural networks for language modeling. IEEE/ACM Trans. Audio Speech Lang. Process. (TASLP) **23**(3), 517–529 (2015)
8. Wang, M., Song, L., Yang, X., Luo, C.: A parallel-fusion RNN-LSTM architecture for image caption generation. In: 2016 IEEE International Conference on Image Processing (ICIP), pp. 4448–4452. IEEE (2016)

Representation and Classification

Classification of Categorical Data in the Feature Space of Monotone DNFs

Mirko Polato[✉], Ivano Lauriola, and Fabio Aiolli

Department of Mathematics, University of Padova,
Via Trieste, 63, 35121 Padova, Italy
{mpolato,aiolli}@math.unipd.it, ivanolauriola@gmail.com

Abstract. Nowadays, kernel based classifiers, such as SVM, are widely used on many different classification tasks. One of the drawbacks of these kind of approaches is their poor interpretability. In the past, some efforts have been devoted in designing kernels able to construct a more understandable feature space, e.g., boolean kernels, but only combinations of simple conjunctive clauses have been proposed.

In this paper, we present a family of boolean kernels, specifically, the Conjunctive kernel, the Disjunctive kernel and the DNF-kernel. These kernels are able to construct feature spaces with a wide spectrum of logical formulae. For all of these kernels, we provide a description of their corresponding feature spaces and efficient ways to calculate their values implicitly. Experiments on several categorical datasets show the effectiveness of the proposed kernels.

Keywords: Kernel methods · Boolean kernels · DNF · SVM

1 Introduction

The SVM classifier is one of the widest used machine learning method. Its high accuracy in many classification problems has meant that, nowadays, it is applied on very different domains, such as text categorization, diagnoses information classification and so on. However, one of the weakest points of the SVM model is its black-box nature. Specifically, since it is based on the, so called, kernel trick, it is very difficult to give an understandable interpretation of what the features represent. For example, one of the most famous kernel, the Radial Basis Function (RBF) kernel, also known as Gaussian kernel, maps input vectors into a space with infinite dimensions. Even though some efforts have been spent in order to extract rules from it [1,2], there is no a really successful method.

On the other hand, Decision Trees (DT), thanks to their easy logical interpretation, are very appreciated especially by non-expert users. The drawback of DTs is that, in general, they are not as accurate as more complex methods.

One of the possible approach to make SVM more interpretable is to design feature spaces which are easy to relate to human-friendly rules, and this can be easily done through the use of boolean kernels. The idea behind these kind of

© Springer International Publishing AG 2017
A. Lintas et al. (Eds.): ICANN 2017, Part II, LNCS 10614, pp. 279–286, 2017.
https://doi.org/10.1007/978-3-319-68612-7_32

kernels is to map vectors into a space made of logical formulae. In literature, as far as we know, all the proposed boolean kernels have embeddings made of conjunctive clauses of the input variables, which, however, represents only part of the whole spectrum of all the possible logical formulae.

In this paper we propose a family of boolean kernels, in particular we introduce a kernel, called (monotone) Disjunctive kernel, in which the embedding is made of disjunctive clauses, of a certain degree, of the input variables. We also propose another boolean kernel, the (monotone) DNF-kernel, which has a feature space made of monotone Disjunctive Normal Form formulae of the input variables. For both of these kernels we give a very efficient closed formula in order to implicitly calculate them. We finally assess their effectiveness against the linear kernel and the RBF kernel on several categorical datasets.

2   Related Works

Boolean kernels are those kernel functions which take in input binary vectors of dimension n and apply the dot product in a feature space, of dimension N (generally $N \gg n$), where each dimension represents a logical formula over the input variables.

Formally, a generic boolean kernel κ can be defined as $\kappa : \mathbb{B}^n \times \mathbb{B}^n \to \mathbb{N}$, where $\mathbb{B} \equiv \{0, 1\}$. Anytime $\mathbf{x}, \mathbf{z} \in \mathbb{B}^n$, the linear kernel, that is $\kappa_{LIN}(\mathbf{x}, \mathbf{z}) = \langle \mathbf{x}, \mathbf{z} \rangle$, where $\langle \cdot, \cdot \rangle$ is the dot-product, can be interpreted as a particular case of boolean kernel, in which the features simply correspond to the boolean literals. The kernel counts how many active literals the input vectors have in common.

A more complex special case of boolean kernel is the polynomial kernel [12,13], $\kappa_{POLY}^d(\mathbf{x}, \mathbf{z}) = (\langle \mathbf{x}, \mathbf{z} \rangle + c)^d, c \in \mathbb{N}$. In this case the feature space contains all possible monomials up to the degree d. From a logical stands point, a monomial can be seen as a conjunction of boolean variables.

It is worth to notice that the polynomial kernel contains sets of equivalent features in its embedding, e.g., with $d = 3$ and $\mathbf{x} \in \mathbb{B}^2$ we would have the features $x_1^2 x_2, x_1 x_2^2$ which are indeed the same feature $x_1 x_2$.

However, the all-subset kernel [5,11], $\kappa_{\subseteq}(\mathbf{x}, \mathbf{z}) = \prod_{i=1}^{n}(x_i z_i + 1) = 2^{\langle \mathbf{x}, \mathbf{z} \rangle}$, overcomes this duplicate issue. This kernel generates all combination of features but, each factor in the monomial has degree at most one.

In [4,9] the DNF-kernel (Disjunctive Normal Form), $\kappa_{\subseteq}'(\mathbf{x}, \mathbf{z}) = 2^{\langle \mathbf{x}, \mathbf{z} \rangle} - 1$, is presented, which is very similar to the all-subset kernel. In fact, it is easy to note that $\kappa_{\subseteq}'$ and $\kappa_{\subseteq}$ are the same kernel up to the constant -1.

By fixing the degree of the monomials of the all-subset kernel to a single d, we obtain the so called ANOVA kernel (κ_A^d) [11]. In [9], the non-monotone version of $\kappa_{\subseteq}'$ is also proposed, $\kappa_{\subseteq}^*(\mathbf{x}, \mathbf{z}) = 2^{\langle \mathbf{x}, \mathbf{z} \rangle + \langle \bar{\mathbf{x}}, \bar{\mathbf{z}} \rangle} - 1$, where $\bar{\mathbf{x}}$ and $\bar{\mathbf{z}}$ are the complements of the binary vectors $\mathbf{x}, \mathbf{z} \in \mathbb{B}^n$. The core difference between $\kappa_{\subseteq}'$ and $\kappa_{\subseteq}^*$ is that the former considers also variables in their negate version. So, for instance, the feature $x_1 \wedge \bar{x}_2 \wedge x_3$ is inside the feature space of $\kappa_{\subseteq}^*$ but not inside the one of $\kappa_{\subseteq}'$. A generalization of both $\kappa_{\subseteq}'$ and $\kappa_{\subseteq}^*$ is presented by Zhang et al. [13]. [7,10] present a reduced variation of $\kappa_{\subseteq}'$ and $\kappa_{\subseteq}^*$ in which only conjunctions with up to d variables are considered: $\kappa'^d_\subseteq(\mathbf{x}, \mathbf{z}) = \sum_{i=1}^d \binom{\langle \mathbf{x}, \mathbf{z} \rangle}{i}$ and $\kappa^{*d}_\subseteq(\mathbf{x}, \mathbf{z}) = \sum_{i=1}^d \binom{\langle \mathbf{x}, \mathbf{z} \rangle + \langle \bar{\mathbf{x}}, \bar{\mathbf{z}} \rangle}{i}$. In [12] the authors propose a Decision Rule Classifier based on boolean kernels which mines interesting rules from the solution of the SVM.

In this work we present two new boolean kernels, the (monotone) Disjunctive kernel and the (monotone) DNF-kernel, in which monomials in the feature space are interpreted as disjunctions and as disjunctions of conjunctions of boolean variables, respectively. We reuse the name (m) DNF-kernel with a different meaning: our kernel constructs features that are DNFs of the input variables, so the solution of a kernel machine using this kernel would be a weighted summation of verified DNFs formulae.

In the experimental section we compare these new kernels, along with the (monotone) Conjunctive kernel, against the linear and the RBF kernel, using a standard Support Vector Machine (SVM), on many categorical datasets.

3   Boolean Kernels

3.1   Monotone Conjunctive Kernel

As mentioned in Sect. 2, since we are working inside a binary input space, monomials of degree c can be interpreted as conjunctions of boolean variables, e.g., $x_1 x_3 x_7 \equiv x_1 \wedge x_3 \wedge x_7$, assuming 1 as *true* and 0 as *false*.

Using this logical interpretation, we can define the ANOVA kernel [11], of degree c, between $\mathbf{x}$ and $\mathbf{z}$ as the number of *true* conjunctions of c literals in common between $\mathbf{x}$ and $\mathbf{z}$. We call this kernel monotone Conjunctive kernel (or simply mC-kernel for brevity). The prefix "monotone" specifies the fact that the variables in the conjunctions are always considered in their affirmative (non-negative) form. Formally, the embedding of the mC-kernel of degree c is given by

$$\phi^c_\wedge : \mathbf{x} \mapsto (\phi^{(\mathbf{b})}_\wedge(\mathbf{x}))_{\mathbf{b} \in \mathbb{B}_c},$$

where $\mathbb{B}_c = \{ \mathbf{b} \in \mathbb{B}^n \mid \|\mathbf{b}\|_1 = c \}$, and

$$\phi^{(\mathbf{b})}_\wedge(\mathbf{x}) = \prod_{i=1}^n x_i^{b_i} = \mathbf{x}^{\mathbf{b}},$$

where the notation $\mathbf{x}^{\mathbf{b}}$ means $x_1^{b_1} x_2^{b_2} \cdots x_n^{b_n}$.

The dimension of the resulting feature space is $\binom{n}{c}$, that is the number of all combinations of c different variables. A conjunction is satisfied if and only if all the monomials by which it is formed are *true*. So, in order to count all the possible conjunctions of c variables satisfied in both $\phi^c_\wedge(\mathbf{x})$ and $\phi^c_\wedge(\mathbf{z})$ we have to calculate the number of combinations of c monomials that can be formed by using all the active variables in both $\mathbf{x}$ and $\mathbf{z}$.

Formally, the kernel ($\kappa^c_\wedge$) is calculated by

$$\kappa^c_\wedge(\mathbf{x}, \mathbf{z}) = \langle \phi^c_\wedge(\mathbf{x}), \phi^c_\wedge(\mathbf{z}) \rangle = \sum_{\mathbf{b} \in \mathbb{B}_c} \mathbf{x}^{\mathbf{b}} \mathbf{z}^{\mathbf{b}} = \binom{\langle \mathbf{x}, \mathbf{z} \rangle}{c}.$$

It is worth to notice that the mC-kernel generalizes the linear kernel, in fact, by fixing $c = 1$ we obtain $\kappa_\wedge^1(\mathbf{x}, \mathbf{z}) = \binom{\langle \mathbf{x}, \mathbf{z} \rangle}{1} = \langle \mathbf{x}, \mathbf{z} \rangle = \kappa_{LIN}(\mathbf{x}, \mathbf{z})$.

3.2   Monotone Disjunctive Kernel

In the previous section we described a kernel which computes conjunctions of variables in the feature space. With a similar approach, in this section we present a kernel which computes disjunctions of variables in the feature space.

The embedding of the monotone Disjunctive kernel (mD-kernel) is the same as the mC-kernel, because it forms all the possible combinations of a certain degree d. The difference is the logical interpretation: in the mD-kernel the combinations of variables represent disjunctions, e.g., $x_1 x_2 x_5 \equiv x_1 \vee x_2 \vee x_5$. A disjunction is satisfied if and only if at least one of its literals is *true*, so, in the feature space, a feature is active if and only if one of its (input) variables is active.

Formally, the embedding of the mD-kernel of degree d is given by

$$\phi_\vee^d : \mathbf{x} \mapsto (\phi_\vee^{(\mathbf{b})}(\mathbf{x}))_{\mathbf{b} \in \mathbb{B}_d},$$

with

$$\phi_\vee^{(\mathbf{b})}(\mathbf{x}) = H(\langle \mathbf{x}, \mathbf{b} \rangle) = H\left(\sum_{i=1}^n x_i b_i \right),$$

where $H : \mathbb{R} \to \mathbb{B}$ is the Heaviside step function.

The dimension of the mD-kernel embedding is $\binom{n}{d}$. It is clear that computing the kernel is not feasible in an explicit way because of the combinatorial explosion. However, we can rely on the analogy between binary vectors and sets.

Let $\mathcal{U} \equiv \{1, \ldots, n\}$ be the universal set and let $\mathcal{X} \equiv \{i \mid x_i = 1\}$ and $\mathcal{Z} \equiv \{i \mid z_i = 1\}$ be the sets interpretation of the vectors $\mathbf{x}$ and $\mathbf{z}$, respectively. An active disjunction of d literals can be defined as a set of d elements taken from $\mathcal{U}$, let us call it $\mathcal{U}_d$, such that $\exists a, b \in \mathcal{U}_d \mid a \in \mathcal{X} \wedge b \in \mathcal{Z}$ and potentially $a = b$. We will call $\mathcal{U}_d$ an *active subset* for $\mathcal{X}$ and $\mathcal{Z}$. Using this interpretation, we can define the mD-kernel between $\mathbf{x}$ and $\mathbf{z}$, $\kappa_\vee^d(\mathbf{x}, \mathbf{z}) = \langle \phi_\vee^d(\mathbf{x}), \phi_\vee^d(\mathbf{z}) \rangle$, as the number of active subsets $\mathcal{U}_d \subseteq \mathcal{U}$ for both $\mathcal{X}$ and $\mathcal{Z}$.

We can count the number of these subsets $\mathcal{U}_d$ in a negative fashion. Starting from the number of all possible subsets $\mathcal{U}_d$, which is $\binom{|\mathcal{U}|}{d}$, we have to remove the number of inactive subsets for $\mathcal{X}$ and for $\mathcal{Z}$. An inactive subset for $\mathcal{X}$ is the set $\mathcal{U}_d$ such that $\forall a \in \mathcal{U}_d, a \notin \mathcal{X}$, and the number of this kind of sets is $\binom{|\mathcal{U} \smallsetminus \mathcal{X}|}{d}$. Analogously, we can do the same for $\mathcal{Z}$. Now, we have removed twice the subsets formed by elements taken from $\overline{\mathcal{X} \cup \mathcal{Z}} \equiv \mathcal{U} \smallsetminus (\mathcal{X} \cup \mathcal{Z})$ and hence we have to add its contribution once, that is $\binom{|\mathcal{U} \smallsetminus (\mathcal{X} \cup \mathcal{Z})|}{d}$. Formally:

$$
\begin{aligned}
\kappa_\vee^d(\mathbf{x}, \mathbf{z}) &= \binom{|\mathcal{U}|}{d} - \binom{|\mathcal{U} \smallsetminus \mathcal{X}|}{d} - \binom{|\mathcal{U} \smallsetminus \mathcal{Z}|}{d} + \binom{|\mathcal{U} \smallsetminus (\mathcal{X} \cup \mathcal{Z})|}{d} \\
&= \binom{n}{d} - \binom{n - \|\mathbf{x}\|_2^2}{d} - \binom{n - \|\mathbf{z}\|_2^2}{d} + \binom{n - \|\mathbf{x}\|_2^2 - \|\mathbf{z}\|_2^2 + \langle \mathbf{x}, \mathbf{z} \rangle}{d}.
\end{aligned}
$$

It is worth to notice that, as for the mC-kernel, the mD-kernel is a generalization of the linear one. Fixed $d = 1$, then:

$$\kappa_\vee^1(\mathbf{x}, \mathbf{z}) = \binom{|\mathcal{U}|}{1} - \binom{|\mathcal{U} \smallsetminus \mathcal{X}|}{1} - \binom{|\mathcal{U} \smallsetminus \mathcal{Z}|}{1} + \binom{|\mathcal{U} \smallsetminus (\mathcal{X} \cup \mathcal{Z})|}{1}$$

$$= n - (n - |\mathcal{X}|) - (n - |\mathcal{Z}|) + (n - |\mathcal{X}| - |\mathcal{Z}| + |\mathcal{X} \cap \mathcal{Z}|)$$

$$= |\mathcal{X} \cap \mathcal{Z}| := \langle \mathbf{x}, \mathbf{z} \rangle = \kappa_{LIN}(\mathbf{x}, \mathbf{z}).$$

3.3   Monotone Disjunctive Normal Form (DNF) Kernel

In boolean logic, a Disjunctive Normal Form (DNF) is a normalization of a logical formula which is a disjunction of conjunctive clauses, e.g., $(x_1 \wedge x_2) \vee (x_3 \wedge x_5) \vee x_4$.

The idea of the monotone DNF kernel (mDNF-kernel) is to compute the dot product of vectors in a feature space composed by monotone DNF (mDNF) formulae of the input variables. In particular, the variables are mapped into the space containing all the monotone DNF formulae composed by disjunction of exactly d conjunctive clauses formed by c literals. For example, by fixing $d = 2$ and $c = 3$ a possible mDNF would be $(x_1 \wedge x_3 \wedge x_5) \vee (x_2 \wedge x_3 \wedge x_4)$.

Formally, the embedding map is the composition of the embedding maps of the mC-kernel and the mD-kernel, $\phi_{\vee\wedge}^{d,c} : \mathbf{x} \mapsto \phi_\vee^d(\phi_\wedge^c(\mathbf{x}))$.

From the embedding map definition we can see that in order to calculate this kernel we have to compute the mD-kernel of degree d in the space formed by all conjunctions of degree c. Using the same sets analogy as in Sect. 3.2, the mDNF-kernel between the vectors $\mathbf{x}, \mathbf{z} \in \mathbb{B}^n$ is calculated by:

$$\kappa_{\vee\wedge}^{d,c}(\mathbf{x}, \mathbf{z}) = \binom{\mathcal{U}|_c}{d} - \binom{\mathcal{U}|_c - \mathcal{X}|_c}{d} - \binom{\mathcal{U}|_c - \mathcal{Z}|_c}{d} + \binom{\mathcal{U}|_c - \mathcal{X}|_c - \mathcal{Z}|_c + (\mathcal{X} \cap \mathcal{Z})|_c}{d}$$

$$= \binom{\binom{n}{c}}{d} - \binom{\binom{n}{c} - \binom{\|\mathbf{x}\|_2^2}{c}}{d} - \binom{\binom{n}{c} - \binom{\|\mathbf{z}\|_2^2}{c}}{d}$$

$$+ \binom{\binom{n}{c} - \binom{\|\mathbf{x}\|_2^2}{c} - \binom{\|\mathbf{z}\|_2^2}{c} + \binom{n - \|\mathbf{x}\|_2^2 - \|\mathbf{z}\|_2^2 + \langle \mathbf{x}, \mathbf{z} \rangle}{c}}{d}$$

where $\mathcal{A}|_c = \binom{|\mathcal{A}|}{c}$. In this case the dimension of the embedding is $\binom{\binom{n}{c}}{d}$.

As for the previous kernels, it is easy to see that for $d = c = 1$ the mDNF-kernel generalizes the linear kernel:

$$\kappa_{\vee\wedge}^{1,1}(\mathbf{x}, \mathbf{z}) = \binom{\mathcal{U}|_1}{1} - \binom{\mathcal{U}|_1 - \mathcal{X}|_1}{1} - \binom{\mathcal{U}|_1 - \mathcal{Z}|_1}{1} + \binom{\mathcal{U}|_1 - \mathcal{X}|_1 - \mathcal{Z}|_1 + (\mathcal{X} \cap \mathcal{Z})|_1}{1}$$

$$= n - (n - |\mathcal{X}|) - (n - |\mathcal{Z}|) + (n - |\mathcal{X}| - |\mathcal{Z}| + |\mathcal{X} \cap \mathcal{Z}|)$$

$$:= \kappa_\vee^1(\mathbf{x}, \mathbf{z}) = \kappa_{LIN}(\mathbf{x}, \mathbf{z}).$$

4   Experiments and Results

All the experiments are conducted using the datasets reported in Table 1. The datasets are freely available from the UCI repository [6]. We selected datasets with binary or categorical features and for each of them the following preprocessing steps have been performed:

– instances with missing attributes have been removed;
– categorical features have been mapped into binary features by means of the *one-hot* encoding [3];
– non binary tasks have been artificially transformed into binary ones, by arranging the classes into two groups while trying to keep the number of instances balanced.

Table 1. Datasets information: name, number of instances, number of features, classes distribution and features type.

Dataset	#Instance	#Features	Distribution (%)	Features type
dna_bin	2000	180	48/52	Binary
house-votes	232	16	53/47	Binary
spect	267	23	79/21	Binary
audiology	92	84	50/50	Categorical
connect-4	30554	126	73/27	Categorical
kr-vs-kp	3196	38	53/47	Categorical
primary-tumor	132	24	45/55	Categorical
promoters	106	228	50/50	Categorical
soybean	266	88	55/45	Categorical
splice	3175	240	49/51	Categorical
tic-tac-toe	958	27	66/34	Categorical
zoo	101	21	59/41	Categorical

We evaluated the effectiveness of the proposed kernels against twelve datasets using SVM as the kernel method classifier. For each dataset, we performed 30 runs of a 5-fold nested cross validation and the average accuracies (with standard deviations) are reported in Table 3. Table 2 shows, for each kernel, the validated parameters, while the regularization parameter C have been validated in the set of values $\{2^{-5}, 2^{-4} \ldots, 2^{4}\}$.

The experiments have been implemented in Python, in particular with the machine learning module Scikit-learn [8]. The source code is freely available at https://github.com/makgyver/pyros.

We compared the proposed kernels against the linear kernel and the RBF kernel. In every experiment all the kernels are normalized. On average the best performing kernel is the mDNF-kernel, followed by the mC-kernel and the mD-kernel. For all the binary datasets (the ones which did not require the one-hot

Table 2. Validated parameters for the kernels.

Kernel	Parameters
Linear	-
RBF	$\gamma \in \{10^{-4}, \dots, 10^{3}\}$
mC-kernel	$c \in [1, 2, 3, 4, 5]$
mD-kernel	$d \in [1, 2, 3, 4, 5]$
mDNF-kernel	$d \in [1, 2, 3, 4, 5], c \in [1, 2, 3, 4, 5]$

Table 3. Accuracy results: best for each dataset are highlighted in **bold**. The mD-kernel have been validated with $1 \leq d \leq 5$, the mC-kernel with $1 \leq c \leq 5$, the DNF-kernel with $1 \leq d, c \leq 5$, while for the RBF kernel $\gamma \in \{10^{-4}, \dots, 10^{3}\}$. For all the tested kernels the SVM has been validated with $C \in \{2^{-5}, \dots, 2^{4}\}$. Inside the parenthesis the average degrees chosen during the validation over the 30 runs are reported.

Dataset	LIN	RBF	$\text{mD}_{(d)}$		$\text{mC}_{(c)}$		$\text{mDNF}_{(d,c)}$	
dna_bin	93.54 ±0.35	95.1 ±0.29	95.46 ±0.30	(4.7)	95.65 ±0.23	(2.7)	**95.78** ±0.21	(3.5, 2.7)
house-votes	**96.92** ±0.20	96.74 ±0.25	**96.92** ±0.20	(1)	**96.92** ±0.20	(1)	**96.92** ±0.20	(1, 1)
spect	83.43 ±0.66	83.12 ±1.54	83.47 ±0.97	(2.3)	83.51 ±0.73	(1.3)	**83.61** ±0.78	(2.2, 1.1)
audiology	99.93 ±0.27	99.82 ±0.40	**100** ±0.00	(1.1)	99.93 ±0.27	(1)	99.93 ±0.27	(1, 1)
connect-4	83.52 ±0.05	91.68 ±0.08	89.14 ±0.06	(4.9)	92.00 ±0.09	(5)	**92.01** ±0.1	(3.9, 5)
kr-vs-kp	96.57 ±0.14	99.55 ±0.1	99.11 ±0.13	(4.6)	99.57 ±0.09	(3.3)	**99.60** ±0.08	(2.4, 2.8)
primary-tumor	70.04 ±2.83	**70.87** ±2.27	70.26 ±2.73	(2.4)	69.84 ±3.08	(1.4)	70.14 ±2.89	(2.1, 1.3)
promoters	91.43 ±2.04	**91.84** ±1.87	91.15 ±2.01	(1.6)	91.27 ±2.06	(1.2)	91.15 ±2.09	(1.2, 1.2)
soybean	97.62 ±0.56	97.66 ±0.65	97.75 ±0.58	(1.4)	**97.8** ±0.61	(2.3)	97.77 ±0.63	(1.1, 2.3)
splice	94.31 ±0.18	96.02 ±0.17	96.24 ±0.19	(4.9)	**96.95** ±0.13	(3.1)	**96.95** ±0.14	(1.5, 3.1)
tic-tac-toe	98.29 ±0.07	99.16 ±0.22	98.41 ±0.21	(4.4)	**99.59** ±0.19	(3.2)	**99.59** ±0.19	(1.2, 3.2)
zoo	**99.87** ±0.34	99.61 ±0.65	**99.87** ±0.34	(1)	**99.87** ±0.34	(1)	**99.87** ±0.34	(1, 1)
Avg. rank	3.67±1.60	3.58±1.38	2.75±1.16		1.83±1.11		**1.58**±0.95	

encoding) the mDNF-kernel achieves the best accuracies. On the other set of datasets both the mDNF-kernel and the mC-kernel achieve the best accuracy in five, and four out of nine datasets, respectively. Only on two datasets, namely primary-tumor and promoters, the RBF kernel is the best performing one, even though on average it is weaker than the kernels proposed in this paper.

It is worth to notice that anytime the linear kernel had the best results, during the validation the chosen degrees (on average) for the proposed kernels are very close to 1. This means that the validation phase worked properly.

5   Conclusions

In this paper, we have introduced a family of boolean kernels able to achieve, on categorical datasets, a significant improvement in performance with respect to the state-of-the-art RBF kernel. We have also presented efficient ways to compute these kernels by means of simple operations over binomial coefficients. In the future we aim to build an efficient and effective algorithm able to extract from these kernels the most relevant features, namely the most relevant boolean rules. In this way we will be able to provide explanations of the solutions given by a kernel machine, e.g., SVM.

References

1. Barakat, N., Bradley, A.P.: Rule extraction from support vector machines: a review. Neurocomputing **74**(1–3), 178–190 (2010)
2. Fu, X., Ong, C., Keerthi, S., Hung, G.G., Goh, L.: Extracting the knowledge embedded in support vector machines. In: 2004 IEEE International Joint Conference on Neural Networks, vol. 1, p. 296, July 2004
3. Harris, D.M., Harris, S.L.: Digital Design and Computer Architecture, 2nd edn. Morgan Kaufmann, Boston (2013)
4. Khardon, R., Roth, D., Servedio, R.A.: Efficiency versus convergence of boolean kernels for on-line learning algorithms. J. Artif. Intell. Res. (JAIR) **24**, 341–356 (2005)
5. Kusunoki, Y., Tanino, T.: Boolean kernels and clustering with pairwise constraints. In: 2014 IEEE International Conference on Granular Computing (GrC), pp. 141–146, October 2014
6. Lichman, M.: UCI machine learning repository (2013). http://archive.ics.uci.edu/ml
7. Nguyen, S.H., Nguyen, H.S.: Applications of Boolean kernels in rough sets. In: Kryszkiewicz, M., Cornelis, C., Ciucci, D., Medina-Moreno, J., Motoda, H., Raś, Z.W. (eds.) RSEISP 2014. LNCS, vol. 8537, pp. 65–76. Springer, Cham (2014). doi:10.1007/978-3-319-08729-0_6
8. Pedregosa, F., Varoquaux, G., Gramfort, A., Michel, V., Thirion, B., Grisel, O., Blondel, M., Prettenhofer, P., Weiss, R., Dubourg, V., Vanderplas, J., Passos, A., Cournapeau, D., Brucher, M., Perrot, M., Duchesnay, E.: Scikit-learn: machine learning in python. J. Mach. Learn. Res. **12**, 2825–2830 (2011)
9. Sadohara, K.: Learning of Boolean functions using support vector machines. In: Abe, N., Khardon, R., Zeugmann, T. (eds.) ALT 2001. LNCS, vol. 2225, pp. 106–118. Springer, Heidelberg (2001). doi:10.1007/3-540-45583-3_10
10. Sadohara, K.: On a capacity control using Boolean kernels for the learning of Boolean functions. In: Proceedings of the 2002 IEEE International Conference on Data Mining, pp. 410–417 (2002)
11. Shawe-Taylor, J., Cristianini, N.: Kernel Methods for Pattern Analysis. Cambridge University Press, New York (2004)
12. Zhang, Y., Li, Z., Cui, K.: *DRC-BK*: mining classification rules by using Boolean kernels. In: Gervasi, O., Gavrilova, M.L., Kumar, V., Laganà, A., Lee, H.P., Mun, Y., Taniar, D., Tan, C.J.K. (eds.) ICCSA 2005. LNCS, vol. 3480, pp. 214–222. Springer, Heidelberg (2005). doi:10.1007/11424758_23
13. Zhang, Y., Li, Z., Kang, M., Yan, J.: Improving the classification performance of Boolean kernels by applying Occam's razor (2003)

DeepBrain: Functional Representation of Neural In-Situ Hybridization Images for Gene Ontology Classification Using Deep Convolutional Autoencoders

Ido Cohen[1], Eli (Omid) David[1(✉)], Nathan S. Netanyahu[1,2], Noa Liscovitch[3], and Gal Chechik[3]

[1] Department of Computer Science, Bar-Ilan University, Ramat-Gan, Israel
cido15@gmail.com, mail@elidavid.com, nathan@cs.biu.ac.il,
nathan@cfar.umd.edu
[2] Center for Automation Research, University of Maryland, College Park, MD, USA
[3] Gonda Multidisiplinary Brain Research Center, Bar-Ilan University,
Ramat-Gan, Israel
noalis@gmail.com, gal.chechik@mail.biu.ac.il

Abstract. This paper presents a novel deep learning-based method for learning a functional representation of mammalian neural images. The method uses a *deep convolutional denoising autoencoder* (CDAE) for generating an invariant, compact representation of *in situ hybridization* (ISH) images. While most existing methods for bio-imaging analysis were not developed to handle images with highly complex anatomical structures, the results presented in this paper show that functional representation extracted by CDAE can help learn features of functional *gene ontology categories* for their classification in a highly accurate manner. Using this CDAE representation, our method outperforms the previous state-of-the-art classification rate, by improving the average AUC from 0.92 to 0.98, i.e., achieving 75% reduction in error. The method operates on input images that were downsampled significantly with respect to the original ones to make it computationally feasible.

1 Introduction

A very large volume of high-spatial resolution imaging datasets is available these days in various domains, calling for a wide range of exploration methods based on image processing. One such dataset has become recently available in the field of Neuroscience, thanks to the Allen Institute for Brain Science. This dataset contains *in situ hybridization* (ISH) images of mammalian brains, in unprecedented amounts, which has motivated new research efforts [3,11,12]. ISH is a powerful technique for localizing specific nucleic acid targets within fixed tissues and cells; it provides an effective approach for obtaining temporal and spatial information about gene expression [16]. Images now reveal highly complex patterns of gene expression varying on multiple scales.

© Springer International Publishing AG 2017
A. Lintas et al. (Eds.): ICANN 2017, Part II, LNCS 10614, pp. 287–296, 2017.
https://doi.org/10.1007/978-3-319-68612-7_33

However, analytical tools for discovering gene interactions from such data remain an open challenge due to various reasons, including difficulties in extracting canonical representations of gene activities from images, and inferring statistically meaningful networks from such representations. The challenge in analyzing these images is both in extracting the patterns that are most relevant functionally, and in providing a meaningful representation that allows neuroscientists to interpret the extracted patterns.

One of the aims at finding a meaningful representation for such images, is to carry out classification to *gene ontology* (GO) categories. GO is a major Bioinformatics initiative to unify the representation of gene and gene product attributes across all species [5]. More specifically, it aims at maintaining and developing a controlled vocabulary of gene and gene product attributes and at annotating them. This task is far from done; in fact, several gene and gene product functions of many organisms have yet to be discovered and annotated [14]. Gene function annotations, which are associations between a gene and a term of controlled vocabulary describing gene functional features, are of paramount importance in modern biology. They are used to design novel biological experiments and interpret their results. Since gene validation through in vitro biomolecular experiments is costly and lengthy, deriving new computational methods and software for predicting and prioritizing new biomolecular annotations, would make an important contribution to the field [20]. In other words, deriving an effective computational procedure that predicts reliably likely annotations, and thus speed up the discovery of new gene annotations, would be very useful [9].

Past methods for analyzing brain images had to reference a brain atlas, and based on smooth non-linear transformations [10,13]. These types of analyses may be insensitive to fine local patterns, like those found in the layered structure of the cerebellum[1], or to spatial distribution. In addition, most machine vision approaches address the challenge of providing human interpretable analysis. Conversely, in bioimaging usually the goal is to reveal features and structures that are hardly seen even by human experts. For example, one of the new functions that follow this approach is presented in [17], using a histogram of local *scale-invariant feature transform* (SIFT) [8] descriptors on several scales.

Recently, many machine learning algorithms have been designed and implemented to predict GO annotations [1,7,15,18,22]. In our research, we examine an *artificial neural network* (ANN) with many layers (also known as *deep learning*) in order to achieve functional representations of neural ISH images.

In order to find a compact representation of these ISH images, we explored *autoencoders* (AE) and *convolution neural networks* (CNN), and found the *convolutional autoencoder* (CAE) to be the most appropriate technique. Subsequently, we use this representation to learn features of functional GO categories for every image, using a simple *support vector machine* (SVM) classifier [4], as in [17]. As a result, each image is represented as a point in a lower-dimensional space whose axes correspond to meaningful functional annotations. A similar example

---

[1] The cerebellum is a region of the brain. It plays an important role in motor control, and has some effect on cognitive functions [23].

to ours is the work of Krizhevsky and Hinton [2], who used deep autoencoders to create short binary codes for content-based images. The resulting representations define similarities between ISH images which can be easily explained, hopefully, by such functional categories.

Our experimental results demonstrate that a so-called *convolutional denoising autoencoder* (CDAE) representation (see Subsect. 3.2) outperforms the previous state-of-the-art classification rate, by improving the average AUC from 0.92 to 0.98, i.e., achieving 75% reduction in error. The method operates on input images that were downsampled significantly with respect to the original ones to make it computationally feasible.

2   Background

2.1   FuncISH - Learning Functional Representations

ISH images of mammalian brains reveal highly complex patterns of gene expression varying on multiple scales. Our study follows [17], which we pursue using deep learning. In [17] the authors present *FuncISH*, a learning method of functional representations of ISH images, using a histogram of local descriptors on several scales.

They first represent each image as a collection of local descriptors using SIFT features. Next, they construct a standard bag-of-words description of each image, giving a 2004-dimension representation vector for each gene. Finally, given a set of predefined GO annotations of each gene, they train a separate classifier for each known biological category, using the SIFT bag-of-words representation as an input vector. Specifically, they used a set of 2081 L_2-regularized logistic regression classifiers for this training. A scheme representing the work flow is presented in Fig. 2 (see Sect. 4).

Applying their method to the genomic set of mouse neural ISH images available from the Allen Brain Atlas, they found that most neural biological processes could be inferred from spatial expression patterns with high accuracy. Despite ignoring important global location information, they successfully inferred ~700 functional annotations, and used them to detect gene-gene similarities which were not captured by previous, global correlation-based methods. According to [17], combining local and global patterns of expression is an important topic for further research, e.g., the use of more sophisticated non-linear classifiers.

2.2   Deep Learning Techniques

Pursuing further the above classification problem poses a number of challenges. First, we cannot define a certain set of rules that an ISH image has to conform to in order to classify it to the correct GO category. Therefore, conventional computer vision techniques, capable of identifying shapes and objects in an image, are not likely to provide effective solutions to the problem. Thus, we use deep learning to achieve better results, as far as functional representations of the

ISH images. This yields an interpretable measure of similarity between complex images that are difficult to analyze and interpret.

Deep learning techniques that support this kind of problems use AE and CNN, as well as CAE, which are successful in preforming feature extraction and finding compact representations for the kind of large ISH images we have been dealing with. While traditional machine learning is useful for algorithms that learn iteratively from the data, our second issue concerns the type of data we possess. Our data consist of 16K images, representing about 15K different genes, i.e., an average of one image per gene. This prevents us from extracting features from each gene independently, but rather consider the data in their entirety. Moreover, not only is there only one image per gene, there are merely a few genes in every examined GO category, and the genes are not unique to one category, i.e., each gene may belong to more than one category. Despite these difficulties, machine learning is capable of capturing underlying "insights" without resorting to manual feature selection. This makes it possible to automatically produce models that can analyze larger and more complex data, achieving thereby more accurate results.

In the next section we present our convolutional autoencoder approach, which operates solely on raw pixel data. This supports our main goal, i.e., learning representations of given brain images to extract useful information, more easily, when building classifiers or other predictors. The representations obtained are vectors which can be used to solve a variety of problems, e.g., the problem of GO classification. For this reason, a good representation is also one that is useful as input to a supervised predictor, as it allows us to build classifiers for the biological categories known.

3   Feature Extraction Using Convolutional Autoencoders

3.1   Auto-Encoders (AE)

While convolutional neural networks (CNN) are effective in a supervised framework, provided a large training set is available, this is incompatible to our case. If only a small number of training samples is available, unsupervised pre-training methods, such as *restricted Boltzmann machines* (RBM) [21] or autoencoders [24], have proven highly effective.

An AE is a neural network which sets the target values (of the output layer) to be equal to those of the input, using hidden layers of smaller and smaller size, which comprise a bottleneck. Thus, an AE can be trained in an unsupervised manner, forcing the network to learn a higher-level representation of the input. An improved approach, which outperforms basic autoencoders in many tasks is due to *denoising autoencoders* (DAEs) [24,25]. These are built as regular AEs, where each input is corrupted by added noise, or by setting to zero some portion of the values. Although the input sample is corrupted, the network's objective is to produce the original (uncorrupted) values in the output layer. Forcing the network to recreate the uncorrupted values results in reduced network overfitting (also due to the fact that the network rarely receives the same input twice), and in extraction of more high-level features. For any autoencoder-based approach, once training is complete, the decoder layer(s) are removed, such that a given input passes through the network and yields a high-level representation of the data. In most implementations (such as ours), these representations can then be used for supervised classification.

3.2 Convolutional Autoencoders (CAE)

CNNs and AEs can be combined to produce CAEs. As with CNNs, the CAE weights are shared among all locations in the input, preserving spatial locality and reducing the number of parameters. In practice, to combine CNNs with AEs (or DAEs), it is necessary for each encoder layer to have a corresponding decoder layer. *Deconvolution* layers are essentially the same as convolutional layers, and similarly to standard autoencoders, they can either be learned or set equal to (the transpose of) the original convolution layers, as with tied weights in autoencoders (both work well). For the *unpooling* operation, more than one method exists [6,19]. In the CAE we use, during unpooling all locations are set to the maximum value which is stored in that layer (Fig. 1).

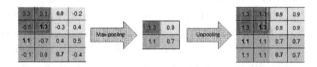

Fig. 1. Pooling and unpooling layers; for each pooling layer, the max value is kept, and then duplicated in the unpooling layer.

Similarly to an AE, after training a CAE, the unpooling and deconvolution layers are removed. At this point, a neural net, composed from convolution and pooling layers, can be used to find a functional representation, as in our case, or initialize a supervised CNN. Similarly to a DAE, a CAE with input corrupted by added noise is called a *convolutional denoising autoencoders* (CDAE).

4   CDAE for GO Classification

Figure 2 depicts a framework for capturing the representation of FuncISH. A SIFT-based module was used in [17] for feature extraction. Alternatively, our scheme learns a CDAE-based representation, before applying a similar classification method as in [17], where two layers of 5-fold cross-validation were used, one for training the classifier and the other for tuning the logistic regression regularization hyperparameter.

For unsupervised training of our CDAE we use the genomic set of mouse neural ISH images available from the Allen Brain Atlas, which includes 16,351 images representing 15,612 genes. These JPEG images have an average resolution

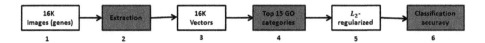

Fig. 2. (1) 16K grayscale images indicating level of gene expression, (2) SIFT- or CDAE-based feature extraction for a compact vector representation of each gene, (3) vector representation due to feature extraction, (4) 16K vectors trained with respect to each of 15 GO categories with best AUC classification in [17], (5) L_2-regularized logistic regression classifiers for top 15 GO categories, and (6) classification accuracy measured.

of $15,000 \times 7,500$ pixels. To get a representation vector of size $\sim 2,000$, the images were downsampled to 300×140 pixels.

The CDAE architecture for finding a compact representation for these downsampled images is as follow: (1) **Input layer**: Consists of the raw image, resampled to 300×140 pixels, and corrupted by setting to zero 20% of the values, (2) three sequential convolutional layers with 32 9×9 filters each, (3) max-pooling layer of size 2×2, (4) three sequential convolutional layers with 32 7×7 filters each, (5) max-pooling layer of size 2×2, (6) two sequential convolutional layers with 64 5×5 filters each, (7) convolutional layer with a single 5×5 filter, (8) unpooling layer of size 2×2, (9) three sequential deconvolution layers with 32 7×7 filters each, (10) unpooling layer of size 2×2, (11) three sequential deconvolution layers with 32 9×9 filters each, (12) deconvolution layer with a single 5×5 filter, and (13) **output layer** with the uncorrupted resampled image.

After training the CDAE, all layers past item 8 are removed, so that item 7 (the convolutional layer of size $1 \times 2,625$) becomes the output layer. Therefore, each image is mapped to a vector of 2,625 functional features. Given a set of predefined GO annotations for each gene (where each GO category consists of 15–500 genes), we trained a separate classifier for each biological category. Training requires careful consideration, in this case, due to the vastly imbalanced nature of the training sets. Similarly to [17], we performed a weighted SVM classification using 5-fold cross-validation.

This network yields remarkable AUC results for every category of the top 15 GO categories reported in [17]. Figure 3 illustrates the AUC scores achieved for various representation vectors. While the average AUC score (of the top 15 categories) reported in [17] was **0.92**, the average AUC using our CDAE scheme was **0.98**, i.e., a **75%** reduction in error.

4.1   Reducing Vector Dimensionality

The above improvement was achieved with a vector size of 2,625, which is larger than the 2004-dimensional vector obtained by SIFT. In an attempt to maintain, as much as possible, the scheme's performance for a comparable vector size, we explored the use of smaller vectors, by resampling the images to different scales, and constructing CDAEs with various numbers of convolution and pooling layers.

Figure 3(b) shows the average AUC for the top 15 categories mentioned earlier, with the same CDAE structure and the images resampled to smaller scales, thus obtaining lower-dimensionality representation vectors.

Downsampling to 240 × 120 images, we obtained a 1800-dimensional representation vector, for which the AUC scores are still superior (relatively to [17]) for each of the top 15 GO categories (as shown in Fig. 3(a)). The **10%**-dimensionality reduction results only in a slightly lower AUC average of **0.97** (see Fig. 3(b)).

The CDAE network for the more compact representation is shown in Fig. 4. The architecture consists of the following layers: (1) **Input layer**: consists of the raw image, resampled to 240 × 120 pixels, and corrupted by setting to zero 20% of the values, (2) four sequential convolutional layers with 16 3 × 3 filters each, (3) max-pooling layer of size 2 × 2, (4) four sequential convolutional layers with 16 3 × 3 filters each, (5) max-pooling layer of size 2 × 2, (6) three sequential convolutional layers with 16 3×3 filters each, (7) convolutional layer with a single 3 × 3 filter, (8) unpooling layer of size 2 × 2, (9) four sequential deconvolution layers with 16 3 × 3 filters each, (10) unpooling layer of size 2 × 2, (11) four sequential deconvolution layers with 16 3 × 3 filters each, (12) deconvolution layer with a single 3 × 3 filter, and (13) **output layer** with the uncorrupted resampled image.

We used the ReLU activation function for all convolution and deconvolution layers, except for the last deconvolution layer, which uses tanh.

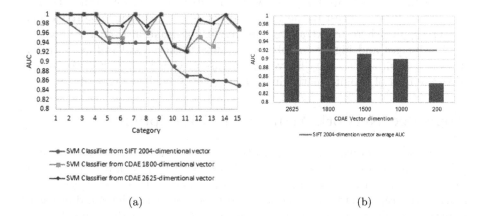

(a)   (b)

Fig. 3. AUC results using convolutional denoising autoencoder for feature extraction: (a) AUC obtained from training a SVM classifier for each GO category, using a compact representation vector for every gene; representation vector dimensionality depends on method used and image resampling rate; (b) average AUC for top 15 classifiers, trained on different representation vectors due to CDAE (as in Fig. 4), for different resampling of brain images.

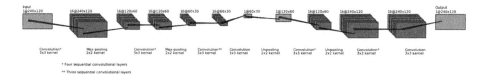

Fig. 4. Illustration of our convolutional denoising autoencoder, achieving a compact representation for each gene.

The learning rate starts from 0.05 and is multiplied by 0.9 after each epoch, and the denoising effect is obtained by randomly removing 20% of the pixels every image in the input layer. We used the AUC as a measure of classification accuracy.

5   Conclusion

Many machine learning algorithms have been designed lately to predict GO annotations. For the task of learning functional representations of mammalian neural images, we used deep learning techniques, and found convolutional denoising autoencoder to be very effective. Specifically, using the presented scheme for feature learning of functional GO categories improved the previous state-of-the-art classification accuracy from an average AUC of 0.92 to 0.98, i.e., a 75% reduction in error. We demonstrated how to reduce the vector dimensionality by 10% compared to the SIFT vectors, with very little degradation of this accuracy. Our results further attest to the advantages of deep convolutional autoencoders, as were applied here to extracting meaningful information from very high resolution images and highly complex anatomical structures. Until gene product functions of all species are discovered, the use of CDAEs may well continue to serve the field of Bioinformatics in designing novel biological experiments.

Appendix: Network Architecture Description

We provide a brief explanation as to the choice of the main parameters of the CDAE architecture. Our objective was to obtain a more compact feature representation than the 2,004-dimensional vector used in FuncISH. Since a CNN is used, the representation along the grid should capture the two-dimensional structure of the input, i.e., the image dimensions should be determined according to the intended representation vector, while maintaining the aspect ratio of the original input image. Thus, we picked an 1,800-dimensional feature vector, corresponding to an (output) image of size 60×30. Taking into account the characteristic of max-pooling (i.e., that at each stage the dimension is reduced by 2), the desire to keep the number of layers as small as possible, and the fact that the encoding and decoding phases each contains the same number of layers (resulting in twice the number of layers in the network), we settled for two max-pooling layers, namely an input image of size 240×120. Between each two max-pooling layers, which eliminate feature redundancy, there is an "array" of 16 convolution layers, each with the purpose of detecting locally connected features from its previous layer. The number of convolution layers (i.e., different filters used) was determined after experimenting with several different layers, all of which gave similar results. Choosing 16 layers (as shown in Fig. 4) provided the best result. We experimented also with various filter sizes for each layer, ranging from 3×3 to 11×11; while increasing the filter size significantly increased the amount of network parameters learned, it did not contribute much to the feature extraction or the improvement of the results. Using a learning rate decay in the training of large networks (where there is a large number of randomly generated parameters) has proven helpful in the network's convergence. Specifically, the combination of a 0.05 learning rate parameter with a 0.9 learning rate decay resulted in an optimal change of the parameter value. In this case, too, small changes in the parameters did not result in significant changes in the results.

References

1. Kordmahalleh, M.M., Homaifar, A., Dukka, B.K.C.: Hierarchical multi-label gene function prediction using adaptive mutation in crowding niching. In: Proceedings of IEEE International Conference on Bioinformatics and Bioengineering, pp. 1–6 (2013)
2. Krizhevsky, A., Hinton, G.E.: Using very deep autoencoders for content-based image retrieval. In: Proceedings of European Symposium on Artificial Neural Networks (2011)
3. Henry, A.M., Hohmann, J.G.: High-resolution gene expression atlases for adult and developing mouse brain and spinal cord. Mamm. Genome **23**, 539–549 (2012)
4. Cortes, C., Vapnik, V.: Support vector networks. Mach. Learn. **20**(3), 273–297 (1995)
5. The Gene Ontology Consortium: The gene ontology project in 2008. Nucleic Acids Res. **36**, D440–D444 (2008)
6. Masci, J., Meier, U., Cireşan, D., Schmidhuber, J.: Stacked convolutional autoencoders for hierarchical feature extraction. In: Honkela, T., Duch, W., Girolami, M., Kaski, S. (eds.) ICANN 2011. LNCS, vol. 6791, pp. 52–59. Springer, Heidelberg (2011). doi:10.1007/978-3-642-21735-7_7
7. Pinoli, P., Chicco, D., Masseroli, M.: Computational algorithms to predict gene ontology annotations. BMC Bioinform. **16**(6), S4 (2015)
8. Lowe, D.G.: Distinctive image features from scale-invariant keypoints. Int. J. Comput. Vis. **60**(2), 91–110 (2004)
9. Skunca, N., du Plessis, L., Dessimoz, C.: The what, where, how and why of gene ontology-a primer for bioinformaticians. Briefings Bioinform. **12**(6), 723–735 (2011)
10. Hawrylycz, M., Ng, L., Page, D., Morris, J., Lau, C., Faber, S., Faber, V., Sunkin, S., Menon, V., Lein, E., Jones, A.: Multi-scale correlation structure of gene expression in the brain. Neural Netw. **24**, 933–942 (2011)
11. Lein, E.S., et al.: Genome-wide atlas of gene expression in the adult mouse brain. Nature **445**, 168–176 (2007)
12. Ng, L., et al.: An anatomic gene expression atlas of the adult mouse brain. Nat. Neurosci. **12**, 356–362 (2009)

13. Davis, F.P., Eddy, S.R.: A tool for identification of genes expressed in patterns of interest using the allen brain atlas. Bioinformatics **25**, 1647–1654 (2009)
14. Ashburner, M., Ball, C.A., Blake, J.A., Botstein, D., Butler, H., Cherry, J.M.: Gene ontology: tool for the unification of biology. Nat. Genet. **25**(1), 25–29 (2000)
15. King, O.D., Foulger, R.E., Dwight, S.S., White, J.V., Roth, F.P.: Predicting gene function from patterns of annotation. Genome Res. **13**(5), 896–904 (2013)
16. Puniyani, K., Xing, E.P.: GINI: from ISH images to gene interaction networks. PLoS Comput. Biol. **9**, 10 (2013)
17. Shalit, U., Liscovitch, N., Chechik, G.: FuncISH: learning a functional representation of neural ISH images. Bioinformatics **29**(13), i36–i43 (2013)
18. Zitnik, M., Zupan, B.: Matrix factorization-based data fusion for gene function prediction in baker's yeast and slime mold. In: Proceedings of Pacific Symposium on Biocomputing, pp. 400–411 (2014)
19. Zeiler, M.D., Fergus, R.: Visualizing and understanding convolutional networks. In: Fleet, D., Pajdla, T., Schiele, B., Tuytelaars, T. (eds.) ECCV 2014. LNCS, vol. 8689, pp. 818–833. Springer, Cham (2014). doi:10.1007/978-3-319-10590-1_53
20. Bork, P., Thode, G., Perez, A.J., Perez-Iratxeta, C., Andrade, M.A.: Gene annotation from scientific literature using mappings between keyword systems. Bioinformatics **20**(13), 2084–2091 (2004)
21. Hinton, G.E., Osindero, S., Teh, Y.W.: A fast learning algorithm for deep belief nets. Neural Comput. **18**(7), 1527–1554 (2006)
22. Vembu, S., Morris, Q.: An efficient algorithm to integrate network and attribute data for gene function prediction. In: Proceedings of Pacific Symposium on Biocomputing, pp. 388–399 (2014)
23. Rapoport, M.J., Wolf, U., Schweizer, T.A.: Evaluating the affective component of the cerebellar cognitive affective syndrome. J. Neuropsychol. Clin. Neurosci. **21**(3), 245–253 (2009)
24. Vincent, P., Larochelle, H., Bengio, Y., Manzagol, P.A.: Extracting and composing robust features with denoising autoencoders. In: Proceedings of the 25th International Conference on Machine learning, pp. 1096–1103 (2008)
25. Vincent, P., Larochelle, H., Lajoie, I., Bengio, Y., Manzagol, P.: Stacked denoising autoencoders: learning useful representations in a deep network with a local denoising criterion. J. Mach. Learn. Res. **11**, 3371–3408 (2010)

Mental Workload Classification Based on Semi-Supervised Extreme Learning Machine

Jianrong Li and Jianhua Zhang[⊠]

School of Information Science and Engineering,
East China University of Science and Technology, Shanghai 200237, China
zhangjh@ecust.edu.cn

Abstract. The real-time operator's mental workload (MWL) monitoring system is crucial for the design and development of adaptive operator-aiding/assistance systems. Although the data-driven approach has shown promising performance for MWL recognition, its major challenge lies in the difficulty in acquiring extensive labeled data. This paper attempts to apply the semi-supervised extreme learning machine (ELM) to the challenging problem of operator's mental workload classification based only on a small number of labeled physiological data. The real data analysis results show that the semi-supervised ELM method can effectively improve the accuracy and computational efficiency of the MWL pattern classification.

Keywords: Mental workload · Physiological signals · Feature extraction · Semi-Supervised Learning · Extreme learning machine

1 Introduction

In recent years, automation technology has been widely used in various fields, but the development of automation technology and artificial intelligence technology are not yet mature, fully automated control can't be achieved, therefore, Human Machine System (HMS) was born [1]. Compared with machines, operators are more susceptible to external factors or their own physiological and psychological impact [2], which will affect the performance of HMS. It is the focus of experts both at home and abroad that how to maintain the best Operator Function State (OFS) [3] to ensure the completion of the planning tasks in the HMS.

The operator's MWL level is an important part in OFS research area. The MWL is considered as a potential variable to measure mental status [4], which reflects the mental needs of operators participating task. For operators, too high or too low psychological load isn't conducive to the performance of HMS. In order to avoid this situation, scholars have proposed an Adaptive Automation (AA) system. The system can reasonably allocate the tasks between operators and the machines according to the levels of operators' MWL. Operators MWL measurement methods are usually divided into three categories [5]: (1) subjective assessment, (2) task performance based assessment, (3) physiological data based assessment. Compared with the first two methods, the third measurement

© Springer International Publishing AG 2017
A. Lintas et al. (Eds.): ICANN 2017, Part II, LNCS 10614, pp. 297–304, 2017.
https://doi.org/10.1007/978-3-319-68612-7_34

method has the advantages of uninterrupted, on-line measurement and easy access, so this paper evaluates the operators' MWL by using psychophysiological signals. Electroencephalogram (EEG), Electrocardiogram (ECG) and Electro-Oculogram (EOG) are widely used in WML recognition.

The structure of this paper is as follows. In Sect. 2, we describe the operator's MWL detection system based on the Semi-Supervised Learning (SSL). The operator's physiological signal acquisition and processing is described in Sect. 3. Section 4 shows the results of the algorithm in six subjects. Section 5 explains the conclusions drawn in this paper.

2 Semi-Supervised Mental Workload Recognition

Operator's MWL classification is a multi-class issue. Figure 1 shows the operator's MWL classification flow chart. The process is divided into two parts, off-line training part and on-line detection part. The data used in the off-line training part consists of two parts: labeled data and unlabeled data. These two parts of the data are used as training samples for the Semi-Supervised Extreme Learning Machine (SS-ELM) [6–8, 14]. The best model is constructed under the off-line part, and then, the physiological signal is detected in the case of on-line.

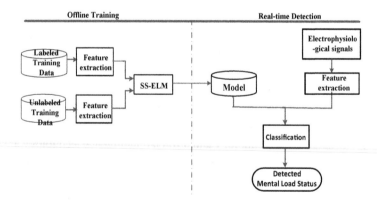

Fig. 1. Flowchart of SSL-based high-risk MWL detection algorithm

3 Data Acquisition and Preprocessing

3.1 Experimental Task Environment

The simulation task platform is "automated-enhanced Cabin Air Management System (aCAMS)", which consists of four subsystems closely related to the enclosed cabin environment, representing oxygen concentration (O2), pressure (P), carbon dioxide concentration (CO2), and temperature (T). In the experiment, we used the aCAMS to simulate the environment in the sealed cabin and affect the operator's MWL by the

Number Of Subsystems (NOS) and the Actuator Sensitivity (AS). The aCAMS simulation platform and Nihon Kohden® signal measurement system together constitute a complex HMS task simulation platform software and hardware environment.

3.2 Experimental Subjects

There were 6 subjects (22–24 years old, male, numbers: A, B, C, D, E, F) participated in the experiments. All subjects were healthy, normal vision, and used right hand regularly. Before the experiment, all subjects were informed by the experimenter of goals and procedures of the experiments, and they were trained more than 10 h of aCAMS simulation exercises.

3.3 Experimental Procedure

The aCAMS system has four subsystems, each subsystem has two control strategies: automatic control and manual control. The two strategies can be switched arbitrarily. The control objective of this experiment is to maintain the control variables of the four subsystems within the target range by automatic control or manual control. In order to further investigate changes in MWL, manual control is set to two different actuators: Standard Level (SL) and High Level (HL). The HL indicates that the sensitivity of the control variables of the subsystem is greater than SL [9, 11].

Each session lasts 50 min and is divided into 10 stages. The stage 1, 4, 7, 10 are the automatic control phase. Operators manually control two subsystems (O2 and P) in the 2 and 3 stages, the difference between the two stages is that the sensitivity of the control variables is different. Similarly, Fig. 2 shows the situation at each stage. At the last 10 s of each stage, the operators perform self-assessment, so the actual data acquisition time is 290 s. Based on the international standard 10–20 electrode configuration method [10], 15 electrodes most relevant to MWL studies were selected, namely, F3, F4, Fz, C3, C4, Cz, CPz, P3, P4, Pz, O1, O2, AFz, CPz, POz, Oz. In addition, EOG data and ECG data are also measured.

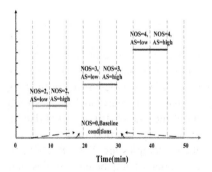

Fig. 2. Task-load conditions in an experimental session

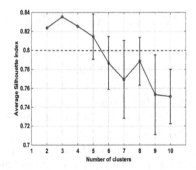

Fig. 3. The average Silhouette index vs. the number of clusters in *k*-means clustering algorithm

3.4 Determination of Target Classes

The data is divided by the time window of 1 s (without overlapping). Each stage is divided into 290 samples. In addition to measuring physiological data, this experiment also records the performance data of the control subsystem. Through the performance data, we can get two important performance indicators PI_m and PI_s:

$$\begin{cases} PI_m = c_1([r_{O_2}(t) + r_P(t) + r_{CO_2}(t) + r_T(t)]/4) + c_2 NOS \\ PI_s = c_1([d_{O_2}(t) + d_P(t) + d_{CO_2}(t) + d_T(t)]/4) + c_2 NOS \end{cases} \tag{1}$$

where, c_1 and c_2 are empirical weights, NOS describes the difficulty of the task. $r_{O_2}(t)$, $r_P(t)$, $r_{CO_2}(t)$, $r_T(t)$ are Boolean variables of the corresponding subsystem at time t (when the control variable of the corresponding subsystem is within the target range at time t, $r(t) = 1$, otherwise $r(t) = 0$). $d(t)$ represents the absolute value of the deviation between the actual value of the controlled variable of the corresponding subsystem and the set-point at the sampling time t. Finally, based on these two indicators, we use K-means to cluster them to determine the corresponding label for the data. According to Fig. 3, when the number of clusters is 2, 3, 4, 5, the average Silhouette index (six subjects) is greater than 0.8. The classification of the two cases has no practical significance in the OFS study, so, we believe that there are three classes (baseline, low, high), four classes (baseline, low, normal, high) and five classes (baseline, low, normal, high, higher).

3.5 Physiological Feature Extraction

In this experiment, The Hilbert-Huang Transform (HHT) is used to extract the characteristics of physiological signals [12, 13]. The original signal is decomposed into several Intrinsic Modal Function (IMF) components by Empirical Mode Decomposition (EMD) algorithm. The sample entropy of the three IMF components with most relevant to the original signal and the Hilbert marginal spectral entropy and energy spectrum entropy are taken as the characteristics of the sample,so each sample will have 85 features (17 channels * 5 features).

4 MWL Classification Results and Analysis

According to the data acquisition and processing methods mentioned in Sect. 3, we can get 2900×85 (2900, sample number; 85, sample dimension) data for each subject. As the data of this experiment have been correctly marked. We can delete some of the tags to get unlabeled data. Usually unlabeled data is much more than label data, so we divide the data into labeled data and unlabeled data at the rate of 1:9. Labeled data is divided into test data and training data according to the proportion of 1:4. So, the number of training samples, test samples and unlabeled samples are 232, 58, 2610. In particular, due to space constraints, the effect of number of unlabeled samples and labeled samples on the accuracy of the algorithm and comparison of algorithms are studied in the case of three classes.

4.1 Results of Semi-Supervised ELM

In this paper, the SS-ELM is applied to classify operator's MWL. As it is showed in Fig. 4, the proposed algorithm has better performance in OFS data set. Specifically, the accuracy of the algorithm is 93.00% (three classes), 90.43% (four classes), 88.93% (five classes). Overall, the results of the three classes are better than the four classes, better than the accuracy of the five classes. When the number of classes becomes large, the difficulty of classification is increased. In addition, the difference between the subjects is quite obvious in the MWL classification test.

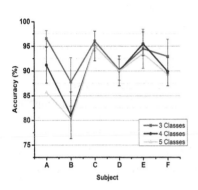 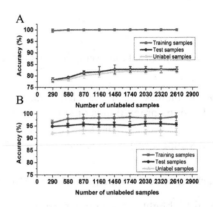

Fig. 4. MWL classification accuracy for each of the six subjects

Fig. 5. The change of subject-average classification accuracy with the number of unlabeled data. (A) 58 training samples; (B) 232 training samples

4.2 Effect of Number of Unlabeled Data

In order to explore the ability of semi-supervised methods in unlabeled data, we evaluate the classifier model by increasing the number of unlabeled samples. In the case of three classes, the average classification accuracy is shown in Fig. 5 (mean ± standard deviation). When the number of training samples is 58, the testing accuracy increases as the number of unlabeled samples increases, and the accuracy of classification does not increase significantly when the number of labeled samples continues to increase. When the number of labeled samples is 232, with the increasing of unlabeled data, the effect on the accuracy of the algorithm changed little. This shows that the semi-supervised algorithm has a significant effect when the labeled samples are few.

4.3 Effect of Number of Labeled Data

We set the number of unlabeled samples set to 1450 and increase the size of the labeled samples set. In the case of three classes, the average accuracy of all subjects was reported in Fig. 6 (mean ± standard deviation).

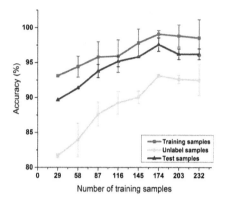

Fig. 6. The change of subject-averaged classification accuracy with the number of labeled data.

With the increase of the labeled data, the accuracy of the three classes has been improved and the promotion is obvious. When the number of labeled data continues to increase, the accuracy of the three data sets (Training samples set, Test samples set, Unlabeled samples set) is no longer increasing.

4.4   Performance Comparison of Five Different Classifiers

In order to highlight the superior performance of the SS-ELM on OFS data set, the feature extraction algorithm adopts Hilbert-Huang algorithm. The classifiers are Naive Bayesian (NB), Random Forest (RF), Support Vector Machines (SVM), ELM, and SS-ELM. As the number of label samples increases, the accuracy of each algorithm is shown in Fig. 7.

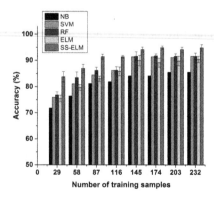

Fig. 7. The change of subject-averaged classification accuracy with the number of labeled data for five different classifiers.

With the increase of the number of trained training samples, the accuracy of the test sample gradually increases, the tag data continues to increase, the accuracy of the test sample will not be significantly improved; When the number of labels is small (the number of labels is 29), the advantage of SS-ELM is the most obvious. Compared with supervised learning, the improvement of accuracy is 12.05% (NB), 7.99% (SVM), 7.08% (RF), 8.39% (ELM). When the number of labeled data is large, the advantage of semi-supervised learning is smaller than that of other algorithms. Overall, the proposed SS-ELM is relatively best classifier in MWL classification issue.

5 Conclusion

The main contributions of this paper are as follows: (1) Most previous work on operator functional state (OFS) analysis was mainly based on various supervised learning techniques. This paper successfully applies semi-supervised learning technique to the mental workload (MWL) recognition problem. (2) Our results show that accurate MWL classification can be achieved using only a small number of labeled data, which overcomes the difficulty in acquiring enough labeled data in real-world applications. (3) Our results also show that the further increase of the number of the labeled training samples does not necessarily improve the classification accuracy if the existing labeled training data is basically representative of the inherent data structure.

All in all, the results presented in this paper demonstrate that the SSL is a promising approach to MWL recognition based on the operator's physiological signals. By taking full advantage of cheap and easy-to-obtain unlabeled data, the SSL algorithm can improve the classification accuracy requiring only a relatively small number of labeled physiological data. When only a smaller number of labeled data are available in practical MWL pattern recognition application, the SSL algorithm seems more applicable and advantageous than supervised learning schemes. Therefore, how to select valuable data from a large number of unlabeled data will be the focus of our further research.

References

1. Lal, S.K., Craig, A.: A critical review of the psychophysiology of driver fatigue. Biol. Psychol. 55(3), 173–194 (2001)
2. Bobko, N., Karpenko, A., Gerasimov, A., Chernyuk, V.: The mental performance of shiftworkers in nuclear and heat power plants of Ukraine. Int. J. Ind. Ergon. 21(3–4), 333–340 (1998)
3. Hollender, N., Hofmann, C., Deneke, M., Schmitz, B.: Integrating cognitive load theory and concepts of human–computer interaction. Comput. Hum. Behav. 26(6), 1278–1288 (2010)
4. Cain, B.: A review of the mental workload literature. Defence Research and Development Toronto (Canada) (2007)
5. Mahfouf, M., Zhang, J., Linkens, D.A., Nassef, A., Nickel, P., Hockey, G.R.J., Roberts, A.C.: Adaptive fuzzy approaches to modelling operator functional states in a human-machine process control system. In: Fuzzy Systems Conference, FUZZ-IEEE 2007, pp. 1–6. IEEE International, July 2007
6. Huang, G.B., Zhu, Q.Y., Siew, C.K.: Extreme learning machine: theory and applications. Neurocomputing 70(1), 489–501 (2006)

7. Huang, G.B., Zhou, H., Ding, X., Zhang, R.: Extreme learning machine for regression and multiclass classification. IEEE Trans. Syst. Man Cybern. Part B (Cybern.) **42**(2), 513–529 (2012)
8. Liu, T., Yang, Y., Huang, G.B., Yeo, Y.K., Lin, Z.: Driver distraction detection using semi-supervised machine learning. IEEE Trans. Intell. Transp. Syst. **17**(4), 1108–1120 (2016)
9. Wang, Y., Zhang, J., Wang, R.: Mental workload recognition by combining wavelet packet transform and kernel spectral regression techniques. IFAC-PapersOnLine **49**(19), 561–566 (2016)
10. Okamoto, M., Dan, H., Sakamoto, K., Takeo, K., Shimizu, K., Kohno, S., Oda, I., Isobe, S., Suzuki, T., Kohyama, K., Dan, I.: Three-dimensional probabilistic anatomical cranio-cerebral correlation via the international 10–20 system oriented for transcranial functional brain mapping. Neuroimage **21**(1), 99–111 (2004)
11. Zhang, J., Yin, Z., Wang, R.: Recognition of mental workload levels under complex human–machine collaboration by using physiological features and adaptive support vector machines. IEEE Trans. Hum.-Mach. Syst. **45**(2), 200–214 (2015)
12. Sharma, P., Ray, K.C.: Efficient methodology for electrocardiogram beat classification. IET Sig. Process. **10**(7), 825–832 (2016)
13. Wang, R., Wang, Y., Luo, C.: EEG-based real-time drowsiness detection using Hilbert-Huang transform. In: 7th International Conference on Intelligent Human-Machine Systems and Cybernetics (IHMSC), vol. 1, pp. 195–198. IEEE, August 2015
14. Huang, G., Song, S., Gupta, J.N.D., et al.: Semi-supervised and unsupervised extreme learning machines. IEEE Trans. Cybern. **44**(12), 2405–2417 (2012)

View-Weighted Multi-view K-means Clustering

Hong Yu$^{(\boxtimes)}$, Yahong Lian, Shu Li, and JiaXin Chen

School of Software, Dalian University of Technology, Dalian, China
hongyu@dlut.edu.cn, lianyahong1@163.com, ann_ssdut@163.com,
jiaxin_chen@163.com

Abstract. In many clustering problems, there are dozens of data which are represented by multiple views. Different views describe different aspects of the same set of instances and provide complementary information. Considering blindly combining the information from different views will degrade the multi-view clustering result, this paper proposes a novel view-weighted multi-view k-means method. Meanwhile, to reduce the adverse effect of outliers, $l_{2,1}$ norm is employed to calculate the distance between data points and cluster centroids. An alternative iterative update schema is developed to find the optimal value. Comparative experiments on real world datasets reveal that the proposed method has better performance.

Keywords: Multi-view clustering · $l_{2,1}$ norm · Weighting · k-means

1 Introduction

In our daily life, more and more instances have representations in the form of multiple views [3,13]. Typical examples include web pages, which can be represented by two main attribute sets. One is page contents, another is anchor texts of inbound hyperlink. The appearance of such data has induced the clustering of technique called multi-view clustering [1].

The traditional clustering methods note as single view clustering just utilize one of the feature sets to learn. The goal of multi-view clustering is to take advantage of information from all views so that it can obtain more stable and accurate clustering result than single-view clustering. Recent years, the research on multi-view clustering has attracted a lot of attention [10–12].

Kumar and Daumé [9] presented a co-training based multi-view spectral clustering method. It uses the spectral embedding from one view to constrain the similarity graph used for the other view. Xia et al. [15] proposed a robust Markov chain based multi-view spectral clustering method which has low-rank and sparse constraint. In the study [4], authors delivered a multi-view normalized cut approach which fuses the spectral clustering with local search procedure. The common problem of the above mentioned methods is that they lose sight of discriminating views from one another. As a result, some views that contain noise may degrade the clustering result.

© Springer International Publishing AG 2017
A. Lintas et al. (Eds.): ICANN 2017, Part II, LNCS 10614, pp. 305–312, 2017.
https://doi.org/10.1007/978-3-319-68612-7_35

To discriminate the importance of different views in multi-view data, it is necessary to assign an appropriate weight for each view. Multi-view kernel k-means (MVKKM) algorithm [14] assigns a weight for each view according to the view's contribution to the clustering result and then combines the kernels derived from the weighted views together. Weighted multi-view convex mixture model [7] allocates weights to each view. Then, a similarity matrix is built using these weights, as a weighted sum of the individual view kernels. In comparison with most of the other multi-view clustering methods, the view weighting approach performs competitive clustering result, strong robustness and good scalability [8,16].

As a popular clustering algorithm k-means has been extensively studied on account of its computational easiness and satisfactory result. When formulating classical k-means as matrix problem, it becomes Frobenius norm of matrix, and this brings about k-means a higher sensitivity to data outliers. To tackle the problem, $l_{2,1}$ norm is used. In detail, l_2 norm is imposed on all features and l_1 norm is imposed among data points. By this way, the side effect of data outliers can be reduced and a more robust result can be expected [2,6].

Inspired by the above analysis, we propose a view-weighted multi-view k-means clustering method which combines $l_{2,1}$ norm and weighting scheme.

It is worthwhile to highlight the main contribution of our work:

1. We propose a novel view-weighting schema which can discriminate views from one to another according to the views' contribution to clustering process.
2. To recap the effectiveness of our weighting schema, we present a view-weighted multi-view k-means clustering algorithm. It can get more efficient clustering result.
3. Besides, in order to optimize objective function, an efficient iterative update method is developed.

2   View-Weighted Multi-view K-means Clustering

The proposed view-weighted k-means clustering algorithm is elaborated in this section.

According to [5], k-means for single-view data can be formulated as:

$$min||X^T - ZC^T||_F^2 \quad s.t. Z_{ik} \in \{0,1\}, \sum_{k=1}^{K} Z_{ik} = 1, \forall i = 1, 2, \ldots, n \quad (1)$$

where $X \in R^{d \times n}$ is the input data matrix with n instances and d-dimensional attributes, $C \in R^{d \times K}$ is the cluster centroids matrix, and $Z \in R^{n \times K}$ is the cluster assignment matrix.

Extending to multi-view scene, objective function can be overwritten as:

$$min||X^{(v)^T} - ZC^{(v)^T}||_F^2 \quad s.t. Z_{ik} \in \{0,1\}, \sum_{k=1}^{K} Z_{ik} = 1, \forall i = 1, 2, \ldots, n \quad (2)$$

where $X^{(v)} \in R^{d_v \times n}$ is the input matrix with n instances and d-dimensional attributes in view v, $C^{(v)} \in R^{d_v \times K}$ is the cluster centroid matrix in view v, and $Z \in R^{n \times K}$ is defined like Eq. (1).

Due to F-norm in the objective function, k-means is sensible to data outliers. To tackle this problem, we use the $l_{2,1}$ norm to measure the reconstruction error, combine with entropy-based weighting scheme which can avoid overfitting and we can get the following optimization formula:

$$\min_{C^{(v)}, Z, w^{(v)}} \sum_{v=1}^{V} w^{(v)} ||X^{(v)^T} - ZC^{(v)^T}||_{2,1} + \lambda \sum_{v=1}^{V} w^{(v)} \ln(w^{(v)})$$

$$s.t. Z_{ik} \in \{0,1\}, \sum_{k=1}^{K} Z_{ik} = 1, \sum_{v=1}^{V} w^{(v)} = 1 \tag{3}$$

where $w^{(v)}$ is the view weight variable which is limited in range 0 to 1. The parameter $\lambda \geq 0$ is used to control the view distribution.

3 Optimization Algorithm

Solving optimal objective (3) is not so easy, the hard problem has two folds. One is each row vector of cluster indicator matrix Z must satisfy the 1-of-K coding scheme. Another is $l_{2,1}$ norm is non-smooth. So it cannot be directly optimized. Therefore, we propose the iterative algorithm to deal with them efficiently.

3.1 Algorithm Derivation

For convenience, we rewrite the optimization problem:

$$\min_{C^{(v)}, D^{(v)}, Z, w^{(v)}} \sum_{v=1}^{V} w^{(v)} A^{(v)} + \lambda \sum_{v=1}^{V} w^{(v)} \ln(w^{(v)}) \tag{4}$$

where

$$A^{(v)} = Tr\{(X^{(v)} - C^{(v)} Z^T) D^{(v)} (X^{(v)} - C^{(v)} Z^T)^T\} \tag{5}$$

$D^{(v)} \in R^{n \times n}$ is the diagonal matrix which represents the v-th view. The i-th element of the diagonal matrix is defined as:

$$D_{ii}^{(v)} = \frac{1}{2||e^{(v)i}||}, \forall i = 1, 2, \dots n, \tag{6}$$

where $e^{(v)i}$ is the i-th row of the following matrix:

$$E^{(v)} = X^{(v)^T} - ZC^{(v)^T}. \tag{7}$$

To solve this problem, we developed the following iterative stages.

Updating the Cluster Centroid for Each View $C^{(v)}$. Taking derivative of Eq. (5) with respect to $C^{(v)}$, we get:

$$-2X^{(v)}\widetilde{D}^{(v)}Z + 2C^{(c)}Z^T\widetilde{D}^{(v)}Z \tag{8}$$

where $\widetilde{D}^{(v)} = w^{(v)}D^{(v)}$. Let the derivative equal zero, we can compute $C^{(v)}$:

$$C^{(v)} = X^{(v)}\widetilde{D}^{(v)}Z(Z^T\widetilde{D}^{(v)}Z)^{-1}. \tag{9}$$

Updating the Cluster Indicator Matrix Z. It can be concluded that

$$\sum_{v=1}^{V} Tr\{(X^{(v)} - C^{(v)}Z^T)\widetilde{D}^{(v)}(X^{(v)} - C^{(v)}Z^T)^T\}$$
$$= \sum_{i=1}^{N}(\sum_{v=1}^{V}\widetilde{D}_{ii}^{(v)}||\mathbf{x}_i^{(v)} - C^{(v)}\mathbf{z}_i||_2^2) \tag{10}$$

For the specific fixed i, with respect to vector $\mathbf{z}=[z_1, z_2, \ldots z_K]^T \in R^{K \times 1}$, Eq. (4) equals to

$$\min_{\mathbf{z}} \sum_{v=1}^{V} \widetilde{d}^{(v)}||\mathbf{x}^{(v)} - C^{(v)}\mathbf{z}||_2^2 \quad s.t. z_k \in \{0,1\}, \sum_{k=1}^{K} z_k = 1 \tag{11}$$

where $\widetilde{d}^{(v)} = \widetilde{D}_{ii}^{(v)}$ is the i-th element of the diagonal of the matrix $\widetilde{D}^{(v)}$. Equation (11) has K candidate solutions because $\mathbf{z}$ should satisfy 1-of-K coding scheme. And each candidate is exactly the *k-th* column of matrix $I_K = [e_1, e_2, \ldots e_K]$. So, we can choose k that satisfy:

$$k = \underset{j}{argmin} \sum_{v=1}^{V} \widetilde{d}^{(v)}||\mathbf{x}^{(v)} - C^{(v)}e_j||_2^2, \tag{12}$$

And then

$$\mathbf{z}^* = \mathbf{e}_k. \tag{13}$$

Updating View Weight $w^{(v)}$. As Eq. (4) equals to

$$\min_{w^{(v)}} \sum_{v=1}^{V} w^{(v)}A^{(v)} + \lambda \sum_{v=1}^{V} w^{(v)}\ln(w^{(v)}) \quad s.t. \sum_{v=1}^{V} w^{(v)} = 1, w^{(v)} \geq 0. \tag{14}$$

where $A^{(v)}$ is also defined as in Eq. (5). To find the optimal $w^{(v)}$, we bring in Lagrange multiplier $\beta \geq 0$, and take the constraint into account, we have:

$$L = \sum_{v=1}^{V} w^{(v)}A^{(v)} + \lambda \sum_{v=1}^{V} w^{(v)}\ln(w^{(v)}) + \beta(\sum_{v=1}^{V} w^{(v)} - 1). \tag{15}$$

Taking derivative with respect to $w^{(v)}$, and setting it to zero, we can get:

$$w^{(v)} = e^{\frac{-\beta - A^{(v)} - \lambda}{\lambda}} \tag{16}$$

Considering the constraint $\sum_{v'=1}^{V} w^{(v')} = 1$, we get:

$$w^{(v)} = \frac{e^{\frac{-A^{(v)}}{\lambda}}}{\sum_{v'=1}^{V} e^{\frac{-A^{(v')}}{\lambda}}} \tag{17}$$

Obviously, the less the intra-cluster differences $A^{(v)}$ of view v, the larger its weight is. And the larger λ induces the flatter view distribution. If $\lambda = 0$ it turns to the single best view situation. The complete algorithm is described as Algorithm 1.

Algorithm 1. The algorithm of view-weighted multi-view k-means

---

Input:
 1: Data for V views $X^{(1)}, ... X^{(V)}$ and $X^{(v)} \in R^{n \times d_v}$.
 2: cluster number K.
 3: Predefined parameter λ.
Output:
 4: The common cluster indicator matrix Z.
 5: The learned view weighted $w^{(v)}$.
Initialization:
 6: Set iter=0
 7: Randomly generate the common cluster indicator matrix $Z \in R^{n \times K}$, such that Z satisfy 1-of-K coding scheme.
 8: Initialize the diagonal matrix $D^{(v)}$ as $n \times n$ identity matrix, that is $D^{(v)} = I_n$.
 9: Initialize the view weight variable $w^{(v)} = \frac{1}{V}$ for each view.
10: **repeat**
11:     Calculate the diagonal matrix $\widetilde{D}^{(v)}$ according to $\widetilde{D}^{(v)} = w^{(v)} D^{(v)}$
12:     Update the centroid matrix $C^{(v)}$ for each view according Eq. (9)
13:     Update the cluster indicator vector z for each data one by one according to Eq. (12) and Eq. (13)
14:     Update the diagonal matrix $D^{(v)}$ for each view according to Eq. (6) and Eq. (7).
15:     Update the view weight variable $w^{(v)}$ for each view according to Eq. (17)
16:     Update iter=iter+1
17: **until** convergence.

3.2   Time Complexity Analysis

For k-means clustering, the estimated time complexity is $Q(IKnd)$, where I represents the number of iteration, K is the cluster number, n is the number of instances and d is the dimension number. Similar to k-means, the time complexity of our method is $Q(IKVnd)$, where V is the view number and others are the same as those of traditional multi-view k-means.

4   Experiment and Evaluation

4.1   Experimental Settings

Five real world datasets are used to evaluate the performance of our algorithm. Brief description is given in Table 1.

Table 1. The properties of real world datasets

Dataset	Size	View num	Cluster num
Digit	2000	5	10
SensIT	300	2	3
3-Sources	169	3	6
Animal	1800	4	9
NUS	900	4	6

Our method is compared with a number of baseline algorithms. In particular, we compare with:

Single-Best is single view clustering algorithm which chooses the best view;
SMKM is simple multi-view k-means that based on Frobenius norm.
RSMKM is robust simple multi-view k-means by imposing the $l_{2,1}$-norm.
WSMKM is based on view weight technique and utilizing F-norm.
MVKKM [14] is a weighted combination of kernel which is learned to conduct clustering.
Co-trainSC [9] learns the clustering in one view and uses it to label the data in other view so as to modify the graph structure (similarity matrix).

For every algorithm, 50 tests run with different random initializations were conducted and the average performances are given. To the experiment, λ chooses from $\{1, 2, 4, 8, 12, 16, 24, 32\}$.

4.2   Experimental Results

Tables 2 and 3 report the clustering quality of the compared algorithms by F1 score and normalized mutual information (NMI). From the tables, we can summarize the following:

(1) Compared with single-best, most of the multi-view clustering methods gain better performance which means that utilizing the complementary information of instances is meritorious.
(2) In most cases, the performance of RSMKM is better than SMKM, which shows that imposing $l_{2,1}$ norm to calculate k-means's reconstruction error is more robust and accurate than using F-norm.
(3) Our method (VWMKM) can boost the clustering results in most of the datasets, which is brought about mainly by the proposed weighting schema and $l_{2,1}$ norm.

Table 2. Clustering results evaluated by **F1** score

F1	Handwritten	sensIT	3-Sources	Animal	NUS
Single-Best	0.6720	0.5387	0.4413	0.1601	0.2239
SMKM	0.6823	0.5404	0.4437	0.1621	0.2542
RSMKM	0.7211	0.5515	0.4693	0.1630	0.2593
WSMKM	0.6901	0.5430	0.4527	0.1628	0.2586
MVKKM	0.6766	0.5765	0.5133	0.1613	0.2311
Co-trainSC	0.7150	0.5659	0.5092	0.1607	0.2342
VWMKM	0.7617	0.5888	0.5236	0.1641	0.2632

Table 3. Clustering results evaluated by **NMI**

NMI	Handwritten	sensIT	3-Sources	Animal	NUS
Single-Best	0.6823	0.3134	0.3663	0.0793	0.0801
SMKM	0.7169	0.3301	0.4095	0.0842	0.0888
RSMKM	0.7350	0.3323	0.4426	0.0860	0.0844
WSMKM	0.7652	0.3321	0.4098	0.0852	0.0813
MVKKM	0.6963	0.3385	0.4769	0.0862	0.0949
Co-trainSC	0.7630	0.3207	0.4754	0.0876	0.0833
VWMKM	0.7914	0.3623	0.4870	0.0886	0.1152

5   Conclusion

In this paper, we proposed a novel view-weighted multi-view k-means clustering algorithm. It can automatically learn the weight of different views. Moreover, by utilizing the structured sparsity $l_{2,1}$ norm on the objective function, our method is more stable and robust to the data outliers. An iterative update algorithm is introduced in detail. Experimental results on five data sets show the proposed methods have the comparable or even better accuracy than the state-of-the-art methods. It is possible to apply the view weighting schema to other multi-view clustering algorithms.

Acknowledgment. Research reported in this publication was supported by the National Natural Science Foundation of China (61602081) and Natural Science Foundation of Liaoning Province (201602180).

References

1. Bickel, S., Scheffer, T.: Multi-view clustering. In: ICDM, pp. 19–26 (2004)
2. Cai, X., Nie, F., Huang, H.: Multi-view k-means clustering on big data. In: IJCAI, pp. 2598–2604 (2013)

3. Chaudhuri, K., Kakade, S.M., Livescu, K., Sridharan, K.: Multi-view clustering via canonical correlation analysis. In: ICML, pp. 129–136 (2009)

4. Chikhi, N.F.: Multi-view clustering via spectral partitioning and local refinement. Inf. Process. Manag. **52**(4), 618–627 (2016)

5. Ding, C., He, X., Simon, H.D.: Nonnegative Lagrangian relaxation of K-means and spectral clustering. In: Gama, J., Camacho, R., Brazdil, P.B., Jorge, A.M., Torgo, L. (eds.) ECML 2005. LNCS (LNAI), vol. 3720, pp. 530–538. Springer, Heidelberg (2005). doi:10.1007/11564096_51

6. Du, L., Zhou, P., Shi, L., Wang, H., Fan, M.: Robust multiple kernel k-means using l21-norm. In: IJCAI (2015)

7. Ioannidis, A., Chasanis, V., Likas, A.: Key-frame extraction using weighted multi-view convex mixture models and spectral clustering. In: ICPR, pp. 3463–3468 (2014)

8. Jiang, B., Qiu, F., Wang, L.: Multi-view clustering via simultaneous weighting on views and features. Appl. Soft Comput. **47**, 304–315 (2016)

9. Kumar, A., Daumé, H.: A co-training approach for multi-view spectral clustering. In: ICML, pp. 393–400 (2011)

10. Kumar, A., Rai, P., Daumé, H.: Co-regularized multi-view spectral clustering. In: Advances in Neural Information Processing Systems, pp. 1413–1421 (2011)

11. Son, J.W., Jeon, J., Lee, A., Kim, S.J.: Spectral clustering with brainstorming process for multi-view data. In: AAAI (2017)

12. Sun, J., Lu, J., Xu, T., Bi, J.: Multi-view sparse co-clustering via proximal alternating linearized minimization. In: ICML, pp. 757–766 (2015)

13. Sun, S.: A survey of multi-view machine learning. Neural Comput. Appl. **23**(7–8), 2031–2038 (2013)

14. Tzortzis, G., Likas, A.: Kernel-based weighted multi-view clustering. In: ICDM, pp. 675–684 (2012)

15. Xia, R., Pan, Y., Du, L., Yin, J.: Robust multi-view spectral clustering via low-rank and sparse decomposition. In: AAAI, pp. 2149–2155 (2014)

16. Xu, Y.M., Wang, C.D., Lai, J.H.: Weighted multi-view clustering with feature selection. Pattern Recogn. **53**, 25–35 (2016)

Indefinite Support Vector Regression

Frank-Michael Schleif[1,2]([✉])

[1] University of Applied Sciences Wuerzburg-Schweinfurt, 97074 Wuerzburg, Germany
`frank-michael.schleif@fhws.de`
[2] School of Computer Science Edgbaston, University of Birmingham,
Birmingham B15 2TT, UK

Abstract. Non-metric proximity measures got wide interest in various domains such as life sciences, robotics and image processing. The majority of learning algorithms for these data are focusing on classification problems. Here we derive a regression algorithm for indefinite data representations based on the support vector machine. The approach avoids heuristic eigen spectrum modifications or costly proxy matrix approximations, as used in general. We evaluate the method on a number of benchmark data using an indefinite measure.

1 Introduction

The relationship between data and response values is always interesting as it can be used to explain the structure or mechanism of a complicated system or to construct a predictive model. This analysis is typically done via a regression analysis, where least squares regression (LSR) is the most popular one.

With kernelization of LSR, a major restriction of regression, where data points and estimated values have to be in linear relation, are relaxed by selecting a more expressive feature transforms or kernel functions. Due to the flexibility and simplicity of the regression model, it is widely applied in various domains such as image processing, bioinformatics and other [1]. A recent review about regression methods and applications is given in [2].

In traditional practice, the construction of kernel is based on applying a valid kernel function over feature vectors. Valid refers to kernel functions satisfying the Mercer's conditions [3]. Under this context, the resulting kernels are always positive semidefinite (psd) and work fine in most kernelized learning methods.

Nowadays non-metric proximity measures receive substantial interest with the advent of domain specific similarity measures, non-standard- and (semi-) structured data, leading to indefinite (non-psd) kernels [4–7]. A recent review is given in [1]. The use of divergence measures [8] is very popular for spectral data analysis in chemistry, geo- and medical sciences [9], and are in general not metric. Also the popular Dynamic Time Warping (DTW) [10] algorithm provides a non-metric alignment score which is often used as a proximity measure between two one-dimensional functions of different length. In image processing and shape retrieval indefinite proximities are often obtained by means of the inner distance [5] - another non-metric measure.

© Springer International Publishing AG 2017
A. Lintas et al. (Eds.): ICANN 2017, Part II, LNCS 10614, pp. 313–321, 2017.
https://doi.org/10.1007/978-3-319-68612-7_36

Indefinite kernels are a severe problem for most kernel based learning algorithms because classical mathematical assumptions such as positive definiteness, used in the underlying optimization frameworks are violated. As a consequence e.g. the classical support vector machine (SVM) [11] has no longer a convex solution - in fact, most standard solvers will not even converge for this problem [12].

As shown in different works in psychology, image analysis [13, 14] and machine learning [15] a restriction to Mercer kernels and metric similarity measures is often inappropriate.

In [15] it is shown that many real life problems are better addressed by e.g. kernel functions which are not restricted to be based on a metric.

Many studies on indefinite kernel methods focus on classification techniques such as support vector machine (SVM) and only few are considering regression models. As indicated in [1] there are two major approaches to address the indefiniteness in a kernel, both leading to a direct or indirect alternative representation of the data by means of a psd kernel. One strategy is focusing on modifications of the eigenspectrum (clipping, flipping, shifting, squaring) (see [1]), another is generating a psd proxy kernel which should be similar to the original indefinite kernel. Both strategies are easy to implement but costly. Further the out of sample extension to new samples is either very costly due to recalculations of the model or inaccurate. Some work on indefinite regression following these concepts was discussed in [1].

A novel alternative concept was proposed in [12], by means of a stabilization approach[1] calculating a valid SVM model in the Kreĭn space which can be directly applied on indefinite kernel matrices. This approach shows great promise but was presented for classification problems only and is extended to regression in the following.

In Sect. 2 we briefly review the novel indefinite SVM approach proposed in [12], with some basic notation. We present the indefinite Support Vector Regression (iSVM) in Subsect. 2.2 and summarize the results of our empirical studies in Sect. 4.

2   Background and Basic Notation

Consider a collection of N objects $\mathbf{x}_i$, $i = \{1, 2, \ldots, N\}$, in some input space $\mathcal{X}$. Given a similarity function or inner product on $\mathcal{X}$, corresponding to a metric, one can construct a proper Mercer kernel acting on pairs of points from $\mathcal{X}$. For example, if $\mathcal{X}$ is a finite dimensional vector space, a classical similarity function is the Euclidean inner product (corresponding to the Euclidean distance) - a core component of various kernel functions such as the famous radial basis function (RBF) kernel. Now, let $\phi : \mathcal{X} \mapsto \mathcal{H}$ be a mapping of patterns from $\mathcal{X}$ to a Hilbert space $\mathcal{H}$ equipped with the inner product $\langle \cdot, \cdot \rangle_{\mathcal{H}}$. The transformation ϕ is in general a non-linear mapping to a high-dimensional space $\mathcal{H}$ and may in

---

[1] A mathematical construct detailed in [16].

general not be given in an explicit form. Instead, a kernel function $k : \mathcal{X} \times \mathcal{X} \mapsto \mathbb{R}$ is given which encodes the inner product in $\mathcal{H}$. The kernel k is a positive (semi) definite function such that $k(\mathbf{x}, \mathbf{x}') = \langle \phi(\mathbf{x}), \phi(\mathbf{x}') \rangle_{\mathcal{H}}$, for any $\mathbf{x}, \mathbf{x}' \in \mathcal{X}$. The matrix $K_{i,j} := k(\mathbf{x}_i, \mathbf{x}_j)$ is an $N \times N$ kernel (Gram) matrix derived from the training data. The motivation for such an embedding comes with the hope that the non-linear transformation of input data into higher dimensional $\mathcal{H}$ allows for using linear techniques in $\mathcal{H}$. Kernelized methods process the embedded data points in a feature space utilizing only the inner products $\langle \cdot, \cdot \rangle_{\mathcal{H}}$ (kernel trick) [3], without the need to explicitly calculate ϕ. The kernel function can be very generic. Most prominent are the linear kernel with $k(\mathbf{x}, \mathbf{x}') = \langle \phi(\mathbf{x}), \phi(\mathbf{x}') \rangle$ where $\langle \phi(\mathbf{x}), \phi(\mathbf{x}') \rangle$ is the Euclidean inner product and ϕ identity mapping, or the RBF kernel $k(\mathbf{x}, \mathbf{x}') = \exp\left(-\frac{||\mathbf{x} - \mathbf{x}'||^2}{2\sigma^2}\right)$, with $\sigma > 0$ as a free scale parameter. In any case, it is always assumed that the kernel function $k(\mathbf{x}, \mathbf{x}')$ is positive semi definite (psd). This assumption is however not always fulfilled, and the underlying similarity measure may not be metric and hence not lead to a Mercer kernel. Examples can be easily found in domain specific similarity measures as mentioned before and detailed later on. Such similarity measures imply *indefinite* kernels, preventing standard "kernel-trick" methods developed for Mercer kernels to be applied.

2.1 Support Vector Regression

Suppose we are now given training data with a continuous output label $\{(\mathbf{x}_1, y_1), \ldots, (\mathbf{x}_N, y_N)\} \subset \mathcal{X} \times \mathcal{R}$. The values in y could be some outcome variable such as the level of protein in a biological measure, the expected costs for buying a product or other econometric indicators. We define $Y = [y_1, \ldots, y_N]^\top$ as the values of the output function.

In ϵ-SV regression [17], our goal is to find a function $f(x)$ that has at most ϵ deviation from the actually obtained targets y_i for all the training data, and at the same time is as flat as possible. In its simplest from $f(x)$ may be given as $f(x) = <\mathbf{w}, \mathbf{x}>$ where $\mathbf{w} \in \mathcal{X}$. We skip the explicit use of the bias term $b \in \mathcal{R}$ in f. The aim is to fit the data to the output function such that $f(x_i) - \hat{f}(x_i) \leq \pm\epsilon$, where $\hat{f}(x_i)$ is the prediction for a given x_i and ϵ is a user defined parameter controlling the permitted error of the prediction. Using the so called epsilon-loss this can be formalized as:

$$\min \frac{1}{2}||\mathbf{w}||^2 \qquad s.t. \begin{cases} y_i - <\mathbf{w}, \mathbf{x_i}> - b \leq \epsilon \\ <\mathbf{w}, \mathbf{x_i}> + b - y_i \leq \epsilon \end{cases} \tag{1}$$

As shown e.g. in [17] the parameter vector $\mathbf{w}$ can be completely described as a linear combination of the training patterns $\mathbf{x}_i$. In Eq. 1 the data and parameters occur only by means of inner products which permits the use of the kernel trick. Accordingly the problem can be formulated using the kernel function k only (for detailed deviations see e.g. [17]). The kernelized SVR problem can be solved using a quadratic problem solver, providing a unique solution given the kernel function k is psd. Before we derive the indefinite Support Vector Regression we review the main concepts for the Krĕin Space SVM, which provides the relevant concepts.

2.2 Indefinite Support Vector Classification

Lets assume (for this section) that the training points in the input space X are labeled with labels $y_i \in \{-1, 1\}$, representing the class of the respective point $\mathbf{x}_i$. For a given positive C, SVM is the minimum of the following regularized empirical risk functional, employing the hinge loss:

$$J_C(f,b) = \min_{f \in \mathcal{H}, b \in \mathbb{R}} \frac{1}{2}\|f\|_{\mathcal{H}}^2 + CH(f,b) \quad H(f,b) = \sum_{i=1}^{N} \max(0, 1 - y_i(f(\mathbf{x}_i) + b)) \quad (2)$$

Using the solution of Eq. (2) as $(f_C^*, b_C^*) := \arg\min J_C(f,b)$ one can introduce $\tau = H(f_C^*, b_C^*)$ and the respective convex quadratic program (QP)

$$\min_{f \in \mathcal{H}, b \in \mathbb{R}} \frac{1}{2}\|f\|_{\mathcal{H}}^2 \quad s.t. \sum_{i=1}^{N} \max(0, 1 - y_i(f(\mathbf{x}_i) + b)) \leq \tau \quad (3)$$

As outlined in [12], this QP can be also seen as the problem of retrieving the orthogonal projection of the null function in a Hilbert space $\mathcal{H}$ onto the convex feasible set. The view as a projection will help to link the original SVM formulation in the Hilbert space to a KSVM formulation in the Krein space, or the respective SVM regression problem. First we need to repeat a few definitions, widely following [12]: A Krĕin space is an *indefinite* inner product space endowed with a Hilbertian topology.

Definition 1 (Inner products and inner product space). Let $\mathcal{K}$ be a real vector space. An inner product space with an indefinite inner product $\langle \cdot, \cdot \rangle_{\mathcal{K}}$ on $\mathcal{K}$ is a bi-linear form where all $f, g, h \in \mathcal{K}$ and $\alpha \in \mathbb{R}$ obey the conditions: Symmetry: $\langle f, g \rangle_{\mathcal{K}} = \langle g, f \rangle_{\mathcal{K}}$, linearity: $\langle \alpha f + g, h \rangle_{\mathcal{K}} = \alpha \langle f, h \rangle_{\mathcal{K}} + \langle g, h \rangle_{\mathcal{K}}$, $\langle f, g \rangle_{\mathcal{K}} = 0 \quad \forall g \in \mathcal{K}$ implies $f = 0$.

An inner product is positive definite if $\forall f \in \mathcal{K}$, $\langle f, f \rangle_{\mathcal{K}} \geq 0$, negative definite if $\forall f \in \mathcal{K}$, $\langle f, f \rangle_{\mathcal{K}} \leq 0$, otherwise it is indefinite. A vector space $\mathcal{K}$ with inner product $\langle \cdot, \cdot \rangle_{\mathcal{K}}$ is called inner product space.

Definition 2 (Krĕin space). An inner product space $(\mathcal{K}, \langle \cdot, \cdot \rangle_{\mathcal{K}})$ is a Krĕin space if we have two Hilbert spaces $\mathcal{H}_+$, $\mathcal{H}_-$ and spanning $\mathcal{K}$ such that $\forall f \in \mathcal{K}$ we have $f = f_+ + f_-$ with $f_+ \in \mathcal{H}_+$, $f_- \in \mathcal{H}_-$ and $\forall f, g \in \mathcal{K}$, $\langle f, g \rangle_{\mathcal{K}} = \langle f_+, g_+ \rangle_{\mathcal{H}_+} - \langle f_-, g_- \rangle_{\mathcal{H}_-}$.

If $\mathcal{H}_+$ and $\mathcal{H}_-$ are reproducing kernel hilbert spaces (RKHS), $\mathcal{K}$ is a reproducing kernel Krĕin space (RKKS). For details on RKHS and RKKS see e.g. [18]. In [16] the reproducing property is shown for a RKKS $\mathcal{K}$.

As shown in [16] for any symmetric non-positive kernel k that can be decomposed as the difference of two positive kernels k_+ and k_-, a RKKS can be associated to it. In [12] it was shown how the classical SVM problem can be reformulated by means of a stabilization problem. This is necessary because a classical norm as used in Eq. (3) does not exist in the RKKS, but instead an alternative projection based SVM was derived, providing an **equivalent** solution to the SVM in the RKHS. Instead of the norm the projection operator is used as a regularization technique [12]. The detailed mathematical formalism behind this concept is provided in [12,16]. As detailed in [12] one finally gets a stabilization problem, allowing to calculate a SVM in a Krĕin space.

$$\text{stab}_{f\in\mathcal{K},b\in\mathbb{R}}\frac{1}{2}\langle f,f\rangle_{\mathcal{K}} \quad \text{s.t.} \sum_{i=1}^{l}\max(0,1-y_i(f(\mathbf{x}_i)+b))\leq\tau \tag{4}$$

where stab means stabilize and refers to finding a stationary point. Note that the norm is replaced by a projection operator in the Krĕin space. In [12] it is further shown that the stabilization problem Eq. (4) can be written as a minimization problem using a semi-definite kernel matrix. By defining projection matrices it is also shown how the dual RKKS problem for the SVM can be related to the dual in the RKHS. Especially the later one permits a reasonable simple algorithmic implementation. This permits to used standard solvers for this classification problems.

3   Indefinite Support Vector Regression

Comparing the derivation in Subsect. 2.2 with the formulation of the Support Vector Regression in Eq. (1), we see that only the conditions on SVR have changed with respect to SVM. As addressed in [12] the crucial part with the Krĕin space SVM is the minimization of a norm, which is not available in the Krĕin space. The SVR contains a norm operator in the objective but not in the constraints. Accordingly, we can use the same derivation as for the Krĕin space SVM and obtain the following optimization problem for iSVR (SVR in Krĕin space)[2]

$$\text{stab}_{f\in\mathcal{K},b\in\mathbb{R}}\frac{1}{2}\langle f,f\rangle_{\mathcal{K}} \qquad \text{s.t.} \begin{cases} y_i - f(\mathbf{x}_i) - b \leq \epsilon \\ f(\mathbf{x}_i) + b - y_i \leq \epsilon \end{cases} \tag{5}$$

Similar as for the Krĕin space SVM (see [12], Sect. 3.3) the algorithm for the iSVR consists of the following five steps:

1. An eigen-decomposition of the full kernel matrix is calculated.
2. A flipping operation is applied on the kernel matrix and the signs of the eigenvalues are stored. The flipping operator is a consequence of the derivation of the Krein SVM which transfers to the iSVR.

---

[2] Details are skipped due to lack of space, but follow analogous to the derivation of the Krein SVM. Instead we provide an adapted pseudo code with descriptions.

3. The solution of an SV regression solver is calculated on the flipped kernel with parameter C and ϵ.
4. The application of the projection operator obtained from the eigen-decomposition on the α vector of the SVR model. This is needed to permit the usage of the **unmodified** input kernel to the optimized SVR model (linking the Krĕin space solution with the Hilbert space solution).
5. The bias b has to be recalculated as the average of the modified α-vector weighted by the labels Y This is necessary because b is not included in f and the calculation of the projection matrices.

A pseudo code roughly related to a Matlab notation is shown in Algorithm 1.

Algorithm 1. Indefinite SVR (iSVR).

SVR in the Krĕin space:

$[U, D] = \text{EigenDecomposition}(K)$ U-Eigenvectors, D-Eigenvalues (on a diagonal matrix)

$\hat{K} = USDU^{\top}$ with $S = sign(D)$

$[\alpha] = \text{KernelSVRSolver}(\hat{K}, Y, C, \epsilon)$ α's from the dual solution of SVR

$\tilde{\alpha} = USU^{\top}\alpha$ $\tilde{b} = \frac{1}{N^2}Y\tilde{\alpha}$ linking to the Krĕin space solution

return $\tilde{\alpha}, \tilde{b}$;

Prediction function:

$f(x') = \frac{1}{2} \cdot \sum_{i=1}^{m} \tilde{\alpha}_i k(x_i, x') + \tilde{b}$ $k(\cdot, \cdot)$ - **indefinite** kernel function

---

4 Experiments

We show the effectiveness of iSVR on a number of simulated and real life bench-mark regression problems and compare with solutions as obtained by using standard SVR but for flipped (all signs of the eigenspectrum become positive) and clipped eigenspectra (negative einvalues are set to 0) of the respective kernel matrices. Data are given as $X \in \mathbb{R}^D$. Target function values $y_i \in \mathbb{R}^1$. The following one-dimensional simulated datasets have been used:

- (SIM1) basic sinc sample, with 200 samples, $f(x) = sinc(x/\pi) + 0.05 \cdot \sigma$ where σ is Gaussian noise and x is linearly spread in $[-30, 30]$
- (SIM2) Friedman function, with 200 samples, $f(x) = 10 \cdot \sin(\pi \cdot \sigma_1 \cdot \sigma_2) + 20 \cdot (\sigma_3 - 0.5)^2 + 10 \cdot \sigma_4 + 5 \cdot \sigma_5 + \sigma$; and uniform noise $\sigma_1, \ldots, \sigma_5$, σ is Gaussian noise
- (SIM3) The Mackey glass data, with 12000 samples (down-sampled to 1500 points), in 1 dimension

Further we used the following real life regression datasets.

- (DS1) Carsmall, with 100 samples, $D = 2$ (horse power, weight) (part of Matlab)
- (DS2) Abalone, with 4177 samples, $D = 8$ taken from [19]

- (DS3) Forest fires, with 517 samples, $D = 13$, dimension 13 was used as output variable, taken from [20]
- (DS4) Diabetis, with 569 samples, $D = 32$, dimension 3 was used as output variable, taken from [19]
- (DS5) White wine quality, with 4898 samples, $D = 12$, dimension 12 was used as output variable, taken from [21]
- (DS6) Tecator, with 240 samples, $D = 122$, dimension 123 was used as output variable (fat content), taken from [22]

All regression functions (outputs) have been z-transformed. The indefiniteness was caused using a Manhattan kernel $K_m = -||X - X^\top||$. The regression profiles for SIM1-SIM3 and DS1, DS2 and DS6 are depicted in Fig. 1. In the experiments we apply the indefinite SVR approach on the given datasets and compare it with the standard SVR algorithm were the indefinite input kernel was corrected by applying a flip or clip eigenspectrum transformation. In Fig. 2 a plot of the output function for DS6 and its prediction using iSVR and SVR on a clipped kernel is shown. The plot shows substantial prediction errors on the clipped kernel in contrast to the prediction of iSVR with the indefinite mahalanobis kernel (Table 1).

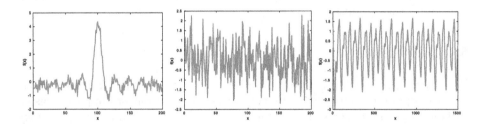

Fig. 1. Plots of the SIM1, SIM2 and SIM3 data.

Table 1. Mean square error (mean ± std-dev.) in the 10-fold crossvalidation. Best results are highlighted in bold, significant results worst↔best (t-test, $p < 0.05$) are marked with a *

Dataset	iSVR (K_m)	SVR-flip (K_m)	SVR-clip (K_m)
SIM1	**0.09 ± 0.02**	0.11 ± 0.01	0.11 ± 0.03
SIM2	**0.15 ± 0.03**	0.17 ± 0.04	0.18 ± 0.05
SIM3	≈0± ≈0	≈0± ≈0	0.01± ≈0
DS1	0.42 ± 0.25	0.42 ± 0.05	**0.40 ± 0.22**
DS2	0.49 ± 0.05	**0.49 ± 0.04**	0.70 ± 0.34*
DS3	**1.42 ± 0.26**	1.47 ± 0.23	1.85 ± 1.00*
DS4	**0.01± ≈0**	**0.01± ≈0**	0.50 ± 0.31*
DS5	0.68 ± 0.06	**0.67 ± 0.03**	0.70 ± 0.03
DS6	0.04 ± 0.02	**0.04 ± 0.01**	0.10 ± 0.01*

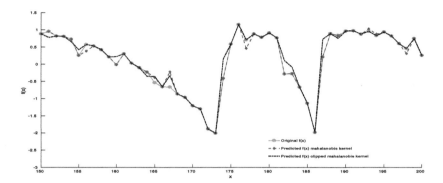

Fig. 2. Zoom in a plot of the tecator output function (green, line + circle). We also show the predicted output using SVR on a clipped mahalanobis kernel (black dashed) and a prediction of the output function using iSVR on the indefinite mahalanobis kernel (red, dashed + diamond). (Color figure online)

It should be noted that an application of the standard SVR on the indefinite kernels is not possible, which was also experimentally verified, because the obtained problem becomes non-convex and the solver is unable to provide a solution to the optimization problem.

5   Conclusions

Here we proposed a formulation for *indefinite Support Vector Regression*. The algorithm permits to use indefinite kernels and a direct out of sample extension without any modifications of the eigenspectrum or the calculation of a psd proxy kernel on the test data. As the experiments showed the iSVR performs well on a number of different datasets, accordingly also data representation employing non-metric measures can now be used easily for regression tasks[3].

References

1. Schleif, F.-M., Tiño, P.: Indefinite proximity learning: a review. Neural Comput. **27**(10), 2039–2096 (2015)
2. Stulp, F., Sigaud, O.: Many regression algorithms, one unified model: a review. Neural Netw. **69**, 60–79 (2015)
3. Shawe-Taylor, J., Cristianini, N.: Kernel Methods for Pattern Analysis and Discovery. Cambridge University Press, Cambridge (2004)
4. Neuhaus, M., Bunke, H.: Edit distance based kernel functions for structural pattern classification. Pattern Recogn. **39**(10), 1852–1863 (2006)
5. Ling, H., Jacobs, D.W.: Shape classification using the inner-distance. IEEE Trans. Pattern Anal. Mach. Intell. **29**(2), 286–299 (2007)

---

[3] Note: iSVR can be applied on non-psd as well as on psd kernels.

6. Gisbrecht, A., Schleif, F.-M.: Metric and non-metric proximity transformations at linear costs. Neurocomputing **167**, 643–657 (2015)
7. Gnecco, G.: Approximation and estimation bounds for subsets of reproducing kernel Krein spaces. Neural Process. Lett. **39**(2), 137–153 (2014)
8. Zhang, Z., Ooi, B.C., Parthasarathy, S., Tung, A.K.H.: Similarity search on Bregman divergence: towards non-metric indexing. PVLDB **2**(1), 13–24 (2009)
9. Mwebaze, E., Schneider, P., Schleif, F.-M., Aduwo, J.R., Quinn, J.A., Haase, S., Villmann, T., Biehl, M.: Divergence based classification in learning vector quantization. Neurocomputing **74**, 1429–1435 (2010)
10. Sakoe, H., Chiba, S.: Dynamic programming algorithm optimization for spoken word recognition. IEEE Trans. Acoust. Speech Sig. Process. **26**(1), 43–49 (1978)
11. Vapnik, V.N.: The Nature of Statistical Learning Theory. Statistics for Engineering and Information Science. Springer, New York (2000)
12. Loosli, G., Canu, S., Ong, C.S.: Learning SVM in Krein spaces. IEEE Trans. Pattern Anal. Mach. Intell. **PP**(99), 1 (2015)
13. Xu, W., Wilson, R.C., Hancock, E.R.: Determining the cause of negative dissimilarity eigenvalues. In: Real, P., Diaz-Pernil, D., Molina-Abril, H., Berciano, A., Kropatsch, W. (eds.) CAIP 2011. LNCS, vol. 6854, pp. 589–597. Springer, Heidelberg (2011). doi:10.1007/978-3-642-23672-3_71
14. Scheirer, W.J., Wilber, M.J., Eckmann, M., Boult, T.E.: Good recognition is nonmetric. Pattern Recogn. **47**(8), 2721–2731 (2014)
15. Duin, R.P.W., Pekalska, E.: Non-Euclidean dissimilarities: causes and informativeness. In: Proceedings of Structural, Syntactic, and Statistical Pattern Recognition, Joint IAPR International Workshop, SSPR&SPR 2010, Cesme, Izmir, Turkey, 18–20 August 2010. pp. 324–333 (2010)
16. Ong, C.S., Mary, X., Canu, S., Smola, A.J.: Learning with non-positive kernels. In: Brodley, C.E. (ed.) Proceedings of 21st International Conference on Machine Learning (ICML 2004), vol. 69. ACM (2004)
17. Smola, A.J., Schölkopf, B.: A tutorial on support vector regression. Stat. Comput. **14**(3), 199–222 (2004)
18. Pekalska, E., Duin, R.: The Dissimilarity Representation for Pattern Recognition. World Scientific, Singapore (2005)
19. Lichman, M.: UCI Machine Learning Repository (2013)
20. Cortez, P., Morais, A.: A data mining approach to predict forest fires using meteorological data. In: Neves, J., Santos, M.F., Machado, J. (eds.) Proceedings of EPIA 2007, pp. 512–523 (2007)
21. Cortez, P., Cerdeira, A., Almeida, F., Matos, T., Reis, J.: Modeling wine preferences by data mining from physicochemical properties. Decis. Support Syst. **47**(4), 547–553 (2009)
22. Thente, K.: Tecator dataset. http://lib.stat.cmu.edu/datasets/tecator. Accessed 01 Feb 2017

Instance-Adaptive Attention Mechanism for Relation Classification

Yao Lu[⊠], Chunyun Zhang, and Weiran Xu

PRIS, Beijing University of Posts and Telecommunications, Beijing, China
luyao_bupt@outlook.com

Abstract. Recently, attention mechanism has been transferred to relation classification task. Since relation classification is a sequence-to-label task, the challenge is how to generate the deciding factor to calculate attention weights. The previous solution randomly initializes a global deciding factor, which is easy to suffer from over-fitting. To solve the problem, we propose instance-adaptive attention mechanism, which generates a specially designed deciding factor for each sentence. The experimental result on SemEval-2010 Task 8 dataset shows that our method can outperform most state-of-the-art systems without external linguistic features.

Keywords: Relation classification · Instance-adaptive · Attention mechanism

1 Introduction

Relation classification plays an important role in natural language processing (NLP), and are of great significance for many other NLP researches, such as information retrieval [2], question answering system [4] and knowledge base complementation [3]. Given a specific pair of entities marked in a sentence, relation classification system tries to identify the semantic relation between these two entities correctly. For instance, the following sentence is an example of relation *Cause-Effect(e2,e1)* between nominals *burst* and *pressure*.

"The *burst* has been caused by water hammer *pressure*".

Traditional relation classification methods use handcrafted features that are artificially constructed or come from NLP tools [15]. These methods have achieved good results. However, NLP tools, which are utilized to extract higher level features, require large computational cost and may cause the problem of error propagation. What's more, designing and selection of features is time-consuming and difficult to generalize. In order to alleviate the issues, in recent years, many deep learning-based methods have been proposed. First, the original sentence is mapped into a sequence of word vectors. Then, the neural network takes the sequence as input and is trained to extract abstract features automatically. These methods avoid complex feature engineering and are currently more effective than

© Springer International Publishing AG 2017
A. Lintas et al. (Eds.): ICANN 2017, Part II, LNCS 10614, pp. 322–330, 2017.
https://doi.org/10.1007/978-3-319-68612-7_37

traditional ones. Convolutional neural networks (CNN), recurrent neural networks (RNN) and their variants are currently the most commonly used framework [7,8]. Recently, the Attention mechanism has been extensively studied and applied in the field of deep learning. Imitating people focusing on key information while reading, researchers want to align larger weights to words that are more informative for the training target. Compared with max-pooling, attention mechanism is more flexible. By weighting each word, it not only emphasizes key information but also avoids the information loss caused by rigid max-pooling rule. Attention mechanism was first used in sequence-to-sequence learning. Taking the translation task as an example, attention weights are calculated based on the hidden state of the predicted word (**deciding factor**), and exerted on the hidden states of source language word sequence [1]. However, relation classification is a sequence-to-label task. How to obtain the attention deciding factor is a problem to be solved.

In this paper, we propose an instance-adaptive attention mechanism. Specifically, the model can automatically generate an adaptive deciding factor for each instance to calculate the attention weights. We try to make the deciding factor contain the main relation-related information of the sentence. We evaluate the proposed method on the SemEval-2010 benchmark and achieve F1-score of 84.6%, higher than most existing methods in the literature.

2   Related Works

Over the years, a variety of methods have been proposed for relation classification. At first, most of them are based on pattern matching. Later, supervised models with complex handcrafted features are proposed to solve the problem. One related work is the support vector machine (SVM) model which utilizes various features from NLP tools and external resource [15]. Recently, the end-to-end deep neural networks have gradually replaced the traditional ones. Zeng et al. [10] used CNN to obtain the abstract features of sentence-level and achieved a good result. While CNN can better learn local features, it is not suitable to learn inconsecutive patterns. To overcome this issue, RNN is applied in relation classification task. To further solve the biased problem of single RNN, bi-directional RNN structure is introduced. The typical models include BRNN [11] and BLSTM [12]. In the proposed method, we continue use this framework. To eliminate irrelevant words in sentence, SDP-LSTM [6] leverages the shortest dependency path (SDP) between two entities as input and picks up semantic information with long short term memory unit (LSTM). It also combines external linguistic features to make another step forward in performance, such as part-of-speech (POS), grammatical relations and WordNet hypernyms.

Attention mechanism was proposed by [1] in machine translation, and currently attracts lots of interest. It is widely applied in a variety of tasks, including question answering, machine translation, speech recognition et al. Recently, this mechanism is transferred to relation classification. Zhou et al. proposed Att-BLSTM [13], which takes raw sentences as input. The model randomly initializes an equal-length vector as the global deciding factor and calculates the similarity between this vector and each word-level vector as corresponding attention weight. By training, this vector is properly adjusted to effectively improve the results on the limited dataset. But it can not adapt to the rich relationship expression outside the training set and thus has the risk of over-fitting. What's more, this method itself is difficult to explain from the logic. Comparing to this model, our model is robuster for leveraging better designed deciding factor, which is generated adaptively according to each individual sentence.

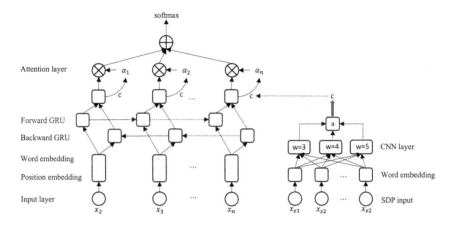

Fig. 1. Bidirectional GRU network with SDP-attention

3   Methodology

Given an input sentence with annotated entity pairs, the relation classification model is to calculate the probabilities of all candidate relations and choose the relation with the highest probability as output. In general, the proposed model mainly contains the following four parts:

(1) Input embedding layer: each token of input sentence is mapped into a fixed-size real-valued vector, including word vector and position vector;
(2) Bi-directional gated recurrent unit (GRU) layer: utilize bi-directional GRU to get word-level features;
(3) Attention layer: calculate weight vector based on the special deciding factor for each sentence. Weighted by this vector, word-level features from each time step are merge into a sentence-level feature vector;
(4) Output layer: use the obtained sentence-level vector to identify relation type.

3.1   Embedding Layer

With regard to relation classification, every input sentence is actually a word sequence $S = \{x_1, x_2, \ldots, x_n\}$, in which the annotated entities are $[x_{e1}, x_{e2}]$.

In embedding layer, each word x_i is converted into a real-valued vector w_i^*, which is the concatenation of its corresponding word embedding w_i^d and position embedding w_i^p:

$$w_i^* = [(w_i^d)^{\mathrm{T}}, (w_i^p)^{\mathrm{T}}]^{\mathrm{T}} \tag{1}$$

Word Embedding: For each word x_i in S, we search for w_i^d in the word embedding matrix $W^{word} \in \mathbb{R}^{d^w|V|}$, where V is a fixed-sized vocabulary and d^w is the size of word embedding. Here, we utilize pre-trained word vectors to initialize W^{word} in order to speed up model training and introduce prior semantic information of each word. In the process of training, W^{word} is updated as parameters after each epoch.

Position Embedding: Crucial words for identifying relation tend to appear close to the target entity pair in sentences. Therefore, position information is used to enrich word representation. Position embedding transforms the relative distance from word to each target entity as distributed representation. For word x_i and entity pair $[x_{e1}, x_{e2}]$, the two partial distance vectors are p_1 and p_2, which are concatenated together to form position embedding $w_i^p = [p_1^{\mathrm{T}}, p_2^{\mathrm{T}}]^{\mathrm{T}}$. Here, p_1 and p_2 are initialized randomly with the same dimension of d^p and modified via model training.

3.2   Bidirectional GRU

LSTM is firstly proposed by [16], aiming to alleviate gradient vanishing and exploding problem in basic RNN. In LSTM, an adaptive gating mechanism is introduced to control the flow of information between adjacent units. GRU is a simplified version of LSTM, which can achieve equivalent performance. It inherits the gating mechanism but greatly reduces the number of parameters [14]. There is no separate memory cell for each time step. Instead, it purely uses states of hidden units and current inputs to control information transfer. Consequently, hidden layer operations are mainly controlled by two gates: the update gate z_t and reset gate r_t. While r_t determines to what extent previous hidden state h_{t-1} influences the generation of new state $\widetilde{h}_t$, z_t defines the ratio of h_{t-1} and $\widetilde{h}_t$ in current hidden state h_t. Just as these following equations demonstrate:

$$z_t = \sigma\left(W_z x_t + U_z h_{t-1} + b_z\right) \tag{2}$$
$$r_t = \sigma\left(W_r x_t + U_r h_{t-1} + b_r\right) \tag{3}$$
$$h_t = (1 - z_t)h_{t-1} + z_t \widetilde{h}_t \tag{4}$$
$$\widetilde{h}_t = \tanh\left(W_h x_t + U_h\left(h_{t-1} \odot r_t\right) + b_h\right) \tag{5}$$

where x_t denotes current input and σ is logistic sigmoid function.

Standard GRU processes sequences in temporal order, which ignores the influence of future context. Hence, we adopt bi-directional GRU (Bi-GRU). Here, forward GRU processes sequences the same way as standard GRU while backward GRU does it in opposite temporal order. Then, at each time step t, hidden states $\overrightarrow{h_t} \in \mathbb{R}^{d^r}$ and $\overleftarrow{h_t} \in \mathbb{R}^{d^r}$ of two directions are concatenated together to form the final hidden state h_t.

3.3   Attention Mechanism

Theoretically speaking, the deciding factor for each sentence should be unique and relevant to the training target. Ideally, treating the distributed representation of the target relation type as the deciding factor can get the most reasonable attention weights. Since we can not make the cause and effect upside down, we try to find a substitution. Our solution is to build another neural network to generate a relation-related vector. Previous studies have proven that SDP from entity e_1 to entity e_2 can retain most relation semantics while eliminating the interference of irrelevant words. However, SDP also may lose some useful information. Hence, previous studies tend to make another step forward in performance by appending additional linguistic features. Here, we build an SDP-based neural network to generate the deciding factor. As showed in Fig. 1, we apply CNN of multi window length $(3, 4, 5)$ on SDP, then get the output vector a through operations of max-pooling and concatenation. To achieve dimension consistency with the hidden states of Bi-GRU, a full-connected layer is applied later to get final deciding factor c.

Let H be a matrix consisting of output vectors $[h_1, h_2, \ldots, h_n]$ that Bi-GRU produced. Through inner product with deciding factor and a softmax operation, we get a normalized attention weight vector α. The representation $r \in \mathbb{R}^{2d^r}$ of the sentence is formed by a weight sum of H.

$$\alpha = softmax\left(c^T H\right) \tag{6}$$
$$r = H\alpha^T \tag{7}$$

3.4   Classifying

We use a softmax classifier to predict the semantic relation type $\hat{y}$ of the target entity pair in sentence S. Before the last classification layer, the sentence representation r is fed into a full-connected layer and get $r^* \in \mathbb{R}^{d^m}$:

$$r^* = \tanh\left(W_m r + b_m\right) \tag{8}$$

Then, a softmax classifier is used to get the probability for each candidate relation y. The relation with the highest probability is identified as final result:

$$p\left(y|S\right) = softmax\left(W_s r^* + b_s\right) \tag{9}$$
$$\hat{y} = \arg\max_{y} p\left(y|S\right) \tag{10}$$

3.5   Regularization

Dropout [17] is proved to be a good regularization technique. It randomly omits units in hidden layers during forward propagation, so as to prevent co-adaptation of some units. Here, we employ dropout on embedding layer, attention layer and penultimate layer, where the corresponding dropout rates are ρ_w, ρ_c, ρ_o respectively. We additionally utilize Max-norm to constrain L2-norms of parameters. After a gradient descent step, rescale ω to have $\|\omega\| = \varepsilon$, whenever $\|\omega\| > \varepsilon$.

4   Dataset and Experimental Set

Experiments are conducted on SemiEval-2010 Task 8 dataset. The dataset has 10717 sentences, including 8000 examples for training and 2717 for testing. Each sentence is annotated with a target entity pair and a relation label. There are 9 relationship types with two directions and an undirected Other type. So, the total number of relation labels is 19. We adopt the official evaluation metric, which is based on macro-averaged F1-score for the 9 actual relations (excluding the Other type) and takes the directionality into consideration.

We use the released word embedding set GoogleNews-vectors-negative300. bin to initialize our embedding layer, which is trained by Mikolov's word2vec[1] tool [9]. For words not contained in the word embedding set, we randomly initialize their word embeddings following a Gaussian distribution. Our model is trained using AdaDelta with a minibatch size of 20 and learning rate of 1.0. The size of position vector is 25 and other vector sizes d^r, d^m, d^a are set as $100, 200, 100$ respectively. Dropout rate ρ_w, ρ_c, ρ_o are $0.7, 0.7, 0.3$ respectively. We randomly select 800 sentences in training set for validation.

5   Results and Discussion

Table 1 compares our proposed SDP-Att-BiGRU with other state-of-the-art methods of relation classification.

SVM: This is the top performed traditional feature-based method. It leverages a large variety of handcrafted features and uses SVM as the classifier. The model achieves an F1-score of 82.2%.

CNN: Treat an input sentence as sequence data and utilize CNN to extract sentence-level features. The model also exploits position embedding to identify the position of words. Then extra lexical features and sentence-level features are concatenated together and fed into a softmax classifier for prediction. The achieved F1-score is 82.7%.

SDP-LSTM: Let LSTM process the shortest dependency path between entity pair to get sentence-level features. The external linguistic features are integrated via multichannel architecture. Based on this, it achieves an F1-score of 83.7%.

---

[1] http://code.google.com/p/word2vec/.

Table 1. Result comparison. PF and PI stand for position features and position indicators.

Model	Feature set	F1
SVM	POS, prefixes, morphological, WordNet, dependency parse, Levin classed, ProBank, FramNet, NomLex-Plus, Google n-gram, paraphrases,TextRunner	82.2
CNN	Word embeddings+PF+WordNet, words around nominal	78.9
		82.7
BRNN	Word embeddings	82.5
CR-CNN	Word embeddings+PF	82.8
		84.1
SDP-LSTM	Word embeddings+POS+GR+WordNet embeddings	82.4
		83.7
BLSTM	Word embeddings+PF+POS+NER+WNSYN+DEP	82.7
		84.3
Att-BLSTM	Word embeddings+PI	84.0
Att-BiGRU	Word embeddings+PF	83.4
SDP-Att-BiGRU	Word embeddings+PF	**84.6**

CR-CNN [5]: The main contribution of this model is that it gives special treatment for class *Other* and proposes a new pair-wise ranking function to substitute softmax. It obtains a F1-score of 84.0%.

BRNN, BLSTM, Att-BLSTM: Similar to our proposed model, this three models utilize bidirectional RNN architecture. BRNN leverages basic RNN and max-pooling operation to learn sentence-level features. It also introduces position indicator (like $<e1> \ldots </e1>$) and gets a F1-score of 82.5%. BLSTM adopts bidirectional LSTM and employs many external lexical features. This model learns sentence-level features by piece-wise max pooling and raises F1-score to 84.3%. Att-BLSTM introduces attention mechanism to relation classification for the first time. Through randomly initializing a common deciding factor, the model generates weight for each word and gets a F1-score of 84.0%.

Our proposed model SDP-Att-BiGRU obtains F1-score of 84.6%. It is worth noting that our proposed model does not use any external lexical feature. In order to compare with previous attention mechanism, which randomly initializes a global deciding factor, we make the experiment of Att-BiGRU under the same conditions. The result shows that our proposed model works better. We attribute it to the specially designed deciding factor, which contains corresponding key relation-related information of each sentence and thus reduces the risk of over-fitting that single global deciding factor may suffer. Meanwhile, the proposed mechanism can also be treated as a special way of model blending, which utilizes one model to generate deciding factors for the other model to calculate attention weights. We also try to replace GRU with LSTM in the experiment but can not achieve the same good result. We haven't figured out the reason yet.

6   Conclusion

In this paper, we improve the attention mechanism applied in relation classification task by generating instance adaptive deciding factors. Based on this, we construct a novel neural network, named SDP-Att-BiGRU. In addition to the dependency parse tool, the model does not rely on any other NLP tool or external lexical resource. The experiment results on SemEval-2010 relation classification task demonstrate that our model achieves state-of-the-art performance.

Acknowledgments. This work was supported by 111 Project of China under Grant No. B08004, National Natural Science Foundation of China (61273217, 61300080, 61671078), the Ph.D. Programs Foundation of Ministry of Education of China (20130005110004).

References

1. Bahdanau, D., Cho, K., Bengio, Y.: Neural machine translation by jointly learning to align and translate. Comput. Sci. (2014)
2. Luo, Z., Osborne, M., Petrovi, S., et al.: Improving Twitter retrieval by exploiting structural information. In: Twenty-Sixth AAAI Conference on Artificial Intelligence (2012)
3. Bienvenu, M., Bourgaux, C., Goasdou, F.: Explaining inconsistency-tolerant query answering over description logic knowledge bases. In: AAAI Conference on Artificial Intelligence (2016)
4. Yao, X., Durme, B.V.: Information extraction over structured data: question answering with freebase. In: Meeting of Association for Computational Linguistics, pp. 956–966 (2014)
5. Santos, C.N.D., Xiang, B., Zhou, B.: Classifying relations by ranking with convolutional neural networks. Comput. Sci. (2015)
6. Yan, X., Mou, L., Li, G., et al.: Classifying relations via long short term memory networks along shortest dependency path. In: Conference on Empirical Methods in Natural Language Processing. 56–61, arXiv (2015)
7. Xu, Y., Jia, R., Mou, L., et al.: Improved relation classification by deep recurrent neural networks with data augmentation. In: COLING, arXiv (2016)
8. Xu, K., Feng, Y., Huang, S., et al.: Semantic relation classification via convolutional neural networks with simple negative sampling. Comput. Sci. **71**(7), 941–949 (2015)
9. Mikolov, T., Sutskever, I., Chen, K., et al.: Distributed representations of words and phrases and their compositionality. Adv. Neural Inf. Process. Syst. **26**, 3111–3119 (2013)
10. Zeng, D., Liu, K., Lai, S., et al.: Relation classification via convolutional deep neural network (2014)
11. Zhang, D., Wang, D.: Relation classification via recurrent neural network. Comput. Sci. (2015)
12. Zhang, S., Zheng, D., Hu, X., et al.: Bidirectional long short-term memory networks for relation classification (2015)

13. Zhou, P., Shi, W., Tian, J., et al.: Attention-based bidirectional long short-term memory networks for relation classification. In: Meeting of Association for Computational Linguistics, pp. 207–212 (2016)

14. Cho, K., Merrienboer, B.V., Gulcehre, C., et al.: Learning phrase representations using RNN encoder-decoder for statistical machine translation. Comput. Sci. (2014)

15. Rink, B., Harabagiu, S.: Classifying semantic relations by combining lexical and semantic resources. In: International Workshop on Semantic Evaluation, pp. 256–259. Association for Computational Linguistics (2010)

16. Hochreiter, S., Schmidhuber, J.: Long short-term memory. Neural Comput. **9**(8), 1735–1780 (1997)

17. Hinton, G.E., Srivastava, N., Krizhevsky, A., et al.: Improving neural networks by preventing co-adaptation of feature detectors. Comput. Sci. **3**(4), 212–223 (2012)

ReForeSt: Random Forests in Apache Spark

Alessandro Lulli, Luca Oneto$^{(\boxtimes)}$, and Davide Anguita

DIBRIS - University of Genoa, Via Opera Pia 13, 16145 Genova, Italy
alessandro.lulli@dibris.unige.it, {luca.oneto,davide.anguita}@unige.it

Abstract. Random Forests (RF) of tree classifiers are a popular ensemble method for classification. RF are usually preferred with respect to other classification techniques because of their limited hyperparameter sensitivity, high numerical robustness, native capacity of dealing with numerical and categorical features, and effectiveness in many real world classification problems. In this work we present ReForeSt, a Random Forests Apache Spark implementation which is easier to tune, faster, and less memory consuming with respect to MLlib, the de facto standard Apache Spark machine learning library. We perform an extensive comparison between ReForeSt and MLlib by taking advantage of the Google Cloud Platform (https://cloud.google.com). In particular, we test ReForeSt and MLlib with different library settings, on different real world datasets, and with a different number of machines equipped with different number of cores. Results confirm that ReForeSt outperforms MLlib in all the above mentioned aspects. ReForeSt is made publicly available via GitHub (https://github.com/alessandrolulli/reforest).

Keywords: Random Forests · Apache Spark · Open source software

1 Introduction

It is well known that combining the output of several classifiers results in a much better performance than using any one of them alone [11]. In [4] Breiman proposed the Random Forests (RF) of tree classifiers, one of the state-of-the-art learning algorithm for classification which has shown to be one of the most effective tool in this context [9,16]. RF combine bagging to random subset feature selection. In bagging, each tree is independently constructed using a bootstrap sample of the dataset [8]. RF add an additional layer of randomness to bagging. In addition to constructing each tree using a different bootstrap sample of the data, RF change how the classification trees are constructed. In standard trees, each node is split using the best division among all variables. In RF, each node is split using the best among a subset of predictors randomly chosen at that node. Eventually, a simple majority vote is taken for prediction.

The challenge today is that the size of data is constantly increasing making infeasible to analyze it with classic learning algorithms or their naive implementations [14]. Data is often distributed, since it is collected and stored by distributed platforms like the Hadoop-based ones [7]. Apache Spark [19] is currently

© Springer International Publishing AG 2017
A. Lintas et al. (Eds.): ICANN 2017, Part II, LNCS 10614, pp. 331–339, 2017.
https://doi.org/10.1007/978-3-319-68612-7_38

gaining momentum for distributed processing because it enables fast iterative in-memory computation with respect to classical disk-based MapReduce jobs. MLlib [14] is the de facto standard for the use of RF learning algorithm in a distributed environment. It is built-in Spark, implemented by the very same authors. They follow a common approach to distributed computation. The initial data is divided into a number of partitions, which is in general larger with respect to the number of machines. Each machine maintains a subset of the partitions. Therefore, in order to construct the forest (i) the needed information must be collected inside a partition, (ii) it is aggregated locally in the machine, and (iii) all the machines' information is aggregated in order to complete the computation. The main downside is that for each node an amount of memory proportional with the number of partitions handled by the machine is allocated.

In addition to the already mentioned MLlib [14] other RF implementations exist, but they show analogous drawbacks. For instance, Chung [6] presents an optimization of MLlib that switches from distributed to local computation when the size of the data relative to a sub-tree is below a threshold, but no source code is available. In [10] it is proposed to send each chunk of data to an independent job and then aggregate the information of each chunk. However, this approach requires the transmission of the entire subsamples to all the machines in the cluster. Wakayama et al. [17] construct in each machine a candidate random forest. Such forests are then aggregated and just the trees which show the best accuracy are kept. The major drawback is that many trees are discarded resulting in wasting computation time. Chen et al. [5] propose to vertically partition the data. The training dataset is split into several feature subsets and then each subset is allocated to a different distributed data structure. Unfortunately, this approach requires a large shuffling phase at the beginning and the comparisons are performed against an old implementation of MLlib.

In this paper we present ReForeSt, a distributed, scalable implementation of the RF learning algorithm which targets fast and memory efficient processing. ReForeSt main contributions are manifold: (i) it provides a novel approach for the RF implementation in a distributed environment targeting an in-memory efficient processing, (ii) it is faster and more memory efficient with respect to the de facto standard MLlib, (iii) the level of parallelism is self-configuring, and (iv) its source code is made publicly available. With respect to current approaches we provide several benefits. With respect to MLlib we avoid the use of multiple data structures requested by the partitioning-based distributed computation, since each machine maintains only one data structure to collect the information of the data stored in it. Contrarily to [14] we grow all the trees in parallel in order to reduce the number of scans of the data. With respect to [17] and [5,10] we avoid to generate trees that are not useful for the final result and to perform too many communications in each iteration respectively. Finally, we do not occupy memory with repetitions of the same data as opposed to [5].

2   ReForeSt: Random Forests in Apache Spark

Let us recall the multi-class classification problem [3] where a set of labeled samples $\mathcal{D}_n = \{(X_1, Y_1), \cdots, (X_n, Y_n)\}$ drawn according to an unknown probability distribution μ over $\mathcal{X} \times \mathcal{Y}$ are available and where $X \in \mathcal{X} = \{\mathcal{X}_1 \times \mathcal{X}_2 \times \cdots \times \mathcal{X}_d\}$ and $Y \in \mathcal{Y} = \{1, 2, \cdots, c\}$. A learning algorithm $\mathscr{A}$ maps $\mathcal{D}_n$ into a function belonging to a possibly unknown set of functions $f \in \mathcal{F}$ according to some criteria $\mathscr{A} : \mathcal{D}_n \rightarrow \mathcal{F}$. The error of f in approximating μ is measured with reference to a loss function $\ell : \mathcal{Y} \times \mathcal{Y} \rightarrow \mathbb{R}$. Since we are dealing with classification problems we choose the loss function which counts the number of misclassified samples $\ell(f(X), Y) = [f(X) \neq Y]$, where the Iverson bracket notation is exploited. The expected error of f in representing μ is called generalization error [15] and it is defined as $L(f) = \mathbb{E}_{(X,Y)}\ell(f(X), Y)$. Since μ is unknown $L(f)$ cannot be computed, but we can compute its empirical estimator, the empirical error, defined as $\widehat{L}(f) = 1/n \sum_{i=1}^{n} \ell(f(\widehat{X}_i), \widehat{Y}_i)$ where $\mathcal{I}_n = \{(\widehat{X}_1, \widehat{Y}_1), \cdots, (\widehat{X}_n, \widehat{Y}_n)\}$ must be a different set with respect to $\mathcal{D}_n$ which has been used to build f in order to ensure that the estimator of the quality of the model is unbiased [1].

In our case $\mathscr{A}$ are RF. We briefly describe the learning phase of each of the n_t trees composing the RF. From $\mathcal{D}_n$, $\lfloor bn \rfloor$ samples are sampled with replacement and $\mathcal{D}'_{\lfloor bn \rfloor}$ is built. A tree is constructed with $\mathcal{D}'_{\lfloor bn \rfloor}$ but the best split is chosen among a subset of n_v predictors over the possible d predictors randomly chosen at each node. The tree is grown until its depth reaches the maximum value of n_d or all the samples in $\mathcal{D}_n$ are correctly classified. During the classification phase of a previously unseen $X \in \mathcal{X}$, each tree classifies X in a class $Y_{i \in \{1, \cdots, n_t\}} \in \mathcal{Y}$, and then the final classification is the majority vote of all the answers of each tree of the RF. If $b = 1$, $n_v = \sqrt{n}$, and $n_d = \infty$ we get the original RF formulation [4] where n_t is usually chosen to tradeoff accuracy and efficiency [12].

ReForeSt is a distributed, scalable algorithm for RF computation targeting fast and memory efficient processing. Our main idea is to create only one data structure, called *matrix*, on each machine. This is used for local data aggregation and to concurrently aggregate information to compute the best cuts. The goal is to reduce the memory requirements and the computational time with respect to alternative approaches. For example, MLlib uses one data structure for each partition in order to collect the information resulting in an inefficient memory management.

Our proposal (see Algorithm 1) counts two main phases. The first phase is called *data preparation*. The output of the first phase is the *working data*, a statically allocated collection of items. Each item is an optimized representation of the original data coupled with how much it contributes to each of the trees. The second phase performs the *tree generation*. The working data is iteratively processed to grow each tree of the forest.

2.1   Data Preparation

Starting from the raw data $\mathcal{D}_n$ we build the *working data*. Such working data is kept in memory for the entire duration of the second phase statically. For performance reasons, similarly to [6,14], the domain of each feature is discretized. We call this operation *binning* and the number of bin n_b is configurable. For each feature, we search for the n_b values for splitting the domain (see L:3, namely Line 3 of Algorithm 1) using a sample $\mathcal{D}''_s \subset \mathcal{D}_n$ where $s \approx 10^4$. Than, each bin is constructed to have approximately the same number of samples $\mathcal{D}''_s/n_b$. Finally, each sample $(X_j, Y_j) \in \mathcal{D}_n$ is converted in a working data item $(X_j^{n_b}, Y_j, B_j)$ which belongs to the dataset of converted data items $\mathcal{D}_n^{n_b} = \{(X_j^{n_b}, Y_j, B_j) : j \in \{1, \cdots, n\}\}$. $X_j^{n_b}$ is the discretized version of X_j, while $B_j \in \mathbb{N}^{n_t}$ is a vector which contains in $B_{j,i}$ the contribution of $(X_j, Y_j) \in \mathcal{D}_n$ to the i-th tree built based on $\mathcal{D}'_{\lfloor bn \rfloor}$.

Algorithm 1. ReForeSt pseudo-code.

Input: $\mathcal{D}_n$, n_t, b, n_b, n_v and n_d
Output: A set of tree $\{T_1, \cdots, T_{n_t}\}$
// Data Preparation
1 $\mathcal{D}_n \leftarrow loadData()$;   /* Parallelized over the n samples */
2 $\mathcal{D}''_s \leftarrow sample(\mathcal{D}_n)$;   /* Parallelized over the d features */
3 $\mathcal{S} \leftarrow findSplit(n_b, \mathcal{D}''_s)$;   /* Parallelized over the d features */
4 $\mathcal{D}_n^{n_b} \leftarrow convertInWorkingData(\mathcal{D}_n, \mathcal{S}, b)$;   /* Parallelized over the n samples */
   // Tree Generation
5 $\{T_1, \cdots, T_{n_t}\} \leftarrow initializeEmptyTrees(n_t)$;
6 **for** $i \leftarrow 0, \cdots, (n_d - 1)$ **do**
       // Local Information Collection
7 | **for** $j \leftarrow 1, \cdots, N_m$ **do in parallel**
8 | | $M^j \leftarrow$ instantiate a matrix $\mathbb{N}^{2^i n_t \times n_b c n_v}$;
9 | | **for** $(X^{n_b}, Y, B) \in (\mathcal{D}_n^{n_b})^j$ **do**   /* $(\mathcal{D}_n^{n_b})^j \subset \mathcal{D}_n^{n_b}$ which resides on machine j */
10 | | | **for** $t \leftarrow 1, \cdots, n_t$ **do**
11 | | | | $node \leftarrow getNode(t, X^{n_b})$;
12 | | | | **if** $\neg isLeaf(node)$ **then**
13 | | | | | **for** $f \leftarrow \mathcal{R}_{n_v}$ **do**
14 | | | | | | $p \leftarrow getColumnInM(t, node, f, X^{n_b}, Y)$;
15 | | | | | | $r \leftarrow getRowOfMFromNode(node)$;
16 | | | | | | $M^j_{r,p} \leftarrow M^j_{r,p} + B_t$;
       // Distributed Information Aggregation
17 | $M \leftarrow mergeByNode(\forall M^j, \; j \in \{1, \cdots, N_m\})$;
       // Trees Update
18 | **for** $r \leftarrow 1, \cdots, 2^i n_t$ **do in parallel** /* Every machine handles a subset of the nodes */
19 | | $node \leftarrow getNodeFromRowOfM(r)$;
20 | | $bestCut \leftarrow findBestCut(M_{r,\{1,\cdots,n_b c n_v\}})$;
21 | | $\{T_1, \cdots, T_{n_t}\}.growTreeBasedOnNode(node, bestCut)$;

2.2 Tree Generation

The *tree generation* phase proceeds breadth-first and each tree is computed in parallel. An iteration is divided in three steps: local information collection, distributed information aggregation, and trees update. At each iteration $i \in \{0, \cdots, n_d - 1\}$ all the nodes at the i-th level are computed by each machine $j \in \{1, \cdots, N_m\}$ in parallel. In particular, we exploit the matrix $M^j \in \mathbb{N}^{2^i \times n_t \times n_b \times c \times n_v}$ which resides on the j-th machine. M^j contains the contributions, needed to select the best split based on the information gain criteria, to the different n_v randomly selected subset of the d original features and to the c classes of the subset of items $\mathcal{D}_n^{n_b}$ handled by the j-th machine to the 2^i nodes at i-th level of the n_t trees of the forest. Note that M^j is flattened from a five-dimensional matrix to a two-dimensional matrix $M^j \in \mathbb{N}^{2^i n_t \times n_b c n_v}$ for performance reasons. Then all the matrices are aggregated in order to collect the information needed to find the best cuts and update the trees of the forest. If M^j does not fit in the memory of the machine, since M^j can become very large, the iterations are automatically divided in many sub-iterations based on the available memory and the number of nodes processed at the i-th iteration.

Local Information Collection. This step does not require any communication between the machines. It operates on the working data saved in each machine j and collects the information in M^j which is instantiated at the beginning of the iteration. All the partitions are processed concurrently by the machine which stores them. In the following we describe how an item $(X^{n_b}, Y, B) \in \mathcal{D}_n^{n_b}$ contributes to M^j for one tree $t \in \{1, \cdots, n_t\}$ with its weight B_t. Each (X^{n_b}, Y, B) is stored in a Spark partition and it contributes to all the trees in the forest as follows. First we have to recall that (X^{n_b}, Y, B) can contribute to only one node per tree since we are processing all the nodes at a particular depth of all the trees. Then, given (X^{n_b}, Y, B) and the t-th tree we can navigate it until we reach the right node where (X^{n_b}, Y, B) contributes (see L:11). For each feature $f \in \mathcal{R}_{n_v}$, where $\mathcal{R}_{n_v}$ is a set of n_v indexes randomly sampled without replacement from $\{1, \cdots, d\}$, the proper element of M^j to be updated is found (see L:14). The row of M^j is the specified node index. The column of M^j is computed as $n_b c f + c X_f^{n_b} + Y$. B_t is added to the aforementioned position of M^j (see L:16). At the end of this step, each machine has one matrix populated with the contributions of each item of the working data stored in it.

Distributed Information Aggregation. In this step the information stored in each M^j is aggregated as follows. The rows of each M^j are shuffled in the machines. In particular, the rows belonging to the same node are collected in a same machine thanks to the Spark hashing function. At the end of this step, each machine stores a subset of the nodes processed at the particular iteration i. The number of nodes in each machine is approximately $2^i n_t / N_m$ thanks to the hashing function that distributes the nodes to the machines uniformly. The matrix instantiated at the beginning of the iteration is freed during the shuffling phase.

Trees Update. In the last step of each iteration each machine, having the complete knowledge about the nodes stored in it, searches the best cuts (see L:20). The best cut is chosen in such a way to maximize the information gain in the sub-tree. All the computed cuts are then exploited to update the n_t trees in the forest (see L:21).

3   Experimental Evaluation

In this Sect. ReForeSt and MLlib [14] are compared through a comprehensive set of experiments. We run the experiments on the Google Cloud Platform (GCP) making use of Linux shell scripts for automatically deploying the clusters of virtual machines (VMs). Each VM runs Debian 8.7 and is equipped with Hadoop 2.7.3 and Apache Spark 2.1.0. To evaluate the ReForeSt and MLlib scalability we tested them on different cluster configurations. In particular, one master node is deployed and a different number of worker machines $N_m \in \{4, 8, 16\}$ equipped with different number of cores $N_c \in \{4, 8, 16\}$ is handled by the master. For this purpose, we used the n1-standard-4, n1-standard-8, and n1-standard-16 machine types from GCP with approximately 15, 30, and 60 GB of RAM respectively and 500 GB of SSD disk space. For every combination of parameters we run the experiments 10 times. Different datasets have been exploited to conduct the experiments: *Susy*, *Epsilon*, *Higgs*, and *Infimnist*. Their descriptions are reported in Table 1. The 70% of each dataset is used as $\mathcal{D}_n$ whereas the remaining 30% as $\mathcal{T}_m$.

Table 1. Dataset exploited in the paper.

Name	Ref.	n	d	c	Size (GB)
Susy	[2]	$5 \cdot 10^6$	18	2	3
Epsilon	[18]	$5 \cdot 10^5$	$2 \cdot 10^3$	2	11
Higgs	[2]	$11 \cdot 10^6$	28	2	8.4
Infimnist	[13]	$14 \cdot 10^6$	784	10	20

Figure 1 depicts the average memory consumption of ReForeSt and MLlib for the Higgs dataset. We collect the memory used by the Java Virtual Machine (JVM) in each second of computation for the environment with $N_m = 4$, $N_c = \{4, 8\}$, $n_b = 32$, $n_d = 10$ and $b = 1$. The JVM Garbage Collector has been invoked periodically in order to avoid artifacts in the results. On the x-axis we report the normalized computational time with respect to the total time in order to better compare the ReForeSt and MLlib memory usage. Figure 1 shows the memory usage picks due to the allocation of the matrices used to collect the information at each iteration of ReForeSt and MLlib. From Fig. 1 it is possible to observe that:

- ReForeSt requires always less memory with respect to MLlib to perform the computation. In particular it requires always less than 3 GB of RAM while MLlib requires 16 GB of RAM;
- the MLlib memory usage linearly increases with the number of cores, whereas the ReForeSt memory usage does not depend on the number of cores.

Results over the other datasets present a similar behavior.

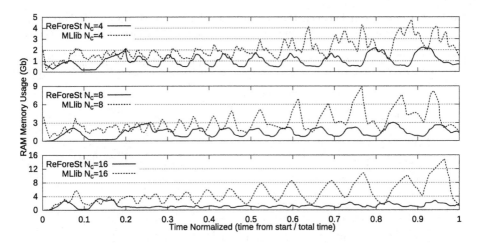

Fig. 1. Memory usage of MLlib and ReForeSt over the Higgs dataset with $N_m = 4$, $N_c = \{4, 8, 16\}$, $n_t = 100$, $n_b = 32$, $n_d = 10$, $b = 1$.

Table 2 reports a series of metrics for the complete sets of experiments run over the different cluster architectures and datasets and by changing n_t. These metrics are: the computation time of ReForeSt and MLlib in seconds, respectively t_R and t_M, the speed-up of ReForeSt and MLlib with respect to the base scenario $N_m = 4$ and $N_c = 4$, respectively S_R and S_M, and $\Delta = t_M/t_R$. n_b and n_d have been fixed to the default MLlib values ($n_b = 32$ and $n_d = 10$) and standard deviation is not reported because of space constraints. However changing n_b and n_d does not substantially change the outcomes and the standard deviation of the results is always less than 5%. Based on Table 2 it is possible to observe that:

- from a computational point of view, ReForeSt is much more efficient than MLlib. We obtain a speed-up with respect to MLlib of at least $\Delta = 1.48$ with a maximum of $\Delta = 3.05$. On average, ReForeSt is two times faster than MLlib;
- ReForeSt scales better with n_t with respect to MLlib as one can observe trough the values of Δ. For instance, on the Epsilon dataset when $N_m = 16$ and $N_c = 16$ we obtain $\Delta = 2.08$ with $n_t = 100$ and $\Delta = 3.05$ with $n_t = 400$;
- ReForeSt scales better with N_c. This effect is easier to observe when the size of the dataset is larger. For instance, in the Infimnist dataset with $N_m = 16$ and $n_t = 400$ we obtain $\Delta = 1.87, 2.15, 2.78$ respectively for $N_c = 4, 8, 16$;
- ReForeSt exhibits comparable or better speed-up, when N_m or N_c are increased, with respect to MLlib;
- ReForeSt requires considerable less memory with respect to MLlib; In fact MLlib is not able to finish the computation on several clusters because of memory constraints. For instance, with $N_m = 4$ and $N_c = 4$ we got the following error "There is insufficient memory for the Java Runtime Environment to continue" since MLlib fails to provide a solution for the Infimnist dataset and for Higgs with $n_t = 400$.

Table 2. Comparison between the computational time of MLlib and ReForeSt. (∗) JVM out of memory error, (-) value cannot be computed because of the JVM error.

N_m	N_c	n_t	Susy (3GB)					Higgs (8GB)					Epsilon (11GB)					Infimnist (20GB)				
			t_R	t_M	S_R	S_M	Δ	t_R	t_M	S_R	S_M	Δ	t_R	t_M	S_R	S_M	Δ	t_R	t_M	S_R	S_M	Δ
4	4	100	178	287	1	1	1.61	399	685	1	1	1.72	197	348	1	1	1.77	1064	∗	1	1	-
		200	319	570	1	1	1.79	756	1306	1	1	1.73	264	543	1	1	2.06	1847	∗	1	1	-
		400	665	1163	1	1	1.75	1598	∗	1	1	-	400	959	1	1	2.4	3635	∗	1	1	-
4	8	100	104	173	1.7	1.7	1.66	223	400	1.8	1.7	1.79	123	192	1.6	1.8	1.56	581	1106	1.8	-	1.9
		200	175	357	1.8	1.6	2.04	429	788	1.8	1.7	1.84	155	304	1.7	1.8	1.96	1013	2095	1.8	-	2.07
		400	370	688	1.8	1.7	1.86	903	1662	1.8	-	1.84	246	543	1.6	1.8	2.21	1935	∗	1.9	-	-
4	16	100	78	138	2.3	2.1	1.77	142	275	2.8	2.5	1.94	94	172	2.1	2	1.83	380	799	2.8	2.8	2.1
		200	118	280	2.7	2	2.37	250	617	3	2.1	2.47	107	285	2.5	1.9	2.66	654	1460	2.8	2.9	2.23
		400	226	608	2.9	1.9	2.69	521	1256	3.1	2.6	2.41	172	519	2.3	1.8	3.02	1284	2842	2.8	-	2.21
8	4	100	107	160	1.7	1.8	1.5	238	408	1.7	1.7	1.71	122	192	1.6	1.8	1.57	659	1078	1.6	2.1	1.64
		200	182	317	1.8	1.8	1.74	437	752	1.7	1.7	1.72	168	303	1.6	1.8	1.8	1040	∗	1.8	-	-
		400	365	619	1.8	1.9	1.7	930	1530	1.7	2.2	1.65	257	526	1.6	1.8	2.05	1912	∗	1.9	-	-
8	8	100	65	97	2.7	3	1.49	133	239	3	2.9	1.8	78	151	2.5	2.3	1.94	354	639	3	3.5	1.81
		200	106	213	3	2.7	2.01	249	452	3	2.9	1.82	100	256	2.6	2.1	2.56	586	1170	3.2	3.6	2
		400	210	410	3.2	2.8	1.95	478	897	3.3	3.7	1.88	162	458	2.5	2.1	2.83	1164	2235	3.1	5.1	1.92
8	16	100	54	80	3.3	3.6	1.48	78	168	5.1	4.1	2.15	66	128	3	2.7	1.94	234	513	4.5	4.3	2.19
		200	72	162	4.4	3.5	2.25	140	328	5.4	4	2.34	78	194	3.4	2.8	2.49	392	963	4.7	4.4	2.46
		400	139	375	4.8	3.1	2.7	275	722	5.8	4.6	2.63	129	371	3.1	2.6	2.88	776	1927	4.7	5.9	2.48
16	4	100	67	102	2.7	2.8	1.52	135	222	3	3.1	1.64	83	162	2.4	2.1	1.95	364	629	2.9	3.5	1.73
		200	109	193	2.9	3	1.77	252	423	3	3.1	1.68	109	265	2.4	2	2.43	610	1138	3	3.7	1.87
		400	223	381	3	3.1	1.71	512	860	3.1	3.9	1.68	174	488	2.3	2	2.8	1167	2177	3.1	5.2	1.87
16	8	100	47	80	3.8	3.6	1.7	74	135	5.4	5.1	1.82	57	115	3.5	3	2.02	216	435	4.9	5.1	2.01
		200	79	175	4	3.3	2.22	150	263	5	5	1.75	73	185	3.6	2.9	2.53	381	823	4.8	5.1	2.16
		400	130	270	5.1	4.3	2.08	261	519	6.1	6.4	1.99	118	342	3.4	2.8	2.9	686	1477	5.3	7.7	2.15
16	16	100	44	64	4	4.5	1.45	50	101	8	6.8	2.02	53	110	3.7	3.2	2.08	132	339	8.1	6.5	2.57
		200	50	127	6.4	4.5	2.54	89	212	8.5	6.2	2.38	62	179	4.3	3	2.89	230	636	8	6.6	2.77
		400	102	250	6.5	4.7	2.45	172	441	9.3	7.5	2.56	104	317	3.8	3	3.05	455	1266	8	9	2.78

Finally, we do not include in the table the accuracies since the differences between ReForeSt and MLlib are not statistically relevant. For instance, for the Infimnist dataset with $n_t = 400$, with ReForeSt we obtain an error of $\widehat{L}_R(f) = 0.082 \pm .001$ while with MLlib we obtain an error of $\widehat{L}_M(f) = 0.083 \pm .001$. With the Higgs dataset the errors are $\widehat{L}_R(f) = 0.029 \pm .001$ and $\widehat{L}_M(f) = 0.028 \pm .001$.

4   Conclusion

In this work we developed ReForeSt, an Apache Spark implementation of the RF learning algorithm that we made publicly available through GitHub. ReForeSt is easier to tune, faster, and less memory consuming with respect to MLlib, the de-facto standard Apache Spark machine learning library. An extensive comparison between ReForeSt and MLlib performed by taking advantage of the GCP and different big data problems confirms the quality of the proposal.

As future works, we plan to further develop ReForeSt by introducing the possibility to conclude the construction of the sub-tree on a single machine when the cardinality of the data relative to a sub-tree is below a certain threshold similarly to [6] and we will take care to develop an ad-hoc computationally inexpensive model selection strategy for the purpose of automatically tuning the hyperparameters of the RF over the available data.

References

1. Anguita, D., Ghio, A., Oneto, L., Ridella, S.: In-sample and out-of-sample model selection and error estimation for support vector machines. IEEE Trans. Neural Netw. Learn. Syst. **23**(9), 1390–1406 (2012)
2. Baldi, P., Sadowski, P., Whiteson, D.: Searching for exotic particles in high-energy physics with deep learning. Nature Commun. **5**(4308), 1–9 (2014)
3. Bishop, B.M.: Neural Networks for Pattern Recognition. Oxford University Press, Oxford (1995)
4. Breiman, L.: Random forests. Mach. Learn. **45**(1), 5–32 (2001)
5. Chen, J., et al.: A parallel random forest algorithm for big data in a spark cloud computing environment. IEEE Transactions on Parallel and Distributed Systems (2016, in press)
6. Chung, S.: Sequoia forest: random forest of humongous trees. In: Spark Summit (2014)
7. Dean, J., Ghemawat, S.: MapReduce: simplified data processing on large clusters. Commun. ACM **51**(1), 107–113 (2008)
8. Efron, B.: Bootstrap methods: another look at the jackknife. Ann. Stat. **7**(1), 1–26 (1979)
9. Fernández-Delgado, M., Cernadas, E., Barro, S., Amorim, D.: Do we need hundreds of classifiers to solve real world classification problems? JMLR **15**(1), 3133–3181 (2014)
10. Genuer, R., Poggi, J., Tuleau-Malot, C., Villa-Vialaneix, N.: Random forests for big data. arXiv preprint arXiv:1511.08327 (2015)
11. Germain, P., Lacasse, A., Laviolette, A., ahd Marchand, M., Roy, J.F.: Risk bounds for the majority vote: from a PAC-Bayesian analysis to a learning algorithm. JMLR **16**(4), 787–860 (2015)
12. Hernández-Lobato, D., Martínez-Muñoz, G., Suárez, A.: How large should ensembles of classifiers be? Pattern Recogn. **46**(5), 1323–1336 (2013)
13. Loosli, G., Canu, S., Bottou, L.: Training invariant support vector machines using selective sampling. In: Large Scale Kernel Machines (2007)
14. Meng, X., et al.: Mllib: Machine learning in apache spark. J. Mach. Learn. Res. **17**(34), 1–7 (2016)
15. Vapnik, V.N.: Statistical Learning Theory. Wiley, New York (1998)
16. Wainberg, M., Alipanahi, B., Frey, B.J.: Are random forests truly the best classifiers? J. Mach. Learn. Res. **17**(110), 1–5 (2016)
17. Wakayama, R., et al.: Distributed forests for MapReduce-based machine learning. In: Asian Conference on Pattern Recognition (2015)
18. Yuan, G., Ho, C., Lin, C.: An improved GLMNET for l1-regularized logistic regression. J. Mach. Learn. Res. **13**, 1999–2030 (2012)
19. Zaharia, M., Chowdhury, M., Franklin, M.J., Shenker, S., Stoica, I.: Spark: cluster computing with working sets. HotCloud **10**(10–10), 1–9 (2010)

Semi-Supervised Multi-view Multi-label Classification Based on Nonnegative Matrix Factorization

Guangxia Wang, Changqing Zhang$^{(\boxtimes)}$, Pengfei Zhu, and Qinghua Hu

School of Computer Science and Technology, Tianjin University, Tianjin, China
{wangguangxia,zhangchangqing,zhupengfei,huqinghua}@tju.edu.cn

Abstract. Many real-world applications involve multi-label classification where each sample is usually associated with a set of labels. Although many methods have been proposed, most of them are just applicable to single-view data neglecting the complementary information among multiple views. Besides, most existing methods are supervised, hence they cannot handle the case where only a few labeled data are available. To address these issues, we propose a novel semi-supervised multi-view multi-label classification method based on nonnegative matrix factorization (NMF). Specifically, it explores the complementary information by adopting multi-view NMF, regularizes the learned labels of each view towards a common consensus labeling, and obtains the labels of the unlabeled data guided by supervised information. Experimental results on real-world benchmark datasets demonstrate the superior performance of our method over the state-of-the-art methods.

Keywords: Multi-view · Multi-label · Semi-supervised · Nonnegative matrix factorization

1 Introduction

Multi-label classification aims at predicting the proper label sets for the unseen samples. It is ubiquitous in many real-world applications, such as image classification, text categorization and gene function prediction [1]. For example, the image shown in Fig. 1 has three labels, i.e., "person", "car", "motorbike". Many methods have been developed to tackle the multi-label classification problem. Binary relevance (BR) trains a classifier for each label straightforwardly, but it neglects the label correlations [2]. Label powerset (LP) explores all possible label subsets and transforms multi-label classification problem into single-label problem. Although LP addresses the disadvantage of BR, it cannot be applied when the number of labels is very large [3]. Recently, researchers have proposed some ensemble methods [4,5] which overcome the drawbacks of BR and LP. Besides, there are several adaptation methods that adopt existing algorithms for the task of multi-label classification [6,7].

© Springer International Publishing AG 2017
A. Lintas et al. (Eds.): ICANN 2017, Part II, LNCS 10614, pp. 340–348, 2017.
https://doi.org/10.1007/978-3-319-68612-7_39

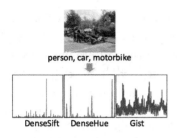

person, car, motorbike

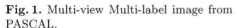

DenseSift   DenseHue   Gist

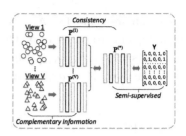

Fig. 1. Multi-view Multi-label image from PASCAL.

Fig. 2. Framework of NMF-SSMM.

Moreover, real-world data often consist of multiple views. For example, image data can be represented by multiple heterogenous features in the form of multiple views. As shown in Fig. 1, the image has three different feature views: DenseSift, DenseHue and Gist. Since each view describes the particular aspect of the data and often provides complementary information to each other, jointly utilizing all views could improve the overall classification performance. As above mentioned, there are many multi-label classification methods, however, most of them are confronted with the limitation that they are only designed for single view data and cannot be used to deal with multi-view case directly. Another limitation is that they are supervised methods which require sufficient labeled training data. Unfortunately, in real-world applications, since labeling data is rather expensive, there are only a small number of labeled data available. Therefore, how to deal with a small number of labeled data and a large number of unlabeled data simultaneously is a key issue. Recently, to handle the aforementioned limitations, multi-view matrix completion and multi-view vector-valued manifold regularization (MV3MR) algorithm are introduced in the semi-supervised approaches [8,9], respectively. However, they do not take into account the consistency of multi-view data as in our method.

In this paper, we propose a novel Semi-Supervised Multi-view Multi-label classification method based on Nonnegative Matrix Factorization (NMF), named NMF-SSMM. As shown in Fig. 2, it exploits the complementary information of multi-view data by multi-view NMF and then acquires the label matrix $\mathbf{P}^{(v)}$ of each view. To guarantee the consistency of multi-view data, it regularizes $\mathbf{P}^{(v)}$ towards a common consensus labeling $\mathbf{P}^{(*)}$. Moreover, it utilizes labeled data and unlabeled data simultaneously, and obtains the labels of the unlabeled data through minimizing the label loss of the labeled data.

2 The Proposed Method: NMF-SSMM

2.1 Notations

Throughout this paper, matrices are written as boldface capital letters and vectors are denoted as boldface lowercase letters. For matrix $\mathbf{A} = (\mathrm{A}_{i,j})$, its i-th row,

j-th column are defined as $\mathbf{A}_{i,\cdot}$, $\mathbf{A}_{\cdot,j}$ respectively. $\|\mathbf{A}\|_F$ is the Frobenius norm of $\mathbf{A}$, and $\mathrm{Tr}(\mathbf{A})$ is the trace of $\mathbf{A}$. Given N samples with V views, $\mathcal{X} = \{x_i, y_i\}_{i=1}^N$, the first L samples $\{x_i, y_i\}_{i=1}^L$ are labeled data and the rest are unlabeled data. Denote the v-th view data matrix as $\mathbf{X}^{(v)} = [\mathbf{x}_1^{(v)}, \mathbf{x}_2^{(v)}, \ldots, \mathbf{x}_N^{(v)}] \in \mathcal{R}^{D_v \times N}$ where $\mathbf{x}_i^{(v)} \in \mathcal{R}^{D_v}$. Supposing these N samples are draw from K classes, denote $\mathbf{Y} = [\mathbf{y}_1; \mathbf{y}_2; \ldots; \mathbf{y}_N] \in \{0,1\}^{N \times K}$ as the label matrix. For labeled data, $\{\mathbf{y}_i\}_{i=1}^L \in \{0,1\}^K$, where $\mathbf{y}_{ij} = 1$ means that $\mathbf{x}_i$ is assigned into the j-th class and vice versa. For unlabeled data, $\mathbf{y}_i$ is set to a vector with all zeros $(i > L)$.

2.2   Formulation

Nonnegative matrix factorization (NMF) [10] is a technique which was originally used to address dimensionality reduction problem. Due to its simplicity and flexibility, NMF has been widely used in many areas of machine learning, such as image classification [11], feature selection [12]. Recently, the researchers adopt NMF in multi-view data [13]. There are some differences between [13] and our methods: (1) [13] is an unsupervised method for clustering, while ours simultaneously utilizes unlabeled and labeled samples for multi-label classification; (2) Our method could automatically weight different views thus balances the importance of multiple views. NMF is a matrix factorization algorithm which aims to find two non-negative matrices $\mathbf{B} \in \mathcal{R}^{D \times K}$ and $\mathbf{P} \in \mathcal{R}^{N \times K}$ where their product can well approximate the original data matrix $\mathbf{X}$, i.e., $\mathbf{X} \approx \mathbf{B}\mathbf{P}^T$. To explore the complementary information of multi-view data, we adopt multi-view NMF :

$$\min_{\mathbf{B}^{(v)}, \mathbf{P}^{(v)}} \sum_{v=1}^V \|\mathbf{X}^{(v)} - \mathbf{B}^{(v)}(\mathbf{P}^{(v)})^T\|_F^2 \quad \text{s.t.} \quad \mathbf{B}^{(v)}, \mathbf{P}^{(v)} \geq 0, \qquad (1)$$

where $\mathbf{B}^{(v)}$, $\mathbf{P}^{(v)}$ are basis matrix and label matrix of the v-th view, respectively.

Following the strategy which is generally adopted in multi-view learning, NMF-SSMM assumes that there exists a common consensus labeling $\mathbf{P}^{(*)}$ which is the desired labeling. It constrains the learned labels matrix $\mathbf{P}^{(v)}$ in each view towards the common consensus labeling $\mathbf{P}^{(*)}$ to preserve the consistency of multi-view data:

$$\min_{\mathbf{P}^{(*)}, \mathbf{P}^{(v)}} \sum_{v=1}^V \|\mathbf{P}^{(v)} - \mathbf{P}^{(*)}\|_F^2 \quad \text{s.t.} \quad \mathbf{P}^{(v)}, \mathbf{P}^{(*)} \geq 0. \qquad (2)$$

To predict the labels of the unlabeled data, NMF-SSMM minimizes the loss between the common consensus labeling $\mathbf{P}^{(*)}$ and the ground truth labels $\mathbf{Y}$ on the labeled data:

$$\min_{\mathbf{P}^{(*)}} \|(\mathbf{P}^{(*)} - \mathbf{Y}) \circ \mathbf{S}\|_F^2 \quad \text{s.t.} \quad \mathbf{P}^{(*)} \geq 0, \qquad (3)$$

where $\circ$ is the hadamard product of two matrices and $\mathbf{S}$ is the matrix that the values of the first L rows's entries are set to be one while the rest entries are set as zero.

Hence, the objective function of the NMF-SSMM is defined as follows:

$$\min_{\mathbf{P}^{(*)}, \mathbf{B}^{(v)}, \mathbf{P}^{(v)}, \alpha} \sum_{v=1}^{V} \alpha_v^r ||\mathbf{X}^{(v)} - \mathbf{B}^{(v)}(\mathbf{P}^{(v)})^T||_F^2 + \beta \sum_{v=1}^{V} ||\mathbf{P}^{(v)} - \mathbf{P}^{(*)}||_F^2$$
$$+ \gamma ||(\mathbf{P}^{(*)} - \mathbf{Y}) \circ \mathbf{S}||_F^2 \qquad (4)$$
$$\text{s.t.} \qquad \mathbf{B}^{(v)}, \mathbf{P}^{(v)}, \mathbf{P}^{(*)}, \alpha \geq 0, \sum_{v=1}^{V} \alpha_v = 1, ||\mathbf{B}_{\cdot,k}^{(v)}||_1 = 1,$$

where $v = 1, \ldots V$, $k = 1, \ldots K$, and both β and γ are tradeoff parameters. Meanwhile, as different views characterize distinct aspect of the data, the contributions of different views are different. Hence, we utilize nonnegative view-weight vector α to adaptively adjust the importance of different views. Moreover, we impose the ℓ_1 normalization with respect to the basis vectors $\mathbf{B}_{\cdot,k}^{(v)}$ to make the comparison between the label matrix $\mathbf{P}^{(v)}$ and the common consensus labeling matrix $\mathbf{P}^{(*)}$ more reasonable [13,14].

Similar to [13], we can simplify the computation by introducing auxiliary variables. Denote the auxiliary matrix as:

$$\mathbf{Q}^{(v)} = \text{Diag}(\sum_{i=1}^{D_v} \mathbf{B}_{i,1}^{(v)}, \sum_{i=1}^{D_v} \mathbf{B}_{i,2}^{(v)}, \ldots, \sum_{i=1}^{D_v} \mathbf{B}_{i,K}^{(v)}). \qquad (5)$$

Then the problem of minimizing Eq. 4 is equivalent to minimizing the following objective function:

$$\min_{\mathbf{P}^{(*)}, \mathbf{B}^{(v)}, \mathbf{P}^{(v)}, \alpha} \sum_{v=1}^{V} \alpha_v^r ||\mathbf{X}^{(v)} - \mathbf{B}^{(v)}(\mathbf{P}^{(v)})^T||_F^2 + \beta \sum_{v=1}^{V} ||\mathbf{P}^{(v)}\mathbf{Q}^{(v)} - \mathbf{P}^{(*)}||_F^2$$
$$+ \gamma ||(\mathbf{P}^{(*)} - \mathbf{Y}) \circ \mathbf{S}||_F^2 \qquad (6)$$
$$\text{s.t.} \qquad \mathbf{B}^{(v)}, \mathbf{P}^{(v)}, \mathbf{P}^{(*)}, \alpha \geq 0, \sum_{v=1}^{V} \alpha_v = 1, v = 1, \cdots, V.$$

2.3 Optimization Algorithm for NMF-SSMM

In this subsection, we present an iterative updating algorithm to solve the optimization problem of NMF-SSMM. There are four sub-problems to be solved and the following four steps are repeated until convergence is achieved.

Fixing $\mathbf{P}^{(v)}$, $\mathbf{P}^{(*)}$, and α, update $\mathbf{B}^{(v)}$: By introducing Lagrange multiplier matrix $\mathbf{\Phi} = [\phi_{ij}]$, the Lagrange function over $\mathbf{B}^{(v)}$ is defined as follows:

$$\alpha_v^r ||\mathbf{X}^{(v)} - \mathbf{B}^{(v)}(\mathbf{P}^{(v)})^T||_F^2 + \beta ||\mathbf{P}^{(v)}\mathbf{Q}^{(v)} - \mathbf{P}^{(*)}||_F^2 + \text{Tr}(\mathbf{\Phi}^T \mathbf{B}^{(v)}). \qquad (7)$$

Setting the derivative of Eq. 7 to be zero and according to the Karush-Kuhn-Tucker (KKT) condition, i.e., $\phi_{ik} B_{ik}^{(v)} = 0$, we can get the following updating rule:

$$B_{i,k}^{(v)} \leftarrow B_{i,k}^{(v)} \frac{(\alpha_v^r \mathbf{X}^{(v)} \mathbf{P}^{(v)})_{i,k} + \beta \sum_{j=1}^{N} P_{j,k}^{(v)} P_{j,k}^{(*)}}{(\alpha_v^r \mathbf{B}^{(v)} (\mathbf{P}^{(v)})^T \mathbf{P}^{(v)})_{i,k} + \beta \sum_{l=1}^{D_v} B_{l,k}^{(v)} \sum_{j=1}^{N} (P_{j,k}^{(v)})^2}. \tag{8}$$

Fixing $\mathbf{P}^{(*)}$, $\mathbf{B}^{(v)}$ and α, update $\mathbf{P}^{(v)}$: First, we normalize the column vectors of $\mathbf{B}^{(v)}$ with $\mathbf{Q}^{(v)}$ in Eq. 5: $\mathbf{B}^{(v)} \leftarrow \mathbf{B}^{(v)} (\mathbf{Q}^{(v)})^{-1}, \mathbf{P}^{(v)} \leftarrow \mathbf{P}^{(v)} \mathbf{Q}^{(v)}$. Similar to $\mathbf{B}^{(v)}$, we can get the updating rule as follows:

$$P_{j,k}^{(v)} \leftarrow P_{j,k}^{(v)} \frac{(\alpha_v^r (\mathbf{X}^{(v)})^T \mathbf{B}^{(v)})_{j,k} + \beta P_{j,k}^{(*)}}{(\alpha_v^r \mathbf{P}^{(v)} (\mathbf{B}^{(v)})^T \mathbf{B}^{(v)})_{j,k} + \beta P_{j,k}^{(v)}}. \tag{9}$$

Fixing $\mathbf{P}^{(v)}$, $\mathbf{B}^{(v)}$ and α, update $\mathbf{P}^{(*)}$: We need to minimize the objective function with respect to $\mathbf{P}^{(*)}$:

$$\beta \sum_{v=1}^{V} \|\mathbf{P}^{(v)} \mathbf{Q}^{(v)} - \mathbf{P}^{(*)}\|_F^2 + \gamma \|(\mathbf{P}^{(*)} - \mathbf{Y}) \circ \mathbf{S}\|_F^2 \quad \text{s.t.} \quad \mathbf{P}^{(*)} \geq 0. \tag{10}$$

Taking the derivative of Eq. 10 to be zero, the updating rule of $\mathbf{P}^{(*)}$ is obtained:

$$P_{j,k}^{(*)} = \frac{\beta \sum_{v=1}^{V} (\mathbf{P}^{(v)} \mathbf{Q}^{(v)})_{j,k} + \gamma Y_{j,k} S_{j,k}}{\gamma S_{j,k} + \beta V} \geq 0. \tag{11}$$

Fixing $\mathbf{P}^{(v)}$, $\mathbf{P}^{(*)}$ and $\mathbf{B}^{(v)}$, update α: Similar to $\mathbf{B}^{(v)}$ and $\mathbf{P}^{(v)}$, we have the updating rule of α:

$$\alpha_v = \frac{\left(\frac{1}{\|\mathbf{X}^{(v)} - \mathbf{B}^{(v)} (\mathbf{P}^{(v)})^T\|_F^2}\right)^{1/r-1}}{\sum_{v=1}^{V} \left(\frac{1}{\|\mathbf{X}^{(v)} - \mathbf{B}^{(v)} (\mathbf{P}^{(v)})^T\|_F^2}\right)^{1/r-1}}. \tag{12}$$

2.4   Complexity and Convergence Analysis

Generally, we have $V \ll N$, $V \ll D$, and $V \ll K$ in practice. For simplicity, we suppose the dimension of each view is D. For these sub-problems, the complexities are $O(NDK)$, $O(NDK)$, $O(NK^2)$ and $O(N^2D + NDK)$ to update $\mathbf{B}^{(v)}$, $\mathbf{P}^{(v)}$, $\mathbf{P}^{(*)}$ and α, respectively. Thus the overall cost of our method is $O(T(N^2D + NK^2 + NDK))$ where T is the number of iterations. Since there are closed-form (optimal) solution when solving each step, our algorithm is guaranteed to convergence to a stationary point.

3   Experiment

In this section, we evaluate the proposed NMF-SSMM on three real-world benchmark multi-label datasets: Corel5K [15], PASCAL VOC' 07 [16] and Esp Game [17]. The Corel5K dataset consists of 4,999 images (4,500 training, 499 test) in 260 categories. The PASCAL VOC' 07 dataset contains 9,963 images (5,011 training, 4,952 test) with 20 categories. There are around 20,000 images (18,689 training, 2,081 test) from 268 categories in the Esp Game dataset. For all the three datasets, we choose one globe feature (Gist) and two local feature (Dense-Hue, DenseSift). Here, we regard each kind of feature as a single view. The dimension of DenseHue, GIST, and DenseSift are 100, 512, and 1,000, respectively. All the datasets and features used are from Lear website[1]. For all methods, we randomly select 20% data from training data as labeled data while use the whole test data as unlabeled data. We repeat each experiment 20 times to avoid randomness. The average results with standard deviation are reported. Five evaluation criteria (Hamming loss, One-error, Coverage, Ranking loss and Average precision (Ave-Pre)) widely used in multi-label classification are employed in this paper [7].

We compare our method with closely related works: **(1)** six single-view multi-label methods: BR [2], LP [3], RAndom k-labELsets (RAkEL) [4], Ensemble of Pruned Sets (EPS) [5], the multi-label version of AdaBoost based on Hamming loss (AdaBoost.MH) [6] and multi-label k-nearest neighbors (ML-kNN) [7]; **(2)** one semi-supervised multi-view multi-label classification method: MV3MR [9]. For single-view methods, we conduct experiments on each view and report their performance on the best single view for the sake of fairness. In our method, we tune β and γ from the set $\{10^{-5}, 10^{-4}, \cdots, 10^4, 10^5\}$, and r is tuned from the set $\{2, 4, 6, 8, 10\}$. We report the best result.

Table 1. Results (mean ± standard deviation) of different algorithms on *Corel5K*. The bolded numbers indicate the best performance among all comparisons.

Method	Hamming loss ↓	One-error ↓	Coverage ↓	Ranking loss ↓	Ave-Pre ↑
BR	.016 ± .001	.722 ± .006	.606 ± .015	.284 ± .004	.228 ± .010
LP	.024 ± .000	.974 ± .003	.905 ± .001	.697 ± .003	.040 ± .002
EPS	.014 ± .001	.782 ± .023	.729 ± .033	.428 ± .029	.185 ± .017
ML-kNN	**.013 ± .000**	.674 ± .004	.392 ± .005	.175 ± .002	.285 ± .004
AdaBoost.MH	.014 ± .000	.768 ± .000	.852 ± .000	.551 ± .000	.144 ± .002
RAkEL	.017 ± .001	.755 ± .024	.741 ± .008	.415 ± .002	.208 ± .007
MV3MR	.014 ± .000	.685 ± .009	.351 ± .010	**.148 ± .003**	.291 ± .001
Ours	.014 ± .000	**.642 ± .004**	**.338 ± .031**	.151 ± .017	**.315 ± .004**

---

[1] http://lear.inrialpes.fr/people/guillaumin/data.php.

Table 2. Results (mean ± standard deviation) of different algorithms on *PASCAL*. The bolded numbers indicate the best performance among all comparisons.

Method	Hamming loss ↓	One-error ↓	Coverage ↓	Ranking loss ↓	Ave-Pre ↑
BR	.104 ± .000	.736 ± .019	.464 ± .000	.425 ± .015	.361 ± .008
LP	.112 ± .000	.798 ± .004	.469 ± .001	.424 ± .001	.291 ± .002
EPS	**.071 ± .000**	.610 ± .003	.354 ± .003	.296 ± .002	.443 ± .004
ML-kNN	**.071 ± .000**	.600 ± .003	.338 ± .000	.279 ± .001	.444 ± .002
AdaBoost.MH	**.071 ± .000**	.595 ± .000	.419 ± .013	.353 ± .010	.414 ± .002
RAkEL	.081 ± .000	.617 ± .002	.334 ± .003	.277 ± .003	.460 ± .003
MV3MR	**.071 ± .000**	.595 ± .000	.305 ± .021	.239 ± .017	.456 ± .006
Ours	**.071 ± .000**	**.592 ± .001**	**.288 ± .002**	**.234 ± .004**	**.465 ± .002**

Table 3. Results (mean ± standard deviation) of different algorithms on *Esp Game*. The bolded numbers indicate the best performance among all comparisons.

Method	Hamming loss ↓	One-error ↓	Coverage ↓	Ranking loss ↓	Ave-Pre ↑
BR	.019 ± .000	.677 ± .002	.623 ± .007	.270 ± .000	.209 ± .005
LP	.031 ± .000	.924 ± .002	.791 ± .001	.488 ± .001	.057 ± .000
EPS	.018 ± .000	.608 ± .018	.721 ± .000	.382 ± .001	.190 ± .003
ML-kNN	**.017 ± .000**	.647 ± .018	.489 ± .000	.205 ± .001	.239 ± .004
AdaBoost.MH	**.017 ± .000**	.757 ± .000	.766 ± .000	.449 ± .000	.118 ± .000
RAkEL	.018 ± .000	.634 ± .009	.733 ± .001	.393 ± .002	.187 ± .006
MV3MR	.018 ± .000	.702 ± .000	.423 ± .002	**.169 ± .000**	.245 ± .004
Ours	.018 ± .000	**.605 ± .021**	**.401 ± .001**	.180 ± .006	**.268 ± .003**

Tables 1, 2 and 3 show the classification performance of different algorithms on the three real-world benchmark datasets. Figure 3 shows the statistical information in terms of average precision for competitive methods. It is clear that our method almost consistently outperforms other methods. The superiority of our method may arise in the following aspects: (**1**) NMF-SSMM learns class labels by nonnegative matrix factorization correctly; (**2**) NMF-SSMM exploits the complementary information of multi-view data and guarantees the consistency by learning the common consensus labeling effectively; (**3**) NMF-SSMM utilizes the small number of labeled data and the large number of unlabeled data simultaneously and properly. Besides, we also experimentally study the speed of the convergence of NMF-SSMM. We can see that our algorithm converges within 40 iterations from Fig. 4, which demonstrates that the proposed optimization algorithm is effective and can converge fast.

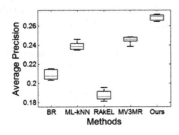

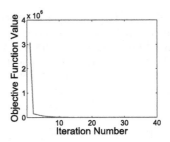

Fig. 3. Boxplot on Esp Game.   **Fig. 4.** Convergence curve on Esp Game.

4 Conclusion

In this paper, we have developed a novel semi-supervised multi-view multi-label classification method based on nonnegative matrix factorization (NMF-SSMM). The proposed method has two appealing properties. First, it leverages complementary information of multi-view data while guarantees the consistency among multiple views. Second, it handles the problem that there exist a small number of labeled data and a large number of unlabeled data simultaneously. An efficient alternating optimization algorithm is developed to solve the optimization problem of NMF-SSMM. Experiment results on the real-world datasets demonstrate the effectiveness of our method.

Acknowledgement. This work was supported in part by the National Natural Science Foundation of China under Grants 61602337, 61432011, U1435212 and 61502332.

References

1. Bi, W., Kwok, J.T.: Multilabel classification with label correlations and missing labels. In: Proceedings of 28th AAAI Conference on Artificial Intelligence, pp. 1680–1686 (2014)
2. Tsoumakas, G., Katakis, I.: Multi-label classification: an overview. Int. J. Data Warehouse. Min. **3**(3), 1–13 (2006)
3. Boutell, M.R., Luo, J., Shen, X., et al.: Learning multi-label scene classification. Pattern Recogn. **37**(9), 1757–1771 (2004)
4. Tsoumakas, G., Katakis, I., Vlahavas, I.: Random k-labelsets for multilabel classification. IEEE Trans. Knowl. Data Eng. **23**(7), 1079–1089 (2011)
5. Read, J., Pfahringer, B., Holmes, G.: Multi-label classification using ensembles of pruned sets. In: 8th IEEE International Conference on Data Mining, pp. 995–1000 (2008)
6. Schapire, R.E., Singer, Y.: BoosTexter: a boosting-based system for text categorization. Mach. Learn. **39**(2–3), 135–168 (2000)
7. Zhang, M.L., Zhou, Z.H.: ML-KNN: a lazy learning approach to multi-label learning. Pattern Recogn. **40**(7), 2038–2048 (2007)
8. Luo, Y., Liu, T., Tao, D., et al.: Multiview matrix completion for multilabel image classification. IEEE Trans. Image Process. **24**(8), 2355–2368 (2015)

9. Luo, Y., Tao, D., Xu, C., et al.: Vector-valued multi-view semi-supervsed learning for multi-label image classification. In: Proceedings of 27th AAAI Conference on Artificial Intelligence, pp. 647–653 (2013)
10. Lee, D.D., Seung, H.S.: Learning the parts of objects by non-negative matrix factorization. Nature **401**(6755), 788–791 (1999)
11. Guillamet, D., Vitria, J., Schiele, B.: Introducing a weighted non-negative matrix factorization for image classification. Pattern Recogn. Lett. **24**(14), 2447–2454 (2003)
12. Qian, M., Zhai, C.: Robust unsupervised feature selection. In: International Joint Conference on Artificial Intelligence. pp. 1621–1627. Citeseer (2013)
13. Liu, J., Wang, C., Gao, J., et al.: Multi-view clustering via joint nonnegative matrix factorization. In: Proceedings of 2013 SIAM International Conference on Data Mining, pp. 252–260. SIAM (2013)
14. Hofmann, T.: Probabilistic latent semantic indexing. In: Proceedings of 22nd Annual International ACM SIGIR Conference on Research and Development in Information Retrieval, pp. 50–57. ACM (1999)
15. Duygulu, P., Barnard, K., de Freitas, J.F.G., Forsyth, D.A.: Object recognition as machine translation: learning a lexicon for a fixed image vocabulary. In: Heyden, A., Sparr, G., Nielsen, M., Johansen, P. (eds.) ECCV 2002. LNCS, vol. 2353, pp. 97–112. Springer, Heidelberg (2002). doi:10.1007/3-540-47979-1_7
16. Everingham, M., Van Gool, L., Williams, C.K.I., et al.: The PASCAL Visual Object Classes Challenge 2007 (VOC 2007) Results (2007). http://www.pascalnetwork.org/challenges/VOC/voc2007/workshop/index.html
17. Von Ahn, L., Dabbish, L.: Labeling images with a computer game. In: Proceedings of SIGCHI Conference on Human Factors in Computing Systems, pp. 319–326. ACM (2004)

Masked Conditional Neural Networks for Audio Classification

Fady Medhat[✉], David Chesmore, and John Robinson

Department of Electronic Engineering, University of York, York, UK
{fady.medhat,david.chesmore,john.robinson}@york.ac.uk

Abstract. We present the ConditionaL Neural Network (CLNN) and the Masked ConditionaL Neural Network (MCLNN) designed for temporal signal recognition. The CLNN takes into consideration the temporal nature of the sound signal and the MCLNN extends upon the CLNN through a binary mask to preserve the spatial locality of the features and allows an automated exploration of the features combination analogous to hand-crafting the most relevant features for the recognition task. MCLNN have achieved competitive recognition accuracies on the GTZAN and the ISMIR2004 music datasets that surpass several state-of-the-art neural network based architectures and hand-crafted methods applied on both datasets.

Keywords: Restricted Boltzmann Machine (RBM) · Conditional Restricted Boltzmann Machine (CRBM) · Music Information Retrieval (MIR) · Conditional Neural Network (CLNN) · Masked Conditional Neural Network (MCLNN) · Deep Neural Network

1 Introduction

The success of the deep neural network architectures in image recognition [1] induced applying these models for audio recognition [2,3]. One of the main drivers for the adaptation is the need to eliminate the effort invested in hand-crafting the features required for classification. Several neural networks based architectures have been proposed, but they are usually adapted to sound from other domains such as image recognition. This may not exploit sound related properties. The Restricted Boltzmann Machine (RBM) [4] treats sound as static frames ignoring the inter-frame relation and the weight sharing in the vanilla Convolution Neural Networks (CNN) [5] does not preserve the spatial locality of the learned features, where *limited weight sharing* was proposed in [2] in an attempt to tackle this problem for sound recognition.

The Conditional Restricted Boltzmann Machine (CRBM) [6] in Fig. 1 extends the RBM [7] to the temporal dimension. This is applied by including conditional links from the previous frames $(\hat{v}_{-1}, \hat{v}_{-2}, \ldots, \hat{v}_{-n})$ to both the hidden nodes $\hat{h}$ and the current visible nodes $\hat{v}_0$ using the links $(\hat{B}_{-1}, \hat{B}_{-2}, \ldots, \hat{B}_{-n})$ and the autoregressive links $(\hat{A}_{-1}, \hat{A}_{-2}, \ldots, \hat{A}_{-n})$, respectively as depicted in Fig. 1. The

© Springer International Publishing AG 2017
A. Lintas et al. (Eds.): ICANN 2017, Part II, LNCS 10614, pp. 349–358, 2017.
https://doi.org/10.1007/978-3-319-68612-7_40

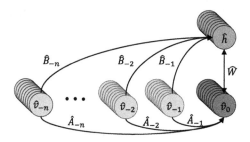

Fig. 1. Conditional Restricted Boltzmann Machine

Interpolating CRBM (ICRBM) [8] achieved a higher accuracy compared to the CRBM for speech phoneme recognition by extending the CRBM to consider both the previous and future frames.

The CRBM behavior (and similarly this work) overlaps with that of a Recurrent Neural Network (RNN) such as the Long Short-Term Memory (LSTM) [9], an architecture designed for sequence labelling. The output of an RNN at a certain temporal instance depends on the current input and the hidden state of the network's internal memory from the previous input. Compared to an LSTM, a CRBM does not require an internal state, since the influence of the previous temporal input states is concurrently considered with the current input. Additionally, increasing the order n does not have the consequence of the vanishing or exploding gradient related to the Back-Propagation Through Time (BPTT) as in recurrent neural networks that LSTM was introduced to solve, since the back-propagation in a CRBM depends on the number of layers as in normal feed-forward neural networks.

Inspired by the human visual system, the Convolutional Neural Network (CNN) depends on two main operations namely the convolution and pooling. In the convolutional operation, the input (usually a 2-dimensional representation) is scanned (convolved) by a small-sized weight matrix, referred to as a filter. Several small sized filters, e.g. 5×5, scan the input to generate a number of feature maps equal to the number of filters scanning the input. A pooling operation generates lower resolution feature maps, through either a mean or a max pooling operation. CNN depends on weight sharing that allows applying it to images of large sizes without having a dedicated weight for each pixel, since similar patterns may appear at different locations within an image. This is not optimally suitable for time-frequency representations, which prompted attempts to tailor the CNN filters for sound [2,10,11].

2   Conditional Neural Networks

In this work, we introduce the ConditionaL Neural Network (CLNN). The CLNN adaptes from the Conditional RBM the directed links between the previous visible and the hidden nodes and extends to future frames as in the ICRBM.

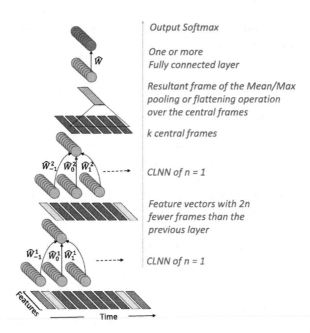

Output Softmax

One or more
Fully connected layer

Resultant frame of the Mean/Max
pooling or flattening operation
over the central frames

k central frames

CLNN of n = 1

Feature vectors with 2n
fewer frames than the
previous layer

CLNN of n = 1

Fig. 2. Two CLNN layers with $n = 1$.

Additionally, the CLNN adapts a global pooling operation [12], which behaves as an aggregation operation found to enhance the classification accuracy in [13]. The CLNN allows the sequential relation across the temporal frames of a multi-dimensional signal to be considered collectively by processing a window of frames. The CLNN has a hidden layer in the form of a vector having e neurons, and it accepts an input of size $[d, l]$, where l is the feature vector length and $d = 2n + 1$ (d is the number of frames in a window, n is the order for the number of frames in each temporal direction and 1 is for the window's middle frame). Figure 2 shows two CLNN layers each having an order $n = 1$, where n is a tunable hyper-parameter to control the window's width. Accordingly, each CLNN layer in the figure has a 3-dimensional weight tensor composed of one central matrix $\hat{W}_0^m$ and two off-center weight matrices, $\hat{W}_{-1}^m$ and $\hat{W}_1^m$ (m is the layer id). During the scanning of the signal across the temporal dimension, a frame in the window at index u is processed with its corresponding weight matrix $\hat{W}_u^m$ of the same index. The size of each $\hat{W}_u^m$ is equal to the feature vector length × hidden layer width. The number of weight matrices is $2n + 1$ (the 1 is for the central frame), which matches the number of frames in the window. The output of a single CLNN step over a window of frames is a single representative vector.

Several CLNN layers can be stacked on top of each other to form a deep architecture as shown in Fig. 2. The figure also depicts a number of k extra frames remaining after the processing applied through the two CLNN layers. These k extra frames allow incorporating an aggregation operation within the network by pooling the temporal dimension or they can be flattened to form a single vector before feeding them to a fully connected network. The CLNN is trained over segments following (1)

$$q = (2n)m + k \qquad , n, \, m \, and \, k \geq 1 \tag{1}$$

where q is the segment size, n is the order, m is the number of layers and k is for the extra frames. The input at each CLNN layer has $2n$ fewer frames than the previous layer. For example, for $n = 4$, $m = 3$ and $k = 5$, the input is of size 29 frames. The output of the first layer is $29 - 2 \times 4 = 21$ frames. Similarly, the output of the second and third layers is 13 and 5 frames, respectively. The 5 remaining frames of third layer are the extra frames to be pooled or flattened. The activation at a hidden node of a CLNN can be formulated as in (2)

$$y_{j,\,t} = f \left(b_j + \sum_{u=-n}^{n} \sum_{i=1}^{l} x_{i,\,u+t} \; W_{i,\,j,\,u} \right) \tag{2}$$

where $y_{j,\,t}$, the activation at node j of a hidden layer, for frame t in a segment of size q, which is also the window's middle frame at $u = 0$, is given by the value of the activation function f when applied on the summation of the bias b_j of node j and the multiplication of $W_{i,\,j,\,u}$ and $x_{i,\,u+t}$. The input $x_{i,\,u+t}$ is the ith feature in a single feature vector of size l at index $u + t$ within a window and $W_{i,\,j,\,u}$ is the weight between the ith input of a feature vector and the jth hidden node. The u index (in $W_{i,\,j,\,u}$ and $x_{i,\,u+t}$) is for the temporal window of the interval of frames to be considered within $[-n + t, n + t]$. Reformulating (2) in a vector form is given in (3).

$$\hat{y}_t = f \left(\hat{b} + \sum_{u=-n}^{n} \hat{x}_{u+t} \cdot \hat{W}_u \right) \tag{3}$$

where $\hat{y}_t$ is activation vector observed at the hidden layer for the central frame conditioned on the input vectors in the interval $[\hat{x}_{-n+t}, \hat{x}_{n+t}]$ is given by the activation function f applied on the summation of the bias vector $\hat{b}$ and the summation of the multiplication between the vector $\hat{x}_{u+t}$ at index $u + t$ (t is for the window's middle frame at $u = 0$ and the index of the frame in the segment) and the corresponding weight matrix $\hat{W}_u$ at the same index, where u takes values in the range of the considered window from $-n$ up to n. The conditional distribution can be captured using a logistic function as in $p(\hat{y}_t | \hat{x}_{-n+t}, ..., \hat{x}_{-1+t}, \hat{x}_t, \hat{x}_{1+t}, ..., \hat{x}_{n+t}) = \sigma(...)$, where σ is the hidden layer sigmoid function or the output layer softmax.

3   Masked Conditional Neural Networks

The Mel-Scaled analysis applied in MFCC and Mel-Scaled spectrograms, both used extensively as intermediate signal representation by sound recognition systems, exploit the use of a filterbank (a group of signal processing filters).

Considering a sound signal represented in a spectrogram, the energy of a certain frequency bin may smear across nearby frequency bins. Aggregating the energy across neighbouring frequency bins is a possible representation to overcome the frequency shifts, which is tackled by filterbanks. More general mixtures across the bins could be hand-crafted to select the most prominent features for the signal under consideration.

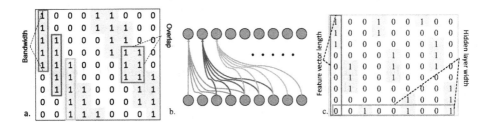

Fig. 3. Masking patterns. (a) *Bandwidth* = 5 and *Overlap* = 3, (b) the active links following the masking pattern in a. (c) *Bandwidth* = 3 and *Overlap* = −1

The Masked ConditionaL Neural Network (MCLNN), we introduce in this work embeds a filterbank-like behaviour and allows the exploration of a range of feature combinations concurrently instead of manually hand-crafting the optimum mixture of features. Figure 3 depicts the implementation of the filterbank-like behaviour through the binary mask enforced over the network's links that activate different regions of a feature vector while deactivating others following a band-like pattern. The mask is designed based on two tunable hyper-parameters: the bandwidth and the overlap. Figure 3a. shows a binary mask having a bandwidth of 5 (the five consecutive ones in a column) and an overlap of 3 (the overlapping ones between two successive columns). A hidden node will act as an expert in a localized region of the feature vector without considering the rest of it. This is depicted in Fig. 3b. The figure shows the active connections for each hidden node over a local region of the input feature vector matching the mask pattern in Fig. 3a. The overlap can be assigned negative values as shown in Fig. 3c. The figure shows a mask with a bandwidth of 3 and overlap of −1, depicted by the non-overlapping distance between the 1's of two successive columns. Additionally, the figure shows an additional role introduced by the mask through the presence of shifted versions of the binary pattern across the first set of three columns compared to the second and third sets. The role involves the automatic exploration of a range of feature combinations concurrently. The columns in the figure map to hidden nodes. Therefore, for a single feature vector, the input at the 1st node (corresponding to the 1st column) will consider the first 3 features in the feature vector, the 4th node will consider a different combination involving the first 2 features and the 7th node will consider even a different combination using the first feature only. This behaviour embeds the mix-and-match operation within the network, allowing the hidden nodes to learn different properties through the different combinations of feature vectors meanwhile preserving the spatial locality. The position of the binary values is specified through a linear index lx following (4)

$$lx = a + (g - 1)(l + (bw - ov)) \qquad (4)$$

where lx is given by bandwidth bw, the overlap ov and the feature vector length l. a takes the values in $[\,0,\ bw-1\,]$ and g is in the interval $[\,1, \lceil (l \times e)/(l + (bw - ov)) \rceil\,]$. The binary masking is enforced through an element-wise multiplication following (5).

$$\hat{Z}_u = \hat{W}_u \circ \hat{M} \qquad (5)$$

where $\hat{W}_u$ is the original weight matrix at a certain index u and $\hat{M}$ is the masking pattern applied. $\hat{Z}_u$ is the new masked weight matrix to replace the weight matrix in (3).

4   Experiments

We performed the MCLNN evaluation using the GTZAN [32] and the ISMIR2004 datasets widely used in the literature for benchmarking several MIR tasks including genre classification. The GTZAN consists of 1000 music files categorized across 10 music genres (blues, classical, country, disco, hip-hop, jazz, metal, pop, reggae and rock). The ISMIR2004 dataset comprise training and testing splits of 729 files each. The splits have 6 unbalanced categories of music genres (classical, electronic, jazz-blues, metal-punk, rock-pop and world) of full length recordings. All files were resampled at 22050 Hz and chunks of 30 s were extracted. Logarithmic Mel-Scaled 256 frequency bins spectrogram transformation was applied using an FFT window of 2048 ($\approx$100 ms) and an overlap of 50%. The feature-wise z-score parameters of the training set was applied to both the validation and test sets. Segments of frames following (1) were extracted.

The network was trained to minimize the categorical cross entropy between the segment's predicted label and the target one. The final decision of the clip's genre is decided based on a majority voting across the frames in the clip. The experiments for both datasets were carried out using a 10-fold cross-validation that is repeated for 10 times. An additional experiment was applied using the ISMIR2004 dataset original split (729 training, 729 testing) that was also repeated for 10 times. We adapted a two layered MCLNN, as listed in Table 3, followed by a single dimensional global mean pooling [12] layer to pool across $k = 10$ extra frames and finally a 50 node fully connected layer before the softmax output layer. Parametric Rectified Linear Units (PReLU) [28] were used for all the model's neurons. We applied the same model to both datasets to gauge the generalization of the MCLNN to datasets of different distributions. Tables 1 and 2 list the accuracy achieved by the MCLNN among other methods widely cited in the literature for the genre classification task on the GTZAN and the ISMIR2004 datasets. MCLNN surpasses several state-of-the-art methods that are dependent on hand-crafted features or neural networks, achieving

Table 1. Accuracies on the GTZAN

Classifier and features	Acc. %
CS + Multiple feat. sets [14][2]	92.7
SRC + LPNTF + Cortical features [15][2]	92.4
RBF-SVM + Scattering Trans. [16][2]	91.4
MCLNN + Mel−Spec. (this work)[2]	**85.1**
RBF-SVM + Spec.−DBN [4][4]	84.3
MCLNN + Mel−Spec. (this work)[3]	**84.1**
Linear SVM + PSD on Octaves [17][3]	83.4
Random Forest + Spec.−DBN [18][5]	83.0
AdaBoost + Several features [13][1]	83.0
RBF SVM + Spectral Covar. [19][2]	81.0
Linear SVM + PSD on frames [17][3]	79.4
SVM + DWCH [20][2]	78.5

Table 2. Accuracies on the ISMIR2004

Classifier and features	Acc. %
SRC + NTF + Cortical features [15][9]	94.4
KNN + Rhythm&timbre [21][2]	90.0
SVM + Block-Level features [22][8]	88.3
MCLNN + Mel−Spec. (this work)[2]	**86.0**
MCLNN + Mel−Spec. (this work)[3]	**84.8**
MCLNN + Mel−Spec. (this work)[9]	**84.8**
GMM + NMF [23][1]	83.5
MCLNN + Mel−Spec. (this work)[6]	**83.1**
SVM + Symbolic features [24][2]	81.4
NN + Spectral Similarity FP [25][7]	81.0
SVM + High-Order SVD [26][2]	81.0
SVM + Rhythm and SSD [27][6]	79.7

[1] 5-fold cross-validation   [4] 50% training, 20% validation and 30% testing   [7] leave-one-out cross-validation
[2] 10-fold cross-validation   [5] 4×50% training, 25% validation and 25% testing   [8] Not referenced
[3] 10× 10-fold cross-validation   [6] 10×(Train 729 file , test 729 file)   [9] Train 729 files, test 729 files

Table 3. MCLNN parameters

Layer	Hidden nodes	MCLNN order	Mask bandwidth	Mask overlap
1	220	4	40	−10
2	200	4	10	3

Table 4. GTZAN random and filtered

Model	Random acc. %	Filtered acc. %
MCLNN (this work)	84.4	**65.8**
DNN [25]	81.2	42.0

an accuracy of 85.1% and 86% over a 10-fold cross-validation for the GTZAN and ISMIR2004, respectively. We repeated the 10-fold cross-validation 10 times to validate the accuracy stability of the MCLNN, where the MCLNN achieved 84.1% and 84.83% over the 100 training runs for each of the GTZAN and the ISMIR2004, respectively.

To further evaluate the MCLNN performance, we adapted the publicly available splits released by Kereliuk et al. [29]. In their work, they released two versions of splits for the GTZAN files: a randomly stratified split (50% training, 25% validation and 25% testing) and a fault filtered version, where they cleared out all the mistakes in the GTZAN as reported by Sturm [30], e.g. repetitions, distortion, etc. As listed in Table 4, MCLNN achieved 84.4% and 65.8% compared to Kereliuk's attempt that achieved 81.2% and 42% for the random and fault-filtered, respectively, in their attempt to reproduce the work by Hamel and Eck [4]. The experiments show that MCLNN performs better than several neural networks based architectures and comparable to some other works dependent on hand-crafted features. MCLNN achieved these accuracies irrespective of the rhythmic and perceptual properties [31] that were used by methods that reported higher accuracies than the MCLNN. Finally, we wanted to tackle the problem of the data size used in training, referring to the works in [4,13,17,19,29], an FFT window of 50 ms was used. On the other hand, the MCLNN achieved the mentioned accuracies using a 100 ms window, which decreases the number of feature vectors to be used in classification by 50% and consequently the training complexity allowing the MCLNN to scale for larger datasets.

5   Conclusions and Future Work

We have introduced the ConditionaL Neural Network (CLNN) and its extension the Masked ConditionaL Neural Network (MCLNN). The CLNN is designed to exploit the properties of the multi-dimensional temporal signals by considering the sequential relationship across the temporal frames. The mask in the MCLNN enforces a systematic sparseness that follows a frequency band-like pattern. Additionally, it plays the role of automating the exploration of a range of feature combinations concurrently analogous to the exhaustive manual search for the hand-crafted feature combinations. We have applied the MCLNN to the problem of genre classification. Through an extensive set of experiments without any especial rhythmic or timbral analysis, the MCLNN have sustained accuracies that surpassed neural based and several hand-crafted feature extraction methods referenced previously on both the GTZAN and the ISMIR2004 datasets, achieving 85.1% and 86%, respectively. Meanwhile, the MCLNN still preserves the generalization that allows it to be adapted for any temporal signal. Future work will involve optimizing the mask patterns, considering different combinations of the order across the layers. We will also consider applying the MCLNN to other multi-channel temporal signals.

Acknowledgments. This work is funded by the European Union's Seventh Framework Programme for research, technological development and demonstration under grant agreement no. 608014 (CAPACITIE).

References

1. Krizhevsky, A., Sutskever, I., Hinton, G.E.: ImageNet classification with deep convolutional neural networks. In: Neural Information Processing Systems, NIPS (2012)
2. Abdel-Hamid, O., Mohamed, A.-R., Jiang, H., Deng, L., Penn, G., Yu, D.: Convolutional neural networks for speech recognition. IEEE/ACM Trans. Audio Speech Lang. Process. **22**(10), 1533–1545 (2014)
3. Schlter, J.: Unsupervised audio feature extraction for music similarity estimation. Thesis (2011)
4. Hamel, P., Eck, D.: Learning features from music audio with deep belief networks. In: International Society for Music Information Retrieval Conference, ISMIR (2010)
5. LeCun, Y., Bottou, L., Bengio, Y., Haffner, P.: Gradient-based learning applied to document recognition. Proc. IEEE **86**(11), 2278–2324 (1998)
6. Taylor, G.W., Hinton, G.E., Roweis, S.: Modeling human motion using binary latent variables. In: Advances in Neural Information Processing Systems, NIPS, pp. 1345–1352 (2006)
7. Smolensky, P.: Information processing in dynamical systems: foundations of harmony theory, pp. 194–281 (1986)

8. Mohamed, A.-R., Hinton, G.: Phone recognition using restricted Boltzmann machines. In: IEEE International Conference on Acoustics Speech and Signal Processing, ICASSP (2010)

9. Hochreiter, S., Schmidhuber, J.: Long short-term memory. Neural Comput. **9**(8), 1735–80 (1997)

10. Pons, J., Lidy, T., Serra, X.: Experimenting with musically motivated convolutional neural networks. In: International Workshop on Content-Based Multimedia Indexing, CBMI (2016)

11. Piczak, K.J.: Environmental sound classification with convolutional neural networks. In: IEEE International Workshop on Machine Learning for Signal Processing (MLSP) (2015)

12. Lin, M., Chen, Q., Yan, S.: Network in network. In: International Conference on Learning Representations, ICLR (2014)

13. Bergstra, J., Casagrande, N., Erhan, D., Eck, D., Kgl, B.: Aggregate features and AdaBoost for music classification. Mach. Learn. **65**(2–3), 473–484 (2006)

14. Chang, K.K., Jang, J.-S.R., Iliopoulos, C.S.: Music genre classification via compressive sampling. In: International Society for Music Information Retrieval, ISMIR (2010)

15. Panagakis, Y., Kotropoulos, C., Arce, G.R.: Music genre classification using locality preserving non-negative tensor factorization and sparse representations. In: International Society for Music Information Retrieval Conference, ISMIR (2009)

16. Anden, J., Mallat, S.: Deep scattering spectrum. IEEE Trans. Sig. Process. **62**(16), 4114–4128 (2014)

17. Henaff, M., Jarrett, K., Kavukcuoglu, K., LeCun, Y.: Unsupervised learning of sparse features for scalable audio classification. In: International Society for Music Information Retrieval, ISMIR (2011)

18. Sigtia, S., Dixon, S.: Improved music feature learning with deep neural networks. In: International Conference on Acoustics, Speech, and Signal Processing, ICASSP (2014)

19. Bergstra, J., Mandel, M., Eck, D.: Scalable genre and tag prediction with spectral covariance. In: International Society for Music Information Retrieval, ISMIR (2010)

20. Li, T., Ogihara, M., Li, Q.: A comparative study on content-based music genre classification. In: ACM SIGIR Conference on Research and Development in Information Retrieval, SIGIR (2003)

21. Pohle, T., Schnitzer, D., Schedl, M., Knees, P., Widmer, G.: On rhythm and general music similarity. In: International Society for Music Information Retrieval, ISMIR (2009)

22. Seyerlehner, K., Schedl, M., Pohle, T., Knees, P.: Using block-level features for genre classification, tag classification and music similarity estimation. In: Music Information Retrieval eXchange, MIREX (2010)

23. Holzapfel, A., Stylianou, Y.: Musical genre classification using nonnegative matrix factorization-based features. IEEE Trans. Audio Speech Lang. Process. **16**(2), 424–434 (2008)

24. Lidy, T., Rauber, A., Pertusa, A., Inesta, J.M.: Improving genre classification by combination of audio and symbolic descriptors using a transcription system. In: International Conference on Music Information Retrieval (2007)

25. Pampalk, E., Flexer, A., Widmer, G.: Improvements of audio-based music similarity and genre classification. In: International Conference on Music Information Retrieval, ISMIR (2005)

26. Panagakis, I., Benetos, E., Kotropoulos, C.: Music genre classification: a multilinear approach. In: International Society for Music Information Retrieval, ISMIR (2008)

27. Lidy, T., Rauber, A.: Evaluation of feature extractors and psycho-acoustic transformations for music genre classification. In: International Conference on Music Information Retrieval, ISMIR (2005)
28. He, K., Zhang, X., Ren, S., Sun, J.: Delving deep into rectifiers: surpassing human-level performance on ImageNet classification. In: IEEE International Conference on Computer Vision, ICCV (2015)
29. Kereliuk, C., Sturm, B.L., Larsen, J.: Deep learning and music adversaries. IEEE Trans. Multimedia **17**(11), 2059–2071 (2015)
30. Sturm, B.L.: The state of the art ten years after a state of the art: future research in music information retrieval. J. New Music Res. **43**(2), 147–172 (2014)
31. Bello, J.P.: Machine Listening of Music, pp. 159–184. Springer, New York (2014)
32. Tzanetakis, G., Cook, P.: Musical genre classification of audio signals. IEEE Trans. Speech Audio Process. **10**(5) (2002)

A Feature Selection Approach Based on Information Theory for Classification Tasks

Jhoseph Jesus[1], Anne Canuto[1], and Daniel Araújo[2(✉)]

[1] Department of Informatics and Applied Math, Federal University of Rio Grande do Norte, Campus Universitário, Lagoa Nova, Natal, RN, Brazil
jhoseph.kelvin@gmail.com, anne@dimap.ufrn.br
[2] Digital Metropolis Institute, Federal University of Rio Grande do Norte, Campus Universitário, Lagoa Nova, Natal, RN, Brazil
daniel@imd.ufrn.br

Abstract. This paper proposes the use of a Information Theory measure in a dynamic feature selection approach. We tested such approach including elements of Information Theory in the process, such as Mutual Information, and compared with classical methods like PCA and LDA as well as Mutual Information based algorithms. Results showed that the proposed method achieved better performance in most cases when compared with the other methods. Based on this, we could conclude that the proposed approach is very promising since it achieved better performance than well-established dimensionality reduction methods.

1 Introduction

In recent days, the amount of data is exponentially growing due to several reasons, like popularization of smart devices, social media, sensors (like cameras, for instance), etc. With the advance of Internet of Things and Smart Cities initiatives, the number of devices and applications that constantly capture and generate data is enormous. Most of this data is created, used for a specific and punctual purpose, and stored without further analysis. With such amount of data, it is very likely that there is far more underlying information in this data that needs exploration.

Due to its complexity, real world data analysis is usually achieved by Machine Learning algorithms [13] which extract useful information from the huge amount of data. In order to do so, we can use feature selection [4] algorithms, which try to filter the data in order to choose the best features that represents the data.

This kind of approach is important in two aspects [4]: it can drastically reduce the amount of data providing a faster processing; and it eliminates non useful data that can disturb the whole information extraction process. In this context, Information-theoretic descriptors, initially used to measure the efficiency of data transmission, are being used to perform feature selection in complex datasets. For instance, [2] proposed several Mutual Information based techniques to select the most relevant features of a dataset. Methods based on Mutual Information have the advantage over traditional linear methods because it can actually measure

© Springer International Publishing AG 2017
A. Lintas et al. (Eds.): ICANN 2017, Part II, LNCS 10614, pp. 359–367, 2017.
https://doi.org/10.1007/978-3-319-68612-7_41

the dependency of two variables, including non-linear correlation, which are very common in real world situations. On the other hand, some papers are successfully using clustering algorithms as a previous step to classification tasks, like [16].

Based on that, this paper proposes an exploratory study on a dynamic feature selection approach in the context of classification tasks. This method is an extension of the approach proposed in [14], since the original paper used only Spearman correlation, we included some Information-theoretical descriptors as similarity measures in order to increase robustness. The proposed selection approach uses clustering to select the best attributes for an instance rather than to the entire dataset.

2   Related Works

The main purpose of feature selection algorithms is to find a subset of the feature set that optimizes a given criteria. Usually this is made using a heuristic, since testing all possible subsets of features is not feasible for most situations. Based on that, a great variety of feature selection algorithms were proposed in the past years, both for pattern classification and clustering tasks. A review of the most used algorithms can be found in [4].

In the clustering context, many other studies were conducted to analyze how feature selection algorithms can be used to improve clustering results. For example, [8] used feature selection algorithms with k-means and Expectation Maximization to improve its accuracy or the running time of these algorithms.

From the studies mentioned before, we can see that most papers are mainly concerned with the application of feature selection algorithms as a pre-processing step for pattern classification or clustering algorithms. To the best of our knowledge, little has been done to explore the use of clustering algorithm in the feature selection process itself. Examples of this kind of approach can be found in [16] and [14] where clustering algorithms are used to determine the most relevant features of the dataset. With the exception of [14], all other methods perform a static selection process based exclusively on the feature space instead of considering the particularity of the instances in the dataset. In this paper, we explore the approach proposed in [14] introducing an information-theoretic measure to extract the underlying information present in the data, since the use of this kind of measure has achieved good results in previous works like [1,5].

3   The Feature Selection Approach

The most common feature selection algorithms consider the entire dataset to choose a subset of the attributes to represent the feature space. This can be very suitable for a set of instances but not for others, which should be better represented by another subset of features. So, in order to overcome this global drawback of usual feature selection algorithm, this paper uses a strategy to select features considering groups of individual instances of the dataset.

In fact, this paper brings an extension of the approach proposed in [14], where we use the benefits of information-theoretic measures to extract the underlying information of the data and select the best features considering some characteristics present in groups of instances. This means that, individual instances behaviors are considered when selecting the features. Fig. 1 shows the overall approach.

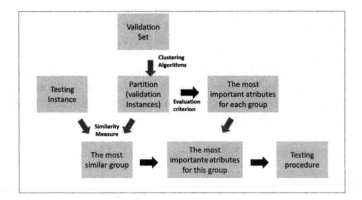

Fig. 1. The general structure of the feature selection approach [14].

The original paper used correlation to determine the best features for each cluster of instances, which is suitable for linear relations between data. When there is a non-linear relation in the data, correlation measures cannot deliver good quality values and lead the overall process to fail. In this paper, we decided to use measures from the Information Theory which, as mentioned before, can capture high order statistical information about the data. In this case, we used Mutual Information [2] as the similarity measure during the clustering and feature selection tasks. As we can see in Fig. 1, a clustering algorithm is applied to a validation set, which creates a partition $C = c1, \ldots, cj$ with similar instances divided into clusters. After that, for each cluster, all attributes have an importance value assigned to them based on a specific evaluation criterion. This is done considering the importance of the attribute to the cluster it belongs. We used Mutual Information to measure the importance of the attributes. The goal in this step is to capture the amount of information shared by each feature and the class label. Once we selected the most important attributes for each cluster, j classifiers are trained, one for each cluster. But instead of using all attributes, we only use the attributes selected to represent each cluster. To test the model, a new instance is provided and, in order to know which features are valid for that instance, it is compared with the clusters in the partition. Once this is done, this instance is assigned to the most similar cluster using the smallest euclidean distance between the instance and the centroids of each cluster and it is classified using the model defined by that cluster. All further details of this approach can be found in [14].

4   Material and Methods

This section brings a brief description of material and techniques used to evaluate the proposed approach. As part of the proposed method of dynamic feature selection, one important phase is the choice of the similarity measure to be used. Unlike [14] that used Spearman Correlation as the similarity measure, we used mutual information [2] as the similarity measure in this paper. This measure allows us to deal with problems that the correlation suffers in solve. Including problems of non-linear correlation and sparse-data in very large datasets, which are very common in real world scenarios. The Mutual Information (MI) descriptor calculates the amount of information shared by two random variables. In other words, it quantifies the amount of information obtained about one variable, through other variable. Let X and Y be random variables and p be a probability function, where we assume the normality of the data. Based on that, Mutual Information can be defined as:

$$I(X, Y) = \sum_{y \in Y} \sum_{x \in X} p(x, y) \log \left(\frac{p(x, y)}{p(x)p(y)} \right) \tag{1}$$

We selected the following algorithms to perform feature selection in our experiments: Conditional Infomax Feature Extraction (CIFE) [11], Mutual Information Feature Selection (MIFS) [2] and Maximum Relevance Minimum Redundancy (MRMR) [15]. We selected these algorithms to perform a comparison between our approach, when using mutual information as similarity measure, with other feature selection algorithms that use the same measure. It is important to notice that, during the experiments, all dimensionality reduction algorithms have performed a 90% reduction of attributes (or 10% selection) for all datasets.

In addition to feature selection algorithms based on mutual information, we also used two feature extraction algorithms widely used by machine learning community, PCA (unsupervised) [6] and LDA (supervised) [12], in order to compare their performance with our proposed approach.

In this empirical analysis, we used three different methods of classification, which are: search-based method (Decision Tree) [13], optimization-based method (SVM) [13] and distance-based method (k-NN) [13]. These classifiers were chosen because they are widely used in the Machine Learning community and each one has a distinct approach to find the best solution. Based on this, we tried to cover a wide range of heuristics of classification to avoid a possible bias to a specific approach. Additionally, with the purpose of performing the clustering task of the proposed approach, we chose to use the k-Means clustering algorithm [7].

In order to compare the effectiveness of the proposed approach, two statistical tests were applied: Friedman's Test [3] and post-hoc Wilcoxon Rank-Sum Test [3]. The second one was applied when the p-value of Friedman's test was lower than 0.05. Both tests were used with a confidence level of 95% ($\alpha = 0.05$).

In our experiments we used twelve datasets from different natures, these datasets were selected aiming to cover different ranges of number of samples, features and contexts. The datasets are distributed in distinct areas, such as: Bioinformatics, text data, face pictures, handwriting images and signal processing. They were collected in three different repositories: UCI Machine Learning [10], Arizona State University repository [9] and Bioinformatics Research Group of Seville repository [17]. The main characteristics of each dataset will be described in the ID, name(n, C, d) format, where n is the number of samples, C is the number of classes and d is the number of features (dimensionality). The used datasets are: B1, LSVT$(126, 2, 310)$; B2, Lung Cancer$(181, 2, 12533)$; B3, Breast Cancer$(569, 2, 30)$; B4, Connectionist Bench$(208, 2, 60)$; B5, Ionosphere$(351, 2, 32)$; B6, Lymphoma$(96, 9, 4026)$; B7, USPS$(9298, 10, 256)$; B8, PCMAC$(1943, 2, 3289)$; B9, Friedman$(1000, 2, 100)$; B10, Colon Cancer$(62, 2, 2000)$; B11, COIL-20 $(1440, 20, 1024)$; B12, Arrhythmia$(452, 16, 279)$;

All algorithms used in this paper were implemented using Matlab software. In this empirical analysis, with the purpose to achieve more robust results, a 10-fold cross-validation approach will be applied for all analyzed methods. One fold is defined to belong to the validation set, one fold to the testing set and eight folds to the training set. Once the dataset is divided, we use the validation fold to create the groups to be used in the k-means clustering algorithm, with the parameter k equals to the number of classes of the corresponding dataset in execution. After the clustering process, we train the classification method using all eight folds of the training set, according to the attributes selected by the dynamic feature selection measure. The remaining fold is used to evaluate the performance of the proposed approach. Finally, as the analyzed approach are non-deterministic methods, all algorithms are performed 10 times, making a total of 100 accuracy values that are averaged to provide the values used in this paper.

5   Results and Discussion

This experimental analysis is divided in two parts; the first one aims to compare the performance of the proposed method to some information theory-based feature selection methods. The other one compares the performance of the proposed method to two well-known feature extraction methods, as well as the original dataset, trying to assess the performance of the proposed method.

Keeping in mind that different datasets with different accuracy levels are being evaluated in this analysis, the direct use of these values can lead to a mistaken analysis of the obtained results. In order to address this issue, in this paper, the performance of the feature selection methods will be assessed taking into consideration the mean ranking of the obtained results. These rankings are based on their accuracy levels, always assigning 1 to the best value, followed by 2, 3 and/or 4 in ascending order according to its performance. This ranking is calculated for each configuration, taking all 3 classification algorithms used in this analysis. The average score for each method is then calculated and the final classification is made according to their average score for each dataset.

5.1 Analysis of Some MI-Based Methods

In this section, we aim to compare the performance of the proposed method (DFS-MI) to three information theory-based feature selection methods, which are: CIFE, MIFS and MRMR. Table 1 describes the average ranking values for all four analyzed methods for all datasets. In this table the shaded cells with bold numbers represent the best performance (lowest ranking), for each dataset.

Table 1. Results using MI-based methods

Approaches	Average Ranking - MI-based Methods				
	DFS-MI	CIFE	MIFS	MRMR	Friedman
Metrics	Mean±Std	Mean±Std	Mean±Std	Mean±Std	p-value
B1	**1.6±1.0**	2.5±0.8(<)	3.3±0.8(<)	2.3±0.9(<)	5.14E-69
B2	**2.0±1.3**	2.1±0.9(=)	3.2±0.9(<)	1.8±1.0(=)	1.00E-40
B3	1.9±1.3	2.9±0.8(<)	**1.8±0.7(>)**	3.1±0.7(<)	7.03E-63
B4	**1.7±1.2**	2.5±0.8(<)	3.4±0.7(<)	2.1±0.8(<)	1.96E-71
B5	**1.6±1.1**	2.5±0.8(<)	2.9±0.8(<)	2.7±1.0(<)	1.00E-49
B6	2.2±1.1	3.1±1.0(<)	2.9±0.7(<)	**1.5±0.7(>)**	8.35E-86
B7	4.0±0.0	2.3±0.5(>)	**1.0±0.0(>)**	2.6±0.5(>)	1.13E-218
B8	2.8±0.6	3.9±0.2(<)	**1.6±0.6(>)**	1.6±0.6(>)	4.08-180
B9	**1.5±1.0**	2.4±0.7(<)	3.5±0.7(<)	2.4±0.7(<)	2.3E-104
B10	2.4±1.2	2.8±1.1(<)	2.5±0.9(=)	**1.9±0.9(>)**	5.21E-24
B11	3.2±1.2	2.1±0.9(>)	**1.9±0.9(>)**	2.3±1.0(>)	2.34E-37
B12	2.5±0.9	2.2±0.6(>)	3.8±0.4(<)	**1.3±0.6(>)**	3.36E-144

From Table 1, we can observe that the proposed method (DFS-MI) achieved the best performance (lowest ranking values) in five datasets, while MIFS achieved the best performance in 4 datasets, MRMR in 3 datasets and CIFE has not achieved the best performance in any dataset. The last column of Table 1 presents the results of the statistical test, comparing all four feature selection methods (Friedman test). In order to compare the the proposed method to the MI-based methods, for each dataset there are three possible signals, $>$, $=$ or $<$ between brackets to define whether the corresponding method is better, similar or worse than DFS-MI, respectively, according to the post-hoc Wilcoxon test.

As can be detected in Table 1, the performance of all four feature selection methods are different, from a statistical point of view, in all 12 datasets. When comparing the proposed method in the post-hoc test, we can observe that, from a statistical point of view, the proposed method had better performance in 8 datasets, similar performance in one dataset and worse performance in only 3 datasets, when compared to CIFE. When compared to MIFS, the performance of the proposed method was higher in 7 datasets, similar in one dataset and worse in 4 datasets. Finally, when compared to MRMR, the performance of the proposed method was either similar or higher, from a statistical point of view, in 6 dataset, while it achieved worse performance in 6 datasets.

In summarizing, the results obtained in Table 1 are very promising since it shows a competitive performance of the proposed method, in which it had an overall better performance than CIFE and MIFS and similar performance to MRMR.

5.2   Comparative Analysis

In this section, we will describe an analysis comparing the performance of the proposed method to some well-known feature extraction methods (PCA and LDA) as well as the original dataset (no feature selection). Table 2 presents the average ranking for all four methods, for all datasets.

Table 2. Results using feature extraction methods and original dataset

Approaches	\multicolumn{5}{c}{Average Ranking - Comparative Analysis}				
Approaches	DFS-MI	PCA	LDA	Original	Friedman
Metrics	Mean±Std	Mean±Std	Mean±Std	Mean±Std	p-value
B1	1.8±0.8	3.4±0.6(<)	**1.3±0.4(>)**	3.1±0.6(<)	1.17E-160
B2	1.9±1.1	2.6±0.4(<)	**1.2±0.5(>)**	3.0±1.0(<)	7.64E-82
B3	**1.8±1.0**	3.2±0.8(<)	2.5±1.1(<)	2.3±1.0(<)	2.41E-51
B4	**1.7±0.9**	2.9±0.8(<)	3.0±0.9(<)	2.2±1.0(<)	5.88E-53
B5	**1.7±1.2**	3.6±0.6(<)	1.7±0.5(<)	2.7±0.6(<)	2.35E-114
B6	2.9±1.2	2.6±0.8(>)	**1.0±0.1(>)**	2.9±0.8(=)	3.47E-120
B7	4.0±0.0	2.1±0.6(>)	2.3±0.9(>)	**1.4±0.5(>)**	1.33E-167
B8	2.7±0.8	2.9±0.9(<)	**2.0±1.4(>)**	2.2±0.8(>)	1.89E-26
B9	**1.4±0.8**	3.6±0.5(<)	1.9±0.7(<)	2.9±0.8(<)	1.08E-136
B10	**2.1±1.1**	2.5±0.9(<)	2.7±1.1(<)	2.3±1.2(<)	8.78E-08
B11	3.1±1.0	**1.6±0.7(>)**	2.0±1.4(>)	2.0±1.1(>)	5.85E-48
B12	2.6±1.0	2.8±0.9(=)	2.7±1.2(<)	**1.7±0.8(>)**	9.37E-32

In analyzing Table 2, we can state that the proposed method surpasses the performance of some well-established feature selection methods, as well the use of no feature selection, since it obtained the best performance (shaded cells with bold numbers) in 5 datasets, out of 12. Then, we have LDA with the best performance in only 4 datasets, the original dataset with the best performance in 2 datasets and, finally, PCA with only 1 best performance.

From the last column of Table 2, it is possible to observe that the performance of all four analyzed methods are different, from a statistical point of view, in all 12 datasets. When comparing the proposed method in the post-hoc test, we can observe that, from a statistical point of view, the proposed method had better performance in 8 datasets, similar performance in one dataset and worse performance in only 3 datasets, when compared to PCA. When compared to LDA, the performance of the proposed method was higher in 6 datasets and worse in 6 datasets. Finally, when compared to the original dataset, the performance of the proposed method was either similar or higher, from a statistical point of view, in 8 datasets, while it achieved worse performance in 4 datasets.

Based on the results obtained in Table 2, we can state that the proposed methods showed a competitive performance, in which it had an overall better performance than PCA and the original dataset and similar performance to LDA.

6   Final Remarks

This paper presented and evaluated a dynamic feature selection method which can be applied to classification tasks. This proposed method (DFS-MI) is an extension of the one used in [14] which uses a clustering algorithm as the basis of the feature selection process. In order to assess the feasibility of the proposed method, an empirical analysis was conducted. In this analysis, we applied three different classification algorithms to receive the subset of attributes selected by the feature selection methods, using 12 datasets. We analyzed the performance of the proposed method, compared to three other Mutual Information (MI-based) feature selection algorithms (CIFE, MIFS and MRMR) as well as two existing feature extraction methods PCA and LDA along with the use of the original dataset (no feature selection).

Through this empirical analysis, we could observe that the DFS-MI method obtained competitive results, since it surpassed the performance of most of the feature selection methods. The results provided in this paper are very promising since the proposed method achieved better performance than well-established dimensionality reduction methods. Additionally, the use of the proposed method achieved better performance than using the original datasets, showing that the reduction of noisy and/or redundant attributes can have a positive effect in the performance of a classification task.

References

1. Araújo, D., Jesus, J., Neto, A.D., Martins, A.: A combination method for reducing dimensionality in large datasets. In: Villa, A.E.P., Masulli, P., Pons Rivero, A.J. (eds.) ICANN 2016. LNCS, vol. 9887, pp. 388–397. Springer, Cham (2016). doi:10.1007/978-3-319-44781-0_46
2. Battiti, R.: Using mutual information for selecting features in supervised neural net learning. Trans. Neural Netw. 5(4), 537–550 (1994)
3. Gibbons, J., Chakraborti, S.: Nonparametric Statistical Inference. Statistics, Textbooks and Monographs. Marcel Dekker Incorporated, New York (2003)
4. Guyon, I., Elisseeff, A.: An introduction to variable and feature selection. J. Mach. Learn. Res. 3, 1157–1182 (2003)
5. Jesus, J., Arajo, D., Canuto, A.: Fusion approaches of feature selection algorithms for classification problems. In: 2016 5th Brazilian Conference on Intelligent Systems (BRACIS), pp. 379–384, October 2016
6. Jolliffe, I.T.: Principal Component Analysis. Springer, New York (1986). doi:10.1007/978-1-4757-1904-8
7. Kanungo, T., Mount, D.M., Netanyahu, N.S., Piatko, C.D., Silverman, R., Wu, A.Y.: An efficient k-means clustering algorithm: analysis and implementation. IEEE Trans. Pattern Anal. Mach. Intell. 24(7), 881–892 (2002)
8. Law, M.H., Figueiredo, M.A., Jain, A.K.: Simultaneous feature selection and clustering using mixture models. IEEE Trans. Pattern Anal. Mach. Intell. 26, 1154–1166 (2004)
9. Li, J., Cheng, K., Wang, S., Morstatter, F., Robert, T., Tang, J., Liu, H.: Feature selection: a data perspective. arXiv:1601.07996 (2016)
10. Lichman, M.: UCI Machine Learning Repository (2013)
11. Lin, D., Tang, X.: Conditional infomax learning: an integrated framework for feature extraction and fusion. In: Leonardis, A., Bischof, H., Pinz, A. (eds.) ECCV 2006. LNCS, vol. 3951, pp. 68–82. Springer, Heidelberg (2006). doi:10.1007/11744023_6

12. McLachlan, G.: Discriminant Analysis and Statistical Pattern Recognition. Wiley Series in Probability and Statistics. Wiley, Hoboken (2004)
13. Mitchell, T.M.: Machine Learning, 1st edn. McGraw-Hill Inc., New York (1997)
14. Nunes, R.O., Dantas, C.A., Canuto, A.M.P., Xavier-Junior, J.C.: An unsupervised-based dynamic feature selection for classification tasks. In: 2016 International Joint Conference on Neural Networks (IJCNN), pp. 4213–4220, July 2016
15. Peng, H., Long, F., Ding, C.: Feature selection based on mutual information: criteria of max-dependency, max-relevance, and min-redundancy. IEEE Trans. Pattern Anal. Mach. Intell. **27**(8), 1226–1238 (2005)
16. Santhanam, T., Padmavathi, M.: Application of k-means and genetic algorithms for dimension reduction by integrating SVM for diabetes diagnosis. Procedia Comput. Sci. **47**(Complete), 76–83 (2015)
17. BioInformatics Group Seville: BIGS Bioinformatics Research Group of Seville Repository (2004)

Two-Level Neural Network for Multi-label Document Classification

Ladislav Lenc[1,2(✉)] and Pavel Král[1,2]

[1] Department of Computer Science and Engineering, Faculty of Applied Sciences,
University of West Bohemia, Plzeň, Czech Republic
{pkral,llenc}@kiv.zcu.cz
[2] NTIS - New Technologies for the Information Society, Faculty of Applied Sciences,
University of West Bohemia, Plzeň, Czech Republic

Abstract. This paper deals with multi-label document classification using neural networks. We propose a novel neural network which is composed of two sub-nets: the first one estimates the scores for all classes, while the second one determines the number of classes assigned to the document. The proposed approach is evaluated on Czech and English standard corpora. The experimental results show that the proposed method is competitive with state of the art on both languages.

Keywords: Convolutional neural networks · Czech · Deep neural networks · Document Classification · Multi-label

1 Introduction

This paper is focused on multi-label document classification using neural networks. This task can be seen as the problem to find a model M which assigns a document $d \in D$ a set of appropriate classes $c \in C$ as follows $M : d \to c$ where D is the set of all documents and C is the set of all possible document classes (labels).

In our previous work [7], we have used standard feed-forward networks and popular convolutional networks (CNNs) with thresholding to obtain the final classification result. We have shown the superior accuracy of these networks without any manually defined features against the state-of-the-art methods.

In this paper, we propose an alternative multi-label document classification approach which uses another neural classifier to identify the number of labels assigned to the document. An original neural network architecture which is composed of two sub-nets is thus proposed: the first one estimates the scores for all classes, while the second one is dedicated to determine the number of classes. To the best of our knowledge, this approach has never been used for multi-label document classification before.

The proposed approach is evaluated on Czech and English standard corpora. The Czech language has been chosen as a representative of highly inflectional

© Springer International Publishing AG 2017
A. Lintas et al. (Eds.): ICANN 2017, Part II, LNCS 10614, pp. 368–375, 2017.
https://doi.org/10.1007/978-3-319-68612-7_42

Slavic language with a free word order. These properties decrease the performance of usual methods and therefore, sophisticated methods are beneficial. English is used to compare the results of our method with state of the art.

The following section contains a short review of the usage of neural networks for document classification with a particular focus on multi-label classification approaches. Section 3 describes the proposed model. Section 4 deals with experiments realized on the ČTK and Reuters corpora and then analyzes and discusses the obtained results. In the last section, we conclude the experimental results and propose some future research directions.

2 Related Work

Nowadays, "deep" neural nets outperform majority of the state-of-the art natural language processing (NLP) methods on many tasks with only very simple features. These include for example POS tagging, chunking, named entity recognition and semantic role labelling.

Recurrent convolutional neural nets are used for text classification in [5]. The authors demonstrated that their approach outperforms the standard convolutional networks on four corpora in single-label document classification task.

On the other hand, traditional feed-forward neural net architectures are not used for multi-label document classification very often. These models were popular previously as shown for instance in [8]. They build a simple multi-layer perceptron with three layers (20 inputs, 6 neurons in hidden layer and 10 neurons in the output layer, i.e. number of classes) which gives F-measure about 78% on the standard Reuters dataset.

The feed-forward neural networks were used for multi-label document classification in [15]. The authors have modified standard backpropagation algorithm for multi-label learning which employs a novel error function. This approach is evaluated on functional genomics and text categorization.

Le and Mikolov propose in [6] so called *Paragraph Vector*, an unsupervised algorithm that addresses the issue of necessity of a fixed-legth document representation. This algorithm represents each document using a dense vector. This vector is trained to predict words in the document. The results show that this approach for creating text representations outperforms many other methods including bag-of-words models. The authors obtain new state-of-the-art results on several text classification and sentiment analysis tasks.

A recent study on multi-label text classification was presented by Nam et al. in [10]. The authors use cross-entropy algorithm instead of ranking loss for training and they also further employ recent advances in deep learning field, e.g. rectified linear units activation, AdaGrad learning with dropout [9,13]. The TF-IDF representation of documents is used as network input. The multi-label classification is done by thresholding of the output layer. The approach is evaluated on several multi-label datasets and reaches results comparable or better than the state-of-the-art.

Another method [4] based on neural networks leverages the co-occurrence of labels in the multi-label classification. Some neurons in the output layer capture the patterns of label co-occurrences, which improves the classification accuracy. The architecture is basically a convolutional network and utilizes word embeddings as inputs. The method is evaluated on the natural language query classification in a document retrieval system.

An alternative multi-label classification approach is proposed by Yang and Gopal in [14]. The conventional representations of texts and categories are transformed into meta-level features. These features are then utilized in a learning-to-rank algorithm. Experiments on six benchmark datasets show the abilities of this approach in comparison with other methods.

For additional information about multi-label document classification, please refer the survey [12].

3   Network Architecture

We use two types of neural networks that were proposed in [7] as the first sub-net. The first one is a convolutional neural network (CNN) while the second one is a standard feed-forward neural network (FNN). Therefore, using the feature vector F, both networks learn a function $S = f_1(F)$ which assigns a score S to each of possible labels. The values of the output layer were usually thresholded [10] using a fixed threshold. The labels with values higher than this threshold are then assigned to a document.

In this paper, we replace the thresholding method by another neural classifier and then we merge both nets together. Therefore, the output of the first network is used as an input of the second-level feed-forward network which is used to estimate the number of relevant labels l. Finally, the l labels with the highest scores are assigned to the classified document.

(1a) Convolutional Neural Network

The input (vector F) of the CNN is a sequence of word indexes from a dictionary. The network requires fixed-length inputs and the documents thus must be shortened or padded to a specified length N. The following layer is an embedding layer which maps the words to real-valued vectors of the size K. In the convolutional layer we employ N_C kernels of the size $k \times 1$. Rectified linear unit (ReLU) activation is used. The next layer performs the max-over-time pooling. The dropout [13] is then applied due to regularization. The output of this layer is fed to a fully-connected layer with ReLU activation function. The output layer of the size C is another fully connected layer which gives the scores for each possible label. We use either *sigmoid* or *softmax* activation function in this layer.

(1b) Feed-forward Neural Network

This network is an alternative to the CNN described previously. The input (vector F) is a bag-of-words (BoW) representation of the documents. It is followed by two fully connected layers. Each of them has a ReLU activation with a subsequent dropout regularization. We use the *softmax/sigmoid* activation in the output layer of the size $|C|$.

(2) 2nd-Level Feed-forward Neural Network

This network is a multi-layer perceptron with one hidden layer. It takes the output from the underlying network (CNN or FNN) S and learns a function $l = f_2(S)$ that maps the vector S to the number of relevant labels l. The output layer has the *softmax* activation.

Figure 1 shows the architecture of the whole network where the CNN and 2nd-level FNN are merged. Due to the space limits, the architecture of the second network which merges together the two FNNs is not depicted.

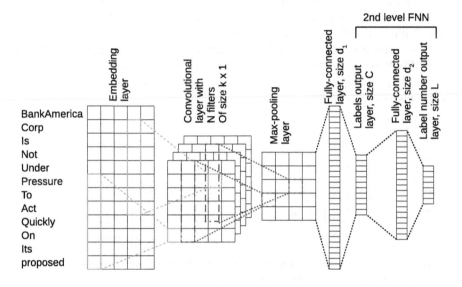

Fig. 1. The architecture of the proposed network - CNN + FNN

The whole network learns the complex function $l, S = f(F) = f_2(f_1(F))$ When we trained the whole network at once, unfortunately, the convergence was not very good. Therefore, we decided to train both sub-nets independently. First, we train the CNN (or FNN) which gives the score S for all labels, then the connected 2nd-level FNN is trained using these scores S. Both sub-nets are learned using adaptive moment estimation (Adam [3]) optimization algorithm.

4 Experiments

4.1 Tools and Corpora

For implementation of all neural nets we used Keras tool-kit [2] which is based on the Theano deep learning library [1]. It has been chosen mainly because of good performance and our previous experience with this tool. For evaluation of the multi-label document classification results, we use the standard recall, precision and F-measure (*F1*) metrics [11]. The values are micro-averaged. To measure the performance of the second sub-net we utilize label accuracy (L-ACC) and mean absolute error (MAE).

Czech Text Document Corpus v 1.0. This corpus is composed of 11,955 documents provided by ČTK and contains 2,974,040 words. The documents are annotated from a set of 60 categories as for instance agriculture, weather, politics or sport out of which we used 37 most frequent ones. The category reduction was done to allow comparison with previously reported results on this corpus where the same set of 37 categories was used. Average number of categories per document is 2.55. 500 randomly chosen documents are reserved for development set while the remaining part is used for training and testing. Left part of Fig. 2 illustrates the distribution of the documents depending on the number of labels, while the right part shows the distribution of the document lengths (in word tokens). This corpus is freely available for research purposes at http:// home.zcu.cz/~pkral/sw/. We use the five-folds cross validation procedure for all experiments on this corpus.

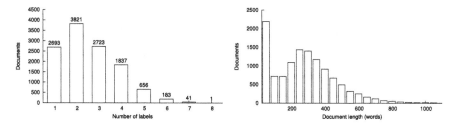

Fig. 2. Distribution of documents depending on the number of labels (left) and distribution of the document lengths (right)

Reuters-21578 English Corpus. The Reuters-21578[1] corpus is a collection of 21,578 documents. As suggested by many authors, the training part is composed of 7769 documents, while 3019 documents are reserved for testing. The number of possible categories is 90 and average label/document number is 1.23. This dataset is used in order to compare the performance of our method with state-of-the-art approaches.

4.2   System Configuration

In this section we summarize the important parameters that we used in our system configuration. The preprocessing was the same for both Czech and English corpora. We convert all texts to lowercase and replace all numbers by one common token.

---

[1] http://www.daviddlewis.com/resources/testcollections/reuters21578/.

The dictionary size is set to 20,000 for both networks. The document length is unified to 400 tokens and the embedding size is 300 for the CNN. The convolutional layer utilizes 40 kernels of the size 16×1. The fully connected layer in CNN has 256 neurons. The two hidden layers of FNN have 1024 and 512 neurons respectively. All dropout rates are set to 20%. In the case of the 2nd-level FNN we use hidden layer with 100 neurons. All the networks are trained for 20 epochs and with the mini-batch size 32.

4.3   Results on the Czech Corpus

The first experiment (see Table 1) shows the performance of the individual networks with the thresholding method. It is realized in order to compare the results of the proposed neural net with state of the art[2]. The threshold values are set on the development data. This table shows that CNN with sigmoid activation function gives the best classification results.

Table 1. Results on Czech corpus with thresholding method, thresholds set on the development corpus

Method	Prec.	Recall	F1 [%]	Threshold
CNN sigmoid	87.68	79.09	**83.17**	0.19
CNN softmax	80.84	80.54	80.69	0.06
MLP sigmoid	80.03	83.35	81.66	0.15
MLP softmax	67.78	90.99	77.69	0.04

The second experiment (see Table 2) presents the results obtained with the proposed neural network method. This table shows that this approach performs better when the sigmoid activation function is used. This behavior is not surprising because sigmoid function usually suits better for the multi-label classification problems. This table further shows that this approach outperforms the reference thresholdind method (see Table 1). This experiment also shows that both network topologies (CNN + FNN or FNN + FNN) are comparable. Note

Table 2. Results on the Czech corpus using the proposed neural network approach

Method	Prec.	Recall	F1 [%]	L-ACC	MAE
CNN sigmoid	87.20	81.13	**84.06**	63.54	0.46
CNN softmax	84.13	80.20	82.12	60.96	0.53
MLP sigmoid	85.61	82.82	**84.19**	64.47	0.48
MLP softmax	77.28	85.30	81.09	57.11	0.62

---

[2] This approach has been proposed in [7].

that L-ACC is the label accuracy of the second level FNN and MAE is its mean absolute error. It is obvious that there is still room for improvement in the 2nd-level FNN performance.

4.4 Results on Reuters-21578

The third experiment (see Table 3) shows the performance of the proposed approach on standard English Reuters dataset. This experiment was realized in order to show its robustness across languages and to compare our method with state of the art (SoTa). The results show that especially CNN with the sigmoid activation has very good performance and is comparable with the best performing approach of Nam et al. [10] (SoTa). Note that the authors use TF-IDF representation of documents which is slightly more sophisticated than ours.

Table 3. Results on English Reuters corpus using the proposed neural network approach

Method	Prec.	Recall	F1 [%]	L-ACC	MAE
CNN sigmoid	89.79	84.99	**87.32**	88.17	0.17
CNN softmax	87.52	83.96	85.70	85.80	0.19
MLP sigmoid	85.16	83.22	84.18	86.27	0.19
MLP softmax	81.52	83.24	82.37	81.29	0.23
BR_R [10] (SoTa)	89.82	86.03	**87.89**	-	-

5 Conclusions and Perspectives

In this paper, we have proposed a novel neural network for multi-label document classification. This network is composed of two sub-nets where the first one estimates the scores for all classes, while the second one is used to determine the number of classes. We have evaluated the proposed approach on Czech and English standard corpora. We have experimentally shown that the proposed method is competitive with state-of-the-art methods on both languages

The experiments have shown that the 2nd-level FNN performance could be further improved. This is thus the first perspective. Another possibility for improvement is using manually pre-trained embeddings. However, in this paper, we did not concentrate on this issue and it will thus be solved in our future work. We also would like to experiment with different network types, as for instance LSTM or recurrent CNNs.

Acknowledgements. This work has been supported by the project LO1506 of the Czech Ministry of Education, Youth and Sports.

References

1. Bergstra, J., Breuleux, O., Bastien, F., Lamblin, P., Pascanu, R., Desjardins, G., Turian, J., Warde-Farley, D., Bengio, Y.: Theano: a CPU and GPU math expression compiler. In: Proceedings of Python for Scientific Computing Conference (SciPy), Austin, TX, vol. 4, p. 3 (2010)
2. Chollet, F.: Keras (2015). https://github.com/fchollet/keras
3. Kingma, D., Ba, J.: Adam: a method for stochastic optimization. arXiv preprint arXiv:1412.6980 (2014)
4. Kurata, G., Xiang, B., Zhou, B.: Improved neural network-based multi-label classification with better initialization leveraging label co-occurrence. In: Proceedings of NAACL-HLT, pp. 521–526 (2016)
5. Lai, S., Xu, L., Liu, K., Zhao, J.: Recurrent convolutional neural networks for text classification (2015)
6. Le, Q.V., Mikolov, T.: Distributed representations of sentences and documents. In: ICML, vol. 14, pp. 1188–1196 (2014)
7. Lenc, L., Král, P.: Deep neural networks for Czech multi-label document classification. In: 17th International Conference on Intelligent Text Processing and Computational Linguistics (CICLing 2016). Springer, Konya, 3–9 April 2016
8. Manevitz, L., Yousef, M.: One-class document classification via neural networks. Neurocomputing **70**(7–9), 1466–1481 (2007). http://www.scopus.com/inward/record.url?eid=2-s2.0-33847410597&partnerID=40&md5=3d75682f283e19695f2857dea9d9f03f
9. Nair, V., Hinton, G.E.: Rectified linear units improve restricted Boltzmann machines. In: Proceedings of 27th International Conference on Machine Learning (ICML-2010), pp. 807–814 (2010)
10. Nam, J., Kim, J., Loza Mencía, E., Gurevych, I., Fürnkranz, J.: Large-scale multi-label text classification - revisiting neural networks. In: Calders, T., Esposito, F., Hüllermeier, E., Meo, R. (eds.) ECML PKDD 2014. LNCS, vol. 8725, pp. 437–452. Springer, Heidelberg (2014). doi:10.1007/978-3-662-44851-9_28
11. Powers, D.: Evaluation: from precision, recall and F-measure to ROC., informedness, markedness & correlation. J. Mach. Learn. Technol. **2**(1), 37–63 (2011)
12. Sebastiani, F.: Machine learning in automated text categorization. ACM Comput. Surv. (CSUR) **34**(1), 1–47 (2002)
13. Srivastava, N., Hinton, G.E., Krizhevsky, A., Sutskever, I., Salakhutdinov, R.: Dropout: a simple way to prevent neural networks from overfitting. J. Mach. Learn. Res. **15**(1), 1929–1958 (2014)
14. Yang, Y., Gopal, S.: Multilabel classification with meta-level features in a learning-to-rank framework. Mach. Learn. **88**(1–2), 47–68 (2012)
15. Zhang, M.L., Zhou, Z.H.: Multilabel neural networks with applications to functional genomics and text categorization. IEEE Trans. Knowl. Data Eng. **18**(10), 1338–1351 (2006)

Ontology Alignment with Weightless Neural Networks

Thais Viana[1], Carla Delgado[1,2]([✉]), João C.P. da Silva[2], and Priscila Lima[1]

[1] Prog. de Pós Graduação em Informática, Universidade Federal do Rio de Janeiro,
Rio de Janeiro, Brazil
{thaisviana,priscila.lima}@ppgi.ufrj.br, {carla,jpcs}@dcc.ufrj.br
[2] Dep. Ciência da Computação, IM, Universidade Federal do Rio de Janeiro,
Av. Athos da Silveira Ramos, 274, Cidade Universitária, Rio de Janeiro 68530, Brasil
http://www.ppgi.ufrj.br, http://www.dcc.ufrj.br

Abstract. In this paper, we present an ontology matching process based on the usage of Weightless Neural Networks (WNN). The alignment of ontologies for specific domains provides several benefits, such as interoperability among different systems and the improvement of the domain knowledge derived from the insights inferred from the combined information contained in the various ontologies. A WiSARD classifier is built to estimate a distribution-based similarity measure among the concepts of the several ontologies being matched. To validate our approach, we apply the proposed matching process to the knowledge domain of algorithms, software and computational problems, having some promising results.

Keywords: Weightless Neural Network · WiSARD · Ontology alignment · Ontology matching

1 Introduction

An ontology typically provides a vocabulary describing a domain of interest and a related specification of the meaning of the terms used in this vocabulary. According to the granularity of the specification, the notion of ontology encompasses several data and conceptual models, including sets of terms, classifications, taxonomies, thesauri and database schemas [13]. As disparate backgrounds are a major barrier to communication among people, organizations and software systems, the conception and implementation of an ontology in a given domain should provide an explicit account of a shared understanding, thus improving communication, software interoperability and enhancing reuse and sharing [18].

Interoperability and communication are also an issue when different applications use even slightly different ontologies. Most often, these applications cannot interact sound and smoothly, unless the ontologies used are aligned [7]. The alignment of ontologies for domains that intercept or even touch each other

T. Viana—Thanks to CNPq for the financial support received.

A. Lintas et al. (Eds.): ICANN 2017, Part II, LNCS 10614, pp. 376–384, 2017.
https://doi.org/10.1007/978-3-319-68612-7_43

has benefits beyond interoperability, as new insights can be inferred by combining information from various sources. Such insights can be valuable to advance the domain knowledge. Besides, human users could access the knowledge from numerous ontologies in a transparent way.

An alignment between two (or even more) ontologies is the output of a hard and challenging process, which is called *ontology matching* [8]. This paper tackles ontology alignment by proposing a matching process using a Weightless Neural Network (WNN) model. A WiSARD classifier [2] is built and used to estimate a distribution-based similarity measure among the concepts of the ontologies being matched. We consider that our approach has two strong points. First, new patterns can be learned without the need to retrain the complete neural network. Second and most important, other information besides class and property names are taken into account in order to obtain a more significant alignment, which is generally not the case with other approaches.

We apply the proposed matching process to the knowledge domain of algorithms, software and computational problems, having some promising results which we compare to results obtained by other classifiers. We also discuss the conceptual difficulties to apply our matching process to benchmarks used in ontology matching competitions, what we believe will bring insights also to the evaluation process of ontology matching approaches in general.

In Sect. 2 we provide a brief description of related works. Section 3 presents the proposed approach to ontology matching using WNNs. Section 4 describes the application of our approach to the software knowledge domain. Sections 5 and 6 state respectively our results and conclusions.

2   Related Works

Several ontology alignment methods attempt to identify the semantic similarity between the entities of two or more ontologies. The strengths and weaknesses of the proposed approaches have been discussed in several publications [6]. The Ontology Alignment Evaluation Initiative (OAEI) is a coordinated international initiative which organizes the evaluation of the increasing number of ontology alignment systems [4]. Carefully observing the results from past OAEIs, we can see that there is no definite method or system for all existing alignment problems.

AgreementMakerLight (AML) was the top performing system in five tracks from OAEI 2016 [1], including the Instance and instance-based Process Model tracks, and one of the top performing systems in three others. AML is based mainly on element-level matching and on the use of external resources as background knowledge [9]. By the time we ran our experiments, the 2016 benchmark was not available anymore. In OAEI 2015 benchmark we can not find the comments associated with class names, which is an essential input for the proper functioning of our algorithm. In this way, our approach has not performed very well classifying this benchmark. We can say that a fair comparison between OAEI results to our approach is not feasible, as our system is supposed to work with ontologies that do have descriptions of their properties and classes.

[5] tackles the automatic matching of ontologies by using recursive neural networks, an extension to the recurrent neural networks capable of efficiently process structured data. [5] considers an ontology as a graph, with the ontology concepts (relations) corresponding to the nodes (edges) of the graph. The method was tested on small-scale datasets with promising initial results, which are considered intuitively correct. Different from [5], our approach does not consider the structure of the ontologies being aligned. As we will present, we use a bag of words approach, considering the descriptions of properties and classes of each ontology being considered. This approach captures information that is neither explicitly available through the properties specification nor the instances data. Matching two ontologies just based on terms, which would be the general case of names of properties and classes, is not enough. Therefore, we take advantage of longer pieces of text in order to obtain a more satisfactory alignment.

3   A Weightless Neural Network for Ontology Alignment

Ontology alignment is an important task in heterogeneous models as for example, database schemas and ontologies. Usually these models are analyzed and matched either manually or semi-automatically at design time [16]. Given two ontologies O_1 and O_2, an alignment between O_1 and O_2 is a set of correspondences $\langle e_1, e_2, r, n \rangle$ with $e_1 \in O_1$ and $e_2 \in O_2$ being the two matched entities, r being a relationship holding between e_1 and e_2, and $n \in [0, 1]$ represents the level of confidence in this correspondence [8].

Our system handles input ontologies both in OWL and RDF formats, and the algorithm used is a string-based classifier. String-based classifiers are divided into two main categories, regarding the method used for comparing terms: either they only consider character strings; or use some linguistic knowledge to interpret these strings [8]. Our approach is of the second kind. The technique we use comes from information retrieval and considers a string as a (multi)set of words (bag of words), i.e., a set in which a particular item can appear several times [8].

We used the Natural Language ToolKit (NLTK) [3] to tokenize the textual description of each ontology class we want to align, and a process known as stemming for removing morphological affixes from words[1]. Next, we created the word incidence matrix, where each line represents a binary vector indicating whether the word of that column appears or not in the textual description of the respective ontology class. The final result of the concatenation of these vectors in array format is used by a WiSARD[2] neural network during training and classification.

WiSARD [2] is a RAM based neural network, composed of a set of individual classifiers, called *discriminators*, each one assigned to learn binary patterns belonging to a particular category. Therefore, a typical WiSARD architecture has as many discriminators as the number of categories it should be able to distinguish [17]. The binary input vector in a discriminator, traditionally called

---

[1] In this project, we adopted the Lancaster Stemmer implementation available in [3].
[2] We developed our python project using the open source PyWaNN library from [15].

retina[3], is of size m (in bits), and is usually divided into m/n addresses of n bits each. These addresses are used to access RAMs of 2^n positions, for writing during training and for reading during classification. The mapping of the address bits is usually random and exclusive. In an ontology matching scenario, WiSARD has the benefit of being a one shot classifier, allowing incremental online learning.

During the training of a class, the input pattern bits define addresses to access the RAMs. Each RAM updates the value in the position addressed. When predicting the class of a new pattern, WiSARD uses the same mapping to access the contents of the positions addressed. If the position addressed contains an integer higher than a predefined value (threshold), 1 is added to the discriminator's response [11]. WiSARD decides the class of the pattern by choosing the discriminator which returns the highest response. The threshold can be incremented to filter lower RAMs' values in case of a draw between two or more discriminators, or when these values are too close [15]. This process is called *bleaching*.

Despite bleaching successful results as a general classification technique, when applied to bag of words many pieces of text can be classified by terms they do not have in common rather than by their proximity. This way, text categorization requires another adaptation of WiSARD due to the sparsity of the feature vector. As many RAMs would access the zero position (those which all address bits are zeros), the prediction would happen based on absent features. To work around this issue, on full-zero patterns the memory does not contribute to the discriminator response. Those digits equally compose the addresses that will indicate which position in each of the discriminator's RAMs will be accessed (written in the case of training or read in the case of classification). In many applications, zero means the absence of a given feature, and that is our case. In our ontologies alignment approach, zero indicates the absence of the document of a term present in the dictionary. In dictionaries relatively larger than the documents analyzed, it is expected that many RAMs will have their position of address zero accessed many times during training, thus rendering an out of proportion emphasis on the absence of terms, rather than on the terms that characterize a particular document. Thus, in the classification mode, zero-addressed positions will not be taken into consideration [15].

After we calibrated all parameters described above, the algorithm returns a map of classifications for all given inputs. The main result is composed by a label of discriminator, the number of memories accepted ($\#accept_{Mem}$) and total number of memories ($\#total_{Mem}$) by that pattern. We calculated this relation rate dividing those two values. So WiSARD classifies a new relation with rate:

$$ratio = \frac{\#accept_{Mem}}{\#total_{Mem}}$$

This *ratio* is used to compare our method with other similarity-based methods described in the results section.

After the classification phase, we used the value *ratio*. To refine the results, we analyze all the classifications generated and create the triple

---

[3] Due to its initial applications to graphical pattern classification.

($class_{ont_A}$, $is\_related\_to$, $class_{ont_B}$) only for the classifications that return a percentage above the mean added to the standard deviation. Thus, all other classifications are discarded. All triples created inside the same ontology are also eliminated. This is what we call *cut statistical filter*.

4   Case Study - Software Ontologies

The domain of software is an interesting candidate for being formalized through an ontology. It is a complex domain with different paradigms (object orientation, procedural, functional, etc.) and different aspects (security, legal information, interface descriptions, etc.). Despite its complexity, this is a sufficiently stable domain where new paradigms and aspects tend to occur rather seldomly [12]. That choice of domain was motivated by an ongoing project that aims to build an encyclopedia in a wiki format with information about computational problems, algorithms and implementations. The Algpedia project is accessible in http:// algpedia.dcc.ufrj.br/.

We selected four ontologies, and used WiSARD to generate a unique cohesive ontology from the matching of them, where new relations between classes of different ontologies could be presented to a specialist to be validated. The source ontologies are:

- *Core Software Ontology* (CSO) defines fundamental concepts of the software domain such as software itself, data, classes and methods. The purpose of this ontology is to provide a reference by specifying the intended meanings of software terms as precisely as possible [12].
- *Core Ontology of Programs and software* (COPS) is a core ontology proposing a set of main concepts in the field of computer programs and software. COPS specializes in the DOLCE foundational ontology [10] and is composed of several modules (sub-ontologies). Unfortunately, this ontology was not available on the internet during the execution of this work, so all classes were extracted from a non-formal descriptive document.
- *Core Ontology of Software Components* (COSC) [14] is based on CSO, but devoted to the paradigm of software componentry. It tackles concepts like libraries and licenses, component profiles, and component taxonomies.
- *AlgPedia Ontology* is the basic ontology from Algpedia [19,20], a free collaborative encyclopedia about algorithms and programs in a wiki format released in 2014. Algpedia was initially fed with information from Wikipedia and since it was launched Algpedia's users collaborate by adding new or editing information about algorithms and implementations.

We expect that the ontology generated in this matching will expand the initial ontology created for Algpedia in such a way to better structure its semantic database, turning the process of querying information more meaningful and smooth both to human and to non-human intelligent agents. Table 1 presents the number of instances, properties and classes in the four ontologies.

Table 1. Number of instances, properties and classes in each ontology

Ontology	Instances	Properties	Classes
CSO	0	12	17
COPS	0	0	245
COSC	0	24	6
Algpedia	122	4	4

From each ontology, we used the names of classes, instances and properties and also the respective descriptions contained in the *rdf:comment* properties. The names became the labels of incidence vectors extracted during the tokenization process of *rdf:comment* properties, as was mentioned in Sect. 3. In order to obtain a resulting cohesive ontology, we did not consider any alignment between classes of the same ontology.

After the tokenization process, each vector was presented to our WNN that learns the associated patterns. In case a pattern shown to the WNN is perceived as completely different from those already presented, the WNN creates a new discriminator and splits this pattern among its memories. Once all vectors were presented, the WiSARD architecture is ready to classify new ontologies in the same domain due to its online learning characteristics.

5   Results

The goal of ontology matching is to find the relations between elements from different ontologies. Normally these relations are identified using a measure of similarity between the elements of the ontologies [8]. To validate our results, we used three classifiers based on similarities (*Euclidean distance, cosine similarity* and *Manhattan distance*), which are indicated in the literature as classical approaches.

The total number of alignments discovered by our WNN was 246 pairs being 108 connecting classes from different ontologies. After applying the statistical filter described in Sect. 3, we cut off all pairs with a *ratio* lower than the mean plus the standard deviation (in our case, respectively, 0.05075329064917711 and 0.07454194887862817). The final number of alignments was 24 pairs. Table 2 shows the number of alignments between the different ontologies. Note that Algpedia and COSC had no alignment between them. This was expected since they are very distinct ontologies, the former concerning algorithms and the later concerning software license.

Using the string-based strategies present in the literature and the statistical filter, the number of alignments obtained was: (i) 37 for Euclidean distance, (ii) 34 for cosine distance and (iii) 56 for Manhattan distance. All 24 alignments obtained by our WNN appear in each one of the others approaches. Considering the alignments obtained by string-based approaches, we observed that 4 meaningful pairs were not identify by our WNN. Such pairs appeared in all

Table 2. Number of matches between each pair of ontologies

Onto. alignment	# of matches	Onto. alignment	# of matches
CSO-COPS	10	COPS-COSC	2
CSO-COSC	3	COPS-AlgPedia	8
CSO-AlgPedia	1	AlgPedia-COSC	0

string-based approaches: 3 in Euclidean, 4 in cosine and 2 in Manhattan distance. The remaining alignments, as for example *software license* and *low level language*, were considered meaningless, which suggests that such approaches generate more false-positives than true-negatives.

6   Conclusions

In this paper, we presented a process for ontology alignment based on Weightless Neural Networks. We described its implementation and application to perform the matching of four ontologies for the knowledge domain of algorithms, software and computational problems.

From a technical perspective, our approach has the advantage that new patterns can be learned without the need to retrain the complete neural network. This constitutes a leverage particularly if further ontologies (or parts of other ontologies) are to be aligned after a previous alignment has already taken place, thus making an incremental improvement of the ontology feasible.

From a semantic perspective, our approach takes into account more information besides class and property names, as it also considers the descriptions of properties and classes. Descriptions are usually longer pieces of text that contain information that is neither explicitly available through the properties' specification nor through the data instances, so we believe this may stand for a significant improvement in the quality and the consistency of the relations identified.

Our approach was able to find a more cohesive set of alignments than those found by all three classical methods we compared. For our case study, the number of false negatives was very low, and no false positives were generated. Besides, when we took a closer look at the false negatives, we get the feeling that the description texts from the corresponding entities of at least one of the ontologies should be improved. As said before, no existing automatic method or system can successfully handle all existing alignment problems. This suggests that more than one method should be used, and a human expert should then have a closer look at the discrepancy in the outcomes. When the expert analyzed the results from our case study, the conclusions were favorable to the output of our WNN, as all alignments found were validated, and the false negatives showed the expert points from the original ontologies that needed improvement.

References

1. Achichi, M., Cheatham, M., Dragisic, Z., Euzenat, J., Faria, D., Ferrara, A., Flouris, G., Fundulaki, I., Harrow, I., Ivanova, V., et al.: Results of the ontology alignment evaluation initiative 2016. In: 11th ISWC Workshop on Ontology Matching (OM), pp. 73–129. No commercial editor (2016)
2. Aleksander, I., Thomas, W., Bowden, P.: Wisard a radical step forward in image recognition. Sens. Rev. **4**(3), 120–124 (1984)
3. Bird, S.: NLTK: the natural language toolkit. In: Proceedings of COLING/ACL on Interactive Presentation Sessions, COLING-ACL 2006, pp. 69–72 (2006)
4. Cheatham, M., Dragisic, Z., Euzenat, J., Faria, D., Ferrara, A., Flouris, G., Fundulaki, I., Granada, R., Ivanova, V., Jiménez-Ruiz, E., et al.: Results of the ontology alignment evaluation initiative 2015. In: 10th ISWC Workshop on Ontology Matching (OM), pp. 60–115. No commercial editor (2015)
5. Chortaras, A., Stamou, G., Stafylopatis, A.: Learning ontology alignments using recursive neural networks. In: Duch, W., Kacprzyk, J., Oja, E., Zadrożny, S. (eds.) ICANN 2005. LNCS, vol. 3697, pp. 811–816. Springer, Heidelberg (2005). doi:10. 1007/11550907_128
6. Djeddi, W.E., Khadir, M.T.: Ontology alignment using artificial neural network for large-scale ontologies. Int. J. Metadata Semant. Ontol. 16 **8**(1), 75–92 (2013)
7. Ehrig, M.: Ontology Alignment: Bridging the Semantic Gap (Semantic Web and Beyond). Springer-Verlag New York, Inc., Secaucus (2006)
8. Euzenat, J., Shvaiko, P.: Ontology Matching. Springer-Verlag New York, Inc., Secaucus (2007)
9. Faria, D., Pesquita, C., Balasubramani, B.S., Martins, C., Cardoso, J., Curado, H., Couto, F.M., Cruz, I.F.: OAEI 2016 results of AML. In: Ontology Matching, p. 138 (2016)
10. Gangemi, A., Guarino, N., Masolo, C., Oltramari, A., Schneider, L.: Sweetening ontologies with DOLCE. In: Gómez-Pérez, A., Benjamins, V.R. (eds.) EKAW 2002. LNCS, vol. 2473, pp. 166–181. Springer, Heidelberg (2002). doi:10.1007/ 3-540-45810-7_18
11. Grieco, B.P.A., Lima, P.M.V., De Gregorio, M., França, F.M.G.: Producing pattern examples from "mental" images. Neurocomputing **73**(7–9), 1057–1064 (2010)
12. Oberle, D., Grimm, S., Staab, S.: An ontology for software. In: Staab, S., Studer, R. (eds.) Handbook on Ontologies, pp. 383–402. Springer, Berlin (2009). doi:10. 1007/978-3-540-92673-3_17
13. Oberle, D., Grimm, S., Staab, S.: What is an ontology? In: Handbook on Ontologies, pp. 383–402 (2009)
14. Oberle, D., Lamparter, S., Grimm, S., Vrandečić, D., Staab, S., Gangemi, A.: Towards ontologies for formalizing modularization and communication in large software systems. Appl. Ontol. **1**(2), 163–202 (2006)
15. Rangel, F., Vieira, P.L.M., Oliveira, J.: Semi-supervised classification of social textual data using wisard. In: Proceedings of ESANN 2016 (2016)
16. Shvaiko, P., Euzenat, J.: Ontology matching: state of the art and future challenges. IEEE Trans. Knowl. Data Eng. **25**(1), 158–176 (2013)
17. Staffa, M., Rossi, S., Giordano, M., Gregorio, M.D., Siciliano, B.: Segmentation performance in tracking deformable objects via WNNs. In: 2015 IEEE International Conference on Robotics and Automation (ICRA), pp. 2462–2467 (2015)
18. Uschold, M., Gruninger, M.: Ontologies: principles, methods and applications. Knowl. Eng. Rev. **11**, 93–136 (1996)

19. Viana, T.N., Abdelhay, P., da Silva, J.C.P., Delgado, C.A.D.M.: AlgPedia: the free algorithms encyclopedia (2014). http://algpedia.dcc.ufrj.br/
20. Viana, T., da Silva, J.C.P., Delgado, C., Martins, C.E.S., Gouvêa, F.R.: Collaborative encyclopedia of algorithms - AlgPedia. In: 25° WEI - Workshop sobre Educação em Computação - CSBC, 2017, São Paulo - SP. Anais do 25° WEI - Workshop sobre Educação em Computação - CSBC, pp. 2277–2286 (2017)

Marine Safety and Data Analytics: Vessel Crash Stop Maneuvering Performance Prediction

Luca Oneto[1](✉), Andrea Coraddu[2], Paolo Sanetti[1], Olena Karpenko[3], Francesca Cipollini[1], Toine Cleophas[3], and Davide Anguita[1]

[1] DIBRIS, University of Genoa, Genoa, Italy
{luca.oneto,paolo.sanetti,francesca.cipollini,davide.anguita}@unige.it
[2] School of Marine Science and Technology, Newcastle University,
Newcastle upon Tyne, UK
andrea.coraddu@newcastle.ac.uk
[3] DAMEN Shipyards Gorinchem, Gorinchem, The Netherlands
{olena.karpenko,toine.cleophas}@damen.com

Abstract. Crash stop maneuvering performance is one of the key indicators of the vessel safety properties for a shipbuilding company. Many different factors affect these performances, from the vessel design to the environmental conditions, hence it is not trivial to assess them accurately during the preliminary design stages. Several first principal equation methods are available to estimate the crash stop maneuvering performance, but unfortunately, these methods usually are either too costly or not accurate enough. To overcome these limitations, the authors propose a new data-driven method, based on the popular Random Forests learning algorithm, for predicting the crash stopping maneuvering performance. Results on real-world data provided by the DAMEN Shipyards show the effectiveness of the proposal.

Keywords: Marine safety · Vessel maneuvering · Crash stop · Data-driven methods · Random forests · Performance assessment · Performance estimation

1 Introduction

Shipping is one of the most safety critical industry [15]. For this reason, as reported in [16,17], the vessel's design has to ensure that the craft should be controllable and be capable of maneuvering securely up to the critical design conditions. In this paper, the authors focus their attention on a particular safety related maneuver which is the crash stop. The goal is to predict, at design stage, the crash stop main characteristics, for the preliminary assessment of safety requirement imposed by the classification society [14]. The crash stop maneuvering is usually performed to avoid any collision or crashing of a ship into any other ship or structure. During this maneuver, the main engine is subjected to severe stress and loading since it involves slowing, stopping and reversing the direction as fast as possible.

© Springer International Publishing AG 2017
A. Lintas et al. (Eds.): ICANN 2017, Part II, LNCS 10614, pp. 385–393, 2017.
https://doi.org/10.1007/978-3-319-68612-7_44

The assessment of the ship crash stop maneuver plays a crucial role in the marine engineering field. Several first principal equation methods are available to estimate the crash stop performance [12,18,20,21,25], but the latter are either too complex [18,25] or not accurate enough [20] due to the complexity of the system. To increase their accuracy, several parameters need to be provided by the different manufacturer of the vessel components, and finally, models need to be fine tuned based on the outcomes of several sea trials which makes the process costly, time-consuming, and not applicable at design stage [18]. Moreover, suppliers are usually not willing to share technical details which may harm their industrial competitive advantages.

In this paper, the authors propose a new fully data-driven method based on Random Forests (RF), a state-of-the-art powerful learning algorithm, first developed in [4] and then recently improved in [3], for predicting the crash stopping performance. Data-driven methods, instead of relying on the physical knowledge about the system, build upon historical data collected about a phenomenon to build a model which can easily take into account many different sources of information which cannot be easily modeled with first principle equations. RF are usually preferred to other classification techniques, because of their high numerical robustness, their innate capacity of dealing with numerical and categorical features, and their effectiveness in many real-world problems [10,24]. By carefully tuning the RF hyperparameters [22] and by assessing the performance of the final learned model with state-of-the-art resampling techniques [2], authors will show the effectiveness of the proposal.

In summary, the paper contribution is twofold. From a marine engineering perspective, the paper deals with the problem of the prediction of the crash stop main characteristics without taking into account the physical laws that are governing the phenomenon. In fact, authors proposal does not require any a-priory knowledge about the problems and allows to exploit information sources which cannot be modeled with conventional approaches. From a data analytics perspective, this paper proposes an alternative RF formulation and shows that a careful tuning procedure of the RF hyperparameters can remarkably improve its performance. Results on real-world data coming from the DAMEN Shipyards demonstrate the effectiveness of the proposal. In particular, DAMEN, in its many years of vessels production, conducted several sea trials to measure vessels general seaworthiness and performance. For this application, the authors used a particular cluster of DAMEN vessels, the High-Speed Craft family [8], as a test case.

2   Vessel Crash Stop Maneuvering

As reported in [1] the stopping ability of a vessel is measured by three main parameters: the Track Reach (TR), the Head Reach (HR) and the Time for Full Maneuver (or time to dead in water) TFM. Also the Lateral Deviations (LD), Lateral Deviation Direction (LDD), and Heading Deviation Direction (HDD) are parameters of interest, but they are more sensitive to initial conditions and wind disturbances. The crash stop maneuver consists in a stop engine full astern performed after a steady approach at the test speed until the vessel starts going backwards. TR is defined as a distance along the vessel track that the vessel covers from the moment that the full astern command is given until ahead speed changes sign. The HR, instead, is the distance along the direction of the course at the moment when the full astern command is given. The distance is measured from the moment when the full astern command is given until the vessel is stopped dead in the water. The LD is defined as the distance perpendicular to the direction of the course at the moment when the full astern command is given. Also this distance is measured from the moment when the full astern command is given until the vessel is stopped dead in the water. Figure 1 shows the meaning of each parameter.

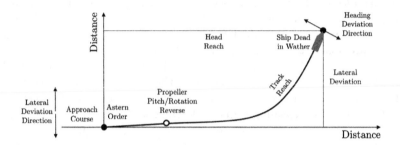

Fig. 1. Crash stop maneuver performance indexes.

The main parameters of the crash stop maneuver are evaluated by means of the full-scale trials. At design stage, in order to assess the maneuvering characteristics both in trail and full load conditions, reliable methods should be applied. These methods should ensure satisfactory accuracies for the prediction of new vessels and satisfactory extrapolation of trial results to the full load condition. As reported in [12], the factors which affect the stopping ability of vessels are the vessel displacement, the initial speed, the block coefficient, the vessel hull fouling degree, the main engine full astern power, the time taken to effect changes in engine telegraph settings, the propeller category, and the environmental conditions (e.g. wind, stream, and the depth of water). During this maneuvers, the interactions between hull and propeller(s) are quite complex to be modeled. For this reason, empirical calculations of its characteristics are used when adequate motion equation coefficients are not available for simulation [18,20]. In this paper the authors focused their attention only on the crash stop from maximum operational speed and any transient mode speed according to the available data provided to DAMEN Shipyards. To prove the effectiveness of the new data-driven approach, authors focused on a particular cluster of DAMEN vessels, the High-Speed Craft (HSC) family [8], but the method is general and the data can be easily retrieved by any shipbuilder. The total amount of the vessels is 230 divided into four product clusters: Fast Crew Supplier, Search And Rescue, Stan

Pilot and Stan Tender. For each product cluster, different products (vessel type) are available, each one characterized by several yard numbers. Every single yard number can perform several crash stop maneuvers. For each of the vessels, the information reported in Table 1 is available. During the trials, the maneuvers are digitally recorded using advanced portable measurement equipment. Therefore, the goal is to predict, based on the information of Table 1, available at design stages, the crash stop maneuver performance indexes (TR, HR, TFM, LD, LDD, and HDD).

3   Proposed Data Driven Approach

In this section, the authors will present the proposed data-driven vessel crash stop maneuvering performance prediction system.

Let authors consider the supervised learning framework where an input space $\mathcal{X} = \mathcal{X}_1 \times \cdots \times \mathcal{X}_d$, composed of d features, and an output space $\mathcal{Y}$ are available [23]. $\mathcal{X}_i$ can be a categorical feature space $\mathcal{X}_i = \{c_i^1, \cdots, c_i^{n_{c_i}}\}$ or a real valued feature space $\mathcal{X}_i \subseteq \mathbb{R}$ (see Table 1). Analogously, also $\mathcal{Y}$ can be a binary valued output space $\mathcal{Y} = \{\pm 1\}$ (LDD and HSS) or real valued output space $\mathcal{Y} \subseteq \mathbb{R}$ (TR, HR, TFM, and LD). Based on the type of output space the associated learning problem is called binary classification or regression respectively [23]. In the supervised learning framework, the goal is to estimate the unknown rule $\mu : \mathcal{X} \rightarrow \mathcal{Y}$ which associates an element $Y \in \mathcal{Y}$ to an element $X \in \mathcal{X}$. Note that, in general, μ can be non-deterministic [23] and some components of X may be missing (errors in the measurements, careless operators, etc.) [9]. In this case, if the missing value is located in a categorical feature, an additional category for missing values is introduced on those features. If, instead, the missing value is associated to a numerical feature, as suggested in [9], that missing value is replaced with the mean value of that feature and an additional logical feature is introduced to indicate if the value of that feature for a particular sample is missing or not. An ML technique estimates μ through a learning algorithm $\mathscr{A}_\mathcal{H} : \mathcal{D}_n \times \mathcal{F} \rightarrow f$, characterized by its set of hyperparameters $\mathcal{H}$, which maps a series of examples of the input/output relation, contained in a datasets of n samples $\mathcal{D}_n : \{(X_1, Y_1), \cdots, (X_n, Y_n)\}$ sampled i.i.d from μ, into a function $f : \mathcal{X} \rightarrow \mathcal{Y}$. The error that f commits, in approximating μ, is measured with reference to a loss function $\ell : \mathcal{X} \times \mathcal{Y} \times \mathcal{F} \rightarrow [0, \infty)$ through the empirical error. Note that, for binary classification problems, authors will make use of the hard loss function which counts the number of errors $\ell_H(f(X), Y) = [f(X) \neq Y] \in \{0, 1\}$ [23] and for regression the truncated relative absolute error $\ell_{TRAE}(f(X), Y) = \min[1, |f(X) - Y|/|Y|] \in [0, 1]$ will be exploited [7]. The purpose of any learning procedure is to select the best set of hyperparameters $\mathcal{H}$ such that the expected error $L(f) = \mathbb{E}_\mu \ell(f(X), Y)$, which unfortunately is unknown since μ is unknown, is minimum. Since $L(f)$ is unknown, the empirical error $\widehat{L}^{\mathcal{D}_n}(f) = 1/n \sum_{(X, Y) \in \mathcal{D}_n} \ell(f(X), Y)$ must be exploited in order to estimate it.

In this paper $\mathscr{A}$ is a RF because of their high numerical robustness, native capacity of dealing with numerical and categorical features, and effectiveness in

Table 1. Available vessels information.

Variable name	Unit	Variable name	Unit	Variable name	Unit
Product Cluster	[]	Draught aftmark	[m]	Waterplane area	$[m^2]$
Product	[]	Draught foremark	[m]	Waterplane area inertia (x-axis)	$[m^4]$
Yard Number	[]	Static trim	[m]	Waterplane area inertia (y-axis)	$[m^4]$
Location	[]	Displacement	[tons]	Waterline length	[m]
Country	[]	Longitudinal center of gravity	[m]	Waterline breadth	[m]
Trial Engineer	[]	Number of driveline	[]	Midship section area	$[m^2]$
Orientation	[]	Propeller diameter	[m]	Wetted surface	$[m^2]$
Crash Stop type	[]	Number of propeller blades	[]	Midship draught	[m]
Initial vessel speed	[knots]	Blade area ratio	[]	Roll angle	[deg]
Initial heading	[]	Engine break power	[kW]	Pitch angle	[deg]
Initial Engine Speed	[rpm]	Engine speed	[rpm]	Longitudinal center of floatation	[m]
Heading Deviation	[deg]	Gearbox reduction ratio	[]	Transversal center of floatation	[m]
Propeller mass	[kg]	Propeller inertia in air	$[\frac{kg}{m^4}]$	Propeller inertia in water	$[\frac{kg}{m^4}]$
Under Keel Clearance	[m]	Water Density	$[\frac{kg}{m^3}]$	Main engine type	[]
Rotative efficiency (design)	[]	Design vessel speed	[knots]	Main engine nominal power	[kW]
Wave Height	[m]	Design wake factor	[]	Gearbox manufacturer	[]
Wave Direction	[deg]	Design propeller pitch	[]	Gearbox type	[]
Wind Velocity	[m/s]	Volume	$[m^3]$	Main engine nominal speed	[rpm]
Wind Direction	[bar]	Longitudinal center of buoyancy	[m]	Propeller manufacturer	[]
Current velocity	[knots]	Transversal center of buoyancy	[m]	Propeller type	[]
Current direction	[deg]	Vertical center of buoyancy	[m]	Propeller diameter	[m]
Loading condition	[]	Vertical center of gravity	[m]	Propeller number of blades	[]

many real-world classification problems [3,4]. The original RF learning phase of each of the n_t trees $\{T_1, \cdots, T_{n_t}\}$ composing the RF is quite simple [4]. From $\mathcal{D}_n$, $\lfloor bn \rfloor$ samples are sampled with replacement and $\mathcal{D}'_{\lfloor bn \rfloor}$ is built. A tree is constructed with $\mathcal{D}'_{\lfloor bn \rfloor}$ but the best split is chosen among a subset of n_v features over the possible d features randomly chosen at each node. The tree is grown until the node contains a maximum of n_l samples. During the classification phase of a previously unseen X, each tree classifies X in a class $Y_{i \in \{1, \cdots, n_t\}}$, and then the final classification is the $\{p_1, \cdots, p_{n_t}\}$-weighted combination of all the answers of each tree of the RF. The empirical error of the tree T built based on $\mathcal{D}'_{\lfloor bn \rfloor}$ over the out of bag data $\mathcal{D}_n \backslash \mathcal{D}'_{\lfloor bn \rfloor}$ is defined as $\widehat{L}^{\mathrm{oob}}(T)$. $p_{\{i \in 1, \cdots, n_t\}}$ are of paramount importance for the accuracy of an ensemble classifier [11,19] and for this reason authors will exploit a state-of-the-art alternative proposed in [5] and recently further developed in [19,22] where $p_i = e^{-\gamma \widehat{L}^{\mathrm{oob}}(T)}$ with $\gamma \in [\gamma, \infty)$. If $\gamma = 0$, $b = 1$, $n_v = \sqrt{n}$, and $n_l = 1$ we get the original RF formulation [4]. RF have been recently improved in [3] which proposes to avoid the initial bootstrapping and the subset feature selection at each node construction of the trees by replacing it with a random rotation of the numerical feature space before learning each tree of the forest. Note that, since rotations can be sensitive to scale in general and to outliers in particular, the RF developed in [3] need to scale the numerical feature space. As suggested by the results in [3], the simple scaling of each feature in the range $[0, 1]$ should be adopted. In this paper, authors propose to use the RF learning algorithm reported in Algorithm 1 which merges the original RF formulation [4] with the most recent one of [3]. In particular, authors propose to use the learning strategy proposed in [4] by also including the random rotation proposed in [3] in order to get the benefits of both approaches. Note that in Algorithm 1 the rotation does not change at each tree but every n_r trees in order to reduce the computational requirements of the RF with respect to [3].

In order to tune, in a data dependent manner, the different hyperparameters of the RF of Algorithm 1 and to estimate the performance of the final model,

Algorithm 1. RF learning algorithm: learning and forward phases.

```
/* Learning phase                                                              */
Input: 𝒟ₙ, nₜ, γ, b, nᵥ, nᵣ, and nₗ
Output: A set of tree {T₁, ⋯ , T_{nₜ}}
1  for i ← 1 to nₜ do
2  |    if i − ⌊i/nᵣ⌋nᵣ = 1 then
3  |    |    Θ = random rotation matrix defined in [3];
4  |    |    𝒟ⁿʳ = rotate the numerical features space 𝒟ₙ based on Θ;
5  |    𝒟'_{⌊bn⌋} sample with replacement ⌊bn⌋ sample from 𝒟ⁿʳ;
6  |    Tᵢ.Θ = Θ; Tᵢ.T = DT(𝒟'_{⌊bn⌋}, nᵥ, nₗ); Tᵢ.p = Exp[−γL̂ᵒᵒᵇ(Tᵢ.T)];
/* Forward phase                                                               */
Input: X, nₜ
Output: Y
7  for i ← 1 to nₜ do
8  |    Xʳ = rotate X based on Tᵢ.Θ; Yᵢ = Tᵢ.T(Xʳ);
9  if Classification Task then  Y = arg max_{j∈{1,⋯,c}} Σ_{i∈{1,⋯,nₜ}:Yᵢ=j} Tᵢ.p ;
10 if Regression Task then  Y = Σ_{i=1}^{nₜ} Yᵢ · Tᵢ.p ;
/* Functions                                                                   */
11 function T = DT(𝒟ₙ, nᵥ, nₗ);
12 if n ≤ nₗ then
13 |    T.l = mode({Y ∈ 𝒟ₙ}) ;
14 else
15 |    Split 𝒟ₙ in 𝒟'_{n'} and 𝒟''_{n''} based on the best split over a random subset of size nᵥ of all the features ;
16 |    T.s = s; T.T' = DT(𝒟'_{n'}, nᵥ, nₗ); T.T'' = DT(𝒟''_{n''}, nᵥ, nₗ);
```

the nonparametric Bootstrap (BOO) is exploited [2]. BOO relies on a simple idea: the original dataset $\mathcal{D}_n$ is resampled once or many (n_o) times with replacement, to build three independent datasets called training, validation, and test sets, respectively $\mathcal{L}_l^o$, $\mathcal{V}_v^o$, and $\mathcal{T}_t^o$, with $o \in \{1, \cdots, n_o\}$. Note that $\mathcal{L}_l^o \cap \mathcal{V}_v^o = \varnothing$, $\mathcal{L}_l^o \cap \mathcal{T}_t^o = \varnothing$, and $\mathcal{V}_v^o \cap \mathcal{T}_t^o = \varnothing$. Then, in order to select the best set of hyperparameters $\mathcal{H}$ in the set of possible ones $\mathfrak{H} = \{\mathcal{H}_1, \mathcal{H}_2, \cdots\}$ for the algorithm $\mathscr{A}_\mathcal{H}$ or, in other words, to perform the performance tuning phase, the following procedure needs to be applied:

$$\mathcal{H}^* : \arg\min_{\mathcal{H} \in \mathfrak{H}} \frac{1}{n_o} \sum_{o=1}^{n_o} \widehat{L}^{\mathcal{V}_v^o}(\mathscr{A}_\mathcal{H}(\mathcal{L}_l^o)). \tag{1}$$

Since the data in $\mathcal{L}_l^o$ are i.i.d. with respect to the ones in $\mathcal{V}_v^o$, the idea is that $\mathcal{H}^*$ should be the set of hyperparameters which allows to achieve a small error on a data set that is independent from the training set. The uncertainty quantification, instead, is performed as follows [2,13]:

$$L(\mathscr{A}_{\mathcal{H}^*}(\mathcal{D}_n)) \leq \widehat{L}(\mathscr{A}_{\mathcal{H}^*}(\mathcal{D}_n)) + \sqrt{\frac{\log(\frac{1}{\delta})}{2t}}, \widehat{L}(\mathscr{A}_{\mathcal{H}^*}(\mathcal{D}_n)) = \frac{1}{n_o}\sum_{o=1}^{n_o} \widehat{L}^{\mathcal{T}_t^o}(\mathscr{A}_{\mathcal{H}^*}(\mathcal{L}_l^o \cup \mathcal{V}_v^o)) \tag{2}$$

where the bound holds with probability $(1 - \delta)$. Note that after the best set of hyperparameters is found, one can select the best model by training the algorithm with the whole data set $\mathscr{A}_{\mathcal{H}^*}(\mathcal{D}_n)$ [2] and since the data in $\mathcal{L}_l^o \cup \mathcal{V}_v^o$ are i.i.d. with respect to $\mathcal{T}_t^o$ it follows that $\widehat{L}^{\mathcal{T}_t^o}(\mathscr{A}_{\mathcal{H}^*}(\mathcal{L}_l^o \cup \mathcal{V}_v^o))$ is an unbiased estimator of $L(\mathscr{A}_{(\mathcal{D}_n, \mathcal{H}^*)})$. Then, any concentration result can be used, like the Hoeffding inequality [13], for bounding the bias between the expected value and its empirical estimator. Note that, in the BOO, $l = n$ and $\mathcal{L}_l^o$ must be sampled with replacement from $\mathcal{D}_n$, while $\mathcal{V}_v^o$ and $\mathcal{T}_t^o$ are sampled without replacement from $\mathcal{D}_n \setminus \mathcal{L}_l^o$.

Finally, note that in this paper authors set n_t as large as possible. Since the performance of the RF always increases by increasing n_t [3,4] we stop increasing n_t when the performance of the RF stops to increase.

4 Results

In this section, authors report the results of applying the techniques proposed in Sect. 3 to the problem described in Sect. 2, based on the data provided by DAMEN Shipyards and outlined in the same section. In particular three approaches have been compared:

- ORF: the original RF proposed in [4];
- RFR: the RF proposed in [3] which improve over the ORF;
- PRF: the RF algorithms proposed in this paper (see Algorithm 1) where their hyperparameters have been tuned with the BOO procedure described in Sect. 3.

For what concerns PRF authors set $\mathcal{H} = \{\gamma, b, n_v, n_r, n_l\}$ and $\mathfrak{H} = \{10^{-4.0}, 10^{-3.5}, \cdots, 10^{3.0}\} \times \{0.7, 0.8, \cdots, 1.2\} \times d^{\{0.0, 0.1, \cdots, 1\}} \times \{1, 10, 100\} \times n \cdot \{0.0, 0.01, 0.05, 0.1\}$, $n_o = 100$ in the BOO procedure, and $n_t = 10^3$ since larger values did not produce any improvement in the accuracies of ORF, RFR, and PRF in any of the experiments.

Moreover, three different scenarios have been investigated:

- S1: authors kept different yard number in each of the sets $\mathcal{L}_l^o$, $\mathcal{V}_v^o$, and $\mathcal{T}_t^o$. In this way in the training set both examples of different products and different product clusters are present;
- S2: authors kept different products in each of the sets $\mathcal{L}_l^o$, $\mathcal{V}_v^o$, and $\mathcal{T}_t^o$. In this way the case when a new product needs to be designed is simulated;
- S3: authors kept different product clusters in each of the sets $\mathcal{L}_l^o$, $\mathcal{V}_v^o$, and $\mathcal{T}_t^o$. In this way, the case when a new series of products needs to be designed is simulated.

Note that S1 is a simpler task with respect to S2, which is again a simpler task with respect to S3. In fact, authors try to simulate the increasingly difficult task to extrapolate the performance indexes of a vessel, which is more and more different with respect to the vessels contained in the training set.

In Table 2 is reported $\hat{L}(\mathscr{A}_{\mathcal{H}^*}(\mathcal{D}_n))$ and $L(\mathscr{A}_{\mathcal{H}^*}(\mathcal{D}_n))$ in percentage respectively for ORF, RFR, and PRF in S1, S2, and S3 where $\delta = 0.05$. From the results it is possible to observe that:

- PRF mostly outperform ORF and RFR as expected;
- $\hat{L}(\mathscr{A}_{\mathcal{H}^*}(\mathcal{D}_n))$ and $L(\mathscr{A}_{\mathcal{H}^*}(\mathcal{D}_n))$ are close with each other and this means that it is possible to guarantee a quality of the estimation which is close enough to the expected quality of the produced data-driven model;
- as expected, the performances in S1 are better than the ones in S2 and S3. Nevertheless, even in S2 an S3 the performances of PRF are quite satisfying since the errors are around 5%. Note, instead, that for S3, ORF and RFR cannot be used in a real-world application because of their low accuracies.

Table 2. $\hat{L}(\mathscr{A}_{\mathcal{H}^*}(\mathcal{D}_n))$ and $L(\mathscr{A}_{\mathcal{H}^*}(\mathcal{D}_n))$ of ORF, RFR, PRF in S1, S2, S3 (in %).

$\hat{L}(\mathscr{A}_{\mathcal{H}^*}(\mathcal{D}_n))$	Loss Function	S1			S2			S3		
		ORF	RFR	PRF	ORF	RFR	PRF	ORF	RFR	PRF
TR	ℓ_{TRAE}	3.9±0.4	3.1±0.3	2.7±0.3	10.2±1.0	4.0±0.4	3.1±0.4	12.9±1.4	3.9±0.4	3.7±0.4
HR	ℓ_{TRAE}	3.7±0.4	3.0±0.3	2.7±0.3	10.8±1.1	4.3±0.4	3.3±0.3	13.3±1.1	4.0±0.4	4.0±0.4
LD	ℓ_{TRAE}	30.8±3.2	12.2±1.1	2.9±0.3	37.1±3.9	14.9±1.6	5.0±0.5	36.1±3.7	14.5±1.4	5.4±0.5
TFM	ℓ_{TRAE}	3.8±0.4	3.1±0.3	2.7±0.3	12.2±1.2	4.9±0.5	4.9±0.5	12.6±1.2	5.0±0.5	5.0±0.5
LDD	ℓ_H	7.1±0.8	5.7±0.6	4.3±0.5	10.3±1.1	6.2±0.7	5.3±0.6	26.7±3.1	8.0±0.7	3.9±0.4
HDD	ℓ_H	8.2±0.9	5.7±0.6	4.1±0.4	11.7±1.2	7.1±0.7	4.7±0.4	25.6±2.4	7.7±0.9	3.9±0.4

$L(\mathscr{A}_{\mathcal{H}^*}(\mathcal{D}_n))$	Loss Function	S1			S2			S3		
		ORF	RFR	PRF	ORF	RFR	PRF	ORF	RFR	PRF
TR	ℓ_{TRAE}	7.1±0.7	5.8±0.5	5.2±0.6	14.2±1.3	7.1±0.7	5.8±0.6	17.6±1.7	7.1±0.7	6.5±0.6
HR	ℓ_{TRAE}	6.5±0.7	5.8±0.6	5.2±0.4	15.3±1.7	7.7±0.8	6.5±0.6	18.1±1.9	7.1±0.8	7.1±0.8
LD	ℓ_{TRAE}	36.8±3.7	16.5±1.7	5.8±0.5	43.0±3.7	19.8±2.0	8.3±0.9	42.0±4.6	19.2±1.9	8.9±0.9
TFM	ℓ_{TRAE}	7.1±0.6	5.8±0.6	5.2±0.5	16.5±1.6	8.3±1.1	8.3±0.9	17.0±1.8	8.3±0.9	8.3±0.8
LDD	ℓ_H	10.7±1.2	8.9±0.8	7.7±0.7	14.8±1.5	9.5±0.9	8.9±1.0	32.1±3.6	11.9±1.3	7.1±0.8
HDD	ℓ_H	11.9±1.3	8.9±0.9	7.1±0.7	15.9±1.7	10.7±1.0	7.7±0.7	31.1±3.7	11.3±1.2	7.1±0.8

5   Conclusions

In this paper, authors developed a series of data-driven models able to estimate the vessel safety properties during the preliminary design stages. In particular, authors have proposed a vessel crash stop maneuvering performance prediction which can accurately predict the results of this safety test. To achieve this goal, authors proposed to use a recent improvement of the RF learning algorithm and show that an accurate tuning procedure can remarkably improve their predictive power. Results on real-world data, collected and provided by the DAMEN Shipyards, demonstrate the effectiveness of the proposal which is already exploited in DAMEN for the realization of new High-Speed Craft vessels. This work is a step forward in the direction of a smart and safe ship design since it allows to better forecast the safety properties of a ship before its production. As a future work, authors plan to derive new predictive models able to both take into account the principal equation methods and the data driven ones, analogously to [6], to obtain even more accurate models able to provide more insights on the ship safety properties.

References

1. ABS: Guide for vessel manoeuvrability (2006)
2. Anguita, D., Ghio, A., Oneto, L., Ridella, S.: In-sample and out-of-sample model selection and error estimation for support vector machines. IEEE TNNLS **23**(9), 1390–1406 (2012)
3. Blaser, R., Fryzlewicz, P.: Random rotation ensembles. JMLR **2**, 1–15 (2015)
4. Breiman, L.: Random forests. Mach. Learn. **45**(1), 5–32 (2001)
5. Catoni, O.: Pac-Bayesian Supervised Classification. Institute of Mathematical Statistics (2007)
6. Coraddu, A., Oneto, L., Baldi, F., Anguita, A.: Ship efficiency forecast based on sensors data collection: Improving numerical models through data analytics. In: OCEANS 2015-Genova (2015)
7. Coraddu, A., Oneto, L., Baldi, F., Anguita, D.: Vessels fuel consumption forecast and trim optimisation: a data analytics perspective. Ocean Eng. **130**, 351–370 (2017)

8. Damen: http://products.damen.com/en/clusters/crew-supply-vessel

9. Donders, A.R.T., van der Heijden, G.J.M.G., Stijnen, T., Moons, K.G.: Review: a gentle introduction to imputation of missing values. J. Clin. Epidemiol. **59**(10), 1087–1091 (2006)

10. Fernández-Delgado, M., Cernadas, E., Barro, S., Amorim, D.: Do we need hundreds of classifiers to solve real world classification problems? JMLR **15**(1), 3133–3181 (2014)

11. Germain, P., Lacasse, A., Laviolette, F., Marchand, M., Roy, J.F.: Risk bounds for the majority vote: from a PAC-Bayesian analysis to a learning algorithm. JMLR **16**(4), 787–860 (2015)

12. Harvald, S.A.: Factors affecting the stopping ability of vessels. J. Int. Shipbuild. Prog. **23**(260), 106–121 (1976)

13. Hoeffding, W.: Probability inequalities for sums of bounded random variables. J. Am. Stat. Assoc. **58**(301), 13–30 (1963)

14. Hoppe, H.: International regulations for high-speed craft an overview. In: International Conference on Fast Sea Transportation (2005)

15. IMO: Maritime safety. http://www.imo.org/

16. IMO: Resolution MSC.36(63). International Code of Safety for High-Speed Craft (1994)

17. IMO: Resolution MSC.97(73). International Code of Safety for High-Speed Craft (2000)

18. Langxiong, G., Liangming, L., Yuangzhou, Z., Baogang, Z.: A new method for accurate prediction of ship's inertial stopping distance. Res. J. Appl. Sci. Eng. Technol. **18**(6), 3437–3440 (2013)

19. Lever, G., Laviolette, F., Shawe-Taylor, F.: Tighter PAC-Bayes bounds through distribution-dependent priors. Theoret. Comput. Sci. **473**, 4–28 (2013)

20. Ming, L., Liu, J.X., Yang, S.: A new method on calculation of vessels stopping distance and crash stopping distance. Adv. Mater. Res. **779**, 800–804 (2013)

21. Okamoto, H., Tanaka, A., Nozawa, K., Saito, Y.: Stopping abilities of vessels equipped with controllable pitch propeller. J. Int. Shipbuild. Prog. **21**(235), 53–69 (1974)

22. Orlandi, I., Oneto, L., Anguita, D.: Random forests model selection. In: ESANN (2016)

23. Vapnik, V.N.: Statistical Learning Theory. Wiley, Hoboken (1998)

24. Wainberg, M., Alipanahi, B., Frey, B.J.: Are random forests truly the best classifiers? JMLR **17**(110), 1–5 (2016)

25. Wirz, D.I.F.: Optimisation of the crash-stop manoeuvre of vessels employing slow-speed two-stroke engines and fixed pitch propellers. J. Mar. Eng. Technol. **11**(1), 35–43 (2012)

Combining Character-Level Representation for Relation Classification

Dongyun Liang$^{(\boxtimes)}$, Weiran Xu, and Yinge Zhao

PRIS, Beijing University of Posts and Telecommunications, Beijing, China
{dongyunliang,xuweiran}@bupt.edu.cn, yingezhao@outlook.com

Abstract. Word representation models have achieved great success in natural language processing tasks, such as relation classification. However, it does not always work on informal text, and the morphemes of some misspelling words may carry important short-distance semantic information. We propose a hybrid model, combining the merits of word-level and character-level representations to learn better representations on informal text. Experiments on the SemEval-2010 Task8 dataset for relation classification show that our model achieves a competitive result.

Keywords: Word embedding · Character-level representation · Relation classification · Recurrent neural network · Highway network

1 Introduction

Deep learning has made significant progress in natural language processing, and most of approaches treat word representation as the cornerstone. Though it is effective, word-level representation is inherently problematic: it assumes that each word type has its own vector that can vary independently; most words only occur once in training data and out-of-vocabulary (OOV) words cannot be addressed. A word may typically include a root and one or more affixes (*rock-s, red-ness, quick-ly, run-ning, un-expect-ed*), or more than one root in a compound (*black-board, rat-race*). It is reasonable to assume that words which share common components (root, prefix, suffix) may be potentially related, while word-level representation considers each word separately. On the other hand, new words enter English from every area of life, e.g. *Chillaxing* - Blend of *chilling* and *relaxing*, represent taking a break from stressful activities to rest or relax. Whereas the vocabulary size of word-level model is fixed beforehand, out-of-vocabulary or rare words in training data are mapped to a common type 'UNKNOWN' to constrain memory requirements when training neural network models, and the lack of these word representations may lose important semantic information.

Especially on informal text, the problems of word-level representation will be amplified and hard to ignore. Some approaches use lexical resources, such as WordNet [1], or segment each word to infer its components (root, prefix, suffix) to build orthographically aware model, however, it entailed extra work

© Springer International Publishing AG 2017
A. Lintas et al. (Eds.): ICANN 2017, Part II, LNCS 10614, pp. 394–401, 2017.
https://doi.org/10.1007/978-3-319-68612-7_45

to increase handcrafted features. Recently, character-level representation, which takes characters as atomic units to derive the embeddings, demonstrates that it can memorize the arbitrary aspects of word orthography. Parameters of these simple model are less, and it will be not ideal when processing long sentence. Combining word-level and character-level representations attempts to overcome the weaknesses of the two representations.

We utilize a Bidirectional Gated Recurrent Unit (Bi-GRU) [2] and Convolutional Neural Networks (CNN) to capture two-level semantic representations respectively. While character-level information is likely to be drowned out by word-level information if simply connected, we adopt Highway Networks [3] to balance both. To evaluate our model, we evaluate on a public benchmark: SemEval-2010 Task8.

2 Related Work

Some works [4,5] started to learn semantic representations of word by unsupervised approaches. Recently, relation classification has focused on neural networks. CNN [6,7] is used to learn patterns of relations from raw text data to make representative progress, but a potential problem of that is that CNN is not suitable for learning long-distance semantic information. Some models [8,9] leveraged the shortest dependency path (SDP) between two nominals. Others [10,11] employed attention mechanism to capture more important semantic information.

Working to a new dataset KBP37, Zhang and Wang [12] proposed a framework based on a bidirectional Recurrent Neural Network (RNN). However, all these methods depend on learning word-level distributed representation without utilizing morphological feature.

Recent work captures word orthography using character-based neural networks. Zhang et al. demonstrated the effectiveness of character-level CNN [13] in text classification. Kim et al. [14] employed CNN and a highway network to learn rich semantic and orthographic features from encoding characters. There were some models [15,16] based on RNN structures, which can memorize arbitrary aspects of word orthography over characters.

Nakov and Tiedemann [17] combined character-based transliteration with a word-level translation model for machine translation, but their work still trained on n-gram aligned characters.

Inspired by these, our model uses multi-channel GRU units and CNN architecture to learn the representations of word-level and character-level, and project it to a softmax output layer for relation classification.

3 Model

As shown in Fig. 1, the architecture of our model contains four components:

1. Input: look up the embedding matrices of words and characters in sequence respectively to obtain input vectors;

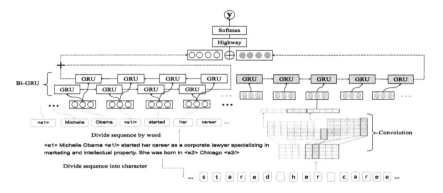

Fig. 1. Hybrid model that combines character-level representation.

2. Word-level representation: process word vector of the sequence by a Bi-GRU layer;
3. Character-level representation: apply convolution to character vector of the sequence, and followed by a GRU layer;
4. Combination: concatenate the word-level representation with character-level representation, and pass them through a Highway Network [3].

The model learns word-level and character-level representations respectively, and combines them with interaction to get the final representation.

3.1   Word-Level

Given a relation sentence consisting of words $w_1, w_2, \ldots, w_m$, each w_i is defined as a one hot vector 1_{w_i}, with value 1 at index w_i and 0 in all other dimensionality. We multiply a matrix $P_W \in \mathbb{R}^{d_w \times |V|}$ by 1_{w_i} to project the word w_i into its word embedding x_i, as with a lookup table:

$$x_i = P_W w_i \qquad (1)$$

where d_w is the size of word embedding and V is the vocabulary of training set. Then input the $x_1, x_2, \ldots, x_m$ sequence to a Bi-GRU network iteratively. Each GRU unit applies the following transformations:

$$
\begin{aligned}
r_t &= \sigma(W_r x_t + U_r h_{t-1} + b_r) \\
z_t &= \sigma(W_z x_t + U_z h_{t-1} + b_z) \\
h_t &= (1 - z_t) \odot h_{t-1} + z_t \odot \tilde{h}_t \\
\tilde{h}_t &= \tanh(W_h x_t + U_h(r_t \odot h_{t-1}) + b_h)
\end{aligned}
\qquad (2)
$$

where z_t is a set of update gates, r_t is a set of reset gates and $\odot$ is an element-wise multiplication. W_r, W_z, W_h and U_r, U_z, U_h are weight matrices to be learned, and $\tilde{h}_t$ is the candidate activation. We use element-wise sum to combine the forward and backward pass final states as word-level representation: $h_m^w = [\overrightarrow{h_m} + \overleftarrow{h_0}]$.

3.2   Character-Level

To capture morphological features, we use convolutions to learn local n-gram features at the lower network layer. At the higher layer, we build a GRU to obtain the long range dependency.

As character-level input, original sentence is decomposed into a sequence of characters, including special characters, such as white-space. We first project each character into a character embedding x_i by a lookup table whose mechanism is exactly as Eq. 1.

Given the $x_1, x_2, \ldots, x_n$ embedding sequence, we compose the matrix $D^k \in \mathbb{R}^{kd_c \times n}$ to execute convolutions with same padding:

$$C^k = \tanh(W^k_{con} D^k) \tag{3}$$

where d_c is the size of word embedding and each column i in D^k consists of the concatenation of vectors (i.e. k embeddings centered at the i-th character), W^k_{con} is a weight matrix of convolution layer, and $C^k \in \mathbb{R}^{c \times n}$ is the output of the convolution with c filters. We use p groups of filters with varying widths to obtain n-gram feature, and concatenate them by column:

$$C = C^{k_1} \oplus C^{k_2} \oplus \ldots \oplus C^{k_p} \tag{4}$$

The next step, $c_i, \ldots, c_n$ denoted by the column vector of C are fed as input sequence to a forward-GRU network (Eq. 2), and we pick up final states activation h^c_n as character-level representation.

3.3   Combination

Instead of fully connected network layer, we utilize Highway Networks to emphasize impact of character level. Highway can be used to adaptively copy or transform representations, even when large depths are not required. We apply this idea to retain some independence of word and character when merging with interaction. Let h^* be the concatenation of h^w_m and h^c_n, The combination z is obtained by the Highway Network:

$$z = t \odot g(W_H h^* + b_H) + (1 - t) \odot h^*$$
$$t = \sigma(W_T h^* + b_T) \tag{5}$$

where g is a nonlinear function (tanh), t is referred to as the transform gate, and $(1 - t)$ as the carry gate. W_T and W_H are square weight matrices, and b_T and b_H are bias vectors.

3.4   Training

Training our model for classifying sentence relation is a processes to optimizing the whole parameters θ of network layers. Given an input sentence

X and the candidate set of relation Y, the classifier returns output $\hat{y} = \arg\max_{y \in Y} p(y|X, \theta)$.

We let the combination vector z through a softmax layer to give the distribution $y = softmax(W_f z + b_f)$.

The training objective is the penalized cross-entropy loss between predicted and true relation:

$$J(\theta) = -\frac{1}{N} \sum_{i=1}^{N} \sum_{j=1}^{m} t_{i,j} \log(y_{i,j}) + \lambda \|\theta\|_F^2 \tag{6}$$

where N is the mini-batch size, m is the size of relation set, $t \in \mathbb{R}^m$ denotes the one-hot represented ground truth, $y_{i,j}$ is the predicted probability that the i-th sentence belongs to class j, and λ is a coefficient of L2 regularization.

4   Experiments

4.1   Dataset

We evaluate our model on SemEval-2010 Task8 dataset. This dataset is an established benchmark for relation classification containing 9 directional relations and an Other class. For instance, *Cause-Effect(e1,e2)* and *Cause-Effect(e2,e1)* are distinct relations with directionality taken into account.

The following sentence contains an example of the *Cause-Effect* relation between the nominals *singer* and *commotion*, and there are four position indicators which specify start and end of the nominals.

The <e1> singer <e1/>, who performed three of the nominated songs, also caused a <e2> commotion <e2/> on the red carpet.

The former 9 relations are directed, the Other class is undirected, so we have 19 different classes for 10 relations as follows:

- Cause-Effect
- Component-Whole
- Content-Container
- Entity-Destination
- Entity-Origin
- Message-Topic
- Member-Collection
- Instrument-Agency
- Product-Agency
- Other

There are 8,000 examples for training that consists of 86 unique characters and 2,717 for testing. We randomly split 800 samples out of the training set for validation, and adopt the official evaluation metric in terms of macro-averaged F1 score (excluding Other class) to evaluate our model.

4.2 Setup

We employ some tricks to assist training, such as pre-trained embedding and dropout [18]. Firstly, we initialize the word embedding with 100-dimensional vectors pre-trained by [5]. Character embeddings are being trained from a simple Bi-RNN network on the principle of [19], and are set to size 100. The width of convolution filter's group is chosen to be $[2, 3, 4, 5]$, and each group contains 40 separate filters. L2 regularization coefficient is set to 10^{-5}.

Dropout can prevents co-adaptation of hidden units by randomly omitting feature detectors from the network during forward propagation. We employ dropout on the embedding layer and the penultimate layer, and the dropout rate is set as 0.3. Then we learn the parameters using AdaDelta [20] on a learning rate of 1.0 by a mini-batch size 30.

As average sentence length of relation classification is long, we take the characters of the sentence between two nominals with position indicators as character-level input.

4.3 Results

Table 1 compares our model with other previous state-of-the-art methods on SemEval-2010 Task8 dataset. The SVM classifier [21] on a variety of handcrafted features achieved an F1-score of 82.2%. Zeng et al. [6] utilized CNN and constructed lexical features by WordNet, making representative progress. Xu et al. [8] achieved an F1-score of 83.7% via heterogeneous information along the SDP. BRCNN [9] combined CNN and two-channel LSTM units to learns features along SDP, and made use of POS tags, NER and WordNet hypernyms. Att-BLSTM [10] only operated attention mechanism on Bidirectional Long Short-Term Memory (BLSTM) units with word vector.

Table 1. Comparison on SemEval-2010 Task8.

Model	F1
SVM [21]	82.2
CNN [6]	82.7
SDP-LSTM [8]	83.7
BRCNN [9]	86.3
Att-BLSTM [10]	84.0
Character-level Only [16]	82.1
Full connected network	83.9
Our architecture	84.1

Our model yields an F1-score of 84.1%, and outperforms most of the existing competing approaches. Compared with the BRCNN [9], our model learns good representations to get a competitive result without using any human-designed features and relying on any lexical resources.

Then, we illustrate Bi-GRU architecture of Tweet2Vec [16], a pure character-level composition model, to show the effectiveness of character-level representation. Next, we get rid of the impact of characters to do word-level only experiment, and replace the highway with a fully connected layer. These clean comparisons demonstrate that the character-level and Highway network help to learn a better representation for classification.

5   Conclusion

In this paper, we propose a hybrid model that combines character-level representation. This model encodes characters by a cascade of CNN and GRU units, encodes words by Bi-GRU units, and uses Highway Network to combine. We demonstrate that our model achieves competitive results on the popular benchmark SemEval-2010 Task8 and achieves a great performance at learning character features without relying on any lexical resources. In future, we plan to release a appropriate dataset to demonstrate further effectiveness of the combination and add interactions for each word with the corresponding positional characters.

Acknowledgments. This work was supported by 111 Project of China under Grant No. B08004, National Natural Science Foundation of China (61273217, 61300080, 61671078), and the Ph.D. Programs Foundation of Ministry of Education of China (20130005110004).

References

1. Miller, G.A.: WordNet: a lexical database for English. Commun. ACM **38**(11), 39–41 (1995)
2. Chung, J., Gulcehre, C., Cho, K., Bengio, Y.: Empirical evaluation of gated recurrent neural networks on sequence modeling. arXiv preprint (2014). arXiv:1412.3555
3. Srivastava, R.K., Greff, K., Schmidhuber, J.: Training very deep networks. In: Advances in Neural Information Processing Systems (2015)
4. Mikolov, T., Chen, K., Corrado, G., Dean, J.: Efficient estimation of word representations in vector space. arXiv preprint. arxiv:1301.3781 (2013)
5. Pennington, J., Socher, R., Manning, C.D.: Glove: global vectors for word representation. In: EMNLP, vol. 14, pp. 1532–1543 (2014)
6. Zeng, D., Liu, K., Lai, S., Zhou, G., Zhao, J., et al.: Relation classification via convolutional deep neural network. In: COLING, pp. 2335–2344 (2014)
7. dos Santos, C.N., Xiang, B., Zhou, B.: Classifying relations by ranking with convolutional neural networks. arXiv preprint. arxiv:1504.06580 (2015)
8. Xu, Y., Mou, L., Li, G., Chen, Y., Peng, H., Jin, Z.: Classifying relations via long short term memory networks along shortest dependency paths. In: EMNLP (2015)
9. Cai, R., Zhang, X., Wang, H.: Bidirectional recurrent convolutional neural network for relation classification. In: ACL, vol. 1, pp. 756–765 (2016)

10. Zhou, P., Shi, W., Tian, J., Qi, Z., Li, B., Hao, H., Bo, X.: Attention-based bidirectional long short-term memory networks for relation classification. In: ACL, p. 207 (2016)
11. Wang, L., Cao, Z., de Melo, G., Liu, Z.: Relation classification via multi-level attention CNNs. In: ACL, vol. 1, pp. 1298–1307 (2016)
12. Zhang, D., Wang, D.: Relation classification via recurrent neural network. arXiv preprint (2015). arxiv:1508.01006
13. Zhang, X., Zhao, J., LeCun, Y.: Character-level convolutional networks for text classification. In: Advances in Neural Information Processing Systems, pp. 649–657 (2015)
14. Kim, Y., Jernite, Y., Sontag, D., Rush, A.M.: Character-aware neural language models. arXiv preprint (2015). arxiv:1508.06615
15. Ling, W., Luís, T., Marujo, L., Astudillo, R.F., Amir, S., Dyer, C., Black, A.W., Trancoso, I.: Finding function in form: compositional character models for open vocabulary word representation. arXiv preprint (2015). arxiv:1508.02096
16. Dhingra, B., Zhou, Z., Fitzpatrick, D., Muehl, M., Cohen, W.W.: Tweet2vec: character-based distributed representations for social media. arXiv preprint (2016). arxiv:1605.03481
17. Nakov, P., Tiedemann, J.: Combining word-level and character-level models for machine translation between closely-related languages. In: ACL, pp. 301–305 (2012)
18. Hinton, G.E., Srivastava, N., Krizhevsky, A., Sutskever, I., Salakhutdinov, R.R.: Improving neural networks by preventing co-adaptation of feature detectors. arXiv preprint (2012). arxiv:1207.0580
19. Mou, L., Meng, Z., Yan, R., Li, G., Yan, X., Zhang, L., Jin, Z.: How transferable are neural networks in NLP applications? In: ACL (2016)
20. Zeiler, M.D.: ADADELTA: an adaptive learning rate method. arXiv preprint (2012). arxiv:1212.5701
21. Rink, B., Harabagiu, S.: UTD: classifying semantic relations by combining lexical and semantic resources. ACL, p. 256 (2010)

On Combining Clusterwise Linear Regression and K-Means with Automatic Weighting of the Explanatory Variables

Ricardo A.M. da Silva and Francisco de A.T. de Carvalho[✉]

Centro de Informatica - CIn, Universidade Federal de Pernambuco, Recife, Brazil
{rams,fatc}@cin.ufpe.br
http://www.cin.ufpe.br

Abstract. This paper gives a clusterwise linear regression method aiming to provide linear regression models that are based on homogeneous clusters of observations w.r.t. the explanatory variables. To achieve this aim, this method combine the standard clusterwise linear regression and K-Means with automatic computation of relevance weights for the explanatory variables. Experiments with benchmark datasets corroborate the usefulness of the proposed method.

1 Introduction

Regression modeling includes a set of well-known methodologies used for describing (predicting) one dependent (response) variable, by fitting a mathematical regression model to the observed data so that the theoretical relationship with one or more independent (explanatory) variables can be explained in a reasonable way. The most widely used method of regression is the Multivariate Linear Regression (MLR) [11] where one or many explanatory variables are related to one response variable according to a parametric linear model.

Often, when the number of observations and explanatory variables are almost the same, only one regression model may be sufficient to achieve a good data modeling. However, when this is not the case, it is reasonable to assume that more than one regression model will be needed to get a good data modeling [13]. As a consequence of the heterogeneity in the data [2,14], different kind of relationships are supposed to exist between the predictive and the explanatory variables into different groups of observations, so that a number of linear regression models should be fitted, one for each group, to fully describe all the relations present in the data.

The classical approach to address the problem of establishing multiple linear regression models for heterogeneous data is called Clusterwise Linear Regression (CLR) [13] where the aim is to find a partition of the dataset in a way that the sum of squared residuals for each within-cluster regression model is minimized for all clusters.

The authors would like to thanks CNPq and FACEPE (Brazilian agencies) for their financial support.

A. Lintas et al. (Eds.): ICANN 2017, Part II, LNCS 10614, pp. 402–410, 2017.
https://doi.org/10.1007/978-3-319-68612-7_46

As stated by Brusco et al. [2] and Vicari and Vichi [14], the CLR method is not designed to identify the linear relationships within homogeneous clusters, with respect to the explanatory variables, that exhibit an internal cohesion and an external separation. The clustering process just follow the minimum residual requirement which can assign very far observations, in terms of their explanatory variables, to the same group just because they have the smallest residual on the regression model associated with this group. Consequently, it is very difficult the choice of the appropriated regression model for an unknown observation using the explanatory variables measurements. To overcome these difficulties, following [9,14], in this paper we propose a clusterwise regression method aiming to provide linear regression models that are based on homogeneous clusters of observations w.r.t. the explanatory variables and that are well fitted w.r.t. the response variable.

Although the methods described in [9,14] fulfill these requirements, they do not take into account the relevance of the variables, i.e., these methods consider that all explanatory variables are equally important to the clustering process in the sense that all have the same relevance weight. However, in most areas we typically have to deal with high dimensional datasets. Therefore, some explanatory variables may be irrelevant and, among the relevant ones, some may be more or less relevant than others [4,6,10].

A better strategy is to consider that there may exist differences in the relevance among explanatory variables. By considering these relevances, the performance of the clustering process can be improved. We use an adaptive distance metric [4] to assess the relevance of the variables during the clustering process. This approach allows us to cluster the dataset into homogeneous groups w.r.t. the relevant explanatory variables. A related approach was developed in the framework of fuzzy clusterwise linear regression [5], where the simultaneous determination of a data partition and regression equations is modified in such a way that the shapes of clusters are changed dynamically and adaptively in the clustering process [12].

To summarize, the proposed method combine the standard clusterwise linear regression and K-Means with automatic computation of relevance weights to the explanatory variables. This method aims to form homogeneous clusters based simultaneously on the relevant explanatory variables and on the minimization of the sum of the squared residuals of the response variable. Because it learns simultaneously a prototype and a linear regression model for each cluster it is able to provide an appropriated regression model for unknown observations based on their description by the explanatory variables.

The paper is organized as follows. Section 2 provides a detailed description of the method. Section 3 presents the experiments with benchmark datasets. Finally, Sect. 4 gives the final remarks of the paper.

2   Clusterwise Linear Regression and K-Means with Automated Weighting of the Explanatory Variables

This section presents the Weighted Clusterwise Linear Regression method, hereafter named WCLR, that aims to provide homogeneous clusters w.r.t. the relevant explanatory variables and linear regression models, one for each cluster. This method is able to select the important explanatory variables in the clustering process and therefore provides linear regression models of better quality.

Let $E = \{e_1, \ldots, e_n\}$ be a set of n objects described by a real-valued response variable y and by p real-valued explanatory variables $x_1, \ldots, x_p$. Each object e_i $(i = 1, \ldots, n)$ is described by a tuple $(\mathbf{x}_i, y_i)$, where $\mathbf{x}_i = (x_{i1}, \ldots, x_{ip}) \in \mathbb{R}^p$ is the vector of explanatory variables and $y_i \in \mathbb{R}$ is the corresponding value of the response variable. The WCLR method provides a partition $\mathcal{P} = (P_1, \ldots, P_K)$ of E into K clusters, a vector of relevance weights $\boldsymbol{\lambda} = (\lambda_1, \ldots, \lambda_p)$, one for each explanatory variable, a matrix of cluster representatives (prototypes) $\mathbf{G} = (\mathbf{g}_1, \ldots, \mathbf{g}_K)$, and K linear regression models.

2.1   WCLR Method

In the WCLR method, the matrix of prototypes $\mathbf{G}$, the vector of relevance weights of the explanatory variables $\boldsymbol{\lambda}$, the vector of parameters of the linear regression models $\boldsymbol{\beta}_{(k)}$ $(k = 1, \ldots, K)$ and the partition $\mathcal{P}$ are obtained iteratively in four steps (representation, weighting, modeling and assignment) by the minimization of a suitable objective function that combines the total homogeneity of the partition, obtained according to the explanatory variables, and the total sum of squared residuals:

$$J_{WCLR} = \sum_{k=1}^{K} \sum_{e_i \in P_k} \left[\sum_{j=1}^{p} \lambda_j (x_{ij} - g_{kj})^2 + \alpha(y_i - \hat{y}_{i(k)})^2 \right] \tag{1}$$

subject to $\prod_{j=1}^{p} \lambda_j = 1$, where

- $\hat{y}_{i(k)} = \hat{\beta}_{0(k)} + \sum_{j=1}^{p} \hat{\beta}_{j(k)} x_{ij}$ is the ith predicted value provided by the kth linear regression model;
- $\alpha > 0$ is a user defined parameter that decides the relative weight of the two terms.

From an initial random partition $\mathcal{P}$, four steps are repeated until the convergence of the WCLR algorithm. These four steps are:

Representation Step. This step provides the optimal solution to the computation of the clusters representatives $\mathbf{g}_k = (g_{k1}, \ldots, g_{kp})$ $(k = 1, \ldots, K)$. During the representation step, the vector of relevance weights of the explanatory variables $\boldsymbol{\lambda}$, the vector of parameters of the linear regression models $\boldsymbol{\beta}_{(k)}$, and the partition $\mathcal{P}$ are kept fixed. The objective function J is optimized with respect to the prototypes.

Thus, from $\frac{\partial J}{\partial g_{kj}} = 0$, and after some algebra, the component g_{kj} of the cluster prototype $\mathbf{g}_k$ is obtained as follows:

$$g_{kj} = \frac{\sum_{e_i \in P_k} x_{ij}}{\sum_{e_i \in P_k}} = \frac{\sum_{e_i \in P_k} x_{ij}}{n_k} \quad k = 1, 2, \ldots, K, \, j = 1, 2, \ldots, p.$$

where n_k is the cardinal of cluster P_k.

Weighting Step. This step provides the optimal solution to the computation of the vector of relevance weights of the explanatory variables $\boldsymbol{\lambda} = (\lambda_1, \ldots, \lambda_p)$. During the weighting step, the matrix of prototypes $\mathbf{G}$, the vector of parameters of the linear regression models $\boldsymbol{\beta}_{(k)}$ and the partition $\mathcal{P}$ are kept fixed. We use the method of Lagrange multipliers with the restriction that [4] $\prod_{j=1}^{p} \lambda_j = 1$ and, after some algebra, we obtain

$$\lambda_j = \frac{\left\{ \prod_{h=1}^{p} \left[\sum_{k=1}^{K} \sum_{e_i \in P_k} (x_{ih} - g_{kh})^2 \right] \right\}^{\frac{1}{p}}}{\sum_{k=1}^{K} \sum_{e_i \in P_k} (x_{ij} - g_{kj})^2} \quad j = 1, 2, \ldots, p. \tag{2}$$

Model Step. This step provides the optimal solution to the computation of the vector of parameters of the linear regression models $\boldsymbol{\beta}_k = (\beta_{0(k)}, \ldots, \beta_{p(k)})$ $(k = 1, \ldots, K)$. During the model step the matrix of prototypes $\mathbf{G}$, the vector of relevance weights $\boldsymbol{\lambda}$, and the partition $\mathcal{P}$ are kept fixed.

Thus, from $\frac{\partial J}{\partial \beta_{0(k)}} = 0$, $\frac{\partial J}{\partial \beta_{j(k)}} = 0 \, (k = 1, \ldots, K)$, and after some algebra, one obtain the following system of equations:

$$\beta_{0(k)} n_k + \sum_{j=1}^{p} \beta_{j(k)} \sum_{e_i \in P_k} x_{ij} = \sum_{e_i \in P_k} y_i$$

$$\beta_{0(k)} \sum_{e_i \in P_k} x_{ij} + \sum_{l=1}^{p} \beta_{l(k)} \sum_{e_i \in P_k} x_{ij} x_{il} = \sum_{e_i \in P_k} x_{ij} y_i \quad k = 1, 2 \ldots, K. \tag{3}$$

This system can be solved similarly to the ordinary linear least squares method [11].

Assignment Step. This step provides the optimal solution for the cluster partition $\mathcal{P} = (P_1, \ldots, P_K)$. During the assignment step, the matrix of prototypes $\mathbf{G}$, the vector of relevance weights of the explanatory variables $\boldsymbol{\lambda}$, and the vector of parameters of the linear regression models $\boldsymbol{\beta}_{(k)} = (\beta_{0(k)}, \beta_{1(k)}, \ldots, \beta_{p(k)})^T$ $(k = 1, \ldots, K)$, are kept fixed.

The partition P_k $(k = 1, \ldots, K)$, that minimizes the clustering criterion J, is updated according the following assignment rule:

$$P_k = \left\{ e_i \in E : k = arg \min_{h=1}^{K} \sum_{j=1}^{p} \left[\lambda_j (x_{ij} - g_{hj})^2 \right] + \alpha \epsilon_{i(h)}^2 \right\} \tag{4}$$

The K-Means algorithm can be viewed as an Expectation-Maximization (EM) algorithm and it is convergent because each EM algorithm is convergent [3]. As the WCLR algorithm is a modified version of the classical K-Means algorithm, its convergence can be proved. The final solution provided by this kind of algorithm depends on the initial partition. It converges to a solution that is locally optimal. Therefore, it is recommended to repeat the process from multiple initial partitions and then select the best one.

3   Experimental Analysis

The aim of this session is to evaluate the performance of the proposed method, WCLR, for a *prediction* task. The standard Multiple Linear Regression (MLR) [11], the Clusterwise Linear Regression (CLR) [13] and the "Modified K-plane" [9], hereafter named KPLANE, methods were also considered for comparison purposes.

3.1   Benchmark Datasets

We assess the performance of the tested methods on several selected benchmarks datasets from the UCI Machine Learning repository [8] (Table 1). These datasets have a single response variable. Moreover, the variables were normalized (by scaling [0,1]) at a preprocessing phase.

Table 1. UCI repository datasets

Dataset	Number of explanatory variables	Number of observations
Wine Quality (Red)	11	1599
Auto-mpg	7	392
Concrete	8	1030
Forest Fires	11	517
Glass	9	214
Housing	13	452
Wine	12	178
Yacht Hydrodynamics	6	252

3.2   Hyper-Parameters Setting

The number of clusters K must be fixed *a priori* for CLR, KPLANE and WCLR methods. The parameters γ and α have a similar role in, respectively, KPLANE and WCLR methods. They are responsible for deciding the relative influence of the two terms of their respective cost functions. This value is extremely dependent on the dataset used and on the absolute value the two terms of the objective function. Following [2,9], we search for the best value of $K \in \{1, 2, 3, 4\}$, and $\alpha, \gamma \in \{0.01, 0.1, 1.0, 10.0, 100.0\}$ for all datasets.

3.3 Assignment Criterion

In order to predict the value of a new observation we need to choose one regression model among the K generated models. We use the cluster's centers provided by WCLR and KPLANE methods and, for CLR, we use the center of the clusters computed after the training process. Thus, for an observation $\mathbf{x}$ we use the hth regression model to predict its value as follows:

$$\text{WCLR: } h = arg \min_{k=1}^{K} \sum_{j=1}^{p} \left[\lambda_j (x_j - g_{kj})^2 \right]$$

$$\text{CLR and KPLANE: } h = arg \min_{k=1}^{K} \sum_{j=1}^{p} \left[(x_j - g_{kj})^2 \right]$$

3.4 Performance Measure

The prediction accuracy of the fitted regression models were measured by the Root Mean Squared Error [11]: $RMSE = \sqrt{\frac{1}{n} \sum_{i=1}^{n} (y_i - \hat{y}_i)^2}$.

3.5 Model Selection

Following [7], we used a 5×10-fold grid-search cross validation procedure to make the best cross-validatory choice for the hyper-parameter set in a prediction context. Table 2 shows the obtained optimal (with respect to the given grid and the given search criterion) parameters for CLR, KPLANE and WCLR methods.

Table 2. Cross-validatory choice for the K, γ and α

Dataset	CLR	KPLANE	WCLR
Wine Quality (red)	$K = 1$	$K = 2, \gamma = 1.0$	$K = 3, \alpha = 0.01$
Auto-mpg	$K = 1$	$K = 4, \gamma = 100.0$	$K = 3, \alpha = 0.01$
Concrete	$K = 2$	$K = 3, \gamma = 10.0$	$K = 4, \alpha = 0.01$
Forest Fires	$K = 1$	$K = 1, \gamma = 0.01$	$K = 1; \alpha = 0.01$
Glass	$K = 1$	$K = 2, \gamma = 10.0$	$K = 2, \alpha = 0.01$
Housing	$K = 1$	$K = 3, \gamma = 10.0$	$K = 2, \alpha = 10.0$
Wine	$K = 1$	$K = 1, \gamma = 0.01$	$K = 1, \alpha = 0.01$
Yacht Hydrodynamics	$K = 2$	$K = 3, \gamma = 0.01$	$K = 3, \alpha = 1.00$

3.6 Model Assessment

The use of predictive models depends on reliable model assessment. Following [7], a repeated nested Kfold cross-validation procedure was used in order to assess the expected prediction loss (RMSE) of the tested models. The cross-validatory assessment was made, for each dataset individually, with 5 repetition of a 10-Fold cross-validation resulting in a sample of 50 values for each tested method.

To assess the statistical significance of the sampled RMSE measures obtained by the cross-validatory assessment protocol we proceed with nonparametric tests. Following [1], we did the Kruskall-Wallis test (nonparametric version of ANOVA) to compare the RMSE samples from each tested method and a post hoc pairwise comparison using the Tukey and Kramer (Nemenyi) test with a confidence level of 0.95. Table 3 shows the mean, standard deviation, minimum and maximum RMSE values obtained from the model assessment procedure. The methods with the lowest average RMSE values are in bold. The difference in performance between a given method and WCLR is marked (*) if it is statistically significant.

Table 3. Comparison results on UCI datasets

Method	Stat	Mean	sd	Min	Max	Method	Stat	Mean	sd	Min	Max
Wine Quality (red)						Auto-mpg					
MLR		0.1144	0.0063	0.1019	0.1298	MLR	*	0.1725	0.0222	0.1227	0.2182
CLR		0.1146	0.0070	0.0969	0.1299	CLR	*	0.1726	0.0213	0.1212	0.2252
KPLANE		0.1133	0.0068	0.0981	0.1263	**KPLANE**		0.1531	0.0254	0.1045	0.2190
WCLR		0.1134	0.0076	0.0998	0.1307	WCLR		0.1536	0.0250	0.1116	0.2060
Concrete						Forest Fires					
MLR	*	0.2640	0.0185	0.2233	0.3112	MLR		0.7379	0.6653	0.2561	2.3800
CLR	*	0.2152	0.0169	0.1715	0.2468	CLR		0.7195	0.6858	0.2189	2.8200
KPLANE		0.2084	0.0167	0.1763	0.2471	**KPLANE**		0.6778	0.6519	0.2265	2.8540
WCLR		0.2029	0.0161	0.1578	0.2409	WCLR		0.7404	0.6638	0.2399	2.4160
Glass						Housing					
MLR		0.3182	0.0771	0.1730	0.5560	MLR	*	0.2028	0.0394	0.1370	0.3163
CLR		0.3215	0.0877	0.1580	0.5045	CLR	*	0.2010	0.0435	0.1169	0.3048
KPLANE		0.3273	0.0810	0.1731	0.4951	**KPLANE**		0.1649	0.0325	0.1249	0.3041
WCLR		0.3296	0.0734	0.1799	0.5025	WCLR		0.1690	0.0285	0.1191	0.2251
Wine						Yacht Hydrodynamics					
MLR		0.0424	0.0077	0.0277	0.0616	MLR	*	0.4920	0.0770	0.3776	0.6820
CLR		0.0425	0.0070	0.0229	0.0566	CLR	*	0.2416	0.0971	0.1245	0.4703
KPLANE		0.0440	0.0085	0.0280	0.0761	KPLANE	*	0.1888	0.0948	0.0561	0.3877
WCLR		0.0445	0.0063	0.0303	0.0582	**WCLR**		0.0858	0.0191	0.0438	0.1367

The WCLR method obtained the best result (lowest average RMSE) in 2 (Concrete and Yacht) of the 8 datasets evaluated. For the datasets where WCLR did not obtain the lowest average RMSE (Wine Quality (red), Auto-mpg, Forest Fires, Glass, Housing and Wine), the observed difference in performance between WCLR and the method of best performance was not statistically significant. Moreover, in the Yacht dataset, WCLR had the best performance and the observed difference in performance regarding the others methods was significant.

Finally, the results obtained from real datasets demonstrate that the inclusion of an additional step of weighting the explanatory variables on the WCLR method does not decreases its prediction performance and can result in more meaningful clusters of individuals based on the explanatory variables and also provides better fitted regression models for a predictive task.

4   Conclusion

This paper presented a Weighted Clusterwise Linear Regression method, WCLR, with automatic weighting of the explanatory variables, that considers differences in relevance among the explanatory variables aiming to obtain meaningful homogeneous clusters, w.r.t. these explanatory variables, and improved regression models. For this purpose, the proposed method combine the standard clusterwise linear regression and a K-Means with automatic computation of relevance weights to the variables. Because it learns simultaneously a prototype and a linear regression model for each cluster, WCLR is able to provide an appropriated regression model for an unknown observation, based on the comparison between each cluster prototype with the unknown observation, both described by the explanatory variables.

The performance and usefulness of the WCLR method was shown with several benchmarks datasets with a varied number of instances and variables. Overall, the proposed method behaved competitively relative to previous proposed methods CLR and KPLANE considered in this paper. The results obtained with the benchmark datasets demonstrate that the inclusion of an additional weighting step, produced more meaningful clusters of individuals based on the explanatory variables and thus provided better fitted regression models. In conclusion, on the considered datasets, the regression models provided by WCLR presented a better or a similar performance in comparison with the regression models provided by MLR, CLR and KPLANE methods.

References

1. Alpaydin, E.: Introduction to machine learning. In: Adaptive Computation and Machine Learning. MIT Press (2014)
2. Brusco, M.J., Cradit, J.D., Steinley, D., Fox, G.L.: Cautionary remarks on the use of clusterwise regression. Multivar. Behav. Res. **43**(1), 29–49 (2008)
3. Camastra, F., Verri, A.: A novel kernel method for clustering. IEEE Trans. Neural Netw. **27**, 801–804 (2005)
4. Diday, E., Govaert, G.: Classification automatique avec distances adaptatives. R.A.I.R.O. Informatique Comput. Sci. **11**(4), 329–349 (1977)
5. Hathaway, R.J., Bezdek, J.C.: Switching regression models and fuzzy clustering. IEEE Trans. Fuzzy Syst. **1**(3), 195–204 (1993)

6. Huang, J., Ng, M., Rong, H., Li, Z.: Automated variable weighting in k-means type clustering. IEEE Trans. Pattern Anal. Mach. Intell. **27**(5), 657–668 (2005)
7. Krstajic, D., Buturovic, L.J., Leahy, D.E., Thomas, S.: Cross-validation pitfalls when selecting and assessing regression and classification models. J. Chem-inform. **6**(1), 10 (2014)
8. Lichman, M.: UCI machine learning repository (2013). http://archive.ics.uci.edu/ml
9. Manwani, N., Sastry, P.: K-plane regression. Inf. Sci. **292**, 39–56 (2015)
10. Modha, D.S., Spangler, W.S.: Feature weighting in k-means clustering. Mach. Learn. **52**(3), 217–237 (2003)
11. Montgomery, D.C., Peck, E.A., Vining, G.G.: Introduction to linear regression analysis (2001)
12. Ryoke, M., Nakamori, Y., Suzuki, K.: Adaptive fuzzy clustering and fuzzy prediction models. In: Proceedings of 1995 IEEE International Fuzzy Systems, pp. 2215–2220. IEEE (1995)
13. Späth, H.: Algorithm 39 clusterwise linear regression. Computing **22**(4), 367–373 (1979)
14. Vicari, D., Vichi, M.: Multivariate linear regression for heterogeneous data. J. Appl. Stat. **40**(6), 1209–1230 (2013)

PSO-RBFNN: A PSO-Based Clustering Approach for RBFNN Design to Classify Disease Data

Ramalingaswamy Cheruku[1(✉)], Damodar Reddy Edla[1],
Venkatanareshbabu Kuppili[1], and Ramesh Dharavath[2]

[1] Department of Computer Science and Engineering,
National Institute of Technology Goa, Ponda, India
{rmlswamygoud,dr.reddy,venkatanaresh}@nitgoa.ac.in
[2] Department of Computer Science and Engineering,
Indian Institute of Technology (ISM), Dhanbad, India
ramesh.d.in@ieee.org

Abstract. The Radial Basis Function Neural Networks (RBFNNs) are non-iterative in nature so they are attractive for disease classification. These are four layer networks with input, hidden, output and decision layers. The RBFNNs require single iteration for training the network. On the other side, it suffers from growing hidden layer size on par with training dataset. Though various attempts have been made to solve this issue by clustering the input data. But, in a given dataset estimating the optimal number of clusters is unknown and also it involves more computational time. Hence, to address this problem in this paper, a Particle Swarm Optimization (PSO)-based clustering methodology has been proposed. In this context, we introduce a measure in the objective function of PSO, which allows us to measure the quality of wide range of clusters without prior information. Next, this PSO-based clustering methodology yields a set of High-Performance Cluster Centers (HPCCs). The proposed method experimented on three medical datasets. The experimental results indicate that the proposed method outperforms the competing approaches.

Keywords: Particle Swarm Optimization · Clustering · Disease classification · Radial Basis Function Neural Networks · Optimal hidden layer neurons

1 Introduction

In disease diagnosis procedure, a doctor has to analyze the data obtained from patients reports for making decision. These evaluations are critical for early diagnosis of disease and sometimes lead to erroneous diagnosis [1]. Hence, the disease diagnosis is a key challenging task. There is a growing need for early detection of diseases using classification systems with good accuracy. To address

© Springer International Publishing AG 2017
A. Lintas et al. (Eds.): ICANN 2017, Part II, LNCS 10614, pp. 411–419, 2017.
https://doi.org/10.1007/978-3-319-68612-7_47

this need, Artificial Neural Networks (ANNs) are widely used in classification systems. ANNs have proven useful in the analysis of disease specific dataset [2–4].

Classification systems are reliable in the health care sector to explore hidden patterns in the medical data. These classification systems aid medical professionals to enhance their diagnosis procedure. Multi-Layer Perceptron Network (MLPNs) are most popular techniques for classification and use iterative process for training. The Radial Basis Function Neural Network (RBFNN) are non-iterative in nature and requires single iteration for training [5]. Hence, a lot researchers are used RBFNN for classification and pattern recognition tasks in the literature. The performance of these neural networks are on par with the more widely used MLPN model. Moreover, RBFNNs learn applications quickly and good at modelling non-linear data [6].

RBFNNs are made up of four layers namely input layer, hidden layer, output layer and decision layer. The size of the input layer is determined by the dimensionality of training patterns and output layer is by number of distinct classes in training patterns. The size of the decision layer is one. The actual problem lies in figure out hidden layer size. In most simple approach the size of the hidden layer is determined by the size of training dataset, i.e., each pattern in training dataset is assigned to single neuron. Even though this approach is simple, it is not implementable in practical applications where the dataset size is big and dimensionality of data is high [5].

So many researchers found the solution for above problem by clustering input data. Once we create a group (cluster) we can assign a neuron to each group. Tagliafen et al. [7] have used supervised fuzzy clustering and Pedrycz [8] have used conditional fuzzy clustering for the determination of hidden layer neuron positions. Cruz et al. [9] and Qasem et al. [10] have used bio-inspired algorithms to find the clusters centers. Cheruku et al. [6] have used cluster validity index to identify the best cluster center locations. In [11] authors have used fisher ratio class separability measure in RBFNN for center selection.

1.1 Radial Basis Function Neural Network

The RBFNN [6] is a four layer feed forward architecture as shown in Fig. 1. The construction of this type of network involves determination of number of neurons in each layer.

- **Input layer:** The input layer is made up of D neurons where D is the dimensionality of input vector. The input layer is usually completely linked to hidden layer neurons. There is no transformation happen at the input layer, this layer simply forward the whatever inputs are present to it.
- **Hidden layer:** The hidden layer is made up of H (H $<<$ size of training dataset) neurons. These hidden layer neurons are complexly connected with output layer of size N neurons. At each hidden layer neuron, it is a nonlinear transformation because of Gaussian activation function. The output value of each hidden layer neuron is computed using Eqs. (1) and (2).

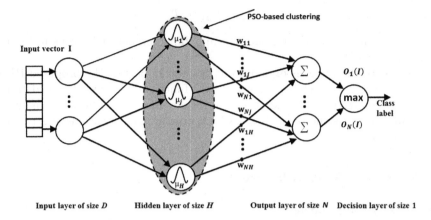

Fig. 1. The RBFNN for classification task.

$$\varphi_i(I) = \frac{1}{\sqrt{2\Pi}\sigma_i}e^{-\frac{||I - \mu_i||}{2(\sigma_i)^2}}, i = 1, 2, \ldots, H. \tag{1}$$

$$||I - \mu_i|| = \sqrt{\sum_{j=1}^{D}(I_j - \mu_i^j)^2} \tag{2}$$

- **Output layer:** The output layer is made up of N neurons, where N is the number of distinct classes in input data. Transformation at output layer is linear because response of the output layer neuron is a weighted sum of hidden layer outputs, which is computed using Eq. (3).

$$0_j(I) = \sum_{i=1}^{H} w_{ji}\phi_i(I), i = 1, 2, \ldots, H, j = 1, 2, \ldots, N \tag{3}$$

- **Decision layer:** The size of this layer is one. This layer determines the class label of given input vector (I) present at input layer using Eq. (4).

$$class - label(I) = arg\max_j O_j(I), j = 1, 2, \ldots, N. \tag{4}$$

The weight vector $w = [w_{11}, w_{12}, \ldots, \ldots, w_{1H}]_{1 \times H}^T$ between ouput layer and hidden layer is given by

$$w = \phi_{L \times H}^{+} * T \tag{5}$$

where ϕ^+ is the pseudoinverse of the ϕ matrix

$$\phi = \begin{bmatrix} \phi_1(I_1) & \cdots & \phi_{H-1}(I_1) & \phi_H(I_1) \\ & \vdots & & \\ \phi_1(I_L) & \cdots & \phi_{H-1}(I_L) & \phi_H(I_L) \end{bmatrix}_{L \times H} \tag{6}$$

$$\phi^+ = (\phi^T \phi)^{-1} \phi^T \tag{7}$$

where L is number of training patterns and H is number of neurons in hidden layer [5].

The rest of the paper is organized as follows: In Sect. 2, the proposed PSO-based clustering approach with new criterion function is discussed. The detailed analysis, which includes the experimental results discussed in Sect. 3. Finally, in Sect. 4 we concludes the paper based on experimental observations and provide future directives.

2   Proposed Methodology

2.1   PSO Preliminaries

Particle Swarm Optimization (PSO) [12,13] is population based meta-heuristic optimization algorithm. It is inspired from the behavior of bird flocking. We encoded each particle in PSO to represent a set of cluster centers. Each particle is evaluated using fitness function. For a better set of cluster positions the fitness function need to be minimized. In every iteration each particle is updated using $pBest$ and $gBest$ values, where $pBest$ is the best solution of a particle obtained so far and $gBest$ is the best solution obtained so far by any particle in the population. After obtaining these two best values, each particle velocity and positions are updated using Eqs. (8) and (9) respectively.

$$v_i^{t+1} = v_i^t + c_1 * U_1^t(pBest_i^t - p_i^t) + c_2 * U_2^t(gBest_i^t - p_i^t) \tag{8}$$

$$p_i^{t+1} = p_i^t + v_i^{t+1} \tag{9}$$

where, v is the particle velocity, p is the current particle (solution). $pBest$ and $gBest$ are defined as stated before. c1 and c2 are learning factors.

2.2   Fitness Function

The fitness function used here is DaviesBouldin Index (DBI) [14,15], which is introduced by David et al. in 1979. This DBI is a measure used to evaluating how well the clusters centers are formed. For a high performance cluster centers this value need to minimized.

$$fitness\,function = arg \min_M \frac{1}{M}(\sum_{i=1}^{M} D_i) \tag{10}$$

where,

$$D_i = arg \max_{j \neq i} R_{i,j}, \tag{11}$$

$$R_{i,j} = \frac{s_i + s_j}{d_{i,j}}, \tag{12}$$

$$s_i = \sqrt{\sum_{j=1}^{T}(A_j - C_i)^2},\tag{13}$$

$d_{i,j}$ is the Euclidean distance between cluster centers C_i and C_j, A_j is the pattern assigned to cluster C_i, and T is the total number of patterns assigned to cluster C_i.

Algorithm 1. Pseudo code for PSO-based clustering

Input: A finite set $C = \{c_1, c_2, \ldots, c_k\}$ of initial centers
Output: The K High Performance Cluster Centers (HPCCs) for the dataset

1 $K \leftarrow$ number of clusters
2 $gBest \leftarrow [\ ]$
3 **for** $i \leftarrow 1$ **to** *Population* **do**
4 $\quad$ Initialize each particle
5 $\quad$ $P_{velocity} = \text{rand}()$
6 $\quad$ $P_{position} = \text{rand}(K)$
7 $\quad$ $pBest \leftarrow P_{position}$
8 $\quad$ Compute the each particle's best position
9 $\quad$ **if** *fitness(pBest)* $<$ *fitness(gBest)* **then**
10 $\quad\quad$ $gBest \leftarrow pBest$

11 **while** *maximum iterations or minimum error* **do**
12 $\quad$ **for** $i \leftarrow 1$ **to** *Population* **do**
13 $\quad\quad$ $P_{velocity} \leftarrow$ Updated particle velocity using Eq. (8)
14 $\quad\quad$ $P_{position} \leftarrow$ Updated particle position using Eq. (9)
15 $\quad\quad$ **if** *fitness($P_{position}$)* $<$ *fitness(pBest)* **then**
16 $\quad\quad\quad$ $pBest \leftarrow P_{position}$
17 $\quad\quad$ **if** *fitness(pBest)* $<$ *fitness(gBest)* **then**
18 $\quad\quad\quad$ $gBest \leftarrow pBest$

19 **return** *gBest*

2.3   PSO-Based Clustering

The pseudo code for PSO-based clustering algorithm shown in Algorithm 1. This Algorithm 1 takes number of clusters (K) as input and outputs K-HPCCs using training dataset.

3   Experimental Results and Discussion

We have used three medical datasets obtained from UCI machine learning repository [16] whose detail specifications are shown in Table 1. For experimental purpose all the datasets are partitioned into training and testing datasets. The training dataset is constituted with 70% of patterns of each class and testing dataset is constituted with remaining patterns.

Table 1. Characteristics of datasets used in this paper.

Feature	# patterns	# features	# classes
Pima Indian Diabetes (PID)	758	8	2
Wisconsin Breast Cancer (WBC)	683	10	2
Statlog Heart Disease (SHD)	297	13	2

In order to find HPCCs, PSO-based clustering approach shown in Algorithm 1 is repeatedly executed until maximum number of clusters reached. Every time Algorithm 1 is run with specific number of clusters (K). At the termination of this algorithm, outputs the minimum fitness value corresponds to best K clusters. This represents a point in the performance plot. This above procedure repeated until K reaches *max-clusters-count*. The values obtained for each value of K is denoted as point in the performance graph. This graph is shown in Fig. 2 and find tuned parameters are listed in Table 2.

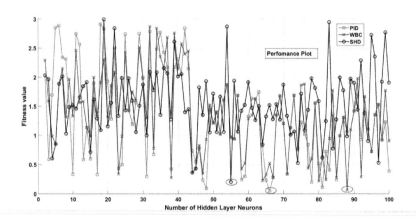

Fig. 2. Performance plot.

From the Fig. 2 it is clear that proposed PSO-based clustering approach using training dataset obtained 66 HPCCs (minimum value is highlighted in Fig. 2). After obtaining the HPCCs clusters, RBFNN classifier is designed. This PSO-RBFNN classifier is experimented with testing dataset. In Table 3 listed the performance of RBFNN classifier on three disease testing datasets.

Next, proposed method has been compared with conventional neural network classifiers, such as Probabilistic Neural Network (PNN), Time Delay Neural (TDN) network etc. These comparison results are shown in Table 4. It is observed from the table results that the proposed PSO-RBFNN performed better in terms of accuracy when compared to other conventional neural network classifiers.

Further, the proposed PSO-RBFNN is compared with other state-of-the-art techniques in the same domain. These results are furnished in Table 5. From

Table 2. Fine tuned parameters of PSO algorithm.

Parameter	Value	Explanation
Population	50	Population of particles
C_1	2	Importance of personal best value
C_2	2	Importance of neighborhood best value
Dimesnion of particles	1 to 150	Each particle dimension
max-clusters-count	150	maximum number of clusters

Table 3. Proposed method performance.

Model	Dataset	Accuracy (%)	Sensitivity (%)	Specificity (%)	# HPCCs
PSO-RBFNN	PID	72.60%	77.34%	63.75%	66
PSO-RBFNN	WBC	97.86%	97.34%	98.15%	87
PSO-RBFNN	CHD	85.76%	84.28%	88.12%	56

Table 4. Comparison of proposed method with conventional classifiers.

	Model	Accuracy (%)	Ref
PID	FFN	68.80	[2]
	CFN	68.00	[2]
	PNN	72.00	[2]
	TDN	66.80	[2]
	GINI	65.97	[2]
	AIS	68.80	[2]
	PSO-RBFNN	**72.60**	
WBC	RBF	96.18	[17]
	PNN	97.00	[17]
	GRNN	98.18	[17]
	MLP	95.74	[17]
	PSO-RBFNN	**97.86**	
SHD	RBF	79.10	[18]
	CART	80.80	[18]
	LDA	84.50	[18]
	MLP+BP	81.30	[18]
	PSO-RBFNN	**85.76**	

the table results it is clear that the proposed PSO-RBFNN obtained highest accuracy and sensitivity, and competitive specificity for all three datasets. It is also observed that the proposed method obtained slightly more number of hidden layer neurons as compared to others.

Table 5. Comparison of proposed method with other RBFNN variants of same domain.

Dataset	Model	Accuracy (%)	Sensitivity (%)	Specificity (%)	# HPCCs	Year [Ref]
PID	MEPGANf1f3	68.35	20.37	94.00	31	2013 [10]
	Bee-RBF	71.13 ±1.06	–	–	35	2016 [9]
	RBFNN+CVI	70.00	77.34	56.25	43	2017 [6]
	PSO-RBFNN	72.60	77.34	63.75	66	This study
WBC	MEPSON	97.66	97.08	97.07	58	2013 [10]
	MGAN	96.78	96.25	97.08	66	2013 [10]
	Bee-RBF	96.79	–	–	72	2016 [9]
	PSO-RBFNN	97.86	97.34	98.15	87	This study
CHD	MEPGANf1f2	80.79	67.69	91.88	56	2011 [19]
	MEPDENf1f3	87.54	83.19	91.25	30	2011 [19]
	Bee-RBF	59.10	–	–	40	2016 [9]
	PSO-RBFNN	85.76	84.28	88.12	56	This study

3.1 A Discussion

In terms of accuracy the proposed PSO-RBFNN is competitive with other methods. Whereas, in terms of number of HPCCs it is not parsimonious (generates larger networks). It is due to the methods used for comparison in Table 5 employ a multi-objective fitness function that takes into account the accuracy, parsimony in terms of number of centers and the network regularization where as proposed method uses single objective as fitness function i.e., DBI. Moreover, DBI index used in this paper is dependent on both the dataset as well as the clustering algorithm.

4 Conclusion and Future Work

In this paper, to design the effective RBFNN classifier we have used PSO-based clustering approach along with DBI index as fitness function. The proposed model experimented on three medical datasets. The experimental results proved that PSO-RBFNN achieved highest accuracy when compared to conventional neural network classifiers. The proposed PSO-RBFNN also achieved highest accuracy and sensitivity at the cost of some more HPCCs when compared to other RBFNN variants in the literature. As a future work we can use other meta-heuristic algorithms, such as Spider Monkey Algorithm (SMO), Bat Algorithm (BA) etc. for effective clustering approach.

References

1. Assal, J., Groop, L.: Definition, diagnosis and classification of diabetes mellitus and its complications. World Health Organization, pp. 1–65 (1999)
2. Bozkurt, M.R., Yurtay, N., Yilmaz, Z., Sertkaya, C.: Comparison of different methods for determining diabetes. Turk. J. Electr. Eng. Comput. Sci. **22**(4), 1044–1055 (2014)
3. Amato, F., López, A., Peña-Méndez, E.M., Vaňhara, P., Havel, J.: Artificial neural networks in medical diagnosis. J. Appl. Biomed. **11**, 47–58 (2013)
4. Fukuoka, Y.: Artificial neural networks in medical diagnosis. In: Schmitt, M., Teodorescu, H.N., Jain, A., Jain, A., Jain, S., Jain, L.C. (eds.) Computational Intelligence Processing in Medical Diagnosi, pp. 197–228. Springer, Heidelberg (2002). doi:10.1007/978-3-7908-1788-1_8
5. Yegnanarayana, B.: Artificial Neural Networks. PHI Learning Pvt. Ltd., Delhi (2009)
6. Cheruku, R., Edla, D.R., Kuppili, V.: Diabetes classification using radial basis function network by combining cluster validity index and bat optimization with novel fitness function. Int. J. Comput. Intell. Syst. **10**(1), 247–265 (2017)
7. Tagliaferri, R., Staiano, A., Scala, D.: A supervised fuzzy clustering for radial basis function neural networks training. In: 2001 Joint 9th IFSA World Congress and 20th NAFIPS International Conference, vol. 3, pp. 1804–1809. IEEE (2001)
8. Pedrycz, W.: Conditional fuzzy clustering in the design of radial basis function neural networks. IEEE Trans. Neural Netw. **9**(4), 601–612 (1998)
9. Cruz, D.P.F., Maia, R.D., da Silva, L.A., de Castro, L.N.: BeeRBF: a bee-inspired data clustering approach to design RBF neural network classifiers. Neurocomputing **172**, 427–437 (2016)
10. Qasem, S.N., Shamsuddin, S.M., Hashim, S.Z.M., Darus, M., Al-Shammari, E.: Memetic multiobjective particle swarm optimization-based radial basis function network for classification problems. Inf. Sci. **239**, 165–190 (2013)
11. Mao, K.: RBF neural network center selection based on Fisher ratio class separability measure. IEEE Trans. Neural Netw. **13**(5), 1211–1217 (2002)
12. Kennedy, J.F., Kennedy, J., Eberhart, R.C., Shi, Y.: Swarm Intelligence. Morgan Kaufmann, Burlington (2001)
13. Zhang, Y., Wang, S., Ji, G.: A comprehensive survey on particle swarm optimization algorithm and its applications. Math. Prob. Eng. **2015**, 931256 (2015)
14. Davies, D.L., Bouldin, D.W.: A cluster separation measure. IEEE Trans. Pattern Anal. Mach. Intell. **2**, 224–227 (1979)
15. SOM-Tollbox: dBi Matlab implementation code. http://www.cis.hut.fi/somtoolbox/package/docs2/db_index.html. Accessed 30 Sept 2016
16. Lichman, M.: UCI machine learning repository (2013)
17. Swathi, S., Rizwana, S., Babu, G.A., Kumar, P.S., Sarma, P.: Classification of neural network structures for breast cancer diagnosis. Int. J. Comput. Sci. Commun. **3**(1), 227–231 (2012)
18. University of North Carolina: Comparison results for datasets. http://fizyka.umk.pl/kis-old/projects/datasets.html. Accessed 20 May 2017
19. Qasem, S.N., Shamsuddin, S.M.: Memetic elitist Pareto differential evolution algorithm based radial basis function networks for classification problems. Appl. Soft Comput. **11**(8), 5565–5581 (2011)

Clustering

Modularity-Driven Kernel k-means
for Community Detection

Felix Sommer$^{(\boxtimes)}$, François Fouss, and Marco Saerens

LSM – LouRIM & ICTEAM, Université catholique de Louvain,
Chaussée de Binche 151, 7000 Mons, Belgium
{felix.sommer,francois.fouss,marco.saerens}@uclouvain.be

Abstract. The k-means algorithm is probably the most well-known and most popular clustering method in existence today. This work evaluates if a new, autonomous, kernel k-means approach for graph node clustering coupled with the modularity criterion can rival, e.g., the well-established Louvain method. We test the algorithm on social network datasets of various sizes and types. The new method estimates the optimal kernel or distance parameters as well as the natural number of clusters in the dataset based on modularity. Results indicate that this simple black-box algorithm manages to perform on par with the Louvain method given the same input.

Keywords: Clustering · Graph theory · Modularity · Kernel k-means · Community detection

1 Introduction

Identifying user- or item-clusters has been of interest in many fields for various reasons [45]. Specifically, in data mining and data analysis applications, grouping similar items or users together can lead to interesting and useful insights (see, e.g., [1]). Moreover, in social network analysis, researchers more and more use segmentation to analyze groups, direct contacts, indirect relationships, etc. Social network analysis shows connections between nodes with ties, edges, or links. The nodes can be individual users or items linked in the network; the ties or links are relationships and interactions [23].

A very popular clustering method is the k-means algorithm, as it is easy to understand, implement, and able to run with reasonably limited computational resources. To address the shortcomings of using a k-means on a graph structure, approaches such as kernel k-means were developed [46]. Kernel k-means can use various kernels derived from the distance-based or proximity-based data, and is particularly useful in community detection, that is, finding similar nodes in a given graph and grouping them together [46,47].

Today, the k-means algorithm is probably the most popular clustering algorithm in existence. In this work we evaluate if a simple kernel k-means coupled with modularity criterion—introduced by Newman and Girvan [36,38]—can choose parameters and the natural number of clusters on its own, such that

© Springer International Publishing AG 2017
A. Lintas et al. (Eds.): ICANN 2017, Part II, LNCS 10614, pp. 423–433, 2017.
https://doi.org/10.1007/978-3-319-68612-7_48

it manages to rival the Louvain method. We show that with a properly chosen distance used for the clustering, k-means indeed does just as well (but not better) than the Louvain method, when compared using statistical measures and rank-comparison on a set of community detection tasks.

Brief Related Work and Contributions. Varying the graph node distance between a graph's nodes can have a substantial influence on clustering effectiveness. As shown in prior work [26,43], modern graph distances can improve clustering solutions. However, clustering the nodes using a kernel k-means approach still suffers a major drawback, in that the k-means algorithm always requires that the number of clusters is given.

The modularity criterion is a standard measure for community detection in various fields, including social network analysis [16]. While modularity has its limitations (see, e.g., [19]), it is generally accepted that, by maximizing modularity, a reasonable good community structure can often be obtained [32]. Furthermore, there are attempts to alleviate its limitations [32,39]. As such, modularity is of interest for clustering tasks and, indeed, there have been many proposals to use the modularity criterion in clustering (see, e.g., [3,5]). However, combining the modularity criterion with recent developments in graph distances and applying this combination in order to empirically analyze the effects this could have on nodes clustering has—to the best of our knowledge—not yet been done.

Following up on our prior work of empirically testing new distances [43], we address the discussed shortcomings of using kernel k-means clustering typically encountered. In this work we therefore (i) propose automatic kernel parameter tuning, in order to improve clustering quality, without requiring user interaction, using the modularity criterion, (ii) identify the natural number of clusters present in a dataset, using also the modularity criterion, without knowledge of the (correct) number of clusters beforehand, (iii) finally, compare this improved kernel k-means approach, using the kernels presented in our previous work [43], as well as additional kernels [26], to the Louvain method [2].

2   Background and Notation

Let $G = (V, E)$ be a weighted undirected graph consisting of a set of n vertices V and an edge set E. The graph is assumed to be connected and non-periodic (regular). A cost matrix $\mathbf{C}$ consists of non-negative scalars $c_{ij} \geq 0$, which represent the cost of following the edge linking nodes i and j. If not defined in our problem, we can compute a cost matrix from an adjacency matrix $\mathbf{A}$, using the relation $c_{ij} = 1/a_{ij}$, where a_{ij} are the elements in $\mathbf{A}$ indicating the affinity between nodes i and j. Also, we can derive G's Laplacian matrix as $\mathbf{L} = \mathbf{D} - \mathbf{A}$, where the diagonal matrix $\mathbf{D} = \mathbf{Diag}(\mathbf{Ae})$ contains the row sums of $\mathbf{A}$ with a column vector full of ones, $\mathbf{e}$.

In the following we give an overview of the kernels and distances used in our experiments. We transform distances and dissimilarities into a kernel $\mathbf{K}$ using the relationship $\mathbf{K} = -\frac{1}{2} \mathbf{H} \boldsymbol{\Delta}^{(2)} \mathbf{H}$, with the centering matrix $\mathbf{H} = \mathbf{I} - \frac{\mathbf{E}}{n}$ (see

[4]); $\mathbf{E}$ is an $n \times n$ matrix full of ones and n is the number of nodes; $\mathbf{\Delta}^{(2)}$ is a squared distance or dissimilarity matrix.

Shortest-Path (SP) Distance. This distance is one of the most popular distances available. It is defined as the distance of the shortest-path between two nodes. For details on this distance, please refer to the literature (e.g., [13]).

Due to space restrictions, for the following four distances and (dis-)similarities already investigated in our previous work [43], we refer to this paper (Eq. (1) through (4) in Sect. 3) or to [20] for details.

Randomized Shortest-Path (RSP) Dissimilarity. See also [29,40,48].

Free Energy (FE) Distance. See also [22,29].

Sigmoid Commute-Time (SCT) Similarity. See also [46,47].

Sigmoid Corrected Commute-Time (CCT) Distance. See also [44].

Communicability (Com) Kernel. This kernel is also known as the adjacency-based exponential diffusion kernel and is based on the communicability distance [18,21,30]. The communicability between a graph's two nodes i and j is the weighted sum of all walks starting at node i and ending in node j. As for most kernels on a graph, more importance is attributed to shorter walks than to longer ones. The kernel is defined by the following equation:

$$\mathbf{K}_{\text{Com}} = \text{expm}(t\mathbf{A}), \quad t > 0 \tag{1}$$

Matrix-Forest (For) Kernel. This kernel is also known as the Regularized Laplacian kernel and is based on the regularization of the graph Laplacian [9, 10,42]. It is defined as follows:

$$\mathbf{K}_{\text{For}} = (\mathbf{I} + t\mathbf{L})^{-1}, \quad t > 0 \tag{2}$$

Heat Kernel (Heat). This kernel is also known as the Laplacian exponential diffusion kernel [11]. The idea of the heat kernel stems from classical physics where the diffusion of, e.g., heat is described by the heat equation, from which this kernel can be derived:

$$\mathbf{K}_{\text{Heat}} = \text{expm}(-t\mathbf{L}), \quad t > 0 \tag{3}$$

Plain Walk Kernel (Walk). This kernel is also known as the Neumann kernel and has originally been proposed to compute document similarity [27], but has equally been applied in the context of link analysis in social network analysis [25]. It is also closely related to the Katz similarity [28] and the walk distance [8]. Note that ρ is the spectral radius of the adjacency matrix $\mathbf{A}$, i.e., the absolute value of $\mathbf{A}$'s largest eigenvalue $\rho(\mathbf{A}) = \max_i(|\lambda_i|)$ for $\mathbf{A}$'s eigenvalues $\lambda_1, \ldots, \lambda_n$:

$$\mathbf{K}_{\text{Walk}} = (\mathbf{I} - t\mathbf{A})^{-1}, \quad 0 < t < \rho^{-1} \tag{4}$$

Logarithmic Kernels. The four kernels presented just beforehand equally exist in logarithmic form. We refer to [6–8, 26] as well as the indicated references for details. Note that ln indicates application of element-wise natural logarithm.

$$\text{Log. Communicability [26]:} \quad \mathbf{K}_{\text{lCom}} = \ln(\text{expm}(t\mathbf{A})), \quad t > 0 \tag{5}$$

$$\text{Log. Heat [26]:} \quad \mathbf{K}_{\text{lHeat}} = \ln(\text{expm}(-t\mathbf{L})), \quad t > 0 \tag{6}$$

$$\text{Log. Forest [7]:} \quad \mathbf{K}_{\text{lFor}} = \ln(\mathbf{I} + t\mathbf{L})^{-1}, \quad t > 0 \tag{7}$$

$$\text{Log. Walk [8]:} \quad \mathbf{K}_{\text{lWalk}} = \ln(\mathbf{I} - t\mathbf{A})^{-1}, \quad 0 < t < \rho^{-1} \tag{8}$$

3   Methodology

In this section we present the investigated clustering methods as well as their runtime parameters used in the experiments. We test the following techniques:

- an enhanced kernel k-means approach inspired from [46,47], that employs the modularity criterion to estimate the optimal kernel or distance parameters as well as the natural number of clusters,
- the Louvain method [2], which also estimates the natural number of clusters on its own,

on 15 graph datasets, the smallest of which (Zachary's Karate club, [49]) contains 34 nodes. The largest graph (a Newsgroup graph, [34,46] with five classes) contains 999 nodes. We analyze a total of nine Newsgroup datasets (400 to 999 nodes). The remaining are the classical Football [23], Political blogs [31] datasets, and three artificial Lancichinetti-Fortunato-Radicchi (LFR) graphs [33].

3.1   Kernel k-means Coupled with Modularity Criterion

This method is a simple extension of the kernel k-means algorithm for community detection [46,47]. This extended method optimizes kernel parameters and automatically estimates the natural number of clusters present in the dataset. The kernel k-means algorithm itself is the same as in our previous work, see [43], and corresponds to a two-step iterative algorithm based on a distance—or dissimilarity—matrix instead of features. Given a meaningful, symmetric distance matrix $\boldsymbol{\Delta}$, containing the distances Δ_{ij}, the goal is to partition the nodes by minimizing the total *within-cluster sum of squared distances*. For details, see [20,46,47].

The change between the standard kernel k-means and the kernel k-means coupled with modularity criterion is found in the two-step approach of the latter, which is more easily explained using the flowchart in Fig. 1. As shown in this flowchart, prior to the *actual clustering* step, the *optimize parameters* step is executed. For the present case we (very verbosely) test 77 kernel parameters and 2 to 18 clusters per kernel and dataset. We then identify the optimum by choosing the kernel

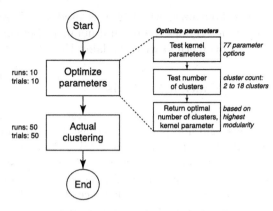

Fig. 1. Kernel k-means coupled with modularity criterion flowchart.

parameter and number of clusters combination which shows the highest modularity. The chosen kernel parameter and the identified number of clusters are passed to the kernel k-means algorithm, which is run in the *actual clustering* step. The results obtained from the *actual clustering* step are analyzed and discussed in Sect. 4.

Let us briefly elaborate on the details of the kernel k-means approach. For both the *optimize parameters* and the *actual clustering* steps it is important to keep in mind that as the kernel k-means approach depends on a random initialization of prototypes, it is necessary to test multiple trials with different initializations. Among these trials we keep the partition showing the lowest *within-cluster sum-of-distances*. It is furthermore necessary to average the results to account for variance in the results and we thus repeat the trials procedure multiple times. As shown in Fig. 1 for the *optimize parameters* step, we execute 10 runs, consisting of 10 trials each, while for the *actual clustering* step, which generates the final results, we conservatively choose to take the average of 50 runs, each of which consists of 50 trials.

The kernel k-means coupled with modularity criterion approach is tested using the 13 different kernels, described in Sect. 2. The aforementioned 77 kernel parameters are tested for each of the 13 kernels. Note that all the compared methods find a natural number of clusters.

3.2 Louvain Method

The idea behind the Louvain method [2] is to first perform an *iterative local optimization* (as in, e.g., [17]) for seeking local minimum of a specific criterion (step 1) – in our case, the modularity criterion [35–38]. Then, the second phase, called the *nodes aggregation* or *coarsening*, step whose purpose is to build a new agglomerated graph (step 2), is performed. These two steps are repeated until no further improvement of the employed criterion (modularity) can be achieved. The details are described in the original work [2].

The Louvain method [2] was used as a baseline comparison method and it equally determines the natural number of clusters for each dataset by itself. We denote this method with the label LVN.

3.3   Evaluation Methods

To compare the algorithms' performance, we compute three metrics for all datasets and methods: the adjusted rand index (ARI) [24], the normalized mutual information criterion (NMI) [12,15] as well as the classification rate (CR). Furthermore, we run a Friedman-Nemenyi test-based [14,15] multiple comparison test [15], which allows for the aggregation of results over multiple datasets, therefore comparing the differences for all algorithms simultaneously. Similarly, we perform two-by-two Wilcoxon signed-rank tests (see, e.g., [41]) to ascertain individual algorithms' performances in a one-on-one rank comparison to identify in a meaningful manner if one algorithm statistically significantly outperforms another. We compare the kernel k-means coupled with modularity criterion with its different kernels to the Louvain method.

4   Results and Discussion

Both clustering methods—kernel k-means coupled with modularity criterion and the Louvain method—were run on the graph-based community datasets and ARI, NMI, and CR metrics were computed for all of them. It is important to stress that all methods were run in a totally unsupervised way, and thus evaluate automatically the natural number of clusters in each dataset. We give the raw numbers for the NMI in Table 1, the results for the ARI and CR show a very similar pattern and we thus omit those here. The results of the Friedman-Nemenyi multiple comparison test are shown in Figs. 2 and 3, and discussed below, as are the results of the two-by-two Wilcoxon signed-rank tests.

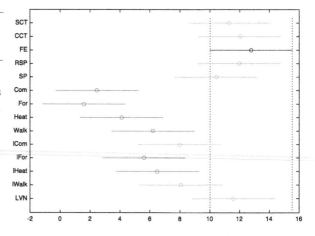

Fig. 2. Friedman-Nemenyi multiple comparison test aggregating results on all datasets for the individual algorithms, based on NMI. A higher rank, i.e., a bar shifted to the right, indicates better results; the length of the bars shows the significance interval. If these bars do not overlap the rank is considered significantly different.

In the following we discuss the results based on an analysis of the NMI. As mentioned before, the results from the NMI, ARI, as well as CR metrics show very similar patterns, and we thus restrict the analysis to NMI-based results.

Table 1. Normalized mutual information (NMI).

Dataset	SCT	CCT	FE	RSP	SP	Com	For	Heat	Walk	lCom	lFor	lHeat	lWalk	LVN
football	**0.908**	0.889	0.884	0.884	0.812	0.545	0.293	0.492	0.749	0.598	0.424	0.583	0.249	0.698
lfr1	0.976	**0.990**	0.981	0.983	0.890	0.052	0.027	0.051	0.003	0.475	0.500	0.511	0.485	0.962
lfr2	**1.000**	**1.000**	**1.000**	**1.000**	0.986	0.147	0.164	0.266	0.694	0.481	0.478	0.449	0.682	0.823
lfr3	**1.000**	0.997	**1.000**	**1.000**	0.989	0.087	0.130	0.159	0.502	0.520	0.379	0.376	0.729	0.827
news2cl1	0.608	**0.638**	0.584	0.581	0.434	0.018	0.032	0.032	0.249	0.291	0.243	0.253	0.462	0.573
news2cl2	0.356	0.396	0.359	0.346	0.296	0.008	0.027	0.100	0.394	**0.584**	0.123	0.207	0.233	0.432
news2cl3	0.579	0.584	0.590	0.598	0.616	0.333	0.053	0.117	0.357	**0.682**	0.553	0.611	0.496	0.586
news3cl1	0.697	0.706	0.702	0.696	0.660	0.096	0.032	0.125	0.245	0.489	0.471	0.478	**0.748**	0.699
news3cl2	0.656	0.689	**0.711**	0.706	0.572	0.068	0.035	0.040	0.294	0.345	0.343	0.281	0.572	0.661
news3cl3	0.642	0.605	0.681	0.678	**0.720**	0.067	0.031	0.033	0.380	0.295	0.255	0.248	0.423	0.673
news5cl1	0.641	0.643	0.648	0.651	0.614	0.087	0.019	0.032	0.284	0.259	0.273	0.291	0.504	**0.684**
news5cl2	0.616	0.630	**0.643**	0.633	0.596	0.185	0.026	0.024	0.291	0.345	0.214	0.234	0.374	0.634
news5cl3	0.573	**0.624**	0.615	0.571	0.480	0.034	0.021	0.021	0.369	0.300	0.337	0.281	0.383	0.572
polblogs	0.556	0.556	0.567	0.568	0.549	0.423	0.322	**0.641**	0.298	0.511	0.550	0.527	0.577	0.597
zachary	0.832	0.724	0.838	0.832	**1.000**	0.262	0.395	**1.000**	0.875	**1.000**	0.866	**1.000**	0.697	0.982

It remains difficult to identify one "best" clustering distance. Not surprisingly, the results in Table 1 show that the datasets have a significant impact on clustering quality. Overall, it is however safe to say that based on the multiple comparison using all methods—with the exception of the logarithmic communicability (lCom) and logarithmic walk (lWalk) kernels—the modern FE, CCT, RSP, SCT kernels outperform the competition to a statistically significant degree. Comparing only these best kernels amongst each other (cf. Fig. 3) confirms, that the most modern kernels (FE, CCT, and RSP) have a (short) edge on the competition. A two-by-two

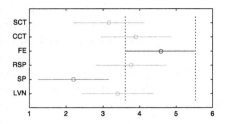

Fig. 3. Friedman-Nemenyi multiple comparison test aggregating the results of all datasets for the six best algorithms. A higher rank, i.e., a bar shifted to the right, indicates better results; the length of the bars shows the significance interval. If these bars do not overlap the rank is considered significantly different.

Wilcoxon signed-rank test, comparing the NMI for the FE-distance to the five best competitors (that is, SCT, CCT, RSP, SP, and LVN) shows, that the FE-distance based kernel manages to outperform the SCT- and SP-distance to a statistically significant degree (both $p < 5 \times 10^{-2}$), but not the others (CCT, RSP, and LVN).

Comparing the results in Table 1 to those in [43] shows that, as expected, the lack of knowledge of the true number of clusters has a detrimental effect on clustering quality, which also cannot be compensated by optimizing kernel parameters per dataset. This behavior should however be expected, as thus far no method has been found to deliver consistently good clustering results, especially with limited to no knowledge on the data.

However, when comparing to the Louvain method, given the same information, i.e., the lack of the true number of clusters, the kernel k-means with modularity criterion approach manages to perform on par, or even outperform the Louvain method, albeit not to a statistically significant level. When comparing only the six best algorithms in a multiple comparison as shown in Fig. 3, the simple FE kernel based k-means obtains results equivalent to the Louvain method.

5   Conclusion and Future Work

This work presents a simple method for executing clustering in a black-box fashion, while making use of recent advances in graph distances. We compare 13 different graph kernels and the Louvain method. The k-means clustering performance depends on the dataset, but obtains results equivalent to, and thus rivals, the Louvain method almost all of the time on the investigated datasets, without needing additional input parameters. The method simply optimizes each kernel's parameters and predicts the number of clusters in the dataset based on modularity. The results are strongly influenced by the choice of kernel, with the most modern FE, CCT, and RSP kernels showing the best results. However, these methods do not scale well on large datasets, while the Louvain method does.

Future work will focus on (1) refining kernel parameters' search space in order to increase estimation speeds, and (2) further confirm the results on other, but also larger, datasets.

Acknowledgements. This work was supported in part by the FNRS and UCL (FSR) through a PhD scholarship. This work was also partially supported by the Immediate and the Brufence projects funded by InnovIris (Brussels Region). We thank these institutions for giving us the opportunity to conduct both fundamental and applied research.

References

1. Berkhin, P.: A survey of clustering data mining techniques. In: Kogan, J., Nicholas, C., Teboulle, M. (eds.) Grouping Multidimensional Data, pp. 25–71. Springer, Heidelberg (2006). doi:10.1007/3-540-28349-8_2
2. Blondel, V.D., Guillaume, J.L., Lambiotte, R., Lefebvre, E.: Fast unfolding of communities in large networks. J. Stat. Mech.: Theory Exp. **10**, P10008 (2008)
3. Bolla, M.: Penalized versions of the Newman-Girvan modularity and their relation to normalized cuts and k-means clustering. Phys. Rev. E **84**(1), 016108 (2011)

4. Borg, I., Groenen, P.: Modern Multidimensional Scaling: Theory and Applications, 2nd edn. Springer, Heidelberg (1997)
5. Brandes, U., Delling, D., Gaertler, M., Görke, R., Hoefer, M., Nikoloski, Z., Wagner, D.: On modularity clustering. IEEE Trans. Knowl. Data Eng. **20**, 172–188 (2008)
6. Chebotarev, P.: A class of graph-geodetic distances generalizing the shortest-path and the resistance distances. Discrete Appl. Math. **159**(5), 295–302 (2011)
7. Chebotarev, P.: The graph bottleneck identity. Adv. Appl. Math. **47**(3), 403–413 (2011)
8. Chebotarev, P.: The walk distances in graphs. Discrete Appl. Math. **160**(10–11), 1484–1500 (2012)
9. Chebotarev, P., Shamis, E.: The matrix-forest theorem and measuring relations in small social groups. Autom. Remote Control **58**(9), 1505–1514 (1997)
10. Chebotarev, P., Shamis, E.: The forest metric for graph vertices. Electron. Notes Discrete Math. **11**, 98–107 (2002)
11. Chung, F., Yau, S.T.: Coverings, heat kernels and spanning trees. J. Comb. **6**, 163–184 (1998)
12. Collignon, A., Maes, F., Delaere, D., Vandermeulen, D., Suetens, P., Marchal, G.: Automated multi-modality image registration based on information theory. Inf. Process. Med. Imaging **3**, 263–274 (1995)
13. Cormen, T., Leiserson, C., Rivest, R., Stein, C.: Introduction to Algorithms, 3rd edn. The MIT Press, Cambridge (2009)
14. Daniel, W.W.: Applied Non-parametric Statistics. The Duxbury Advanced Series in Statistics and Decision Sciences. PWS-Kent Publishing Company, Boston (1990)
15. Demšar, J.: Statistical comparisons of classifiers over multiple data sets. J. Mach. Learn. Res. **7**, 1–30 (2006)
16. Devooght, R., Mantrach, A., Kivimaki, I., Bersini, H., Jaimes, A., Saerens, M.: Random walks based modularity: application to semi-supervised learning. In: Proceedings of the 23rd International World Wide Web Conference (WWW 2014), pp. 213–224 (2014)
17. Duda, R.O., Hart, P.E.: Pattern Classification and Scene Analysis. Wiley, Hoboken (1973)
18. Estrada, E.: The communicability distance in graphs. Linear Algebra Appl. **436**(11), 4317–4328 (2012)
19. Fortunato, S., Barthelemy, M.: Resolution limit in community detection. Proc. Natl. Acad. Sci. U.S.A. **104**(1), 36–41 (2007)
20. Fouss, F., Saerens, M., Shimbo, M.: Algorithms and Models for Network Data and Link Analysis. Cambridge University Press, Cambridge (2016)
21. Fouss, F., Yen, L., Pirotte, A., Saerens, M.: An experimental investigation of graph kernels on a collaborative recommendation task. In: Proceedings of the 6th International Conference on Data Mining (ICDM 2006), pp. 863–868 (2006)
22. Françoisse, K., Kivimäki, I., Mantrach, A., Rossi, F., Saerens, M.: A bag-of-paths framework for network data analysis. Neural Netw. **90**, 90–111 (2017)
23. Girvan, M., Newman, M.E.J.: Community structure in social and biological networks. Proc. Natl. Acad. Sci. **99**, 7821–7826 (2002)
24. Hubert, L., Arabie, P.: Comparing partitions. J. Classif. **2**(1), 193–218 (1985)
25. Ito, T., Shimbo, M., Kudo, T., Matsumoto, Y.: Application of kernels to link analysis. In: Proceedings of the eleventh ACM SIGKDD International Conference on Knowledge Discovery and Data Mining, pp. 586–592 (2005)

26. Ivashkin, V., Chebotarev, P.: Do logarithmic proximity measures outperform plain ones in graph clustering? In: Proceedings of 6th International Conference on Network Analysis (2016)
27. Kandola, J., Cristianini, N., Shawe-Taylor, J.: Learning semantic similarity. In: Advances in Neural Information Processing Systems (NIPS 2002), vol. 15, pp. 657–664 (2002)
28. Katz, L.: A new status index derived from sociometric analysis. Psychmetrika **18**(1), 39–43 (1953)
29. Kivimäki, I., Lebichot, B., Saerens, M.: Developments in the theory of randomized shortest paths with a comparison of graph node distances. Phys. A: Stat. Mech. Appl. **393**, 600–616 (2014)
30. Kondor, R.I., Lafferty, J.: Diffusion kernels on graphs and other discrete structures. In: Proceedings of the 19th International Conference on Machine Learning (ICML 2002), pp. 315–322 (2002)
31. Krebs, V.: New political patterns (2008). http://www.orgnet.com/divided.html
32. Lancichinetti, A., Fortunato, S.: Limits of modularity maximization in community detection. Phys. Rev. E **84**(6), 066122 (2011)
33. Lancichinetti, A., Fortunato, S., Radicchi, F.: Benchmark graphs for testing community detection algorithms. Phys. Rev. E **78**(4), 46–110 (2008)
34. Lang, K.: 20 newsgroups dataset. http://bit.ly/lang-newsgroups
35. Newman, M.E.J.: Finding community structure in networks using the eigenvectors of matrices. Phys. Rev. E **74**(3), 036104 (2006)
36. Newman, M.E.J.: Modularity and community structure in networks. Proc. Natl. Acad. Sci. **103**, 8577–8582 (2006)
37. Newman, M.E.J.: Networks: An Introduction. Oxford University Press, Oxford (2010)
38. Newman, M.E.J., Girvan, M.: Finding and evaluating community structure in networks. Phys. Rev. E **69**, 026113 (2004)
39. Reichardt, J., Bornholdt, S.: Detecting fuzzy community structures in complex networks with a Potts model. Phys. Rev. Lett. **93**(21), 218701 (2004)
40. Saerens, M., Achbany, Y., Fouss, F., Yen, L.: Randomized shortest-path problems: two related models. Neural Comput. **21**(8), 2363–2404 (2009)
41. Siegel, S.: Non-parametric Statistics for the Behavioral Sciences. McGraw-Hill, New York city (1956)
42. Smola, A.J., Kondor, R.: Kernels and regularization on graphs. In: Schölkopf, B., Warmuth, M.K. (eds.) COLT-Kernel 2003. LNCS, vol. 2777, pp. 144–158. Springer, Heidelberg (2003). doi:10.1007/978-3-540-45167-9_12
43. Sommer, F., Fouss, F., Saerens, M.: Comparison of graph node distances on clustering tasks. In: Villa, A.E.P., Masulli, P., Pons Rivero, A.J. (eds.) ICANN 2016. LNCS, vol. 9886, pp. 192–201. Springer, Cham (2016). doi:10.1007/978-3-319-44778-0_23
44. von Luxburg, U., Radl, A., Hein, M.: Getting lost in space: large sample analysis of the commute distance. In: Proceedings of the 23th Neural Information Processing Systems conference (NIPS 2010), pp. 2622–2630 (2010)
45. Xu, R., Wunsch, D.: Survey of clustering algorithms. IEEE Trans. Neural Netw. **16**(3), 645–678 (2005)
46. Yen, L., Fouss, F., Decaestecker, C., Francq, P., Saerens, M.: Graph nodes clustering based on the commute-time kernel. In: Zhou, Z.-H., Li, H., Yang, Q. (eds.) PAKDD 2007. LNCS (LNAI), vol. 4426, pp. 1037–1045. Springer, Heidelberg (2007). doi:10.1007/978-3-540-71701-0_117

47. Yen, L., Fouss, F., Decaestecker, C., Francq, P., Saerens, M.: Graph nodes clustering with the sigmoid commute-time kernel: a comparative study. Data Knowl. Eng. **68**(3), 338–361 (2009)
48. Yen, L., Mantrach, A., Shimbo, M., Saerens, M.: A family of dissimilarity measures between nodes generalizing both the shortest-path and the commute-time distances. In: Proceedings of the 14th ACM SIGKDD International Conference on Knowledge Discovery and Data Mining (KDD 2008), pp. 785–793 (2008)
49. Zachary, W.W.: An information flow model for conflict and fission in small groups. J. Anthropol. Res. **33**, 452–473 (1977)

Measuring Clustering Model Complexity

Stefano Rovetta$^{(\boxtimes)}$, Francesco Masulli, and Alberto Cabri

DIBRIS, University of Genova, Via Dodecaneso 35, 16146 Genoa, Italy
{stefano.rovetta,francesco.masulli,alberto.cabri}@unige.it

Abstract. The capacity of a clustering model can be defined as the ability to represent complex spatial data distributions. We introduce a method to quantify the capacity of an approximate spectral clustering model based on the eigenspectrum of the similarity matrix, providing the ability to measure capacity in a direct way and to estimate the most suitable model parameters. The method is tested on simple datasets and applied to a forged banknote classification problem.

Keywords: Spectral clustering · Model complexity · Model selection

1 Introduction

The control of model complexity has always been a central focus in statistics and machine learning. In supervised learning, this view has generated some of the most fruitful lines of research, for instance statistical learning theory [15]. Unsupervised methods, however, still lack a similarly complete treatment, especially in the case of clustering where the objective itself is not so well-defined.

Model complexity has been defined in several ways in the realm of supervised learning, but in the case of clustering the most usual definition is simply in terms of the number of model parameters.

In [13] an approach to model complexity control was applied to an approximated spectral clustering method based on landmarks. In this contribution, we introduce a method to quantify the ability of the same model based on the eigenspectrum of the similarity matrix. This provides the ability to measure, in a direct way, the *capacity* of the model to represent complex spatial data distributions and to estimate the most suitable model parameters.

2 Previous Work on Clustering Complexity

The study of the spectrum of particular proximity matrices is a vast area of research. Spectral graph theory [2] is entirely devoted to the spectrum of normalised graph Laplacians, while the older field of data mapping studies the eigendecomposition of distance matrices [14]. However, the spectrum of a similarity matrix has in some sense nicer properties than that of a distance matrix,

© Springer International Publishing AG 2017
A. Lintas et al. (Eds.): ICANN 2017, Part II, LNCS 10614, pp. 434–441, 2017.
https://doi.org/10.1007/978-3-319-68612-7_49

and while the graph Laplacian enhances the separability of clusters, its normalisation destroys some useful insight into their diversity. For this reason, here we consider spectra of similarity matrices with a *normal* similarity function, $w \leq 1$.

In the literature, most approaches to unsupervised model complexity focus on vector quantization (VQ) rather than clustering. These are often understood as two applications of the same technique to different problems. In fact, the most popular approaches to each of these problems, namely codebook-based unconstrained vector quantization and central (k means) clustering, start from the same objective, the average square distance from the nearest representative

$$J = \frac{1}{n} \sum_{l=1}^{n} \|\mathbf{x}_l - \mathbf{y}(\mathbf{x}_l)\|^2 \tag{1}$$

where $\mathbf{x}_l \in \{\mathbf{x}_1, \dots, \mathbf{x}_n\} \subset \mathbb{R}^d$ are the input vectors and $\mathbf{y} \in \{\mathbf{y}_1, \dots, \mathbf{y}_c\} \subset \mathbb{R}^d$ are cluster representatives (centroids), with $\mathbf{y}(\mathbf{x}_l)$ the nearest centroid to $\mathbf{x}_l$.

The goal of VQ, however, is to minimize this objective only; model complexity is bounded only by the maximum allowable codebook size [7]. In this framework, the capacity of a clustering model was studied by Buhmann, who proposed an Empirical Risk Approximation framework [1] along the lines of Vapnik's Empirical Risk Minimization theory. Conversely, the objective of clustering is *summarization*: clusters are required to be meaningful [9], highlighting actual structure in the data or classes. As a consequence, for instance, the number of centroids in k means clustering is normally assessed by maximizing some additional cluster validity criterion [8]. A good clustering solution has the *minimum* number of centroids that provides a sufficiently low distortion, whereas VQ exploits the *maximum* codebook size allowed by resource constraints [6].

One line of research addressing the expressive capacity of clusters, as opposed to the number of degrees of freedom of the model, is related to the "additive clustering" framework [10]. To the best of our knowledge, this is the only work that deals with this perspective.

3   Approximated Spectral Clustering

One well-known limit of spectral clustering, shared with all proximity-based methods, is the n^2 space complexity. Given a training set $\mathcal{X}$ of n observations, spectral clustering consists of building the $n \times n$ similarity matrix W^{xx} and then the Laplacian matrix, built using W^{xx} and the degree matrix D, defined as $D_{ij} = \delta_{ij} \sum_{k=1}^{n} W^{xx}_{ik}$ (δ_{ij} = Kronecker delta). The leading eigenvectors of the Laplacian, starting from the second one, are either used directly as cluster indicators, or clustered with a quick-and-dirty method (e.g., k means or spherical k means) that converges easily due to the enhanced separation of clusters.

Several versions of the Laplacian matrix are in use: the unnormalized Laplacian $L = D - W^{xx}$, the symmetrically normalized Laplacian $L^{sym} = I - D^{-1/2}W^{xx}D^{-1/2}$, the asymmetrical "random walk" Laplacian $L^{rw} = I - D^{-1}W^{xx}$.

Algorithm 1 [13]. ASC - Approximate Spectral Clustering

- · select suitable $w()$, c, k
- · generate landmarks Y by vector quantization on $\mathcal{X}$ with c centroids
- · compute similarity matrix W^{xy} between data $\mathcal{X}$ and landmarks Y using $K()$
- · compute correlation matrix $R = W^{xy}W^{xy^\top}$
- · compute degree matrix $D = \text{diag}(R)$
- · compute the desired form of Laplacian L from R and D (unnormalized, sym, rw)
- · compute E, first $k+1$ (column) eigenvectors of L
- · discard first eigenvector by removing first column from E
- · cluster rows of E with k-means, obtaining a cluster membership for each row E_i
- · attribute pattern x_i to the cluster of row E_i

Our Approximated Spectral Clustering (ASC) method is shown in Algorithm 1. It builds on the results of Tan et al. [17] who applied perturbation analysis to bound the clustering errors when the $n \times n$ data-data proximity matrix W^{xx} is replaced with a $c \times c$ landmark-landmark proximity matrix W^{yy}, where landmarks are found by vector quantization or k means clustering. The method proposed in [13] uses instead a $n \times c$ data-landmark matrix W^{xy} which reflects more accurately the input data, as well as allowing an incremental operation. To measure model capacity, however, we exploit the properties of the landmark-landmark matrix W^{yy} which, as proven in [17], is a good proxy for W^{xx}. Note that, in a different setting (multidimensional scaling), the landmark-landmark *distance* matrix was also employed in [3].

4   Measuring the Clustering Capacity of ASC

A central property of the ASC method is that cluster complexity is decoupled from the number of clusters. The two main factors influencing complexity are:

1. The number of landmarks c;
2. The similarity function $w(\cdot, \cdot)$.

Note that, in the algorithm, the number of desired clusters k is selected as an independent parameter with respect to c.

4.1   Role of c

A measure of model complexity is the number of possible, distinct model configurations. Spectral clustering embeds n-dimensional data in a similarity space, at most n-dimensional. This space is given by the rows of the similarity matrix. In this subsection we assume for the moment a binary similarity function (either two patterns are similar, or they are not). In this case there are in principle 2^n possible configurations for standard spectral clustering. For the approximated ASC method, where the similarity is computed against landmarks only, this number reduces to 2^c for both W^{xy} and W^{yy}, which have rank c.

Let $U\Sigma V^{\top}$ be the singular value decomposition of a similarity matrix. In the case of W^{yy}, which is square, symmetric, and positive definite, this is an eigendecomposition, so $V = U$ (eigenvectors), U and Σ are $c \times c$, and $\Sigma : \Sigma_{ij} = \delta_{ij}\sigma_i$ are the eigenvalues. Additionally, $\sum_{i=1}^{c} \sqrt{\sigma_i} = \text{tr}(W^{yy}) = c$.

The eigenvalues of a distance matrix have interesting properties. Those of the leading one (Perron-Frobenius eigenvalue, or *spectral radius*) have been extensively studied [18]. Here we explore the *similarity* matrix W^{yy}, whose eigenvalues in the case of a normal similarity function ($w(\mathbf{x}, \mathbf{y}) \leq 1$, $w(\mathbf{x}, \mathbf{x}) = 1$) have a clear interpretation in terms of clustering capacity, and are most commonly studied in the case of adjacency matrices of graphs or networks [2].

The following are simple linear algebra facts about similarity matrices in the case of a normal, binary similarity function.

- **First limiting case** – When $W^{yy} = 1_c =$ the $c \times c$ matrix of all ones, then $\sigma_1 = c$ and $\sigma_i = 0$ for all $i : 2 \ldots n$.

  Proof. Since 1_c has rank 1 there is only one non-zero eigenvalue, corresponding to the constant eigenvector. The value is c because

  $$\begin{pmatrix} 1 & 1 & \ldots & 1 \\ 1 & 1 & \ldots & 1 \\ & & \vdots & \\ 1 & 1 & \ldots & 1 \end{pmatrix} \begin{pmatrix} 1 \\ 1 \\ \vdots \\ 1 \end{pmatrix} = c \begin{pmatrix} 1 \\ 1 \\ \vdots \\ 1 \end{pmatrix} \tag{2}$$

- **Second limiting case** – When $W^{yy} = I_c$, the identity matrix of order c, then $\sigma_i = 1$ for all $i : 1 \ldots n$.
  Proof. I_c is diagonal, so its diagonal values are the eigenvalues.
- **General case** – σ_i is the size of the i-th largest cluster.
  Proof. Since $w(\cdot, \cdot)$ is normal, $\text{tr}(W^{yy}) = c$ and therefore $\sum_i \sigma_i = c$ as well. Reorder the rows and columns of W^{yy} to make it block-diagonal. The eigenvalues of a block-diagonal matrix are the eigenvalues of the blocks (this can be verified by decomposing the characteristic polynomial). Since the blocks are composed of all ones, each block corresponds to the first limiting case above, and the eigenvalue of each block is equal to its size.

4.2   Role of w

Although the number of landmarks c imposes a theoretical maximum of 2^c to the number of distinct configurations that can characterize a clustering, with non-binary similarities several configurations may define a single cluster because they happen to be "similar enough," and "different enough" from the rest. So the effective number of configurations is smaller than the theoretical maximum. For concreteness, from here on we focus on the "heat kernel"

$$w(\mathbf{x}_i, \mathbf{y}_j) = e^{-\beta\|\mathbf{x}_i - \mathbf{y}_j\|^2}. \tag{3}$$

Here coefficient β can be related to the inverse of a time parameter governing diffusion, so that, for small β, $\mathbf{x}_i$ and $\mathbf{y}_j$ are more similar than for high β.

In general, the similarity function w decays with distance. This decay is usually controlled by some parameter; in Eq. (3) this is the inverse diffusion coefficient β. While the rank of a matrix is an integer, this coefficient influences the value of the leading eigenvalue by making the rows of W^{yy} more or less similar to each other. As a consequence, the first eigenvalue will have real values, anywhere between 1 and c.

The mechanism by which the similarity function induces groupings between similar real-valued rows, and the limiting regimes by which this can or cannot occur, have been studied in the context of spectral community detection in networks [4]. Essentially, this involves the presence of a gap between the noise-like distribution of trailing eigenvalues, which are distributed according to Wigner's semicircle law [16], and the position of the leading eigenvalues which should be sufficiently distinguishable from the noise-like background.

In the present work this behaviour is studied experimentally and demonstrated in the experimental section.

4.3   Spectral Measures of Clustering Model Capacity

Since the sum of all eigenvalues is constant, the leading eigenvalue σ_1 (spectral radius) measures the degree of imbalance between the largest cluster and the remaining ones, since an eigengap develops as soon as $\sigma_1 > 1$.

A model with the tendency toward many clusters of similar size will have a lower value of the leading eigenvector than another model that favours fewer larger clusters. On the other hand, the overall distribution of cluster sizes is reflected in the similarity matrix spectrum.

As a result of the previous discussion, indexes of clustering capacity could be defined. One based on the leading eigenvalue of W^{yy} shows a particularly informative behaviour, and is presented in an absolute and a relative version:

$$h = c - \sigma_1; \qquad \overline{h} = 1 - \frac{\sigma_1}{c}. \tag{4}$$

The absolute version directly measures the number of effective bits required to express the leading cluster size, and indirectly the balance between clusters. The relative version is independent of the model dimensionality and is the fraction of total theoretical model capacity actually expressed by a particular model implementation, as fixed by the number and position of landmarks and by the similarity function and its parametrisation.

The graphs in the following section show the index $\overline{h}$ as well as its variation from sample to sample (approximating a derivative), with peaks corresponding to values of maximum sensitivity.

5   Experiments

5.1   Datasets

In this section the properties discussed above are demonstrated on some training sets, shown in Fig. 1. These datasets are sufficiently low-dimensional ($d = 2, 4$) to be easily visualized, but they are quite structured, with different scales.

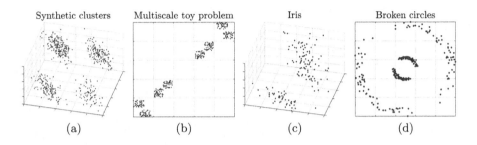

Fig. 1. Four simple datasets used in the experiments.

a. Synthetic clusters. A simple dataset with convex but noisy clusters. Clusters: 4. Dimensions: 4. Observations: 560. Source: Matlab as "kmeansdata".
b. Multi-scale toy problem. Several clusters separated by different-sized gaps. Clusters: 2 or 4 or 8 (depending on resolution). Dimensions: 2. Observations: 400. Source: original.
c. Iris. The standard benchmark dataset since 1936. Clusters: 2 (one is actually two partly overlapping classes). Dimensions: 4. Observations: 150. Source: originally from [5], available in Matlab as "fisheriris."
d. Broken circles. Two noisy concentric circles, broken into two arcs each, with structure at multiple scales and nonlinearly separable shapes. Clusters: 2 or 4 (depending on resolution). Dimensions: 2. Observations: 280. Source: original.

A real-world application is also presented. The data, "banknote authentication" from the UCI repository [11], consist of 4 wavelet features from 1372 images of authentic and forged banknotes.

5.2   Results on Toy Data

The toy datasets have been chosen to verify the behaviour of the capacity indexes as a function of β. To make the results comparable, the graphs in Fig. 2 are based on the relative capacity $\bar{h}$. The dashed lines are the measure of capacity, or model complexity (i.e., $h(\beta_i)$ for $i = 1 \ldots 100$ values of β), while the solid lines represent the absolute delta or variation in the capacity graph (i.e., $|h(\beta_{i+1}) - h(\beta_i)|$) which highlights the region(s) of higher and lower sensitivity to variations of β. These regions have been compared to phase transitions in physics due to the discontinuity (or rapid change) in a measured quantity [4,12], such as the layout of clusters. The criterion for choosing β is that of minimum sensitivity, so that the system is far from phase transitions.

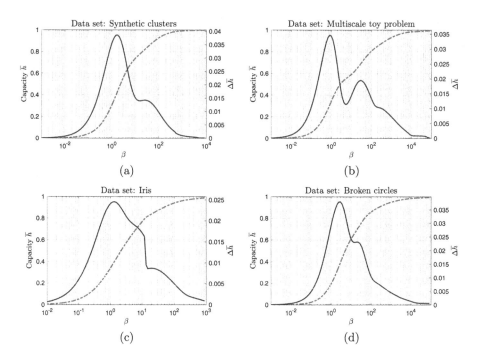

Fig. 2. Value of $\overline{h}$ (dashed) and its absolute variation $|\overline{h}(\beta_{i+1}) - \overline{h}(\beta_i)|$ (solid) for (a) synthetic clusters, (b) multiscale toy problem, (c) iris, and (d) broken circles.

5.3   Results on Banknote Classification

The same analysis was used for dimensioning the ASC model for banknote classification. The number of clusters was chosen to be 2 and the optimal number of landmarks, as indicated by the analysis exemplified in the previous subsection (Fig. 2) to find the regions of maximum sensitivity to variations in β, was found to be 20. The peak of $\Delta \overline{h}$ was at $\beta = 100$. After clustering with these parameters, an external validation against the target classification was performed.

The validation yielded accuracy $= 0.97$, sensitivity 0.95, specificity >0.99. These results are quite good, and yet obtained in an entirely unsupervised fashion. In particular, only one forged banknote was not recognized. High specificity is a desirable behaviour in this kind of application.

5.4   Discussion and Conclusion

The graphs for the toy problems clearly show the behaviour of $\overline{h}$ as a function of β. The plots relative to the variation show peaks in correspondence of values for which clusters change their shape ("phase transitions").

The banknote classification problem is quite well separated, and therefore easy as a supervised task, but the class distributions are elongated. This proves challenging for centroid-based clustering, and makes parameter selection critical. The good results obtained, comparable to supervised classification, indicate that the parameter selection procedure is effective.

Differently from most other available approaches, capacity, as represented by indexes $h/\bar{h}$, is not directly related to the number of cluster centroids. Rather, it refers to cluster shape and geometry. In the case studied, with "heat kernel" similarity, the main model parameters influencing these indexes are the number of landmarks c and the inverse diffusion coefficient β.

Such a measure can be exploited to correctly dimension these model parameters in standard spectral clustering. Due to the ability of the ASC method to work incrementally, it also has the potentiality to allow online adaptation of parameters in time-varying stream clustering.

References

1. Buhmann, J., Tishby, N.: Empirical risk approximation a statistical learning theory of data clustering. NATO ASI Ser. Ser. F: Comput. Syst. Sci. 57–68 (1998)
2. Chung, F.R.K.: Spectral Graph Theory (CBMS Regional Conference Series in Mathematics, No. 92). American Mathematical Society, Providence (1997)
3. De Silva, V., Tenenbaum, J.B.: Sparse multidimensional scaling using landmark points. Technical report, Stanford University (2004)
4. Decelle, A., Krzakala, F., Moore, C., Zdeborová, L.: Inference and phase transitions in the detection of modules in sparse networks. Phys. Rev. Lett. **107**(6), 065701 (2011)
5. Fisher, R.A.: The use of multiple measurements in taxonomic problems. Annu. Eugen. **7**(Part II), 179–188 (1936)
6. Gersho, A., Gray, R.M.: Vector Quantization and Signal Compression. Kluwer, Boston (1992)
7. Gray, R.: Vector quantization. IEEE Acoust. Speech Signal Process. Mag. **1**, 4–29 (1984)
8. Halkidi, M., Batistakis, Y., Vazirgiannis, M.: On clustering validation techniques. J. Intell. Inf. Syst. **17**(2–3), 107–145 (2001)
9. Handl, J., Knowles, J., Kell, D.B.: Computational cluster validation in postgenomic data analysis. Bioinformatics **21**(15), 3201 (2005)
10. Lee, M.D.: On the complexity of additive clustering models. J. Math. Psychol. **45**(1), 131–148 (2001)
11. Lichman, M.: UCI machine learning repository (2013). http://archive.ics.uci.edu/ml
12. Rose, K., Gurewitz, E., Fox, G.: Statistical mechanics and phase transitions in clustering. Phys. Rev. Lett. **65**, 945–948 (1990)
13. Rovetta, S.: Model complexity control in clustering. In: Bassis, S., Esposito, A., Morabito, F.C., Pasero, E. (eds.) Advances in Neural Networks. SIST, vol. 54, pp. 111–120. Springer, Cham (2016). doi:10.1007/978-3-319-33747-0_11
14. Torgerson, W.S.: Theory and Methods of Scaling. Wiley, New York (1958)
15. Vapnik, V.N.: Statistical Learning Theory. Wiley, New York (1998)
16. Wigner, E.P.: Characteristic vectors of bordered matrices with infinite dimensions. Ann. Math. **62**, 548–564 (1955)
17. Yan, D., Huang, L., Jordan, M.I.: Fast approximate spectral clustering. In: Proceedings of the 15th ACM SIGKDD International Conference on Knowledge Discovery and Data Mining, pp. 907–916. ACM (2009)
18. Zhou, B., Trinajstić, N.: On the largest eigenvalue of the distance matrix of a connected graph. Chem. Phys. Lett. **447**(4), 384–387 (2007)

GNMF Revisited: Joint Robust k-NN Graph and Reconstruction-Based Graph Regularization for Image Clustering

Feng Gu[1,2], Wenju Zhang[1,2], Xiang Zhang[1,2(✉)], Chenxu Wang[2],
Xuhui Huang[3], and Zhigang Luo[1,2(✉)]

[1] Science and Technology on Parallel and Distributed Processing Laboratory,
College of Computer, National University of Defense Technology, Changsha, China
[2] Institute of Software, College of Computer, National University of Defense
Technology, Changsha, China
[3] Department of Computer Science and Technology, College of Computer,
National University of Defense Technology, Changsha, China
gufengnudt@gmail.com, zhangxiang_43@aliyun.com, zgluo@nudt.edu.cn

Abstract. Clustering has long been a popular topic in machine learning and is the basic task of many vision applications. Graph regularized NMF (GNMF) and its variants as extensions of NMF decompose the whole dataset as the product of two low-rank matrices which respectively indicate centroids of clusters and cluster memberships for each sample. Although they utilize graph structure to reveal the geometrical structure within datasets, these methods completely ignore the robustness of graph structure. To address the issue above, this paper jointly incorporates a novel Robust Graph and Reconstruction-based Graph regularization into NMF (RG^{2}NMF) to promote the gain in clustering performance. Particularly, RG^{2}NMF stabilizes the objective of GNMF through the reconstruction regularization, and meanwhile exploits a learning procedure to derive the robust graph. Experiments of image clustering on two popular datasets illustrate the effectiveness of RG^{2}NMF compared with the baseline methods in quantities.

Keywords: k-NN graph · Graph regularization · Nonnegative matrix factorization · Clustering

1 Introduction

As the basic task of many vision applications, clustering seeks to divide data points into several groups composed of similar subjects. Up to now, it is still a popular and challenging topic in machine learning for lack of prior information. K-means is one of the most representative clustering methods, which assigns each sample to the nearest cluster centroid. Due to its simplicity and effectiveness, it has been widely applied in various applications like text and image clustering [1].

© Springer International Publishing AG 2017
A. Lintas et al. (Eds.): ICANN 2017, Part II, LNCS 10614, pp. 442–449, 2017.
https://doi.org/10.1007/978-3-319-68612-7_50

Recent works [2] show that K-means can be treated as a constrained matrix factorization problem.

Nonnegative matrix factorization (NMF, [3]) as a powerful matrix factorization method has proven to be effective in clustering [4]. It decomposes an original data matrix into the product of two lower-rank nonnegative matrices, where the two matrices indicate centroids of clusters and cluster memberships of each sample respectively. NMF can induce the parts-based representation by a nonnegativity constraint and provide the psychological intuition of a whole composed of parts. Although NMF has enjoyed reasonable performance, it neglects important prior knowledge for clustering such as the geometrical structure within the datasets. To address this issue, Zhang et al. [5] minimized the gradient distance to preserve the topology structure of samples. Cai et al. [6] explored the graph regularized NMF (GNMF) to encode the geometric structure within the datasets into k-NN graph. Yang et al. [7] proposed nonnegative graph embedding (NGE) in the frame of graph-embedding framework. Apparently, their graph construction is completely independent of NMF and the clustering results may be not optimal. To remedy this deficiency, Peng et al. [8] integrated graph and feature learning procedures into a unified NMF model. Pei et al. [9] developed a concept factorization with adaptive neighbors (CFANs) which performs dimensionality reduction and finds the neighbor graph weights matrix simultaneously. However, the constructed graph as noted above is fragile to noisy data to some extent. Moreover, these methods regard the coefficient-based graph regularization term as the part of the objective. And the objective value would obviously burden the instability resulting from the fluctuation of coefficient matrix.

In order to defeat the preceding problems, this paper proposes a novel method which jointly incorporates an ingenious Robust Graph and Reconstruction-based Graph regularization into NMF (RG^{2}NMF). Concretely speaking, RG^{2}NMF employs the reconstruction regularization to stabilize the objective of GNMF, and meanwhile exploits the learning fashion to generate the robust graph. Although our robust graph construction is formally independent of feature learning, it induces no performance degeneration in clustering for the sake of removing the effect of the irrelevant features. The experimental results on two image datasets including Yale [10] and Webcam [11] show that RG^{2}NMF outperforms the representative baseline methods.

2   Robust k-NN Graph

In graph regularization, the quality of graph plays an important role in manifold learning, and has a significant effect on related tasks like clustering. There are several universal graph weight methods such as binary k-Nearest Neighbours (k-NN) graph and heat kernel k-NN graph. However, k-NN graph is not robust to noisy data since its construction relies on the pair-wise Euclidean distance which is known to be sensitive to outliers. In this section, we propose a novel robust k-NN graph construction method to overcome the aforementioned deficiency.

Let A_{*i} denote the i-th column and A_{j*} denote the j-th row of the matrix A. Given a data matrix $X \in R^{m \times n}$, where m and n denote the number of features and samples respectively, the construction of traditional k-NN graph of X can be reformulated as a learning procedure as follows:

$$\min_{S_{pq}\in\{0,1\},\ \|S_{p*}\|_0=k} \sum_{p=1}^{n}\sum_{q=1}^{n} \|X_{*p} - X_{*q}\|_2^2 S_{pq} \tag{1}$$

where S is the weight matrix of the graph. It can be verified that k-NN graph is identical to the symmetrized result of the solution to (1) using $S \leftarrow \max\left(S, S^T\right)$. For clarity, we rewrite (1) as

$$\min_{S_{pq}\in\{0,1\},\ \|S_{p*}\|_0=k} \|Y\|_{\mathbb{F}}^2 = \sum_{i=1}^{m} \|Y_{i**}\|_F^2 = \sum_{i=1}^{m}\sum_{p=1}^{n}\sum_{q=1}^{n} Y_{ipq}^2 \tag{2}$$

where $\|\cdot\|_{\mathbb{F}}$ denotes the tensor Frobenius norm, $\|\cdot\|_F$ denotes the matrix Frobenius norm, and Y is a 3-dimensional tensor whose entries are defined as $Y_{ipq} = S_{pq}\left(X_{ip} - X_{iq}\right)$. It is not difficult to find that the tensor Frobenius norm loss function in (2) is sensitive to outliers. To enhance the robustness of $\|\cdot\|_{\mathbb{F}}$, we detect the outliers by enforcing the non-outlier support constraint as follows:

$$\min_{S_{pq}\in\{0,1\},\ \|S_{p*}\|_0=k,\delta_i\in\{0,1\},\|\delta\|_0=m-c} \sum_{i=1}^{m} \delta_i \|Y_{i**}\|_F^2 \tag{3}$$

where c denotes the number of outliers and the binary vector δ denotes the non-outlier support, namely, $\delta_i = 0$ if $\|Y_{i**}\|_F$ is outlier and $\delta_i = 1$ otherwise.

We alternatively update S and δ with the other variable fixed. To optimize S when δ is fixed, (3) can be recast as

$$\min_{S_{pq}\in\{0,1\},\ \|S_{p*}\|_0=k} \sum_{p=1}^{n}\sum_{q=1}^{n} \left\|\widetilde{X}_{*p} - \widetilde{X}_{*q}\right\|_2^2 S_{pq} \tag{4}$$

where $\widetilde{X} = diag\left(\delta\right)X$ and the diagonal matrix $diag\left(\delta\right)$ contains the entries of δ along its diagonal. Thus, the optimal solution of (4) is

$$S_{pq} = \begin{cases} 1, & \text{if } \widetilde{X}_{*q} \in N_k\left(\widetilde{X}_{*p}\right) \\ 0, & \text{otherwise} \end{cases} \tag{5}$$

where $N_k(\widetilde{X}_{*p})$ denotes the k nearest neighbors of $\widetilde{X}_{*p}$. Finally, we conduct a symmetrizing step by using $S \leftarrow \max\left(S, S^T\right)$.

To optimize δ when S is fixed, assuming S is symmetric, the optimization problem in (3) can be rewritten as

$$\min_{\delta_i\in\{0,1\},\|\delta\|_0=m-c} \text{Tr}\left(diag\left(\delta\right)X\left(D - S\right)X^T diag\left(\delta\right)\right) \tag{6}$$

where D denotes a diagonal matrix whose element is $D_{ii} = \sum_{j=1}^{n} S_{ij}$. And the optimal solution of (6) can be obtained by

$$\delta_i = \begin{cases} 0, & \text{if } X_{i*}\left(D - S\right)X_{i*}^T \text{ belongs to the } c \text{ largest values} \\ 1, & \text{otherwise} \end{cases} \tag{7}$$

In summary, we present the total construction procedure of robust k-NN graph in Algorithm 1, which is considered to have converged when $\|S^t - S^{t-1}\|_F^2 / \|S^{t-1}\|_F^2$ is less than the tolerance or t is greater than the maximum number of iterations.

As demonstrated above, the robust k-NN graph adopts the outlier detection procedure. However, we can also give another interpretation from the perspective of feature selection. The variable δ in (3) can be explained as feature indicator, that is, $\delta_i = 1$ signifies the corresponding feature to be kept. Moreover, (4) can be interpreted as constructing graph based on data samples after feature selection. We alternate graph construction and feature selection until stopping criterion is satisfied. Since feature selection removes the noisy features, we can learn a robust graph in the end.

Algorithm 1: Robust k-NN graph
Input: k, c
Output: S
Initialize $\forall i$, $\delta_i = 1$;
$t = 1$;
repeat
$\quad$ Update S via (5);
$\quad$ $S \leftarrow \max\left(S, S^T\right)$;
$\quad$ Update δ via (7);
$\quad$ $t \leftarrow t + 1$;
until *convergence*;

Algorithm 2: MUR for RG^{2}NMF
Input: X, r, k, c
Output: W and H
Construct graph S using **Alg. 1**;
Randomly initialize W, H;
$t = 1$;
repeat
$\quad$ Update W via (11);
$\quad$ Update H via (12);
$\quad$ $t \leftarrow t + 1$;
until *convergence*;

---

3   Joint Reconstruction-Based Graph Regularization and Robust k-NN Graph

Although GNMF [6] has attracted increasing attention in recent years, it still suffers from several problems. The objective of GNMF is

$$\min_{W \geq 0, H \geq 0} \|X - WH\|_F^2 + \lambda \operatorname{Tr}\left(H\left(D - G\right)H^T\right) \tag{8}$$

where G denotes a graph weight matrix and D is a diagonal matrix whose entries are column sums of G. (8) is instable in evidence since it is dominated by the second term, i.e., graph regularized term, with the reconstruction error term fixed. It implies that we can yield any solution to (8). For purpose of tackling the problem, we jointly introduce a reconstruction-based graph regularization to replace the coefficient-based graph regularization. The reconstruction-based graph regularization can be written as

$$\operatorname{Tr}\left(WH\left(D - G\right)H^T W^T\right) \tag{9}$$

Clearly, the value of (9) remains no change with the reconstruction error term fixed. This can guarantee the resultant solution to be suboptimal other than any feasible solution. To illustrate this point, we compared the coefficient-based GNMF (C-GNMF) and reconstruction-based GNMF (R-GNMF) on Yale dataset. Figure 1 displays that clustering capability of (9) outperforms the

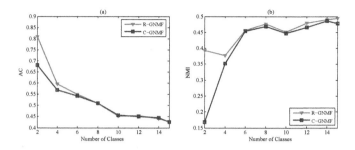

Fig. 1. Average accuracy (AC) and normalized mutual information (NMI) versus different numbers of classes on Yale dataset.

coefficient-based graph regularization in the case both regularization terms employ traditional k-NN graph.

However, the traditional k-NN graph used in GNMF is sensitive to outliers as mentioned earlier. Our robust k-NN graph is a great substitute for it. Similar to that, we can embed our robust k-NN graph into the reconstruction-based regularization term and obtain the resultant GNMF model termed RG^{2}NMF. Accordingly, the objective function of RG^{2}NMF is

$$\min_{W \geq 0, H \geq 0} F(W, H) = \|X - WH\|_F^2 + \lambda \operatorname{Tr}\left(WH(D - S)H^T W^T\right) \quad (10)$$

where λ is a positive parameter. We can derive the following multiplicative update rules (MUR) for W and H:

$$W = W \frac{XH^T + \lambda WHSH^T}{WHH^T + \lambda WHDH^T} \quad (11)$$

$$H = H \frac{W^T X + \lambda W^T WHS}{W^T WH + \lambda W^T WHD} \quad (12)$$

The total optimization procedure of RG^{2}NMF is summarized in Algorithm 2, for which the convergence criterion is set as $\left\|F^t - F^{t-1}\right\|_F^2 / \left\|F^{t-1}\right\|_F^2 \leqslant \varepsilon$ or $t \geqslant t_{\max}$, where ε is the tolerance and $t_{\max}$ denotes the maximum number of iterations.

4   Experiments

This section verifies the effectiveness by comparing the clustering performance of our method with the representative clustering methods including K-means, NMF [3], GNMF [6], local coordinate concept factorization (LCF, [12]), nonnegative local coordinate factorization (NLCF, [13]) on Yale [10] and Webcam [11] datasets. In clustering tasks, we learned the coefficients of examples and chose K-means to cluster the coefficients. Each experiment was independently conducted 5 times and then we validated the clustering performance in terms of average accuracy (AC) and normalized mutual information (NMI).

For fair comparison, we searched the best average result under combinations of different parameter settings. For GNMF and RG^{2}NMF, the parameter k was set by $\{2, 3, 4, 5, 6, 8, 10\}$, and the regularization parameter was selected from $\{0.01, 0.05, 0.1, 0.5, 1, 5, 10, 50, 100, 150, 200, 250\}$. As to LCF and NLCF, they involved a regularization parameter whose proper value was selected from the range $\{0.01, 0.03, 0.05, 0.08, 0.1, 0.3, 0.5, 0.8, 1, 1.3, 1.5, 1.8, 2, 5, 8, 10\}$. And for RG^{2}NMF, the number of the outliers c was set from $\{0, 50, 100, 150, 200, 250, 300, 350, 400, 450, 500, 550, 600\}$.

4.1 Case Study

To verify the effectiveness of our robust k-NN graph, we learned the robust graph on Yale dataset and visualized δ according to its meaning of the feature indicator. The parameters in Algorithm 1 were set as $k = 3$ and $c = 130$. Figure 2 illustrates that our graph construction can remove the background features and ensure that the selected features are reasonable, considering the background features is definitely useless to cluster faces.

Fig. 2. Demonstration of selected images from Yale dataset (in blue box) and reshaped δ (in red box). (Color figure online)

Moreover, we compared our robust k-NN graph with different graphs including k-NN graph, l_1-graph [14], low-rank graph [15] in the frame of our reconstruction-based graph regularization on Yale dataset. As we can see from Fig. 3, our robust k-NN graph is significantly superior to others in terms of average accuracy (AC) and normalized mutual information (NMI).

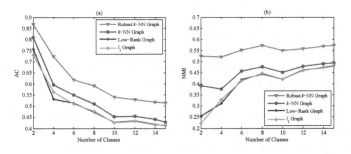

Fig. 3. Average accuracy (AC) and normalized mutual information (NMI) versus different numbers of classes on Yale dataset.

4.2   Image Clustering

We used Yale face dataset and Webcam object dataset for comparison in this section. The former contains 165 images of 15 individuals. The images were cropped and resized to vectors with 32×32 pixels. And the latter contains 795 images of 31 categories. We extracted their SURF features and quantized them into 800-bin histogram with codebooks. Figure 4 shows the AC and NMI on Yale and Webcam datasets under different numbers of classes. It is observed that our RG^{2}NMF consistently outperforms the baseline methods in all cases.

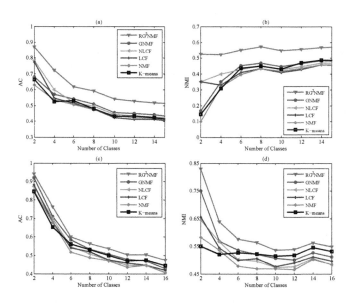

Fig. 4. Average accuracy (AC) and normalized mutual information (NMI) versus different numbers of classes on Yale (a, b) and Webcam (c, d) datasets.

5   Conclusion and Discussion

This paper devises a new GNMF model termed RG^{2}NMF by jointly integrating a robust graph and reconstruction-based graph regularization into NMF. RG^{2}NMF considers both the geometric structure of clean reconstruction data space and robust k-NN graph to boost clustering performance. Experimental results of image clustering on two popular image datasets verify the effectiveness of RG^{2}NMF. Furthermore, as a variant of NMF, it is still a promising method to tackle the non-image data like text data. We plan to study the applicability of our method on data of different nature in the future work.

Acknowledgments. This work was partially supported by National High-tech R&D Program (under grant No. 2015AA020108) and National Natural Science Foundation of China (under grant No. U1435222).

References

1. Wu, X., Kumar, V., Quinlan, J.R., Ghosh, J., Yang, Q., Motoda, H., McLachlan, G.J., Ng, A., Liu, B., Philip, S.Y., et al.: Top 10 algorithms in data mining. Knowl. Inf. Syst. **14**(1), 1–37 (2008)
2. Bauckhage, C.: K-means clustering is matrix factorization. CoRR abs/1512.07548 (2015)
3. Lee, D.D., Seung, H.S.: Learning the parts of objects by non-negative matrix factorization. Nature **401**(6755), 788–791 (1999)
4. Shahnaz, F., Berry, M.W., Pauca, V.P., Plemmons, R.J.: Document clustering using nonnegative matrix factorization. Inf. Process. Manag. **42**(2), 373–386 (2006)
5. Zhang, T., Fang, B., Tang, Y.Y., He, G., Wen, J.: Topology preserving non-negative matrix factorization for face recognition. IEEE Trans. Image Process. **17**(4), 574–584 (2008)
6. Cai, D., He, X., Han, J., Huang, T.S.: Graph regularized nonnegative matrix factorization for data representation. IEEE Trans. Pattern Anal. Mach. Intell. **33**(8), 1548–1560 (2011)
7. Yang, J., Yang, S., Fu, Y., Li, X., Huang, T.S.: Non-negative graph embedding. In: 2008 IEEE Conference on Computer Vision and Pattern Recognition, pp. 1–8. IEEE (2008)
8. Peng, C., Kang, Z., Hu, Y., Cheng, J., Cheng, Q.: Nonnegative matrix factorization with integrated graph and feature learning. ACM Trans. Intell. Syst. Technol. **8**(3), 42 (2017)
9. Pei, X., Chen, C., Gong, W.: Concept factorization with adaptive neighbors for document clustering. IEEE Trans. Neural Netw. Learn. Syst. **PP**(99), 1–10 (2016)
10. Belhumeur, P.N., Hespanha, J.P., Kriegman, D.J.: Eigenfaces vs. fisherfaces: recognition using class specific linear projection. IEEE Trans. Pattern Anal. Mach. Intell. **19**(7), 711–720 (1997)
11. Saenko, K., Kulis, B., Fritz, M., Darrell, T.: Adapting visual category models to new domains. In: Daniilidis, K., Maragos, P., Paragios, N. (eds.) ECCV 2010. LNCS, vol. 6314, pp. 213–226. Springer, Heidelberg (2010). doi:10.1007/978-3-642-15561-1_16
12. Liu, H., Yang, Z., Yang, J., Wu, Z., Li, X.: Local coordinate concept factorization for image representation. IEEE Trans. Neural Netw. Learn. Syst. **25**(6), 1071–1082 (2014)
13. Chen, Y., Zhang, J., Cai, D., Liu, W., He, X.: Nonnegative local coordinate factorization for image representation. IEEE Trans. Image Process. **22**(3), 969–979 (2013)
14. Cheng, B., Yang, J., Yan, S., Fu, Y.: Learning with ℓ^1-graph for image analysis. IEEE Trans. Image Process. **19**(4), 858–866 (2010)
15. Liu, G., Lin, Z., Yu, Y.: Robust subspace segmentation by low-rank representation. In: 27th International Conference on Machine Learning, pp. 663–670 (2010)

Two Staged Fuzzy SVM Algorithm and Beta-Elliptic Model for Online Arabic Handwriting Recognition

Ramzi Zouari[✉], Houcine Boubaker, and Monji Kherallah

National School of Engineers of Sfax (ENIS), University of Sfax, Sfax, Tunisia
ramzi.zouari@gmail.com, houcine-boubaker@ieee.org,
monji.kherallah@enis.rnu.tn

Abstract. Online handwriting recognition has been gaining more interest in the field of document analysis due to the growth of data entry technology. In this context, we propose a new architecture for online Arabic Word recognition based on a pre-classification of their handwriting trajectory segments delimited by pen-down and pen-up actions. To characterize these segments, we extract their kinematic and geometric profiles characteristics according to the overlapped beta-elliptic approach. The main contribution in this work consists on combining two stages of Support Vector Machines (SVM). The first one is developed in fuzzy logic (Fuzzy SVM) and allows computing the membership probabilities of pseudo-words in different sub-groups. The second stage consists on gathering the membership probabilities vectors of pseudo-words belonging to the same word in order to predict the word label. The tests are performed on 937 classes which represent the Tunisian town names from the ADAB database. The obtained results show the effectiveness of the proposed architecture which reached the rate of 99.89%.

Keywords: Online · Fuzzy · Pseudo-words · Beta-elliptic · Velocity · Unsupervised · Clustering

1 Introduction

During the two last decades, several researches have been made on online handwriting analysis field thanks to the emergence of new technologies in the field of data entry (tablet PC, electronic pen, PDA, etc.). In this context, many approaches have been done like writer identification, signature verification and word recognition [1–3]. Unlike offline analysis, where only a scanned image of the handwriting is available, online analysis provides dynamic informations such as velocity profile and temporal order of the trajectory [4]. Among online handwriting systems, Arabic word recognition is one of the most important areas to deal with, because the cursive style of the Arabic writing. Indeed, Arabic characters change shapes according to their location in the word (beginning, middle, isolate

© Springer International Publishing AG 2017
A. Lintas et al. (Eds.): ICANN 2017, Part II, LNCS 10614, pp. 450–458, 2017.
https://doi.org/10.1007/978-3-319-68612-7_51

and at the end). Furthermore, there are delayed strokes written above or below the character which may be a single or multi dots, Hamza or Chadda [5].

In the Arabic handwriting recognition process, a segmentation step is required. It consists on dividing a word into sub-units. Different segmentation techniques have been proposed which are generally based on geometric approaches. Sternby et al. [6] proposed a method that consists on segmenting trajectory at the vertical extreme points. Boubaker et al. [7] presented a graphemes segmentation technique based on the detection of two types of topologically particular points (Bottom of the ligature valleys and Angular points). In the other hand, segmentation can be made according to the kinematic profile. Tagougui et al. [8] decomposed the trajectory into segments representing pen up or pen-down moments. Kherallah et al. [9] segmented the word into strokes delimited between two consecutives extremums velocity points. The reliability of a system is given by its recognition rate. It depends on several factors like segmentation technique, extracted features and architecture of the system. In some researches, a combination between online and offline features is investigated [10,11]. The test results of this technique are conducted on ADAB database and reached a recognition rates of 93.33% and 91.8% respectively. In other works, the uses of multiple classifiers improves system performance. Tagougui et al. [12] proposed a hybrid MLP/HMM model. The segmented strokes are trained with a Multi-Layer Perceptron (MLP) to extract class script probabilities. Then, the MLP outputs are decoded through HMMs to provide script level recognition. This method achieved 96.4% recognition accuracy. Another hybrid TDNN-SVM architecture has been proposed in [13]. The fuzzy outputs of the Time Delay Neural Network (TDNN) are forwarded to the SVM classifier to predict the true label class. This architecture was tested on LMCA database and achieved a rate of 99.52%.

In this paper, we present a new architecture for online Arabic word recognition based on the association of two fuzzy SVM stages with beta-elliptic model. The first stage aims to compute the pseudo-words probability memberships within K groups, whereas the second puts the probabilities of pseudos-words belonging to the same word in order to find its true label class.

The rest of the paper is organized as follows: in the Sect. 2 we present beta-elliptic model. In the next part, the framework for online word recognition is presented. The Sect. 4 presents experiments and results and finally we give a conclusion with some future works.

2 Beta-Elliptic Modeling

Handwriting movement is generated by neurophysiologic excitations which may be characterized by its velocity and trajectory profiles [14]. As for the sigma-lognormal model [15] where the production of a handwriting trajectory is seen as the vectorial superposition in time of concatenated strokes engendered by lognormal shaped neuromuscular impulses [16], The beta-elliptic approach returns the generation of a handwriting trajectory to the mobilisation of N neuromuscular subsystems whose effects in the velocity domain are modeled by the sum of overlapped Beta impulses [17–19]. In fact, during each trajectory segment, executed between two successive extrema speed times, two neuromuscular subsystems S_i and S_{i+1} are mobilized to deputize progressively the dynamic of the movement drive. In the geometric profile, the model predicts that the neurophysiologic Beta shaped allure of the velocity tangential components $V_i(t)$ and $V_{i+1}(t)$ engendered by the neuromuscular subsystems S_i and S_{i+1} respectively, combined with constrains imposed by the relationship between the curvilinear velocity and radius of curvature in handwriting trajectory (known as the power law) lead to design an elliptic allure to the handwriting trajectory segment [20,21].

2.1 Handwriting Trajectory Segmentation

Curvilinear velocity profile $V_\sigma(t)$ represents the resulting response to the finished impulses. It can be calculated through the following formula:

$$V_\sigma(t) = \sqrt{\left(\frac{dx}{dt}\right)^2 + \left(\frac{dy}{dt}\right)^2}. \tag{1}$$

The curvilinear velocity curve shows a signal that alternates between extremums of velocity (minima, maxima and inflexion points). These specific points define the number of strokes (Fig. 1b).

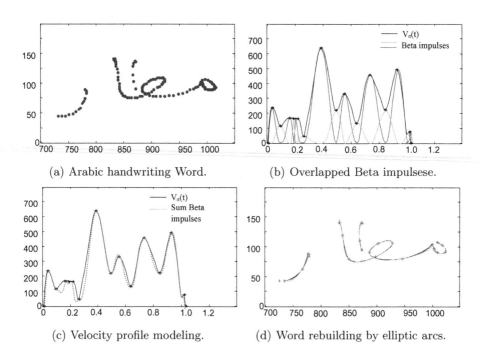

(a) Arabic handwriting Word.

(b) Overlapped Beta impulsese.

(c) Velocity profile modeling.

(d) Word rebuilding by elliptic arcs.

Fig. 1. Beta-elliptic modeling.

2.2   Velocity Profile Modeling

According to the works of Alimi et al. [18], each stroke converges with a beta impulse. Then, the curvilinear velocity can be approximated by an algebraic addition of the successive overlapped beta impulses (Fig. 1c)

$$V_\sigma(t) \approx \sum_{i=1}^{n} K_i \times \beta_i(t, q_i, p_i, t_{0i}, t_{1i}).$$ (2)

with

$$\beta_i(t, q_i, p_i, t_{0i}, t_{1i}) = \left\{ \begin{array}{ll} \left(\frac{t-t_{0i}}{t_{ci}-t_{0i}}\right)^{p_i} \left(\frac{t_{1i}-t}{t_1 t_{ci}}\right)^{q_i} & \text{if } t \in [t_{0i}, t_{1i}] \\ 0 & \text{elsewhere.} \end{array} \right\}$$ (3)

$$t_{ci} = \frac{(p_i \times t_{1i}) + (q_i \times t_{0i})}{p+q}$$ (4)

- K_i: amplitude of ith beta impulse,
- p_i, q_i are intermediate parameters,
- t_{0i}, t_{ci}, t_{1i} are the moments witch correspond respectively to the start, the maximum amplitude and the end of the Beta function ($t_{0i} < t_{ci} < t_{1i}$).

2.3   Trajectory Modeling

In the space domain, each stroke located between two successive extrema speed times can be modeled by an elliptic arc that represents a simple quarter of ellipse [19]. Boubaker et al. [20] have proposed two novel approaches of rebuilding trajectory based on five points and oblique projection methods. They allow using arcs of ellipses which are not limited by tops in order to reduce the error of rebuilding (Fig. 1d).

3   Framework for Online Arabic Handwriting Recognition

3.1   Data Processing and Script Segmentation

In the preprocessing step, we have applied a Chebyshev second type low pass filter to eliminate the noise generated by spatial and temporal sampling. Furthermore, the vertical dimension of the script lines is adjusted to obtain a normalized script size. The script segmentation principle consists on decomposing the signal into segments, called pseudo-words, defined as a continuous handwriting trajectory delimited between pen-up and pen-down moments.

3.2   Features Extraction

The feature extraction step consists on calculating the dynamic and geometric profiles of all pseudo-words. For each one, we calculate the beta-elliptic parameters of the set of strokes that constitute it. In fact, each stroke is represented by a number of 7 parameters (Table 1). So, the pseudo-word feature vector X is the concatenation of the beta-elliptic parameters of its strokes.

Table 1. Beta-elliptic parameters

	Parameters	Explanation
Dynamic profile	K	Beta impulse amplitude
	$\delta t = (t_1 - t_0)$	Beta impulse duration
	$Rap = \frac{p}{p+q}$	Rapport of beta impulse asymmetry or culminating time
	P	Beta shape parameters
Geometric profile	a	Ellipse major axis half length
	b	Ellipse small axis half length
	θ	Ellipse major axis inclination angle

3.3   Pre-classfication Stage

This stage aims to classify all database pseudo-words into groups according to their feature vectors X. Since the developed recognition algorithm is addressed for multi-writer application, the pseudo-word trajectory shape and length change from one person to another depending to the handwriting style. For this reason, we can not manually associate a label for each pseudo word. We have apply the K-means algorithm to classify automatically all pseudo-words into K groups [22] (Fig. 2a). These groups are trained using Fuzzy SVM in order to associate for each pseudo-word a set of scores $S_{i=1,...,K}(X)$ that represents the distance separating it from the hyperplanes [23]. To turn these scores into probabilites,

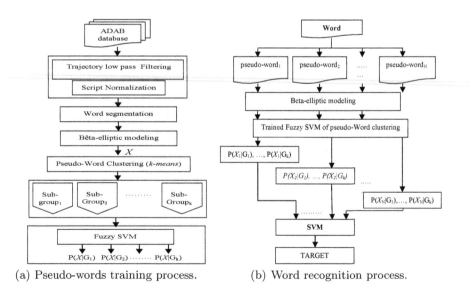

(a) Pseudo-words training process.   (b) Word recognition process.

Fig. 2. Online handwriting recognition process.

we applied the Platt algorithm [24]. So, a pseudo word will be modeled by a vector of size K that contains the membership probabilities to the K sub-groups.

3.4 Word Recognition Process

This step consists of recognizing a word from its pseudo-words. For this reason, we gathered for each word the membership probabilities vectors of its pseudo-words to form the input data to the second SVM which allows to establish a relation between the fuzzy outputs obtained from the first stage and the desired output (target) (Fig. 2b).

4   Experiments and Results

The experiments have been made on ADAB database. It is a multi-writer database that was written by 166 writers. It includes a total of 21575 online Tunisian towns names belonging to 937 different classes (Table 2). After the segmentation process, we obtained a total of 114924 pseudo-words which are classified into K groups according to the K-means algorithm. The number of clusters K is fixed at 100 since it returns the least within-cluster sums of points-to-centroid distances. To check the effectiveness of the clustering algorithm, we chose randomly two thirds of sub-groups samples for the training step and we associated the pseudo-word from the test set to a sub-group with the higher membership probability. Experiments have been made on Fuzzy SVM with different kernel functions and the best results have been obtained with Radial Basis Function (Table 3).

Table 2. ADAB database description

	Number of words	Number of pseudo words	Writers
Set1	5037	40296	56
Set2	5090	25450	37
Set3	5031	15093	39
Set4	4417	22085	25
Set5	1000	4000	6
Set6	1000	8000	3
Total	**21575**	**114924**	**166**

Following the pevious stage, we have stored for each pseudo word a vector of size K that contains its membership probabilities to the K sub-groups. The word recognition step consists on gathering the vectors of pseudo-words belonging to the same word in order to recognize the word label. The experiments were carried out on a second SVM with different kernel functions. The best result has been obtained with RBF kernel and have reached the impressive recognition rate of 99.89% (Table 4).

Table 3. Pseudo-word classification results

	Kernel function			
	Linear	Polynomial	Sigmoid	RBF
Recognition rate	84.14%	87.74%	89.99%	**92.33%**

Table 4. Word recognition Rates

	Kernel function			
	Linear	Polynomial	Sigmoid	RBF
Recognition rate	96.52%	96.92%	97.12%	**99.89%**

Compared to other works from the literature, the proposed system performs better than the others which are conducted on ADAB database and based on HMM, MLP and CNN networks (Table 5).

Table 5. Results comparison

Systems	Architecture	Database	Recognition rate
Khlif et al. [10]	HMM	ADAB	93.33%
Tagougui et al. [11]	MLP-HMM	ADAB	96.45%
Elleuch et al. [12]	CNN	ADAB	91.8%
Best ICDAR 2011 [25]	AUC-HMM1	ADAB	98.45%
Present work	**FSVM-SVM**	ADAB	**99.89%**

5   Conclusions and Future Works

We presented in this paper a new architecture for online Arabic handwriting recognition. The beta-elliptic approach was used to model the dynamic and geometric profiles of handwriting trajectory. The proposed system proceeds by using the fuzzy logic in order to identify the membership probabilities of the pseudo-words in different sub-groups. Thereafter, the membership probabilities vectors of pseudo-word belonging to the same word are gathered to form the input data to the second SVM in order to recognize the handwriting script. The obtained result demonstrates the effectiveness of the proposed system compared to others already exists in literature. As future work, we will interested to test the proposed method also on other forms of script like digits and Latin handwriting since the beta-elliptic model does not specific to Arabic handwriting.

References

1. Chaabouni, A., Boubaker, H., Kherallah, M., Alimi, A.M., El Abed, H.: Multi-fractal modeling for on-line text-independent writer identification. In: International Conference on Document Analysis and Recognition, pp. 623–627 (2011)

2. Hassaïne, A., Al-Maadeed, S.: An online signature verification system for forgery and disguise detection. In: Huang, T., Zeng, Z., Li, C., Leung, C.S. (eds.) ICONIP 2012. LNCS, vol. 7666, pp. 552–559. Springer, Heidelberg (2012). doi:10.1007/978-3-642-34478-7_67

3. El-Sana, J., Biadsy, F.: Online Arabic handwriting recognition. U.S. Patent and Trademark Office, vol. 1, no. 8, pp. 131–615 (2013)

4. Chaabouni, A., Boubaker, H., Kherallah, M., Alimi, A.M., El Abed, H.: Combining of off-line and on-line feature extraction approaches for writer identification. In: International Conference on Document Analysis and Recognition, pp. 1299–1303 (2011)

5. Tagougui, N., Kherallah, M., Alimi, A.M.: Online Arabic handwriting recognition: a survey. Int. J. Document Anal. Recogn. (IJDAR), **16**(3), 209–226 (2013)

6. Sternby, J., Morwing, J., Andersson, C.: On-line Arabic handwriting recognition with templates. Pattern Recogn. **42**(12), 3278–3286 (2009)

7. Boubaker, H., El Baati, A., Kherallah, M., Alimi, A.M., Elabed, H.: Online Arabic handwriting modeling system based on the graphemes segmentation. In: 20th International Conference on In Pattern Recognition (ICPR), pp. 2061–2064. IEEE (2010)

8. Tagougui, N., Boubaker, H., Kherallah, M., Alimi, M.A.: A hybrid NN/HMM modeling technique for online Arabic handwriting recognition, arXiv preprint arXiv 1401.0486 (2014)

9. Kherallah, M., Haddad, L., Alimi, M.: A new approach for online Arabic handwriting recognition. In: Proceedings of the Second International Conference on Arabic Language Resources and Tools, pp. 22–23 (2009)

10. Khlif, H., Prum, S., Kessentini, Y., Kanoun, S.: Fusion of explicit segmentation based system and segmentation-free based system for on-line Arabic handwritten word recognition. In: 15th International Conference on Frontiers in Handwriting Recognition (ICFHR), pp. 399–404. IEEE (2016)

11. Elleuch, M., Zouari, R., Kherallah, M.: Feature extractor based deep method to enhance online Arabic handwritten recognition system. In: Villa, A.E.P., Masulli, P., Pons Rivero, A.J. (eds.) ICANN 2016. LNCS, vol. 9887, pp. 136–144. Springer, Cham (2016). doi:10.1007/978-3-319-44781-0_17

12. Tagougui, N., Boubaker, H., Kherallah, M., Alimi, A.M.: A hybrid MLPNN/HMM recognition system for online Arabic handwritten script. In: World Congress on Computer and Information Technology (WCCIT), pp. 1–6. IEEE (2013)

13. Zouari, R., Boubaker, H., Kherallah, M.: Hybrid TDNN-SVM algorithm for online Arabic handwriting recognition. In: Abraham, A., Haqiq, A., Alimi, A.M., Mezzour, G., Rokbani, N., Muda, A.K. (eds.) HIS 2016. AISC, vol. 552, pp. 113–123. Springer, Cham (2017). doi:10.1007/978-3-319-52941-7_12

14. Boubaker, H., Chaabouni, A., Tagougui, N., Kherallah, M., Alimi, A.M.: Handwriting and hand drawing velocity modeling by superposing beta impulses and continuous training component. Int. J. Comput. Sci. **10**(5(1)), 57–63 (2013)

15. Reilly, C.O., Plamondon, R.: Development of a sigma-lognormal representation for on-line signatures. Pattern Recogn. **42**(12), 3324–3337 (2009)

16. Plamondon, R.: A kinematic theory of rapid human movements. Part I. Movement representation and generation. Biol. Cybern. **72**(4), 295–307 (1995)
17. Alimi, A.M.: Evolutionary neuro-fuzzy approach to recognize on-line Arabic handwriting. In: Proceedings of the International Conference on Document Analysis and Recognition (ICDAR), vol. 1, pp. 382–386 (1997)
18. Bezine, H., Alimi, A.M., Sherkat, N: Generation and analysis of handwriting script with the beta-elliptic model. In: 9th International Workshop on Frontiers in Handwriting Recognition, pp. 515–520. IEEE (2004)
19. Kherallah, M., Haddad, L., Alimi, A.M., Mitiche, A.: On-line handwritten digit recognition based on trajectory and velocity modeling. Pattern Recogn. Lett. **29**(5), 580–594 (2008)
20. Boubaker, H., Kherallah, M., Alimi, A.M.: New strategy for the on-line handwriting modelling. In: 9th International Conference on Document Analysis and Recognition (ICDAR), vol. 2, pp. 1233–1247 (2007)
21. Boubaker, H., Rezzoug, N., Kherallah, M., Gorce, P., Alimi, A.M.: Spatio-temporal representation of 3D hand trajectory based on beta-elliptic models. Comput. Methods Biomech. Biomed. Eng. J. (CMBBE) **18**(15), 1632–1647 (2015)
22. MacQueen, J: Some methods for classification and analysis of multivariate observations. In: Proceedings of the Fifth Berkeley Symposium on Mathematical Statistics and Probability, vol. 1, no. 14, pp. 281–297 (1967)
23. Zadrozny, B., Elkan, C.: Transforming classifier scores into accurate multiclass probability estimates. In: Proceedings of the 8th ACM SIGKDD International Conference on Knowledge Discovery and Data Mining, pp. 694–699 (2002)
24. Platt, J.: Probabilistic outputs for support vector machines and comparisons to regularized likelihood methods. Adv. Large Margin Classifiers **10**(3), 61–74 (1999)
25. Kherallah, M., Tagougui, N., Alimi, A.M., Elabed, H., Mrgner, V.: Online Arabic handwriting recognition competition. In: Proceeding of 11th International Conference on Document Analysis and Recognition, pp. 1454–1459 (2011)

Evaluating the Compression Efficiency of the Filters in Convolutional Neural Networks

Kazuki Osawa[1](✉) and Rio Yokota[2]

[1] School of Computer Science, Tokyo Institute of Technology, Tokyo, Japan
oosawa.k.ad@m.titech.ac.jp
[2] Advanced Computing Research Division,
Advanced Applications of High-Performance Computing Group,
Global Scientific Information and Computing Center,
Tokyo Institute of Technology, Tokyo, Japan
rioyokota@gsic.titech.ac.jp
http://www.titech.ac.jp/english/, http://www.gsic.titech.ac.jp/en

Abstract. Along with the recent development of Convolutional Neural Network (CNN) and its multilayering, it is important to reduce the amount of computation and the amount of data associated with convolution processing. Some compression methods of convolutional filters using low-rank approximation have been studied. The common goal of these studies is to accelerate the computation wherever possible while maintaining the accuracy of image recognition. In this paper, we investigate the trade-off between the compression error by low-rank approximation and the computational complexity for the state-of-the-arts CNN model.

Keywords: Convolutional neural networks · Low-rank approximation

1 Introduction

In recent years, a lot of deep learning models have demonstrated high accuracy in many tasks of machine learning including image classification tasks. Since the Convolutional Neural Network (CNN) of Krizhevsky et al. [1] showed overwhelming performance in ILSVRC [2] held in 2012, CNNs have received wide attention in the field of image recognition and in many other field, and excellent models have been developed and researched by many researchers. As a recent trend, state-of-the-arts CNNs have more layers than before and improves the performance to more complex tasks. Meanwhile, with the multilayering of networks, the computational complexities and the space requirements involved in model training and inference are increasing. It has been reported that it takes several days or weeks for training the model, and convolution processing in multiple convolutional layers occupies most of these times [3].

In order to solve this problem, several methods utilizing the resistance to noise of CNN have been proposed. Courbariaux et al. [4] constrained the weights and activities to +1 or −1, and Gupta et al. [5] used half precision fixed point

© Springer International Publishing AG 2017
A. Lintas et al. (Eds.): ICANN 2017, Part II, LNCS 10614, pp. 459–466, 2017.
https://doi.org/10.1007/978-3-319-68612-7_52

for calculation. They show that accuracy does not degrade. Several compression methods for convolutional filters using low-rank approximation have also been proposed [6–10]. By reducing the rank of the tensor (matrix) constituting each filter and compressing it, the computational complexity and the space requirement involved in the convolution process are reduced. However, quantitative investigations on the compressibility of convolution filters have not been reported in such studies. In this work, we investigate the compression efficiency of the filter of the convolution layer for the state-of-the-arts CNN models.

2   Related Work

2.1   Convolutional Neural Networks

As a research field of artificial intelligence that finds consistent rules out of a large amount of data, the development of machine learning is remarkable. Deep learning is one of the most attractive machine learning methods in recent years due to high recognition accuracy. Deep learning has a multilayered neural network model inspired by the neural circuits of the human brain, and this "deep" structure provides an effective solution to problems that require complex judgment. In the field of image recognition, Convolutional Neural Networks (CNN), which is one type of deep learning, exercises the highest recognition performance in many benchmarks and contests [2,11], finally exceeding the image recognition accuracy by human beings (called *superhuman*) [12].

ILSVRC. ImageNet Large Scale Visual Recognition Challenge (ILSVRC) [2] is a large-scale object recognition and image classification benchmark held since 2010. In this work, we are targeting state-of-the-arts CNNs that demonstrated the best performance with ILSVRC 2014 and ILSVRC 2015. In ILSVRC 2014, VGG ConvNet (VGG) [13] demonstrated the best performance in one of the tasks of the object detection department (DET), and GoogLeNet [14] demonstrated the best performance in the tasks of both DET and object classification, localization department (LOC).

2.2   CNN with Low-Rank Approximation

Parameters of the deep learning model including CNN have redundancy. In recent years, several studies exploiting this property by compressing the convolution filter to a low-rank for accelerating convolution have been reported. Rigamonti et al. [6] separates the image convolution filter used in the field of machine learning and computer vision, not only to CNN, to a smaller linear filter (rank-1) and approximates it. Denil et al. [7] focuses on the redundancy of the parameters of the deep learning model and accurately estimates the remaining values from a given part of the weights. In the model for MNIST [15] and CIFAR-10 [16], they succeeded in estimating the maximum 95% weight without degrading recognition accuracy. Denton et al. [17] speed up the computation of each layer by the CPU and the GPU twice without damaging the recognition accuracy of CNN for ILSVRC 2012 dataset by 1%. Jaderberg et al. [8] has achieved a speedup of 4.5 times for pre-trained CNNs for scene text character recognition at the expense of 1% recognition accuracy. Lebedev et al. [9] compresses the 4 dimensional filter of the convolution layer of the large scale CNN to the low-rank using CP-decomposition. They achieves 8.5 times faster speed on CPU, overwhelming the method of Denton et al., and Jaderberg et al. Also, by merely impairing the recognition accuracy of AlexNet [1] by 1%, it has achieved 4 times faster than the second convolved layer. Tai et al. [10] applied a low-rank approximation method of the convolutional layer filters to AlexNet, NIN, VGG, GoogLeNet that are state-of-the-arts CNNs for CIFAR-10 and ILSVRC 12 dataset, achieved high speed. In addition, it reports the result of achieving higher recognition accuracy than the model without filter compression. However, in this study, they consider only the speed-up in each convolutional layer.

3   Compression of the Filters

3.1   Singular Value Decomposition

The Singular Value Decomposition (SVD) of a real matrix $A \in \mathbb{R}^{m \times n}$ is a matrix decomposition technique that transforms A into the product of three matrices, such as $A = U \Sigma V^{\mathrm{T}}$, using orthogonal matrices $U \in \mathbb{R}^{m \times m}$ and $V \in \mathbb{R}^{n \times n}$. Here we think about a real symmetric matrix $AA^{\mathrm{T}} \in \mathbb{R}^{m \times m}$. Assume the eigenvalues λ_i $(i = 1, 2, \ldots, m)$ of AA^{T} are in order, $\lambda_1 \geq \cdots \geq \lambda_r > \lambda_{r+1} = \cdots = \lambda_m = 0$, then, $\sigma_i := \sqrt{\lambda_i} > 0$ $(i = 1, \ldots, r)$ are called singular values of A. By using the singular values of A, the matrix Σ is defined as,

$$\Sigma := \begin{cases} \begin{bmatrix} \Delta & O \end{bmatrix} & if \ (m > n) \\ \Delta & if \ (m = n) \\ \begin{bmatrix} \Delta \\ O \end{bmatrix} & if \ (m < n) \end{cases}, \quad \begin{array}{l} \Delta := \mathrm{diag}(\sigma_1, \ldots, \sigma_r), \\ O : \text{zero matrix.} \end{array} \tag{1}$$

Because $\sigma_1 \geq \cdots \geq \sigma_r > 0$, Σ is uniquely determined (U and V are not uniquely determined). By using the eigenvectors $\mathbf{u}_j \in \mathbb{R}^m (j = 1, \ldots, r)$ of AA^{T} corresponding to eigenvalues λ_j $(j = 1, \ldots, r)$ and the eigenvectors $\mathbf{v}_j := \frac{1}{\sigma_j} A^{\mathrm{T}} \mathbf{u}_j \in \mathbb{R}^n$ of $A^{\mathrm{T}} A$) corresponding to eigenvalue λ_j $(j = 1, \ldots, r)$, A is also represented as, $A = \sum_{i=1}^{r} \sigma_i \mathbf{u}_i \mathbf{v}_i^{\mathrm{T}}$.

3.2   Low-Rank Approximation Using SVD

Then, think about lowering the rank of matrix $A \in \mathbb{R}^{m \times n}$ using SVD of it. Suppose the SVD of A is $A = \sum_{i=1}^{r} \sigma_i \mathbf{u}_i \mathbf{v}_i^{\mathrm{T}}$, by using $1 \leq k \leq r$, the matrix is approximated as $A \approx \sum_{j=1}^{k} \sigma_j \mathbf{u}_j \mathbf{v}_j^{\mathrm{T}} =: \tilde{A}_k$. This is called low-rank approximation. The space requirement of A is $\mathcal{O}(mn)$, and that of $\tilde{A}_k$ is $\mathcal{O}(k(m + n + k))$.

Suppose k are small enough, the space requirement of the approximated matrix can be kept lower than that of the original. For a certain rank k, this approximate form minimize the Frobenius norm $\|A - \tilde{A}_k\|_F$ which is the index of approximation error.

3.3   Compressing Filters in CNNs

We apply the low-rank approximation method using SVD to the 4 dimensional filter in each convolutional layer of CNN. Our method respects C. Tai et al's method [10]. First, convert 4-dimensional tensor $\mathcal{W} \in \mathbb{R}^{C \times d \times d \times K}$ to matrix $W \in \mathbb{R}^{Cd \times dK}$. Here, C represents the number of input channels of the convolutional layer, K represents the number of output channels, and d represents the size of the kernels. Let $j_1 := (i_1 - 1)d + i_2$ and $j_2 := (i_4 - 1)d + i_3$, then (j_1, j_2) component of W is (i_1, i_2, i_3, i_4) component of $\mathcal{W}$. Now, we calc the low-rank approximation of matrix $W \in \mathbb{R}^{Cd \times dK}$ for certain rank k. We can get the low-rank matrix $\tilde{W}_k := U_{W,k} \Sigma_{W,k} V_{W,k}^{\mathrm{T}}$.

3.4   Compression Efficiency

Our goal is to reduce computational complexity as much as possible without degrading CNN recognition accuracy. Therefore, we are interested in how much the filter after the low-rank approximation ($\tilde{W}_k$) deteriorates compared with the original one (W) and the computational amount that can be reduced at that time. In order to quantitatively measure the error of the filter after the approximation, the following relative norm using the Frobenius norm is adopted,

$$E(W, k) := \frac{\|W - \tilde{W}_k\|_F}{\|W\|_F}. \tag{2}$$

This is because the sizes of the filters (Frobenius norm) are different in each convolutional layer.

Let $Z \in \mathbb{R}^{X \times Y \times K}$ be the output feature map to a convolutional layer. Then, the computational complexity of normal convolution using $\mathcal{W} \in \mathbb{R}^{C \times d \times d \times K}$ is $\mathcal{O}(d^2 KCXY)$. In Tai et al's method [10], the computational complexity of the convolution using rank k approximated filter $\tilde{W}_k \in \mathbb{R}^{Cd \times dK}$ is $\mathcal{O}(dk(K + C)XY)$. Therefore, the difference in computational amount relative to original convolution is represented by

$$D(W, Z, k) := dk(K + C)XY - d^2 KCXY$$
$$= dXY(k(K + C) - dKC). \tag{3}$$

Here if $D(W, Z, k) < 0$, the computational amount of the convolution with approximation is lower than that without approximation.

Using (2) and (3), we examine the compressibility of the filter W, in the convolutional layer its output is Z, for a desired approximation error e, by calculating the smallest rank k_{min} as following,

$$k_{min} := \min\{k \mid E(W, k) < e\}, \tag{4}$$

and calculating the value of $D(W, Z, k_{min})$.

4 Experiments

4.1 CNN Model

We apply the low-rank approximation method to the pre-trained filters of VGG-16 which is state-of-the-arts CNN model demonstrated the best performance in ILSVRC, and investigated the relationship between rank k, approximation error, and speeding-up. Specifically, we used pre-trained filters (https://github.com/tensorflow/models/tree/master/slim) which is trained by ILSVRC2012 datasets. The configuration of the convolutional layers, the filters before/after approximation, and the output sizes in VGG-16 are showed in Table 1 ($k_{1\_1}, \ldots, k_{5\_3}$ are the rank k for low-rank approximation method for conv1_1, . . . , conv5_3).

Table 1. Configuration of VGG-16 (convolutional layers)

Layer	Original filter $C \times d \times d \times K$	Approximated filter $C \times d \times d \times K$	Output size $X \times Y$
conv1_1	$3 \times 3 \times 3 \times 64$	$3 \times 3 \times 1 \times k_{1\_1}$ $k_{1\_1} \times 1 \times 3 \times 64$	224×224
conv1_2	$64 \times 3 \times 3 \times 64$	$3 \times 3 \times 1 \times k_{1\_2} k_{1\_2} \times 1 \times 3 \times 64$	224×224
conv2_1	$64 \times 3 \times 3 \times 128$	$64 \times 3 \times 1 \times k_{2\_1}$ $k_{2\_1} \times 1 \times 3 \times 128$	112×112
conv2_2	$128 \times 3 \times 3 \times 128$	$128 \times 3 \times 1 \times k_{2\_2}$ $k_{2\_2} \times 1 \times 3 \times 128$	112×112
conv3_1	$128 \times 3 \times 3 \times 256$	$128 \times 3 \times 1 \times k_{3\_1}$ $k_{3\_1} \times 1 \times 3 \times 256$	56×56
conv3_2	$256 \times 3 \times 3 \times 256$	$256 \times 3 \times 1 \times k_{3\_2}$ $k_{3\_2} \times 1 \times 3 \times 256$	56×56
conv3_3	$256 \times 3 \times 3 \times 256$	$256 \times 3 \times 1 \times k_{3\_3}$ $k_{3\_3} \times 1 \times 3 \times 256$	56×56
conv4_1	$256 \times 3 \times 3 \times 512$	$256 \times 3 \times 1 \times k_{4\_1}$ $k_{4\_1} \times 1 \times 3 \times 512$	28×28
conv4_2	$512 \times 3 \times 3 \times 512$	$512 \times 3 \times 1 \times k_{4\_2}$ $k_{4\_2} \times 1 \times 3 \times 512$	28×28
conv4_3	$512 \times 3 \times 3 \times 512$	$512 \times 3 \times 1 \times k_{4\_3}$ $k_{4\_3} \times 1 \times 3 \times 512$	28×28
conv5_1	$512 \times 3 \times 3 \times 512$	$512 \times 3 \times 1 \times k_{5\_1}$ $k_{5\_1} \times 1 \times 3 \times 512$	14×14
conv5_2	$512 \times 3 \times 3 \times 512$	$512 \times 3 \times 1 \times k_{5\_2}$ $k_{5\_2} \times 1 \times 3 \times 512$	14×14
conv5_3	$512 \times 3 \times 3 \times 512$	$512 \times 3 \times 1 \times k_{5\_3}$ $k_{5\_3} \times 1 \times 3 \times 512$	14×14

4.2 Approximation Error and Computational Complexity

For several approximate error $e \in \{0.01, 0.02, \ldots, 0.49, 0.50\}$, we calculate (4) and (3) for each convolutional layer of VGG-16 (Fig. 1). By considering the total computational amount of all convolutions and the compression efficiency of each convolution, we can select the ranks for low-rank approximation. Possible strategies for selecting ranks are

- If the computational amount that can be reduced is small relative to the total amount, then we select HIGH rank in order to lower the approximation error.
- Otherwise, we select LOW rank in order to accelerate the convolution.
- HIGH or LOW ranks are determined by comparing with the ranks used by Tai et al. [10].

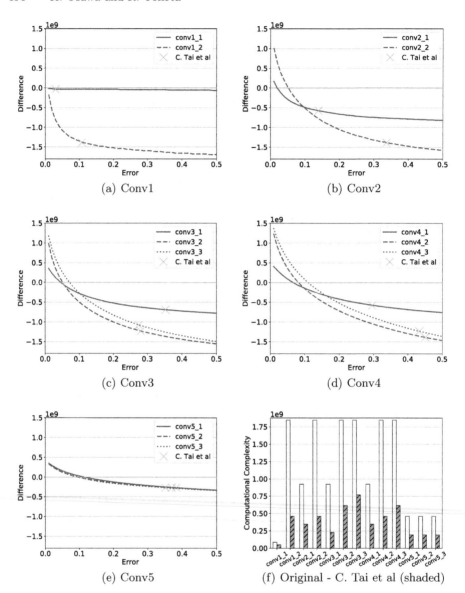

Fig. 1. (a)–(e): Trade-off between the approximation error (2) and the difference in computational amount relative to original convolution (3) in each layer by using k_{min} (4) for several error $e \in \{0.01, 0.02, \ldots, 0.49, 0.5\}$ (f): Comparison of computational complexity with original convolution (while bar) and that with convolution by Tai et al's method (shaded bar)

For example, in conv1_1 (Fig. 1(a)), we cannot reduce the computational complexity very much even if we set LOW rank (high approximation error). In addition, in all layers of Conv5 (Fig. 1(e)) have same feature as conv1_1. So we can understand that we should select HIGH ranks for these convolutional layers. Similarly, for the remaining layers, we can select relatively LOW ranks.

5   Conclusions and Future Work

We evaluated the compressibility of the CNN filter in the low-rank approximation quantitatively, which was not done in previous studies. As a result of investigations conducted on the VGG-16 model which is one of the CNNs of state-of-the-arts, we could know the characteristics of the compression efficiency of the filters of each convolutional layer. As a future possibility, by carefully considering the characteristics of the CNN model obtained in this work, it is expected to acquire the optimum ranks in the low-rank approximation. For future work, we have to compare the results of this work and the low-rank approximation strategies used in previous researches. Also, we have to examine the relationship between the relative norm and the classification accuracy.

Acknowledgments. This work was supported by JST CREST Grant Number JPMJCR1687, Japan.

References

1. Krizhevsky, A., Sutskever, I., Hinton, G.E.: Imagenet classification with deep convolutional neural networks. In: Bartlett, P., Pereira, F.C.N., Burges, C.J.C., Bottou, L., Weinberger, K.Q. (eds.) Advances in Neural Information Processing Systems, vol. 25, pp. 1106–1114 (2012)
2. Russakovsky, O., Deng, J., Hao, S., Krause, J., Satheesh, S., Ma, S., Huang, Z., Karpathy, A., Khosla, A., Bernstein, M., Berg, A.C., Fei-Fei, L.: ImageNet large scale visual recognition challenge. Int. J. Comput. Vis. (IJCV) **115**(3), 211–252 (2015)
3. Jia, Y.: Learning semantic image representations at a large scale. Ph.D. thesis, EECS Department, University of California, Berkeley, May 2014
4. Courbariaux, M., Bengio, Y.: Binarynet: training deep neural networks with weights and activations constrained to +1 or -1. CoRR, abs/1602.02830 (2016)
5. Gupta, S., Agrawal, A., Gopalakrishnan, K., Narayanan, P.: Deep learning with limited numerical precision. CoRR, abs/1502.02551 (2015)
6. Rigamonti, R., Sironi, A., Lepetit, V., Fua, P.: Learning separable filters. In: The IEEE Conference on Computer Vision and Pattern Recognition (CVPR), June 2013
7. Denil, M., Shakibi, B., Dinh, L., Ranzato, M., de Freitas, N.: Predicting parameters in deep learning. In: Neural Information Processing Systems (NIPS) (2013)
8. Jaderberg, M., Vedaldi, A., Zisserman, A.: Speeding up convolutional neural networks with low rank expansions. In: BMVC 2014 (2014)
9. Lebedev, V., Ganin, Y., Rakhuba, M., Oseledets, I., Lempitsky, V.: Speeding-up convolutional neural networks using fine-tuned cp-decomposition. arXiv preprint arXiv:1412.6553 (2014)
10. Tai, C., Xiao, T., Zhang, Y., Wang, X., et al.: Convolutional neural networks with low-rank regularization. arXiv preprint arXiv:1511.06067 (2015)

11. Lin, T.-Y., Maire, M., Belongie, S.J., Bourdev, L.D., Girshick, R.B., Hays, J., Perona, P., Ramanan, D., Dollár, P., Zitnick, C.L.: Microsoft COCO: common objects in context. CoRR, abs/1405.0312 (2014)

12. Schmidhuber, J.: Deep learning in neural networks: an overview. Neural Netw. **61**, 85–117 (2015)

13. Simonyan, K., Zisserman, A.: Very deep convolutional networks for large-scale image recognition. CoRR, abs/1409.1556 (2014)

14. Szegedy, C., Liu, W., Jia, Y., Sermanet, P., Reed, S., Anguelov, D., Erhan, D., Vanhoucke, V., Rabinovich, A.: Going deeper with convolutions. In: Computer Vision and Pattern Recognition (CVPR) (2015)

15. LeCun, Y., Cortes, C.: MNIST handwritten digit database (2010)

16. Krizhevsky, A., Nair, V., Hinton, G.: Cifar-10 (canadian institute for advanced research)

17. Denton, E.L., Zaremba, W., Bruna, J., LeCun, Y., Fergus, R.: Exploiting linear structure within convolutional networks for efficient evaluation. In: Ghahramani, Z., Welling, M., Cortes, C., Lawrence, N.D., Weinberger, K.Q. (eds.) Advances in Neural Information Processing Systems, vol. 27, pp. 1269–1277. Curran Associates Inc (2014)

Dynamic Feature Selection Based on Clustering Algorithm and Individual Similarity

Carine A. Dantas, Rômulo O. Nunes, Anne M.P. Canuto$^{(\boxtimes)}$,
and João C. Xavier-Júnior

Federal University of Rio Grande do Norte - UFRN, Natal, RN, Brazil
carine-cad@hotmail.com, romulo.ciencomp@gmail.com, anne@dimap.ufrn.br,
jcxavier@imd.ufrn.br

Abstract. This paper introduces a new dynamic feature selection to classification algorithms, which is based on individual similarity and it uses a clustering algorithm to select the best features for an instance individually. In addition, an empirical analysis will be performed to evaluate the performance of the proposed method and to compare it with existing feature selection methods, applying to classification problems. The results shown in this paper indicate that the proposed method had better performance results than the existing methods compared, in most cases.

Keywords: Feature selection · Clustering algorithm · Classification task

1 Introduction

Classification techniques have been widely applied in different real world applications in the last decades. Basically, a classification model assigns a given instance to a specific class considering that this instance has not been previously seen [1]. Nowadays, the number of features in different problem domains has grown enormously. The majority of classification tasks explore domains with hundreds to thousands of features [2]. Furthermore, an important question always needs to be considered when dealing with a high number of features, which is the selection of features to be used during the classification process [2]. A feature selection method proposes to obtain a subset of attributes that replaces an original data set, aiming at reducing dimensionality and at improving the model performance.

Several feature selection methods have been proposed in the literature, however, most of the existing methods select one subset of features and use this subset to the whole testing set. In this paper, we propose a new dynamic feature selection technique based on individual similarity and using data clustering algorithms to select features for classification tasks. In [15], an initial effort was made in which a dynamic feature selection was proposed. However, in [15], a subset of features is defined for a group of patterns. Unlike [15], this paper proposes a real dynamic feature selection method, in which one subset of features

© Springer International Publishing AG 2017
A. Lintas et al. (Eds.): ICANN 2017, Part II, LNCS 10614, pp. 467–474, 2017.
https://doi.org/10.1007/978-3-319-68612-7_53

is selected for each test instance rather than to the entire data set. In order to build this dynamic method, a clustering algorithm and a similarity measure are used to select the best subset of features for an instance. In order to evaluate the feasibility of the proposed method, an analysis will be conducted, evaluating an important parameter of the proposed methods as well as comparing it to some classical feature selection methods.

2   Related Work

Feature Selection methods applied to classification tasks has been widely studied in the Machine Learning area. Its main aim is to reduce the data set dimensionality, finding a more compact representation of the problem, without affecting the performance of the classification algorithms. Several Feature Selection methods have been proposed in the literature for classification tasks and can be found in [7–10]. Surveys can be found on [11].

Many studies can be found Feature Selection methods for clustering techniques, where the feature selection methods are used as a pre-processing step for the clustering algorithms [12–14]. However, To the best of the authors knowledge, very little has been done to explore the use of clustering algorithms in the feature selection process for classification algorithms. In this paper, we will use a feature selection method that uses a clustering algorithm during the feature subset selection and the selected subset will be used for a classification algorithm.

Additionally, all feature selection methods presented above make a static selection process, selecting a single subset to represent an entire data set. Unlike them, the proposed method has a dynamic selection process, selecting one feature subset to represent each instance individually.

3   The Proposed Method

In this section, the functioning of the proposed method will be presented. The functioning of the proposed method can be summarized as follows. Suppose that D is data set composed of i (instances) and a (attributes), where i is divided in three sets: train set $TR = \{tr_1, tr_2, ..., tr_{ntr}\}$, validation set $V = \{v_1, v_2, ..., v_{nv}\}$ and test set $T = \{t_1, t_2, ..., t_{nt}\}$, where ntr, nv, and nt are the number of instances for training, validation, and test, respectively.

1. A clustering algorithm Alg is applied in V, that will group the validation instances, that is represented by the following equation.

$$G = Alg(V) \tag{1}$$

   Where $G = \{g_1, g_2, ..., g_j\}$ and each group g_j has central point p_j, that is defined with the group's center of mass.
2. A function $F_{g_j} = cr(g_j)$ is applied for each group g_j as evaluation criterion to define the important attributes of this group. In this stage any evaluation criterion can be applied as F.

3. Based on the evaluation criterion function F_{g_j}, all attributes are ranked, based on its evaluation within g_j.

$$R_j = rank(F_{g_j}) \tag{2}$$

4. When a testing instance t_i needs to be classified, it is compared to the partition G, through a distance measure $DIST$:

$$DIST = dist_y(t_i, p_y)|y = \{1, .., j\}. \tag{3}$$

The main aim of $DIST$ is to calculate the distance between the testing instance and the group centroid.

5. A function P is applied to each value of $DIST$, $dist_y$, to define probability, $prob_y$, of t_i belong g_y.

$$prob_y = P(t_i, dist_y). \tag{4}$$

This probability function is based on the test instance and its distance to the group centroids. The probability will be high for small distances. This probability will represent the proportion of features selected for each group to compose the instance's feature subset.

6. The feature subset NV_i for each test pattern t_i, is obtained picking the N_j most important attributes for each group g_j, as follows.

$$NV_i = select(N_j, Prob_j) \tag{5}$$

The values of N_j will be defined by the proportion for each group in $Prob_j$. Suppose that a test instance t_i has $PROB = \{30, 60, 10\}$ for a problem with 100 features. If we will select a subset with 50% of the attributes, we will select a subset of size 50. Based on $PROB$, 30% of the selected features will be picked from group 1 (15 attributes), 60% of the selected features will be picked from group 2 and 30% of the selected features will be picked from group 3.

7. Finally, t_i will be trained by classifier C_i using the NV_i subset. The accuracy is obtained through application of the test patterns in the trained classifier C_i.

In using this method, each instance has a different feature subset. As a result, we will have a dynamic feature selection method.

4 Methods and Materials

In order to analyze the performance of the proposed method, an experimental analysis will be conducted. In this analysis, we will use the k-means clustering algorithm [1] in the feature selection method, with k equals to the number of classes of a data set. In addition, the obtained subsets will be applied in four classifiers: k-NN (k-Nearest Neighbors), Decision Tree, SVM (Support Vector Machine) and Naive Bayesian [1]. The evaluation criterion, F_{g_j}, used in step 2 of the proposed method (Sect. 3) is Pearson Correlation [6]. Finally, all algorithms of this analysis were developed using MATLAB language.

For this analysis, we will use 15 data sets from UCI repository, varying the number of attributes (A), instances (I) and class labels (C). Each database will be represented by an identifier (Id). The data sets are: **Ionosphere** (Id: b1, A: 34, I: 351 and C: 2);**Gaussian** (Id: b2, A: 600, I: 60 and C: 3); **Lung Cancer** (Id: b3, A: 56, I: 32 and C: 3); **Breast Cancer Prognostic** (Id: b4, A: 34, I: 198 and C: 2); **Spam** (Id: b5, A: 58, I: 4601 and C: 2); **Arrhythmia** (Id: b6, A: 279, I: 452 and C: 13); **Parkinsons** (Id: b7, A: 23, I: 195 and C: 2); **Jude** (Id: b8, A: 985, I: 248 and C: 6); **Libras Movement** (Id: b9, A: 91, I: 160 and C: 15); **Simulated** (Id: b10, A: 600, I: 60 and C: 6); **Micromass** (Id: b11, A: 1301, I: 931 and C: 2); **ADS** (Id: b12, A: 1559, I: 3279 and C: 2); **Semeion Handwritten Digit** (Id: b13, A: 256, I: 1593 and C: 2); **Protein** (Id: b14, A: 121, I: 583 and C: 5) and **Hill-Valley** (Id: b15, A: 101, I: 606 and C: 2).

For comparison purposes, the performance of the proposed method will be compared to six existing dimensionality reduction methods (feature selection and extraction), which are: Random, PCA [3], LDA [3], CFS [3], LLCFS [4] and FSV [5]. In addition, we will compare the performance of the proposed method to the use of the original data set (no feature selection).

In this paper, in order to obtain a better estimation of the accuracy rates, a 10-fold cross validation method is applied to all classification algorithms. As the clustering algorithm is a non-deterministic one, 10 runs will be performed. Therefore, the values presented in this papers are the average of 100 cases (10 folds of 10 runs). In order to validate the performance of the proposed method from a statistical point of view, we will apply the Friedman test which will be used to identify if the obtained results in different methods will be detected by a statistical test.

5   Results

This section presents the results of the empirical analysis and will be done in two different ways. In the first analysis, one important parameter of the proposed method will be evaluated, which is the size of the selected subset. In this paper, we will use three different subset sizes, 25%, 50% and 75% of the original data set. The purpose of this analysis is to evaluate the impact of the subset size in the performance of the proposed method and to select the best size to be used in the following analysis. In the second analysis, a comparative analysis between the proposed method and some existing dimensionality reduction methods will be made.

In both analyses, the performance is measured taking into consideration the average ranking of the obtained results. These rankings are based on their accuracy, always assigning 1 to the best value (highest accuracy), followed by $2, ..., m$ (where m is the number of analyzed methods) in descending order according to its classification accuracy.

5.1   An Analysis of the Subsets Size

Table 1 presents the results of the average ranking of the different subsets size, 25%, 50% and 75% of the original data set, for each data set. In this table, each column represents the results of each subset size. In addition, the best results (achieved the lowest average ranking), for each data set (line), is highlighted in shaded cells.

From Table 1, it can be observed that the best results were obtained when using the subset size 75% was used in proposed method, since this size achieved the best results in 7 of the 15 used data sets. It means that the best results are obtained when a 75% of the features are selected. This is an expected result since the best result was obtained by the largest feature subset.

Table 1. Ranking results and standard deviation of comparative between proportions

ID	25%	50%	75%
b1	**2.09±0.800**	2.13±0.786	2.18±0.817
b2	**2.55±0.709**	2.67±0.614	2.75±0.536
b3	2.42±0.714	**2.41±0.719**	2.46±0.714
b4	**1.95±0.833**	2.15±0.719	2.06±0.804
b5	2.29±0.897	**1.72±0.734**	2.04±0.710
b6	2.12±0.827	2.10±0.819	**1.85±0.776**
b7	2.33±0.776	2.10±0.802	**2.08±0.772**
b8	**2.75±0.486**	2.83±0.380	2.90±0.301
b9	2.59±0.646	1.975±0.726	**1.67±0.738**
b10	2.74±0.565	2.69±0.576	**2.67±0.623**
b11	2.70±0.557	1.96±0.699	**1.60±0.707**
b12	2.32±0.771	2.00±0.788	**1.83±0.781**
b13	2.46±0.755	2.00±0.712	**1.70±0.762**
b14	2.59±0.521	**1.08±0.370**	2.42±0.538
b15	2.78±0.518	**2.76±0.484**	2.80±0.473
Numb	4	4	7

In order to analyze the performance of the impact of the subset size in the proposed method from a statistical point of view, we have applied the Friedman test to compare the performance of the different subset sizes. Table 2 presents the p-values of the Friedman test in which the shaded cells represent the statistically significant performances. When the p-value is less than 0.05, then we applied the post-hoc Friedman test for each pair of subset sizes. In addition, the last line of Table 2 is the number of statistically significant results (first column) as well as the number of wins of the compared methods, always in the A/B format, where represents the number of wins of the first method and B represents the number of wins of the second method.

From Table 2, we can observe that the difference in performance was statistically significant for the majority of data sets (11 out of 15 data sets). Furthermore, when we compare as subsets sizes among themselves, is observed that

Table 2. Friedman test results (p-values) for comparative between 3 subsets size

ID	FRIEDMAN	25%-50%	25%-75%	50%-75%
b1	0.411	-	-	-
b2	0.001	0.020	0.001	0.168
b3	0.496	-	-	-
b4	0.004	0.009	0.015	0.098
b5	0.001	0.001	0.001	0.001
b6	0.001	0.910	0.001	0.034
b7	0.001	0.001	0.001	0.804
b8	0.001	0.012	0.001	0.001
b9	0.001	0.001	0.001	0.001
b10	0.088	-	-	-
b11	0.001	0.001	0.001	0.001
b12	0.001	0.001	0.001	0.413
b13	0.001	0.001	0.001	0.001
b14	0.001	0.001	0.034	0.001
b15	0.766	-	-	-
Numb	11	3/7	3/8	3/4

50% and 75% obtain better results than 25%. In addition, 50% was statistically better than 25% in 7 data sets and 75% better than 25% in 8 data sets. When we compare 50% with 75%, the subset size 75% is statistically better than 50% in 4 data sets, while 50% is statistically better than 75% in 3 data sets.

Based on the results obtained in Tables 2 and 1, we can conclude that 25% achieved the worst performance and 50% and 75% obtained similar performance. In this sense, we decided to use 50% in the second part of this empirical analysis, since 50% and 75% had similar performance and there is a larger reduction in the number of features with 50%, providing a smaller representation of the original problem.

5.2   Comparative Analysis: Classical Methods

As mentioned previously, a comparative analysis between the proposed method and some existing dimensionality reduction methods will be made. For this comparative analysis, the proposed method with 50% of subset size will be used, together with the use of random feature selection (RD), no feature selection (NoFS) as well as well-known feature reduction methods, such as: PCA, LDA, CFS, LLCFS and FSV, respectively.

For simplicity reasons, in this paper, we will only present the results of the Friedman test, in order to present only the results of a statistical test. Table 3 presents the p-values of the Friedman test as well the pairwise post-hoc test, for the cases the Friedman test proved to be statistically different.

When observing Table 3, we can observe that the performance of the different dimensionality reduction methods proved to be statistically significant, in all 15 data sets. Additionally, we can see that the proposed method achieved better results, when compared to all other analyzed methods. When comparing the proposed method, in a two-by-two basis, the proposed method surpassed the random method in 10 data sets, while also it surpasses NoFS, PCA, LDA, CFS, LLCFS and FSV in 5, 11, 7, 8, 6 and 6 data sets, respectively.

In summary, this paper presented promising results, since the proposed method achieved better performance than well-established dimensionality reduction methods.

Table 3. Friedman test results (p-values) of comparative with existing dimensionality reduction methods

ID	Fried	MP-NFS	MP-RD	MP-PCA	MP-LDA	MP-CFS	MP-LLCFS	MP-FSV
b1	0.001	0.001	0.001	0.001	0.001	0.044	0.003	0.002
b2	0.001	0.001	0.001	0.001	0.001	0.666	0.296	0.321
b3	0.001	0.001	0.001	0.001	0.001	0.756	0.612	0.001
b4	0.001	0.007	0.001	0.029	0.001	0.001	0.001	0.001
b5	0.001	0.001	0.884	0.001	0.966	0.001	0.001	0.001
b6	0.001	1	0.001	0.001	0.001	0.001	0.991	0.997
b7	0.001	0.682	0.998	0.001	1	0.041	0.336	0.004
b8	0.001	0.071	0.822	0.001	0.001	0.064	0.208	0.061
b9	0.001	0.866	0.001	1	0.001	0.001	0.869	0.360
b10	0.001	0.628	0.001	0.001	0.001	0.002	0.001	0.996
b11	0.001	0.001	0.001	0.001	0.001	0.001	0.001	0.001
b12	0.001	0.999	0.001	0.001	0.899	0.465	1	0.922
b13	0.001	0.001	0.001	0.295	1	0.001	0.001	0.001
b14	0.001	0.001	1	0.001	0.001	0.001	0.001	0.001
b15	0.001	0.686	0.603	0.001	0.343	0.001	0.001	0.001
Numb	15	5/2	10/0	11/2	7/3	8/3	6/2	6/3

6 Final Remarks

This paper presented a new dynamic feature selection method based on individual similarity. The aim of this proposed method is to select the best feature subset for each instance rather than just one feature set for the entire data set. An experimental analysis was necessary to evaluate the feasibility of the proposed method, applying the obtained subsets in four classifiers (k-NN, Decision Tree, SVM and Naive Bayesian) with 15 different data sets.

In the first part of the empirical analysis, the proposed method was evaluated with different subset sizes. The proposed method obtained better results when using 50% or 75% of the total number of features. Then, the proposed method was compared with other dimensionality reduction methods (Random, PCA, LDA, CFS, LLCFS, FVS). As a result of this comparative analysis, we could observe that the proposed method provided the best results, when compared to all feature selection methods. In addition, the use of the proposed method achieved better performance than using the original data sets (no feature selection). Therefore, we can conclude that the proposed method is an efficient choice for feature selection.

References

1. Mitchell, T.: Machine Learning. McGraw Hill, New York (1997)
2. Motoda, H., Liu, H.: Feature selection, extraction and construction. Commun. Inst. Inf. Comput. Mach. Taiwan **5**, 67–72 (2002)
3. Liu, H., Motoda, H.: Computational Methods of Feature Selection. CRC Press, Boca Raton (2007)
4. Zeng, H., Cheung, Y.: Feature selection and kernel learning for local learning-based clustering. IEEE Trans. Pattern Anal. Mach. Intell. **33**, 1532–1547 (2011)
5. Bradley, P.S., Mangasarian, O.L.: Feature selection via concave minimization and support vector machines. In: ICML, vol. 98, pp. 82–90 (1998)
6. Pearson, K.: Mathematical contributions to the theory of evolution. III. Regression, heredity, and panmixia. Philos. Trans. Roy. Soc. London **187**, 253–318 (1896)
7. Chu, C., Hsu, A., Chou, K., Bandettini, P., Lin, C.: Alzheimer's disease neuroimaging initiative and others: does feature selection improve classification accuracy? Impact of sample size and feature selection on classification using anatomical magnetic resonance images. Neuroimage **60**, 59–60 (2012)
8. Bolón-Canedo, V., Porto-Díaz, I., Sánchez-Maroño, N., Alonso-Betanzos, A.: A framework for cost-based feature selection. Pattern Recogn. **647**, 2481–2489 (2014)
9. Wang, J., Zhao, P., Hoi, S.C., Jin, R.: Online feature selection and its applications. IEEE Trans. Knowl. Data Eng. **26**, 698–710 (2014)
10. Chen, Z., Wu, C., Zhang, Y., Huang, Z., Ran, B., Zhong, M., Lyu, N.: Feature selection with redundancy-complementariness dispersion. Knowl.-Based Syst. **89**, 203–217 (2015)
11. Chandrashekar, G., Sahin, F.: A survey on feature selection methods. Comput. Electr. Eng. Nagel **40**, 16–28 (2014). Elsevier
12. Maldonado, S., Carrizosa, E., Weber, R.: Kernel penalized K-means: a feature selection method based on kernel K-means. Inf. Sci. **322**, 150–160 (2015)
13. Boutsidis, C., Magdon-Ismail, M.: Deterministic feature selection for k-means clustering. IEEE Trans. Inf. Theory **59**, 6099–6110. IEEE (2013)
14. Bhondave, R., Kalbhor, M., Shinde, S., Rajeswari, K.: Improvement of expectation maximization clustering using select attribute. Int. J. Comput. Sci. Mob. Comput. **3**, 503–508 (2014)
15. Nunes, R.O., Dantas, C.A., Canuto, A.M.P., Xavier-Jnior, J.C.: An unsupervised-based dynamic feature selection for classification tasks. In: 2016 International Joint Conference on Neural Networks, pp. 4213–4220. IEEE (2016)

Learning from Data Streams
and Time Series

Dialogue-Based Neural Learning to Estimate the Sentiment of a Next Upcoming Utterance

Chandrakant Bothe[✉], Sven Magg, Cornelius Weber, and Stefan Wermter

Department of Informatics, Knowledge Technology, Universität Hamburg
Vogt-Kölln-Str. 30, 22527 Hamburg, Germany
{bothe,magg,weber,wermter}@informatik.uni-hamburg.de
www.informatik.uni-hamburg.de/wtm/

Abstract. In a conversation, humans use changes in a dialogue to predict safety-critical situations and use them to react accordingly. We propose to use the same cues for safer human-robot interaction for early verbal detection of dangerous situations. Due to the limited availability of sentiment-annotated dialogue corpora, we use a simple sentiment classification for utterances to neurally learn sentiment changes within dialogues and ultimately predict the sentiment of upcoming utterances. We train a recurrent neural network on context sequences of words, defined as two utterances of each speaker, to predict the sentiment class of the next utterance. Our results show that this leads to useful predictions of the sentiment class of the upcoming utterance. Results for two challenging dialogue datasets are reported to show that predictions are similar independent of the dataset used for training. The prediction accuracy is about 63% for binary and 58% for multi-class classification.

1 Introduction

In human-robot interaction, one of the primary concerns is safety. In this paper, we address safety as the condition of being protected from or unlikely to cause danger or injury. A mobile robot serving a wrong drink, coffee instead of water, in a cup might be an acceptable mistake, whereas serving the drink in a broken cup might be an unacceptable risk. When the robot is verbally instructed to perform this action, most probably the user also tells the robot that there is a danger or a chance of risky situation.

Early recognition of hazards is crucial for safety-related control systems, such as protective or emergency stop, which is an essential feature for personal care robots [21]. The main goal of our research is to study the early detection of safety-related cues through language processing. In the case of a wrong robot action, the user might respond with an utterance which, although often not easily understandable for the robot, carries feedback information for the last action performed, which can help to understand the situation [12,23].

A possible conversation is shown in Fig. 1, the robot (R) perceives a sentence from the person (P) with neutral sentiment and responds with a query whether this means it should continue. Expecting a positive reply in case everything is

© Springer International Publishing AG 2017
A. Lintas et al. (Eds.): ICANN 2017, Part II, LNCS 10614, pp. 477–485, 2017.
https://doi.org/10.1007/978-3-319-68612-7_54

ok, the next utterance has a negative sentiment. Without understanding the meaning of a sentence, the robot can stop or revert the last action just on the basis of a failed response sentiment prediction. Furthermore, an estimate of the user's response sensitivity is necessary when the robot needs to ask safety-critical questions [7].

R: Hello, how can I help you?	Neutral
P: Can you bring me tea?	Neutral
R: Yes, I can make some tea.	Positive (context)
P: Oh, that cup seems broken.	Neutral
R: Shall I continue the action.	Neutral
P: No, don't use the broken cup.	Negative (context)
R: Okay, I will find another one.	Neutral

Fig. 1. Example for preparing the contexts: labeled by sentiment analyser, previous two utterances of the positive and negative class are taken as context.

Our goal is, as a first step, to learn from spoken language dialogues to predict the sentiment of the next upcoming utterance. As shown in Fig. 1, we use two utterances as context, capturing a sequence with both speakers, to predict the next utterance sentiment from the first speaker. Long short-term memory networks (LSTM) have shown good performance on the text-classification tasks (e.g. [2]) learning long-term dependencies. Since we want to extend our model to longer contexts, we choose those networks and show that they could successfully learn to estimate the sentiment of the next upcoming utterance.

2   Related Work

Responses from humans in an interaction have been used in various ways in human-robot scenarios. In student/teacher learning scenarios, to facilitate learning, a teacher gives positive and negative feedback depending on the success of the student [12]. Weston [23] has shown that the positive-negative sentiment in the teacher's response helps to guide the learning process. Other work [20] describes context-sensitive response generation in the field of language understanding and generation. They report that there is a lack of reflecting the agents intent and maintaining the consistency with the sentiment polarity. This consistency of polarity means that unpredicted changes in polarity may be cues for changing situations, so monitoring the sentiment over a dialogue can not only be used for simple feedback signals but give evidence on, maybe not yet otherwise perceivable, changes in the environment.

Sentiment analysis is an important aspect of the decision-making process [17] and thus has received much attention in the scientific community. With vast amounts of data available for analysis, many methods have been explored recently, e.g. [10,22]. Deep learning has given rise to some new methods for the sentiment analysis task, outperforming traditional methods [5,19]. Different NLP tasks have been performed independently and in a unified way using deep neural networks [4]. Especially in the field of text classification, the strength of neural network approaches is evident, e.g. convolutional neural networks [11] or recursive and recurrent neural networks [2,19]. A fixed-size context window can solve the problem of the variable length of language text sequences, but this fails to capture the dependencies longer than the window size. Recurrent neural networks have the ability to use variable sequence length, and especially LSTM networks have shown good performance [5].

The accessibility of large unlabelled text data can be utilised to learn the meaning of words and the structure of sentences and this has been attempted by word2vec [16]. The learned word embeddings are used for creating lexicons and have a reduced dimensionality compared to traditional methods. This approach has also been used for learning sentiment-specific word embedding for sentiment classification [14]. Our approach utilises word embeddings to feed an LSTM network similar to [2] in order to learn sentiment prediction.

3   Approach

3.1   Datasets

We have used two spoken interaction corpora for training our model from two very different sources, child-adult interaction and movie subtitles. The first is the child language component of the TalkBank system, called CHILDES[1] [15], where different child and adult speakers converse on daily issues. In this dataset, we selected the conversations with children of age 12 and above, which have significant verbal interaction and less grammatical mistakes [3]. The other corpus is the Cornell Movie-Dialogues corpus [6], which is more structured, i.e. it is more grammatically correct, and is also larger than the child-interaction corpus.

As our goal is to predict sentiment from a context as shown in Fig. 1, we need sentiment annotation of the utterances. The child-interaction corpus (CHI) already has word-level sentiment annotation, while the movie dialogues corpus (MDC) has none. We thus used the natural language toolkit's [13] Vader sentiment analysis tool [9] to create sentiment labels for each utterance. To avoid imbalanced classes in our data, we empirically adjusted the thresholds of the sentiment level to 0.2 and 0.6 on the scale of 0 to 1 for both positive and negative classes. Data samples were now extracted by selecting an utterance with a given sentiment as ground truth and saving the previous two utterances as context. We have created datasets for two experiments, creating contexts from utterances with either negative/positive, or negative/neutral/positive classes. The dataset details are shown in Table 1. While taking the previous utterances for each sample, we have the overlapping of utterances in the contexts, i.e. one utterance may appear in two contexts. The two data-sets are processed for binary (pos-neg) and multi-class (pos-neu-neg) classification.

---

[1] http://childes.talkbank.org or http://childes.psy.cmu.edu.

Table 1. Dataset details

Datasets	CHI	MDC
Raw utterances	11.1k	304k
Contexts (pos-neg)	4.1k	189k
Contexts (pos-neu-neg)	6.2k	283k

3.2   Model

For the experiments, we used the well-established recurrent long short-term memory (LSTM) neural network [8], a special form of recurrent neural network, shown in Fig. 2(a). The sequence of the words, represented by their numeric indices in a dictionary, is first fed into the embedding layer which is implemented as standard MLP layer, as shown in Fig. 2(b). The embedding layer randomly initializes the normalised vectors, or can utilize already pretrained embeddings, to represent each word index by a real-valued vector of a given size of the embedding dimension which is then fed into the LSTM layer.

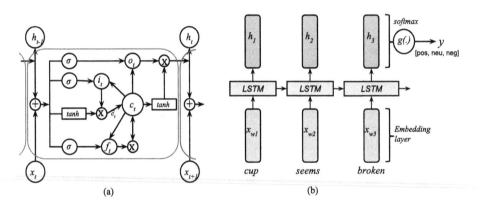

(a)   (b)

Fig. 2. (a) The long short-term memory unit with (b) our classification setup. Biases are ignored for simplicity.

The LSTM unit receives an embedded word x as an input and outputs a sentiment prediction y. It maintains a hidden vector h and a memory vector in cell c responsible for controlling state updates and outputs. The LSTM consists of a memory cell c, an input gate i, a forget gate f, and an output gate o, which are updated at time step t as follows:

$$f_t = \sigma \left(W_f * h_{t-1} + I_f * x_t + b_f \right) \tag{1}$$

$$i_t = \sigma \left(W_i * h_{t-1} + I_i * x_t + b_i \right) \tag{2}$$

$$o_t = \sigma \left(W_o * h_{t-1} + I_o * x_t + b_o \right) \tag{3}$$

$$\tilde{c}_t = tanh\left(W_c * h_{t-1} + I_c * x_t + b_c\right) \tag{4}$$

$$c_t = f_t \odot c_{t-1} + \tilde{c}_t \tag{5}$$

$$h_t = o_t \odot tanh\left(c_t\right) \tag{6}$$

where σ is the *sigmoid* function, W_f, W_i, W_o, W_c are recurrent weight matrices, I_f, I_i, I_o, I_c are the corresponding projection matrices and b_f, b_i, b_o, b_c are learned biases. The weight-projection matrices and bias vectors are initialized randomly and learned during training. The gating functions of the LSTM helps this RNN to mitigate the vanishing and exploding gradient problems and to train the model smoothly. As an output, we get a hidden vector representation (h) of the entire sequence of words which is then used as an input to a classifier. In the sequence classification setup as shown in Fig. 2(b), given the current activation function in the hidden state h_t, the RNN generates the output according to the following equation:

$$y_t = g\left(W_{out} * h_t\right) \tag{7}$$

where $g(.)$ denotes an output activation function, in our case a *softmax* function that gives the normalized probability distribution over the possible classes, and W_{out} is an output weight matrix which can be stored to make the predictions.

3.3   Experiments and Results

Our aim is to recognise the sentiment polarity of the upcoming utterance, given the recent utterances as the context. We have trained our classifier by concatenating the context utterances and using the label of the utterance following this context as the training signal. The utterances have been labeled by the sentiment analysis for either binary or multi-class classification as shown in Table 1. The input to the network was always concatenated utterances and the prediction for the upcoming utterance was taken from the classified output of an LSTM at the end of the input sequence. The model was implemented using the Keras Python library and Theano [1]. The input sequence length was fixed to the maximum length in the utterances and padding was used to make them of the same length.

Table 2. Prediction accuracy on test data

Different setups	Random guess	Trained embeddings			GloVe embeddings (100D)	
		CHI (10D and 100D)		MDC (100D)	CHI	MDC
Binary	50.00%	59.30%	59.06%	52.44%	63.36%	54.97%
Multi-class	33.33%	54.60%	54.56%	48.36%	58.13%	51.71%

The training was done using categorical crossentropy as the loss function, using stochastic gradient descent as the optimization method. Learning rate and the number of hidden units were empirically determined for both datasets. The hidden layer dimension was 64 for CHILDES and 512 for Movie-Dialogues corpus. We randomly initialized the word embedding vectors with the dimension of 10 and 100 for CHILDES and 100 for the other, and we also used the pre-trained GloVe vectors of dimension 100 [18]. We trained the model on both the datasets as described before and for two different set-ups. Each dataset was split into training, validation and test data with a 60%-20%-20% split. The summary of the test data prediction accuracies is shown in Table 2.

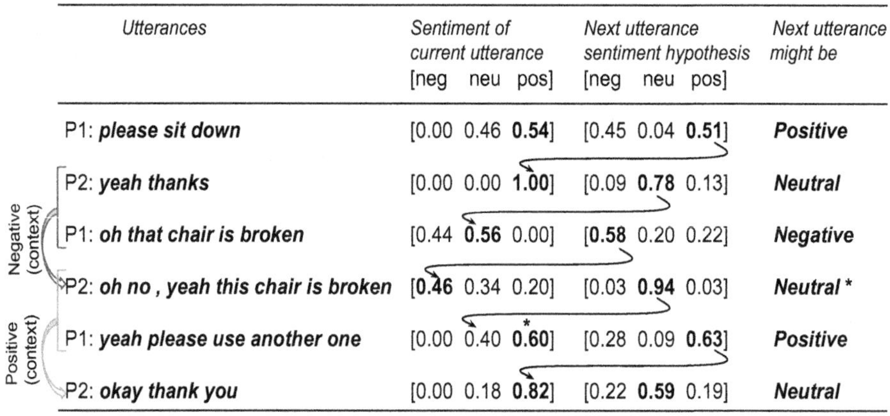

	Utterances	Sentiment of current utterance [neg neu pos]	Next utterance sentiment hypothesis [neg neu pos]	Next utterance might be
	P1: **please sit down**	[0.00 0.46 **0.54**]	[0.45 0.04 **0.51**]	**Positive**
Negative (context)	P2: **yeah thanks**	[0.00 0.00 **1.00**]	[0.09 **0.78** 0.13]	**Neutral**
	P1: **oh that chair is broken**	[0.44 **0.56** 0.00]	[**0.58** 0.20 0.22]	**Negative**
	P2: **oh no , yeah this chair is broken**	[**0.46** 0.34 0.20]	[0.03 **0.94** 0.03]	**Neutral ***
Positive (context)	P1: **yeah please use another one**	[0.00 0.40 **0.60**]*	[0.28 0.09 **0.63**]	**Positive**
	P2: **okay thank you**	[0.00 0.18 **0.82**]	[0.22 **0.59** 0.19]	**Neutral**

Fig. 3. Test example: prediction on some utterances. * indicates that the sentiment recognition does not match the actual. (Color figure online)

The use of pre-trained embedding shows more accuracy than the random initialization, also using different embedding dimensions produced very similar results. We also implemented a simple chat-bot in Python, that receives the utterances sequentially, to evaluate the trained model on a dialogue and monitor the changing hypothesis of the sentiment of the upcoming utterances.

In Fig. 3, we present an example from test data. The utterances from the conversation are processed one by one, and the progression of the statements is shown with the predicted hypothesis and the ground-truths. Bold values in the array [neg neu pos] represent the detected class, for the sentiment hypothesis of the current and the next utterance. We also show two related contexts, positive (green) and negative (red). For example, the utterance *"oh no, yeah this chair is broken"* has a negative sentiment label and the model has the correct prediction hypothesis. We can also see that the model failed to predict the positive class for the utterance *"yeah please use another one"*.

Looking at the details of the distributions, the unpredicted increase in negative sentiment for the sentence *"oh that chair is broken"*, although overall still classified as neutral (negative), could have been used already to detect a change in sentiment and thus be aware of a possible change in the environment, the safety situation, or just the user's perception of the robot's current action. The same can be said for the misclassified utterance where P2 perceived a negative situation and might have no solution, interpreting the suddenly positive sentiment of P1 in the next utterance to understand that the situation has a solution or has been solved and nothing bad has happened. Overall, the results show that it is possible to derive valuable cues by estimating the sentiment of the next upcoming utterance, and the model can learn to keep track of the sentiment through dialogues. The corpora used were auto-annotated with the standard sentiment analysis tool which led to comprehensible results, although a human-annotated corpus might still lead to better results.

4   Conclusion and Future Work

We have presented a learning approach to estimate the sentiment of the next upcoming utterance within a dialogue. We have shown that the model can predict the sentiment of an upcoming utterance to a certain degree, taking into account that the used corpora are noisy and no system would be able to reliably predict the upcoming sentiments simply due to the changing nature of human dialogues. Detecting safety-related cues as early as possible is crucial, and a number of false-positives can be accepted (or quickly resolved through a query within the dialogue) if dangers can be avoided when they occur. We think that tracking even a noisy sentiment through a dialogue can have a positive impact on the safety of a robot, especially when combined with a multi-modal system.

While this work focuses on keeping track of the sentiment in dialog-based context learning, our aim is to extend this to different language features containing safety-related cues. Using not only simple auto-annotated sentiment as labels but including annotations based on prosodic features might lead to a better prediction since humans often involuntarily change their voice when perceiving a dangerous situation while speaking. This work presents already a promising step towards the main goal and can provide useful dialogue-based information regarding the current safety context in human-robot interaction.

Acknowledgement. This project has received funding from the European Union's Horizon 2020 research and innovation programme under the Marie Sklodowska-Curie grant agreement No. 642667 (SECURE).

References

1. Bastien, F., Lamblin, P., Pascanu, R., Bergstra, J., Goodfellow, I.J., Bergeron, A., Bouchard, N., Bengio, Y.: Theano: new features and speed improvements. 2012 Workshop on Deep Learning and Unsupervised Feature Learning NIPS (2012)
2. Biswas, S., Chadda, E., Ahmad, F.: Sentiment analysis with gated recurrent units. Adv. Comput. Sci. Inf. Technol. (ACSIT) **2**(11), 59–63 (2015)
3. Clark, E.V.: Awareness of language: some evidence from what children say and do. In: Sinclair, A., Jarvella, R.J., Levelt, W.J.M. (eds.) The Child's Conception of Language, pp. 17–43. Springer, Heidelberg (1978). doi:10.1007/978-3-642-67155-5_2

4. Collobert, R., Weston, J.: A unified architecture for natural language processing. In: Proceedings of the 25th International Conference on Machine Learning - ICML 2008. vol. 20, pp. 160–167 (2008)
5. Dai, A.M., Le, Q.V.: Semi-supervised sequence learning. In: Neural Information Processing Systems (NIPS), pp. 3079–3087. No. 28, Curran Associates, Inc. (2015)
6. Danescu-Niculescu-Mizil, C., Lee, L.: Chameleons in imagined conversations: a new approach to understanding coordination of linguistic style in dialogs. In: Proceedings of the Workshop on Cognitive Modeling and Computational Linguistics. ACL (2011)
7. Fong, T., Thorpe, C., Baur, C.: Collaboration, dialogue, and human-robot interaction. In: Jarvis, R.A., Zelinsky, A. (eds) 10th International Symposium of Robotics Research (Springer Tracts in Advanced Robotics), pp. 255–266 (2003). doi:10.1007/3-540-36460-9_17
8. Hochreiter, S., Schmidhuber, J.: Long short-term memory. Neural Comput. **9**, 1735–1780 (1997)
9. Hutto, C.J., Gilbert, E.: VADER: A parsimonious rule-based model for sentiment analysis of social media text. In: Association for the Advancement of Artificial Intelligence (Proceedings of Eighth International AAAI Conference on Weblogs and Social Media), pp. 216–225 (2014)
10. Kim, S.M., Hovy, E.: Determining the sentiment of opinions. In: COLING 2004 Proceedings of 20th International Conference on Computational Linguistics, p. 1367 (2004)
11. Kim, Y.: Convolutional neural networks for sentence classification. In: Proceedings of the Conference on EMNLP, pp. 1746–1751 (2014)
12. Latham, A.S.: Learning through feedback. Educ. Leadersh. **54**(8), 86–87 (1997)
13. Loper, E., Bird, S.: NLTK: the Natural Language Toolkit. In: Proceedings of ACL-2 Workshop on Effective Tools and Methodologies for Teaching Natural Language Processing and Computational Linguistics. vol. **1**, pp. 63–70 (2002)
14. Maas, A.L., Daly, R.E., Pham, P.T., Huang, D., Ng, A.Y., Potts, C.: Learning word vectors for sentiment analysis. In: Proceedings of 49th Annual Meeting of the Association for Computational Linguistics, pp. 142–150 (2011)
15. MacWhinney, B.: The CHILDES project: tools for analyzing talk. Lawrence Erlbaum Associates, Inc (1991). http://childes.psy.cmu.edu/
16. Mikolov, T., Corrado, G., Chen, K., Dean, J.: Efficient estimation of word representations in vector space. In: Proceedings of International Conference on Learning Representations (ICLR 2013), pp. 1–12 (2013)
17. Pang, B., Lee, L.: Opinion mining and sentiment analysis. Found. Trends Inf. Retr. **2**(12), 1–135 (2008)
18. Pennington, J., Socher, R., Manning, C.D.: GloVe: global vectors for word representation. In: Proceedings of Conference on EMNLP, pp. 1532–1543 (2014)
19. Socher, R., Perelygin, A., Wu, J.Y., Chuang, J., Manning, C.D., Ng, A.Y., Potts, C.: Recursive deep models for semantic compositionality over a sentiment treebank. In: Proceedings of Conference on EMNLP, pp. 1631–1642. Association for Computational Linguistics (2013)
20. Sordoni, A., Galley, M., Auli, M., Brockett, C., Ji, Y., Mitchell, M., Nie, J.Y., Gao, J., Dolan, B.: A neural network approach to context-sensitive generation of conversational responses. In: Association for Computational Linguistics (Human Language Technologies: The 2015 Annual Conference of North American Chapter of the ACL), pp. 196–205 (2015)

21. Tadele, T.S., de Vries, T., Stramigioli, S.: The safety of domestic robotics: a survey of various safety-related publications. IEEE Robot. Autom. Mag. **21**(3), 134–142 (2014)
22. Wang, S., Manning, C.D.: Baselines and bigrams: simple, good sentiment and topic classification. In: Proceedings of 50th Annual Meeting of the Association for Computational Linguistics, pp. 90–94 (2012)
23. Weston, J.: Dialog-based language learning. In: Lee, D.D., Sugiyama, M., Luxburg, U.V., Guyon, I., Garnett, R. (eds.) Advances in Neural Information Processing Systems (NIPS) 29, pp. 829–837. Curran Associates, Inc. (2016)

Solar Power Forecasting Using Pattern Sequences

Zheng Wang[1], Irena Koprinska[1(✉)], and Mashud Rana[2]

[1] School of Information Technologies, University of Sydney, Sydney, Australia
{zheng.wang, irena.koprinska}@sydney.edu.au
[2] Sydney Informatics Hub, University of Sydney, Sydney, Australia
mashud.rana@sydney.edu.au

Abstract. We consider the task of predicting the solar power output for the next day from solar power output and weather data for previous days, and weather forecast for the next day. We study the performance of pattern sequence methods which combine clustering and sequence similarity. We show how the standard PSF algorithm can be extended to utilize data from more than one data source by proposing two extensions, PSF1 and PSF2. The performance of the three PSF methods is evaluated on Australian data for two years and compared with three neural network models and a baseline. Our results show that the extensions were beneficial, especially PSF2 which uses a 2-tier clustering and sequence matching. We also investigate the robustness of all methods for different levels of noise in the weather forecast.

Keywords: Solar power output · Pattern sequence similarity · Neural networks

1 Introduction

Solar energy is clean, renewable, easily available and cost-effective. PhotoVoltaic (PV) solar panels are especially promising – they are easy to install and maintain, and their cost continues to fall due to advances in PV technology. By 2050 it is expected that Australia will produce 30% of its electricity using PV systems [1].

The generated solar power is dependent on meteorological factors such as solar irradiance, rainfall and temperature. This makes its large-scale integration into the power grid more difficult than the traditional energy sources and motivates the need for accurate prediction of the produced solar power, to ensure reliable electricity supply.

In this paper we focus on simultaneously predicting the PV power output for the next day at half-hourly intervals. Specifically, given: (1) a time series of PV power outputs up to the day d: $[P^1, \ldots, P^d]$ where P^i is a vector of half-hourly power outputs for day i, (2) a time series of weather vectors for the same days: $[W^1, \ldots, W^d]$, where W^i is the weather vector for day i, and (3) the weather forecast vector for the next day $d + 1$: WF^{d+1}, our goal is to forecast P^{d+1}, the half-hourly power output for day $d + 1$.

Different approaches for PV power forecasting have been proposed. They use statistical methods such as liner regression and autoregressive moving average [2, 3], and machine learning methods such as: Neural Networks (NNs) [2, 4, 5], nearest

© Springer International Publishing AG 2017
A. Lintas et al. (Eds.): ICANN 2017, Part II, LNCS 10614, pp. 486–494, 2017.
https://doi.org/10.1007/978-3-319-68612-7_55

neighbor [2, 5, 6] and support vector regression [7, 8]. In this paper we study the application of Pattern Sequence Forecasting (PSF) methods, which have been very successful in other energy time series forecasting tasks such as predicting electricity demand and prices [9, 10] but haven't been applied for solar power forecasting. The original PSF method was proposed by Martínez-Álvarez et al. [9] and one of its distinct features is that it predicts all values for the next day simultaneously, as opposed to iteratively as in other methods.

While the original PSF algorithm uses only the time series of interest, PV data in our case, we propose two extensions which utilize also the weather data for the previous days and the weather forecast for the next day. The importance of these three data sources was studied in [6] and it was shown that the weather forecast was the most useful source, followed by the weather data and the PV data. We investigate if the proposed extensions can improve the accuracy of the traditional PSF algorithm. Specifically, the contributions of this paper are:

1. We evaluate the performance of the standard PSF algorithm for solar power fore-casting. We propose two extended versions, PSF1 and PSF2, which utilize also the historical weather data and weather forecast data, and a 2-tier clustering and sequence matching method in PSF2 to refine the prediction. More generally, we show how PSF can be extended to use data from more than one data source.
2. We evaluate the performance of the three PSF methods on Australian PV and weather data for two years. We compare the PSF methods with three NN methods and a persistence forecasting model used as a baseline. NNs were chosen as they are the most popular method for solar power forecasting.
3. We investigate the performance of all methods for three different levels of noise in the weather forecast.

2   Data and Data Preprocessing

We use PV power and weather data for two years - from 1 January 2015 to 31 December 2016. The data is summarized in Table 1.

PV Data. It was collected from a rooftop PV plant, located at the University of Queensland in Brisbane, Australia. The data is publicly available from http://www.uq.edu.au/solarenergy/. For each day, we only selected the data during the daylight period from 7 am to 5 pm.

Weather Data. It was collected from the Australian Bureau of Meteorology and is available from http://www.bom.gov.au/climate/data/. For each day, we collected 14 meteorological variables. There are two weather feature sets – W1 and W2. W1 includes all 14 feature while W2 is a subset of W1 and includes only 4 features, the ones used in weather forecasts.

Weather Forecast Data. The weather forecast feature set WF includes the same four features as the weather set W2. This reduced set is the set of features typically available from meteorological bureaus as weather forecast. Since the weather forecasts were not

Table 1. Data sources and feature sets

Data source	Feature set	Description
PV data for the current day d and previous days	P 20 features	Half-hourly PV values between 7am and 5pm
Weather data for the current day d and previous days	W1 14 features	(1–6) Daily: min and max temperature, rainfall, sun hours, max wind gust and average solar irradiance; (7–14) At 9am and 3pm: temperature, relative humidity, cloudiness and wind speed
Weather data for the current day d and previous days	W2 4 features	Daily: min and max temperature, rainfall and solar irradiance. W2 is a subset of W1.
Weather forecast for the next day $d + 1$	WF 4 features	Daily: min and max temperature, rainfall and average solar irradiance

available retrospectively for 2015 and 2016, we used the actual weather data with added noise at three different levels: 10%, 20% and 30%.

Data Preprocessing. The original PV power data was measured at 1-min intervals and was aggregated to 30-min intervals by taking the average value of the interval. Both the PV power and weather data we normalized to [0, 1].

There was a small number of missing values − 0.82% for the weather data and 0.02% for the PV data. They were replaced using the following nearest neighbor method, applied firstly to the weather data and then to the PV data: (1) if a day d has missing values in its weather vector W^d, we find its nearest neighbor with no missing values, day s, using the Euclidean distance and the available values in W^d. The missing values in W^d are replaced with the corresponding values in W^s; (2) if day d has missing values in its PV vector P^d, we find its nearest neighbor day s, by comparing weather vectors, and then replace the missing values in P^d with the corresponding values in P^s.

3   Pattern Sequence Forecasting Methods

PSF [9] combines clustering with sequence matching and is illustrated in Fig. 1. Let P^i be the 20-dimensional vector of the half-hourly PV output for day i. PSF firstly clusters all vectors P^i from the training data into k_1 clusters and labels them with the cluster number, e.g. *C1, C2,* etc. as shown in Fig. 1. To make a prediction for a new day $d + 1$, it extracts a sequence of consecutive days with length w, starting from the previous day d and going backwards, and matches the cluster labels of this sequence against the previous days to find a set of equal sequences ES_d. It then follows a nearest neighbor approach - finds the post-sequence day for each sequence in ES_d and averages the PV vectors for these days, to produce the final half-hourly PV predictions for day $d + 1$. PSF was applied to electricity demand and electricity prices data in [9]; the results showed that it is a very competitive approach outperforming ARIMA, support vector regression and NNs.

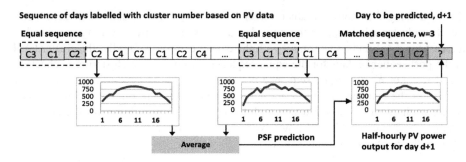

Fig. 1. The standard PSF method

PSF1 is the first extension of PSF that we developed and is shown in Fig. 2. In contrast to PSF, where the clustering and sequence matching are done using the PV data only, in PSF1 this is done using the W2 weather data for the previous days and the weather forecast WF for the new day. The training data is clustered using the 4-dimensional W2 data into k_2 clusters. To make a prediction for a new day $d + 1$, PSF1 firstly uses the weather forecast for $d + 1$ (also a 4-dimensional vector containing the same features as W2, which facilitates the comparison) to find the cluster label for $d + 1$ by comparing it with the cluster centroids of the existing clusters, and assigning it to the cluster of the closest centroid. It then extracts a sequence of consecutive days with length w, from day $d + 1$ backwards (including $d + 1$), and matches the cluster labels of this sequence against the previous days to find a set of equal sequences. It then obtains the PV power vector for the last day of each equal sequence and averages these vectors, to produce the prediction for $d + 1$.

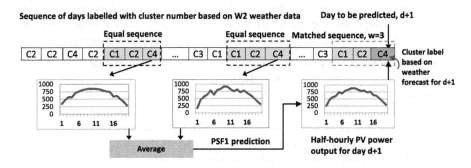

Fig. 2. The proposed PSF1 method

PSF2 is the second extension of the traditional PSF that we propose. As Fig. 3 shows it involves clustering of the days in two different ways: based on the W1 and W2 weather data. Firstly, the training data is clustered using the W1 data (the full weather data, containing 14 features) into k_1 clusters. The days are labelled with the cluster number, e.g. $C1$, $C2$, etc. as shown in Fig. 3. A sequence of consecutive days with length w, from day d backwards (including d), is found. Secondly, the training data is clustered using the shorter weather vector W2 into k_2 clusters, denoted with $K1$, $K2$, etc. The cluster label K_x for the new day $d + 1$ is found by obtaining the weather forecast for $d + 1$ and comparing it with the cluster centroids. Thirdly, the cluster label of the post-sequence days for the equal sequences from the first clustering is checked, and if it is not K_x, the equal sequence is not included in obtaining the prediction for $d + 1$. For the example in Fig. 3, the left most equal sequence is not included as the cluster of the post-day is $K1$ which is different from $K2$, the cluster for the new day. Finally, PSF2 averages the PV power vectors of the chosen the post-sequence days, to produce the prediction for day $d + 1$.

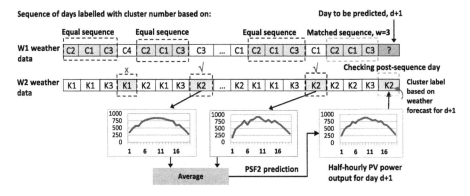

Fig. 3. The proposed PSF2 method

In summary, PSF2 is an extension of PSF1. It utilizes better the available weather data than PSF1 by using the full weather vector WF for the initial clustering (available for the previous days) and the shorter weather vector W2 to match the weather forecast for the new day, and refine the equal sequence selection from the previous step.

Parameter Selection. We follow the procedure described in the original PSF paper [9] which uses the data for the first year (2015).

To select the number of clusters (k_1 and k_2), the clustering algorithm (k-means) is run for different values (from 1 to 5) and the results are evaluated by computing the Silhouette, Dunn and Davies-Bouldin indexes, and then taking the by majority vote.

To select the sequence length w, different values are evaluated (from 1 to 10) using 12-fold cross validation, where one fold corresponds to one month. The best w is the one that minimizes the average error for the 12 folds. The selected parameters are: PSF: $k_1 = 2$, $w = 2$, PSF1: $k_2 = 2$, $w = 4$, PSF2: $k_1 = 2$, $k_2 = 2$, $w = 2$.

4 Methods Used for Comparison

We compare the PSF methods with three NN methods and a persistence model commonly used as a baseline.

NN Models. The NN prediction models are multi-layer NNs with one hidden layer, trained with the Levenberg-Marquardt version of the backpropagation algorithm. The three NN models correspond to the three PSF models in terms of data source used, e.g. NN and PSF use only PV data while NN2 and PSF2 use data from all three data sources. The inputs and outputs for each model are shown in Table 2. For example, NN2 uses as inputs the PV power for the previous day, the weather data for the previous day and the weather forecast for the next day and predicts the PV power for the next day; it has $20 + 14 + 4 = 38$ input neurons and 20 output neurons.

Table 2. Input and output of the neural models used for comparison

NN model	Input	Output
NN	P^d (20)	P^{d+1} (20)
NN1	P^d (20), WF^{d+1} (4)	P^{d+1} (20)
NN2	P^d (20), W^d (14), WF^{d+1} (4)	P^{d+1} (20)

The number of hidden neurons h was selected experimentally by varying it from 5 to 30, with an increment of 5, evaluating the performance on the validation set and selecting the best NN. The selected h are: NN: $h = 5$; NN1: $h = 15$ for 10% and 20% WF noise and $h = 30$ for 30% WF noise; NN2: $h = 30$ for 10%, 20% and 30% WF noise.

Persistence Baseline. This baseline B_{per} considers the half-hourly PV power output from the previous day d as the prediction for the next day $d + 1$, i.e. $\widehat{P}^{d+1} = P^d$.

5 Experiment Setup

Data Sets. We divided the PV power and the corresponding weather data into three non-overlapping subsets: training – the first 70% of the 2015 data, validation: the remaining 30% of the 2015 data and testing – the 2016 data. For the PSF models, the whole 2015 data was used for determining the parameters (number of clusters and sequence length) as in the original PSF paper [9]. For the NN models, the training data was used to build the model, the validation set - to select the number of hidden neurons and other parameters. The testing set was used to evaluate the accuracy of all models.

Evaluation Measures. We used two standard performance measures: Mean Absolute Error (MAE) and Root Mean Squared Error (RMSE):

$$\text{MAE} = \frac{1}{D \times n} \sum_{i=1}^{n} \left| P^i - \widehat{P}^i \right|, \text{RMSE} = \sqrt{\frac{\sum_{i=1}^{n} \left(P^i - \widehat{P}^i \right)^2}{D \times n}}$$

where P^i and $\widehat{P}^i$ are the actual and forecasted half-hourly PV power outputs for day i, D is the number of days in the testing set and n is the number of predicted daily values.

6 Results and Discussion

Table 3 shows the accuracy results of all prediction models, for the three noise levels in the weather forecast. Figure 4 presents graphically the MAE results in sorted order for visual comparison. Table 4 shows the pair-wise comparison for statistically significant differences in accuracy. The main results can be summarized as follows:

- Among the PSF methods, PSF2 is the most accurate for all three noise levels. PSF2 outperforms PSF in all cases and the improvements are statistically significant. Thus, the extensions introduced in PSF2 – the use of weather and weather forecast data, and the 2-tier clustering and sequence matching – were beneficial.
- PSF2 outperforms PSF1 in all cases. It uses a more refined sequence matching and an additional data source – the full weather vector W1.
- PSF1 performs similarly to PSF. PSF1 uses the weather forecast for sequence matching, while PSF uses the PV data. When the weather forecast is more accurate (10% noise), PSF1 performs slightly better than PSF, but as the accuracy of the weather forecast decreases (20% and 30% noise), PSF performs better. However, the differences are statistically significant only for 20% noise, hence overall the two methods perform similarly. An advantage of PSF1 over PSF is the faster training and prediction as it uses a feature vector with smaller dimensionality (4 vs 20 features).
- In all cases NN2 is the most accurate model. It uses all data sources directly as inputs – PV data, weather and weather forecast. The second best model PSF2 also uses all data sources but in a different way. The core part, sequence matching, is done using the weather and weather forecast data only, while the PV data is used only in the last step. PSF2, however, is faster to train than NN2.
- All prediction models outperform the persistence baseline in all cases, except one (NN1 for 30% WF noise) but the difference in this case is not statistically significant.
- The last graph in Fig. 4 compares only the prediction models that are affected by WF noise. We can see that as the noise increases, the accuracy decreases but this decrease is smaller for NN2 and PSF2, as these models rely less on WF data – NN2 uses all three data sources as inputs and PSF2 uses WF only for refining the solution.

Table 3. Accuracy of all methods

Method	10% noise in WF		20% noise in WF		30% noise in WF	
	MAE (kW)	RMSE (kW)	MAE (kW)	RMSE (kW)	MAE (kW)	RMSE (kW)
PSF	119.17	149.52	119.17	149.52	119.17	149.52
PSF1	118.12	151.52	120.05	156.61	123.04	154.10
PSF2	109.19	139.75	109.63	140.79	112.17	142.70
NN	116.64	154.16	116.64	154.16	116.64	154.16
NN1	111.16	149.33	117.47	158.86	126.14	173.85
NN2	94.75	133.65	95.76	134.62	96.89	135.69
B_{per}	124.80	184.29	124.80	184.29	124.80	184.29

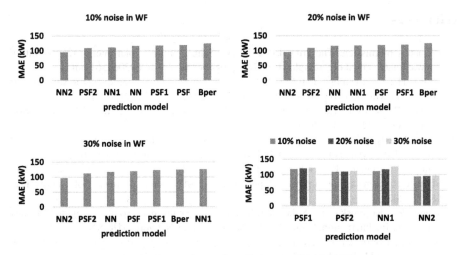

Fig. 4. Comparison of prediction models (MAE)

Table 4. Pair-wise statistical comparison of MAE (two-sample t-test); * - stat.sign. at $p \leq 0.05$, x – no stat.sign. difference. The three values in each cell correspond to 10%, 20%, 30% noise in WF respectively.

Method	PSF1	PSF2	NN	NN1	NN2	B_{per}
PSF	x*x	***	xxx	*x*	***	***
PSF1		***	xx*	*x*	***	***
PSF2			***	x**	***	***
NN				*x*	***	***
NN1					***	**x
NN2						**

7 Conclusion

In this paper we study the application of pattern sequence methods for solar power prediction from previous PV power and weather data, and weather forecast for the new day. We show how the standard PSF algorithm can be extended to utilize data from more than one data source by proposing two extensions, PSF1 and PSF2. We evaluate the performance of the three PSF methods on Australian data for two years, and compare them with three NN methods and a baseline. Our results show that the extensions were beneficial - PSF2, which uses a 2-tier clustering and sequence matching, was more accurate than PSF in all cases. PSF1 performed similarly to PSF but was faster due to its smaller feature vector. Overall PSF2 was the second most accurate method, after NN2 - a neural network that uses directly the data from the three sources as inputs. However, PSF2 was faster to train than NN2. PSF2 and NN2 were also the most robust methods to higher levels of noise in the weather forecasts. Hence, we conclude that both PSF2 and NN2 are promising methods for solar power forecasting.

References

1. Climate Commission: The critical decade: Australia's future - solar energy (2013). http://www.climatecouncil.org.au/uploads/497bcd1f058be45028e3df9d020ed561.pdf
2. Pedro, H.T.C., Coimbra, C.F.M.: Assessment of forecasting techniques for solar power production with no exogenous inputs. Sol. Energy **86**, 2017–2028 (2012)
3. Bacher, P., Madsen, H., Nielsen, H.A.: Online short-term solar power forecasting. Sol. Energy **83**, 1772–1783 (2009)
4. Rana, M., Koprinska, I., Agelidis, V.G.: Forecasting solar power generated by grid connected PV systems using ensembles of neural networks. In: IJCNN (2015)
5. Chu, Y., Urquhart, B., Gohari, S.M.I., Pedro, H.T.C., Kleissl, J., Coimbra, C.F.M.: Short-term reforecasting of power output from a 48 MWe solar PV plant. Sol. Energy **112**, 68–77 (2015)
6. Wang, Z., Koprinska, I.: Solar power prediction with data source weighted nearest neighbors. In: International Joint Conference on Neural Networks (IJCNN) (2017)
7. Rana, M., Koprinska, I., Agelidis, V.G.: 2D-interval forecasts for solar power production. Sol. Energy **122**, 191–203 (2015)
8. Shi, J., Lee, W.-J., Lin, Y., Yang, Y., Wang, P.: Forecasting power output of photovoltaic systems based on weather classification and support vector machines. IEEE Trans. Ind. Appl. **48**, 1064–1069 (2012)
9. Martínez-Álvarez, F., Troncoso, A., Riquelme, J.C., Aguilar-Ruiz, J.S.: Energy time series forecasting based on pattern sequence similarity. IEEE Trans. Knowl. Data Eng. **23**, 1230–1243 (2011)
10. Koprinska, I., Rana, M., Troncoso, A., Martínez-Álvarez, F.: Combining pattern sequence similarity with neural networks for forecasting electricity demand time series. In: International Joint Conference on Neural Networks (IJCNN) (2013)

A New Methodology to Exploit Predictive Power in (Open, High, Low, Close) Data

Andrew D. Mann$^{(\boxtimes)}$ and Denise Gorse

Department of Computer Science, University College London,
London WC1E 6BT, UK
{A.Mann,D.Gorse}@cs.ucl.ac.uk

Abstract. Prediction of financial markets using neural networks and other techniques has predominately focused on the close price. Here, in contrast, the concept of a mid-price based on an Open, High, Low, Close (OHLC) data structure is proposed as a prediction target and shown to be a significantly easier target to forecast, suggesting previous works have attempted to extract predictive power from OHLC data in the wrong context. A prediction framework incorporating a factor discovery and mining process is developed using Randomised Decision Trees, with Long Short Term Memory Recurrent Neural Networks subsequently demonstrating remarkable predictive capabilities of up to 50.73% better than random (75.42% accuracy) on hourly data based on the FGBL German Bund futures contract, and 42.5% better than random (72.04% accuracy) on a comparison Bitcoin dataset.

Keywords: Machine learning · LSTMs · Decision Trees · Factor Mining · OHLC data · Financial forecasting · Mid-price

1 Introduction

The accurate prediction of an asset's direction has long been the goal of many academics and industry practitioners, with predictive methodologies ranging from the use of traditional technical analysis (TA) to more recent machine learning (ML) techniques. This paper utilises ML technology in the form of Randomised Decision Trees (RDTs) [1] and Long Short Term Memory Recurrent Neural Networks (LSTM RNNs) [2] as a key component in a process for trend detection which takes advantage of the relative ease of prediction of the *mid-price* (defined in terms of OHLC candlestick levels in Sect. 2.2) when compared to the traditional close price prediction target. RDTs are used to identify the most important factors from a rich factor universe generated from all possible combinations of OHLC lagged levels given L lags, using differences, ratios, and pairwise operations. Within this context it is demonstrated that OHLC levels have a remarkably high predictive potential, in contrast to the negative view espoused by a majority of academics and some practitioners [3–5].

© Springer International Publishing AG 2017
A. Lintas et al. (Eds.): ICANN 2017, Part II, LNCS 10614, pp. 495–502, 2017.
https://doi.org/10.1007/978-3-319-68612-7_56

2 Background

2.1 Literature Review

There exists no prior literature relating to a mid-price based on a candlestick structure, as proposed here. The common definition of a mid-price is the price halfway between the bid and ask; this has no relevance to the current work. There have, however, been many studies focusing on the predictive power of candlestick patterns. These studies have reported varying results, with most evidencing little or no value in these patterns as predictors of close price movements.

On the negative side, Marshall et al. [3] find that the relationships between OHLC levels have no useful information when applied to stocks in the Dow Jones Industrial Average. Horton [4] confirms there is little to no value in candlestick charting. Interestingly, Fock et al. [5] present negative results for both the DAX stock index and the FGBL German Bund futures contract, which latter the current work conflicts with (though it should be noted both that our target is different– mid-price rather than close price– and that our OHLC-derived patterns are not traditional candlesticks but data-mined constructions).

On the positive side, Xie et al. [6] find that candlestick patterns have significant predictive power to forecast US equity returns. Lu et al. [7] find predictive power in several patterns, but these are rare and the research in addition did not sufficiently address the distinction between candlestick patterns being able to yield profit and their being able to predict trends. One study, that of Lu [8], finds that traditional patterns have little value but that novel ones may do so; this finding is in line with observations made in the current work, though it should again be emphasised that our use of the mid-price as target creates a very different context.

Overall the evidence in the literature favours the dominant academic belief that candlestick patterns have little value. The results presented below, albeit in the context of mid-price prediction and utilising novel OHLC patterns as input factors, may thus be somewhat of a surprise.

2.2 A Mid-Price Definition and Motivation

Two definitions of mid-price are used in the current work. Mid-price-1 is defined as the price mid-way between a time interval's high and low,

$$mid\text{-}price\text{-}1 = \frac{high + low}{2}, \tag{1}$$

while mid-price-2 focuses on the real body of a candlestick (area of the candlestick between open and close) and is defined as

$$mid\text{-}price\text{-}2 = \frac{open + close}{2}. \tag{2}$$

The predominant reason for investigating the use of a mid-price as a prediction target was the observation that mid-price time series display far less noise than close price series. As an example, the time series of close price, mid-price-1, and mid-price-2 were examined for 27,927 samples of the German Bund futures data set used here. The standard deviation of price movements in this example data set shows the close price has a standard deviation of 13.71 ticks[1] compared to 11.64 and 10.52 ticks for mid-price-1 and mid-price-2 respectively. Similar results were obtained for many other examples of financial time series data, confirming the mid-price (in particular mid-price-2) as a less noisy target.

2.3   Machine Learning Models Used

Factor Importance Mining. Randomised Decision Trees [9] are used to rank the importance of a factor to its target using the Gini impurity metric which measures the frequency of an incorrect classification of an element in a feature set if it was randomly allocated a classification; a higher value is thus a measure of a more significant level of correlation between factor and target.

Mid-Price Prediction. LSTM RNNs are selected as the prediction model due to their ability to detect persistent statistical patterns in sequences while avoiding issues with vanishing gradients[2]; the addition of LSTM units to a RNN allows the network to selectively remember and forget information while retaining long and short term dependencies. The LSTM RNN is here trained to minimise a mean square error loss function using residual back-propagation (RPROP) [10]. RPROP is a first-order optimisation algorithm acting independently over each weight and accounting only for the sign of the partial derivative (ignoring magnitude); this results in a computationally cheap locally adaptive scheme allowing fast convergence in binary classification (here, to predict whether a price movement is up or down).

2.4   Performance Metrics

Normalised Percentage Better than Random (NPBR) and a simple accuracy were used as evaluation metrics. The latter measures the proportion of correctly predicted directional movements; it has the advantage of simplicity but the weakness of being an unreliable indicator of performance in a strongly trending market, where there may be a tendency to overpredict the majority class. NPBR (also known as the Kappa Statistic [11]) is a more robust performance metric for imbalanced data sets, with a range of -100% to 100%, a score of 0% being equivalent to chance. The metric is formalised as

$$t = n_{00} + n_{01} + n_{10} + n_{11}, \tag{3}$$

---

[1] A tick is the minimum movement in a price series, which for the FGBL futures contract is equivalent to 10 EUR.

[2] Gradient calculations in layers further from the output accumulate progressively more fractional derivative factors, which results in weight changes tending to zero in lower layers and thus vanishing.

$$R_{total} = \frac{(n_{11} + n_{01})(n_{11} + n_{10}) + (n_{00} + n_{01})(n_{00} + n_{10}))}{t}, \qquad (4)$$

$$NPBR = \frac{(n_{11} + n_{00}) - R_{total}}{t - R_{total}}. \qquad (5)$$

In this n_{00} represents true negatives, n_{01} false positives, n_{10} false negatives, and n_{11} true positives, these four quantities summing to the total number of predictions, t. This measure allows a comparison against random, which is a valuable metric to state.

3   Methodology

3.1   OHLC Factor Mining

All possible combinations are generated of one hour OHLC bars using differences and ratios given L lags. This rich factor universe is then ranked for importance in relation to a target (mid-price direction at $t + 1$) using Randomised Decision Trees deriving their importance values from the Gini metric. The top N factors are then selected. In this instance $N = 100$ as beyond the top 100 factors the Gini metric curve flattens, as can be observed in Fig. 1.

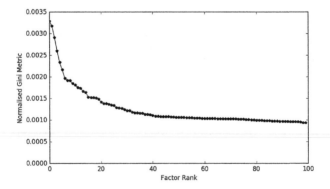

Fig. 1. Ranked Factor Importance Curve

It is notable that the top ranked factors using this machine learning methodology do not include simple lags of the kind considered in the baseline experiments of Sect. 4.1; in fact conventional lagged inputs do not appear anywhere in the top 100 factors. This supports the later observation that factor mining in itself, without further filtering as described below, gives rise to a large improvement in prediction performance over that seen in the baseline experiments.

The top N factors are then filtered based on correlation to target and factor-to-factor correlation, selecting factors which pass the tests $|corr_{ft}| \leq c_1$ and $|corr_{ff}| \geq c_2$ respectively, with c_1 and c_2 optimised on the training set.

3.2   Mid-Price Directional Prediction

Once the optimal factors have been selected they were standardised and used to train the LSTM RNN with outputs in the range $[-1, +1]$ and targets of -1 (down) and $+1$ (up). The net used to produce the results of the next section had eight hidden units and a 2% weight decay; experiments were carried out using other numbers of hidden units and differing amounts of weight decay, but results were found to be robust to reasonable variations of these parameters. It was decided to avoid the risk of overfitting by not optimising these network parameters; the results below, for an out-of-sample dataset, may thus be regarded as generally indicative of the level of predictive power that can be achieved.

4   Results

4.1   Baseline Performance: Use of Close and OHLC Lags as Inputs

A baseline performance was established by investigating the prediction of both close and mid (see Table 1) from close price lags and OHLC lags (defined as a full set of OHLC lags, for two preceding time steps, a total of eight factors in all). Lagged inputs are defined by the equation below,

$$\delta_i = \frac{(p_i - p_{i-1})}{p_{i-1}}, \tag{6}$$

where p_i is the current price and p_{i-1} is the previous price.

Table 1. Baseline performance results

I/O configuration	Accuracy	NPBR
Close from Close Lags	51.74%	1.89%
Mid-1 from Close Lags	66.15%	32.27%
Mid-2 from Close Lags	69.64%	39.25%
Close from OHLC Lags	51.44%	0.60%
Mid-2 from OHLC Lags	71.34%	42.69%

The first line of Table 1 corresponds to traditional directional prediction; as can be seen from the table results are poor, with only a 51.74% accuracy. However it should be noted that the poor performance derives primarily from the use of close price as a target rather than as a single lagged input. Replacing the target at $t+1$ by either of the mid-prices, but retaining the simple close lag as input, results in an immediate and large improvement in directional accuracy, with an accuracy of 66.15% and 69.64% for mid-price-1 and mid-price-2 respectively. It is thus possible to predict a mid-price to a high accuracy while continuing to use traditional baseline close price lags as factors.

It can also be seen from the table that using additional open, high, and low (OHL) lagged inputs has only a very small effect on the network's ability to predict close direction; this may well explain why many traditional candlestick patterns appear not to be predictive [3–5]. There is however a somewhat more noticeable improvement in mid-price-2 prediction when additional OHL lagged inputs are used; this suggests that mid-price-2 predictions might be improved by a more intelligent selection of OHLC based factors.

At this point only two lags have been considered. The number of lags of OHLC data could have an impact on predictive power and certainly has an impact on the complexity of the model (fewer parameters being preferred).

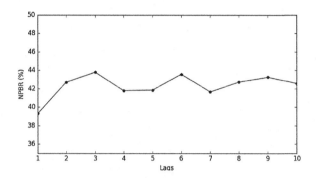

Fig. 2. Factor Lag Experimental Results

Figure 2 shows training data NPBR peaks at three, six and nine OHLC lags. However the maximum is reached at three, implying three lags of OHLC data is sufficient in this context. (Interestingly, many candlestick patterns are created from three lags of OHLC data, such as the Three Line Strike.)

4.2   Use of Mined OHLC Factors as Inputs

Table 1 was suggestive of the possibility that suitably configured OHLC data might enhance mid-price-2 prediction. In the experiments below mined data as described in Sect. 3.1 were used. The term *Importance Mining* in Table 2 refers to test results using the top 100 importance-ranked factors, and *Correlation Subset* to a reduced input set with those same factors now filtered.

Table 2. Factor mining performance results

I/O configuration	Accuracy	NPBR
Mid-2: Importance Mining	74.48%	48.75%
Mid-2: Correlation Subset	75.42%	50.73%

It can be seen from Table 2 that factor importance mining does substantially improve the LSTM RNN net's performance, resulting in an increase in NPBR from 42.69% (see OHLC input result in Table 1) to 48.75%. However from Table 2 correlation based filtering adds only a further 1.98% to the NPBR. In addition the optimal values of the correlation thresholds c_1 and c_2 (see Sect. 3.1) were found to be 0.2 and 1.0, respectively. These observations indicate both that it is the use of the mined factors per se that is predominantly leading to the improvement in performance, and that the LSTM RNN is able to operate effectively without correlation based input screening.

At this point it might appear that the mid-price predictive power could be an artifact of the FGBL futures contract. To allay this concern we apply the same methodology to predict mid-price-2 (with no additional parameter optimisation). Bitcoin was chosen due to its having very different dynamics, being an emerging market highly sensitive to news, exhibiting high volatility, showing the effects of price manipulation, and with low liquidity constraints.

Table 3. German bund vs. bitcoin performance

I/O configuration	Close from close lags		Mid-2 from correlation subset	
	Accuracy	NPBR	Accuracy	NPBR
FGBL futures	51.74%	1.89%	75.42%	50.73%
Bitcoin	51.47%	0.64%	72.04%	42.5%

As can be seen in Table 3 the performance of Close from Close Lags is similarly poor for Bitcoin as for FGBL futures. However the factor mining methodology (incorporating correlation based filtering with the same thresholds c_1 and c_2 as for FGBL futures) produces a remarkable 42.5% NPBR on Bitcoin, even though it was threshold-optimised on FGBL futures. Thus the predictive value of the mid-price appears to be consistent across vastly different markets.

5   Discussion

It has been shown that use of the proposed mid-price (Eq. 2) as target can result in up to a 75.42% prediction accuracy (50.73% NPBR) using appropriate machine learning techniques. OHLC data was used to generate candlestick factors via Randomised Decision Trees which increased the predictive power of an LSTM RNN from an initial 39.25% (Mid-2 from Close Lags) to this maximum of 50.73% NPBR, showing OHLC data does have a high predictive value in relation to the mid-price. However it was demonstrated also that OHLC data did not increase predictive power when forecasting the traditional close price target, which is in line with [3–5]. Hence the results here, while they may be surprising, are not at odds with the conclusions drawn in other work. The usefulness of

OHLC data is not in predicting the close price, but predicting the mid-price, which has been neglected in past research.

The discovery of the high predictive power of the mid-price is in itself a significant result given the prevailing sentiment that no aspect of an asset's price behaviour can be predicted substantially above random. It is not immediately obvious how to harness this high predictive power within a trading strategy, as a mid-price prediction is not located at a specific moment in time but only within an interval. However a trading strategy built around the mid-price is by no means impossible, though it would necessarily require more for its execution than the simple prediction of this value.

References

1. Geurts, P., Ernst, D., Wehenkel, L.: Extremely randomized trees. Mach. Learn. **63**, 3–42 (2006)
2. Hochreiter, S., Schmidhuber, J.: Long short-term memory. Neural Comput. **9**(8), 1735–1780 (1997)
3. Marshall, B., Young, M., Rose, L.: Candlestick technical trading strategies: can they create value for investors. J. Bank. Financ. **30**, 2303–2323 (2005)
4. Horton, M.: Stars, crows, and doji: the use of candlesticks in stock selection. Q. Rev. Econ. Financ. **49**, 283–294 (2009)
5. Fock, J., Klein, C., Zwergel, B.: Performance of candlestick analysis on intraday futures data. J. Deriv. **13**(1), 28–40 (2005)
6. Xie, H., Zhao, X., Wang, S.: A comprehensive look at the predictive information in Japanese candlesticks. In: International Conference on Computational Science (2012)
7. Lu, T., Chen, Y., Hsu, Y.: Trend definition or holding strategy: what determines the profitability of candlestick charting. J. Bank. Financ. **61**, 172–183 (2015)
8. Lu, T.: The profitability of candlestick charting in the Taiwan stock market. Pac.-Basin Financ. J. **26**, 65–78 (2014)
9. Breiman, L., Friedman, R.A., Olshen, R.A., Stone, C.G.: Classification and Regression Trees. Wadsworth, Pacific Grove (1984)
10. Riedmiller, M., Braun, H.: A direct adaptive method for faster backpropagation learning: the RPROP algorithm. In: IEEE International Conference on Neural Networks, pp. 586–591 (1993)
11. Smeeton, N.C.: Early history of the kappa statistic. Biometrics **41**, 795 (1985). JSTOR 2531300

Recurrent Dynamical Projection for Time Series-Based Fraud Detection

Eric A. Antonelo$^{(\boxtimes)}$ and Radu State

Interdisciplinary Centre for Security, Reliability and Trust,
University of Luxembourg, Luxembourg City, Luxembourg
ericaislan.antonelo@uni.lu

Abstract. A Reservoir Computing approach is used in this work for generating a rich nonlinear spatial feature from the dynamical projection of a limited-size input time series. The final state of the Recurrent neural network (RNN) forms the feature subsequently used as input to a regressor or classifier (such as Random Forest or Least Squares). This proposed method is used for fraud detection in the energy distribution domain, namely, detection of non-technical loss (NTL) using a real-world dataset containing only the monthly energy consumption time series of (more than 300 K) users. The heterogeneity of user profiles is dealt with a clustering approach, where the cluster id is also input to the classifier. Experimental results shows that the proposed recurrent feature generator is able to extract relevant nonlinear transformations of the raw time series without a priori knowledge and perform as good as (and sometimes better than) baseline models with handcrafted features.

Keywords: Recurrent neural networks · Reservoir computing · Non-technical loss · Eletricity fraud detection · Clustering · Energy distribution networks

1 Introduction

In the context of energy distribution networks, frauds are non-technical losses (NTL) that may account for up to 40% of the total energy distributed in some developing countries. Fraudsters alter (or bypass) the eletricity meter in order to pay less than the right amount. Many different methods have been used for devising fraud detection models [4,5]. These methods usually require feature engineering on the consumptions time series data in order to train classifiers for fraud detection. Other features can also be employed such as the ones derived from customer data (e.g., spatial coordinates, neighborhood, type of residence, etc.) and textual notes written by employees of the energy distribution network responsible for reading the meters monthly - however, these notes are scarce. Whenever a note is written with respect to a customer's meter, there is a high probability of fraud. In order to verify the fraud, an inspector is sent to the field, i.e., a specialist makes a visit to the customer's residence in order to check

© Springer International Publishing AG 2017
A. Lintas et al. (Eds.): ICANN 2017, Part II, LNCS 10614, pp. 503–511, 2017.
https://doi.org/10.1007/978-3-319-68612-7_57

the eletricity meter and confirm the fraud. Three outcomes are possible out of an inspection: the fraud is confirmed, there is an anomaly incurring NTL (e.g. faulty meter or fraud not affirmed), or there was no fraud (there may also be some mislabeled data for the cases of bribery or other causes). Thus, the remaining non-inspected customers are not used in the supervised learning of the model (which can cause the so-called sample selection bias [6]). In this context, the discovery or detection of frauds is necessary to decrease the NTL of the energy distribution networks. Predictive models devised to this end have to be used with parsimony since the cost to send a inspector to confirm the fraud is expensive. Thus, only the most certain predictions (those with highest score) could be used for sending inspections, for instance. Previous work on NTL detection has employed different approaches, types of inputs and dataset sizes. For instance, [9] focuses on feature engineering with random forest, logistic regression and support vector machine as classifiers. A survey on this field is presented in [5], citing also other approaches based on fuzzy systems, genetic algorithms, etc.

This work proposes a new general purpose temporal feature extraction based on recurrent neural networks (RNNs) that projects the input stream $\mathbf{u}(t)$ into a high-dimensional dynamic space $\mathbf{x}(t)$. This projector is called *reservoir* as in Reservoir Computing (RC), whose recurrent weights are randomly initialized [11]. The states $\mathbf{x}(t)$ of the resulting dynamical system form a trajectory in the high-dimensional space that exhibits a short-term memory. This means that when a snapshot is taken from the dynamical system (i.e., at $t = t_s$), the states $x(t_s)$ sums up the recent history of the input stream. The main idea is to transform the temporal dimension of $\mathbf{u}(t)$ into a spatial dimension of the snapshoted state $x(t_s)$. In this work, this last state is used as a feature for a predictive model, which can be a regressor or a classifier. The proposed method is applied to fraud detection in the energy distribution domain where million of users with heterogeneous energy consumption profiles exist. Our work considers that the short-length time series consumption data from each user is the sole input available to the model. The proposed model also employs k-means clustering to preprocess the heterogeneous input time series as well as to provide cluster information as an additional relevant input. The resulting method is novel as far as the authors know, specially in the fraud detection domain. The experiments presented in this work show that the general-purpose recurrent feature generator achieves predictive performance at least as good as models considering handcrafted input features, and that large reservoirs and cluster information is useful mainly when using Least Squares training.

2   Methods

2.1   Recurrent Dynamical Projection

Our proposed method views an RNN as an automatic temporal feature generator. It transforms an input stream into a set of spatial nonlinear features that sums up the trajectory of the underlying input-driven dynamical system (see

Fig. 1(a)). The RNN model we use is based on the Echo State Network (ESN) approach [7,8]. The state update equation for the reservoir is given by:

$$\mathbf{x}(t+1) = f(\mathbf{W}_{in}\mathbf{u}(t) + \mathbf{W}_{res}\mathbf{x}(t) + \mathbf{W}_{bias}) \tag{1}$$

where: $\mathbf{u}(t)$ represents the input at time t; $\mathbf{x}(t)$ is the M-dimensional reservoir state; and $f() = \tanh()$ is the hyperbolic tangent activation function; $\mathbf{W}_{in}$ and $\mathbf{W}_{bias}$ are the weight matrices from input and bias to reservoir, respectively and $\mathbf{W}_{res}$ represents the recurrent connections between internal nodes of the reservoir. The initial state is $\mathbf{x}(0) = \mathbf{0}$. The non-trainable weights $\mathbf{W}_{in}$, $\mathbf{W}_{res}$ and $\mathbf{W}_{bias}$ are randomly generated from a Gaussian distribution $N(0,1)$ or a uniform discrete set $\{-1,0,1\}$. After this random initialization, the matrix $\mathbf{W}_{in}$ ($\mathbf{W}_{bias}$) is scaled by the parameter called input scaling v_{inp} (bias scaling v_{bias}). Additionally, the $\mathbf{W}_{res}$ matrix is rescaled so that the reservoir has the echo state property [7], that is, the spectral radius $\rho(\mathbf{W}_{res})$ (the largest absolute eigenvalue) of the linearized system is smaller than one [7]. This means that the reservoir should have a fading memory such that if all inputs are zero, the reservoir states also approach zero within some time period. The configuration of the reservoir parameters are given in Sect. 3.

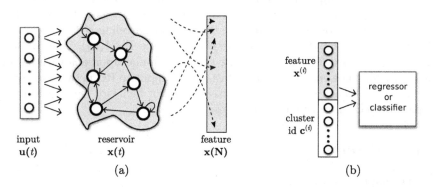

Fig. 1. (a) Recurrent Feature Generator (RFG). The reservoir is a non-linear dynamical system usually composed of recurrent sigmoid units. Solid lines represent fixed, randomly generated connections. The dashed lines show a hypothetical reservoir trajectory, ending up into a final state $\mathbf{x}(N)$ that sums up the recent history of the signal. (b) The learning machine with the temporal feature generated by RFG and the cluster id as input. We call *Temporal Machine* the conjunction of RFG + the learning module.

In this work, the reservoir is used to generate a high-dimensional feature at $t = N^{(i)}$, i.e., the reservoir states $\mathbf{x}(N^{(i)})$, where $N^{(i)}$ is the size of the ith input time series $\mathbf{u}^{(i)}(t)$, which in our case is the unidimensional monthly energy consumption series. We should care that this input time series is short enough compared to the size of the reservoir such that the reservoir has enough memory to generate a dynamical state $\mathbf{x}(N^{(i)})$ summing up the main characteristics of the input stream throughout time. For each ith time series, there is a feature vector $\mathbf{x}(N^{(i)})$ generated using (1) and a corresponding label $y^{(i)}$ indicating the class of the ith sample - fraud (1) or non-fraud (0). The mapping $\mathbf{x}(N^{(i)}) \rightarrow y^{(i)}$ is then learned by any regression or classification algorithm (Fig. 1(b)), such as Regularized Least Squares (Ridge Regression) or Random Forest.

2.2   Clustering and Normalization

The time series data $(\mathbf{u}^{(i)}(t))$ may contain very heterogeneous streams that vary on different scales. In our current application, this means that some customers consume 1000 times more energy than others (e.g., industrial or commercial customers in relation to residential clients). Even only using normalization, the results would be sub-optimal since some samples (from high energy consumption profiles) would drive the reservoir near the saturation region of the tanh function, while others would take it to linear area around zero. We would like that the ith sample $(\mathbf{u}^{(i)}(t), t = 0, \dots, N^{(i)})$ be in a scale not very different from the rest of the samples. At the same time, we can keep the information from the original scale of the sample (consumption profile of the user) that might be lost after rescaling. Both of these things can be easily accomplished by using a clustering method such as k-means. The method work as follows: compute the mean $m^{(i)}$ of $\mathbf{u}^{(i)}(t)$; use k-means to group the samples into clusters $\beta^{(i)}$ based on the value $m^{(i)}$; rescale each sample $\mathbf{u}^{(i)}(t)$ by dividing it over the value of the center of the cluster $\beta^{(i)}$. Now, all the samples will have less disparate scales. To compensate the loss of information, we concatenate the one-hot encoding $\mathbf{c}^{(i)}$ of the cluster $\beta^{(i)}$ into the total input vector for the classifier (see Fig. 1(b)). The resulting architecture is called *Temporal Machine* (TM). A similar approach with respect to using the one-hot encoding of the cluster id as input to RC networks is taken in [2]. In [1], a binary input vector is used for robot behavior learning through subspace projection in the dynamical reservoir space.

3   Experiments

3.1   Datasets

The complete dataset obtained from a certain energy distribution network in Brazil contains 3.6 M customers, from which at least 800 K were inspected for fraud. In this work, we only consider samples that span at least $N = 24$ months of collected energy consumption, while having a mean consumption over this time period greater than zero. These constraints reduce the dataset to $313,297$ samples, each one consisting of a time series $\mathbf{u}^{(i)}(t), t = 0, \dots, N - 1$.

3.2   Settings and Results

We made experiments using regularized Least Squares (LS) (ridge regression) [3], and random forest (RF)[1] as the regressor/classifier in the learning module of TM (Fig. 1(b)). These models are called TM-LS and TM-RF, respectively.

---

[1] RF uses the method provided in the *sklearn* Python toolbox (version 0.17.1).

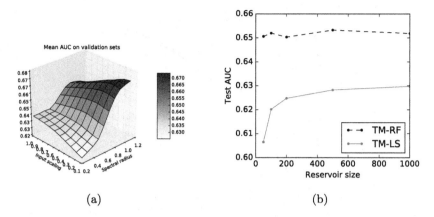

Fig. 2. (a) Grid search on spectral radius vs. input scaling showing the AUC on validation sets averaged over 10 runs each with different randomly initialized reservoirs. (b) AUC test performance vs. reservoir size for TM-RF and TM-LS in dashed and solid lines, respectively.

The RF method always uses 30 trees in the forest and a maximum depth of 20. Furthermore, comparisons to baseline models are made: instead of $\mathbf{x}^{(i)}$ being generated by the RFG, it is manually computed as an 8-dimensional feature vector composed of the means and the standard deviations of the time series over the following periods: the previous 24 months, 12 months, 6 months, and 3 months. Their corresponding acronyms are LS and RF (without *TM*) for Least Squares and Random Forest, respectively. The reservoir size is $M = 100$, unless otherwise stated. Two parameters of the reservoir in the RFG are optimized with a grid search on a validation set: the spectral radius and the input scaling. This is done ten times with reservoirs whose weights are randomly initialized each time. The average AUC (area under the ROC curve) is shown in Fig. 2(a). The maximum performance is achieved for high values of the spectral radius ($\rho(\mathbf{W}_{res}) = 1$) but low values of the input scaling ($v_{inp} = 0.3$). With this optimal set of parameters, the TMs were trained using Least Squares and Random Forest on the first 80% samples and tested on the most recent 20% of the samples. The resulting ROC curves on the test set are computed using each trained model and also the baseline models LS and RF (Fig. 3). We can note that the TMs using the RFG achieves comparable performance to the baseline models with handcrafted simple features (*mean* and *std*). Additionally, the Random Forest training method seems to have better test performance than the Least Squares method. This can also be seen in Fig. 2(b), where M is varied while keeping other parameters fixed, showing that greater reservoirs matter more to Least Squares training (improving performance) than to the Random Forest method. Table 1 shows the same test AUC of the models in Fig. 3 plus two models where the reservoirs have 500 neurons (TM500-LS and TM500-RF) and other two models LS and RF without the cluster id as input. Note that the cluster id is important when LS is used, but not as much as when RF is used as training method.

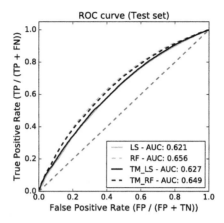

Fig. 3. (a) ROC curves on test sets (20% of the data) for 4 models: LS, RF, TM-LS and TM-RF.

Table 1. AUC - fixed test set

Model	Test AUC
LS (no cluster input)	0.604
RF (no cluster input)	0.654
LS	0.621
RF	0.656
TM-LS	0.627
TM-RF	0.649
TM500-LS	0.630
TM500-RF	0.653

Table 2. Average test AUC over sliding evaluation

Model	Average test AUC
LS	0.671
TM-LS	0.672
TM500-LS	0.678
RF	0.701
TM-RF	0.688

Another type of evaluation was made in order to observe how the predictive model would perform on a sliding-through-time iterative train and test procedure. Figure 4(a) shows the results of this evaluation considering the Least Squares method for training the models LS, TM-LS, and TM500-LS. Each point is one iteration of the procedure, in which a grid search on spectral radius vs input scaling is run with a validation set to find the best parameter configuration, and then the model is evaluated on a different test set corresponding to the *current month*. The next iteration will slide the current month into the training dataset, and the new test set will be formed by samples of the following month. On average, we can see that the first two models have equal performance (the horizontal lines represent the average AUC). The latter uses a greater, more complex reservoir ($M = 500$) that can perform a little better due to its increased power for representation and temporal processing. The same procedure now with Random Forest as learning method can be visually checked in Fig. 4(b). The TM-RF model with 100 neurons in the reservoir is not as performant as the RF model. However, both of them are better then the models based

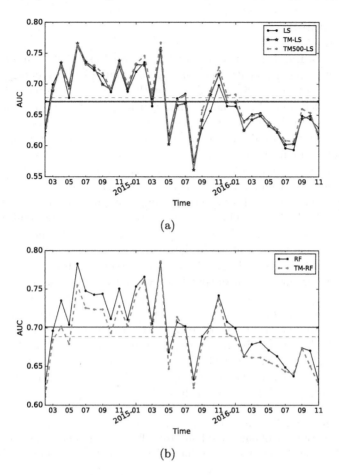

Fig. 4. Sliding evaluation: iterative training on data starting in 2015 throughout 2016, testing each time on the following month (using AUC). Average AUC given by horizontal lines. (a) All models trained by ridge regression (regularized Least Squares estimate). (b) All models trained by Random Forest.

on LS, on average (Table 2). The results of the sliding evaluation show that the performance is better throughout 2014 until the first quarter of 2015. In 2016, the performance drops relative to the mean AUC. One possible explanation is that detection of frauds may have explanatory variables other than the energy consumption time series not considered in this work. As a matter of comparison, [9] achieves AUC of 0.729 using random forests and handcrafted feature engineering. Their dataset is similar to the one used in this work, although being bigger, filtered and preprocessed differently, without sliding evaluations performed.

4   Conclusion

In this paper, a fraud detection method based on Reservoir Computing is proposed for detecting electricity theft having as input solely the energy consumption time series of each customer. To deal with the heterogeneous user consumption profiles, k-means clustering is employed for normalization of all the time series according to the cluster it was assigned to. The RC approach allows us to extract relevant temporal features from short-length time series by projecting the input into a high-dimensional nonlinear space. The trajectory of this input-driven dynamical system ends up into a final state which sums up the input time series behavior over time. The input feature used for the classifier is exactly this last state of the reservoir, showing comparable performance with baseline models using handcrafted features. The method effectively converts the temporal dimension into a spatial one, and although it was used for detecting non-technical loss in electricity grids (with real-world data) in this paper, it can also be used for general-purpose time series-based classification tasks (e.g. fraud detection). However, as the reservoir without output feedback has a limited short-term memory [7], the time series can not be indefinitely long. Furthermore, future work will research methods to optimize the reservoir dynamics (e.g., Intrinsic Plasticity [10]) in order to generate even better features. In the context of the real-world task of NTL detection, the next crucial step is to consider additional input variables such as user neighborhood, type of connection, etc. into a integrated framework which corrects the existing sample selection bias, currently considered an obstacle to the optimal use of such models.

Acknowledgments. The authors would like thank Jorge Meira and Patrick Glauner from University of Luxembourg, and Lautaro Dolberg, Yves Rangoni, Franck Bettinger and Diogo M. Duarte from Choice Technologies for useful discussions on NTL.

References

1. Antonelo, E.A., Schrauwen, B.: On learning navigation behaviors for small mobile robots with reservoir computing architectures. IEEE Trans. Neural Netw. Learn. Syst. **26**(4), 763–780 (2015)
2. Antonelo, E.A., Flesch, C., Schmitz, F.: Reservoir computing for detection of steady state in performance tests of compressors. Neurocomputing (in press)
3. Bishop, C.M.: Pattern Recognition and Machine Learning. Information Science and Statistics. Springer, New York (2006)
4. Depuru, S.S.S.R., Wang, L., Devabhaktuni, V., Green, R.C.: High performance computing for detection of electricity theft. Int. J. Electr. Power Energy Syst. **47**, 21–30 (2013)
5. Glauner, P., Meira, J., Valtchev, P., State, R., Bettinger, F.: The challenge of non-technical loss detection using artificial intelligence: a survey. Int. J. Comput. Intell. Syst. (IJCIS) **10**(1), 760–775 (2017)
6. Heckman, J.J.: Sample selection bias as a specification error. Econometrica **47**(1), 153–161 (1979). http://www.jstor.org/stable/1912352

7. Jaeger, H.: The "echo state" approach to analysing and training recurrent neural networks. Technical report GMD Report 148, German National Research Center for Information Technology (2001)
8. Jaeger, H., Haas, H.: Harnessing nonlinearity: predicting chaotic systems and saving energy in wireless telecommunication. Science **304**(5667), 78–80 (2004)
9. Meira, J.A., Glauner, P., Valtchev, P., Dolberg, L., Bettinger, F., Duarte, D., et al.: Distilling provider-independent data for general detection of non-technical losses. In: Power and Energy Conference, Illinois, 23–24 February 2017 (2017)
10. Schrauwen, B., Warderman, M., Verstraeten, D., Steil, J.J., Stroobandt, D.: Improving reservoirs using intrinsic plasticity. Neurocomputing **71**, 1159–1171 (2008)
11. Verstraeten, D., Schrauwen, B., D'Haene, M., Stroobandt, D.: An experimental unification of reservoir computing methods. Neural Netw. **20**(3), 391–403 (2007)

Transfer Information Energy: A Quantitative Causality Indicator Between Time Series

Angel Caţaron[1] and Răzvan Andonie[1,2(✉)]

[1] Electronics and Computers Department, Transilvania University, Braşov, Romania
cataron@unitbv.ro
[2] Computer Science Department, Central Washington University,
Ellensburg, WA, USA
andonie@cwu.edu

Abstract. We introduce an information-theoretical approach for analyzing cause-effect relationships between time series. Rather than using the Transfer Entropy (TE), we define and apply the Transfer Information Energy (TIE), which is based on Onicescu's Information Energy. The TIE can substitute the TE for detecting cause-effect relationships between time series. The advantage of using the TIE is computational: we can obtain similar results, but faster. To illustrate, we compare the TIE and the TE in a machine learning application. We analyze time series of stock market indexes, with the goal to infer causal relationships between them (i.e., how they influence each other).

1 Introduction

Causal analysis is not merely a search for statistical correlations, but an investigation of cause-effect relationships. Although, in general, statistical analysis cannot distinguish genuine causation from spurious covariation in every conceivable case, this is still possible in many cases [15]. Causality is usually posed using two alternative scenarios: the Granger causality and the information-theoretical approach (based on the Kullback-Leibler divergence or the TE).

The Granger[1] causality test [5] is a statistical hypothesis test for determining whether one time series is useful in forecasting another. According to Granger, causality could be reflected by measuring the ability of predicting the future values of a time series using past values of another time series. The Granger test is based on linear regression modeling of stochastic processes. More complex extensions to nonlinear cases exist, but these extensions are more difficult to apply in practice [6].

The TE, introduced by Schreiber [17], has been used to quantify the statistical coherence between time-series. It is able to distinguish driving and responding elements and to detect asymmetry in the interaction of time-series. For instance, in the financial market, based on the TE concept, Kwon and Oh [12] found that the amount of information flow from index to stock is larger than from stock to

---

[1] Clive Granger, recipient of the 2003 Nobel Prize in Economics.

© Springer International Publishing AG 2017
A. Lintas et al. (Eds.): ICANN 2017, Part II, LNCS 10614, pp. 512–519, 2017.
https://doi.org/10.1007/978-3-319-68612-7_58

index. It indicates that the market index plays a role of major driving force to individual stock. Barnett *et al.* proved that Granger causality and TE causality measure are equivalent for time series which have a Gaussian distribution [1]. Hlaváčková-Schindler [8] generalized this result.

Our main contribution is an information-theoretical approach for analyzing cause-effect relationships between time series. Rather than using the relatively well-known Kullback-Leibler divergence and the TE (both based on a measure of uncertainty - the Shannon entropy), we introduce the TIE, which is based on a measure of certainty - the Onicescu Information Energy (IE) [14]. In general, any monotonically growing and continuous probability function can be considered as a measure of certainty and the IE is such a function. The IE is a special case of Van der Lubbe *et al.* certainty measure [18] and was interpreted by several authors as a measure of expected commonness, a measure of average certainty, or as a measure of concentration, and is not related to physical energy. We claim that the TIE can substitute the TE for detecting cause-effect relationships between time series, with the advantage of being faster to compute.

An hot application area of causal relationships is finance. Most investors in the stock market consider various indexes to be important sources of basic information that can be used to analyze and predict the market perspectives. We may be interested in the correlation (and beyond that, causality as well) between two time series such as a market/bench index and an individual stock/ETF products. An ETF (Exchange Traded Fund), is a marketable security that tracks an index, a commodity, bonds, or a basket of assets like an index fund. In our application, we compare the TIE and the TE in a machine learning application, analyzing time series of stock market indexes with the goal to infer how they influence each other.

The paper is organized as follows. First, we refer to previous work (Sect. 2). Section 3 introduces the TIE. The financial application is presented in Sect. 4. The paper is concluded in Sect. 5.

2   Related Work: TE for Financial Time-Series

An overview of causality detection based on information-theoretic approaches in time series analysis can be found in [9]. Most of the information-theoretic approaches in time series analysis are based on the TE. The recent literature on TE applications is rich.

TE measures the directionality of a variable with respect to time base on the probability density function (PDF). For two discrete stationary processes I and J, TE relates k previous samples of process I and l previous samples of process J and is defined as follows [17]:

$$TE_{J \to I} = \sum_{t=1}^{n-1} p(i_{t+1}, i_t^{(k)}, j_t^{(l)}) \, log \frac{p(i_{t+1}|i_t^{(k)}, j_t^{(l)})}{p(i_{t+1}|i_t^{(k)})}, \tag{1}$$

where i_t and j_t are the discrete states at time t of I and J, respectively; $i_t^{(k)}$ and $j_t^{(k)}$ are the k and l dimensional delay vectors of time series I and J, respectively.

$T_{J \to I}$ measures the extend to which time series J influences time series I. The TE is asymmetric under the exchange of i_t and j_t, and provides information regarding the direction of interaction between the two time series. In fact, the TE is an equivalent expression for the conditional mutual information [9].

Accurate estimation of entropy-based measures is notoriously difficult and there is no consensus on an optimal way for estimating TE from a dataset [4]. Schreiber proposed the TE using correlation integrals [17]. The histogram estimation approach with fixed partitioning is the most widely used. This method is simple and efficient, but not scalable for more than three scalars. It also has another drawback - it is sensible to the size of bins used. Since estimating the TE reduces to the non-parametric entropy estimation, other entropy estimation methods have been also used for computing the TE [4,7,19]: kernel density estimation methods, nearest-neighbor, Parzen, neural networks, etc.

Without intending to be exhaustive, we mention two papers which describe time-series information flow analysis with TE. Other recent results can be found in [3,13].

Kwon and Yang [11] computed the information flow between 25 stock markets to determine which market serves as a source of information for global stock indexes. They analyzed the daily time series for the period of 2000 to 2007 using TE in order to examine the information flow between stock markets and identify the hub. They concluded that the American and European markets are strongly clustered and they are able to be regarded as one economic region, while Asia/Pacific markets are economically separated from American and European market cluster. Therefore, they could infer that American and European stock markets fluctuate in tune with a common deriving mechanism. The considerable quantity of the TE from American and European market cluster to the Asia/Pacific markets is the strong evidence that there is an asymmetry of information flow between the deriving mechanisms.

Sandoval [16] used the stocks of the 197 largest companies in the world, in terms of market capitalization, in the financial area, from 2003 to 2012. He studied the causal relationships between them using TE. He could assess which companies influence others according to sub-areas of the financial sector. He also analyzed the exchange of information between those stocks and the network formed by them based on this measure, verifying that they cluster mainly according to countries of origin, and then by industry and sub-industry.

3   Transfer Information Energy

The information entropy of a discrete random variable I with possible values $\{i_1, i_2, \ldots, i_n\}$ is the expected value of the information content of I [2], $H(I) = -\sum_{t=1}^{n} p(i_t) \, log \, p(i_t)$, whereas the IE is the expected value of the probabilities of the possible values of I [14], $IE(I) = \sum_{t=1}^{n} p(i_t) \cdot p(i_t)$.

We define the TIE:

$$TIE_{J \to I} = \sum_{t=1}^{n-1} p(i_{t+1}, i_t^{(k)}, j_t^{(l)}) \left(p(i_{t+1} | i_t^{(k)}, j_t^{(l)}) - p(i_{t+1} | i_t^{(k)}) \right), \qquad (2)$$

to quantify the increase in certainty (energy) of process I, knowing k previous samples of process I and l previous samples of process J. Like the TE, the TIE is non-symmetric and measures cause-effect relationships between time series I and J. For computational reasons, we take $k = l = 1$.

Both (1) and (2) can be rewritten substituting the conditional probabilities:

$$TE_{J \to I} = \sum_{i_{t+1}, i_t, j_t} p(i_{t+1}, i_t, j_t) \log \frac{p(i_{t+1}, i_t, j_t)p(i_t)}{p(i_{t+1}, i_t)p(i_t, j_t)}, \qquad (3)$$

$$TIE_{J \to I} = \sum_{i_{t+1}, i_t, j_t} p(i_{t+1}, i_t, j_t) \left(\frac{p(i_{t+1}, i_t, j_t)}{p(i_t, j_t)} - \frac{p(i_{t+1}, i_t)}{p(i_t)} \right). \qquad (4)$$

Comparing formulas (3) and (4), we observe that for TE we have 4 multiplications/divisions and one logarithm, whereas for TIE we have 3 multiplications/divisions and 1 subtraction. Considering all operations equivalent, the TIE is theoretically 20% faster, which is obviously a rough theoretical estimate.

The histogram estimation of TE and TIE between two time series can be computed in three steps: *(a)* Transformation of the continuous valued time series into series with discrete values by binning; the result is a sequence of tokens selected from an alphabet with as many symbols as the number of bins; *(b)* Evaluation of the probabilities $p(i_{t+1}, i_t, j_t)$, $p(i_t)$, $p(i_{t+1}, i_t)$, and $p(i_t, j_t)$, for all i_t and j_t; and *(c)* Computation of TE and TIE by using Eqs. (3) and (4).

4   Transfer Energy Between Financial Time Series

We illustrate with all details the estimation of TI and TIE on a real-world data set, to make the procedure reproducible.

Table 1. The 20 stock market indexes, obtained from the finance.yahoo.com web site. We estimate the TE and TIE of all pairs from the 20 stock market symbols. Each symbol represents a time series of daily closing prices recorded between Jan. 3, 2000– Feb. 14, 2017.

Americas	Asia/Pacific	Europe
1: MERV	8: AORD	16: ATX
2: BVSP	9: SSEC	17: BFX
3: GSPTSE	10: HSI	18: GDAXI
4: MXX	11: BSESN	19: AEX
5: GSPC	12: JKSE	20: SSMI
6: DJA	13: N255	
7: DJI	14: KS11	
	15: TWII	

For 20 stock market indexes from Americas, Asia/Pacific and Europe (Table 1), we estimate the TE and TIE for all pairs. The working days of the markets across the world may vary from one country to another. Therefore, the time series are aligned by time stamp and the missing values are replaced with the previous available ones. We estimate TE and TIE as follows:

(a) *Discretization: binning the time series*

We slice the domain limited by the minimum and maximum values from the whole data set into equally sized intervals which are then labeled by assigning a symbol to each of them. The result is a sequence of characters, for which we compute the probabilities needed in Eqs. (3) and (4).

When the binning is applied on the first log-returns of stocks, the narrow bins provide more information content, thus a higher value of entropy H then the large bins. Nevertheless, the correlation between the two choices of binning is high in general, reflecting an important similarity of the approaches [16]. In general, for shorter time series it is advisable to use larger bins in order to avoid the excessive fragmentation (and thus very low or uniform probabilities of symbols). We use 24 bins, noting that the binning strategy is less relevant in our case, since we are not interested in absolute values for TE and TIE, but in their relative values (for comparison). Fig. 1 depicts the binning and Table 2 shows a numerical example of binning based on the first values of the DJI and HSI stock indexes.

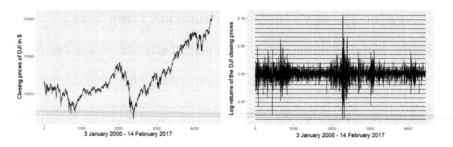

Fig. 1. Binning the time series. The left graph presents the raw values of the DJI stock ranging between Jan. 3, 2000–Feb. 14, 2017. On the right side, we represent the log-returns of closing prices and the slicing of the values domain, with 24 equal intervals between minimum and maximum values. Each interval is labeled with a symbol (a letter).

(b) *Compute the marginal and joint probabilities in Eqs. (3) and (4)*

We denote by TE_t the term under the sum sign in (3) and by TIE_t the term under the sum sign in Eq. (4). The next step is to evaluate TE_t and TIE_t by counting the number of each occurrence (Table 2). The string obtained by binning the log-returns of the DJI stock starts with the symbols "g l m n l j k k m k ...". Therefore, $p(i_1) = 0.00673$ is the probability of occurrence of symbol "g", $p(i_2) = 0.21054$ is the probability of occurrence of symbol "l",

Table 2. Illustration of the step by step calculation of TE and TIE. Binning the log-returns of the DJI values is subject to slicing the values interval, limited by -0.082 and 0.105. The limits of log-returns of HSI are -0.135 and 0.134. The probabilities are the relative frequencies of symbols or combination of symbols, while TE and TIE can be calculated from the intermediary values TE_i and TIE_i, which are obtained from the probabilities listed on column t_i.

	t_0	t_1	t_2	t_3
Closing prices of DJI	11357.51	10997.93	11122.65	11253.26
Log-returns of DJI		-0.0321	0.0112	0.0116
Binned log-returns of DJI		$i_1 : g$	$i_2 : l$	$i_3 : m$
Closing prices of HSI	17369.63	17072.82	15846.72	15153.23
Log-returns of HSI		-0.0172	-0.0745	-0.0447
Binned log-returns of HSI		$j_1 : k$	$j_2 : f$	$j_3 : i$
(i_{t+1}, i_t)		$(i_2, i_1) : lg$	$(i_3, i_2) : ml$	$(i_4, i_3) : nm$
(i_t, j_t)		$(i_1, j_1) : gk$	$(i_2, j_2) : lf$	$(i_3, j_3) : mi$
(i_{t+1}, i_t, j_t)		$(i_2, i_1, j_1) : lgk$	$(i_3, i_2, j_2) : mlf$	$(i_4, i_3, j_3) : nmi$
$p(i_t)$		$p(i_1)$	$p(i_2)$	$p(i_3)$
$p(i_{t+1}, i_t)$		$p(i_2, i_1)$	$p(i_3, i_2)$	$p(i_4, i_3)$
$p(i_t, j_t)$		$p(i_1, j_1)$	$p(i_2, j_2)$	$p(i_3, j_3)$
$p(i_{t+1}, i_t, j_t)$		$p(i_2, i_1, j_1)$	$p(i_3, i_2, j_2)$	$p(i_4, i_3, j_3)$
$TE = \sum(TE_t)$		TE_1	TE_2	TE_3
$TIE = \sum(TIE_t)$		TIE_1	TIE_2	TIE_3

etc. The probability $p(i_2, i_1) = 0.00179$ is the probability of the sequence "gl", $p(i_3, i_2) = 0.00942$ is the probability of "lm", etc. The string obtained by binning the log-returns of the HSI stock starts with the symbols "k f i n o m l l l m ...". We obtain the probability of "gk": $p(i_1, j_1) = 0.00224$, the probability of "gk": $p(i_2, j_2) = 0.00224$, etc. Next, $p(i_2, i_1, j_1) = 0.00067$ is the probability of "lgk", $p(i_3, i_2, j_2) = 0.00022$ is the probability of "mlf", etc. For an accurate estimation, a larger number of decimals is preferred.

(c) *Estimate TE and TIE*
We calculate TE_t and TIE_t. For the first step, $TE_1 = 0.000011$ and $TIE_1 = 0.0000022$, etc. Finally, we compute $TE = 47.76$ and $TIE = 17.85$, summing-up the partial results.

The results are summarized in the heatmaps (Fig. 2). The lighter shaded pixels are associated with a higher values of TE and TIE. We visually observe that the two heatmap correlate well. In fact, Pearson correlation coefficient is 0.973, showing a strong correlation.

Figure 3 illustrates the execution time for computing TIE and TI. For time series with more than 1,000 values, the execution time for TIE becomes clearly shorter. For an increasing number of values, the ratio TIE/TE of the executions times decreases.

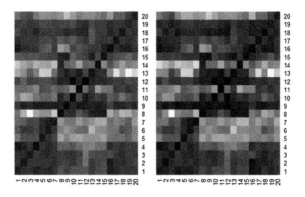

Fig. 2. The two heatmaps are calculated for TE (left) and TIE (right), between all combinations of the 20 stock indexes.

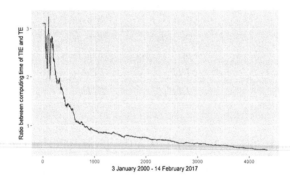

Fig. 3. Execution time. The graph shows the ratio TIE/TE of the executions times, for an increasing number of values. The time is computed for the DJI and HSI stocks ranging between Jan. 3, 2000–Feb. 14, 2017. The relative efficiency of TIE increases for larger time series. For 4357 points, the ratio is 0.49918.

5   Conclusions

According to our preliminary results, the TIE can substitute the TE for detecting cause-effect relationships between time series, with the advantage of a computational complexity reduction. This result is very interesting, since the TE is already a standard concept (Scheiber's paper [17] has at this moment 842 citations.

Even if its use as an information flow measure is debatable (see [10]), the TE can be used as a measure of the reduction in uncertainty about one time series given another. Symmetrically, the TIE may be viewed as a measure of the increase in certainty about one time series given another. It is an open problem if the TIE is an appropriate energy flow measure.

References

1. Barnett, L., Barrett, A.B., Seth, A.K.: Granger causality and transfer entropy are equivalent for Gaussian variables. Phys. Rev. Lett. **103**, 238701 (2009)
2. Borda, M.: Fundamentals in Information Theory and Coding. Springer, Heidelberg (2011). doi:10.1007/978-3-642-20347-3
3. Dimpfl, T., Peter, F.J.: Using transfer entropy to measure information flows between financial markets. SFB 649 Discussion Papers SFB649Dpp. 2012-051, Sonderforschungsbereich 649, Humboldt University, Berlin, Germany, August 2012
4. Gencaga, D., Knuth, K.H., Rossow, W.B.: A recipe for the estimation of information flow in a dynamical system. Entropy **17**(1), 438–470 (2015)
5. Granger, C.W.J.: Investigating causal relations by econometric models and cross-spectral methods. Econometrica **37**(3), 424–438 (1969)
6. Guisan, M.C.: A comparison of causality tests applied to the bilateral relationship between consumption, GDP in the USA. Mexico. Int. J. Appl. Econom. Quant. Stud.: IJAEQS **1**(1, (1/3)), 115–130 (2004)
7. Hlaváčková-Schindler, K.: Causality in time series: its detection and quantification by means of information theory. In: Emmert-Streib, F., Dehmer, M. (eds.) Information Theory and Statistical Learning, pp. 183–207. Springer, Boston (2009). doi:10.1007/978-0-387-84816-7_8
8. Hlaváčková-Schindler, K.: Equivalence of granger causality and transfer entropy: a generalization. Appl. Math. Sci. **5**(73), 3637–3648 (2011)
9. Hlaváčková-Schindler, K., Palu, M., Vejmelka, M., Bhattacharya, J.: Causality detection based on information-theoretic approaches in time series analysis. Phys. Rep. **441**(1), 1–46 (2007)
10. James, R.G., Barnett, N., Crutchfield, J.P.: Information flows? A critique of transfer entropies. Phys. Rev. Lett. **116**(23), 238701 (2016)
11. Kwon, O., Yang, J.-S.: Information flow between stock indices. EPL (Europhys. Lett.) **82**(6), 68003 (2008)
12. Kwon, O., Oh, G.: Asymmetric information flow between market index and individual stocks in several stock markets. EPL (Europhys. Lett.) **97**(2), 28007 (2012)
13. Mao, X., Shang, P.: Transfer entropy between multivariate time series. Commun. Nonlinear Sci. Numer. Simul. **47**, 338–347 (2017)
14. Onicescu, O.: Theorie de l'information energie informationelle. C. R. Acad. Sci. Paris Ser. A–B **263**, 841–842 (1966)
15. Pearl, J.: Causality: Models, Reasoning and Inference, 2nd edn. Cambridge University Press, New York (2009)
16. Sandoval, L.: Structure of a global network of financial companies based on transfer entropy. Entropy **16**(8), 4443–4482 (2014)
17. Schreiber, T.: Measuring information transfer. Phys. Rev. Lett. **85**, 461–464 (2000)
18. van der Lubbe, J.C.A., Boxma, Y., Bockee, D.E.: A generalized class of certainty and information measures. Inf. Sci. **32**(3), 187–215 (1984)
19. Zhu, J., Bellanger, J.-J., Shu, H., Le Bouquin Jeannès, R.: Contribution to transfer entropy estimation via the k-nearest-neighbors approach. Entropy **17**(6), 4173–4201 (2015)

Improving Our Understanding of the Behavior of Bees Through Anomaly Detection Techniques

Fernando Gama[1], Helder M. Arruda[2], Hanna V. Carvalho[3], Paulo de Souza[4], and Gustavo Pessin[2(✉)]

[1] Institute of Exact and Natural Sciences, Federal University of Pará,
Belém, PA, Brazil
fernando.mata@pq.itv.org
[2] Applied Computing Lab, Instituto Tecnológico Vale, Belém, PA, Brazil
{helder.arruda,gustavo.pessin}@itv.org
[3] SENAI Institute of Innovation in Minerals Technologies, Belém, PA, Brazil
hanna.carvalho@pq.itv.org
[4] Data61, CSIRO, Sandy Bay, TAS, Australia
paulo.desouza@data61.csiro.au

Abstract. Bees are one of the most important pollinators since they assist in plant reproduction and ensure seed and fruit production. They are important both for pollination and honey production, which benefits small and large-scale agriculturists. However, in recent years, the bee populations have declined significantly in alarming ways on a global scale. In this scenario, understanding the behavior of bees has become a matter of great concern in an attempt to find the possible causes of this situation. In this study, an anomaly detection algorithm is created for data labeling, as well as to evaluate the classification models of anomalous events in a time series obtained from RFID sensors installed in bee hives.

Keywords: Machine learning · Bees · Anomaly detection · Pollination

1 Introduction

Bees play a very important role in pollinating plant species. Basically, the pollinating process consists of exchanging gametes between vegetable species, which lead to the production of fruit of higher quality and greater abundance. Worker bees are responsible for carrying the pollen of flowers, which remains held between their bristles. More than one hundred thousand flowers can serve a single hive [6]. In economic terms, bees are responsible for crop pollination which is worth over USD 19 billion and earns about USD 385 million worth of honey per year just in the United States. In Australia, the industry makes USD 92 million from bee production [2]. Small to large-scale farmers are interested in breeding these insects. Estimates show that one-third of all food consumed by mankind depends on the activities of pollinators [8,9].

Despite a global growth in the number of domestic beehives, the number of bees has been declining in the United States since the 1940s, and in some European countries since the 1960s [10]. It is believed that there is a set of factors

© Springer International Publishing AG 2017
A. Lintas et al. (Eds.): ICANN 2017, Part II, LNCS 10614, pp. 520–527, 2017.
https://doi.org/10.1007/978-3-319-68612-7_59

responsible for this, such as the emergence of new types of parasites, pesticides, the cultivation of monocultures, electromagnetic waves generated by cell towers, genetically-modified vegetation and the inappropriate management of hives [11].

In an attempt to find a clearer explanation of this situation, several research groups have carried out investigations into bees. For example, the digital beehive project designed by [2], seeks to enable beekeepers to remotely monitor the temperature and levels of humidity in hives, as well as to undertake a weight control of honey bees GPS for the spatial location of beehives and bee counts. The scheme is also able to transmit and interpret data from a set of tools that can assess the health of the colony.

In a context of vulnerability, [4] adopts a approach that seeks to distinguish between real medical conditions and false alarms through detecting sensor anomalies that employ prediction- based methods to compare and detect anomalies. These anomaly detection methods establish the spatio-temporal correlation that exists between the physiological parameters. In a theoretical field, [13] examines the main design principles related to the anomaly detection techniques employed in WSNs. It carries out analysis and makes comparisons of approaches that belong to a similar technical category. In addition, it includes a brief discussion about research areas that offer good prospects in the near future. Anomaly detection is also examined by [3] who carry out a theoretical-practical study that includes an evaluation of 19 unsupervised algorithms for anomaly detection which reveals the strengths and weaknesses of the different approaches. In addition, there is an investigation of questions such as performance, computational effort, the impact of configuration parameters, as well as global and local anomaly detection.

Knowing the behavior of bees is important because it can help producers to have a better understanding of their activities. In a broader context, it is hoped that this work can be beneficial to agriculture, biology and other related fields. Detecting anomalies in a time series will automatically allow beekeepers to take the necessary steps to understand which factors are causing the stress (degree of disturbance) of a beehive. According to [5], an anomaly (*outlier*) is an observation that greatly deviates from other observations. Another definition defines anomalies as being patterns in data that do not conform to a well-defined notion of normal behavior. In addition, [7] defines *outlier* as an observation in a dataset that is inconsistent with other observations.

Thus, the objective of this article is to employ a proximity-based anomaly detection method based on the Local Outlier Factor (LOF) algorithm for data labeling and then to evaluate supervised models for the classification of anomalous events in a time series involving the data on bee activity obtained from RFID sensors. Section 2 will outline the methodology adopted for this work. Section 3 will show the preliminary results based on the different sizes of time windows as well as the best window and the model that obtained the greatest degree of precision. Finally, Sect. 4 concludes the study and makes suggestions for future work.

2   Methodology

2.1   Data Collection

This work forms a part of the Swarm Sensing project set out by [12]. Electronic tags (RFID) were glued on bees to improve our knowledge of their behavior. The data collection is carried out through an instrumental system shown in Fig. 1, and covers a period from 1st–31st August 2015 when 1280 bees were analyzed, 160 in each hive. From the moment a bee passes through the RFID reader, a movement is recorded and altogether, we recorded a total of 127,758 activities. In this experiment, data were condensed as hourly, making a total of 744 records. The level of activity was examined in an attempt to evaluate the bees behavior. This consists of the ratio between the total number of movements in a given period and the number of live bees at that time. If the activity level is 0.0, it means no bee is carrying out any activity at that time. If it is 1.0, it means that there is a single activity per bee at that time. During the experiment there were between 240 and 320 live bees per day.

Fig. 1. Left: (1) *Melipona fasciculata* hive, (2) Intel Edison for RFID controlling and data storage, (3) PVC box for storing electronic items, (4) RFID reading antenna, (5) Plastic tube for bees' passage. Right-top: The 8 hives overview. Right-bottom: Bee with RFID tag attached to the chest.

After the selection of the variable for the activity level, we conducted research in the database. It was noticed that although the temporal period had many noises, there were few anomalies. In view of this, we decided to create a disturbance in the dataset from the original database to force more anomalies to appear (which was the main purpose of the investigation). Figure 2 illustrates a part of a time window generated within a specified range that shows the data level of bee activities within the time frame.

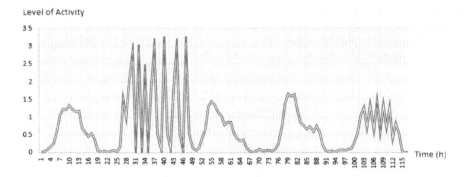

Fig. 2. The figure illustrates one section of the time series. The average number of activities carried out by each active bee in the system in a time window of 3 h.

An unsupervised detection algorithm was employed to validate the data labeling which was called Local Outlier Factor (LOF) [1]. Basically, the algorithm shows as output a score that indicates the outlier value. Scores with values close to 1 indicate that the point belongs to the cluster and is in a region of homogeneous density. In contrast, values of density distant from 1, suggest that the point is in a sparse region compared with its neighbors. Therefore, it can be regarded as an outlier. In this work, the values of density above 1.5 are treated as outliers; otherwise the instance is not an anomaly.

In making the density calculations of the algorithm, it is reasonable to choose a good interval for k, that ranges from a minimum and maximum value defined by the user. It is not recommended to use a much lower value for k in case there are undesirable statistical fluctuations [1]. Table 1 shows the summarized test cases for each window. The intervals were tested with regard to the limits on the maximum size of neighbors relative to the time window (window size minus 1). For example, the 12 h window displays the first test case with a minimum value of k equal to 1 and maximum of k equal to 11.

We applied the LOF algorithm that generated a score for each of the 744 instances of the dataset to each test set in the table. As this involved intervals of k, we obtained the density value for each instance in function of each k. A heuristic was adopted to select the maximum value of the interval. For example, in the case of window k1:k5, we obtained 6 values of density (score) for that instance and the highest value among these 6 is selected. After labeling the data for all the instances, the points classified by the algorithm were compared with the points classified by non-specialists, by following the same procedure for all the remaining test cases. Finally, i the best k interval was chosen for each time window in accordance with the highest percentage of correct points suggested by the algorithm compared with that suggested by non-specialists. After this last task had been carried out, we obtained the datasets for each time window as a basis for evaluating the models.

Table 1. A summary of test cases for the determination of the k value (:) follows a sequence, for example, k1:k5 is equivalent k1, k2, k3, k4, k5. The intervals for setting the value of k are determined for different sizes of the time windows. The cells highlighted in yellow represent the ranges chosen for each window.

Test cases			
3h	6h	12h	24h
k1:k2	k1:k5	k1:k11	k1:k23
	k2:k4	k2:k10	k5:k10
	k2:k5	k3:k9	k10:k20
	k3:k5	k4:k8	k11:k20
	k4:k5	k5:10	k12:k20
		k6:k10	...
			k21:23
			...

2.2 Modeling

Multilayer Perceptron (Bagging), Random Forest (RF) and Support Vector Machines (SVM) are models of machine-learning models that were tested in each time window and the performances of each model were evaluated. Minimal changes were made in the parameters of the models in accordance with the Table 2. Moreover, we perform 10 runs for each model in all of the time windows.

Table 2. Parameter setting of the models. These parameters were applied to all the time windows studied.

RandomForest	Value	MLP (Bagging)	Value	SVMachine	Value
NumberIterations	100				
NumberAttributes	0	BatchSize	100	C	1
NumberSlots	1	HiddenLayers	1	Degree	3
		LearningRate	0.3	Gamma	0
		Momentum	0.2	Coef0	0
		Epochs	500	Tolerance	0.001
		ValidationSet	20	Episolon	0.1

The models were evaluated by means of the Precision measurement that corresponds to the ratio of the number of true positives (TP) (that is, the number of items that were correctly classified as belonging to the positive class) and the total number of elements labeled as belonging to the positive class (including not only true positives but also false positives (FPs)). Since we were faced with a binary classification problem, we decided to evaluate the models on the basis of the results obtained by the ROC curve. The ROC analysis is conducted as an alternative to supplement the evaluation of the model. It is based on the rate of true positives and the rate of false positives. The leave-one-out cross-validation method was employed for partitioning the dataset. This method includes a specific case of another cross-validation method: k-fold. However, leave-one-out uses k as the total that is equal to the total number of samples N (744 instances). We believe that this method allows an in-depth investigation of the model and it was found that the computational cost was not as significant as in our dataset.

3   Results

The results were obtained by running 10 executions for each of the assessment measurements (precision and the ROC curve) and calculating the mean and standard deviation from Fig. 3. The graph shows a greater variation in the results of the models for the time windows of 3 h and 24 h. In the first window, the RF obtained the best result (about 60%) followed by the MLP (Bagging) that reached about 54% and SVM where the result was below expectations (about 29%). In the following windows (6 h, 12 h) the models behaved in a similar way with results that were very close. RF obtain the highest result (about 59%) the 6 h window and MLP (Bagging) to the 12 h window (about 68%). However, the models were very well suited to the 24 h temporal window where they achieved the best results. The MLP (Bagging) obtained 96.66% followed by the SVM with 83.06% and RF with 81%.

We also calculated the mean and standard deviation of the models from Fig. 4. It was found that in terms of accuracy, in the first time window (3 h), SVM and MLP had the same result (50.4%), whereas the RF, in relation to

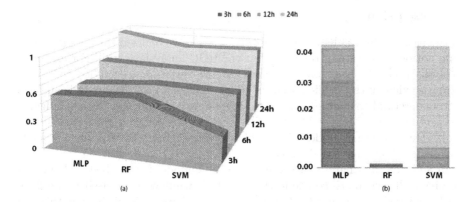

Fig. 3. (a) 3D area plot with axis (levelPrecision, model, timeWindow). The growth of MLP (Bagging) was achieved when the time window was extended. Although the progress of the SVM obtained a poor result of 28.62% in the first window (3 h), when we increased the time window, the SVM achieved the second best result of 83.09%, which was only lower than the MLP (Bagging) that had the best result of 96.62%. (b) Standard Deviation Sampling in each of the models that involved the 10 executions. In addition, the RF obtained the lowest variability in all the windows. In contrast, the SVM model had the widest variation in the larger window (24 h).

these, obtained 64.33%. With regard to the second window, in the three models, from the third time window (12 h), where MLP (Bagging), RF and SVM had the following degrees of precision 73.72%, 65.33%, 75.17%, respectively. However, the last time window (24 h) had the best results and a similar behavior and was able to achieve the same level of precision (98.4%).

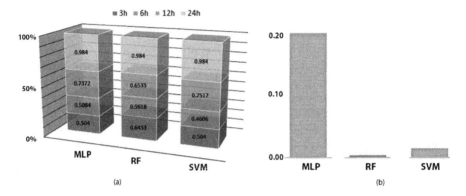

Fig. 4. (a) Degree of precision in the 3 models studied. The actual increase in degrees of accuracy occurred after the third window (12 h). The highest degree of accuracy is given in Window 24, where the three models obtained similar results. (b) The sample standard deviation was higher in the second window (6 h) whereas in the other windows variation was minimal.

3.1 Discussion

On the basis of the results achieved from our work, we realized the importance of using not only the rate of precision but the ROC analysis as well. For example, when the precision level was increased for the three models, it led to a very optimistic view of the studied scenario. The addition of a ROC analysis enabled us to understand that although the three models had achieved the same degree of precision, the bagging of MLPs is the most suitable, since it achieved a better result than the other models. The difference was about 13.56% for the SVM model and 15.62% for the RF algorithm.

In addition, an analysis of the most suitable model for the bees behavior in the hives, allowed us to conclude that the best window to be used is the 24 h, which achieved better results than the other windows. It is likely that this can be explained by the behavior of the bees which work in a pattern that is related to sunrise and sunset.

4   Conclusion and Suggestion for Future Work

In this study, three classification models were evaluated: a bagging of Multilayer Perceptron (MLP), Support Vector Machines (SVM) and the Random Forest

(RF), in distinct time windows. It was found that MLP achieved the best result and that 24 h was the best time window and the one which conformed best to all the evaluated methods. It should also be underlined that an anomaly detection algorithm can be used to label the dataset gathered from RFID sensors. This extra kind of labeling was important to ratify the labeling by a non-specialist.

In future work, we believe that environmental variables, such as air temperature and barometric pressure can assist in designing a robust model to help obtain a better understanding of bee behavior. Although the initial results of this work have been promising, we believe that the model needs to be strengthened by testing other methods which could be combined with our approach, as well as the tuning of the parameters of the studied models.

References

1. Breunig, M.M., Kriegel, H.P., Ng, R.T., Sander, J.: LOF: identifying density-based local outliers. In: ACM Sigmod Record, vol. 29, pp. 93–104. ACM (2000)
2. Foth, M., Blackler, A., Cunningham, P.: A digital beehive could warn beekeepers when their hives are under attack (2016). http://theconversation.com/a-digital-beehive-could-warn-beekeepers-when-their-hives-are-under-attack-54375
3. Goldstein, M., Uchida, S.: A comparative evaluation of unsupervised anomaly detection algorithms for multivariate data. PLOS ONE **11**(4), 1–31 (2016). doi:10.1371/journal.pone.0152173
4. Haque, S., Rahman, M., Aziz, S.M.: Sensor anomaly detection in wireless sensor networks for healthcare. Sensors **15**(4), 8764–8786 (2015)
5. Hawkins, D.: Identification of Outliers. Chapman and Hall, London (1980)
6. Henein, M., Langworthy, G., Erskine, J.: Vanishing of the bees (2009). http://www.vanishingbees.com
7. Johnson, J.: Applied Multivariate Statistical Analysis. Prentice Hall, Upper Saddle River (1992)
8. Klein, A.M., Vaissire, B.E., Cane, J.H., Steffan-Dewenter, I., Cunningham, S.A., Kremen, C.: Importance of pollinators in changing landscapes for world crops. Proc. R. Soc. London B: Biol. Sci. **274**(1608), 303–313 (2007)
9. Kluser, S., Peduzzi, P.: Global pollinator decline: a literature review (2007)
10. Potts, S.G., Biesmeijer, J.C., Kremen, C., Neumann, P., Schweiger, O., Kunin, W.E.: Global pollinator declines: trends, impacts and drivers. Trends Ecol. Evol. **25**(6), 345–353 (2010)
11. Ratnieks, F.L.W., Carreck, N.: Clarity on honey bee collapse? Science **327**(5962), 152–153 (2010)
12. Souza, P.A., Williams, R.N., Quarrell R.S., Budi, S., Susanto, F., Vincent, B., Allen, G.R.: Agent-based modelling of honey bee forager flight behaviour for swarm sensing applications. Environmental Modelling and Software (2017, under review)
13. Xie, M., Han, S., Tian, B., Parvin, S.: Anomaly detection in wireless sensor networks: a survey. J. Netw. Comput. Appl. **34**(4), 1302–1325 (2011)

Applying Bidirectional Long Short-Term Memories (BLSTM) to Performance Data in Air Traffic Management for System Identification

Stefan Reitmann[1(✉)] and Karl Nachtigall[2]

[1] Department of Air Transportation, Institute of Flight Guidance, German Aerospace Center (DLR), Cologne, Germany
stefan.reitmann@dlr.de
[2] Chair of Traffic Flow Sciences, Institute of Logistics and Aviation, TU Dresden, Dresden, Germany
karl.nachtigall@tu-dresden.de
http://www.dlr.de/fl/

Abstract. The performance analysis of complex systems like Air Traffic Management (ATM) is a challenging task. To overcome statistical complexities through analyzing non-linear time series we approach the problem with machine learning methods. Therefore we understand ATM (and its identified system model) as a system of coupled and interdependent sub-systems working in time-continuous processes, measurable through time-discrete time series.

In this paper we discuss the requirements of a system identification process and the attached statistical analysis of ATM emitted performance data based on discussed benchmarking frameworks. The superior aim is to show, that neural networks are able to handle complex non-linear time-series, to learn how to rebuild them considering multidimensional inputs and to store knowledge about the observation data set's behavior.

Keywords: Key performance indicator · Neural networks · LSTM · RNN · Time series analysis

1 Introduction

1.1 Ease of Use

Understanding and controlling the inner workings of a complex systems like ATM at performance level regularly requires to understand the relationships and interactions between all observed data points. These introduce interdependencies which basically states that no single system operates without affecting other, which might also affect the relationships of the time series at performance level. Because of these bidirectional relationships local decisions or performance measurements are often problematic. To achieve a global multidimensional (>1 point of measurement) optimum or quantification of a system the local system's

© Springer International Publishing AG 2017
A. Lintas et al. (Eds.): ICANN 2017, Part II, LNCS 10614, pp. 528–536, 2017.
https://doi.org/10.1007/978-3-319-68612-7_60

emitted performance data's influence on other parts of the whole needs to be accounted. In the light of an increasing interest in research on performance based airport management (PBAM) and today's importance of Key Performance Indicators (KPI) [1] in decision support systems (DSS) [2] this paper focuses on the role of multivariate non-linear time series analysis at performance level.

This necessity is known in general and simplified in [3], implemented as a trade-off-operation to balance performance in regard to different target values within the system. The process takes place after determining if there are conflicting objectives that need to be balanced and involves several types of multicriteria decision-making techniques (MCDM). To avoid such a downstream adaptation of interdependencies via trade-offs the here described adaptive model is executed online within the analysis. A similar approach is introduced in [4], where so called "core-KPIs" are identified, which have an assumed relation to a set of exogenous KPIs. Nevertheless, this connection is not proven mathematically.

1.2 Mathematical Background

The problem of analyzing KPI interdependencies in ATM is describable as inverse problem by processing the causal factors of time series patterns from a set of $n \in \mathbb{N}$ observations $\{y(t)\}$ for a given set of inputs $\{x(t)\}$ with $t \in \mathbb{N}, 0 \leq t \leq n$ [3]. Our statistical approach via neural networks represents a self-trained admittance function $G(z)$ for further analysis of the problem as time-discrete control system, which contains dependencies between input factors (KPIs). Training and creating $G(z)$ enables the ability to make predictions and use the knowledge as an time-discrete controller. The requirements catalog in Table 1 shows up the necessity of using neural networks for the given task. Also other mathematical

Table 1. Requirements catalog

Category	Type	Short description
General	Adaptive character	No certain system structure given
General	Characteristic type	Event based and periodic measurements
General	Complexity	Irregular, nonlinear time series handling
Measurement	Time-delay	Time-parallel and -delayed measurements
Measurement	Pattern recognition	Regularities identification
Measurement	Own dynamics	Separation of processes
System knowledge	Transitivity	System reducing to principle components
System knowledge	Interdependencies	Bidirectional relationships
System knowledge	Level-of-Detail (LoD)	Micro and macro views

methods are able to handle complex non-linear data, but they mostly lack certain features to get preferred to LSTM (e.g. Gaussian Processes and Multivariate adaptive regression splines (MARS)). The most important advantage of LSTM is their ability to handle long-term dependencies between several time series, which is very important for the recognition of interdepencies between them.

2   Machine Learning Approach

2.1   Long Short-Term Memory (LSTM)

The LSTM structure is implemented through the following functions:

$$i(t) = \sigma(W_{xi}x(t) + W_{hi}h(t-1) + W_{ci}c(t-1) + b_i) \tag{1}$$

$$f(t) = \sigma(W_{xf}x(t) + W_{hf}h(t-1) + W_{cf}c(t-1) + b_f) \tag{2}$$

$$c(t) = f(t) * c(t-1) + i(t) * tanh(W_{xc}x(t) + W_{hc}h(t-1) + b_c) \tag{3}$$

$$o(t) = \sigma(W_{xo}x(t) + W_{ho}h(t-1) + W_{co}c(t-1) + b_o) \tag{4}$$

$$h(t) = o(t) * tanh(c(t)) \tag{5}$$

σ and $tanh$ represent the specific, element-wise applied activation functions of the LSTM. i, f, o and c denote the mentioned inner-cell gates, respectively the input gate, forget gate, output gate, and cell activation vectors. c need to be equal to the hidden vector h. The W terms denote weight matrices [4,5].

2.2   Bidirectional LSTM (BLSTM)

As we need to consider dependencies/correlations in both forward and backward direction the conventional LSTM needs to get adjusted. Bidirectional LSTM (BLSTM) are introduced, which are able to process data in both directions with two separate hidden layers. Both hidden layers are connected to the same output layer. A BLSTM computes the forward hidden sequence h and the backwards hidden sequence h separately, the output layer y by iterating the backward layer from $t = T$ to 1 and the forward layer from $t = 1$ to T. To shorten the representation a BRNN is represented in (6) to (8), where H could be implemented by the composite function (1) to (5) as done in [8,9].

$$\overrightarrow{h}(t) = H(W_{x\overrightarrow{h}}x(t) + W_{\overrightarrow{hh}}\overrightarrow{h}(t-1) + b_{\overrightarrow{h}}) \tag{6}$$

$$\overleftarrow{h}(t) = H(W_{x\overleftarrow{h}}x(t) + W_{\overleftarrow{hh}}\overleftarrow{h}(t-1) + b_{\overleftarrow{h}}) \tag{7}$$

$$y(t) = W_{\overrightarrow{h}y}\overrightarrow{h}(t) + W_{\overleftarrow{h}y}\overleftarrow{h}(t) + b_y \tag{8}$$

3   Application

3.1   Experimental Setup

We implemented the given BLSTM structure in Python 3.5 using the deep learning library KERAS with theano back-end. Training and testing were done on GPU (NVIDIA Geforce 980 TI) using CUDA.

The used data for our simulation derived from the DLR-tool RUCSim (Runway Capacity Simulation) to recreate an ATM-scenario. The used flight schedules are acquired from EC DDR2 data of Heathrow Airport (LHR) for period March 2013. Only arrivals at Runway 27R are considered. In Table 2 a segment of the RUCSim output header is depicted showing up the important PIs for the application: flow, delay and demand.

Table 2. RUCSim output header

Flight ID	...	Average delay[s]	...	Flow	Delay	Demand

The BLSTM are characterized by the number of hidden layers ($n_{hiddenlayer}$, not KERAS layers), number of samples propagated through the network (batchsize), the number of trained epochs (n_{epoch}) and the fuzz factor (η).

Some of these parameters were compressed in pre-defined optimizers in KERAS. For the following experiments the optimizers Adagrad ($\eta = 0.01$, $\epsilon = 1e{-}08$) and Adam ($\eta = 0.001$, $\epsilon = 1e{-}08$) were used.

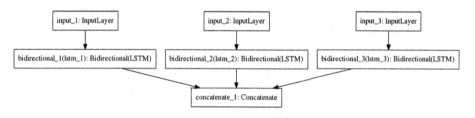

Fig. 1. Model conception in KERAS.

Figure 1 shows up the basic structure of the implemented network in KERAS. Three input layers (Flow, Demand, Delay) connected to single BLSTM layers were merged through an concatenate layer. The given structure is interpreted as consistent BLSTM network with a multiple input - single output setting by KERAS.

Furthermore we added a dropout layer to the merged BLSTM block with a fraction rate of 0.2, which helps prevent overfitting.

3.2 Data Preparation

The mentioned neural networks use, like majority of practical machine learning approaches, supervised learning. For a given set of input variables $\{x(t)\}$ and an output variable $\{y(t)\}$ one uses an algorithm to learn the mapping function from the input to the output. The goal is to approximate the real underlying mapping so well that one can predict output variables $y \in \{y(t)\}$ by just having input variables $x \in \{x(t)\}$.

Therefore and adjustment of the described datasets to a *sliding window representation for multivariate time series* is needed. When phrased as a regression problem the input variables are $t - 2, t - 1, t$ and the output variable is $t + 1$ (Table 3).

Table 3. Adjusted multi-to-one dataset

X1	X2	X3	Y
?	?	Demand (1)	Flow (1)
Demand (1)	Flow (1)	Demand (2)	Flow (2)
Demand (2)	Flow (2)	Demand (3)	Flow (3)
Demand (3)	Flow (3)	?	?

To train the supervised model, one may need to remove the first and last rows in order to provide enough data for prediction.

As we work with bidirectional relationships these sliding window techniques need to be applied in both directions. Forwards (prediction of $t + 1$) with $\{t - 2, t - 1, t\}$, backwards with $\{t + 2, t + 3, t + 4\}$. Training the model with historical data enables the availability of prospective data.

Table 4. Bidirectional time series influences

Time	Observation1	Observation2	Observation3
1	*Demand (1)*	*Flow (1)*	*Delay (1)*
2	*Demand (2)*	**Flow (2)**	*Delay (2)*
3	*Demand (3)*	Flow (3)	*Delay (3)*

Depicting Table 4 the influences among the whole viewed dataset on the prediction of one certain data point is shown. In the given example the predicted value is Flow (2), which depends on the its own past ($t < 2$, here Flow (1)) and on the other observed KPIs Demand and Delay, here both future and past states as well as the current value at $t = 2$, but not Flow (3), the future state and just one further step of prediction.

3.3   Simulation Results

The original datasets (solid line) were normalized ($\mu = 0$ and $\sigma = 1$) and divided into BLSTM training sets (2/3, ongoing learning process) and test sets (1/3, independent prediction) with a total amount of 19324 data rows. For both scenarios A: $n_{epoch} = 20$ and B: $n_{epoch} = 2000$ the best network results are shown in a segment of training data, a segment of test data and an overview about the network outputs $Flow_{BLSTM}$ with a calculate Root-Mean-Square Error (RMSE) without weighting over time.

Table 5. Overview optimizer-related results scenario A and B

Optimizer	n_{layer}	Window$_{width}$	A: RMSE	A: t_{Calc}[s]	B: RMSE	B: t_{Calc}[min]
Adagrad	4	5	22.68	23	14.48	05:38
Adagrad	4	50	34.96	22	33.05	05:56
Adagrad	40	5	31.66	25	7.36	07:02
Adagrad	40	50	33.51	25	34.21	07:29
Adam	4	5	29.34	26	5.18	07:32
Adam	4	50	34.39	21	41.37	07:19
Adam	40	5	31.95	23	4.94	07:42
Adam	40	50	32.70	27	39.13	08:39

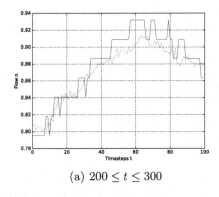
(a) $200 \leq t \leq 300$

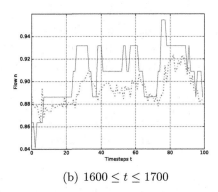
(b) $1600 \leq t \leq 1700$

Fig. 2. A: Flow$_{training}$ (t, Demand, Delay) and Flow$_{test}$ (t, Demand, Delay), $n_{epoch} = 20$

As shown in Table 5 optimizer Adagrad delivers the best results with a 4 hidden layer inlay and a window size of 5. No improvements could be made with an enlargement of the network structure, still less with an enlargement of the window size. This might be reasoned in the simple network structure in connection with a higher learning rate by optimizer Adagrad. The calculation

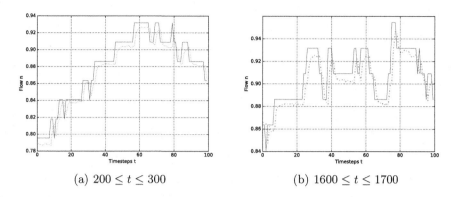

(a) $200 \leq t \leq 300$ (b) $1600 \leq t \leq 1700$

Fig. 3. B: Flow$_{training}$ (t, Demand, Delay) and Flow$_{test}$ (t, Demand, Delay), $n_{epoch} =$ 2000

Table 6. Overall flow time series results for A and B

Dataset	Time	A: Flow$_{BLSTM}$	Flow$_{Observation}$	B: Flow$_{BLSTM}$
Train	0	0.4442	0.273	0.295
Train	100	0.879	0.909	0.882
Train	200	0.804	0.796	0.789
Train	300	0.879	0.886	0.882
...	...	...	...	
Train	1100	0.889	0.864	0.850
Train	1200	0.929	0.909	0.905
Test	0	0.663	0.568	0.572
Test	100	0.856	0.886	0.874
Test	200	0.837	0.841	0.834
Test	300	0.892	0.886	0.903
Test	400	0.904	0.932	0.925
Test	500	0.799	0.886	0.858
Test	600	0.844	0.909	0.873

time is lower than half a minute for all examples because of the low number n_{epoch}. Unlike scenario A optimizer Adam delivers in B the best results with a more complex network structure covering 40 hidden layers and a window size of 5. A RMSE of 4.94 towards the best value 22.68 for $n_{epoch} = 20$ shows the model parametrization improvements through a more complex learning process. Nevertheless the network shows for both Adam and Adagrad inadequate results with an increased window size of 50. The network might struggle from the high number of inputs at a lower η.

Both Fig. 2(a) and (b) show the network not matching the flow curve, but recognizing its basic structure. A noisy tracing of the flow path over time, recognizing peaks (like in Fig. 2 (b) at $t = 30$), is already realizable with a simple structure and a low number n_{epoch}.

More than the scenario A the trained model of B is able to rebuild an stepwise change of the flow considering the side effects demand and delay. As depicted in Fig. 3 the independent prediction basing on the model's own outputs can basically trace the curve. A higher number of hidden layers and more n_{epoch} might affect an improved reaching of the peaks as the tested curve is always below the observation (Table 6).

4 Conclusion

We could show that BLSTM are able to rebuild non-linear time series and make meaningful and valid predictions. In the current step of the research is focused on understanding the BLSTM as a time-discrete control system of time-continuous processes like in ATM.

Solid State Representation. As prior representations of BLSTM are made in the first canonical form it is not possible to observe them for further studies. A transformation of the given formulas (1)–(8) to a Solid State Representation (SSR) needs to be done. As BLSTM are enrolled RNN structures the structure of the SSR describes an iterative control system formalization over different levels of time. Therefore knowledge about the initial state is essential.

Stability. In further steps we want to divide the derived SSR into a linear part and the non-linearity of the time-discrete system. For the evaluation of a control system an analysis of its stability is essential, because such a system is only useful if it is able to process interference and to reach its initial state. For both linear and non-linear part a Lyapunov stability analysis can be applied.

Dimension. Next to stability other properties of the BLSTM might be interesting for understanding and value the network's behavior. For the given application cases of bifurcation might be dangerous. A detailed search for triggering parameter sets might be useful to avoid oscillation in learning and prediction behavior of the BLSTM. Capacity should be quantified through dimension theory approaches describing sufficient sets of coordinates for describing the system relevant outputs.

References

1. Parmenter, D.: Key Performance Indicators - Developing, Implementing and Using Winning KPIs, p. 3. Wiley, Hoboken (2007)
2. Reitmann, S., Gillissen, A., Schultz, M.: Performance benchmarking in interdependent ATM systems. In: International Conference on Research in Air Transportation, Philadelphia, USA (2016)

3. ICAO: Manual on Global Performance of the Air Navigation System, Doc 9883, 1st edn. (2009)
4. Airports Council International: Guide to Airport Performance Measures, pp. 6–16 (2012)
5. Reitmann, S., Nachtigall, K.: Pattern recognition and prediction of multivariate time series with long short-term memory (LSTM). In: International Science & Progress Conference, St. Petersburg, Russia (2016)
6. Hochreiter, S., Schmidhuber, J.: Long short term-memory. Neural Comput. **9**(8), 1735–1780 (1997)
7. Hochreiter, S., Schmidhuber, J.: Learning to forget: continual prediction with LSTM. Neural Comput. **12**, 2451–2471 (2000)
8. Graves, A., Jaitly, N., Mohamed, A.: Hybrid speech recognition with deep bidirectional LSTM. In: Automatic Speech Recognition and Understanding (ASRU) (2013)
9. Graves, A., Schmidhuber, J.: Framewise phoneme classification with bidirectional LSTM and other neural network architecures. Neural Netw. **18**(5), 602–610 (2005)

Image Processing and Medical Applications

A Novel Image Tag Completion Method Based on Convolutional Neural Transformation

Yanyan Geng[1]([✉]), Guohui Zhang[2], Weizhi Li[3], Yi Gu[4], Ru-Ze Liang[5],
Gaoyuan Liang[6], Jingbin Wang[7], Yanbin Wu[8], Nitin Patil[9],
and Jing-Yan Wang[10]

[1] Provincial Key Laboratory for Computer Information Processing Technology,
Soochow University, Suzhou 215006, China
yanyangeng@outlook.com
[2] Huawei Technologies Co., Ltd., Shanghai, China
[3] Suning Commerce R&D Center USA, Inc., Palo Alto, CA 94304, USA
[4] Analytics and Research, Travelers, Hartford, CT 06183, USA
[5] King Abdullah University of Science and Technology, Thuwal, Saudi Arabia
[6] Jiangsu University of Technology, Jiangsu 213001, China
[7] Information Technology Service Center, Intermediate People's Court of Linyi City,
Linyi, China
jingbinwang1@outlook.com
[8] Hebei University of Economics and Business, Shijiazhuang 050061, China
[9] Savitribai Phule Pune University, Pune 411007, Maharashtra, India
[10] Jiangsu Key Laboratory of Big Data Analysis Technology/B-DAT, Collaborative
Innovation Center of Atmospheric Environment and Equipment Technology,
Nanjing University of Information Science and Technology, Nanjing, China

Abstract. In the problems of image retrieval and annotation, complete textual tag lists of images play critical roles. However, in real-world applications, the image tags are usually incomplete, thus it is important to learn the complete tags for images. In this paper, we study the problem of image tag complete and proposed a novel method for this problem based on a popular image representation method, convolutional neural network (CNN). The method estimates the complete tags from the convolutional filtering outputs of images based on a linear predictor. The CNN parameters, linear predictor, and the complete tags are learned jointly by our method. We build a minimization problem to encourage the consistency between the complete tags and the available incomplete tags, reduce the estimation error, and reduce the model complexity. An iterative algorithm is developed to solve the minimization problem. Experiments over benchmark image data sets show its effectiveness.

Keywords: Convolutional neural filtering · Image representation · Tag completion · Image retrieval · Image annotation

J.-Y. Wang—The study was supported by the open research program of Jiangsu Key Laboratory of Big Data Analysis Technology, Nanjing University of Information Science and Technology, China (Grant No. KBDat1602).

A. Lintas et al. (Eds.): ICANN 2017, Part II, LNCS 10614, pp. 539–546, 2017.
https://doi.org/10.1007/978-3-319-68612-7_61

1 Introduction

Image tagging problem is defined as assigning a set of textual tags to an targeted set of images, and it has becoming more and more important for both image retrieval and annotation applications [8]. In the ideal case, the tags of an image should be accurate and complete. However, in the real-world applications, the tags of images are usually incomplete, and it is necessary to complete the tags of images. The problem of completing the tags of images are called image tag completion [36]. To solve this problem, many approaches have been proposed [7,15,18,19,33,34], but the performance of these works are not satisfying yet. Meanwhile, convolutional neural network (CNN) has been shown to be an effective tool to represent images [9,20,21,35]. However, surprisingly, CNN has not been applied to the problem of image tag completion.

In our paper, we propose a novel image tag completion method based on the convolutional representation of the images and the linear prediction of the tag assignment vectors. We first use a CNN model to represent the images to the convolutional vectors, and then apply a linear predictive model over the convolutional representations to obtain the complete tag assignment vectors of the images. The possible effect of using convolutional transformation lies on the potential of finding effective visual features for the task of tag prediction. To learn the parameters of the CNN and the linear predictive model, we impose the learned tag assignment vectors to be consistent to the available elements of the incomplete tag vectors, minimize the prediction errors of the linear predicative model over the image set. We also minimize the distance between tag assignment vectors images which have large convolutional similarities. Finally, we apply the sparsity penalty to the tag assignment vectors. To solve argued minimization problem, we use gradient descent method. The experimental results over some benchmark data sets show that the proposed convolutional representation-based tag completion method outperforms the state-of-the-art tag completion methods.

2 Proposed Method

We suppose we have a set of images, denoted as $\mathcal{I} = \{I_1, \cdots, I_n\}$, and a set of candidate tags of these images, $\mathcal{T} = \{T_1, \cdots, T_m\}$. To denote the assigning relation between the images and the tags, we define a matrix of assignment, $T = [t_{ji}] \in \{1,0\}^{m \times n}$, and its (j,i)-th entity t_{ji} is set to 1 if T_j is assigned to I_i, and 0 otherwise. T is the output of the model, and in our learning process, it has been relaxed to realtime value matrix $T \in \mathbb{R}^{m \times n}$. We have a existing assignment matrix $\widehat{T} = [\widehat{t}_{ji}] \in \{1,0\}^{m \times n}$, and its entities are of the same meaning as T, but it is incomplete. We further define a binary matrix $\Phi = [\phi_{ji}] \in \{1,0\}^{m \times n}$, where its (j,i)-th entity is defined to indicate if $\widehat{t}_{ji}$ is missing, $\phi_{ji} = 0, if\ \widehat{t}_{ji}\ is\ missing,\ and\ 1, otherwise.$ The problem of image tagging is transformed to the learning of a complete assignment matrix T from $\mathcal{I}, \widehat{T}$, and Φ.

To complete the tags of an image, I, we propose to learn its convolutional representation and the complete tag assignment vector jointly. Given the image

I we use a sliding window to split the image to n_I over-lapping small image patches, $I \rightarrow [\mathbf{x}_1, \cdots, \mathbf{x}_{n_I}]$, where $\mathbf{x}_i$ is the visual feature vector of the i-th image patch. The convolutional representation of I is given as $\mathbf{y} = \max(G) = [y_1, \cdots, y_r]^\top$, $where$ $G = g\left(W^\top X\right)$, where $W = [\mathbf{w}_1, \cdots, \mathbf{w}_r]$ is the matrix of r filters, $g(\cdot)$ is a element-wise non-linear transformation function, and $\max(\cdot)$ gives the row-wise maximum elements, and y_k is the maximum entity of the k-th row of G, $y_k = \max(G_{k,:})$. To learn the tag assignment vector $\mathbf{t}$ of an image from its convolutional representation vector $\mathbf{y}$, we use a linear function to predict $\mathbf{t}$ from $\mathbf{y}$, $\mathbf{t} \leftarrow f(\mathbf{y}) = U\mathbf{y} - \mathbf{b}$, where $U \in \mathbb{R}$ and $\mathbf{b}$ are the parameters of the predictive model for the assignment vector. To the learn the CNN parameter W, linear predictor parameter U and $\mathbf{b}$, and the complete tag matrix T, we consider propose the following minimization problem,

$$\min_{T,U,\mathbf{b},W} \left\{ O(T,U,\mathbf{b},W) = \sum_{i=1}^{n} Tr\left((\mathbf{t}_i - \widehat{\mathbf{t}}_i)^\top diag(\boldsymbol{\phi}_i)(\mathbf{t}_i - \widehat{\mathbf{t}}_i)\right) \right.$$

$$\left. + \lambda_1 \sum_{i=1}^{n} \|\mathbf{t}_i - (U\mathbf{y}_i - \mathbf{b})\|_F^2 + \lambda_2 \sum_{i,i'=1}^{n} S_{ii'} \|\mathbf{t}_i - \mathbf{t}_{i'}\|_F^2 + \lambda_3 \sum_{i=1}^{n} \|\mathbf{t}_i\|_1 \right\}. \tag{1}$$

The objective function terms are introduced as follows.

- The first term of the objective is to encourage the consistency between the available tags of $\widehat{\mathbf{t}}_i$ and the estimated tag vector $\mathbf{t}_i$ of an image I_i. It is defined as the squared Frobenius norm distance between t_{ji} and $\widehat{t}_{ji}$ weighted by the ϕ_{ji} is minimized with regard to t_{ji}. This term is popular in other tag completion works.
- The second term is the squared Frobenius norm distance to measure the prediction error of the linear model of linear predictor. This loss term is novel and it has not been used in other works.
- The third term is the visual similarity regularization term. For a images I_i, we seek its k-nearest neighbor set to present its visually similar images, denoted as $\mathcal{N}_i$. To measure the similarity between I_i and a neighboring image $I_{i'} \in \mathcal{N}_i$ is measured by the normalized Gaussian kernel of the Frobenius norm distance between their convolutional representation vectors, $S_{ii'} = \exp\left(-\gamma\|\mathbf{y}_i - \mathbf{y}_{i'}\|_F^2\right) / \sum_{i'' \in \mathcal{N}_i} \exp\left(-\gamma\|\mathbf{y}_i - \mathbf{y}_{i''}\|_F^2\right)$, if $I_{i'} \in \mathcal{N}_i$, and 0 otherwise. If $S_{ii'}$ is large, the I_i and $I_{i'}$ are visually similar, we expect their complete tag assignment vectors to be close to each other, and minimize the squared Frobenius norm distance between $\mathbf{t}_i$ and $\mathbf{t}_{i'}$ weighted by $S_{ii'}$. This term is not used by other tag completion works and it is novel in our work.
- The last term is a sparsity term of the learned tag vectors, and it is also imposed by other works to seek the sparsity.

λ_1, λ_2, and λ_3 are the weights of different regularization terms of the objective.

To solve the problem in (1), we use the gradient descent method and the alternate optimization strategy. In iterative algorithm, we first fix the variables to calculate the similarity measure $S_{ii'}$, and then fix the similarity measures to calculate the sub-/gradient regarding to different variables. The sub-/gradient functions with regard to the variables are calculated as

$$
\nabla_{\mathbf{t}_i} O(\mathbf{t}_i) = 2 diag(\phi_i)(\mathbf{t}_i - \widehat{\mathbf{t}}_i) + 2\lambda_1 (\mathbf{t}_i - (U\mathbf{y}_i - \mathbf{b})) + 2\lambda_2 \sum_{i'=1}^{n} S_{ii'} (\mathbf{t}_i - \mathbf{t}_{i'})
$$

$$
+ 2\lambda_3 \sum_{i=1}^{n} diag\left(\frac{1}{|t_{1i}|}, \cdots, \frac{1}{|t_{mi}|}\right) \mathbf{t}_i,
$$

$$
\nabla_U O(U) = -2\lambda_1 \sum_{i=1}^{n} (\mathbf{t}_i - U\mathbf{y}_i + \mathbf{b})\, \mathbf{y}_i^\top, \ \nabla_\mathbf{b} O(\mathbf{b}) = 2\lambda_1 \sum_{i=1}^{n} (\mathbf{t}_i - U\mathbf{y}_i + \mathbf{b}),
$$

$$
\nabla_{\mathbf{w}_k} O(\mathbf{w}_k) = \sum_{i=1}^{n} \left[\nabla_{\mathbf{y}_i} O(\mathbf{y}_i)\right]_k \nabla_{\mathbf{w}_k} y_i(\mathbf{w}_k), \nabla_{\mathbf{y}_i} O(\mathbf{y}_i) = -2\lambda_1 U^\top (\mathbf{t}_i - (U\mathbf{y}_i - \mathbf{b})),
$$

$$
\nabla_{\mathbf{w}_k} y_i(\mathbf{w}_k) = \nabla_{\mathbf{w}_k} g(\mathbf{w}_k^\top \mathbf{x}_{ij^*})\mathbf{x}_{ij^*}, \ where \ \mathbf{x}_{ij^*} = \arg\max_{\mathbf{x}_i \in X_i} \mathbf{w}^\top \mathbf{x}_{ij}.
$$

$$(2)$$

For a variable, $x \in \{T, U, \mathbf{b}, W\}$, the updating rule is $x \leftarrow x - \eta \nabla O_x(x)$.

3   Experiments

In the experiments, we use three benchmark data sets of image, including Corel data set, Labelme data set, Flickr data set. The Corel data set has 4,993 images tagged by 260 unique tags, Labelme data set is composed of 2,900 of 495 tags, while Flickr data set has 1 million images of over 1,000 tags. We perform two groups of experiments, one group of image retrieval, and another group of image annotation.

Image Annotation. Given an image, and a set of candidate tags, the problem of image annotation is to predict its true complete list of tags relevant to the image. This is an special case of image tag completion. We use the four-fold cross-validation protocol to split the training/test subsets. We rank the tags for each image according to the tag scores output of our model, and the top-ranked tags are returned as the tags of the candidate image. The performance measures of Precision@5 is used to evaluate the results. We compare our method to the existing stat-of-the-art methods, including the methods proposed by Lin et al. [19], Wu et al. [33], Feng et al. [7], Lin et al. [18], and Li et al. [15]. The results are reported in Table 1. From the results reported in Table 1, the proposed method outperforms the compared methods over all the three data sets on the four performance measures. This is an strong evidence of the advantage of the CNN model for the tag completion and annotation of images. This is not surprising because we use an effective convolutional reforestation method to extract features from the images, and the CNN parameters are tuned especially for the tag completion problem.

Image Retrieval. Then we evaluate the proposed method over the problem of tag-based image retrieval [16]. This problem uses tags as queries to retrieve the

Table 1. Results of image annotation measured by Precision@5.

Data sets	Corel	Labelme	Flickr
Proposed	0.47	0.30	0.28
Lin et al. [19]	0.35	0.22	0.18
Wu et al. [33]	0.37	0.23	0.19
Feng et al. [7]	0.40	0.24	0.20
Lin et al. [18]	0.43	0.23	0.23
Li et al. [15]	0.44	0.25	0.24

Table 2. Results of image retrieval experiments measured by Pos@Top.

Methods	Corel	Labelme	Flickr
Proposed	0.73	0.67	0.66
Lin et al. [19]	0.64	0.57	0.54
Wu et al. [33]	0.65	0.58	0.55
Feng et al. [7]	0.65	0.59	0.57
Lin et al. [18]	0.61	0.59	0.58
Li et al. [15]	0.68	0.62	0.60

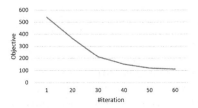

Fig. 1. Convergence curve over Corel data set.

images from the database of images. In each data set of images, we remove some tags of the images to set up the image tag completion problem, and then apply the image tag completion algorithm to complete the missing tags. We measure the retrieval performance by the positive at top (Pos@Top). The usage of this performance measure is motivated by the works of Liang et al. [16]. The works of Liang et al. [12,16] show that the Pos@Top is a robust and parameter-free performance measure, which is suitable for most database retrieval problems. Following the works of Liang et al. [12,16], we adapt this performance measure to evaluate the results of the image retrieval problem in our experiments. The retrieval results of different methods are reported in Table 2. We can observe from this table that the proposed method outperforms the other methods over all the three data sets.

Convergence of the Alternating Gradient Descent. We also plot the curve of the objective values with regard to increasing iterations for the alternating gradient descent algorithm. The curve of experiments over the Corel data set is shown in Fig. 1. According to Fig. 1, the algorithm converge after 40 iterations.

4   Conclusion and Future Works

In this paper, we proposed a novel image tag completion method. We use the CNN model to represent the image, and then predict the complete image tags from the CNN representations. The complete tag assignment score vectors are also regularized by the visual similarities calculated from the CNN representations. We develop an iterative algorithm to learn the parameters of the CNN model, the linear predictive model, and the complete tags. The experiments of the problems of image annotation and image retrieval based on image tag completion over three benchmark data sets show the advantage of the proposed method. In the future, we will extend our work of CNN model to other machine learning problems beside image tag completion, such as computer vision [17,23,31,37–39], portfolio choices [25–29], big data [5,6], and biomedical engineering [1–4,10,11,13,14,22,24,30,32].

References

1. Cai, W.: Class D power amplifier for medical application. Inf. Eng. Int. J. (IEIJ) **4**(2), 9–15 (2016)
2. Cai, W.: Low power SI based power amplifier for healthcare application. Int. J. Pharm. Pharm. Sci. **8**(9), 307–309 (2016)
3. Cai, W., Huang, L., Wen, W.: 2.4 GHZ class AB power amplifier for healthcare application. Int. J. Biomed. Eng. Sci. (IJBES) (2016). arXiv preprint arXiv:1605.02455
4. Cai, W., Zhou, X., Cui, X.: Optimization of a GPU implementation of multi-dimensional RF pulse design algorithm. In: 2011 5th International Conference on Bioinformatics and Biomedical Engineering, (iCBBE), pp. 1–4. IEEE (2011)
5. Cheng, L., Kotoulas, S., Ward, T.E., Theodoropoulos, G.: Robust and efficient large-large table outer joins on distributed infrastructures. In: Silva, F., Dutra, I., Santos Costa, V. (eds.) Euro-Par 2014. LNCS, vol. 8632, pp. 258–269. Springer, Cham (2014). doi:10.1007/978-3-319-09873-9_22
6. Cheng, L., Kotoulas, S., Ward, T.E., Theodoropoulos, G.: Robust and skew-resistant parallel joins in shared-nothing systems. In: Proceedings of the 23rd ACM International Conference on Conference on Information and Knowledge Management, pp. 1399–1408. ACM (2014)
7. Feng, Z., Feng, S., Jin, R., Jain, A.K.: Image tag completion by noisy matrix recovery. In: Fleet, D., Pajdla, T., Schiele, B., Tuytelaars, T. (eds.) ECCV 2014. LNCS, vol. 8695, pp. 424–438. Springer, Cham (2014). doi:10.1007/978-3-319-10584-0_28
8. Fu, J., Wu, Y., Mei, T., Wang, J., Lu, H., Rui, Y.: Relaxing from vocabulary: robust weakly-supervised deep learning for vocabulary-free image tagging. In: Proceedings of the IEEE International Conference on Computer Vision, vol. 11–18-December-2015, pp. 1985–1993. doi:10.1109/ICCV.2015.230 (2016)

9. Geng, Y., Liang, R.Z., Li, W., Wang, J., Liang, G., Xu, C., Wang, J.Y.: Learning convolutional neural network to maximize pos@top performance measure. In: ESANN (2016)
10. Hobbs, K.H., Zhang, P., Shi, B., Smith, C.D., Liu, J.: Quad-mesh based radial distance biomarkers for alzheimer's disease. In: 2016 IEEE 13th International Symposium on Biomedical Imaging (ISBI), pp. 19–23. IEEE (2016)
11. King, D.R., Li, W., Squiers, J.J., Mohan, R., Sellke, E., Mo, W., Zhang, X., Fan, W., DiMaio, J.M., Thatcher, J.E.: Surgical wound debridement sequentially characterized in a porcine burn model with multispectral imaging. Burns 41(7), 1478–1487 (2015)
12. Li, Q., Zhou, X., Gu, A., Li, Z., Liang, R.Z.: Nuclear norm regularized convolutional max pos@top machine. Neural Comput. Appl. 1–10 (2016)
13. Li, W., Mo, W., Zhang, X., Lu, Y., Squiers, J.J., Sellke, E.W., Fan, W., DiMaio, J.M., Thatcher, J.E.: Burn injury diagnostic imaging device's accuracy improved by outlier detection and removal. In: SPIE Defense+ Security, p. 947206. International Society for Optics and Photonics (2015)
14. Li, W., Mo, W., Zhang, X., Squiers, J.J., Lu, Y., Sellke, E.W., Fan, W., DiMaio, J.M., Thatcher, J.E.: Outlier detection and removal improves accuracy of machine learning approach to multispectral burn diagnostic imaging. J. Biomed. Optics 20(12), 121305 (2015)
15. Li, X., Zhang, Y.J., Shen, B., Liu, B.D.: Low-rank image tag completion with dual reconstruction structure preserved. Neurocomputing 173, 425–433 (2016)
16. Liang, R.Z., Shi, L., Wang, H., Meng, J., Wang, J.J.Y., Sun, Q., Gu, Y.: Optimizing top precision performance measure of content-based image retrieval by learning similarity function. In: 2016 23st International Conference on Pattern Recognition (ICPR). IEEE (2016)
17. Liang, R.Z., Xie, W., Li, W., Wang, H., Wang, J.J.Y., Taylor, L.: A novel transfer learning method based on common space mapping and weighted domain matching. In: 2016 IEEE 28th International Conference on Tools with Artificial Intelligence (ICTAI), pp. 299–303. IEEE (2016)
18. Lin, Z., Ding, G., Hu, M., Lin, Y., Sam Ge, S.: Image tag completion via dual-view linear sparse reconstructions. Comput. Vis. Image Underst. 124, 42–60 (2014)
19. Lin, Z., Ding, G., Hu, M., Wang, J., Ye, X.: Image tag completion via image-specific and tag-specific linear sparse reconstructions. In: Proceedings of the IEEE Computer Society Conference on Computer Vision and Pattern Recognition, pp. 1618–1625 (2013)
20. Lopes, A., de Aguiar, E., De Souza, A., Oliveira-Santos, T.: Facial expression recognition with convolutional neural networks: coping with few data and the training sample order. Pattern Recogn. 61, 610–628 (2017)
21. Ma, J., Wu, F., Zhu, J., Xu, D., Kong, D.: A pre-trained convolutional neural network based method for thyroid nodule diagnosis. Ultrasonics 73, 221–230 (2017)
22. Mao, H., Liu, H., Shi, P.: Neighbor-constrained active contour without edges. In: Mathematical Methods in Biomedical Image Analysis, pp. 1–7 (2008)
23. Mao, H., Liu, H., Shi, P.: A convex neighbor-constrained active contour model for image segmentation, pp. 793–796 (2010)
24. Mo, W., Mohan, R., Li, W., Zhang, X., Sellke, E.W., Fan, W., DiMaio, J.M., Thatcher, J.E.: The importance of illumination in a non-contact photoplethysmography imaging system for burn wound assessment. In: SPIE BiOS, p. 93030M. International Society for Optics and Photonics (2015)

25. Shen, W., Wang, J.: Transaction costs-aware portfolio optimization via fast löwner-john ellipsoid approximation. In: Proceedings of the Twenty-Ninth AAAI Conference on Artificial Intelligence, pp. 1854–1860. AAAI Press (2015)

26. Shen, W., Wang, J.: Portfolio blending via Thompson sampling. In: Proceedings of the Twenty-Fifth International Joint Conference on Artificial Intelligence, pp. 1983–1989. AAAI Press (2016)

27. Shen, W., Wang, J.: Portfolio selection via subset resampling. In: Proceedings of the Thirty-First AAAI Conference on Artificial Intelligence. AAAI Press (2017)

28. Shen, W., Wang, J., Jiang, Y.G., Zha, H.: Portfolio choices with orthogonal bandit learning. In: Proceedings of the Twenty-Fourth International Conference on Artificial Intelligence, pp. 974–980. AAAI Press (2015)

29. Shen, W., Wang, J., Ma, S.: Doubly regularized portfolio with risk minimization. In: Proceedings of the Twenty-Eighth AAAI Conference on Artificial Intelligence, pp. 1286–1292. AAAI Press (2014)

30. Shi, B., Chen, Y., Zhang, P., Smith, C.D., Liu, J., Initiative, A.D.N., et al.: Nonlinear feature transformation and deep fusion for alzheimer's disease staging analysis. Pattern Recogn. **63**, 487–498 (2017)

31. Tan, M., Hu, Z., Wang, B., Zhao, J., Wang, Y.: Robust object recognition via weakly supervised metric and template learning. Neurocomputing **181**, 96–107 (2016)

32. Thatcher, J.E., Li, W., Rodriguez-Vaqueiro, Y., Squiers, J.J., Mo, W., Lu, Y., Plant, K.D., Sellke, E., King, D.R., Fan, W., et al.: Multispectral and photoplethysmography optical imaging techniques identify important tissue characteristics in an animal model of tangential burn excision. J. Burn Care Res. **37**(1), 38–52 (2016)

33. Wu, L., Jin, R., Jain, A.: Tag completion for image retrieval. IEEE Trans. Pattern Anal. Mach. Intell. **35**(3), 716–727 (2013)

34. Xia, Z., Feng, X., Peng, J., Wu, J., Fan, J.: A regularized optimization framework for tag completion and image retrieval. Neurocomputing **147**(1), 500–508 (2015)

35. Yang, W., Chen, Y., Liu, Y., Zhong, L., Qin, G., Lu, Z., Feng, Q., Chen, W.: Cascade of multi-scale convolutional neural networks for bone suppression of chest radiographs in gradient domain. Med. Image Anal. **35**, 421–433 (2017)

36. Yang, X., Yang, F.: Completing tags by local learning: a novel image tag completion method based on neighborhood tag vector predictor. Neural Comput. Appl. **27**(8), 2407–2416 (2016)

37. Zhang, P., Kong, X.: Detecting image tampering using feature fusion. In: International Conference on Availability, Reliability and Security, ARES 2009, pp. 335–340. IEEE (2009)

38. Zhang, P., Shi, B., Smith, C.D., Liu, J.: Nonlinear metric learning for semi-supervised learning via coherent point drifting. In: 2016 15th IEEE International Conference on Machine Learning and Applications (ICMLA), pp. 314–319. IEEE (2016)

39. Zhao, J.Y., Tang, M., Tong, R.F.: Connectivity-based segmentation for GPU-accelerated mesh decompression. J. Comput. Sci. Technol. **27**(6), 1110–1118 (2012)

Reducing Unknown Unknowns with Guidance in Image Caption

Mengjun Ni[✉], Jing Yang[✉], Xin Lin[✉], and Liang He[✉]

Institute of Computer Applications, East China Normal University, No. 3663
Zhongshanbei Road, Putuo District, Shanghai, China
{mengjunni,jyang,xlin,lhe9191}@ica.stc.sh.cn

Abstract. Deep recurrent models applied in Image Caption, which link up computer vision and natural language processing, have achieved excellent results enabling automatically generating natural sentences describing an image. However, the mismatch of sample distribution between training data and the open world may leads to tons of hiding-in-dark Unknown Unknowns (UUs). And such errors may greatly harm the correctness of generated captions. In this paper, we present a framework targeting on UUs reduction and model optimization based on recurrently training with small amounts of external data detected under assistance of crowd commonsense. We demonstrate and analyze our method with currently state-of-the-art image-to-text model. Aiming at reducing the number of UUs in generated captions, we obtain over 12% of UUs reduction and reinforcement of model cognition on these scenes.

Keywords: Image Caption · Recurrent neural network · Crowdsourcing · Commonsense

1 Introduction

Computer Vision (CV) applications with high accuracy such as Image Caption can be widely used in Image Retrieval, Visual Disorder Assistance and so on. With involvement of deep recurrent models, many technologies performing extremely well compared to those in traditional ways, are hopeful to be available in wild. However, there is still a huge gap between the performance of machine and human in many scenarios of CV, especially those are rare in training dataset. This kind of problem can be categorized as Unknown Unknowns (UUs), a kind of mistakes that may arise when training data used for model is not representative of instances that appear at test time [1] and greatly decline the accuracy of pattern recognition applications.

To demonstrate UUs in Image Caption, consider a task where the goal is to generate natural description for a random image. Assume that training data includes none male with long hair. Given a new image shown in Fig. 1 with a person wearing both long hair and bushy beard, with standard description "A man with his laptop sitting on the couch", a well trained image-to-text model,

© Springer International Publishing AG 2017
A. Lintas et al. (Eds.): ICANN 2017, Part II, LNCS 10614, pp. 547–555, 2017.
https://doi.org/10.1007/978-3-319-68612-7_62

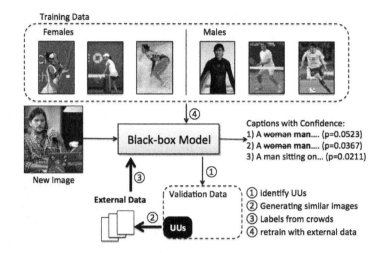

Fig. 1. The flow in horizontal direction shows an example of UUs, while vertically, a toy framework process eliminating UUs is displayed in numerical order.

even with deep recurrent, is very likely to describe the person as woman. Indicators, like BLEU-4, METEOR and CIDEr [2,3], only measure the similarity and consensus [4] between translated sentences and standard answers, may give the description a high score by mistake for fitting all words except "woman". These UUs, hard to eliminate for the lack of commonsense that males can wear long hair, greatly harm the correctness of generated captions and call for reduction. In Image Caption, most of the UUs are hard to eliminate due to ubiquity and unpredictability. Not clearly shown in traditional indicators like BLEU-4, UUs can do much harm to the accuracy of CV applications in dark, and thus become one of the serious obstacles to carry out CV applications in the open world.

We address the problem of eliminating UUs in Image Caption deployed in the open world and formulate it as an optimization problem from outside of the model with small amounts of external data carrying hints from crowds on different scenarios to reinforce the model cognition from scene to scene. The formulation assumes no knowledge of inner structure of the initial model is needed.

In this paper, we present a framework, with which optimization of a deep recurrent model can be seen as crowds polishing a black box in a few separated procedures with commonsense they are born with. In a few rounds of training cycles, tons of UUs hiding in dark can be eliminated by system designers or even end users with no understanding of model inner structures.

To address this task, we take NIC [2] as our black-box model with MSCOCO dataset for training and validation. A four-step approach is proposed, which first partitions the validation data where images with similar captions are grouped together and then choose scenarios from these partitions with UUs we are interested in. The second step is to pre-screen candidate training data and validate candidate images with rapid-crowdsourcing [5] for ultimate retraining and polishing of initial model. For standard descriptions, we collect true labels relying on the combination of templates and crowd labor for simplified crowdsourcing task and minimum cost. The final step is to add those images with true labels for model retraining and cognition enhancing.

Main Contributions:

- Propose and illustrate that the framework can be used to optimize deep recurrent models with small amounts of external data from outside without inner understanding. To the best of our knowledge, this is the first work dealing with reduction of UUs with crowd commonsense knowledge as hints in deep recurrent models.
- Demonstrate the effectiveness of our framework with experiments on the state-of-the-art NIC model and achieve 12% to 26% UUs eliminated on chosen scenes respectively.

2   Related Work

Unknown Unknowns. The challenge of capturing Unknown Unknowns, which always hide in dark and are hard to detect, has become a critical issue, since the day utility of AI technologies came into open world seems nearer [6]. The problem of identifying UUs experienced the simplification from depending totally on mankind for error search [7], to relying on machine-generated partitions with features and confidence data to lighten the labor of oracle [1]. Still the problem of how to make good use of these labeled data in UUs reduction on model deployed in wild remains unsolved.

Commonsense in Image Caption. Commonsense is the kind of knowledge we human beings take for granted, but hard for machines to acquire, represent and apply [8,9]. In image caption tasks, we define the problems, such as detecting a flying frisbee as football and being unable to tell the number of people in an image, impacting the correctness of generated captions greatly and calling for reduction as UUs due to lack of commonsense and work on elimination of those errors.

Current State-of-the-Art Models. Although recent deep recurrent models have a mainstream trend of using LSTMs [10,11] and RNNs [12], claiming to perform better than traditional models in the field of Image Caption, UUs remain covering the "eyes" of model from seeing truth behind camouflages. For instance, yellow vehicle does not always mean school bus, but probably a private car judging from its volume. These false perceptions are common in deep recurrent models like NIC [2], for that traditional evaluation indicators aim at the fluency of the generated sentence, and the correlation of captions with images, but not much attention paid to components obviously inconsistent with the facts. Human beings, unlike machine, rely on commonsense to cognise the open world, with which current models need urgently to narrow the gap with human performance.

In this paper, we present a framework relying on hints given by crowd during the optimization of model in a way papa and mama teaching their own babies knowledge. In the process of cognition reinforcement, initial model relies on external knowledge from crowd to strength their understanding from scene to scene, at the same time, reduce the number of UUs produced in captions.

3   Problem Definition

Conventional image caption tasks can be abstracted as translating images to texts. Indicators such as BLEU-4 reflects the quality of generated captions compared to standard answers. Avoiding common mistakes, however, is not comprehensively considered with these indicators. In generated captions, there are still a great number of errors that are easy for people to prevent but difficult for machines to find. UUs such as detecting a young boy as woman or old as young are not rare. Reducing these mistakes may positively impact caption representations for given images.

In this paper, we take NIC as our original black-box model M, which is a deep recurrent model with complex inner structures, taking image data point x as input and sentences $R = \{r_1, r_2, ..., r_n\}$ generated with scores $S = \{s_1, s_2, ...s_n\}$ in order of confidence as output where $s_i \in (0, 1)$. In the training process of M, a set of N images $X = \{x_1, x_2, ..., x_N\}$ with standard captions $C = \{c_1, c_2, ..., c_N\}$ are given as training data. The validation set V, as given to check the model performance, contains standard caption set G. Our goal is to dispel UUs in captions of M on targeted scenes with a small amount of external dataset $D = \{d_1, d_2, ..., d_m\}$ labeled by crowds, $m << $N. This process can be circulated along with the discovery of UUs and optimize M from scene to scene, with UUs eliminated step by step.

4   Proposed Method

In this section, we present a framework in four steps to address the problem of reducing UUs, which occurs due to mismatch between distribution of training data and the open world, with assistances of commonsense from crowds as hints.

Identifying Unknown Unknowns. The first step is to identify the UUs from the validation set V. With none feature of clear meaning due to complex network paths, we take key words extracted from standard captions G as classification conditions. To simplify the task and concentrate our attention on the problem of reducing UUs found in captions and optimization of M, we simply divide V with apparent conditions. For instance, we separate images with people appearing from those with none, and divide those with three and more as "a group of people". After scanning these rough partitions, the problem of "gender confusion" emerges containing tons of UUs to be eliminated. We choose four typical scenes, with most problems of mistaking girls as boys and boys as girls, as subjects of study for further investigation.

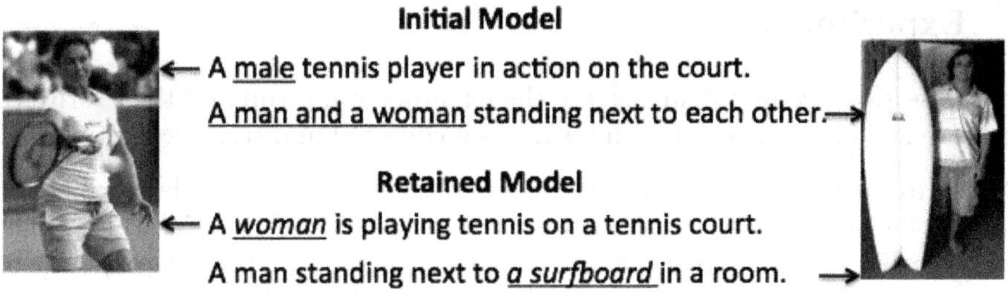

Initial Model

← A <u>male</u> tennis player in action on the court.

A <u>man and a woman</u> standing next to each other.→

Retained Model

← A <u>*woman*</u> is playing tennis on a tennis court.

A man standing next to *a surfboard* in a room. →

Fig. 2. Comparison between initial generated captions and the ones with assistance of crowd commonsense.

Generating Similar Images. Having identified target scenes with UUs, we then retrieve the images satisfying key words that appear in captions of chosen scenes. The candidate images for training data may contain many unrelated scenes. After being tested on M, these candidate images with none related component can be removed from the dataset. Still, the candidate set contains irrelevant scenes and calls for assistance from crowds. Considering the amount of human labour called for within the process, we manage to use rapid crowdsourcing [5], with which one can easily remove the unrelated candidate images within a short period of time and less labour cost. Left images that survive three rounds of selection with similar scene are kept for later usage.

Labels from Crowds. In order to get true labels for captions, we design crowdsourcing tasks with templates of captions to lighten the workload of crowd workers. In the tasks we release, crowd workers need only fill in the blanks with main components of the images they see on the screen, relying on human commonsense. For instance, a sentence with subject missing may calls for worker to fill in words such as "woman" and "young boy". In case the template does not match up with the image, workers may choose to report the unrelated image, or rewrite the sentence for the image strongly correlated. Each image has five templates with different expressions, thus needs five true labels. Since we solve separate scenes one by one, images in each round of UUs reduction share the same templates with different main components. We rely on templates to simplify the tasks and make it easier for workers to carry on for a longer period before they lose interest. Also, much simpler tasks come with lower costs and less supervision from crowd.

Reinforcement of Model. Chosen images with captions generated with the combination of templates and crowd commonsense are then incorporated into the training set. With the injection of a certain amount of data, we can compensate for the problem of uneven distribution on training set. (Fig. 2 shows an example) Experiments are focused on both the quantity of the injected data and the effectiveness of our framework in both single and mixed scenes.

5   Experiments

In this section, we first demonstrate the experimental setup and then verify the effectiveness of our method with result data collected and statistically obtained.

Experimental Preparations. We run our experiment on a node of supercomputing cluster with Tesla K80 GPU, 2 cores, 64-bit Red Hat Enterprise Linux Server release 6.7. For experimental validation, we firstly repeat the experiments shown in [2] on MSCOCO dataset and achieve similar evaluation results on NIC model (Table 1 shows the evaluation results with varying iteration times, in which MM stands for million times). The repeating experiment takes over two weeks to train and fine tune the model with 2 million iterations on a single Tesla K80, in the case of CPU ten times slower. Thus, we attempt to compress the experimental cycle and try training model with fewer iterations. After a series of attempts, we finally chose 0.2MM(200,000 iterations) version with no fine tune as our baseline which converges to 2.0 on loss function.

Table 1. Selection of the number of iterations.

Iterations	BLEU-4	METEOR	CIDEr
NIC-2MM	32.1	25.7	99.8
2MM	32.0	25.7	95.9
1MM	29.5	24.5	87.8
0.2MM	27.9	23.4	81.4

Dataset. We choose MSCOCO dataset which is frequently used in Image Caption. The diversity of image themes adapt to our experiment assumptions of complex scenes with variable components and distribution of features which may lead to appearance of UUs all over the dataset.

Evaluating Model Performance. In this section, we evaluate the performance of our learning pattern for UUs reduction on both separate and mixed scenes. As for the single scenes, we test our model on three different scenarios for "gender confusion" UUs reduction. We assume that there is only one UU in each image. In order to save time and computing resources, we compare the performance of our model with the original model NIC within 0.2MM iterations.

As to the problem of "gender confusion", we compare the model performance on original training data and the ones with external added ones. Due to space limitations, we only display the result of tennis scenario to represent other single scenes. Data in Table 2 shows the number of UUs reduced with different number of extra images, from 50 to 300. The model achieve best effect with 100 external images, which can reduce 21 UUs from 89 wrongly captioned validation images. With the increase of external data after it reaches 150, the improvement of model begin to decline due to the data bias. Take tennis scene as an example, the model

Table 2. Number of fixed captions in tennis scene with "gender confusion" UUs.

	Original	50	100	150	200	250	300
Male	/	6	5	12	8	5	2
Female	/	3	16	8	7	9	13
Total	/	9	21	20	15	14	15
Impro-Ratio	/	10.11%	23.6%	22.47%	16.85%	15.73%	16.85%

may caption each image as "woman" and cause the problem of overfitting if we add too many images labeled with "woman".

In this paper, we concentrate on validating the effectiveness of our framework. The problem of correlation between the number of external data m and the origin distribution of training data is left for further studies. However, we make it clear that the order of magnitude of external data is negligible compared to the one of training set ($m << N$). Within the example of tennis scene, we only choose 300 images for extension of training set which has over 800,000 images.

As to the problem of mixed scenes, we train the model with different permutations and combinations among tennis, surfing, football scenarios respectively. As is shown in Table 3, we both consider the evaluation indicators of the original model and evaluate the ability of our framework in eliminating UUs. Compared with the captions from original NIC model on three main indicators [2], as shown in the first column, external data from single source of different scenes achieves over 12% of elimination on UUs with the indicators basically unchanged. Under the condition of two or more scenes combined, the model gains over 13% of UUs reduction. Also, mixing different scenarios together may promote CIDEr and BLEU-4 over the whole validation set to a certain extent. Last column of Table 3 shows that, with over 26% of UUs eliminated, our method can still maintain, even promote, the performance of the model on original validation indicators in mixed scenarios. And this promotion among mixed scenes is a great inspiration to our future work, since the pattern of our framework is based on the assumption of reducing UUs constantly found within the open world.

Table 3. Comparison on reduction of UUs in separate and mixed scenes.

	Origin	Tennis	Surf	Football	tenSur	tenFoo	surFoo	tenSurFoo
Modified	/	15	14	23	28	38	27	65
Improv-Ratio	/	16.85%	12.07%	58.97%	13.66%	29.69%	17.42%	26.64%
BLEU-4	27.9	27.9	28.1	27.7	28.1	27.7	27.9	**28.2**
METEOR	23.5	23.4	23.5	23.6	23.5	23.7	23.4	**23.7**
CIDEr	81.4	80.7	81.1	82.0	81.1	82.6	81.9	**83.0**

6   Conclusions

In this paper, we present a framework for UUs reduction and performance improvements for deep recurrent models. The approach assumes that no knowledge of model inner structures is needed, which can be seen as a black box deployed in wild. The process of polishing mainly relies on human commonsense as hints for external data labeling and promote the model's cognition on targeted scenes with only a small amount of additional data. On both separate and mixed scenarios, over 12% UUs are eliminated with cognition ability improved on corresponding scenes and original evaluation indicators promoted in mixed scenarios.

Problem of determining optimal value for m needs further studies, which relates to the distribution of training and external data. Also in this paper, simultaneous occurrence of multi UUs is not concerned and may emerge in use. Above all, our framework is not smart enough due to notable amount of supervision which is difficult to eliminate. Fortunately, the discovery and elimination of UUs with our framework may help system designers and end users, to improve the model performance without even understanding model inner structures, which conforms to the trend of AI solutions being used in the open world. We hope our current job, though naive, on discovering new ways pushing AI application into use while facing unpredictable new circumstances in open world will stimulate more relevant researches.

Acknowledgement. This research is funded by the National Key Technology Support Program (No. 2015BAH01F02), the National Nature Science Foundation of China (No. 61602179) and the Natural Science Foundation of Shanghai (No. 17ZR1444900).

References

1. Lakkaraju, H., Kamar, E., Caruana, R., et al.: Identifying unknown unknowns in the open world: representations and policies for guided exploration. In: AAAI 2017, pp. 2124–2132 (2017)
2. Vinyals, O., Toshev, A., Bengio, S., et al.: Show and tell: lessons learned from the 2015 MSCOCO image captioning challenge. IEEE Trans. Pattern Anal. Mach. Intell. **39**(4), 652–663 (2016)
3. Devlin, J., Gupta, S., Girshick, R., et al.: Exploring nearest neighbor approaches for image captioning. arXiv preprint arXiv:1505.04467 (2015)
4. Vedantam, R., Lawrence Zitnick, C., Parikh, D.: CIDEr: consensus-based image description evaluation. In: Proceedings of the IEEE Conference on Computer Vision and Pattern Recognition, pp. 4566–4575 (2015)
5. Krishna, R.A., Hata, K., Chen, S., et al.: Embracing error to enable rapid crowdsourcing. In: CHI Conference on Human Factors in Computing Systems, pp. 3167–3179. ACM (2016)
6. Horvitz, E.: Artificial intelligence in the open world. Presidential Address. AAAI (2008). http://bit.ly/2gCN7t9
7. Attenberg, J., Ipeirotis, P., Provost, F.: Beat the machine: challenging humans to find a predictive model's unknown unknowns. J. Data Inf. Qual. **6**(1), 1–17 (2015)

8. Davis, E., Marcus, G.: Commonsense reasoning and commonsense knowledge in artificial intelligence. Commun. ACM **58**(9), 92–103 (2015)
9. Cambria, E., Olsher, D., Rajagopal, D.: SenticNet 3: a common and common-sense knowledge base for cognition-driven sentiment analysis. In: AAAI, pp. 1515–1521 (2014)
10. Donahue, J., Hendricks, L.A., Guadarrama, S., et al.: Long-term recurrent convolutional networks for visual recognition and description. AB initto calculation of the structures and properties of molecules, pp. 85–91. Elsevier (2014)
11. Fang, H., Platt, J.C., Zitnick, C.L., et al.: From captions to visual concepts and back. In: Computer Vision and Pattern Recognition, pp. 1473–1482. IEEE (2015)
12. Karpathy, A., Li, F.F.: Deep visual-semantic alignments for generating image descriptions. In: Computer Vision and Pattern Recognition, pp. 3128–3137. IEEE (2015)

A Novel Method for Ship Detection and Classification on Remote Sensing Images

Ying Liu[1(✉)], Hongyuan Cui[1], and Guoqing Li[2]

[1] University of Chinese Academy of Sciences, Beijing 100049, China
yingliu@ucas.ac.cn, hongyuancui@163.com
[2] Institute of Remote Sensing and Digital Earth, Chinese Academy of Sciences,
Beijing 100094, China
ligq@radi.ac.cn

Abstract. Ship detection and classification is critical for national maritime security and national defense. As massive optical remote sensing images of high resolution are available, ship detection and classification on optical remote sensing images is becoming a promising technique, and has attracted great attention on applications including maritime security and traffic control. Some image processing-based methods have been proposed to detect ships in optical remote sensing images, but most of them face difficulty in terms of accuracy, performance and complexity. Therefore, in this paper, we propose a novel ship detection and classification approach which utilizes deep convolutional neural network (CNN) as the ship classifier. Next, in order to overcome the divergence problem of deep CNN-based classifier, a residual network-based ship classifier is proposed. In order to deepen the network without excessive growth of network complexity, inception layers are used. In addition, batch normalization is used in each convolution layer to accelerate the convergence. The performance of our proposed ship detection and classification approach is evaluated on a set of ship images downloaded from Google Earth, each in 256×64 pixels at the resolution 0.5 m. Ninety-five percent classification accuracy is achieved. A CUDA-enabled residual network is implemented in model training which achieved $75\times$ speedup on 1 Nvidia Titan X GPU.

Keywords: Ship detection · Ship classification · Deep convolutional neural network · Residual learning

1 Introduction

Ship detection and classification in remote sensing images is of vital importance for maritime security and other applications, e.g., traffic surveillance, protection against illegal fisheries and sea pollution monitoring. With the increasing volume of satellite image data, automatic ship detection and classification from remote sensing images is a crucial application for both military and civilian fields. However, most of the conventional methods face difficulty in accuracy, performance and complexity.

In recent years, deep learning, or deep neural network has shown great promise in many practical applications. Since the early work of ship detection and classification, it

© Springer International Publishing AG 2017
A. Lintas et al. (Eds.): ICANN 2017, Part II, LNCS 10614, pp. 556–564, 2017.
https://doi.org/10.1007/978-3-319-68612-7_63

has been known that the variability and the richness of image data make it almost impossible to build an accurate detection and classification system entirely by hand.

In this paper, ship candidates are coarsely extracted by image segmentation methods first, then actual ships are detected from all the ship candidates and finally classified into 10 different ship classes by deep learning. The proposed method consists of preprocessing (ship candidates extraction), ship detection and ship classification model training. The specific contributions of this paper are as follows: (1) ship candidates were extracted by conducting image enhancement, target-background segmentation and ship locating based on shape criteria; (2) a CNN model was implemented for ship detection and 99% accuracy was achieved; (3) using the proposed residual learning network, 95% classification accuracy was achieved; (4) inception module and batch normalization were proposed to use to optimize the training efficiency. The flow diagram of the proposed ship detection and classification approach is shown in Fig. 1.

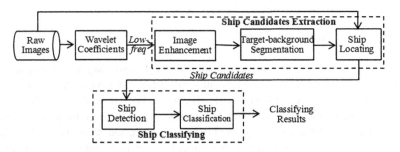

Fig. 1. Flow diagram of the proposed ship detection and classification approach.

The reminder of this paper is organized as follows. Section 2 overviews the related work about this research; Sect. 3 describes the processing of ship candidates extraction; Sect. 4 explains our proposed CNN model for ship detection; Sect. 5 explains the proposed residual learning network of ship classification; Sect. 6 demonstrates the experiments and analysis about the results; Sect. 7 conducts this paper.

2 Related Work

As SAR images have advantages which mainly include relatively little influence of weather and time, ship detection in SAR images has extensively been studied [1–5]. The most common algorithms of ship detection are based on a constant false-alarm rate (CFAR) detector with a certain SAR image background distribution such as Gauss distribution [2], k-distribution and Gamma distribution [4] or other combination [5]. Han and Chong [1] took a brief review of ship detection algorithms in polarimetric SAR images. Greidanus et al. [3] compared the performance of eight ship detection systems based on spaceborne systems by running a benchmark test on RADARSAT images of various modes. However, ship detection based on SAR has limitations. First, it cannot meet the needs of the application of real-time ship monitoring because of the relative long revisit cycle of SAR. Second, the resolution of most satellite SAR images is often not high enough to extract detailed ship information.

For ship detection and classification on optical images, traditional methods were widely studied [6–9]. Zhu et al. [6] and Antelo et al. [7] extracted manually designed features from images such as shapes, textures and physical properties. Chen and Gao [8] and Wang et al. [9] exploited Dynamic Bayesian Network to classify different kinds of ships. However, they cannot overcome the images' variability and big volume problems. Recently, as the emergence of deep learning architectures, an autoencoder-based deep neural network combined with extreme learning machine was proposed [10]. It outperformed some other methods in detection accuracy. However, it has some limitations: (1) as the image resolution is 5 m, the extracted features are good enough to detect ships from waves, clouds and islands. It cannot recognize different types of ships; (2) as autoencoder model uses full connection totally which leads to a large number of nodes and large computation.

3   Ship Candidates Extraction

First of all, CDF 9/7 wavelet coefficients are extracted from images. The original image is decomposed into a low-frequency subband (LL) and several horizontal/vertical/diagonal high-frequency subbands (LH, HL, and HH). Generally speaking, the low frequency contains most of the global information, while the high frequency represents local or detail information. Ship candidates are extracted from the low-frequency subband LL by conducting image enhancement, target-background segmentation and shape criteria-based ship locating.

In image enhancement, in order to remove uneven illumination, a morphological operator, i.e., top-hat transform (THT), is used for ship candidates extraction and background suppression. As ships are usually brighter than their surroundings, the white THT is employed in the proposed work [shown in Fig. 2(a)].

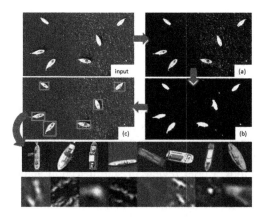

Fig. 2. The process of ship candidates extracting.

In target-background segmentation, each input image is binarized by the Otsu algorithm [11]. After that, connected regions are labelled. As the binarized image usually remains small holes in sea waves or clouds, then the median filtering, morphology dilation and erosion (circular structuring element with a radius of three) are applied to fill the isolated holes. Finally, the masks of sea waves, clouds, islands and ship candidates are segmented [shown in Fig. 2(b)]. In the following, ship candidates will be further extracted by using the unique shape properties of ships.

In ship locating, the ship candidates are further extracted by using the unique shape properties of ships, including the area, the major minor axis ratio and the compactness [10]. Area equals the number of pixels in the corresponding connected region. Area is used to cut off the clouds, sea waves and other obviously large/small false targets. By using these shape criteria, we can obtain the coarse locations of ship candidates [shown in Fig. 2(c)].

Note that some of the pseudo-targets may be included in the extracted regions; however, they can be removed in the process of ship detection by CNN in Sect. 4.

4 Ship Detection by CNN

Ship detection by deep learning is the next step of our proposed method. It detects actual ships from all the ship candidates and then the actual ships are classified into different types by CNN.

In training, firstly, we solve a two-class (ship and non-ship) classification problem. We constructed a CNN consisting of four convolutional, three max-pooling and a fully-connection layer with a final 2-way softmax classifier for ship detection. Its structure is shown in Fig. 3. After ship detection, all the actual ships are detected. To classify all the ships into 10 different types, this model is used for ship classification by changing the number '2' to '10' at the right end.

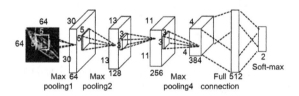

Fig. 3. Our proposed CNN model.

5 Ship Classification by Residual Learning Network

The above mentioned CNN exists some disadvantages: (1) with the network depth increasing, accuracy gets saturated and then degrades rapidly; (2) as stacking more layers, problem of vanishing/exploding gradients might appear, which hampers convergence. Therefore, in order to improve the feature extraction ability and learning ability of the model, a ship classifier based on residual learning network (ResNet) is proposed in this section. In order to overcome the problem of vanishing/exploding gradients, we propose to use residual function learned by using 'shortcut'; for reducing the computation, we propose to use 'Inception' model; for accelerating the convergence speed of the iterative training, we propose to use Batch Normalization (BN) method to normalize each layer.

5.1 Residual Learning Network

Theory and practice prove that the depth is very important to the success of neural network, and deep networks can represent certain function classes far more efficiently than shallow ones. However, as networks get deeper, some problems appear: (1) back propagated gradients disappear; (2) training cost increases. Srivastava et al. [13] proposed to modify the architecture of very deep feedforward networks such that information flow across layers becomes much easier. This is accomplished through an adaptive gating mechanism that allows for computation paths along which information can flow across many layers without attenuation. The results of the layer can be mapped to its subsequent layer directly, the training error keeps unchanged instead of increased in a deepened network model. So, [14] introduces the concept of residual, making the training converge easier.

Two types of underlying mappings are defined in this paper, *Identity_block* and *Conv_block* shown in Fig. 4. Thus depth and width of the network are both increased.

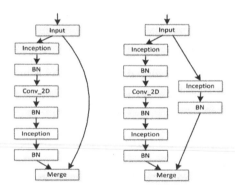

Fig. 4. Diagram of *Identity_block* (left) and *Conv_block* (right)

5.2 Optimization of the Residual Learning Network

Batch Normalization (BN)
Training Deep Neural Networks is complicated because of the fact that the distribution of each layer' s inputs changes, as the parameters of the previous layers change during training. This slows down the training by requiring lower learning rates. Therefore, we propose to use the BN method in this section. In this way, a higher learning rate can be used directly, which leads to faster training speed.

Inception Module

From AlexNet [12] in 2012 to GoogleNet [15] in most recent years, the main idea is to make the network deeper and wider. However, increasing the network blindly has two shorcomings: (1) over fitting; (2) large amount of computation. Inception refers to adding a 1 × 1 convolutional layer behind the normal convolutional layer [14, 15]. As increasing the scale of the network, the feature presentation increases with less computation and parameters.

5.3   Ship Classifier Using Residual Learning Network

A ship classifier based on residual learning network proposed in this section is composed of 5 *Identity_block* and 2 *Conv_block* alternately, as shown in Fig. 5.

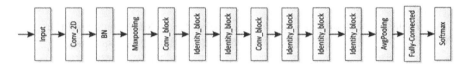

Fig. 5. Proposed residual network for ship classification.

6   Experiments

We conducted the training on a server with Intel Core i5-4460 CPU @3.20 GHz, 8.00 GB RAM and Titan X card. Matlab2014a and cuda 7.0 were used.

Images shown in Fig. 6(1) were downloaded from Google Earth and after ship candidates extraction, a dataset consisting 1200 images (containing ships, clouds, sea waves and islands) were obtained and used for performance evaluation each in 64 × 64 pixels, 4/5 used for network training and 1/5 for testing.

Fig. 6. Datasets

In order to be more convincing, another dataset shown in Fig. 6(2), consisting 1500 images (10 categories of ships) and each in 256 × 64 pixels with higher resolution were also downloaded and used for performance evaluation.

After ship candidates extraction on Dataset (1), 1200 images were obtained containing ships and nonships. Ship detection model in Sect. 4 was used to separate all the ships. Then using the same model, ships were classified into different types. Finally, ship detection and classification accuracy on dataset (1) are 99% and 93%.

In dataset (2), with the same classification model, even higher classification accuracy 95% was achieved, which is closely related to the higher spatial resolution. Classifying error rate of each type of ship by CNN is shown in Table 1. With equivalent number of parameters, ship classifier based on ResNet proposed in Sect. 5 was used to classify dataset (2), the same classification accuracy 95% was obtained. The error rate of each type of ship is shown in Table 2.

Table 1. Misclassification rate in each type of ship by CNN on dataset (2).

Ship class	C0	C1	C2	C3	C4	C5	C6	C7	C8	C9
Error rate	6.5%	3.3%	10%	13%	6.5%	6.5%	13%	3.3%	0%	3.3%

Table 2. Misclassification rate in each type of ship by ResNet on dataset (2).

Ship class	C0	C1	C2	C3	C4	C5	C6	C7	C8	C9
Error rate	13%	6.5%	3.3%	10%	10%	6.5%	3.3%	0%	3.3%	3.3%

The results show that, when the numbers of parameters in ResNet and CNN are comparable, deep residual learning network can converge faster than simply stacked CNN. ResNet converged at about 20th epoch, while CNN converged at about 50th epoch (shown in Figs. 7 and 8).

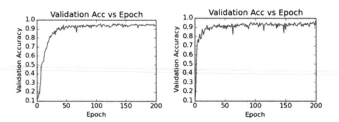

Fig. 7. Accuracy of CNN (left) and ResNet (right)

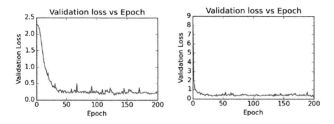

Fig. 8. Loss value of CNN (left) and ResNet (right)

Seventy-five times ($75\times$) speedup was achieved on a Titan X card.

So when data becomes complex, using deep residual learning network has advantages.

As a comparison, Support Vector Machine (SVM) and Neural Network (NN) were used for classification on dataset (2), and achieved 87% and 81% accuracy respectively shown in Table 3.

Table 3. Classifying accuracy on dataset (2)

Method	CNN	SVM	Neural network
Accuracy	95%	87%	81%

7 Conclusion

In this paper, we proposed a ship detection and classification method on remote sensing optical images. Ship candidates are extracted by conducting image enhancement, target-background segmentation and ship locating based on shape criteria. Note that there are still nonship targets in the ship candidates, so in the next step a CNN was trained to detect actual ships from all candidates. Finally, using the proposed ResNet model with the optimization techniques (Batch Normalization and Inception module), we classified all the actual ships into different ships. The model was trained on remote sensing images downloaded from Google Earth. Eventually, 99% detection accuracy and 95% classification accuracy were achieved, which is comparable with some state-of-the-art algorithms such as SVM and NN. Experiments showed that CNN, as a deep neural network is a good model for automatically feature learning and extraction and when dataset becomes complex, residual learning network has more advantages. Up to $75\times$ speedup was achieved on a server with a Titan X GPU which indicates its potential for real-time processing.

Acknowledgments. This project was partially supported by Grants from Natural Science Foundation of China #71671178/#91546201. It was also supported by Hainan Provincial Department of Science and Technology under Grant No. ZDKJ2016021, and by Guangdong Provincial Science and Technology Project 20162016B010127004.

References

1. Han, Z.Y., Chong, J.S.: A review of ship detection algorithms in polarimetric SAR images. In: Proceedings of the 7th ICSP, 31 August–4 September, vol. 3, pp. 2155–2158 (2004)
2. Eldhuset, K.: An automatic ship and ship wake detection system for spaceborne SAR Images in coastal regions. IEEE Trans. Geosci. Remote Sens. **34**(4), 1010–1019 (1996)
3. Greidanus, H., Clayton, P., Indregard, M.: Benchmarking operational SAR ship detection. In: Proceedings of the IGARSS, vol. 6, pp. 4215–4218 (2004)
4. Wackerman, C.C., Friedman, K.S., Li, X.: Automatic detection of ships in RADARSAT-1 SAR imagery. Can. J. Remote. Sens. **27**(5), 568–577 (2001)

5. Crisp, D.J.: The state of the art in ship detection in synthetic aperture radar imagery. Australian Government Department of Defence, Edinburgh, Australia, DSTO-RR-0272 (2004)
6. Zhu, C.-R., Zhou, H., Wang, R.-S., Guo, J.: A novel hierarchical method of ship detection from space-borne optical image based on shape and texture features. IEEE Trans. Geosci. Remote Sens. (2010)
7. Antelo, J., Ambrosio, G., Gonzalez, J., Galindo, C.: Ship detection and recognition in high-resolution satellite images. In: Proceedings of the IEEE International Geoscience and Remote Sensing Symposium. IEEE (2009)
8. Chen, H.Y., Gao, X.G.: Ship recognition based on improved forwards-backwards algorithm. In: Proceedings of the 6th International Conference on Fuzzy Systems and Knowledge Discovery. IEEE (2009)
9. Wang, Q.J., Gao, X.G., Chen, D.Q.: Pattern recognition for ship based on Bayesian networks. In: Proceedings of the 4th International Conference on Fuzzy Systems and Knowledge Discovery. IEEE (2007)
10. Tang, J., Deng, C., Huang, G.-B., Zhao, B.: Compressed-domain ship detection on spaceborne optical image using deep neural network and extreme learning machine. IEEE Trans. Geosci. Remote Sens. (2014)
11. Gonzalez, R.C., Woods, R.E.: Digital Image Processing, 3rd edn, pp. 742–745. Gatesmark Publishing, Knoxville (2007)
12. Krizhevsky, A., Sutskever, I., Hinton, G.: ImageNet classification with deep convolutional neural networks. In: NIPS (2012)
13. Srivastava, R.K., Greff, K., Schmidhuber, J.: Highway networks. Computer Science (2015)
14. He, K., Zhang, X., Ren, S., et al.: Deep residual learning for image recognition. Computer Science (2015)
15. Szegedy, C., Liu, W., Jia, Y., et al.: Going deeper with convolutions. In: Proceedings of the IEEE Conference on Computer Vision and Pattern Recognition, pp. 1–9 (2015)

Single Image Super-Resolution by Learned Double Sparsity Dictionaries Combining Bootstrapping Method

Na Ai[1,2(✉)], Jinye Peng[2], Jun Wang[2], Lin Wang[1,2], and Jin Qi[2]

[1] Northwestern Polytechnical University, Xian 710129, China
aina@nwu.edu.cn
[2] Northwest University, Xian 710127, China

Abstract. A novel single image super-resolution (SISR) method using learned double sparsity dictionaries combining bootstrapping method is proposed in this paper. The bootstrapping method we used is proposed by Zeyde et al. in [1], which uses the input low-resolution (LR) image (as high-resolution image) and its own scaled-down version (as LR image) as the training images. In our previous work [15], with the output image obtained by the bootstrapping method, two difference images can be computed and are used to learn a pair of dictionaries as proposed in [1]. In this paper, we further improve the SISR method by using four wavelet sub-bands of the two difference images as extra information when learning the sparse representation model. We use the K-singular value decomposition (K-SVD) method to obtain the dictionary and the orthogonal matching pursuit (OMP) method to derive the sparse representation coefficients. Comparative experimental results show that our proposed method perform better in terms of both visual effect and Peak Signal to Noise Ratio (PSNR) improvements.

Keywords: Single image super-resolution · Bootstrapping method · Sparse representation model · Double sparsity dictionaries

1 Introduction

The goal of single image super-resolution (SISR) is to restore a high-resolution (HR) image $y_h \in \mathbb{R}^{N_h \times M_h}$ from the observed low-resolution (LR) image $\mathbf{z}_l \in \mathbb{R}^{N_l \times M_l}$. $\mathbf{z}_l$ is defined to be the LR version of the original image as $\mathbf{z}_l = S^{\downarrow}(h * \mathbf{y}_h)$. It is assumed that h is the blurring kernel which applies a low-pass filter to the original image, and $S^{\downarrow}$ is the down-sampling operator which performs a decimation by a factor of s by discarding rows and columns from $\mathbf{y}_h$. Given $\mathbf{z}_l$, the task is to estimate an output image $\hat{y} \in \mathbb{R}^{N_h \times M_h}$ such that $\hat{y} \approx y_h$. It is treated as a resolution enhancement method which can be applied to many practical applications such as surveillance systems and medical imaging systems, where high-resolution images are urgently needed while low cost digital imaging sensors are often used.

This SISR problem is usually considered to be an ill-posed inverse problem with much more unknowns than the observed data. So an effective image prior is needed to

© Springer International Publishing AG 2017
A. Lintas et al. (Eds.): ICANN 2017, Part II, LNCS 10614, pp. 565–573, 2017.
https://doi.org/10.1007/978-3-319-68612-7_64

reconstruct a HR image from a single LR image. By using various priors to regularize the inversion, existing SISR approach can be roughly classified into three categories: the interpolation-based [3–7], example-based [8] and sparse representation model-based [1, 9–13] methods. Nearest, bilinear and bicubic are conventional interpolation schemes with the simple image "smoothness" prior. As images contain strong discontinuities, as edges and corners, the interpolated results often suffer from artifacts such as jaggies, ringing and blurring. Therefore, more sophisticated priors considering the varying structure of pixels, ranging from robust statistics [3, 4], Total-Variation [5] and auto-regression model [6, 7] are adopted to overcome this drawback. The example-based SISR methods use a training set which consists a large number of known LR and HR image patch pairs as the prior [8]. The corresponding relationships between LR and HR image patches are learned to reconstruct a new HR image.

The sparse representation model [9–11] is introduced to super-resolution (SR) work firstly by Yang et al. in [12] by assuming a local Sparse-Land model on image patches which serves as the regularization. Based on the assumption that each patch in a natural image can be well represented by a linear combination of few atoms from a dictionary, Yang et al. construct the dictionaries by using the randomly sampled patches of LR and HR training images. This work is improved by themselves with an advanced dictionary training strategy, where the LR and HR dictionaries are trained simultaneously, ensuring that the LR image patch and its corresponding HR image patch have the same sparse representation coefficients [13]. Zeyde et al. modified Yang et al.'s algorithm by using the K-SVD method in dictionary training stage and the OMP algorithm in sparse coding stage [1] which significantly reduce the computational complexity. In our previous work [2], we propose to train a dictionary using the wavelet sub-bands of the LR image instead of the first and second derivatives as proposed by Zeyde et al. [1]. Our trained dictionaries have the property of double sparsity and are proved to have better generalization ability to various kind of natural images.

In recent years, the structural self-similarity based SR methods, which can overcome the deficiency of the example-based learning methods to some extent, have been proposed in several researches to solve the SR problem by using the LR image itself instead of the database. Based on the observation that patches in a natural image tend to redundantly recur many times inside the image, both within the same scale, as well as across different scales, Glasner et al. [14] proposed a single unified approach which combines the classical example-based SR methods with the information exploited by the patch redundancies across all image scales. Zeyde et al. pointed out in [1] that by exploiting the "scale invariant" patch redundancy property, one can learn a dictionary pair by using the given LR image (as the HR image) and its own scaled-down version (as the LR image) as the training sample images. Thus by learning the sparse representation model, we can easily bootstrap the super-resolution task from the given LR image itself. This is the so-called bootstrapping method in [1]. In our previous work [15], we adopt the bootstrapping approach to get a scaled-up version of LR training image, which is better than the bicubic scaled-up image. Then the difference image between the bootstrapping result and the bicubic scaled-up image, and the difference image between the HR training image and the bootstrapping result are computed and used as the feature maps to train a pair of dictionary. The proposed method shows to gain better visual and Peak Signal to Noise Ratio (PSNR) improvement than Zeyde et al.'s method in [1].

In this paper, we aim to propose a SISR framework that combines the sparse representation model with the bootstrapping method more effectively. Two difference images suggested in [15] are still used as the extra information but we further modify the SISR method to taking full advantage of the double sparsity dictionary by learning the sparse representation model proposed in [2]. The major improvement lies in the four wavelet sub-bands of each difference image are used as the feature maps when training the dictionary.

The remainder of this paper is organized as follows. Section 2 details the SISR method based on sparse representation model and the bootstrapping approach. Section 3 presents how we apply bootstrapping method in the sparse representation framework. Section 4 provides a number of comparative experimental results. Finally, we conclude this paper in Sect. 5.

2 Sparse Representation Model and Self-learning Based SISR

2.1 Sparse Representation Model-Based SISR

The sparse representation model assumes that each patch in a natural image can be well represented by a linear combination of few atoms from a dictionary. The key to success of sparse representation model based SISR method is to learn a dictionary pair $\{D_l, D_h\}$ which establishes adequate relationship between the corresponding LR and HR patches.

Suppose $X_l = \{x_1, x_2, \ldots, x_q\}$ is the LR data set in which every column represents a signal. The K-SVD method [15] is used to obtain the LR dictionary D_l by solving the following minimization problem:

$$D_l, A = \min_{D_l, A} \|X_l - D_l A\|_F^2$$
$$\text{s.t. } \|\alpha^k\|_0 \leq K_0, \forall k \tag{1}$$

where K_0 denotes the sparsity constraint. A side product of this training phase is the representation matrix $A = \{\alpha_1, \alpha_2, \ldots, \alpha_q\}$ which is corresponding to the LR data set X_l. The HR dictionary D_h can be inferred directly from HR data set X_h and the sparse representation matrix A as follows:

$$D_h = X_h A^T (A A^T)^{-1}. \tag{2}$$

The LR data set used in [1] is formed by the patches collected from four feature maps, which resulted from four derivatives $[\partial_x, \partial_y, \partial_{xx}, \partial_{yy}]$ applied to the LR image y_l. The HR data set is constructed by the patches taken from e_h, which is the difference between the HR image y_h and LR image y_l. The derivative operators are chosen to be the feature extractor which will extract the local features (edges and texture content) that correspond to the high-frequency content of the LR image. The reason for this step is the desire to focus the training on characterizing the relation between the LR patches and the HR ones.

The optimization of feature extractor problem is still challenging and open as stated in [1]. Inspired by this, one level *stationary wavelet transform* is chosen to be the feature extractor in our previous work in [2] which have been shown to have better performance than the simple derivative operators used by Zeyde et al. in [1].

With the dictionary pair $\{D_l, D_h\}$, the OMP algorithm [15] is used to compute the sparse representation matrix A of the test image data set over the LR dictionary D_l. Then the reconstructed HR data is obtained by

$$X_{out} = D_h A. \tag{3}$$

Reshaping each column vector in X_{out} into a $\sqrt{n} \times \sqrt{n}$ patch, putting it in proper location, and averaging in overlapped pixels, the reconstructed difference image $\hat{e}$ is obtained. Finally adding y_l to $\hat{e}$, we get the SR output image $\hat{y}$.

2.2   Bootstrapping Method

It was also pointed out in [1] that by exploiting the "scale invariant" property [14], one can learn a dictionary pair directly from the given LR image itself. Note that in order to train the dictionary pair $\{D_l, D_h\}$, the proposed algorithm needs only access to pairs of LR and HR images. Using the given LR image z_l as the HR image and its scaled-down version z_{ll} as the LR image, the dictionary is learned, based on the relation between these two images reflects also the relationship that should be used to scale-up z_l to y_h. Thus by learning the sparse representation model proposed in [1], we can easily bootstrap the super-resolution task from the given LR image z_l itself. The bootstrapping results is proved to be better than the conventional interpolation methods (e.g. bicubic).

Aiming at further improvement of SISR performance, our previously proposed method in [15] integrate the bootstrapping approach into the sparse representation model. We use the difference images between the bootstrapping results and the LR and HR training images as the feature maps when training the dictionary. Then a super-resolution image can be get by learning the sparse representation model proposed in [1]. In this paper, we take a step further to use the four sub-bands of the difference images as the extra information when training the dictionary. Hoping that by taking full advantage of the double sparsity dictionary as proposed in [2], we can further improve the SISR method's performance.

3   Proposed Method

3.1   Preparation of Sample Images

We collect several high quality natural images as the training sample images. For each HR training sample image y_h, applying blurring kernel h_1 and down-sampling operator by a factor s, we get a corresponding LR image z_l.

3.2   Bootstrapping and Interpolation

LR image $\mathbf{z}_l$ is further scaled-down by a factor of s, resulting the image $\mathbf{z}_{ll}$. The image pair $\{\mathbf{z}_l, \mathbf{z}_{ll}\}$ is used for dictionary training. The training phase, interpolation and feature extraction within this subroutine are as same as described in [2] but a smaller patch size is used. The trained dictionary is used to enable the reconstruction phase which scales up $\mathbf{z}_l$ to y_m, the result of the bootstrapping algorithm which is better than the result of conventional interpolations. The reconstruction phase of the bootstrapping approach is exactly the same as the reconstruction phase of the example-based learning approach as described in Sect. 2.1 which we need not to repeat.

On the other hand, $\mathbf{z}_l$ is scaled-up using bicubic interpolation, generating the LR image y_l. As y_m and y_l have the same size as the original image y_h, two difference images can be computed by:

$$\begin{aligned} e_h &= y_h - y_m \\ e_l &= y_m - y_l \end{aligned}. \tag{4}$$

3.3   Gather Data and Dictionary Learning

To form the LR data set, we decompose e_l with one level *stationary wavelet transform* (SWT) into four sub-bands as suggested in [2]. We slide a $\sqrt{n} \times \sqrt{n}$ window on the four feature maps from left to right, top to bottom. The four $\sqrt{n} \times \sqrt{n}$ patches extracted inside the window at the same location k are now represented as four n dimensional vectors. Then stacking those four vectors to form a $4n$ dimensional vector x_l^k. By putting them column by column, the LR training data set $X_l = \{x_l^k\} \in \mathbb{R}^{n \times c}$ (where c denotes the total number of patches) is obtained. The HR training data set $X_h = \{x_h^k\} \in \mathbb{R}^{n \times c}$ is constructed by the same way as gathering X_l. The K-SVD algorithm is used to learn the LR dictionary D_l and the sparse representation matrix A can be obtained by the OMP method [16]. Then the corresponding HR dictionary D_h can be computed directly by Eq. (2).

3.4   Sparse Coding and Reconstruction

For a given LR test image, following the same interpolation and bootstrapping procedure, one can get the image y_l and y_m. By applying stationary wavelet transform to $e_l = y_m - y_l$, four wavelet sub-bands of e_l are obtained. Extracting four $\sqrt{n} \times \sqrt{n}$ patches from the feature maps at location k, which can be presented as four n dimensional column vectors, then stacking the four column vectors to form the test LR signal vector x_l^k. Sparse coding x_l^k over the trained dictionary D_l by OMP algorithm, we can get the representation vector α^k. Then a corresponding HR column vector can be reconstructed by $p_h^k = D_h \alpha^k$. Reshaping p_h^k to a $\sqrt{n} \times \sqrt{n}$ patch and putting it back to location k, averaging the overlapped pixels and finally adding it to y_m, the output image

$$\hat{y} = y_m + \left[\sum_k R_k^T R_k\right]^{-1} \left[\sum_k R_k^T D_h \alpha^k\right] \tag{5}$$

is obtained [1] (where $R \in \mathbb{R}^{n \times N}$ denotes the data extraction operator). The major difference between the proposed method and our previous work in [15] is that we take a new step to extract more local features in the two difference images that correspond to the high-frequency content. The reason for this step is to focus the training on characterizing the relationship between the LR patches and their corresponding HR ones more adequately.

In brief, our proposal can be considered as an extension of our previous work in [15]. It is also a two-step resolution enhancement technique. The first step of bootstrapping exploits the information learned from the input LR image itself. The second step of sparse coding and reconstruction merges the information learned from external HR images.

4 Experimental Results

In this section, a number of experimental results are given to evaluate the performance of the proposed SISR method. Several SISR approaches including the example-based learning method and the bootstrapping method proposed by Zeyde et al. in [1], and our previously proposed method in [15] are compared to the method proposed in this paper both visually and quantitatively. To make a fair comparison between the performances of the selected SISR methods, all the dictionaries used are retrained in accordance with our degradation model.

4.1 Training Phase

We randomly select five natural grey images (shown in Fig. 1) to be the training images. Each training image y_h^j is blurred using a 5×5 Gaussian filter h_1 with a standard deviation 3 and down-sampled by a factor of s (s can be 2 or 3) to generate the z_l. Scale-up z_l with the bicubic interpolation, the degraded LR image y_l is created.

Fig. 1. Training images

The parameters of dictionary training are set as follows: the patch size used is 7×7, the dictionary training procedure applied 50 iterations of the K-SVD algorithm, with $K = 512$ atoms in the dictionary, and allocating $K_0 = 3$ atoms for each representation vector. The parameters involved in the bootstrapping subroutine are exactly the same as described above except the atom number K is 144 and a smaller patch size 5×5 is used.

4.2 Testing Phase

The blurring kernel h_2 used in test phase is the Kronecker product of a 1-D filter [4, 4.5, 5, 4.5, 4]/22, which is slightly different from h_1 in training phase. The reconstruction algorithm is tested on 15 test images shown in Fig. 2. Part of the SR results are presented in Fig. 3. The PSNR values and improvements for up-sample factor $s = 2$ can be found in Table 1.

Fig. 2. 15 test images

Fig. 3. Visual comparison of SR results (upsample factor 2) on test image (8) by different SISR methods. (a) Bicubic. (b) Zeyde et al.'s method [1]. (c) Bootstrapping method [1]. (d) Our previously proposed method [15]. (e) Proposed method in this paper. (f) Original HR image.

From the SR image results presented in Fig. 3, we can see that our method produces sharp edges and recovers more details, such as the head and the eye of the parrot shown in Fig. 3(e). Although visual effect differences between the reconstructed images might not be very obvious, the PSNR values of our SR results are almost the highest as listed in Table 1. The average gains of PSNR values over Zeyde et al.'s example-based learning method in [1] and our previously proposed model in [15] are 0.2882 dB and 0.0456 dB for s = 2, 0.2761 dB and 0.0277 dB for s = 3 respectively.

Table 1. PSNR (dB) values of SR images using different methods (upsample factor $s = 2$)

Test images	Bicubic	Zeyde et al.'s method in [1]	Bootstrapping method [1]	Our previously proposed method in [15]	Proposed method in this paper
(1)	24.3399	26.4468	26.3388	26.8058	26.8912
(2)	20.9412	22.5122	22.4220	22.7229	22.7692
(3)	26.2802	28.0098	27.7941	28.2498	28.2894

(continued)

Table 1. (*continued*)

Test images	Bicubic	Zeyde et al.'s method in [1]	Bootstrapping method [1]	Our previously proposed method in [15]	Proposed method in this paper
(4)	26.9922	30.4620	29.8660	30.4912	30.4898
(5)	20.8722	22.6106	22.5286	22.9884	23.0505
(6)	25.3656	27.4640	27.3123	27.7503	27.7774
(7)	21.7853	24.8364	24.7411	25.5971	25.7780
(8)	25.7524	28.0133	27.9512	28.2774	28.2506
(9)	24.7153	26.7310	26.8078	27.1747	27.2723
(10)	24.9187	27.5101	27.3119	27.9207	28.0079
(11)	25.3411	27.3493	27.2318	27.7348	27.7943
(12)	27.5332	29.1333	28.9924	29.2377	29.2760
(13)	30.7498	32.1457	32.0275	32.2796	32.3228
(14)	26.5626	27.7127	27.6479	27.8014	27.8210
(15)	24.0617	25.2955	25.0660	25.3176	25.3145

5   Conclusion and Discussion

In this paper, we propose a two-step SISR method based on sparse representation model-based method and the self-example based bootstrapping method. With the output of bootstrapping method, two difference images can be computed as suggested in [15] and their four wavelet sub-bands are treated as LR and HR data source. Then the double sparsity dictionaries are learned using the sparse representation model proposed in [2] to take full advantage of double sparsity dictionaries. Experimental results demonstrate the effectiveness of our method. How to achieve better SISR results using a better optimization method during the dictionary training procedure is an important issue to be considered in our future research.

References

1. Zeyde, R., Elad, M., Protter, M.: On single image scale-up using sparse-representations. In: Boissonnat, J.-D., Chenin, P., Cohen, A., Gout, C., Lyche, T., Mazure, M.-L., Schumaker, L. (eds.) Curves and Surfaces 2010. LNCS, vol. 6920, pp. 711–730. Springer, Heidelberg (2012). doi:10.1007/978-3-642-27413-8_47
2. Ai, N., Peng, J.Y., Zhu, X., Feng, X.Y.: SISR via trained double sparsity dictionaries. Multimed. Tools Appl. **74**, 1997–2007 (2015)
3. Li, X., Orchard, M.T.: New edge-directed interpolation. IEEE Trans. Image Process. **10**(10), 1521–1527 (2001)
4. Schultz, R.R., Stevenson, R.L.: A Bayesian approach to image expansion for improved definition. IEEE Trans. Image Process. **3**(3), 233–242 (1994)
5. Marquina, A., Osher, S.J.: Image super-resolution by TV-regularization and Bregman iteration. J. Sci. Comput. **37**(3), 367–382 (2008)

6. Dong, W., Zhang, L., Shi, G., Wu, X.: Image deblurring and super-resolution by adaptive sparse domain selection and adaptive regularization. IEEE Trans. Image Process. **20**(7), 1838–1857 (2011)
7. Zhang, X., Wu, X.: Image interpolation by adaptive 2-D autoregressive modeling and soft-decision estimation. IEEE Trans. Image Process. **17**(6), 887–896 (2008)
8. Elad, M., Datsenko, D.: Example-based regularization deployed to super resolution reconstruction of a single image. Comput. J. **50**(4), 1–16 (2007)
9. Elad, M., Aharon, M.: Image denoising via learned dictionaries and sparse representation. In: IEEE Computer Society Conference on Computer Vision and Pattern Recognition, vol. 1, no. 1, pp. 895–900 (2006)
10. Elad, M., Aharon, M.: Image denoising via sparse and redundant representations over learned dictionaries. IEEE Trans. Image Process. **15**(12), 3736–3745 (2006)
11. Rubinstein, R., Zibulevsky, M., Elad, M.: Double sparsity: learning sparse dictionaries for sparse signal approximation. IEEE Trans. Signal Process. **58**(3), 1553–1564 (2010)
12. Yang, J., Wright, J., Huang, T., Ma, Y.: Image super-resolution as sparse representation of raw image patches. In: IEEE Conference on Computer Vision and Pattern Recognition (CVPR), pp. 1–8 (2008)
13. Yang, J., Wright, J., Huang, T., Ma, Y.: Image super resolution via sparse representation. IEEE Trans. Image Process. **19**(11), 2861–2873 (2010)
14. Glasner, D., Bagon, S., Irani, M.: Super-resolution from a single image. In: Proceedings of the 12th ICCV, pp. 349–356 (2009)
15. Ai, N., Peng, J.Y., Zhu, X., Feng, X.Y.: Single image super-resolution by combining self-learning and example-based learning methods. Multimed. Tools Appl. **75**(11), 6647–6662 (2016)
16. Aharon, M., Elad, M., Bruckstein, A.M.: The K-SVD: an algorithm for designing of over-complete dictionaries for sparse representation. IEEE Trans. Signal Process. **54**(11), 4311–4322 (2006)

Attention Focused Spatial Pyramid Pooling for Boxless Action Recognition in Still Images

Weijiang Feng, Xiang Zhang$^{(\boxtimes)}$, Xuhui Huang, and Zhigang Luo$^{(\boxtimes)}$

College of Computer, National University of Defense Technology, Changsha, China
zhangxiang_43@aliyun.com, zgluo@nudt.edu.cn

Abstract. Existing approaches for still image based action recognition rely heavily on bounding boxes and could be restricted to specific applications with bounding boxes available. Thus, exploring the boxless action recognition in still images is very challenging for lack of any supervised knowledge. To address this issue, we propose an attention focused spatial pyramid pooling (SPP) network (AttSPP-net) free from the bounding boxes by jointly integrating the soft attention mechanism and SPP into a convolutional neural network. Particularly, soft attention mechanism automatically indicates relevant image regions to be an action. Besides, AttSPP-net further exploits SPP to boost the robustness to action deformation by capturing spatial structures among image pixels. Experiments on two public action recognition benchmark datasets including PASCAL VOC 2012 and Stanford-40 demonstrate that AttSPP-net can achieve promising results and even outweighs some methods based on ground-truth bounding boxes, and provides an alternative way towards practical applications.

Keywords: Action recognition · Convolutional neural network · Soft attention · Spatial pyramid pooling

1 Introduction

Recognizing human action in still images (such as a biker and a runner with the green bounding boxes in Fig. 1 (a)) is still challenging due to large changes in appearance and clutter background. Recently, although amounts of deep learning models [4,5,7,13] have been explored to do that with reasonable accuracy, they highly depend on ground-truth bounding boxes and are not tailored for practical situations where bounding boxes are not available just like Fig. 1 (b)). Consequently, can we successfully recognize actions in Fig. 1 (b) without the supervision of bounding boxes? This task of boxless still image based action recognition is obvious more challenging than before because this requires us to locate the actors just like the bounding boxes do meanwhile reducing the negative effect of action deformation without any supervised knowledge. Tackling both issues are the key factors of boxless action recognition.

For human beings, we are easily attracted to the most salient regions of an image such as the rider shown in Fig. 1 (b). Inspired by this insight, we can resort

© Springer International Publishing AG 2017
A. Lintas et al. (Eds.): ICANN 2017, Part II, LNCS 10614, pp. 574–581, 2017.
https://doi.org/10.1007/978-3-319-68612-7_65

Fig. 1. Training instances of actions with and without bounding boxes.

to the mechanism to highlight the salient image regions. Soft attention mechanism was originally applied in machine translation [1] in order to automatically find out relevant anchors of a source sentence to a predicted target word. This property seamlessly meets the demand of boxless action recognition which plans to locate image regions of an action. Thus, we exploit soft attention to replace bounding boxes by assigning large weights to candidate regions of actions in an unsupervised manner.

To bring into play the efficacy of soft attention, we have to incorporate the spatial structures among pixels to reduce the negative effect of action deformation before that. Spatial pyramid pooling (SPP, [12]) can achieve this goal by partitioning the whole image into spatial patches from fine to coarse levels and then aggregating features from these local spatial bins. It was first applied for hierarchical feature representation and now has been introduced into convolutional neural networks (CNNs) such as SPP-net [6]. He *et al.* [6] developed SPP-net to tackle the inconsistent image size problem in traditional CNNs for the purpose of reducing information loss. Similar to SPP-net, we adopt the SPP layer on top of the last convolutional layer to respect spatial structures among pixels. But the big difference from SPP-net lies in that we assign weights to each spatial bin with soft attention and then aggregate local spatial features based on weighted summation. Obviously, our goal greatly differs from SPP-net as well.

Motivated by the observations above, this paper proposes an attention focused SPP network (AttSPP-net) free from the bounding boxes by jointly integrating the soft attention mechanism and SPP into a convolutional neural network (CNN). Benefitting from soft attention, AttSPP-net can readily locate the salient image regions of different actions. Furthermore, AttSPP-net exploits SPP to boost robustness to action recognition as well as respect spatial structures among image pixels. This nontrivial joint way is simple yet effective and can effectively address two issues above. To validate such claim, experiments of still image based boxless action recognition on two public action benchmark datasets including PASCAL VOC 2012 [3], and Stanford-40 [17] show the promise of AttSPP-net compared with the state-of-the-art methods.

2   Related Work

Still image based action recognition has long been a popular topic in visual applications. For a comprehensive study on this topic, we refer interested readers to the survey paper [14]. Here, we focus on convolutional neural network based methods. Oquab *et al.* [13] utilized a CNN to extract features of the bounding boxes and further obtain a small gain in performance against previous methods. Hoai [7] employed the *fc7* features of a network trained on ImageNet dataset to weight different image regions. Gkioxari *et al.* [4] train body part detectors based on the *pool5* features and then combine them with the bounding box to jointly train a CNN. Later on, they use a CNN to extract features from the bounding box region and the candidate regions generated by the bottom up region proposals method, and then combine the features of the bounding box region and the most informative candidate region to make the final prediction [5].

The previous studies on still image based action recognition strongly rely on the prior knowledge of the ground-truth bounding boxes. They can be regarded as weak supervised methods and may be fragile in real-world applications. Reversely, we explore effective AttSPP-net network with both soft attention and spatial pyramid pooling layers free from the ground-truth bounding boxes in a completely unsupervised manner.

Yu *et al.* [18] also conduct action recognition in still images without utilizing human bounding boxes. They first utilize a five-step iterative optimization pipeline for unsupervised discovery of a foreground action mask of current image, then design good and dedicated feature representation from the action mask for recognition purpose. Compared with their complexity, the proposed AttSPP-net makes straightforward and lightweight modification to the existing deep CNN architecture.

3   Attention Focused SPP Network

In this section, we are readily to detail our network model, i.e., AttSPP-net. By assigning large weights to feature bins of spatial pyramid pooling layer which corresponds to salient image regions through a soft attention layer, AttSPP-net can readily locate the action performer of interest, thus conducts action recognition without the supervision of ground-truth bounding boxes. The structure is illustrated in Fig. 2. To facilitate the success of deep models in computer vision community, we construct AttSPP-net based on the 19-layer VGGNet [16] with the following novel modifications: (1) we replace the last pooling layer *pool5* with a SPP layer, and (2) we bypass a soft attention layer to the SPP layer. Particularly, given an image I, AttSPP-net first extracts features with the convolutional layers, and then pools the extracted features using three-level spatial pyramid pooling. Subsequently, the soft attention assigns a weight to each spatial bin, and AttSPP-net derives the aggregated features by weighted summation. Then, AttSPP-net takes as the input of the fully-connected layers the aggregated features, and in the final softmax layer outputs probabilities of each action.

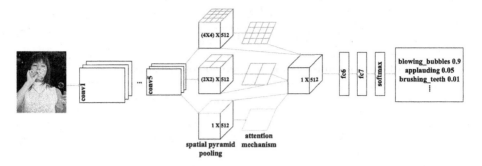

Fig. 2. The schematic structure of our AttSPP-net. AttSPP-net is built based on VGG19 with a SPP layer replacing the last pooling layer *pool5* and a soft attention layer bypassing the SPP layer.

3.1 The Spatial Pyramid Pooling Layer

AttSPP-net extracts features using convolutional layers of the 19-layer VGGNet [16] trained on ImageNet [2] dataset. The last convolutional layer of VGGNet has D (512 in our experiments) convolutional maps. On top of the last convolutional layer, AttSPP-net applies SPP with h (3 in our experiments) levels. The SPP layer here captures the spatial structures among pixels to reduce the negative effect of action deformation. On each level i, SPP applies pooling in a unique scale and obtains $\left(2^{i-1}\right)^2$ spatial bins. Thus, at the SPP layer, AttSPP-net represents each image as a feature matrix:

$$X = [X_{1,1}, X_{2,1}, \cdots, X_{h,4^{h-1}}] \in \mathbb{R}^{s \times D}, \tag{1}$$

where $s = 4^0 + \cdots + 4^{h-1} = \frac{4^h - 1}{3}$ denotes total number of spatial bins, D denotes feature dimensionality of each spatial bin, and $X_{i,j}$ $\left(i \in [1, h], j \in [1, 4^{h-1}]\right)$ corresponds to the i−th scale and j−th region of each image. We refer to this feature matrix X as the SPP features. Since each spatial feature column $X_{i,j}$ is mapped to different overlapping spatial regions in the input image space, AttSPP-net can perform soft attention on these s features. This layer is same to that of SPP-net [6], and the difference between AttSPP-net and SPP-net is the following soft attention layer.

3.2 The Soft Attention Layer

AttSPP-net utilizes the soft attention mechanism to automatically focus on salient image regions. For each spatial feature column $X_{i,j}$, the soft attention layer generates a positive weight $\alpha_{i,j}$ representing the relative importance to give to the spatial bin when aggregating $X_{i,j}$ together. To compute α, the soft attention layer uses a perceptron network taking the SPP feature X as input:

$$e_{i,j} = W^T X_{i,j} + b$$
$$\alpha_{i,j} = \frac{\exp(e_{i,j})}{\sum_{i=1}^{h} \sum_{j=1}^{4^h - 1} \exp(e_{i,j})}, \tag{2}$$

where W and b are parameters for the perceptron network.

Once the weights α are computed, AttSPP-net computes the aggregated feature vector $x \in \mathbb{R}^D$ by taking the expectation of x directly:

$$\mathrm{E}_{p(\alpha|X)}[x] = \sum_{i=1}^{h} \sum_{j=1}^{4^h - 1} \alpha_{i,j} X_{i,j}. \tag{3}$$

AttSPP-net then feeds x to the fully-connected layer *fc6*. AttSPP-net is smooth and differentiable under the deterministic soft attention mechanism, and the end-to-end learning can be optimized by standard back-propagation.

3.3 Learning

To train AttSPP-net, we use cross-entropy loss together with weight decay. The loss over a mini-batch of training examples $B = \{I_i, y_i\}_{i=1}^{M}$ is given by

$$\mathrm{loss}(B) = -\frac{1}{M} \sum_{i=1}^{M} \sum_{c=1}^{C} y_{i,c} \log \hat{y}_{i,c} + \lambda \sum_{j} \theta_j^2, \tag{4}$$

where y_i and $\hat{y}_i$ are the one hot label vector and class probabilities vector of image I_i respectively, C is the number of action classes, λ is the weight decay coefficient, and θ represents all the model parameters.

We train our model with stochastic gradient descent (SGD) using back-propagation. Based on the learned model parameters of 19-layer VGGNet, we first fine-tune our network on the ImageNet dataset for the image classification task. We set the learning rate to 0.001, the batch size to 32, and the weight decay coefficient to 0.0002. We fine-tune for 100 K iterations on ImageNet dataset using two K80 GPUs under Caffe [8] framework. After the fine-tuning, we train our model on each action recognition dataset for 50 K iterations with a batch size of 20 using one K80 GPU core.

4   Experimental Results

In this section, we evaluate the effectiveness of AttSPP-net for action recognition in still images on the PASCAL VOC 2012 Actions dataset [3] and the Stanford-40 dataset [17] by comparing with two variants of AttSPP-net. One is VGG19_SPP that removes attention layer of AttSPP-net, while the other is the baseline VGG19 model which removes both the attention and SPP layer of AttSPP-net. During test time, we estimate probabilities for all actions for every example, and compute AP for each action and the mean AP.

4.1 PASCAL VOC 2012 Actions Dataset

The PASCAL VOC 2012 Action dataset consists of 10 different actions, *Jumping, Phoning, Playing Instrument, Reading, Riding Bike, Riding Horse, Running, Taking Photo, Using Computer, Walking*. Since AttSPP-net can only recognize one action from one image for this moment, we ignore images occurred more than one action in the same image. The final training dataset consists of 1865 images and the testing dataset contains 1848 images.

For this dataset, we use the validation set for testing and AttSPP-net obtains a mean AP of 76.2%. We show the comparison of AttSPP-net with its variants and the state-of-the-art in Table 1. Our experiments show that AttSPP-net performs effectively, and achieves higher mean AP compared with its two variants. In spite of no ground-truth bounding boxes available, AttSPP-net obtains higher AP for some action categories like "Phoning" and "Reading", though lower AP for "Running", "Walking" compared with Hoai [7] and Oquab *et al.* [13]. In terms of mean AP, AttSPP-net behaves comparably with these two methods.

Table 1. Comparison of different approaches on the PASCAL VOC dataset.

AP(%)	Jumping	Phoning	Playing instru- ment	Reading	Riding bike	Riding horse	Running	Taking photo	Using com- puter	Walking	Mean AP
Oquab *et al.* [13]	74.8	46.0	75.6	45.3	93.5	95.0	86.5	49.3	66.7	69.5	70.2
Hoai *et al.* [7]	82.3	52.9	84.3	53.6	95.6	96.1	89.7	60.4	76.0	72.9	76.3
Zhang *et al.* [18]	86.68	72.22	**93.97**	71.30	95.37	97.63	88.54	72.42	88.81	65.31	83.23
Gkioxari *et al.* [4]	84.7	67.8	91.0	66.6	96.6	97.2	90.2	76.0	83.4	71.6	82.6
Gkioxari *et al.* [5]	**91.5**	**84.4**	93.6	**83.2**	**96.9**	**98.4**	**93.8**	**85.9**	**92.6**	**81.8**	**90.2**
VGG19	74.86	66.34	82.33	66.21	82.35	84.82	67.63	56.38	78.19	48.67	71.27
VGG19_SPP	80.33	68.78	83.26	73.97	82.35	89.53	72.66	64.36	77.13	58.67	75.49
AttSPP-net	75.41	73.17	83.26	74.43	86.47	91.1	71.22	61.7	79.26	62	76.19

4.2 Stanford-40 Dataset

The Stanford-40 dataset contains images of humans performing 40 different actions such as *applauding, climbing, cooking, drinking, fishing, gardening, jumping, phoning, running, and walking the dog*. There are 9532 images in total with 180–300 images per action class, 4000 images for training, and 5532 images for testing.

AttSPP-net achieves a mean AP of 81.62% on the test set, with performance varying from 47.31% for *texting message* to 95.9% for *climbing*. Figure 3 shows the AP performance per action on the test set. In Table 2 we compare our methods with other approaches on the Stanford-40 test set. The SB [17] method jointly models the attributes and parts by learning a set of sparse bases and

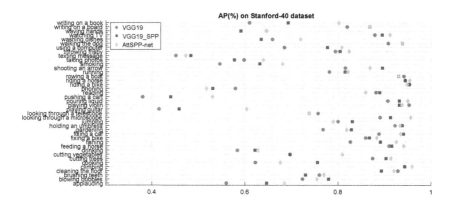

Fig. 3. AP (%) of AttSPP-net on the Stanford-40 dataset per action.

obtains a mean AP of 45.7%. The EPM [15] method based on part based information obtains a mean AP of 45.2%. The CF [9] method fuses multiple color descriptors and obtains a mean AP of 51.9%. The SMP [10] method constructs pyramids on different body parts and obtains a mean AP of 53.0%. The PD [11] method does not use the bounding boxes but uses an action specific person detector and obtains a mean AP of 75.4%. The R*CNN [5] method obtains a mean AP of 90.9%, the best published result. Again, AttSPP-net achieves higher mean AP than its variants. Similar to the results reported in Table 1, AttSPP-net yields reasonable performance compared with the baseline methods in terms of mean AP.

Table 2. Comparison of different approaches on the Stanford-40 dataset.

Method	SB	EPM	CF	SMP	PD	Zhang	R*CNN	VGG19	VGG19_SPP	AttSPP-net
Mean AP(%)	45.7	45.2	51.9	53.0	75.4	82.64	**90.9**	77.21	79.92	81.62 (3rd place)

5   Conclusion

This paper develops a simple yet effective model termed AttSPP-net for action recognition in still images. It is able to automatically pay attention to image regions of the action without the supervision of the ground-truth bounding boxes and also provides an alternative way for real-world situations. Experiments show that AttSPP-net achieves higher mean action recognition accuracy than its variants VGG19 and VGG19_SPP, demonstrating the effectiveness of soft-attention and spatial pyramid pooling. More importantly, AttSPP-net achieves promising boxless action recognition performance in still images.

Acknowledgments.. This work is supported by National High Technology Research and Development Program (under grant No. 2015AA020108) and National Natural Science Foundation of China (under grant No. U1435222).

References

1. Bahdanau, D., Cho, K., Bengio, Y.: Neural machine translation by jointly learning to align and translate. arXiv preprint (2014). arXiv:1409.0473
2. Deng, J., Dong, W., Socher, R., Li, L.J., Li, K., Fei-Fei, L.: Imagenet: a large-scale hierarchical image database. In: IEEE Conference on Computer Vision and Pattern Recognition, pp. 248–255 (2009)
3. Everingham, M., Van Gool, L., Williams, C.K., Winn, J., Zisserman, A.: The pascal visual object classes (VOC) challenge. Int. J. Comput. Vis. **88**(2), 303–338 (2010)
4. Gkioxari, G., Girshick, R., Malik, J.: Actions and attributes from wholes and parts. In: IEEE International Conference on Computer Vision, pp. 2470–2478 (2015)
5. Gkioxari, G., Girshick, R., Malik, J.: Contextual action recognition with r*cnn. In: IEEE International Conference on Computer Vision, pp. 1080–1088 (2015)
6. He, K., Zhang, X., Ren, S., Sun, J.: Spatial pyramid pooling in deep convolutional networks for visual recognition. IEEE Trans. Pattern Anal. Mach. Intell. **37**(9), 1904–1916 (2015)
7. Hoai, M.: Regularized max pooling for image categorization. J. Br. Inst. Radio Eng. **14**(3), 94–100 (2014)
8. Jia, Y., Shelhamer, E., Donahue, J., Karayev, S., Long, J., Girshick, R., Guadarrama, S., Darrell, T.: Caffe: convolutional architecture for fast feature embedding. In: ACM International Conference on Multimedia, pp. 675–678 (2014)
9. Khan, F.S., Anwer, R.M., van de Weijer, J., Bagdanov, A.D., Lopez, A.M., Felsberg, M.: Coloring action recognition in still images. Int. J. Comput. Vis. **105**(3), 205–221 (2013)
10. Khan, F.S., van de Weijer, J., Anwer, R.M., Felsberg, M., Gatta, C.: Semantic pyramids for gender and action recognition. IEEE Trans. Image Process. **23**(8), 3633–3645 (2014)
11. Khan, F.S., Xu, J., Van De Weijer, J., Bagdanov, A.D., Anwer, R.M., Lopez, A.M.: Recognizing actions through action-specific person detection. IEEE Trans. Image Process. **24**(11), 4422–4432 (2015)
12. Lazebnik, S., Schmid, C., Ponce, J.: Beyond bags of features: spatial pyramid matching for recognizing natural scene categories. In: IEEE Conference on Computer Vision and Pattern Recognition, pp. 2169–2178 (2006)
13. Oquab, M., Bottou, L., Laptev, I., Sivic, J.: Learning and transferring mid-level image representations using convolutional neural networks. In: IEEE Conference on Computer Vision and Pattern Recognition, pp. 1717–1724 (2014)
14. Poppe, R.: A survey on vision-based human action recognition. Image Vis. Comput. **28**(6), 976–990 (2010)
15. Sharma, G., Jurie, F., Schmid, C.: Expanded parts model for human attribute and action recognition in still images. In: IEEE Conference on Computer Vision and Pattern Recognition, pp. 652–659 (2013)
16. Simonyan, K., Zisserman, A.: Very deep convolutional networks for large-scale image recognition. arXiv preprint (2014). arXiv:1409.1556
17. Yao, B., Jiang, X., Khosla, A., Lin, A.L., Guibas, L., Fei-Fei, L.: Human action recognition by learning bases of action attributes and parts. In: IEEE International Conference on Computer Vision, pp. 1331–1338 (2011)
18. Yu, Z., Li, C., Wu, J., Cai, J., Do, M.N., Lu, J.: Action recognition in still images with minimum annotation efforts. IEEE Trans. Image Process. **25**(11), 5479–5490 (2016)

The Impact of Dataset Complexity on Transfer Learning over Convolutional Neural Networks

Miguel D. de S. Wanderley$^{(\boxtimes)}$, Leonardo de A. e Bueno, Cleber Zanchettin, and Adriano L.I. Oliveira

Centro de Informática - Universidade Federal de Pernambuco, Recife, PE, Brazil
{mdsw,lab6,cz,alio}@cin.ufpe.br

Abstract. This paper makes use of diverse domains' datasets to analyze the impact of image complexity and diversity on the task of transfer learning in deep neural networks. As the availability of labels and quality instances for several domains are still scarce, it is imperative to use the knowledge acquired from similar problems to improve classifier performance by transferring the learned parameters. We performed a statistical analysis through several experiments in which the convolutional neural networks (LeNet-5, AlexNet, VGG-11 and VGG-16) were trained and transferred to different target tasks layer by layer. We show that when working with complex low-quality images and small datasets, fine-tuning the transferred features learned from a low complexity source dataset gives the best results.

Keywords: Convolution neural networks · Transfer learning · Dataset complexity

1 Introduction

Transfer Learning is the process of reusing an already trained model on a given source domain and continue the training on a target domain aiming to execute a new but similar classification task [1]. As a result, the training time and complexity may be reduced and problems with a small number of examples of the target domain may be mitigated as the parameters previously learned can be reused. Combined with the recent success of Convolutional Neural Networks (CNNs) on image classification tasks [2–5], transfer learning has the potential to improve research on several domains.

Yosinski *et al.* [6] and Soekhoe *et al.* [7] investigated the impact of layer specialization and dataset size on transfer learning. Though extensive, these studies did not evaluate the effect of image complexity during the transfer learning process. The definition of image complexity is mainly subjective and hard to automatically treat or predict. A useful definition is that image complexity is a rating of the quantity and density of details or intricacy of lines in the image [8].

The image size predictably influences the classifier performance, since it changes the quantity of available data to set the layer's parameters. Likewise,

© Springer International Publishing AG 2017
A. Lintas et al. (Eds.): ICANN 2017, Part II, LNCS 10614, pp. 582–589, 2017.
https://doi.org/10.1007/978-3-319-68612-7_66

image complexity may affect how layers generalize the features information during the training process. Thus, it is pertinent to investigate the ability to reuse features obtained from low quality and diverse datasets (Which are the most common, frequent and available type of training images). It is also important to provide additional insights on the process of network freezing and fine-tuning when transferring knowledge from different datasets.

Our experiments aimed to statistically evaluate the ability to reuse features learned by varying the domain and the complexity of source and target datasets. We also investigate the most appropriate CNN layer to transfer, in either freeze or fine-tuning conditions. The experiments were performed using LeNet [9], AlexNet [2] and VGG networks [3] (with 5, 8, 11 and 16 layers, respectively) on MNIST [10], SVHN [11] and CIFAR-10 [12] datasets.

It is important to highlight that the objective of this work is not to reach state-of-the-art accuracy, which can be done through several epochs of training and with an appropriated learning rate. Our main goal is to investigate transfer learning comparative performance. As a direct extension of previous works, this paper's study is based on the hypothesis that transferring weights from a simpler dataset to a more complex target dataset enables the network to learn features more accurately. This may lead to better results on the classification task, independent of domain.

1.1 Related Works

Demonstrating the potential of transfer mid-level features learned on deep neural networks, Oquab et al. [13], Zeiler et al. [14] and Razavian et al. [15] pre-trained CNNs on ImageNet[1] (normally combined with others classifiers), to perform classification tasks over different datasets (e.g. PASCAL VOC 2012, Caltech-101[2], Caltech-256[3] and MIT-67 Indoor Scenes), the authors observed that the transferred model generalizes well for most of the datasets. Furthermore, investigating how well features are transferred to different domain target tasks, in [16] the authors trained an AlexNet on ImageNet and have conducted transfer experiments on Caltech-101 (see footnote 2), Office[4], Caltech-UCSD birds[5] and SUN-397 Large-Scale Scene Recognition datasets, observing that in all the experiments the benchmark scores were improved, demonstrating that ImageNet features provide generalizable properties.

Analyzing how well transferred features performs among the layers of CNNs, Yosinski et al. [6] used AlexNet network trained on splits of the ImageNet dataset

---

[1] J. Deng et al., "Imagenet: A large-scale hierarchical image database". IEEE Conference on Computer Vision and Pattern Recognition, 2009.

[2] L. Fei-Fei, R. Fergus e P. Perona, "Learning generative visual models from few training examples: an incremental Bayesian approach tested on 101 object categories", Computer Vision and Image Understanding, 2007.

[3] G. Griffin, A. Holub e P. Perona, "Caltech-256 object category dataset", 2007.

[4] K. Saenko, B. Kulis, M. Fritz e T. Darrell, "Adapting visual category models to new domains", Computer Vision-ECCV, pp. 213–226, 2010.

[5] P. Welinder et al., "Caltech-ucsd birds 200", 2010.

containing each one a half of the classes, called baseA and baseB. After training the base models, the features of each layer were transferred to the same or to the other dataset partition tasks. The authors observed that the first three layers of the network represent general filters similar to Gabor filters and color blobs and could be transferred to improve the classifier performance independently from the datasets domains. The deeper layers, however, contain information specific to the task and transferring them decreases the classifier performance, even when applying fine-tuning on the transferred layers [6].

The Soekhoe *et al.* [7] study investigated the effect of the target dataset size in the transfer learning also using the AlexNet model. The hypothesis evaluated was that a transfer approach by freezing the first layers results in a higher classification accuracy if the target set is smaller, in contrast with larger datasets, in which updating all layers gives better results. The authors varied the domain and the size of the target dataset when testing the transferred weights of each layer. They concluded that when transferring the first two or three layers to target datasets with less than a thousand instances per class, freezing the weights boosts the performance over the baseline results.

2   Proposed Methodology

To evaluate our hypothesis, four well known convolutional networks were selected based on their depth. The first network is **LeNet-5** [9]. The second network is **AlexNet** [2], also used on referenced works, winner of the ImageNet Large Scale Visual Recognition Challenge 2012. The next two network architectures chosen were **VGG-11** and **VGG-16**, proposed by Karen Simonyan and Andrew Zisserman (ConvNet configurations 'A' and 'D', respectively) [3], first and second places winners of the localization and classification tasks at the ImageNet Large Scale Visual Recognition Challenge 2014.

2.1   Networks Adjustments

Since our objectives do not cover evaluating the state-of-the-art performance and efficiency, but only the relative performance of the transfer learning process itself, some adjustments were done in the networks in order to better handle with the datasets input shape (28×28 pixels RGB images).

– Input layer setup to 28×28 RGB images, in all networks configurations.
– Resize all convolutional layers and resize the number of units in the first Fully Connected layers, proportionally to the new input layer,
– Amount of units in the last Fully Connected layer set to 10, to match the number of classes in the datasets.

The comparison between the original networks layers configurations and the adjusted layers are shown in the Table 1, the parameters of the convolutional layer are denoted as "conv⟨number of channels⟩-⟨receptive field size⟩". Final

Fully Connected layer and activation function are omitted for brevity. All remaining parameters were kept as the original proposal (Max pooling layers, Local Response Normalization layers, and Activation Functions – ReLU or Hyperbolic Tangent). These new configurations fit better the 28×28 RGB datasets' input since the original configurations were designed for different inputs.

Table 1. Convolutional neural networks layers configurations adjustments

layers (VGG-11/VGG-16)	VGG-11/VGG-16		layers	AlexNet	
	Original	**Adjusted**		**Original**	**Adjusted**
	input image 224x224RGB	input image 28x28RGB		input image 224x224RGB	input image 28x28RGB
1 / 1, 2	conv3-64	conv3-8	1	conv11-96	conv11-12
2 / 3, 4	conv3-128	conv3-16	2	conv5-256	conv5-32
3, 4 / 5, 6, 7	conv3-256	conv3-32	3,4	conv3-384	conv3-48
5,6,7,8 / 8, 9, 10, 11, 12, 13	conv3-512	conv3-64	5	conv3-256	conv3-32
9, 10 / 14, 15	FC-4096	FC-512	6,7	FC-4096	FC-512
11 / 16	FC-1000	FC-10	8	FC-1000	FC-10

layers	Lenet-5	
	Original	**Adjusted**
	input image 32x32 grayscale	input image 28x28RGB
1	conv3-8	conv3-32
2	conv3-16	conv3-64
3	FC-42	FC-128
4	FC-84	FC-256

2.2 Image Datasets

The experiments transfer features from CNNs trained on a source task to a different target task. The scenarios considered include three datasets with different complexities and domains. As resumed on Table 2, the first dataset is the **MNIST** [10] database of handwriting digits (dataset "A"). Since these images were preprocessed, this dataset has a low complexity. The second dataset is **Street View House Number (SVHN)**[11] (dataset "B"), here considered complex, but with the similar domain of MNIST, because of color and structure variation of digits, as well as "distracting digits"close to the digits of interest. The third dataset is the **CIFAR-10** [12] database (dataset "C") which includes images from the real world, also a complex domain.

Dataset Adjustments. The images were reshaped to 28×28 RGB pixels and all pixels' color values were adjusted for variation between $\{0,1\}$, normalizing the color scale for network processing. This preprocess was performed to avoid bias on the training process and posterior harm to experiment results.

– MNIST: Color layers were included, changing the original shape from $28 \times 28 \times 1$ (one gray scale color layer) to $28 \times 28 \times 3$ (RGB colors layers).

Table 2. Datasets overview

	A: MNIST	B: SVHN	C: CIFAR-10
Train instances	60000	73257	50000
Test instances	10000	26032	10000
Original shape	28x28x1(grayscale)	32x32x3 (RGB)	32x32x3 (RGB)
Domain	Simple digits	Complex digits	Real-world
Example			

- SVHN: The original images were cropped (removing the most external borders - 2 pixels) from $32 \times 32 \times 3$ to $28 \times 28 \times 3$, keeping content centered.
- CIFAR-10: The same cropping as SVHN was applied to obtain $28 \times 28 \times 3$ images.

2.3   Transfer Learning

Training was set to 50 epochs (25 epochs for training the base model and 25 for training the transferred model) using a learning rate of 10^{-5}. These values experimentally showed promising results for our intended investigations. With epochs and learning rate fixed, the variables of the transfer experiments are:

- **Source dataset (S):** the base dataset used for training the network, one of {A,B,C} datasets.
- **Target dataset (T):** the second dataset used for training and for evaluation, one of {A,B,C} datasets.
- **Restored layers (n):** first 'n' layers to be restored in the transfer procedure. In the experiments, 'n' depends on the number of layers of the model. The transferred layers sets for each network architecture are: LeNet = {1,2,3,4}, AlexNet = {1,2,3,4,5,6,7}, VGG-11 = {1,2,4,6,8,10}, and VGG-16 = {2,4,7,10,13,15},
- **Freeze/Fine-tuning ($\pm$):** the possibility of keeping the weights of the restored layers without training (denoted as '-') or train/fine-tuning the weights of the restored layers (denoted as '+').

To label each execution combination, the following notation was adopted:

'⟨Source dataset⟩⟨Restored layers⟩⟨Freeze/Fine-tune⟩⟨Target dataset⟩' → '**Sn±T**'.

For instance, a transfer procedure on a network first trained on the MNIST(A) dataset (source), and then retrained on the SVHN(B) dataset (target), with the first four (n = 4) convolutional layers weights restored (the remain layers initialized with random values) and fine-tuning ('+') on the restored layers, is represented as 'A4 + B'.

3   Results and Discussion

The experiments' results are shown in Fig. 1. The accuracy and standard deviations are calculated from ten runs of each transfer scenario with 95% confidence. For comparison, the baseline model without transfer and the model transferred in the same dataset (called a *selfer*) are also included.

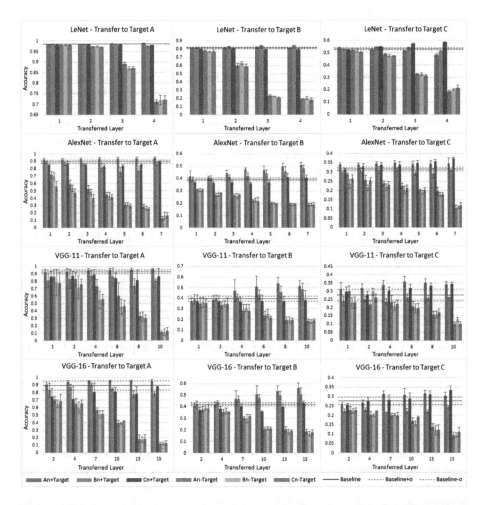

Fig. 1. Transfer results (accuracy, y-axis), with('+') and without('-') Fine-tuning, through different n layers (n restored layers, x-axis) on MNIST(A), SVHN(B) and CIFAR-10(C) datasets.

The results demonstrate how image domain and complexity impact the accuracy of transfer learning with deep convolution neural networks. The experiments (Fig. 1) exhibit the same behavior reported on the Yosinski *et al.* [6]. The effectiveness of feature transfer declines as baseline and target tasks diverge. Also, weights learned on the middle layers are less transferable than those on initial or final layers, as can be seen throughout all 'Sn-Target' bar plottings (orange, yellow and green).

Observing and comparing the freeze and fine-tuning approaches, it becomes easy to notice how freezing loses performance as the transferred layer goes deeper. This phenomenon stands out in contrast to the fine-tuning approach, which keeps a substantial performance (equivalent to baseline dataset performance) through deeper transferred layers, exactly as mentioned by Yosinski et al. [6], sometimes performing better.

We also observed an additional performance improvement from transferring the weights from a less complex source database to a more complex target, as obtained in the VGG-11 and 16 transfers to target B(SVHN), starting from layer 7. This behavior starts to be prominent on deeper networks like AlexNet and VGG-16. Though especially noticeable on a same domain transfer process (MNIST to SVHN transferring), the effect occurs even when transferring weights between different domains. In this scenario, observed on the Target C transfers, only the last one or two fine-tunned self-transfers resulted in significantly better accuracy than $An + C$ transfers.

Interestingly enough, fine-tuning *selfer* transfer performed similarly to the base model until the second layer, from that point on, the transferred model performs better than the baseline model. This can be explained by an improvement in the training process of base layers, where detection of basic features was improved using fine-tuning.

The Yosinski et al. [6] transfer experiments were done over partitions of the same dataset (ImageNet), leading to the conclusion that the $Mn\pm N$ and $Nn\pm M$ transferring scenarios are quite the same. Since we investigated the transferring over distinct datasets (MNIST, SVHN, and CIFAR-10), our results corroborate and expand the findings of [6], pointing out the significant impact of source dataset complexity when transferring knowledge from a pre-trained CNN to another dataset.

4   Conclusion

In this study, the effect of dataset domain and complexity on the generalization of learned weights in CNNs was investigated. To this end, features were transferred from pre-trained models to new networks. The LeNet-5, AlexNet, VGG-11 and VGG-16 networks were trained to evaluate datasets with similar and different domains, on images with different complexity. It was found that transferring initial and middle layers' features of simpler source datasets to complex target datasets results in a significant performance boost over the baseline score even when applied on different domain scenarios. The effect becomes more prominent the deeper the network is. Further research should be done to extend these conclusions to networks with more layers and on CNNs designs diverse from the ones explored in this study as GoogLeNets [4] and ResNets [5].

The source code is available at: http://cin.ufpe.br/~mdsw/icann17/

References

1. Lu, J., Behbood, V., Hao, P., Zuo, H., Xue, S., Zhang, G.: Transfer learning using computational intelligence: a survey. Knowl.-Based Syst. **80**, 14–23 (2015)
2. Krizhevsky, A., Sutskever, I., Hinton, G.E.: ImageNet classification with deep convolutional neural networks. In: Advances in Neural Information Processing Systems, vol. 25 (2012)
3. Simonyan, K., Zisserman, A.: Very deep convolutional networks for large-scale image recognition. In: International Conference on Learning Representations (ICLR), San Diego (2015)
4. Szegedy, C., Liu, W., Jia, Y., Sermanet, P., Reed, S., Anguelov, D., Erhan, D., Vanhoucke, V., Rabinovich, A.: Going deeper with convolutions. In: IEEE Conference on Computer Vision and Pattern Recognition (CVPR), Boston (2015)
5. He, K., Zhang, X., Ren, S., Sun, J.: Deep residual learning for image recognition. In: IEEE Conference on Computer Vision and Pattern Recognition (CVPR) (2016)
6. Yosinski, J., Clune, J., Bengio, Y., Lipson, H.: How transferable are features in deep neural networks?. In: Advances in Neural Information Processing Systems (NIPS 2014), vol. 27, Montral (2014)
7. Soekhoe, D., van der Putten, P., Plaat, A.: On the Impact of data set Size in transfer learning using deep neural networks. In: The 15th International Symposium on Intelligent Data Analysis, Stockholm (2016)
8. Palumbo, L., Ogden, R., Makin, A.D.J.: Examining visual complexity and its influence on perceived duration. J. Vis. **14**, 3 (2014)
9. LeCun, Y., Bottou, L., Bengio, Y., Haffner, P.: Gradient-based learning applied to document recognition. Proc. IEEE **86**, 2278–2324 (1998)
10. LeCun, Y., Cortes, C., Burges, C.J.: The MNIST database of handwritten digits. http://yann.lecun.com/exdb/mnist/
11. Netzer, Y., Wang, T., Coates, A., Bissacco, A., Wu, B., Ng, A.Y.: Reading digits in natural images with unsupervised feature learning. In: NIPS Workshop on Deep Learning and Unsupervised Feature Learning, Granada, Spain (2011)
12. Krizhevsky, A., Hinton, G.: Learning multiple layers of features from tiny images. University of Toronto, Toronto (2009)
13. Oquab, M., Bottou, L., Laptev, I., Sivic, J.: Learning and transferring mid-level image representations using convolutional neural networks. In: 2014 IEEE Conference on Computer Vision and Pattern Recognition, Columbus (2014)
14. Zeiler, M.D., Fergus, R.: Visualizing and understanding convolutional networks. In: Fleet, D., Pajdla, T., Schiele, B., Tuytelaars, T. (eds.) ECCV 2014. LNCS, vol. 8689, pp. 818–833. Springer, Cham (2014). doi:10.1007/978-3-319-10590-1_53
15. Razavian, A., Azizpour, H., Sullivan, J., Carlsson, S.: CNN features off-the-shelf: an astounding baseline for recognition. In: Proceedings of the IEEE Conference on Computer Vision and Pattern Recognition Workshops (2014)
16. Donahue, J., Jia, Y., Vinyals, O., Hoffman, J., Zhang, N., Tzeng, E., Darrell, T.: DeCAF: a deep convolutional activation feature for generic visual recognition. In: International Conference on Machine Learning (2014)

Real-Time Face Detection Using Artificial Neural Networks

Pablo S. Aulestia[1], Jonathan S. Talahua[1], Víctor H. Andaluz[1],
and Marco E. Benalcázar[2(✉)]

[1] Universidad de las Fuerzas Armadas ESPE, Sangolquí, Ecuador
{psaulestia,jstalahua,vhandaluz1}@espe.edu.ec
[2] Departamento de Informática y Ciencias de la Computación, Escuela
Politécnica Nacional, Quito, Ecuador
marco.benalcazar@epn.edu.ec

Abstract. In this paper, we propose a model for face detection that works in
both real-time and unstructured environments. For feature extraction, we applied
the HOG (Histograms of Oriented Gradients) technique in a canonical window.
For classification, we used a feed-forward neural network. We tested the performance of the proposed model at detecting faces in sequences of color images.
For this task, we created a database containing color image patches of faces and
background to train the neural network and color images of 320×240 to test
the model. The database is available at http://electronica-el.espe.edu.ec/
actividad-estudiantil/face-database/. To achieve real-time, we split the model
into several modules that run in parallel. The proposed model exhibited an
accuracy of 91.4% and demonstrated robustness to changes in illumination, pose
and occlusion. For the tests, we used a 2-core-2.5 GHz PC with 6 GB of RAM
memory, where input frames of 320×240 pixels were processed in an average
time of 81 ms.

Keywords: Real-time face detection · Histograms of oriented gradients ·
Feed-forward neural networks

1 Introduction

Computer vision consists of a set of algorithms which allow us to analyze the content
of digital images through mathematical models that emulate the human visual system.
Object detection is one of the main problems of computer vision and is the base to
implement algorithms to interpret and understand the dynamic world using color,
grayscale or binary images. Computer vision represents a great challenge, especially
when we try to interpret or understand an image or sequences of images (i.e., video)
automatically. The main applications of computer vision include the identification and
localization of objects in given space, search and tracking of objects for autonomous
robots, and image restoration. Therefore, computer vision is an important field to do
research and object detection is a key topic for developing new algorithms.

© Springer International Publishing AG 2017
A. Lintas et al. (Eds.): ICANN 2017, Part II, LNCS 10614, pp. 590–599, 2017.
https://doi.org/10.1007/978-3-319-68612-7_67

An object detection system is composed of the following modules: image acquisition and preprocessing, feature extraction, classification and refinement of the detection. The feature extraction problem has been extensively addressed using different methods such as extraction of edges, local binary patterns, segmentation and blending of color spaces [1–3]. For example, in [4] authors propose the use of local binary patterns (LBP). Histograms of oriented gradients (HOG) [5] and discrete-time filters based on the HAAR wavelet transform [6] have also been used. The goal of these methods is to represent a digital image in a given n-dimensional space of characteristics. For a given application, we want the feature extractor module to be robust to changes of illumination, orientation or position [7].

The classification stage implements a decision boundary to separate the different object classes of a given image. The most common and classical methods for classification include the use of support vector machines (SVMs), k-nearest neighbors (kNN), cascade classifiers, and logistic regression. These classifiers combined with the feature extractors described above work well in images whose background is a structured or a partially structured environment [8–13]. On the other hand, when the conditions of the environment change, the performance of the detectors worsen. For example, in [8–11] the performance of the classifiers is less than 94% and the detection accuracy of the whole systems is lower than 90%. In [12, 13] the processing time per image is greater than 200 ms. Additionally, there are other contributions [14–18] that show a performance over 96% using advanced classifiers such as convolutional neural networks (CNN). However, for training and testing these detectors, GPUs have been used to accelerate the computations.

In the literature review presented in this paper, we can see that there exist object detection models with relatively low computational cost. These models with relatively simple structure perform well in structured or partially structured environments. However, when the conditions of the environment change, their performance worsen. On the other hand, there are complex models that exhibit good performance but demand of high computational resources to be trained and tested. Therefore, more research is needed to develop simple object detection models that exhibit both low computational cost and good performance simultaneously.

In this work, we propose a real-time face detection system for unstructured environments. The input to our system is a sequence of images (i.e., video). For feature extraction, we use the HOG descriptor. For classification, we use a feed-forward artificial neural network (ANN). We use a 2-core-2.5 GHz PC with 6 GB of RAM memory to test the proposed model. The algorithm was split into several modules that run in parallel to achieve real-time processing.

Following this introduction, in Sect. 2 we describe the materials and methods used for the feature extraction and classification stages. In Sect. 3, we present the experimental results of the complete system. Finally, in Sect. 4 we present the conclusions and future work.

2 Materials and Methods

2.1 Materials

As an application case of the proposed model, we considered the problem of face detection. To address this problem, we took 7117 photographs to create a database of color images. To train the ANN, we used 5750 color images and the remaining 1367 images were used to validate the system of classification and detection. Out of the 5750 images, 2750 images contain faces with a frontal pose and the remaining 3000 images are background (Fig. 1). The training images are patches with a size of 64 × 64 pixels. The images for testing have a size of 640 × 480 pixels. Both sets of images are represented in the RGB color space and are in the JPG format. These images were taken from students and staff of the Universidad de las Fuerzas Armadas ESPE-Ecuador. The age range of the people that were photographed is between 12 to 50 years. This data set is available at http://electronica-el.espe.edu.ec/actividad-estudiantil/face-database/.

Fig. 1. Examples of faces.

2.2 Face Detection

The first step of the proposed face detection model consists of extracting an image patch I from the original image. We assume this patch belongs to the class $Y \in \{0, 1\}$, where $Y = 1$ and $Y = 0$ represent the face and non-face classes, respectively. The image patch I is obtained by observing the original image through a canonical window W, whose upper left corner is located at the pixel $p = (x, y)$. Second, from the patch I, we extract a feature vector $\mathbf{X}$ using the HOG technique. Third, the vector $\mathbf{X}$ is fed to classifier $\psi : \mathbf{X} \to \{0, 1\}$ based on an ANN. Fourth, if the result of $\psi(\mathbf{X})$ is 1, then a bounding box of the same size as W is placed at $p = (x, y)$ (Fig. 2). Fifth, we shift W to the pixel $p + \Delta p$ in the original image and repeat the previous steps. The value of Δp controls the overlapping between adjacent windows. Finally, to deal with objects of different sizes, we generate a pyramid of images by iteratively resizing the original image until W contains the object of interest within its limits. In Fig. 3, we show a pyramid of six images by reducing the size of the original image by a factor of 1.1.

We chose a canonical window W of 64 × 64 pixels. This size is a tradeoff between the size of the objects that can be detected and the computational cost of the proposed

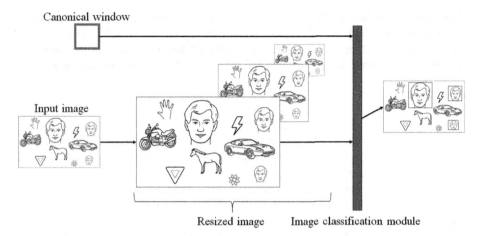

Canonical window

Input image

Resized image   Image classification module

Fig. 2. Illustration of a face detection system, where the faces detected are enclosed in bounding boxes.

i	Width	Height
0	320	240
1	290	218
2	264	198
3	240	180
4	218	163
5	198	149

Original image

Canonical window: 64x64 fits at the tip of the pyramid

Fig. 3. Pyramid of images obtained by reducing the size of the original image by $s = 1.1$

system. We assume the proposed system will operate in scenarios where the objects of interest are located at a maximum distance of 2 m from the camera.

2.3   Histograms of Oriented Gradients

We used the HOG descriptor because it provides information about the orientations of the edges that dominate each position of the image. This method is also invariant to changes of illumination, pose and occlusion of the object to detect.

Gradient Calculation: The vertical and horizontal gradients of a pixel $p = (x, y)$ of an image I are $dx = I(x+1, y) - I(x-1, y)$ and $dy = I(x, y+1) - I(x, y-1)$, respectively. We calculate the orientation and magnitude of these gradients with $\theta(x, y) = arctan(dy/dx)$ and $g(x, y) = \sqrt{dx^2 + dy^2}$, respectively.

Histogram Calculation: We split the input image I into non-overlapping cells of 8×8 pixels each (Fig. 4a). Then, we split the orientation between $0°$ and $180°$ into 9 intervals (Fig. 4b). Next, we calculated the value of the histogram h at the interval k, $h(k)$, by accumulating the gradients of the cell C using the following equation:

$$h(k) = \sum_{(x,y) \in C} w_k(x,y)g(x,y),$$
(1)

where $k = 1, 2, \ldots, 9$, $w_k(x,y) = 1$ if $20 * (k-1) \le \theta(x,y) < 20 * k$ and $w_k(x,y) = 0$ otherwise. Next, we concatenated the histograms of each cell inside a block of 2×2 cells obtaining thus the vector $v' = (h_1, \ldots, h_4)$, where h_i, $i = 1, 2, 3$, and 4, denotes the histogram of the ith cell in a given block (Fig. 4c). Then we normalized the vector v' using the L2 norm obtaining the vector v. Finally, to obtain the one-dimensional HOG vector, we concatenated all the normalized vectors v into the new vector $\mathbf{X} = (v_1, v_2, \ldots, v_n)$, where n is the total number of blocks in a patch I. With these configurations, the length of a HOG vector for an image patch of 64×64 pixels is 1764.

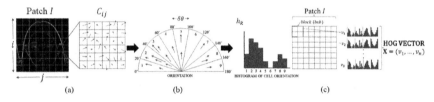

(a)	(b)	(c)

Fig. 4. Illustration of the feature extraction stage using the HOG technique: (a) division of the image patch into non-overlapping cells, (b) histogram of each cell, and (d) feature vector for an image patch.

2.4   Classification

For the classification stage, we used a feed-forward ANN because this model is a universal function approximator [19]. The ANN we used in this work has three layers: input $L^{(0)}$, hidden $L^{(1)}$ and output $L^{(2)}$. The hidden layer is composed of m neurons, and a sigmoid transfer function $f^{(1)}$. The output layer is composed of a single neuron with a sigmoid transfer function. This structure can be seen in Fig. 5. The response $\mathbb{P}(Y = 1|\mathbf{X})$ of the ANN, for an input $\mathbf{X} = (v_1, \ldots, v_n)$, is given by the following expression:

$$\mathbb{P}(Y = 1|\mathbf{X}) = f^{(2)}[W^{(2)}f^{(1)}(W^{(1)}\mathbf{X} + b^{(1)}) + b^{(2)}],$$
(2)

where $\mathbb{P}(Y = 1|\mathbf{X})$ denotes the conditional probability that $\mathbf{X}$ belongs to a face, $W^{(1)}$ and $W^{(2)}$ denote the matrices of weights of the layers $L^{(1)}$ and $L^{(2)}$, respectively, and $b^{(1)}$ denotes the bias vector for neurons of the layer $L^{(1)}$, and $b^{(2)}$ is the bias for the neuron of the layer $L^{(2)}$.

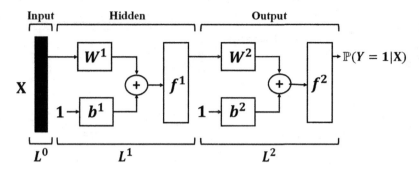

Fig. 5. Architecture of a feed-forward artificial neural network of three layers.

The activation functions that we used in the artificial neural network are $f^{(1)} = f^{(2)} = logsig(z) = 1/(1+e^{-z})$. To train the ANN, we created a database with patches of faces and backgrounds. From these patches, we extracted their corresponding HOG vectors. If a vector $\mathbf{X}$ belongs to a face, we labeled it with $Y = 1$, otherwise, we labeled it with $Y = 0$. In this way, we obtained a training set $\mathcal{D} = \{(\mathbf{X}_1, Y_1), \ldots, (\mathbf{X}_N, Y_N)\}$ composed of N examples. Then, we use the full-batch back-propagation and the gradient-descent algorithms to minimize the cost function $-\ln[\mathbb{P}(\mathcal{D}|\beta)]$, where $\mathbb{P}(\mathcal{D}|\beta)$ denotes the likelihood of the training set $\mathcal{D}$ given the parameters $\beta = \{W^{(1)}, W^{(2)}, b^{(1)}, b^{(2)}\}$ of the ANN [20].

3   Experimental Results

3.1   ANN Training

For training the neural network, we used a training set composed of 5750 image patches. The hidden layer of the ANN was composed of 4 neurons. With these configurations, we obtained a training error of 0.2% after 100 epochs.

3.2   Validation of the Classification Module

To evaluate the performance of the classifier of the proposed approach, we used 959 images divided in two cases: positive (faces) and negative (non-faces). The ROC (Receiver Operating Characteristic) curve was used to analyze the results. The AUC (area under curve) for the classification module has a value of 97.4% (Fig. 6a). The variation step of the threshold to obtain the ROC curve was of 0.001.

3.3   Validation of the Complete System

The system detects faces at six different scales. The input of the system is a video frame of 320×240 pixels (scale 1). To obtain the remaining 5 scales, we reduced the size of the original image by a factor of 1.1. For feature extraction, we used a canonical window of 64×64 pixels. The face detection at each scale was done in parallel to

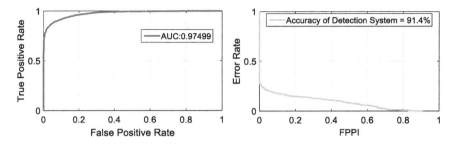

Fig. 6. (a) ROC curve of the classification module AUC = 0.97, (b) error rate versus false positives per image (FPPI) for the whole system.

reduce the computational time and achieve real-time. We tested the system in different environments to verify the robustness of the proposed approach to changes of illumination, pose and occlusion as shown Fig. 7. The first row shows that the system detects the faces in different light conditions. In the second row, the faces were detected even though the light conditions are very low and there are occlusions on the object of interest.

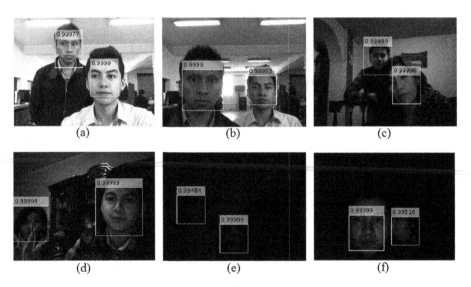

Fig. 7. Face detection results for different lights conditions: (a) high, (b) moderate (c) medium with overlapping of faces, (d) medium with occlusion, (e) low, and (f) low, with overlapping faces.

The performance of the whole system is 91.4% (Fig. 6b). This performance is lower than the performance of the classification module because the complete system is composed of an additional module to refine the detections. This module eliminates all the detections that overlap in more than 10%, except for the one with the highest probability. Additionally, the performance of the whole system also decreases because of an increase in the rate of false negatives. This increase of false negatives occurs because there are faces in the test set that do not fit at any scale within the canonical window of 64 × 64 pixels.

In Table 1, we show the averages of the time that it takes for each module of the system to process a video frame. We can see that the average detection time per video frame is 81 ms. This value shows a relatively high speed compared to other detectors [14, 18].

Table 1. Averages of the time of the modules that compose the proposed system.

Step	Average time
Search of potential faces at different scales	31 ms
Feature extraction	16 ms
Classification	5 ms
Refinement of the detection	29 ms
Total	81 ms

These results obtained in this work evidence that our model is robust to changes of light conditions. Although the detection of the proposed system is limited by the maximum distance to which the object of interest can be located from the camera, the system can correctly detect a face, even when there is occlusion. There are several works that use traditional methods to detect faces, obtaining recognition accuracies higher than 90% [14–18]. However, most of these works evaluate their systems with still images and not with video frames. Additionally, some of these works are tested in highly controlled environments, where the light conditions are roughly the same among all the test images. Therefore, variations of brightness, which are not a problem for our system, are a limiting factor for these models.

4   Conclusions and Future Work

In this work, we have presented a real-time object detection system. We used a feature extractor based on the histograms of oriented gradients. The classifier is a feed-forward neural network with 4 neurons in the hidden layer and 1 neuron in the output layer. We tested this system at detecting faces, showing a detection rate of 91.4%. Even though we used a shallow neural network with only 4 neurons in the hidden layer, we obtained high performance in unstructured environments that included variations in brightness, pose and occlusion. We tested the proposed model using not sophisticated computational resources. The average processing time of the complete algorithm is 81 ms for each video frame of 320 × 240 pixels. To achieve this speed, we ran the different scales of detection in parallel, combining high and low level languages (MATLAB and C++). We also make publicly available the training and testing sets we used for this work at http://electronica-el.espe.edu.ec/actividad-estudiantil/face-database/. Future work includes testing other classifiers different from neural networks. Additionally, we will also test the proposed model at detecting other type of objects different from faces.

Acknowledgment. The authors thank the Consorcio Ecuatoriano para el Desarrollo de Internet Avanzado -CEDIA-, and the Universidad de las Fuerzas Armadas -ESPE- for supporting the development of this work.

References

1. Gil, P., Torres, F., Ortiz, F.: Detección de objetos por segmentación multinivel combinada de espacios de color. Federación Internacional de Automatización, Real (2004)
2. Canny, J.: A computational approach to edge detection. Trans. Pattern Anal. Mach. Intell. **8**, 679–698 (1986). IEEE
3. Zhao, G., Pietikaen, M.: Dynamic texture recognition using local binary patterns with an application to facial expressions. Trans. Pattern Anal. Mach. Intell. **29**, 915–928 (2007). IEEE
4. Wolf, L., Hassner, T., Taigman, Y.: Descriptor based methods in the wild. In: Workshop on Faces in 'Real-Life' Images: Detection, Alignment, and Recognition, pp. 1–14, France (2008)
5. Dalal, N., Triggs, B.: Histograms of oriented gradients for human detection. In: Computer Vision and Pattern Recognition, pp. 886–893. IEEE, Francia (2005)
6. Tang, J., Gongjian, W.: Object recognition via classifier interaction with multiple features. In: 2016 8th International Conference on Intelligent Human-Machine Systems and Cybernetics, pp. 337–340. IEEE, China (2016)
7. Nixon, M., Aguado, A.: Feature Extraction and Image Processing for Computer Vision, pp. 218–220. Academic Press, London (2012)
8. Viola, P., Jones, M.: Robust real-time face detection. Int. J. Comput. Vis. **57**, 137–154 (2004). Springer, The Netherlands
9. Schroff, F., Kalenichenko, D., Philbin, J.: Facenet: a unified embedding for face recognition and clustering. In: The IEEE Conference on Computer Vision and Pattern Recognition, pp. 815–823. IEEE, Boston (2015)
10. Guillaumin, M., Verbeek, J., Schmid, C.: Is that you? Metric learning approaches for face Identification. In: 12th International Conference on Computer Vision, pp. 498–505. IEEE, Kyoto (2009)
11. Cheng, W., Hüllermeier, E.: Combining instance-based learning and logistic regression for multilabel classification. Mach. Learn. **76**, 211–225 (2009). Springer
12. Fasel, I., Fortenberry, B., Movellan, J.: A generative framework for real time object detection and classification. Comput. Vis. Image Underst. **98**, 182–210 (2005). Elsevier
13. Ren, S., He, K., Girshick, R. and Sun, J.: Faster R-CNN: towards real-time object detection. In: Neural Information Processing Systems Conference, pp. 91–99 (2015)
14. Liu, Y., Cao, Y., Li, Y.: Facial expression recognition with PCA and LBP features extracting from active facial patches. In: IEEE International Conference on Real-time Computing and Robotics, pp. 1–6. IEEE, Angkor Wat (2016)
15. Jia, J., Xu, Y., Zhang, S., Xue, X.: The facial expression recognition method of random forest based on improved PCA extracting feature. In: 2016 IEEE International Conference on Signal Processing, Communications and Computing, pp. 1–5. IEEE, Hong Kong (2016)

16. Abdulrahman, M., Gwadabe, T., Abdu, F., Eleyan, A.: Gabor wavelet transform based facial expression recognition using PCA and LBP. In: Signal Processing and Communications Applications Conference, pp. 1–4. IEEE, Trabzon (2014)
17. Taigman, Y., Yang, M., Ranzato, M., Wolf, L.: DeepFace: closing the gap to human-level performance in face verification. In: The IEEE Conference on Computer Vision and Pattern Recognition, pp. 1701–1708. IEEE (2014)
18. Lagerwall, B., Viriri, S.: Robust real-time face recognition. In: Proceedings of the South African Institute for Computer Scientists and Information Technologists Conference, pp. 194–199. ACM New York, East London (2013)
19. Hornik, K., Stinchcombe, M., White, H.: Multilayer feedforward networks are universal approximators. Neural Netw. 2, 359–366 (1989)
20. Hagan, M., Menhaj, M.: Training feedforward networks with the marquardt algorithm. IEEE Trans. Neural Netw. 5, 989–993 (1994)

On the Performance of Classic and Deep Neural Models in Image Recognition

Ricardo García-Ródenas[(⊠)], Luis Jiménez Linares,
and Julio Alberto López-Gómez

Department of Mathematics, University of Castilla la Mancha, Ciudad Real, Spain
{Ricardo.Garcia,Luis.Jimenez,JulioAlberto.Lopez}@uclm.es

Abstract. Deep learning has arisen in the last years as a powerful and ultimate tool for machine learning problems. This article analyses the performance of classic and deep neural network models in a challenging problem like face recognition. The aim of this article is to study what the main advantages and disadvantages deep neural networks provide and when they will be more suitable than classic models, which have also obtained really good results in some complex problems. Is it worth using deep learning? The results show that deep models increase the learning capabilities of classic neural networks in problems with high non-linearities features.

Keywords: Deep neural networks · Convolutional neural networks · Face recognition · Object recognition

1 Introduction

Face recognition is a very popular research topic in artificial intelligence, computer vision and machine learning. That is not a coincidence, since it can be explained by two main reasons: On the one hand, face recognition is a problem with a large amount of practical applications ranging from user authentication [2,19], security [17] and video-games [7,12] to augmented reality [9,14]. Nowadays, plenty of private enterprises invest a lot of money in these kind of applications, which explains face recognition continues being studied today and it is one of the most promising areas in artificial intelligence. On the other hand, face recognition exhibits loads of interesting features to the previously mentioned fields of computer science. For example, this problem has very strong non-linear features. Therefore, image recognition and its classification is a complex computational problem. Furthermore, images are usually represented by multidimensional arrays which increase the complexity of the computation and time needed to process them, which is critical in real-time applications. Finally, the different features of an image and its strong dependence on them (for example background, resolution or scale) make this problem so challenging. For all these reasons, face recognition is a key topic in artificial intelligence since

© Springer International Publishing AG 2017
A. Lintas et al. (Eds.): ICANN 2017, Part II, LNCS 10614, pp. 600–608, 2017.
https://doi.org/10.1007/978-3-319-68612-7_68

this area from computer science has tried to retrieve all the information and knowledge from images. Besides, computer vision is in charge of building, representing and reconstructing images with the purpose of understanding a scene and programming tasks that the human visual system can do. Some applications of face recognition in computer vision are: 3D modeling [5,20], virtual and augmented reality [9,14] and even craniofacial superimposition [8,11] among others. Moreover, this problem is very famous and popular in the context of machine learning, since images can be represented as matrixes which can be the input to classifiers and clustering algorithms. In this way, there is a great variety of works about machine learning applied to face recognition to detect emotions [10], intrusions [15], classify images [16], among others. Furthermore, neural networks have been widely used to solve face and object recognition problems. In this article, classic and deep neural network methodologies have been analysed in order to study the main features of each one, when classic or deep models are preferred and if deep learning really improves classic neural model's results and deserves further consideration.

The rest of the document is structured as follows: Sect. 2 makes a set of experiments using classic neural networks in order to pose the results of these methods. Section 3 explains the deep neural networks methodology in order to study its main features. After that, Sect. 4 shows the experiments and the results obtained using deep models, and finally, Sect. 5 exposes some conclusions and further works.

2 Classic Neural Networks for Face and Object Recognition Problems

In this section, some experiments using classic neural networks applied to face and object recognition problems are carried out. To do that, two different datasets have been selected. On the one hand, cars dataset has been used [3,4]. This is a common dataset used for benchmarking in object recognition and applications of neural networks. It contains 1050 images where it is possible to find or not a car. The problem is to classify the images into positive and negative classes, where positive are those that contain a car, and negative those that do not. Then, it is a binary classification problem. On the other hand, a face database has been made taking photos of the members of MAT (Models and Algorithms for Transportation Systems) research group. In this case, the problem is to recognize the member of the group in each photo. This problem is a multi-class problem, since there is a total of seven members in the group and within each one, twenty five photos were taken. After that, with the purpose of obtaining a similar dataset, concerning to size of cars dataset, the images obtained have been replicated and transformed through movements and rotations in order to provide a larger dataset using the keras image data generator module. After that, faces dataset had 1256 images. These datasets have been chosen deliberately, since it is intended to study the performance of classic neural networks in different classification problems.

The experiments have been made using the 70% of the data for training and the rest for testing. The images have been compressed into an array of twenty-one statistical features, which have been extracted for each image. These include: maximum, minimum and mean of the pixels, variance, standard deviation, quartiles, kurtosis, etc. Thus, each image from the dataset can be represented as an array which include all the computed features and the class attribute, reducing the complexity of managing images as multi-dimensional arrays. This process is shown in Fig. 1. The features extraction process can be as complex as it is wanted, existing different kinds of statistical features in order to improve the image compression. Usually, this process is the most expensive in terms of computational and temporary cost in classic methodologies and it is highly dependent on the problem features, which is an important drawback of classic neural networks. In this case, to reduce the time needed to this process, these easy features have been chosen.

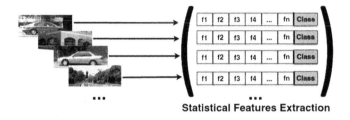

Statistical Features Extraction

Fig. 1. Image processing sample

Nine neural network models have been trained for both datasets: eight of them are variations of a multilayer perceptron (MLP), changing the number of hidden layers, neurons per hidden layer and iterations of the training algorithm. In these cases, Resilient Propagation (RProp) [18] algorithm has been used to train the networks. This algorithm proposes a local adaption of the weight-updates according to the behaviour of error function and the sign of the derivatives. The last neural network is a probabilistic neural network (PNN) which employs constructive training [1] as underlying training algorithm. The main advantage of this algorithm is that it does not need a network topology, since it adds hidden layers according to the training process and avoids misclassifications.

The results of the nine networks applied to both datasets are shown in Table 1. Accuracy and Cohen's Kappa index κ have been shown. The first one defines the percentage of well-classified instances, while the second one measures the agreement between two raters who classify the data. If there is not agreement, $\kappa \leq 0$ and if they are in complete agreement, $\kappa = 1$. It is calculated as it is shown in Eq. (1),

$$\kappa = \frac{p_0 - p_e}{1 - p_e} \tag{1}$$

Table 1. Experiments using classic neural models

Neural network		Cars dataset		Faces dataset	
		Accuracy (%)	Cohen's Kappa	Accuracy (%)	Cohen's Kappa
MLP_1	1 hidden layer 10 neurons/hidden layer 100 iterations RProp	73.968	0.476	50.398	0.422
MLP_2	5 hidden layers 10 neurons/hidden layer 100 iterations RProp	77.46	0.544	42.971	0.335
MLP_3	1 hidden layer 100 neurons/hidden layer 100 iterations RProp	73.651	0.466	55.172	0.477
MLP_4	5 hidden layers 100 neurons/hidden layer 100 iterations RProp	69.206	0.39	44.562	0.354
MLP_5	1 hidden layer 10 neurons/hidden layer 1000 iterations RProp	80.317	0.605	55.172	0.477
MLP_6	5 hidden layers 10 neurons/hidden layer 1000 iterations RProp	66.032	0.313	50.398	0.421
MLP_7	1 hidden layer 100 neurons/hidden layer 1000 iterations RProp	<u>80.635</u>	<u>0.611</u>	<u>61.008</u>	<u>0.545</u>
MLP_8	5 hidden layers 100 neurons/hidden layer 1000 iterations RProp	73.016	0.458	45.358	0.366
PNN	Theta minus = 0.2 Theta plus = 0.4	80.317	0.604	51.194	0.43

where p_0 is the observed probability of agreement and p_e is the expected probability of chance agreement. Analysing the results, it is possible to see that the best model for both problems is MLP_7. It is a shallow MLP with a large number of hidden neurons and iterations to train the network. The second best model is MLP_5. It has only ten neurons in the hidden layer but employs 1000 iterations to train the model. In the case of car dataset, the results of this model are similar to the results provided by PNN model. Thus, it can be noticed that the parameters which impact more in the performance of the models are the number of hidden neurons in the hidden layer and the number of training iterations. In this case, the number of hidden layers does not provide any improvement. Furthermore, the third best model is different now. In the case of cars dataset, it is MLP_2. It uses only ten neurons in the hidden layer and 100 Rprop iterations. In the case of faces dataset, the third best model is MLP_3, which uses the same training iterations but 100 neurons in the hidden layer. Here, we can notice that it is possible to see that in cases of binary classification it is not necessary as many neurons as in the case of a multi-class classification problem. Finally, the probabilistic neural network appears in both cases as a good approximation without the need of checking different configurations of a MLP, which are usually chosen by trial and error. In the case of cars dataset, it provides the second best result together with MLP_5 while in the face dataset, it provides a good mean result. However, in both cases, there is a threshold that is difficult to improve. In cars dataset it is an 80% of accuracy and a 60% in the case of faces dataset.

3   Deep Neural Networks in Object and Face Recognition

One of the main drawbacks of image compression by feature extractors is the loss of information. Although a lot of different engineering mechanisms to extract features in images have been developed, they are unable to detect features from different abstraction levels, obtaining only a general representation highly dependent on each individual image.

In order to solve this problem, deep neural models appear. They are composed by different processing layers which will detect and learn representations and features of different abstraction levels [13]. Now, the input data of the classifier will be the multi-dimensional array which represent each image of the dataset, and each layer of the network will learn different image characteristics in multiple abstraction levels.

One of the most popular deep learning models are convolutional neural networks (CNNs). They are mainly used in image and video recognition, since they usually receive multi-dimensional arrays as input and not a linear features representation like it happens in classic models. CNNs are composed by convolutional layers, which have a receptive field which deals with a portion of the real image. In this way, the neurons in a convolutional layer are organised in feature maps in such a way that each layer has the features extracted by the previous layers [6]. Thus, this portion of image, so called convolutional frame, is moving through the rest of the dataset in order to learn image characteristics. The activation function in these layers is usually the ReLU activation function. After convolutional layers, pooling layers are added to the model. These layers use the maximum function value for each receptive field. In this manner, the activation is the maximum value of the output neurons, avoiding overfitting. Thus, in the example of car dataset, the first layer will detect the edges of the image, the next one can detect a component like a wheel, and finally, the last layer will determine if the image contains or not a car. Using this approach, solving this problem do not require expert knowledge or an expensive engineering process for feature extraction according with problem characteristics, in contrast with what happens in classic models. An example of a CNN network is shown in Fig. 2.

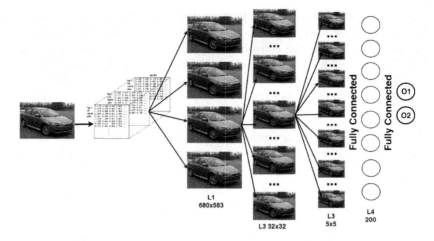

Fig. 2. An example of a convolutional neural network

4   Experiments and Results

This section defines the computational experiments carried out in order to check the performance and capabilities of deep neural networks in face and object recognition problems. To do that, cars and face datasets have been used again. Four experiments based on CNNs have been defined which are called C1,C2,C3 and C4. They have been trained for one hundred epochs, using the same train and test sets that in the experiments carried out in Sect. 2. The experiments have been repeated ten times in order to normalize the results reached. Each configuration has the following features:

- **C1:** It is a simple CNN which has one convolutional layer with a convolutional frame of 5 × 5 pixels. After this layer, a max pooling and a dropout layer are added in order to retrieve the results of the convolutional layer and prevent from overfitting. Dropout is a regularization technique which disable certain neurons in each layer using a Bernouilli probability distribution. Finally the feature maps is flatten out into a fully-connected layer adding a dense layer of 128 neurons.
- **C2:** This model is a variation of the previous one. In this case, the convolutional frame is larger. In the case of the faces dataset it has 50 × 50 pixels while in the case of cars is 10 × 10 (since the images from cars dataset are smaller). The dense layer of this model has 200 neurons in comparison with the dense layer of C1 configuration.
- **C3:** The third configuration is a convolutional network which contains two convolutional layers, in order to check the performance of these networks when multiple convolutional layers are added in order to extract different features from various abstraction levels. In this way, the network has one convolutional layer followed by the max pooling and dropout layers. Later, the output of the dropout layer will be the input of the second convolutional

layer, which will have again its max pooling and dropout layers. Finally, the feature maps obtained here is flatten out into a dense layer with 128 neurons. In this configuration, the convolutional frame has 5×5 pixels in both layers.

- **C4:** The last model is a variation of the third one. In this case, the convolutional frame is augmented like in C2 configuration. Thus, it has 50×50 pixels in the case of faces dataset and 10×10 pixels in the case of cars. The dense layer has again 200 neurons.

Table 2 shows the four configurations chosen in this article, the amount of parameters to be fixed in each model and the results obtained for each network in terms of error (loss), accuracy and standard deviation.

Table 2. Experiments using convolutional neural networks

	Cars dataset				Faces dataset			
	N° parameters	Loss	Accuracy	Std	N° parameters	Loss	Accuracy	Std
C1	3,541,762.0	0.1465	94.36%	0.1904	4,330,234.0	1.6061	70.55%	0.0283
C2	4,330,234.0	0.2378	91.46%	0.1492	2,322,443.0	1.6872	68.35%	0.0277
C3	659,234.0	0.2837	87.32%	0.1337	1,381,291.0	1.6674	67.03%	0.0247
C4	333,634.0	0.2285	89.37%	0.1502	613,451.0	1.8403	65.18%	0.0233

The results are very positive. On the one hand, in the case of cars dataset, the four proposed models improve the results achieved by classic neural networks models. However, the best model is C1, since it is the model which has the best accuracy and it does not imply the largest number of parameters to optimize. On the other hand, for the case of faces dataset, the results also improve the performance of classic models, although these kind of deep networks need more iterations to learn different features and obtain better results. In this case, the best model is also C1, in terms of accuracy, but depending on the kind of application it will be necessary to consider the rest of the models, which do not have the best accuracy, but implies less parameters to optimize.

5   Conclusions

In conclusion, this article has studied the performance of deep learning methods, concretely, convolutional neural networks, in face and object recognition problems in comparison with classical neural networks based on feature extractors. Although classic models remove the problem of managing images as multi-dimensional array, using a linear representation based on features extracted from images, they need a lot efforts in developing feature extractors adapted to the problem at hand. Besides, these linear representations have the disadvantage of loss information. In contrast, deep learning and CNNs provide a new tool to solve this kind of problems without the need to have expert knowledge about the problem, since the features extracted by features extractors and others appear in the convolution process to enrich the classification and they run very well in multiclassification and large-scale problems. Furthermore, this approach can be applied to other problems, without replacing the feature extractor.

Acknowledgment. The authors would like to express his thanks to the project with number PEIC-2014- 003-P and to the authorities that give their support to its development, the FEDER and the *Junta de Comunidades de Castilla la Mancha*.

References

1. Berthold, M.R., Diamond, J.: Constructive training of probabilistic neural networks. Neurocomputing **19**(1–3), 167–183 (1998)
2. Abate, A., Nappi, M., Riccio, D., Sabatino, G.: 2d and 3d face recognition: a survey. Pattern Recogn. Lett. **28**(14), 1885–1906 (2007)
3. Agarwal, S., Awan, A., Roth, D.: Learning to detect objects in images via a sparse, part-based representation. IEEE Trans. Pattern Anal. Mach. Intell. **26**(11), 1475–1490 (2004)
4. Agarwal, S., Roth, D.: Learning a sparse representation for object detection. In: Heyden, A., Sparr, G., Nielsen, M., Johansen, P. (eds.) ECCV 2002. LNCS (including LNAI and LNB), vol. 2353, pp. 113–127. Springer, Heidelberg (2002). doi:10.1007/3-540-47979-1_8
5. Barr, J., Bowyer, K., Flynn, P., Biswas, S.: Face recognition from video: a review. Int. J. Pattern Recogn. Artif. Intell. **26**(5), 1266002 (2012)
6. Bengio, Y.: Learning deep architectures for AI. Found. Trends Mach. Learn. **2**(1), 1–27 (2009)
7. Candès, E., Li, X., Ma, Y., Wright, J.: Robust principal component analysis? J. ACM **58**(3), 11:1–11:37 (2011)
8. Damas, S., Cordón, O., Ibáñez, O., Santamaría, J., Alemán, I., Botella, M., Navarro, F.: Forensic identification by computer-aided craniofacial superimposition: a survey. ACM Comput. Surv. **43**(4), 27:1–27:27 (2011)
9. Dantone, M., Bossard, L., Quack, T., Van Gool, L.: Augmented faces, pp. 24–31 (2011)
10. Fasel, B., Luettin, J.: Automatic facial expression analysis: a survey. Pattern Recogn. **36**(1), 259–275 (2003)
11. Ibáñez, O., Ballerini, L., Cordón, O., Damas, S., Santamaría, J.: An experimental study on the applicability of evolutionary algorithms to craniofacial superimposition in forensic identification. Inf. Sci. **179**(23), 3998–4028 (2009)
12. Ilves, M., Gizatdinova, Y., Surakka, V., Vankka, E.: Head movement and facial expressions as game input. Entertain. Comput. **5**(3), 147–156 (2014)
13. Lecun, Y., Bengio, Y., Hinton, G.: Deep learning. Nature **521**(7553), 436–444 (2015)
14. Lee, J.D., Huang, C.H., Huang, T.C., Hsieh, H.Y., Lee, S.T.: Medical augment reality using a markerless registration framework. Expert Syst. Appl. **39**(5), 5286–5294 (2012)
15. Li, Y., Li, W., Wu, G.: An intrusion detection approach using SVM and multiple kernel method. Int. J. Adv. Comput. Technol. **4**(1), 463–469 (2012)
16. Lu, D., Weng, Q.: A survey of image classification methods and techniques for improving classification performance. Int. J. Remote Sens. **28**(5), 823–870 (2007)

17. Ma, L., Tan, T., Wang, Y., Zhang, D.: Efficient Iris recognition by characterizing key local variations. IEEE Trans. Image Process. **13**(6), 739–750 (2004)
18. Riedmiller, M., Braun, H.: A direct adaptive method for faster backpropagation learning: the RPROP algorithm. In: IEEE International Conference on Neural Networks, vol. 1, pp. 586–591 (1993)
19. Snelick, R., Uludag, U., Mink, A., Indovina, M., Jain, A.: Large-scale evaluation of multimodal biometric authentication using state-of-the-art systems. IEEE Trans. Pattern Anal. Mach. Intell. **27**(3), 450–455 (2005)
20. Yin, L., Wei, X., Sun, Y., Wang, J., Rosato, M.: A 3d facial expression database for facial behavior research, pp. 211–216 (2006)

Winograd Algorithm for 3D Convolution Neural Networks

Zelong Wang$^{(\boxtimes)}$, Qiang Lan, Hongjun He, and Chunyuan Zhang

Computer Science Department, National University of Defense Technology,
Changsha 410003, China
{wangzelong15,cyzhang}@nudt.edu.cn, lanqiang_nudt@163.com, hhj_hi@sina.com

Abstract. Three-dimensional convolution neural networks (3D CNN) have achieved great success in many computer vision applications, such as video analysis, medical image classification, and human action recognition. However, the efficiency of this model suffers from great computational intensity. In this work, we reduce the algorithmic complexity of 3D CNN to accelerate this model with Winograd's minimal algorithm. We benchmark a net model on GPU platform, resulting in a speed-up by a factor of 1.2× compared with cuDNN, which is commonly used in many current machine learning frameworks.

Keywords: Winograd algorithm · 3D CNN · Algorithmic complexity

1 Introduction

Recently, 3D image processing has been an important task in computer vision and medical diagnosis. 3D CNN has shown good performance in human action recognition [5] and video classification [16], revealing good ability for 3D image processing. Nevertheless, the remarkable ability of 3D CNN's extracting features is accompanied by a large computational cost. In a 3D CNN model, convolution layers dominate the computation consumption, taking the most computing time. The computational complexity of 3D convolution layers grows cubically and becomes a bottleneck in this model; therefore, it is necessary to reduce the computation complexity of the 3D convolution layers, which is the largest part of the calculation in 3D CNN.

In this work, we present an algorithm to accelerate 3D CNN using Winograd's minimal algorithm. In addition, we represent the algorithmic complexities of several convolution layers with various parameter configurations. After this, practical experiments are conducted and the result reveals that our method obtains a considerable speed-up by a factor of 1.4× compared with cuDNN in our test CNN model.

Related Work. Recent work exploited CNN algorithmic complexity to make this model fast. Denton et al. [3] focused on decreasing the redundancy of CNN

© Springer International Publishing AG 2017
A. Lintas et al. (Eds.): ICANN 2017, Part II, LNCS 10614, pp. 609–616, 2017.
https://doi.org/10.1007/978-3-319-68612-7_69

models by linear compression techniques and reported experiments on Imagenet [7], showing a considerable speed-up on convolution layers by a factor of two to three times. Jaderberg et al. [4] demonstrated some tensor decomposition schemes. They obtained a remarkable speed-up by a factor of 4.5×. Based on previous work, Tai et al. [14] made progress on tensor decomposition ideas, proposing an approach for training low-rank constrained CNNs. They illustrated a good speed-up (1.5×) on a NIN [9] model.

Vasilache et al. [17] implemented convolution with fast fourier transform (FFT) on a Torch [1] framework, decreasing the time for convolution operation. Mathieu et al. [10] presented an algorithm with the Convolution Theorem, accelerating the training and inference processes in CNN models. Wang et al. [18] reduced the algorithmic complexity of a special CNN model by combining the FFT algorithm with a spectral pooling technique, which is proposed by Rippel et al. [12]

Exploration on reducing convolution algorithmic complexity has been carried out since the early years [2,15]. By developing the previous work of Cook [2] and Toom [15], Winograd [19] presented a minimal filtering algorithm to reduce the arithmetic complexity of a convolution operation. His invention made great progress on signal processing technology. Creatively, Lavin and Gray [8] utilised the Winograd algorithm on 2-dimensional (2D) CNN and benchmarked a GPU implementation with the VGG [13] network. They obtained a state-of-art performance.

2 Three-Dimensional Winograd Algorithm

2.1 Winograd Algorithm

In CNN models, convolution operation is extraordinarily similar to the finite impulse response (FIR) filter. Let $x_0, x_1, x_2, \cdots$ be the signal sequence at times $0, t, 2t, \cdots$, and we would like to compute the first m outputs with an n-tap filter: $z_i = \sum_{j=0}^{n-1} x_{i+j} w_j$, $i = 0, 1, 2, \cdots, m-1$, where $w_0, w_1, w_2, \cdots, w_{n-1}$ are the weights of the taps of the filter. We denote this computation by $F(m, n)$. The ordinary algorithm for $F(2,3)$ needs $2 \times 3 = 6$ multiplications; however, Winograd [19] developed an artful minimal algorithm to reduce the amount of multiplications for $F(m, n)$. Now we consider the minimal algorithm for $F(2,3)$, which is used as an important kernel in the high-dimension case:

$$F(2,3) = \begin{pmatrix} z_0 \\ z_1 \end{pmatrix} = \begin{pmatrix} x_0 \ x_1 \ x_2 \\ x_1 \ x_2 \ x_3 \end{pmatrix} \begin{pmatrix} w_0 \\ w_1 \\ w_2 \end{pmatrix} = \begin{pmatrix} m_1 + m_2 + m_3 \\ m_2 - m_3 - m_4 \end{pmatrix} \tag{1}$$

where $m_1 = (x_0 - x_2)w_0$, $m2 = (x_1 + x_2)\frac{w_0+w_1+w_2}{2}$, $m_3 = (x_2 - x_1)\frac{w_0-w_1+w_2}{2}$, and $m_4 = (x_1 - x_3)w_2$. This algorithm needs only four multiplications for computing m_i $(i = 1, 2, 3, 4)$. Theoretically, it has been proven that the amount of multiplications for $F(m, r) = m+r-1$ [19]. Note that it also needs two additions for m_1 and m_4, seven additions ($w_0 + w_2$ can be reused) and two multiplications by a constant for m_2 and m_3.

Generally, the minimal algorithm for $F(2,3)$ can be written in matrix form as $Z = M[(X\boldsymbol{x}) \odot (W\boldsymbol{w})]$, where $\odot$ is denoted as element-wise multiplication, $\boldsymbol{x}, \boldsymbol{w}$ are column vectors, and the specific matrices are:

$$M = \begin{pmatrix} 1 & 1 & 1 & 0 \\ 0 & 1 & -1 & -1 \end{pmatrix}, X = \begin{pmatrix} 1 & 0 & -1 & 0 \\ 0 & 1 & 1 & 0 \\ 0 & -1 & 1 & 0 \\ 0 & 1 & 0 & -1 \end{pmatrix}, W = \begin{pmatrix} 1 & 0 & 0 \\ \frac{1}{2} & \frac{1}{2} & \frac{1}{2} \\ \frac{1}{2} & -\frac{1}{2} & \frac{1}{2} \\ 0 & 0 & 1 \end{pmatrix} \quad (2)$$

Note that the transformation matrices X, W, M are left multiplied by $\boldsymbol{x}, \boldsymbol{w}$, and the intermediate result, respectively. According to the knowledge of linear algebra, left multiplication by a matrix is equivalent to row transformation, and right multiplication by a matrix is equivalent to column transformation. In other words, the transformation matrices make row transformations for $\boldsymbol{x}, \boldsymbol{w}$ and the intermediate result. This observation indicates how to develop a one-dimension Winograd algorithm to multi-dimension cases.

2.2 Nesting Technique for $F(2 \times 2, 3 \times 3)$ and $F(2 \times 2 \times 2, 3 \times 3 \times 3)$

Minimal 2D algorithms for computing $m \times n$ outputs with an $r \times s$ filter is denoted by $F(m \times n, r \times s)$. It has been documented in Lavin et al. [8] that $F(m \times n, r \times s)$ can be nested by minimal 1D algorithms $F(m, r)$ and $F(n, s)$. Specifically, $F(m \times m, r \times r)$ are obtained by nesting $F(m, r)$ with itself and can be expressed as: $Z = M[(X\boldsymbol{x}X^T) \odot (W\boldsymbol{w}W^T)]M^T$, where $\boldsymbol{w}$ is an $\mathbf{r} \times \mathbf{r}$ filter, $\boldsymbol{x}$ is an $(\mathbf{m + r - 1}) \times (\mathbf{m + r - 1})$ image tile, and X, W, M are transformation matrices. Using the similar notation above, we denote $F(m \times n \times l, r \times s \times t)$ as a minimal 3D algorithm for computing $m \times n \times l$ outputs with an $r \times s \times t$ filter. In practice, we just considered $F(m \times m \times m, r \times r \times r)$. Given an $r \times r \times r$ filter and an $m \times m \times m$ image tile, $F(m \times m \times m, r \times r \times r)$ can be generated by nesting $F(m, r)$ with itself on column, row and depth direction. We illustrated the process in Fig. 1:

Generally, $F(2 \times 2 \times 2, 3 \times 3 \times 3)$ is an important kernel when computing large image size convolution layers due to the common usage of the filter size of $3 \times 3 \times 3$ in many 3D networks. However, there are other kernels such as $F(3 \times 3 \times 3, 2 \times 2 \times 2)$ and $F(4 \times 4 \times 4, 3 \times 3 \times 3)$. Computation for these kernels can be obtained by utilising our nesting technique demonstrated in Fig. 1, with corresponding transformation matrices (X, W, M), which can be found in Lavin et al. [8]

It has been proven that the minimal filtering algorithm for computing $F(m \times n, r \times s)$ requires $\mu(F(m \times n, r \times s)) = \mu(F(m, r))\mu(F(n, s)) = (m+r-1)(n+s-1)$ multiplications. [20] With the similar idea, it is easy to prove that $\mu(F(m \times n \times l, r \times s \times t)) = \mu(F(m, r))\mu(F(n, s))\mu(F(l, t)) = (m+r-1)(n+s-1)(l+t-1)$. Therefore, the standard algorithm for computing $F(2 \times 2 \times 2, 3 \times 3 \times 3)$ uses $2 \times 2 \times 2 \times 3 \times 3 \times 3 = 216$ multiplications, while the minimal algorithm just uses $(2 + 3 - 1)^3 = 64$ multiplications. It is obviously a significant reduction in the algorithmic complexity.

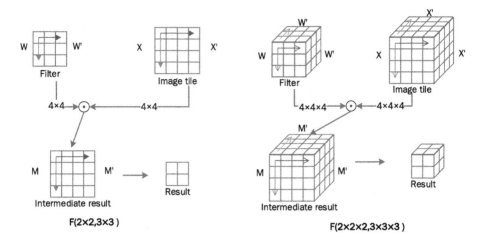

Fig. 1. The nesting skills for generating a minimal algorithm for a 3D case using transformation matrices. For simplicity, we just considered $F(2 \times 2 \times 2, 3 \times 3 \times 3)$. As for the other choices for m and r, the procedure is the same as above, while the W, X, M are different. Matrices and directions with the same colour are corresponding. The matrices are responsible for leading transformation in the corresponding directions.

3   3D Convolution Network

A 3D convolution layer correlates an input image tensor $\mathcal{X} \in \mathbb{R}^{N \times D \times H \times W \times C}$ and a filter tensor $\mathcal{W} \in \mathbb{R}^{C \times R \times S \times T \times K}$, where N, C, K denote the batch size of images, input channels, and output channels, respectively. D, H, W and R, S, T denote the size of input images and filters. The output image $\mathcal{O}$ is given by the expression: $\mathcal{O}_{n,\hat{d},\hat{h},\hat{w},k} = \sum_{c=1}^{C} \sum_{r=1}^{R} \sum_{s=1}^{S} \sum_{t=1}^{T} \mathcal{X}_{n,\hat{d}+r,\hat{h}+s,\hat{w}+t,c} \mathcal{W}_{c,r,s,t,k}$ where $\mathcal{O} \in \mathbb{R}^{N \times (D-R+1) \times (H-S+1) \times (W-T+1) \times K}$.

3.1   Winograd Algorithm for 3D Convolution Network

The Winograd minimal algorithm for $F(m \times m \times m, r \times r \times r)$ can be utilised to compute the output of a 3D convolution layer, where the size of the kernels in the convolution layer is exactly $r \times r \times r$. In each channel, the input image is divided into a range of tiles, whose sizes are all $\alpha \times \alpha \times \alpha$ ($\alpha = m + r - 1$). Neighbouring tiles overlap each other with $r - 1$ elements. The number of tiles in every channel is $P = \lceil \frac{D}{m} \rceil \lceil \frac{H}{m} \rceil \lceil \frac{W}{m} \rceil$. For each tile, we can use the minimal algorithm to compute $F(m \times m \times m, r \times r \times r)$, then the results are merged over all the channels. We denote $x_{c,b} \in \mathbb{R}^{\alpha \times \alpha \times \alpha}$ as the input tile b in channel c, $w_{k,c} \in \mathbb{R}^{r \times r \times r}$ as the filter k in channel c, and $\mathcal{O}_{k,b} \in \mathbb{R}^{m \times m \times m}$ as the output tile b in filter k, where $b \in \{1, \ldots, P\}, c \in \{1, \ldots, C\}, k \in \{1, \ldots, K\}$. The minimal algorithm for computing convolution layers is demonstrated in Algorithm 1. Note that there are many optimisations which can be used in this algorithm. In each **for-loop**, there are no data hazards, hence we can compute the transformation

Algorithm 1. Compute Convolution Layer with Winograd Algorithm $F(m \times m \times m, r \times r \times r)$

1: **for** $k = 1, \cdots, K, c = 1, \cdots, C$ **do**
2:     Transform $w_{k,c}$ to $u_{k,c}$;
3: **end for**
4: **for** $c = 1, \cdots, C, b = 1, \cdots, P$ **do**
5:     Transform $x_{c,b}$ to $v_{k,c}$;
6: **end for**
7: **for** $k = 1, \cdots, K, b = 1, \cdots, P$ **do**
8:     Compute $y_{k,b} = \sum_{c=1}^{C} u_{k,c} \odot v_{c,b}$
9: **end for**
10: **for** $k = 1, \cdots, K, b = 1, \cdots, P$ **do**
11:     Transform $y_{k,b}$ to $\mathcal{O}_{k,b}$
12: **end for**

---

in parallel using GPU architecture. Moreover, the element-wise multiplication can be converted to a matrix multiplication, which is suitable for GPU and FPGA architectures due to their computational ability.

3.2 Algorithmic Complexity Analysis

In our fast convolution layer, the algorithmic complexity for multiplication is: $\mathfrak{C}_{fast} = NCK\lceil\frac{H}{m}\rceil\lceil\frac{W}{n}\rceil\lceil\frac{D}{l}\rceil(m+r-1)(n+s-1)(l+t-1)$. In order to simplify the equations, we assumed that $\frac{H}{m}, \frac{W}{n}$ and $\frac{D}{l}$ have no remainders. Also, we assumed cubic filters and blocks, that is, $r = s = t$ and $m = n = l$. With the hypothesis above, the fast convolution layer's algorithmic complexity for multiplication is $\mathfrak{C}_{fast} = NCKHWD\frac{(m+r-1)^3}{m^3}$ while the standard convolution layer's algorithmic complexity for multiplication is $\mathfrak{C}_{std} = NCK(H-r+1)(W-r+1)(D-r+1)r^3$. We compared the complexity of a variety of convolution layers that use the minimal algorithm and the standard algorithm. The results are presented in Table 1.

Table 1. Theoretical algorithmic complexity of convolution layers with variety of parameter configurations. We assumed the kernel size is $3 \times 3 \times 3$ and use $F(2 \times 2 \times 2, 3 \times 3 \times 3)$ as the minimal algorithm.

I/O channels		Size of input and filter		Comparison		
Input	Output	$D \times H \times W$	$R \times S \times T$	$\mathfrak{C}_{fast}$	$\mathfrak{C}_{std}$	$\frac{\mathfrak{C}_{fast}}{\mathfrak{C}_{std}}$
3	64	$224 \times 224 \times 224$	$3 \times 3 \times 3$	1.73×10^{10}	5.7×10^{10}	0.30
64	64	$224 \times 224 \times 224$	$3 \times 3 \times 3$	3.68×10^{11}	1.21×10^{12}	0.31
64	128	$112 \times 112 \times 112$	$3 \times 3 \times 3$	9.21×10^{10}	2.94×10^{11}	0.31
128	256	$56 \times 56 \times 56$	$3 \times 3 \times 3$	4.604×10^{10}	1.39×10^{11}	0.33
256	512	$28 \times 28 \times 28$	$3 \times 3 \times 3$	2.302×10^{10}	6.22×10^{10}	0.37
512	512	$28 \times 28 \times 28$	$3 \times 3 \times 3$	4.604×10^{10}	1.24×10^{11}	0.37
512	512	$14 \times 14 \times 14$	$3 \times 3 \times 3$	5.75×10^{9}	1.22×10^{10}	0.47

4   Experiments

In this section, some practical experiments are conducted to evaluate our models. First of all, we implemented the convolution using the matrix-multiplication method (Convolutional MM), which is used in some recent machine learning frameworks [6,11]. We implemented 3D convolution layers with Convolution MM using *blas* on CPU architecture and *cublas* on GPU architecture. Then the run time of convolution layers implemented with Convolutional MM and Winograd minimal algorithm were reported. After that we evaluated the 3D minimal algorithm with a 3D CNN model on GPU architecture.

4.1   Implement Convolution Layer with Matrices Multiplication

In this evaluation, batch numbers were set at 32; there were 64 input channels, 128 output channels and the kernel size was $3 \times 3 \times 3$. We fixed the above parameters and recorded the run time with different input image sizes. The result is presented on the left of Fig. 2.

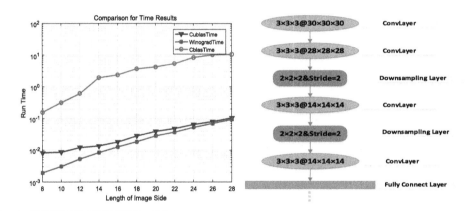

Fig. 2. Left: the run time (seconds) of three methods. When the image size becomes large, *cublas* has an advantage. But the Winograd algorithm holds the best performance in all cases. Right: the architecture of our CNN model. The model is composed of four convolution layers, two down-sampling layers, and some following layers (full connection and softmax).

4.2   Evaluation of the 3D CNN Model

We further experimented with the 3D Winograd algorithm with cuDNN on a 3D CNN model, whose architecture is shown on the right of Fig. 2. The filter size in the convolution layers was always $3 \times 3 \times 3$. Down-sampling layers took the maximum value in every $2 \times 2 \times 2$ cube with a stride of 2. A comparison of the results is illustrated in Table 2. It should be pointed out that the experiment was performed on Nvidia GEFORCE GTX 1080 architecture with Intel Xeon CPU E5-2620 v3 @ 2.40 GHz.

Table 2. Details of our 3D CNN model using the Winograd minimal algorithm on GPU and cuDNN. We implemented our model with the two methods and compared the run time (seconds). The result reveals good speed-up.

Convolution layers	Input tensors				Comparison of the methods		
	N	C	K	$D \times H \times W$	3D Winograd	3D cuDNN	Speed-up
Conv1	32	32	64	$30 \times 30 \times 30$	0.084879	0.0944664	111%
Conv2	32	64	64	$28 \times 28 \times 28$	0.094	0.15013	118%
Conv3	32	64	128	$14 \times 14 \times 14$	0.0113349	0.0207535	183%
Conv4	32	128	128	$7 \times 7 \times 7$	0.00448214	0.00697034	156%
Total					0.19469604	0.27232024	140%

5   Conclusion

In this paper, we introduced a new algorithm for 3D CNN based on the Winograd minimal filter algorithm. We presented in detail a generic nesting technique to generate three-dimensional computing kernels with one-dimensional computing kernels in detail. The algorithm computes the minimal arithmetic complexity convolution over small tiles of the input data. Using the algorithm on 3D CNN leads to a significant reduction in multiplication and efficient GPU implementation due to the natural parallelism. We evaluated this algorithm on convolution layers with a variety of parameter configurations and a specific CNN model. The results show that our implementation on GPU is faster than both Convolution MM with *cublas* and cuDNN(v5 GEMM).

Acknowledgements. This research is supported by the National Key Research and Development program under No. 2016YFB1000401, the National Nature Science Foundation of China under NSFC Nos. 61502509, 61402504, and 61272145; the National High Technology Research and Development Program of China under No. 2012AA012706; and the Research Fund for the Doctoral Program of Higher Education of China under SRFDP No. 20124307130004.

References

1. Collobert, R., Kavukcuoglu, K., Farabet, C.: Torch7: a matlab-like environment for machine learning. In: BigLearn, NIPS Workshop, no. EPFL-CONF-192376 (2011)
2. Cook, S.A.: On the minimum computation time for multiplication. Doctoral dissertation, Harvard U., Cambridge, Mass, 1 (1966)
3. Denton, E.L., Zaremba, W., Bruna, J., LeCun, Y., Fergus, R.: Exploiting linear structure within convolutional networks for efficient evaluation. In: Advances in Neural Information Processing Systems, pp. 1269–1277 (2014)
4. Jaderberg, M., Vedaldi, A., Zisserman, A.: Speeding up convolutional neural networks with low rank expansions. arXiv preprint arXiv:1405.3866 (2014)
5. Ji, S., Xu, W., Yang, M., Kai, Y.: 3d convolutional neural networks for human action recognition. IEEE Trans. Pattern Anal. Mach. Intell. **35**(1), 221–231 (2013)

6. Jia, Y., Shelhamer, E., Donahue, J., Karayev, S., Long, J., Girshick, R., Guadarrama, S., Darrell, T.: Caffe: convolutional architecture for fast feature embedding. In: Proceedings of the 22nd ACM International Conference on Multimedia, pp. 675–678. ACM (2014)

7. Krizhevsky, A., Sutskever, I., Hinton, G.E.: Imagenet classification with deep convolutional neural networks. In: Advances in Neural Information Processing Systems, pp. 1097–1105 (2012)

8. Lavin, A., Gray, S.: Fast algorithms for convolutional neural networks. In: Proceedings of the IEEE Conference on Computer Vision and Pattern Recognition, pp. 4013–4021 (2016)

9. Lin, M., Chen, Q., Yan, S.: Network in network. arXiv preprint arXiv:1312.4400 (2013)

10. Mathieu, M., Henaff, M., LeCun, Y.: Fast training of convolutional networks through FFTs. arXiv preprint arXiv:1312.5851 (2013)

11. Redmon, J.: Darknet: open source neural networks in C (2013–2016). http:// pjreddie.com/darknet/

12. Rippel, O., Snoek, J., Adams, R.P.: Spectral representations for convolutional neural networks. In: Advances in Neural Information Processing Systems, pp. 2449–2457 (2015)

13. Simonyan, K., Zisserman, A.: Very deep convolutional networks for large-scale image recognition. arXiv preprint arXiv:1409.1556 (2014)

14. Tai, C., Xiao, T., Zhang, Y., Wang, X., et al.: Convolutional neural networks with low-rank regularization. arXiv preprint arXiv:1511.06067 (2015)

15. Toom, A.L.: The complexity of a scheme of functional elements realizing the multiplication of integers. In: Soviet Mathematics Doklady, vol. 3, pp. 714–716 (1963)

16. Tran, D., Bourdev, L., Fergus, R., Torresani, L., Paluri, M.: Learning spatiotemporal features with 3d convolutional networks. In: Proceedings of the IEEE International Conference on Computer Vision, pp. 4489–4497 (2015)

17. Vasilache, N., Johnson, J., Mathieu, M., Chintala, S., Piantino, S., LeCun, Y.: Fast convolutional nets with fbfft: a GPU performance evaluation. arXiv preprint arXiv:1412.7580 (2014)

18. Wang, Z., Lan, Q., Huang, D., Wen, M.: Combining FFT and spectral-pooling for efficient convolution neural network model (2016)

19. Winograd, S.: Arithmetic complexity of computations. SIAM, Philadelphia (1980)

20. Winograd, S.: On multiplication of polynomials modulo a polynomial. SIAM J. Comput. $9(2)$, 225–229 (1980)

Core Sampling Framework for Pixel Classification

Manohar Karki[1(✉)], Robert DiBiano[2], Saikat Basu[1],
and Supratik Mukhopadhyay[1]

[1] Louisiana State University, Baton Rouge, LA, USA
mkarki6@lsu.edu
[2] Autopredictive Coding LLC, Baton Rouge, LA, USA

Abstract. The intermediate map responses of a Convolutional Neural Network (CNN) contain contextual knowledge about its input. In this paper, we present a framework that uses these activation maps from several layers of a CNN as features to a Deep Belief Network (DBN) using transfer learning to provide an understanding of an input image. We create a representation of these features and the training data and use them to extract more information from an image at the pixel level, hence gaining understanding of the whole image. We experimentally demonstrate the usefulness of our framework using a pretrained model and use a DBN to perform segmentation on the BAERI dataset of Synthetic Aperture Radar (SAR) imagery and the CAMVID dataset with a relatively smaller training dataset.

1 Introduction

Pixel-wise prediction/classification has applications [9] in scene understanding. The rise of machine learning has led to novel and automatic segmentation techniques that require very little user input [2,8,15]. Deep learning in particular, has enabled this as it makes it possible to learn data representations without supervision. *Core sampling* has been used in engineering and science extensively where a sample section from the cores used to understand the properties of natural materials [16], climatic record from ice cores [11] etc. The lower layers of a Convolutional Neural Networks (CNN) encode the pixels, while the higher layers provide representation of objects comprising of those pixels that eventually help in understanding the entire image. Pixel wise classification and image understanding can be improved with the local and global information that are encoded in the different layers of a CNN; this information, stacked at different pyramidal levels, can be viewed as a *core sample* that can enable better understanding of an image. Figure 2 shows map responses when an input image of a cow is passed through the layers of a pretrained CNN.

In this paper[1], we present a framework that is able to use the activation maps from several layers as features for a Deep Belief Network (DBN) for using transfer

---

[1] A previous version of this paper can be found at: https://arxiv.org/pdf/1612.01981.pdf.

© Springer International Publishing AG 2017
A. Lintas et al. (Eds.): ICANN 2017, Part II, LNCS 10614, pp. 617–625, 2017.
https://doi.org/10.1007/978-3-319-68612-7_70

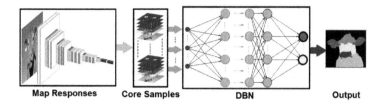

Fig. 1. Architecture of the core sampling framework.

learning to provide an understanding of an entire input image. Our framework creates a representation that combines features from the test data and the contextual knowledge gained from the responses of a pretrained network, processes it and feeds it to a separate DBN. We use this representational model to extract more information from an image at the pixel level, thereby gaining understanding of the whole image. Transfer Learning allows the use of the knowledge gained from solving one problem to improve the solution to another [21]. Our framework makes use of transfer learning, where core samples acquired from a previously trained CNN is used to train a DBN. This strategy helps increase the overall performance and speeds up training by avoiding training a very large network on a huge dataset. The two-stage architecture of our core sampling framework is given in Fig. 1. We use the VGG-16 [19] model to bootstrap our framework. This model has been trained on the ImageNet dataset [12] comprising of an excess of a million training images and 1000 classes. A *core* is a collection of pixels along with their map responses stacked together (i.e. a collection of hypercolumns [9]). It consists of vectors, each with k columns, where k is the number of intermediate maps in the VGG-16 model, with each component of the vector being a map. The spatial correlation between the pixels and the constituent maps are not maintained by the core. A random sample drawn from a core is called *a core sample*. Core samples generated from input images are fed to the second stage of our framework.

At the second stage, our framework consists of a Deep Belief Network (DBN) for classification. DBNs are unsupervised deep learning models [10]. Since no spatial correlation among the maps is preserved when we treat each pixel as a separate data point, a CNN cannot be used in the second stage as the filters in a CNN presume spatial correlation between adjacent maps. The DBN interprets the input core samples to provide an understanding of the original input image. Training VGG-16 on any reasonably large dataset takes a long time [19]. In our core sampling framework we avoid training VGG-16, we only need to train the DBN. This paper makes the following contributions:

1. We present a novel core sampling framework that uses a random samples of activation maps from several layers of a CNN as features to a DBN using transfer learning to provide an understanding of an input image. It combines features from the test data and the contextual knowledge gained from the responses of a pretrained network and then utilizes the representational and discriminative ability of a DBN for pixel level classification.

2. We demonstrate the utility of our framework by showing its ability to automatically segment two distinct types of datasets by using transfer learning: the BAERI dataset [7] of Synthetic Aperture Radar (SAR) imagery and the CAMVID dataset [5].

2   Related Work

Within the deep learning community, CNNs have been used extensively for image recognition; deep CNNs have enabled recognition of objects in images with high accuracy without any human intervention [3,12,14,18]. There has been some research in using the information acquired from the intermediate layers of a CNN to solve tasks such as classification, recognition, segmentation or a combination of these [2,9,15]. Girshick et al. [8] use Region-based CNNs (R-CNNs) where category-independent region proposals are defined during the pre-processing stage, that are input to a CNN to generate feature vectors. A linear Support Vector Machine (SVM) is then used to classify the regions. Unsupervised Sparse auto-encoders have been used in [6] on Synthetic Aperture Radar (SAR) data to classify different types of vehicles. They only deal with classification of images already segmented into smaller regions containing the objects. We deal with segmentation by classification at pixel level.

While introducing hypercolumns, [9] use maps from intermediate layers of a CNN to segment and localize objects. They use a linear combination of K x K classifiers across different positions of the images to classify each pixel. Ladický et al. [13] use a Conditional Random Fields (CRF) based approach to aggregate results from different recognizers. Zhang et al. [24] recover dense depth map images and other information about the frames in video sequences such as height above ground, global and local parity, surface normal, etc. They use graph cut based optimization and decision forests to evaluate their features. The need of video sequences limits their application. Both the previous approaches need manual feature extraction. Another approach is to use deconvolution layers after the convolution layers as a way to reconstruct segmented images as done in [17] and [2]. SegNet [2] uses an encoder architecture similar to VGG-16. The decoder is constructed by removing the fully connected layers and adding deconvolution layers. It is used to transform low resolution maps to high resolution ones.

3   Core Sampling Framework for Pixel Classification

The first few layers of a CNN are used for accurate localization of an object and the layers close to the output layer help to distinguish between different objects. We use the pre-trained VGG-16 [19] model for bootstrapping the core sampling framework. This network is trained on the ImageNet dataset which contains a large variety of objects. This makes it a perfect model to construct a framework that works for a variety of datasets [22]. The first layer of the network learns Gabor Filters or Color blobs [22]. The deeper layers help to discriminate objects and parts of objects while losing spatial and local information [23]. Hence, the

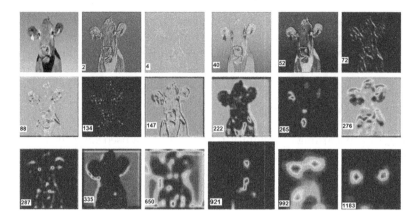

Fig. 2. Response maps resized to original image size. Higher number indicates maps from deeper layers.

combination of maps at different layers helps to capture the spatial as well as the discriminative features. We can see from Fig. 2 that the deeper maps extract abstract features but lose the detalied spatial information about the objects. Each pixel's value, combined with the map response values produced using the pretrained model, is used as a data point. The map values are thus the features for their respective pixels. The size of the core sampling data (processed output data from the pretrained network, described in Sect. 3.2) gets large with the use of response maps from multiple layers of the CNN. For this reason we use a randomly sampled subset of pixels to train the DBN in the second stage.

3.1 Preprocessing and Data Augmentation

The BAERI dataset [7] consists of raw images at inconsistent intensity levels and variable image sizes. Resizing the images would create images that are at different scales which is undesirable. And because the pretrained network needs images with dimensions 224×224, we added padding around images smaller than that. For the same reason, we created sub-images (tiles) from larger images before extracting the map responses. There is no resizing of images; hence no scale normalization is done. We also generated more data by varying contrast to improve robustness. The map responses are individually normalized and the same normalization parameters are used for the corresponding features during testing. All the images in the CAMVID dataset are of the same size (480×360) and are at the same scale, being a standard dataset; hence not much preprocessing or data augmentation needs to be done.

3.2 Core Sample: Intermediate Data Representation

The input images are normalized with the mean Red, Green and Blue (RGB) values (the same procedure that was used while training the pretrained model).

From each image, we acquire map responses from each layer. Most of the map responses are n × n shapes (n ∈ 2^i, i = positive integer). The map responses, which are of various sizes, are resized to original image size using bilinear interpolation. These map responses are then stacked along with original input image. From this point onwards, each pixel is a distinct data point with the map response values as its features. We are expecting a data point to have a single label value, when we train on this data in the second stage of our framework. The map responses from each layer of the CNN are normalized using standard feature scaling. We define a *core* as a collection of such map response values, one per pixel for an input image. *Core samples* are random samples drawn from a core. We feed the core samples to the second stage of our framework. Depending upon the size of the image and the number of response maps on the pretrained network, the number of features for the DBN can be high. We are limited by the amount of data points that can be processed by our Graphical Processing Unit (GPU). We define a hyperparameter χ, which is the total core samples that we can process. The value of χ can be adjusted to provide a trade-off between computational power and classification accuracy.

3.3   Pixel Level Prediction Using Deep Belief Network

DBNs consist of several layers of stochastic, latent variables that are first updated with unsupervised training and then later with supervised learning phase [10]. During the unsupervised learning phase, a Restricted Boltzmann Machine (RBM) is used to train the layers. We use unsupervised pretraining using RBMs followed by supervised learning using DBNs for the final pixel-wise prediction. The unsupervised training helps us to cluster the features together further, and helps to converge the training faster.

Why DBN: If we cluster images by average map response, we can see a CNN gets more organized every layer as larger chunks are recognized. In simple cases where many high level features/object parts are recognized, a standard two layer network should be enough. In a standard CNN, the convolutional layers handle the bulk of the data abstraction, and the fully connected layers are only receiving the very abstracted data from the bottom layer. If the maps from the upper layers are a major part of solving the problem, a DBN should be used to ensure the data is properly abstracted. In [22], the authros showed how CNNs lose generality as data travels through them; so this would certainly be the case when trying to make predictions about images that differ significantly from those in the original CNN training set (as is the case for our data). Similarly, the more the classification problem diverges from simple object recognition, the less our desired output distributions will resemble the internal distributions in the CNN, and the more additional levels of abstraction will be desirable.

4   Experimental Results and Discussion

The BAERI dataset [7] consists of imagery collected from a Synthetic Aperture Radar (SAR). The input single channel image consists of SAR values and the labels are the ground truth values at each of the pixels. Labels were obtained by morphological image processing techniques for noise removal, i.e., opening and closing. There are certain areas in the ground truth images that still contain some noise with incorrect labels. As, we are classifying each pixel separately, the noise must be taken into account during training. The values in the training images were in the range between -40 and 25. In this dataset, the pixel classes are those belonging to the ship class and the rest. There are only 55 images of variable sizes available in this dataset with the total size of 68 megabytes. This dataset is quite different from ImageNet because it contains SAR data not present in ImageNet. As a result of transfer learning, the knowledge acquired from ImageNet based on the wide variety of features abstracted at various levels by the pretrained VGG-16 network prevented the sparsity of the BAERI dataset [7] from creating any problem in training the DBN in the second stage. On this dataset, our frame work was able to slightly outperform SegNet (see Table 1). The output images of SegNet had less blobs that could be classified as noise but it also missed a few of the smaller "ships" and had a larger area of pixels incorrectly classified as ships around the main clusters compared to our algorithm. All results images can be seen at [1].

Table 1. Results on BAERI dataset [7]

Metric	Our method	SegNet [2]
Accuracy (%)	**99.24**	98.08
Mean Squared Error (MSE)	**.0115**	.0142

The CAMVID dataset [4,5] consists of 32 semantic classes of objects out of which, like most of the other approaches [13,24], we evaluate our algorithm on the 11 major classes and 1 class that includes the rest. These classes are Building, Sky, Car, Road, Pedestrian, Column-Pole, Fence, Side-walk, Bicyclist, Tree and Sign Symbol [5]. The training set includes input images, that are regular three channel color images and the targets are segmented single channel images (Fig. 3).

These consist of labeled images with 367 training, 101 validation and 233 test images of consistent sizes at the same scale. On the CAMVID dataset, our framework outperformed both [13,24] on 10 of the 11 classes in terms of accuracy and had a better per class accuracy (see Table 2). Both [13,24] and our framework were trained on 367 labeled training images. As can be seen from Table 2, our framework could not match the performance of SegNet on the CAMVID dataset in terms of accuracy except for the Sky, Column-Pole, and Bicyclist classes where it outperformed SegNet. However, while our framework was trained on 367 labeled images, SegNet was trained on 3500 labeled images. Compared to the other approaches that only use 367 training images, our approach did better on classes (underlined in Table 2) with limited pixels such as Column-Pole, Bicyclist, Pedestrian and Sign-Symbol as well as the overall class average. We used the theano [20] deep learning library and an Intel i7 six core server with TITAN X GPU for our experiments. On this processor, the maximum χ value was 1003520

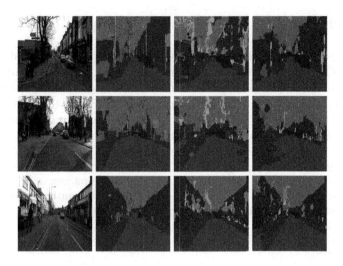

Fig. 3. Results on the CAMVID dataset [4,5]. The images from left to right: (a) original image (b) ground truth (c) our alogrithm (d) SegNet [2]

Table 2. Results on CAMVID dataset [4,5]

Classes	Our method	Boosting (CRF + Detectors) [13]	Dense depth maps [24]	SegNet [2]
	367 Training images			3.5 K Images
Building	71.0	81.5	<u>85.3</u>	**89.6**
Tree	62.6	<u>76.6</u>	57.3	**83.4**
Sky	**96.8**	96.2	95.4	96.1
Car	72.2	<u>78.7</u>	69.2	**87.7**
Sign-Symbol	<u>52.3</u>	40.2	46.5	**52.7**
Road	80.4	93.9	**98.5**	96.4
Pedestrian	<u>56.4</u>	43.0	23.8	**62.2**
Fence	<u>48.1</u>	47.6	44.3	**53.5**
Column-Pole	**39.5**	14.3	22.0	32.1
Sidewalk	77.3	<u>81.5</u>	38.1	**93.3**
Bicyclist	**38.5**	33.9	28.7	36.5
Class Avg.	<u>63.2</u>	62.5	55.4	**71.2**

core samples (approximately the same number of pixels as 20 full input images), which is only 1.58% of the total available pixels on the CAMVID dataset. We can expect improvements with a better processor by increasing this percentage.

5   Conclusions

We presented a framework that takes activation maps from several layers of a pretrained CNN as features to a DBN using transfer learning to aid pixel level classification. We experimentally demonstrate the usefulness of our framework by performing segmentation on Synthetic Aperture Radar (SAR) imagery and the CAMVID dataset [4,5]. We intend to use the core sampling framework to facilitate compression of images and texture synthesis.

Acknowledgement. The project is partially supported by Army Research Office (ARO) under Grant #W911-NF1010495. Any opinions, findings, and conclusions or recommendations expressed in this material are those of the authors and do not necessarily reflect the views of the ARO or the United States Government.

References

1. Results, baeri images. https://drive.google.com/open?id=0B0gFcrqVCm9pUy01 bWpheGs3RlU
2. Badrinarayanan, V., Handa, A., Cipolla, R.: Segnet: a deep convolutional encoder-decoder architecture for robust semantic pixel-wise labelling. arXiv preprint arXiv:1505.07293 (2015)
3. Bengio, Y.: Learning deep architectures for AI. Found. Trends® Mach. Learn. **2**(1), 1–127 (2009)
4. Brostow, G.J., Fauqueur, J., Cipolla, R.: Semantic object classes in video: a high-definition ground truth database. Pattern Recogn. Lett. **30**(2), 88–97 (2008)
5. Brostow, G.J., Shotton, J., Fauqueur, J., Cipolla, R.: Segmentation and recognition using structure from motion point clouds. In: Forsyth, D., Torr, P., Zisserman, A. (eds.) ECCV 2008. LNCS, vol. 5302, pp. 44–57. Springer, Heidelberg (2008). doi:10. 1007/978-3-540-88682-2_5
6. Chen, S., Wang, H.: Sar target recognition based on deep learning. In: 2014 International Conference on Data Science and Advanced Analytics (DSAA), pp. 541–547. IEEE (2014)
7. Ganguly, S.: Baeri dataset. Personal Communication. https://drive.google.com/ open?id=0B0gFcrqVCm9peTdMdndTV0pQMFE
8. Girshick, R., Donahue, J., Darrell, T., Malik, J.: Region-based convolutional networks for accurate object detection and segmentation. IEEE Trans. Pattern Anal. Mach. Intell. **38**(1), 142–158 (2016)
9. Hariharan, B., Arbeláez, P., Girshick, R., Malik, J.: Hypercolumns for object segmentation and fine-grained localization. In: Proceedings of IEEE Conference on Computer Vision and Pattern Recognition, pp. 447–456 (2015)
10. Hinton, G.E., Osindero, S., Teh, Y.W.: A fast learning algorithm for deep belief nets. Neural Comput. **18**(7), 1527–1554 (2006)
11. Kotlyakov, V.: A 150,000-year climatic record from Antarctic ice. Nature **316**, 591–596 (1985)
12. Krizhevsky, A., Sutskever, I., Hinton, G.E.: Imagenet classification with deep convolutional neural networks. In: Advances in Neural Information Processing Systems, pp. 1097–1105 (2012)

13. Ladický, Ľ., Sturgess, P., Alahari, K., Russell, C., Torr, P.H.S.: What, where and how many? combining object detectors and CRFs. In: Daniilidis, K., Maragos, P., Paragios, N. (eds.) ECCV 2010. LNCS, vol. 6314, pp. 424–437. Springer, Heidelberg (2010). doi:10.1007/978-3-642-15561-1_31

14. LeCun, Y., Jackel, L., Bottou, L., Cortes, C., Denker, J.S., Drucker, H., Guyon, I., Muller, U., Sackinger, E., Simard, P., et al.: Learning algorithms for classification: a comparison on handwritten digit recognition. Neural Netw. Stat. Mech. Perspect. **261**, 276 (1995)

15. Long, J., Shelhamer, E., Darrell, T.: Fully convolutional networks for semantic segmentation. In: Proceedings of IEEE Conference on Computer Vision and Pattern Recognition, pp. 3431–3440 (2015)

16. Lotter, N., Kowal, D., Tuzun, M., Whittaker, P., Kormos, L.: Sampling and flotation testing of sudbury basin drill core for process mineralogy modelling. Miner. Eng. **16**(9), 857–864 (2003)

17. Noh, H., Hong, S., Han, B.: Learning deconvolution network for semantic segmentation. In: Proceedings of IEEE International Conference on Computer Vision, pp. 1520–1528 (2015)

18. Russakovsky, O., Deng, J., Su, H., Krause, J., Satheesh, S., Ma, S., Huang, Z., Karpathy, A., Khosla, A., Bernstein, M., et al.: Imagenet large scale visual recognition challenge. Int. J. Comput. Vis. **115**(3), 211–252 (2015)

19. Simonyan, K., Zisserman, A.: Very deep convolutional networks for large-scale image recognition. arXiv preprint (2014). arXiv:1409.1556

20. Theano Development Team: Theano: a Python framework for fast computation of mathematical expressions. arXiv e-prints abs/1605.02688. http://arxiv.org/abs/1605.02688

21. Torrey, L., Shavlik, J.: Transfer learning. In: Handbook of Research on Machine Learning Applications and Trends: Algorithms, Methods, and Techniques. **1**, p. 242 (2009)

22. Yosinski, J., Clune, J., Bengio, Y., Lipson, H.: How transferable are features in deep neural networks? In: Advances in Neural Information Processing Systems, pp. 3320–3328 (2014)

23. Zeiler, M.D., Fergus, R.: Visualizing and understanding convolutional networks. In: Fleet, D., Pajdla, T., Schiele, B., Tuytelaars, T. (eds.) ECCV 2014. LNCS, vol. 8689, pp. 818–833. Springer, Cham (2014). doi:10.1007/978-3-319-10590-1_53

24. Zhang, C., Wang, L., Yang, R.: Semantic segmentation of urban scenes using dense depth maps. In: Daniilidis, K., Maragos, P., Paragios, N. (eds.) ECCV 2010. LNCS, vol. 6314, pp. 708–721. Springer, Heidelberg (2010). doi:10.1007/978-3-642-15561-1_51

Biomedical Data Augmentation Using Generative Adversarial Neural Networks

Francesco Calimeri[1], Aldo Marzullo[1(✉)], Claudio Stamile[2],
and Giorgio Terracina[1]

[1] Department of Mathematics and Computer Science,
University of Calabria, Rende, Italy
{calimeri,marzullo,terracina}@mat.unical.it
[2] Department of Electrical Engineering (ESAT), STADIUS,
Katholieke Universiteit Leuven, Leuven, Belgium
Claudio.Stamile@esat.kuleuven.be

Abstract. Synthesizing photo-realistic images is a challenging problem with many practical applications [15]. In many cases, the availability of a significant amount of images is crucial, yet obtaining them might be not trivial. For instance, obtaining huge databases of images is hard, in the biomedical domain, but strictly needed in order to improve both algorithms and physicians' skills. In the latest years, new deep learning models have been proposed in the literature, called Generative Adversarial Neural Networks (GANNs) [7], that turned out as effective at synthesizing high-quality image in several domains. In this work we propose a new application of GANNs to the automatic generation of artificial Magnetic Resonance Images (MRI) of slices of the human brain; both quantitative and human-based evaluations of generated images have been carried out in order to assess effectiveness of the method.

Keywords: Generative Adversarial Networks · MRI · Biomedical imaging

1 Introduction

The availability of a large amount of data is a crucial issue for applications in many domains. Indeed, proper data are essential in order to understand specific scenarios (for instance, useful information are extracted for predicting the evolution of systems or environments) and develop effective applications. This is especially the case of the biomedical domain; however, in such context collecting a significant amount of "good" data is not always an easy task, due, for instance, to the high costs in terms of money and time required to perform screenings and

The work is partially funded by an EU MC ITN TRANSACT 2012 (316679) project and the European Union's Horizon 2020 research and innovation programme under the Marie Skłodowska-Curie grant agreement No. 690974. Authors thank the Nvidia GPU Education Center of the University of Calabria for the kind support.

© Springer International Publishing AG 2017
A. Lintas et al. (Eds.): ICANN 2017, Part II, LNCS 10614, pp. 626–634, 2017.
https://doi.org/10.1007/978-3-319-68612-7_71

analyses, or, as in the case of certain pathologies, to the number of case study which is too limited for the creation of data banks large enough to train physicians, experts, or artificial models. A possible way to overcome limited availability, in some domains, is to artificially *create new data*. For many tasks, indeed, this can be achieved by modifying initially available data [8]. As an example, new instance images can be obtained by applying linear transformations (i.e., rotation, reflection, scaling, etc.) to already available ones. Unfortunately, the same approach is not straightforwardly applicable to any task: for example, it is difficult to generate new "artificial" data for a density estimation, unless one has already solved the density estimation problem.

One of the most interesting alternatives, when dealing with image data, consists of learning the latent manifold on which the input images lie, and then sample realistic pictures (and their labels) from this manifold. We refer to *Generative* models as a class of machine learning algorithms which start from a training set consisting of samples drawn from a distribution, and learn how to represent an estimate of that distribution, or samples of it, to some extent. One of the goals of this work is to apply such techniques to new *generative* areas, not explored so far. In particular, we present the application of a specific type of Generative Models, namely *Generative Adversarial Neural Networks* (GANNs), to the generation of new, unseen, MRI (Magnetic Resonance Imaging) slices of the human brain. Interestingly, the model produces samples very similar to real MRI slices, which present realistic features. To the best of our knowledge, this is one of the first attempts to apply GANNs to biomedical imaging, and brain images in particular. We validated the generated images both analytically and via an ad-hoc web platform, where human physicians and experts have been invited to distinguish whether an image is real or artificially generated.

The remainder of the paper is structured as follows. In Sect. 2 we provide a detailed description of our approach, and then illustrate related literature in Sect. 3. Section 4 presents our experimental evaluation and eventually, in Sect. 5 we draw our conclusion.

2 Proposed Approach

In the following, we describe the background techniques and methods, and provide further details on the proposed approach.

2.1 Generative Adversarial Neural Networks

Generative Adversarial Neural Network is a generative model approach based on differentiable generator networks [8]. GANNs are conceived for scenarios in which the generator network must compete against an adversary, in a sort of forger-police relation. Two actors are involved: the *Generator* network (the "forger"), which directly produces samples $x = g(z, \theta^{(g)})$, where g is a given probability distribution that describes the training set; the *Discriminator* (the "police"), that attempts to distinguish between samples taken from the original data and samples drawn from the Generator; in other words, it estimates a probability value given by $d(x, \theta^{(d)})$, indicating the probability that x is a real training example rather than an artificial sample drawn from the model. The best way to describe the GANN training process is as a zero-sum game as defined in game theory, in which the Discriminator's Generator's payoffs are $v(\theta^{(g)}, \theta^{(d)})$ and $-v(\theta^{(g)}, \theta^{(d)})$, respectively. During the learning process, each player attempts to maximize its own payoff; in such a scenario, the Discriminator is called examine an image and estimate whether it is "real" (i.e., taken from the training set) or "artificial" (i.e. generated by the algorithm). This means that it must learn some general rules that govern the distribution until, at convergence, the Discriminator is no more able to distinguish Generator's samples from real data, so its output is $\frac{1}{2}$ everywhere. On the other side, the Generator should learn how to generate images that look more and more similar to the samples from the training set, in order to fool the Discriminator and make it believe that they are real.

2.2   Laplacian Pyramid of Adversarial Networks

Several GANN models exist. As a first attempt, we take advantage from a recent optimization method which uses a cascade of convolutional networks within a Laplacian pyramid framework (LAPGAN), in order to generate images in a coarse-to-fine fashion [4]. The goal is achieved by building a series of generative models, each one able to capture image structure at a particular scale of a Laplacian pyramid[1]. This approach allows to first generate a very low-resolution version of an image, and then incrementally add details to it. The Generator (G) and the Discriminator (D), indeed, are not trained directly on full-sized images: the training starts with a downsampling at a minimum size which is increased (e.g., doubled) during multiple steps, until the final size is reached. During these steps another pair of G and D are trained to learn good refinements of the upscaled images. This means that G learns how to improve the quality of its input, adding good refinements, and, at the same time, D learns how refined images look like. It is worth noting that this methodology is very closely related to the one a human being typically employ to draw images: start with a rough sketch, and then progressively add more and more details.

2.3   Generating MRI Slices of the Brain

Our approach uses a GANN to automatically generate MRI slices of the brain; in our work the architecture described in [4], public available on github[2], was maintained "as is", except for the size of the output, which has been increased by adding one more convolutional layer. The framework makes use of another convolutional neural network, the *Validator*, in charge of assigning validation scores to generated images and trained once before the Generator network. Artificial

---

[1] Due to space constraints we omit a detailed description of Laplacian pyramid; we refer the reader to [1].

[2] https://github.com/aleju/sky-generator.

images used to train the Validator are created by applying some transformations to real images. These techniques are sometimes combined with each other.

Both the Generator and the Discriminator are convolutional networks trained with stochastic gradient descent, where Adaptive Moment Estimation is used as optimizer. The architecture of the Generator is basically a full laplacian pyramid in one network; it starts with a linear layer, which generates 16×8 images, followed by upsampling layers, which increase the image size to 32×16, 64×32 and then 128×64 pixels. The Discriminator is a convolutional network with multiple branches. Rotations are removed by means of spacial transformer at the beginning; three out of the four branches have also spatial transformers (for rotation, translation and scaling), so they can learn to focus on specific areas of the image. The fourth branch is intended to analyze the whole image.

3   Related Works

Artificial generation of natural images is a widely studied task in machine learning, and constituted an ambitious goal for many years [8]. Several efforts have been spent to solve the problem of generating realistic high-resolution images, and several novel approaches [5,6] have already been proven to be well-suited for generating realistic images which look very similar to the ImageNet dataset [11], also achieving impressive results at high resolutions.

As for the biomedical domain, the problem of automatically generated unseen instances has been addressed by means of many different techniques. Many studies focussed on the reconstruction or the synthesis of an image starting from some initial data [9], on the synthesis of a source MRI modality to another target MRI modality [13], on the generation of multi-modal medical images of pathological cases based on a single label map, also outperforming the state-of-the-art methods it has been compared against. Closer to our proposal, in [3], the Authors tested the capability of GANNs in generating high quality retinal fundus images from pairs of retinal vessel trees and corresponding retinal images. We use the method proposed in [4], as an attempt to generate high-quality MRI slices in order to augment biomedical datasets with a fast and inexpensive method.

4   Experimental Analysis

4.1   Dataset Description

The dataset consists of $46,737$ images representing MRI slices extracted from 77 subjects. Each subject underwent 8 MR scans. The MR protocol consisted in the acquisition of a sagittal 3D-T1 sequence $(1 \times 1 \times 1\,\text{mm}^3, TE/TR = 4/2000\,\text{ms})$. In order to have "pure" MRI images, no post-processing was applied to the images.

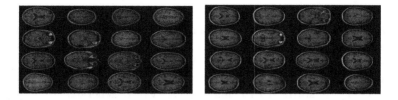

Fig. 1. Real (left) images compared with artificial (right) images

4.2 Training Phase

The training process consists of multiple steps: at first, the Validator and the Generator are trained for a predefined number of steps, 50 and 10, respectively; then, the real training process, i.e., the zero-sum game, starts. Results shown in the following refer to 800 epochs of training (Fig. 1). Since images are defined on a grayscale, the framework was used with the *grayscale* parameter enabled, so that only one input channel was used during the operations. In order to perform all the tests, the following workstation was used: x86_64 CPU(s), Intel(R) Xeon(R) CPU E5440 @ 2.83 GHz, Linux Debian 4.8.4-1, CUDA compilation tools, release 7.5, V7.5.17, NVIDIA Corporation GK110GL on Tesla K20c.

4.3 Evaluation

Rigorous performance evaluation of GANNs is an important research area, since is not clear how to quantitatively evaluate generative models [8]. Indeed, finding an images evaluation method in such a context is not straightforward. When using statistical methods, for instance, it might not be sufficient to look at probability distributions among pixels or part of the images, as "geometric" relations are crucial. Also, the task is quite different from a clustering or classification problem, as the point is to find what kind of "features" allow one to tell if an image is eligible to stay within a given group or not, and not only judge "similarities". This is why, besides quantitative tests, we also conduct human evaluation to evaluate the quality of the generated images [15].

4.4 Quantitative Image Quality Assessment

We evaluate our approach by means of two different quantitative methods: *(i)* Estimating the distributions of the real and the generated datasets by means of the Kernel Density function and comparing their likelihood; *(ii)* comparing the Inception Score of the two datasets. For the sake of the present work, for each metric we considered two distributions similar if their distance, in terms of score, is below the empirical threshold of 10%.

Kernel Density Function. The approach based on Kernel Density function to evaluate generative models was originally introduced in [2] and applied on

Table 1. Likelihood comparison

Samples	Real	Generated
100	37.31	33.90
1000	34.30	33.92
10000	34.02	33.93

Table 2. Inception score comparison (± standard deviation in parenthesis)

Test	Real	Generated
100	1.92 (±0.26)	1.80 (±0.29)
1000	1.79 (±0.06)	1.89 (±0.08)
10000	1.80 (±0.03)	1.93 (±0.03)

GANNs in [7]. The method estimates the probability of the generated dataset, by fitting a Gaussian Parzen window to the generated samples and reporting the likelihood under this distribution. The bandwidth of the Gaussians is obtained by cross-validating the validation set. In our approach, we compute the similarity between the two datasets estimating their distribution by means of the Kernel Density function, so that similar datasets should be represented by similar distributions. Figure 2 shows the comparison of the density distribution and the estimated Cumulative Density function under real and generated datasets.

Inception Score. Inception Score [12] is an automatic method to evaluate samples which is found to correlate well with human judgement. The probability $p(y \mid x)$ is estimated by applying the Inception model [14] to every image in the dataset, so that images belonging to the same distribution should have low entropy. Consequently, if the generated images are distant from the estimated distribution, the marginal should present high entropy. These assumption are used to compute the Inception Score according to the equation $IS = exp(\mathbb{E}_x KL(p(y \mid x) \| p(y))))$, where KL is the Kullback-Leibler divergence and results are exponentiated so the values are easier to compare. In this work we compare the Inception Score computed on both generated and real dataset. Tables 1 and 2 report a comparison of the likelihood and the Inception Score between both the estimated distributions over 100, 1000 and 10000 samples.

4.5 Human Evaluation of Generated Images

The quality assessment of the generated images are evaluated by means of a web platform[3], where physicians and experts are called to distinguish between real and artificial images. More in detail, two sets of 100 images (both 100 real and 100 artificial) was prepared. Each user is proposed, one at a time, images from a set of 20 randomly extracted from the two sets with, probability $\frac{1}{2}$. During each trial, true positive (TP), true negative (TN), false positive (FP) and false negative (FN) are collected, where *positive* is used to indicate real images and *negative* is referred to artificial ones. In order to assess the quality of the delineation, we compute Accuracy ($Acc = \frac{TP}{P+N}$), Precision ($Prec = \frac{TP}{TP+FP}$), Recall ($Rec = \frac{TP}{TP+FN}$) and F1-score ($F1 = \frac{2*Prec*Rec}{Prec+Rec}$) where P is the number

---
[3] www.tinyurl.com/mrichallenge.

of positive samples and N the number of negative ones. We collected 15 tests performed by different experts in neuroimaging field; they achieved (on average) an accuracy, precision, recall and F1-score, to discriminate between real and "artificial" images, of 0.52 ± 0.16, 0.55 ± 0.23, 0.58 ± 0.21, and 0.53 ± 0.17, respectively. A detailed report of the performances obtained by each expert can be found on the project website[4].

Results obtained after human evaluation show the capability of our method to generate "artificial" MR images similar to real one. The difficulty to differentiate between the two is well underlined by the low values of F1-score obtained by humans in the tests. Furthermore, in order to have a more detailed feedback, we also asked our experts to write down comments describing how did they tell the difference between real and "artificial" images. Among others, we received two interesting observations: the first is about grey and white matter tissues contrast, while and the second about image symmetry. Those two limitations are indeed noticeable in the generated images: they present a low level of contrast between the two tissues, and an high symmetry between the two hemispheres. Based on the quantitative results and the comments obtained from the experts, we can say that our method is definitely appropriate, and still features significant room for improvement.

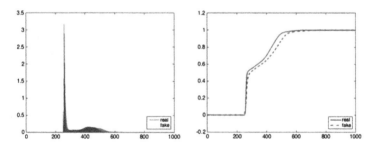

Fig. 2. Density function (left) and Cumulative Density function (right) comparison of generated (orange ▬) and real (blue ▬) datasets (Color figure online).

5   Conclusion

In this paper we show the feasibility of learning to perform the synthesization of unseen high-quality MRI slices of the human brain by means of Generative Adversarial Neural Network (GANNs). The aim of the work is to ease inexpensive and fast augmentation of biomedical datasets, in order to overcome the lack of real images and allow physicians and machine learning algorithms to take advantage from new instances for their training.

Applications of GANNs have been just started to be studied in literature, and a large variety of applications are still open. As future work, we aim to

---

[4] www.tinyurl.com/mrichallenge-reports.

improve the quality of the generated images, to be more and more similar to real MRI scans; to this aim, a comparison with alternatives models, such as Deep Convolutional Generative Adversarial Networks (DCGAN) [10], will be of clear interest, as they are currently emerging in literature. Furthermore, the generation may be improved by allowing the network to add pathological symptoms and provide unseen data of synthesized patients; this might also improve the study of rare diseases. Another perspective is the combination of the generated slices in order to compose a three-dimensional MRI. Eventually, we are planning to better investigate quality and use of quantitative measures for the assessment of the methods.

References

1. Burt, P.J., Adelson, E.: The laplacian pyramid as a compact image code. IEEE Trans. Commun. **31**, 532–540 (1983)
2. Breuleux, O., Bengio, Y., Vincent, P.: Quickly generating representative samples from an RBM-derived process. Neural Comput. **23**(8), 2053–2073 (2011)
3. Costa, P., Galdran, A., Meyer, M.I., Abrmoff, M.D., Niemeijer, M., Mendonça, A.M., Campilho, A.: Towards adversarial retinal image synthesis. arXiv preprint arXiv:1701.08974 (2017)
4. Denton, E.L., Chintala, S., Fergus, R.: Deep generative image models using a Laplacian pyramid of adversarial networks. In: Advances in Neural Information Processing Systems, pp. 1486-149 (2015)
5. Dosovitskiy, A., Springenberg, J.T., Brox, T.: Learning to generate chairs with convolutional neural networks. In: Computer Vision and Pattern Recognition, CVPR (2015)
6. Dosovitskiy, A., Brox, T.: Generating images with perceptual similarity metrics based on deep networks. arXiv preprint arXiv:1602.02644 (2016)
7. Goodfellow, I.J., Pouget-Abadie, J., Mirza, M., Xu, B., Warde-Farley, D., Ozair, S., Courville, A., Bengio, Y.: Generative adversarial nets. Advances in Neural Information Processing Systems (2014)
8. Bengio, Y., Goodfellow, I.J., Courville, A.: Deep Learning Book. MIT Press (2015, in preparation). http://www.iro.umontreal.ca/bengioy/dlbook
9. Nie, D., Trullo, R., Petitjean, C., Ruan, S., Shen, D.: Medical image synthesis with context-aware generative adversarial networks. arXiv preprint arXiv:1612.05362 (2016)
10. Radford, A., Metz, L., Chintala, S.: Unsupervised representation learning with deep convolutional generative adversarial networks. arXiv preprint arXiv:1511.06434 (2015)
11. Russakovsky, O., Deng, J., Su, H., Krause, J., Satheesh, S., Ma, S., Huang, Z., Karpathy, A., Khosla, A., Bernstein, M., Berg, A.C., Fei-Fei, L.: Imagenet large scale visual recognition challenge. IJCV **115**(3), 211–252 (2015)
12. Salimans, T., Goodfellow, I.J., Zaremba, W., Cheung, V., Radford, A., Chen, X.: Improved techniques for training gans.In: Advances in Neural Information Processing Systems, pp. 2226–2234 (2016)
13. Sevetlidis, V., Giuffrida, M.V., Tsaftaris, S.A.: Whole image synthesis using a deep encoder-decoder network. In: Tsaftaris, S.A., Gooya, A., Frangi, A.F., Prince, J.L. (eds.) SASHIMI 2016. LNCS, vol. 9968, pp. 127–137. Springer, Cham (2016). doi:10.1007/978-3-319-46630-9_13

14. Szegedy, C., Vanhoucke, V., Ioffe, S., Shlens, J., Wojna, Z.: Rethinking the Inception Architecture for Computer Vision. arXiv:1512.00567, pp. 2818–2826 (2016)
15. Zhang, H., Xu, T., Li, H., Zhang, S., Huang, X., Wang, X., Metaxas, D.: Stack-GAN: text to photo-realistic image synthesis with stacked generative adversarial networks. arXiv preprint arXiv:1612.03242 (2016)

Detection of Diabetic Retinopathy Based on a Convolutional Neural Network Using Retinal Fundus Images

Gabriel García[1], Jhair Gallardo[1], Antoni Mauricio[2], Jorge López[2(✉)], and Christian Del Carpio[1]

[1] Medical Image Processing Group, Department of Mechanical Engineering, Universidad Nacional de Ingeniería, Bldg. A - Off. A1-221, 210 Tupac Amaru Ave., Lima, Peru
gabrconatabl@gmail.com, jhairgallardo@gmail.com, cdelcarpiod@gmail.com
[2] Department of Computer Science, Research Institute of Computer Science, Universidad Católica de San Pablo, Bldg P. José de Acosta, 4th Floor, Urb. Campi ña Paisajista s/n, Arequipa, Peru
{manasses.mauricio,jorge.lopez}@ucsp.edu.pe

Abstract. Diabetic retinopathy is one of the leading causes of blindness. Its damage is associated with the deterioration of blood vessels in retina. Progression of visual impairment may be cushioned or prevented if detected early, but diabetic retinopathy does not present symptoms prior to progressive loss of vision, and its late detection results in irreversible damages. Manual diagnosis is performed on retinal fundus images and requires experienced clinicians to detect and quantify the importance of several small details which makes this an exhaustive and time-consuming task. In this work, we attempt to develop a computer-assisted tool to classify medical images of the retina in order to diagnose diabetic retinopathy quickly and accurately. A neural network, with CNN architecture, identifies exudates, micro-aneurysms and hemorrhages in the retina image, by training with labeled samples provided by EyePACS, a free platform for retinopathy detection. The database consists of 35126 high-resolution retinal images taken under a variety of conditions. After training, the network shows a specificity of 93.65% and an accuracy of 83.68% on validation process.

Keywords: Diabetic retinopathy · Deep learning · Convolutional neural network · Medical image classification

1 Introduction

The recent success of convolutional neural network algorithms in natural imaging applications is due to the fact that it is inspired by the hierarchical organization of the human visual cortex, the use of database images on a scale of millions and the development of hardware (GPU) fast enough to process the training of millions of parameters. The results obtained have shown that in basic visual

© Springer International Publishing AG 2017
A. Lintas et al. (Eds.): ICANN 2017, Part II, LNCS 10614, pp. 635–642, 2017.
https://doi.org/10.1007/978-3-319-68612-7_72

tasks (from the point of view of human vision) these algorithms are capable of having a precision very close to that of a human. These facts have also allowed to open many possibilities in medical applications in different areas.

Although deep learning has reduced the time of analysis in medical imaging, including the diabetic retinopathy test, its computational cost far exceeds established previous methods. According to [1], prior algorithms to intensive use of convolutional neural networks can be categorized into 5 groups: preprocessing, location and segmentation of the optic disc, segmentation of the retinal vasculature, location of the macula and fovea, location and segmentation of pathologies of diabetic retinopathy. In [2], an automatic system for the detection of diabetic retinopathy was presented using fundus images extracting characteristics such as the area of blood vessels, area of microaneurysms and texture. The selected characteristics were trained using Naive Bayes to classify the disease in 3 states: Normal, Nonproliferative Diabetic Retinopathy (NPDR) and Proliferative Retinopathy. While [3] focuses on detecting changes in the retina that indicate diabetic retinopathy. Retinal images are first subjected to preprocessing techniques by color normalization and then image segmentation in order to detect blood vessels, microaneurysms, haemorrhages, the optic disc and lipid clusters. In that line, [4] presents a new algorithm for detecting blood vessels in the fundus images. The enhancement of the blood vessels in the image is carried out using a pretreatment stage, followed by transformations on curves which is applied to the equalized image. This improved image is used for removal of blood vessels. The estimation of the exudates is obtained from the blood vessels and the optical disc extracts from the image. The results show that the retinal images improved by this method have a better PSNR and the area of exudates shows the severity of the disease. By using an SVM classifier, [5] focuses on the automatic detection of diabetic retinopathy by detecting exudates in the background color of the retinal eye images and also classifies the severity of the lesions. [6] performs its work with the same classifier but using the sequential minimal optimization algorithm.

The works presented in [7] and [8] are among the first to solve the problem through neural networks, focusing on learning changes in blood vessels and lipid clusters. In [9], the authors classify different states of Diabetic Retinopathy (NPDR) and differentiate them from a healthy eye by analyzing fundus images. A feature extraction stage is performed and then use a multi-layer perceptron or "MLP algorithm" achieving 94.11% accuracy. More recently with the inclusion of CNN architectures, works like [10–12] have improved the learning ratios marked by other neural network architectures. In [10], is proposed the use of a deep neural network (DNN) by means of the use of auto-encoders to obtain an initialization model. Then they perform a supervised training using "random forest" for the detection of blood vessels in the fundus images. They obtained an accuracy of 93.27% and an area under the ROC curve of 0.9195. While [11] presents a method using deep learning to perform the detection of blood vessels in the fundus images. The structure or "ConvNet" that they propose is trained to segment the areas where the blood vessels of the areas that do not contain them are located. Their experiments were carried out using the "DRIVE" database, obtaining an average accuracy of 94.7% and an area under the ROC curve of 0.9283. [12] propose a CNN approach to diagnosing diabetic retinopathy from digital fundus images and accurately classifying its severity. Developing a network with CNN architecture and data augmentation which can identify the intricate features involved in the classification task such as micro-aneurysms, exudate and haemorrhages on the retina and consequently provide a diagnosis automatically and without user input. By using a high-end graphics processor unit (GPU) on the publicly available Kaggle dataset and demonstrate outstanding results, particularly for a high-level classification task. On the data set of 80,000 images used its proposed CNN achieves a sensitivity of 95% and an accuracy of 75% on 5,000 validation images.

2   Preprocesssing

Retinal images were provided by EyePACS [13], a free platform for retinopathy detection. The database consists of high-resolution retinal images taken under a variety of conditions. Both eyes images are provided to us for each patient. Each case is rated on a scale of 0 to 4, depending on the level of degeneration and these scales are used as labels in the algorithm. Figure 1, shows the illumination variability and size in different images of the database.

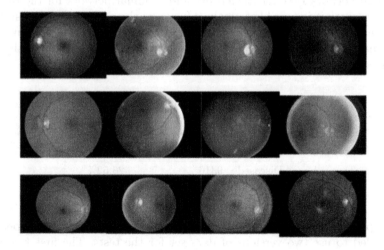

Fig. 1. Sample of the EyePACS image bank.

It can be noticed that the images in Fig. 1 are not standardized. In other words, each contains an non-regular black border, different aspect ratio, different lighting and different color average. In images pre-processing, each one was scaled by standardizing the size of the eyeball; then we 'subtract the color mean', and

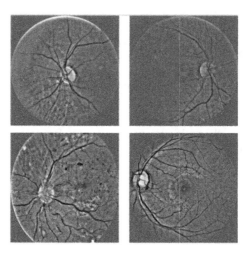

Fig. 2. Retinal fundus images after preprocessing.

thus map the mean to gray (128). Finally, we re-scaled the image to 256×256. The results are shown in Fig. 2.

We decided to separate the images into two sections: the right and the left eye. The same network model will be used in each section and thus, we achieve an specialized network type for the left eye and a similar network for the right eye. In a future work it is possible to make a fusion of these two networks using their fully connected layers. Another detail of the set of images is the class imbalance. So for that, it was decided to perform a binary classification. Table 1 shows the new division in classes.

Table 1. Binary classification labels of the data.

Class	Name	Number of images	Percentage
0	Healthy	25810	73.48%
1	Diseased	9316	26.52%

The proportion between healthy and diseased cases is 2.74 to 1, respectively. We decided to use two versions of data set for the tests. The first has a ratio of 2.74 to 1, and the second has a ratio of 1 to 1 called 50/50. For this second version, we simply took all the diseased cases and the same number of healthy cases were chosen randomly. In both versions a data augmentation method was used, which consists on flips and take parts of the images. A probability of 50% was given for each image, If it gets positive, it is taken the 80% of the image in length and height from a random border inside. In a similar way was performed the flips.

3   Neural Networks

Different configurations of neural networks architectures were tested, all based on convolutional networks. Table 2 shows the networks, number of layers and training mode.

Table 2. Different neural network architectures

Network	Distribution	Layers	Training mode	Learning rate
$Model_1$	50/50	6	From scratch	0.01
$Model_2$	50/50	9	From scratch	0.01
VGG16	50/50	16	Pre-train	0.0001
$VGG16noFC_1$	50/50	15	Pre-train	0.0001
$VGG16noFC_2$	Original	15	Pre-train	0.0001

These models are inspired in the "Alex-net" model [14], they are convolutional layers followed by "max-polling" layers and finally by a set of fully connected layers. Moreover, all networks have a fixed momentum of 0.9, and the fully-connected layer has a dropout of 0.65, making it highly robust, but with low performance possibility in classification process.

Models 1 and 2 were trained from scratch. By testing of said model it was analyzed the capacity of a convolutional network to learn the corresponding filters to classify the data. When trained from scratch, the networks must learn basic filtering such as edge detection or corners in their first layers. A pre-trained network already contains such filters, so the models VGG16, $VGG16noFC_1$ and $VGG16noFC_2$ are based on the model VGG-net [15] already trained in the ImageNet database [16]. The two latter ones allows the network to re-adjust the filters according to the data used, resulting in a more robust result. Also, they don't have two Fully Connected Layers, but they have just one.

From the first four networks, $VGG16noFC_1$ has a good performance, so we decide to use a similar network, but this time using the Original distribution. To equilibrate this difference, we use Class Weight, which consists in assign a weight in the cost function of the data depending on the class. As we talked before, the distribution was from 2.74 to 1, so the weight assigned are 1 to the healthy Cases and 2.74 for the diseased ones. Furthermore, we assign it a decay of 0.00005. This new network is called $VGG16noFC_2$.

4   Results

After performing the tests to configure the hyperparameters of each network in Table 2, we obtained the following results.

In Fig. 4, we can see that the network $VGG16noFC_2$ is highly noised and not uniform in the test set, although in the training set, it has a continuous and

Table 3. Results of the training in the test set.

Network	Epochs	Accuracy	Sensitivity	Specificity
Model$_1$	45	63.6%	-	-
Model$_2$	91	66.4%	-	-
VGG16	80	74.3%	62%	86%
VGG16noFC$_1$	75	72.70%	68%	77.60%
VGG16noFC$_2$	80	83.68%	54.47%	93.65%

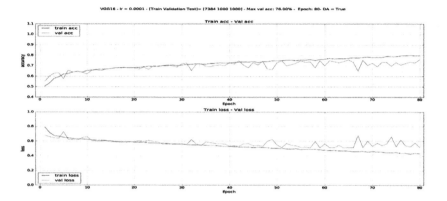

Fig. 3. Epochs vs accuracy and loss function for VGG16.

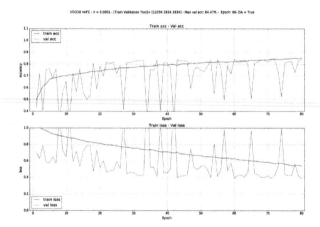

Fig. 4. Epochs vs accuracy and loss function for VGG16noFC$_2$.

non-noise graphics. So it can be deduced that it has a low value of sensitivity, and a high value of specificity, which can be verified in Table 3. As we can see in Fig. 3, the graphics generated in the train set are continuous and they don't have noise, and in contrast, the test graphics has little noise, but it isn't so high. In Table 3 we can see that, although it is 9 points in percentage accuracy below from VGG16noFC$_2$, it is not so highly sensible as it. We can see it in the sensitivity value of 62% in contrast with the 54.47%.

5   Conclusions and Future Work

In this work, we have implemented the most efficient CNN architectures to detect diabetic retinopathy, beginning with a pre-processing stage that included the normalization of the saturation values of each figure, as well as normalization of measurements and elimination of noise. The second stage included training by applying various values of hyperparameters and data distributions. At the end, a 93.65% efficiency in specificity and 83.68% accuracy were obtained in VGG16noFC$_2$ but just 54.47% in sensitivity. Which means that true positive rate is lower than true negative rate. These results leave a possibility of using work as an effective method of discarding the disease in the future. For future work, we will seek to expand the retina imaging database, make a fusion of the two networks (right and left eye) using their fully connected layers as well as improve the network architecture and develop cost functions that fit the database model more closely.

Acknowledgments. The present work would not be possible without the funds of the General Research Institute (IGI - UNI), The Office of Research (VRI - UNI), The Research Institute of Computer Science (RICS - UCSP) and the support of the Artificial Intelligence and Robotics Lab.

References

1. Prentasic, R.P.: Detection of diabetic retinopathy in fundus photographs (2013)
2. Maher, R., Kayte, S., Dhopeshwarkar, D.M.: Review of automated detection for diabetes retinopathy using fundus images. Int. J. Adv. Res. Comput. Sci. Softw. Eng. **5**(3) (2015)
3. Thomas, N., Mahesh, T.: Detecting clinical features of diabetic retinopathy using image processing. Int. J. Eng. Res. Technol. (IJERT) **3**(8) (2014)
4. Singh, B., Jayasree, K.: Implementation of diabetic retinopathy detection system for enhance digital fundus images. Int. J. Adv. Technol. Innov. Res. **7**(6), 0874–0876 (2015)
5. Gandhi, M., Dhanasekaran, R.: Diagnosis of diabetic retinopathy using morphological process and SVM classifier. In: 2013 International Conference on Communications and Signal Processing (ICCSP). IEEE (2013)
6. Sangwan, S., Sharma, V., Kakkar, M.: Identification of different stages of diabetic retinopathy. In: 2015 International Conference on Computer and Computational Sciences (ICCCS). IEEE (2015)
7. Shahin, E.M., et al.: Automated detection of diabetic retinopathy in blurred digital fundus images. In: 2012 8th International Computer Engineering Conference (ICENCO). IEEE (2012)
8. Karegowda, A.G., et al.: Exudates detection in retinal images using back propagation neural network. Int. J. Comput. Appli. **25**(3), 25–31 (2011)

9. Kanth, S., Jaiswal, A., Kakkar, M.: Identification of different stages of diabetic retinopathy using artificial neural network. In: 2013 Sixth International Conference on Contemporary Computing (IC3). IEEE (2013)
10. Maji, D., et al.: Deep neural network and random forest hybrid architecture for learning to detect retinal vessels in fundus images. In: 2015 37th Annual International Conference of the IEEE Engineering in Medicine and Biology Society (EMBC). IEEE (2015)
11. Maji, D., et al. : Ensemble of deep convolutional neural networks for learning to detect retinal vessels in fundus images. arXiv preprint arXiv:1603.04833 (2016)
12. Pratt, H., et al.: Convolutional neural networks for diabetic retinopathy. Procedia Comput. Sci. **90**, 200–205 (2016)
13. Christine, N.: Your diabetic patients: look them in the eyes. Which ones will lose their sight? (2015). http://www.eyepacs.com/diabeticretinopathy/
14. Krizhevsky, A., Sutskever, I., Hinton, G.E.: ImageNet classification with deep convolutional neural networks. In: 26th Advances In Neural Information Processing Systems (2012)
15. Simonyan, K., Zisserman, A.: Very deep convolutional networks for large-scale image recognition. In: International Conference on Learning Representations (ICRL), 114 (2015)
16. Deng, J., Dong, W., Socher, R., Li, L., Li, K., Fei-fei, L.: ImageNet: a large-scale hierarchical image database. In: IEEE Computer Vision and Pattern Recognition (CVPR) (2009)

A Comparison of Machine Learning Approaches for Classifying Multiple Sclerosis Courses Using MRSI and Brain Segmentations

Adrian Ion-Mărgineanu[1,2,3]([⊠]), Gabriel Kocevar[1], Claudio Stamile[1,2,3],
Diana M. Sima[2,3,4], Françoise Durand-Dubief[1,5], Sabine Van Huffel[2,3],
and Dominique Sappey-Marinier[1,6]

[1] CREATIS CNRS UMR5220 & INSERM U1206, Université de Lyon,
Université Claude Bernard-Lyon 1, INSA-Lyon, Villeurbanne, France
adrian@esat.kuleuven.be
[2] Department of Electrical Engineering (ESAT),
STADIUS Center for Dynamical Systems,
Signal Processing and Data Analytics, KU Leuven, Leuven, Belgium
[3] imec, Leuven, Belgium
[4] R&D Department, icometrix, Leuven, Belgium
[5] Service de Neurologie A, Hôpital Neurologique, Hospices Civils de Lyon,
Bron, France
[6] CERMEP - Imagerie du Vivant, Université de Lyon, Bron, France

Abstract. The objective of this paper is to classify Multiple Sclerosis courses using features extracted from Magnetic Resonance Spectroscopic Imaging (MRSI) combined with brain tissue segmentations of gray matter, white matter, and lesions. To this purpose we trained several classifiers, ranging from simple (i.e. Linear Discriminant Analysis) to state-of-the-art (i.e. Convolutional Neural Networks). We investigate four binary classification tasks and report maximum values of Area Under receiver operating characteristic Curve between 68% and 95%. Our best results were found after training Support Vector Machines with gaussian kernel on MRSI features combined with brain tissue segmentation features.

Keywords: Machine learning · Convolutional neural networks · Multiple sclerosis · Magnetic resonance spectroscopic imaging · Brain segmentation

1 Introduction

Multiple sclerosis (MS) is an inflammatory disorder of the brain and spinal cord [1], affecting approximately 2.5 million people worldwide.

The majority of MS patients (85%) usually experience a first attack defined as Clinically Isolated Syndrome (CIS), and will develop a relapsing-remitting (RR) form [2]. Two thirds of the RR patients will develop a secondary progressive (SP) form, while the other third will follow a benign course [3]. The rest of MS patients (15%) will start directly with a primary progressive (PP) form.

© Springer International Publishing AG 2017
A. Lintas et al. (Eds.): ICANN 2017, Part II, LNCS 10614, pp. 643–651, 2017.
https://doi.org/10.1007/978-3-319-68612-7_73

The criteria to diagnose MS forms were originally formulated by McDonald in 2001 [4] and revised by Polman in 2005 [5] and 2011 [6]. They all rely on using conventional magnetic resonance imaging techniques (MRI), such as T1 and FLAIR, due to high sensitivity in visualizing MS lesions. More recently [7], ^{1}H-Magnetic Resonance Spectroscopic Imaging (MRSI) has been shown to provide a better understanding of the pathological mechanisms of MS.

The objective of this study is to fully explore the potential of MRSI for automatic classification of MS courses. To this purpose we use four different machine learning approaches to classify individual spectroscopic voxels inside the brain. We start by using simple machine learning methods (i.e. Linear Discriminant Analysis (LDA)) trained on low-level features commonly used in MRSI, and advance up to state-of-the-art methods (e.g. Convolutional Neural Networks (CNN)) trained on high-level MRSI features.

2   Materials and Methods

2.1   Patient Population

This longitudinal study includes 87 MS patients who were scanned multiple times over several years between 2006 and 2012. Diagnosis and disease course were established according to the McDonald criteria [4,8]. This study was approved by the local ethics committee (CPP Sud-Est IV) and the French national agency for medicine and health products safety (ANSM), and written informed consents were obtained from all patients prior to study initiation. More details for each MS group can be found in Table 1.

Table 1. MS population details

	CIS	RR	PP	SP
Number of patients	12	30	17	28
Total number of scans	60	212	117	192
Total number of voxels	5916	18682	10830	17377

2.2   Magnetic Resonance Data Acquisition and Processing

All patients underwent magnetic resonance (MR) examination using a 1.5 Tesla MR system (Sonata Siemens, Erlangen, Germany) and an 8 elements phased-array head-coil.

MRI Acquisition. Conventional MRI protocol consisted of a 3 dimensional T1-weighted (magnetization prepared rapid gradient echo-MPRAGE) sequence with repetition time/echo time/time for inversion $TR/TE/TI = 1970/3.93/1100$ ms, flip angle $= 15°$, matrix size $= 256 \times 256$, field of view $(FOV) = 256 \times 256$ mm, slice thickness = 1 mm, voxel size = 1 × 1 × 1 mm, and a fluid attenuated inversion recovery (FLAIR) sequence with TR/TE/TI = 8000/105/2200 ms, flip angle = 150°, matrix size = 192 × 256, FOV = 240 × 240 mm, slice thickness = 3 mm, voxel size = 0.9 × 0.9 × 3 mm.

MRSI Acquisition. MRSI data was acquired from one slice of 1.5 cm thickness, placed above the corpus callosum and along the anterior commissure - posterior commissure (AC-PC) axis, encompassing the centrum semioval region. A point-resolved spectroscopic sequence (PRESS) with TR/TE = 1690/135 ms was used to select a volume of interest (VOI) of 105 × 105 × 15 mm^3 during the acquisition of 24 × 24 (interpolated to 32 × 32) phase-encodings over a FOV of 240 × 240 mm^2.

MRI Processing. Three tissues of the brain, gray matter (GM), white matter (WM), and lesions, were segmented based on T1 and FLAIR, using the MSmetrix software [9] developed by ico**metrix** (Leuven, Belgium).

MRSI Processing. MRSI data processing was performed using SPID [10] in MatLab 2015a (MathWorks, Natick, MA, USA). Three metabolites well-studied in MS, N-acetyl-aspartate (NAA), Choline (Cho), and Creatine (Cre), were quantified with AQSES [10] (**A**utomated **Q**uantitation of **S**hort **E**cho time MR **S**pectra), using a synthetic basis set which incorporates prior knowledge of the individual metabolites. Maximum-phase finite impulse response filtering was included in the AQSES procedure for residual water suppression, with a filter length of 50 and spectral range from 1.7 to 4.2 ppm.

Quality Control. First, we removed a band of two voxels at the outer edges of each VOI in order to avoid chemical shift displacement artifacts and lipid contamination artifacts. Second, for each voxel inside a grid, we performed three outlier detections, corresponding to each metabolite, using the median absolute deviation filtering. Final selection includes voxels with a maximum Cramer Rao Lower Bound of 20% for each metabolite, preserved by all three outlier detection mechanisms. In the end, average voxel exclusion rate was 31% ± 6% standard deviation, and only 2 out of 581 spectroscopy grids had an exclusion rate higher than 50%.

2.3   Classification Tasks and Performance Measures

We study four binary classification tasks, relevant from a clinical point of view: CIS vs. RR, CIS vs. PP, RR vs. PP, and RR vs. SP. For each task we set the less represented class between the two to be the positive class, or the class of interest. Therefore, we set the positive class to CIS, CIS, PP, and SP, corresponding to each task. When classifying, we perform a 2-fold stratified cross-validation at the patient level, meaning that each patient will be assigned once to training, and once to testing. The training dataset includes all voxels from all patients assigned to training. When testing, a voxel will be assigned to one of the two classes. For each grid, we compute the probability to be assigned to the positive class by measuring the percentage of voxels assigned to the positive class.

We compute and report three performance measures widely used in classification: AUC (**A**rea **U**nder receiver operating characteristic (ROC) **C**urve), sensitivity, and specificity. The last two measures were computed for the optimal operating point of the ROC curve. Using the general formulation of the confusion matrix from Table 2, sensitivity, or true positive rate (TPR), is defined as $\frac{TP}{TP+FN}$. Specificity, or true negative rate (TNR), is defined as $\frac{TN}{TN+FP}$.

Table 2. General confusion matrix.

Confusion matrix		Predicted condition	
		Predicted negative	Predicted positive
True condition	Condition negative	True Negative (TN)	False Positive (FP)
	Condition positive	False Negative (FN)	True Positive (TP)

The ROC curve can be created when the classification model gives probability values of test points belonging to the positive class, by plotting Sensitivity (y-axis) against 1-Specificity (x-axis) at various probability thresholds. A random classifier has an AUC of 0.5 or 50%, while a perfect classifier will have an AUC of 1 or 100%.

2.4   Feature Extraction Models

Model nr.1 (M1). We use the absolute values of the complex frequency spectrum cut by a pass-band filter between 1.2 and 4.2 ppm, so that we retain the most useful information. In order to have a perfect alignment of all spectra for all patients, we detect the highest peak in the low frequencies (NAA) and shift to the NAA peak of a randomly assigned reference voxel. In this case, each voxel is represented by the filtered frequency vector, which has 81 points. We normalize each vector to its L_2-norm.

Model nr.2 (M2). We use the three quantified metabolite concentrations (NAA, Cho, Cre) to compute three ratios: NAA/Cho, NAA/Cre, and Cho/Cre. Mean values and standard deviations for each MS group can be found in Table 3.

Model nr.3 (M3). For each voxel, we measure the percentage of each tissue of the brain (GM, WM, lesions). In this case, each voxel is represented by 6 features: three metabolic ratios and three tissues percentages.

Table 3. MS population: metabolite ratios - mean (standard deviation).

	CIS	RR	PP	SP
NAA/Cho	2.21 (0.24)	2.02 (0.25)	1.83 (0.18)	1.86 (0.32)
NAA/Cre	1.36 (0.1)	1.35 (0.11)	1.27 (0.11)	1.22 (0.12)
Cho/Cre	0.63 (0.07)	0.69 (0.08)	0.72 (0.1)	0.69 (0.1)

Model nr.4 (M4). For each voxel, we compute the spectrogram of its time-domain signal. First, we interpolate the time-domain signal to 1024 points. We compute the spectrogram using a moving window of 128 points, with an overlap of 112 points. In the end, each voxel will be represented by a 128×57 image. These values have been especially selected such that the final image is large enough to be used as input in CNNs.

2.5   Classifiers

For each classification task and for each of the first three feature extraction models, we used three supervised classifiers: (1) LDA [11] without adjusting for class unbalance, (2) Random Forest [12] (RF) with 1000 trees, adjusted for class unbalance by setting the *class_weight* parameter to *balanced_subsample*, and (3) Support Vector Machines with radial basis function (SVM-rbf) [13], adjusted for class unbalance by setting the *class_weight* parameter to *balanced*, and tuned the misclassification cost "C" by selecting its optimal value out of four values (0.1, 1, 10, and 100) over a 5-fold cross-validation loop. The *gamma* parameter was set to *auto*. All classifiers were built in Python 2.7.11 with scikit-learn 0.17.1 [14]. Feature scaling was learned using the training set and applied on both training and test sets, only for the second and third model.

For the last feature extraction model and for each classification task, we built a CNN inspired by [15] using the Keras package [16] based on Theano [17]. Our architecture consists of 8 weighted layers: 6 convolutional (conv) and 2 fully connected (FC). All convolutional layers have a receptive field of 3×3 and the *border_mode* parameter set to 'same'. All weighted layers are equipped with the rectification non-linearity (ReLU). Spatial pooling is carried out by 3 max-pooling (MP) layers over a 2×2 window with stride 2. The first FC layer has 64 channels, while the second one has only 2, because it performs the two-class classification. The final layer is the sigmoid layer. To regularise the training, we used a Dropout layer (D) between the two FC layers, with ratio set to 0.8. A simplified version of our architecture is (conv-conv-MP-conv-conv-MP-conv-conv-MP-FC(64)-D(0.8)-FC(2)-Sigmoid). When training each CNN, we used the 'adadelta' optimizer, the 'categorical_crossentropy' loss function, and we split the training dataset into 70-30 training-validation data. We stopped training after 200 epochs, and for each classification task, validation accuracy was at a stable value over 85%, signalling that training was performed correctly.

3   Results and Discussion

All performance measures can be found in Table 4. Maximum AUC values for each classification task are highlighted in bold.

Table 4. AUC, Sensitivity, and Specificity values for all classifiers, feature extraction models (M1-M4), and classification tasks.

Percentage [%]		M1			M2			M3			M4
		LDA	RF	SVM-rbf	LDA	RF	SVM-rbf	LDA	RF	SVM-rbf	CNN
CIS vs. RR	AUC	65	50	63	53	55	66	63	76	**77**	71
	Sensitivity	0	0	38	2	0	13	2	28	25	17
	Specificity	100	100	83	100	100	99	100	96	100	98
CIS vs. PP	AUC	89	92	88	87	90	90	88	91	**95**	83
	Sensitivity	68	68	63	67	72	78	65	77	83	73
	Specificity	93	95	94	91	90	89	91	87	90	82
RR vs. PP	AUC	66	62	**68**	64	64	**68**	55	54	57	**68**
	Sensitivity	21	17	50	29	37	56	0	0	0	28
	Specificity	93	94	78	87	82	76	100	100	100	92
RR vs. SP	AUC	72	72	**73**	**73**	71	72	**73**	71	71	69
	Sensitivity	60	54	57	40	43	48	51	38	29	56
	Specificity	75	84	77	90	86	81	82	92	97	75

For CIS vs. RR we obtain a maximum AUC of 77% when combining metabolite ratios with GM, WM, and lesions percentage. The increase in AUC for both SVM-rbf and RF is higher than 10% when we compare M3 to M1 or M2, therefore we can safely conclude that adding GM, WM, and lesions percentage, is indeed beneficial when classifying CIS vs. RR courses. This is most probably due to the fact that RR patients have more lesions than CIS patients. It is worth mentioning that the CNN, which takes as input only the MRSI spectrogram, performs better than all other classifiers based on spectroscopic features.

For CIS vs. PP we obtain a maximum AUC of 95% when combining metabolite ratios with GM, WM, and lesion percentages in each voxel. The increase in AUC for SVM-rbf is higher than 5% when we compare M3 to M1 or M2. This task is not too interesting from the medical point of view, because we know that PP patients have a more aggressive form of MS and a higher lesion load than CIS patients. Our results confirm the clinical background and provide an accurate classification with high sensitivity for PP.

For RR vs. PP we obtain the lowest AUC value of the four classification tasks, only 68%. It is interesting to see that adding GM, WM, and lesion percentages did not improve the results, but on the contrary. This indicates an opposing effect between brain segmentation percentages and metabolic ratios. Another interesting fact is that maximum results obtained with M1, M2, or M4, are exactly the same, indicating that spectroscopy is not sensitive enough to classify these two MS courses.

For RR vs. SP we obtain a maximum AUC value of 73%, if we use M1, M2, or M3. There are two main observations to be made: (1) LDA trained on metabolic ratios can be regarded as the best classifier for this task, due to a simple feature extraction model and high computational speed, and (2) adding brain segmentation percentages did not improve the results.

To our knowledge, there are only two other studies which report classification results between MS courses, and both are based on diffusion MRI. Muthuraman et al. [18] report almost a perfect accuracy of 97% for 20 CIS vs. 33 RR patients, and Kocevar et al. [19] report F1-scores of 91.8% for 12 CIS vs. 24 RR patients, 75.6% for 24 RR vs. 17 PP patients, and 85.5% for 24 RR vs. 24 SP patients. These results show that features extracted from diffusion MRI are clearly better than MRSI features at discriminating MS courses.

The main goal of this study was to compare different levels of extracting information from the MRSI voxels. To that extent, at the low-level we used only 3 metabolite ratios, at the mid-level we used the entire absolute frequency spectrum of 81 points, and at the high-level we used the MRSI spectrograms, of size 128×57. To boost the low-level features, we added the brain tissue segmentations percentages of WM, GM, and lesions. We used spectrograms as input to state of the art classifiers (e.g. CNNs), and compared the results with widely used machine learning algorithms (e.g. LDA, RF, SVM-rbf) trained on features commonly used in MRSI. We observe that results obtained with CNNs are not significantly worse or better than the rest. Thus, it means that there is an inherent limitation of our particular MRSI protocol to classify MS courses.

Our results show that combining low-level MRSI features with brain tissue segmentations percentages can improve classification between the least aggressive MS course (CIS) and the moderate-severe courses (RR and PP). However, there are obvious limitations on any level of the MRSI features when classifying moderate (RR) from severe MS courses (PP and SP). In the future we will incorporate diffusion MRI features and perform multi-class classification.

4   Conclusions

In this paper we performed four binary classification tasks for discriminating between MS courses. We report AUC, sensitivity, and specificity values, after training simple and complex classifiers on four different types of features. We show that combining metabolic ratios with brain tissue segmentation percentages can improve classification results between CIS and RR or PP patients. Our best results are always obtained with SVM-rbf, so we can safely conclude that building complex architectures of convolutional neural networks do not add any improvement over classical machine learning methods.

Acknowledgments.. This work was funded by European project EU MC ITN TRANSACT 2012 (No. 316679) and the ERC Advanced Grant BIOTENSORS nr.339804. EU: The research leading to these results has received funding from the

European Research Council under the European Union's Seventh Framework Programme (FP7/2007–2013). This paper reflects only the authors' views and the Union is not liable for any use that may be made of the contained information.

References

1. Compston, A., Coles, A.: Multiple sclerosis. Lancet **372**(9648), 1502–1518 (2008)
2. Miller, D.H., Chard, D.T., Ciccarelli, O.: Clinically isolated syndromes. Lancet Neurolog. **11**(2), 157–169 (2012)
3. Scalfari, A., Neuhaus, A., Degenhardt, A., Rice, G.P., Muraro, P.A., Daumer, M., Ebers, G.C.: The natural history of multiple sclerosis, a geographically based study 10: relapses and long-term disability. Brain **133**(7), 1914–1929 (2010)
4. McDonald, W.I., Compston, A., Edan, G., Goodkin, D., Hartung, H.P., Lublin, F.D., McFarland, H.F., Paty, D.W., Polman, C.H., Reingold, S.C., et al.: Recommended diagnostic criteria for multiple sclerosis: guidelines from the international panel on the diagnosis of multiple sclerosis. Ann. Neurolog. **50**(1), 121–127 (2001)
5. Polman, C.H., Reingold, S.C., Edan, G., Filippi, M., Hartung, H.P., Kappos, L., Lublin, F.D., Metz, L.M., McFarland, H.F., O'Connor, P.W., et al.: Diagnostic criteria for multiple sclerosis: 2005 revisions to the McDonald criteria. Ann. Neurolog. **58**(6), 840–846 (2005)
6. Polman, C.H., Reingold, S.C., Banwell, B., Clanet, M., Cohen, J.A., Filippi, M., Fujihara, K., Havrdova, E., Hutchinson, M., Kappos, L., et al.: Diagnostic criteria for multiple sclerosis: 2010 revisions to the McDonald criteria. Ann. Neurolog. **69**(2), 292–302 (2011)
7. Rovira, À., Auger, C., Alonso, J.: Magnetic resonance monitoring of lesion evolution in multiple sclerosis. Ther. Adv. Neurolog. Disord. **6**(5), 298–310 (2013)
8. Lublin, F.D., Reingold, S.C., et al.: Defining the clinical course of multiple sclerosis results of an international survey. Neurology **46**(4), 907–911 (1996)
9. Jain, S., Sima, D.M., Ribbens, A., Cambron, M., Maertens, A., Van Hecke, W., De Mey, J., Barkhof, F., Steenwijk, M.D., Daams, M., et al.: Automatic segmentation and volumetry of multiple sclerosis brain lesions from MR images. NeuroImage Clin. **8**, 367–375 (2015)
10. Poullet, J.B.: Quantification and classification of magnetic resonance spectroscopic data for brain tumor diagnosis. Katholic University of Leuven (2008)
11. Fisher, R.A.: The use of multiple measurements in taxonomic problems. Ann. Eugen. **7**(2), 179–188 (1936)
12. Breiman, L.: Random Forests. Mach. Learn. **45**(1), 5–32 (2001)
13. Cortes, C., Vapnik, V.: Support-vector networks. Mach. Learn. **20**(3), 273–297 (1995)
14. Pedregosa, F., Varoquaux, G., Gramfort, A., Michel, V., Thirion, B., Grisel, O., Blondel, M., Prettenhofer, P., Weiss, R., Dubourg, V., Vanderplas, J., Passos, A., Cournapeau, D., Brucher, M., Perrot, M., Duchesnay, E.: Scikit-learn: machine learning in Python. J. Mach. Learn. Res. **12**, 2825–2830 (2011)
15. Simonyan, K., Zisserman, A.: Very deep convolutional networks for large-scale image recognition. arXiv preprint (2014). arXiv:1409.1556
16. Chollet, F.: Keras (2015). https://github.com/fchollet/keras
17. Theano Development Team: Theano: a Python framework for fast computation of mathematical expressions. arXiv e-prints abs/1605.02688. http://arxiv.org/abs/1605.02688

18. Muthuraman, M., Fleischer, V., Kolber, P., Luessi, F., Zipp, F., Groppa, S.: Structural brain network characteristics can differentiate CIS from early RRMS. Front. Neurosci. **10** (2016). Article no. 14
19. Kocevar, G., Stamile, C., Hannoun, S., Cotton, F., Vukusic, S., Durand-Dubief, F., Sappey-Marinier, D.: Graph theory-based brain connectivity for automatic classification of multiple sclerosis clinical courses. Front. Neurosci. **10**, 478 (2016)

Advances in Machine Learning

Parallel-Pathway Generator for Generative Adversarial Networks to Generate High-Resolution Natural Images

Yuya Okadome[✉], Wenpeng Wei, and Toshiko Aizono

Intelligent Information Research Department, Hitachi, Ltd., 1-280,
Higashi-koigakubo, Kokubunji-shi, Tokyo 185-8601, Japan
{yuya.okadome.qj,wenpeng.wei.bo,toshiko.aizono.jn}@hitachi.com

Abstract. Generative Adversarial Networks (GANs) can learn various generative models such as probability distribution and images, while it is difficult to converge training. There are few successful methods for generating high-resolution images. In this paper, we propose the parallel-pathway generator network to generate high-resolution natural images. Our parallel network are constructed by parallelly stacked generators with different structure. To investigate the effect of our structure, we apply it to two image generation tasks: human-face image and road image which does not have square resolution. Results indicate that our method can generate high-resolution natural images with few parameter tuning.

Keywords: Generative Adversarial Networks · Deep learning · Generative models · Parallel structure

1 Introduction

Generative Adversarial Networks (GANs) [1,2] is an easily implementable and powerful generative model. GANs is not only applied to the approximation of probability distribution but also to the task of image generation [3], grasping in the robotics field [4], and aging of the face image [5]. Many applications of GANs are used for the task of image generation based on the success of many deep convolutional neural networks. However, in order to generate a high-resolution image, it is not easy to stably train networks due to the difficulty of tuning to adjust many initial parameters by network designer. Generation of high-resolution image based on the GANs has not been realized.

In this research, we propose the parallel-pathway structure of generation to generate high-resolution natural images. Our parallel structure is capable of generating the image with different aspect ratio by only changing the input of generator and output of discriminator. In addition, while the number of parameters does not dramatically increase [8], the proposed network prevents the collapse which is caused by conversion to "undesired" local optima, since each network has different conversion speed.

© Springer International Publishing AG 2017
A. Lintas et al. (Eds.): ICANN 2017, Part II, LNCS 10614, pp. 655–662, 2017.
https://doi.org/10.1007/978-3-319-68612-7_74

We applied our method to two different image generation tasks: human face and road. The generation task of human face includes different background, and we show that our network allows for separation of the face and background. In addition, we then demonstrate that our network with same parameter and structure of hidden layers cound be applied generate road images with different aspect ratio.

2   Related Work

Generating images are one of the important problems in computer vision. Recently, image generation has become popular with a development of GANs [1]. However, since the learning of original GANs is unstable [6], it is not easy to generate high-resolution images. Therefore, some methods for stable learning and generating high-resolution images are studied and proposed.

DCGAN [3] is proposed to improve the learning of GANs and generate various images. In DCGAN, full-connection layers of GANs are replaced with convolution layers, and the learning is stabilized by setting the network structure, initial weight of convolution layers, and activation function. However, collapse of images is occurred when the condition of experiment is changed such as a different resolution of images.

To stabilize the learning of GANs, some techniques such as minibatch discrimination for preventing collapse of image are proposed [6]. By employing these techniques, it is possible to achieve a stable and fast conversion. However, efficiency of these techniques for image of different aspect ratio is not investigated.

StackGAN [7] is a method of conditional GANs [2] for image generation by converting sentences to numeric vector and input it to generator. This GANs has a structure of connecting two generators in series to generate high-resolution images, and there are discriminator for each generator, i.e., this method has to learn four networks. Therefore, the number of parameters and iterations for learning dramatically increases.

3   Parallel-Pathway Generator Network

In this section, we introduce the structure of the parallel-way generator network. To generate a high-resolution picture, we propose the network structure which has the following properties:

– Parallel-way generator
– The structure of discriminator is same as previous work
– Robustness w.r.t. changing the resolution and aspect ratio of input image.

Since our proposed method does not have a structure connecting in series, the increase in number of parameter become moderate [8]. It is expected that the conversion of learning is not too slow while the capacity of the network increases.

3.1 Preliminaries of GANs

In GANs, the generator network (G) and discriminator network (D) are alternatively trained. D is a classifier and it classifies whether the input image is from training dataset or fake generated by G. G is learned to deceive the D. By competing D and G, generation distribution p of training dataset can be approximated by G. This is the similar setting of two-player min-max with non-cooperative game in the game theory [6].

In two-player min-max setting like GANs, the objective function becomes:

$$\min_G \max_D V(D,G) = E_{x \sim p_{data}}[\log D(x)] + E_{z \sim p_z}[\log(1 - D(G(z)))], \quad (1)$$

where x and z are the true image obtained from data distribution p_{data} and noise vector obtained from certain distribution p_z (e.g., uniform distribution and Gaussian distribution). The updates of D and G are based on following equation:

$$\nabla_{\theta_d} V(D,G) = \nabla_{\theta_d} E_{x \sim p_{data}}[\log D(x)] + E_{z \sim p_z}[\log(1 - D(G(z)))], \quad (2)$$
$$\nabla_{\theta_g} V(D,G) = \nabla_{\theta_g} E_{z \sim p_z}[\log(1 - D(G(z)))]. \quad (3)$$

By using mini-batch, each expectation becomes average of each mini-bach.

Conditional GAN [2,7,9] which condition c is added to z is the one of large research area of GANs. By adding certain condition (e.g., word vector), the generated image can be controlled. However, we don't consider about the conditional GANs since our aim is to generate a high-resolution natural image. The extension of out proposed method to conditional GANs is one of our future work.

Fig. 1. Examples of human face with background. These figures are drawn from [12].

3.2 Structure of Our Network

To generate high-resolution natural images, it is necessary to separate various objects. If the human and background cannot be separated in the case of the structured images such as a human with various backgrounds (Fig. 1), it is not possible to generate naturally looking images. To overcome this, our parallel-way network is composed of networks to generate rough feature and detailed feature (e.g., eye, heir, and bear).

Figure 2 shows the structure of our proposed network. The generator is composed of two networks with different structure described above. Figure 2(A)

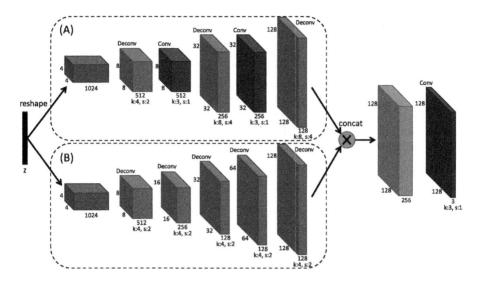

Fig. 2. The structure of our network. Generator is constructed as multiple-way network. The red and blue layers show the transposed convolution (Deconv) and convolution layer (Conv). The green layer shows the concatenation of result of each generator. The k and s show the kernel size and stride. (Color figure online)

shows the network for generating rough feature. To handle the rough feature, the stride of later two transposed convolution layers is set to 4. Note that, a convolution layer is put after a transposed convolution layer to improve the capacity of this network.

Figure 2(B) shows the network for generating detailed feature. This network is constructed by only transposed convolution layer. The kernel size and stride of transposed convolution layers are set to 4 and 2, respectively. By using this setting, detailed feature compared to Fig. 2(A) can be generated. A batch normalization layer [10] is put after each convolution and transposed convolution layer in Fig. 2(A), (B).

The networks in Fig. 2(A) and (B) are concatenated after their own process. The last convolution layer outputs the resulting image. In the last layer, there are not any activation functions (e.g., tanh and sigmoid), i.e., the output is directly estimated. Our network structure does not have full-connection layer and is constructed by fully convolution layer. The advantage of this structure is to reduce the number of parameters.

The structure of D is basically same as DCGANs. Since the image size is different in our research, we added one convolution layer, and sigmoid activation function is not used in the output layer.

4   Image Generation

We applied our network structure to the experiment of large-size image generation. In this experiment, we conducted two tasks: human-face image generation and road image generation. The resolutions of human face and road generation were set to 128×128 and 256×128, respectively.

We used the computer with CPU: Xeon 2.4 GHz, Memory: 64 GB, GPU: Nvidia Quadro M6000 12 GB for the experiments. The optimizer for training networks was Adam [11], and the learning rate and momentum were set to $\alpha = 0.002$ and $\beta_1 = 0.5$ for all experiment. We didn't adjust the initial weight of networks for our proposed network. Because of the limitation of graphics memory, the number of networks of our parallel-way is two (the same structure of Fig. 2), and mini-batch size for task of human face and road are set to 50 and 30, respectively.

4.1   Generation of Human Faces with Various Backgrounds

In this experiment, we used the celebA dataset [12] as the face image dataset. This dataset included 202,600 face with various backgrounds images. Since the original resolution of this dataset was 178×218, images were cropped 178×178 and downsized to 128×128. We implemented a DCGAN structure which was similar to the Fig. 2(B) for comparison, and the weights of G and D networks were randomly initialized by the Gaussian distribution with standard deviation 0.2 [3].

Figure 3 shows the results of the face image generation task. The collapse is occurred in the result of DCGAN structure (Fig. 3(a)) since the only few variations of face images are generated. Our network structure can generate various face and more natural images (Fig. 3(b)) since the shadow, lighting, and heir details are expressed. The separation of the face and background can be achieved since sharp outline of the face is generated by our method. Our network structure permits us to generate the high-resolution images.

4.2   Generation of Road Images

In this experiment, we used the DETRAC dataset [13] as a road image dataset. The dataset included 83,792 road images. Since the original resolution of this dataset was 960×540, images were cropped 960×480 and downsized to 256×128. The input reshapes of G (Fig. 2) were changed to $8 \times 4 \times 1024$, and input of output full-connection layer of D was also changed to $8 \times 4 \times 1024$. Other parameters were same as the previous face generation task.

Figure 4 shows the result of the road image generation task. The collapse is also occurred in the result of DCGAN structure (Fig. 4(a)). Our method can generate nearly natural road images (Fig. 4(b)) while some images has crossing road. In generated images, it is clear on the shape of car, divisional strip, and road sign. From this experiment, we show our method can generate the image with different aspect ratio with out many parameter tuning.

(a) The result of DCGAN structure.

(b) The result of our structure.

Fig. 3. The results of face image generation. Results are extracted from the generator after 10 epochs training.

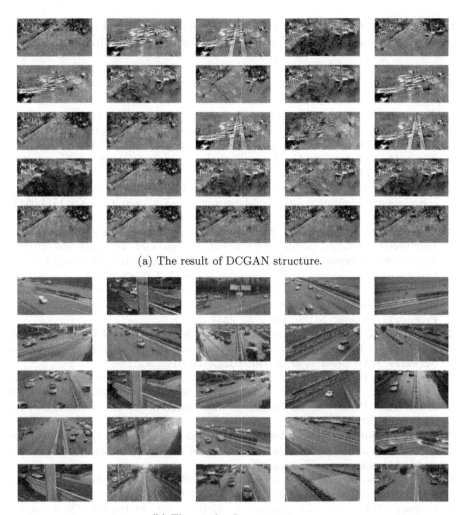

(a) The result of DCGAN structure.

(b) The result of our structure.

Fig. 4. The results of road generation. Results are extracted from the generator after 20 epochs training.

5   Conclusion

In this research, we proposed a parallel-pathway generator which parallelly stacks networks of different structure. The experimental results of human face and road image generation indicate high-resolution natural images without collapse of training reducing the hand-tuned parameters.

Our future work is to investigate the theoretical aspects of parallel-way structure such as the stability and the conversion speed. Intuitively, it seems that our structure stacks networks with different conversion speed and this prevents to converge the "undesired" local optima which leads to unsense images.

References

1. Goodfellow, I., Pouget-Abadie, J., Mirza, M., Xu, B., Warde-Farley, D., Ozair, S., Courville, A., Bengio, Y.: Generative adversarial nets. In: Advances in Neural Information Processing Systems (NIPS 2014), pp. 2672–2680 (2014)
2. Mirza, M., Osindero, S.: Conditional generative adversarial nets. arXiv preprint arXiv:1411.1784 (2014)
3. Radford, A., Metz, L., Chintala, S.: Unsupervised representation learning with deep convolutional generative adversarial networks. arXiv preprint arXiv:1511.06434 (2015)
4. Veres, M., Moussa, M., Taylor, G.W.: Modeling grasp motor imagery through deep conditional generative models. IEEE Robot. Autom. Lett. **2**(2), 757–764 (2017)
5. Antipov, G., Baccouche, M., Dugelay, J.-L.: Face Aging with Conditional Generative Adversarial Networks. arXiv preprint arXiv:1702.01983 (2017)
6. Salimans, T., Goodfellow, I., Zaremba, W., Cheung, V., Radford, A., Chen, X.: Improved techniques for training GANs. In: Advances in Neural Information Processing Systems (NIPS), pp. 2226–2234 (2016)
7. Zhang, H., Xu, T., Li, H., Zhang, S., Huang, X., Wang, X., Metaxas, D.: Stack-GAN: Text to Photo-realistic Image Synthesis with Stacked Generative Adversarial Networks. arXiv preprint arXiv:1612.03242 (2016)
8. Szegedy, C., Liu, W., Jia, Y., Sermanet, P., Reed, S., Anguelov, D., Erhan, D., Vanhoucke, V., Rabinovich, A.: Going deeper with convolutions. In: Proceedings of the IEEE Conference on Computer Vision and Pattern Recognition (CVPR), pp. 1–9 (2015)
9. Reed, S., Akata, Z., Yan, X., Logeswaran, L., Schiele, B., Lee, H.: Generative adversarial text to image synthesis. In: Proceedings of The 33rd International Conference on Machine Learning, vol. 3 (2016)
10. Ioffe, S., Szegedy, C.: Batch normalization: accelerating deep network training by reducing internal covariate shift. arXiv:1502.03167 (2015)
11. Kingma, D.P., Ba, J.: Adam: A Method for Stochastic Optimization. arXiv:1412.6980 (2014)
12. Liu, Z., Luo, P., Wang, X., Tang, X.: Deep learning face attributes in the wild. In: Proceedings of International Conference on Computer Vision (ICCV) (2015)
13. Wen, L., Du, D., Cai, Z., Lei, Z., Chang, M., Qi, H., Lim, J., Yang, M., Lyu, S.: DETRAC: A New Benchmark and Protocol for Multi-Object Detection and Tracking. arXiv CoRR (2015)

Using Echo State Networks for Cryptography

Rajkumar Ramamurthy(✉), Christian Bauckhage, Krisztian Buza,
and Stefan Wrobel

Department of Computer Science, University of Bonn, Bonn, Germany
`ramamurt@iai.uni-bonn.de`

Abstract. Echo state networks are simple recurrent neural networks
that are easy to implement and train. Despite their simplicity, they show
a form of memory and can predict or regenerate sequences of data. We
make use of this property to realize a novel neural cryptography scheme.
The key idea is to assume that Alice and Bob share a copy of an echo
state network. If Alice trains her copy to memorize a message, she can
communicate the trained part of the network to Bob who plugs it into his
copy to regenerate the message. Considering a byte-level representation
of in- and output, the technique applies to arbitrary types of data (texts,
images, audio files, etc.) and practical experiments reveal it to satisfy the
fundamental cryptographic properties of diffusion and confusion.

1 Introduction

The emerging field of *neural cryptography* is a sub-field of cryptography that
deals with artificial neural networks for encryption and cryptanalysis.

Early contributions in this area considered cryptographic systems based on
recursive auto encoders and showed that feed-forward networks trained via back-
propagation can encrypt plain-text messages in the activation patterns of hidden
layer neurons [3]. Later work introduced key-exchange systems where coupled
neural networks synchronize to establish common secret keys [6]; while the original approach was not completely secure [7], more recent work showed that modern convolutional interacting neural networks can indeed learn to protect their
communication against adversary eaves-droppers [1]. Another popular idea is to
combine chaotic dynamics and neural networks [8,9,13–15]. For example, chaotic
neural networks were found to be able to generate random binary sequences for
encryption.

Given this short survey, the novel idea for neural cryptography proposed in
this paper can be seen as a hybrid approach that harnesses chaotic dynamics
and the deterministic outcome of a training procedure. Namely, we propose to
use echo state networks [4] both for encryption and decryption.

Considering the classic scenario where Alice and Bob exchange messages and
want to protect their communication against Eve's eavesdropping, we assume
that both share an identical copy of an echo state network whose internal states
evolve according to a non-linear dynamical system. To encrypt a message (a
text, an image, etc.), Alice feeds it into her copy of the network and trains the

© Springer International Publishing AG 2017
A. Lintas et al. (Eds.): ICANN 2017, Part II, LNCS 10614, pp. 663–671, 2017.
https://doi.org/10.1007/978-3-319-68612-7_75

output weights such that the network reproduces the input. She then sends these output weights to Bob who uses them to run his copy of the network which will regenerate the message. Eve, on the other hand, may retrieve the communicated output weights, but without the corresponding echo state network (its structure, input weights, and internal weights), she will not be able to decipher the message. Our experiments with this kind of private-key or symmetric cryptography system reveal the approach to be easy to use, efficient, scalable, and secure. Our work differs considerably from [8,9,13–15] in which chaotic neural networks generate binary sequences which are then mapped on to the given data whereas we train echo state networks to reproduce the given data directly. A preliminary draft of this paper has been made available on arXiv repository [11].

Next, we briefly summarize the basic theory behind echo state networks and how to use them as auto encoders that memorize their input. We then discuss how to harness them for cryptography and present experiments which underline that our approach satisfies the fundamental cryptographic properties of diffusion and confusion.

2   Echo State Networks as Memories

Echo state networks (ESNs) follow the paradigm of reservoir computing where a large reservoir of recurrently interconnected neurons processes sequential data. The central idea is to randomly generate weights $\boldsymbol{W}^i \in \mathbb{R}^{n_r \times n_i}$ between input and reservoir neurons as well as weights $\boldsymbol{W}^r \in \mathbb{R}^{n_r \times n_r}$ between reservoir neurons. Only the weights $\boldsymbol{W}^o \in \mathbb{R}^{n_o \times n_r}$ between reservoir and output neurons are trained in order to adapt the network to a particular task.

At time t, the states of the input, output, and reservoir neurons are collected in $\boldsymbol{x}_t \in \mathbb{R}^{n_i}$, $\boldsymbol{y}_t \in \mathbb{R}^{n_o}$, and $\boldsymbol{r}_t \in \mathbb{R}^{n_r}$, respectively, and their evolution over time is governed by the following non-linear dynamical system

$$r_t = (1 - \alpha)r_{t-1} + \alpha\, f_r\big(\boldsymbol{W}^r r_{t-1} + \boldsymbol{W}^i \boldsymbol{x}_t\big) \tag{1}$$

$$y_t = f_o\big(\boldsymbol{W}^o r_t\big) \tag{2}$$

where $\alpha \in [0, 1]$ is called the leaking rate. The function $f_r(\cdot)$ is understood to act component-wise on its argument and is typically a sigmoidal activation function. For the output layer, however, $f_o(\cdot)$ is usually just a linear or softmax function depending on the application context.

To train an echo state network, one provides a training sequence of input data $\boldsymbol{x}_1, \boldsymbol{x}_2, \ldots, \boldsymbol{x}_T$ gathered in a matrix $\boldsymbol{X} \in \mathbb{R}^{n_i \times T}$ together with a sequence of desired outputs $\boldsymbol{y}_1, \boldsymbol{y}_2, \ldots, \boldsymbol{y}_T$ gathered in $\boldsymbol{Y} \in \mathbb{R}^{n_o \times T}$. The training sequence is fed into the network and the internal activations that result from iterating Eq. (1) are recorded in a matrix $\boldsymbol{R} = [\boldsymbol{r}_1, \boldsymbol{r}_2, \ldots, \boldsymbol{r}_T] \in \mathbb{R}^{n_r \times T}$. Appropriate output weights $\boldsymbol{W}^o$ can then be determined using least squares

$$\boldsymbol{W}^o = \boldsymbol{Y}\boldsymbol{R}^T(\boldsymbol{R}\boldsymbol{R}^T + \beta\boldsymbol{I})^{-1} \tag{3}$$

where β is a regularization constant. However, for a good practical performance, the scale a of $\boldsymbol{W}^i$ and the spectral radius ρ of $\boldsymbol{W}^r$ have to be chosen carefully. Together with the leaking rate α, these parameters are rather task specific, yet, useful, commonly adhered to general guidelines are given in [10].

Because of its recurrent connections, the reservoir of an echo state network can be understood as a non-linear high-dimensional expansion of the input data that has a memory of the past. The temporal reach of this memory is called "memory capacity" and bounded by the number of reservoir neurons [5]. An entire input sequence (e.g. a text file) can therefore be stored in- and retrieved from the reservoir provided the reservoir is large enough. Hence, our idea in this paper is to produce an echo state network with a large reservoir and to train it to memorize an input sequence. Once the training is complete, we let the network run freely to (re)generate the memorized sequence.

3   ESN-Based Encryption and Decryption

We consider the classic cryptographic scenario where Alice and Bob want to secure their communication against Eve's eavesdropping. Using a *secret key*, Alice converts her messages known as *plaintexts* into encrypted messages known as *ciphertexts*. She then sends the ciphertexts to Bob who uses the same key to convert them back into plaintexts.

Given this setup, our idea is to "memorize" a given message using an echo state network at one end of a communication channel and to "recall" it at the other end using the same network. If Alice and Bob share an identical copy of the network, Alice can train it to memorize the data and transmits only the resulting weights $\boldsymbol{W}^o$ over the insecure channel. Bob then plugs these weights into his copy of the network and runs it to reconstruct Alice's message. In other words, the weight matrices $\boldsymbol{W}^i$ and $\boldsymbol{W}^r$ and leaking rate α of the echo state network constitute the secret key of our cryptographic system. Without it Eve can not decipher the transmitted ciphertext $\boldsymbol{W}^o$.

3.1   Representing Data

In our practical implementations of the above scheme, we consider byte-level representations of messages. This allows for flexibility and wide applicability because, in the memory of a computer, texts or images are represented as a byte-stream after all. To further increase flexibility, we consider a "one hot" encoding of individual bytes where each of the 256 possible values is represented as a 256-dimensional binary vector.

3.2   Memorizing Data

Given any byte sequence $\boldsymbol{B} = [b_1, b_2, \ldots, b_N]$ of input data, we train and apply an echo state network as follows: First, we append a dummy byte b_0 at the beginning of the original sequence $\boldsymbol{B}$ so as to make the later recall process independent of the value of the original first byte in the sequence. Second, we encode the resulting sequence to obtain $H = [h_0, h_1, \ldots, h_N]$ where each h_i is a binary vector of length 256. Given H, we then set the in- and output sequence for an echo state network to

$$X = [h_0, h_1, \ldots, h_{N-1}] \tag{4}$$
$$Y = [h_1, h_2, \ldots, h_N] \tag{5}$$

where the indices of the vectors in sequences X and Y differ by one time step. Given an echo state network with input weights W^i and reservoir weights W^r, we then iterate the system in (1) and (2) and learn appropriate output weights W^o according to (3).

3.3   Recalling Data

Once W_o has been determined, it can be plugged into an identical copy of the echo state network at the other end of a communication channel. This network can then regenerate the encoded message one element at a time. To this end, we consider the dummy byte b_0 and "one hot" encode it to obtain $x_0 = h_0$. Using this as the first input to the network, we run the system in (1) and (2) to obtain y_t from x_t. At each time step, we consider the network output y_t, which is not necessarily a binary vector, as a vector of probabilities for different bytes. We thus subject it to the softmax function which returns a 1 for the most likely entry and 0 s for all others. The resulting binary vector is then used as the input x_{t+1} for the next iteration of the network. Moreover, we decode the binary vectors obtained in each iteration into bytes b_t and collect them in a matrix S, which is exactly the original sequence B memorized by the echo state network.

3.4   Working with "Data Chunks"

As the size N of data sequence increases, the size $n_r \in \mathcal{O}(N)$ of a reservoir that can memorize it increases, too. This makes the matrix multiplications $W^r r_t$ required for the network's state updates expensive. In fact, the total cost for N internal updates will be of order $\mathcal{O}(N^3)$ and, to reduce this cost, we adopt a "divide-and-conquer" strategy where we split the data into chunks of size m and employ a small reservoir to memorize each chunk at an effort of $\mathcal{O}(m^3)$. Hence, for an entire sequence, i.e. for $\frac{N}{m}$ chunks, efforts reduce to $\mathcal{O}(\frac{N}{m} \times m^3) = \mathcal{O}(Nm^2)$.

4   Experiments and Security Analysis

In our practical experiments, we found that echo state networks used as described above can indeed memorize and perfectly recall different types of data such as texts, images, audio files, videos, archives, etc. In this section we report results obtained from different kinds of security analysis of our cryptographic scheme. The parametrization of the echo state networks considered in these experiments is summarized in Table 1.

Table 1. Echo state network configuration

Parameter	Value
Chunk size m	200 (reservoir size n_r chosen as $0.95 \times m$)
Leaking rate α	0.07
Spectral radius ρ of W^r	1.0
Input scaling a of W^i	0.5
Random seed	Randomly chosen
Input connectivity	Input neurons are connected to 30% of reservoir neurons
Reservoir connectivity	Reservoir neurons are connected to 30% of reservoir neurons
Activation function f	Logistic for the reservoir and softmax for the output

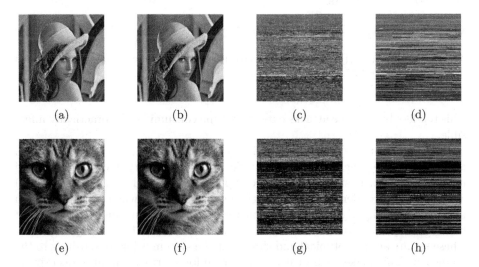

(a)   (b)   (c)   (d)

(e)   (f)   (g)   (h)

Fig. 1. Key sensitivity: (a), (e) original images; (b), (f) decrypted images using the same key (echo state network) as used for encryption; both decrypted images are identical to the originals; (c), (d), (g), (h) decrypted images using slightly modified keys, i.e. slightly modified echo state networks; here, all decrypted images differ considerably from the original images.

Next, we discuss security analysis of the proposed scheme by following a standard framework [2] which provides basic guidelines for testing fundamental cryptographic properties.

Any cryptography system should be robust against common types of attacks such as brute force attacks, chosen-plaintext attacks, and ciphertext-only attacks. In a brute force attack, an attacker attempts to find the keys of the system through trial and error. It is evident from the Table 1 that the key space of our proposed system is very large and most of the parameters are unbounded.

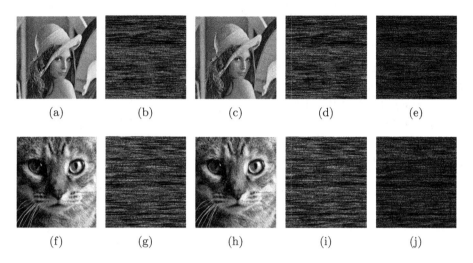

Fig. 2. Plaintext sensitivity: (a), (f) original images; (b), (g) encrypted images; (c), (h) original images with 1% of their pixels randomly distorted; (d), (i) encryptions of the modified images; (e), (j) difference between encrypted original and encrypted modified images (33.22% and 37.78%, respectively).

This renders brute force attacks extremely time consuming and practically infeasible.

Figure 1(a) and (e) show two original images one of which (Lena) was given as a tiff file, the other (cat) as a png file. Both were encrypted and decrypted using the same echo state network. Decryption produced the images in Fig. 1(b) and (f) which are identical to the original ones. However, when decrypting with networks with slightly modified parameters, i.e. when using slight variations of the secret key, we obtained useless images as shown in Fig. 1(c), (d), (g), and (h). These results are prototypical and show that the system is highly sensitive to the secret key. This makes it robust against brute force attacks because decryption is only possible if all the parameters of the secret key are set precisely.

Chosen-plaintext attacks are ones where an attacker has access to a set of pairs of plaintext (a message) and corresponding ciphertext (weight matrix $\boldsymbol{W}^o$) and attempts to crack the secret key via a comparative analysis of changes between them. For instance, by analyzing changes in the ciphertexts of images which differ by just a few pixels, it might possible to obtain part of the mapping involved in encryption. Figure 2(a) and (f) show original images and Fig. 2(c) and (h) show slightly distorted versions where 1% of the pixels were randomly changed. The corresponding encrypted images (matrices $\boldsymbol{W}^o$) are visualized in Fig. 2(b), (g), (d), and (i). Only small changes in the plaintext led to considerable changes in the ciphertext; these differences are visualized in Fig. 2(e) and (j) and amount to about 35%. Thus, our system is sensitive to slight modification of the plaintext and therefore renders chosen-plaintext attacks very difficult.

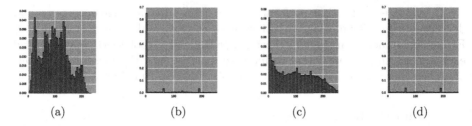

(a)	(b)	(c)	(d)

Fig. 3. Ciphertext sensitivity: (a), (b) plaintext distribution of the Lena image and its ciphertext distribution; (c), (d) plaintext distribution of the cat image and its ciphertext distribution. Since the ciphertext distributions are almost identical, this system is robust against frequency analysis and ciphertext-only attacks.

In ciphertext-only attacks, an attacker has access to a set of ciphertexts, however has some knowledge about statistical distribution of plaintexts. Using frequency analysis of ciphertexts, for instance, exploiting the fact that "e" is the most frequent character in English texts, one can map the most frequent parts in a ciphertext to corresponding plaintexts. Figure 3 shows frequency distributions for the plaintexts and ciphertexts of the images "Lena" and "cat". Although the plaintext distributions of two images differ, their ciphertext distributions are very similar. From these distributions it is evident that most of the elements ($\approx 50\%$) in the ciphertext (W^o) are zero and that the non-zero elements are uniformly distributed. Thus, frequency analysis will be ineffective and the proposed system is robust against ciphertext-only attacks.

According to Shannon [12], diffusion and confusion are the two fundamental properties of a good cryptography system. A system that has the diffusion property is one where a small change in either plaintext or key causes a large change in the ciphertext. A system with the confusion property is one where the mapping between plaintext and ciphertext is complex. Our experimental results indicate that the proposed system has both these properties. Also, our approach satisfies similar cryptographic properties as satisfied by [9,13,14] and offers better security than [15] which is prone to chosen-plaintext attacks [8].

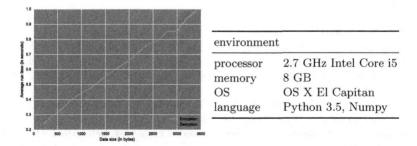

environment	
processor	2.7 GHz Intel Core i5
memory	8 GB
OS	OS X El Capitan
language	Python 3.5, Numpy

Fig. 4. Run times for encryption and decryption for different message sizes.

To evaluate the runtime performance, we determined average encryption and decryption times for messages of different sizes. Our results are shown in Fig. 4. For instance, encrypting and decrypting a 3KB message took less than one second each and runtimes were found to increase linearly with the message size. Our approach therefore scales well and can be used in real-time applications.

5   Conclusion

In this paper, we proposed a novel neural cryptography scheme based on the capability of echo state networks to memorize and reproduce sequences of input data. The proposed system was found to be robust against common security attacks and satisfies the fundamental cryptographic properties of diffusion and confusion. Moreover, our approach is scalable, suitable for real-time applications, and does not require special purpose hardware (such as GPUs) for computation.

References

1. Abadi, M., Andersen, D.G.: Learning to protect communications with adversarial neural cryptography. arXiv:1610.06918 (2016)
2. Alvarez, G., Li, S.: Some basic cryptographic requirements for chaos-based cryptosystems. Int. J. Bifurcat. Chaos **16**(08), 2129–2151 (2011)
3. Clark, M., Blank, D.: A neural-network based cryptographic system. In: Proceedings of the Midwest Artificial Intelligence and Cognitive Science Conference (1998)
4. Jäger, H.: The "echo state" approach to analysing and training recurrent neural networks. Technical report 148, GMD (2001)
5. Jäger, H.: Short term memory in echo state networks. Technical report 152, GMD (2002)
6. Kanter, I., Kinzel, W., Kanter, E.: Secure exchange of information by synchronization of neural networks. Europhys. Lett. **57**(1), 141–147 (2002)
7. Klimov, A., Mityagin, A., Shamir, A.: Analysis of neural cryptography. In: Zheng, Y. (ed.) ASIACRYPT 2002. LNCS, vol. 2501, pp. 288–298. Springer, Heidelberg (2002). doi:10.1007/3-540-36178-2_18
8. Li, C., Li, S., Zhang, D., Chen, G.: Chosen-plaintext cryptanalysis of a clipped-neural-network-based chaotic cipher. In: Wang, J., Liao, X.-F., Yi, Z. (eds.) ISNN 2005. LNCS, vol. 3497, pp. 630–636. Springer, Heidelberg (2005). doi:10.1007/11427445_103
9. Lian, S.: A block cipher based on chaotic neural networks. Neurocomputing **72**(46), 1296–1301 (2009)
10. Lukoševičius, M.: A practical guide to applying echo state networks. In: Montavon, G., Orr, G.B., Müller, K.-R. (eds.) Neural Networks: Tricks of the Trade. LNCS, vol. 7700, 2nd edn, pp. 659–686. Springer, Heidelberg (2012). doi:10.1007/978-3-642-35289-8_36
11. Ramamurthy, R., Bauckhage, C., Buza, K., Wrobel, S.: Using Echo State Networks for Cryptography. arXiv:1704.01046 (2017)
12. Shannon, C.E.: Communication theory of secrecy systems. Bell Labs Tech. J. **28**(4), 656–715 (1949)
13. Wang, X.Y., Yang, L., Liu, R., Kadir, A.: A chaotic image encryption algorithm based on perceptron model. Nonlinear Dyn. **62**(3), 615–621 (2010)

14. Yu, W., Cao, J.: Cryptography based on delayed chaotic neural networks. Phys. Lett. A **356**(45), 333–338 (2006)
15. Zhou, T., Liao, X., Chen, Y.: A novel symmetric cryptography based on chaotic signal generator and a clipped neural network. In: Yin, F.-L., Wang, J., Guo, C. (eds.) ISNN 2004 Part II. LNCS, vol. 3174, pp. 639–644. Springer, Heidelberg (2004). doi:10.1007/978-3-540-28648-6_102

Two Alternative Criteria for a Split-Merge MCMC on Dirichlet Process Mixture Models

Tikara Hosino[(✉)]

Nihon Unisys, Ltd., 1-1-1 Toyosu, Koto-ku, Tokyo 135-8560, Japan
Chikara.Hoshino@unisys.co.jp

Abstract. The free energy and the generalization error are two major model selection criteria. However, in general, they are not equivalent. In previous studies, for the split-merge algorithm on conjugate Dirichlet process mixture models, the complete free energy was mainly used. In this work, we propose, the new criterion, the complete leave one out cross validation which is based on the approximation of the generalization error. In numerical experiments, our proposal outperforms the previous methods with the test set perplexity. Finally, we discuss the appropriate usage of these two criteria taking into account the experimental results.

1 Introduction

When we choose a statistical inference method, there are two main purposes: the one is to get a good description of given samples and the other is a good prediction of future samples. Obviously, these two purposes are not completely orthogonal, for example, if we find the good description of data, we will create better predictive models by using the findings. Additionally, in the process of statistical inference, we need to iteratively formulate each hypothesis as a statistical model and compare them. The model selection criteria have a fundamental role to this model comparison.

There are two famous model selection criteria, which are the free energy and the generalization error. The free energy is a minus logarithm of the probability of the hypothesis. Under the given triplet which are samples $x^n \equiv \{x_1, \ldots, x_n\}$, the model $p(x|\theta)$ and the prior of the parameters $\varphi(\theta)$, the free energy is defined by

$$F \equiv -\log \int \prod_{i=1}^{n} p(x_i, |\theta)\varphi(\theta)d\theta. \tag{1}$$

The free energy is also called the minus of marginal log likelihood or the evidence [7] and it is well known that, in some case, it has 'consistency' which is the property that if the model contains the true distribution, when the number of samples goes to infinity, the criteria can select the true model that has minimum parameters. Except for simple models, the integration of Eq. (1) cannot be analytically obtained and we need to use an approximation. The 'BIC' [11], 'MDL' [9], 'WBIC' [14] are well studied approximations.

© Springer International Publishing AG 2017
A. Lintas et al. (Eds.): ICANN 2017, Part II, LNCS 10614, pp. 672–679, 2017.
https://doi.org/10.1007/978-3-319-68612-7_76

On the other hand, the generalization error is the direct measure of prediction accuracy which is the distance of the true distribution $q(x)$ and the estimated predictive distribution $p(x|x^n)$. Under the same condition of the free energy, it is defined by

$$G \equiv \int q(x) \log \frac{q(x)}{p(x|x^n)} dx,$$

$$p(x|x^n) = \int p(x|\theta)p(\theta|x^n)d\theta,$$

$$p(\theta|x^n) = \frac{\prod_{i=1}^{n} p(x_i|\theta)\varphi(\theta)}{\int \prod_{i=1}^{n} p(x_i|\theta)\varphi(\theta)d\theta},$$

where $p(\theta|x^n)$ is the posterior distribution. In most cases, the generalization error cannot be obtained because we do not know the true distribution $q(x)$. However, in some case, the approximation of the generalization error such as 'AIC' [1], 'WAIC' [13] or 'Leave one out cross validation' [13] has 'efficiency' which is the property that if the true distribution is the out of the model distribution, the criteria can select the model which minimizes the generalization error.

We should use properly two criteria for our purpose because of their different characteristics. In this paper, in order to focus this problem, we choose conjugate Dirichlet process mixture model which has efficient approximation of these criteria. Our contributions of the paper are as follows.

- For split-merge MCMC on conjugate Dirichlet process mixture model, we propose novel criteria 'complete leave one out cross validation (LOO_c)' which is based on the approximation of generalization error.
- We experimentally show that the proposed criteria is consistently superior to the test set perplexity over previous methods.
- We discuss the appropriate usage of two criteria by considering the experimental results.

2   Problem Settings

Dirichlet process mixture model is a non parametric Bayesian extension of finite mixture models which simultaneously estimates model parameters and the number of mixtures. The definition is as follows,

$$\begin{aligned}
G &\sim DP(G_0, \alpha) \\
\theta_i | G &\sim G, \\
x_i | \theta_i &\sim F(x_i | \theta_i),
\end{aligned} \tag{2}$$

where G is a base distribution and $\alpha (> 0)$ is the concentration parameter. When G is integrate over its prior distribution in Eq. (2), we see that the model parameters θ_i follows a generalized Polya urn scheme [2]. The prior distribution of θ_i is given by the following conditional distributions,

$$\theta_1 \sim G_0,$$

$$\theta_i | \theta_1, \ldots, \theta_{i-1} \sim \frac{\sum_{j=1}^{i-1} \delta(\theta_j) + \alpha G_0}{i - 1 + \alpha},$$

where $\delta(\theta_j)$ is the distribution which is a point mass at θ_j. For each observation x_j, we introduce latent variable y_j which indicates latent class k. Then, the Polya urn scheme for sampling θ_i is equivalent for sampling y_i from the distribution,

$$p(y_i = k | y^{i-1}) = \frac{n_k}{i - 1 + \alpha},$$

$$p(y_i = k^* | y^{i-1}) = \frac{\alpha}{i - 1 + \alpha},$$

where n_k is the number of samples for which $y_j = k$ $(j < i)$ holds and k^* is the new class which is not appear in the previous $i - 1$ samples. Moreover, in the case of $G_0(\theta)$ is a conjugate prior for the likelihood $F(x|\theta)$, the simple Gibbs sampling of y_i from the posterior distribution is obtained [8],

$$p(y_i = k | x^n, y_{-i}^n) = \frac{n_k - 1}{n - 1 + \alpha} \int F(x_i|\theta) dH_{(x_{-i}^n, y_{-i}^n)}(\theta),$$

$$p(y_i = k^* | x^n, y_{-i}^n) = \frac{\alpha}{n - 1 + \alpha} \int F(x_i|\theta) dG_0(\theta),$$

where (x^n, y^n) are so called "complete-data" and (x_{-i}^n, y_{-i}^n) means excluding ith sample (x_i, y_i) from (x^n, y^n). Furthermore, $H_{(x_{-i}^n, y_{-i}^n)}(\theta)$ is the posterior distribution of θ based on the prior G_0, the likelihood F and samples (x_{-i}^n, y_{-i}^n).

Next, we define two criteria, the first, the complete free energy is defined by

$$F_c(x^n, y^n) \equiv -\log p(x^n, y^n) = -\log \left(\int \prod_{i=1}^{n} p(x_i, y_i|\theta) \varphi(\theta) d\theta \right). \tag{3}$$

The second, the complete leave one out cross validation is defined by

$$LOO_c(x^n, y^n) \equiv -\sum_{i=1}^{n} \log p(x_i | x_{-i}^n, y_{-i}^n) = -\sum_{i=1}^{n} \log \sum_{y_i} p(x_i, y_i | x_{-i}^n, y_{-i}^n)$$

$$= -\sum_{i=1}^{n} \log \sum_{y_i} \exp \left(- \left((F_c(x^n, y^n) - F_c(x_{-i}^n, y_{-i}^n) \right) \right). \tag{4}$$

In conjugate exponential models with complete data (x^n, y^n), the integration of the parameters (3) can be performed analytically which enables us to construct an efficient approximation algorithm. Moreover, it is noted that F_c and LOO_c have a relation indicated by Eq. (4) and we use this relation later.

3   Related Works

In Bayesian case, the asymptotic property of the free energy and the generalization error are clarified and efficient numerical approximation are proposed

[13,14]. In these works, it was probed that Bayesian leave one out cross validation is asymptotically equivalent to mean of generalization error. Using these works, MCMC method with leave one out cross validation was proposed [6].

At complete data methods, which use joint distribution with hidden variables, the asymptotic $F_c(x^n, y^n)$ was revealed [16]. Additionally, for model selection of clustering, minimizing F_c instead of the negative likelihood was proposed [15]. Hyperparameter estimation of latent Dirichlet allocation by LOO_c was proposed and smaller test set perplexities than previous studies was reported [10].

Specifically, MCMC for the conjugate Dirichlet process, trying to large move than the local Gibbs samplers, split-merge algorithm which uses F_c was proposed [3,5]. However, for hierarchical Dirichlet process, their method reported no gain of test set perplexity on real world data set [12].

4   Proposed Algorithm

We describe the proposed LOO_c split-merge MCMC algorithm. The acceptance probability of the proposed merge (split) state from the current state is described by the following Eq. [5],

$$A(\text{current} \rightarrow \text{merge}) = \min\left(1, \frac{p(\text{merge})g(\text{merge} \rightarrow \text{current})}{p(\text{current})g(\text{current} \rightarrow \text{merge})}\right),$$

$$A(\text{current} \rightarrow \text{split}) = \min\left(1, \frac{p(\text{split})g(\text{split} \rightarrow \text{current})}{p(\text{current})g(\text{current} \rightarrow \text{split})}\right),$$

where $p(\text{current})$, $p(\text{merge})$ and $p(\text{split})$ are the probability of each state. In our algorithm, we change these state probabilities $p(\text{state})$ from $\exp(-F_c(state))$, which is used by previous studies, to $\exp(-LOO_c(state))$. For transition kernel $g(\text{state} \rightarrow \text{state}')$, we use the same method as Dahl [3].

4.1   Concrete Example (Diagonal Gaussian Case)

We describe the concrete example of the proposed method where the components of the mixture are diagonal Gaussian distributions. In the form of canonical exponential family, the Gaussian distribution is given by the equation

$$p(x|s, \mu) = \frac{1}{(2\pi)^{\frac{1}{2}}} \exp\left(-\frac{s}{2}x^2 + s\mu x - \frac{s}{2}\mu^2 + \frac{1}{2}\log s\right),$$

where s and μ are model parameters. The conjugate prior of the distribution is given by the equation

$$p(s, \mu) = \frac{1}{Z} \exp\left(-\frac{s}{2}\phi_1 + s\mu\phi_2 + (-\frac{s}{2}\mu^2 + \frac{1}{2}\log s)\phi_3\right), \quad (5)$$

where ϕ_1, ϕ_2, ϕ_3 are the prior hyperparameter and Z is the normalizing constant. In the conjugate exponential family which includes Gaussian distribution, the integration of the parameters μ, s are analytically executed and Z is explicitly given by

$$Z(\phi 1, \phi 2, \phi 3) = \frac{(2\pi)^{\frac{1}{2}}\Gamma(\frac{\phi_3+1}{2})}{\phi_3^{\frac{1}{2}}(\frac{1}{2}(\phi_1 - \frac{\phi_2^2}{\phi_3}))^{\frac{\phi_3+1}{2}}}.$$

The posterior probability of parameters s, μ is obtained by the same form of the prior distribution (5) by changing the each hypeparameter ϕ with the sufficient statistics,

$$\hat{\phi}_1 = \phi_1 + \sum_{i=1}^{n} x_i^2, \ \hat{\phi}_2 = \phi_2 + \sum_{i=1}^{n} x_i, \ \hat{\phi}_3 = \phi_3 + n.$$

Then, the free energy is given by

$$F_g(x^n) = \frac{n}{2} \log 2\pi - \log \frac{Z(\hat{\phi}_1, \hat{\phi}_2, \hat{\phi}_3)}{Z(\phi_1, \phi_2, \phi_3)}. \tag{6}$$

Using above Eq. (6), on Gaussian Dirichlet process mixture which has K components and concentration parameter α, the complete free energy is given by

$$F_c(x^n, y^n)$$
$$= -K \log \alpha + \log \Gamma(n + \alpha) - \log \Gamma(\alpha) - \sum_{k=1}^{K} (\log \Gamma(n_k) - F_{g_k}(x^n)), \tag{7}$$

where $F_{g_k}(x^n)$ is the free energy of kth Gaussian component. Furthermore, $LOO_c(x^n, y^n)$ is derived using the Eqs. (7) and (4).

5   Experiment

To compare the different characteristics of each criterion, we conducted two experiments, the one is the model selection experiment for toy data set and the other is the prediction error experiment for real world data set. In both experiments, one MC step is composed by one Gibbs sampler and randomly selected split or merge proposal. We execute 1000 MC steps for burn-in period and collect 10000 samples after the burn-in period.

5.1   Experiment 1

Toy Data. The toy data are collected from two dimensional four components mixture of Gaussian whose means are given by $(3.0, 3.0)$, $(-3.0, 3.0)$, $(3.0, -3.0)$, $(-3.0, -3.0)$ and all variances are 1.0. In this example, the approximation of F_c is appropriate, because the support of each component does not overlap [16]. We use 200 samples which are collected 50 samples from each component and repeat the trial 10 times. To compare model selection abilities, we measure the number of component which attain the best (minimum) of F_c and LOO_c and the mean number of components of posterior distribution for F_c and LOO_c. We set hyperparameter $\alpha = 1.0$, $\phi_1 = \phi_3 = 0.001$ and $\phi_2 = 0$ in this experiment.

Table 1. Estimated number of components (mean $\pm$ std). True is 4.

F_c best	F_c all posterior	LOO_c best	LOO_c all posterior
4.0 $\pm$ 0.0	4.69 $\pm$ 0.83	8.3 $\pm$ 0.95	6.3 $\pm$ 1.45

Result. The results are shown by Table 1. It indicates that the minimum F_c achieves the best performance, which is the perfect, for this experiment.

5.2 Experiment 2

Real World Data. We obtain the real world data set from LIBSVM: Data [4][1]. The dimension and the number of samples of each data set and the model hyperparameters are shown by Table 2. These hyperparameters are determined by preliminary experiments. On each data set, we repeat the trial 10 times. In one trial, we divided samples randomly in half with a training and validation set. For experimental statistics, we collect the test set perplexities and the mean number of components from the posterior distribution. The test set perplexity (TSP) is the estimation of the generalization error and defined by

$$TSP(x^{test}) \equiv -\sum_{i=1}^{n} \log \frac{1}{M} \sum_{m=1}^{M} p(x_{test_i}|x^{train}, y^{train_m}),$$

where n is the number of the test samples, x^{train} are training samples, y^{train_m} are corresponding hidden variables of mth MC step, and M is the number of collected MC samples.

Table 2. Real world data attributes and used hyperparameters

Data set	Number of samples	Dimension	α	$\phi 1$	$\phi 2$	$\phi 3$
iris	150	3	1.0	0.001	0	0.001
wine	178	13	1.0	0.1	0	0.1
svmguide1	7089	4	1.0	0.001	0	0.001
svmguide2	391	20	1.0	0.1	0	0.1
svmguide3	1284	21	1.0	0.001	0	0.001

Result. The test set perplexities are described by Table 3. It is shown that the proposed split-merge by LOO_c are consistently outperform conventional no split-merge and split-merge by F_c. Moreover, we observe that, in all cases of the experiments, the proposed algorithm attains the minimum test set perplexities. Additionally, the mean numbers of components of each algorithm are shown by Table 4. It is shown that the mean number of components of proposed algorithm are consistently larger than ordinary methods.

---

[1] https://www.csie.ntu.edu.tw/~cjlin/libsvmtools/datasets/.

Table 3. Test set perplexities (mean ± std). The bold is minimum.

Data set	No S-M	S-M by F_c	S-M by LOO_c (proposed)
iris	17.46 ± 17.38	16.65 ± 16.24	**2.5 ± 18.86**
wine	248.80 ± 45.19	243.32 ± 40.73	**205.11 ± 26.50**
svmguide1	−4870.55 ± 138.46	−5015.47 ± 52.76	**−5204.01 ± 54.18**
svmguide2	699.05 ± 89.53	681.68 ± 86.72	**583.57 ± 72.65**
svmguide3	−16446.2 ± 675.44	−18883.4 ± 172.10	**−19928.9 ± 244.96**

Table 4. Number of components (mean ± std)

Data set	No S-M	S-M by F_c	S-M by LOO_c (proposed)
iris	4.47 ± 0.73	4.48 ± 0.72	**6.81 ± 0.72**
wine	4.10 ± 0.94	4.27 ± 0.88	**6.74 ± 0.50**
svmguide1	24.34 ± 1.73	27.65 ± 1.30	**38.95 ± 1.20**
svmguide2	4.05 ± 0.61	4.40 ± 0.73	**7.36 ± 0.68**
svmguide3	9.54 ± 1.45	15.55 ± 0.88	**31.78 ± 2.38**

6   Discussion

As suggested by Table 1, the proposed LOO_c has slightly larger estimate of the number of components. On the contrary, as suggested by Table 3, the ordinary F_c is slightly conservative for minimizing the generalization errors on real world data set. These results suggest that, in the model selection problem, if our purpose is the description of the given data, we prefer the maximum of F_c, which has accurate estimation of number of components in the separable case and better interpretation capability because of each sample point belongs to a distinct cluster. On the other hand, if our purpose is small prediction errors, the ensemble estimation with proposed LOO_c has advantage which minimizes the generalization error more directly than F_c.

7   Conclusion

In Split-Merge MCMC on Dirichlet process mixture, we proposed novel criteria LOO_c which is designed for the minimizing the generalization error. In numerical experiments, we shows that our proposed algorithm consistently achieves the smaller test set perplexities than existing free energy based methods. Moreover, the experiment clearly shows the difference of two alternative criteria and suggests that we should use properly for our purpose. To clarify the theoretical property of these criteria and comparing the other approximation methods such as variational Bayes are future works.

References

1. Akaike, H.: Information theory and an extension of the maximum likelihood principle. In: 2nd International Symposium on Information Theory. Academiai Kiado (1973)
2. Blackwell, D., MacQueen, J.B.: Ferguson distributions via pólya urn schemes. Ann. Stat. **1**(2), 353–355 (1973)
3. Dahl, D.B.: An improved merge-split sampler for conjugate dirichlet process mixture models. Technical report 1, 086 (2003)
4. Hsu, C.W., Chang, C.C., Lin, C.J., et al.: A practical guide to support vector classification. Technical report, Department of Computer Science, National Taiwan University (2003)
5. Jain, S., Neal, R.M.: A split-merge markov chain monte carlo procedure for the dirichlet process mixture model. J. Comput. Graph. Stat. **13**(1), 158–182 (2004)
6. Kenji, N., Jun, K., Shin-ichi, N., Satoshi, E., Ryoi, T., Masato, O.: An exhaustive search and stability of sparse estimation for feature selection problem. IPSJ Trans. Math. Model. Appl. **8**(2), 23–30 (2015)
7. MacKay, D.J.: Information Theory, Inference and Learning Algorithms. Cambridge University Press, Cambridge (2003)
8. Neal, R.M.: Markov chain sampling methods for dirichlet process mixture models. J. Comput. Graph. Stat. **9**(2), 249–265 (2000)
9. Rissanen, J.: Modeling by shortest data description. Automatica **14**(5), 465–471 (1978)
10. Sato, I., Nakagawa, H.: Stochastic divergence minimization for online collapsed variational Bayes zero inference of latent Dirichlet allocation. In: Proceedings of the 21th ACM SIGKDD International Conference on Knowledge Discovery and Data Mining, pp. 1035–1044. ACM (2015)
11. Schwarz, G., et al.: Estimating the dimension of a model. Ann. Stat. **6**(2), 461–464 (1978)
12. Wang, C., Blei, D.M.: A split-merge MCMC algorithm for the hierarchical dirichlet process. arXiv preprint arXiv:1201.1657 (2012)
13. Watanabe, S.: Asymptotic equivalence of Bayes cross validation and widely applicable information criterion in singular learning theory. J. Mach. Learn. Res. **11**(Dec), 3571–3594 (2010)
14. Watanabe, S.: A widely applicable Bayesian information criterion. J. Mach. Learn. Res. **14**(Mar), 867–897 (2013)
15. Welling, M., Kurihara, K.: Bayesian k-means as a "maximization-expectation" algorithm. In: Proceedings of the 2006 SIAM International Conference on Data Mining, pp. 474–478. SIAM (2006)
16. Yamazaki, K.: Asymptotic accuracy of Bayes estimation for latent variables with redundancy. Mach. Learn. **102**(1), 1–28 (2016)

FP-MRBP: Fine-grained Parallel MapReduce Back Propagation Algorithm

Gang Ren[1,2(✉)], Qingsong Hua[3], Pan Deng[1,2(✉)], and Chao Yang[1,2,4]

[1] Institute of Software, Chinese Academy of Sciences, Beijing 100190, China
[2] University of Chinese Academy of Sciences, Beijing 100190, China
{rengang2013,dengpan}@iscas.ac.cn
[3] School of Mechanical and Electrical Engineering,
Qingdao University, Qingdao 266071, China
[4] State Key Laboratory of Computer Science,
Chinese Academy of Sciences, Beijing 100190, China

Abstract. MRBP algorithm is a training algorithm based on the MapReduce model for Back Propagation Network Networks (BPNNs), that employs the data parallel capability of the MapReduce model to improve the training efficiency and has shown a good performance for training BPNNs with massive training patterns. However, it is a coarse-grained pattern parallel algorithm and lacks the capability of fine-grained structure parallelism. As a result, when training a large scale BPNN, its training efficiency is still insufficient. To solve this issue, this paper proposes a novel MRBP algorithm, Fine-grained Parallel MRBP (FP-MRBP) algorithm, which has the capability of fine-grained structure parallelism. To the best knowledge of the authors, it is the first time to introduce the fine-grained parallelism to the classic MRBP algorithm. The experimental results show that our algorithm has a better training efficiency when training a large scale BPNN.

Keywords: BPNN training · MapReduce model · Fine-grained Parallelism

1 Introduction

BPNNs are a class of artificial neural networks that update connection weights by back propagation of error [1–3]. Due to the excellent function approximation ability, they are one of the most popular artificial neural networks. MRBP algorithm is a training algorithm based on MapReduce model [4], a parallel programming model on Hadoop cluster [5], for BPNN. This algorithm uses the data parallel capability of MapReduce model to improve the training efficiency and has shown a good performance for training BPNN with massive training data [6–8].

However, it adopts the coarse-grained pattern parallel strategy to train BPNN, that divides training patterns into multiple sub-groups and train BPNN in parallel by these sub-groups [9–11]. This way lacks the capability of fine-grained structure parallelism, that partitions the network into multiple small

© Springer International Publishing AG 2017
A. Lintas et al. (Eds.): ICANN 2017, Part II, LNCS 10614, pp. 680–687, 2017.
https://doi.org/10.1007/978-3-319-68612-7_77

structures and trains these structures in parallel [12–14]. Thus, when training a large scale BPNN, the training efficiency of the classic MRBP algorithm is still insufficient. On the other hand, the existing structure parallel strategies are only suitable for message passing clusters, where computing nodes can directly communicate each other at any time [15] whilst there is only one global communication chance in MapReduce model on Hadoop clusters [4].

To address this issue, in this paper, we attempt to propose a fine-grained structure parallel strategy suitable for Hadoop cluster and introduce fine-grained structure parallelism into the classic MRBP algorithm to improve its training efficiency. The main contributions of this paper are listed below.

(1) We propose a fine-grained structure parallel strategy, Layer-wise Parallelism, Layer-wise Integration (LPLI) strategy, that is suitable for training BPNN on Hadoop cluster.
(2) We propose a novel MRBP algorithm, FP-MRBP algorithm, that implements LPLI strategy on Hadoop cluster. To the best knowledge of the authors, it is the first time to introduce the fine-grained structure parallelism to the MRBP algorithm.
(3) A set of experiments are conducted to compare the performance of our algorithm with the classic MRBP algorithm. The experimental results show our algorithm has better training efficiency.

The remainders of this paper proceed as follows. Section 2 introduces the training process of BPNN. The proposed FP-MRBP is introduced in Sect. 3. Section 4 compares the performance of our algorithm with the classic MRBP algorithm. In the end, we draw some conclusions about this paper.

2   BPNN

BPNN is a multi-layer network including an input layer, several hidden layers, and an output layer. Figure 1 shows a BPNN with L layers. The l-th layer contains n_l neurons. Each neuron in a layer is connected to all neurons in the next layer. Associated with each neuron i on layer l are an activation value $a_i(l)$ and a threshold value $\theta_i(l)$, and attached to each connection, connecting neuron i on layer l to neuron j on layer $l + 1$, is a weight $w_{ij}(l, l + 1)$.

As shown in Fig. 3, a typical BPNN training process includes three phases: feed-forward execution, back-propagation of error, and weight update. In feed-forward phase, input portion of a training pattern is fed to the input layer. It is propagated through layers to calculate activation values of all neurons in each layer. For neuron i in the l-th layer, its activation value can be calculated as follows:

$$a_i(l) = f(\sum_{j=1}^{n_{l-1}} a_j(l-1) + \theta_i(l)), \tag{1}$$

where $f(.)$ is a non-linear sigmoid function.

In the back-propagation of error phase, error between network output and target value is back-propagated to all the neurons through output weights. The error of i-th neuron in the output layer can be calculated by:

$$\delta_i(L) = (d_i - a_i(L))f'(.), i = 1, 2, \cdots, n_L, \tag{2}$$

where d_i is the desired output pattern, $f'(.)$ is the first derivative of activation function.

The error of i-th neuron in the l-th hidden layer can be calculated by:

$$\delta_i(l) = f'(.) \sum_{j=1}^{n_{l+1}} w_{ij}(l, l+1)\delta_j(l+1), \tag{3}$$

The third phase updates weights in the light of error $\delta_i(l+1)$ and activation value $a_j(l)$. The new $w_{ij}(l, l+1)$ can be calculated as follow:

$$w_{ij}(l, l+1) = w_{ij}(l, l+1) + \eta\delta_i(l+1)a_j(l), \tag{4}$$

where, η denotes the learning rate.

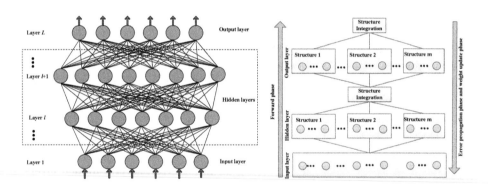

Fig. 1. BPNN   **Fig. 2.** LPLI strategy

3   FP-MRBP Algorithm

3.1   Fine-grained Parallel Strategy

We propose a fine-grained parallel strategy, Layer-wise Parallelism, Layer-wise Integration (LPLI) strategy. As shown in Fig. 2, we divide the hidden and output layer into multiple parallel structures, each of which has multiple neurons, whilst the input layer remains unchanged.

In the feed-forward phase, each parallel structure of the hidden layer first calculates the activation values of its neurons according to Formula 1. Then all the results are integrated together to prepare for calculation of activation values

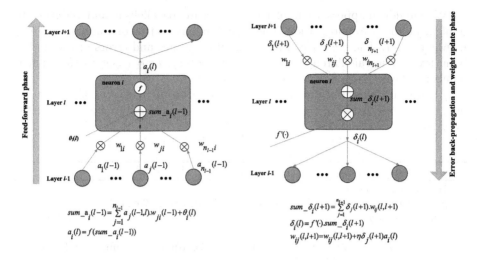

Fig. 3. Training process of BPNN

of neurons in the next layer. Repeat this iteration process until all the activation values are worked out. The back-propagation phase adopts the same strategy to calculate the errors of the output layer and hidden layer according to Formulas 2 and 3. Finally, we use the obtained errors to calculate and update the weights according to Formula 4.

3.2 Parallel Implementation Using MapReduce on Hadoop Cluster

A job of MapReduce model includes two phases, map and reduce. Each phase has several parallel tasks, called mappers and reducers, respectively. The input data are first divided into multiple splits and then processed in parallel by different mappers. A mapper reads each line in the input split successively. Each line is seen as one key/value pair, the key is the line number and the value is the line itself. It processes these pairs according to specific businesses, generating a list of new key/value pairs. The transformation is listed as follow:

$$Mapper :: (key_1, value_1) \longrightarrow list(key_2, value_2). \tag{5}$$

These new key/value pairs will be sent into reducers on other computing nodes and these pairs with the same key_2 will be merged by system as follows.

$$Merge :: list(key_2, value_2) \longrightarrow (key_2, list(value_2)). \tag{6}$$

Next, the merged pairs are processed according to specific businesses, and the calculated results are emitted. Conceptually, a reducer has the following type:

$$Reducer :: (key_2, list(value_2)) \longrightarrow (key_3, value_3). \tag{7}$$

We employ mappers to implement structure parallelism and reducers to implement structure integration. The main implementation of a mapper is given in Algorithm 1. The $value_1$ contains activation values and errors of the underlying layer. The calculated results is put to $value_2$. key_2 is set to the current number of layer.

Algorithm 2 presents the main implementation of a reducer for structure integration. We let $key_3 = key_2$ and add all the $value_2$ to $value_3$. Finally, $(key_3, value_3)$ is emitted.

Algorithm 1. Mapper for parallel structure$_k$ of Layer l

Input: $(key_1, value_1)$.
phase: current training phase, its range is {Feed, Error, Weight}.
Output: $(key_2, value_2)$.
1   **if** $phase == Feed$ **then**
2   Use $value_1$ to calculate activation values according to Formula 1 and assign the obtained results to $value_2$.
3   **else**
4   **if** $phase == Error$ **then**
5   Use $value_1$ to calculate error values according to Formulas 2 and 3 and assign the obtained results to $value_2$.
6   **else**
7   Use $value_1$ to calculate and update the weights according to Formula 4 and assign the obtained results to $value_2$.
8   **end**
9      $key_2 = l$;
10   EMIT$(key_2, value_2)$;
11 **end**

Algorithm 2. Reducer for Structure Integration of Layer l

Input: $(key_2, list(value_2))$.
Output: $(key_3, value_3)$.
1   $key_3 = key_2$;
2   **for** $each\ value_2\ in\ list(value_2)$ **do**
3      $value_3 = value_3 \bigcup value_2$;
4   EMIT$(key_3, value_3)$;
5   **end**

---

4   Experiments

We perform 4 groups of experiments to evaluate performance of our algorithm. The first is to illustrate effect of different number of of parallel structures on performance of our algorithm. The other 3 groups compare our algorithm with the classic MRBP algorithm in [6], the MBNN algorithm in [7] and the MRBPNN_3 algorithm in [8] for scalability in computing node, network and pattern size.

4.1 Scalability of Parallel Structure Size

The experimental data includes 1 million training patterns, the number of computing nodes is 16. We consider three neural networks with 3 layers, [50, 50, 50], [100, 100, 100] and [200, 200, 200]. We increase the number of parallel structures from 1 to 16. As shown in Fig. 4, initially, the training times for three different networks gradually decrease as more parallel structures are used. However, as the number of parallel structures increases, the decrease tends to diminished. Sometimes, the training times slightly increase. There are two reasons for this: First, the increasing number of parallel structures will lead to higher communication costs. Second, the increased parallel structures cause the total number of mappers to go beyond the maximum number of concurrency. At the same time, we observe that the larger the network, the later the occur of performance bottleneck. It shows that our algorithm is more effective for large-scale networks.

4.2 Scalability of Computing Node Size

This experiment is used to evaluate scalability of our algorithm in computing node size. We increase the number of computing nodes from 1 to 16. From the results shown in Fig. 5, we can see that as the number of computing nodes increases, the training times of the 4 algorithms decrease. But the training times of our algorithm are always less than the other 3 algorithms. Also, we observe that when the number of computing nodes is small, the training times of the 4 algorithms are similar. But, with the increasing number of computing nodes, the training times of the other 3 algorithms no longer decline whilst our algorithm still maintains a downward trend. This illustrates that our algorithm has better scalability in terms of the number of computing nodes.

4.3 Scalability of Pattern Size

This experiment is used for testing effect of different pattern size on performance of our algorithm. We increase the number of training patterns from 100 thousand to 1 million. From the results shown in Fig. 6, we can see that the training times of our algorithm are always less than the other 3 algorithms. Moreover, the growth rate of our algorithm is smaller and more stable. This illustrates that our algorithm has a higher performance as the number of training patterns increases.

4.4 Scalability of Network Size

This experiment is used to compare performance of our algorithm with the other 3 algorithms in term of scalability of network size. The number of neurons per layer is increased from 50 to 500. As shown in Fig. 7, the training times of all the algorithms increase exponentially as the number of neurons per layer increases. But the growth rate of our algorithm is smaller than the other 3 algorithms. This is because the amount of computation can be equally distributed into parallel structures in our algorithm. This shows the effectiveness of fine-grained structure parallelism of our algorithm.

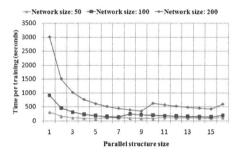

Fig. 4. Scalability of parallel structure size.

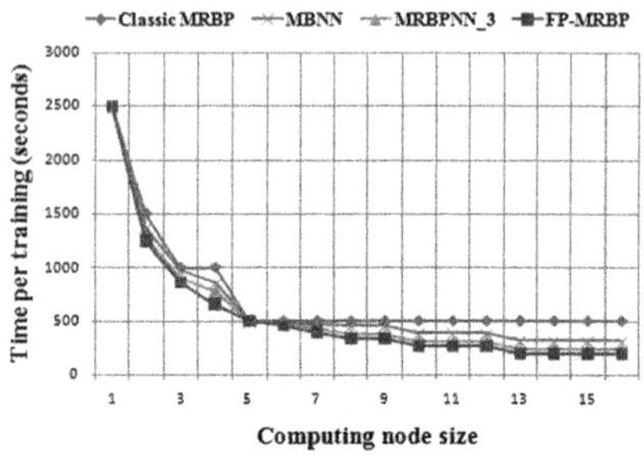

Fig. 5. Scalability of computing node size.

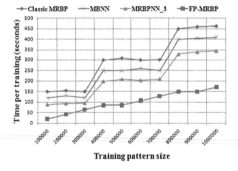

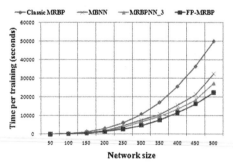

Fig. 6. Scalability of training pattern size.

Fig. 7. Scalability of network size.

5   Conclusion

In this paper we propose a novel MRBP algorithm, FP-MRBP algorithm, which has the capability of fine-grained structure parallelism. To the best knowledge of the authors, it is the first time to introduce fine-grained parallelism to the classic MRBP algorithm. The experimental results show that our algorithm has a better training efficiency when training a large scale BPNN.

Acknowledgment. This work was supported by National Science Foundation of China (Nos. 61100066, 91530323), National Key R&D Plan of China (No. 2016YFB0200603). The authors would like express sincere gratitude to all the authors of the references in this paper. The authors also extend their thanks to all anonymous referees for providing valuable comments on this paper.

References

1. Gupta, J.N.D., Sexton, R.S.: Comparing backpropagation with a genetic algorithm for neural network training. Omega **27**(6), 679–684 (1999)
2. Yang, S.E., Huang, L.: Financial crisis warning model based on BP neural network. Syst. Eng.-Theory Pract. **25**(12), 12–19 (2005)
3. Li, J., Cheng, J., Shi, J., Huang, F.: Brief introduction of back propagation neural network algorithm and its improvement. In: Jin, D., Lin, S. (eds.) Advances in Computer Science and Information Engineering. AINSC, vol. 169, pp. 553–558. Springer, Heidelberg (2012). doi:10.1007/978-3-642-30223-7_87
4. Dean, J., Ghemawat, S.: MapReduce: simplified data processing on large clusters. In: Proceedings of the Conference on Symposium on Opearting Systems Design & Implementation, pp. 107–113 (2004)
5. White, T.: Hadoop: The Definitive Guide. O'Reilly Media Inc., Sebastopol (2012)
6. Chu, C., Kim, S.K.: Map-Reduce for machine learning on multicore. In: Advances in Neural Information Processing Systems, vol. 19, pp. 281–288 (2006)
7. Liu, Z., Li, H., Miao, G.: MapReduce-based backpropagation neural network over large scale mobile data. In: International Conference on Natural Computation, ICNC 2010, 10–12 August 2010, Yantai, Shandong, China, pp. 1726–1730 (2010)
8. Liu, Y., Yang, J., Huang, Y., Xu, L., Li, S., Qi, M.: MapReduce based parallel neural networks in enabling large scale machine learning. Comput. Intell. Neurosci. **1–13**, 2016 (2015)
9. Turchenko, V.: Computational grid vs. parallel computer for coarse-grain parallelization of neural networks training. In: Meersman, R., Tari, Z., Herrero, P. (eds.) OTM 2005. LNCS, vol. 3762, pp. 357–366. Springer, Heidelberg (2005). doi:10.1007/11575863_55
10. Turchenko, V., Paliy, I., Demchuk, V.: Coarse-grain parallelization of neural network-based face detection method. In: Proceedings of the 4th IEEE Workshop on Intelligent Data Acquisition, 6–8 September 2007, pp. 155–158 (2007)
11. Turchenko, V., Grandinetti, L.: Efficiency analysis of parallel batch pattern NN training algorithm on general-purpose supercomputer. In: Proceedings of the International Work-Conference on Artificial Neural Networks, pp. 223–226 (2009)
12. Sudhakar, V., Murthy, C.S.R.: Efficient mapping of backpropagation algorithm onto a network of workstations. IEEE Trans. Syst. Man Cybern. **28**(6), 841–848 (1998)
13. Suresh, S., Omkar, S.N., Mani, V.: Parallel implementation of back-propagation algorithm in networks of workstations. IEEE Trans. Parallel Distrib. Syst. **16**(1), 24–34 (2005)
14. Ganeshamoorthy, K., Ranasinghe, D.N.: On the performance of parallel neural network implementations on distributed memory architectures. In: Proceedings of the IEEE International Symposium on Cluster Computing, pp. 90–97 (2008)
15. Chu, L., Wah, B.W.: Optimal mapping of neural-network learning on message-passing multicomputers. J. Parallel Distrib. Comput. **14**(3), 319–339 (1992)

IQNN: Training Quantized Neural Networks with Iterative Optimizations

Shuchang Zhou[1,2,3(✉)], He Wen[3], Taihong Xiao[3], and Xinyu Zhou[3]

[1] University of Chinese Academy of Sciences, Beijing 100049, China
shuchang.zhou@gmail.com
[2] State Key Laboratory of Computer Architecture,
Institute of Computing Technology, Chinese Academy of Sciences,
Beijing 100190, China
[3] Megvii Inc., Beijing 100190, China
{wenhe,xiaotaihong,zxy}@megvii.com

Abstract. Quantized Neural Networks (QNNs) use low bitwidth numbers for representing parameters and intermediate results. The lowering of bitwidths saves storage space and allows for exploiting bitwise operations to speed up computations. However, QNNs often have lower prediction accuracies than their floating point counterparts, due to the extra quantization errors. In this paper, we propose a quantization algorithm that iteratively solves for the optimal scaling factor during every forward pass, which significantly reduces quantization errors. Moreover, we propose a novel initialization method for the iterative quantization, which speeds up convergence and further reduces quantization errors. Overall, our method improves prediction accuracies of QNNs at no extra costs for the inference. Experiments confirm the efficacy of our method in the quantization of AlexNet, GoogLeNet and ResNet. In particular, we are able to train a GoogLeNet having 4-bit weights and activations to reach 11.4% in top-5 single-crop error on ImageNet dataset, outperforming state-of-the-art QNNs. The code will be available online.

Keywords: Quantized Neural Network · Uniform quantization · Iterative quantization · Alternating least squares · Bitwise operation

1 Introduction

Deep Neural Networks have found wide-spread applications due to their ability to model nonlinear relationships in massive amount of data and robustness to real world noises. However, the modeling capacities of DNNs are roughly proportional to their computational complexities. For example, DNNs that are widely used in computer vision applications, like AlexNet [9], GoogLeNet [15] and ResNet [5], require billions of multiply-and-add operations for an input image of scale of 224. Such high resource requirements impede applications of DNNs to embedded devices and interactive scenarios.

Quantized Neural Networks (QNNs) [7,8,12] have been proposed as less resource-intensive variants of DNNs. By quantizing some of weights, activations

© Springer International Publishing AG 2017
A. Lintas et al. (Eds.): ICANN 2017, Part II, LNCS 10614, pp. 688–695, 2017.
https://doi.org/10.1007/978-3-319-68612-7_78

and gradients to low bitwidth numbers, QNNs typically require less memory, storage space and computation, and have found applications in Image Classification, Segmentation, etc [16]. However, as the quantization introduces approximation errors, QNNs are in general worse than their floating point counterparts in terms of prediction accuracies.

In this paper, we focus on reducing the quantization errors of parameters of QNNs to improve prediction accuracies. We first propose an optimization formulation for the multi-bit quantization of weight parameters. As no closed-form solutions exist for the optimization, we construct Iterative Quantization, an Alternating Least Squares (ALS) [11] algorithm, to find the optimal scaling factors for the quantization. The iterative algorithm is designed to use only simple matrix operations, and can be readily integrated into the training process. Because the iterative optimization is only performed during training, there will be no overhead added to the inference. Moreover, we propose to initialize the optimization with values based on statistics of weights, to further reduce quantization errors and number of iterations required for the optimization.

Numerical experiments on the quantization of weights of neural networks confirm the efficacy of our method in reducing quantization errors. We also train QNNs by Iterative Quantization from scratch on the large-scale ImageNet [2] dataset, and outperform the state-of-the-art QNNs in terms of prediction accuracies.

2   Quantized Neural Networks

We first introduce some notations. We define a utility function quant_k that converts floating point numbers in the closed interval $[-\frac{1}{2}, \frac{1}{2}]$ to fixed point numbers as follows:

$$\mathrm{quant}_k(\mathbf{W}) \overset{\mathrm{def}}{=} \frac{1}{2^k-1}\mathrm{round}((2^k-1)(\mathbf{W}+\frac{1}{2})) - \frac{1}{2}, \quad -\frac{1}{2} \le w_{i,j} \le \frac{1}{2} \; \forall i,j, \tag{1}$$

where $w_{i,j}$ are entries of matrix $\mathbf{W}$, and the outputs of quant_k are among $-\frac{1}{2}, -\frac{1}{2}+\frac{1}{2^k-1}, -\frac{1}{2}+\frac{2}{2^k-1}, \cdots, \frac{1}{2}$.

When quantizing parameters of a Neural Network, we would need first map the parameters $\mathbf{W}$ to the closed interval $[-\frac{1}{2}, \frac{1}{2}]$ before applying quant_k:

Definition 1 (k-bit Uniform Quantization [7,17]).

$$\mathrm{uniform\text{-}quant}_k(\mathbf{W}) \overset{\mathrm{def}}{=} 2\max(|\mathbf{W}|)\,\mathrm{quant}_k(\frac{\mathbf{W}}{2\max(|\mathbf{W}|)}),$$

where the subscript k stands for k-bit quantization, and $|\mathbf{W}|$ is a matrix with values being the absolute values of corresponding entries in $\mathbf{W}$.

As $-\max(|\mathbf{W}|) \le w_{i,j} \le \max(|\mathbf{W}|)$, we have $-\frac{1}{2} \le \frac{w_{i,j}}{2\max(|\mathbf{W}|)} \le \frac{1}{2}$. We can then apply quant_k to get the fixed point values. Finally we restore the value range back to $[-\max(|\mathbf{W}|), \max(|\mathbf{W}|)]$ by multiplying $2\max(|\mathbf{W}|)$.

As its outputs are discrete values, any quantization function will have zero gradients, which invalidates the Back Propagation algorithm. To circumvent this problem, we need convert *quant* to a Straight Through Estimator [6], by substituting the gradients with respect to the quantized value for the gradients of the original value.

3   Iterative Quantization of Neural Network

QNNs often incur significant degradations in prediction accuracies when bitwidths are below 4-bit [7,12,17]. We note that for the uniform quantization defined in Definition 1, the scaling factors are determined from extremal values in one shot, which may be suboptimal. In this section we propose an algorithm that iteratively optimizes the scaling factors, which generalizes the uniform quantization method and reduces quantization errors.

3.1   Quantization as Optimization

To reduce quantization errors measured in Frobenius norm, we investigate the following optimization formulation for k-bit quantization:

$$\min_{\boldsymbol{\Lambda}, \mathbf{Q}} \| \boldsymbol{\Lambda} \mathbf{Q} - \mathbf{W} \|_F \qquad (2)$$

where $\mathbf{W}$ contains weights of a fully-connected (convolutional) layer of a neural network, $\boldsymbol{\Lambda}$ is a diagonal matrix containing floating point scaling factors[1], and $\mathbf{Q}$ contains fixed-point values in the closed interval $[-\frac{1}{2}, \frac{1}{2}]$. Determining the scaling factor $\boldsymbol{\Lambda}$ is important as it affects the value of the fixed point part $\mathbf{Q}$. The product $\boldsymbol{\Lambda} \mathbf{Q}$ will be used to replace $\mathbf{W}$ during the inference.

3.2   Solution by Iterative Algorithm

The objective function of Formula 2 is non-convex and lacks a closed-form solution except for the special case of 1-bit [12]. Nevertheless, it can be solved by the Alternating Least Squares algorithm, detailed in Algorithm 1.

It can be observed that only simple matrix operations are used in Algorithm 1. Hence the iterative optimization can be readily integrated into the computation graph of a QNN as a unrolled loop. Alternatively, as $(\boldsymbol{\Lambda}_i, \mathbf{Q}_i)$ are iteratively updated, the iterations can be implemented as a Recurrent Neural Network layer with $(\boldsymbol{\Lambda}_i, \mathbf{Q}_i)$ as state variables, which reduces memory footprint during training.

The uniform quantization method from Definition 1 can be formulated as a special case of Algorithm 1, by setting all entries of $\boldsymbol{\Lambda}_0$ to be $2 \max(|\mathbf{W}|)$ and having the number of iterations $N = 1$.

---

[1]   Floating point multiplication with $\boldsymbol{\Lambda}$ during inference can be avoided [17].

Algorithm 1. Iterative quantization for matrix $\mathbf{W} \in \mathbb{R}^{I \times J}$

Require: Initialization values Λ_0
Ensure : Quantized weights $\Lambda_N \mathbf{Q}_N \approx \mathbf{W}$

1 **for** $t = 1 \rightarrow N$ **do**
2      $\mathbf{Q}_t \leftarrow \text{quant}_k(\text{clip}((\Lambda_{t-1})^{-1}\mathbf{W}, -\frac{1}{2}, \frac{1}{2}))$;
       // The clipping function $\text{clip}(x, l, h) = \max(\min(x, h), l)$ is used to
       limit the value range to $[l, h]$.
3   **for** $i = 1 \rightarrow I$ **do**
4          $(\Lambda_t)_i \leftarrow \frac{<(\mathbf{W})_i, (\mathbf{Q}_t)_i>}{\epsilon + <(\mathbf{Q}_t)_i, (\mathbf{Q}_t)_i>}$;
           // $< \cdot, \cdot >$ computes the inner product.
           // $(\mathbf{W})_i, (\mathbf{Q}_t)_i$ are the i-th row of $\mathbf{W}$ and $\mathbf{Q}_t$ respectively.
           $(\Lambda_t)_i$ is the i-th diagonal entry of Λ_t.
           // ϵ is a small constant thas is used to avoid division by
           zero.
5   **end**
6 **end**

3.3 Distribution of Weights and Initialization

When weights follow a well known distribution, the scaling factors Λ may be determined from theoretical results of optimal uniform quantizers [14], which we list in Table 1. As the theoretical optima are fixed points of Iterative Quantization, when they are used as initialization values, the convergence of the iterative algorithm can be accelerated.

Table 1. Comparison of maximal quantized value of optimal uniform quantizers for uniform (over $[-1, 1]$) and standard normal distributions [14].

Statistics	Uniform	Normal
Maximum after optimal 2-bit quantization	0.5	0.798
Maximum after optimal 4-bit quantization	0.938	2.513
Mean of absolute value	0.5	0.798

However, the distribution of weights of Neural Networks may be quite complex. Two illustrative examples are given in Fig. 1, where the second one has many peaks. Hence it is not in general possible to determine optimal initialization values Λ_0. Nevertheless, we observe that the ratio between mean of absolute value and maximal quantized value is quite stable across different distributions and different bitwidths. For example, when performing 2-bit quantization, the ratios are 1 for both Uniform and Normal distributions.

We propose to initialize Λ_0 with mean of absolute values scaled by an coefficient γ when performing k-bit quantization as follows:

$$(\Lambda_0)_i = \gamma \, \text{mean}((|\mathbf{W}|)_i), \tag{3}$$

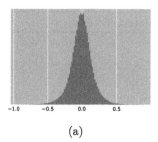 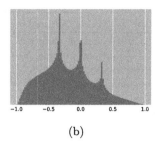

(a)   (b)

Fig. 1. (a) Distribution of weights from a convolution layer in a GoogLeNet model. (b) Distribution of weights before quantization from the last fully-connected layer in a QNN version of AlexNet.

where $(|\mathbf{W}|)_i$ is the i-th row of $|\mathbf{W}|$ and $(\mathbf{\Lambda}_0)_i$ is the i-th diagonal entry of $\mathbf{\Lambda}_0$. For 2-bit case we set $\gamma_{opt} = 2 = 2 \times \frac{0.5/0.5 + 0.798/0.798}{2}$, and for 4-bit we set $\gamma_{opt} = 5.02 \approx 2 \times \frac{0.938/0.5 + 2.513/0.798}{2}$. The γ coefficient is 2 times the average of ratios for Uniform and Normal distributions, as the maximual quantized values are mapped to $\frac{1}{2}$ in Definition 1.

4   Experiments

In this section, we conduct experiments to compare the performance of Iterative Quantization with the non-iterative method (Definition 1). Experiments are performed on machines equipped with Intel Xeon CPUs and NVidia TitanX Graphics Processing Units.

4.1   Iterative Quantization of Weights of a Layer

We first experiment on the quantization of weights of the last fully-connected layer of AlexNet, and test the convergence of our algorithm. Results are listed in Fig. 2. It can be seen that the quantization errors decrease monotonically with more iterations, which is a property of ALS. However, the initialization values significantly impact the speed of convergence. In fact, initialization with the approximate optimum $\gamma_{opt} = 5.02$ significantly reduces the number of iterations required for convergence. On the other hand, quantization errors are still substantially reduced even when initializing with γ_{opt}, which justifies performing the iterative optimization during training.

We will set $\#iter = 8$ in remaining experiments unless noted, to strike a balance between the training speed and the prediction accuracy.

4.2   Iterative Quantization for Training Neural Networks

We also apply Iterative Quantization to train QNNs from scratch. We use ImageNet dataset that contains 1.2 M images for training and 50 K images for validation. While testing, images are first resized so that the shortest edge contains

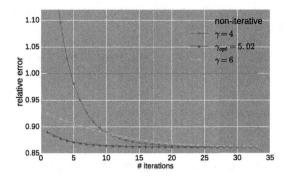

Fig. 2. Relative errors against number of iterations for the 4-bit quantization. Weights are from the last fully-connected layer of AlexNet. The errors are scaled so that the error of non-iterative method is 1.

256 pixels, then the center 224-by-224 crops will be used as inputs. Following the conventions, we report results in two measures: single-crop top-1 error rate and top-5 error rate over ILSVRC12 validation sets [13].

For all QNNs in this section, weights and activations of all convolutional and fully-connected layers have been quantized by specified bitwidths unless noted. The activations are quantized by the method of DoReFa-net [17].

Table 2. Comparison of classification errors of QNNs trained with different methods. FP stands for neural networks with floating point weights and activations. "FP weights + 2-bit activations" refers to models that have floating point weights and activations quantized to 2-bit numbers. Results in rows prefixed with "non-iterative" are produced from non-iterative uniform quantization.

Method	AlexNet		ResNet-18	
	Top-1 error	Top-5 error	Top-1 error	Top-5 error
FP	42.9%	20.6%	31.8%	12.5%
FP weights + 2-bit activations	43.5%	21.0%	38.9%	17.3%
Non-iterative 2-bit	45.3%	22.3%	42.3%	19.2%
Iterative 2-bit	**43.2%**	**20.8%**	**41.8%**	**19.0%**

Table 2 demonstrates the efficacy of Iterative Quantization for training QNNs, exhibited by the improved prediction accuracies. For AlexNet, the QNN trained with our method has almost the same top-5 error rate as the floating point one.

Table 3 compares the GoogLeNet quantized with our method against the state-of-the-art. The row marked with "QNN 4-bit" is from Hubara *et al.* [7]. To rule out factors like Image Augmentation, we also list the accuracies of their

Table 3. Comparison of classification errors of our method with the state-of-the-art for the quantization of GoogLeNet.

Method	Top-1 error	Top-5 error
FP [7]	28.4%	8.8%
Our FP	28.5%	10.1%
Ristretto [4] 8-bit	33.4%	-
QNN 4-bit [7]	33.5%	16.6%
Our 4-bit (#iter=4)	31.6%	11.9%
Our 4-bit (#iter=16)	**31.2%**	**11.4%**

floating point model. It can be seen that their FP model has better accuracies than our FP model. In contrast, our quantized model outperforms their quantized model. In particular, our method reduces the top-5 accuracy degradation, which is the difference in accuracy between a QNN and its floating point version, from 7.8 percentages to 1.3 percentages. In addition, with our initialization method, the top-5 error rate only slightly increases by 0.5 percentages if we reduce the number of iterations from 16 to 4.

5   Related Work

Our iterative quantization method is different from that of Gong *et al.* [3], because QNNs restrict the transformation of weights to scaling. Lin *et al.* [10] investigated optimal uniform quantization but did not integrate it into the training of DNNs, hence their method incurred severe accuracy degradations when bitwidths are below 6. Anwar *et al.* [1] investigated an iterative algorithm for quantization of pre-trained networks, which were later fine-tuned. However, such operations were only performed a few times during the whole training process. To the best of our knowledge, we are the first to integrate the iterative quantization into training of QNNs and perform experiments on a dataset of the scale of ImageNet.

6   Conclusion

In this paper, we propose the method of Iterative Quantization for training QNNs. We formulate the multi-bit quantization of weights of Neural Networks as an optimization problem, which is solved by an iterative algorithm to minimize quantization errors, during each forward pass of the training. Moreover, we propose a method to use statistics of weights as initial values, which further reduces quantization errors and the overhead added to training.

References

1. Anwar, S., Hwang, K., Sung, W.: Fixed point optimization of deep convolutional neural networks for object recognition. In: 2015 IEEE International Conference on Acoustics, Speech and Signal Processing, ICASSP 2015, South Brisbane, Queensland, Australia, April 19–24, 2015, pp. 1131–1135 (2015)
2. Deng, J., Dong, W., Socher, R., Li, L.J., Li, K., Fei-Fei, L.: Imagenet: a large-scale hierarchical image database. In: IEEE Conference on Computer Vision and Pattern Recognition, CVPR 2009, pp. 248–255. IEEE (2009)
3. Gong, Y., Lazebnik, S., Gordo, A., Perronnin, F.: Iterative quantization: a procrustean approach to learning binary codes for large-scale image retrieval. IEEE Trans. Pattern Anal. Mach. Intell. **35**(12), 2916–2929 (2013)
4. Gysel, P., Motamedi, M., Ghiasi, S.: Hardware-oriented approximation of convolutional neural networks. CoRR abs/1604.03168 (2016)
5. He, K., Zhang, X., Ren, S., Sun, J.: Deep residual learning for image recognition. In: 2016 IEEE Conference on Computer Vision and Pattern Recognition, CVPR 2016, Las Vegas, NV, USA, June 27–30, 2016, pp. 770–778, June 2016
6. Hinton, G., Srivastava, N., Swersky, K.: Neural networks for machine learning. Coursera Video Lect. vol. 264 (2012)
7. Hubara, I., Courbariaux, M., Soudry, D., El-Yaniv, R., Bengio, Y.: Quantized neural networks: training neural networks with low precision weights and activations. CoRR abs/1609.07061 (2016)
8. Kim, M., Smaragdis, P.: Bitwise neural networks. CoRR abs/1601.06071 (2016)
9. Krizhevsky, A., Sutskever, I., Hinton, G.E.: Imagenet classification with deep convolutional neural networks. In: Advances in Neural Information Processing Systems, pp. 1097–1105, December 2012
10. Lin, D.D., Talathi, S.S., Annapureddy, V.S.: Fixed point quantization of deep convolutional networks. In: International Conference on Machine Learning (ICML2016) (2015)
11. Lloyd, S.P.: Least squares quantization in PCM. IEEE Trans. Inf. Theor. **28**(2), 129–136 (1982)
12. Rastegari, M., Ordonez, V., Redmon, J., Farhadi, A.: XNOR-Net: imagenet classification using binary convolutional neural networks. In: Leibe, B., Matas, J., Sebe, N., Welling, M. (eds.) ECCV 2016. LNCS, vol. 9908, pp. 525–542. Springer, Cham (2016). doi:10.1007/978-3-319-46493-0_32
13. Russakovsky, O., Deng, J., Su, H., Krause, J., Satheesh, S., Ma, S., Huang, Z., Karpathy, A., Khosla, A., Bernstein, M., et al.: Imagenet large scale visual recognition challenge. Int. J. Comput. Vision **115**(3), 211–252 (2015)
14. Shi, Y.Q., Sun, H.: Image and Video Compression for Multimedia Engineering: Fundamentals, Algorithms, and Standards. CRC Press, Boca Raton (1999)
15. Szegedy, C., Liu, W., Jia, Y., Sermanet, P., Reed, S.E., Anguelov, D., Erhan, D., Vanhoucke, V., Rabinovich, A.: Going deeper with convolutions. In: IEEE Conference on Computer Vision and Pattern Recognition, CVPR 2015, Boston, MA, USA, June 7–12, 2015, pp. 1–9, June 2015
16. Wen, H., Zhou, S., Liang, Z., Zhang, Y., Feng, D., Zhou, X., Yao, C.: Training bit fully convolutional network for fast semantic segmentation. CoRR abs/1612.00212 (2016)
17. Zhou, S., Wu, Y., Ni, Z., Zhou, X., Wen, H., Zou, Y.: DoReFa-Net: training low bitwidth convolutional neural networks with low bitwidth gradients. CoRR abs/1606.06160 (2016)

Compressing Neural Networks by Applying Frequent Item-Set Mining

Zi-Yi Dou, Shu-Jian Huang$^{(\boxtimes)}$, and Yi-Fan Su

National Key Laboratory for Novel Software Technology,
Nanjing University, Nanjing 210023, China
141242042@smail.nju.edu.cn, huangsj@nju.edu.cn, suyf@nlp.nju.edu.cn

Abstract. Deep neural networks have been widely used contemporarily. To achieve better performance, people tend to build larger and deeper neural networks with millions or even billions of parameters. A natural question to ask is whether we can simplify the architecture of neural networks so that the storage and computational cost are reduced. This paper presented a novel approach to prune neural networks by frequent item-set mining. We propose a way to measure the importance of each item-set and then prune the networks. Compared with existing state-of-the-art pruning algorithms, our proposed algorithm can obtain a higher compression rate in one iteration with almost no loss of accuracy. To prove the effectiveness of our algorithm, we conducted several experiments on various types of neural networks. The results show that we can reduce the complexity of the model dramatically as well as enhance the performance of the model.

Keywords: Neural networks · Frequent item-set mining · Deep learning

1 Introduction

In recent years, neural networks have been proven to be a powerful tool in many fields, including object classification [1] and speech recognition [2]. Typically, people have a tendency to build deeper and larger neural networks. In the field of computer vision, starting with LeNet-5 which requires 431 thousand parameters [3], Krizhevsky *et al.* designed AlexNet with 60 million parameters in 2012 [4] and Sermanet *et al.* won the ImageNet competition using 144 million parameters in 2013 [1]. For natural language processing tasks, a recent state-of-the-art neural machine translation system requires over 200 million parameters [5].

It is true that enormous amount of parameters dramatically improve the performance ,but we should be aware that there is significant redundancy in the parameterization of several deep learning models [6]. Over-parametrization can also lead to problems like over-fitting which can result in low generalization ability. In addition , training and using such large neural networks requires

This work is supported by NSFC No. 61672277, 61472183 and the Collaborative Innovation Center of Novel Software Technology and Industrialization, China.

A. Lintas et al. (Eds.): ICANN 2017, Part II, LNCS 10614, pp. 696–704, 2017.
https://doi.org/10.1007/978-3-319-68612-7_79

long running time and costs much energy and memory. The trend of applications of machine learning shifting toward embedded devices, which have limited storage size and computational ability, makes the problem of utilizing so many parameters more severe.

All these issues have motivated the idea of neural network compression, which aims to reduce the storage and energy required to run inference on large neural networks without losing any accuracy. Several methods have been proposed to tackle this problem and here we introduce a rather novel way to compress neural networks based on frequent item-set mining which can be implemented easily and achieve relatively high compression rate in one iteration.

2   Related Work

Network Pruning. Pruning the parameters from a neural network have been investigated for several decades. Basically, many of the traditional algorithms, such as penalty term methods or magnitude based methods, defines a measure of each connection or node and remove the element with the least effect [7].

In recent years, the deep learning renaissance has prompted a re-investigation of network pruning for modern models and tasks [8]. Admittedly, a lot of traditional pruning algorithms can achieve great performance. However, when it comes to large deep neural networks, the high computational complexity cannot be tolerated. In 2015, Han *et al.* proposed an algorithm that can remain efficient in deep neural networks [9].

Inspired by Han *et al.*'s paper, several methods have been put forward to prune the neural networks. DropNeuron [10] adds two more regularization terms into the objective function and thus makes it possible to delete more neurons in neural networks. Network Trimming prunes the neurons with zero activation [11].

To our knowledge, no one has ever applied association rule or frequent item-set generation into pruning neural networks. In addition, only a few papers [8] discuss their applications in recurrent neural networks, which are widely used in areas like sentiment analysis or language models.

Frequent Item-Set Mining. Nowadays there are many sophiscated algorithms for frequent item-set mining. One of the most popular algorithm is Apriori [12]. However, Apriori is inefficient in some scenarios. To resolve the issue, Lin *et al.* use MapReduce to accelerate the algorithm [13]. Cut-Both-Ways (CBW) algorithm first finds all frequent item-sets of a pre-defined length and then employs search in both directions [14]. However, these methods all have exponential complexity and thus cannot be applied in large scale problem.

3   Our Proposed Methods

In this section, we first give a brief overview of frequent item-set mining. Then we illustrate how to apply it in neural networks. Finally we propose our algorithm based on frequent item-set mining.

3.1   Frequent Item-Set Mining Task

Frequent item-set mining is often regarded as the first part of association rule mining. the problem of frequent item-set mining can be defined as [15]:

Let $IT = \{it_1, it_2, ..., it_n\}$ be a set of n binary attributes called *items*. and $D = \{t_1, t_2, ..., t_m\}$ be a set of transactions called the *database*.

Each *transaction* in D has a unique transaction ID and contains a subset of the items in IT. Suppose T is a set of transactions of a given database, then the *support* of an item-set X with respect to T is defined as the proportion of transactions t in the database which contains item-set X, which can be expressed as

$$Supp(X) = \frac{|\{t \in T; X \subset t\}|}{|T|}. \tag{1}$$

The task of frequent item-set mining is to discover all item-sets that satisfy a user-specified minimum support $minsup$.

3.2   Frequent Item-Set Mining in Neural Networks

Symbols and Definitions. In this section, we first introduce some symbols and definitions which will be used in later parts of the paper. Since our strategy prunes the neural networks layer by layer, without loss of generality, the following parts all consider one single layer.

Suppose the layer consists of m input nodes $I = \{i_1, i_2, ..., i_m\}$ and n outputs nodes $O = \{o_1, o_2, ..., o_n\}$, its weight matrix can be represented as a $m \times n$ matrix W. In order to express whether there exists an connection between two nodes, we need an extra connection matrix C, where C is an $m \times n$ boolean matrix and $C_{ab} = 1$ if and only if the output node o_b is connected to the input node i_a.

Therefore, the layer L can be represented as a tuple $< I, O, W, C >$. Normally, for a fully connected layer, the elements of C all equal to one and our mission is to turn as many elements in C into zero as possible without the loss of accuracy.

Item-Sets in Neural Networks. In order to apply frequent item-set mining into pruning neural networks, we must first construct item-sets in neural networks. Based on the definition above, given a layer $L = < I, O, W, C >$, each input node is connected to several output nodes S_i, namely a subset of O. Each element o_i in O can be considered as an item. Thus, we can delete some nodes from S_i and take the rest of the nodes as an item-set. In the end, we can construct m item-sets in total, which is then viewed as our set of transactions T. In our approach, we specify a constant ϵ in advance and delete the nodes whose absolute value of weights of connections to the input node are smaller than ϵ, i.e.

$$o_i \in t_j \Leftrightarrow |W_{ij}| > \epsilon, for\ each\ t_j \in T$$

In order to make this point clear, let's consider a fully connected layer whose $m = 5$ and $n = 4$. The weight matrix is shown in Fig. 1.

	Output		
0.32	0.44	0.53	-0.11
-0.25	-0.36	0.42	0.12
0.14	-0.22	0.15	0.25
-0.12	-0.34	-0.10	0.09
0.23	0.27	0.02	-0.01

(Input on left axis)

→

0.32	0.44	0.53	-0.11
-0.25	-0.36	0.42	0.12
0.14	-0.22	0.15	0.25
-0.12	-0.34	-0.10	0.09
0.23	0.27	0.02	-0.01

→

1	1	1	0
1	1	1	0
0	1	0	1
0	1	0	0
1	1	0	0

→

0	1	0	0
1	0	0	0
1	1	0	0
1	1	1	0
0	0	1	0

Fig. 1. Three steps to apply frequent item-set mining in neural networks: separate each row of W, view each o_k as an item; construct set of transactions T; applying frequent item-set mining algorithm directly.

We view each output node as an item. First, we consider each row separately and those connections whose weights less than $\epsilon = 0.2$ are removed from the item-sets. In the end, we get five item-sets from this layer.

Frequent Item-Set Mining in Neural Networks. Once we have constructed the item-sets, we can directly use current frequent item-set mining algorithms like Apriori to find out all the item-sets whose support is greater than the pre-defined *minsup*. Then we can select the top m item-sets with the highest support so that the basic architecture of neural networks remain the same.

Again, let us consider the previous example. After applying frequent item-set mining, the result is shown in Fig. 1.

Importance Measure of Item-Sets. The support of one item-set cannot be the only measure. If one item-set is frequent, *i.e.* its support is greater than a constant, then all its subsets are frequent. Therefore, the sets with few elements always have the highest support. As we can see from the figure, three out of five frequent item-sets only consist of one element. To fix the issue, we should measure the importance of an item-set not only in terms of its support. Here we propose an importance measure of an item-set S:

$$Importance(S) = \frac{|\{t \in T; S \subset t\}|}{|T|} + \lambda * e^{|S|/n} \qquad (2)$$

Here n denotes the total number of output nodes, T represents the item-sets constructed from neural networks and λ is a pre-defined hyper-parameter. The first term on the right side is the original definition of support and the second term tries to model the effect of the size of one item-set. In this way, we hope the length of item-sets will counteract the influence of support.

3.3   FIMP Algorithm

The naive idea is to first use frequent item-set mining algorithm such as Apriori to calculate the support of each item-set and then re-rank all the remaining item-set according to their importance as defined in Eq. 2. Finally, we select m item-set with the highest importance.

However, we should be aware that this simple idea has some potential draw-backs. First, the computational cost is growing exponentially. Second, the item-sets cannot be repetitive, which means that in extreme cases where $m >> n$, there will be not enough item-sets.

Here we improve our former idea and propose an algorithm that can solve all the drawbacks mentioned above. We call it FIMP algorithm, which is short for Frequent Item-set Mining based Pruning.

In the first step, we construct all the item-sets in every layer as described in Sect. 3.2, corresponding to the third matrix from the left in Fig. 1. Then, for every item-set, we apply greedy search or beam search to calculate the importance of its subsets. Then we choose the subset with largest importance and continue the above procedure until during the search no subset has higher importance than the current item-set. The full procedure is shown in Algorithm 1. S_i is a subset of S with $size(S_i) >= size(S) - k$, where k is a hyper-parameter.

Algorithm 1. FIMP Algorithm

Input: Neural Network N, ϵ
Output: Pruned Neural Network PN
1: **for** each layer with $m_i \times n_i$ nodes **do**
2:    Construct item-sets following the procedure described in Sect. 3.2
3:    **for** each item-set S **do**
4:      **while** $Importance(S_i) > Importance(S)$ **do**
5:        $max\_id = argmax_{1 \leq i \leq m_i} Importance(S_i)$
6:        $S = S_{max\_id}$
7:      **end while**
8:    **end for**
9: **end for**

---

4   Experiment

4.1   Baseline Models

We compare our model with two baseline methods: (1) The method proposed by Han *et al.*, where they simply remove the connection with least weight [9]. (2) *DropNeuron* proposed by Pan *et al.* where they add two more regularization terms so that more neurons can be removed [10].

We list the percentage of connections left after pruning for each layer L, represented as $W^L\%$, and the performance of the model before and after pruning.

4.2   Deep Antoencoder

First we conducted experiment on deep autoencoder. We considered the image dataset of MNIST [16]. The number of training examples and test examples are

60000 and 10000 respectively, the image sizes are 28×28 digit images and 10 classes. We used the same setting as [10], where they use $784 \rightarrow 128 \rightarrow 64 \rightarrow 128 \rightarrow 784$ autoencoder and all units were logistic with mean square error as loss.

Table 1. Results of pruning autoencoder

	$W^{FC1}\%$	$W^{FC2}\%$	$W^{FC3}\%$	$W^{FC4}\%$	$W^{total}\%$	NMSE (before)	NMSE (pruned)
Han *et al.*∗	15.18%	46.29%	52.53%	17.54%	18.86%	0.011	0.011
Pan *et al.*∗	16.00%	44.47%	54.11%	18.14%	19.50%	0.012	0.012
FIMP	14.27%	29.00%	39.94%	8.95%	13.34%	0.009	0.007

∗ Means the result is cited from Pan *et al.* [10]

The results can be seen at Table 1. Here we use the standard normalized mean square error (NMSE) metric, *i.e.* $NMSE = \frac{\sum_{t=1}^{N}(y_t - \hat{y}_t)^2}{\sum_{t=1}^{N} y_t^2}$, to evaluate the prediction accuracy of the model. From the table, we can see that our method can achieve greater compression rate compared with [9] and [10].

4.3   Fully Connected Neural Networks

We also implemented our algorithm on fully connected neural networks. Here we mainly focus on the representative neural networks LeNet. LeNet-300-100 is a fully connected network with two hidden layers, with 300 and 100 neurons each, which achieves 1.6% error rate on MNIST. Unfortunately, we could not find any pre-trained model of LeNet-300-100 on TensorFlow and it is hard for us to get 1.6% error rate. So we just use the best model we can find with 98.24% accuracy and prune it. As we can see from Table 2, our compression rate is still higher than the other two pruning strategies. Even though our accuracy is a little bit lower, we should notice that the accuracy is actually higher after pruning, which suggests that the relatively lower accuracy may result from the unsatisfied initial model.

Table 2. Results of pruning LeNet-300-100

	$W^{FC1}\%$	$W^{FC2}\%$	$W^{FC3}\%$	$W^{total}\%$	Accuracy (before)	Accuracy (pruned)
Han *et al.* ∗∗	8%	9%	26%	8%	98.36%	98.41%
Pan *et al.*∗	9.56%	11.16%	54.5%	9.91%	98.13%	98.17%
FIMP	6.19%	19.00%	38.50%	7.76%	98.24%	98.27%

∗ Means the result is cited from Pan *et al.* [10]
∗∗ Means the result is cited from Han *et al.* [9]

Figure 2 shows the sparsity pattern of the first fully connected layer of LeNet-300-100 after pruning. The matrix size is $784 * 300$ and the white regions of the figure indicate non-zero parameters. The figure demonstrates how FIMP affects the network. Since digits are written in the center of image, it is no surprising that the graph is concentrated in the middle and sparse on the left and right.

Fig. 2. Visualization of the first FC layer's sparsity pattern of Lenet-300-100.

4.4   Convolutional Neural Networks

LeNet-5 is a convolutional network that has two convolutional layers and two fully connected layers, which achieves 0.8% error rate on MNIST. Actually, our algorithm is the same as the other strategy when pruning convolutional layers, thus we can just compare the performance of three algorithms on the fully connected layers.

Table 3. Results of pruning LeNet-5

	$W^{FC1}\%$	$W^{FC2}\%$	$W^{total}\%$	Accuracy(before)	Accuracy(pruned)
Han *et al.* **	8%	19%	8%	99.20%	99.23%
Pan *et al.*.*	1.44%	16.82%	1.49%	99.07%	99.14%
FIMP	2.95%	17.42%	3.00%	99.05%	99.12%

* Means the result is cited from Pan *et al.* [10]
** Means the result is cited from Han *et al.* [9]

The results are shown in Table 3. As we can see from the table, the second algorithm did quite well in this task, however, our algorithm can still obtain a similar result which is far better than the first algorithm.

4.5   Recurrent Neural Networks

In this experiment we turn our attention to a recurrent neural network and use it on a challenging task of language modeling. The goal is to fit a probabilistic model which assigns probabilities to sentences. It does so by predicting next words in a text given a history of previous words. We use the Penn Tree Bank (PTB) dataset and perplexity, a common way of evaluating language models, to evaluate the performance of models. We use LSTM model with 2 layers and the hidden size is set to 200 (Table 4).

Table 4. Results of pruning LSTM on language model

	$W^{total}\%$	Perplexity(before)	Perplexity(pruned)
Han *et al.*	10.21%	115.910	109.032
Pan *et al.*	11.37%	115.910	109.724
FIMP	9.33%	115.910	108.999

As we can see from the table, the perplexity after pruning is clearly lower than the original one, which indicates better performance of the model.

5   Discussion and Conclusion

In this paper we present a novel way to prune neural network motivated by the intuition that frequent pattern should be more important. We hope this method could provide the reader with a new perspective toward pruning neural networks. Although FIMP has shown promising results, there are still some unfinished work. For example, we could add constraints that favor the emergence of repeating connectivity patterns so that higher compression rate could be achieved. Also, we could try different measure of importance. Right now larger λ in Eq. 2 means more connections would be pruned and more time would be cost. In this work we set λ to a small value like $1e - 5$ and it now takes about half an hour to prune a fully connected layer on a PC while the other two algorithms only cost a few seconds. Although compared with training a large neural network this amount of time is negligible, we may still find some way to speed up FIMP.

References

1. Sermanet, P., Eigen, D., Zhang, X., Mathieu, M., Fergus, R., LeCun, Y.: Overfeat: Integrated recognition, localization and detection using convolutional networks. arXiv preprint arXiv: 1312.6229 (2013)
2. Hinton, G., Deng, L., Yu, D., Dahl, G.E., Mohamed, A.R., Jaitly, N., Kingsbury, B.: Deep neural networks for acoustic modeling in speech recognition: the shared views of four research groups. IEEE Signal Process. Mag. **29**(6), 82–97 (2012)

3. LeCun, Y., Boser, B., Denker, J.S., Henderson, D., Howard, R.E., Hubbard, W., Jackel, L.D.: Backpropagation applied to handwritten zip code recognition. Neural Comput. **1**(4), 541–551 (1989)

4. Krizhevsky, A., Sutskever, I., Hinton, G.E.: Imagenet classification with deep convolutional neural networks. In: Advances in Neural Information Processing Systems, pp. 1097–1105 (2012)

5. Luong, M.T., Pham, H., Manning, C.D.: Effective approaches to attention-based neural machine translation. arXiv preprint arXiv:1508.04025 (2015)

6. Denil, M., Shakibi, B., Dinh, L., de Freitas, N.: Predicting parameters in deep learning. In: Advances in Neural Information Processing Systems, pp. 2148–2156 (2013)

7. Augasta, M.G., Kathirvalavakumar, T.: Pruning algorithms of neural networks—a comparative study. Cent. Eur. J. Comput. Sci. **3**(3), 105–115 (2013)

8. See, A., Luong, M.T., Manning, C.D.: Compression of Neural Machine Translation Models via Pruning. arXiv preprint arXiv:1606.09274 (2016)

9. Han, S., Pool, J., Tran, J., Dally, W.: Learning both weights and connections for efficient neural network. In: Advances in Neural Information Processing Systems, pp. 1135–1143 (2015)

10. Pan, W., Dong, H., Guo, Y.: DropNeuron : Simplifying the Structure of Deep Neural Networks. arXiv preprint arXiv:1606.07326 (2016)

11. Hu, H., Peng, R., Tai, Y.W., Tang, C.K., Trimming, N.: A Data-Driven Neuron Pruning Approach towards Efficient Deep Architectures. arXiv preprint arXiv:1607.03250 (2016)

12. Borgelt, C.: Frequent item set mining. Wiley Interdisc. Rev.: Data Min. Knowl. Discov. **2**(6), 437–456 (2012)

13. Lin, M.Y., Lee, P.Y., Hsueh, S.C.: Apriori-based frequent itemset mining algorithms on MapReduce. In: Proceedings of the 6th International Conference on Ubiquitous Information Management and Communication, p. 76. ACM (2012)

14. Su, J.H., Lin, W.: CBW: an efficient algorithm for frequent itemset mining. In: Proceedings of the 37th Annual Hawaii International Conference on System Sciences, 2004, p. 9. IEEE (2004)

15. Agrawal, R., Imieliski, T., Swami, A.: Mining association rules between sets of items in large databases. In: ACM SIGMOD Record, vol. 22, no. 2, pp. 207–216. ACM (1993)

16. Lecun, Y., Cortes, C.: The mnist database of handwritten digits (2010)

Applying the Heavy-Tailed Kernel to the Gaussian Process Regression for Modeling Point of Sale Data

Rui Yang$^{(\boxtimes)}$ and Yukio Ohsawa$^{(\boxtimes)}$

Graduate School of Engineering, The University of Tokyo, Tokyo, Japan
yangruiacademic@gmail.com, ohsawa@sys.t.u-tokyo.ac.jp

Abstract. Heavy-tailed distributions such as student's t distribution have a special position in the statistical machine learning research due to their robustness when handling Gaussian noise model or other models within unknown types of noise. In this paper, we focus on using the robust kernel as an alternative to the wildly used squared exponential kernel for promoting the model's robustness. Furthermore, we apply the heavy-tailed kernel to the Gaussian process with Bayesian regression for predicting the daily turnover of merchandises based on learning *Point of Sale (PoS)* data. The experiment results show better and more robust performs when comparing with other kernels.

Keywords: Heavy-tailed kernel · Robustness · Gaussian process · Bayesian regression · *PoS* data

1 Introduction

How to eliminate noise from real data confuses researchers for a long time. So far, many researchers proposed various tools and theorems for defibrillating the abnormal data sets. Such as Fourier transform [1] can transfer the wave from the time domain to frequency domain, and high-frequency harmonic waves will be treated as noise. Or classical Principal Component Analysis [2], this linear algebraical method decomposes the covariance matrix, and orthogonal vectors within lower eigenvalues will be treated as noise. In probability and statistics domain, heavy-tailed distributions can also neglect noise, with their tails heavier than exponential distributions'. Such as the *Student's T Distribution* has more stable mean value with unsmooth observations rather than *Gaussian distribution*. On account of such features, heavy-tailed distributions perform well again the noise data.

Naturally, various kernel functions generated from different distributions. For instance, the Gaussian distribution without normalization coefficient is similar to the equation of Gaussian kernel. Kernel functions observe the linear or non-linear inner products, which can transfer absolute value to other target weights by different definitions. Once a kernel function can satisfy the Mercers theorem

© Springer International Publishing AG 2017
A. Lintas et al. (Eds.): ICANN 2017, Part II, LNCS 10614, pp. 705–712, 2017.
https://doi.org/10.1007/978-3-319-68612-7_80

and is positive semi-defined, it can be judged as a legal kernel [9]. Common kernels include Linear, Polynomial, Gaussian, Exponential, Generalized T-student kernels, etc. They exhibit different performances in Support Vector Machine [10] and other machine learning algorithms.

One technique utilizing the kernel function is Gaussian process [3]. It demonstrates excellent performance since Rasmussen and Carl Edward published it. This Bayesian nonparametric algorithm with general applicability has been further developed over recent years. It assumes that all output $f(x_n)$ are following the joint Gaussian distribution, which means $f(x_n) \sim \mathcal{GP}(\mathbf{0}, \boldsymbol{\Sigma})$, and Σ is the covariance obtained from kernel function $f(x, x')$. Kernels can transfer the distance between every input to a covariance matrix for representing the weight of importance between every input value, and normally treat this matrix as the covariance parameter in the joint Gaussian distribution. As the core part of the Gaussian process, the performance of kernel function can affect the final result of Gaussian process indeed.

Recently, other stochastic process methods such as student-t process [4,5], the log-normal process [6] and some amelioration of Gaussian process [7,8] based on various promoting methods were proposed. In our work, we prefer to use the plain Gaussian Process due to its universality. In our assumption, the noise of the data should be neglected at the parameter optimization step via the heavy-tailed kernel, because the kernel function in these stochastic processes handles the input data at the first step. If we don't eliminate noise at first step, it will hard to interpret the final performance is reasoning from which step.

In this paper, we focus on using a parameter-optimized robust kernel to replace the wildly used RBF kernel to obtain a reliable result based on the *point of sale data*. We highlight three major tasks in our work:

1. Apply the heavy-tailed kernel to Gaussian process.
2. Optimize kernel parameters by parameter optimizer.
3. Infer the regression result and predict new outputs of test data.

2   Gaussian Process

We give a brief review of the Gaussian process [3] here. Given a data set $D = (\mathbf{x}_n, \mathbf{y}_n)_{n \in \mathbb{R}}^{c,d}$, for an unknown function $f : \mathbb{R}^c \to \mathbb{R}^d$ (c and d represent for input and output dimensions respectively), the hypothesis of Gaussian process is a multivariate joint Gaussian distribution over function f, which can be written in the following equation:

$$f \sim \mathcal{GP}(m, k) \tag{1}$$

where m refers to the mean function and k is the covariance function. Usually, we will use a kernel function to define the covariance function, such as the squared exponential kernel:

$$\Sigma_{ij} = k(x_i, x_j) = exp(-0.5(x_i - x_j)^2) \tag{2}$$

Except for squared exponential kernel, there are many other kernel functions with various features, and we emphasize heavy-tailed kernel in our work.

3   Heavy-Tailed Kernel

For a heavy-tailed distribution, when the variable's absolute value tends to a large number, the corresponding probability also becomes higher than exponential distribution's, which means that $P_h(x) > P_e(x)$ when $|x| >> 0$. As for the kernel function, this particular feature will lead to a higher value for $k_h(x, x')$ than $k_e(x, x')$, which leads to a higher weight for those x' far away from current x in the covariance matrix.

In another word, a point far from the current position will have a higher importance in heavy-tailed kernels than light-tailed kernels. In recent year, another work in dimensionality reduction domain called t-SNE [14] which uses student's t kernel for embedding learning, has proved the strong performance of t kernel with its robustness. So in this paper, we choose the *Student's T Kernel*, a robust kernel derived by *Student's T Distribution*, to exemplify our hypothesis.

The Non-standardized student's t distribution can be written as the following equation [11],

$$p(x) = t(\nu, \mu, \sigma^2) \equiv \frac{\Gamma((\nu+1)/2)}{\Gamma(\nu/2)\sqrt{\nu\pi\sigma^2}}(1 + \frac{(x-\mu)^2}{\nu\sigma^2})^{-\frac{\nu+1}{2}} . \tag{3}$$

And specialize for the kernel function, similar to the relationship between *Gaussian Kernel* and *Gaussian Distribution*, the normalization coefficient is no more needed and the mean value parameter is set as zero. The freedom parameter ν is set as one (which degenerates into the standard *Cauchy Distribution*) for reducing the calculation complexity and improving robustness.

So the only parameter is σ^2, and the kernel function can be written as

$$k(x, x') = \frac{1}{1 + \tau \left\| x - x' \right\|^2} , \tag{4}$$

where τ stands for the precision parameter which equals to σ^{-2}.

The student's t kernel has been proved as a *Mercer kernel* [9] and satisfies properties above.

3.1   Optimization

We now consider the optimization of *Student's t Distribution*. There exist some approximate inference [15] and marginal likelihood maximization methods such as variational inference, Laplace Approximation, Expectation Propagation and MCMC sampling which are very famous and influential to different kinds of tasks. Its a pity that some inference methods require the conjugate prior of parameter distribution, but *EM algorithm* can be qualified for the *Student's t Distribution*.

3.2   EM Algorithm for Student's T Kernel

EM algorithm and its extensions [12] are famous parameter optimization methods. Through mean-field inference is invalid on non-exponential family distributions, the likelihood functions can be optimized by other algorithms. The universal Expectation-Maximization method is adequate can be used for optimizing the parameter of student's t distribution. However, it is difficult to maximize the likelihood function of the student's t distribution, so we need to rewrite the distribution equation and use EM algorithm to optimize its hyper-parameter [12]. Due to the deviation of student's t distribution from the Gaussian distribution [16], the probability of a zero-mean student's t distribution with freedom equals to one can be transferred to the following equation:

$$P(x_{ij}|\sigma, w_{ij}) \sim \mathcal{N}(0, \sigma^2 w_{ij}^{-1}) , \qquad (5)$$

where x_{ij} means the distance between input x_i and x_j and $w_{ij} \sim Gam(\frac{1}{2}, \frac{1}{2})$.
$\mathbf{E - Step}$: Evaluate the hyper-parameter by finding the expectation,

$$w_*^{(i,j)} = \mathbb{E}[N(x_{ij}, \sigma^2)] = \frac{2\sigma^2}{\sigma^2 + x_{ij}^2} \qquad (6)$$

$\mathbf{M - Step}$: Substitute hyper-parameter back to log-likelihood function and update σ_*,

$$\sigma_*^2 = \frac{\sum_{ij} w_{ij} x_{ij}^2}{n} \qquad (7)$$

Repeat E-step and M-step until convergence. By now, we can observe the optimized parameter of student's t distribution, and for the kernel function, the only difference is the normalization coefficient; thus the kernel function is

$$k(x_i, x_j) = \frac{1}{1 + \tau_{ij}||x_i - x_j||^2} , \qquad (8)$$

where $\tau_{ij} = w_*^{(i,j)}/\sigma_*^2$ is the parameter of kernel function optimized from probability distribution via EM-algorithm.

4   Bayesian Regression

Once we obtained the covariance matrix from the kernel function, we can use a uniform distribution to make new inputs for testing the joint Gaussian distribution and store it discretely. Then we can sample the observed result for several times and approximate the real mapping function from inputs to outputs. The Bayesian regression for a Gaussian process can be derived from the posterior distribution conditioning on new inputs and training dataset D naturally [3]:

$$\begin{bmatrix} \mathbf{y} \\ \mathbf{y}_* \end{bmatrix} \sim \mathcal{N}\left(\begin{bmatrix} \mu \\ \mu_* \end{bmatrix}, \begin{bmatrix} \Sigma & \Sigma_* \\ \Sigma_*^\top & \Sigma_{**} \end{bmatrix} \right) , \qquad (9)$$

where, $\mathbf{y}$ and x_i in $\mu = m(x_i)$ are from D; Σ is the kernel function with parameter optimized by EM algorithm, lay out μ_* and Σ_* from the new input $x_*^{(i)} \sim \mathcal{U}(0, \theta), \theta \in \mathbb{R} \setminus \{\mathbf{X}\}$ (X is the set of training input), and prediction target is new output $\mathbf{y}_*$. Thus, the posterior probability is [13]:

$$p(y_*^{(i)}|x_*^{(i)}, x_i, y_i) \sim \mathcal{N}(m_*^{(i)}, k_*^{(i)}) , \tag{10}$$

where $m_*^{(i)} = m(x_*^{(i)}) + \Sigma_{(X_*, x_*^{(i)})}^{\top} \Sigma^{-1}(y_i - m(x_i))$, mean function m commonly set as zero mean, and $k_*^{(i)} = \Sigma_{**} - \Sigma_{(X_*, x_*^{(i)})}^{\top} \Sigma^{-1} \Sigma_{(X_*, x_*^{(i)})}$, whose $\Sigma_{(X_*, x_*^{(i)})}$ and its transfer are weight vectors between all new input $\mathbf{X}_*$ and current input $x_*^{(i)}$.

5   Experiment

We designed an experiment to test kernel performances based on PoS data. PoS data plays a significant role in financial activities, which is a time series data by recording the retail transaction. Primary variables include date, barcode scanning moment, name and brand of merchandise, amount, price, etc. Mining the implicit consumption willing from PoS data always attract researchers' eyesight. In our experiment, we select typical merchandises and test days with intervals for avoiding statistical errors. We test different kernels in the Gaussian Process regression model and observe their performance in regression and prediction.

In our experiment, we analysis the number of commodities per day for turnover volume prediction by comparing with other kernels.

We use "potato" to exemplify the performance of different kernels in Gaussian Process regression, and then apply them onto other merchandises.

5.1   Data Processing and Analysis

First, we test t-kernel with freedom parameter equals to one to show the regression curve. Once the regression result was observed from t-kernel based on Gaussian process, we do same experiments for other two kernels, $k_{Gaussian}(x, x') = exp(-\frac{\|x-x'\|^2}{2\sigma^2})$ and $k_{Exponential}(x, x') = exp(-\frac{\|x-x'\|}{2\sigma^2})$, to compare the regression and prediction performances.

Figure 1(a), (b) and (c) show the transaction tendency of "potato" from 2016-07-31 to 2016-08-29 for blue points, and red points are the turnover volumes in next several days. Red curve describes the predicting mean values, and the gray area represents the mean value standard deviation of predicting distribution.

Figure 1(a), (b) and (c) represent for Gaussian kernel, Student's T kernel and Exponential kernel separately. From all three figures, we obtained some interesting result. All three kernels can fit training data, but a small difference between adjacent points. In last two days of training data, exponential kernels red curve links two points directly. However G-kernel and T-kernel both have a small zigzag. Other continuous points closed in y-axis also have similar phenomenon, which demonstrate a better performance in G-kernel and T-kernel about

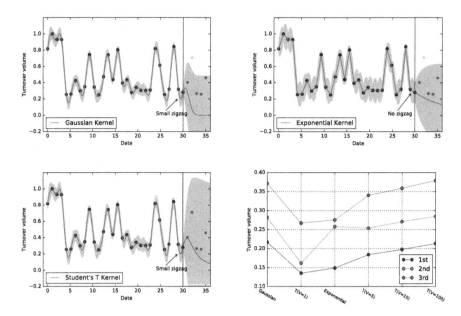

Fig. 1. Experiment results of "Potato" (Color Figure Online)

the over-fitting problem. Prediction curve in G-kernel tends to zero rapidly. In contrast, T-kernel and E-kernel can fit several points in the following days.

Based on such results, we made further explorations. We count the transaction volumes per day of "potato" from 2016-01-01 until 2016-12-15 (351 days). Then, pick out thirty consecutive days randomly 10 times (each period allows partially overlap) as training data to predict the turnover volumes in next three day. The predictive error rate function is defined as below:

$$Error(p, r) = \frac{|T_p - T_r|}{max(\mathbf{T})} , \qquad (11)$$

where, T_p refers to the predicted turnover volume in one day, and T_r is the real volume. $max(\mathbf{T})$ means the maximum turnover volume in one day during the whole year. Then we compute the average mean error rate of the prediction in following three days via different kernels (Gaussian, T with freedom parameter equals to 1, Exponential, T with 5, T with 10, T with 100) and plot out their average ranks. Figure 1(d) clearly demonstrates that, in the second and third day, without out data support, the prediction results tend to a higher bias. So we focus on exploring the first day's performance for other merchandises, for comparing kernels' performances in predictive error rate.

5.2   Rank of Results

Figure 2 shows the rank of different kernels for the turnover volumes of nine merchandises (bread, canned liqueur, cup noodle, green tea, milk, onigiri, onion,

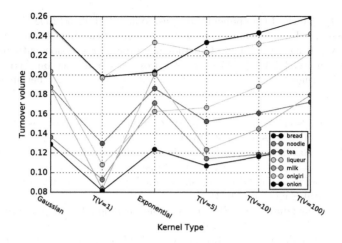

Fig. 2. Rank of different kernels

salad and raw seaweed). Broken lines in Fig. 2 refer to the mean values of the absolute difference between prediction results and real data values of these merchandises. We can observe that $T_{\nu=1}$-kernel performs better than the G-kernel and E-kernel in most of these merchandises.

Otherwise, when freedom parameter grows to a high value, the kernel performance in the T-kernel performs analogously to the G-kernel. This is corresponding to the phenomenon that Student's t distribution becomes closer to the Normal distribution as ν increases.

6   Conclusion and Future Work

The Gaussian process exhibit various performance with different kernel functions. However, real data sets can hardly follow the ideal probability models. Without assuming the distribution of noise, it is better to filter the noise via a robust kernel. In this paper, we demonstrate significant preference of *Student's t kernel*, which is one of the heavy-tailed kernel, on the Point of Sale data.

In future, we will try to discover further optimization methods for robust kernels. We use the universal EM algorithm for kernel optimization, but inference methods perform very well in other models and data sets. How to combine heavy-tailed kernel and inference methods together will become an attractive topic.

Acknowledgments. This work was supported by JST CREST Grant Number JPMJCR1304, JSPS KAKENHI Grant Numbers JP16H01836, and JP16K12428. The *Point of Sale data* was provided by KASUMI CO., LTD.

References

1. Brigham, E.O., Brigham, E.O., Rey Pastor, J.J., et al.: The Fast Fourier Transform and its Applications. Prentice Hall, New Jersey (1988)

2. Jolliffe, I.: Principal Component Analysis. Wiley, Hoboken (2002)
3. Rasmussen, C.E.: Gaussian Processes for Machine Learning (2006)
4. Wang, Y., Tang, Q., Xia, S.-T.: Student-t process regression with independent student-t noise. In: ECAI 2016: 22nd European Conference on Artificial Intelligence, 29 August – 2 September 2016, The Hague, The Netherlands-Including Prestigious Applications of Artificial Intelligence (PAIS 2016). vol. **285**, IOS Press (2016)
5. Shah, A., Wilson, A.G., Ghahramani, Z.: Student-t processes as alternatives to Gaussian processes. AISTATS (2014)
6. Zvyagin, P., Sazonov, K.: Analysis and probabilistic modeling of the stationary ice loads stochastic process with lognormal distribution. In: ASME 2014 33rd International Conference on Ocean, Offshore and Arctic Engineering. American Society of Mechanical Engineers (2014)
7. Tran, D., Ranganath, R., Blei, D.M.: The variational Gaussian process. arXiv preprint arXiv:1511.06499 (2015)
8. Bauer, M., van der Wilk, M., Rasmussen, C.E.: Understanding probabilistic sparse Gaussian process approximations. In: Advances in Neural Information Processing Systems, pp. 1525–1533 (2016)
9. Souza, C.R.: Kernel functions for machine learning applications. Creat. Commons Attrib. Noncommerc. Share Alike **3**, 29 (2010)
10. Scholkopf, B., Smola, A.J.: Learning with Kernels: Support Vector Machines, Regularization, Optimization, and Beyond. MIT press, Cambridge (2001)
11. Figueiredo, M.A.T.: Lecture Notes on the EM Algorithm. http://www.stat.duke.edu/courses/Spring06/sta376/Support/EM/EM.Mixtures., Figueiredo (2004)
12. McLachlan, G., Krishnan, T.: The EM Algorithm and Extensions. vol. **382**, Wiley, Hoboken (2007)
13. Ebden, M.: Gaussian processes for regression: a quick introduction. In: The Website of Robotics Research Group in Department on Engineering Science, University of Oxford (2008)
14. Jylanki, P., Vanhatalo, J., Vehtari, A.: Robust Gaussian process regression with a student-t likelihood. J. Mach. Learn. Res. **12**, 3227–3257 (2011)
15. Van Der Maaten, L.: Accelerating t-SNE using tree-based algorithms. J. Mach. Learn. Res. **15**(1), 3221–3245 (2014)
16. Ogunnaike, B.A.: Random Phenomena: Fundamentals of Probability and Statistics for Engineers. CRC Press, Boca Raton (2011)

Chaotic Associative Memory with Adaptive Scaling Factor

Tatsuuya Okada and Yuko Osana$^{(\boxtimes)}$

Tokyo University of Technology, 1404-1 Katakura, Hachioji, Tokyo 192-0982, Japan
osana@stf.teu.ac.jp

Abstract. In this paper, we propose a Chaotic Associative Memory with Adaptive Scaling Factor. In the proposed model, the scaling factor of refractoriness is adjusted according to the maximum absolute value of the internal state up to that time as similar as the conventional Chaotic Multidirectional Associative Memory with Adaptive Scaling Factor. Computer experiments are carried out and we confirmed that the proposed model has the same dynamic association ability as the conventional model, and the proposed model also has recall capability similar to that of the conventional model, even for the number of neurons not used for automatic adjustment of parameters.

Keywords: Chatic associative memory · Dynamic association · Scaling factor

1 Introduction

In recent years, various researches on neural networks have been conducted as a method for performing flexible information processing found in the brains of living organisms. Among them, researches on associative memory models simulating associative memory functions of humans have also been conducted, and many associative memories have been proposed.

On the other hand, chaos is attracting attention as one of methods for performing flexible information processing. Chaos is a phenomenon that can not be predicted over a long term occurring in a nonlinear system with deterministic time evolution. It is observed in the brain and nervous system of living organisms and is thought to play an important role in memories and learning in the brain [1]. Chaotic neuron model [1] introducing chaos by considering spatio-temporal summation, refractoriness, continuous output function seen in real neurons is also proposed in artificial neural network research. In addition, the chaotic associative memory composed of the chaotic neuron model is an auto-associative memory having the same structure as the Hopfield network [2], and it is known that it can recall the stored binary/bipolar patterns dynamically [1,3]. It is also known that dynamic association ability improves by temporally changing scaling factor of refractoriness which is a parameter of chaotic neuron model [4].

© Springer International Publishing AG 2017
A. Lintas et al. (Eds.): ICANN 2017, Part II, LNCS 10614, pp. 713–721, 2017.
https://doi.org/10.1007/978-3-319-68612-7_81

However, dynamic association ability depends on parameters of chaotic neuron model. Since appropriate parameters vary depending on the number of neurons, the number of training patterns and so on, there is a problem that appropriate parameters have to be determined by trial and error.

We have proposed some methods to automatically adjust parameters in hetero associative memories such as the Chaotic Multidirectional Associative Memory [5] and the Chaotic Complex-Valued Multidirectional Associative Memory [6] composed of the chaotic complex-valued neurons [7]. However, the tendency of appropriate parameters of chaotic neuron model is considered to be different between hetero-associative memories and auto-associative memories.

In this paper, we propose a Chaotic Associative Memory with Adaptive Scaling Factor. In this model, automatic parameter adjustment method are determined based on the relationship between the internal state and the parameters in which the high dynamic association ability is obtained in the Chaotic Associative Memory with Variable Scaling Factor. In the proposed model, the connection weight is normalized by dividing by the number of neurons so that the range that internal value does not depend on the number of neurons.

2   Chaotic Associative Memory with Variable Scaling Factor

Here, we explain the conventional Chaotic Associative Memory with Variable Scaling Factor [4] that is the basis of the proposed Chaotic Associative Memory with Adaptive Scaling Factor. This model is an auto-associative memory composed of a chaotic neuron model having a scaling factor of refractoriness that varies with time. It can realize dynamic association of binary stored patterns by internal state change by chaos.

2.1   Structure

The Chaotic Associative Memory with Variable Scaling Factor has the similar structure as the Hopfield network [2] as shown in Fig. 1. Each neuron is a chaotic neuron model with a scaling factor of refractoriness that varies with time and are coupled to each other.

2.2   Learning Process

In the learning process of the Chaotic Associative Memory wit Variable Scaling Factor, the connection weight is determined using correlation learning as similar as the Hopfield network. When P patterns are memorized into the network consisting of N neurons, the weight matrix $\boldsymbol{w}$ is determined as follows:

$$\boldsymbol{w} = \sum_{p=1}^{P} \boldsymbol{x}^{(p)} \boldsymbol{x}^{(p)T} - P \boldsymbol{I}_N \tag{1}$$

where $\boldsymbol{x}^{(p)}$ is the p-th stored bipolar pattern vector, $\boldsymbol{I}_N$ is a unit matrix $(N \times N)$, and T represents transposition.

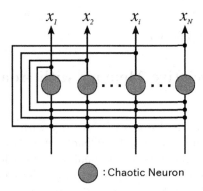

Fig. 1. Structure of chaotic associative memory with variable scaling factor.

2.3   Recall Process

The recall process of the Chaotic Associative Memory wit Variable Scaling Factor has following four steps.

Step 1 : Input of Pattern
    A pattern is given to the network. The input pattern is treated as it is as output at time $t = 0$.

Step 2 : Calculation of Internal States
    The internal states of the neuron i at the time $t + 1$, $u_i(t + 1)$ is given by

$$u_i(t + 1) = \sum_{j=1}^{N} w_{ij} \sum_{d=0}^{t} k_m^d x_j(t - d) - \alpha(t) \sum_{d=0}^{t} k_r^d x_i(t - d) \tag{2}$$

where N is the number of neurons, k_m is the damping factor of the mutual coupling term, k_r is the damping factor of the refractoriness term, w_{ij} is the connection weight between the neuron i and the neuron j, and $x_j(t)$ is the output of the neuron j at the time t. $\alpha(t)$ is the scaling factor of the refractoriness at the time t and is given by

$$\alpha(t) = a + b \sin \left(c \cdot \frac{\pi}{12} \cdot t \right) \tag{3}$$

where a, b, c are parameters that determine how to change the scaling factor of refractoriness. a is the average value, b is the amplitude, and c affects the cycle.

Step 3 : Calculation of Output
    The output of the neuron i at the time $t + 1$, $x_i(t + 1)$ is given by

$$x_i(t + 1) = f(u_i(t + 1)) \tag{4}$$

where $f(\cdot)$ is output function. Here, we use the following sigmoid function.

$$f(u) = \tanh \left(\frac{u}{\varepsilon} \right) \tag{5}$$

where ε is a steepness parameter.

Step 4 : Repeat
   Steps 2 and **3** are repeated.

3   Chaotic Associative Memory with Adaptive Scaling Factor

Here, the proposed Chaotic Associative Memory with Adaptive Scaling Factor is explained. This model is based on the Chaotic Associative Memory with Variable Scaling Factor [4], and can realize dynamic association of bipolar patterns. In this model, the scaling factor of refractoriness is determined based on the maximum absolute value of the internal state up to the time t as similar as in the conventional Chaotic Multidirectional Associative Memory with Adaptive Scaling Factor [5]. In the proposed model, the connection weights are normalized by dividing by the number of neurons so that the range of possible values of the internal state does not depend on the number of neurons.

3.1   Structure

The structure of the proposed model is the same as the conventional Chaotic Associative Memory with Variable Scaling Factor [4] mentioned in Sect. 2.1.

3.2   Learning Process

In the learning process of the proposed model, the connection weight is determined using correlation learning as similar as the conventional Chaotic Associative Memory with Variable Scaling Factor. In this model, each neuron receives a signal from all neurons other than itself via its weight, so that as the number of neurons constituting the network increases, the absolute value of the internal state of the neuron increases. Therefore, in this model, normalization is performed by dividing the connection weight matrix by the number of neurons so that the range of possible values of the internal state does not depend on the number of neurons.

In the proposed model, the connection weight matrix w is determined as follows.

$$w = \frac{1}{N} \left(\sum_{p=1}^{P} x^{(p)} x^{(p)T} - P I_N \right) \tag{6}$$

3.3   Recall Process

In the proposed model, recall is realized using the same method as described in Sect. 2.3, but instead of the scaling factor of refractoriness at the time t ($\alpha(t)$) which varies depending on time, the scaling factor of refractoriness at the time t when the maximum absolute value of the internal state up to the time t is $I(t)_{max}$ ($\alpha(t, I(t)_{max})$) is used.

The scaling factor of refractoriness $\alpha(t, I(t)_{max})$ is given by

$$\alpha(t, I(t)_{max}) = a(I(t)_{max}) + b(a(I(t)_{max})) \sin\left(c \cdot \frac{\pi}{12} \cdot t\right) \tag{7}$$

where $I(t)_{max}$ is the maximum absolute value of the internal state up to the time t, and it is given by

$$I(t)_{max} = \max\{I(t), I(t-1)_{max}\}. \tag{8}$$

Here, $I(t)$ is the average of the absolute values of internal states excluding the refractoriness term at time t, and it is given by

$$I(t) = \frac{1}{N} \sum_{i=1}^{N} \left| \sum_{j=1}^{N} w_{ij} \sum_{d=0}^{t} k_m^d x_j(t-d) \right| \tag{9}$$

$a(I(t)_{max})$ and $b(a(I(t)_{max}))$ are given by

$$a(I(t)_{max}) = \begin{cases} 2.97 & (I(t)_{max} \leq 3.4106) \\ -4.7006 I(t)_{max} + 19.002 & (3.4106 < I(t)_{max} \leq 3.634) \\ 1.92 & (3.634 < I(t)_{max}) \end{cases} \tag{10}$$

and

$$b(a(I(t)_{max})) = 0.9532 a(I(t)_{max}) - 0.0516. \tag{11}$$

These equations are determined based on the relationship between the internal state and the parameters a and b in the parameter in which the high dynamic association ability is obtained in the Chaotic Associative Memory with Variable Scaling Factor composed of 100 to 600 neurons (See Figs. 2 and 3).

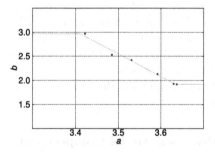

Fig. 2. Relation between internal state and a.

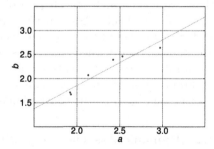

Fig. 3. Relation between a and b

4   Computer Experiment Results

Here, we show the computer experiment results to demonstrate the effectiveness of the proposed model under the condition shown in Table 1. The following experiments are the average of 100 trials.

Table 1. Experimental conditions

	Proposed model	Conventional model
Coefficient in scaling factor a	Eq. (10)	2.42 ($N = 100$) 2.97 ($N = 200$)
		2.53 ($N = 300$) 2.13 ($N = 400$)
		1.92 ($N = 500$) 1.93 ($N = 600$)
		2.11 ($N = 700$) 2.15 ($N = 800$)
Coefficient in scaling factor b	Eq. (11)	2.39 ($N = 100$) 2.64 ($N = 200$)
		2.46 ($N = 300$) 2.07 ($N = 400$)
		1.71 ($N = 500$) 1.67 ($N = 600$)
		1.85 ($N = 700$) 1.91 ($N = 800$)
Coefficient in scaling factor c	2	
Recall time	100000	
Damping factor k_m	0.81	
Damping factor k_r	0.96	
Steepness parameter ε	0.013	

4.1   Comparison of Dynamic Association Ability with Proposed Model and Conventional Model

Here, we compare the recall rate of the proposed model with the well-tuned conventional Chaotic Associative Memory with Variable Scaling Factor [4]. The coefficients a, b and the damping factors k_m and k_r of the conventional model use valuesobtained when the highest recall rate is obtained. Figure 4 shows the recall rate when 2 to 20 patterns are memorized in each model.

From Fig. 4, it can be seen that the proposed model has the same dynamic association ability as the conventional model.

4.2   Dynamic Association Ability of Proposed Model Composed of 700 and 800 Neurons

Here, we investigated whether a high recall rate can be obtained also in the case of the number of neurons not used for determining the parameter automatic adjustment method in the proposed model. Figure 5 shows the recall rate when 2 to 20 patterns are memorized in each model. From Fig. 5, it can be seen that

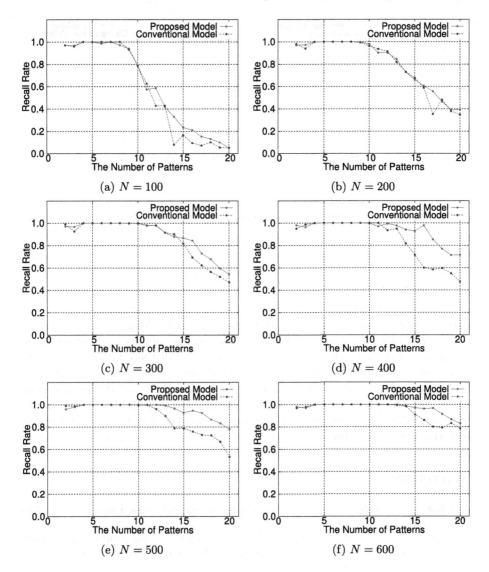

Fig. 4. Dynamic association ability of the proposed model and the conventional model ($N = 100$–600).

the proposed model also has recall capability similar to that of the conventional model, even for the number of neurons not used for automatic adjustment of parameters.

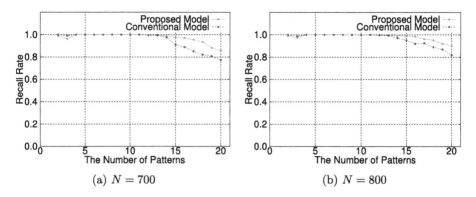

Fig. 5. Dynamic association ability of the proposed model and the conventional model ($N = 700, 800$)

5   Conclusions

In this paper, we have proposed the Chaotic Associative Memory with Adaptive Scaling Factor. In the proposed model, the scaling factor of refractoriness is adjusted according to the maximum absolute value of the internal state up to that time. Computer experiments are carried out and we confirmed that the proposed model has the same dynamic association ability as the conventional model, and the proposed model also has recall capability similar to that of the conventional model, even for the number of neurons not used for automatic adjustment of parameters.

References

1. Aihara, K., Takabe, T., Toyoda, M.: Chaotic neural networks. Phys. Letter A **144** (6 and 7), 333–340 (1990)
2. Hopfield, J.J.: Neural networks and physical systems with emergent collective computational abilities. In: Proceedings of National Academy of Sciences of the USA, vol. 79, pp. 2554–2558 (1982)
3. Osana, Y., Hagiwara, M.: Separation of superimposed pattern and many-to-many associations by chaotic neural networks. In: Proceedings of IEEE and INNS International Joint Conference on Neural Networks, Anchorage, vol. 1, pp. 514–519 (1998)
4. Osana, Y.: Recall and separation ability of chaotic associative memory with variable scaling factor. In: Proceedings of IEEE and INNS International Joint Conference on Neural Networks, Hawaii (2002)
5. Hayashi, N., Osana, Y.: Chaotic multidirectional associative memory with adaptive scaling factor of refractoriness. In: Proceedings of IEEE and INNS International Joint Conference on Neural Networks, Killarney (2015)

6. Chino, T., Osana, Y.: Generalization ability of chaotic complex-valued multidirectional associative memory with adaptive scaling factor. In: Lee, M., Hirose, A., Hou, Z.-G., Kil, R.M. (eds.) ICONIP 2013. LNCS, vol. 8227, pp. 291–298. Springer, Heidelberg (2013). doi:10.1007/978-3-642-42042-9_37
7. Nakada, M., Osana, Y.: Chaotic complex-valued associative memory. In: Proceedings of International Symposium on Nonlinear Theory and its Applications, Vancouver, pp. 16–19 (2007)

Short Papers

EvoCNN: Evolving Deep Convolutional Neural Networks Using Backpropagation-Assisted Mutations

Eli (Omid) David$^{(\boxtimes)}$ and Nathan S. Netanyahu

Department of Computer Science, Bar-Ilan University, Ramat-Gan, Israel
mail@elidavid.com, nathan@cs.biu.ac.il

Abstract. In this abstract we present our initial results with a novel genetic algorithms based method for evolving convolutional neural networks (CNN). Currently, standard backpropagation is the primary training method for neural networks (NN) in general, including CNNs. In the past several methods proposed using genetic algorithms (GA) for training neural networks. These methods involve representing the weights of the NN as a chromosome, creating a randomly initialized population of such chromosomes (each chromosome represents one NN), and then evolving the population by performing the steps (1) measure the fitness of each chromosome (the lower the average loss over the training set, the better), (2) select the fitter chromosomes for breeding, (3) perform crossover between the parents (randomly choose weights from the parents to create the offspring), and (4) mutate the offspring. While in smaller NNs these methods obtained results comparable with backpropagation, their results deteriorate as the size of NN grows, and are impractical for training deep neural nets. Nowadays these methods have largely been abandoned due to this inefficiency.

We propose a combination of GA-based evolution and backpropagation for evolving CNN as follows. Similar to the abovementioned methods we create an initial population of N chromosomes, each representing the weights of one CNN, and then evolve the chromosomes by applying fitness evaluation, crossover, and mutations, but with several key differences: **(1) During crossover, instead of randomly selecting weights from each of the two parents, randomly select entire filters from each parent** (this ensures that a useful filter is copied in its entirety, rather than being disrupted), **(2) During mutation, modify weights by performing standard backpropagation, instead of random changes; and then randomly set a small portion of weights to zero** (these steps allow for a more goal-oriented evolution, and zeroing some weights encourages sparsity in the network and has a regularizing effect). We refer to this method as EvoCNN.

To measure the performance of our method, we ran several experiments on the MNIST handwritten digit recognition dataset. A standard CNN architecture was used containing the following layers: [Input size 28×28]–[convolution with 128 filters of size 5×5]–[max-pooling]–[convolution with 256 filters of size 3×3]–[max-pooling]–[fully connected layer of size 1000]–[softmax layer of size 10].

© Springer International Publishing AG 2017
A. Lintas et al. (Eds.): ICANN 2017, Part II, LNCS 10614, pp. 725–726, 2017.
https://doi.org/10.1007/978-3-319-68612-7

For a baseline to compare against, the CNN with backpropagation alone resulted in test error of **0.82%**. Training 20 separate CNNs and then performing model averaging reduced the test error to **0.75%**. Using the EvoCNN method described above, we trained a population of 20 CNNs, with a crossover rate of 0.75 and mutation rate of 0.005. The test result in this case was **0.51%**, a new state-of-the-art for MNIST without preprocessing, dataset augmentation (e.g., by distortions), and without pretraining. Note that the entire time required for training a population of 20 CNNs is similar to the time required for training 20 separate CNNs, so the comparison shows a substantial improvement due to our method.

Stage Dependent Ensemble Deep Learning for Dots-and-Boxes Game

Yipeng Zhang$^{(\boxtimes)}$, Shuqin Li, Meng Ding, and Kun Meng

Sensing and Computational Intelligence Joint Lab, Beijing Information Science
and Technology University, Beijing, China
bipedalbit@gmail.com, {lishuqin2005,dmm,mengkurt}@bistu.edu.cn

Abstract. Depth first search based $\alpha - \beta$ search and stochastic Monte
Carlo tree search (MCTS) are two major solutions for computer gaming. Since DeepMind introduced deep learning into Go gaming, ensemble
deep learning is widely noticed in the field. Dots-and-boxes game has
been contested in Computer Olympiad for years, and its largest solved
game size is of 4×5 boxes to date [2].

Complete $\alpha - \beta$ search offers the most accurate game state evaluation but costs too much time for early game stages. For turns earlier
than 33 in 5×5 boxes dots-and-boxes game, it cost at least a minute to
finish a complete search with our python program. MCTS offers controllable time cost but worse accuracy while a convolutional neural network
(CNN) could evaluate any game state in a few microseconds with promising accuracy depends on how well it trained. So it comes a demand to
combine CNN with existing algorithms with different form for different
game stages.

We format each game state into 17 stacked rich-meaning matrixes.
And after labeling randomly generated game state with 36–60 turn number by complete $\alpha - \beta$ searches, we run an algorithm based on game rules
and backstepping $\alpha - \beta$ search, to label more game state with 24–35 turn
number, making up the lack of real gaming data for CNN training and
validation. CNN is combined with $\alpha - \beta$ search by staightly acting as the
game state evaluating method. And for MCTS, we modify the balancing strategy namely the UCB1-TUNED fomula [1] by adding weighted
simulation win rate and CNN output together instead of just win rate.

$$v(s_i) = (1 - \lambda)E_s + \lambda E_c + c\sqrt{\frac{2lnN}{n_s(s_i)}}min\{0.25, D_s\} \qquad (1)$$

Experiment confirms that $\alpha - \beta$ search and MCTS are both improved
in earlier game stages than endgame with the same search depth and
simulation sum. However when time limit for each turn is set 20 s, only
CNN combined MCTS beats tradition algorithms in 0–24 turns.

Keywords: Ensemble deep learning · Stage dependent · Computer
gaming

© Springer International Publishing AG 2017
A. Lintas et al. (Eds.): ICANN 2017, Part II, LNCS 10614, pp. 727–728, 2017.
https://doi.org/10.1007/978-3-319-68612-7

References

1. Auer, P., Cesa-Bianchi, N., Fischer, P.: Finite-time analysis of the multiarmed bandit problem. Mach. Learn. **47**(2–3), 235–256 (2002)
2. Barker, J.K., Korf, R.E.: Solving dots-and-boxes. In: AAAI (2012)

Conditional Time Series Forecasting with Convolutional Neural Networks

Anastasia Borovykh[1(✉)], Sander Bohte[2], and Cornelis W. Oosterlee[3]

[1] Dipartimento di Matematica, Università di Bologna, Bologna, Italy
borovykh_a@hotmail.com
[2] Centrum Wiskunde and Informatica, Amsterdam, The Netherlands
s.m.bohte@cwi.nl
[3] Delft University of Technology, Delft, The Netherlands
c.w.oosterlee@cwi.nl

Abstract. Forecasting financial time series using past observations has been a significant topic of interest. While temporal relationships in the data exist, they are difficult to analyze and predict accurately due to the non-linear trends and noise present in the series. We propose to learn these dependencies by a convolutional neural network. In particular the focus is on multivariate time series forecasting. Effectively, we use multiple financial time series as input in the neural network, thus conditioning the forecast of a time series $x(t)$ on both its own history as well as that of a second (or third) time series $y(t)$. Training a model on multiple stock series allows the network to exploit the correlation structure between these series so that the network can learn the market dynamics in shorter sequences of data. We show that long-term temporal dependencies in and between financial time series can be learned by means of a deep convolutional neural network based on the WaveNet model [2]. The network makes use of dilated convolutions applied to multiple time series so that the receptive field of the network is wide enough to learn both short and long-term dependencies. The architecture includes batch normalization and uses a $1 \times k$ convolution with parametrized skip connections from the input time series as well as the time series we condition on, in this way learning long-term interdependencies in an efficient manner [1]. This improves the forecast, while at the same time limiting the requirement for a long historical price series and reducing the noise. Knowing the strong performance of CNNs on classification problems we show that they can be applied successfully to forecasting financial time series, without the need of large samples of data. We compare the performance of the WaveNet model to a state-of-the-art fully convolutional network (FCN), and an autoregressive model popular in econometrics and show that our model is much better able to learn important dependencies in between financial time series resulting in a more robust and accurate forecast.

Keywords: Convolutional neural network · Financial time series

© Springer International Publishing AG 2017
A. Lintas et al. (Eds.): ICANN 2017, Part II, LNCS 10614, pp. 729–730, 2017.
https://doi.org/10.1007/978-3-319-68612-7

References

1. Borovykh, A., Bohte, S., Oosterlee, C.: Conditional time series forecasting with convolutional neural networks. ArXiv e-prints (2017)
2. van den Oord, A., Dieleman, S., Zen, H., Simonyan, K., Vinyals, O., Graves, A., Kalchbrenner, N., Senior, A., Kavukcuoglu, K.: WaveNet: a generative model for raw audio. ArXiv e-prints (2016)

A Convolutional Neural Network Based Approach for Stock Forecasting

Haixing Yu[1(✉)], Lingyu Xu[1], and Gaowei Zhang[2]

[1] Department of Computer Science, Shanghai University, Shanghai, China
sceptic@i.shu.edu.cn
[2] Shanghai Advanced Research Institute,
Chinese Academy of Sciences, Beijing, China

Abstract. The Artificial Neural Network is widely applied to the forecasting of financial time series, and has got certain effects. The problem, however, is that most of these methods is based on daily trading data. When facing the high frequency trading data which is more powerful in short-term forecasting, these methods become incapable. Inspired by the development of Convolutional Neural Network in image recognition tasks, this paper tries to apply the Convolutional Neural Network on the high frequency financial trading data, and has achieved good results. We collect the close price of Shanghai Composite Index from 2006 to 2008 and from 2014 to 2015, about 1000 trading days in total. The frequency of the trading data is 5 min. The paper intends to forecast the stock's future trend of the next day from historical data, namely, go up or down. First, we apply Hodrick-Prescott decomposition [1] on the original time series. The Hodrick-Prescott filter(decomposition) is a mathematical tool used in macroeconomics to separate the cyclical component c_t and trend component τ_t from a time series. After preprocessing, the proposed method novelly transforms the time series into pictures. We apply GASF, GADF and MTF algorithm [2] on the time series respectively, forming the R, G and B channels of a picture. By transforming each of the time series into picture mode, the trading time series produces a picture library. Finally, the proposed method uses AlexNet architecture as feature extractor and classifier. The net has five convolution layers, three pooling layers, and two fully-connected layers.

In data set of time series from 2006 to 2008, we choose the training data and the testing data randomly, and the proposed method can keep the accuracy at about 0.55 on the binary classification problem. In data set of time series from 2014 to 2015, we choose the last 16 training days of the data set as testing data and the accuracy can reach up to 0.60.

Keywords: Stock forecasting · Convolutional neural network

"A convolutional neural network based approach for stock forecasting" Set as article note.

References

1. Hodric, R.J., Prescott, E.C.: Postwar U.S. business cycles: an empirical investigation. J. Money Credit Bank. **29**(1), 1–16 (1997)
2. Wang, Z., Oates, T.: Imaging time-series to improve classification and imputation. Int. Conf. Artif. Intell. **1043**(1), 3939–3945 (2015)

The All-Convolutional Neural Network with Recurrent Architecture for Object Recognition

Yiwei Gu and Xiaodong Gu$^{(\boxtimes)}$

Department of Electronic Engineering, Fudan University, Shanghai 200433, China
xdgu@fudan.edu.cn

Abstract. Convolutional Neural Networks (CNNs) is a successful deep learning model for many computer vision tasks, due to many properties it shares with the visual system of brain. In this paper, we proposed an all-convolutional neural network with recurrent architecture (AR-ConvNet) for object recognition. There are two mainly differences between our model and standard CNNs. We replaced all pooling layers in traditional CNNs by convolution layers with strides 2. Thus we constructed a network that solely consists convolution operations. Besides, inspired by the succeed of recurrent neural networks in modeling of sequential data, we introduced a recurrent architecture into convolution layers in the model. The input of a convolution operation at time step t consists of both the output of the previous layer and the output of the convolution operation at time step $(t-1)$ in the same layer. Our model is tested on an object recognition of small pictures benchmark, CIFAR-10. Result in Table 1 shows that, with replacing pooling by convolution operations and introduction of recurrent architecture in convolution layer, our AR-ConvNet can achieve very competitive performance and outperforms some well-known state-of-art object recognition models on classification error. The experiments we conducted illustrated that, with enough data and carefully training, convolution layer can learn the pooling function and all necessary in-variances itself without losing performance. And with recurrent connecting, the structure of CNN involved kind of memory ability and can go deeper without a huge increase on model parameters.

Table 1. CIFAR-10 classification error.

Model	Maxout	Prob Maxout	NIN	DSN	AR-ConvNet
Error	11.68%	11.35%	10.41%	9.69%	**8.94%**
#params	>6M	>5M	1M	1M	1.2M

Keywords: Object recognition · Convolutional neural networks · Recurrent architecture

© Springer International Publishing AG 2017
A. Lintas et al. (Eds.): ICANN 2017, Part II, LNCS 10614, pp. 733–734, 2017.
https://doi.org/10.1007/978-3-319-68612-7

Acknowledgments. This work was supported in part by National Natural Science Foundation of China under grant 61371148.

Reference

1. Liang, M., et al.: Convolutional neural networks with intra-layer recurrent connections for scene labeling. In: Advances in Neural Information Processing Systems (2015)

Body Measurement and Weight Estimation for Live Yaks Using Binocular Camera and Convolutional Neural Network

Siqi Liu[1(✉)], Chun Yu[1], Yuan Xie[2], Zhiqiang Liu[3], Pin Tao[1], and Yuanchun Shi[1]

[1] Department of Computer Science and Technology,
Tsinghua University, Beijing, China
liusiqi14@mails.tsinghua.edu.cn, {chunyu,taopin,shiyc}@tsinghua.edu.cn
[2] Computer Science Department,
Indiana University Bloomington, Bloomington, USA
xieyuan@iu.edu
[3] Computer Technology and Application Department,
Qinghai University, Xining, China
2009990040@qhu.edu.cn

Abstract. Determining yaks' live weight (LW) and body measurements (BMs) which are important indicators of yaks' growth status, health condition and economic value is very costly when using scales and tapes. Existing computer-aided studies [1, 2] are basically limited to restricted space and fixed equipments, which cannot be widely applied. To address this, we demonstrate a handheld, contact-less, accurate, real-time and vision-based approach to automatically or semi-automatically measure yaks' LW and BMs in open spaces.

Using a binocular stereo camera, we capture 50,000 color and depth images for 120 yaks (side images) from farms in Qinghai, China, together with their actual weights obtained by scales. From each raw frame, we extract yak's foreground image by point cloud segmentation algorithms. Due to the difficulty of collecting large number of observations, we utilize data augmentation [3] to increase the dataset size to 300,000.

To calculate the BMs, we define and manually label 16 pivotal points on yak's body. Leveraging both these points and raw images, we extract 10 yak's BMs, 6 of which are traditional features (body length, hip height, belly width, back height, body diagonal length and heart girth). Besides, we design 4 new features (average body height, body thickness, leg length and surface area). Afterwards we build a random decision forest according to the relevance between BMs and LW [4] to predict yak's LW by the 10 extracted features and the labeled points. The error rate observed is 10.7% in terms of root mean square error (RMSE).

Furthermore, to acquire BMs and LW fully automatically, we train and tune a five-layer convolutional neural network (CNN) to predict LW directly from images of yaks, achieving a relatively lower error rate of 8.4% which is significantly better than that of artificial estimation. Additionally, we build another seven-layer CNN to recognize yak's body pivotal points from images. Each input image of the two CNNs above has

© Springer International Publishing AG 2017
A. Lintas et al. (Eds.): ICANN 2017, Part II, LNCS 10614, pp. 735–736, 2017.
https://doi.org/10.1007/978-3-319-68612-7

6 channels including 3D world coordinates and RGB values. The average RMSE of pivotal point prediction on test set is 6.34 cm, which, according to local husbandry standards, is acceptable for calculating BMs.

This study is supported by Significant Science and Technology Projects of Qinghai Province, China under Grant No. 2015-SF-A4-3.

Keywords: Convolutional neural network · Random decision forest · Computer vision · Binocular camera

References

1. Menesatti, P., Costa, C., Antonucci, F., Steri, R., Pallottino, F., Catillo, G.: A low-cost stereovision system to estimate size and weight of live sheep. Comput. Electron. Agric. **103**, 33–38 (2014)
2. Tasdemir, S., Urkmez, A., Inal, S.: Determination of body measurements on the Holstein cows using digital image analysis and estimation of live weight with regression analysis. Comput. Electron. Agric. **76**(2), 189–197 (2011)
3. Su, H., Qi, C.R., Li, Y., Guibas, L.J.: Render for CNN: viewpoint estimation in images using cnns trained with rendered 3d model views. In: IEEE International Conference on Computer Vision, pp. 2686–2694 (2015)
4. Heinrichs, A.J., Rogers, G.W., Cooper, J.B.: Predicting body weight and wither height in Holstein heifers using body measurements. J. Dairy Sci. **75**(12), 3576–3581 (1992)

A Modified Resilient Back-Propagation Algorithm in CNN for Optimized Learning of Visual Recognition Problems

Sadaqat ur Rehman[1(✉)], Shanshan Tu[2], and Yongfeng Huang[1]

[1] Department of Electronic Engineering, Tsinghua University, Beijing, China
z-sun15@mails.tsinghua.edu.cn, yfhuang@tsinghua.edu.cn
[2] Faculty of IT, Beijing University of Technology, Beijing, China
sstu@bjut.edu.cn

Abstract. Training of convolution neural network (CNN) is a problem of global optimization. We hypothesize that the more smooth and optimize the training of CNN goes, the more efficient the end rsult becomes. Therefore, in this short paper, we propose a modified resilient back-propagation (MRPROP) algorithm to improve the convergence and efficiency of CNN, in which global best concept is introduced in weight updating criteria, to allow the training algorithm of CNN to optimize its weights more swiftly and precisely to find a good solution. Experimental results demonstrate that MRPROP outperforms previous benchmark algorithms and helps in improving training speed and classification accuracy on a public face and skin dataset [1] up to 4X (four times) and 2% respectively. In RPROP [2], the change in weight δw depends on the updated value $\delta_{x,y}$ increased or decreased according to the error, in order to reach a better solution. However, the previously updated values are neglected after every iteration. It means that all the best values previously achieved in weight change would not be referring back. Hence, there is no information sharing between the best values that have been achieved at the previous iterations with the current result. Therefore, by using the term "global best" concept in MRPROP, the information of previous weight change is the only guide for the accurate results. Thus, the past best value is selected in term of optimized solution from all updated values of the current weight change and is used to update the process. This variable is called global best "$gbst$". The $gbst$ selection procedure in MRPROP is: First, select two best updated values randomly from all the current change in weight δw. Then, compare these two values in term of optimized solution and choose the better one as $gbst$.

Keywords: Modified RPROP · Training algorithm · CNN optimization

© Springer International Publishing AG 2017
A. Lintas et al. (Eds.): ICANN 2017, Part II, LNCS 10614, pp. 737–738, 2017.
https://doi.org/10.1007/978-3-319-68612-7

References

1. Phung, S.L., Bouzerdoum, A., Chai, D.: Skin segmentation using color pixel classification: analysis and comparison. IEEE Trans. Pattern Anal. Mach. Intell. **27**(1), 148–154 (2005)
2. Riedmiller, M., Braun, H.: A direct adaptive method of faster back propagation learning: The RPROP algorithm. In: Proceedings of the IEEE International Conference NN, CA, pp. 586–591 (1993)

Learning in Action Game by Profit Sharing Using Convolutional Neural Network

Kaichi Murakami[$\boxtimes$] and Yuko Osana

Tokyo University of Technology, Hachioji, Japan
osana@stf.teu.ac.jp

Abstract. In recent years, deep learning is attracting attention as one that shows better performance than the conventional method in the field of image recognition and speech recognition. Moreover, various studies on reinforcement learning are being conducted as a learning method to acquire an appropriate behavior sequence by interaction with the environment [1]. The deep Q network [2] which is a combination of convolutional neural network [3] which is a representative method of deep learning and the Q learning [4] which is a typical method of reinforcement learning has been proposed. In the deep Q network, learning is realized that can obtain scores equal to or higher than humans for multiple games. In this research, Q Learning is used as a reinforcement learning method, but it can be considered that it is possible to combine a convolution neural network with another method such as Profit Sharing [5].

In this paper, we propose Profit Sharing using convolutional neural network and realize learning of 2D action game. In the proposed method, the value of each action corresponding to the input observation (game play screen) is learned using the convolutional neural network. Here, the value function in Profit Sharing is used. In the proposed method, play every 5 seconds is handled as one episode. 2D action game shown in Fig. 1 are trained in the proposed method, we confirmed that an agent can learn actions that can reach the goal.

Keywords: Convolutional neural network · Profit Sharing · Action game

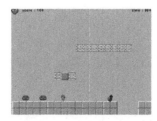

Fig. 1. 2D Action Game.

© Springer International Publishing AG 2017
A. Lintas et al. (Eds.): ICANN 2017, Part II, LNCS 10614, pp. 739–740, 2017.
https://doi.org/10.1007/978-3-319-68612-7

References

1. Sutton, R.S., Barto, A.G.: Reinforcement Learning: An Introduction. The MIT Press (1998)
2. Mnih, V., et al.: Human-level control through deep reinforcement learning. Nature **518**, 529–533 (2015)
3. LeCun, Y., Bottou, L., Bengio, Y., Haffner, P.: Gradient-based learning applied to document recognition. Proc. IEEE **86**(11), 2278–2324 (1998)
4. Watkins, C.J.C.H., Dayan, P.: Technical note: Q-learning. Mach. Learn. **8**, 55–68 (1992)
5. Grefenstette, J.J.: Credit assignment in rule discovery systems based on genetic algorithms. Mach. Learn. **3**, 225–245 (1988)

Deep Learning for Adaptive Playing Strength in Computer Games

Eli (Omid) David$^{(\boxtimes)}$ and Nathan S. Netanyahu

Department of Computer Science, Bar-Ilan University, Ramat-Gan, Israel
mail@elidavid.com, nathan@cs.biu.ac.il

Abstract. In this abstract we present our initial results on the first successful attempt to train computer chess programs to realistically exhibit different playing strengths.

While the main target of research in computer chess has always been achieving stronger playing strength, the seemingly easier task of creating *realistically weaker* programs remains challenging. Nowadays human chess players from novice to grandmaster are easily defeated by state-of-the-art chess programs, and thus gain little enjoyment or experience by playing against such an overwhelmingly superior opponent. As a result, commercial chess programs have always tried to allow the human user to adjust their strength to best match theirs. Previous attempts used by commercial chess programs involved either limiting the amount of time or search depth used by the program, or randomly playing inferior moves with some probability. All these methods have resulted in unrealistic playing style, which yields little benefit and enjoyment for the human opponents (i.e., the computer program does not pass a Turing test).

In our work, we train the chess program to exhibit a targeted playing strength realistically, without any artificial handicap. To do so, we build on our previous DeepChess [1] work which allowed us to train an end-to-end neural network from scratch, achieving a state-of-the-art chess program.

Here, instead of training the deep neural network on datasets of grandmaster chess players only, we train two separate neural networks using DeepChess architecture. Using the ChessBase Mega Database, we extract two hundred thousand positions from games where both players were rated above 2500 Elo, and train the first neural network (to which we refer as DEEPCHESSSTRONG). Similarly, we train a second neural network that using two hundred thousand positions from games where both players were rated below 2300 (to which we refer as DEEPCHESSWEAK).

To compare the performance of these two chess programs, we conducted 100 games at a time control of 30 min per game for each side. The result was DEEPCHESSSTRONG defeating DEEPCHESSWEAK by of 78.5% to 21.5%, corresponding to a rating difference of 225 Elo in favor of DEEPCHESSSTRONG.

These results present the first successful attempt at adaptive adjustment of playing strength in computer chess, while producing realistic playing style. This method can be extended to additional games in order to achieve realistic playing style at different playing strength levels.

© Springer International Publishing AG 2017
A. Lintas et al. (Eds.): ICANN 2017, Part II, LNCS 10614, pp. 741–742, 2017.
https://doi.org/10.1007/978-3-319-68612-7

Reference

1. David, O.E., Netanyahu, N.S., Wolf, L.: DeepChess: End-to-end deep neural network for automatic learning in Chess. In: Villa, A.E.P., Masulli, P., Pons Rivero, A.J. (eds.) ICANN 2016. LNCS, vol. 9887, pp. 88–96. Springer, Cham (2016). doi:10. 1007/978-3-319-44781-0_11

Benchmarking Reinforcement Learning Algorithms for the Operation of a Multi-carrier Energy System

J. Bollenbacher$^{(\boxtimes)}$ and B. Rhein

TH Köln – University of Applied Sciences, Cologne, Germany
{jan.bollenbacher,beate.rhein}@th-koeln.de

Abstract. Nowadays common energy infrastructures such as electricity, natural gas and local district heating systems are mostly planned and operated independently. There are several reasons to couple these energy infrastructures and to optimize the resulting system as unit. One approach is based on the concept of "energy hubs" (EH), which can be considered as functional units to convert, store and dissipate multiple energy carriers [1]. Recent research combines the concept of EH with machine learning concepts such as Reinforcement Learning (RL) and introduce the Smart Energy Hub (SEH). There are approaches to use RL to operate a SEH [2] and also to find the components' optimal sizing [3].

A SEH consists of a transformer, a gas turbine, a furnace and a heat storage. It is feasible to choose a configuration out of a set of devices or to operate without particular devices. Every device has different efficiencies and costs. The load of electricity and heat must be provided by purchasing and processing the proper amount of electricity and gas units. We are facing two different problems, finding the optimal configuration and the optimal policy w.r.t. the chosen configuration.

To solve these problems, we implemented a SEH as an RL environment. The application of RL enables us to find an optimal policy by exploring the state space without any prior knowledge of the underlying physical model. The used RL framework is very flexible and can be adapted to other EH systems easily.

As our problem is a Continuous Control problem, we benchmarked different RL algorithms using RLLab [4]. We were able to find a set of optimal configurations and corresponding operation policies.

Keywords: Reinforcement learning · Smart engergy hub · Smart grids

References

1. Geidl, M., Andersson, G.: Optimal coupling of energy infrastructures. In: PowerTech, pp. 1398–1403 (2007)
2. Rayati, M., Sheikhi, A., Ranjbar, A.M.: Applying reinforcement learning method to optimize an energy hub operation in the smart grid. In: ISGT (2015)

© Springer International Publishing AG 2017
A. Lintas et al. (Eds.): ICANN 2017, Part II, LNCS 10614, pp. 743–744, 2017.
https://doi.org/10.1007/978-3-319-68612-7

3. Sheikhi, A., Rayati, M., Ranjbar, A.M.: Energy hub optimal sizing in the smart grid. Machine learning approach. In: ISGT (2015)
4. Duan, Y., Chen, X., Houthooft, R., Schulman, J., Abbeel, P.: Benchmarking deep reinforcement learning for continuous control. CoRR (2016)

Differentiable Oscillators in Recurrent Neural Networks for Gradient-Based Sequence Modeling

Sebastian Otte$^{(\boxtimes)}$ and Martin V. Butz

Cognitive Modeling Group, University of Tübingen,
Sand 14, 72076 Tübingen, Germany
sebastian.otte@uni.tuebingen.de

Abstract. Long Short-Term Memories (LSTMs) [1] trained with Back Propagation Through Time (BPTT) are very powerful sequence learners, particularly for sequence labeling tasks, for which they are the most commonly used technique nowadays. However, while sequences that consist of multiple superimposed waves can be easily learned by approaches such as Echo State Networks (ESNs) [2, 3], this task remains difficult for gradient-based learning models, including LSTMs. One major reason for this issue is that the latter networks are forced to interpret the data in a sequentially, temporally correlated manner, which typically results in learning the data along the sequence, that is, approximating the shape of the signal. As a consequence, a typical LSTM network can learn a single sine wave easily, but it will perform significantly worse than ESNs on two or more waves in terms of long-range generalizations.

In this work, we have developed a simple pre-structured RNN that consists of multiple independent recurrent submodules with only a few cells per module, showing that such an architecture can learn such problems much better than fully connected RNNs. Next, we introduced neurally implemented oscillator units, which are differentiable, and which can be integrated in conventional RNNs and trained with BPTT in the time-domain. As a result, these RNNs can compose their outputs from multiple oscillating basis components, where learning effectively tunes the frequencies, amplitudes, and phase-shifts of the wave generators. This results in an entirely different, temporally more "global" learning behavior. To evaluate our approach, we studied two architectures, namely, LSTMs with integrated wave generators and LSTMs with wave generators that are encapsulated in a separate hidden layer. Our results show that such RNNs, trained with plain BPTT, can learn signals of superimposed waves and even acoustic tones orders of magnitudes better than LSTMs.

Keywords: Recurrent neural networks (RNNs) · Long short-term memories (LSTMs) · Sequence modeling · Oscillating RNNs

© Springer International Publishing AG 2017
A. Lintas et al. (Eds.): ICANN 2017, Part II, LNCS 10614, pp. 745–746, 2017.
https://doi.org/10.1007/978-3-319-68612-7

References

1. Hochreiter, S., Schmidhuber, J.: Long short-term memory. Neural Comput. **9**(8), 1735–1780 (1997)
2. Koryakin, D., Lohmann, J., Butz, M.V.: Balanced echo state networks. Neural Netw. **36**, 35–45 (2012)
3. Otte, S., Butz, M.V., Koryakin, D., Becker, F., Liwicki, M., Zell, A.: Optimizing recurrent reservoirs with neuro-evolution. Neurocomputing **192**, 128–138 (2016)

Empirical Study of Effect of Dropout in Online Learning

Kazuyuki Hara$^{(\boxtimes)}$

College of Industrial Technology, Nihon University,
1-2-1 Izumi-cho, Narashino-shi, Chiba 275-8575, Japan
hara.kazuyuki@nihon-u.ac.jp

Abstract. We analyze the behavior of dropout used in online learning. Previously, we analyzed the behavior of dropout learning using the soft-committee machine [1]. In this work, we use a three-layer network that shows slow dynamics called a quasi-plateau. Quasi-plateaus are caused by singular subspaces of hidden-to-output weights that do not exist in the soft-committee machine [2]. The Fig. 1 shows the effect of the slow dynamics of a three-layer network by using stochastic gradient descent (SGD; left) and that of dropout (right) in a simulation. The overlap (R) shows the similarity of the teacher and student network weights. From the results, SGD converged slowly to a fixed point indicated by the circle, and the hidden-to-output weights show that the network was in a quasi-plateau state. Dropout converged to a fixed point quickly and the weights show that the network was not in a quasi-plateau state. Therefore, dropout did not fall into a quasi-plateau state. Dropout selects and neglects the hidden unit weights of the student network in every learning iteration. It is expected that a more intermittent interval of dropout may reduce the effect. We performed 20 trials in which we changed the initial weights of the student network and found that the effect of dropout remained until an interval dropout of N iterations was reached ($N = 1000$).

Keywords: Dropout · Quasi-plateau · Interval dropout

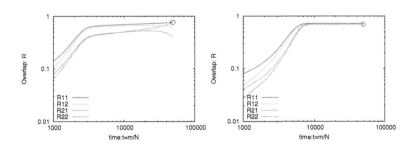

Fig. 1. Comparison of SGD (left), and that of dropout (right).

© Springer International Publishing AG 2017
A. Lintas et al. (Eds.): ICANN 2017, Part II, LNCS 10614, pp. 747–748, 2017.
https://doi.org/10.1007/978-3-319-68612-7

References

1. Hara, K., Saitoh, D., Kondou, T., Suzuki, S., Shouno, H.: Group Dropout inspired by ensemble learning. In: Hirose, A., Ozawa, S., Doya, K., Ikeda, K., Lee, M., Liu, D. (eds.) ICONIP 2016. LNCS, vol. 9948, pp. 66–73. Springer, Cham (2016). doi:10.1007/978-3-319-46672-9_8
2. Park, H., Inoue, M., Okada, M.: Slow dynamics due to singularities of hierarchical learning machines. Prog. Theoret. Phys. Suppl. **157**, 275–279 (2005)

Context Dependent Input Weight Selection for Regression Extreme Learning Machines

Yara Rizk[(✉)] and Mariette Awad

Department of Electrical and Computer Engineering,
American University of Beirut, Beirut, Lebanon
{yar01,mariette.awad}@aub.edu.lb

Abstract. Extreme learning machine (ELM) is a popular machine learning algorithm due to its fast non-iterative training and good generalization [2]. However, it randomly assigns input weights and biases from a uniform distribution regardless of the characteristics of the training data. Exploiting this data would produce a more specialized model, instead of adopting a "one size fits all" approach. This could result in better generalization while preserving ELM's fast training.

Hence, we developed a context dependent input weight selection for regression ELM (CDR-ELM) which is a non-iterative training algorithm for supervised regression. First, k-means clusters input data into P clusters based on the number of hidden layer neurons. Then, cluster head differences are assigned to input weights as described in (1), and biases are computed from cluster sizes as $b_i = \frac{N_j}{N_k}$. Finally, ELM is trained using least squares.

$$w_i = \frac{|E[x_{\in cluster_i}] - E[x_{\in cluster_j}]|}{|E[y_{\in cluster_i}] - E[y_{\in cluster_j}]|} \qquad (1)$$

Six publicly available regression datasets were used to compare CDR-ELM to ELM [2], backpropagation-trained ANN (ANN-BP), support vector regression (SVR) and low discrepancy sequence (LDS)-ELM [1]. Relevant existing classification algorithms (C-ELM [5], C^{2}ELM [3], CIW-ELM [4]) were also extended to regression problems and compared to CDR-ELM.

In general, CDR-ELM's training time increased due to the additional computations but it was still faster than SVR, ANN-BP and CIW-ELM, especially on larger data sets. Furthermore, CDR-ELM's repeatability decreased compared to ELM (up to 60% higher variance on some data) due to the k-means' random initialization, but it still achieved the lowest variance for some data (25% less than C-ELM and 50% less than ELM).

Finally, CDR-ELM achieved a lower testing MSE than ELM on some datasets (e.g. concrete compress, housing and slump) but worse on others. For example, CDR-ELM achieved a 19.4% reduction in MSE compared to ELM but required twice as long to train the model. CDR-ELM also achieved 11% reduction in MAE compared to ELM on the housing data and was slower by a factor of 1.23. Therefore, we concluded that CDR-ELM is not suitable for all types of problems. The algorithm's lack of randomness can lead to over-fitting

© Springer International Publishing AG 2017
A. Lintas et al. (Eds.): ICANN 2017, Part II, LNCS 10614, pp. 749–750, 2017.
https://doi.org/10.1007/978-3-319-68612-7

on highly noisy data. Furthermore, sparsely distributed data would result in unsuitable clusters which will negatively impact the quality of ELM input weights.

Keywords: Extreme learning machines · Non-iterative training · Supervised learning · Regression

Acknowledgments. Supported by the National Council of Scientific Research in Lebanon (CNRS-L).

References

1. Cervellera, C., Macciò, D.: Low-discrepancy points for deterministic assignment of hidden weights in extreme learning machines. IEEE Trans. Neural Netw. Learn. Syst. **27**(4), 891–896 (2016)
2. Huang, G.B., Zhu, Q.Y., Siew, C.K.: Extreme learning machine: a new learning scheme of feedforward neural networks. In: Proceedings of the International Joint Conference on Neural Networks, vol. 2, pp. 985–990. IEEE (2004)
3. Liu, X., Miao, J., Qing, L., Cao, B.: Class-constrained extreme learning machine. In: Proceedings of ELM-2015, vol. 1, pp. 521–530. Springer (2016)
4. Tapson, J., de Chazal, P., van Schaik, A.: Explicit computation of input weights in extreme learning machines. In: Proceedings of ELM-2014, vol. 1, pp. 41–49. Springer (2015)
5. Zhu, W., Miao, J., Qing, L.: Constrained extreme learning machine: a novel highly discriminative random feedforward neural network. In: IEEE International Joint Conference on Neural Networks, pp. 800–807 (2014)

Solution of Multi-parameter Inverse Problem by Adaptive Methods: Efficiency of Dividing the Problem Space

Alexander Efitorov[1]([✉]), Tatiana Dolenko[1,2], Sergey Burikov[1,2],
Kirill Laptinskiy[1,2], and Sergey Dolenko[1]

[1] D.V. Skobeltsyn Institute of Nuclear Physics, M.V. Lomonosov Moscow State
University, Moscow, Russia
sasha.efitorov@gmail.com, dolenko@srd.sinp.msu.ru
[2] Physical Department, M.V. Lomonosov Moscow State University, Moscow, Russia

Abstract. The considered multi-parameter inverse problem (IP) is determination of concentrations of salts or ions in multi-component water solutions of inorganic salts by Raman spectroscopy with subsequent spectra analysis by a non-linear adaptive method (multilayer perceptron type artificial neural networks (ANN)) or by a linear adaptive method (partial least squares (PLS) method based on principal component analysis) [1]. Dividing the problem space into parts by data clustering simplifies the problem within each cluster but reduces the number of samples. This study compares efficiency of application of this approach for problems with various complexity (determination of concentrations of five salts, or ten salts, or ten ions) and with various distributions of samples over concentration range of the components [2].

It has been demonstrated, that the approach is efficient for IP with medium complexity (5 salts). The best clustering method was Kohonen self organized map (SOM). However, division into physically grounded sections of problem space by classification followed by applying a linear PLS regressor within each class provided better results than clustering; uniform sample distribution over the concentration range also required nonlinear data preprocessing within each class. For a more complex problem (10 salts or 10 ions), the single regressor approach with strongly non-linear ANN regressors turned out to perform better. The main reason of the observed effects is decreasing representativity of data within each section with increasing number of sections; so the results should be checked on other problems with much larger amount of data available.

This study has been conducted at the expense of Russian Science Foundation grant no. 14-11-00579.

Keywords: Inverse problems · Artificial neural networks · Partial least squares · Clustering · Raman spectroscopy

© Springer International Publishing AG 2017
A. Lintas et al. (Eds.): ICANN 2017, Part II, LNCS 10614, pp. 751–752, 2017.
https://doi.org/10.1007/978-3-319-68612-7

References

1. Efitorov, A.O., et al.: Optical Memory & Neural Networks (Information Optics), vol. 24, no. 2, pp. 93–101 (2015)
2. Dolenko, S., Efitorov, A., Burikov, S., Dolenko, T., Laptinskiy, K., Persiantsev, I.: Neural network approaches to solution of the inverse problem of identification and determination of the ionic composition of multi-component water solutions. In: Iliadis, L., Jayne, C. (eds.) EANN 2015. CCIS, vol. 517, pp. 109–118. Springer, Cham (2015). doi:10.1007/978-3-319-23983-5_11

Hopfield Auto-Associative Memory Network for Content-Based Text-Retrieval

Vandana M. Ladwani[1], Y. Vaishnavi[2], and V. Ramasubramanian[1(✉)]

[1] International Institute of Information Technology -
Bangalore (IIIT-B), Bangalore, India
{vandana.ladwani,v.ramasubramanian}@iiitb.org
[2] PES Institute of Technology - Bangalore
South Campus (PESIT-BSC), Bangalore, India
vaishnaviy2@gmail.com

Abstract. We examine how the Hopfield auto-associative memory network [1] can be adapted for text retrieval to realize its ideal functionality as a content-based information retrieval system. Towards this, we examine various issues such as (i) how the capacity of the Hopfield net is limited (far below the theoretical limit) for correlated patterns, and how its capacity is significantly enhanced by the Pseudo-inverse learning rule, and (ii) the performance characterization of retrieval under two types of queries, namely, queries with substitution errors and partial queries. We present results on large text databases and establish the practical scalability of both the storage capacity and the retrieval robustness of the Hopfield network for content-based retrieval of text data.

In this work, we use two data sets of text patterns (sentences made of sequence of letters from the English alphabet and special characters, with each character binarized by its 8-bit ASCII code), as shown in Fig. 1.

Capacity Performance: Figure 2 shows the 'capacity performance' using Data-Set-1: y-axis is the number of sentences retrieved from the Hopfield storage (on being presented with the full sentence as a probe pattern) plotted against the number of sentences stored (in the x-axis), ranging up to 10000 sentences (as defined above) within a specified error-tolerance measured as the Hamming distance between the retrieved sentence and the original sentence (that the query is) and for two learning rules: (i) Hebbian and, (ii) Pseudo-inverse rule. While the capacity of Hebbian learning can be seen to be very poor (being significantly lower than the theoretical capacity of $0.14N$), the capacity of Pseudo-inverse rule is very significant, yielding close to the theoretical capacity of $N-1$, i.e., up to 8500 sentences even with 0% error tolerance (or, in general, close to N patterns for a Hopfield of size N neurons). This is a significant result, particularly on actual large text corpus, hitherto neither attempted nor reported.

Query Performances: Figure 3 shows retrieval performances characterizing the following two types of query patterns, for the Pseudo-inverse learning rule using Data-Set-2.

Query with Substitution Errors: Figure 3 (Left-panel) shows the retrieval performance (% retrieved sentences) for a range of 'substitution errors' (with respect to a full target sentence) for substitution error

A. Lintas et al. (Eds.): ICANN 2017, Part II, LNCS 10614, pp. 753–755, 2017.
https://doi.org/10.1007/978-3-319-68612-7

rates up to 40% as a family of curves for different 'error tolerances' (0 to 10%). The network retrieves 100% of the 2400 sentences stored with 0% error tolerance for up to 15% substitution errors, gracefully degrading for substitution errors in the range of 15% to 30%. This indicates the robustness of the content-based retrieval mechanism of the Hopfield network to retrieve 100% of the stored patterns from a large text database with 0% errors, under significant substitution errors, representative of queries commonly typed, or derived from spoken queries after speech recognition, as in spoken-term detection or spoken document retrieval [2].

Partial Query: Figure 3 (Right-panel) shows an important performance of the Hopfield network, where the query is a partial query, centrally located within a target sentence. The retrieval performance (% retrieved sentences) is shown for partial query lengths 50–100% (of the full sentence length) for error tolerances 0 to 10%. While the retrieval performance expectedly drops as the query length reduces from 100% (i.e., the full sentence, as stored), the network gives 100% retrieval down to 85% partial lengths, gracefully degrading as the partial query length lowers down to 70–75%, clearly establishing how the content-based retrieval property of Hopfield network copes with partial queries.

Keywords: Hopfield network · Auto-associative memory · Text retrieval · Content-based retrieval

	# Sentences	Sentence Length (# Characters C)	# Bits / Sentence ($8 \times C$)	Hopfield network size	
				# Neurons (N)	# Interconnection weights (N^2)
Data–set-1	10000	1250	10000	10000	100 million
Data–set-2	2400	300	2400	2400	5.76 million

Fig. 1. Data sets used and Hopfield network sizes

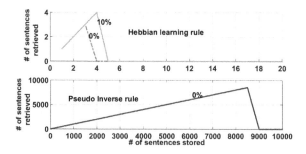

Fig. 2. Hopfield capacity performance

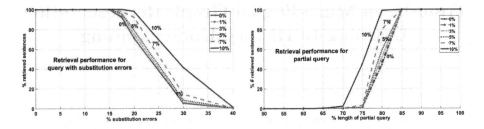

Fig. 3. Retrieval performance under substitution errors and partial query

References

1. Hopfield, J.J.: Neural networks and physical systems with emergent collective computational capabilities. Proc. Natl. Acad. Sci. (USA) **79**, 2554–2558 (1982)
2. http://trec.nist.gov/

From Deep Multi-lingual Graph Representation Learning to History Understanding

Sima Sharifirad[1](✉), Stan Matwin[1], and Witold Dzwinel[2]

[1] Department of Computer Science, Dalhousie University, Halifax, Canada
s.sharifirad@dal.ca, stan@cs.dal.ca
[2] Department of Computer Science, AGH University of Science and Technology,
Krakow, Poland
dzwinel@agh.edu.pl

Abstract. This research aims at understanding and developing a knowledge representation that will show the differences and similarities between two different languages and cultures around one concept in history considering the structure information of the two Wikipedia graphs. World war II was considered as the concept of interest in two languages, English and German. The solution was proposed and divided into different steps of learning. Primarily, Positive Pointwise Mutual Information (PPMI) and then Random Surfing were used to capture the structure information of the undirected weighted Wikipedia graphs. After that, the correlation between the two views were considered and complex features were extracted using deep canonical correlation autoencoder (DCCAE). For each language under consideration, the top one hundred most similar pages to the page of interest in the other language were considered using Jaccard similarity. Topics were extracted using Latent Dirichlet Allocation (LDA) from those pages and the topics were considered along with highly correlated words from DCCAE were fed into SVM for sentiment classification task. We compare our method with previous proposed methods on word similarity tasks after deploying DCCAE for evaluation. Based on our best knowledge, it is the first application of DCCAE in this context.

Keywords: Deep canonical correlation autoencoder · Graph representation

References

1. Alexei, V., Nello, C., John, S.T.: Inferring a semantic representation of text via cross-language correlation analysis. Adv. Neural Inf. Proc. Syst. (NIPS) **15**, 1497–1504 (2003)
2. David, R.H., Sandor, S., John, S.T.: Canonical correlation analysis: An overview with application to learning methods. Neural Comput. **16**(12), 2639–2664 (2004)
3. Paramveer, D., Dean, F., Lyle, U.: Multi-view learning of word embeddings via CCA. Adv. Neural Inf. Proc. Syst. (NIPS) **24**, 199–207 (2011)
4. Mathew, B.B., Christoph, H.L.: Correlational spectral clustering. In: Proceedings of the 2008 IEEE Computer Society Conference Computer Vision and Pattern Recognition, pp. 1–8 (2008)

© Springer International Publishing AG 2017
A. Lintas et al. (Eds.): ICANN 2017, Part II, LNCS 10614, p. 756, 2017.
https://doi.org/10.1007/978-3-319-68612-7

Adaptive Construction of Hierarchical Neural Network Classifiers: New Modification of the Algorithm

Sergey Dolenko$^{(\boxtimes)}$, Vsevolod Svetlov, and Igor Isaev

D.V. Skobeltsyn Institute of Nuclear Physics, M.V. Lomonosov Moscow State
University, Moscow, Russia
dolenko@srd.sinp.msu.ru

Abstract. Multiple classification problems are usually hard to solve. With increasing number of classes, classification algorithms rapidly degrade, both by error rate and by computational cost. Multi-layer perceptron (MLP) type neural networks (NN) solving such problems are subject to the same effect: greater number of classes requires increasing the number of neurons in the hidden layer(s) (HL) to build a more complex separation surface, making the NN more prone to overtraining. An alternative way is to build a hierarchical classifier system, uniting the target classes into several groups and solving the recognition problem within each group recursively at the lower-lying levels of hierarchy.

The authors of this study are developing an algorithm for adaptive construction of such a hierarchical NN classifier (HNNC) [1]. Each node of the constructed hierarchical tree is an MLP with a single HL consisting of only a few neurons. Such an MLP is knowingly unable to recognize all the required classes in a multiple classification problem. So after it has been trained for a specified number of epochs, it is applied to all the samples of the training set, and its output is analyzed. If the majority of samples from some class k "vote" at the MLP output as belonging to another class m, the desired output for class k is changed to be the same as for class m. In this way, classes are united into groups, and as this modification is performed in the way favorable for the MLP, we obtain a system with positive feedback, rapidly converging to a trained NN with a high rate of recognition into several adaptively formed groups of classes. Afterwards, each group is subject to further recognition in an iterative way, thus providing adaptive construction of a HNNC.

In this study, a new modification has been introduced into the algorithm. Now the target classes may not only unite, but under some conditions any target class may split into two new classes, possibly simplifying class separation borders, increasing efficiency and stability of the algorithm.

The presentation displays the results of the algorithm without and with the new modification on several well-known benchmark problems.

This study was supported by RFBR grant no.15-07-08975-a.

Keywords: Multiple classification · Hierarchial classifier

© Springer International Publishing AG 2017
A. Lintas et al. (Eds.): ICANN 2017, Part II, LNCS 10614, pp. 757–758, 2017.
https://doi.org/10.1007/978-3-319-68612-7

Reference

1. Svetlov, V.A., Dolenko, S.A.: Opt. Mem. Neur. Netw. (Inform.Opt.) **26**(1) 40–46 (2017)

Automobile Insurance Claim Prediction Using Distributed Driving Behaviour Data on Smartphones

Chalermpol Saiprasert[(⊠)], Pantaree Phumphuang,
and Suttipong Thajchayapong

National Electronics and Computer Technology Center (NECTEC),
112 Pahonyothin Road, Klong Luang, Pathum Thani, Thailand
{chalermpol.saiprasert,suttipong.thajchayapong}@nectec.or.th

Abstract. Recently, a new disruptive technology known as insurance telematics has been gaining market share in the car insurance industry. It relies on insurance premiums calculated based on the risk profile of individual driver which is measured via smartphones sensors. More dynamic parameters such as mileage, driving behaviour and type of roads driven are being used instead of the traditional parameters. With this approach of using a more fine-grained and personalised driving data, we are able to create a more granular risk differentiation for each driver based on actual driving behaviour. As a result, policy holders who drive more cautiously will possess lower risk profiles reflecting in lower insurance premium and less likelihood to make a claim.

This paper proposes a preliminary study of a neural network based algorithm to predict car insurance claims based on driving behaviour data. A smartphone based driving behaviour evaluation tool is used to collect driving data of users who subscribed to a policy with insurance telematics. The algorithm is distributed to all drivers who have the application installed on their smartphones. This is a previous work of the authors proposed in [1]. Driving behaviour computations are performed on the client smartphone in real-time where a driver will be able to assess their own driving style in a distributed manner. The processed driving data from each vehicle is then sent to a central server via 3G/4G channels where all sudden driving events along with their geo-location are stored into the main database. The input parameters used in this paper are as follows: Average distance driven per trip, Average Speed, Number of sudden braking per km., Number of sudden acceleration per km., Number of sudden left lane change per km., Number of sudden right lane change per km., Number of sudden left turn per km., Number of sudden right turn per km. and percentage of driving over speed limit per km. Feed-forward neural network (FFNN) with back propagation is used for the classification model. As FFNN is one of the least complex neural network models, it would enable more flexibility in adjusting and interpreting the experimental results. To minimise computational complexity, only one hidden layer is used, while the number of nodes is selected empirically to find the fewest number of nodes that give the highest accuracy. The number

© Springer International Publishing AG 2017
A. Lintas et al. (Eds.): ICANN 2017, Part II, LNCS 10614, pp. 759–760, 2017.
https://doi.org/10.1007/978-3-319-68612-7

of nodes in the input layer is equal to the number of input parameters. For the output layer, two nodes are used for 2-class prediction, while three nodes are used for 3-classed prediction. We have divided the classification into two settings. One is to have 2 predicted classes which are 'claim' and 'no claim'. The second setting is to have 3 classes which are 'no claim', 'claim 1-2 times' and 'claim more than 2 times'.

The experiment is performed on a real-world dataset insurance policies of over 600 actual policy holders over a 3 month period. Fine grained driving behaviour such as braking, accelerating, turning and changing lanes are used in this paper. Within the same time period, the number of accident claims of the participated drivers are recorded accordingly to be used in the prediction model. For performance evaluation, a comparison is made between our proposed approach and three fundamental machine learning algorithms often used in predicting automobile insurance policies namely, Decision Tree, Naive Bays and K-Nearest Neighbor. For overall performance in both the 2 classes and 3 classes prediction, the proposed approach with attribute selection produces the highest prediction accuracy of 76.12% and 77.61% respectively. On the other end of the scale, the model with the poorest performance is Naive Bayes with considerably lower accuracy for both 2 and 3 classes prediction. Naive Bayes's lower accuracies are due to the imbalance amongst classes, where approximately 60% of drivers do not claim at all, while only 7% claim for than twice.

Overall, the proposed algorithm can utilise driving behaviour data alone to achieve more than 70% prediction accuracy. Preliminary results in this paper have shown the potential of using driving behaviour data to predict automobile insurance claim. Improvement can be further achieved by incorporating with more usage-based insurance data [2]. Also, as driving behaviours can be influenced by traffic conditions, incorporating traffic transition information [3] would help improve the prediction capability. These are subject to further investigation.

Keywords: Smartphone sensors · Insurance telematics · Driving behaviours · Prediction models

References

1. Saiprasert, C., Pholprasit, T., Thajchayapong, S.: Detection of driving events using sensory data on smartphone. Int. J. Intell. Transp. Syst. Res. **15**, 17–28 (2017)
2. Handel, P., Skog, I., Wahlstrom, J., Bonawiede, F., Welch, R., Ohlsson, J., Ohlsson, M.: Insurance telematics: opportunities and challenges with the smartphone solution. IEEE Intell. Transp. Syst. Mag. **8**, 1238–1248 (2014)
3. Thajchayapong, S., Barria, J.: Spatial inference of traffic transition using micro-macro traffic variables. IEEE Trans. Intell. Transp. Syst. **16**, 854–864 (2015)

A Fault-Tolerant Indoor Localization System with Recurrent Neural Networks

Eduardo Carvalho[1], Bruno Ferreira[1], Geraldo P. R. Filho[2], Jó Ueyama[2], and Gustavo Pessin[3(✉)]

[1] SENAI Institute of Innovation in Minerals Technologies, Belém, PA, Brazil
{eduardo.isi,bruno.isi}@sesipa.org.br
[2] University of São Paulo, São Carlos, SP, Brazil
{geraldop,joueyama}@icmc.usp.br
[3] Instituto Tecnológico Vale (ITV), Belém, PA, Brazil
gustavo.pessin@itv.org

Abstract. This paper proposes a fault-tolerant indoor localization system that employs Recurrent Neural Networks (RNNs) for the localization task. A decision module is developed to identify failures and it is responsible for the allocation of adequate RNNs for each situation. Besides of the proposal of the fault-tolerant system, we exploit several architectures and models of RNNs in the system: Gated Recurrent Unit, Long Short-Term Memory and Simple RNN [1]. In this work we extend [2] by means of the evaluation of fault-tolerant policies and the use of RNNs instead of Convolution Neural Networks. The system uses as inputs a collection of Wi-Fi Received Signal Strength Indication (RSSI) signals, and the RNN classifies the position of an agent according to this collection. A fault-tolerant mechanism has been developed to support two types of failures: (i) momentary failures, and (ii) permanent failures. Two are the research questions we aim to answer: (1) "Can we locate agents in indoor environments with Recurrent Neural Networks?", and (2) "How different types of failure impact the accuracy of the localization of the agents in indoor environments". For answering the first question, we ran GRU, LSTM and SimpleRNN with 5, 10, 30 and 50 recurrent neurons. The best accuracy was found with the GRU using 50 recurrent neurons. For the second question, the investigation figured out that the architectures with GRU were also the most suitable. Related to momentary failures, we obtained an accuracy of 87% and for permanent failures, although it depends on the affected node, the accuracy were between 73% and 81%.

Keywords: Fault tolerant · Indoor localization · Recurrent neural networks · Gated recurrent unit · Long short-term memory

© Springer International Publishing AG 2017
A. Lintas et al. (Eds.): ICANN 2017, Part II, LNCS 10614, pp. 761–762, 2017.
https://doi.org/10.1007/978-3-319-68612-7

Reference

1. Chung, J., Gulcehre, C., Cho, K., Bengio, Y.: Empirical evaluation of gated recurrent neural networks on sequence modeling. arXiv preprint (2014). arxiv:1412.3555
2. Ferreira, B.V., Carvalho, E., Ferreira, M.R., Vargas, P.A., Ueyama, J., Pessin, G.: Exploiting the use of convolutional neural networks for localization in indoor environments. Appl. Artif. Intell. **31**(3), 279–287 (2017)

SNN Model for Highly Energy and Area Efficient On-Chip Classification

Anmol Biswas[✉], Aditya Shukla, Sidharth Prasad, and Udayan Ganguly

Department of Electrical Engineering, Indian Institute of Technology Bombay,
Bombay, India
anmolbiswas@gmail.com, aditya.adi2293@gmail.com, sidharth52@gmail.com,
udayan@gmail.com

Abstract. Classification is a common problem addressed in Spiking Neural Network literature, but the models developed are often too complex for hardware implementation, or on-chip learning. We present a simplified model to an LIF-neuron differential equation [1] to convert current to voltage spikes, synapses for voltage to current conversion and a modified-STDP learning rule [2] to enable hardware implementation (demonstrated by circuit-level simulation [3]). In this paper, we develop a 2-layered SNN model in MATLAB, based on Population Coding [4] and laterally inhibiting output neurons - implementing a Winner-Take-All mechanism [5] and train it under Supervision with our modified-STDP learning rule [2]. Supervision is provided in the form of negative bias currents to output neurons of the incorrect class(es). The network is tested on Fisher Iris and Wisconsin Breast Cancer databases, giving accuracy results (95.3% and 96.5% respectively) comparable to literature in SNN [6, 7]. The model is also simulated in a circuit simulator (SPICE) [3] to show software-equivalent performance (i.e. no performance degradation due to hardware implementation). For state-of-art SNN performance, the smaller size of our network (about 3x fewer neurons) translates to improved hardware density. Further, combination of the greater speed of convergence (i.e. 18x fewer epochs) and 3x fewer neurons and synapse, translates to equivalently reduced energy of learning.

Keywords: Spiking neural networks · Supervised learning · Two-layer networks · Energy efficient implementation

References

1. Koch, C., Segev, I.: Methods in Neuronal Modeling; From Ions to Networks, 2nd edn., p. 687. MIT Press, Cambridge (1999). ISBN0-262-11231-0
2. Guetig, R., Aharonov, R., Rotter, S., Sompolinsky, H.: Learning input correlations through non-linear temporally asymmetric Hebbian plasticity (2003)
3. Shukla, A., Kumar, V., Ganguly, U.: A Software-equivalent Hardware approach to Spiking Neural Network based Real-time Learning using RRAM array demonstration in SPICE (Submitted for IJCNN 2017)

© Springer International Publishing AG 2017
A. Lintas et al. (Eds.): ICANN 2017, Part II, LNCS 10614, pp. 763–764, 2017.
https://doi.org/10.1007/978-3-319-68612-7

4. Bohte, S.M., Kok, J.N., La Poutre, H.: Error Backpropagation in Temporally Encoded Networks of Spiking Neurons (2002)
5. Gupta, A., Long, L.N.: Character recognition using spiking neural. In: IEEE Neural Networks Conference, Orlando, FL (2007)
6. Xu, Y., Zeng, X., Zhong, S.: A new supervised learning algorithm for spiking neurons. Neural Comput., 1472–1511 (2013)
7. Xin, J., Embrechts, M.: Supervised learning with spiking neural networks. In: IJCNN (2001)

A Highly Efficient Performance and Robustness Evaluation Method for a SNN Based Recognition Algorithm

Sidharth Prasad$^{(\boxtimes)}$, Anmol Biswas, Aditya Shukla, and Udayan Ganguly

Department of Electrical Engineering,
Indian Institute of Technology Bombay, Mumbai, India
sidharth52@gmail.com, anmolbiswas@gmail.com, aditya.adi2293@gmail.com,
udayan@gmail.com

Abstract. We have recently demonstrated a SNN based classifier that enabled state-of-the-art performance with 3× area efficiency and 60× energy efficiency for standard datasets (e.g. Wisconsin Cancer Database) [1]. A hardware implementation was also demonstrated using a 2-array scheme with a cross-bar of memristors with asynchronous signals to show software equivalent performance [2]. Both learning and recognition (testing) were done with spiking neurons. However, simulating the neural dynamics for testing is computationally expensive which translated to high energy consumption in hardware. Also, the output is only a digital decision, namely the predicted class, which does not reflect the confidence of the decision. In this paper, we present a methodology for a quick and efficient performance evaluation - based on a DC analysis scheme termed as "Current Space" method implemented in hardware with a cross bar array. Here the input neurons produce analog dc voltage inputs for the crossbar array with learnt resistances (weights) to produce analog current levels at the output neurons. The relative current levels provide an analog measure of the decision i.e. extent of separation of classes (i.e. robustness) in the current space of the different output neurons as opposed to a digital decision based on vigorous vs. no spiking in the SNN network. This output signal is essentially equivalent to a software dot-product of input signals with the learnt weight matrix, as is done for ANNs. This method accurately reflects the classification accuracy of SNNs (correlation of 0.98). It enables fast testing (i.e. 15000× faster) in software which translates to a 25× energy reduction for recognition in hardware by our method compared to SNN based recognition. We show that robustness metric can be used to evaluate noise tolerance in the network to produce a training completion criterion based on immunity to noise.

Keywords: Spiking neural networks · Supervised hebbian learning · Crossbar arrays · Two-layer networks · Recognition · Robustness · Noise-tolerance

© Springer International Publishing AG 2017
A. Lintas et al. (Eds.): ICANN 2017, Part II, LNCS 10614, pp. 765–766, 2017.
https://doi.org/10.1007/978-3-319-68612-7

References

1. Biswas, A., Prasad, S., Shukla, A., Ganguly, U.: SNN model for highly energy and area efficient on-chip classification. Submitted to ICANN (2017)
2. Shukla, A., Kumar, V., Ganguly, U.: A software-equivalent hardware approach to spiking neural network based real-time learning using RRAM array demonstration in SPICE. In: IJCNN (2017)

Metric Entropy and Rademacher Complexity of Margin Multi-category Classifiers

Khadija Musayeva[(✉)], Fabien Lauer, and Yann Guermeur

LORIA, University of Lorraine, CNRS, Nancy, France
{khadija.musayeva,fabien.lauer,yann.guermeur}@loria.fr

Abstract. This communication introduces a new bound on the probability of error of margin multi-category classifiers. We consider classifiers based on classes of vector-valued functions with one component function per category. The γ-dimensions [3] of the classes of component functions are supposed to grow no faster than polynomially with γ^{-1}. We adopt a standard approach which starts with a bound on the risk in terms of a Rademacher complexity [4]. In [5], this Rademacher complexity is upper bounded by the sum of the ones of the component function classes. This yields a bound at least linear in the number C of categories. In [1, 2], the Rademacher complexity is bounded by a function of the metric entropy using the chaining method [6] to obtain a sublinear dependency on C. Then, the quality of the final result depends on the generalized Sauer-Shelah lemma used. We establish that dimension-free lemmas (yielding metric entropy bounds independent of the sample size) do not improve the final convergence rate. Thus, we choose the lemma most favorable with respect to C. In this way, we obtain a confidence interval growing as the square root of C with convergence rate similar to those in [1, 2]. This behaviour holds true irrespective of the degree of the polynomial.

Keywords: Margin multi-category classifiers · Guaranteed risks · Rademacher complexity · Metric entropy

References

1. Guermeur, Y.: L_p-norm Sauer-Shelah lemma for margin multi-category classifiers (2016). arxiv:1609.07953
2. Guermeur, Y.: Rademacher complexity of margin multy-category classifiers. In: WSOM+ (2017) (to appear)
3. Kearns, M., Schapire, R.: Efficient distribution-free learning of probabilistic concepts. J. Comput. Syst. Sci. **48**(3), 464–497 (1994)
4. Koltchinskii, V., Panchenko, D.: Empirical margin distributions and bounding the generalization error of combined classifiers. Ann. Stat. **30**(1), 1–50 (2002)
5. Kuznetsov, V., Mohri, M., Syed, U.: Multi-class deep boosting. In: NIPS, vol. 27, pp. 2501–2509 (2014)
6. Talagrand, M.: Upper and Lower Bounds of Stochastic Processes. Springer, Berlin (2014)

© Springer International Publishing AG 2017
A. Lintas et al. (Eds.): ICANN 2017, Part II, LNCS 10614, p. 767, 2017.
https://doi.org/10.1007/978-3-319-68612-7

A Fuzzy Clustering Approach to Non-stationary Data Streams Learning

A. Abdullatif[1], F. Masulli[1,2(✉)], S. Rovetta[1], and A. Cabri[1]

[1] DIBRIS - Department of Informatics, Bioingengering, Robotics and Systems Engineering, University of Genoa, Via Dodecaneso 35, 16146 Genoa, Italy
francesco.masulli@unige.it
[2] Sbarro Institute for Cancer Research and Molecular Medicine, College of Science and Technology, Temple University, Philadelphia, PA, USA

Abstract. Multidimensional data streams are a major paradigm in data science. They are always related to time, albeit to different degrees. They may represent actual time series or quasi-stationary phenomena that feature longer-term variability, e.g., changes in statistical distribution or a cyclical behavior. In these non-stationary conditions, a given model is expected to be appropriate only in a temporal neighborhood of the time when it has been validated/learned. Its validity may decrease smoothly with time (*concept drift*), or there may be sudden changes, for instance when switching from one operating condition to a new one (*concept shift*). The proposed approach consists in studying a clustering process able to adapt to streaming data, by implementing a continuous learning exploiting the input patterns as they arrive. Based on this idea we specifically exploit the ability of possibilistic clustering [2] to cluster iteratively using both batch (sliding-window) and online (by-pattern) strategies that track and adapt to concept drift and shift in a natural way. Measures of fuzzy "outlierness" and fuzzy outlier density are obtained as intrinsic by-products of the possibilistic clustering technique adopted. These measures are used to modulate the amount of incremental learning according to the different regimes required by non-stationary data stream clustering. The proposed method is used as a generative model to assess and improve the accuracy of a forecaster based of a neural network ensemble [1]. The generative model provides two kinds of information: The first is used to partition the data for obtaining a specialized forecaster for each cluster; the second allows us to provide a soft rejection, i.e., a fuzzy evaluation of outlierness that is a symptom of a possibly anomalous pattern.

Keywords: Data streams learning · Graded possibilistic clustering

© Springer International Publishing AG 2017
A. Lintas et al. (Eds.): ICANN 2017, Part II, LNCS 10614, pp. 768–769, 2017.
https://doi.org/10.1007/978-3-319-68612-7

References

1. Abdullatif, A., Rovetta, S., Masulli, F.: Layered ensemble model for short-term traffic flow forecasting with outlier detection. In: 2016 IEEE 2nd International Forum on Research and Technologies for Society and Industry Leveraging a Better Tomorrow (RTSI), pp. 1–6, September 2016
2. Masulli, F., Rovetta, S.: Soft transition from probabilistic to possibilistic fuzzy clustering. IEEE Trans. Fuzzy Syst. **14**(4), 516–527 (2006)

Data Stream Classification by Adaptive Semi-supervised Fuzzy Clustering

Giovanna Castellano$^{(\boxtimes)}$ and Anna Maria Fanelli

Computer Science Department, University of Bari Aldo Moro, Bari, Italy
{giovanna.castellano,annamaria.fanelli}@uniba.it

Abstract. The analysis and classification of data streams has attracted much attention recently due to the increasing amount of applications that produce streaming data. Most of the existing work relevant to data stream classification assume that all data are completely labeled. However in many applications, labeled data are difficult or expensive to obtain, meanwhile unlabeled data are relatively easy to collect. Semi-supervised learning algorithms can solve this problem by using unlabeled samples together with a few labeled ones to build classification models. In [1] we introduced a data stream classification method based on an incremental semi-supervised fuzzy clustering algorithm. The method assumes that data belonging to different classes are continuously available during time and processed as chunks. The clusters are formed from a chunk via the SSFCM (Semi-Supervised FCM) clustering and when the next chunk becomes available the clustering is run again starting from cluster prototypes inherited from the previous chunk. The algorithm creates a fixed number of clusters that is set equal to the number of classes. In real-world contexts the underlying distribution of data may change over the time, hence a fixed number of clusters may not capture adequately the evolving structure of streaming data. To overcome this limitation in this work we extend the method proposed in [1] by introducing the capability to adapt dynamically the number of clusters. When the cluster quality deteriorates from one data chunk to another, the number of clusters is increased (by splitting some clusters) or also decreased (by merging some clusters). The cluster quality is evaluated in terms of the *reconstruction error* [2] that measures the difference between the original data and their "reconstructed" counterpart derived using the clustering outcome (prototypes and membership degrees). Preliminary experimental results on the benchmark data set KDD-CUP99 show that the proposed adaptive version of the data stream classification method outperforms the previous static version and is more robust in presence of outliers.

Keywords: Data stream classification · Semi-supervised clustering

© Springer International Publishing AG 2017
A. Lintas et al. (Eds.): ICANN 2017, Part II, LNCS 10614, pp. 770–771, 2017.
https://doi.org/10.1007/978-3-319-68612-7

References

1. Castellano, G., Fanelli, A.M.: Classification of data streams by incremental semi-supervised fuzzy clustering. In: Petrosino, A., Loia, V., Pedrycz, W. (eds.) WILF 2016. LNCS, vol. 10147, pp. 185–194. Springer, Cham (2017). doi:10.1007/978-3-319-52962-2_16
2. Pedrycz, W.: A dynamic data granulation through adjustable fuzzy clustering. Pattern Recogn. Lett. **29**, 2059–2066 (2008)

The Discovery of the Relationship on Stock Transaction Data

Wanwan Jiang[✉], Lingyu Xu, Gaowei Zhang, and Haixing Yu

Shanghai University, No.99 Shangda Road, Baoshan District, Shanghai, China
jiangwanwan0327@163.com

Abstract. Recently, the discovery of relationship in financial markets attracts much attention, however, there has been little work studying the relationship on stock transaction data. Since it is essential for us to have a deeper understanding of stock's internal mechanism, we intend to explore more relevant relations among the stocks determinants.

Based on the time series characteristics of the stock, we adopt a sequence-to-sequence mapping method [1] to study the correlation among any two properties of the stock. The traditional methods can only deal with problems whose inputs and targets can be sensibly encoded with vectors of fixed dimensionality, however, in many scenarios we can not determine the length of sequence in advance, hence these methods are impractical. In this paper we explore using the encoder-decoder-based neural network for extracting the relationship of any two properties of the stock. The advantage of that model is that it is good at dealing with the mapping problem of variable-length sequences, which is characterized as follows: (1) both input and output are sequences; (2) the length of the sequence is not fixed; (3) there is no correspondence between the input and output sequence length.

First, we segment the time series D_A and D_B of stock properties according to the length of the segment. Second, we obtain the corresponding segmented time series sets $D_A^{'}$ and $D_B^{'}$. Third, we take $D_A^{'}$ as the input sequence of the model, through training, we can predict the corresponding output sequence, which is expressed as $D_B^{''}$. Finally, we determine whether there is a certain relationship between A and B based on the degree of similarity between $D_B^{''}$ and $D_B^{'}$. We believe that the higher the degree of similarity, the greater the correlation between them.

The experimental results demonstrate that there are certain correlations between four stock properties, among which the correlation between $Close\&\%Tuv$ and $\%Chg\&\%Tuv$ are more prominent. In addition, we also conclude that the correlation strength is not the same when we use different length of time series for testing, and the time series, whose length are greater than 5, are more suitable to reflect the correlation between the two attributes.

Keywords: Correlation coefficient · Time series · Neural network

© Springer International Publishing AG 2017
A. Lintas et al. (Eds.): ICANN 2017, Part II, LNCS 10614, pp. 772–773, 2017.
https://doi.org/10.1007/978-3-319-68612-7

Reference

1. Sutskever, I., Vinyals, O., Le, Q.V.: Sequence to sequence learning with neural networks. Adv. Neural Inf. Process. Syst. **4**, 3104–3112 (2014)

Confirmation of the Effect of Simultaneous Time Series Prediction with Multiple Horizons at the Example of Electron Daily Fluence in Near-Earth Space

Irina Myagkova[(⊠)] and Sergey Dolenko

D.V. Skobeltsyn Institute of Nuclear Physics, M.V. Lomonosov Moscow State
University, Moscow, Russia
{irina,dolenko}@srd.sinp.msu.ru

Abstract. It is often necessary to make time series (TS) predictions
for several values of the prediction horizon. Usually such predictions are
made in autonomous mode, i.e. separately for each horizon value. Meanwhile, it is also possible to make simultaneous predictions for all the
desired horizons, or group prediction for several horizons at once.

In the preceding studies [1], it has been demonstrated that group
determination of parameters in solving multi-parameter inverse problem
with a multi-layer perceptron (MLP) may outperform autonomous determination if the approximated dependences of the grouped parameters on
the input features of the problem are similar and if the sets of significant
input features largely intersect. Last year it has been demonstrated, that
the effect also holds for MLP TS prediction with multiple horizons [2].

In the present study, efficiency of group prediction of TS with MLP
has been checked at the example of TS of electron daily fluence in near-
Earth space, which is characterized by rapid degradation of prediction
quality with increasing horizon. Relativistic electrons (RE) of the outer
Earth's radiation belt are sometimes called "killer electrons" since they
can damage electronic components, resulting in temporary or even complete loss of spacecraft. Daily fluence is summary daily flux of these
electrons; at geosynchronous orbit of about 35,000 km altitude it is of
interest due to the large number of satellites populating this region, and
it is predictable thanks to long TS of experimental data available.

For this problem, group prediction with average size of groups proved
to outperform autonomous and simultaneous prediction. Thus, the positive effect of group determination of outputs in multi-output problem
has been confirmed as a property of MLP as data processing algorithm.

This study has been performed at the expense of Russian Science
Foundation, project no. 16-17-00098.

Keywords: Time series prediction · Prediction horizon · Multi-output
problem · Mlti-layer perceptron · Electron daily fluence

© Springer International Publishing AG 2017
A. Lintas et al. (Eds.): ICANN 2017, Part II, LNCS 10614, pp. 774–775, 2017.
https://doi.org/10.1007/978-3-319-68612-7

References

1. Dolenko, S., Isaev, I., Obornev, E., Persiantsev, I., Shimelevich, M.: Study of influence of parameter grouping on the error of neural network solution of the inverse problem of electrical prospecting. In: Iliadis, L., Papadopoulos, H., Jayne, C. (eds.) EANN 2013. CCIS, vol. 383, pp. 81–90. Springer, Heidelberg (2013). doi:10.1007/978-3-642-41013-0_9
2. Myagkova, I., Shiroky, V., Dolenko, S.: Effect of simultaneous time series prediction with various horizons on prediction quality at the example of electron flux in the outer radiation belt of the earth. In: Villa, A.E.P., Masulli, P., Pons Rivero, A.J. (eds.) ICANN 2016. LNCS, vol. 9887, pp. 317–325. Springer, Cham (2016). doi:10.1007/978-3-319-44781-0_38

A Neural Attention Based Approach for Clickstream Mining

Chandramohan T.N.$^{(\boxtimes)}$ and Balaraman Ravindran

IIT Madras, Chennai, India
{chandramohan,ravi}@cse.iitm.ac.in

Abstract. E-commerce has seen tremendous growth over the past few years, so much so that only those companies which analyze browsing behaviour of users, can hope to survive the stiff competition in the market. Analyzing customer behaviour helps in modeling and recognizing purchase intent which is vital to e-commerce for providing improved personalization and better ranking of search results. In this work, we make use of user clickstreams to model browsing behaviour of users. But clickstreams are known to be noisy and hence generating features from clickstreams and using them in one go for building a prediction model may not always capture the purchase/intent characteristics. There are multiple aspects within the clickstreams which are to be taken in such as the sequence (path taken) and temporal behaviour of users. Hence we see clickstreams as having multiple *views*, each view concentrating on one aspect or a component of clickstream. In this work, we develop a Multi-View learning (MVL) framework that predicts whether users would make a purchase or not by analyzing their clickstreams. Recent advances in deep learning allow us to build neural networks that are able to extract complex latent features from the data with minimal human intervention. Separate models known as *experts* are trained on each view. The experts are then combined using an Expert-Attention (EA) network, where the *attention* part of the network tries to learns when to attend to which view of the data. Multiple variants have been proposed based on how EA network is trained. They are (1) Update only the weights of the attention network while backpropagating the errors. (2) Update the weights of both expert and attention networks while backpropagating the errors. (3) A context of each expert is fed to the attention network at intermediate layer besides the input fed at input layer. (4) Learn the EA network from scratch. Yet another challenge is the extreme *class imbalance* present in the data since only a small fraction of clickstreams correspond to buyers. We propose a well informed undersampling strategy using autoencoders. This simple undersampling technique was able to reduce the imbalance to such levels that the performance improvement was observed to be in the order of hundreds. Experimental results show that using EA networks there is an improvement of 13% over single view methods. Moreover, it was also noticed that MVL using EA network was found to perform better than conventional MVL methods such as Multiple Kernel Learning.

© Springer International Publishing AG 2017
A. Lintas et al. (Eds.): ICANN 2017, Part II, LNCS 10614, pp. 776–777, 2017.
https://doi.org/10.1007/978-3-319-68612-7

Keywords: Clickstream · LSTM · Attention · Multi-view learning · Class-Imbalance

Classification of Quantitative Light-Induced Fluorescence Images Using Convolutional Neural Network

Sultan Imangaliyev[1,4]($\boxtimes$), Monique H. van der Veen[2],
Catherine M.C. Volgenant[2], Bruno G. Loos[2], Bart J.F. Keijser[2],
Wim Crielaard[2], and Evgeni Levin[3,4]

[1] VU University Medical Center Amsterdam, Amsterdam, The Netherlands
s.imangaliyev@vumc.nl
[2] Academic Centre for Dentistry Amsterdam, Amsterdam, The Netherlands
[3] Academic Medical Center, Amsterdam, The Netherlands
[4] Horaizon BV, Rotterdam, The Netherlands

Abstract. Images are an important data source for diagnosis of oral diseases. The manual classification of images may lead to suboptimal treatment procedures due to subjective errors. In this paper an image classification algorithm based on Deep Learning framework is applied to Quantitative Light-induced Fluorescence (QLF) images [4]. The Convolutional Neural Network [3] (CNN) outperforms other state of the art shallow classification models in predicting labels derived from three different dental plaque assessment scores. Such result is possible because our model directly learns invariant feature representations from raw pixel intensity values without any hand-crafted feature engineering. The model benefits from multi-channel representation of the images resulting in improved performance when, besides the Red colour channel, additional Green and Blue colour channels are used. Previous studies on this topic either focused on only single plaque scoring system without providing detailed analysis of results [1] or used a smaller dataset of non-QLF images and a shallow network architecture [2] to address the problem. We expect that Deep Learning of QLF-images can help dental practitioners to perform efficient plaque assessments and contribute to the improvement of patients' oral health. An extended version of the manuscript with detailed description of the experimental setup and the obtained results can be found at http://arxiv.org/abs/1705.09193 or http://learning-machines.com/.

Keywords: Deep learning · Quantitative light-induced fluorescence

References

1. Imangaliyev, S., van der Veen, M.H., Volgenant, C.M.C., Keijser, B.J.F., Crielaard, W., Levin, E.: Deep learning for classification of dental plaque images. In: Pardalos, P.M., Conca, P., Giuffrida, G., Nicosia, G. (eds.) MOD 2016. LNCS, vol. 10122, pp. 407–410. Springer, Cham (2016). doi:10.1007/978-3-319-51469-7_34

© Springer International Publishing AG 2017
A. Lintas et al. (Eds.): ICANN 2017, Part II, LNCS 10614, pp. 778–779, 2017.
https://doi.org/10.1007/978-3-319-68612-7

2. Kang, J., et al.: Dental plaque quantification using cellular neural network-based image segmentation. In: Huang, D.-S., Li, K., Irwin, G.W. (eds.) Intelligent Computing in Signal Processing and Pattern Recognition. LNCIS, vol. 345, pp. 797–802. Springer, Heidelberg (2006)
3. LeCun, Y., et al.: Deep learning. Nature **521**(7553), 436–444 (2015)
4. van der Veen, M.H., et al.: Dynamics of red fluorescent dental plaque during experimental gingivitis - a cohort study. J. Dent. **48**, 71–76 (2016)

Deep Residual Hashing Network for Image Retrieval

Edwin Jimenez-Lepe$^{(\boxtimes)}$ and Andres Mendez-Vazquez

CINVESTAV Guadalajara, Guadalajara, Mexico
{eejimenez,amendez}@gdl.cinvestav.mx
http://www.gdl.cinvestav.mx

Abstract. Conventional methods in Content-Based Image Retrieval use hand-crafted visual features as input but sometimes such feature vectors do not preserve the similarity between images. Taking advantage of the improvements in the Convolutional Neural Networks (CNN) area we propose a Deep Residual Hashing Network (DRHN) based in the work of [1] that generates binary hash codes based on the features learned.

The base of our model is a residual block which is formed by the following operations: Convolution, Rectified Linear Unit (ReLU), Batch normalization (BN) [2] and Element-wise addition. A Residual Group is the join of n Residual Blocks. The architecture of the proposed model is the next: Input $\rightarrow$ (Convolution $\rightarrow$ ReLU $\rightarrow$ BN) $\rightarrow$ six residual blocks $\rightarrow$ Average Pooling Layer (APL) $\rightarrow$ Hash Layer $\rightarrow$ Fully Connected Layer with Softmax, where the APL calculates the average of all values in a channel and Hash Layer length is denoted by h.

We exploit a previous proposed idea in the field [3]: in a supervised manner the binary codes can be learned adding an extra hidden layer to represent the main features that identifies the classes in a database, hence to generate the binary code of h bits related to an image we binarize the activation of the Hash Layer according to some threshold t.

The experimental results outperforms the state-of-the-art hashing algorithms on the CIFAR-10 dataset, using a DRHN with $n = 15$ and $h = 48$ we obtained a mean average precision (mAP) of 92.91 in the image retrieval task, previous best known result for the same number of bits was 89.73 [3].

Keywords: Convolutional neural networks · Content-based image retrieval · Computer vision · Deep learning

References

1. He, K., Zhang, X., Ren, S., Sun, J.: Deep residual learning for image recognition. In: Proceedings of the IEEE Conference on Computer Vision and Pattern Recognition, pp. 770–778 (2016)
2. Ioffe, S., Szegedy, C.: Batch normalization: accelerating deep network training by reducing internal covariate shift. arXiv preprint (2015). arxiv:1502.03167

© Springer International Publishing AG 2017
A. Lintas et al. (Eds.): ICANN 2017, Part II, LNCS 10614, pp. 780–781, 2017.
https://doi.org/10.1007/978-3-319-68612-7

3. Lin, K., Yang, H.F., Hsiao, J.H., Chen, C.S.: Deep learning of binary hash codes for fast image retrieval. In: Proceedings of the IEEE Conference on Computer Vision and Pattern Recognition Workshops, pp. 27–35 (2015)

Model Evaluation Improvements for Multiclass Classification in Diagnosis Prediction

Adriana Mihaela Coroiu$^{(\boxtimes)}$

Babes-Bolyai University, Cluj-napoca, Romania
adrianac@cs.ubbcluj.ro

Abstract. We are living in an age in which we are invaded by the amount of available data. These data are increasing in an exponential way. The art of making sense of all the data represent an issues nowadays. Moreover, the ability to deal with different types of these data require new approaches in the field of exploratory analysis. Therefore the extraction of relevant information, the discovery of relations between data and the ability to generalize to new data represent a continuous challenge.

Exploratory data analysis becomes an impressive area of concern for certain domains such as education, healthcare, biology, economics, geography, geology, history or agriculture. Particularly, the purpose of this paper is related to medicine and psychology. Some machine learning advantages are being investigated in order to improve a treatment, a diagnosis of a patient.

This paper, presenting a work in progress, discusses an approach to a relevant supervised learning method from the art of machine learning field: classification. Various aspects are considered, as preprocessing of the input data; selection of the model applied to the data; evaluation of the model; improving the performance of a model, selection of the most relevant features to be included in the model and also learning a model that is able to perform well on new data [1]. The computed metrics for performance evaluation of a model are also highlighted.

The data sets (mixed data) used in our analysis are data from medical field (kidney and lung disease: pulmonar-renal syndrome) and also are suitable for multiclass classification. In this paper, the selected models are ensembles of decision trees such as Random Forest and Gradient Boosted Regression Trees.

The model evaluation, the model improvements and feature selection ultimately lead to building models able to generalize to new data with a high value of accuracy. All these represent an added value in fields such us medicine and psychology, where a physician or a psychologist may use pattern and information as input in the treatment of a patient.

Keywords: Multiclass classification · Evaluation model · Features selection

© Springer International Publishing AG 2017
A. Lintas et al. (Eds.): ICANN 2017, Part II, LNCS 10614, pp. 782–783, 2017.
https://doi.org/10.1007/978-3-319-68612-7

Reference

1. Varoquaux, G., Buitinck, L., Louppe, G., Grisel, O., Pedregosa, F., Mueller, A.: Scikit-learn: machine learning without learning the machinery. GetMobile: Mobile Comp. and Comm. **19**(1), 29–33 (2015)

MMT: A Multimodal Translator for Image Captioning

Chang Liu[1(✉)], Fuchun Sun[1], and Changhu Wang[2]

[1] Department of Computer Science, Tsinghua University, Beijing, China
[2] Toutiao AI Lab, Beijing, China

Abstract. Image captioning is a challenging problem. Different from other computer vision tasks such as image classification and object detection, image captioning requires not only understanding the image, but also the knowledge of natural language. In this work, we formulate the problem of image captioning as a multimodal translation task. Analogous to machine translation, we present a sequence-to-sequence recurrent neural network (RNN) model for image caption generation. Different from most existing work where the whole image is represented by a convolutional neural network (CNN) feature, we propose to represent the input image as a sequence of detected objects to serve as the source sequence of the RNN model. In this way, the sequential representation of an image can be naturally translated into a sequence of words, as the target sequence of the RNN model. To obtain the source sequence from the image, objects are first detected by pre-trained detectors and then converted to a sequential representation using heuristic ordering strategies, that is, by the saliency scores of the detected objects. We propose three ordering methods, descending, ascending and random, according to the saliency scores, in order to study the influence of ordering over RNN cells. To obtain the target sequence, the language words are represented as one-hot feature vector. The representations of the objects and the words are then mapped into a common hidden space. The translation from the source sequence to the target sequence is done by leveraging LSTM. Extensive experiments are conducted to evaluate the proposed approach on benchmark dataset, i.e., MSCOCO, and achieve the state-of-the-art performance. The proposed approach is also evaluated by the evaluation server of MS COCO captioning challenge and achieves very competitive results. For example, we achieve CIDEr of 93.2, RougeL of 53.2 and BLEU4 of 31.1. We validate the contribution of each idea, that is, sequential representation and ordering method, by comparison studies, and show that sequential representation indeed improves the performance compared to vanilla CNN + RNN based methods, and ascending ordering outperforms the other two ordering methods.

Keywords: Image captioning · Deep learning · Natural language generation

Acknowledgment: This paper is jointly supported by National Natural Science Foundation of China under with Grant No.61621136008, 61327809, 61210013, 91420302 & 91520201.

A. Lintas et al. (Eds.): ICANN 2017, Part II, LNCS 10614, p. 784, 2017.
https://doi.org/10.1007/978-3-319-68612-7

A Multi-Channel and Multi-Scale Convolutional Neural Network for Hand Posture Recognition

Jiawen Feng[1(✉)], Limin Zhang[1], Xiangyang Deng[1,2], and Zhijun Yu[3]

[1] Naval Aeronautical and Astronautical University, Yantai, China
fengjiawen777@163.com, iamzlm@163.com, xavior2012@aliyun.com
[2] Institute of Electronic Engineering, Naval Engineering University, Wuhan, China
[3] Naval Aeronautical and Astronautical University Training Base, Yantai, China
15684082191@163.com

Abstract. Hand posture recognition is a popular research topic in computer vision, on account of its important real-world applications such as sign language recognition. Understanding human gestures is hard because of several challenges like feature extracting. Various algorithms have been employed in gesture recognition, but many of the best results were achieved by Convolutional neural networks (CNN), which are powerful visual models that are widely applied to many fields of pattern recognition, such as image classification [1], face recognition, speech recognition, including hand posture recognition.

Inspired by [2] this paper proposes a multi-channel and multi-scale convolutional neural network (MMCNN), provided by two channels with diverse convolution kernel sizes, meanwhile, the input pictures are pre-processed into different sizes. MMCNN could accept the different features of the image as input, and then combines these features for image classification. The multi-channel structure is able to extract image features from multiple spatial scales using convolutional kernels with different sizes, and multi-scale structure input ensures the richness of the input image characteristics.

Experiments were performed using two gesture databases, the proposed MMCNN classifies 24 gesture classes with 98.4% accuracy, better than the nearest competitor, enhancing the generalization ability of convolution neural networks.

Keywords: Convolution neural networks · Hand posture recognition · Multi-channel · Multi-scale · Convolution kernel

References

1. Le, Q.V.: Building high-level features using large scale unsupervised learning. In: 2013 IEEE International Conference on Acoustics, Speech and Signal Processing (ICASSP), pp. 8595–8598. IEEE (2013)
2. Barros, P., Magg, S., Weber, C., et al.: A multichannel convolutional neural network for hand posture recognition. In: International Conference on Artificial Neural Networks, Springer International Publishing, pp. 403–410 (2014)

© Springer International Publishing AG 2017
A. Lintas et al. (Eds.): ICANN 2017, Part II, LNCS 10614, p. 785, 2017.
https://doi.org/10.1007/978-3-319-68612-7

Semi-supervised Model for Feature Extraction and Classification of Fashion Images

Seema Wazarkar[1]([⊠]), Bettahally N. Keshavamurthy[1], and Shitala Prasad[2]

[1] National Institute of Technology, Ponda, Goa, India
{wazarkarseema,bnkeshav.fcse}@nitgoa.ac.in
[2] NTU, Singapore, Singapore
shitala@ieee.org

Abstract. Fashion forecasting plays an important role in the growth of fashion and textile industries. Popularity of social network provides a statistical way to predict the upcoming and outgoing fashion trends through social content data analysis. Social image data is a most expressive form of content data which is useful to get the fashion related information. But, characteristics of social data such as heterogeneity, large volume, etc. make this problem challenging. Hence, in this paper semi-supervised feature extraction and classification model is proposed based on the joint probability of multiple features. We conducted experiments on *Fashion 10000* dataset [1] having images from Flickr.

First, feature extraction is done where Convolutional Neural Network (CNN) based matching points (using labelled and unlabelled images) along with five other features i.e. color, texture, regional, geometric and face detection (using unlabelled image) are obtained. Due to the consideration of multiple significant features, proposed approach is able to deal with the heterogeneity in given images. Linear convolution is performed to get the representative image with prominent features and it is compared with labelled representative images of each class to get the number of matching points for that class. Color and texture features are extracted with the help of RGB components and gray level co-occurrence matrix, respectively. Values of extent, eccentricity and orientation are considered as regional features and Euler number as geometric feature. As most of the social images with person consist fashion related information, face detection is also carried out to show the presence of person in given image and stored it as a feature. Then, class-conditional probabilities of all the extracted features are computed and the maximum joint probability is used while assigning the class label to the given image.

Obtained results show that incorporation of matching points using CNN with other features, improves the accuracy than using only other five features. In [2], search based classification using twelve global features is carried out by B. Loni et al. on same fashion dataset where 0.7421 f1-score for *visual only* method is obtained. Using only six features, approximately similar results are achieved with our proposed approach.

© Springer International Publishing AG 2017
A. Lintas et al. (Eds.): ICANN 2017, Part II, LNCS 10614, pp. 786–787, 2017.
https://doi.org/10.1007/978-3-319-68612-7

Keywords: Classification · Feature extraction · Fashion images · Social data

References

1. Loni, B., et al.: Fashion 10000: an enriched social image dataset for fashion and clothing. In: ACM Multimedia Systems Conference, pp. 41–46 (2014)
2. Loni, B., et al.: Getting by with a little help from the crowd: practical approaches to social image labeling. In: IWCM, pp. 69–74 (2014)

Identification of Differential Flat Systems with Artifical Neural Networks

J. Hoedt$^{(\boxtimes)}$, J. Kaste$^{(\boxtimes)}$, K. Van Ende$^{(\boxtimes)}$, and F. Kallmeyer$^{(\boxtimes)}$

Vehicle Dynamics, Volkswagen Group Resarch, Wolfsburg, Germany
{jens.hoedt,jonas.kaste,kristof.van.ende}@volkswagen.de

Abstract. The property of differential flatness in dynamic systems leads to advantages in the field of analysis and control. These properties are widely elaborated [1]. Flatness means, that the whole system dynamics can be described by a flat output and a finite number of its derivatives. The flatness property defines a diffeomorphism from the system manifold to a trivial one. We use the bijective property of this map to design artifical neuronal networks accordingly. The weights of the designed networks directly correspond to the parameterization of the diffeomorphism. Training these networks result in a parameter estimation of the observed system. One main objective is to get more insights in how to choose network topologies for a given problem formulation. Parameter estimation of mechanical models with neural networks is performed in [2], where the authors estimate parameters of a dynamic aircraft system model directly from the weights of a feed forward neural network. Using a flatness based method leads in practice often to a static diffeomorphism which can exactly be reproduced by feed forward neural networks. The considered hidden layers correspond to the parameterization of measurements by the flat output. Therefore several learning algorithms (e.g. Levenberg-Marquardt, gradient descent with and without momentum, ADAM) and initialisation values of the weights are evaluated. It can be shown that it is not suitable to use a constant and overall learning rate if parameters are not in similar domains. To overcome the necessity of using all flat outputs and their derivatives as inputs for the neural networks we integrate an algebraic derivative estimation into the net. Several models have been tested to show the potential of this approach, for example, a first order linear system up to a single track model of a vehicle. Finally the method has been compared to a model based machine learning linear regression approach.

Keywords: Differential flatness · Artificial neuronal networks · Parameter estimation

© Springer International Publishing AG 2017
A. Lintas et al. (Eds.): ICANN 2017, Part II, LNCS 10614, pp. 788–789, 2017.
https://doi.org/10.1007/978-3-319-68612-7

References

1. Fliess, M., Lévine, J., Martin, P., Rouchon, P.: A lie-bäcklund approach to equivalence and flatness of nonlinear systems. IEEE Trans. Autom. Control **44**, 922–937 (1999)
2. Kirkpatrick, K., May Jr., J., Valasek, J.: Aircraft system identification using artifcial neural networks. In: AIAA, pp. 2013–0878 (2013)

Adaptive Weighted Multiclass Linear Discriminant Analysis

Haifeng Zhao[1], Wei He[1], and Feiping Nie[2(✉)]

[1] Key Lab of Intelligent Computing and Signal Processing of MOE
and School of Computer Science and Technology, Anhui University, Hefei 230601,
People's Republic of China
{senith,Xiaohw}@ahu.edu.cn
[2] School of Computer Science and Center for OPTical IMagery Analysis
and Learning(OPTIMAL), Northwestern Polytechnical University, Xi'an 710072,
Shanxi, People's Republic of China
feipingnie@gmail.com

Abstract. In this paper, we propose a novel linear dimension reduction method called Adaptive Weighted Multiclass Linear Discriminant Analysis (AWMLDA). The proposed approach is based on the Fisher's linear discriminant analysis (FLDA), which maximizes the ratio of the sum of the between-class scatter and the within-class scatter. Since the projection direction of FLDA overemphasized the large class distances that causing the classes with small distances are still closed in the subspace, the solution of FLDA is suboptimal for the multiclass problem. In the proposed method, firstly our method learn the transform matrix by measuring the between-class scatter and the within-class scatter of every pairwise classes rather than the sum measurement, and we use the square root of the inverse covariance matrix $\sum^{-1/2}$ to replace the original within-class matrix. The method of AWMLDA considers every distances of each pairwise, unlike MMDA [1] and WLDA [2] considered the minimum between/maximum within class distances respectively. Secondly, we assign the weights for each pairwise to balance the distances between each pairwise in the subspace and they can be updated with the Cauchy-Schwarz inequality adaptively. The distances of weighted pairwise are more close in the subspace such that the neighboring classes can be separated as well. Finally, we derive an efficient algorithm to solve the optimization problem, and give the theoretical analysis in detail. Experimental results demonstrate the effectiveness of AWMLDA when compared with some other well-known multiclass LDA methods.

Keywords: Linear dimension reduction · Multiclass · Fisher's linear discriminant analysis · Adaptive weighted

© Springer International Publishing AG 2017
A. Lintas et al. (Eds.): ICANN 2017, Part II, LNCS 10614, pp. 790–791, 2017.
https://doi.org/10.1007/978-3-319-68612-7

References

1. Bian, W., Tao, D.: Max-min distance analysis by using sequential SDP relaxation for dimension reduction. IEEE Trans. Pattern Anal. Mach. Intell. **33**(5), 1037–1050 (2011)
2. Zhang, Y., Yeung, D.-Y.: Worst-case linear discriminant analysis. In: Advances in Neural Information Processing Systems, vol. 23, pp. 2568–2576. MIT Press, Cambridge (2010)

Efficient Graph Construction Through Constrained Data Self-Representativeness

L. Weng[1,2], F. Dornaika[1(✉)], and Z. Jin[2]

[1] University of the Basque Country & IKERBASQUE, San Sebastian, Spain
[2] Nanjing University of Science and Technology, Nanjing, China

Recently, graph-based semi-supervised learning (SSL) becomes a hot topic in machine learning and pattern recognition[1]. Constructing an informative graph is one of the most important steps in SSL. In this paper, we introduce an efficient graph construction algorithm named constrained data self-representativeness graph construction (CSRGC). It is known that data self-representation can provide a relationship between one data sample and other samples which also can be regarded as a similarity measurement. Our proposed CSRGC graph exploits data self-representation. It also integrates constraints that stipulate that similar samples should also have similar edge weights. We propose to construct an affinity matrix $\mathbf{B}$ that simultaneously exploits data self-representation and Laplacian smoothness of the graph coefficients by solving the following minimization problem:

$$\mathbf{B} = \arg \min_{\mathbf{B}} \|\mathbf{X} - \mathbf{X}\,\mathbf{B}\|_F^2 + \lambda \|\mathbf{B}\|_F^2 + \rho\,\text{Trace}\left(\mathbf{B}\,\mathbf{L_B}\,\mathbf{B}^T\right) \qquad (1)$$

where $\mathbf{X}$ is the data matrix, $\mathbf{L_B}$ is the Laplacian matrix of the affinity matrix $\mathbf{B}$, and λ and ρ are two positive balance parameters. $\| \bullet \|_F$ is Frobenius norm. Equation (1) is efficiently and iteratively solved by fixing the Laplacian matrix and then solving for the affinity matrix. In practise, three iterations were found enough to get a stable graph. To evaluate the performance of our proposed method, we compare it with several other competing methods including KNN graph and LLE graph, ℓ_1 graph, the simple linear coding graph (ℓ_2 graph) and the Weighted Regularized Least Square (WRLS) method. For every graph construction method, several values for the parameter are used. We then report the best recognition accuracy. Table 1 shows the mean recognition rates on PF01 face dataset over ten random splits (Asian Face Image Database PF01. Database, Intelligent Multimedia Lab, Dept of CSE, POSTECH, 2001) (103 Asian persons each 17 images). Several labelled images per class are used (2–10 samples). Future work may apply the proposed method to other types of data such as music and speeches.

---

[1] Dornaika, F., Bosaghzadeh, A.: Adaptive graph construction using Data self-representativeness for pattern classification. Inf. Sci. **325** (2015).

© Springer International Publishing AG 2017
A. Lintas et al. (Eds.): ICANN 2017, Part II, LNCS 10614, pp. 792–793, 2017.
https://doi.org/10.1007/978-3-319-68612-7

Table 1. Recognition rates (%) on PF01 by label propagation over data driven graphs.

Graph construction method $\backslash l$	2	4	6	8	10
kNN	35.5	43.3	47.0	50.6	53.8
LLE	34.6	43.6	51.2	64.9	73.7
ℓ_1	40.3	50.4	55.9	59.3	63.6
ℓ_2	54.3	69.8	76.6	80.7	85.1
WRLS	54.7	69.6	75.5	79.7	85.1
CSRGC	**57.2**	**71.6**	**77.4**	**81.2**	**85.8**

Author Index

Printed in the United States
By Bookmasters